Studying Teacher Education:
The Report of the AERA Panel
on Research and Teacher Education

Studying Teacher Education:
The Report of the AERA Panel
on Research and Teacher Education

Edited by

Marilyn Cochran-Smith
Boston College

Kenneth M. Zeichner
University of Wisconsin at Madison

Published for the American Educational Research Association
by Lawrence Erlbaum Associates, Inc.

AMERICAN EDUCATIONAL RESEARCH ASSOCIATION
Washington, D.C.

LAWRENCE ERLBAUM ASSOCIATES, PUBLISHERS
2005   Mahwah, New Jersey   London

Senior Acquisitions Editor:	Naomi Silverman
Assistant Editor:	Erica Kica
Cover Design:	Kathryn Houghtaling Lacey
Textbook Production Manager:	Paul Smolenski
Full-Service Compositor:	TechBooks
Text and Cover Printer:	Hamilton Printing Company

This book was typeset in 10/12 pt. Palatino Roman, Bold, and Italic.
The heads were typeset in Korinna, Korinna Bold, and Korinna Bold Italic.

The American Educational Research Association (AERA) publishes books and journals based on the highest standards of professional review to ensure their quality, accuracy, and objectivity. Findings and conclusions in publications are those of the authors and do not reflect the position or policies of the Association, its Council, or officers.

Lawrence Erlbaum Associates, Inc., Publishers
10 Industrial Avenue
Mahwah, New Jersey 07430
www.erlbaum.com

American Educational Research Association
1230 Seventeenth Street, NW
Washington, DC 20036-3078
www.aera.net

Library of Congress Cataloging-in-Publication Data

AERA Panel on Research and Teacher Education.
   Studying teacher education : the report of the AERA Panel on Research and Teacher
Education / edited by Marilyn Cochran-Smith, Kenneth M. Zeichner.
      p.   cm.
   Includes bibliographical references and index.
   ISBN 0-8058-5592-0 (case : alk. paper) – ISBN 0-8058–5593-9 (pbk. : alk. paper)
   1. Teachers—Training of—United States.   2. Education—Research—
United States.   I. Cochran-Smith, Marilyn, 1949-   II. Zeichner, Kenneth M.   III. Title.

   LB1715.A47   2006
   370'.71'1—dc22   2005011015

Books published by Lawrence Erlbaum Associates are printed on
acid-free paper, and their bindings are chosen for strength and durability.

Printed in the United States of America
10   9   8   7   6   5   4   3   2

Contents

Foreword

This is a volume whose time has come. Issues related to teacher quality and quality teacher education are always a priority in a democratic society committed to excellence in teaching and learning for all of its participants. These issues, however, are seldom as central to public policy concerns and decisions as they are today. As the Preface points out, this book was conceived as a project in the late 1990s, at a time when teacher education reform policies were becoming highly controversial and politicized. We are pleased that the American Educational Research Association (AERA) did what a national research organization can do best—that is, serve the public good by ensuring that research knowledge is rigorously assessed and made accessible in a timely way to inform discussion and decisionmaking.

There were several fundamental premises underlying AERA's decision to pursue this project, each in keeping with the Association's goal of advancing research on education and promoting its sound application to policy and practice. First, through action of its governing Council, the Association determined that the debate over teacher education required thoughtful analysis of the relevant research and established a study panel to undertake this exploration. Second, the Association gave the panel independence to undertake this activity without further approval of the work product by its Council. Third, the panel was charged with building in internal processes of peer review so that each of the chapters of the report were vetted by scholars who brought independent expertise to the work and who had no stake in the panel or its report.

That the journey of the AERA Panel on Research and Teacher Education took only four years from its first organizational meeting to AERA's putting a book into production with Lawrence Erlbaum Associates, is a tribute to the fine leadership of the Panel's Co-Chairs and Co-Editors, Marilyn Cochran-Smith and Kenneth Zeichner. They, along with an exceptional roster of panel members, authors, graduate student assistants, and reviewers emulated the best in scholarly practice to assess what is known and what needs to be known in order to reform the preparation of quality teachers. In completing this project, the co-editors demonstrated an open-mind to diverse information and critique, the capacity to conceptualize and analyze a broad field of research, high standards of evidence, and a heavy dose of motivation and perseverance. The result is a volume—*Studying Teacher Education*—that will become an essential resource in addressing today's very compelling concerns about the education and preparation of the nation's teachers.

The strength of the book lies in both the specific issues that are addressed through topical chapters and the overarching chapters that knit together a wide-ranging set of topics in teacher education. In an era when both the research and policy communities are taking very seriously the importance of research-based guidance in professional practices of all types, this volume takes just the right tack in providing information and insights that derive from research. Through research syntheses, charts that map the extant research literature, and discussion of the areas where knowledge is non-existent or thin, this book does the "heavy lifting" for a wide number of audiences seeking to understand, improve, and study teacher education and the larger contexts that shape quality teaching.

It is a tremendous advantage for policymakers and scholars to have a volume that offers both a benchmark and a guide to what research on teacher education is and can be. As with all book publications of AERA, *Studying Teacher Education* received a final independent review by three anonymous reviewers not connected to the project as part of the determination to publish this product under AERA's imprimatur. While the substance and recommendations in this volume are solely those of the panel, this book has fully met the quality standards that AERA applies to its published work. We are pleased that the Association is positioned to offer a foundation of knowledge about teacher education for policymakers and practitioners, for scholars, and for those involved in educating and supporting the next generation of teacher education researchers.

Felice J. Levine
Executive Director
Carl Grant
Chair, Publications Committee
2005–2007

American Educational Research Association

Preface

During the mid- to late 1990s, the quality of public schools and of the nation's teaching force reached center stage in federal as well as in state and local politics. During that time, the national discourse about the recruitment, preparation and retention of teachers became increasingly contentious. Competing agendas for teacher education reform were advocated by groups with differing political and professional agendas, all of whom claimed to have empirical support for their positions. During this same time, the two of us served back-to-back terms as Vice President of AERA for Division K (Teaching and Teacher Education), Kenneth Zeichner from 1996 to 1998 and Marilyn Cochran-Smith from 1998 to 2000. In these roles, we participated in multiple AERA Council and committee discussions about the scope and strength of the empirical research base for proposed or existing accountability procedures, structural arrangements, and state and federal policies related to teacher preparation. As scholars who had been long and actively involved in teacher education practice, research, and policy, we grew increasingly concerned about the claims that were being made about evidence related to teacher education and about the assumptions people seemed to have about the role research could or should play in determining teacher education policy and practice. During the AERA Presidency of Lorrie Shepard (1999–2000), an AERA Panel on Research and Teacher Education, which we had proposed to the Council a year or so earlier, was approved, and we were appointed as the Panel's co-chairs. President Shepard appointed eight additional Panel members with different areas of expertise, including not only teacher education but also policy, testing and assessment, curriculum, liberal arts, multicultural education, research design and methods, and school reform: Mary Dilworth, Dan Fallon, Bob Floden, Susan Fuhrman, Drew Gitomer, Jacqueline Jordan Irvine, Ann Lieberman, and Ana Maria Villegas. Designated chapter authors were later invited to join the Panel as well: Renee Clift, Pamela Grossman, Etta Hollins, Marleen Pugach, Suzanne Wilson, and Karen Zumwalt. Kim Fries was named Project Manager.

When we began work on this project in 1999, the many current syntheses of research on teacher education were not yet published (although there have been a dozen or more new reviews with different purposes and sponsors released since 2000). In the midst of claims and counter-claims about which teacher preparation programs and routes were truly effective, our charge was to try to make sense of what the research did and did not say about teacher education and to craft a new research agenda that might begin to answer some of the most important, but previously unanswered, questions. We undertook this challenging task by endeavoring to provide a critical and evenhanded analysis of the weight of the empirical evidence relevant to key practices and policies in preservice teacher education in the United States. Just as important as the nine research syntheses we eventually produced, however, the panel's job was to recommend a new research agenda for teacher education by outlining topics that needed further study, identifying terms and concepts that required clarification and consistent usage, describing promising lines of research, and pointing to the research genres and processes most likely to define new directions and yield useful findings for policy and practice. In translating our charge into a workable set of questions and topics, the Panel was faced with many difficult decisions about what to include and what to omit from consideration. We were guided in part by a sense of what we were *not* doing relative to other related projects. Unlike many large handbook-type projects, we were not constructing a comprehensive analysis of the existing research related to all areas of teacher education, nor were we surveying the state of the field. Most importantly, our goal was *not* to provide a brief on behalf of teacher education that marshaled all of the evidence we could find in favor of policies and practices we already advocated. In fact, given the markedly different perspectives and areas of expertise of panel members, as noted in the following, it was crystal clear that there was no foregone approach or policy that we all advocated in the first place.

What the Panel did do was to select a relatively small number of key questions that policymakers, the public, and the educational community seemed particularly interested in and develop research syntheses that focused on these questions. We also prepared three framing chapters that provide historical and conceptual background information and recommend a new teacher education agenda. In doing so, we knowingly made the decision to leave out of our reviews large bodies of important work, including all of the research in, on, and about teacher education in contexts other than the United States, even though we were (and are) well aware of the relevance of this work to many of our questions and of its importance in the broader field. We also did not systematically review, but were informed by, historical and other scholarship that is not empirical. Again we made these choices knowingly, acknowledging that trade-offs are unavoidable in defining the limits of a research review. In the Executive Summary and introductory chapter of this volume, we have tried to make the decisions, assumptions, and trade-offs that defined this project transparent and explicit.

The AERA Panel on Research and Teacher Education was first convened in November of 2000. Over the next four years, the Panel held seven multiday meetings to deliberate about its charge, specify working assumptions, establish criteria for the inclusion and exclusion of empirical studies, debate the strengths and weaknesses of particular research methods and designs, review multiple outlines and drafts of chapters, and deliberate about the contours of a new agenda for teacher education. Working together as part of this multidisciplinary panel was an unusual experience for everybody involved, sometimes affirming, sometimes exasperating, and always provocative and instructive. There are few contexts in the academic world where one's writing is reviewed and critiqued by as many as 18 scholars with different ideas and areas of expertise. That the members of the Panel eventually completed their work and ultimately "signed off" on each chapter in the volume is a feat in itself. But even more noteworthy is the fact that the members of the Panel argued but also remained collegial, were highly critical of each others' analyses but also respectful of differences in perspectives and paradigms, and were steadfast over a long time in their commitment to constructing an evenhanded critical review of the empirical evidence. As co-chairs of the Panel and co-editors of this volume, we are enormously grateful to all of the Panel members who have become our colleagues.

There is no way this project could have been done without the thoughtful, always positive, and tireless efforts of Kim Fries, Project Manager, who is also co-author of two of its chapters. Kim kept all of us organized and also handled all of the administration, logistics, and finances related to the project over four years. Her efforts were absolutely indispensable, and her cheerful diplomacy and unfailing grace in the most trying circumstances were inspiring. Her organizational and intellectual contributions to the project and to this volume are immense.

We are also grateful to the graduate students and co-authors who worked on these chapters, met on numerous occasions with the panel, and presented along with us at multiple conferences. Their hard work and strong commitments to the profession were always apparent. Our thanks to Melanie Agnew, University of Wisconsin, Milwaukee; Patricia Brady, University of Illinois at Urbana-Champagne; Hilary Conklin, University of Wisconsin, Madison; Elizabeth Craig, Teachers College, Columbia; Byron Delgado, University of Southern California; Kim Fries, University of New Hampshire (formerly Boston College); Danielle Igra, Stanford University; Kimberly Hollins, University of Southern California; Jesse Kass, University of Southern California; Marco Meniketti, Michigan State University; Chancey Monte-Sato, Stanford University; and Peter Youngs, Michigan State University (formerly University of Wisconsin-Madison).

Peer review is at the heart of ensuring scholarly research products of highest merit. We were privileged to have an extraordinary group of colleagues who provided exceptional service at various stages in the development of the chapters that comprise this volume. Their comments, feedback, and critique furthered our work tremendously, adding to its quality, depth, and breadth. We would like to acknowledge and gratefully thank each of those who took the time to review our work: Michael Allen, Education Commission of the States; Michael Andrew, University of New Hampshire; JoMills Braddock, University of Miami; Carol Sue Englert, Michigan State University; Fred Erickson, University of California at Los Angeles; Sharon Feiman Nemser, Brandeis University; Carl Grant, University of Wisconsin-Madison; Dan Humphrey, SRI International; David Imig, American Association for Colleges of Teacher Education; Richard Ingersoll, University of Pennsylvania; Mary Kennedy, Michigan State University; Gloria Ladson-Billings, University of Wisconsin-Madison; Bill McDiarmid, University of Washington; David Monk, Penn State University; Frank Murray, University of Delaware; Martin Nystrom, University of Wisconsin-Madison; Annemarie Palinscar, University of Michigan; Andrew Porter, Vanderbilt University; Jeremy Price, University of Maryland; Christine Sleeter, California State University at Monterey Bay; Brian Stetcher, Rand Corporation; Alan Tom, University of North Carolina; and Linda Valli, University of Maryland. We would also like to thank the three anonymous reviewers who reviewed the entire volume toward the end of its development as well as those who provided us with formative feedback in their roles as conference discussants or commentators: Carol Ames, Michigan State University; David Berliner, Arizona State University; A. Lin Goodwin, Teachers College, Columbia; Carl Grant, University of Wisconsin-Madison; Judith Green, University of California–Santa Barbara; David Imig, American Association of Colleges for Teacher Education; and Fred Korthagen, University of Utrecht, the Netherlands.

Finally we want to acknowledge the generous financial support provided to us by the American Educational Research Association in the form of a grant to launch and complete this project, with special thanks to AERA Past Presidents James Banks, Alan

Schoenfeld, and Lorrie Shepard, whose foresight, wisdom, and support allowed this volume to get off the ground and come to fruition. We also want to thank the Carnegie Corporation of New York, which provided two small grants to fund graduate research assistants for each of the chapter authors. Without this financial support, the volume would certainly not have been possible. Finally we thank Felice Levine, Executive Director of AERA, and the AERA publications staff for encouragement, support, and help during the publication process. Felice's advice, attention to detail, and wealth of experience as a publisher and editor were invaluable, and her unfailing commitment to the value of this work kept us going during its final stages. Likewise Naomi Silverman and her colleagues at Lawrence Erlbaum Associates were excited about publishing this project, and their attention and support were very important to us.

We look forward to discussion and debate about the ideas set forth in this volume. We believe there are few things as important as the quality of the nation's teaching force, which is—to a great extent—entrusted with the future of our democracy.

Marilyn Cochran-Smith, Co-Chair
Kenneth M. Zeichner, Co-Chair

EXECUTIVE SUMMARY

It is now widely agreed that teachers are among the most, if not the most, significant factors in children's learning and the linchpins in educational reforms of all kinds. Despite the growing consensus that teachers matter, however, there are many debates about why and how they matter or how they should be recruited, prepared, and retained in teaching.

Growing recognition that teacher quality is significant coupled with concerns about low standards in the schools prompted a new wave of criticism of teachers and "traditional" teacher preparation that began in the mid-1990s and continued into the 21st century. Several different agendas for reforming teacher preparation emerged and were hotly debated. Advocates of opposing viewpoints claimed to have an empirical research base to support their ideas about how best to recruit, prepare, and retain teachers. In fact, in some of the most important debates about teacher preparation, the central focus—at least on the surface—was research itself, particularly whether there was a methodologically and conceptually strong research base about teacher preparation, and if so, what it suggested for policy and practice. It was within this context that the American Educational Research Association (AERA) formed its Panel on Research and Teacher Education.

The Charge to the Panel

The AERA Panel on Research and Teacher Education was charged with providing a critical and evenhanded analysis of the empirical evidence relevant to practices and policies in preservice teacher education in the United States. Just as importantly, the panel's job was to recommend a new research agenda for teacher education by outlining topics that need further study, identifying terms and concepts that require clarification and consistent usage, describing promising lines of research, and pointing

---

This "Executive Summary" provides an overview of *Studying Teacher Education: The Report of the AERA Panel on Research and Teacher Education*. The summary draws directly from the three general chapters and the nine research reviews included in the report. Although intended to be informative and using some actual passages from the chapters in the report, this summary in no way does justice to the careful and nuanced reviews of the research that are provided in each chapter. Readers are strongly encouraged to read the full report.

to the research genres and processes most likely to define new directions and yield useful findings for policy and practice.

This volume represents a systematic effort to apply a common set of evaluative criteria to a range of important topics in teacher education. It is our intention to provide balanced, thorough, and unapologetically honest descriptions of the state of research on particular topics in teacher education as a field of study. For many of the topics we considered, this meant that we needed to identify and acknowledge the considerable inconsistencies and contradictions that characterize the field. Our reviews were designed not only to note this state of the field but also to explain why this is so and to evaluate both the strengths and the weaknesses of different questions and approaches as we simultaneously identified promising lines of inquiry.

Each of the research syntheses developed by the AERA Panel on Research and Teacher Education points to promising lines of research that we can build on to enhance what we know about the impact of teacher preparation and the influence of various policies and practices. As we state in the conclusion of this summary, we believe that we are at a turning point in the field with more attention than ever before focused on the recruitment, preparation, and retention of teachers for the nation's schools. As a field, we need now to develop a rich portfolio of theory-driven studies that address the questions posed in this report as well as other important questions related to teacher preparation from multiple perspectives and using many different research designs. We need to develop accurate national databases that make many kinds of cross-institutional and multivariate analyses possible. We need to initiate multisite studies that link multiple smaller studies in ways that reveal the impact of differing contexts and conditions. We need to develop reliable and valid outcome measures with consistent language and procedures. Perhaps most importantly, we need studies from differing paradigmatic and epistemological perspectives that examine the links between and among teacher preparation contexts for learning, what teacher candidates actually learn, how their learning is played out in practice in K–12 schools and classrooms, and how this influences pupils' learning—all within the context of varying resource allocation, schools, communities, and programs. To do all of these things, it will take strategic investments in research infrastructure that supports both large-scale studies and in-depth case studies of teacher preparation. It will also take significant improvements in the peer-review process and the preparation of teacher education researchers. Finally it will take many research partnerships among teacher educators themselves and their colleagues in other fields and disciplines, in the schools, and in research and policy institutes.

Working Assumptions About Research, Practice, and Policy

The AERA Panel worked from an empirical perspective on teacher preparation. From the beginning, however, the panel acknowledged that although many empirical questions are important, there are also many important questions that cannot be answered by empirical research alone. We assumed that some of the most contested questions in the history of education deal with fundamental disagreements about the purposes and processes of schooling in a democratic society. The panel took as a working assumption that questions like these cannot be settled simply by assembling good evidence. To be sure, questions can be shaped, reformulated, or understood more profoundly on the basis of evidence; but evidence must always be interpreted, and interpretations are often made in highly politicized contexts. The values and beliefs of the interpreter influence the purposes for which evidence is used. Education and teacher education are social institutions that pose moral, ethical, social, philosophical, and ideological questions. Although questions of value and ideology underlie many of the most contentious disagreements about teacher education, these disagreements are often mistakenly treated as if they were value-neutral and ideology-free. Along the same lines, research is often mistakenly portrayed as if it had the capacity to resolve issues on the basis of evidence alone. The panel assumed from the outset that teacher preparation policies and practices cannot be decided solely on the basis of empirical evidence divorced from values.

It is important to note that the work of the panel is situated both within but also outside of the contemporary policy and political scene. On the one hand, the panel's work responds to the policy context of the time, and our choice to evaluate the empirical evidence about some of the teacher education issues that are of most interest to decision makers has been influenced by current policy debates. On the other hand, explicit in the panel's working assumptions is a critique of the current policy focus and considerable skepticism about the feasibility of producing the kind of evidence that many policymakers now seem to want—research that settles the teacher education "horse race" once and for all and declares a definitive winner.

Our reviews of the literature make clear why the horse race approach to studying teacher education invariably leads to mixed or inconclusive results and at the same time leaves out other very important questions. As this volume suggests, teacher preparation in the United States is enormously complex. It is conducted in local communities and institutions where program components and structures interact with one another as well as with the different experiences and abilities prospective teachers bring with them. Teacher preparation is also affected by local and state political conditions, which create their own accountability demands and other constraints and possibilities. In addition, the outcomes of teacher preparation always depend in part on candidates' interactions with one another and how they make sense of their experiences.

As it began its work, the panel acknowledged the difficulty in producing research that examines the impact of teacher preparation on the eventual achievement of pupils in K–12 classrooms. This kind of research depends on a chain of causal evidence with several critical links: empirical evidence demonstrating the link between teacher preparation programs or structures and teacher candidates' learning (i.e., candidates' knowledge growth, skills, and dispositions); empirical evidence demonstrating the link between teacher candidates' learning and their practices in actual classrooms; and empirical evidence demonstrating the link between the practices of graduates of teacher preparation programs and what their pupils learn. Individually each one of these links is complex and challenging to estimate. When they are combined, the challenges are multiplied: There are often substantial time lags between the teacher preparation period and the eventual measures of pupils' achievement; there are many confounding and intervening variables (which are themselves difficult to measure) that influence what teacher candidates are able to do and what their pupils learn; and, the sites where teacher candidates complete fieldwork and eventually teach are quite different from one another in terms of context, school culture, resources available, students, and communities. Unraveling the complicated relationships between and among these variables and the contexts and conditions in which they occur is exceedingly complex, and of course this entire enterprise assumes in the first place that there is consensus about appropriate and valid outcome measures, an assumption that is arguable.

Taken together, the syntheses in this volume suggest that there are not likely to be good answers to the most important questions about teacher preparation unless they are driven by sophisticated theoretical frameworks about the nature of good teaching and the nature of teachers' learning, unless they are built on rich empirical work from both qualitative and quantitative perspectives and from mixed-methods studies, and unless they are designed to take into account the varying social, organizational, and intellectual contexts and conditions of schools, universities, and communities. In this sense, our analyses differ from some contemporary policy reviews, which refer to research to make claims about already-favored preparation programs and routes. The panel's approach is different. We argue that it is not research that tries to determine "who wins" that is most important, but research that helps to identify and explain what the active ingredients are in teacher preparation programs whose graduates have a positive impact on pupils' learning and other important educational outcomes. Research that identifies these active ingredients and the conditions and contexts in which they are most likely to be present is the kind of research that can guide policy and practice in the 21st century.

What Is the Weight of the Evidence About Teacher Preparation?

The work of the AERA Panel is organized around a number of major topics that concern policymakers, teacher educators, and researchers. These include the entry paths and characteristics of those entering the teaching force; the contributions of subject matter study and of education coursework and fieldwork to desired outcomes; the pedagogical approaches used in teacher preparation; the impact of deliberate efforts to prepare teachers for special needs students and for groups traditionally underserved by the schools; the accountability processes typically used in teacher education; and the effects of different program types, organizational structures, and routes.

Readers will note that there is unequal weight in some of the chapters to different efforts in these areas. As the chapters show, this inequality reflects the history, scope, and depth of study on each topic, rather than the differences in the ways the standards of scholarly critique and assessment were applied.

Our analyses also suggest that some of what are considered serious failings in the research on teacher education are more rightly understood as reflections of the field's relative youth and of its history in terms of research priorities and resource allocation. Research on teacher education emerged as an identifiable field separate from research on teaching only during the last half-century. Some of the strengths and limitations of the research reflect this newness. For example, in the current policy context, there are many calls for increased randomized field trials in all areas of education and sharp criticisms of areas where these are lacking. It is worth noting, however, that randomized field trials—whether in medicine or in other lines of research—are generally appropriate at a point in the maturity of the research where enough theoretical and preliminary empirical work has been completed to permit the design of competing interventions that reflect the most promising combinations of components and conditions known to have an impact on the outcomes in question. In teacher education research—where the outcomes in question include teachers' learning, classroom practice, and pupils' achievement—the preliminary theoretical and empirical work does not fully exist. In addition, it also is worth noting that the newly emerging policy imperative is forcing questions that have not been asked of other professions at all, nor have they been previously asked in teacher education.

In addition, as the chapters show, in several areas of the teacher education research, there are primarily small studies conducted in individual courses or seminars by individual teacher educators functioning as researchers. These studies are often carried out to improve practice at a local level. But there have also been very few longitudinal studies or analyses based on national databases. Again it is worth repeating that this dearth of larger and longer studies is the case, at least in part, because teacher education has rarely been either a research priority for funding agencies or a focus of well-supported programmatic research.

Our syntheses reveal that there are promising lines of research in each of the areas we reviewed. Nonetheless, the body of teacher education research that directly addresses desirable pupil and other outcomes and the conditions and contexts within which these outcomes are likely to occur is relatively small and inconclusive. In posing the following questions about teacher preparation, the intention of the panel was to not only build on the promising research lines but also stake out the territory worth pursuing in a new research agenda for teacher education.

TOPIC 1: TEACHER CHARACTERISTICS: RESEARCH ON THE DEMOGRAPHIC PROFILE

Background

There are many current claims and predictions about the number of teachers the nation needs and will need in the near future, how and where they are being prepared to teach, and what career paths they follow into the profession. In particular, there are competing claims about the long- and short-term retention and effectiveness of teachers with differing characteristics. In posing questions about the demographic profile of teachers, the panel was interested in sorting out conflicting claims and providing an empirically accurate but sufficiently complex profile of the demographic characteristics of those entering teaching. (Readers should note that research comparing the impact of teachers certified through "traditional" and "alternative" routes is reviewed under Topic 9.)

Guiding Questions

Who is going into teaching, how are teachers being prepared, what entry routes did they take, and what career paths do they follow?

What We Have Learned About the Topic

Who Are They? Teachers are predominantly female, White, and monolingual. They are currently more likely to have high-school- and college-educated parents than was the case in previous years. Their average age is in the low 40s, reflecting the aging of the teaching force, the older age of college graduates, and the growth of graduate and alternative programs.

Where Are They Prepared? Although there is a growing number of extended, graduate, and alternative programs, most teachers are prepared in baccalaureate programs at public institutions. There is great regional and institutional variation in the distribution of prospective teachers of color. Graduate and alternative programs attract similar or higher proportions of students of color compared to undergraduate teacher preparation programs.

Where Do They Teach?   New first-time teachers represent an increasing proportion of the teaching force. Currently, they are slightly more likely to be male, older, and more diverse than was the case in previous years. They are more likely to find their first jobs in hard-to-staff, low-performing, rural, and central city schools with higher proportions of minority and low-income students.

Alternately prepared teachers, especially teachers of color, are more likely to teach initially in urban schools serving minority and low-income students. Teachers teaching in the suburbs, in high schools, and in the Northeast are more likely to have master's degrees.

How Long Do They Stay?   Reasons for teaching and expectations about staying in teaching show some variation by gender, race and ethnicity, socioeconomic status (SES), and age. Less than half of those prepared to teach actually teach the next year, with prospective elementary teachers more likely to enter teaching than secondary teachers.

Teacher turnover is the largest single determinant of demand for new teachers. The average annual turnover is about 30%, with about 17% switching teaching assignments, about 7% moving to another school, and about 6% leaving teaching altogether. Of those leaving, more than half return to teaching after taking a "break." Age is the prime demographic factor in the 6% attrition rate, with the highest rates of departure among the youngest and oldest teachers. Generally, secondary-school teachers, special education teachers, and teachers in small, private schools exhibit higher attrition rates than others. Research comparing the attrition rates of teachers prepared through alternative and traditional routes and the attrition rates of those prepared in graduate and undergraduate programs yields mixed results.

Impact of Demographic Variables   Although studies indicate that gender of teachers is not related to differences in pupil achievement, research examining the relationship of teachers' race and ethnicity and pupil achievement yields findings that are more mixed.

What We Have Learned About the Research

Empirical evidence confirms, in broad strokes, commonly held assumptions about the current demographic profile of teachers. Yet the lack of up-to-date demographic data limits our knowledge. We know even less about the impact of race and ethnicity imbalances in the demographic profile on teacher practice and student learning.

Data on school staffing from the National Center for Education Statistics are the most comprehensive, but because of the time lag between collection, release, and analysis, the picture it paints is dated. This directly affects the ability of the research and policy communities to determine whether the teaching force is getting more or less diverse in terms of race and ethnicity. Data on the SES background of teachers are not available. Little is known about the reserve pool of teachers.

The data on prospective teachers are less comprehensive than the data on practicing teachers. A major challenge is developing an accurate national picture of teacher candidates in many different types of undergraduate, graduate, and nondegree certification programs within the complex higher education system in 50 different states with different certification requirements.

The usefulness of demographic research is also limited by changing classifications of race and ethnicity and by inconsistent definitions of education major, alternative program, certification status, and teacher turnover. State and local databases that are not linked to one another limit information about what happens to teachers when they leave a particular jurisdiction.

We have limited knowledge about the interaction of teacher characteristics such as race and ethnicity, gender, SES background, and age because few datasets examine these variables in relation to how teachers are prepared, where they teach, and how long they stay in teaching.

The research evidence about impact on pupil outcomes is much slimmer, and although it is characterized as "impact" research, it is largely correlational. Pupil outcomes are usually defined by student achievement test scores rather than by other variables. We know little about the impact on pupil achievement of the interaction of demographic and quality variables, teacher preparation variables, schools and pupil variables, and teacher retention rates.

The Research We Need

Most important, the research and policy communities need to develop a comprehensive, up-to-date demographic profile about prospective teachers, current teachers, and the reserve pool of teachers. We also need to know how demographic variables— separately and together—are related to how teachers are prepared, where they teach, and how long they stay in teaching.

We need a comprehensive database of who is in the teacher education pipeline, utilizing consistent definitions of types of programs and routes.

Given the growing diversity of the student population, the continuing predominance of White teachers, and the general belief in the desirability of a diverse teaching force, demographic research should focus on the race and ethnicity of prospective, current, and reserve pool teachers. Baseline comparisons with other professions would help us understand the lack of diversity among teachers and indicate different policy implications, particularly if the problem is unique to teaching. Further study is needed about the impact of raising entry and certification standards on the number of teachers of color as well as about what happens to teachers of color at various points along the teacher education pipeline. Given the persistent staffing needs in large urban schools and the desire to ensure a diverse teaching staff in all schools, a clearer understanding of the dynamics of hiring, supporting, and retaining teachers of color is also needed. Research needs to examine and take account of the impact of changing demographics of the teacher workforce.

The persistent achievement gap is particularly pronounced between minority–majority students and students from low versus middle- and high-income groups. Given this situation, research should be designed to find out whether and how the nonrepresentative profile and distribution of teachers affects achievement and other pupil outcomes.

It is particularly important that the research and policy communities have access to large, longitudinal databases that take into consideration related student, family, teacher, and school variables to examine the impact of demographic variables. Correlational studies should be supplemented with qualitative research that probes relationships indicated but not explained by large-scale data analyses.

Research must also look beyond the characteristics of individual teacher variables to consider the external forces, such as the civil rights and women's movements, which shape demographic patterns. The changing economy also provides an opportunity to study such factors. Research is needed about whether and how the ethos of the teaching occupation and the structure of schools shape who is attracted to teaching, who prepares to teach, where they teach, and how long they stay.

TOPIC 2: TEACHER CHARACTERISTICS: RESEARCH ON THE INDICATORS OF QUALITY

Background

This second set of questions directly follows from and is the companion to the first set. The intention of the panel here was to provide an analysis of empirical relationships between the demographic profile, as outlined earlier, and the indicators of teacher quality. It was not the intention with this set of questions to analyze all of the literature related to teacher quality, teacher effectiveness, and teacher attributes. Rather, this was limited to research that sheds light on the relationships between and among demographic characteristics, preparation, career paths, and certain indicators of quality. Readers should note that research on the impact of other indicators of quality, such as content majors, teacher tests, and certification, is considered under Topics 3 and 8.

Guiding Questions

What are the relationships between teacher quality and the demographic profile, including teacher preparation, entry routes, and career paths?

What We Have Learned About the Topic

Academic Ability and Achievement   The bleak picture of teachers' academic ability and achievement painted by earlier reports has been modified by recent studies, probably reflecting improvement in both research methods and teacher education reform.

When academic differences among college students are reported, prospective teachers tend to have lower college entry test scores but higher academic achievement as measured by high school grade point average (GPA) and rank and college GPA than do college students in general. These differences, however, may largely reflect gender imbalance in the teaching pool.

More lower ability students exit the teacher education pipeline at successive stages (e.g., high school graduation, college entry, entry into teacher education programs, graduation from college) than do higher ability students.

By graduation, those who have completed teacher preparation programs have higher average SAT/ACT scores than the general pool of students entering college. Although prospective teachers in general have slightly lower average scores when compared to all college graduates, those preparing for secondary teaching have test scores comparable to other college graduates.

Those in the top SAT/ACT quartile are actually less likely to take jobs as teachers, and once teaching, are less likely to stay.

There are some patterns indicating differences in the academic ability, as indicated by test scores and GPA, between Black and White teachers—those preparing for elementary school teaching and those preparing for secondary school teaching—and between male and female teachers.

Teacher Education Programs Most prospective teachers are still prepared in undergraduate programs. However, as state and institutional requirements have changed, more teachers are graduating with regular content-area majors rather than with education majors.

Currently more prospective teachers are graduating from alternative programs than was the case in previous years. Research on the indicators of quality of alternately prepared candidates is inconclusive. Although they are more likely to have content majors, they are not necessarily more likely to have majored in the subject they are teaching.

Teacher Test Scores The relationship between teacher test scores and teacher attrition is inconclusive. However, studies have documented differences among groups on teacher tests used to both enter teacher preparation programs and gain licensure: When compared to other groups, higher average test scores have been found for White teachers graduating from teacher education programs and private universities.

The overall effect of teacher tests is to enhance the test scores of teachers, which has resulted in restricting the diversity of the teaching force.

Certification Status Given the often-used inclusive definitions of certification, most teachers are counted as being "certified," even though they may hold partial, provisional, probationary, or emergency certification. Under these conditions, viewing certified teachers as being "qualified" can be problematic.

The generally high proportion nationwide of certified teachers drops considerably when data about whether teachers are certified in the area in which they teach most of their classes or in the other areas they teach are taken into account.

Teachers in departmentalized school contexts (e.g., many middle and secondary schools) are less likely to be certified in their teaching areas than are elementary teachers. The least likely to be certified are bilingual and special education teachers.

Schools serving high-poverty and high-minority students have more teachers without full certification and more teaching "out of field" compared to schools serving low-poverty and low-minority schools.

Impact of Academic Ability and Achievement Differences in teachers' academic ability may have an impact on public perceptions about the teaching force. However, whether differences in teachers' academic ability and achievement have an impact on pupil achievement is unclear because empirical research findings are mixed.

Although some recent studies provide strong evidence of the relationship between teacher verbal ability and student achievement, there is no evidence about the relative importance of high ability compared to other indicators of teacher quality.

The research suggests that the goal of increasing the diversity of the teaching force and the goal of increasing the academic achievement of teachers by establishing higher GPA and SAT/ACT scores for entry and graduation may be in conflict. Given historical inequities in opportunities and achievement, minority teacher candidates are less likely to meet higher entry requirements.

What We Have Learned About the Research

Some earlier reports about the low academic quality of teachers were the result of misleading research that compared the academic ability and achievement of high school students who intended to teach with those who intended to go into other fields. These high school students are not the same population of students who actually prepare to teach.

Research following cohorts of students through the teacher education pipeline has been particularly informative in understanding changes in the ability and achievement profile of prospective teachers, as has the recognition that the gender and SES distribution of teachers may explain some of the differences between prospective teachers and college students in general.

Conclusions about quality indicators of teachers is limited by the lack of comprehensive, comparative data. Breakdowns by gender, race and ethnicity, SES, and age are also limited. Because of different state and local requirements, it is difficult to compile comparable data and make meaningful interpretations about education majors, teacher tests, certification status, and alternative programs.

Constructing a quality profile is also limited by the use of current indictors that rely heavily on such variables as college entry test scores, GPAs, college majors, teacher tests, and certification status. Without comparable data from other professions, it is difficult to draw conclusions about the academic ability and achievement of the teaching profession. In addition, questions have been raised about whether teachers' intellectual attributes, narrowly defined and measured, capture the qualities important for good teaching.

The few studies that have examined the impact of differences in teacher ability and achievement, largely measured by test scores, have focused on correlations with pupils' test scores, rather than with other outcomes or with differences in teachers' classroom practices.

The Research We Need

The research and policy communities need to develop a comprehensive, timely database on the quality profile of prospective, current, and reserve pool teachers. This should be broken down by demographic variables as well as by information about how teachers are prepared, where they teach, and how long they stay in teaching.

We need comparative research on the academic ability and achievement of college students, in general, and on those who enter teaching as well as other occupations. This should be broken down by demographic variables.

Research should assess the impact of institutional and state policy changes with regard to minimum GPAs, SAT/ACT, and teacher test cutoff scores on the ability and achievement profile and the demographic profile of teacher education students and entering teachers.

We need to develop quality profiles of teachers based more on broadly defined conceptions of academic ability and other personal qualities than on standardized college entry tests.

Although pipeline and other studies focusing on individual teachers is useful, we also need research that looks at how larger social and economic factors, the ethos of the occupation, and the structure of schools shape the quality profile of teachers.

The research community needs to conduct predictive validity studies of GPA, SAT/ACT, and teacher tests in relation to teacher performance and student achievement. But we also need research on teacher quality that expands the conception of pupil outcomes beyond standardized achievement test scores. We need to know how quality and demographic variables interact with and relate to measures of teachers' knowledge, attitudes, practice, and pupil outcomes.

Of particular importance is research that explores whether and how the nonrepresentative distribution of "quality" teachers contributes to the achievement gap among students of different races and ethnicities and SES backgrounds.

The research and policy communities need longitudinal databases with information about pupils, families, teachers, and school variables. These can be used to examine the impact and interaction of quality indicators, but should also be supplemented with qualitative research that probes the relationships indicated but not explained by large-scale data analyses.

In light of claims that verbal ability and content knowledge are the most important attributes of highly qualified teachers, we especially need research that examines the relative contribution of all of the different quality indicators, including the value of teacher education programs, workplace context factors, and teachers' dispositions and personality traits.

TOPIC 3: RESEARCH ON THE EFFECTS OF COURSEWORK IN THE ARTS AND SCIENCES AND IN THE FOUNDATIONS OF EDUCATION

Background

For many years, collegiate teacher preparation programs and now many alternative route programs have been organized around several key components of preparation, including preparation in subject matter, general arts and sciences, the foundations of education, pedagogy and teaching methods, and classroom teaching. The third and fourth sets of questions the panel investigated are companions to each another, posed to investigate the evidence regarding these components. The third set focuses on the evidence regarding the outcomes of teachers' preparation in subject matter knowledge, other arts and sciences content, and knowledge of the foundations of education. (Readers should note that to avoid redundancy, research dealing with culture, multicultural education, and teaching diverse populations is considered under Topic 6, rather than under Topics 3, 4, and 5. Research dealing with preparing teachers to teach pupils with disabilities and special needs is considered under Topic 7.)

Guiding Questions

What are the outcomes of teachers' subject matter preparation; general arts and sciences preparation; and preparation in the foundations of education for teachers' learning, knowledge, and professional practice; and for pupils' learning?

What We Have Learned About the Topic

The Impact of Subject-Specific Study   There is very little research on the impact of subject-specific study on learning except in the area of mathematics. Studies of secondary-school mathematics teachers show a positive association between prospective teachers' college study of mathematics and the mathematics learning of their high school pupils. The implication is that teachers gain valuable teaching knowledge from college mathematics courses. The details about *what* mathematics prospective teachers should study need further examination. The number of studies in other subject areas and for other grade levels is small and inconclusive.

Studies that examine prospective teachers' knowledge of subject matter indicate that a majority of those studied have only a "mechanical" understanding of the subject they will teach. They know rules to follow, but cannot explain the rationale behind the rules.

Studies of the impact of individual subject matter courses (typically studies of a single course, studied for one semester) on prospective teachers are also few in number, again with mathematics being the most frequently studied subject area. These studies typically examine particular instructional modules or techniques, documenting that students gained knowledge in the area the instructor intended, but not addressing general questions about the impact of subject-specific studies on teachers' knowledge.

The Impact of General Arts and Sciences Coursework   Our literature search did not identify any publications that met the criteria for inclusion and examined the impact on prospective teachers' knowledge of arts and science courses outside of the teaching candidate's teaching field.

Because general arts and science coursework occupies a large part of college-based teacher preparation and is also usually included in alternative certification, we looked outside the studies that met our criteria to get some evidence of the effects of the study of arts and sciences on knowledge that might improve teaching performance. In particular, we looked at two standard references on what students learn from going to college, one of which is a literature review.

These sources report that college attendance leads to increases in areas that might be valuable for teachers, including verbal and mathematical skills, general cognitive skills (e.g., being able to evaluate new ideas and techniques), and written and oral communication. The research indicates that college also has a modest effect on social conscience, humanitarian values, and interest in politics. The influence college has on students is related to their field of study, with quantitative skills enhanced more for those college students majoring in areas such as mathematics or engineering, and verbal skills for those majoring in areas such as the social science. There is evidence that writing and rewriting papers help students develop critical thinking ability.

Impact of Education Foundations Courses   The research on the impact of education foundations courses (e.g., educational psychology, sociology of education, philosophy of education, and history of education) on teachers' knowledge is scant. As with studies of the impact of individual subject matter courses (i.e., single courses, typically studied for a single semester), the studies of foundations courses found that prospective teachers learn the content intended by the instructors in special course modules (e.g., about statistical reasoning) or from particular instructional methods (e.g., from analyzing cases in light of course content). Like the studies of individual subject matter courses, the benefit for those outside the institution is largely as a source of promising practices, where promise is based on success in one context and on the practical judgment of the college faculty members who invested in the development and study of these approaches. Put simply, the studies offer evidence about the effects of a small set of instructional practices used in the context of foundations courses, but do not provide evidence about the overall effect of foundations coursework.

What We Have Learned About the Research

Our literature review revealed that the evidence about the effects of arts and sciences courses and educational foundations courses on teachers' knowledge is extremely thin, with the exception of studies about the connections between secondary-school pupils' mathematics achievement and the amount of college mathematics taken by those pupils' teachers. That thin research base can be explained in part by the absence of datasets that include both explicit information about teachers' education and good measures of the outcomes of that education, whether direct measures of teachers' knowledge or pupil achievement data that can be interpreted as a measure of teachers' effectiveness. The thin research base can also be attributed to the difficulty of studying effects in the complex context of teachers' learning. Natural variations among these are difficult to describe and to study. But the success that scholars have had in the work on content study for teaching secondary mathematics demonstrates that the challenges of data gathering and analysis can be overcome.

The research uses a mix of approaches, from regression analyses of national datasets to small studies of individual students in one course. Across the board, the work has limited implications for major policy questions such as the coursework that should be required for teacher certification or the value of additional arts and science or education foundations courses. Although the studies attempt to account for differences in the characteristics of K–12 pupils, they generally do not account for the differences prospective teachers bring to their preparation programs in the first place. Thus, although one can use the association between study of mathematics and pupil achievement to identify which teachers in the current system are most likely to achieve higher pupil gains, those associations do not offer a strong basis for making predictions about the consequences of increasing the mathematics coursework for all new teachers.

The Research We Need

To build greater understanding of the effects on prospective teachers' knowledge of subject matter courses, other arts and science courses, and educational foundations courses, researchers must work on three fronts.

- **Improving measures of teachers' knowledge, skills, and dispositions**. To accumulate knowledge about college courses' effect on teachers' knowledge, the research community needs greater agreement on what effects should be studied and how these outcomes can be measured. Connection to the learning of K–12 pupils is an important criterion for selecting these measures. The connection to pupil learning can be directly addressed by using "value added" as an outcome measure for teacher education, but the temporal and conceptual distance between teacher education and effects on K–12 pupils makes it difficult to attribute effects to particular components of teacher preparation. Thus, research that uses impact on pupil learning as an outcome measure needs to be coupled with studies that explore the connections between teachers' knowledge and pupil learning and with work that looks at the more immediate effects of teacher education coursework on teachers' knowledge.
- **Creating and making use of national and international datasets**. In the last decade, the strongest empirical research base has come from analyses of large, representative national data bases: NAEP, NELS, LSAY. Existing databases may

support additional analyses, both in mathematics and in other subject areas; creation of additional datasets, within the United States and across nations, will allow exploration of new questions. Work at the course level will likely be more productive than attempts to attribute teachers' learning to entire programs. The challenge will be to improve the sophistication of data systems to reach a level of detail beyond course counts.

- **Drawing on other research on learning to sharpen the vocabulary for describing college coursework.** In national surveys, courses are described only by general content area (biological science vs. physical science) and level (undergraduate vs. graduate). Those differences matter, but each category covers an enormous range of variability. To build understanding, a more precise, commonly shared vocabulary is needed, which can highlight features with the greatest promise for influencing teachers' learning.

TOPIC 4: RESEARCH ON METHODS COURSES AND FIELD EXPERIENCES

Background

As noted previously, the panel approached the fourth set of questions as a companion to the third set. This fourth set focuses on the evidence regarding the outcomes of teacher candidates' preparation in teaching methods and supervised classroom teaching. (Again, readers should note that in order to avoid redundancy, research dealing with methods courses and fieldwork preparing teachers to teach traditionally underserved populations is considered under Topic 6, rather than under Topics 3, 4, and 5. Research dealing with methods courses and fieldwork preparing teachers to teach pupils with disabilities and special needs is considered under Topic 7.)

Guiding Questions

What are the outcomes of preparation in teaching methods and in student teaching and other fieldwork and classroom experiences for teachers' learning and knowledge, teachers' professional practice, and pupils' learning? This set focuses on the evidence regarding the outcomes of preparation in teaching methods and supervised classroom teaching.

What We Have Learned About the Topic

Our literature review revealed that in many instances methods courses and fieldwork experiences are tightly connected aspects of teaching candidates' pre-student teaching experiences. The instructors of methods courses who are reporting on their research often state that they are working from an assumption that prospective teachers' beliefs before they begin a course or field experience must be addressed, particularly when their beliefs run counter to research on student learning. These researchers examine changes in beliefs and the relationships among beliefs and actual teaching methods. Therefore the term *method* has come to signify something more complex than learning a set of teaching techniques.

Methods Courses   Across the studies it is clear that the term *methods course* has evolved from a training environment in which specific strategies are transmitted and practiced or from a text- and lecture-based environment. The researchers see teaching and learning as very interactive and at times even collaborative. Methods courses are seen as complex and unique sites in which instructors work simultaneously with prospective teachers' beliefs, teaching practices, and creation of identities. A methods course is seldom defined as a class that transmits information about particular methods of instruction and ends with a final exam.

Methods courses and field experiences can impact prospective teachers' thoughts about practice and actual teaching practices, but implementing a practice based on one's beliefs is neither linear nor simple. Simply intending to engage in a desirable teaching practice is insufficient. The research documents numerous situations in which prospective teachers and even teacher educators want to teach in desirable ways but are not able to move easily from intention to action.

Across content areas and across elementary- and secondary-school settings, the studies document that prospective teachers often feel conflict among the messages they receive from differing university instructors, field-based teacher educators, and school settings. It is also the case that prospective teachers resist coherent messages when they find it difficult to engage in recommended practices. When field placements reinforce and support the practices advocated by the teacher education program, individuals may still resist changing their own beliefs or practices because they are personally uncomfortable with the competing beliefs and practices. Teaching practices and beliefs are mediated by numerous factors, including their prior beliefs and experiences, coursework, and current perceptions of curriculum, students, and pedagogy.

Field Sites   When the teaching practices that are allowed and encouraged by teachers in field experiences are congruent with the teaching practices advocated by teacher education program instructors, it is much easier to help prospective teachers move from simply wanting to implement a desired practice to actually being able to do so.

Professional development schools and other collaborative models are examples of sites that not only exhibit such congruence but also are perceived as beneficial professional learning opportunities for both experienced teachers and prospective teachers. There is also some indication that the students in professional development schools also benefit from collaborative arrangements.

What We Have Learned About the Research

Research on methods courses and field experiences is increasing over time and across the content areas. Much of the current research on methods and fieldwork is conducted by teacher educators interested in learning about the impact of their own courses.

Researchers have examined teacher candidates' actions, reactions, and beliefs about the nature of subject matter knowledge, such as studies of candidates' understandings of what constitutes mathematics and mathematical learning or studies of their understandings of pupils' reading preferences and abilities. Much of the research is concerned with how new teachers are socialized into the profession or how their beliefs and actions do and do not change as a function of methods courses and field experiences.

There is a growing attempt to study teacher candidates as they begin student teaching, and there are beginning to be more year-long studies of students that begin in methods courses and follow the students as they apply their course work during student teaching, as opposed to studies that begin and end with one course. There are still only very few studies in which the graduates of teacher education programs are followed into the first years of teaching. In addition, there is almost no joint inquiry conducted by university researchers and classroom teachers in professional development schools or other collaborative settings.

Qualitative methods relying on observations and interviews are predominant in the literature. Typically, researchers select one to three preservice students to illustrate dominant trends in students' responses during the course and field experience. Case study designs are the methods researchers use most often, which necessarily limit any causal claims or any efforts to generalize. There are few quantitative studies examining the impact of methods course or field experiences on immediate practice and virtually none that examine impact on long practice over time or on students' learning once the novice teachers are in charge of their own classrooms.

Research within any particular content area is seldom informed by research in a different content area, and researchers across content areas seldom address common questions.

There is wide variation in the extent of detail provided on data collection and analysis procedures, with some studies offering minimal information. This makes following the trail from research questions to conclusions very difficult.

The Research We Need

We need more studies within and across content areas that use similar conceptual or theoretical frameworks, questions, and methods in different settings and with varying populations. We need well-conceptualized, long-term programs of research in this area. Currently there are too few studies investigating similar questions and starting from similar theoretical bases to enable us to learn by aggregating across studies. The ability to aggregate is critical if we hope to learn about more and less effective practices as advocated by teacher education programs.

In addition, there is little research that includes the perspectives, questions and voices of cooperating teachers and prospective teachers. Instead the voices and perspectives of university-based researchers predominate. We need to examine the perspectives of the diverse participants involved in conducting, interpreting, and reporting on research. We need to pay attention to differences in racial and linquistic backgrounds, as well as differences in role groups and research methodologies.

We also need research frameworks that go beyond simply studying teaching techniques or, on the other hand, simply studying teachers' thinking. We need research that examines the interactions of these as well as how they relate to pupil outcomes. We also need frameworks that go beyond a limited focus on the individual, either alone or in a group. These frameworks need to be more complex and be informed by sophisticated knowledge about how practice is shaped not only by what individuals may believe or hope to achieve but also by contexts, materials, and other people.

Many of the studies about the impact of teacher preparation coursework and fieldwork treat teacher candidates' beliefs and attitudes as outcomes. However we need research that examines the impact of coursework and fieldwork on other outcomes, such as on teachers' practices and knowledge growth, and we need well-developed measures to assess these.

An approach to research that would enable several researchers using complementary, but mixed, methodologies that combine internally and externally generated analyses of teaching and learning would not only enable us to discern trends across analyses but also help us guard against the power relations that are obtained when data collection and analysis are only conducted within an instructor's own course or program.

It is important to commit both financial and temporal resources to conduct research across many varieties of teacher education settings, including teaching without any formal preparation, and programs based in universities that are not located in research-intensive universities and departments. We also need teacher education research structures that encourage collaboration and long-term work—structures that are not currently embedded in traditional promotion and tenure arrangements and even less in schools and school districts. Field sites and those who work in them are responsible for far more than participating in research, and an expectation of such may decrease schools' willingness to accept prospective teachers. We do not have institutions (schools or classrooms) dedicated to promoting field-based research, and we have policies that discourage experimental designs or quasiexperimental designs that investigate variations among prospective teachers' learning, development, practice, or impact in varying field settings, teaching methods, or entire teacher education programs.

TOPIC 5: RESEARCH ON PEDAGOGICAL APPROACHES IN TEACHER EDUCATION

Background

There are a number of pedagogical approaches that are widely used in teacher education. The panel's intention with this question was to review the literature on pedagogical approaches in teacher education, particularly the teaching methods, strategies, instructional approaches, assignments, and learning opportunities common to teacher education programs and projects at many institutions and within many program types. The panel was interested in what evidence existed regarding the contributions of particular pedagogical strategies to teacher preparation outcomes and the contexts and conditions under which these occur.

Guiding Questions

What are the outcomes of the pedagogies used in teacher preparation (specifically the various instructional strategies and experiences commonly used in teacher education courses, projects, and programs) for teachers' learning and knowledge and professional practice and for pupils' learning? Under what conditions and in what contexts do these outcomes occur?

What We Have Learned About the Topic

The literature on teacher education pedagogy focuses on how teacher candidates are taught and how various approaches affect what they learn. The research reviewed in this chapter focuses on five approaches: laboratory experiences, case methods, video and hypermedia materials, portfolios, and practitioner research.

Laboratory Experiences The studies of laboratory experiences include both microteaching and computer simulations, with the majority of studies focusing on training preservice teachers in the use of specific skills that researchers posit are related to effective teaching. Studies in this area are strongly rooted in principles of behavioral psychology, reflecting in part the historical context of these studies. The behavioral model also underlies the pedagogical approach, with its emphasis on feedback and targeting of specific skills. The primary outcome investigated in these studies is teacher behavior, although a few more recent studies look at teacher cognition as the outcome. Studies suggest that microteaching and computer simulations can help students develop targeted skills. However, little research has looked at how the preservice teachers might use these skills in the context of actual classrooms.

Case Methods   Despite enthusiasm for "the case idea," there is more descriptive work about what people are doing in their teacher education classrooms than systematic studies of how case-based pedagogy influences teacher candidates' learning. The available studies provide initial evidence that cases may help improve the reasoning skills of preservice teachers, enabling them to identify issues and analyze an educational problem more effectively. It is also clear from the research that the instruction around cases matters not only in the use of case materials per se but also in candidates' learning. This suggests that it may be worthwhile to study the instructional interactions around case methods. A small body of research has looked at the substantive knowledge preservice teachers gain from reading cases. Finally, several researchers argue that case-based analyses and discussions can reveal the thinking of preservice teachers, giving teacher educators a better window into how their students think. Most of the research in this area focuses on cognitive outcomes. Because existing studies have not looked at impact on practice, the field lacks evidence that the use of case-based pedagogy affects preservice teachers' classroom practice.

Video and Hypermedia Materials   A number of studies found that preservice teachers had positive attitudes about the uses of interactive video, and several studies found that viewing videotapes can improve preservice teachers' understanding of a teaching strategy or concept. A few of these studies tried to untangle what preservice teachers learned from videotapes as opposed to what they learned from other approaches, such as role-plays, live observations, or written materials. These studies suggest that video materials can be at least as effective as other approaches in helping teacher candidates learn about instructional approaches. However, the studies do not reveal whether preservice teachers were better able to implement these approaches in classrooms.

Portfolios   The research suggests that the portfolios used in teacher education share some common elements (lesson plans and reflective pieces), and most serve at least the dual purpose of helping teacher candidates reflect on their practice and assessing their learning. The research suggests that how portfolios are used in the context of teacher education influences teacher candidates' perceptions of their value. Even within the same preparation program, teacher candidates had different views of the value of portfolios depending on particular instructors and the quality of the feedback provided. Despite the challenges of constructing portfolios, most teacher candidates seemed to value the process. However, despite the claim that portfolios can contribute to preservice teachers' ability to reflect on their practice, only one study looked at how the portfolio assignment affected the content of teacher candidates' reflections.

Practitioner Research   Although many teacher educators value practitioner research, there is little empirical evidence about the outcomes of engagement in practitioner research during preservice teacher education. Studies suggest that student teachers find it difficult to find the time to engage in sustained inquiry while student teaching and that negotiating their research agendas with their cooperating teachers can be challenging. Placing student teachers with more experienced teacher-researchers can ease the difficulty of these negotiations and provide teacher candidates with not only support but also a perspective on teaching that is inquiry oriented. However, there is little evidence that engaging in practitioner research affects actual classroom practice.

What We Have Learned About the Research

The most recent research in this area is almost exclusively qualitative and consists largely of studies conducted by teacher educators on their own programs. The studies generally examine only one pedagogical approach (e.g., case methods or use of portfolios) and seldom compare the effectiveness of different pedagogical approaches. The studies in this area generally do not provide extensive information on how particular pedagogical approaches are implemented, or on how an approach used in a specific course relates to approaches used in other parts of the curriculum.

The outcomes investigated in these studies range from shifts in perceptions, changes in knowledge and beliefs, changes in the ability to reflect or identify issues—all cognitive outcomes of one form or another—to attitudes toward the pedagogy or feelings of self-efficacy—more affective outcomes. Few, if any, of these studies attempted to investigate the difficult problem of the relationships among pedagogy used in teacher education, the practices of beginning teachers, and the learning of their students (Wilson, Floden, & Ferrini-Mundy, 2001). The shifting nature of outcomes in this research makes any form of meta-analysis or aggregation of results difficult if not impossible. The studies are simply not looking for the same thing. But even when different researchers attempt to study a common outcome, they generally use different instruments or analytic procedures, leading to a wide variability in methodology. Our field does not yet have a tradition of using similar instruments or common ways of analyzing data, and, in fact, few common tools exist for studying student teachers' learning.

Finally, very little research in this area, other than the research on microteaching, is truly programmatic in nature. A few researchers have continued to study facets of case methods over time, but there are relatively few examples of research programs in this area.

The Research We Need

To build a more robust understanding of the outcomes of various pedagogical approaches in teacher education, we will need more programmatic research that is well grounded in theory. The most useful theoretical frameworks would go beyond the particulars of a specific pedagogical approach to help us understand more broadly the relationship between the pedagogies of professional education and those of professional practice.

A program of research in this area should encompass a broader territory than a single instance of a pedagogical approach—such as the use of portfolios in one teacher education program—and then investigate that territory more deeply and systematically. For example, the emerging research on case-based pedagogy might develop into a program of research in which researchers investigate how different kinds of cases—textual, video, and hypermedia cases—used in different contexts influence what prospective teachers learn with regard to a variety of outcomes, including cognitive outcomes such as ability to reason through a classroom dilemma as well as outcomes related to classroom practices. Such programmatic research could also investigate interactions between particular pedagogical approaches and characteristics of either the prospective teachers or the programmatic contexts in which the approaches are used. A program of research might also involve more explicitly comparative work, very little of which currently exists.

Finally, researchers in this area need better tools for studying the outcomes of teacher education. In order to understand more about how different forms of pedagogy result in different kinds of outcomes, we need better tools for understanding distinct facets of teacher learning. If researchers could borrow from a common set of toolkits for looking at teacher learning as a field, we might find ourselves working on the same problem in ways that allow us more easily to build on each other's work. As a field, research on teacher education has spent relatively little time developing the tools of the trade. Yet, if researchers want to be able to build on each other's work, they may also need to use more common tools for both data collection and data analysis.

TOPIC 6: RESEARCH ON PREPARING TEACHERS FOR DIVERSE POPULATIONS

Background

A major challenge facing teacher education today is preparing teachers with the knowledge, skills, and dispositions to work successfully with an increasingly diverse pupil population, particularly with those whose cultural, language, racial, and ethnic backgrounds differ from those of the mainstream and with those who live in poor urban and rural areas. The panel wanted to know what evidence existed about the contributions to teacher preparation outcomes of deliberate efforts to prepare teachers to work with these groups and in these settings and the contexts and conditions under which these outcomes occur.

Guiding Questions

What is the research base for preparing teachers to be effective in teaching traditionally underserved student populations and students in traditionally underserved areas? What is known about the conditions and contexts under which specific efforts to prepare teachers for work with these populations contribute to teacher education outcomes?

What We Have Learned About the Topic

The literature on preparing teacher candidates to teach underserved populations has been organized in this chapter around four aspects of the preparation of preservice teachers: candidates' predispositions, preservice preparation of prospective teachers, the experiences of teacher candidates of color, and program evaluations.

Candidates' Predispositions   Studies of candidates' predispositions are based on the premise that teachers' knowledge frames and belief structures are the filters through which their practices, strategies, actions, interpretations, and decisions are made. This means that knowledge and beliefs play an important mediating role in what candidates learn during their teacher education programs and also how and what they teach once they are in classrooms. Studies reveal that in addition to being White and middle-class females, the majority of teacher candidates are from suburbs or small towns and have limited experience with those from cultures or areas different from their own. Although many have negative attitudes and beliefs about those different from themselves, they often say they are willing to teach in urban areas.

Preparation of Teacher Candidates   Many of the studies about the preparation of teacher candidates for work with underserved populations can be grouped according to their focus on prejudice reduction, equity pedagogy, field experiences, and the experiences of candidates of color. Studies of prejudice reduction reveal that prior experiences, early socialization, and ways of thinking influence teacher candidates' attitudes and beliefs. A variety of teacher education practices intended to reduce prejudice in teacher candidates have been studied. The majority yield short-term positive impacts on candidates' attitudes and beliefs. However, none of these studies is longitudinal and none includes followups of candidates' beliefs and attitudes.

Equity pedagogy refers to the use of students' cultural and experiential background to facilitate learning and to provide students with the skills necessary to support the development of a more equitable society. This includes creating curriculum and instruction based on students' backgrounds, fostering self-determination, and attending to oppressed and underserved groups. Studies in science methods courses and in language arts methods courses suggest that how candidates understand subject matter can either interfere with or support their openness to equity pedagogy. In some methods courses, teacher candidates can learn and apply knowledge of equity pedagogy to their planning of classroom instruction. Studies that focus on teacher candidates' learning about equity pedagogy do not reveal the extent to which candidates are actually able to implement equity pedagogy to improve the academic performance of students of color.

Studies about field experiences intended to prepare candidates to work with underserved populations focus on community-based fieldwork, relocating candidates to urban settings, candidates' responses and emphases in urban settings, the use of biographies and storytelling, and the application of multicultural knowledge to classroom practice. Most of these studies indicate short-term positive impacts, including enhanced awareness, sensitivity, and acceptance of those from other cultural backgrounds. The studies also identify candidates' concerns about understanding, instructing, motivating, and developing relationships with their students and mentors. Studies suggest there are limited opportunities for candidates to implement or observe multicultural practices in classrooms.

Studies about the experiences of teacher candidates of color reveal that teacher candidates currently find teaching a less attractive career, as apposed to how it was regarded in previous years, and they confront more barriers to admission than do their White counterparts. They also often face financial, social, and personal difficulties and are hindered by inadequate academic preparation. Candidates of color are more likely to come from working-class backgrounds and have a better understanding of inequities in the society and a stronger commitment to social justice than do their

White counterparts. There is some evidence that candidates of color benefit from cohort placements or programs with a focus on social justice and preparation for diversity.

Program Evaluations   Studies of programs reveal that a small number of university programs offer carefully crafted programs that prepare candidates to teach students from diverse populations. However, many programs do not yet have the capacity to address cultural and linguistic diversity. Studies that followed teacher candidates once they left the program found that program emphases did not necessarily translate to school practices.

What We Have Learned About the Research

The majority of studies on the preparation of candidates for diverse students are qualitative. Most of these qualitative studies are conducted in a single course or field experience, drawing on narrative data from course assignments, field notes, and transcriptions of classroom observations. Because most of these studies do not include much information about the larger context of the teacher education program, it is difficult to account for the impact of the program and other variables. This is especially true of self-studies conducted by instructors in their own courses. In the research on field experiences, little information is provided about the field site or the experiences and preparation of the supervising practitioners. This information is important in accounting for the impact of a particular intervention and for looking at the impact of an intervention across studies.

The majority of the quantitative studies employ surveys or questionnaires focused on candidates' beliefs and attitudes. These follow traditional survey research designs for data collection, analysis, and reporting. Some researchers used self-constructed surveys and questionnaires that had not been validated, or the validation procedures were not described. The majority of the quantitative studies addressed the predispositions of candidates upon entering a teacher preparation program and upon completion. Limitations characteristic of many of the studies on the preparation of candidates for diverse students included short-term investigations of candidates' behaviors, experiences and attitudes during teacher preparation programs without followup to practice in the field; small sample sizes that may not have been representative of the larger population from which the sample was drawn; and self-studies in courses taught by the researcher. These characteristics limit the trustworthiness and transferability of the findings from these studies.

The Research We Need

Research is needed to identify particular attributes, prior knowledge, and background experiences that increase the probability for learning to teach diverse students. The existing research shows the short-term impact of specific approaches used during teacher preparation on candidates' attitudes, beliefs, and classroom practices; however, this research does not track candidates based on their characteristics upon entering teacher preparation programs to determine whether some candidates are more likely than others to learn to teach diverse students based on the characteristics they bring to teacher preparation. Also, research is needed on the academic and experiential preparation needed by teacher educators to support candidates in learning to teach diverse students. More needs to be known about approaches to professional development for teacher educators who have had little contact with diverse students in elementary and secondary schools and who have not spent a great deal of time in diverse and urban communities.

Much of the research on prejudice reduction indicates short-term benefits; however, there is need for longitudinal and follow-up studies that investigate the sustainability of these gains in actual teaching situations with diverse student populations. We need to inquire into how candidates who receive training in prejudice reduction accompanied by training in traditional content methodology compare with their peers who receive training in prejudice reduction combined with training in content-specific equity pedagogy in their ability to adapt instruction to the needs of diverse and underserved student populations. Also, more research is needed to determine the impact of training in general multicultural concepts on candidates' classroom practices.

The majority of the studies on the preparation of candidates for diverse students were qualitative; however, most were lacking rich descriptions of the context of the teacher preparation programs. Rich descriptive studies are needed that clearly document the internal operation of teacher education programs and that show how courses within a program are related to one another and to field experiences. Survey studies and qualitative studies employing informal and structured interviews with cooperating teachers and other practitioners who support candidates' field experiences that reveal their academic and professional preparation, their understanding of the teacher preparation program with which they are affiliated, and their attitudes and beliefs related to diverse populations are needed to better inform practices related to field experiences. Such studies can be used as a basis for understanding how to construct programs that better prepare candidates for diverse students. Studies employing mixed methodological approaches are needed to show the relationship between the preparation of candidates and learning outcomes of the diverse student.

Finally, studies on the preparation of teachers of color reveal differences in their background experiences and in the challenges they face in gaining entrance into the profession, when compared to White candidates. A few studies found that candidates of color had limited opportunities during student teaching to use their cultural insider knowledge when teaching students with similar cultural and experiential backgrounds; however, these studies did not indicate how candidates of color were supported in learning to apply their cultural insider knowledge to professional practice. Experimental studies are needed to provide a comparison of the performance of candidates of color, to provide support for learning, and to apply cultural insider knowledge to professional practice with candidates of color who have not had such training.

TOPIC 7: RESEARCH ON PREPARING TEACHERS TO WORK WITH STUDENTS WITH DISABILITIES

Background

Nearly all teachers currently teach classes comprised of pupils with a wide range of abilities and disabilities. The panel wanted to know what evidence existed about the contributions of deliberate efforts to prepare teachers to work with pupils with disabilities and the contexts and conditions under which these outcomes occur. The focus of this set of questions was not on the preparation of educational specialists whose particular area of expertise is working with pupils with disabilities, but on the preparation of general education teachers to teach groups of pupils that include those with disabilities.

Guiding Questions

What is the research base for preparing teachers to be effective in teaching students with disabilities? What is known about the conditions and contexts under which specific efforts to prepare teachers for work with pupils with disabilities contribute to teacher education outcomes?

What We Have Learned About the Topic

In general, the field of teacher education has demonstrated a commitment to including preparation for teaching students with disabilities as a normative expectation for preservice programs. This commitment is visible in requirements in the majority of states that prospective teachers study special education and in national standards for individual teacher candidates and teacher education programs that address teaching students with disabilities. Preservice students are concerned with acquiring the knowledge and skills to help them work well with students with disabilities and view this as part of their professional responsibility.

Preservice students expect their preservice programs to provide experiences and instruction that will ensure they have the range of knowledge and skills needed to teach students with disabilities. Although there is evidence that preservice students can gain confidence in this regard, they do not uniformly believe they are well prepared for this responsibility.

Relatively few studies of pedagogy for preparing general education teachers to work with students with disabilities have been conducted. Among them, modest indications are emerging that cases and problem-based learning are starting to be implemented to address this issue.

Often teacher education programming relies on the delivery of special education content and application by general teacher education faculty, either alone or in collaboration with special education faculty. General teacher education faculty who have responsibility for providing instruction in working with students with disabilities do not always feel prepared for or confident in their roles delivering instruction on topics related to teaching students with disabilities.

Understanding the relationship between disability as a form of diversity and diversity of race, class, culture, and language is limited. Special educators who are concerned about diversity of race, class, culture, and language present these topics in the teacher education literature in special education as a means of providing a general understanding of the issues for professionals in the field. The specific, complex relationship among diversities is not typically addressed.

What We Have Learned About the Research

The attitudes teacher education candidates hold toward working with students with disabilities is a dominant focus of the research. Studies indicate that preservice students' attitudes are concerned with acquiring the knowledge and skills to be successful with students with disabilities. These studies contrast with early studies of teacher attitudes, which focused on the global disposition to support or reject inclusive education.

It appears that for the most part prospective teachers accept this responsibility but are worried about how to carry it out.

Research is most often conducted within instructors' preservice classes as a form of self-study by teacher educators. This small-scale research is often conducted by faculty in special education and sometimes by teams of special and general teacher educators. In these studies, outcomes are often measured in terms of preservice students' perceptions on a variety of issues related to working with students with disabilities.

Despite the trend toward preparing prospective teachers to work with students with disabilities, few studies of program effects have been conducted. When they have, measures of P-12 student learning for students with disabilities are not usually selected as outcome measures.

The Research We Need

There is a pressing need to conduct longitudinal research on program effects so that we can begin to answer the question: How well are programs preparing graduates to foster learning for their students who have disabilities? These studies need to include not only measures of pre-service candidates' knowledge and skills, but also outcome measures for P-12 students with disabilities.

The growing number of programs based on collaboration across general and special education provide an opportunity for joint, cross-institutional programmatic research that is aligned and that uses the same variables and the same instruments across several institutions of higher education. Research consortia should be considered as a major focus of future efforts.

We do not have documentation on what actually takes place in general teacher education classes with regard to working with students with disabilities. How do general teacher education faculty actually address this topic? To unpack this black box phenomenon, qualitative studies of faculty discourse across general teacher education classes are needed. For example, what is actually said or done in the name of accommodation and modification within general methods classes? How are general education pedagogies connected and applied specifically to working with students with disabilities?

As a function of longitudinal research, qualitative studies of preservice student decision making about pedagogies and curriculum for students with disabilities are needed. What pedagogies are considered to be appropriate for students with disabilities, and what pedagogies are actually implemented? What choices are being made with regard to the complexity of the curriculum?

In addition to studies about how disability is addressed in methods classes, qualitative studies are also needed on how disability is addressed in classes on multicultural education. How is the relationship between diversity of race, class, culture, and language, on the one hand, and disability, on the other, presented? We also need research that tracks how teacher education grapples with changes in classification regulations.

As the use of portfolios continues to increase, qualitative studies of portfolio entries on diversity are needed to document the choices teacher education students make in portraying their knowledge and skills. Do they address diversity generally? Do they use disability as the only example of diversity? Do they address issues of race, class, culture, and language and not of disability, or vice versa? What practices are described as evidence of meeting the needs of students with disabilities? A critical research-related issue is the development of frameworks that organize and conceptualize how we ought to consider outcomes for different students with different needs.

TOPIC 8: RESEARCH ON ACCOUNTABILITY PROCESSES IN TEACHER EDUCATION

Background

Teacher preparation across the nation is governed by a number of governmental and nongovernmental accountability processes and procedures. The most common of these are state-regulated initial certification of new teachers, state-required teacher tests for initial licensing, and voluntary professional accreditation of teacher preparation programs and institutions. The panel wanted to know what evidence existed about the effectiveness of these accountability processes and their impacts on various measures of teacher quality. (Readers should note that research comparing teachers certified through "traditional" and "alternative" routes is considered under Topic 9, rather than under Topic 8. Research about the relationship between accountability procedures and teacher quality indicators—for example, between teacher tests and the academic ability of teacher candidates—is considered under Topic 2 rather than under Topic 8.)

Guiding Questions

What is the research base for the range of accountability processes currently used in teacher preparation, specifically certification, teacher testing, and accreditation? What is known about the outcomes of these processes for teachers' learning and knowledge and teachers' professional practice and for pupils' learning?

What We Have Learned About the Topic

Certification   Certification is the process by which states assess the qualifications of individuals to teach. Individual states are responsible for certifying and licensing teachers; most states award an initial teaching certificate after successful completion of an approved preparation program. All states require that teacher candidates possess a B.A. in education or in a content area. Most states also require that teacher candidates have some supervised student teaching experience, which varies from 9 to 18 weeks. The literature on certification is limited, but the weight of the evidence generally favors certification over noncertification or undercertification, as measured by student achievement.

Testing   Forty-two states require some form of teacher testing. Teacher tests can include tests of basic skills, general knowledge, subject matter knowledge, or professional knowledge. Unlike other professions where the same test is used across most states, over 600 tests are currently used in the United States. The research on teacher testing is outdated, focusing primarily on tests that are no longer in use. The research that does exist suggests that such tests have content and concurrent validity. However, there is very little evidence that such tests have predictive validity—that is, there is little evidence that there is a relationship between teachers' scores on such tests and their teaching success (measured in terms of teacher behavior, principal ratings, or student achievement).

Accreditation   Accreditation is the process by which an institution (a college or university) provides evidence to the public and other institutions of its program's soundness and rigor. All states require that teacher preparation programs receive state approval, which is typically based on state standards. Approval standards and licensure requirements are unique to each state. Unlike other professions such as architecture, medicine, and law, national accreditation is not required in teacher education. Over half of the approximately 1,300 teacher education programs in the United States are regionally accredited by the two national accrediting organizations.

The research on accreditation is primarily informational. Most published articles describe the process of participating in accreditation review and feature recommendations for other institutions as they prepare for reviews. Empirical studies on the impact of accreditation policies and processes are almost nonexistent.

What We Have Learned About the Research

Given the impassioned debates around accountability in teacher education, it is both surprising and troubling that there is so little relevant empirical research. Teacher tests are often locally- or nationally-developed tests that are adapted to state requirements and needs. This makes it difficult to compare teacher testing results across states. The developers of teacher tests do not claim that these tests have predictive validity (that higher scoring candidates will be better teachers), even though the tests are often used in policy environments in which such claims are made.

Typical research on teacher testing has focused on validating the concurrent or content validity of tests, not their predictive validity. Furthermore, because teacher testing is a state level decision, contrasting the effects of teacher tests on the teacher pool—does the use of such tests improve teacher quality?—is nearly impossible: Either everyone in a state takes a test or does not. We found one study that took advantage of a natural experiment—the suspension of the teacher testing requirement for a few years—to examine the effects on the teacher candidate pool.

Typical research in this area attempts to correlate teacher test scores with other measures of college success, for example, grade point average in liberal arts and teacher education classes. A few studies examine the relationship between teacher test scores and locally developed measures of teacher classroom behavior, student achievement, or other measures of teacher effectiveness. In some cases, researchers found significant relationships between teacher test scores and student achievement.

The Research We Need

The use and impact of accountability processes related to teacher preparation is a research domain in need of sustained, intensive work. First, we need research about the current tests being used, including research on their content, and concurrent, predictive, and consequential validity. Further, we need research that explores alternative formats and arrangements for teacher testing. All of the research on teacher testing needs to be much more subtle and sophisticated in its recognition of important variations in tests and their use. In particular, we need to do research on whether and how different state policies concerning teacher testing have an impact on student achievement and effective instruction.

In terms of future research on teacher certification, we need to understand the multiple forms of certification that exist within and across states. This includes understanding the variability in what one form of certification (e.g., emergency credentials) might exist. In addition, we have almost no research on the impact of teacher certification in areas other than mathematics teaching. We need to broaden the fields investigated to include both the full range of subject matters in which teachers are certified and the grade levels. We also need research that compares teacher certification processes with those of other professions and examines the impact of these.

Given the often fuzzy line between certification and licensure, it is important to separate the two processes in research and look for the differential effects of one or the other. Finally, because certification is most often the combination of a number of different requirements (completion of a subject matter major or B.A., completion of a teacher education program, teacher testing, and other requirements), research needs to be designed to investigate the relative contributions of the individual proxies that are used to make the certification decision.

With so little existing research, almost any research in the area of program accreditation would help, particularly studies of the impact of accreditation policies and processes. In particular, the field would benefit from studies that linked program accreditation with impact measures, including pupil learning and effective instruction. Given the coexistence of several different models of accreditation (TEAC, NCATE, state reviews that involve primarily paperwork, and state reviews that involve visiting teams), it also seems appropriate to conduct research on the relative effectiveness of different models of accreditation.

TOPIC 9: RESEARCH ON TEACHER EDUCATION PROGRAMS

Background

One of the most heavily debated issues in teacher education has to do with the effectiveness of different kinds of teacher education programs and entry routes into teaching. Many states now permit multiple entry routes into teaching, some of which require very limited professional preparation prior to the assumption of full responsibility for a classroom. This chapter examines the research evidence related to the impact of different structures of preservice teacher education programs on various aspects of teacher recruitment and retention, teacher quality, and student learning.

Guiding Questions

What is the evidence related to the impact of different forms of preservice teacher education on teacher recruitment, teacher retention, teacher quality, and student learning? The comparisons examined in this summary are 4- and 5-year programs, state-sponsored alternative programs and traditional programs (4-year undergraduate or 5-year university-based extended programs), university-sponsored alternative programs and traditional programs, school-district-sponsored alternative programs and traditional programs, and comparisons of multiple programs. Several in-depth case studies of multiple teacher education programs are also examined for what they can teach us about examining teacher education programs and teacher learning during preservice teacher education.

What We Have Learned About the Topic

Though the research has examined the effects of different program structures, because of the significant amount of variation that exists within teacher education institutions, in programs of a given structural type (e.g., 4-year undergraduate program) and in state policy contexts, it does not make sense to attempt to define program effectiveness according to the general structural characteristics of programs alone.

Studies comparing the effectiveness of various kinds of traditional and alternative teacher education programs and 4-year versus 5-year programs in relation to a variety of outcomes generally provide conflicting findings about the efficacy of different forms of teacher preparation and do not enable us to identify the specific program features that are related to the achievement of particular outcomes. Across the studies, there is a lack of information about the programs, about the teachers who enter the programs, and about the places teachers teach after program completion. These omissions, together with the vague criteria often used to assess teaching, limit the value of these studies in helping us understand the relative impact of different kinds of alternative and traditional programs on aspects of teacher quality and student learning.

The four case studies reviewed in this summary represent efforts by researchers to probe more deeply into teacher education programs, the opportunities that they provide for teacher learning, what teachers actually learn, and the identification of program characteristics that are responsible for desired outcomes. Although the researchers do not establish clear links between evidence in their data and characteristics of program excellence, these studies provide examples of how researchers can more carefully study the process of teacher education.

Regardless of the type of teacher education program completed, the subject matter specialization of teachers seems to matter in terms of teacher retention. Specifically secondary mathematics teachers sometimes had lower retention rates than did teachers in other subject areas.

There is some evidence that during the beginning of their first year of teaching, teachers with no or minimal preservice professional preparation prior to becoming teachers of record perform at a lower level of competence than do teachers who have completed either traditional or alternative programs with significant professional preparation. Although the former group appears to "catch up" to the later group by the end of the year, the students who are assigned to teachers during the period of catching up may suffer academic losses by being taught by teachers with minimal professional preparation.

Only four studies were reviewed that attempted to connect teacher education programs to student learning. Although three of these studies used various forms of matching and controls in an attempt to isolate the effects of teacher education programs, none of these studies is free from methodological weaknesses that rule out alternative explanations for the findings. Also, very limited information is provided in these studies about the programs being compared, which makes it impossible to link the findings back to specific program characteristics.

What We Have Learned About the Research

The research examined compares the efficacy of 4- and 5-year programs and different kinds of alternative programs. The outcomes examined in these studies include how many teachers completed different programs and entered teaching and what kind of schools they entered, teachers' ratings of the effectiveness of their preparation in relation to particular tasks of teaching, and the professional teaching knowledge of graduates from different programs.

In addition, various aspects of teaching quality were examined after program completion including the self-ratings by teachers of their own teaching abilities; teacher self-reports of the teaching practices and problems faced in the classroom; observations of teaching by researchers; principals', supervisors', or mentors' ratings of the quality of teaching; and measures of pupil learning. Teachers' commitment to teaching as a career, their sense of efficacy and career satisfaction, involvement in leadership activities, and actual teacher retention were also assessed.

As mentioned previously, few definitive statements can be made about the effects of different structural models for preservice teacher education programs based on this body of research. Inconsistent and contradictory findings across studies and various conceptual and methodological problems with the research reveal limitations that should guide future inquiry. Future research needs to include descriptions of the attributes that teachers bring to their teacher education programs; the curriculum, pedagogy, and social relations in the teacher education programs; the institutional and state policy contexts in which the programs are embedded; the school and community contexts where program graduates teach; and the criteria and comparison groups used in the evaluation of teacher performance.

Generally the research has not distinguished program effects from the influence of the characteristics that teachers bring to their preparation programs (selection effects) and from the effects of the contexts in which teachers teach. Because these studies have not carefully examined the actual process of teacher education, teachers' entering characteristics, and the contexts in which teachers teach, it is not possible to explain the contradictory findings.

It is difficult to aggregate findings across studies because studies used different definitions of alternative and traditional teacher education programs.

The Research We Need

Research on teacher education programs needs to describe the characteristics that teachers bring to their programs, the opportunities for learning that the programs provide and what teachers learn from these opportunities, the institutional and state policy contexts in which programs are embedded, and the characteristics of the schools where program graduates teach. Attention to these things will better enable researchers to disentangle the effects of programs from selection effects and the effects of contexts and to identify the critical features of programs that make a difference in achieving desired outcomes.

It is important that researchers use consistent definitions for alternative and traditional teacher education programs.

Systematic quantitative studies of distinct and carefully described alternative program alternatives are needed. These studies should utilize matching, controls, or random assignment to isolate the effects of particular teacher education program characteristics from other influences. These studies should include specific information about the features of the programs being compared that goes beyond a general label taken from their structural characteristics. These studies also need to compare teachers who are teaching the same subjects to the same kind of students at the same grade levels.

In-depth case studies of teacher education programs are needed that illuminate what teacher education students learn from the opportunities they are provided within their programs. These studies should attempt to link specific program characteristics to various outcomes.

Studies that combine systematic quantitative analyses of distinct preparation alternatives and in-depth qualitative analyses of the nature and meaning of these alternatives are especially needed. These studies will provide both the systematic comparisons and the rich contextual data needed to be able to explain the findings.

More studies on teacher education programs should include attention to the links between teacher education and student learning. In addition to students' growth on standardized achievement tests, other ways of assessing academic learning and assessments of other kinds of learning such as social and civic learning should be addressed.

Better measures of teacher performance are needed in research that attempts to connect preparation programs to the teaching performance of their graduates. Instruments and rating scales to assess teaching performance should use clear, specific criteria and address broader definitions of teaching performance that incorporate multiple aspects of teaching performance.

A RESEARCH AGENDA FOR TEACHER EDUCATION

The main recommendation of the panel, elaborated in the remainder of this summary, is that research about teacher education needs now to be undertaken using methods that will increase our knowledge about important features of teacher education and its connections to the outcomes that are important in a democratic society. We recommend attention to the full variety of research approaches available, recognizing that multidisciplinary and multimethodological approaches are necessary.

We caution, however, that although empirical research can inform important decisions about research and policy, it cannot tell us what to do. Simply because something has been researched does not tell us much about what people actually do or should do in preparation programs. Indeed, we see many instances where the same research is interpreted to justify dramatically different practices and policy decisions. As we note throughout this report, education and teacher education pose many kinds of questions, including those that are grounded in moral, ethical, social, philosophical, and ideological concerns. Although questions like these can be shaped and understood more fully on the basis of evidence, they cannot be settled by empirical evidence alone. Evidence always has to be interpreted, and there are many influences on teacher education practice besides research findings. However well-designed studies, such as natural experiments that take advantage of naturally occurring variations among teacher preparation programs and arrangements, can provide evidence to guide policy and practice decisions.

Of course, the arguments we make about research on teacher education are relevant in any applied field, including medicine and the health professions, where policy decisions depend not only on a synthesis of the empirical evidence but also on local circumstances, costs weighed against benefits, and the availability of personnel, equipment, and technology. This in no way suggests that empirical research related to teacher preparation has no role in policy. On the contrary, the empirical research agenda recommended here can inform policy and practice by providing evidence concerning the outcomes of particular strategies, arrangements, and components of preparation and by providing analyses of the impact of programs and policies at the local level. Decisions about teacher education will always be influenced by a mix of values, experience, politics, and empirical evidence. However, we currently have relatively little evidence about the impact of teacher education and even less agreement about what counts as evidence in the first place. In this volume we are calling for multiple programs of empirical research on teacher education, which will require more sophisticated theoretical frameworks and research designs. Sound empirical research on teacher education can help us better understand the contexts and conditions within which teacher education is associated with enhanced pupil learning and other outcomes, as evidenced by multiple rather than by unitary indicators. This empirical evidence ought to guide decisions about policy and practice.

Recommended Research Designs and Important Methodological Issues

The panel recommends that researchers carefully develop research designs along the lines that follow and also attend to the noted methodological issues noted as they conduct research on teacher education. Some of the standards the panel calls for apply to all good research; others are more specific to teacher education.

Research Situated in Relevant Theoretical Frameworks Particular conceptions of teaching and learning to teach are embedded in the curriculum, instructional strategies, and organizational structures of teacher education programs. Without locating empirical studies in relation to appropriate theoretical frameworks regarding teacher learning, teaching effectiveness, and pupil learning, it will be difficult to explain findings about the effects of particular teacher education practices.

Clear and Consistent Definitions of Terms All aspects of teacher education including instructional approaches, curriculum, and organizational arrangements should be defined clearly, consistently, and with enough specificity to enable the accumulation of knowledge across studies about the nature and impact of different aspects of teacher education.

Fuller Description of Data Collection and Analysis Methods and Research Contexts Studies need to provide detailed information about how data were collected and analyzed, how courses were situated within program and institutional contexts, and the characteristics of the school and community contexts in which teachers work.

Development of More Programs of Research More programs of research in teacher education wherein researchers consciously build on each other's work to pursue particular lines of inquiry are needed. Productive research programs allow researchers to pursue different aspects of particular problems and questions, accumulating and extending knowledge with each new study.

Attention to the Impact of Teacher Education on Teachers' Learning and Professional Practice Researchers should examine the impact of various aspects of teacher preparation programs and routes on teachers' learning, particularly their knowledge and beliefs and their professional practice in classroom and school settings. Especially important are studies that examine these issues over time and studies that examine the connections among teacher preparation, teacher learning, teacher practice, and pupils' learning.

Research That Links Teacher Education to Pupil's Learning   Much more research is needed about the relationships between teacher education components, pathways, and experiences, on one hand, and various aspects of pupil's learning, including but by no means limited to learning as measured by standardized test scores, on the other. We need both more studies that closely examine the outcomes of teacher education for pupils' learning and broader views of what constitutes pupils' learning in the first place. We also need studies that try to sort out the many factors, including teacher preparation, that influence pupils' growth over time.

Multidisciplinary and Mixed-Methods Studies   To generate knowledge that is useful to policymakers and practitioners, we need multidisciplinary research, mixed-methods studies, and a multimethodological approach. Given the complexity of teacher education and its connections to various aspects of both teacher quality and student learning, it is clear that no single methodological approach can provide the knowledge we need. Rather, the field needs experimental and quasiexperimental designs, case studies, ethnographic analyses, and many other approaches to address the array of complex issues that are critical in the field.

Reliable Measures of Teachers' Knowledge and Skills   Researchers need to use better and more consistent measures of teachers' knowledge and skills and how these are linked to teacher preparation programs and routes. Of particular importance are measures that connect particular teacher preparation components to the teaching of candidates and graduates of various programs, especially studies that address multiple aspects of teaching and use multiple indicators of performance.

Experimental Research Comparing Programmatic Alternatives in Terms of Outcomes   Given the large size and scale of teacher education as well as the tremendous natural variation that occurs in programs across the country, there are many opportunities for experimental research designs that compare the impacts of program variations on teachers' knowledge, their professional practice, and pupils' learning.

Recommended Research Topics and Issues

The panel recommends that research be conducted on a number of topics that are especially important and amenable to productive research, but where either little research has been done, or what has been done has been limited to very small samples or short-term study. In addition, there are several important topics that are virtually unexplored.

Preparing Teachers to Help Close the Achievement Gap   The status quo in teacher preparation has failed to prepare teachers to meet the needs of the increasingly diverse population of public school students, thus failing to close the gap in achievement and other school outcomes among White students and their peers of color. In particular, we need research on how to prepare teachers to work with English-language learners, how to work effectively with students with disabilities, how to recruit and retain a more diversified teacher workforce, and how to prepare teachers for particular settings, such as urban and rural areas, where the achievement gap is particularly pronounced.

Contexts and Participants in Teacher Education Much more research is needed regarding the impact of the varying contexts and participants in teacher preparation In particular, we need to know more about who is teaching and supervising teacher education courses and fieldwork experiences and what instructional strategies and texts and programs they are using. We also need more information about the conditions under which these are most effective.

Teacher Education Curriculum, Instruction, and Organization The panel recommends that more research be conducted about the conditions under which different conceptual and structural arrangements within teacher education programs are connected to various outcomes. In particular, we need research about the nature of the instructional interactions that occur in coursework and fieldwork contexts and the impact of these on teachers' learning and performance and on pupils' learning, including the impact of the racial and ethnic composition of participants.

Organizational and Structural Alternatives for Teacher Preparation There are many variations among programs and pathways into teaching in terms of organizational and structural arrangements, timing, and requirements before, during, and after designation as teacher of record with full responsibility for pupils' learning. Much more research is needed regarding the processes, experiences, and impacts of these variations.

Predictive Validity of Teacher Education Program Admission Criteria Current initiatives in teacher education are utilizing a variety of admissions criteria for programs, pathways, and alternatives. We need research that analyzes the predictive validity of these for effective teaching and retention in the teaching profession, particularly in urban, rural, and other hard-to-staff schools.

National Databases on Teacher Candidates, Teachers, and Reserve Pools The panel strongly recommends that national databases be established that include accurate longitudinal data on how the demographic and quality profiles of the nation's teachers are interrelated as well as on how teachers with different quality and demographic characteristics are prepared for teaching and where and whether they enter, stay, or leave the teaching profession.

Research on Teacher Preparation in Various Subject Areas We need more research on the impact of preparation in various subject areas on teachers' performance and knowledge as well as on their pupil's learning. In particular, we need to know the impact of arts and sciences study and engagement on teachers' performance and knowledge and on their pupils' learning. In particular, we need research that disentangles the effects of programs from those of subject areas.

Systematic Analyses of Alternative Preparation Programs and Routes The panel recommends an array of research designs intended to explore the impacts of clearly identifiable alternative routes, programs, and organizational structures in teacher education. Although this array could include randomized trials, the panel recommends that various forms of matching and controls are better alternatives for research in teacher education, because random assignment of pupils to teachers with no preparation carries important ethical considerations.

In-Depth Case Studies of Programs Although expensive and complicated to carry out, the panel recommends that more in-depth, large-scale, and multi-institutional case studies of teacher education programs and components are needed. Targeted resource allocation would make this kind of study possible.

Research That Links Preparation With Practice and Pupils' Learning Although it is exceedingly complex and difficult to do, the panel recommends that a series of well-designed, theory-grounded studies examine the complex links among teacher preparation programs and contexts, teacher candidates' knowledge growth, teachers' professional practices, and pupils' learning within the contexts of schools and classrooms.

Unexplored Topics Related to Teacher Preparation There are many important aspects of teacher preparation that are virtually unexplored in the research literature. Although many small-scale studies during the last decade focused on teacher candidates' beliefs, there has been almost no research that examines connections between those beliefs and graduates' performance as teachers, let alone the connections among beliefs, teacher performance, and the performance of their pupils. Research is needed that systematically explores the relationships among teacher candidates' beliefs, attitudes, skills, and practices and pupil's learning opportunities, attitudes, achievement, and growth. In addition, research is needed on the impact of subject matter and general education preparation of teachers, the role of psychological and social foundations, and the impact of these on teachers' and pupil's performance. We also need to know how different policies and accountability processes affect teacher education's impact on pupils' learning. Although there are major national reform initiatives calling for greater university responsibility for teacher preparation and greater engagement of the arts and sciences in teacher preparation, there is virtually no research in this area. In addition, there has been little research on the impact of different accountability systems and different state and federal policies on teacher education outcomes.

A Needed Infrastructure for Research on Teacher Education

To develop the body of research that is needed to inform policy and practice in teacher education, a number of investments in infrastructure need to be made.

Funding and Other Resources for Research on Teacher Education Especially in light of the fact that much of teacher education research has been conducted by individuals using small samples, the panel recommends that federal and other funds be provided so that large-scale and other kinds of systematic studies can be carried out. This is needed in areas other than mathematics and science. Federal and foundation funding should be targeted for specific areas with the potential for important results.

Preparing Educational Researchers and the Peer-Review Process The panel recommends that the preparation of researchers in the area of teacher education be made a top priority for foundations and government training grants so that researchers understand the complexity and interdisciplinarity of research in this area and gain the methodological, substantive, and theoretical education needed to carry out productive research. In addition, the panel suggests that rigorous standards for evaluating research on teacher education be established by the educational research community and applied in the peer-review process for refereed journals as well as for books. In particular, clear criteria need to be established for describing the teacher education students, components, and policy contexts under study as well as describing the research protocols, instruments, and terms that are used.

Research Partnerships   The panel recommends the development and support of research partnerships and collaborations that cut across institutions and involve focused assessment agendas related to teacher preparation and desirable outcomes, especially pupil learning outcomes. In addition the panel recommends that the databases generated through self-studies used for state program approval and national accreditation be linked and made available to researchers engaged in national assessments, comparisons, and evaluation studies. Comprehensive national datasets on teacher education students, teacher educators, curriculum, and instruction would allow analysis of the impact of components, pathways, and learning opportunities on pupil learning and other desirable school and pupil outcomes. Research partnerships that pool resources and researchers can alleviate the limitations of individual researchers studying single courses or program aspects and move toward understanding the larger patterns involved in teacher education and various outcomes.

The syntheses developed by the AERA Panel on Research and Teacher Education point to many promising lines of research that can be built on to expand what we know about the impact of various kinds of teacher preparation and the impact of various local and larger policy decisions. We are at a turning point, however, with more attention than ever before focused on the recruitment, preparation, and retention of highly qualified teachers. As a field, we need to develop a rich portfolio of studies that addresses many of the most important questions about teacher education from multiple perspectives and uses many different research designs. The panel recommends that some of the most promising places to start are the construction of accurate national databases, strategic investments to support both large-scale studies and indepth case studies, and significant improvement in the peer-review process and the preparation of teacher education researchers.

REFERENCE

Wilson, S., Floden, R., & Ferrini-Mundy, J. (2001). Teacher preparation research: Current knowledge, gaps and recommendations. Washington, DC: Center for the Study of Teaching and Policy.

1

The AERA Panel on Research
and Teacher Education: Context
and Goals

Marilyn Cochran-Smith
Boston College

Kim Fries
University of New Hampshire

This book reports the work of the American Educational Research Association's (AERA's) Panel on Research and Teacher Education,[1] which began preliminary discussions in 1999. At that time, there was growing concern in the educational community about the vagueness of much of the research claimed to support certain policies and practices related to teacher preparation. Sometimes the same research was cited to support conflicting positions. Sometimes close scrutiny revealed that particular studies provided no clear evidence for the claims being made. Often it was apparent that quite different assumptions were operating about what constituted good research, what research questions ought to be addressed, and what role research could be

---

[1] AERA constituted this panel to bring clarity to research on teacher education drawing on the work of a team of experts in the field. In doing so, AERA wished to have a project that would add to and advance research knowledge and considerations of future research directions. However, the volume itself is not endorsed by nor does it represent the view of AERA on matters of substance.

expected to play in policy and practice. It was clear to the panel that careful and unbiased analysis of the empirical evidence supporting various practices and suggesting new directions for research in teacher education was needed.

The situation has changed somewhat since this project began. Debates about research and teacher preparation have intensified. Major federal education legislation has been implemented with far-reaching implications for how we define well-prepared teachers and appropriate professional development; how we recruit, prepare, support, retain, test, certify, and license teachers; how we evaluate and accredit teacher preparation programs and providers; and how we make judgments about the effectiveness of teachers, schools, and the overall enterprise of teacher education. Since we began, there have been dozens of new reports, surveys, research syntheses, policy reviews, and empirical studies about teacher preparation. Blue ribbon panels have weighed in about the future of teacher preparation, and foundations and professional groups have pursued new initiatives. Notwithstanding the considerable debate about the meanings of "teacher quality" and "highly qualified teachers," it is no exaggeration to say that the national focus on these issues is more intense now than ever. There are also more claims than ever before about the relationships that do and do not exist among teacher qualifications, the policies and practices governing teacher preparation, teaching performance, and educational outcomes.

Having said all this, we want to make a point of noting that the work of the AERA Panel on Research and Teacher Education is situated within but also outside of the contemporary policy and political scene. In other words, as discussed in the following section, it is clear that the panel's work has been influenced by and responsive to the contentious policy context of the time, and that our choice to evaluate the empirical evidence about some of the teacher education issues that are of most interest to decision makers has to a great extent been determined by current policy debates. There is no question that we took on the current task in the interest of providing a dispassionate and careful rendering of fairly traditional forms of empirical research that speak to educational outcomes and are responsive to current demands for accountability in teaching and teacher education.

On the other hand, our analyses look and feel quite different from many contemporary policy reviews, which often use research to forward policy and political arguments that have already been made by their authors. Reviews of this kind are likely to conclude with definitive recommendations for policies, positions, or practices with the claim that they are drawn from the research literature. Our reviews are decidedly different. They are intended to provide balanced, thorough, and unapologetically honest descriptions of the state of research on particular topics in teacher education as a field of study. In many areas this means that our analysis includes the considerable inconsistencies and even contradictions that characterize some aspects of the field. Our reviews are designed not simply to note that this is the state of the field in some areas, but to explain why this is so and to evaluate both the strengths and weaknesses of different questions and approaches as we simultaneously identify promising lines of inquiry. The panel's analyses also differ from typical policy reviews in that we have stood back from the current prevailing viewpoint that the right kind of research can definitively guide policy by determining the "winners" in the teacher education horse race. Implicit in our analyses and explicit in the panel's stated working assumptions is a critique of the current policy focus and considerable skepticism that there will be definitive answers about teacher preparation unless they are driven by sophisticated theoretical frameworks, built on empirical work from rich qualitative and quantitative perspectives, and designed to take into account the varying social, organizational, and intellectual contexts and conditions of schools, universities, and communities.

TEACHER EDUCATION IN THE 21ST CENTURY: POLICY AND POLITICS

This chapter offers an analysis of the complex policy, political and professional issues that constrained and supported teacher education research during the mid- to late 1990s and into the mid-2000s. Next, the chapter provides background about the work of the panel, including a rationale for the major questions and an overview of procedures. (See the "Executive Summary" for an overview of the specific findings and recommendations of each chapter.) The chapter also describes the panel's charge, outlines working assumptions, describes criteria used to select and critique empirical research, and comments on how the panel constructed its research agenda.

During the latter years of the 20th century and the early years of the 21st, momentous changes occurred that affected teacher education research, policy, and practice. These included shifting population patterns, major swings in the political pendulum, the growth of a complex global economy, and a number of educational and political movements. Among them were the standards movement, the accountability movement, initiatives to privatize education and other public services, the press for market-based education reform, and the emergence of access to quality education as a civil rights issue. Contemporary research on teacher education is affected by and connected to all of these.

As the 21st century began, there was wide agreement that teacher quality is essential to educational reform but disagreement about what teacher quality is and which teacher characteristics are linked with desirable outcomes. Acknowledgment of the importance of teachers coupled with widespread concern about low standards in the schools prompted criticism of "traditional" teacher education and multiple agendas for reform. Exacerbating these difficulties is the fact that the 1,300 colleges and universities that prepare teachers in the United States face difficult financial times with rising tuitions, diminished resources, and increased competition for enrollments.

In most states, many alternate providers of teacher preparation have emerged, including school-based teacher preparation projects, computer-based distance learning programs, and alternate entry and certification routes. Some are attached to universities, whereas others bypass them altogether. In addition, for-profit teacher preparation is a growing trend in higher education, wherein proprietary, degree-granting, and accredited institutions offer occupational training for entry-level positions in a variety of areas rather than simply offering training in specialized trades, which was previously the case. With market demand for teachers strong and the number of traditional college students interested in teaching declining, proprietary institutions are keen on developing the market for adult teacher preparation. All providers face mounting pressure to demonstrate that the teachers they produce can prepare all members of the school population to pass standardized tests. We suggest that the contemporary scene is characterized by five major trends: heightened attention to teacher quality, the changing demographic profile of the nation's schoolchildren coupled with growing disparities in educational resources and outcomes, criticism of traditional teacher preparation coupled with pressure to demonstrate impact on pupil learning, multiple agendas for teacher education reform, and the ascendance of the science of education as the presumed solution to educational problems.

Teacher Quality Matters

Nationwide there is an emerging consensus that teacher quality makes a significant difference in schoolchildren's learning and in overall school effectiveness. Politicians, policymakers, and researchers of all stripes increasingly use the term "teacher quality" to emphasize that teachers are a critical influence (if not the single most important influence) on how, what, and how much students learn. Recent polls suggest that the public agrees (Hart & Teeter, 2002; Rose & Gallup, 2003). The *No Child Left Behind Act* (NCLB; P.L. 107–110, 2002) cemented into law the assumption that teacher quality matters by guaranteeing that all schoolchildren have "highly qualified teachers" who receive "high-quality" professional development. As pointed out in chapter 4 (this volume), researchers have traditionally investigated proxies for teacher quality such as college entrance test scores, college majors and grade point averages (GPAs), status of college or university attended, scores on teacher tests, and teacher certification status. These have been used to assess the presumed strength of the teaching force, for example, by comparing how the test scores of teacher candidates compared with those of other college graduates or those entering other professions.

Since the late 1990s, however, the phrase "teacher quality," has taken on new meaning and is increasingly attached to an array of purposes. Nevertheless, educational researchers and policymakers do not agree on a single definition of teacher quality. Within the general guidelines mandated by NCLB, the states are defining teacher quality differently from one another and putting different policies into place. In the research community, there are two broad approaches to conceptualizing teacher quality with different implications: teacher quality defined as student achievement and teacher quality defined as teacher qualifications. Although these are not necessarily mutually exclusive from one another, they represent different relative emphases.

When teacher quality is defined as student achievement, the premise is that although there is measurable variation in effectiveness across teachers, this variation is not captured by the common indicators of quality, such as teachers' preparation, experience, and test scores, but is captured in pupils' performance. For example, based on 2 decades of research on the impact of school inputs on students' achievement (Hanushek, 1996, 1997; Rivkin, Hanushek, & Kain, 1998), Hanushek (2002) defined teacher quality quite simply: "good teachers are ones who get large gains in student achievement for their classes; bad teachers are just the opposite" (p. 3). The work of William Sanders and colleagues (Rivers & Sanders, 2002; Sanders, 1998; Sanders & Horn, 1994, 1998) is consistent with this approach. Sanders concluded that individual teachers are the single largest factor that adds value to student learning, overshadowing students' previous achievement, class size, and ethnic and socioeconomic status (Rivers & Sanders). What the work of Hanushek and Sanders have in common is defining and operationalizing teacher quality in terms of pupil performance. With this approach, the point is to identify major differences in student achievement gains that are linked to teachers and then suggest implications regarding incentives, school accountability systems, and policies regarding the placement of teachers and students.

The second approach defines teacher quality in terms of teacher qualifications. The point is to determine which (if any) of the characteristics, attributes, and qualifications generally considered indicators of teacher quality are actually linked to student achievement or other outcomes, such as principal evaluations of teachers or teachers' sense of efficacy. For example, based on multiple analyses of the impact of teacher preparation policy (Darling-Hammond, 2000, 2000b; Darling-Hammond, Chung, & Frelow, 2002; Darling-Hammond & Youngs, 2002), Darling-Hammond (2000b) concluded that pupil learning "depends substantially on what teachers know and can do" (p. 11), most importantly on teacher preparation and certification. This approach was also evident in Rice's (2003) recent analyses of the impact of teacher characteristics on effectiveness, which concluded that despite gaps in the literature, many teacher characteristics do have an impact on performance. In a related review that examined the relationship between teacher characteristics and pupil achievement, Wayne and Youngs (2003) concluded that pupils learn more from teachers with certain characteristics, including certain college characteristics and tested skills and knowledge, although results were inconclusive about the impact of coursework, degrees, and certification. As with the first approach, there is an emphasis here on pupil achievement. However, with this second approach to teacher quality, the point is to identify which characteristics of teachers impact pupil achievement and then to suggest policy implications.

The Demographic Imperative

The phrase "the demographic divide" (Gay & Howard, 2000; Hodgkinson, 2002) has been used to refer to the marked disparities in educational opportunities, resources, and achievement among student groups that differ from one another racially, culturally, linguistically, socioeconomically, and geographically. Others have used the phrase "the demographic imperative" (Banks, 1995; Dilworth, 1992) to draw attention to these sharp disparities and emphasize that the educational community must take action.

Hodgkinson (2001) drew on Census 2000 data to point out that 40% of the school population came from racially and culturally diverse groups. Although this varies by state (Hodgkinson, 2002), it is strikingly different from the school population 30 years ago when nearly 80% were White (Villegas & Lucas, 2002). If projections are accurate, children of color will constitute the majority of the student population by 2035 and account for 57% by 2050 (U.S. Department of Commerce, 1996; Villegas & Lucas, 2002). Meanwhile, the nation's teaching force has quite a different profile, with White teachers accounting for 86% of the teaching force and teachers of color only 14% (National Center for Education Statistics, 1997), a pattern that reflects a modest increase in minority teachers since a low of 7% in 1993. Information about who is currently preparing to teach indicates a pattern that is generally similar to the current teaching force (American Association of Colleges for Teacher Education [AACTE], 1997, 1999; Dilworth, 1992; Howey, Arends, Galluzzo, Yarger, & Zimpher, 1994) with White college students representing 80% to 93% of those enrolled.

Hodgkinson (2002) suggests that declines since the 1960s in enrollments among African Americans in teacher education programs are related to proportionate increases in other opportunities. The decline is also related to the increased use of standardized tests for entry into the profession (Gitomer & Latham, 2000), ongoing under funding of teacher education programs at historically Black colleges and universities (Freeman, 2001), and the alienation many teacher candidates of color experience in majority White institutions (Villegas & Lucas, 2004). Although there is evidence that some teacher education programs are becoming somewhat more diverse (AACTE, 1999) and some alternate route programs are attracting more minorities (Wilson & Floden, 2003; Zeichner & Schulte, 2001), it seems clear that the teaching force will remain primarily White and primarily Americans of European ancestry for the foreseeable future (see also chaps. 3 and 9, this volume). The demographic implications are far greater than the obvious differences between pupil and teacher populations. There are also marked differences in the biographies of most White teachers from middle-class backgrounds who speak only English, on the one hand, and the experiences of many pupils of color, those who live in poverty, and those whose first language is not English (Gay, 1993; Irvine, 1997) on the other. Perhaps most serious, many White, middle-class teachers understand diversity as a deficit and have low expectations about students different from themselves, especially those in urban schools (Gay, 2000; Irvine, 1990; Valenzuela, 2002; Weiner, 1993; Yeo, 1997).

The third part of the demographic imperative has to do with the disparities in educational outcomes and conditions for pupils with and without the advantages conferred by race, culture, language, and socioeconomic status. Villegas and Lucas (2002) pointed out that in the United States the percentage of Black and Hispanic children living in poverty (42% and 40%, respectively) far exceeds the percentage of White children (16%; Kilborn, 1996). Further, the achievement levels of Black and Hispanic pupils on the National Assessment of Educational Progress (NAEP) are markedly lower than levels for White students (National Center for Education Statistics, 1997, 1998, 1999) as are high school graduation rates (Educational Research Service, 1995; National Education Goals Panel, 1994). In addition, there are major discrepancies in allocation of resources among urban, suburban, and rural schools (Darling-Hammond, 1995; Kozol, 1991), and there is growing evidence that children of color and children who live in urban or poor areas are the most likely to have teachers who are not fully qualified or licensed to teach (Darling-Hammond & Sclan, 1996; Ingersoll, 1995, 1999). This is partly the case because low-resourced urban schools are at a competitive disadvantage for hiring teachers (Oakes, Franke, Quartz, & Rogers, 2002). Urban schools, which have often suffered from severe teacher shortages, have tended to fill open positions with unlicensed teachers, substitute teachers, or teachers with temporary credentials (Darling-Hammond, 1999; Ingersoll, 1995, 1999). In addition, urban schools are less likely to provide strong support for teachers and ongoing professional opportunities for advancement, two of the central reasons teachers state for leaving schools (Ingersoll, 2001). Based on analyses similar to this one, many people have concluded that the education system needs to change and that teachers need to be prepared in fundamentally different ways. As the next sections of this chapter reveal, however, their conclusions about how to do this are often very different.

Dissatisfaction With "Traditional" Teacher Preparation

Coupled with pressure to raise school standards has been growing dissatisfaction with "traditional" approaches to teacher preparation. In many contexts, the term "traditional" is used to refer to undergraduate-college- and university-based initial teacher preparation programs. It is important to note that the critiques come from both inside and outside teacher education. Some are intended fundamentally to strengthen teaching and university-based teacher preparation as professions with high standards and a research-based curriculum, whereas others are intended to do away with university-based preparation altogether.

Criticisms of teacher education, far from being unprecedented, are part of a long history that reflects lack of consensus about many enduring questions about the schools and those who teach in them. Many of these were reflected in the critique of teacher education issued by U.S. Secretary of Education Rodney Paige in his first and second reports to Congress on how the nation was meeting the "highly qualified teachers" challenge (U.S. Department of Education, 2002, 2003). The conclusion of the first report was "Schools of education and formal teacher training programs are failing to produce the types of highly qualified teachers that the *No Child Left Behind Act* demands" (p. viii). The report asserted that states' academic standards for teachers were low, whereas the barriers that kept qualified prospective teachers who had not completed collegiate teacher preparation out of teaching were high. The report concluded that states should transform certification requirements, base programs on academic content, get rid of requirements not based on scientific evidence, and recruit candidates from other fields. With regard to research evidence, the report drew the following conclusion: "In summary, we have found that rigorous research indicates that verbal ability and content knowledge are the most important attributes of highly qualified teachers. In addition there is little evidence that education school coursework leads to improved student achievement" (p. 19). The report advocated alternate route programs as the "model" option, which, if widely implemented, would simultaneously solve the teacher quality and supply problems. The Secretary's second report (U.S. Department of Education, 2003) was consistent with the first, calling for continued research on teacher quality and preparation as well as studies that identify "interventions that [will] raise effectiveness for all teachers" (p. 3).

Several researchers have challenged the empirical grounds for the conclusions in the Secretary's reports (e.g., Cochran-Smith, 2002b, 2003; Darling-Hammond & Youngs, 2002; Heap, 2002) and argued that some of the so-called "research-based" conclusions listed were false. Notwithstanding debates about the evidence, it is clear that devastating public critiques of "traditional" teacher preparation are influencing how the educational community conducts and uses research in, on, and for teacher education. In conjunction with the push for evidence-based policies and practices, there is intense pressure on teacher educators and others to measure the impact of teacher preparation on pupil learning and to assemble persuasive evidence that teacher preparation makes a difference.

Multiple Agendas for Teacher Education Reform

Almost everyone agrees that teacher education needs to be improved, but there is vast disagreement about how, why, and for what purposes. Calls for change stem from complex social, political, and organizational goals that are quite different from one another in history and tradition. Some are strategies to control teaching politically, whereas others reflect long-term struggles for professional autonomy and equity. Although these are different, they are referred to here as *agendas* to highlight major distinctions: the professionalization agenda, the deregulation agenda, the regulation agenda, and the social justice agenda.[2] These agendas are competing and even contradictory in certain ways, but they are not mutually exclusive. Rather they overlap and collide with one another, depending on state regulations, how the agendas are positioned by proponents and opponents, and the professional relationships among state agencies, particular institutions, and accrediting agencies. Each has implications for the research that is funded, conducted, cited, and heeded in teacher education.

The Professionalization Agenda. Although the professionalization agenda has been around since the beginning of formal teacher education in normal schools in the 1800s, the current iteration was prompted by criticisms of teaching and teacher education in the 1980s and by early work about teachers' thinking (Clark & Peterson,

---

[2]For related discussions of some of these agendas, see Cochran Smith (2001), Cochran-Smith and Fries (2001, 2002), and Zeichner (2003).

1986) and knowledge (Shulman, 1986, 1987). The current agenda aims to make teaching and teacher education a profession with a research-base and formal body of knowledge that distinguishes professional educators from lay persons (Gardner, 1989; Murray, 1996), has jurisdictional responsibility for defining and acting on professional problems (Yinger, 1999; Yinger & Hendricks-Lee, 2000), and works from clear and consistent standards for professional practice (Darling-Hammond, Wise, & Klein, 1999; National Commission on Teaching & America's Future, 1996).

The major goal of the professionalization agenda is to ensure that all teachers are fully prepared and fully certified in accordance with professional standards (National Commission on Teaching & America's Future, 1996; 1997). This agenda is linked to the K–12 curriculum standards movement (Darling-Hammond & Sykes, 1999) and was influenced by the emerging "learning sciences" (National Research Council, 2000) and other lines of research on human development, language, assessment, pedagogy, and social contexts. Professionalization builds on long efforts by the National Council for the Accreditation of Teacher Education (NCATE), the National Board for Professional Teaching Standards (NBPTS), the Interstate New Teacher Assessment and Support Consortium (INTASC), the Association for Teacher Educators (ATE), and the American Association of Colleges for Teacher Education (AACTE) to make standards for teaching and teacher education consistent and unified across initial preparation, certification, and licensing. The publication of *What Matters Most: Teaching for America's Future* (National Commission on Teaching & America's Future, 1996) was a galvanizing event in shaping the current professionalization agenda. That report asserted strong empirical research demonstrating that professional teachers—prepared in university-based programs and fully licensed—were among the most important factors that determine students' learning and achievement (Darling-Hammond, 2000a, 2000b).[3]

The Deregulation Agenda.   Competing with professionalization is the agenda to reform teacher preparation through deregulation, which aims to eliminate most requirements for entry into the profession. Proponents favor doing away with both collegiate program requirements and the licensing and certification apparatus operating in each state. They advocate opening multiple entry routes into teaching, with pupil test scores the bottom line for determining who should be teaching. Based on the assumption that most entry requirements simply keep bright young people out of teaching and focus on social goals rather than on pupils' achievement (Kanstoroom & Finn, 1999), advocates of deregulation want to break up the "monopoly" of the profession (Abell Foundation, 2001; Kanstoroom & Finn, 1999). Those who favor deregulation argue that research indicates that courses in pedagogy and other experiences associated with university programs and state-licensing agencies have no significant impact on pupil's achievement (Ballou & Podgursky, 2000).[4]

The Thomas B. Fordham Foundation, a leader of the deregulation agenda, explicitly equates the professionalization agenda with state regulation (Kanstoroom & Finn, 1999, p. 3). The deregulation agenda is consistent with other market-based approaches to reform and with the larger movement to privatize health, education, and other services. As Hess (2001) pointed out, the success of market-based approaches is dependent on a strong competitive environment. The assumption is that to improve

---

[3]These claims about the research base have been debated extensively; they are considered in further detail later in this chapter.

[4]This claim has been debated extensively; it is considered in further detail later in this chapter.

teaching and quality of life for the public *writ large*, what schools need most is the freedom to recruit, hire, and keep all teachers who can raise pupils' test scores regardless of their credentials.

The Regulation Agenda.   Concurrent with professionalization and deregulation is what we refer to as the *regulation agenda*, or increased federal and state control of both the "inputs" (e.g., number, kind, and content of courses and fieldwork experiences) and "outputs" or "outcomes" (e.g., assessments of the impact of teacher preparation on professional practice and K–12 students' learning) of teacher preparation. Along these lines, 42 states now require statewide assessments for initial certification, with 32 states requiring tests in one or more subject areas (Whitehurst, 2001). In addition, the 1998 reauthorization of Title II of the Higher Education Act (HEA) put into place unprecedented federal regulation of teacher preparation, including the requirement that all states report annually to Washington on the quality of preparation programs. This requires in turn that all higher education institutions report to the state the qualifications of all candidates recommended for certification.

Leading proponents of deregulation and professionalization often define their approaches as direct opposites. However, the regulation agenda may be linked with or opposed to either deregulation or professionalization. In some places, new state regulations are in sync with professionalization and at odds with deregulation (e.g., requirements for performance-based assessments of teachers that are linked to INTASC and NBPTS professional standards). In these instances, professionalization and regulation appear to be somewhat consistent, although even here critics have suggested that increased state regulation reduces professional autonomy, thus undermining the professionalization agenda. In other places, state regulations are simultaneously at odds with both professionalization and deregulation (e.g., control by the state of allowable arts and sciences majors for students in university-based preparation programs, which undermines the autonomy of the profession but, at the same time, also imposes new barriers to entry into teaching, which is at odds with the position of deregulators). In a number of states there are simultaneous efforts to deregulate and regulate teacher preparation (e.g., tight control of required courses at state-approved teacher preparation institutions coupled with the state's sanctioning alternate routes with few requirements). These contradictions also exist at the federal level, which Cochran-Smith (2004a) has referred to as "tightly regulated deregulation": support for alternate routes that do away with most requirements and make entry into teaching wide open, on the one hand, and centralized federal control that diminishes state and local decisions and greatly limits professional discretion and autonomy, on the other.

The Social Justice Agenda.   Over the last decade or so, conceptualizing teaching and teacher education in terms of social justice has been the central animating idea for educational scholars and practitioners (e.g., Cochran-Smith, 2004b; Gay & Howard, 2000; Hollins, King, & Hayman, 1994; Irvine, 1997; Ladson-Billings, 1999; Villegas & Lucas, 2002; Zeichner, 2003) who connect their work to larger critical movements (Apple, 2001; Aronowitz & Giroux, 1985; Castenell & Pinar, 1993; Oakes, 1988; Sleeter, 1996; Weiner, 2000). Advocates of a social justice agenda want teachers to be professional educators as well as activists committed to diminishing the inequities of American society (Gay, 1993; Sleeter, 1995; Villegas & Lucas, 2001; Zeichner, 1993). They also seek teachers who are more likely to stay in hard-to-staff schools with large numbers of minority and poor students (Haberman, 1988, 1991; Quartz & TEP Research Group, 2003).

The social justice agenda overlaps with but also bumps up against other agendas for teacher education reform. For example, federal mandates that all children have fully qualified teachers explicitly reject the practice of employing teachers on "waivers" of state requirements, a practice more common in poor urban schools than in afflu- ent schools (Darling-Hammond & Sclan, 1996; U.S. Department of Education, 2002). On this point, social justice and regulation advocates agree. However, social justice advocates worry that concerns about the achievement gap and concerns about prepar- ing qualified teachers have been melded together and converged with policymakers' obsession with testing and accountability. The crux of the difference between those who support a social justice agenda and those who support tighter regulation is that the former insist on analyses of differential access to resources based on critical race, culture, and language perspectives coupled with redistributing resources and rein- venting teacher preparation and school structures (King & Castenell, 2001; Ladson- Billings, 1999; Murrell, 2001). Regulation advocates assume that tighter control will compel higher achievement without addressing underlying structural, institutional, and historical inequities.

Although the social justice and professionalization agendas share many goals, the social justice agenda is defined at least in part by its critique of professionalization, particularly its reliance on a universal knowledge base; its avoidance of field experi- ences in urban schools; and its failure to acknowledge the pervasive influences of race, class, and culture on schooling (Grant & Wieczorek, 2000; Irvine & Fraser, 1998; Jenks, Lee, & Kanpol, 2001; King & Castenell, 2001; Murrell, 2001). Finally, it is important to note that some proponents of social justice are also supporters of certain alternate routes and alternate certification programs intended to diversify the teaching force by recruiting teachers of color and teachers with life experiences that support success in urban schools (e.g., Haberman, 1996; Villegas & Lucas, 2002). Although supporters of the social justice agenda generally support strong teacher preparation programs, their advocacy for certain programs intended to recruit teachers of color suggests affinity between at least some aspects of the social justice and deregulation agendas.

The preceding discussion suggests that the varied agendas for the reform of teacher preparation are nuanced and complex. Although they have been presented in the public discourse in terms that are often dichotomized (Cochran-Smith & Fries, 2001), it is more accurate to acknowledge that they are in certain ways consistent with and in other ways competing and even contradictory with one another. It is also important to note that each agenda claims to have an empirical research base, but this has been hotly debated.

The Elevation of the Science of Education

In a growing number of arenas, the "science of education" has been greatly elevated (National Research Council, 2001). Today's rich data sources, powerful analytical tech- niques, and increasingly sophisticated researchers are presumed by some to permit the verification of scientifically based practices and policies that will increase students' achievement, improve teaching and schools, and solve the problems involved in pro- viding universal education to a large and diverse population.

The elevation of science is reflected in the formation of the U.S. Department of Edu- cation's (DOE) Institute of Education Sciences (IES) directed by Russ Whitehurst. IES is explicitly aimed at "reflect[ing] the intent of the President and Congress to advance the field of education research, making it more rigorous in support of evidence-based education" (Institute of Education Sciences, 2003). Shortly after it was established, IES created the What Works Clearinghouse to provide a central reliable source of scientific evidence in education for use by policymakers, practitioners, and the general public. Emphasis on greater scientific rigor is intended to respond to the widespread perception that educational research has been generally low in quality with constantly contested results and little capacity to improve educational policy and practice (Kaestle, 1993; Lagemann, 2000). The "awful reputation" (Kaestle) of educational research motivated the DOE's charge to the National Research Council (NRC) to review the literature on scientific educational research and make recommendations about how to support high-quality science (Shavelson & Towne, 2002). Along related lines, the Strategic Education Research Partnership is envisioned as a bold new partnership among the research, practice, and policy communities intended to marshal new resources to make research-based practice a reality (Donovan, Wigdor, & Snow, 2003).

The notion of "scientifically based research" (SBR) and its complement, "evidence-based education" (EBE), along with the new agencies and partnerships created to foster them reflect renewed confidence in the power of science to solve social and educational problems. This is threaded throughout the language of NCLB, which defined "scientific research" as the application of "rigorous, systematic and objective procedures to obtain reliable and valid knowledge by employing systematic methods of observation or experimentation " (Section 9101, Definitions, 37). Whitehurst (2001) described EBE as "the integration of professional wisdom with the best available empirical evidence in making decisions about how to deliver instruction." He was clear, however, that decisions currently rely far too heavily on professional wisdom and far too little on empirical evidence. He was also clear that all types of evidence are not created equal, with randomized trials the "gold standard" for evidence, followed by quasiexperimental studies, pre–post comparisons, correlational studies, case studies and, finally, anecdotes. The NRC report on scientific research in education (Shavelson & Towne, 2002) supported wider use of randomized trials but also said "there is no one method or process that unambiguously defines science" (p. 16).

Disagreements about what constitutes science are not new, nor is burgeoning faith in the ability of science to solve educational problems. As Lagemann (2000) noted in her history of the scholarship of education, educational research has always been "an elusive science," with debates as early as the 1890s about whether there could truly be a science of education. As Lagemann pointed out about the end of the 19th century, the beginning of the 21st is also a time in which "science is remaking conceptions of truth and knowledge" (p. 19) in education generally and in teacher education particularly. Throughout the educational community, there are many new research initiatives intended to examine scientifically the impact of teacher preparation on pupil, teacher, and school outcomes.

THE AERA PANEL ON RESEARCH AND TEACHER EDUCATION

Located both within and outside of the policy and political contexts described previously and in the face of competing claims about the research base for teacher preparation, the goal of the AERA Panel on Research and Teacher Education was to provide a critical, evenhanded analysis of the empirical research related to preservice teacher education in major areas of interest to researchers, policymakers, and practitioners. Equally important, the panel was designed to recommend a research agenda for teacher education, outlining topics for further study, identifying terms and concepts requiring clarification and consistent usage, describing promising lines of research, and pointing to research genres and designs most likely to define new directions and yield useful findings for policy and practice.

It is our hope that the agenda we recommend will be scrutinized and debated by academic scholars and practitioners, policymakers, school-based educators, and researchers in think tanks and other organizations that provide advice about policy and practice. As noted earlier, we believe our report makes clear that it is pointless to spend further time attempting to prove whether "traditional" teacher education is better or worse than "alternative" preparation or whether master's programs are better than undergraduate programs. It is unlikely that there will ever be a clear and single "winner" in such match races. This problem is exacerbated when teacher preparation is mistakenly assumed to be a matter of uniformly applied and received "treatments," when effectiveness is defined narrowly (e.g., only in terms of scores on standardized tests), and when empirical research is presumed capable of proving which "treatment" produces better results. Instead, questions need to be posed about the various pathways into teaching that account for the characteristics of both programs and candidates as well as the conditions that are needed to ensure effective teachers.

Our review of the literature makes clear why the horse race approach invariably leads to mixed or inconclusive results and at the same time leaves out other very important questions. As this volume suggests, teacher preparation in the United States is enormously complex. It is conducted in local communities and institutions where program components and structures interact with one another as well as with the different experiences and abilities prospective teachers bring with them. Teacher preparation is affected as well by local and state political conditions, which create their own accountability demands and other constraints and possibilities. In addition, the outcomes of teacher preparation always depend in part on candidates' interactions with one another and how they make sense of their experiences.

This is *not* to say that little has been learned or can be learned from empirical study of teacher preparation programs. Our work underscores that studying teacher education is complicated, but it also suggests that what we need now is to develop new programs of research that acknowledge the limitations of previous questions and research designs while building on the most promising current lines.

The Panel

As noted, in the mid- to late 1990s there were many debates about the research base for teacher education, including conflicting claims about the evidence in support of particular policies and practices. Within this context, there were discussions among AERA committees and boards that raised additional questions about the strength of the research base supporting particular standards and accreditation processes. Growing out of these conversations, which occurred under the presidencies of James Banks and Alan Schoenfeld, the AERA Council constituted a Panel on Research and Teacher Education whose chairs and members were appointed by then-AERA-President Lorrie Shepard. Panel members were appointed with different areas of expertise, including teacher education but also including policy, testing and assessment, curriculum, liberal arts, multicultural education, research design and methods, and school reform. Once the panel translated its charge into specific questions, additional panel members were added who authored the individual syntheses included in this volume.

The intention in constituting the panel (and later, in designating external reviewers) was to include multiple viewpoints from the educational research community and to avoid any suggestion that we started with foregone conclusions about the quality of the research base. Throughout its work, the panel took seriously its charge to produce a synthesis that was not beholden to any reform agenda and did not advocate for or against any particular political position. At no time did the panel approach its task as seeking research evidence to bolster "traditional" teacher education, support "the professionalization agenda," or discredit "alternate" routes. Nor did we intend to denigrate the usefulness of existing research. Rather our intention was to review the full body of empirical evidence on certain key questions and evaluate the weight of the evidence.

Several panel members and many of the external reviewers came from outside the teacher education community, working instead from policy or assessment perspectives. Their outside viewpoints broadened the questions we considered and shaped the form and substance of our work.

Having said this, however, it is also important to acknowledge that the panel was primarily university based (with a few notable exceptions). Several members, including the co-chairs, were active researchers and practitioners within the teacher education community. In this sense, the panel's approach may be regarded as an "inside" one similar to that described by Wilson, Floden, and Ferrini-Mundy (2002) in their review of the gaps in teacher preparation research. Wilson and colleagues subtitled their article "An Insider's View from the Outside" to signal that although they were researchers and teacher educators within a university, it was their intention to step back and provide a sharp critique of their own field. We see the inside perspective as a strength because it deepened the questions asked and prompted us to think hard about the value and the limitations of many kinds of research. There is an admitted tension, however, when insiders look critically at the evidence in their own field. By definition, critical synthesis requires a strong scholarly and analytic voice that avoids editorializing or advocating for one's own agenda. On the other hand, a scholarly, analytic voice may be perceived by others within the teacher education community as too distant and passive, failing to take a stand on important issues. We believe it is this combination of inside and outside perspectives that makes this volume unique. We have analyzed what we know and do not know about key aspects of teacher preparation based on the existing research.

THE PANEL CHARGE AND WORKING ASSUMPTIONS

As noted earlier, the panel's charge was twofold: (a) to create for the larger educational community a critical but evenhanded analysis of the empirical evidence related to practices and policies in preservice teacher education in the United States and (b) to recommend research directions that are most promising for what the educational community needs to know in order to prepare strong teachers for the nation's schoolchildren.

To organize its work, the panel translated the charge into nine key questions. We worked from four sets of assumptions about teacher preparation components and programs, the characteristics of empirical research, desirable outcomes of teacher preparation, and the relationships of research to practice and policy.

The Role of Components and Programs

In constructing its questions, the panel focused on the "components" of teacher preparation rather than on programs themselves. By components, we mean the features, structures, and elements that are often part of teacher preparation, such as arts and sciences background, subject matter majors or minors, supervised fieldwork experiences and mentoring in the classroom, instruction in teaching methods, and certification and licensing requirements. It is important to note that different versions and combinations of these components may be present or absent in traditional university-based undergraduate programs, in alternate-route teacher recruitment programs, and in programs run by for-profit providers.

In focusing on components, the panel worked from the assumption that "teacher preparation" and "teacher education" are neither monolithic nor unitary. To the contrary, we assumed that even in the face of tightly specified policies, teacher education is enacted in ways that are highly local—embedded in the multiple and changing contexts of local institutions and subject to the interpretations and social interactions of individuals and groups. Thus, we assumed complexity and variation between and among teacher education structures, organizational arrangements, program types, institutional categories, and preparation paths or routes. At the same time, we acknowledged that there has been considerable inconsistency in the language used to characterize program and structural types.

For these reasons, the panel decided at the outset not to treat teacher education simply as a broad general policy that could be evaluated empirically as either effective or ineffective. Rather than concentrating only on empirical evidence that reflected larger debates about 4- and 5-year programs, traditional and alternate routes, and undergraduate and graduate degrees, we began with an empirical analysis of the characteristics of the prospective and current teaching force and then focused primarily on teacher preparation components and accountability processes. Our assumption was that a variety of teacher preparation programs, paths, and entry routes could contain one or more of these components. By the same token, we assumed that teacher preparation programs and arrangements characterized by the same labels might or might not contain the same components.

We also acknowledged that none of the components of teacher preparation exists in isolation. We recognized that the myriad components of teacher preparation interact with one another, and that their impact is likely to depend on the conditions and contexts within which they occur. Thus, along with questions about outcomes, we also asked questions about the conditions and contexts in which these outcomes occur. Our thought was that this kind of analysis might allow us to map forward from important components to program structures, routes, and types. In our final synthesis chapter (chap. 11, this volume), however, we went back to the issue of program types and entry routes. In this chapter we attempted to sort out claims about program types and entry routes on the basis of empirical evidence. This analysis also suggested directions for research that maps backward from successful programs to components.

What Counts as High-Quality Empirical Research?

There are very few studies in teacher education that conform to the current demand for randomized experiments. As a consequence, there are almost no studies that demonstrate direct causal links from teacher preparation programs to pupils' achievement, most often defined as scores on standardized tests. Many of the reasons for this are discussed in chapter 2 on the history of research on teacher education. Some are parallel to those that explain the general lack of randomized trials in education research—limited funding, other governmental priorities, politics, the objections of some researchers and practitioners to random assignment studies, and the difficulties of implementing this kind of research (Mosteller & Boruch, 2001). It is important to note, however, that experimental studies of the effects of particular instructional strategies used in teacher preparation programs on prospective teachers' behavior were quite popular during the 1960s and 1970s—indeed, these dominated research on teacher education at the time. Some of these experiments, especially those conducted within large teacher preparation programs with multiple sections of courses and fieldwork, involved random assignment of teacher candidates to treatment and control groups. By today's standards, a weakness of these studies was that they concentrated on candidates' behaviors rather than on pupils' learning.

The lack of randomized trials in teacher preparation may also be partly due to the nature of the teacher education enterprise. In an essay entitled, "What To Do Until the Random Assigner Comes," for example, Weiss (2001) describes the complexities involved in conducting randomized field trials to evaluate community programs. If we substitute "teacher education" for "community programs," Weiss's point is interesting here: "Random assignment has a spare beauty all its own, but the sprawling changeable world of [teacher education] is inhospitable to it" (p. 222). Weiss's caution reminds us that the world of teacher education, like the world of community projects or welfare programs, is sprawling and changeable rather than unitary and fixed. In addition, it is very important to emphasize that causal research about teacher preparation has steep and thorny research challenges. It requires at least two causal links—the first linking teacher preparation with the knowledge, skills, and dispositions teacher candidates learn during the preparation period; and the second linking that repertoire of knowledge, skills, and dispositions—as enacted in classroom practice—with pupils' learning or other outcomes. Either link by itself is complex. Causal research that makes both these links may not be impossible nor even necessarily more difficult to conduct in teacher education than in other complex fields, but it is appropriate only at a point in maturity of a line of work when sufficient theoretical and empirical analyses have been done to make randomized trials possible and advisable. It requires resources that seldom have been available in this field.

For these and other reasons, the panel looked at research intended to answer a number of questions, not just causal questions. Our reviews of the literature included the few experimental studies and quasiexperiments that are available as well as correlational studies using sophisticated statistical analyses. Although some critics have suggested that there has been a qualitative bias in teacher education research that needs to be rectified by more causal research, our assumption was that different paradigms of research have different notions of causality and that many empirical approaches are needed. Although the panel agrees that experimental study constitutes an important form of research that has been ignored, we did not regard it as the "gold standard" of all teacher education research. Rather we assumed that different questions call for different research approaches and yield different insights. Along these lines, for example, we assumed that qualitative forms of research, such as case studies and ethnographic research, could be valuable in exploring the ways teacher preparation is locally enacted, how its multiple and dynamic contexts influence the ways resources are used and interpreted by individuals and groups (Erickson & Gutierrez, 2002), and what meanings and understandings participants construct within different contexts.

Our assumption about the need for different research designs is consistent with the approach of the NRC Committee on Scientific Principles for Education Research (Shavelson & Towne, 2002). The NRC report did not define scientific educational research by method or genre but by principles of inquiry, including significant questions that can be investigated empirically, links to related theoretical or conceptual frameworks, research designs and methods appropriate to the question, coherent and explicit chains of reasoning between evidence and theory, findings that are integrated and synthesized across studies, and public critique and review in the professional community. Although the NRC report had not yet been published when we began this project, its principles for defining scientific research in education are consistent with our approach to selecting empirical research and proved useful in describing the range of empirical work included in our syntheses.

A Focus on Outcomes

The panel reviewed empirical research related to the outcomes of teacher preparation, but we interpreted "outcome" in a broad way. Although panel members were unanimous in their view that pupils' learning is paramount, our assumption was that pupils' learning, especially when defined solely by test scores, is a necessary but insufficient way to conceptualize the outcomes of teacher preparation. Thus, we did not limit our review only to those studies intended to determine linkages between teacher preparation and pupils' achievement. Rather, we looked for empirical studies that investigated the influence of teacher preparation on teachers' own learning, teachers' professional practices, and pupils' learning—in addition to studies that examined workforce outcomes such as teacher recruitment and retention.

In treating "teachers' learning" as an outcome of teacher preparation, we included studies on teachers' knowledge growth and understanding and their beliefs and assumptions, as well as on their attitudes, dispositions, and perceptions. We assumed that beliefs and attitudes were the lenses through which teachers enact and interpret their daily work and also the filters through which they use knowledge to construct practice. In treating teachers' practice as an outcome, we focused on professional performance, including what teachers do in classrooms and schools, how they construct curriculum and instruction, how they work with communities and colleagues, how they pose and answer new questions, how they assess and use information about their students' learning, and also how they are evaluated by others. Our inclusion of teachers' learning and performance as outcomes of teacher preparation reflects the panel's assumption that teaching is both an intellectual and a technical activity wherein teachers must translate subject matter and other knowledge into curricular and instructional actions; establish working relationships with pupils, colleagues, and families; and make decisions within the changing contexts of daily work in schools.

In terms of pupils' learning outcomes, we included but did not limit our attention to their standardized test scores, which we regarded as one among multiple measures of what, how, and how much pupils know. We also considered studies of the influence of teacher preparation on pupils' social and emotional growth, attitudes and dispositions, subject matter knowledge, and problem-solving skills. The panel was particularly interested in the interrelationships among these three kinds of outcomes and how they interact with the contexts and conditions of teacher preparation programs, schools, and communities. As we note in the next section, however, and discuss in more detail in the final chapter, we found little research that considered these issues.

Research, Practice, and Policy

As we have noted, the panel took an empirical perspective on teacher preparation. From the beginning, however, the panel acknowledged that although many empirical questions are important, there are also many important questions that cannot be answered by empirical research alone. As noted in chapter 2 (this volume), for example, some of the most contested issues in the history of education deal with fundamental disagreements about the purposes and processes of schooling in a democratic society: Who should be educated? What should be taught? How should it be assessed? Who should decide? In terms of the preparation of teachers, there have been equally enduring disagreements: What is the purpose of the education of teachers in relation to the purposes of education more broadly? Should teachers be prepared to serve the needs of the existing social order, or should they be prepared to be critical and political? Is part of the purpose of teacher preparation to produce new teachers who are "progressive" or readily in line with the "status quo"? How should the effectiveness of teachers be measured?

Questions like these cannot be settled simply by assembling good evidence. To be sure, questions can be shaped, reformulated, or understood more profoundly on the basis of evidence, but evidence must always be interpreted. The values and beliefs of the interpreter influence the purposes for which evidence is used. Education and teacher education are social institutions that pose moral, ethical, social, philosophical, and ideological questions. Although questions of value and ideology underlie many of the most contentious disagreements about teacher education, these disagreements are often mistakenly treated as if they were value-neutral and ideology-free. Along the same lines, research is often mistakenly portrayed as if it had the capacity to resolve issues on the basis of evidence alone. The panel assumed from the outset that teacher preparation policies and practices can never be decided solely on the basis of empirical evidence divorced from values.

The panel assumed that there is a loose coupling between research and actual practice and that research is shaped by the same changing policy and political contexts as is practice (Kennedy, 1997). Simply because something has been researched does not tell us much about what people actually do or should do in preparation programs. Indeed, we see many instances where the same research is interpreted to justify dramatically different practices and policies. In addition, the panel assumed that there are many influences on teacher education practice besides research findings—including ideological commitments, faculty autonomy and academic freedom, the desire to avoid costly disruptions of established practices, the limits of fiscal and other resources, and external regulations. The relationship between research and policy in teacher education is also loose, not tightly coupled. In part because research informs but does not resolve values questions and in part because research problems are constructed by researchers rather than existing independently, the panel worked from the assumption that empirical research cannot generate nomothetic or universal knowledge claims capable of explicitly charting policy (Florio-Ruane, 2002; Liston & Zeichner, 1991). This, of course, is true in every applied field, including medicine and the health professions, where policy decisions depend not only on a synthesis of the empirical evidence but also on local circumstances, costs weighed against benefits, and the availability of personnel, equipment, and technology.

KEY TOPICS AND GUIDING QUESTIONS

To organize its work, the panel translated its charge into nine key topics, each with guiding questions. Some reflect issues that have endured since the preparation of teachers first became a matter of concern in the middle part of the 19th century. Others reflect pressing contemporary issues. Many of the questions refer to the conditions and contexts within which desired outcomes occur. This line of questioning is intended to emphasize the panel's assumption that particular components, programs, and pedagogies do not exist in isolation but in dynamic interrelationship with other components and with the conditions of local environments, the characteristics of prospective teachers in the first place, and the constraints as well as resources of larger political and accountability contexts. Although we found little research that addresses the intricate relationships of conditions, components, and outcomes, it was our intention to stake these questions out as markers for new territories worth pursuing and to guide our formulation of needed research agendas.

For each topic area in the following sections, when teacher education *outcomes* are mentioned, this term is used in its general sense, including teachers' learning outcomes (e.g., teachers' subject matter knowledge, beliefs, and sense of efficacy), teachers' professional practice and performance outcomes (e.g., teachers' skills, instructional strategies, and job evaluations), and pupils' learning outcomes (e.g., achievement test scores, problem-solving strategies, understandings of disciplines, and attitudes toward learning), as well as supply and longevity outcomes such as teacher recruitment, service in hard-to-staff schools and subjects, and retention, as defined earlier.

The background for each of these questions, including detailed discussion about how they have been conceptualized and investigated over time and why they are important currently, is analyzed in the chapters that follow. Readers will need to refer to each chapter for discussion of how and why the issues are framed as they are, including what aspects of the topics are not considered. Here we simply list the overall topics and questions and provide a few explanatory notes. In the following section, we talk about the importance of this set of questions.

Topics 1 and 2 ask questions about the characteristics and entry paths of those entering the teaching force.

TOPIC 1: TEACHER CHARACTERISTICS: RESEARCH ON THE DEMOGRAPHIC PROFILE

Guiding Questions

Who goes into teaching, how are teachers being prepared, what entry routes do they take, and what career paths do they follow?

There are many current claims and predictions about the numbers of teachers the nation needs and will need in the near future, how and where they are being prepared to teach, and what career paths they follow into the profession. In particular, there are competing claims about the long- and short-term retention of teachers with differing characteristics. In posing this set of questions, the panel was interested in sorting out the conflicting claims and providing an empirically accurate but sufficiently complex profile of the demographic characteristics of those entering teaching. (Note that research comparing teachers certified through "traditional" and "alternate" routes was considered with the questions under Topic 9, rather than under Topics 1 or 2.)

TOPIC 2: TEACHER CHARACTERISTICS: RESEARCH ON THE INDICATORS OF QUALITY

Guiding Questions

What are the relationships between teacher quality and the demographic profile, including teacher preparation, entry routes, and career paths?

This second set of questions directly follows from and is the companion to the first set. The intention of the panel here was to provide an analysis of empirical relationships between the demographic profile, as outlined previously, and indicators of teacher quality. It was not the intention with this set of questions to analyze all of the literature related to teacher quality, attributes, and effectiveness. Rather, this topic was limited to research that pertains to preservice teacher preparation per se and that sheds light on the relationships among demographic characteristics, preparation paths, and indicators of quality.

Topics 3, 4, and 5 have to do with the evidence regarding the contributions of the components of teacher preparation programs to desired outcomes.

TOPIC 3: RESEARCH ON THE EFFECTS OF COURSEWORK IN THE ARTS AND SCIENCES AND IN THE FOUNDATIONS OF EDUCATION

Guiding Questions

What are the outcomes of teachers' subject matter preparation, general arts and sciences preparation, and preparation in the foundations of education for teachers' learning and knowledge, teachers' professional practice, and pupils' learning?

For many years, collegiate teacher preparation programs and now many alternate-route programs as well have been organized around key components of preparation, including preparation in subject matter, general arts and sciences, the foundations of education, pedagogy and teaching methods, and classroom teaching. The third and fourth sets of questions the panel investigated are companions, posed to investigate the evidence regarding these components. The third set focuses on the evidence regarding the outcomes of teachers' preparation in subject matter knowledge, general knowledge, and knowledge of the foundations of education. (To avoid redundancy, research dealing with culture, multicultural education, and teaching diverse populations is considered under Topic 6, rather than under Topics 3, 4, and 5. Research dealing with preparing teachers to teach pupils with disabilities and special needs is considered under Topic 7.)

TOPIC 4: RESEARCH ON METHODS COURSES AND FIELD EXPERIENCES

Guiding Questions

What are the outcomes of preparation in teaching methods and in student teaching and other fieldwork and classroom experiences for teachers' learning and knowledge, professional practice, and pupils' learning?

As noted previously, the panel approached the fourth set of questions as a companion to the third set. This fourth set focuses on the evidence regarding the outcomes of teacher candidates' preparation in teaching methods and supervised classroom teaching. (Again, to avoid redundancy, research dealing with methods courses and fieldwork preparing teachers to teach traditionally underserved populations is considered under Topic 6, rather than under Topics 3, 4, and 5. Research dealing with methods courses and fieldwork preparing teachers to teach pupils with disabilities and special needs is considered under Topic 7.)

TOPIC 5: RESEARCH ON PEDAGOGICAL APPROACHES IN TEACHER EDUCATION

Guiding Questions

What are the outcomes of the pedagogies used in teacher preparation (specifically the various instructional strategies and experiences commonly used in teacher education courses, projects, and programs) for teachers' learning and knowledge, professional practice, and pupils' learning? Under what conditions and in what contexts do these outcomes occur?

There are a number of pedagogical approaches that have become quite common, sometimes even referred to as the "signature pedagogies" of teacher education. The panel's intention was to review the literature on pedagogical approaches in teacher education, particularly the teaching methods, strategies, instructional approaches, assignments, and learning opportunities common to teacher education programs and projects at many institutions and within many program types. The panel was interested in what evidence existed regarding the contributions of particular pedagogical strategies to teacher preparation outcomes and the contexts and conditions under which these occur.

Topics 6 and 7 examine the evidence regarding deliberate efforts to prepare teachers to work with populations not traditionally well served by the educational system. We offer a special note here about the research on preparing teachers to work with diverse populations, including children living in poverty, attending hard-to-staff schools, and those from minority racial, cultural, and language backgrounds. The empirical research in these areas is reviewed primarily under Topic 6, although some studies are considered as part of the research on educational foundations (Topic 3), methods courses and fieldwork (Topic 4), and the pedagogy of teacher education (Topic 5). The panel's decision to include the diversity and multicultural research in its own chapter was made partly to avoid redundancy. More to the point, however, we included this literature in its own chapter to call attention to the critical importance of this work given the changing population and continuing disparities in the achievement of groups from different racial and cultural groups. We wanted to mark the fact that this work represents a topic in its own right in teacher education research. There is a paradox here, however. In setting apart the research on teacher education for diversity, we run the risk of marginalizing this work. That certainly is not our intention, but the paradox goes further. To a great extent, the research on preparing teachers for diversity reflects the state of practice in teacher education where issues related to diversity are often relegated to a single course rather than integrated into a coherent program and woven throughout all courses and fieldwork experiences. In following the divisions traditionally made in research and practice in teacher education, then, some people may interpret this volume as implicitly bolstering the status quo. And yet, in constructing a review of the existing research in the field, there are few other options.

TOPIC 6: RESEARCH ON PREPARING TEACHERS FOR DIVERSE POPULATIONS

Guiding Questions

What is the research base for preparing teachers to be effective with traditionally underserved student populations and students in traditionally underserved areas?

What is known about the conditions and contexts under which specific efforts to prepare teachers for work with these populations contribute to teacher education outcomes?

A major challenge facing teacher education today is preparing teachers with the knowledge, skills, and dispositions to work successfully with an increasingly diverse pupil population, particularly those whose cultural, language, racial, and ethnic backgrounds are different from the teachers' backgrounds, and those who live in poor urban and rural areas. The panel wanted to know what evidence existed about the contributions to teacher preparation outcomes of deliberate efforts to prepare teachers to work with these groups and in these settings and the contexts and conditions under which these outcomes occur.

TOPIC 7: RESEARCH ON PREPARING TEACHERS TO WORK WITH STUDENTS WITH DISABILITIES

Guiding Questions

What is the research base for preparing teachers to be effective in teaching students with disabilities? What is known about the conditions and contexts that best prepare teachers for work with pupils with disabilities?

Nearly all teachers today teach classes comprised of pupils with a wide range of abilities and disabilities. The panel wanted to know what evidence existed about the contributions to teacher preparation outcomes of deliberate efforts to prepare teachers to work with pupils with disabilities and the contexts and conditions under which these outcomes occur. The focus here was not on the preparation of specialists whose expertise is working with pupils with disabilities, but the preparation of general education teachers to teach classes that include students with disabilities.

Topics 8 and 9 each stands as its own area, although each is also cross-cutting. Topic 8 includes questions about the accountability processes typically used in teacher education and the evidence regarding the relationship of these processes to teacher education outcomes. Finally Topic 9 explores questions about program and organizational structures as a whole and the evidence regarding their influence on teacher education outcomes.

TOPIC 8: RESEARCH ON ACCOUNTABILITY PROCESSES IN TEACHER EDUCATION

Guiding Questions

What is the research base for the range of accountability processes currently used in teacher preparation, specifically teacher certification, teacher testing, and program accreditation? What is known about the outcomes of these processes for teachers' learning and knowledge, teachers' professional practices, and pupils' learning?

Teacher preparation across the nation is governed by governmental and nongovernmental accountability processes and procedures. The most common are state-regulated initial certification of new teachers, state-required teacher tests for initial licensing, and voluntary professional accreditation of teacher preparation programs and institutions. The panel wanted to know what evidence existed about the effectiveness of these accountability processes and their impacts on teacher quality. (Note that research comparing teachers certified through "traditional" and "alternate" routes was considered with the questions under Topic 9.)

TOPIC 9: RESEARCH ON TEACHER
EDUCATION PROGRAMS

Guiding Questions

What is the research base for recruiting and preparing teachers within particular programmatic or structural arrangements and through alternative certification or recruitment routes? What is known about the conditions, contexts, and outcomes of particular programmatic structures and entry routes for teachers' learning and knowledge, teachers' professional practices, and pupils' learning?

The effectiveness of different teacher education programs, organizational structures, and entry routes to teaching is one of the most hotly contested issues in teacher preparation. Most states now have multiple entry routes, some of which require very limited training prior to full classroom responsibility. In particular there are debates about "traditional" and "alternate" routes, university-based and non-university-based programs and on-the-job versus preparatory teacher education. The panel sought to sort out the conflicting claims about the empirical evidence about these pathways into teaching.

Why These Questions and Not Others?

The panel's questions illuminate many of the most contentious debates about teacher preparation and teacher education reform. These questions are certainly among those that most interest practitioners and policymakers. In the following section, we discuss why we focused on these questions and also consider how the panel's work relates to other current initiatives.

THE AERA PANEL AND OTHER RESEARCH
INITIATIVES IN TEACHER EDUCATION

There are a number of initiatives designed to assess or establish some aspect of the research base for teacher education. Although they often use the same language, they vary considerably in terms of the images of research they convey, how they use research, and the larger purposes to which they are attached. There are at least four different uses and images of research in the current discourse about the research base for teacher education: research as instrument for political reform, research as a warrant for policy decisions, research as foundation for curricular decisions, and research as stance for generating local knowledge (see also, Cochran-Smith, 2002a; Cochran-Smith, 2004c). What appear to be inconsistent conclusions about the quality and strength of the research base may actually reflect different images of research and the fact that different questions were asked in the first place.

For example, in the sharply focused debates about teacher education that emerged in the mid- to late 1990s, research was frequently used as an instrument (and sometimes a weapon—see Cochran-Smith & Fries, 2001) to bolster a particular political agenda, as discussed previously—either professionalization, on the one hand, or deregulation, on the other. In these debates, the person or group reviewing the literature was usually a well-known advocate of one of these reform agendas, and the intention of the review was to gather persuasive research evidence that bolstered that agenda and questioned other agendas (e.g., Abell Foundation, 2001; National Commission on Teaching & America's Future, 1996; Thomas B. Fordham Foundation, 1999). When research is used as a warrant for policy decisions, however, the point is to assess the strength of the empirical evidence about the broad parameters of teacher preparation that policymakers can manipulate. When research is a warrant for policy, the point is not to support an *a priori* agenda (although the reviewer may indeed have a preference), but to present a dispassionate analysis of the weight of the evidence to guide the investment of human and fiscal resources in particular aspects of teacher education (e.g., Allen, 2003; Rice, 2003; Wilson et al., 2001).

Along very different lines, there are also efforts where research is conceptualized as the basic foundation of the teacher education curriculum. When research is evaluated as the foundation of teacher education (e.g., Darling-Hammond & Bransford, in press; Reynolds, 1989), the intention is to identify research-grounded knowledge about pupils' learning, language, pedagogy, and other foundational areas to inform the preparation of new teachers. Finally, there are many local and regional initiatives that regard research as a stance rather than as an instrument or warrant for teacher education. Again the logic is different. The point is to promote teacher education (and teaching) where it is simply part of the culture to engage in research and inquiry that generate local useable knowledge and to make decisions on the basis of evidence and inquiry.

The AERA Panel's intention was to assess the empirical evidence on the components and structures of teacher education of particular interest to the educational community and about which there has been considerable debate. In this sense, the panel's work is similar to other current efforts where research is regarded as the warrant for policy decisions. However, the panel also wanted to critique the assumptions implicit in a policy approach, pointing out strengths and weaknesses in the research of many kinds. The panel also wanted to address a broader range of questions than the causal questions that guide state-level and other governmental policymakers. Finally a main purpose of the panel was to recommend a research agenda for the educational community. Our intent was not simply to draw conclusions about what we know, but to build on what we know and broaden the scope of what we need to know and to consider questions that will generate a richer and more complex research agenda. At the same time, we wanted to acknowledge gaps in our knowledge and understanding of teacher preparation—gaps attributable in part to weaknesses in previous research designs but also to a lack of resources and the research priorities that have guided the distribution of research funds.

What the AERA Panel Project Did Not Do

Our panel did not analyze the full range of conceptual and empirical research related to teacher education. Unlike some previous efforts, particularly those reported in lengthy handbooks of research on teacher education (e.g., Houston, 1990; Sikula, Buttery, & Guyton, 1996), the panel did not attempt to take stock of the field, exploring the array of questions addressed by researchers or taking a comprehensive view of teacher education. In circumscribing its task, the panel knowingly omitted important work related to teacher education. For example, although panel members agreed that teacher education occurs across the career continuum, we limited our review to preservice teacher preparation. Similarly, we did not review the literature on teacher educators themselves, including research on who teaches teachers, the credentials and roles of the professoriate, and other issues related to teacher education providers. In addition, although the panel acknowledges that many issues regarding teacher preparation have global connections, the panel's reviews were limited to research about teacher preparation in the United States.

Furthermore, the panel did not review scholarly work in teacher education unless it addressed the major questions. This means we did not review historical or critical analyses of the foundations of teacher education or writing that was not based on systematic data collection and analysis, such as descriptions of programs and practices, commentaries and opinion pieces, narratives, and reflections. We fully acknowledge, however, that these forms of scholarship significantly shape the ways we think about and do the work of teacher preparation and thus are important contributions to the field. Finally, it is important to note that a wide array of conceptual and theoretical scholarship influenced the ways we conceptualized the problems addressed in this review and also informed our critiques and recommendations for further research. This literature is cited throughout the volume and is reported in a separate bibliography for each synthesis chapter, labeled "other related literature."

CRITERIA FOR SELECTING AND CRITIQUING EMPIRICAL RESEARCH

The nine syntheses in this volume report on original, peer-reviewed empirical studies, including case studies and practitioner studies and, in some chapters, meta-analyses and other syntheses. Although most of the research reviewed was published between 1990 and 2003, the time frames for the nine reviews vary with some chapters reviewing research published over the last 2 decades and others including only more recent research. Variation is the case here because the conditions and contexts that shaped the relevant research differ across the question areas. Each chapter locates its topic within the relevant policy, professional, and historical contexts and specifies reasons for the time frame used.

As a basic selection rule that cuts across the chapters, each review draws on empirical work, as defined in our discussion and consistent with the NRC (Shavelson & Towne, 2002) principles of scientific inquiry. Each chapter describes the process for locating studies, but all combined electronic and hand searches on key words and phrases within the established time period. Studies had to be published in peer-reviewed journals, in books produced by publishers that use peer-review, or in technical reports from research organizations with explicit peer-review procedures.

There are difficulties in determining inclusion and exclusion criteria for teacher preparation research. Some genres of research are regarded differently by different sectors of the educational community. For example, self-study, practitioner inquiry, teacher research, narrative research, the scholarship of teaching and learning, and other emerging forms that take as a research site the practitioner's own professional context and blur the roles of practitioner and researcher are increasingly more common within teacher education (Zeichner, 1999). Many scholars see this work as critical to understanding the processes involved in learning to teach and in teaching teachers (Bullough & Pinnegar, 2001; Hamilton, 1998). However, some reviewers discount this work from inclusion in reviews of "rigorous research" because it is difficult to synthesize studies of "idiosyncratic" courses (Wilson et al., 2001). Other critics suggest that this work does not meet criteria for objectivity and distance between researcher and subject (e.g., Huberman, 1996). In a project like this one, efforts to adjudicate these controversies are exacerbated by the large volume of practitioner research on some of our questions.

In keeping with our working assumption that research designs and genres do not unambiguously define rigor, however, we did not make *a priori* exclusions based on research genres or because practitioner-researchers studied their own students' or single programs. Rather, we stipulated criteria for rigor that were appropriate for each genre, as noted in the following section. In addition, each chapter describes how decision rules were applied and also specifies what can and cannot be generalized, particularly with regard to small studies conducted within one teacher education program or course.

Our criteria were adapted from the guidelines used in Wilson et al.'s (2001) review of the literature on teacher preparation, which was available to the panel in an early form. We revised and adapted these as follows.

- Experimental and quasiexperimental studies were expected to use random assignment to group or some form of matching for entering characteristics.
- Multiple regression studies were expected to control for relevant differences among students, other than the teacher preparation they received, insofar as data on such differences were available.
- Follow-up surveys were expected to be sent to a representative sample with information provided about the return rate; inferences were restricted to alumni perceptions, not allowing for inferences about the effects of programs on other beliefs and knowledge.
- Comparisons of credentialed and noncredentialed teachers were treated like multiple regression studies, including the expectation that they "controlled" for relevant differences between the two groups, other than the characteristic of being credentialed.
- Longitudinal studies of change were expected to check for the effects of attrition and to provide evidence that the changes were not simply due to maturation and teaching experience.
- Interpretive studies were expected to include a description of processes for data collection and analysis and include evidence, such as samples of interview responses or detailed descriptions of events, as part of the report.
- Practitioner inquiries were treated like interpretive studies; they were expected to have clear descriptions of research questions, processes for data collection, and analysis and evidence.

In some chapters, selected studies that did not meet these criteria were included because they were widely cited or represented new efforts in an area of interest. These studies, which were critiqued according to the aforementioned criteria, help to illuminate certain issues, such as the problems that ensue when random assignment or matching of subjects are not used as well as the limitations of single-case studies.

RECOMMENDING A RESEARCH AGENDA

This panel report does not attempt to make pronouncements that can resolve the principal controversies about teacher preparation practice and policy. Teacher education research has rarely enjoyed adequate funding or other resources. It is not at the stage of development that would allow general professional consensus about the conclusions of empirical research and its implications for policy and practice. Research on teacher preparation per se (i.e., empirical research that is identifiable as a body of work related to but separate from research on teaching and research on education in general) is a relatively young field. As chapter 2 points out, research on teacher education began with several large surveys of programs and institutions published in the first half of the 20th century. In the second half of the century, research focused on training and development within programs and then opened up into an array of topics including teachers' knowledge, beliefs, and attitudes; problem solving; professional development over time; and performances in actual classrooms.

As every chapter in this volume makes clear, however, there has been relatively little teacher preparation research that examines the impact of teacher preparation components, pathways, or pedagogies on pupils' learning, an issue at the heart of the most contentious current debates among policymakers, practitioners, and researchers. The panel did not limit its definition of outcomes only to pupils' learning, however, but also considered teachers' learning and professional practices. The panel was particularly interested in the contributions of teachers' learning and practice to pupils' learning and in the complex interrelationships among these three. Unfortunately, we found little research that attempted to make these links, or that explored the impact of curriculum and pedagogy on learning and practice. The research agenda we recommend reflects our identification of this missing program of research on teacher preparation.

Given the historical development of research on teacher education and the strengths and limitations of current research, the panel strove to reach consensus on a new research agenda regarding teacher preparation. As a panel, we agreed on the following points:

- Analysis of the claims that can and cannot be justified on the basis of the empirical research in each area this volume explores
- Identification of important issues and questions in teacher preparation today and how these issues can most usefully be framed and understood
- Criteria for rigorous research
- The directions, questions, and programs of research needed to move the field forward
- The contours of a general research agenda for teacher education that addresses important questions while also responding to the demands of policy and practice

To achieve agreement on this research agenda, the panel deliberated at length over its 4-year life span. We met to conceptualize and elaborate each question and provide feedback on multiple drafts of each chapter. In addition, two panel members served as internal reviewers for each chapter. Following internal review, each chapter was also reviewed by at least two external reviewers differently positioned in policy and education, some affiliated with schools of education and some not, but none affiliated directly with the panel. Finally, in keeping with AERA procedures and our own criteria for rigor, the whole volume was reviewed by three external reviewers who were not involved in the project at any stage prior to the review.

Structure of the Report

Each chapter was authored by a senior researcher (or researchers) in the field, in some cases in collaboration with an advanced doctoral student or recent graduate and in most cases with the help of one or more research assistants. This volume begins with an "Executive Summary" that concisely introduces the nine topics, highlights the findings of each of the reviews, and summarizes recommendations for research on that topic. Chapter 2 provides historical background for the panel's work, locating this work within the history of research on teacher education during the 20th century.

Chapters 3 through 11 contain syntheses of empirical research. Although each chapter raises different issues, each is organized to do the following:

- Introduce the question and discuss its importance historically and currently
- Frame the question in terms of relevant conceptual, policy, and professional issues
- Discuss how the criteria for selection and critique were applied to the review, including the time frame used and the research designs and approaches that were most prevalent
- Organize the relevant research into the major substantive areas studied
- Analyze the relevant empirical research in each area, including claims that can and cannot be made about the topic based on the weight of the empirical evidence
- Recommend a research agenda that builds on but also extends what we know and that addresses the limitations of previous research, including needed research designs, questions that ought to be addressed, and the relationships and contextual factors that ought to be examined

Each chapter includes a detailed chart containing summary information for each of the empirical studies cited as well as two reference lists, one for all of the empirical studies reviewed in the chapter and the other for all other references that informed the chapter.

Chapter 12 lays out a general research agenda for teacher education and suggests the areas of study and the research designs most likely to yield useful findings. This chapter draws on the recommendations made in the preceding chapters but also cuts across the chapters and suggests new directions.

REFERENCES

Abell Foundation. (2001). *Teacher Certification Reconsidered: Stumbling for Quality*, Retrieved October 2001, from http://www.abell.org

Allen, M. (2003). *Eight questions on teacher preparation: What does the research say?* Denver, CO: Education Commission of the States.

American Association of Colleges for Teacher Education. (1997). Selected data from the 1995 AACTE/NCTE joint data collection. Washington, DC: Author.

American Association of Colleges for Teacher Education. (1999). Teacher education pipeline IV: Schools, colleges, and departments of education enrollments by race, ethnicity, and gender. Washington, DC: Author.

Apple, M. (2001). Markets, standards, teaching, and teacher education. *Journal of Teacher Education, 52*(3), 182–195.

Aronowitz, S., & Giroux, H. (1985). *Education under siege.* New York: New World Foundation.

Ballou, D., & Podgursky, M. (2000). Reforming teacher preparation and licensing: What is the evidence? *Teachers College Record, 102*(1), 5–27.

Banks, J. (1995). Multicultural education: Historical development, dimensions, and practice. In J. Banks & C. Banks (Eds.), *Handbook of research on multicultural education* (pp. 3–24). New York: Macmillan.

Bullough, R. V., & Pinnegar, S. (2001). Guidelines for quality in autobiographical forms of self-study research. *Educational Researcher, 30*(3), 13–21.

Castenell, L., & Pinar, W. (Eds.). (1993). *Understanding curriculum as racial text: Representations of identity and difference in education.* Albany, NY: SUNY Press.

Clark, C., & Peterson, P. (1986). Teachers' thought processes. In M. Wittrock (Ed.), *Handbook of research on teaching* (3rd ed., pp. 255–296). New York: Macmillan.

Cochran-Smith, M. (2001). Reforming teacher education: Competing agendas. *Journal of Teacher Education, 52*(4), 263–265.

Cochran-Smith, M. (2002a). The research base for teacher education: Metaphors we live (and die) by. *Journal of Teacher Education, 53*(4), 283–285.

Cochran-Smith, M. (2002b). Reporting on teacher quality: The politics of politics. *Journal of teacher education, 53*(5), 379–382.

Cochran-Smith, M. (2003). Teacher education's Bermuda Triangle: Dichotomy, mythology and amnesia. *Journal of Teacher Education, 54*(4), 275–279.

Cochran-Smith, M. (2004a). Taking stock in 2004: Teacher education in dangerous times. *Journal of Teacher Education, 55*(1), 3–7.

Cochran-Smith, M. (2004b). *Walking the road: Race, diversity and social justice in teacher education.* New York: Teachers College Press.

Cochran-Smith, M. (Ed.). (2004c). *Promises and politics: Images of research in the discourse of teacher education.* Washington, DC: National Reading Conference.

Cochran-Smith, M., & Fries, K. (2001). Sticks, stones, and ideology: The discourse of teacher education. *Educational Researcher, 30*(8), 3–15.

Cochran-Smith, M., & Fries, M. K. (2002). The discourse of reform in teacher education: Extending the dialogue. *Educational Researcher, 31*(6), 26–29.

Darling-Hammond, L. (1999). *Educating teachers for California's future: A report prepared for the Teacher Education Summit of California College and University Presidents.* Los Angeles: The James Irvine Foundation.

Darling-Hammond, L. (Ed.). (2000). *Studies of excellence in teachers.* Washington, DC: National Commission on Teaching and America's Future.

Darling-Hammond, L. (2000a). How teacher education matters. *Journal of Teacher Education, 51*(3), 166–173.

Darling-Hammond, L. (2000b). Teacher quality and student achievement: A review of state policy evidence. *Education Policy Analysis Archives, 8*(1).

Darling-Hammond, L., & Bransford, J. (Eds.). (In press). *Preparing teachers for a changing world. Report of the Committee on Teacher Education of the National Academy of Education.* San Francisco: Jossey-Bass.

Darling-Hammond, L., Chung, R., & Frelow, F. (2002). Variation in teacher preparation: How well do different pathways prepare teachers to teach? *Journal of Teacher Education, 53*(4), 286–302.

Darling-Hammond, L., & Sclan, E. (1996). Who teaches and why. In J. Sikula (Ed.), *Handbook of research on teacher education* (pp. 67–101). New York: Simon & Schuster/Macmillan.

Darling-Hammond, L., & Sykes, G. (Eds.). (1999). *Teaching as the learning profession: Handbook of policy and practice.* San Francisco: Jossey-Bass.

Darling-Hammond, L., Wise, A., & Klein, S. (1999). *A license to teach, raising standards for teaching.* San Francisco: Jossey-Bass.

Darling-Hammond, L., & Youngs, P. (2002). Defining 'Highly Qualified Teachers.' What does 'Scientifically-Based Research' actually tell us? *Educational Researcher, 31*(9), 13–25.

Dilworth, M. E. (Ed.). (1992). *Diversity in teacher education.* San Francisco: Jossey-Bass.

Donovan, M., Wigdor, A., & Snow, C. (Eds.). (2003). *Strategic education research partnership.* Washington, DC: National Academy of Science.

Educational Research Service. (1995). *Demographic factors in American education.* Arlington, VA: Educational Research Service.

Erickson, F., & Gutierrez, K. (2002). Culture, rigor, and science in educational research. *Educational Researcher, 31*(8), 21–24.

Florio-Ruane, S. (2002). More light: An argument for complexity in studies of teaching and teacher education. *Journal of Teacher Education, 53*(3), 205–215.

Gardner, W. (1989). Preface. In M. Reynolds (Ed.), *Knowledge base for the beginning teacher.* Oxford: Pergamon Press.

Gay, G. (1993). Building cultural bridges: A bold proposal for teacher education. *Education and Urban Society, 25*(3), 285–289.

Gay, G. (2000). *Culturally responsive teaching: Theory, research and practice.* New York: Teachers College Press.

Gay, G., & Howard, T. C. (2000). Multicultural teacher education for the 21st century. *The Teacher Educator, 36*(1), 1–16.

Gitomer, D., & Latham, A. (2000). Generalizations in teacher education: Seductive and misleading. Journal of Teacher Education, *51*(3), 215–220.

Grant, C., & Wieczorek, K. (2000). Teacher education and knowledge in "the knowledge society": The need for social moorings in our multicultural schools. *Teachers College Record, 102*(5), 913–935.

Haberman, M. (1988). *Preparing teachers for urban schools.* Bloomington, IN: Phi Delta Kappan Educational Foundation.

Haberman, M. (1991). Rationale for training adults as teachers. In C. Sleeter (Ed.), *Empowerment through multicultural education* (pp. 275–286). Albany: SUNY Press.

Haberman, M. (1996). Selecting and preparing culturally competent teachers for urban schools. In J. Sikula, T. Buttery, & E. Guyton (Eds.), *Handbook of research on teacher education* (2nd ed., pp. 747–760). New York: Macmillan.

Hamilton, M. L. (Ed.). (1998). *Reconceptualizing teaching practice: Self-study in teacher education.* London: Falmer Press.

Hanushek, E. (1996). A more complete picture of school resource policies. *Review of Educational Research, 66*(3), 397–409.

Hanushek, E. (1997). Assessing the effects of school resources on student performance: An update. *Educational Evaluation and Policy Analysis, 19*(2), 141–164.

Hanushek, E. (2002). Teacher quality. In L. Izumi & W. Evers (Eds.), *Teacher quality* (pp. 1–12). Palo Alto, CA: Hoover Institution.

Hart, P. D., & Teeter, R. M. (2002). *A national priority: Americans speak on teacher quality.* Princeton, NJ: Educational Testing Service.

Heap, J. (2002). Personal communication. Memo sent in response to the DOE Secretary's Report: Meeting the highly qualified teachers challenge. Athens, OH: Governor's Commission on Teaching Success.

Hess, F. (2001). *The work ahead [online Web site].* Retrieved March 30, 2001, from the World Wide Web. http://www. educationnext.org

Hodgkinson, H. (2001). Educational demographics: What teachers should know. *Educational Leadership, 58*(4), 6–11.

Hodgkinson, H. (2002). Demographics and teacher education—An overview. *Journal of Teacher Education, 53*(2), 102–105.

Hollins, E., King, J., & Hayman, W. (Eds.). (1994). *Teaching diverse populations: Formulating a knowledge base.* Albany, NY: SUNY Press.

Houston, R. (Ed.). (1990). *Handbook of research on teacher education* (1st ed.). New York: Macmillan.

Howey, K., Arends, R., Galluzzo, B., Yarger, K., & Zimpher, N. (1994). RATE VI: The Context of reform in teacher education. Washington, DC: AACTE.

Huberman, M. (1996). Focus on research moving mainstream: Taking a closer look at teacher research. *Language Arts, 73*(2), 124–140.

Ingersoll, R. (1995). *Teacher supply, teacher quality, and teacher turnover.* Washington, DC: National Center for Education Statistics.

Ingersoll, R. (1999). The problem of underqualified teachers in American secondary schools. *Educational Researcher, 28*(2), 26–37.

Ingersoll, R. (2001). *Teacher turnover, teacher shortages, and the organization of schools.* Seattle, WA: Center for the Study of Teaching and Policy.

Institute of Education Sciences. (2003). *Institute of education sciences*. Retrieved September 12, 2003, from www.ed.gov/about/offices/list/ies/index.html?svc=mr

Irvine, J. (1990). *Black students and school failure: Policies, practice and prescriptions*. Westport, CT: Greenwood.

Irvine, J. (Ed.). (1997). *Critical knowledge for diverse teachers and learners*. Washington, DC: American Association of Colleges for Teacher Education.

Irvine, J., & Fraser, J. (1998, May 13). Warm demanders. *Education Week*, p. 35.

Jenks, C., Lee, J.-O., & Kanpol, B. (2001). Approaches to multicultural education in preservice teacher education: Philosophical frameworks and models for teaching. *The Urban Review, 33*(2), 87–105.

Kaestle, C. (1993). The awful reputation of education research. *Educational Researcher*, 23–31.

Kanstoroom, M., & Finn, C. (1999). *Better teachers, better schools*. Washington, DC: Thomas B. Fordham Foundation.

Kennedy, M. (1997). The connection between research and practice. *Educational Researcher, 26*(7), 4–12.

Kilborn, P. T. (1996, November 30). The welfare overhaul: A special report. *The New York Times*, pp. 1, 10.

King, S., & Castenell, L. (Eds.). (2001). *Racism and racial identity: Implications for teacher education*. Washington, DC: AACTE.

Kozol, J. (1991). *Savage inequalities: Children in America's schools*. New York: Harper & Row.

Ladson-Billings, G. (1999). Preparing teachers for diverse student populations: A critical race theory perspective. In A. Iran-Nejad & D. Pearson (Eds.), *Review of research in education* (Vol. 24, pp. 211–248). Washington, DC: American Educational Research Association.

Lagemann, E. (2000). *An elusive science: The troubling history of education research*. Chicago, IL: University of Chicago Press.

Liston, D., & Zeichner, K. (1991). Research for teaching and teacher education. In D. Liston & K. Zeichner (Eds.), *Teacher education and the social conditions of schooling* (pp. 118–153). New York: Routledge.

Mosteller, F., & Boruch, R. (2001). *Evidence matters, randomized trials in education research*. Washington, DC: Brookings Institution.

Murray, F. (1996). Beyond natural teaching: The case for professional education. In F. Murray (Ed.), *The teacher educator's handbook* (pp. 3–13). San Francisco: Jossey-Bass.

Murrell, P. (2001). *The community teacher*. New York: Teachers College Press.

National Center for Education Statistics. (1997). *Digest of educational statistics*. Washington, DC: U.S. Government Printing Office.

National Center for Education Statistics. (1998). *1998 data file: 1996–1997 common core of data public elementary and secondary school universe*. Washington, DC: U.S. Government Printing Office.

National Center for Education Statistics. (1999). *NAEP 1998 reading report card for the nation*. Washington: DC: U.S. Government Printing Office.

National Commission on Teaching & America's Future. (1996). *What matters most: Teaching for America's future*. New York: Teachers College, Columbia University.

National Commission on Teaching & America's Future. (1997). *Doing what matters most: Investing in quality teaching*. New York: National Commission on Teaching and America's Future.

National Education Goals Panel. (1994). *Data volume for the National Education Goals Report: Volume 1—National data*. Washington, DC: U.S. Government Printing Office.

National Research Council. (2000). *How people learn*. Washington, DC: National Academy Press.

Oakes, J. (1988). *Keeping track: How high-schools structure inequality*. New York: Yale University Press.

Oakes, J., Franke, M., Quartz, K., & Rogers, J. (2002). Research for high-quality urban teaching: Defining it, developing it, assessing it. *Journal of Teacher Education, 53*(3), 228–234.

P.L. 107-110. (2002). *No Child Left Behind Act: Reauthorization of the elementary and secondary act*. Retrieved June, 2002, from http://www.ed.gov

Quartz, K., & TEP Research Group. (2003). Too angry to leave: Supporting new teachers' commitment to transform urban schools. *Journal of Teacher Education, 54*(2), 99–111.

Reynolds, M. (Ed.). (1989). *Knowledge base for the beginning teacher*. Oxford: Pergamon Press.

Rice, J. K. (2003). *Teacher quality: Understanding the effectiveness of teacher attributes*. Washington, DC: Economic Policy Institute.

Rivers, J., & Sanders, W. (2002). Teacher quality and equity in educational opportunity: Findings and policy implications. In L. Izumi & W. Evers (Eds.), *Teacher quality* (pp. 13–23). Palo Alto, CA: Hoover Institution.

Rivkin, S., Hanushek, E., & Kain, J. (1998). *Teachers, schools, and academic achievement* (Working Paper No. 6691). Washington, DC: National Bureau of Economic Research.

Rose, L., & Gallup, A. (2003). The 35th Annual Phi Delta Kappa/Gallup Poll of the public's attitudes toward the public schools. *Phi Delta Kappan,* 41–56.

Sanders, W. (1998). Value-added assessment. *The School Administrator,* 24–27.

Sanders, W., & Horn, S. (1994). The Tennessee Value-Added Assessment System (TVAAS): Mixed-model methodology in educational assessment. *Journal of Personnel Evaluation in Education, 8,* 299–311.

Sanders, W., & Horn, S. (1998). Research findings from the Tennessee Value-Added Assessment System (TVAAS) database: Implications for educational evaluation and research. *Journal of Personnel Evaluation in Education, 12*(3), 247–256.

Shavelson, R., & Towne, L. (Eds.). (2002). *Scientific research in education, Report of the National Research Council's Committee on Scientific Principles in Education Research*. Washington, DC: National Academy Press.

Shulman, L. (1986). Those who understand: Knowledge growth in teaching. *Educational Researcher, 5,* 4–14.

Shulman, L. (1987). Knowledge and teaching: Foundations of the new reform. *Harvard Educational Review, 51,* 1–22.

Sikula, J., Buttery, T., & Guyton, E. (Eds.). (1996). *Handbook of research on teacher education* (2nd ed.). New York: Macmillan.

Sleeter, C. (1995). Reflections on my use of multicultural and critical pedagogy when students are white. In C. Sleeter & P. McAllen (Eds.), *Multicultural education, critical pedagogy: The politics of difference*. Albany: State University of New York Press.

Sleeter, C. (1996). *Multicultural education as social activism*. Albany: State University of New York Press.

Thomas B. Fordham Foundation. (1999). The teachers we need and how to get more of them: A manifesto. In M. Kanstoroom & C. Finn (Eds.), *Better teachers, better schools* (pp. 1–18). Washington, DC: Thomas B. Fordham Foundation.

U.S. Department of Commerce. (1996). *Current population reports: Population projections of the United States by age, sex, race and Hispanic origin, 1995-2050*. Washington, DC: Author.

U.S. Department of Education. (2002). *Meeting the highly qualified teachers challenge: The Secretary's annual report on teacher quality*. Washington, DC: Author.

U.S. Department of Education. (2002). *Meeting the highly qualified teachers challenge, The Secretary's annual report on teacher quality*. Washington, DC: U.S. Department of Education, Office of Postsecondary Education.

U.S. Department of Education. (2003). *Meeting the highly qualified teachers challenge: The Secretary's second annual report on teacher quality*. Washington, DC: U.S. Department of Education, Office of Postsecondary Education.

Valenzuela, A. (2002). Reflections on the subtractive underpinnings of education research and policy. *Journal of Teacher Education, 53*(3), 235–241.

Villegas, A. M., & Lucas, T. (2001). *Preparing culturally responsive teachers: A coherent approach*. Albany, NY: SUNY Press.

Villegas, A. M., & Lucas, T. (2002). *Educating culturally responsive teachers: A coherent approach*. Albany, NY: SUNY Press.

Villegas, A., & Lucas, T. (2004). Diversifying the teacher workforce: A retrospective and prospective account. In M. Smylie & D. Miretzky (Eds.), *Developing the teacher workforce: The 103rd*

Yearbook of the National Society for the Study of Education (pp. 70–104). Chicago: University of Chicago Press.

Wayne, A., & Youngs, P. (2003). Teacher characteristics and student achievement gains: A review. *Review of Educational Research, 73*(1), 89–122.

Weiner, L. (1993). *Preparing teachers for urban schools, lessons from 30 years of school reform.* New York: Teachers College Press.

Weiner, L. (2000). Research in the 90s: Implications for urban teacher preparation. *Review of Educational Research, 70*(3), 369–406.

Weiss, C. (2001). What to do until the random assigner comes. In F. Mosteller & R. Boruch (Eds.), *Evidence matters, randomized trials in education research* (pp. 198–224). Washington, DC: Brookings Institution.

Whitehurst, G. (2001). *Evidence-based education (EBE).* Retrieved September 12, 2003, from www.ed.gov

Wilson, S., & Floden, R. (2003). *Creating effective teachers: Concise answers for hard questions.* Washington, DC: American Association of Colleges for Teacher Education.

Wilson, S., Floden, R., & Ferrini-Mundy, J. (2001). *Teacher preparation research: Current knowledge, gaps, and recommendations.* Washington, DC: Center for the Study of Teaching and Policy.

Wilson, S., Floden, R., & Ferrini-Mundy, J. (2002). Teacher preparation research: An insider's view from the outside. *Journal of Teacher Education, 53*(3), 190–204.

Yeo, F. L. (1997). Teacher preparation and inner-city schools: Sustaining educational failure. *The Urban Review, 29,* 127–143.

Yinger, R. (1999). The role of standards in teaching and teacher education. In G. Griffin (Ed.), *The education of teachers: The 98th yearbook of the NSSE* (pp. 85–113). Chicago: University of Chicago Press.

Yinger, R., & Hendricks-Lee, M. (2000). The language of standards and teacher education reform. *Educational Policy, 14*(1), 94–106.

Zeichner, K. (1993). *Educating teachers for cultural diversity* (National Center for Research on Teacher Learning Special Report No. ERIC Document, ED 359 167). East Lansing, MI: Michigan State University.

Zeichner, K. (1999). The new scholarship in teacher education. *Educational Researcher, 28*(9), 4–15.

Zeichner, K. (2003). The adequacies and inadequacies of three current strategies to recruit, prepare, and retain the best teachers for all students. *Teachers College Record, 105*(3), 490–515.

Zeichner, K., & Schulte, A. (2001). What we know and don't know from peer-reviewed research about alternative teacher certification programs. *Journal of Teacher Education, 52*(4), 266–282.

2

Researching Teacher Education in Changing Times: Politics and Paradigms

Marilyn Cochran-Smith
Boston College

Kim Fries
University of New Hampshire

Teacher education has been a contested enterprise since its emergence in the mid-19th century. From the beginning, research has played a prominent role, particularly in disputes about which disciplines are appropriate to the study of education, what counts as educational scholarship and how evidence should be used to make the case for or against particular approaches to the professional preparation of teachers (Borrowman, 1965; Lagemann, 2000). Although the history of teacher education has been braided with the history of educational research for many years, the role of research is more prominent today than ever before. In many of the most important contemporary debates about teacher quality and teacher preparation, the central focus—at least on the surface—is research itself, particularly on the fundamental question of whether there is a research basis for teacher education and, if so, what that research base suggests.

This chapter analyzes the recursive but nuanced history of research on teacher education over the last half-century, beginning with the 1950s, when research on teacher education emerged as an identifiable field of study in its own right, and ending in the early 2000s. We identify three shifts during this time period in how research on teacher education was conceptualized and studied. We argue that each approach was shaped by the political and professional contexts of the time, particularly public concerns about the schools and calls for the reform of teacher education; the predominant ways teacher education was constructed as a "problem" by researchers and practitioners during the time; and, the major research designs used to study teacher education and make recommendations regarding practice, policy, and further research.

THE "PROBLEM" OF TEACHER EDUCATION

If, as Lagemann (2000) suggests, the history of educational research throughout the 20th century was a troubling one, with "science" a complex and elusive objective, then the history of research on teacher education per se has been at least as troubling and the development of a "science" of teacher education at least as elusive. In 1962 Seymour Sarason, Kenneth Davidson, and Burtor Blatt published *The Preparation of Teachers: An Unstudied Problem in Education.* The title seemed to imply that as of 1962, little research had been done on teacher education, and the book was often cited in the following years as a way to justify new studies of teacher education. Nevertheless, just 2 years after this book appeared, there was enough research for Frederick Cyphert and Ernest Spaights (1964) to publish an entire volume that synthesized 189 studies on teacher education published between 1958 and 1963.[1]

The publication just 2 years apart of these two books—one implying that teacher preparation was "unstudied" and the other reviewing almost 200 studies on the topic—introduces an important point about the history and the current state of research on teacher education. When assessing research on teacher education in terms of quality, quantity, and usefulness, reviewers often work from very different assumptions about what counts as research, what defines research rigor, which research questions are important to study, and what the purposes of research ought to be in terms of its influence on policy and practice.

Looking back to 1962, it becomes apparent that Sarason and his colleagues (1962) were not referring to teacher education research *writ large* when they suggested that the preparation of teachers was an "unstudied problem." Rather they were referring to the lack of systematic attention to the disconnect between teacher preparation and the realities of classrooms and school systems, which was the "problem" they deemed most important. Their book, which actually had very little to say about research on teacher education, made a case for constructing "the problem of teacher education" in accordance with their particular interest. Cyphert and Spaights (1964), on the other hand, were reviewing how teacher education research had been defined over a 5-year period in terms of the topics commonly studied and the methodological approaches employed. Their intent was to provide a broad overview of an emerging field by examining how much and what kind of research had been done on the historical development and scope of teacher preparation, its administration and organization, college and faculty staff, curriculum and instruction, and teacher education students and faculty. The Sarason et al. and the Cyphert and Spaights (1964) reviews reached very different conclusions about the status of teacher education research not

---

[1]As far as we can determine, the Cyphert and Spaights's review was the first attempt to synthesize research focusing specifically on teacher education.

because they necessarily disagreed but because they asked very different questions in the first place.

A Historical Overview of Teacher Education Research

In this chapter, we analyze the background of contemporary research on teacher education by asking what it has meant since the 1950s to study teacher preparation. We limit our historical overview to the last half-century for two reasons. First, the syntheses in chapters 3 through 11 of this volume concentrate primarily on contemporary research published since 1980. This chapter's analysis of the directions of research on teacher education over the last 50 years helps to contextualize the contemporary research, not only revealing the roots of current lines of research but also foreshadowing many contemporary critiques. Second and more importantly, however, we begin our history with the 1950s because it was during this period that research on teacher education (as well as research on teaching) began to mushroom in scope and quantity, due in part to the development of recording technologies that permitted close observations of teachers.

To make this chapter manageable, we used syntheses of research on teacher education as historical artifacts, assuming that they reflected the ways of defining and studying teacher education that prevailed in particular periods. We located 29 syntheses of research on teacher education published between 1950 and 2003. We are not suggesting, however, that there was no research on teacher education prior to the 1950s. Several major surveys of teacher education programs were conducted during the first half of the 20th century as well as a number of commissioned reports. Although we do not consider these in detail, we refer to them briefly in the section that follows.

A number of distinctions have been made over time between research on teaching and research on teacher education. Although closely related, these two are not the same. The latter may best be understood as a subset of the former (Fenstermacher, 1985), and there are important distinctions between them (Zimpher & Ashburn, 1985). In this chapter, we work from the simple distinction that research on teaching primarily refers to investigations of some aspect of teaching in K–12 schools where the learners in question are K–12 pupils, and research on teacher education refers to studies of aspects of the preparation of K–12 teachers where the learners in question are teacher candidates. Based on this distinction, we regard research on teaching as an essential part of the context in which research on teacher education developed.

A Recurring Pattern in the History of Research on Teacher Education

In this chapter, we argue that the history of research on teacher education from the late 1950s to the early 2000s has followed a similar pattern: A confluence of events and blue-ribbon reports reveals that the schools are in trouble and teachers are failing in some way. Teacher preparation is condemned by both internal and external critics for its lack of intellectual rigor, selectivity standards, structural arrangements, research base and failure to achieve positive results in schools and classrooms. There are many calls for reform (that may be, but often are not, research based), including calls for more sharply focused and better funded research. Many initiatives are put into place in teacher education that may or may not have lasting value, and new programs of research develop with and without funding.

Of course this pattern in the history of research on teacher education does not unfold in nearly so linear a way as we just made it sound, and conclusions about the state of research on teacher education have often differed. Our argument is that different conclusions are not dependent so much on who was right or wrong about teacher education research, but on (a) the historical and political context and how research on teacher education is positioned in that larger context; (b) how "the problem" of teacher education is defined; and, (c) how the study of teacher education is worked out methodologically to address the problem. We use these factors to organize our history of research on teacher education.

When we refer to the historical context of an era, we mean the larger political, professional, and policy contexts that influence the development of teacher education research. These include public concern about the economy, the welfare of the nation in a changing society, and the capacity of the schools to meet the needs of future citizens and leaders. Our discussion of the larger context also includes major commissioned reports about the education of elementary and secondary teachers as well as critiques of existing educational research. We also consider governmental and nongovernmental regulations and resources that constrain and support teacher education practice and research. By "the problem" of teacher education, we do not mean problem in a pejorative sense. We use the word as social science researchers do to define "the problem" to be addressed by a particular study, including the issues, questions, and conditions that define a topic of concern to the educational community. Conceptualizing a research problem limits the shape and scope of that problem, delineates important questions, and suggests appropriate research designs. For each period we discuss how "the problem" of teacher education was studied, including the questions researched and the designs used.

In the pages that follow, we outline the historical context for research on teacher education during three overlapping periods: the late 1950s through the early 1980s, the early 1980s and into the early 2000s, and the mid- to late 1990s to the present. Our argument is that during these periods there were different dominant ways of constructing and studying the problem of teacher education: as a training problem, as a learning problem and as a policy problem. Although these three constructions capture the predominant approach of each period, it is important to note that, like the history of educational research generally, the history of research on teacher education was not a steady march over time in which one perspective supplanted another (Lagemann, 2000). Rather, the development of research on teacher education can be characterized more as a "conversation" among alternative viewpoints and approaches (Shulman, 1986a) than as a linear shift from one approach to the next.

PRELUDE: RESEARCH ON TEACHER EDUCATION PRIOR TO THE 1950S

As the 20th century began, industrialization, urbanization, and immigration were strong influences on the American scene. Surging elementary and secondary school enrollments prompted a teacher shortage, and women were hired in large numbers to meet the demand, a phenomenon Lagemann (2000) and others have described as the "feminization" of teaching. Concurrently there were increasing calls for professional teaching standards, including the beginning of certification requirements, the establishment of accrediting organizations and the beginnings of research on attributes related to teaching effectiveness. Educators and policymakers debated the appropriateness of normal schools versus colleges and universities as well as liberal arts colleges versus teachers colleges as the proper location for teacher education. There were deep rifts between "academic" professors in the humanities and letters and professors in the emerging field of education who were referred to by their critics as the "educationists." Partly as a result of the perceived scholarly weakness among education faculty, many critics called for changes in how and where teachers were prepared (Lagemann, 2000; Lucas, 1999).

Notwithstanding the lack of evidence linking time spent in preparation programs with desirable educational outcomes, the time spent by future teachers in preparatory programs steadily increased (Clifford, 1975; Herbst, 1989; Lucas, 1999; Watson, Cottrell, & Lloyd-Jones, 1938). No one could be confident, however, that greater amounts of teacher education, including supervised "practice teaching," had a positive impact on teachers' performance in the classroom (Sedlak, 1989; Warren, 1985; Warren & Ogonowski, 1998). In response to the lack of information about what really made for good teacher education, there was a push between 1920 and 1940 to upgrade the teaching profession with numerous advisory councils and organizations, several national conferences, and multiple institutional self-studies (Bagley, 1939; Borrowman, 1956; Learned & Bagley, 1920; Monroe, 1952; Rugg, 1952).

The push to upgrade the profession also prompted several massive investigations. Using survey as the primary research tool, the Commonwealth Teacher-Training Study (Charters & Waples, 1929) and the National Survey of the Education of Teachers (Evenden, 1933; also see Frazier, 1935) were conducted. The point of the Commonwealth study was to find out "scientifically" what the most important traits of teachers were, isolate and reduce these traits to charts, lists and formulae including minute behavioral components, and then use these to guide teacher preparation. Charters and Waples, the principal investigators, identified 83 traits of "good" teachers, rank-ordered them by importance. They concluded that teacher training institutions should use these to guide the curriculum (Charters & Waples; Condliffe Lagemann, 2000; Kliebard, 1973). In 1929, following the Commonwealth Study, Congress mandated that the U.S. Commissioner of Education undertake a nationwide survey of the education of teachers. This mandate was supported by the American Association of Teachers Colleges (established in 1923), the National Council of State Superintendents and Commissions of Education, the Association of Deans of School of Education and the North Central Association of Colleges and Secondary Schools. The National Survey of the Education of Teachers (Evenden, 1933) called for (a) an increase in the amount of teacher preparation, academic studies, professional studies, and classroom practice; (b) more research on teacher education; and (c) preparation programs that reflected the proven characteristics of effective teaching. As a result, teacher preparation programs increased requirements in general education, separated secondary from elementary methods and deemphasized general methods in favor of subject-specific methods. In addition, coursework in the history of education lost out to courses in philosophy, psychology, and measurement (Cottrell et al., 1956; Cremin, 1953; Frazier, 1935).

Between 1938 and 1944, the American Council on Education (ACE) disseminated 27 publications on teacher education. Moving away from the survey method, the ACE sought to initiate self-improvement of teacher preparation programs. In 1938, for example, ACE's Commission on Teacher Education undertook a project involving experimental action in 20 institutions of higher education and 14 public school systems. The results were largely descriptive of activities or points of view. The commission directed its efforts toward the discovery of processes that would expedite reform and increase cooperation among the agencies involved in teacher education. By emphasizing goal setting, shared commitment, and common principles surrounding teacher education, the commission clearly signaled that the search for a universal formula in teacher education was unproductive and foolish (Commission on Teacher Education, 1946).

Whatever improvement was made as a result of these three major studies, the recession and two World Wars negated much of it. Teachers flocked to war-related efforts, and the number of students enrolled in teacher education programs sagged (Hodenfield & Stinnett, 1961; Rugg, 1952). Alarmed at the growing trend of teachers with emergency certificates, the National Education Association (NEA) established the National Commission on Teacher Education and Professional Standards (TEPS) in 1946. Setting up liaisons in every state, the primary goal of TEPS was to upgrade the status of teaching as a "profession" (Bigelow, 1941, 1958; Conant, 1963; Cottrell et al., 1956; Frazier, 1943; VanEvery, 1979). During the first half of the 20th century, however, the division between liberal arts scholars and teacher educators erupted and escalated a number of times. Extremists on one side proclaimed that teachers were being taught how to teach but not what to teach; extremists on the other side claimed that if one really knew how to teach, one could teach anything.

A decade after the establishment of TEPS and a year before Sputnik, the American Association of Colleges for Teacher Education published *Teacher Education for a Free People*, a study of trends and problems in teacher education. After a 3-year examination of academic preparation, professional studies and laboratory experiences, the panel, chaired by Donald Cottrell (Cottrell et al., 1956), recommended institutional action to remedy deficiencies at the college and university level. Unfortunately, however, the report provided few concrete recommendations of procedures, techniques, or issues of pedagogy at the "practice" level.

The Cottrell et al. (1956) report was quickly followed by three conferences held in Bowling Green, Ohio; Lawrence, Kansas; and San Diego, California, between 1958 and 1960. The conferences brought together teacher educators and professors from liberal arts colleges in an effort to end ongoing debates. The point was to figure out what these two groups agreed upon relative to teacher education. Hodenfield and Stinnett (1961) indicated that the following consensus was reached: (a) prospective teachers needed more and better education; (b) "deadwood and trivia" needed to be cleared out of teacher education programs; (c) establishing higher standards would result in more, not fewer, teachers; (d) knowing "how to teach" and "what to teach" were both important; (e) there was value in "practice teaching"; (f) all schools and departments in a university needed to share in the responsibility for teacher education; (g) early identification of prospective teachers, selective recruitment, and admissions standards and effective guidance policies were needed; (h) a fifth year in college for teachers was a "must"; (i) a substantial part of the total program needed to be devoted to general education; (j) elementary- and secondary-school teachers alike needed a substantial academic specialization; and (k) elementary-school teachers needed more courses in methods than those preparing for high school.

Prior to the 1950s, teacher education moved from normal schools to teachers colleges and eventually to colleges and universities. The idea that teaching and teacher education were "professions" was argued. There were multiple critiques of teacher preparation programs and simultaneous calls for reform (Borrowman, 1956, 1965; Cremin, 1978). During this same period, criticisms also were leveled against other professions, including law, medicine, nursing, the clergy, and engineering, which were attempting to upgrade and enhance their professional status.

RESEARCH ON TEACHER EDUCATION AS A TRAINING PROBLEM: LATE 1950S TO EARLY 1980S

The pattern of critique and reform that shaped teacher education research, policy, and practice began to emerge during the post-World-War II years, although its roots reached further back (Lagemann, 2000). During this time, teacher education was constructed and studied primarily as a training problem.

Political, Professional, and Policy Contexts

The 1957 launch of Sputnik by the Soviets prompted "public hysteria" about the ability of American public schools to prepare the next generation of scientists for graduate study in physics and the other sciences (Lagemann, 2000, p. 172). This exacerbated already-existing public concerns about the quality of the schools following World War II, when, as Lagemann points out, public education was intensely criticized for having become "soft" and "mediocre" (p. 159), placing more emphasis on students' interests and life adjustment than on rigor and excellence.

Not surprisingly, public perceptions of the failure of the schools were linked to similar conclusions about the failure of the "educationists" to prepare the nation's teachers. Arthur Bestor (1953), a leader of the Council for Basic Education that was founded in 1956 to bolster the academic curriculum of schools, had already conveyed the message that educationists were making the public schools into an "educational wasteland" (Clifford & Guthrie, 1988). Following Bestor came influential critiques of teacher education from James Conant (1963) and James Koerner (1963).

Conant's 2-year study (1963), sponsored by The Carnegie Corporation of New York, examined where elementary- and secondary-school teachers received their education. Conant, a former president of Harvard University, concluded that educational requirements for teachers were low, although he found considerable variety across institutions. Conant did not conclude, as was charged, that there was a conspiracy among educators to limit what teachers studied (Goodlad, 1990). However, he did recommend a "radical" new approach to certification and a "redirection of public authority" (Conant, p. 56), that would remove the states from prescribing time spent on education courses. Central to Conant's recommendation that teacher preparation place more emphasis on liberal arts and humanities courses and less on pedagogy and methods was his assessment that the "science of education" had not come of age and was not capable of playing a role in the training of teachers.

James Koerner's study (1963), which focused on the "miseducation" of American teachers, was considerably more damning than Conant's (1963). A leader of the Council for Basic Education, Koerner bluntly declared that "the inferior intellectual quality of the education faculty [was] *the* fundamental limitation of the field" (p. 17). Koerner's critique, like Conant's, focused on the idea of a science of education. Based on a broad review of the literature, commission reports, and institutional transcripts, Koerner concluded that the evidence for teacher preparation was weak, if not nonexistent, and thus there should be less rigidity in programs and multiple entry routes. Unlike those who make similar critiques of teacher education programs and research evidence in the 2000s; however, Koerner emphatically rejected the idea that systematic application of the scientific method, which he referred to as "the trap of scientism" (p. 29), would solve the problems of teacher education. This would only happen, he asserted, by training the intellect and "the moral facility" of teachers through subject matter study and liberal education.

Notwithstanding these sharp critiques, new federal programs sprang up in the 1960s and 1970s that provided direct or indirect support for teacher training and recruitment. The Teacher Corps was enacted in 1965 as part of Title V of the Higher Education Act to address teacher shortages, particularly in high-poverty areas. The Education Professions Development Act of 1967 was also intended to improve educator recruitment and training. These two programs shaped the dominant research agenda on teacher training that emerged (Earley & Schneider, 1996).

Constructing Teacher Education as a Training Problem

Those who conducted research on teacher education during the 1960s and 1970s were no doubt influenced by the critics' conclusions that there was no compelling science of education. In fact the major developments in research on teaching during these years were the end of a program of research seeking to identify the personal characteristics of teachers that were linked to effectiveness—following Ryan's (1960) definitive finding that this research had produced nothing of use (Lanier, 1982)—and the rise of teacher effectiveness research, especially studies that attempted to correlate observed teacher behaviors with pupils' achievement, as measured on end-of-year tests. Known as process–product research, the ultimate intention of this new line of research was to develop "the scientific basis for the art of teaching" (Gage, 1963) by specifying effective teacher behaviors and applying them as treatments to classroom situations. This line of inquiry dominated research on teaching for at least 2 decades (Shulman, 1986a).

It was also during this era that research on teacher education emerged as an identifiable program of empirical study related to, but different from, research on teaching. The federal research and development centers, established in 1963, the regional education laboratories, especially the Far West Labs, and large studies and projects such as Stanford's Program on Teaching Effectiveness, played a major role in developing this line of research. The Research and Development Center for Teacher Education at the University of Texas, Austin, was led by Gene Hall and then Robert Peck and Oliver Brown in partnership with colleagues at the Universities of Houston, Oregon, and Florida. The agenda of the Texas center was the development of innovations in educational settings (Freiberg & Waxman, 1990), particularly inventing technologies for the training of teachers and analyzing the conditions under which these technologies were effective. This line of research led to whole catalogs of "teacher training products" (Gage, 1978) and was linked to the competency-based teacher education movement of the 1970s, which zeroed in on prospective teachers' mastery of specific observable teaching behaviors and competencies (Urban, 1990).

The major line of research that developed in teacher education, which was in keeping with the reasoning of the process–product research on teaching more generally, identified the most effective procedures for training teachers to display teaching behaviors already validated as effective ways to raise pupils' test scores. In his 1971 symposium on teacher education research that helped to shape this emerging field of study, for example, B. O. Smith (1971) defined the purview of research on teacher education this way: "Generally speaking, research on teacher education attempts to answer the question of how the behavior of an individual in preparation for teaching can be made to conform to acceptable patterns" (p. 2). Similarly Turner (1975) characterized the aim of teacher education research in the 1975 National Society for the Study of Education (NSSE) yearbook (Ryan, 1975) as "optimiz[ing] that portion of teacher work success attributable to teacher preparation" (p. 87).

It is important to note that other topics, from recruitment to student teaching, were also studied during this time, and there were discussions about the theoretical foundations of teacher education as well. Much of the research was conducted by researchers whose disciplinary base was psychology and who were not necessarily involved in the actual practice of teacher education. These trends are reflected in the research reviews and syntheses generated during the period (Cyphert & Spaights, 1964; Denemark & Macdonald, 1967; Haberman & Stinnett, 1973; Peck & Tucker, 1973; Turner, 1975; Wilk, Edson, & Wu, 1967). In addition, there were important discussions about the role of research in teacher education (e.g., Collier, 1964; Haskew, 1964; Smith, 1971; Smith & Meux, 1964; Turner, 1971). Nonetheless, as reviewers have noted previously (Lanier & Little, 1986; Wideen, Mayer-Smith, & Moon, 1998; Zeichner, 1999), the major focus of the research during this time period was identification and verification of instructional methods used in teacher-training programs themselves.

The assumptions underlying the construction of teacher education as a training problem mirrored many of the assumptions underlying the process–product research on teaching more generally. With process–product research, teaching was regarded largely as a technical transmission activity, and teaching and learning were assumed to be related in a linear way. Teacher behavior was the beginning point and pupil learning the endpoint of classroom exchanges. Building on these premises, research on teacher education assumed that teacher training was a technical transmission activity and that teacher training and teacher behavior were related to one another in a linear way with training the starting point and teacher behavior the endpoint. It is important to note that within the training model, researchers paid more attention to teacher outcomes than to pupil outcomes. This was the case because the target behaviors for prospective teachers were assumed already to be correlated with pupils' achievement (largely based on the emerging teaching effectiveness research); thus, the targeted teacher behavior was assumed to be a reasonable proxy for pupil outcomes.

Studying Teacher Education as a Training Problem

When teacher education was constructed as a training problem, the ultimate objective of research was to identify transportable training procedures that had an impact on teacher behaviors. The version of the training approach that became prominent in research on teacher education was using the independent variables of process–product research on teaching (i.e., teacher behaviors that had been shown to be effective) as the dependent variable in research on teacher preparation. Teacher-training procedures themselves (i.e., various procedures for training teachers to exhibit these behaviors and policies for selecting teachers most likely to exhibit these behaviors) were regarded as the independent variables. Along these lines, Gage (1964) argued that in the "strictest logic," teacher effectiveness should be the dependent variable in all teacher preparation studies, including research on recruitment and selection policies, personnel decisions, and arrangements of internships.

The independent variables most often studied were specific training procedures (e.g., microteaching, interaction analysis, behavior modification, lecture, and demonstration) or clusters of training procedures (e.g., some version of the aforementioned with and without feedback, with immediate or delayed feedback) used in teacher preparation programs. The dependent variables were demonstrations by teachers that they had mastered desired behaviors (e.g., clearly stated objectives for learning, certain question-asking techniques, and displaying variability in teaching practices) or had developed certain attitudes. Demonstrations were usually based on observers' ratings of videotaped teaching segments, direct observations of teaching where observers looked for specific behaviors, and pupils' and supervisors' judgments about prospective teachers' behaviors. Research methods included correlational and other studies, but the preferred method was experimental design featuring control and one or more treatment groups of prospective teachers who received different training, based on the presence, absence, or combination of specific training techniques. Very few of these studies examined the link between the observed teacher behaviors and the pupil outcomes.

As noted previously, a number of research reviews were published during this time. The early ones agreed with Cyphert and Spaights (1964) that the "extant research in teacher education [was] neither extensive nor profound" (p. 1). A few years later, Denemark and Macdonald (1967) evaluated the research on teacher education in terms of the five aspects identified in Smith's (1962) appraisal of teacher education, which had guided the 39 "breakthrough" teacher education programs supported (at the level of $29 million) by the Fund for the Advancement of Education and the Ford Foundation. Denemark and Macdonald concluded that there was little or no research on three of the five aspects—prospective teachers' general education, prospective teachers' subject matter knowledge, and the role of unifying theories in teacher education. They found that most research focused on the last two aspects—the impact of instructional methods and media on prospective teachers' mastery of behaviors or the impact of student teaching and internships on prospective teachers' attitudes, responses, and observations.

The definitive synthesis of this period was the chapter by University of Texas, Austin, researchers, Peck and Tucker in the second *Handbook of Research on Teaching* (Travers, 1973). Characterizing the "state of the art" of research on teacher education, Peck and Tucker reached this optimistic conclusion:

> Since 1964 there has been a great deal more empirical research performed on one or another operation in the education of teachers than in all the decades before that date. Moreover, it is our strong impression that a quantum leap occurred, somewhere between 1963 and 1965, in the quality of both the design and the reporting of research in this field. One can only speculate about possible causes, but the most likely one would appear to be the influx of substantial federal monetary support for graduate training and research in education, for the first time in American history, starting in the early 1960s. (p. 941)

Based on a synthesis of "experimental research on the process of teacher education" (p. 942), Peck and Tucker concluded that prospective teachers could master specific teaching behaviors during the preservice program and that certain training procedures were more effective than others. Their most important conclusion was that a "systems approach" or an "instructional design" approach improved teacher education's effectiveness at inducing desirable teaching behaviors in both "cognitive and affective respects" (p. 943). Their review cited evidence to support three examples of this approach—training teachers in interaction analysis, microteaching (or learning particular teaching strategies through focused trial lessons with guided supervision and feedback), and behavior modification. They also concluded that prospective teachers were more likely to master teaching behaviors when they were modeled by their instructors, that direct or simulated involvement was more effective than lectures or instructional theory, and that using these procedures improved patterns of learning by teachers and pupils.

Although the training research was dominant during this time, it was not without critics. Haberman and Stinnett (1973), for example, questioned the teacher-training studies at their very core by critiquing the effectiveness research on which they were based. They argued that the empirical research base for specific and generally applicable teaching behaviors was, at best, thin. They concluded that the competency-based teacher-training programs that arose in the late 1960s and early 1970s partly as a result of the effectiveness research on teaching had no greater empirical research support than did other teacher education programs. Popkewitz, Tabachnick, and Zeichner (1979) also critiqued the training studies at their roots, challenging the "empirical–analytic" paradigm, which was the foundation of the training research. They suggested this kind of research not only "dull[ed] the senses" (p. 52) but ultimately was unhelpful:

> The empirical-analytic paradigm makes sense in a world in which it is possible to separate causes from one another so that some causes can be controlled while others are manipulated experimentally or otherwise traced. The world must be one in which causes *preceded* and are *separate* from effects or else the logic (the search for controls over causes that produce desirable effects) breaks down. (emphasis in original, p. 56)

Popkewitz and colleagues suggested that a more critical research stance was needed that made the existing social arrangements of schooling problematic and challenged assumptions about definitions of professional competence.

Turner (1971) raised methodological issues about the research of this time period. He viewed teacher preparation as a policy that should produce teachers more proficient than those "alternately prepared" (p. 10). Turner saw major obstacles to establishing causal relationships between particular aspects of teacher preparation and teacher performance, given the many intervening variables and the long lag between preparation and actual classroom performance. Turner argued that the research situation in teacher education was not like that in experimental psychology; he called for research driven by theory and having the capacity to account for multivariate relationships.

Despite these and other critiques, constructing and studying teacher education as a training problem was the dominant approach until it ebbed in influence by the mid-1980s as researchers became more interested in studying teacher education as a "learning problem," as defined in the following section. Nevertheless, it is important to note that understanding teacher education as a training problem was not completely abandoned any more than research on "the effects of teaching" was abandoned following its heyday in the 1960s and 1970s (Floden, 2001). Although the training research program in teacher education ebbed in influence, it continued and in the early 2000s has reemerged in a somewhat different but closely related version.

The Value of Studying Teacher Education as a Training Problem

The essence of studying teacher education as a "training problem" during the 1960s and 1970s was twofold. It meant conceptualizing teacher preparation as a formal educational process intended to ensure that prospective teachers' behaviors conformed to those of effective teachers. To a large extent, the training research assumed that the behaviors of effective teachers were already clearly identified and well known. That is, these behaviors were presumed to have been empirically established through studies of classroom teaching that defined teacher effectiveness in terms of pupils' scores on achievement tests or other outcomes deemed desirable. Studying teacher preparation this way meant conducting experimental and other empirical research on the training techniques most likely to lead to sustained performance of effective teaching behaviors in prospective teachers. From the training perspective, the link from teacher preparation to pupil achievement was assumed rather than examined in most of these studies. In other words, the training aspects of teacher preparation were not connected directly to pupil outcomes or to measured effects beyond the preparation period. The outcome most often studied was prospective teachers' behavior (or supervisors' and pupils' evaluations of that behavior), which the researchers assumed was correlated with pupil achievement, rather than pupil achievement itself. Prospective teacher behavior and its presumed connection to pupil achievement was the proxy for teacher effectiveness.

To their credit, those who carried out the training research in the 1960s and 70s attempted to develop and disseminate what in the parlance of contemporary policy might be called evidence-based practice in teacher preparation. That is, they concentrated on developing a body of rigorous empirical research about how to produce effective behaviors in prospective teachers so that program and policy decisions could be empirically rather than normatively based. This is precisely what is called for in the early 2000s by the critics of university-based teacher preparation who argue that there is little compelling evidence about the most effective approaches to teacher preparation and also by reform initiatives intended to ensure that decisions about how to prepare teachers are driven by evidence, not ideology.

The research from the training period reveals that prospective teachers can indeed be trained to exhibit targeted teaching behaviors and that some training techniques are more effective than others in producing those behaviors. Assuming that teaching is in part a technical activity, it may well be that research on training can be used to establish evidence-based practices for preparing teachers for some of the routine and technical tasks of teaching, such as certain aspects of classroom management and organization. In addition, because the training research utilized a variety of experimental and correlational research designs, it has the potential to inform current efforts to study the impact of teacher preparation on a variety of educational outcomes, including teachers' professional practice. As the next two sections of this chapter reveal, however, the training research did not connect the technical aspects of teaching to its many intellectual and decision-making aspects nor did it account for how teachers' knowledge and beliefs mediated their behavior in classrooms. Furthermore, the training research did not address the many variations in policy and accountability contexts in which teachers' work is embedded. It may well be, as we discuss in our conclusion, that the research on teacher preparation that is most needed in the contemporary context is that which attempts to link the training, learning, and policy aspects of teacher preparation to one another.

RESEARCH ON TEACHER EDUCATION AS A LEARNING PROBLEM: EARLY 1980S TO EARLY 2000S

Over the last 20 years, the pattern of critique and reform that had shaped teacher education research during the previous 3 decades continued. Concerns about the public schools surfaced again in the 1980s, accompanied and followed by critique of teacher preparation, reform of programs, and development of new lines of research.

Political, Professional, and Policy Contexts

As the 1980s began, the United States was mired in economic difficulties. Concerns escalated that the nation had not kept pace with the changing world economy. Not surprisingly—and rightly or wrongly—concerns about the economy were tightly coupled with concerns about America's schools. Historians and critics of all stripes (e.g., Goodlad, 1990; Lagemann, 2000; Ravitch, 2000) agree that the galvanizing event of the period was the publications of *A Nation at Risk: The Imperative for Educational Reform*, the report of the National Commission on Excellence in Education (1983). It asserted that if the current state of American education had been imposed on the nation by a foreign power, it would have been considered an act of war. The report's blustery language, paired with its clarion call for higher educational standards, triggered a swift array of school reforms that "redefined the politics of education" (Ravitch, p. 411) for the remainder of the century.

To reverse the presumed decline in educational standards and outcomes, such influential groups as the Task Force on Teaching as a Profession of the Carnegie Forum on Education and the Economy (1986) asserted that the situation cried out for "a profession of well-educated teachers prepared to assume new powers and responsibilities to redesign schools for the future" (p. 3). The argument was that redesigning the schools would require a restructured and differentiated teaching force culminating for some in certification from a newly envisioned National Board for Professional Teaching Standards. This vision was consistent with the 1976 report of the American Association of Colleges for Teacher Education (AACTE) Bicentennial Commission on Education for the Profession of Teaching (Howsam, Corrigan, Denemark, & Nash, 1976), which lamented that a valid body of knowledge and skills for the teaching profession was sorely lacking. This vision was also in keeping with Judge's (1982) critique that American graduate schools put a low priority on the preparation of teachers and with Gideonse's (1982) efforts to organize education deans to focus on research.

In 1986, the Holmes Group, an alliance of some 100 research universities, called for dramatic improvements in teacher preparation—education that was rigorous and intellectual (undergraduate liberal arts and graduate-level professional preparation), career ladders for teachers, high entry standards (including examinations and educational requirements), and the creation of professional development schools to link graduate schools of education with K–12 schools (Fullan, Galluzzo, Morris, & Watson, 1998). Its recommendations were consistent with the Carnegie Forum's report (Taskforce on Teaching as a Profession, 1986) and the other efforts noted previously. The Holmes Group agenda focused on establishing a professional knowledge base as well as creating contexts to sustain and support prospective teachers' learning of the knowledge base. The Holmes Group agenda was summarized as follows:

> Reforming the education of teachers depends on engaging in the complex work of identifying the knowledge base for competent teaching, and developing the content and strategies whereby it can be effectively mastered. Although specialized professional knowledge has been under development for some time—and dramatic strides have been made during the past two decades—an amalgam of intuition, unreflective reactions, and personal dispositions still seems to ground the right to teach ... Basically a 'nonprogram' at present, professional studies are rarely interrelated or coherent. (Sedlak, 1987, p. 11)

The second and third Holmes Group reports elaborated on this agenda with attention to schools of education and K–12 schools.

The National Network for Educational Renewal (NNER) was also founded in 1986 as a way to extend the work of the Center for Educational Renewal, established by

John Goodlad, Ken Sirotnik, and Roger Soder in 1985. NNER was based on the premise that school improvement and teacher education renewal needed to proceed simultaneously and in partnership in order to succeed. As its strongest advocates put it, the fundamental operating assumption of NNER members and their affiliated colleges and universities, school districts, and partner schools was that "good schools require good teachers, and good teachers learn their profession in good schools" (Patterson, Michelli, & Pacheco, 1999, p. xv). The NNER and the Holmes Group are best understood as parallel efforts to professionalize teacher education in partnership with arts and sciences faculty and with school-based colleagues.

Committed to the idea that the nation needed a professional teaching force, researchers and organizations tied to teacher preparation worked to codify the professional knowledge base (Gardner, 1989; Houston, 1990; Murray, 1996; Richardson-Koehler, 1987; Shulman, 1983, 1986b) and change teacher education from a "normative" enterprise into one that could justifiably be referred to as a "state of the art" profession (Gardner, p. ix). By "state of the art," Gardner and others involved in AACTE's knowledge base project (Murray; Reynolds, 1989) meant a profession that was "deliberate and rational" with policies and practices established on a common professional knowledge base (Gardner, p. ix) rather than on idiosyncrasies or tradition. The National Council for Accreditation of Teacher Education's (NCATE's) new standards for evaluating teacher preparation programs according to the extent to which they coherently incorporated into the curriculum the professional knowledge bases for teaching and learning (Christensen, 1996) shaped the professionalization agenda of the 1980s. Likewise, a series of RAND studies by Linda Darling-Hammond, Arthur Wise, Barnatt Berry, and others made the case that although teaching had not yet achieved professional stature in terms of salaries, standards and status, there was mounting evidence that well-prepared teachers were more effective (Darling-Hammond, 1984, 1988; Darling-Hammond & Berry, 1987; Wise, 1988).

Goodlad's (1990) 5-year study of teacher education institutions, which was being conducted at roughly the same time as the events noted previously, was among the most publicized critiques of teacher education of this time period. The news it brought about the state of the field, although different in emphasis from Conant's (1963) and Koerner's (1963) more than 25 years earlier, was not much better. According to Goodlad (p. 270), teacher education was certainly not "state of the art."

> It can be concluded . . . that the teacher education train is *not* on the tracks. Further, the engine is not coupled to the cars nor the cars to one another. The board of directors is not even sure where the train should go once it is on the tracks and coupled. Confusing signals have demoralized many of the workers; unsure about what is expected, they do not know where to direct their energies in order to be rewarded.

Goodlad (pp. 290–294) called for more coherent programs with components tightly linked to one another and a focus on preparing teachers to meet the challenges of a changing society. Teachers' ongoing learning was central to this vision:

> Programs for the education of educators must be characterized in all respects by the conditions of learning that future teachers are to establish in their own schools and classrooms . . . and must be conducted in such a way that future teachers inquire into the nature of teaching and schooling . . . [programs] must be infused with understanding of and commitment to the moral obligation of teachers to ensure . . . the best possible K-12 education for *all* children and youths . . . [they] must involve future teachers not only in understanding schools as they are but in alternatives.

Goodlad, the Holmes Group (1986), the Carnegie Task Force (Task Force on Teaching as a Profession, 1986), and other reformers (e.g., Howey & Zimpher, 1989; Sirotnick & Goodlad, 1988; Soder & Sirotnick, 1990), both inside and outside the profession, advocated teacher education reform linked to the economic and social needs of the nation and to school reform and renewal. It was assumed that a well-educated teacher was the linchpin in all of this.

Constructing Teacher Education as a Learning Problem

Much research on teacher education during the 1980s and continuing into the 2000s was shaped by contemporary critiques of teacher education as well as by the emerging agenda to produce knowledgeable professional teachers who were learners, leaders, and school reformers. This research was also shaped by the expanded array of questions, multiple research designs, and broadened problematics of research on teaching, learning, and schooling that came to characterize the time. Lagemann (2000) suggested that the major influences of this time were the development of cognitive science, the application to education of research perspectives from anthropology and other interpretive traditions, new relationships between educational research and practice (such as teacher research and design experiments), and the shift from a linear to a systemic view of how research influenced policy.

Remembering that research on teaching is closely tied to but not the same as research on teacher education, it is important to note that the process–product paradigm of research on teaching had waned in influence by the early 1980s. There was a great deal of interest in what Erickson (1986) calls "a whole family of approaches to participant observational research," which researchers used to study "the ecology of classrooms" (Shulman, 1986a). These concentrated on particular school and classroom contexts, the social organization of classroom life, and how teachers and students together constructed local meanings. Research on teaching focused on pedagogy as a social exchange among participants rather than as simply the transmission of information from teacher to pupils. This same general shift was evident in the research on teacher education.

Again, it is worth noting that research on teaching did not follow a linear path with new and "better" ways of conceptualizing and studying the issues replacing those that had come before (Floden, 2001; Gage, 1989). Rather, the major paradigms of research on teaching evolved and continued rather than appeared and disappeared.

Lagemann (2000) suggested that, "Even though the history of educational scholarship has been filled with contests between and among different groups and individuals, it is always worth remembering that the story is not one in which the soldiers of darkness have been pitted against the soldiers of light" (p. xi). What this suggests for understanding the history of research on teacher education is that programs and paradigms of research that were considered seminal—even revolutionary—during one period often seemed narrow and wrong-headed later. Lagemann's words remind us that although the history of teacher education research is evolutionary rather than episodic, it is always embedded in the politics and debates of its time and influenced by the same pendulum swings as other educational developments.

During the late 1970s and into the early 1980s, research on teacher education shifted away from constructing and studying teacher preparation as a training problem and toward constructing and studying it as a learning problem. Undoubtedly this shift was influenced by the research program on teaching and teacher knowledge spearheaded at Michigan State University (MSU) by Judith Lanier and Lee Shulman in the late 1970s and developed through the work of scholars at MSU, University of Wisconsin, Stanford University, and elsewhere during the 1980s and 1990s.

Sponsored by the federal government's National Institute of Education, which had been established in 1972, a National Conference on Studies of Teaching was organized in 1974 to encourage 10 panels of scholars to develop new ways to conceptualize and analyze patterns of pupil interaction in schools and classrooms. The panel on "teaching as clinical information processing," one of 5 panels that concentrated on teaching, developed a research agenda to examine teacher cognition, including teachers' thinking, reasoning, planning, and decision making. The Panel 5 agenda was the basis for the Institute for Research on Teaching (IRT), established at Michigan State in 1976 to study teachers and teaching. The University of Texas, Austin, initially housed the federal research and development center on teacher education, but MSU won the bidding when the contract was reopened to competition in 1985. Building on the work of the IRT, MSU'S National Center for Research on Teacher Education and later the National Center for Research on Teacher Learning operated for more than a decade, developing a series of projects related to teacher learning, teaching thinking, and teacher knowledge. The research focus on knowledge for teaching, teachers' cognitive processes, how teachers learned to teach, and how they made sense of and used knowledge in classroom situations continued into the 2000s.

If we take as artifacts the major syntheses of research on teacher education published during this time, they clearly reflect the shift noted previously. The research on teacher education moved away from identifying the most effective instructional procedures for training prospective teachers to perform specific behaviors and toward understanding teachers' knowledge development; sources and use of knowledge, beliefs, and attitudes; the teacher education pedagogies that prompted knowledge development; and how people learned to teach over time. The problem of teacher education came to be understood as a "learning problem" rather than as a training problem. Understanding teacher education as a learning problem meant examining the kinds of knowledge, attitudes, and beliefs prospective teachers brought with them when they began formal teacher preparation programs (as well as how these changed over time); how they learned the knowledge, skills, and dispositions needed to teach; and how they interpreted their experiences in teacher preparation courses, fieldwork, and other contexts.

In many research studies and programs of research, the concept and language of "learning to teach" (Feiman-Nemser, 1983) replaced the language of "teacher training." Understanding teachers' work from a "deliberative orientation" (Zumwalt, 1982) replaced a technical orientation. As Feiman-Nemser pointed out in seminal work on this idea, it came to be understood that teacher learning was not equivalent to formal teacher preparation programs. Teacher learning also had to do with the beliefs, knowledge, and experiences prospective teachers brought with them into preparation programs; the ways their knowledge of subject matter changed and were translated into classroom practice over time; the ways teachers interpreted their fieldwork and course experiences in light of their own school experiences; and how they developed professionally by observing and talking with other teachers.

To an extent, constructing teacher education as a learning problem involved explicitly rejecting the technical view of teaching and the training view of teacher education that were prevalent in the training study era. Tom (1980), for example, argued that trying to improve teacher education through the application of the lawlike relationships identified in those studies was a "futile quest" (p. 15) not because of weaknesses in instrumentation, but because of an overly simplified view of teaching and learning that ignored its dynamic, social, and moral aspects of teaching. Along similar lines, Lanier (1982) argued that even though the teacher education research of the previous decades had shown that "teachers could indeed be trained to do most anything, the endless lists of behavior performances lacked coherence in terms of their overall relation to the preparation of more effective teachers" (p. 19). Lanier called for teacher education research that concentrated on teacher knowledge and on the professional decision making of teachers.

In their seminal chapter on teacher education research in the third *Handbook of Research on Teaching* (Wittrock, 1986), Lanier and Little (1986) moved beyond the training approach that had defined the entire synthesis of research on teacher education in the previous handbook in favor of a more "comprehensive, interdisciplinary" view. They stated their rejection of the previous research quite directly:

> Few studies of this nature are referred to or included in this chapter because we already know that teachers, like other normal human beings, are capable of learning new thoughts and behaviors in ways that conform to a set of generally accepted principles of human learning. It is hardly informative to learn that models and modeling (even if called supervising teachers or demonstration teaching) make a difference and that corrective feedback (even if referred to as coaching) enhances learning...Studies emphasizing these general themes have been systematically excluded [in this review]. (p. 528)

Lanier and Little's emphasis was certainly debatable (and fiercely debated) during this period. Carter (1990) correctly pointed out that many of the training-oriented researchers of the previous decade no doubt dismissed Lanier's approach as "too mentalist" because it did not concentrate on teacher behaviors. Notwithstanding the debates, however, by the time Wideen et al.'s (1998) synthesis of empirical research on learning to teach appeared, the general shift from conceptualizing teacher education as a training problem to understanding it as a learning problem was quite evident. Wideen et al. began their comprehensive review with the premise that studies of learning to teach were in large measure studies of prospective teachers' beliefs and how and whether these changed over time.

In the broad way we are defining it here, conceptualizing and studying teacher education as a learning problem included attention to teachers' knowledge, cognition, decision making, attitudes, beliefs, dispositions, development of skills, and performance in classrooms. It also included uses of knowledge, how teachers developed professionally over time, how they posed and solved problems of practice, and how they interpreted their coursework and fieldwork experiences. Clearly all of the aspects of teacher learning that are encompassed by this broad terminology are not the same. Some teacher education programs and research agendas focused heavily on teachers' subject matter knowledge and pedagogical content knowledge, whereas others focused on teachers' knowledge about culture and the role of culture in learning and schooling. Some concentrated on teachers' beliefs and attitudes about, for example, the capacities and needs of particular populations or the purposes of education in a democratic society. As many of the reviews in this volume make clear, in certain areas of research on teacher education during this time period, many researchers focused primarily on beliefs with less attention to knowledge and classroom skill. Although both are part of the larger topic of teacher learning, the shift in attention from knowledge to beliefs is a significant one, which we discuss in the next section.

In addition, it is important to note that there is a wide variety of ways of conceptualizing the process of learning to teach. Some of these are derived from cognitive psychology, whereas others work from sociological and anthropological perspectives. The former focus to a great extent on the knowledge teachers need to have, assuming that the acquisition of knowledge is more or less propositional in nature (Wideen et al., 1998). The latter, on the other hand, challenge the idea that the acquisition of knowledge is propositional and attend much more to the conditions and contexts in which teachers learn to teach and how teachers' interpretations of their experiences are embedded in social and cultural contexts. "Ecological" approaches to studying teaching and learning to teach (Erickson, 1986; Wideen et al.) emphasize the interconnectedness of teachers' learning, teacher educators' perspectives, and the contexts and conditions of teacher education programs, school and classrooms where teacher candidates work, and communities.

From a historical perspective, it is important to note that general approaches to conceptualizing and studying teacher education overlapped with rather than replaced one another. Kennedy (1996), for example, noted several training "experiments" in teacher education, published during the early 1990s, that tested the effects of differing procedures on prospective teachers' behaviors, and Floden (2001) pointed out that there were continuing research models seeking causal connections between teaching and student achievement. In addition, two syntheses (Evertson, Hawley, & Zlotnik, 1985; Haberman, 1985a)[2] explicitly addressed the question of whether teacher education made a difference in pupils' learning, a question that is different from both teacher training and teacher learning questions.

Studying Teacher Education as a Learning Problem

Based on the premise that teacher education was a learning problem, the point of research on teacher education was to build and explore the professional knowledge base, codifying not only how and what teachers should know but also how they learned in preservice programs and in schools and the multiple conditions and contexts that shaped that learning. Not surprisingly, means and methods for studying teacher knowledge and teacher learning were much more diverse than those for studying teacher training. Multiple research questions, methods, and approaches to interpretation and analysis developed rather than adhered to a single dominant paradigm. Although there were still studies that defined teacher effectiveness as the dependent variable and particular program structures or course methods as independent variables, many studies—whether qualitative or quantitative—examined teachers' attitudes, beliefs, knowledge structures, predispositions, perceptions, and understandings; as well as the intellectual, social, and organizational contexts that supported or constrained them.

In addition, in keeping with changes in research on teaching, teacher education research saw what Hamilton and McWilliam (2001) described as many more "ex-centric voices" devoted to "deconstructing" problems related to access, equity, and injustices implicit in the everyday arrangements of teaching, learning, and schooling. A whole

---

[2]We regard these two reviews as forerunners of the many policy-related syntheses produced during the next period and do not include them here. However, they make the point that although there were dominant approaches to research on teacher education during different periods, there were multiple and continuing threads of research in other areas as well.

program of research emerged that explored how teachers learn to teach for diversity; what knowledge, beliefs, and attitudes prospective teachers bring as they begin formal preparation programs; and the pedagogies of teacher preparation that enable new learnings (see, e.g., Bennett, 1995; Ladson-Billings, 1995; Zeichner, 1993; also see chap. 6, this volume). In addition to new research questions and perspectives from disciplines in the social sciences and humanities, there were also new investigators in teacher education research, including teacher educators who studied their own practices (e.g., Hamilton, 1998; Loughran & Northfield, 1998) and how their students made sense of their experiences, as well as new studies from critical and feminist perspectives (e.g., Britzman, 1991; Gore, 1993; Luke, 1992; also see chap. 4, this volume).

Zeichner (1999) suggested that there was a marked difference in the teacher education research prior to and following the mid-1980s. Zeichner used the initiation of the American Educational Research Association's (AERA's) Division K on Teaching and Teacher Education in 1984 as a dividing line. However, the research shift had many forerunners and actually coincided with a host of events that reflected the emerging new focus on teacher learning and teacher knowledge, including the establishment of the federal R&D center on teacher education in 1985 at MSU, the beginning of the Holmes Group and National Network for Educational Renewal (NNER) in 1985, the launching in 1985 of *Teaching and Teacher Education*, the implementation in 1985 of NCATE's knowledge base standards for program accreditation, the release of the third *Handbook of Research on Teaching* (Wittrock, 1986), the establishment of the National Board for Professional Teaching Standards in 1987, and the initiation in 1987 of the Interstate New Teacher Assessment and Support Consortium. As Zeichner observed, the research prior to the 1980s gave little attention to the processes of teacher education or to teachers' cognitive processes nor did it account for the "content, character and quality of particular teacher education programs and experiences" (p. 5). As teacher education came to be defined as processes and structures that would enhance prospective teachers' learning as professionals. the focus of research also shifted.

During the early 1980s to the early 2000s, several syntheses of research on teacher education were widely disseminated, including Lanier and Little's (1986) chapter in the third *Handbook of Research on Teaching*; the Association of Teacher Educators (ATE) sponsored first *Handbook of Research on Teacher Education* (Houston, 1990), which was quickly followed by a second (Sikula, Buttery, & Guyton, 1996); a synthesis of research on learning to teach from psychological perspectives (Borko & Putnam, 1996), published in the *Handbook of Educational Psychology* and the *Review of Educational Research* synthesis of the literature on learning to teach by Wideen et al. (1998). There also were several short reviews that are relevant, such as Koehler's (1985) summary of research on preservice teacher education that appeared in the *Journal of Teacher Education* and Richardson and Placier's (2001) section on preservice education within their longer review of the literature on teacher change in the fourth *Handbook of Research on Teaching* (Richardson, 2001).

Lanier and Little (1986) explicitly excluded experimental research on teacher training procedures and took as their purpose to synthesize interdisciplinary research that provided insights into the seemingly intractable problems of teacher education. They reviewed conceptual and empirical research on teacher educators, prospective teachers and the curriculum of teacher education including field experience, as well as higher education and school policies, structures and resources that had an impact on teacher education. They concluded that teacher preparation was characterized by a "pervasive atmosphere of conservatism" (p. 534) among teacher educators and a student body who expected a technical model and who included large numbers of low scorers on tests of academic ability. They concluded that teacher education curricula did not challenge conservative views of schooling and fostered a "group management" rather than an "intellectual leader" (p. 550) perspective. All this took place in an institutional culture that not only did not foster quality teaching and teacher education but also, worse, constrained them.

Although much longer and organized differently, Houston's (1990) *Handbook of Research* synthesized research in all the areas in Lanier and Little's (1986) review in addition to governance issues, contexts, and models of teacher education, evaluation, and teacher education in particular curricular areas. Houston, in his preface to the 49-chapter *Handbook*, straddled the fence about the strength of the research base for teacher education. He applauded the "tremendous strides toward identifying a research base [made] in the preceding decade" but acknowledged that "little progress" had been made (p. ix) in establishing the research base for educating the nation's teachers. Both Houston's *Handbook* and its second edition (Sikula et al., 1996) pinned the reason for the thin research base, at least in part, to the low priority the nation placed on schooling and teacher education. Both handbooks skirted the issue of the poor quality of some research on teacher education due to limited funding, inadequate attention to research methods, and many studies not linked to one another or to larger research agendas.

The research synthesis by Borko and Putnam (1996) focused explicitly on the psychological aspects of learning to teach. Drawing on constructs from cognitive psychology, their review summarized research on prospective and experienced teachers' general pedagogical knowledge and beliefs, their subject matter knowledge and beliefs, and their pedagogical content knowledge and beliefs. They concluded that learning to teach—across the professional life span—was a complex process requiring multiple knowledge bases, skills, and understandings. They also pointed out that prospective teachers' prior knowledge and beliefs as well as certain contextual aspects of schools and universities act as impediments to learning to teach.

Like Borko and Putnam (1996), the review by Wideen et al. (1998) focused explicitly on the process of learning to teach and did not include the full breadth of research topics covered in the two handbooks. Examining research on beginning teachers' beliefs, preservice program interventions, and student teaching experiences, they concluded not only that beliefs were difficult to change (although changing beliefs is more likely when programs build on current beliefs) but also that there is a fundamental tension between teacher educators' desire to change their students' beliefs and prospective teachers' desire to learn how to "do" teaching. Wideen and colleagues commented explicitly that many studies of teacher education were weak methodologically and, consequently, so were their findings. They commented explicitly on the need for more attention by researchers to data collection and presentation and more explicit links between data and conclusions. They also called for researchers to have a more self-critical stance about the limitations of their own work.

The Value of Studying Teacher Education as a Learning Problem

When teacher education is constructed as a learning problem, it is assumed that teacher preparation, teacher performance, and educational outcomes are related to one another in complex and recursive rather than linear ways. Perhaps most importantly, it is assumed that teachers' beliefs and knowledge as well as the constraints and conditions of schools and school systems mediate between what prospective teachers experience in formal preparation programs and their practice and accomplishments in particular schools and classrooms. The assumptions underlying the study of teacher education as a learning problem are consistent with the major thrust of cognitive psychology over the last quarter century as scientific study of how knowledge is developed, used, and organized by individuals. In a different way, the assumptions of the learning approach to studying teacher education are also consistent with anthropological and other interpretive perspectives on the ecology of classrooms, wherein knowledge is regarded as constructed and fluid; teaching is regarded as an intellectual, decision-making, and professional activity; and teaching and learning are understood to interact dynamically with the social and cultural contexts of schools and classrooms.

In his review of paradigms and research programs in the study of teaching, Shulman (1986a, pp. 25–26) suggested that the missing paradigm was research on how teachers understood and used subject matter knowledge. He wrote:

> The general public and those who set educational policy are in general agreement that teachers' competence in the subjects they teach is a central criterion of teacher quality. They remain remarkably vague, however, in defining what sort of subject-matter knowledge they have in mind . . . Ironically, little is known about such matters empirically because these questions have fallen between the cracks in the research-on-teaching field.

Many researchers shared Shulman's assessment. Over the next 20 years, as we have noted, major programs of research on teaching and teacher education concentrated on teachers' subject matter expertise, pedagogical content knowledge, and the ways teachers transform subject matter knowledge into effective classroom practice. Animated by the idea that knowledge and beliefs are the filters through which all action is mediated, there were also major lines of research about would-be teachers' knowledge of culture and diverse populations as well as their beliefs and dispositions and how these do and do not change over time.

Programs of research on teachers' cognition, knowledge use, and beliefs were so successful over the past 2 decades that a number of scholars (Cochran-Smith, Davis, & Fries, 2004; Wilson, Floden, & Ferrini-Mundy, 2001) have more recently suggested that what is missing now is research that connects teacher knowledge and beliefs to pupils' learning, including scores on achievement tests and other indicators of academic learning as well as social, emotional, and civic learning. Even Shulman (1986a), one of the founders of the influential program of research on teachers' subject matter knowledge, acknowledged this limitation when he recently concluded that research on teachers' knowledge and use "reflects the theoretical importance of the three C's of content, cognition and context [but] continued to ignore a fourth C, consequences for students" (p. 251). Shulman's assessment of the research on teaching also applies to research on teacher education. When teacher education is primarily constructed and studied as a learning problem, understanding teachers' knowledge and beliefs is considered an important research purpose in its own right, and there is often little or no attention to pupil achievement and the link between teachers' knowledge and beliefs and pupils' learning and other desirable educational outcomes.

As we argue in the next section, during the late 1990s and into the 2000s, research on teacher education, as reflected in recent syntheses, shifted from teacher learning issues to educational policy issues, including efforts to document the effectiveness of teacher preparation on pupils' learning. In many policy-related critiques of the literature, research on teacher preparation focusing on knowledge and beliefs was not considered useful because it addressed noncausal questions, did not make the link to pupil achievement, and had limited implications for policy. From our vantage, we need not only to acknowledge the limitations of the research on teacher education as a learning problem but also to consider its value. We need to draw on the research on teacher education as a learning problem to make links between what teachers know and believe and how they develop professional practice in the context of different schools and classrooms. We also need to understand, however, the intricate ways that knowledge, beliefs, and professional practices are related to pupil learning and other outcomes.

RESEARCH ON TEACHER EDUCATION AS A POLICY PROBLEM: MID-1990S TO 2000S

Since the mid-1990s, we have seen the continuation of the cycle of critique and calls for reform that characterized teacher education for at least the previous 40 years. The focus on high standards and accountability has been intense and unremitting. Growing attention to teacher quality was accompanied by scathing critique of "traditional" teacher education. The emphasis in research on teacher education shifted from learning to policy, and the problem of teacher education was constructed as a matter of specifying the policies and practices that were warranted by both empirical evidence and cost–benefit analyses. We suggest in the following section that this emphasis tells only part of the story.

Political, Professional, and Policy Contexts

By the mid-1990s, globalization of the world economy heightened concerns that the United States would not be able to preserve its role as the largest and most productive industrialized nation unless it could prepare more of its citizens to compete for jobs in a knowledge-based society. The shifting global economy coupled with the increasing diversity of the nation's schoolchildren and the continuing achievement gap among groups outside the cultural, economic, and linguistic mainstream contributed to the urgent sense that education was vital to the nation's future. In nearly every state, new curricular frameworks had been implemented, coupled with new standards for K–12 student achievement. In 1996, President Clinton and the nation's governors met with business leaders and education leaders at the National Education Summit to solidify their commitment to holding the schools to internationally competitive standards and assessments (National Education Goals Panel, 1997). In most states, enhanced teaching and learning standards were accompanied by new standardized tests, many with high stakes such as graduation candidacy. These paper-and-pencil assessments were intended to be tightly aligned with new curriculum frameworks, which in turn were to be tightly aligned with new knowledge bases in the subject areas.

As in previous eras, concerns about the economy and education were linked to public demands for reforms in teaching and teacher education. In 1994, the Rockefeller Foundation and the Carnegie Corporation provided support for the new National Commission on Teaching and America's Future (NCTAF). NCTAF's first report (1996) concluded that both a strong body of empirical evidence coupled with rich professional experience showed that teaching and teacher education "mattered most" in improving schoolchildren's achievement and thus in determining America's future. The report identified key obstacles to creating a strong and professionalized teaching force: "major flaws" (p. 31) in traditional teacher education, "slipshod recruitment and hiring" (p. 34) patterns, "continued tolerance for extraordinary turnover among new teachers" (p. 39), little investment in teachers' professional development, and schools "structured for failure instead of success" (p. 44). NCTAF's reports as well as efforts by NCATE, Interstate New Teacher Assessment and Support Consortium (INTASC), and National Board of Professional Teaching Standards (NBPTS) set out a blueprint for redressing the failure of the teacher preparation system by attacking each obstacle through a broad program of professionalization and high standards for teaching and teacher education across the professional life span.

With an intensity that to many observers seemed unprecedented, the interest of the public in teacher quality and accountability deepened. Between 1996 and 2000, *The New York Times* alone printed 1,220 articles about teacher quality and 920 articles about teacher testing (Cochran-Smith, 2001). In many newspaper articles, teacher education was condemned as—at best—out of touch with the interests of "the public" (Farkas & Johnson, 1997) and—at worst—utterly worthless (e.g., Raspberry, 1998). Articles in periodicals for the educated public (e.g., Schrag, 1999) portrayed schools of education as the purveyors of "a lot of stuff called research on trendy or esoteric topics of little consequence to anybody" (p. 31) and the teacher education curriculum was characterized as having changed over the years primarily through the addition of a "heavy dose" of multiculturalism that was mostly "touchy-feely self awareness" (p. 32). In the media, in public policy debates, and within education itself, the push for higher standards for teachers and pupils zeroed in on test results and outcomes. By the end of the decade, accountability—rather than higher standards—had become the bottom line (Elmore, 2002). With the implementation of President Bush's No Child Left Behind (NCLB) Act of 2001, testing had become not only the means but also seemingly the purpose of accountability.

Citing research on teacher quality, certification, and effective teaching, the American Council on Education's President's Task Force on Teacher Education (1999) promoted increased higher education responsibility for teacher preparation and recommended to college and university presidents that teacher education be strengthened through greater collaboration, clear admissions standards, well-articulated offerings, and strong program evaluation and induction programs. Between 1987 and 1998, the number of states requiring tests for entry into the teaching profession greatly increased and became more standardized (SRI International, 2000). Aggregated scores on teacher tests began to be interpreted as a way to grade teacher education institutions and states themselves rather than as a way to assess individual fitness for teaching. High-profile "failures" of teacher education, such as the failure of 59% of Massachusetts' teacher candidates to pass the state's first teacher test in 1998 (Melnick & Pullin, 2000), fanned the debate about teacher quality and teacher preparation that was already going on in Congress and soon led to changes in the Higher Education Act (Earley, 2000). To qualify for federal student aid, institutions and states now must report annually to the U.S. Secretary of Education on the credentials—including test scores—of all teachers they certify.

Conservative foundations were another major voice in teacher education reform during this time, especially the Thomas B. Fordham Foundation, directed by Chester E. Finn, Jr., and particularly its 1999 report, *Better Teachers, Better Schools* (Kanstoroom & Finn, 1999). As noted earlier, the report advocated deregulation of teacher education and redirection of public authority for teacher quality by dismantling or significantly reducing college- and university-based teacher education programs and state-level certification bureaucracies. The Fordham Foundation's "manifesto" asserted that NCTAF and other professionalization education groups were pushing regulatory reforms that had already been proven failures as demonstrated by the disinclination of "able liberal arts graduates" to enter teaching and the reputation of "pedagogical degrees as 'Mickey Mouse' programs" (Kanstroom & Finn, p. 5). Concerned about teacher shortages, Fordham and other foundations called for new and different strategies to reform teacher preparation including alternate routes that allowed college graduates to enter teaching without pedagogical preparation or supervised fieldwork in classrooms and what they referred to as a "relentless" focus on results.

CONSTRUCTING TEACHER EDUCATION
AS A POLICY PROBLEM

Each of the multiple agendas for the reform of teacher education that emerged and sometimes collided during the mid 1990s and into the 2000s claimed to have an empirical base. Numerous and opposing claims were presented about the "evidentiary warrant" (Cochran-Smith & Fries, 2001) that supported these agendas. Debates about the evidence occurred in both scholarly and popular literature and through Congressional testimony and other public forums (e.g., Ballou & Podgursky, 2000; Darling-Hammond, 2000a; Education Commission of the States, 2000; Kanstoroom, 1999; Wise, 1998). One result was to draw new and sharp attention to research on teacher education and to construct teacher education primarily as a policy problem rather than as a training problem or a learning problem as the previous decades had done.

Again, this is not to suggest that research on teacher education as a learning or training problem disappeared (see, e.g., the synthesis of research on teacher change in Richardson & Placier, 2001). By the same token, some recently emerging projects intended to provide teachers with scientifically based professional development, as required by NCLB, seem to reflect a training model of teacher education.

Our point is not that constructing and studying teacher education as a policy problem replaced all other ways of doing so. Rather, we suggest that within the political, social, and professional contexts of a given time, particular ways of framing the problem of teacher education became dominant and others ebbed in prominence or evolved. If the many syntheses of teacher education research disseminated between 2000 and 2003 (Abell Foundation, 2001a; Allen, 2003; Ballou & Podgursky, 2000; Darling-Hammond, 1998, 2000a; Darling-Hammond & Youngs, 2002; Lauer, 2001; Rice, 2003; Whitehurst, 2002; Wilson et al., 2001)[3] and the responses and rejoinders to these (Abell Foundation, 2001b; Darling-Hammond, 2000a, 2001; Wilson & Floden, 2002) are any indication, then constructing teacher education as a policy problem has now become predominant. (See chaps. 3, 4, 5, 6, 8, and 9, this volume, for discussion of many of the individual studies referred to in these larger syntheses.)

Constructing teacher education as a policy problem assumes that one important way policymakers can meet the challenges involved in providing a well-prepared teaching force is by manipulating those broad aspects of teacher preparation (e.g., teacher tests, subject matter requirements, and entry routes) most likely to affect pupil

---

[3]Whether Darling-Hammond's 2000 review of state policy evidence about teacher qualifications and student achievement was a synthesis is arguable. Her article reviewed an extensive amount of previous research and presented a new analysis of state policy evidence. We include it here in our list of syntheses in part because of its extensive literature review but even more so because it was the impetus for many other syntheses, explicitly framed to corroborate or refute its conclusions.

achievement. As noted previously, this policy approach to teacher preparation has not been the norm during most of the long history of critique and calls for reform in teacher education. As Evertson, Hawley, and Zlotnik (1985) pointed out 2 decades ago, "Most proposals for teacher reform are unburdened by evidence that the suggested changes will make a difference in the quality of students preparing to teach in elementary and secondary schools" (p. 2). Constructing teacher education as a policy problem means focusing on large-scale or institutional and programmatic policies and practices that are warranted by empirical evidence demonstrating impact on desired outcomes or by economic analyses that weigh costs and benefits. The evidence sought are empirical studies, preferably experimental studies or correlational studies with sophisticated statistical analyses, indicating which of the broad parameters of teacher preparation have a systematic and positive impact on pupil or other outcomes.

Some of the assumptions underlying the construction of teacher education as a policy problem are similar to those of teacher education as a training problem, particularly the desire for experimental research evidence indicating impact on pupil learning. The primary difference is that the training research focused on specific practices internal to teacher preparation programs, such as microteaching or instructing prospective teachers using videotapes of classrooms versus actual field experiences, whereas the policy research focuses on broader parameters that can be manipulated by state and federal policymakers.

There is some variation in scope and level of the teacher education policy problem considered in recent syntheses. Several of the most debated syntheses examined the impact of teacher education as part of analyses of state-level policies regarding certification, licensure, teacher tests, and other accountability mechanisms (e.g., Ballou & Podgursky, 2000; Darling-Hammond, 2000b). Some used econometric models and techniques, including cost–benefit and other analyses, to draw conclusions about the impact of school resources, including teacher qualifications (e.g., Hanushek, 1997). Other syntheses examined the research base for state or institutional policies regarding teacher requirements such as subject matter preparation, coursework, and field experiences (e.g., Allen, 2003; Rice, 2003). Across analyses that construct teacher education as a policy problem, there was variation about what counted as a desirable outcome in research related to teacher preparation. Some syntheses zero in only on pupil learning defined in terms of scores on achievement tests, whereas others use a broader notion of outcomes including teachers' knowledge and professional practices, evaluators' judgments of teachers, and teachers' attitudes and career paths. Underlying the construction and study of teacher education as a policy problem is an assumption that empirical evidence linking teacher preparation and desirable outcomes can and should shape the policies and practices that govern teacher education.

As noted earlier, almost 2 decades ago, there were 2 research syntheses of research on teacher education (Evertson et al., 1985; Haberman, 1985b) that shared important features with the current spate of policy syntheses. Not surprisingly, these reviews were prompted by some of the same disputes that currently plague the field. In the early 1980s, there were severe criticisms of preparation programs from those outside teacher education along with calls for alternate routes and demands for higher standards. Those inside the profession also proposed higher standards, longer courses of study, and stricter entry requirements.

To weigh the evidence, Evertson et al. (1985) reviewed research that linked teacher education with improvements in teaching or student achievement, concluding—with many caveats about the weak body of evidence—that students with formal preservice preparation were more likely to be effective. Along similar lines, Haberman (1985a) reviewed research that compared teachers who had had liberal arts majors (and were provisionally or temporarily certified) with those who had had teacher education majors (and were regularly certified). He found some evidence that provisionally certified teachers with some education courses and teaching experiences scored as well or better than some regularly prepared teachers on tests. He also concluded, however, that there was much evidence that regularly certified teachers were rated higher than provisionally certified teachers by principals, colleagues, the public, and students. On the other hand, at roughly the same time that Evertson and colleagues and Haberman were synthesizing research on teacher education, Hanushek (1989) was engaged in what became a long line of production–function studies of the differential impact on pupil achievement of school resources and expenditures. He concluded that teachers' education made no difference in school performance.

The mixed conclusions of these reviews are not surprising, given the different definitions of teacher effectiveness and the different notions of outcomes and methodological perspectives that guided the syntheses. To a certain extent, these differences also help explain the mixed conclusions about teacher education as a policy problem among the most recent syntheses. The most important difference between previous syntheses related to teacher education as a policy problem and the current spate of policy-related research syntheses is that the former rarely made their way into the discourse of the professional community responsible for teacher education. As Mary Kennedy (1996) noted, policy-related syntheses have been most familiar to skeptics and critics of teacher education, including economists and policy analysts and least familiar to teacher educators themselves. This situation has changed recently as debates about the research base for teacher education concentrated on the policy-related literature. This has occurred concurrently with an unprecedented and enlarged federal role in education, a major campaign to rely on science to solve educational problems and a movement to privatize many aspects of education, reflecting market-based approaches to reforms. These conditions have boosted sharply the influence of policy studies and moved them into the discourse about teacher education within and outside the education community.

Studying Teacher Education as a Policy Problem

Based on the premise that teacher education is a policy problem, the goal of research is to provide evidence about how teacher education as an overall enterprise can be successful and cost effective. A related goal is unraveling and identifying aspects of teacher education that are not likely to be successful and cost effective when implemented. In useful discussions along these lines, Kennedy (1996, 1999) suggested that the question of whether teacher education "makes a difference" has been studied through several different genres of research, two of which are consistent with the approaches taken in recent syntheses. What Kennedy (1996) called "searches for contributions to student learning" (p. 122) have been conducted primarily using multiple regression analyses that attempt to identify characteristics or aspects of teachers, including their education, that have an impact on pupil achievement. Kennedy's second genre of research, "comparing the haves and have-nots" (p. 127), relied primarily on comparing certified and uncertified teachers in schools and districts. The comparisons are based on classroom observations of teacher behaviors. More recent lines of research also compare the "haves and the have nots" but are more likely to do so using pupils' or teachers' tests scores as outcome measures rather than observations or evaluators' judgments of teacher behavior.

A large number of research syntheses published since the year 2000 have constructed teacher education as a policy problem. The syntheses were similar in focus and methodology but differ primarily in the conclusions they reached. These cluster into three groups.

One group of syntheses includes Darling-Hammond's (2000b) synthesis of state policy evidence regarding teacher quality and achievement and Darling-Hammond and Youngs's (2002) analysis of research on teacher quality as well as responses, rejoinders, and addenda that extend or qualify the conclusions of these syntheses and refute critiques of them (Darling Hammond, 2001; Darling-Hammond, 2000a, 2000b; Darling-Hammond & Youngs) by other scholars, such as Ballou and Podgursky (2000), Walsh (Abell Foundation, 2001a, 2001b), and Whitehurst (2002), all of which are discussed in the following paragraphs. Darling-Hammond's reviews of the literature conclude that teacher preparation and certification, regarded as important aspects of a cluster of variables that comprise teachers' qualifications, contribute at least as much as, if not more than, other variables to educational outcomes including teacher effectiveness and students' achievement. It is not surprising that the reviews in this group reach similar conclusions, given that they are all sponsored by or related to the work of NCTAF and authored or co-authored by its founding director, Linda Darling-Hammond. An ardent advocate of the right of all school children to have fully prepared and fully certified teachers and a tireless supporter of the professionalization agenda, Darling-Hammond defined teacher effectiveness in terms of students' achievement but also included as outcomes teacher performance, strategies used, observations of teachers, attitudes, perceptions of efficacy, and teacher retention. Darling-Hammond's research designs included regression analyses aggregated at the school level. Some of her studies sought to measure teacher qualifications by combining several variables and measuring the impact of that cluster on particular outcomes.

A second group of syntheses, including responses (Abell Foundation, 2001a, 2001b; Ballou & Podgursky, 2000; Whitehurst, 2002), reached a very different conclusion about teacher preparation and teacher certification. This group concluded that although there was evidence that teachers' verbal ability and subject matter knowledge had an impact on pupil achievement, there was little evidence to support teacher education policies that required teacher preparation in university-based programs, the study of pedagogy, teacher certification, or program approval and accreditation. The syntheses and critiques by economist Michael Podgursky, an original signer of the Fordham Foundation's "manifesto," and Dale Ballou, also an economist, and those by Kate Walsh, formerly senior policy analyst of the Abell Foundation and now executive director of the National Council on Teacher Quality, were prepared in direct response to Darling-Hammond's (2001) and the NCTAF's conclusions about the policy-relevant evidence. Ballou and Podgursky concluded that although the evidence was clear that "teacher expertise" is an important factor in student achievement, the research base for NCTAF-recommended reforms that bolster the professionalization of the teaching force was weak due to treatment of teacher characteristics as independent rather than endogenous variables, results aggregated at district levels, and biased selection of studies.

Along similar lines, Walsh (Abell Foundation, 2001a, 2001b) concluded that the evidence offered by Darling-Hammond in support of NCTAF proposals and the professionalization agenda did not support regulations and policies regarding state certification. Walsh refuted Darling-Hammond's (2001) conclusions and policy recommendations on the grounds of selective citation, nonretrievable or unreliable evidence, and failure to conform with standard statistical procedures. Whitehurst's (2002) brief

synthesis reviewed the scientific research evidence that supported the policy recommendations regarding teacher preparation and teacher quality contained in the
Secretary of Education's reports to Congress on teaching quality (U.S. Department of
Education, 2002, 2003). Whitehurst's review, presented at a White House conference
on the preparation of teachers, was included as an appendix to the Secretary's second report. Cautioning that factors related to the identification of certified and other
teachers were often confused or confounded and that aggregation of data at the school
or district level automatically made conclusions suspect, Whitehurst concluded that
"the evidence for the value of certification in general is equivocal at best."

A third group of syntheses, including responses (Allen, 2003; Lauer, 2001; Rice,
2003; Wilson & Floden, 2002; Wilson et al., 2001), concluded that although there was
some evidence that teacher preparation and certification had a positive impact on
educational outcomes in some content areas and at certain school levels, the research
base related to teacher preparation as policy was neither deep nor robust. Results
were mixed in some areas, and there was virtually no reliable research in many other
areas. These syntheses called for greater investments in research on teacher preparation and in developing qualified teachers. All of these syntheses but Rice's were
related. Wilson et al.'s synthesis of research on teacher preparation was sponsored
by the Office of Educational Research and Improvement (OERI); its addendum (Wilson & Floden) was sponsored by Education Commission of the States (ECS) through
funds from OERI. Both were intended to identify the lacunae in the research literature as well as methodological and design issues related to the extant research. Lauer's
(2001) policy-oriented secondary analysis of the Wilson et al. report and Allen's (2003)
synthesis were sponsored by ECS through funds from OERI. Allen's review drew
heavily on Wilson's two reviews as well as on Lauer's to make recommendations to
state policymakers about the degree of confidence they should have in policies regarding teacher preparation based on the extent and depth of empirical evidence. Rice's
(2003) synthesis, which was sponsored by the Economic Policy Institute, focused explicitly on aspects of "teacher background" that could be translated into policy and
practice. Although Wilson, Floden, and Rice are faculty members in schools of education and thus in a certain sense could be said to have a vested interest in teacher
education, as far as we can determine, none of the syntheses in this group emerged
from a preexisting, identifiable ideological position about policy reform in teacher
education.

Although their language and emphases differed, the syntheses in this third group
were generally consistent in their conclusion that the "research base regarding teacher
preparation is thin" (Wilson et al., 2001, p. i), but "there is no merit in large-scale
elimination of all credentialing requirements" (Rice, 2003, p. 2). Our juxtaposition of
conclusions from two different syntheses reflects the fact that all of the reviews in this
category were explicitly intended to assess empirical research evidence as the basis
for policy recommendations. The syntheses in this third group also were consistent
in their conclusions about methodological and design problems and thus in their conclusions about what was needed—uniform measures of "impact" and "effectiveness"
(Allen, 2003), more stable measures of teacher knowledge and behavior (Wilson et
al.), designs that capture the interactions among various aspects of teacher quality
(Rice), designs that directly link aspects of teacher preparation to pupil achievement
(Wilson et al.), direct attention to elementary and middle school teaching and in areas
beyond mathematics (Rice) and data linking information about individual teachers
to actual performance rather than aggregating data at the school or district level
(Allen).

Rice's (2003, p. 2) conclusion about the research base for teacher education as a policy problem was consistent with the other reviews in this group:

Education policy makers and administrators would be well served by recognizing the complexity of the issue and adopting multiple measures along many dimensions to support existing teachers and to attract and hire new, highly qualified teachers. The research suggests that investing in teachers can make a difference in student achievement. In order to implement needed policies associated with staffing every classroom—even the most challenging ones—with high-quality teachers, substantial and targeted investments must first be made in both teacher quality and education research.

Wilson et al. (2001) proposed "strategic investments" in research on teacher preparation, a call echoed by Allen (2003). Recommended investments included building on teacher educators' interest in self-study to establish multisite research initiatives; bolstering capacity within the educational research community for large-scale studies of teacher preparation and certification; and developing research programs to explore the conditions and contexts within which teacher education can increase teacher effectiveness.

Differing conclusions about the empirical evidence for certain policies regarding teacher education have led to contentious disputes among researchers, which have often been arcane and sometimes *ad hominem*. Certainly there are intricate methodological issues, barely mentioned here, that explain some of the sharp differences in the conclusions of these recent syntheses. (Also see chaps. 5, 8, and 9, this volume, for discussion of some of these issues.) Differences in what was operationalized as a desirable educational outcome were also influential. Finally, as suggested previously (Cochran-Smith & Fries, 2002), the stark differences in the conclusions between the first two groups of syntheses may be partly explained by the allegiance of the researchers to particular reform agendas and thus their relative emphases on research that supports their positions. Earley (2000) made an incisive point along these lines about the value-laden nature of educational research and its easy use by policymakers to further their own agendas. She suggested that "data and evidence used in the policy process will have several levels of bias: that embedded in the data or evidence itself, bias associated with analysis, and the biases of those in the policy world who use the information" (p. 35). Policy bias along with differences in research methods and disciplinary perspectives may explain some of the differences highlighted in this discussion of syntheses of research on teacher education as a policy problem.

The Value of Studying Teacher Education as a Policy Problem

The essence of studying teacher education as a policy problem is to identify which broad parameters of teacher education policy that can be controlled by institutional, state, or federal policymakers are most likely to have a positive impact on desirable outcomes, especially student gains on achievement tests. The purpose is to use empirical evidence to guide policymakers in decisions about how to invest limited human and fiscal resources in the preparation and professional development of K–12 teachers. Research designs considered by some (e.g., Hanushek, 1989; Rivkin, Hanushek, & Kain, 1998) best suited to examine teacher education as a policy problem are production function studies of educational resources and other multiple regression analyses that aim to establish correlations between resources—including aspects of teacher preparation (e.g., college majors, certification status, institution attended, advanced degrees, scores on teacher tests, courses taken)—and indicators of teacher effectiveness (e.g., pupil achievement scores). Other researchers (e.g., Rice, 2003; Wilson et al., 2001) take a broader approach, allowing a variety of accepted research methods and a range of indicators of effectiveness, including not only pupil achievement but also professional evaluations of teachers and teachers' sense of efficacy and preparedness, to draw conclusions about what the evidence says about the impact of teacher attributes—including preparation—on outcomes.

In the current accountability context, the value of studying teacher education as a policy problem seems obvious, although this was not always the case, at least within the teacher education research community. It now seems evident that policy decisions, whether state regulations or institutional requirements, should be driven, at least in part, by empirical evidence. Unfortunately, in the absence of clear, consistent evidence, many policymakers ignore research or focus only on evidence that supports their already established positions (Rice, 2003).

From the vantage point of contemporary society, it seems clear that we need to make "strategic investments" (Wilson et al., 2001) in the capacity of the research community to conduct rigorous, thoughtful, and useable research on teacher education as a policy problem. However, we also need to acknowledge the limitations of this approach. As Kennedy (1999) observed, the aspects of teacher education studied from a policy perspective are often "crude quantifiable indicators" (p. 89) of a teacher's educational background that cannot be used to make meaningful distinctions among the extremely varied facets of teacher preparation that exist within the more than 1,300 institutions that prepare teachers.

In addition, studies of teacher education as a policy problem generally do not account for the contexts and cultures of K–12 schools, which also vary widely. They also do not account for how school variations support or constrain teachers' abilities to apply their knowledge and skills. Given strong evidence that school cultures influence teachers' work and ability to make effective use of resources (Cohen, Raudenbush, & Ball, 2002; Little, 1993; McLaughlin & Oberman, 1996; Pressley et al., 2001), it is important to note this limitation of policy studies. Finally, it is worth noting that when teacher education is constructed as a policy problem, the focus almost always is on pupil achievement gains as the most important educational outcome. Although this is certainly an important outcome, it is often not the only outcome that teacher education programs aim for when they prepare teachers. Such outcomes as pupils' social and emotional growth as well as their preparedness to live and work in a democratic society and engage in civic discourse also are important. Teacher preparation programs often have other purposes and goals related, for example, to teacher placement and retention in hard-to-staff schools, teachers' work as advocates for educational equity, and teachers' knowledge of subject matter, pedagogy, and professional practice.

STUDYING TEACHER EDUCATION IN CHANGING TIMES

We have suggested that the history of research on teacher education over the last half-century can be explained at least in part by identifying how "the problem" of teacher education is constructed and how that problem is studied, analyzed, and interpreted. Different ways of constructing and studying the problem are influenced by the political, professional, and policy contexts of the times, particularly by public concerns and policies about teachers and schooling linked to larger economic and social issues, internal and external critiques of teacher education coupled with demands for reform, and new directions in educational research generally and research on teaching more specifically. It is also important to acknowledge that the quality of some published research on teacher education is poor. This judgment holds regardless of methodological and epistemological preferences and regardless of which questions are being addressed. As in any field, poor-quality research contributes to the impression that the research base on teacher education is weak.

It is also important, however, to make it clear that some of those who have concluded that the research base for teacher education is weak have done so because they were interested in a particular construction of the "problem" of teacher education about which there has been little research, even though large amounts of worthwhile research have been conducted on different constructions of the problem. Some reviewers who have reached different conclusions about the breadth and depth of the research base have done so because they worked from quite different constructions of the problem. This means that simply asking a different question about the quality and depth of the research base on teacher education can produce a different answer (Cochran-Smith, 2004). At other times, however, reviewers have asked similar questions but worked from differing assumptions about what counted as research, what levels of data aggregation were appropriate, or what educational outcomes mattered most. Understanding these differences also helps to account for some of the sharply different conclusions about the strengths or weaknesses of the research base that have been noted over time.

For example, Peck and Tucker's 1973 review, discussed earlier, focused almost exclusively on experimental research on the instructional methods used in teacher education courses and programs. They considered this research revolutionary because of the sophisticated statistical methodology it employed, concluding that there had been an "explosive growth of sound research on the education of teachers in just the last 8–10 years" (Peck & Tucker, p. 942). Notwithstanding Peck and Tucker's enthusiasm about experimental teacher education research, Whitehurst commented in his 2002 overview of scientifically based research on teacher quality: "Unfortunately experimental methods have not yet found their way to research on teacher training" (p. 10). At first glance, Peck and Tucker's and Whitehurst's conclusions appear contradictory, and it may well be that Whitehurst was simply unaware of the earlier research on teacher preparation. Besides the decades that divided these two conclusions, however, was the fact that Peck and Tucker were working from the perspective that teacher education was a training problem; thus, they were looking for experimentally verifiable and transportable techniques that could be used to train teachers to perform on demand certain behaviors assumed to help pupils' learning. From this perspective, there was a burgeoning body of experimental research on teacher training. On the other hand, Whitehurst, who also used the language of "teacher training," actually worked from a construction of teacher education as a policy problem. From this perspective, he was looking for causal or correlational evidence about the impact of teacher preparation and certification status on pupils' achievement and thus could be used as a guide for policy decisions about teacher education.

A different example that helps to make the same point is Wideen et al.'s (1998) synthesis of research, mentioned earlier, which constructed teacher education as a learning problem that revolved around what teachers believe. It is clear throughout the review that their focus was on what beliefs beginning teachers held, how beliefs changed over time, how beliefs functioned as a filter for interpreting experiences, and the tensions that existed between the beliefs prominent in the cultures of universities and those in schools. Sharply contrasting with the assumptions that guided Wideen et al.'s review of research on teacher education as a learning problem, however, Allen's (2003) synthesis clearly constructed teacher education as a policy problem. He explicitly stated that "intermediate outcomes" such as teacher beliefs and understandings of subject matter were of little interest to policymakers unless there was solid evidence of their connection to pupils' achievement.

The contrasts in the conclusions of these and other syntheses about the strength and depth of the research base for teacher education reflect both historical and contemporary issues. Some researchers (and reviewers) work from the premise that teachers' learning (e.g., enhanced subject matter knowledge, changes in beliefs and attitudes about working with diverse populations, and development of a disposition or stance toward inquiry) is a justifiable and important outcome of teacher preparation because of its impact on instructional decisions, relationships with pupils and families, and the nature and quality of learning opportunities made available. This is based on the premise that teachers' knowledge frames and belief structures are the filters through which teachers' practices, strategies, actions, interpretations, and decisions are made. The assumption is that knowledge and beliefs always mediate teachers' practices in schools and classrooms and thus knowledge and beliefs greatly influence pupils' learning opportunities, their achievement, and other educational outcomes. One conclusion to this line of reasoning is that a well-educated and competent teaching force is made up of teachers with deep content knowledge, sophisticated pedagogical strategies, rich knowledge of culture and human learning, and positive beliefs about the capacity of all children to learn academic content.

From this perspective, teacher learning itself (including understandings, beliefs, attitudes, and knowledge in many areas including, but not limited to, subject matter) is an important outcome of teacher preparation. Along the same lines, investigating how knowledge and beliefs function as filters for interpretations and actions, under what conditions they do so, and how they in turn have an impact on pupils' learning opportunities and other educational outcomes are critically important questions. When teacher learning itself is the focus of teacher education research, it is not the case, as some have claimed, that pupils' learning is necessarily ignored or considered unimportant. Rather what is the case is that the link between teachers' learning and pupils' learning is not the focus of that particular line of research. Instead the link between teacher preparation components, organizational structures, and conceptual models, on the one hand, and teachers' development of knowledge and rethinking of beliefs and attitudes, on the other, is the focus. In the contemporary scene, some of the most exciting and potentially influential research on teacher preparation is that which examines and untangles the relationships between teachers' knowledge and beliefs, their professional skill and performance in classrooms, and their pupils' learning, including academic achievement, but also including their social and emotional growth and their preparedness for participating in a democratic society.

One final example adds to the point that different constructions of the problem and study of teacher education lead to different conclusions about the strength and depth of the research base. As noted earlier, Wilson et al.'s (2001) synthesis was intended to summarize the rigorous empirical research on teacher preparation from 1980 to 2000. Their purpose was to provide for the policy and research communities a sense of what was currently known about how best to prepare highly qualified teachers for the nation's classrooms. The authors excluded studies they considered insufficiently rigorous or lacking empirical evidence, including those based on a single course in a particular teacher education program. Studies in this last category were excluded "because it was difficult to synthesize studies that were idiosyncratic" (p. 3). The report noted that many studies were found "that examined teacher learning within a particular course, but, given both the limited time frame for this report and the difficulties in comparing specific courses cross institutions [the report] did not include those course-specific studies" (p. 14). Applying these criteria meant that much of the practitioner inquiry in the area of teacher education, conducted by teacher educators engaged in research or self-studies of their own and their students' learning, was excluded. This left out the kind of fine-grained analyses of what happens in particular courses and programs that teacher-learning-oriented constructions of the problem consider highly important.

In his discussion of directions in research on teacher education over the same period as Wilson et al.'s (2001) review, for example, Zeichner (1999) referred to the emergence of practitioner inquiry and self-study in teacher education as one of the promising directions of the "new scholarship" in teacher education. Zeichner suggested that studies of practice, often conducted by individual teacher educators in their own courses and programs, had provided a "deep and critical look at practices and structures in teacher education" (p. 11). Differing viewpoints about whether self-studies and other practitioner-oriented inquiries "count" as rigorous or useful research on teacher education reflect current tensions in the field. On the one hand, there is burgeoning interest among teacher educators in studying their own practice to interrogate and ultimately improve what they and their students learn. This seems a healthy and productive development, reflecting the commitment teacher educators have to getting better at what they do through systematic inquiry and sometimes leading to the development of conceptual frameworks, theories, and practices useful well beyond the original site. On the other hand, there is criticism and sometimes dismissal of practitioner research because it is obviously "biased" in the traditional sense of desired researcher separation from what is being researched (Huberman, 1996), it uses different criteria for making knowledge claims than those used in traditional formal research (Fenstermacher, 1994), the cumulative meaning of many little studies is difficult to assess (Sleeter, 2001), and, as noted previously (Wilson et al.), it is difficult to draw cross-cutting conclusions from analyses of single courses.

This chapter makes the case that historically there have been different constructions of the problem of teacher education coupled with different assumptions about how to study that problem. These not only reflect larger political, professional, and policy contexts but also help to explain some of the differences in the conclusions of contemporaneous syntheses. These divergent conclusions may suggest the need for new initiatives in teacher education research that combine various constructions of the problem of teacher education as training, learning, and policy and examine the relationships among these.

CONCLUSION: DIRECTIONS FORWARD

The purpose of this chapter is to provide the historical context for the work of the AERA Panel on Research and Teacher Education. This chapter provides the historical context, describing the predominant approaches to studying teacher education during three overlapping periods from the 1950s to the present day.

Coupled with chapter 1, which examines the contemporary context in which research on teacher education is located, this chapter suggests three important ideas. First, there are important connections between the contemporary context and the history of research on teacher education. Our analyses in chapters 1 and 2 suggest that many of the current critiques and calls for reform that some people think are unprecedented are the contemporary manifestations of perennial issues in the history of educational research and of public schooling. As we state in these two chapters, failing to account for either the complex current political and professional context or the nuanced history of research on teacher education leads to an unsophisticated and limited understanding of the current state of research on teacher education.

Second, our analysis suggests that some of what are considered serious failings in the research on teacher education are more rightly understood as reflections of the field's relative youth. Research on teacher education emerged as an identifiable field only during the last half-century. Even if we counted the early institutional self-studies and large-scale surveys of normal schools, colleges and universities conducted in the 1920s and 1930s, the field is no more than 70 to 80 years old. Some of the strengths and limitations of the research reflect this newness. Other strengths and weaknesses reflect the priorities and viewpoints of the time. For example, in the early and middle years of the 20th century, there was harsh critique of the "educationists" and the "scientism" they were pursuing, particularly the notion that science rather than philosophy or moral education should suggest solutions to the problems of teacher education. In the early years of the 21st century, however, science has skyrocketed in importance. It now is written into federal law that scientific evidence ought to be the grounding for educational practice, policy, and resource allocation. Although science was apparently considered a ludicrous direction for teacher education by the critics of teacher education 50 years ago, it was simultaneously considered revolutionary and a "quantum leap" by those engaged in the experimental studies of teacher education that emerged in the 1950s. As far as we can determine, this work is either long forgotten or unknown to many of those who are calling today for more scientifically based studies of teacher education.

Finally, our discussion of the shift in research on teacher education from training to learning to policy coupled with our analysis of the value and limits of each approach suggests that studies that link these aspects of teacher preparation could prove worthwhile. A few initiatives in their early stages are attempting to study the impact of teacher education policies that have built into them differing degrees and kinds of support for teacher learning, thus tying together the constructions of teacher education as learning and teacher education as policy in sophisticated and intriguing new ways. The final chapter of this volume discusses the kinds of research that would be needed in order to make these links.

REFERENCES

Abell Foundation. (2001a, October). *Teacher certification reconsidered: Stumbling for quality.* Retrieved 2001, from http://www.abell.org

Abell Foundation. (2001b, November). *Teacher certification reconsidered: Stumbling for quality. A rejoinder.* Retrieved 2001, from http://www.abell.org

Allen, M. (2003). *Eight questions on teacher preparation: What does the research say?* Denver: Education Commission of the States.

American Council on Education. (1999). *To touch the future: Transforming the way teachers are taught: An action agenda for college and university presidents.* Washington, DC: American Council on Education.

Bagley, W. (1939). Basic problems in teacher education. *Teacher Education Journal, 1,* 100–105.

Ballou, D., & Podgursky, M. (2000). Reforming teacher preparation and licensing: What is the evidence? *Teachers College Record, 102*(1), 5–27.

Bennett, C.-I. (1995). Preparing teachers for cultural diversity and national standards of academic excellence. *Journal of Teacher Education, 46,* 259–265.

Bestor, A. (1953). *Educational wastelands: The retreat from learning in our public schools.* Urbana, IL: University of Illinois Press.

Bigelow, K. (1941). Some trends in teacher education. *Childhood Education, 17,* 393–395.

Bigelow, K. (1958). New direction in teacher education appraised. *Teachers College Record, 59,* 350–356.

Borko, H., & Putnam, R. (1996). Learning to teach. In D. Berliner & R. Calfee (Eds.), *Handbook of research on educational psychology* (pp. 673–699). New York: Macmillan.

Borrowman, M. (1956). *The liberal and technical in teacher education: A historical survey of American thought.* New York: Teachers College Press.

Borrowman, M. (1965). *Teacher education in America: A documentary history.* New York: Teachers College Press.

Britzman, D. (1991). *Practice makes practice: A critical study of learning to teach.* Albany, NY: State University of New York Press.

Carter, K. (1990). Teachers' knowledge and learning to teach. In W. Houston (Ed.), *Handbook of research on teacher education* (pp. 291–320). New York: Macmillan.

Charters, W., & Waples, D. (1929). *The commonwealth teacher-training study.* Chicago, IL: University of Chicago Press.

Christensen, D. (1996). The professional knowledge-research base for teacher education. In J. Sikula, T. Buttery, & E. Guyton (Eds.), *The handbook of research on teacher education* (pp. 38–52). New York: Macmillan.

Clifford, G. (1975). *The shape of American education.* Englewood Cliffs, NJ: Prentice Hall.

Clifford, G., & Guthrie, J. (1988). *ED school, a brief for professional education.* Chicago, IL: University of Chicago Press.

Cochran-Smith, M. (2001). Constructing outcomes in teacher education: Policy, practice and pitfalls. *Educational Policy Analysis Archives, 9*(11).

Cochran-Smith, M. (2004). Ask a different question, get a different answer: The research base for teacher Eeucation. *Journal of Teacher Education, 55*(2).

Cochran-Smith, M., Davis, D., & Fries, K. (2004). Multicultural teacher education: Research, practice and policy. In J. Banks (Ed.), *Handbook of research on multicultural education* (3rd ed., pp. 931–975). San Francisco: Jossey-Bass.

Cochran-Smith, M., & Fries, K. (2001). Sticks, stones, and ideology: The discourse of teacher education. *Educational Researcher, 30*(8), 3–15.

Cochran-Smith, M., & Fries, M. K. (2002). The discourse of reform in teacher education: extending the dialogue. *Educational Researcher, 31*(6), 26–29.

Cohen, D., Raudenbush, S., & Ball, D. (2002). Evidence matters: Randomized trials in education research. In F. Mosteller & R. Boruch (Eds.), *Evidence matters: Randomized trials in education research.* Washington: Brookings Institute Press.

Collier, R. (1964). Some strengths and weaknesses of research methodology in teacher education. In F. Cyphert & E. Spaights (Eds.), *An analysis and project of research in teacher education* (pp. 123–148). Columbus, OH: Ohio State University.

Commission on Teacher Education. (1946). *The improvement of teacher education: A final report by the Commission on Teacher Education.* Washington, DC: American Council on Education.

Conant, J. (1963). *The education of American teachers.* New York: McGraw-Hill.

Condliffe Lagemann. (2000). *An elusive science: The troubling history of education research.* Chicago: University of Chicago Press.

Cottrell, D., Cooper, R., Hunt, C., Maaske, R., Sharpe, D., Shaw, J., et al. (Eds.). (1956). *Teacher education for a free people*. Oneonta, NY: AACTE.

Cremin, L. (1953). The heritage of American teacher education. *Journal of Teacher Education, 4*, 163–164.

Cremin, L. (1978). *The education of the educating profession*. Washington, DC: AACTE.

Cyphert, F., & Spaights, E. (1964). *An analysis and projection of research in teacher education*. Columbus, OH: Ohio State University.

Darling-Hammond, L. (1984). *Beyond the commission reports: The coming crisis in teaching* (No. R-3177-RC). Santa Monica, CA: RAND.

Darling-Hammond, L. (1988). Teacher quality and educational equality. *College Board Review, 148*, 16–23, 39–41.

Darling-Hammond, L. (1998). Teachers and teaching: Testing policy hypotheses from a national commission report. *Educational Researcher, 27*(1), 5–15.

Darling-Hammond, L. (2000a). Reforming teacher preparation and licensing: Debating the evidence. *Teachers College Record, 102*(1), 28–56.

Darling-Hammond, L. (2000b). Teacher quality and student achievement: A review of state policy evidence. *Education Policy Analysis Archives, 8*(1).

Darling-Hammond, L. (2001). *The research and rhetoric on teacher certification: A response to "Teacher certification reconsidered."* Retrieved October 2001, from http://www.nctaf.org

Darling-Hammond, L., & Berry, B. (1987). *The evolution of teacher policy* (No. RJRE-01). Santa Monica, CA: RAND.

Darling-Hammond, L., & Youngs, P. (2002). Defining 'Highly Qualified Teachers' what does 'Scientifically-Based Research' actually tell us? *Educational Researcher, 31*(9), 13–25.

Denemark, G., & Macdonald, J. (1967). Preservice and inservice education of teachers. *Review of Educational Research, 37*, 233–247.

DuBois, W. E. B. (1944). The meaning of education. In H. Aptheker (Ed.), *Against racism: Unpublished essays, papers, addresses, 1887–1961, W. E. B. DuBois* (pp. 249–252). Amherst, MA: University of Massachusetts Press.

Earley, P. (2000). Finding the culprit: Federal policy and teacher education. *Educational Policy, 14*(1), 25–39.

Earley, P., & Schneider, E. J. (1996). Federal policy and teacher education. In J. Sikula, T. Buttery, & E. Guyton (Eds.), *Handbook of research on teacher education* (2nd ed., pp. 306–319). New York: Macmillan.

Education Commission of the States. (2000). *Two paths to quality teaching—The debate*. Retrieved from http://www.ecs.org

Elmore, R. F. (2002). Testing trap. *Harvard Magazine, 105*(1), 35.

Erickson, F. (1986). Qualitative methods on research on teaching. In M. Wittrock (Ed.), *Handbook of research on teaching* (3rd ed., pp. 119–161). New York: Macmillan.

Evenden, E. (1933). *National survey of the education of teachers: Volume VI. Summary and interpretation* (Bulletin No. 10). Washington, DC: U.S. Department of the Interior.

Evertson, C., Hawley, W., & Zlotnik, M. (1985). Making a difference in educational quality through teacher education. *Journal of Teacher Education, 36*, 2–10.

Farkas, S., & Johnson, J. (1997). *Different drummers: How teachers of teachers view public education*. New York: Public Agenda.

Feiman-Nemser, S. (1983). Learning to teach. In L. Shulman & G. Sykes (Eds.), *Handbook of teaching and policy* (pp. 150–170). New York: Longman.

Fenstermacher, G. (1985). What counts as research in teacher education. In S. Hord, S. O'Neal, & M. Smith (Eds.), *Beyond the looking glass: Papers from a National Symposium on Teacher Education Policies, Practices, and Research*. Austin: Research and Development Center for Teacher Education at the University of Texas, Austin.

Fenstermacher, G. (1994). The knower and the known: The nature of knowledge in research on teaching. In L. Darling-Hammond (Ed.), *Review of research in education* (Vol. 20, pp. 3–56). Washington, DC: American Educational Research Association.

Floden, R. (2001). Research on effects of teaching: A continuing model for research on teaching. In V. Richardson (Ed.), *Handbook of research on teaching* (4th ed.). Washington, DC: American Educational Research Association.

Frazier, B. (1935). History of the professional education of teachers. In *National survey of the education of teachers* (Bulletin No. 10, Vol. 5, Part I, pp. 42–59). Washington, DC: U.S. Office of Education.

Frazier, B. (1943). Meeting the teacher education shortage problem. *Teacher Education Journal, 5,* 15–20.

Freiberg, H. J., & Waxman, H. (1990). Changing teacher education. In R. Houston (Ed.), *Handbook of research on teacher education* (pp. 617–635). New York: Macmillan.

Fullan, M., Galluzzo, G., Morris, P., & Watson, N. (1998). *The rise and stall of teacher education reform.* Washington, DC: AACTE.

Gage, N. (1963). Paradigms for research on teaching. In N. Gage (Ed.), *Handbook of research on teaching.* Chicago: Rand McNally.

Gage, N. (1964). The evaluation of teaching. *SPATE Journal, 3,* 33–41.

Gage, N. (1978). *The scientific basis of the art of teaching.* New York: Teachers College Press.

Gage, N. (1989). The paradigm wars and their aftermath: A "historical" sketch of research on teaching since 1989. *Teachers College Record, 91*(2), 135–150.

Gardner, W. (1989). Preface. In M. Reynolds (Ed.), *Knowledge base for the beginning teacher.* New York: Pergamon Press.

Gideonse, H. (1982). The necessary revolution in teacher education. *Phi Delta Kappan, 64*(1), 15–18.

Goodlad, J. (1990). *Teachers for our nation's schools.* San Francisco, CA: Jossey-Bass.

Gore, J. (1993). *The struggle for pedagogies: Critical and feminist discourses as regimes of truth.* New York: Routledge.

Haberman, M. (1985a). Does teacher education make a difference: A review of comparisons between liberal arts and teacher education graduates. *Journal of Thought, 20*(2), 25–34.

Haberman, M. (1985b). Does teacher education make a difference? A review of comparisons of liberal arts and teacher education majors. *Journal of Thought, 20*(2), 25–34.

Haberman, M., & Stinnett, T. (1973). *Teacher education and the new profession of teaching.* Berkeley, CA: McCutchen Publishing Company.

Hamilton, M. L. (Ed.). (1998). *Reconceptualizing teaching practice: Self-study in teacher education.* London: Falmer Press.

Hamilton, D., & McWilliam, E. (2001). Ex-centric voices that frame research on teaching. In V. Richardson (Ed.), *Handbook of research on teaching* (4th ed.). Washington, DC: American Educational Research Association.

Hanushek, E. (1989). The impact of differential expenditures on school performance. *Educational Researcher, 18*(3), 45–51, 62.

Hanushek, E. (1997). Assessing the effects of school resources on student perfomance: An update. *Educational Evaluation and Policy Analysis, 19*(2), 141–164.

Haskew, L. (1964). The impact of the research upon the practice of teacher education. In F. Cyphert & E. Spaights (Eds.), *An analysis and projection of research in teacher education* (pp. 149–173). Columbus, OH: Ohio State University.

Herbst, J. (1989). *And sadly teach: Teacher education and professionalization in American culture.* Madison, WI: University of Wisconsin Press.

Hodenfield, G., & Stinnett, T. (1961). *The education of teachers: Conflict and consensus.* Englewood Cliffs, NJ: Prentice Hall.

Holmes Group. (1986). *Teachers for tomorrow's schools.* East Lansing, MI: Author.

Houston, R. (Ed.). (1990). *Handbook of research on teacher education* (1st ed.). New York: Macmillan.

Howey, K., & Zimpher, N. (1989). *Profiles of preservice teacher education: Inquiry into the nature of programs.* Albany, NY: State University of New York Press.

Howsam, R., Corrigan, D., Denemark, G., & Nash, R. (1976). *Educating a profession.* Washington, DC: AACTE.

Huberman, M. (1996). Focus on research moving mainstream: Taking a closer look at teacher research. *Language Arts, 73*(2), 124–140.

Judge, H. (1982). *American graduate schools of education: A view from abroad.* New York: Ford Foundation.

Kanstoroom, M. (1999). *Boosting teacher quality: A common sense proposal, testimony prepared for delivery to the Subcommittee on Postsecondary Education of the Committee on Education and the Workforce, U.S. House of Representatives.* Washington, DC: Thomas B. Fordham Foundation.

Kanstoroom, M., & Finn, C. (1999). *Better teachers, better schools.* Washington, DC: Thomas B. Fordham Foundation.

Kennedy, M. (1996). Research genres in teacher education. In F. Murray (Ed.), *The teacher educator's handbook: Building a knowledge base for the preparation of teachers* (pp. 120–154). San Francisco, CA: Jossey-Bass.

Kennedy, M. (1999). The problem of evidence in teacher education. In R. Roth (Ed.), *The role of the university in the preparation of teachers* (pp. 87–107). Philadelphia: Falmer Press.

Kliebard, H. (1973). The question in teacher education. In D. McCarty (Ed.), *New perspectives on teacher education* (pp. 8–24). San Francisco, CA: Jossey-Bass.

Koehler, V. (1985). Research on preservice teacher education. *Journal of Teacher Education, 36*(1), 23–30.

Koerner, J. (1963). *The miseducation of American teachers.* Boston: Houghton Mifflin.

Ladson-Billings, G. (1995). Toward a theory of culturally relevant pedagogy. *American Educational Research Journal, 32*(3), 465–491.

Lagemann, E. (2000). *An elusive science: The troubling history of education research.* Chicago, IL: University of Chicago Press.

Lanier, J. (1982). Teacher educaton: Needed research and practice for the preparation of teacher professionals. In D. Corrigan (Ed.), *The future of teacher education: Needed research and practice* (pp. 13–36). College Station: College of Education, Texas A&M University.

Lanier, J., & Little, J. (1986). Research on teacher education. In M. Wittrock (Ed.), *Handbook of research on teaching* (3rd ed., pp. 527–569). Washington, DC: American Educational Research Association.

Lauer, P. (2001). *A secondary analysis of a review of teacher preparation research*: Education Commission of the States.

Learned, W., & Bagley, W. (1920). *The professional preparation of teachers for American public schools* (Vol. 14). New York: Carnegie Foundation for the Advancement of Teaching.

Little, J. (1993). Professional community in comprehensive high schools: The two worlds of academic and vocational teachers. In J. Little & M. McLaughlin (Eds.), *Teacher's work: Individuals, colleagues, and contexts* (pp. 137–163). New York: Teachers College Press.

Loughran, J., & Northfield, J. (1998). A framework for the development of self-study practice. In M. L. Hamilton (Ed.), *Reconceptualizing teaching practice: Self-study in teacher education* (pp. 7–18). London: Falmer Press.

Lucas, C. (1999). *Teacher education in America: Reform agendas for the twenty-first century.* New York: St. Martin's Press.

Luke, C. (1992). Feminist politics in radical pedagogy. In C. Luke & J. Gore (Eds.), *Feminisms and critical pedagogy* (pp. 25–53). New York: Routledge.

McLaughlin, M., & Oberman, I. (1996). *Teacher learning: New policies, new practices.* New York: Teachers College Press.

Melnick, S., & Pullin, D. (2000). 'Can you take dictation?' Prescribing teacher quality through testing. *Journal of Teacher Education, 51*(4), 262–275.

Monroe, W. (1952). *Teacher-learning theory and teacher education 1890–1950.* Urbana, IL: University of Illinois Press.

Murray, F. (Ed.). (1996). *The teacher educator's handbook: Building a knowledge base for the preparation of teachers.* Washington, DC: AACTE.

National Commission on Excellence in Education. (1983). *A nation at risk: The imperative for educational reform.* Washington, DC: U.S. Government Printing Office.

National Commission on Teaching & America's Future. (1996). *What matters most: Teaching for America's future.* New York: Teachers College, Columbia University.

National Education Goals Panel. (1997). *National education goals report.* Washington, DC: Author.

Patterson, R. S., Michelli, N., & Pacheco, A. (1999). *Centers of pedagogy, new structures for educational renewal.* San Francisco: Jossey-Bass.

Peck, R., & Tucker, J. (1973). Research on teacher education. In R. Travers (Ed.), *Handbook of research on teaching* (2nd ed., pp. 940–978). Chicago: Rand McNally.

Popkewitz, T., Tabachnick, B., & Zeichner, K. (1979). Dulling the senses: Research in teacher education. *Journal of Teacher Education, 30*(5), 52–60.

Pressley, M., Wharton-McDonald, R., Allington, R. L., Block, C. C., Morrow, L., Tracey, D., et al. (2001). The nature of effective first-grade literacy instruction. *Scientific Studies in Reading, 5,* 35–58.

Raspberry, W. (1998, July 3). A place for teacher tests: The often worthless education courses frequently serve to keep the competent out of teaching.*The Washington Post,* p. A19.

Ravitch, D. (2000). *Left back, a century of failed school reforms.* New York: Simon & Schuster.

Reynolds, M. (Ed.). (1989). *Knowledge base for the beginning teacher.* Oxford: Pergamon Press.

Rice, J. K. (2003). *Teacher quality: Understanding the effectiveness of teacher Attributes.* Washington: Economic Policy Institute.

Richardson, V. (Ed.). (2001). *Fourth handbook of research on teaching.* Washington, DC: American Educational Research Association.

Richardson, V., & Placier, P. (2001). Teacher change. In V. Richardson (Ed.), *Handbook of research on teaching* (4th ed., pp. 905–947). Washington, DC: American Educational Research Association.

Richardson-Koehler, V. (1987). *Educator's handbook: A research perspective.* New York: Longman.

Rivkin, S., Hanushek, E., & Kain, J. (1998). *Teachers, schools, and academic achievement* (No. working paper 6691). Washington: National Bureau of Economic Research.

Rugg, H. (1952). *The teacher of teachers: Frontiers of theory and practice in teacher education.* New York: Harper & Row.

Ryan, K. (1960). *Characteristics of teachers.* Washington, DC: American Council on Education.

Ryan, K. (Ed.). (1975). *Teacher education, 74th Yearbook of the National Society for the Study of Education.* Chicago: University of Chicago Press.

Sarason, S., Davidson, K., & Blatt, B. (1962). *The preparation of teachers: An unstudied problem in education.* New York: Wiley.

Schrag, P. (1999). Who will teach the teachers. *University Business, July 1999,* 29–34.

Sedlak, M. (1987). Tomorrow's teachers: The essential arguments of the Holmes Group Report. In J. Soltis (Ed.), *Reforming teacher education, the impact of the Holmes Group Report* (pp. 4–15). New York: Teachers College Press.

Sedlak, M. (1989). "Let's go and buy a school master": Historical perspectives on the hiring of teachers in the United States, 1750–1980. In D. Warren (Ed.), *American teachers: Histories of a profession at work.* New York: Macmillan.

Shulman, L. (1983). Knowledge and teaching: Foundations of the new reform. *Harvard Educational Review, 51,* 1–22.

Shulman, L. (1986a). Paradigms and research programs in the study of teaching: A contemporary perspective. In M. Wittrock (Ed.), *Handbook of research on teaching* (3rd ed., pp. 3–36). New York: Macmillan.

Shulman, L. (1986b). Those who understand: Knowledge growth in teaching. *Educational Researcher, 5,* 4–14.

Sikula, J., Buttery, T., & Guyton, E. (Eds.). (1996). *Handbook of research on teacher education* (2nd ed.). New York: Macmillan.

Sirotnick, K., & Goodlad, J. (Eds.). (1988). *School-university partnerships in action.* New York: Teachers College Press.

Sleeter, C. (2001). Epistemological diversity in research on preservice teacher preparation for historically underserved children. In W. Secada (Ed.), *Review of research in education* (Vol. 25, pp. 209–250). Washington, DC: American Educational Research Association.

Smith, B. (Ed.). (1971). *Research in teacher education: A symposium.* Englewood Cliffs, NJ: Prentice Hall.

Smith, B., & Meux, M. (1964). Status of research in teacher education research in teacher education: Problems, analysis, and criticism. In F. Cyphert & E. Spaights (Eds.), *An analysis and projection of research in teacher education* (pp. 103–122). Columbus, OH: Ohio State University.

Smith, E. (1962). *Teacher education: A reappraisal.* New York: Harper & Row.

Soder, R., & Sirotnick, K. (1990). Beyond reinventing the past: The politics of teacher education. In J. Goodlad, R. Soder, & K. Sirotnick (Eds.), *Places where teachers are taught* (pp. 385–412). San Francisco, CA: Jossey-Bass.

SRI International. (2000). *Preparing and supporting new teachers: A literature review* (Prepared for the Planning and Evaluation Service of the U.S. Department of Education). Menlo Park, CA: SRI International.

Task Force on Teaching as a Profession. (1986). *A nation prepared: Teachers for the 21st century.* New York: Carnegie Forum on Education and the Economy.

Tom, A. (1980). The reform of teacher education through research: A futile quest. *Teachers College Record, 82*(1), 15–29.

Travers, R. M. W. (1973). *Second handbook of research on teaching.* Chicago: Rand McNally.

Turner, R. (1971). Conceptual foundations of research in teacher education. In B. Smith (Ed.), *Research in teacher education: A symposium* (pp. 10–36). Englewood Cliffs, NJ: Prentice Hall.

Turner, R. (1975). An overview of research in teacher education. In K. Ryan (Ed.), *Teacher education, 74th Yearbook of the National Society for the Study of Education* (pp. 87–110). Chicago: University of Chicago Press.

U.S. Department of Education. (2002). *Meeting the highly qualified teachers challenge: The Secreatry's annual report on teacher quality.* Washington, DC: Author.

U.S. Department of Education. (2003). *Meeting the highly qualified teachers challenge: The Secretary's Second Annual Report on Teacher Quality.* Washington: U.S. Department of Education, Office of Postsecondary Education.

Urban, W. (1990). Historical studies of teacher education. In W. Houston (Ed.), *Handbook of research on teacher education* (pp. 59–71). New York: Macmillan.

VanEvery, I. (1979). Teacher education meeting the needs of society: Past-present-future. *Kappa Delta Pi Record, 15*(3), 72–75.

Warren, D. (1985). Learning from experience: History and teacher education. *Educational Researcher, 14*(10), 5–12.

Warren, B., & Ogonowski, M. (1998). *From knowledge to knowing: An inquiry into teacher learning in science.* Newton, MA: Education Development Center, Inc.

Watson, G., Cottrell, D., & Lloyd-Jones, E. (1938). *Redirecting teacher education.* New York: Teachers College Press.

Whitehurst, G. (2002). *Scientifically based research on teacher quality: Research on teacher preparation and professional development.* Paper presented at the White House Conference on Preparing Tomorrow's Teachers, Washington, DC.

Wideen, M., Mayer-Smith, J., & Moon, B. (1998). A critical analysis of the research on learning to teach: Making the case for an ecological perspective on inquiry. *Review of Educational Research, 68*(2), 130–178.

Wilk, R., Edson, W., & Wu, J. (1967). Student personnel research in teacher education. *Review of Educational Research, 37*, 219–232.

Wilson, S., & Floden, R. (2002). *Addendum to teacher preparation research: Current knowledge, gaps, and recommendations.* Denver: Education Commission of the States.

Wilson, S., Floden, R., & Ferrini-Mundy, J. (2001). *Teacher preparation research: Current knowledge, gaps, and recommendations.* Washington, DC: Center for the Study of Teaching and Policy.

Wise, A. (1988). *Impacts of teacher testing: State educational governance through standard-setting* (No. NIE-G-83-0023). Santa Monica, CA: Rand Corporation.

Wise, A. (1998). *NCATE: Assuring quality for the nation's teachers. Testimony of Arthur E. Wise at the Senate committee on labor and human resources hearing on "Better teachers for today's classroom:*

How to make it happen." Retrieved October 10, 1999 from http://www.ncate.org/specfoc/arttest.html

Wittrock, M. (Ed.). (1986). *Handbook of research on teaching* (3rd ed.). New York: Macmillan.

Zeichner, K. (1993). *Educating teachers for cultural diversity* (National Center for Research on Teacher Learning Special Report No. ERIC Document, ED 359 167). East Lansing, MI: Michigan State University.

Zeichner, K. (1999). The new scholarship in teacher education. *Educational Researcher, 28*(9), 4–15.

Zimpher, N., & Ashburn, E. (1985). Studying the professional development of teachers: How conceptions of the world inform the research agenda. *Journal of Teacher Education, 36*(6), 16–26.

Zumwalt, K. (1982). Research on teaching: Policy implications for teacher education. In A. Leiberman & M. McLaughlin (Eds.), *Policy making in education: 81st yearbook of NSSE* (pp. 215–248). Chicago, IL: University of Chicago Press.

3

Teachers' Characteristics: Research on the Demographic Profile

Karen Zumwalt
Elizabeth Craig
Teachers College, Columbia University

Increasing birthrates, immigration, teacher retirements, and attrition are fueling the projected need for 200,000 new teachers annually over the next decade. The news media regularly predict teacher shortages and raise concerns that teacher education institutions will not be able to meet the demand for new teachers. Educators are apprehensive that the rush to fill vacancies will scuttle recent progress in upgrading standards for the profession. Most importantly, they fear that a shortage of good teachers will undermine attempts to educate all children to meet the challenges of the new century. Hence, issues of quantity, quality, and equity dominate current discussions of the teaching pool.

This chapter looks at what research since 1985 tells us about the characteristics of teachers who are going into teaching, where they are prepared, where they teach, and how long they stay. The focus is the demographic profile (i.e., gender, race and ethnicity, socioeconomic background, and age) and its impact on students. The chapter ends with a discussion of a research agenda based on what we know and do not know about the demographic profile of teachers.

Although this volume focuses on teacher education, research on retention is included because teachers, once recruited, prepared, and placed in schools, make a variety of career choices that affect both the quantity and the quality of the teaching pool. Those choices also affect challenges facing teacher educators. Research on teachers' characteristics related to indicators of quality and the impact on students is reviewed in the next chapter.

DEMOGRAPHIC DATA AND RESEARCH

Demographic data are primarily provided by the U.S. Department of Education's National Center for Educational Statistics (NCES). The Schools and Staffing Survey (SASS) was collected nationwide in 1987 to 1988, 1990 to 1991, 1993 to 1994, and 1999 to 2000. The 1993 to 1994 dataset is the most comprehensive one analyzed by researchers to date. Raw data for 1999 to 2000 were released in May 2002, but researchers have not yet fully analyzed that data. Hence, we look at studies using available NCES data, supplemented by more recent but less comprehensive data from other sources.

The American Association of Colleges of Teacher Education (AACTE) periodically collects demographic data about teacher education students. But as routes into teaching have expanded, the picture of who is preparing to teach is not as definitive as in the past when institutional surveys captured the entire pool of prospective teachers.

The literature reviewed for this chapter and the next was generated through four primary search strategies, an ERIC search, a manual search of educational journals, an online search of Web sites of organizations concerned with teaching and teacher education, and an examination of literature reviews to identify other resources.

The ERIC database was searched using these descriptors: preservice teachers, teacher background, teacher characteristics, minority group teachers, teacher qualifications, teacher certification, institutional characteristics, academic achievement, student achievement, effective teachers, career ladder, teacher persistence, teacher employment, teacher attrition, preservice teacher education and teacher education programs. Combinations of these descriptors were used to identify literature related to patterns such as the impact of teacher quality on career paths.

The electronic search was supplemented by a manual search of several key educational journals. The indices or table of contents of *Action in Teacher Education, Journal of Teacher Education, Review of Educational Research, Review of Research in Education, Sociology of Education, Teacher Educator, Teachers College Record* and *Teaching and Teacher Education* were examined for relevant articles.

In addition, Internet sites were searched for publications. The Web sites of organizations such as AACTE, American Federation of Teachers (AFT), Educational Testing Service (ETS), National Council for Accreditation of Teacher Education (NCATE), NCES, National Commission on Teaching and America's Future (NCTAF), National Education Association (NEA), Office of Educational Research and Improvement (OERI), and the Rand Corporation proved helpful in identifying and accessing resources.

Several overviews of recent literature pertaining to the demographic and quality profiles of current and prospective teachers provided references to other work (Brookhart & Freeman, 1992; Darling-Hammond, 2000; Darling-Hammond & Cobb, 1996; Dill, 1996; Henke, Choy, Chen, Geis, & Alt, 1997). Likewise, the bibliographies of all sources were scanned in an iterative process to locate further studies. Panel members and reviewers of the chapters also suggested additional sources, which were pursued through early summer 2003. Reports using NCES datasets were added as published, through August 2004.

With few exceptions, searches were limited to material published in 1985 and later. Although the original plan was to focus on research in the past 10 years, it seemed more appropriate to look back to the mid-1980s when the current reform efforts in teacher education began. As agreed on by the panel, the focus was on teacher education students and public school teachers in the United States. We did not look at demographic and quality profiles of private school teachers, reserve pool teachers, teachers in other countries, or teacher educators. Issues related to teacher supply and demand provide a context, but such research was beyond the scope of this chapter.

The nature of the topic necessitated inclusion of research that has not undergone the peer-review process common to academic journals for such reports as the NCES School and Staffing Survey or the AACTE Research about Teacher Education (RATE) studies or seminal monographs (e.g. Murnane, Singer, Willett, Kemple, & Olsen, 1991).

Once identified, the literature was classified by key words. Using the bibliographic software Endnote, key word searches produced subsets of literature relevant to the recruitment, preparation, placement, and career paths of teachers.

On closer reading, we discarded studies whose sample size was too small to reasonably support their findings, whose methodology was unclear, or whose findings were not supported by the reported data. Because most demographic data are not analyzed with statistical tests, we did not use statistical tests as a criterion for inclusion of studies. When used, we report whether differences were statistically significant, but leave it up to the reader to judge substantive significance. Details of the studies may be found in Table 4.1 following chapter 4.

WHO IS TEACHING?

Demographic research describes teachers and prospective teachers in terms of gender, race and ethnicity, age, and socioeconomic background.

Gender

In 1999 to 2000, 74.5% of public school teachers were female, according to NCES (2003). Other national surveys support these figures, which have remained fairly consistent over recent years, with women actually increasing their majority slightly (Boe, Cook, Bobbitt, & Terhaian, 1998). Feistritzer (1996) suggested that the trend may be toward even higher proportions of females because 84% of teachers in their 20s were female. The NEA (2003) reported that 79% of teachers it surveyed in 2000 to 2001 were female.

More careers now are open to female college graduates. In 1970, approximately 40% of female college graduates ages 20 to 29 were employed as teachers compared with fewer than 11% in 1990. The proportion of male college graduates who were teaching dropped from 9% to 5.7% (Hanushek & Pace, 1995).

Teacher Education Students.   According to 1996 data, nearly 67% of all teacher education students were female, whereas 74% of Whites were female (AACTE, 1999). In a meta-analysis of 44 studies of teacher education students, Brookhart and Freeman (1992) found 75% to 80% were female. In all studies reviewed for this chapter, females made up the vast majority of elementary candidates, but a lower proportion of secondary candidates. In some studies, the proportion of women in elementary programs was as high as 85% (AACTE). Although early childhood and elementary teacher education students from all racial and ethnic groups were predominantly female, all minority groups had a higher proportion of men in these fields than Whites did. Of African Americans in elementary programs, 21.5% were men, compared to just 15% of Whites (AACTE).

Whether the recent higher percentages of males enrolled in teacher education programs (AACTE, 1999) will translate into a more diverse teaching pool is unknown. The High School and Beyond Study, following students who were high school sophomores in 1980, found that males, from all racial and ethnic groups, were less likely to graduate from college than were females (Vegas, Murnane, & Willett, 2001). Gender composition may also be affected by a tight labor market or war, as it has in the past.

Race and Ethnicity

Although the student population is increasingly diverse, 1999 to 2000 data indicate that public school teachers were predominantly White, non-Hispanic (84%). Of the remaining proportion, 7.8% were African American, 5.7% Hispanic, 1.6% Asian American, and .8% Native American (NCES, 2003).

Historically, teaching has been a popular career among African Americans, although less so among other minorities (Murnane et al., 1991). After World War II, 79% of Black female college graduates were employed as teachers. As other opportunities became available, by the mid-1980s, this number fell to 23% and the proportion of minority teachers in general had dropped considerably (Snyder, 1998). During this period, concerns about the disproportionately small numbers of teachers of color were raised, especially in light of increasing student diversity.

In 1971, the public school teaching force was 88.3% White, 8.1% African American, and 3.6% other minorities (Snyder, 1998). By the mid-1980s, White teachers increased to 92.4%, whereas African Americans fell to 6.9%, and others dropped to .7% in 1986. By 1993, the proportion of teachers of color had increased to 12.8%, including 6.8% African American (Henke, Choy, Geis, & Broughman, 1997). Six years later, minority teachers increased to 16%, including 7.8% African American (NCES, 2003).

Contradictory data exist about recent trends. In 1999 to 2000, Asian and Hispanic teachers were more likely to have 5 or fewer years of experience, whereas African-American teachers were more likely to have 20 or more years of experience (NCES, 2003). The latest NEA study (2003) notes a higher proportion of Whites (89.7%), but Hispanics were not included as a minority. Feistritzer (1996) notes that teachers in their 20s were 86% White, indicating little diversity change among younger teachers. Whatever the actual trend in the diversity of the teaching staff, the diversity gap between students and teachers is large and widening.

Teacher Education Students.   In the late 1960s, 60% of Black college graduates entered teaching within 5 years, compared with 40% of their White peers. By 1981, only 10% of White college graduates entered teaching within 5 years, whereas slightly fewer than 10% of Black college graduates did (Murnane et al., 1991). From 1975 to 1982, the number of bachelor's degrees in education awarded to minorities decreased by 50%, whereas bachelor's degrees in business administration increased 60% (Alston, 1988). Although it is true that degrees in education declined for White students as well, the decrease for African Americans was at nearly twice the rate (AACTE, 1988).

Although the majority of prospective teachers are White, there are differences across institutions and regions. In the studies reviewed by Brookhart and Freeman (1992), the percentage of White students ranged from 80% to 96%. AACTE's RATE studies, which surveyed 30 randomly selected schools, colleges, and departments of education (SCDEs) yearly from 1985 to 1992, reported majorities of White students ranging from 89% to nearly 93% (AACTE, 1987, 1988, 1989, 1990, 1994b). The only variation was found in the RATE VII study that focused on major metropolitan areas; 78% were White and 22.3% were minorities (AACTE, 1994c). Another exception is the low White enrollment at historically Black colleges and universities (HBCU).

Prospective teachers appear to be more diverse. In its most recent data, AACTE (1999) reports that White students made up 80.5% of enrollment in SCDEs, a 2 percentage points decline since their initial study in 1989. African Americans increased their representation over the decade to 9%, a 40% increase, and Hispanics comprised 4.7%, or 80% higher than before. Asian and Pacific Americans and Native Americas comprised 1.7% and 0.7%, respectively. Additionally, studies indicate alternative programs often attract a higher proportion of students of color.

Prospective teachers are different from the K–12 student population in another conspicuous way. Most are English-only speakers, whereas in the last decade, the number of school children with limited English skills doubled to 5 million (Zhao, 2002). The AACTE RATE III study (1989) found that 40% of prospective teachers spoke a language other than English, but only 3% did so fluently. The AACTE RATE VII study (1994c) of colleges in metropolitan areas reported 12% of prospective teachers were fluent in another language.

Socioeconomic Background

Teaching has long been viewed as an upwardly mobile career choice for those from the working and lower middle classes (Lanier & Little, l986; Lortie, 1975). This generalization masks distinctions related to gender, race, and region (Sedlak & Schlossman, 1986). Teachers have always come from a variety of socioeconomic status (SES) backgrounds. Black teachers generally have come from lower income backgrounds than White teachers. White female teachers from higher SES backgrounds were overrepresented in the teaching pool through the l960s until other job opportunities became more widely available. The number of male teachers, especially in secondary schools, grew during the 20th century as larger student enrollments and higher salaries made teaching a more attractive route out of the working class.

Educational attainment of parents (particularly mothers) and occupational level of parents (particularly fathers) are often used as proxies for SES, although this distinction may be increasingly less meaningful. Data suggest the educational attainment and occupational profile of parents of teachers are still relatively modest, but are gradually increasing. In 1981, almost 20% of mothers of teachers had only an elementary school education, and 70% had no college. Although 40% of teachers' fathers were employed in occupations that required some higher education, the majority were from the ranks of skilled and unskilled laborers, clerical, sales, and farm workers (Lanier & Little, l986). In a study of the NELS-72 data, Heyns (1988) found that those teaching in l986 tended to come from lower socioeconomic backgrounds compared to all college graduates. By 2001, however, almost 31% of fathers and 41% of mothers of teachers were high school graduates, and 45% of fathers and 42% of mothers had some college education. The proportion of teachers whose parents had at least some college education was inversely related to teachers' ages and experiences. Some historical differences continue to be true. Male teachers were still less likely to have parents with a college education (NEA, 2003). White teachers were more likely to have both parents with at least some college education (Sedlak & Schlossman, l986).

Some authors speculate that the decrease in the percentage of African Americans, particularly females, who choose teaching is related to the greater proportions of middle-class and upper-middle-class African Americans (Kemple, 1989; King, 1993b). Teaching may be less appealing to them if it is seen not only as a traditional career choice for women and African Americans but also as the traditional route out of the working class.

Teacher Education Students.   Studies of teacher education students follow the pattern noted in the teaching pool. Some recent changes, particularly in the educational attainment of their parents, may reflect the increased educational attainment of the American population.

In a meta-analysis of 44 studies, two thirds of mothers and fathers had no college degree (Brookhart & Freeman, 1992). Book, Freeman, and Brousseau (1985) reported that teacher education candidates came from homes with a lower annual income than noneducation majors. In the AACTE RATE II study (1988), White teachers were more likely to be from higher income families. Recent studies indicate some changes. In the AACTE RATE VII (1994c) study, 51% of students reported that one or both parents graduated from college.

Age

NCES data (Gruber, Wiley, & Broughman, l995; Henke, Choy, Chen, et al., 1997; Smith, 1995) indicate the average age of teachers in public schools increased from 40 in l987 to 1988 to 43 in 1993 to 1994 and dropped to 42.3 in 1999 to 2000. An increasing number of teachers in 1999 to 2000 were 50 or older (29.4%), but the number under 30 (16.9%) also had increased over 6 years earlier (Gruber et al., 2002).

Minority teachers tend to be slightly older than White teachers (AACTE, l999), but there are differences among minority groups. In a study of the teaching force in Texas, Kirby, Naftel, and Berends (1999) found that the median age of Black teachers was higher than that of White or Hispanic teachers. NCES data (Henke, Choy, Chen, et al., 1997) also indicated that Hispanic and Asians were relatively well represented among teachers with less than 3 years experience, whereas African Americans were disproportionately represented among those with more than 20 years of experience.

Teacher Education Students.   College graduates who go on to teach are older on average than classmates with whom they graduated. One study found that nearly 40% of new teachers in 1994 were 25 or older when they graduated from college a year earlier, compared with 34% of other college graduates that year (Henke, Choy, Chen, et al., l997).

New licensees in North Carolina from 1975 to 1982 and in Connecticut from 1980 to 1987 indicated a decreased number under age 24, with larger proportions in their late 20s and over 30. Murnane et al. (l991) speculated that declining job opportunities and salaries had the greatest impact on college students who could change career plans. In addition, "some of the traditional rewards of teaching—such as shorter structured workdays and vacations that coincide with children's vacations—continued to attract somewhat older people with families" (p. 27).

Besides the increasing age of teacher education students, the average age of prospective teachers has also increased in tandem with the growth of graduate programs and alternative programs in the last 15 years. These programs are designed to attract to teaching college graduates who did not prepare to teach during their college years.

HOW ARE THEY PREPARED?

From the 1930s through the 1980s, the structure of teacher education was generally stable. Teachers were prepared primarily in 4-year undergraduate programs terminating in a bachelor's degree with a recommendation for state certification (Arends & Winitzky, 1996; Funkhouser, 1988). Generally, those preparing to teach elementary school majored in education, whereas secondary school teachers were more likely to major in a subject. A smaller proportion of teachers who had not completed undergraduate preparation programs earned master's degrees in education leading to state certification.

Discontent with traditional undergraduate teacher education, which has existed at least since the 1920s, became widespread in the early 1980s. Some critics have argued that the process of obtaining a teaching license should be made more rigorous and professional; others have argued for deregulation of teacher licensing. The first approach is most clearly seen in a series of reports, produced between 1976 and 1986, which criticized the quality of traditional preparation and demanded reforms. Many called for the elimination of the undergraduate major in education and for a 5-year degree or a master's degree (Holmes Group, 1986; National Commission on Excellence in Education, 1983). During the same period, others concerned about the quality and supply of teacher candidates pushed for alternative preparation programs. They hoped to make teaching more accessible to academically able students who did not meet certification requirements or who were deterred by them (Feistritzer, 1993). The two movements have changed the shape of teacher education in the past 15 years, although less perhaps than many would have liked. In this section, we look at demographic data that exist for teachers who prepare through college and university programs and those who prepare through alternative programs. As more colleges sponsor alternative programs, this distinction becomes less clear. We started here with Adelman's (1986) definition of alternative programs: "Any program which enrolls non-certified, post-baccalaureate individuals and offers short-cuts, special assistance or unique curricula leading to eligibility for standard teaching certification" (p. 2). These programs may be offered by a college or university, a state education department, a school district, or a private organization. However, although conceptually useful, this definition proved difficult to apply because studies often used the term ambiguously or to mean different things.

College or university programs are described in two different ways: the type of institution in which the programs are housed and the structure of program offered, such as a bachelor's or master's program. Within each category, we looked at the demographic profiles of students' preparing to teach, when it differed from the general demographic profile.

College and University: Type of Institution

Researchers describe institutions in various ways. Some distinctions are primarily descriptive such as size, region, or public and private control. Other classifications are used as proxies for educational quality such as standards of admission and degree-granting status. Studies use two different kinds of analyses—between those who intend to teach and those who do not, and among demographic groups of teacher candidates.

According to Feistritzer (1999), three fourths of teacher education students attended public institutions, and nearly half attended schools with more than 10,000 students. Only one fourth attended schools with fewer than 5,000 students. Henke, Geis,

Giambattista, and Knepper (1996), using NCES data, found that among 1992 to 1993 college graduates those who prepared to teach or who had taught already by 1994 were more likely to have received their degrees from public, non-doctorate granting universities than those who had not prepared to teach or become teachers. This difference was attributed to the historical connection between public non-doctorate-granting schools and former normal schools and teachers colleges.

When looking at type of institution where prospective teachers prepare to teach, the demographic variables of most interest to researchers have been race and ethnicity and socioeconomic status.

Race and Ethnicity.   Students' racial and ethnic backgrounds are related to where they start their postsecondary education. In general, minority students, including prospective teachers, are more likely first to attend 2-year colleges (Alston, 1988; Irvine, 1988; Smith, Miller, & Joy, 1988). Students of color made up 30% of those receiving associate's degrees in education in 1997 to 1998 (Snyder, 1998), and they were more likely than Whites to transfer to teacher education programs from 2-year colleges (AACTE, 1992). Woods and Williams (1987) found that minority students chose 2-year schools because they were close to home, cost less, and offered a more personal environment.

More than a third of Black students in teacher education programs attended historically Black colleges and universities (HBCU) (AACTE, 1999). Consequently, in 1995, Blacks made up only 6.2% of teacher education students in all non-historically-Black-institution (HBI) teacher education programs. Minority students were not evenly distributed among other schools (Brookhart & Freeman, 1992). Because the majority of students attend college in close proximity to their residences, the proportion of minorities at any institution is a function of the racial and ethnic makeup of the local community (Howey & Zimpher, 1986).

The RATE studies, which divide SCDEs on the basis of the highest degree and size, found that a negligible percentage of African Americans attended small, bachelor's-degree-only schools. The highest proportion (8%) was found at programs within medium size universities offering postbaccalaureate degrees. The reason suggested was that these schools were the least expensive of the three types (AACTE, 1988). A more recent study by the ETS, using a different system of categorization, found that the largest proportion of African-American students (51%) was at small (fewer than 5,000 students) public colleges (Wenglinsky, 2000).

Socioeconomic Background.   In a study of 40,000 prospective teachers at 152 institutions in the southeastern United States, ETS reported that students from higher SES backgrounds were more likely to attend large rather than small institutions, private rather than public ones, and universities rather than colleges (Wenglinsky, 2000).

College and University: Program Structure

Since the early 1980s, reformers have sought to move teacher education in part or wholly to the graduate level. The principal goal is to ensure that future teachers have a strong arts and sciences background, as well as a thorough grounding in professional education and field experience (Darling-Hammond & Cobb, 1996). A second goal is to help professionalize teaching by requiring postbaccalaureate study (Holmes Group, 1986; Wise, 1986). These different aims, along with practical implementation problems, have led to considerable variation even among programs that tried to make these changes (Darling-Hammond, 1998).

According to Arends and Winitzky (1996), four notable forms of extended teacher education have emerged. Integrated 5-year programs culminating in a bachelor's degree offer more time for teacher education without the complication of a graduate component. Integrated 5-year programs culminating in both a bachelor's and a master's degree were suggested by both the Holmes Group (1986) and Carnegie reports as conferring the greater professional status associated with graduate degrees. They were viewed as superior to 1-year master's programs where integration between academic studies and teacher education is more problematic. However, because the 5-year integrated structure does not adequately address the needs of students who do not make a 5-year commitment to one institution at an early stage in their postsecondary careers, 1-year master's programs leading to a degree and certification have also proliferated. Last, the 2-year graduate program culminating in a master's degree was suggested by reformers particularly interested in making graduate teacher education more research oriented rather than merely a professional program. To this list, Feistritzer (1999) added a fifth-year, postbaccalaureate program culminating in certification but not in a master's degree.

Although data on the number of students enrolling in different program structures do not exist, data are available on the offerings of various SCDEs. In a 1999 survey of teacher preparation programs, Feistritzer found that 78% offered at least one 4-year program, 45% offered programs that took between 4 and 5 years to obtain a bachelor's degree, 11% had 5-year programs culminating in bachelor's degrees and certification, 48% offered a postbaccalaureate certification program without a degree, and 43% had postbaccalaureate graduate degree programs that led to certification. The latter two options were found most often at larger, public institutions.

Extended teacher education programs also have proliferated. Over the course of the first four RATE studies, AACTE found large increases in enrollment in bachelor's-, master's-, and doctorate-granting institutions. Noteworthy has been the jump in the number of students at the master's level, even at what historically had been bachelor's-degree-only programs (AACTE, 1988, 1990). According to the National Center for Educational Information (NCEI) (Feistritzer, 1999), 28% of those receiving formal teacher education began preservice work at the postbaccalaureate level in 1998. In 1984, only 3% of schools with teacher education programs offered any initial postbaccalaureate preservice preparation, compared to 65% in 1998. Since 1986, more than 300 institutions have created programs allowing prospective teachers to earn a degree in arts and sciences as well as a master's in teaching (Darling-Hammond, 1998). In 1990, more than a third of institutions with preservice programs offered some form of extended program (AACTE, 1990). Thus, newer teachers are more likely to hold degrees in academic fields rather than education (Lewis, Parsad, Carey, Bartfai, & Farris, 1999).

The majority of SCDEs offer some traditional 4-year programs (Wong & Osguthorpe, 1993). A little over half only offer programs in a 4-year structure. About 10%, mostly located at research, doctorate-granting universities offer only extended programs (AACTE, 1990).

The traditional structure has persisted for institutional reasons as well as for student demands. Graduate education is more expensive for institutions, requiring lower faculty–student ratios (Wong & Osguthorpe, 1993). The more expensive graduate programs are especially difficult to justify when there are competing 4-year programs. Additionally, many colleges depend heavily on tuition from large undergraduate teacher education programs. According to Cyphert and Ryan (1984), fewer than half of teacher education students would choose teaching if it meant a 5-year program. A survey of Washington State teachers who did not seek a master's degree found their reasons centered on the cost, their distance from the institution where the degree was offered, and the perceived lack of the degree's utility. Ten percent felt that they would not meet the requirement for admission (Sherman, 1991). Last, some worry that students who have already invested in a bachelor's degree will be unwilling to pay more to prepare to teach, given the low salaries of teaching in comparison with other professions (Howey & Zimpher, 1986; Tom, 1986). However, as more states require master's degrees for permanent licensure, students' perception about the degree's attractiveness changes.

Because comprehensive data on enrollment in various programs are lacking, there is little research on the different demographic profiles associated with these programs.

Gender. Feistritzer (1999) reported that 29% of graduate students in teacher education were male compared to 25% of undergraduate teacher education students. However, AACTE (1999) found no gender difference in undergraduate and graduate programs.

Race and Ethnicity. A major concern about moving teacher preparation to the graduate level is the potential for increasing elitism and creating another barrier for poor and minority candidates (Howey & Zimpher, 1986; Ryan, 1987). However, so far, those fears have not been borne out. AACTE (1999) reports that minorities made up 20% of postbaccalaureate teacher education students compared to 18.5% of students in undergraduate programs. Feistritzer (1999) reported a wider disparity: 22.5% versus 19%.

Age. The growth of postbaccalaureate teacher education programs, the older age of undergraduates, and an increase in the proportion of students who take more than 4 years to complete their undergraduate degrees has meant that the average age of those entering teaching has risen. A 1999 survey of all teacher education programs found a median age of 22.4 for undergraduate students and 30.2 for graduate students (Feistritzer, 1999).

Alternative Programs

While some educators debated the structure of traditional teacher education, others developed alternatives that circumvented college- and university-based teacher education. The goals behind alternative routes were varied. Some programs, including the earliest ones, were created to alleviate regional or subject-specific teacher shortages (Cornett, 1992; Feistritzer, 1993; Hawk & Schmidt, 1989; Shen, 1998b; Zumwalt, 1991), providing a better option than emergency certification, which allowed the hiring of unlicensed teachers. Other states, less driven by shortages than by concerns about quality, created alternatives to attract "nontraditional" people into teaching by eliminating the barriers of standard certification (Huling-Austen, 1986; Jelmberg, 1996; Kopp, 1994; Zumwalt, 1991). Specific programs were aimed at minorities, career switchers, retirees, and those interested in teaching in urban schools (Zeichner & Schulte, 2001). Hence, Zumwalt made an argument for evaluating these programs in the context of their specific goals rather than as a single group, which is frequently how they are viewed.

Research on alternative programs is complicated by lack of definitional clarity. Some consider everything that is not the traditional 4-year structure an alternative program. Others include all programs that are not university-based undergraduate or graduate programs. Darling-Hammond (1990) separated programs into those that reduced the standards for certification (alternate routes to teaching) and those that held standards constant but offered different approaches for those who already hold a bachelor's degree (alternative certification programs). Cornett (1992) described a similar split between those programs that gave interim certification and allowed teachers to earn standard certification over time and those that created shorter, intensified programs or allowed candidates to meet requirements through tests or other demonstration of competency.

The wide variation in these programs and the inconsistency of researchers' definitions confound efforts to obtain comprehensive data (Miller, McKenna, & McKenna, 1998; Zeichner & Schulte, 2001). The research regarding alternative programs tends to be anecdotal and descriptive, making overall assessments difficult. However, we do know that the number of teachers alternately prepared has steadily increased. Forty-six states in 2003 had approved alternative programs in some form (Feistritzer, 2003). National surveys found an increase between 1993 and 1998 in the number of teachers holding provisionary certification by virtue of participation in alternative programs. In 1998, 3% of teachers in general elementary education classrooms and 4% of those teaching in departmentalized classrooms held this type of certification (Lewis et al., 1999). An analysis of NCES data, using each state's own definition of alternative, suggested that 6.7% of all public elementary teachers and 8.6% of all public secondary teachers certified between 1984 and 1994 were alternately certified (Shen, 1998b). Overall, it is estimated that 125,000 teachers were licensed through alternative programs from 1983 to 1999 (Zeichner & Schulte, 2001).

Some states use alternative programs more extensively than do others. McKibbin and Tyson (2000) reported that California's budget for such programs increased 10-fold from 1993 to 2001. The state hired 7,498 teachers through these routes in 2002 to 2003 (Chin, Young, & Floyd, 2004). Texas gets 16% of its teachers through alternative routes; New York City hired 15% of its teachers in 2000 to 2001 from alternative routes; and Houston fills 50% of annual vacancies this way (Cornett, 1992; Goodnough, 2002; Kirby, Naftel, & Berends, 1999; Stafford & Barrow, 1994). If teacher shortages continue, these numbers will likely increase.

Some research indicates that the demographic profile of those who enter teaching through alternative routes differs from those entering through traditional undergraduate and graduate programs.

Gender.   Some studies found a higher percentage of males in alternative programs. Although traditional programs are approximately 25% to 28% male, some alternative programs had 30% (Wright, McKibbin, & Walton, 1987), 35% (Kopp, 1994), or even 40% (Jelmberg, 1996). This difference may result in part because a larger percentage of those in alternative programs plan to teach in secondary schools. A different phenomenon has been seen in alternative programs for science and math teachers. Kirby, Darling-Hammond, and Hudson (1989) reported that males comprised 40% of such teachers in alternative programs, compared to male majorities in the range of 60% to 70% among existing secondary science faculties. Shen's (1998b) nationwide study of alternately prepared teachers found no significant gender effect (Alternative, 25.7% male vs. Traditional, 23.7% male).

Race and Ethnicity. Alternative programs have reported higher than average rates of minority teachers (Andrew, 1990; Cornett, 1992; Darling-Hammond, Hudson, & Kirby, 1989, Feistritzer, 2003; Kirby, Darling-Hammond, & Hudson, 1989; Kirby, Naftel, & Berends, 1999; Kopp, 1994; Lutz & Hutton, 1989; Natriello & Zumwalt, 1993; Stafford & Barrow, 1994).

Likewise, in an analysis of NCES data, Shen (1998b) found that 21% of teachers alternately prepared in 1984 to 1994 were ethnic or racial minorities, compared with 13% of traditionally prepared teachers. Alternately prepared elementary teachers were considerably more diverse than alternately prepared secondary teachers.

Age. Alternative programs are aimed at those who already have completed undergraduate programs and thus attract older candidates. Moreover, many programs focus on career switchers and retirees likely to be even older than traditional graduate students. Several studies report a median age over 30, with significant numbers over 40 (Cornett, 1992; Hawk & Schmidt, 1989; Lutz & Hutton, 1989). Shen (1998b) found a higher proportion of alternately prepared teachers under 30 and a lower proportion over 50. This profile may result from relative newness of alternative programs. His data suggested that alternative programs are more likely to produce minority teachers over 40.

WHERE DO THEY TEACH?

Where new teachers find their first teaching jobs, and where they end up teaching, depends on both personal choice and the supply and demand of jobs in a specific region and teaching field at that time. This section looks briefly at data describing the demographic profile of new teachers and then at the relationship between teacher demographics and school and student characteristics. Then we turn to the research on the relationship between different preparation programs and teaching assignments.

Demographic Profile of New Teachers

Despite the general aging of the teaching force, the proportion of new teachers is increasing. The percentage of first-time public school teachers who have never taught before increased sharply from 40% of hires in 1988 to 62% in 1994, perhaps indicating that the reserve pool of experienced but inactive teachers had grown smaller (Boe, Cook, et al., 1998). As one might expect, the demographics of new teachers closely resemble those of teacher education students.

Gender. Twenty-seven percent of newly hired, newly prepared teachers in the 1993 to 1994 national database were male, compared with 21% in 1987 and 1991 (Broughman & Rollefson, 2000).

Race and Ethnicity. Eighteen percent of newly prepared public school teachers in 1993 identified themselves as coming from a minority group, compared to 8.7% 6 years earlier (Snyder, 1998). This is higher than the 13.5% of minorities in the teaching force at that time and higher than minority enrollments reported in teacher education programs (AACTE, 1987, 1988, 1989, 1990, 1999; Brookhart & Freeman, 1992). The research does not make clear whether this was the result of a higher rate of entry among minorities or the expanding role of postbaccalaureate and alternative programs. A recent analysis of the HSB 1980 cohort of high school sophomores indicates that as of

1992, a higher proportion of all non-White college graduates, except Asian Americans, entered teaching than White college graduates. Of Black male college graduates, 10.6% entered teaching compared with 5.4% of White males. Of Black female college graduates, 28.7% entered teaching compared to 17.5% of Whites (Vegas et al., 2001).

It is important to note that the increase in minority representation among newer teachers is not true for all groups. Black teachers are disproportionately represented among teachers with 20 or more years of experience, whereas larger proportions of other minorities are found among newer teachers. Among Black teachers, only 8.5% had less than 3 years of experience, compared to 16.7% among Hispanics, 15% among Asians, and 11.3% among American Indians (Snyder, 1998).

Age. Newly prepared teachers are generally older, as compared to previous years. In 1987, the majority of newly prepared teachers were under age 25, but by 1993 the majority was in the 25 to 29 age group. However, these general trends mask gender differences. The median age among men decreased approximately 1 year between 1987 and 1993, whereas there was an opposite trend among women (Broughman & Rollefson, 2000).

School Characteristics: Level, and Subject

Henke, Chen, and Geis (2000) found that more 1992 to 1993 graduates who entered teaching before 1997 had taught only in elementary schools (52%) rather than in middle or high schools, probably reflecting the faster growing elementary student population in the mid-1990s (Snyder, 1998).

Gender. Females are more likely to teach at the elementary level than are males. In 1996, 60% of women taught elementary classes compared to 27% of men (Feistritzer, 1996). The reverse was true at the high school level. Fifty percent of male teachers but only 19% of female teachers taught in high schools. Relatively similar proportions of men and women taught at the middle school level. Higher proportions of females were also found among kindergarten, special education, bilingual education, ESL, and secondary school English teachers (Henke, Choy, Geis, & Broughman, 1997).

Despite the predominance of female elementary teachers, the size of their majority has fluctuated over the past 4 decades. Perhaps reflecting military draft deferments related to the Vietnam War, the proportion of males teaching elementary classes grew from 12.2% in 1961 to 17.7% in 1981, before slipping over the next 15 years to 9.1%. Women were a minority among secondary schools teachers in 1961 (43.2%), but by 1996 they held 58.9% of the secondary school teaching positions. The proportion of males at the secondary level dropped to a record low of 35% in 2001, according to the NEA's annual survey (NEA, 2003).

Race and Ethnicity. Teachers of color are more likely to teach at the elementary level than at the secondary level. In 1996, 75% of Black teachers were at the elementary level compared to 49% of Whites and 66% of other non-Whites, according to Feistritzer (1999). Henke et al. (2000) reported only 29% of new Hispanic teachers entered the profession at the secondary level. This distribution may reflect gender patterns among non-White teachers. For example, in 1996, 89% of Black teachers were female compared to 74% of all teachers (Feistritzer, 1999). Whatever the cause, secondary students of color are less likely to be taught by teacher of color than elementary students. Even in large urban centers, Casserly (1992) found the proportion of

African-American teachers declined from 24.6% at the K–5 level to 19.7% in Grades 9 to 12. Hispanic teachers declined from 2.5% at the K–5 level to 1.8% in Grades 9 to 12.

Age.   On average high school teachers are slightly older than elementary school teachers. Although high school teachers comprised 27% of all teachers, they made up 34% of teachers over 50. Elementary teachers made up 47% of public school teachers, but 55% of teachers in their 20s (Feistritzer, 1999). The median age of male teachers was 2 years older than that of female teachers.

School Characteristics: Region and Location

Regional differences are particularly important when considering the availability of jobs for newly prepared teachers. The supply of teachers in a region is affected by many factors, including where newly prepared teachers grew up, where they attended college and where they desire to work (AACTE, 1987). Many areas of the Northeast and Southeast have teacher surpluses, whereas parts of the West and Alaska are experiencing shortages (American Association for Employment in Education, 2000).

Within regions, central city and rural districts generally have more difficulty filling vacancies than suburban districts (Henke, Choy, Geis, & Broughman, 1997). Darling-Hammond and Cobb (1996) suggested that new teachers may avoid less desirable jobs in city schools to the extent that they may choose not to teach if they cannot find a suburban position. Even when urban districts offer higher salaries, they are unable to compete with the pay, working conditions, and preferred student population in many suburban schools (Grissmer & Kirby, 1997). Rural districts face similar problems because of isolation, limited facilities, and distance from population centers (Matthes & Carlson, 1986).

In a study of 99 teachers newly graduated from the University of Iowa and the University of Vermont, Matthes and Carlson (1986) found that these neophytes were drawn to different areas by different attractions. City teachers pointed to greater social and cultural opportunities, professional autonomy, and benefits. Suburban teachers were more attracted by community emphasis on school achievement, community involvement opportunities, reputation of the school district, starting salary, and access to tenure. Like teachers in urban settings, suburban teachers also valued professional autonomy and social and cultural opportunities. Alternatively, the pace of life, cost of living and size of the school were most important to rural teachers.

The research has found little gender or age difference related to region and location. According to the NCES, the only modest variation from the national average was in rural areas where 28.2% of public school teachers were male compared with a national public average of 27% in 1993 to 1994 (Henke, Choy, Geis, & Broughman, 1997). The rural teachers were also slightly younger, with a median age of 42 years compared to 43.7 years for those in urban or suburban schools, perhaps reflecting the fact that rural areas had slightly more newly prepared teachers.

Race and Ethnicity.   Non-White, non-Hispanic teachers comprised 13.5% of the national teaching force in 1993 to 1994, but they were not evenly distributed among locations. Rural schools had 7.5% teachers of color compared to 10.8% in suburban schools and 25.2% in central cities (Henke, Choy, Geis, & Broughman, 1997). In the larger central cities, 37.9% were teachers of color in 1991 (Casserly, 1992).

The distribution of minority teachers differs by group and location (AACTE, 1994a; Richards & Encarnation, 1986). A Texas study found that Hispanics were more likely to find work in rural, suburban, or smaller central cities, whereas a majority of new African-American teachers found jobs in major urban districts (Kirby, Berends, & Naftel, 1999; TEA, 1995). The generally low proportion of minority teachers in rural settings may be related to different hiring mechanisms or to the trend for prospective teachers to seek jobs in areas where they grew up. According to Pflaum and Abramson (1990), rural schools may depend on informal networks for hiring, whereas minorities depend more on such formal routes such as ads and employment agencies. Some studies suggested that minority teachers were more interested in teaching in urban settings (Shen, 1998b; Su, 1997); others found this not to be the case (Bracey, 2001; Gordon, 1994).

School Characteristics: Size

School size, on its own, is not related to proportion of new teachers. Schools of different sizes have very different experiences in terms of filling vacancies based on their location. For example, central city schools with fewer than 150 students have fewer new teachers on their staffs than do other urban schools. Conversely, in suburban districts, the schools with fewer than 150 students have the highest proportion of new teachers (Henke, Choy, Geis, & Broughman, 1997). The same holds true for small schools in rural districts, although rural schools with enrollments over 750 also have high rates of new teachers. No overall trend can be found regarding school size and new teacher placement.

Student Characteristics: Race and Ethnicity

Schools with high minority enrollments have a disproportionately high number of first-time teachers, and those with less than 3 years' experience. More than one in five teachers at these schools has taught for less than 3 years (Wirt et al., 2001). Of 1992 to 1993 college graduates who became teachers within 4 years, 33% were teaching in schools with 50% or higher minority enrollment compared. That compared to 20% of all teachers (Henke et al., 2000). Only 20% of these new teachers worked in schools with fewer than 5% minority enrollment. This trend was noticeable in public schools in urban, suburban, and rural districts.

Race and Ethnicity. Race and ethnicity of teachers is related to race and ethnicity of students, but gender is not (Henke et al., 2000). More than two thirds of African-American teachers and 79% of Hispanics worked in schools where minority students were the majority (AACTE, 1999; Henke, Choy, Geis, & Broughman, 1997; Henke et al.). Conversely, 67% of White teachers taught in schools with fewer than 30% minority students. Schools with fewer than 10% minority students had almost no minority teachers. This means that nearly half of all schools had no minority teachers (Henke, Choy, Chen, et al.). Pavel (1995) also found that Native American teachers were more likely to be hired at Bureau of Indian Affairs schools than in non-Indian schools.

Although it may appear that minority students are taught by minority teachers, the paucity of minority teachers makes this impossible. At public schools where minority students are in the majority, two thirds of teachers are White (AACTE, 1999). King (1993b), in a review of literature on the decline in the numbers of African-American teachers, reported that through 1960 African-American students were most likely to be taught by African-American teachers. But this changed in the 3 decades that followed. Even in central cities where the proportions of minority students were highest, in 1992, there was one African-American teacher for every 25 African-American students, one Hispanic teacher for every 63 Hispanic students, one Asian teacher for every 46 Asian students in 1992 (Casserly, 1992). By contrast, there was one White teacher for every 7.4 White students.

Student Characteristics: Low Income

New teachers disproportionately teach in schools where large numbers of students qualify for free or reduced price lunch. More than 20% of teachers in schools with a high rate of low-income students had fewer than 3 years experience (Wirt et al., 2001). One quarter of the new teachers in the Henke et al. (2000) study taught in schools where more than half of the students were eligible for the federal lunch program.

Race and Ethnicity. According to Henke et al. (2000), African-American and Hispanic teachers were more likely than Whites to work in schools with a high proportion of students eligible for the federal lunch program. Fifty percent of Black and 63% of Hispanic teachers worked in these schools compared to 21% of White teachers.

In a study of new Texas teachers, Kirby, Naftel et al. (1999) divided districts into low, medium, and high risk based on the percentage of students participating in the school lunch program. Fifty percent of White teachers were hired by low-risk districts compared with 11% of Hispanic and 18% of Black teachers. In contrast, 55% of African Americans were hired in medium-risk districts, whereas 60% of Hispanics were employed in high-risk districts. Hispanic students made up 70% of the students in high-risk districts, whereas Black students comprised 20% in medium and high-risk districts.

Student Characteristics: Achievement

Lankford, Loeb, and Wykoff (2002) examined data on all teachers who worked in New York State schools from 1985 to 2000. They reported that public schools that had no students score in the lowest category on the fourth-grade Language Arts exam had an average of 6% of teachers with no experience compared with 14% in schools where more than one in five students scored in the lowest category. They concluded that new teachers often were hired for their first position in lower performing schools. Likewise, Betts, Reuben, and Danenberg (2000) found that California teachers moved quickly after gaining experience to schools with students who perform better on tests.

Preparation Differences

There is some research related to master's degrees, but more research examines whether alternative teachers are more likely to teach in urban settings because that is one of the promises of alternative programs.

Master's Degrees. Feistritzer (1996) reported that suburban teachers were more likely to have master's degrees (71%) than urban (64%), small town (55%) or rural (41%) teachers. NEA (2003) reported almost half of teachers (49.6%) had master's degrees in 2001. Teachers in the Northeast (63.9%) were more likely to have master's degrees than were teachers in the Midwest (52%), South (40.7%), and West (38.7%). Also, junior high (51.1%) and senior high (55%) teachers were more likely to have master's degrees than were elementary school teachers (46.3%). In 1999, Lewis et al. found that the percentage of students eligible for free lunch was inversely related to the percentage of teachers with master's degrees. Moreover, at schools where more than 60% of students got lunch free, the proportion of teachers with a master's degree decreased from 41% in 1993 to 37% in 1998. In contrast, Parsad, Lewis, and Farris (2000) found no difference between high- and low-poverty schools in teachers with master's degrees.

Alternative Programs.   According to Zeichner and Schulte (2001), many alternative programs are aimed at producing urban teachers, and, hence, they are more likely to be located in urban areas and have a greater proportion of minorities. Although that was true in a longitudinal study of New Jersey's alternative program, Natriello and Zumwalt (1993) reported that the alternative teachers were no closer a match to the students they taught in urban schools than were traditionally prepared teachers. The majority of the alternative teachers were White, suburban, and monolingual. Many studies reported that alternative candidates preferred or were more willing to consider teaching in urban settings (Feistritzer, Hill, & Willett, 1998; McKibbin & Giblin, 2000; Natriello & Zumwalt, 1993).

At least initially, more alternatively prepared teachers take jobs in urban schools (Houston, Marshall, & McDavid, 1993; Huling-Austen, 1986; Natriello & Zumwalt, 1993 Shen, 1998b). According to Shen (1998b), this is especially true for non-White alternative candidates. It was not clear how much of the increased employment in urban schools was based on preference nor how long they will remain once they gain experience. Huling-Austen states that alternative graduates often take hard-to-fill positions because traditional candidates were more likely to land more desirable spots. In a longitudinal study, Natriello and Zumwalt (1993) found the proportion of alternative candidates working in urban settings declined over time.

HOW LONG DO THEY STAY?

Retention is an issue all along the teacher preparation pipeline. Prospective teachers make decisions in college about entering a teacher preparation program, completing the program and entering classroom teaching. Once in the classroom, they make decisions about staying, moving to a new position, school or district, or quitting teaching, temporarily or permanently. Most of these decisions are voluntary and are made for a multitude of reasons. Some, however, are not voluntary. Some prospective teachers do not meet teacher education admissions requirements, do not complete the program, and do not pass their certification tests. Others are not hired or cannot find a job they are willing to take. Some are laid off because of staffing cutbacks or dismissed for unsatisfactory performance. Others leave the profession due to accidents, illness, or death. We examine here what the research tells us about how these decisions—voluntary and involuntary—relate to teachers' demographic profiles, preparation programs, and where they teach.

Teachers' career decisions provide teacher educators with insights about their graduates that can influence program decisions and help them advise students better. They need to know when attrition levels are increasing—as they have from the relatively low levels of the mid-1980s to the mid-1990s—because attrition is the largest single determinant of demand for new teachers (Baker & Smith, 1997; Boe, Cook, et al., 1996; Grissmer & Kirby, 1987; Heyns, 1988). Grissmer and Kirby (1997) predict a dramatic increase in demand for new teachers through 2012 due to retirements and the higher attrition rates among young teachers hired as replacements.

Prospective Teachers

Two ways of assessing teachers' career intentions are to ask why they chose teaching and how long they expect to stay as classroom teachers or in education. As researchers have noted, intentions of high school seniors are not accurate measures of who will enter teacher education programs because adolescents change their minds, have limited knowledge of career options, may not graduate from high school, may not enter college, and may not meet the entry requirements for teacher education programs (Hanushek & Pace, 1995). Those entering teacher preparation programs include students who previously expressed an interest in teaching and those considered "late aspirants." Those who enter graduate or alternative programs are even "later aspirants."

Gender. Women and men generally give similar reasons for entering teaching (NEA, 1997, 2003). Men are more likely to say they chose the profession because they love the subject area or were influenced by a teacher (Hanushek & Pace, 1995), whereas women were more likely to say they were influenced by family (NEA, 2003). Once in teacher education, women and men are equally likely to expect to enter teaching, but women are more likely to plan on staying in the classroom for their career (Biraimah, 1988). Both genders expect to stay in education at approximately the same rate, but males are more likely to expect a move into administration or into college teaching.

Race and Ethnicity. In citing reasons for teaching, minorities were more likely than were Whites to cite the value of education to society as a major motivation (56%–41.6% NEA, 2003). Several qualitative studies provided additional insight into why minorities chose teaching for a career (Gordon, 1994; King, 1993a; Su, 1997). In interviews with 56 teacher education students from diverse racial and ethnic backgrounds, Su (1997) found that although all students said they chose teaching for altruistic and practical reasons, minority students were more likely to subscribe to social reconstructionist or activist notions of teaching. This was particularly true for students who felt their own educational experience was negative. Most wanted to teach in urban schools, change the curriculum, and make a difference in the lives of poor and minority students. Su also found that minority students expressed more enthusiasm and pride than did White students about their choice of profession and felt they had become even more positive about teaching during their teacher education preparation.

Similarly, King (1993a) found 41 African-American prospective and beginning teachers also regarded themselves as activists. More than half mentioned the need for minority teachers, the lack of minority role models for youth, and the poor condition of minority communities as compelling reasons for teaching. King found some differences between prospective and beginning teachers. Students were more likely to say that they chose teaching because of the opportunity to work with diverse students and that teaching contributed to the betterment of society. Beginning teachers also cited those reasons but were more likely to bring up practical considerations (e.g., salary, working conditions, vacations, and job security). The data do not indicate whether these differences reflect the more pragmatic outlook of practicing teachers or differences between those who actually entered teaching and those who did not.

In looking at the reverse question—why minority students might not become teachers—Gordon (1994) asked 40 teachers of color why they thought young minority students did not choose teaching. They speculated that a poor educational background limits some from becoming teachers and gives them negative feelings toward schools and teachers. For others, being a teacher may be seen as "acting White." They also noted that family, friends, and school counselors often discouraged minority students from considering teaching because of low pay and low status. More than half the respondents felt that "professional self-image" was very important among people of color. One fourth of the teachers said that minority students not from urban areas were afraid that they would be placed in high-minority, low-SES schools where they would not feel comfortable.

Other research also pointed to many of these same reasons, but with differences among and within groups (Gordon, 2000; Guyton, Saxton, & Wesche, 1996; Jorgenson, 2000; King, 1993a). For instance, many of the Asian students interviewed by Gordon did not hold teaching in low esteem; they thought that it was a profession deserving the utmost respect and that they were not worthy. Moreover, some felt uncomfortable with the lack of respect shown teachers in this country and were reluctant to teach students from other minority groups. In another study of Asian-American teachers and preservice students, the biggest barrier cited was the perception that teaching is not intellectually challenging (Goodwin, Genishi, Asher, & Woo, 1997).

Socioeconomic Background. According to Pigge and Marso (1992), higher SES families counsel their children away from teaching because of low pay and status. Gordon (1994) found the same phenomena in her study of teachers of color, but also found that low-SES students were steered away from teaching because it was seen as too hard or too expensive for them to pursue. Biraimah (1988), focusing on class and career expectations, found that SES made no significant difference in teacher education students' expectations about entering teaching, but it did in their expectations of how long they would stay in the profession. Prospective teachers from lower SES backgrounds expected to teach longer. Higher SES women and lower SES men were more likely to expect to move on to university teaching jobs.

Age. Among new teachers in New Jersey, Johnson (2001) found that midcareer entrants (average age 33) and first-career entrants (average age 26) were just as likely to expect to stay in education, but midcareer entrants were more likely to expect to be classroom teachers the remainder of their careers (81% vs. 57%).

New Teachers

According to Henke et al. (2000), only 41% of 1992 to 1993 newly graduated education majors, who had not taught before obtaining their degree, entered teaching right away. Some "delayed entrants" eventually enter teaching, but many do not (Heyns, 1988; Murnane & Olsen, 1988). Murnane and Schwinden (1989) found that prospective elementary teachers were more likely to enter teaching than secondary teachers. Entry rates for different secondary subjects varied widely.

The number of first-time teachers increased sharply in 1994 compared to 1988, possibly indicating that the reserve pool of teachers was shrinking (Baker & Smith, 1997; Boe, Cook, et al., 1998). Only half of new teachers, however, came directly out of college. The rest came from delayed entrants and those who entered the profession by alternative routes (Baker & Smith). The greatest increase was in special education, many of whom were not fully certified (Boe, Cook, et al.). Using NLS-72 data, Heyns (1988) found that late-entry teachers were more likely to come from more advantaged backgrounds and have more graduate training and advanced degrees.

Teachers: Staying, Moving, and Leaving

Of those who enter teaching, a growing number are staying longer in their positions, according to a nationwide study by the NEA (2003). Twenty-seven percent of teachers in 2001 had been in their current position for more than 20 years, compared to just 8% in 1976. The mean duration in current position was 12.6 years. The proportion of teachers with 20-plus years' experience was the highest in 3 decades. Although this is explained in part by the aging of the profession, there is some evidence that teacher mobility is declining. In 2001, 2.9% of teachers taught in a different district the previous year; in 1966, 7% had just moved from another district. Those who expected to teach in a different district the next year declined from 5.7% to 2.2% (NEA).

It is difficult to say with precision what the national attrition rate is. Various studies over the past decade, using different definitions and methodology, produced estimates ranging from 5% to 9% annually. After each Schools and Staffing Survey (SASS) survey, the NCES does a teacher follow-up study (TFS) of a sample of the teachers 1 year later. These data are based on actual behavior rather than on intentions and can distinguish between those who move to positions outside a state and those who left teaching. In most state studies, it is impossible to distinguish "movers" from "leavers."

According to the most recent TFS, 7.4% of public school teachers left teaching in 1999 to 2000, compared with 6.6% in 1994 to 1995, 5.1% in 1991 to 1992, and 5.6% in 1988 to 1989 (Luekens, Lyter, & Fox, 2004; Whitener & Gruber, 1997). A large-scale study looking at Texas teachers' career moves between 1992 and 1993 found that 8% did not return to teaching the next year, which may reflect regional differences or the inability to count out-of-state teaching (TEA, 1995). In an NEA study (2003), 5.7% of teachers in 2001 said they did not plan to teach the next year.

One-year follow-up studies, however, have drawn criticism as exaggerating actual attrition rates because they cannot distinguish between those taking breaks and those leaving the profession (Murnane & Schwinden, 1989). Grissmer and Kirby (1987) found that 40% to 60% of teachers who leave eventually return to teaching. Breaks in service have long been a part of the teaching culture. Almost one fourth of teachers surveyed in 1996 had taken a break of a year or more; 13% had taken two or more such breaks (NEA, 1997). These percentages, however, represent a decline in the number of teachers reporting a break in service for the first time in 20 years.

Retirement is the primary reason people leave public school teaching (Luekens et al., 2004). They reported that TFS data from 1999 to 2000 indicated that 29% left for retirement. Other top reasons mentioned were to pursue another career (21%), receive better salary or benefits (19%) , pregnancy or childrearing (16.5%) and family or personal moves (11%). SASS and TFS data indicate that only 5% to 7% leave because they are dissatisfied with teaching as a career (Baker & Smith, 1997; Boe, Bobbitt, Cook, Barkanic, & Maislin, 1998). Those who left dissatisfied cited lack of administrative support (39%), discipline problems or lack of student motivation (36%), salary (11%), and lack of authority in the school (7%). Although only 5% reported dissatisfaction with career as the reason for leaving, combining this category with the 12% who left "to pursue another career" and the 6.5% who left "for better salary or benefits" made dissatisfaction the second top reason for teacher attrition.

Looking at turnover figures presents a different picture. Turnover figures often include both permanent and temporary leavers, those who change schools and districts, and teachers who switch teaching assignments. For instance, Boe, Bobbitt, et al. (1998), citing SASS and TFS data, reported that the average annual turnover rate in teaching positions between 1987 and 1995 was of 30.2%. Their study reported 5.8% of teachers left, 7.4% moved to another school or district, and 17% switched teaching assignments.

About a third of turnovers were involuntary. Ingersoll (1999), counting those who moved and those who left, but not those who switched assignments, placed annual teacher turnover in the last decade between 13% and 15%, compared to 12% in nursing and 11% in the entire U.S. workforce.

Also looking at teacher turnover rather than just leavers, Ingersoll (1999) painted a different picture about the level of teacher dissatisfaction. After controlling for teacher and school effects, he found that "inadequate support from the administration, low salaries, student discipline problems and limited faculty input into school decision-making all contribute to higher rates of turnover" (p. 6). By collapsing categories of dissatisfaction used by others, he found that retirement was a relatively minor reason for teacher turnover; more teachers left because of job dissatisfaction, to change careers, or to move for a better teaching job. "[S]chool staffing problems are not solely a result of shortfalls driven by increasing retirement levels, but also a result of low retention due to organizational conditions," he said (p. 4). Districts need to address this "revolving door" rather than just rely on recruitment efforts to fill vacancies, Ingersoll asserted.

Teachers' Career Paths: Demographic Profile

Decisions about staying, moving, and leaving vary by age, gender, race and ethnicity, and SES.

Age.   Age is the prime demographic factor in attrition. Attrition rates generally form a "u-shaped" pattern with higher rates among the youngest and oldest teachers (Boe, Cook, et al., 1996; Grissmer & Kirby, 1987; Ingersoll, 1999; TEA, 1995; Theopold, 1990; Whitener & Gruber, 1997). According to Theopold, the probability of staying in teaching increases each year to age 44, then decreases each year after 45. The highest attrition rates (26%) in 1999 to 2000 TFS data were among teachers ages 60 to 64 (Luekens et al., 2004). However, this 1999 rate indicates a reversal in the trend of increasing retirements in this age group since 1987. And for teachers over 65 years old, the rate decreased from 34% to 17% compared to 5 years earlier (Luekens et al., 2004; Whitener & Gruber, 1997).

The highest attrition among younger teachers was the 10% rate for those ages 25 to 29 (Luekens et al., 2004). Without combining categories for reasons, the most common reason for leaving under age 40 was pregnancy or childrearing (Whitener & Gruber, 1997). Teachers in their 40s had the lowest attrition rates. When they left, the most common reason was for better salary and benefits or to pursue another career (Luekens et al.). The proportion of teachers who say the reason they stay in teaching is because they have too much invested in it generally increases with age (NEA, 1997).

Years of teaching experience also interacts with age, producing a u-shaped pattern (Boe, Cook, et al., 1996; Boe, Bobbitt, et al., 1998; Heyns, 1988). The highest rates of attrition were among those with more than 25 years' experience (11%) and those in their first year (9.3%; Whitener & Gruber, 1997). Teachers in their first 3 years had the highest attrition rate since the TFS survey began: 8.5% up from 7.4% in 1994. Looking at a cohort 10 years after college, Heyns found the highest rates of attrition in the first 3 or 4 years of teaching. Involuntary attrition due to job actions decreases sharply as years of experience increase (Boe, Bobbitt et al.). The rate of attrition in the first year varies considerably from state to state, depending on how attrition is defined. Texas, which counts all out-of state movers as leavers, reported a first-year attrition rate of 17.2% (TEA, 1995).

In three national surveys between 1987 and 1993, the attrition rate among first-year teachers fell from 11.6% to 9.3% (Whitener & Gruber, 1997). Some researchers have suggested improvements in induction programs as well as the presumed maturity, greater self-knowledge, and experience of older first-year teachers may have contributed to declining attrition rates (Mantle-Bromley, Gould, McWhorter, & Whaley, 2000). Support for the effect of age was found in a study of all new hires in a large urban district in the Southwest over $6\frac{1}{2}$ years (Adams & Dial, 1993). New teachers who entered the classroom before age 40 were 43% more likely to have left the district than those who started teaching after age 40.

Gender. The proportion of women taking breaks in service is higher than that for men (NEA, 1997). The reasons for these breaks also differ. In 1996, the largest group of men (8.4%) took a break to take a position outside of education. Almost one fourth of teachers, mostly women, had left teaching and returned after bearing or caring for a child. Since 1971, far fewer women say they are taking a break to get married or become full-time homemakers than in previous years, likely reflecting economic and societal changes. In a study of teachers from an urban district in Florida, Hall and Carroll (1987) found that gender and marital status were not related to plans to quit or stay in teaching. Using one TFS data set, Boe, Cook, Kaufman, and Danielson (1996) found that attrition rates of general and special education teachers were not associated with gender, but those with children of their own under age 6 were more likely to leave. However, as the number of children in their families increased, teachers were less likely to move. More teachers with children are remaining or returning to the classroom than was the case in previous years. In one NLS cohort, Heyns (1988) found the retention rate for married women with children was higher than that for single women or married women without children.

This pattern of breaks by women leads to some contradictions in the reported attrition numbers. Hanushek and Pace (1995) reported that women were more likely than were men to stay in teaching once they expressed initial interest, even if that interest began in high school. In contrast, Boe, Bobbitt et al. (1998), using three SASS and TFS datasets, found that gender was not predictive of those moving or leaving. Whitener and Gruber (1997), using one SASS and TFS dataset, reported that women left the profession at higher rates than did men (7.1%–5.2%). But 5 years later, the TFS data indicated the attrition rate was 7.4% for both men and women. However, although the rates were equal, men were more likely to report leaving for better salary or a new career, and women were more likely to leave for pregnancy, child care, and health reasons. In the Texas study, men left at a higher rate in a 1-year period, but proportionately more women left over the first 5 years of their career (TEA, 1995). Likewise, Adams and Dial (1993) in looking at teachers hired over $6\frac{1}{2}$ years found that women were 37% more likely to leave than were men. Using National Education Longitudinal Study (NELS) data looking at a cohort 10 years out of college, Heyns (1988) found men were more likely to leave and less likely to consider returning, but if one controlled for school level, women were more likely to leave than men. Murnane (1987) in a mid-1970s study of Michigan teachers, found that women remained in teaching at a lower rate than men (52% to 65%) 6 years after entry, but he raised the need to look at reentry rates.

Noting an age and gender interaction, Theopold (1990) found that younger women were more likely to leave than were younger men, but older men were more likely to leave than were older women.

Race and Ethnicity. The 1994 TFS (Whitener & Gruber, 1997) found that minority attrition was slightly higher than attrition among White teachers (6.8% to 6.5%). High attrition rates among Hispanics (9.1%), who were also entering at higher rates, were a major contributing factor. However, the 1999 TFS data found very similar attrition rates (7.5%) among all groups except Asians (2.1%).

Black and White teachers have had very similar attrition rates nationally over all four SASS and TFS datasets. Race and ethnicity was not a significant factor in either teacher moving or teacher leaving (Boe, Cook, et al., 1996; Boe, Bobbitt, et al., 1998). Although the rates were similar, reasons for leaving were different. The latest TFS data indicated that Blacks were almost twice as likely to say retirement was an important reason for leaving and three times as likely to say they were leaving for a better salary or benefits (Luekens et al., 2004). Whites were much more likely to say that pregnancy or childrearing was an important reason for leaving.

There are regional differences. Murnane et al. (1991) reported that Black teachers in North Carolina and Michigan in the 1970s were more likely to stay in teaching than were Whites. The TEA (1995) also reported lower attrition rates for Black teachers than for White teachers, when taking school characteristics into account. Hispanics left teaching at the lowest rates, whereas Native Americans and Asians left at the highest rates. Adams and Dial (1993), in their study of first-year teachers in a Southwest urban district, found that Blacks had the lowest attrition rates. Whites were four times more likely to leave than were Blacks and 57% more likely to leave than were Hispanics.

Socioeconomic Background. Little research exists on how teachers' SES backgrounds affect career paths. Pigge and Marso (1992), following the careers of 550 teacher education students, found that students from higher socioeconomic backgrounds, as measured by parental educational levels, had higher rates of attrition after 5 years.

Teachers' Career Paths: Preparation Programs

Researchers have compared retention rates and long-term teaching expectations of teachers prepared in college programs and those from alternative programs. They also have looked at the retention rates of those with bachelor's degrees or less and those with graduate degrees.

Traditional Versus Alternative Programs. In their literature review, Wilson, Floden, and Ferrini-Mundy (2001, 2002) found little conclusive evidence regarding the relationship between programs and retention. For instance, Stoddart (1990) reported that 29% of alternatively certified teachers in Los Angeles had dropped out, a rate far higher than that among the traditionally prepared. Other studies reported alternative candidates were more positive about teaching; some found no difference. Houston, Marshall, and McDavid (1993) found that any difference in original commitment to teaching disappeared by 8 months. Kirby, Darling-Hammond, and Hudson (1989) found that alternative programs did not overcome the usual problems of retention of math and science teachers.

These mixed findings may result in part result from comparing traditionally and alternately prepared teachers as undifferentiated groups. In their study of elementary, secondary math, and secondary English teachers, Natriello and Zumwalt (1993) found that retention rates varied by school level and subject. After 3 years, the highest retention rates were among elementary teachers (85%) for both preparation types.

The lowest retention rates were for the alternately prepared math teachers (60%) compared to 80% to 90% among traditionally prepared math teachers. About 75% of the alternately prepared English teachers and 67% of those traditionally prepared were still in the classroom. However, this differential may be related to the fact that traditionally prepared teachers, unlike alternative route teachers, had no guarantee of a job upon graduation. About 25% were still in substitute positions in their third year of teaching.

It is important to distinguish between attrition and those who move to better teaching jobs. In their study of new elementary teachers, Adams and Dial (1993) expected alternately prepared teachers to stay longer because they had made a choice to teach after trying another job and because they needed to stay at least 1 year to gain certification. They found traditionally prepared teachers were 19% more likely to leave the district. They speculated that these teachers had more opportunity to leave the district for higher paying, more competitive school districts than were those who entered through alternative programs. Natriello and Zumwalt (1993) found that although more alternately prepared teachers were still teaching in New Jersey urban districts by the fourth year, the large gap in where the two groups of teachers taught had narrowed. Generally this resulted from the greater migration of alternately prepared teachers from urban to nonurban districts in the third and fourth years of teaching.

In the New Jersey study, career expectations differed by preparation program, school level, and subject taught. Although four out of five of the traditionally prepared elementary teachers expected to make teaching their long-term career; only two of five alternately prepared math teachers had long-range plans to remain in teaching. In a large survey of beginning teachers in New York City, Darling-Hammond, Chung, and Frelow (2002) found alternative teachers felt significantly less well prepared than did peers from teacher education programs, and those who felt less prepared were significantly less likely to expect to stay in teaching. In a national sample, Shen (1998a) found that minority teachers prepared through alternative programs planned to stay in teaching for shorter periods than did their traditionally prepared counterparts.

Undergraduate Versus Graduate Degrees.   Although studies have found differences between those with undergraduate degrees and those with master's degrees, the findings are difficult to interpret because they failed to distinguish whether the graduate degree was a preservice or inservice degree. The use of a confounded category, bachelor degree or less, also complicates the picture.

Andrew and Schwab (1995) found that 5-year graduates entered teaching at a higher rate (90%) than graduates of 4-year programs (60% to 80%) and, after 3 years, remained in teaching at higher rates (80%-plus compared with 50% to 70%). Several researchers, including Hall and Carroll (1987), Boe, Bobbitt, et al. (1998), and NCES, found no difference in intentions to quit or actually leave between those with bachelor's and those with master's degrees (Whitener & Gruber, 1997). In contrast, Heyns (1988) and Adams and Dial (1993) found that those with graduate degrees were more likely to have stayed in teaching or in the district than were those without graduate degrees. The type of graduate degree mattered in Texas (TEA, 1995); teachers with doctorates left at the highest rates, whereas those with only a bachelor's degree left at the lowest rates. Theopold (1990) found a negative relationship between staying 2 years and staying 3 years after receiving a master's degree. Boe, Bobbitt, Cook, Whitener, and Weber (1996) also reported turnover rates related to when the graduate degree was awarded. Turnover was highest for those who received their degrees in the past 2 years; those with graduate degrees of older vintage were more likely to stay in the district. Special education teachers who stayed were more likely to have graduated degrees than were general education teachers who stayed. Also, those with a bachelor's or less were more likely to leave for personal or family reasons, whereas those with graduate degrees were more likely to leave for outside employment or income opportunities. Theopold (1990) found male teachers with advanced degrees were more likely to leave teaching. There was little difference among females with advanced degrees.

Teachers' Career Paths: Teaching Placement

Researchers have studied retention rates in relation to school level (elementary-school vs. secondary-school teachers), subjects taught (special education and secondary school subjects), and student characteristics (proportion minority and low income).

School Level.   Most studies have found that elementary teachers intend to teach or actually stay in teaching longer (Grissmer & Kirby, 1987; Hall & Carroll, 1987; Heyns, 1988; Murnane & Olsen, 1988; Natriello & Zumwalt, 1993). Luekens et al. (2004) reported a greater gap between attrition rates for secondary teachers (8.6%) and those for elementary teachers (6.8%) than in TFS data 5 years earlier. Whitener and Gruber (1997) found that elementary teachers were more likely to change teaching positions (7.6% to 6.7%). In a Texas study, secondary teachers had higher rates in the first 5 years, but elementary teachers had a slightly higher attrition rate over their careers. Middle-school teachers had the highest rates of attrition and mobility (TEA, 1995).

Subjects.   Most research has indicated that special education is the subject area where retention poses the largest challenge (Billingsley, 1993; Boe, Bobbitt et al., 1996; Brownell & Smith, 1992; Ingersoll, 1999). Whitener and Gruber (1997) reported that attrition was higher than average in all special education fields except learning disabilities. The highest rate was among teachers of the mentally retarded (9.2%). Using one SASS and TFS data set, Boe, Bobbitt et al. (1996) reported that special education teachers were not only more likely to leave (7.9% vs. 5.8%) but were especially more likely to move (12.1% vs. 7.1%). Using three SASS and TFS datasets, Boe, Bobbitt et al. (1998) found that special education teachers were the specialists most likely to move, but they left at rates similar to the national average. However, special education teachers were only half as likely to leave for retirement as were other teachers. Using a logistical regression analysis of the same three datasets, Ingersoll (1999) found that special education was the only teaching field with significantly more teacher turnover. A study of special education teachers in Florida found that the turnover rate (movers and leavers) was one and a half times that of general education teachers (Miller et al., 1998). This same pattern was seen in Texas where special education had both the highest attrition and mobility rates (TEA, 1995). Although Billingsley (1993) and Brownell and Smith (1992) offered a variety of possible explanations, they criticized the research explanations for the high attrition of special education teachers. Boe, Bobbitt, et al. (1996) found that similar factors can predict the attrition of special education and general education teachers.

In contrast to this consistent finding about high attrition rates among special education teachers is the most recent TFS dataset (Luekens et al., 2004). They reported an attrition rate of 8.7% for special education teachers, similar to or surpassed by rates for social studies teachers (8.8%) and mathematics teachers (9%). Special education teachers, however, were reported to have the second highest moving rate (10.2%) after arts teachers (11.4%). It is unknown whether this finding represents a changed pattern or is a 1-year exception.

After special education, the greatest concern about attrition has been in science and math. State studies in the 1970s and 1980s found significantly higher attrition among science teachers, especially in chemistry or physics (Kirby & Grissmer, 1993; Murnane, 1987; Murnane & Olsen, 1988; Murnane & Schwinden, 1989; Murnane et al., 1991). However, more recent studies (Ingersoll, 1999; TEA, 1995; Whitener & Gruber, 1997) found that science and math teachers have not left teaching significantly more than have other teachers. Nationally, the attrition rate for science teachers was 6.5%, almost the same as the average for all teachers (Whitener & Gruber, 1997).

Student Characteristics. Summarizing studies from the 1970s through early 1980s, Grissmer and Kirby (1987) noted high attrition rates from districts serving lower SES students and students with lower achievement. In contrast, Heyns (1988), looking at the 1972 NLS cohort, found those no longer teaching in 1986 were more likely to have left suburban schools than rural schools, upper- and upper-middle-class schools than mixed SES schools, high- or average-ability schools than mixed-ability schools. Attrition rates for urban, low-income, and low-ability schools fell in the middle. There were no differences in attrition related to the racial composition of the schools. In contrast to earlier studies, Boe, Bobbitt, et al. (1996) and Boe, Bobbitt, et al. (1998), using SASS and TFS datasets, found that community type was not associated with teachers' moving or leaving. Ingersoll (2001, p. 3) concluded, that while high poverty schools have moderately higher rates (compared to low poverty schools), neither larger schools, large school districts nor urban public schools have high rates of teacher turnover compared to small private schools.

IMPACT OF DEMOGRAPHIC PROFILES

Despite concerns about the gender imbalance of the teaching pool, empirical evidence generally indicates that gender of the teacher is not an important factor in student achievement (Brophy, 1985; Evans, 1992; Gold & Reis, 1982; Humrich, 1988). The impact of the aging teaching force has been studied primarily with a view toward its consequences for potential teacher shortages rather than in terms of its relationship to student achievement. The impacts of the dominant monolingual teaching force, despite the growing number of limited English-proficient students, and the SES background of teachers have not been studied.

The demographic of most concern is the racial and ethnic composition of the teaching force. Although there are indications that prospective teachers, in comparison to the current teaching force, are less likely to be White, the proportion of teachers of color is much lower than the increasingly diverse student population. In light of the unequal opportunities provided many minorities, moves by some states to raise cutoff scores on teacher certification tests have the potential to decrease the pool of minorities who actually enter teaching.

Much of the argument for increasing the racial and ethnic diversity of the teaching force to reflect the diversity of the student population is based on the belief that a diverse teaching force is good for all children and the health of our democracy. The case is made that not only should the authority of knowledge not be seen as the special privilege of Whites, but also that teachers of different races and ethnicities can better prepare children for life in a multicultural society.

This *prima facie* argument for a diverse teaching force is accompanied by the argument that it is especially important for children of color to have as a role model a teacher of their own race or ethnicity who can instill positive attitudes toward school and learning and provide culturally relevant pedagogy (Clewell & Puma, 2003; Dee, 2001; Ladson-Billings, 1992, 1994; King, 1993b; NCTAF, 1996). The predominantly White teaching force is seen as possibly contributing to the continuing "achievement gap" between Whites and Blacks, Hispanics and Native Americans.

In the 1960s and 1970s, many researchers focused on teacher expectations to explain the lower achievement of minority and poor children (Brophy, 1985; Brophy & Good, 1974; Irvine, 1986; Rist, 1970; Rosenthal & Jacobson, 1968). In summarizing this body of research, Ehrenberg, Goldhaber, and Brewer (1995, pp. 547–548) conclude:

> Research on the relative effectiveness of minority teachers in educating minority students ... has focused on teachers attitudes toward, expectations for, and placement of minority students, as well the feedback that they provide to the students. Most of this research has not addressed the students' educational outcomes, has failed to control for other teacher characteristics, such as verbal ability, experience, and degree levels; and has not investigated the effects that under-represented minority teachers have on non-minority students.

To address this lack of empirical data, Ehrenberg, Goldhaber, and Brewer (1995) used the large longitudinal NELS dataset from 1988 to analyze how a teacher's race, gender, and ethnicity (RGE) related to how they evaluated students and how much students learned. They looked at standardized tests the students took in the same subjects in Grades 8 and 10 and correlated the results by the race, gender, and ethnicity of teacher and students.

Using tests in two subject areas, they were able to "estimate gain score equations to ascertain whether teachers' RGE influenced how much their students learned" between the 8th and 10th grades. Tenth-grade teachers' survey responses about their perceptions of each student were aggregated into several teacher subjective evaluation variables. Whereas various personal, family and school variables were used as controls, the race, gender, and ethnicity of the 9th grade teachers was not available.

The study concluded there was little association between the race, gender, and ethnicity of the teacher and students and how much students learned. One exception was in history classes taught by Black males to Black students. Trying to reconcile these findings with earlier findings that teachers' attitudes, expectations, and treatment of students were related to the race, gender, and ethnicity match, the authors looked to see if this relationship existed in the NELS data. They found in several instances a significant relationship between a teacher's subjective evaluation and the race, gender, and ethnicity match, although it was not related to achievement.

Similarly, Farkas, Grobe, Sheehan, and Shuan (1990) using data from seventh- and eighth-grade social studies classes in an urban district, found that African-American students taught by Black teachers not only were absent less from school and were perceived as having better work habits but also engaged in more disruptive behavior. A race match between teacher and students was not related to performance on curriculum tests or student course grades. Ehrenberg and Brewer (1994), using longitudinal data from the HSB study, also found this lack of relationship. They found that teachers' race was not related to the probability of student dropout nor to achievement gain for students who stayed in school between their sophomore and senior years.

Contrary evidence has been found in a reanalysis of the national Coleman et al. (1966) data (Ehrenberg & Brewer, 1995) and in several more recent studies (Clewell & Puma, 2003; Dee, 2001; Evans, 1992; Hanushek, 1992) in relation to Black teachers and students. In reanalyzing the Coleman data, Ehrenberg and Brewer found, in some analyses, that the proportion of Black teachers in a school was associated with higher score gains for Black high school students, but with lower gains for White elementary- and secondary-school students. The authors cautioned that "these findings are for American schools in the mid-1960s ... (and) do not directly apply to our contemporary experience" (p. 14). It should also be noted that their study dealt only with the proportion of Black teachers in a school, not the match between the race of the classroom teacher and that of the student.

Hanushek (1992) did match teacher and student race in studying reading and vocabulary score gains for low-income Black students between second and sixth grades in Gary, Indiana. Although family size and birth order helped explain achievement differences, Hanushek found that adding teacher variables increased the explained variance by one third. Although there was no difference in male and female teachers on student achievement, by holding other teacher variables constant, he found that having a Black teacher enhanced the achievement of these Black pupils. His explanation was that either "Black students do better with teachers of their own race" or that the White teachers "attracted to this setting" are inferior (p. 110).

Likewise, in a study of race and gender role-model effects in high school economic courses surveyed by the Joint Council on Economic Education in 1987, Evans (1992) found a significant role-model effect for African Americans, but none for gender. The positive achievement effect of having Black teachers was particularly strong for Black students whose mothers did not graduate from college. In contrast, using a 3-year longitudinal national sample of 8,427 third-graders, Clewell and Puma (2003) found that having a teacher of the same race or ethnicity had a stronger effect on math scores than on reading scores and a stronger effect for Hispanic students than for other students.

The effect of racial matching was recently explored with an unusual dataset in which teachers and students had been randomly matched within participating schools. Using data from Tennessee's Project STAR class-size experiment, Dee (2001) looked at the match between teacher and student race and student achievement in Grades K to 3. Dee found that assigning a kindergarten student to an "own-race" teacher significantly increased the math and reading achievement scores, by 3 to 4 percentage points, of Black students and White male pupils in regular size classes, but not in the small-size classes. That was similar to the effects of assigning a child to a small class. The cumulative effect of having a same race teacher was estimated at a yearly gain of 2 to 4 percentage points.

The findings may be mixed in part because many of these studies ignored SES. An earlier large cohort study of first-graders in Baltimore (Alexander, Entwisle, & Thompson, 1987) found that the gap between White and Black achievement test scores only existed in classes with high-SES teachers. But only student race, not SES, interacted with teacher SES. In a later analysis reported in Ferguson (1998), Alexander later found that teacher race and SES did interact. The largest verbal and math gains were for White students who had high-SES Black teachers. For Black students, the highest gains in math were for those with Black low-SES teachers and White high-SES teachers.

SUMMARY

Most teachers are female, White, and monolingual. They are currently more likely to have college-educated parents than in previous years, reflecting the increased education level of Americans. Their average age is in the low 40s, reflecting in part the graying of the work force, as well as the older age of college graduates and the growth of graduate and alternative programs.

Although there is a growing number of extended teacher education programs and 46 states now offer alternative programs, most prospective teachers still are prepared in baccalaureate programs at public institutions. Despite fears that extended teacher education programs would create another barrier for students of color, graduate and alternative programs attract similar or higher proportions of students of color.

New first-time teachers represent an increasing proportion of the teaching force; they are older, more diverse, and include more males than in previous years. These new teachers are more likely to find their first jobs in harder-to-staff, lower performing rural and central city schools with high proportions of minority and low-income students.

Teachers with master's degrees are more likely to be found in the suburbs, in high schools, and in the Northeast. Some studies have found that fewer teachers hold master's degrees at schools with large numbers of low-income students. Alternately prepared teachers, especially non-Whites, initially are more likely to take positions in urban schools.

Teachers' reasons for teaching and their expectations show some variation by gender, race and ethnicity, SES, and age. Fewer than half of those prepared to teach actually teach the next year. Some delay entry, but others never teach. Prospective elementary, teachers are more likely to enter teaching than are prospective secondary teachers.

Turnover—switching teaching assignments, moving to different schools and districts, and temporary and permanent leaving—is the largest determinant of demand for new teachers. The average turnover is about 30% with about 17% switching teaching assignments, about 7% moving to another school, and about 6% leaving. Of those leaving, more than half return to teaching after a break. A growing proportion of teachers are staying in their classroom positions for longer periods of time. Attrition is expected to rise as more teachers reach retirement age and younger teachers with higher attrition rates replace them.

Age is the prime demographic contributor to attrition, with the rates highest among youngest and oldest teachers. Attrition rates are confounded by more women taking breaks from teaching, primarily for childbearing and rearing. Findings comparing attrition rates between alternately and traditionally prepared teachers and between those with undergraduate and graduate degrees are mixed, indicating the need to look at school level, subject, type of school, time frame, and race and ethnicity of teacher. Most studies have found that secondary teachers and special education teachers have higher attrition rates. Despite expectations, yearly attrition rates for math and science teachers are near average and the highest attrition rates are in small, private schools, not in large urban public schools.

There are not many studies that assess the impact of teachers' demographics on students. Although studies indicate that the gender of teachers is not related to student achievement, the research on the relationship of teachers' race and student achievement is mixed.

WHAT WE KNOW ABOUT THE DEMOGRAPHIC PROFILE

The evidence confirms, in broad strokes, the demographic profile of teachers commonly held. Claims about the impact of imbalances in the demographic profile are not as clearly supported. After looking at what we do know about the demographic profile of teachers, we turn to what we don't know about the demographic profile as a basis for suggesting a research agenda.

Gender

Approximately 75% of teachers are female. This predominance is even greater at the early childhood and elementary level, and among special education, bilingual, ESL, and secondary English teachers. Beyond these levels and subject differences, the gender of teachers is not related to the race and ethnicity or SES characteristics of schools or students served. Although still predominantly female, there is some evidence that graduate-level and alternative programs attract proportionately more males than do undergraduate teacher education programs. Once in teaching, females take more breaks from teaching, primarily for childbearing and rearing, but findings on overall attrition are mixed. Although attrition rates are higher for secondary teachers who are less likely to be female, they are also higher for special education teachers who are more likely to be female. Whereas the large number of female teachers may have an impact on perceptions about teaching, the evidence indicates that generally it is not related to student learning, as measured by achievement tests.

Race and Ethnicity

Teachers are predominantly White. National data indicate that Whites comprised 84% of teachers in 2000 (NCES, 2003). Although the proportion of teachers of color, especially that of prospective teachers, has increased slightly in recent years, it does not match the increase in student diversity. Although more minorities are graduating from college, a smaller percentage of African-American college graduates now choose teaching than they did in an earlier era when teaching was one of the few professions open to them.

The numbers of prospective and practicing teachers of color vary widely by region and by institution. They are more likely than Whites to start their higher education at 2-year colleges and transfer to 4-year public institutions for teacher preparation. Although prospective teachers in all types of teacher education programs are predominantly White, higher proportions of minorities have been reported in alternative programs and some graduate programs. Minority teachers disproportionately teach at the elementary level and are found more often in central cities and in schools serving high proportions of minority and low-income students. Attrition rates between Black and White teachers are generally similar.

Evidence on what impact the match between teacher and student race and ethnicity has on student learning is mixed.

Socioeconomic Background

Historically, teaching has attracted people from all SES levels. As a middle-class occupation, it has been an upwardly mobile choice for those from the working and lower middle classes. The majority of teachers' parents still do not have high-school or college degrees, but the proportion with high-school- and college-educated parents has risen over the past 25 years. Reflecting the general increase in educational attainment, prospective teachers are even more likely to have parents with high school and college degrees. Although more teachers are coming from higher SES backgrounds, a counter trend is that higher SES females and minorities now have a range of other job possibilities that were not previously available to them and are not choosing teaching in as high proportions.

Teachers with higher SES backgrounds are more likely to have attended private institutions. Although there are few studies, there is some indication that those with higher SES backgrounds are more highly represented in alternative programs that recruit from elite, private institutions; are more likely to be "late entrants" to teaching; are more likely to have graduate degrees at entry; and are more likely to have higher attrition rates.

Age

The average age of current teachers is in the low 40s, and it had been rising until the late 1990s. The average age of prospective teachers has been rising. The majority of teachers now enter teaching between the ages of 25 and 29, rather than under 25. This reflects the older age of college graduates and the growth of graduate and alternative programs.

Females and elementary-school teachers are slightly younger than males and secondary-school teachers. Rural teachers are younger than their counterparts in urban and suburban schools, reflecting the greater proportion of new teachers hired. New teachers are more likely to teach in schools serving high proportions of minority and low-income students. Younger and older teachers are most likely to leave teaching, creating the u-shaped curve consistently found in retention research.

WHAT WE DON'T KNOW ABOUT
THE DEMOGRAPHIC PROFILE

Although data confirm what is commonly believed about the demographic profile of teachers, the lack of current data limit our knowledge. We know less about the impact of the demographic profile on teacher practice and student learning.

Demographic Profile

Although existing research reveals few surprises, the data are neither as detailed nor as current as desired. The most comprehensive data come from the NCES, but the picture the data paint is dated because of the lag among collection, release, and analysis of its surveys. As of April 2002, the most recent final data were from the 1993 to 1994 school year. Although raw data for 1999 to 2000 had been released, analysis was just beginning. Although it is unlikely that major changes take place between collection periods, the knowledge lag is considerable. For instance, we do not know the current number of minority teachers and can only speculate on trends from less comprehensive data sources in the intervening years. This is one reason why there are contradictory reports on whether the teaching force recently has become more or less diverse. Although demographic statistics gathered by states and local school districts often provide useful information, they are limited because of differing definitions and their inability to capture teachers who have left their jurisdiction.

Although the demographic data on current teachers are limited, our knowledge of who is in the teacher preparation pipeline is in worse shape. AACTE's RATE studies provide informative surveys about the demographics of those enrolled in their member institutions, but these surveys are based on samples of different types of institutions in particular years. There is no comprehensive database on all prospective teachers in teacher education programs. Getting a national picture of the different types of undergraduate, graduate, and nondegree certification programs within the complex system of higher education institutions, operating in 50 different states with different certification requirements, is a major challenge. In addition, the use of "education major" as an indicator of who is preparing to teach is increasingly inaccurate as many states and institutions now require an undergraduate subject matter major for all prospective teachers, including elementary teachers.

The proliferation of alternative programs that are not university based also complicates the task of gathering data on who is preparing to teach. These programs are often local, short-lived, and offered by school districts, city or state agencies, or private organization. It is hard to get solid numbers. There is no common definition of alternative programs, so comparing numbers from different studies is difficult. Programs frequently change as state policies change, so even comparing data from the same state across the years is difficult. By design, these programs often blur the difference between those preparing to teach and who is actually teaching, further complicating the compilation of demographic data. In light of anticipated teacher shortages and the increasing number of states' approving alternative programs, this source of future teachers is likely to grow as will the difficulty of knowing who and how many are in the pipeline. Our knowledge of differential retention rates is not definitive. Some expect alternately prepared teachers to have higher attrition rates because of their limited preparation or lack of commitment; others believe attrition will be lower because these candidates are opting to teach at a more mature age and have a more realistic sense of other jobs.

These kinds of difficulties make it hard to interpret the limited data we have about prospective teachers. In some college and alternative programs, there are currently proportionately more males, students of color, and older aspirants than in previous years. How widespread these patterns are and whether they change the demographics of who actually enters and stays in classroom teaching is uncertain. Very little is known about the reserve pool of teachers, who might reenter teaching in larger numbers in a tightening economy. It seems unlikely, however, that the predominance of Whites and females will change in the near future.

We know more about the demographics of teachers than about those of prospective teachers, especially the two most straightforward, routinely collected pieces of data, their gender and age. Researchers in the past 15 years have paid the least attention to teachers' SES background. The greatest challenge, however, has been in getting valid and reliable evidence about the race and ethnicity of prospective, current, and reserve pool teachers. In looking at data over the last 50 years, there is little assurance that the categories used to classify race and ethnicity are comparable. Earlier studies generally looked at White versus non-White teachers, often labeling the latter group as Black. Sometimes other groups were eliminated because of small numbers; sometimes they were included in the non-White group. Only recently have Whites been classified as White, non-Hispanic. How multiracial and ethnic people are reported often is unclear. Hence, comparing race and ethnicity data across studies and across years can be problematic. Additionally, we have limited knowledge about the interaction of race and ethnicity, gender, SES background, and age, as few datasets look at all these variables in relation to how teachers are prepared, where they teach, and how long they stay in teaching.

Impact of Demographic Profile

The predominantly White, female teaching force, coming from relatively modest family backgrounds, engenders two major concerns. One is the messages such a demographic profile sends to students, prospective teachers, and the public about teaching and teachers. We know little about the actual impact these messages have on students, on who is attracted to and stays in teaching, and on the support the public gives to teachers.

Another major concern is that the growing differences between the demographic profiles of teachers and students may contribute to the achievement gap for minority students. Although we know that teachers are not proportionately representative of the population in terms of gender, race and ethnicity, SES, and age, we do not know if this imbalanced profile affects student outcomes.

Looking at the impact on student learning, gender is the only demographic variable that research consistently seems to indicate does not make a difference. Research on the impact of race and ethnicity of teachers has yielded mixed results. Knowledge of the impact of SES background and age of teachers is limited by lack of research on these demographic variables. Likewise, we know little about the impact on student achievement of the interaction of these demographic teacher variables with the quality profile of teachers, type of teacher preparation, characteristics of schools and students, and retention rates. It must also be remembered that even the limited research that is called "impact" research is largely correlational research, indicating relationships but not causality.

Research on the impact of demographic profiles has focused on student learning outcomes, as measured by test scores. Researchers acknowledge the narrowness of this yardstick, but continue to rely on it because test scores are easily obtained and often standardized. We know little about teacher demographics' impact on other cognitive performance measures and such student outcomes as attitudes, self-concept, motivation, cultural identity, graduation, college entry, and avoidance of risky behavior.

Underlying this research is the implication is that demographic profiles of teachers influence teacher practice which in turn influence student learning. Although there was much research on teacher attitudes and expectations as they related to teacher demographics in the 1970s and 1980s, little attention has been paid to how the demographic profile may affect the practice of teaching and how that, in turn, may affect student achievement.

RESEARCH AGENDA

The need is clear for developing a comprehensive, up-to-date demographic profile of prospective teachers, current teachers, and the reserve pool and understanding how demographic variables related to how teachers are prepared, where they teach, and how long they stay in teaching. Such a comprehensive, timely database would be a great asset for policymakers interested in supply-and-demand issues related to the teaching force, both regionally and down to the level of individual schools. Given the ease of reentry, teachers' career paths will probably remain unpredictable. Getting improved data on the reserve pool is important because most "leavers" might potentially return to the classroom, despite their stated intention at the time of leaving. Having better, up-to-date data would alert teacher educators and prospective teachers to expected needs for teachers that might affect state and institutional resource decisions, as well as career decisions for teachers.

For teacher education, the greatest contribution would be developing a comprehensive database of who is in the teacher education pipeline. With the mandatory
reporting associated with Title II, the collection and analysis of demographic and
quality profile data of who is preparing to teach as well as who has graduated in a
particular year seems a reasonable goal. Getting data on when and if graduates actually enter teaching would be more difficult, but it is information institutions already
are encouraged to collect as part of accreditation requirements. Such a database would
move beyond the misleading "education major" in providing a census of students in
undergraduate, graduate, and nondegree programs leading to teacher certification.
Although classifying programs in terms of the array of structural options now available might be a challenge, it would not be as difficult as the data collection and analysis
issues involved in who is enrolled, completing and entering teaching from alternative
programs. The varied definitions of what alternative programs actually entail within
and across the states present a major challenge. Although the easiest way out has been
to accept each state's definition, this has led to lumping of programs and participants
together in ways that impede interpretation and lead to misleading conclusions. A
clear indication of how each alternative program differs from the particular state's
standards for full certification would provide the basis for differentiating and comparing programs.

These database improvements are critical to obtaining more accurate and useful
information about the demographic profile of teachers. Congress should consider
incorporating such a goal into Title II reporting requirements. Because institutions
of higher education are not the sole source of teachers, states could collect agreed
on demographic data, quality indicators, preparation, and job history as part of their
certification process and annual school district reporting process.

Assuming that better and more complete demographic profiles become available,
we now turn to some important questions that researchers could mine from these
improved databases.

Demographic Profile

Given the growing diversity of the student population, the predominance of White
teachers, and the belief that a diverse teaching force is desirable, the demographic
variable needing most attention is race and ethnicity of prospective, current, and
reserve pool teachers. Teacher educators also could gain insight from knowing more
about age, gender, and SES background, particularly how they interact with types of
preparation, placement, and retention.

Race and Ethnicity.   Nationally, the teaching force has ranged from 84% to 92%
White in the last 30 years, with the highest percentage in the mid-1980s. There is
some indication that prospective teachers now in undergraduate programs are more
diverse and that master's and alternative programs are attracting a higher proportion
of minorities. The proportion of newly prepared minority hired doubled between
1987 and 1993 (Snyder, 1998). But as states implement tests for teacher certification
with increasingly higher cutoff scores and minorities are more actively recruited by
other professions, there is renewed concern that the number of minorities actually
entering classroom teaching will decline once again. Timely, comprehensive, comparable data about the race and ethnicity of teachers in the preparation pipeline,
in the classroom, and in the reserve pool would address the conflicting claims and
concerns about the diversity of the teaching force. Baseline comparisons with other

professions would not only help us understand the dynamics of the problem but also indicate different policy implications, particularly if the problem is unique to teaching.

For teacher educators, knowing and understanding what happens to students of color throughout the teacher education pipeline could help them define and address the problem. Vegas et al. (2001) concluded, using 1992 data, that the major problem is not necessarily that minority graduates are less attracted to teaching but that they are less likely to graduate from college. Others fear that even more will be denied entry as institutions raise standards for admission into teacher education programs and as states raise passing scores on certification tests. Seeking evidence to support or disprove these claims at the institutional, state, or national level would be worthy of study. Research that followed cohorts of students through intentions expressed on admission to college, entry into teacher preparation programs, graduation from teacher education programs, obtaining certification, and entry into teaching would be particularly helpful in identifying particular pipeline barriers. Because prospective teachers of color are more likely to start at 2-year colleges and transfer to 4-year colleges to complete their preparation, special attention to transfer students would be appropriate. Also, because HBIs prepare a disproportionate number of Black teachers, research that looks at pipeline movement through HBIs into teaching would be useful. Another area for further exploration would be to look more closely at the strong motivations, as well as at ambiguities, related to race and ethnicity expressed by many students of color about going into teaching. Gaining a better handle on these students' motivations would be helpful not only for recruitment and retention efforts but also for teacher educators who work with these candidates.

Similarly, because studies indicate that graduate and alternative programs attract more non-Whites, we need to examine the entering cohorts closely to see if there are racial and ethnic differences as students enter these programs, complete them, seek certification, and get their first jobs. Research exploring reasons for programmatic and institutional variation in participation of teachers of color also could add to our understanding of ways to increase the diversity of the teaching force.

Currently, teachers of color are more likely to be found in elementary schools, in central city schools, and in schools serving higher proportions of minority and low-income students. Although this leaves many schools and students with no or few minority teachers, the supply of minority teachers is so small that even students in predominantly minority schools usually have mostly White teachers. Research examining whether this results from self-selection or differential hiring practices would be useful, as well as studying ways to diversify the teaching force in schools with no or few minority teachers.

Fears that teachers of color are leaving at a higher rate than are White teachers need to be addressed by empirical evidence, particularly in light of contradictory findings. Although Black and White attrition rates appear similar, there is some indication that rates for Hispanics may be higher. In some recent studies, contrary to expectations, teachers left small private schools, suburban schools, and schools serving advantaged students at higher rates. Also unexpected were studies that indicated that dissatisfaction with teaching and working conditions, often found in large urban schools, were not a major reason for attrition. By contrast, other studies indicate that these were major factors for moving from one school or district to another. It is not clear whether these different findings can all be attributed to the use of different response categories in the studies, as well as to the different definitions of attrition. Given the persistent staffing needs in large, urban schools and the desire for a diverse teaching staff in all schools, a clearer understanding of the dynamics of hiring, supporting, and retaining teachers, particularly those of color, is needed.

Age. Teacher educators—in undergraduate, graduate, and alternative programs—are all working with students older than 18 to 22. Undergraduates are taking more than 4 years to complete their programs, and older adults, many with parenting experience, are returning to college to start or complete their bachelor's degrees. Graduate and alternative programs are designed for older adults who did not prepare for teaching in college; these prospective teachers range from new college graduates to retirees.

Although data about mean ages are useful, they may mask differences among different types and structures of preparation programs. Such information could give us a better idea about the attractiveness of different options and provide useful information to teacher educators. Age is not a perfect proxy for maturity and experience, but if the candidates are getting older, teacher educators might want to reconsider elements of preparation programs that were appropriate for unmarried, college-age students but less so for older students with children of their own.

As the age of prospective teachers increases, research about the initial attractions of teaching and the career paths for teachers needs to be updated. Teacher educators need to become familiar with the expectations and career decisions facing older adults preparing to teach. Researchers, in studying retention, need to consider that new teachers no longer are necessarily "young" and often are in places in their life and career different from those of entering teachers in the past. Childbearing may be behind some and may approach more quickly for others. Researchers need to look at age and years of experience to provide a more accurate picture of the relationship between age and retention.

Claims about teacher retention most in need of evidence—undergraduate versus graduate versus alternative programs—call for research that controls for teachers' age. Differences in retention might have more to do with the ages of new teachers rather than with the attributes of their preparation programs. Or perhaps, certain preparation options may be more effective in preparing older candidates who will stay in teaching longer. Older adults in traditional undergraduate programs could be compared with similar-aged adults in graduate and alternative programs. Information on the relationships among age, program completion, certification, entry into teaching, and retention would be particularly useful for those running alternative programs who might want to adjust the balance among recent college graduates, second careerists, and retirees.

Gender. Even if the gender imbalance of teachers has no impact on student achievement, some believe that gender diversity is not only intrinsically valuable, but important for the symbolic messages it sends about teachers and education. The perception that teaching is a "female" career is seen by some as having a negative impact on efforts to improve working conditions and the status of the profession, as well as possibly discouraging half the population from considering teaching when making career choices.

The evidence that males are disproportionately attracted to graduate and alternative programs is worth exploring further. Are there elements of these programs more attractive to males considering teaching, or is age the critical factor here? It might be much harder for a young college male than for an older male to make this career decision.

Socioeconomic Background. We know the least about teachers' SES backgrounds. We know that they are currently more likely to have parents who completed high school and college than in previous years, but we do not know how these changes relate to general demographic trends. Are prospective teachers now coming from a different SES background? How does SES interact with race and ethnicity, gender, age, type of preparation program, placement, and retention?

For teacher educators, the answers to these questions do more than satisfy intellectual curiosity and provide grist for recruitment strategies. The SES of their teacher education students is likely to be highly correlated with the quality and types of teaching they experienced in their own K–12 education (Popkewitz, Tabachnick, & Wehlage, 1982). Such knowledge could affect the content and strategies teacher educators use in their programs if they want students to enact teaching that goes beyond that which they have experienced.

Research is also needed that looks beyond individual teacher variables at the external forces that shape the demographic patterns. The civil rights and women's movements and the Vietnam war are recent examples of societal forces that affected who went into teaching. The changing economy and graying of the population are current examples of such factors. The ethos of the teaching occupation and the structure of schools also shape who is attracted to teaching, who prepares to teach, where they teach, and how long they stay. More research here will inform both teacher educators and policymakers.

Impact of Demographic Profile

One concern about the predominantly White, female demographic profile of teachers is that it may send male and minority students a discouraging message about equal access, knowledge, and achievement. One could argue that in a democratic society, the profile of teachers should mirror the profile of the student population for these reasons alone.

More research is needed about the impact of teacher demographics on student outcomes. Given the persistent achievement gap that is pronounced among different race and ethnicity groups and among students from lower SES backgrounds, more studies are warranted to determine whether the nonrepresentative profile and distribution of teachers contribute to educational inequalities for children.

Researchers have difficulty capturing the impact of demographic variables. This work demands large, longitudinal studies that take into consideration multiple and related student, family, teacher, and school variables. Because most studies yield correlational rather than causal findings, substantial qualitative research is needed to probe relationships that are indicated but not explained by large-scale data analysis. It is also challenging because it could lead to uncomfortable findings that certain groups of teachers might be more effective with students in general or students of particular gender, race and ethnicity, SES background, age, or in particular subjects. That, however, is not a reason to avoid research of this type nor to conclude that such evidence should be used to support discriminatory policies in admission to teacher education programs and hiring. Rather, a focus on how demographic variables relate to teacher knowledge and attitudes and teaching practice might provide new insights into some intractable issues related to student achievement and help educators better prepare prospective teachers who can meet the diverse needs of all students.

Race and Ethnicity.   Given concern about achievement gaps among different racial and ethnic groups, the mixed findings on the relationship of teachers' race and ethnicity and student achievement underscore the need for further research. The current upsurge in standardized testing should provide large, longitudinal databases. If student data (e.g., race and ethnicity, gender, age, SES, and prior test scores), teacher data (e.g., race and ethnicity, gender, SES, age, teaching experience, and type of preparation program), and school data (e.g., location, student race and ethnicity, and family SES) are collected at the same time, researchers can better control for related factors as they seek evidence on the impact of teachers' race and ethnicity on achievement. Two kinds of relationships could be explored. One is the proportion of minority teachers in a school, district, or state, aggregated and broken down by different races and ethnicities, in relation to student achievement, by and across groups. The other involves the match between the race and ethnicity of teachers and students. At the secondary level, this would involve a match by subjects. In both cases—proportions and matches—it would be important to collect data over time to assess the impact of diverse teachers over a child's school career. Although it is overly ambitious to include all these elements in one study, the more that are included, the greater the confidence in the findings about the impact of the race and ethnicity of teachers.

Researchers will continue to use using student achievement as the dependent variable, because test scores provide easily obtainable, standardized measures. Obviously, it does not capture other goals of public education. Additionally, claims for the importance of students' having teachers of the same race and ethnicity as positive role models go beyond its impact on student achievement. Studies looking at the impact of race and ethnicity of teachers on other student outcomes, such as self-concept, motivation, cultural identity, graduation, college entry, and avoidance of risky behavior would broaden our knowledge about the possible impact of teachers' race and ethnicity.

If relationships are found between race and ethnicity of teachers and student outcomes, knowing more about teacher knowledge, attitudes and practice would be useful for teacher educators to help all teachers better meet the needs of diverse students. Given the difficulty of capturing the complexity of teaching in quantifiable terms, there is a need for qualitative studies of teachers' and students' interacting in classrooms to provide further insight into these relationships and to aid teacher educators in working with prospective teachers. There is also a need for research syntheses of existing qualitative studies. Findings of such studies, based on their limited but intensive samples, are beyond the scope of most reviews, including this one, and the knowledge rarely accumulates.

Besides informing teacher educators and prospective teachers about addressing the needs of diverse learners, evidence about the impact of teachers of diverse races and ethnicities could add further impetus to current efforts to recruit, prepare, and retain teachers of color. Another research agenda involves the evaluation of different strategies and programs to increase the numbers of minority teachers.

Socioeconomic Background.   Despite the high correlation between student SES and achievement, the SES background of teachers has been neglected in impact studies. Although confounded with race and ethnicity, it may make a separate contribution to student outcomes. The SES background of teachers may affect the quality of teachers' own K–12 education and the types of teaching they were exposed to as pupils. Teachers from different SES backgrounds may bring different knowledge, attitudes, and practices to the classroom that affect students differentially. If more information about teacher SES background were collected, a research agenda parallel to the one exploring the impact of teachers' race and ethnicity could be mounted.

Age. The aging of the teaching pool has been cause for both concern and celebration. On one hand, the greater maturity, experience, and stability of the teaching pool and the ability of graduate and alternative programs to attract older candidates are viewed as positive. On the other hand, the "graying" of the teaching pool is seen as alarming—too many burned-out teachers' holding on to old (e.g., progressive or traditional) ways of teaching, resisting change and new demands for accountability. A research agenda parallel to the one exploring teachers' race and ethnicity could be mounted. Given the greater range in age of prospective teachers, it would be important to collect data on years of teaching experience along with age.

Gender. Of the four demographic variables, research on the impact of gender has been the most conclusive. Recent studies show that teacher gender is not related to student achievement, as measured by test scores. The impact of gender on other student outcomes needs further study. Gender could also interact with race and ethnicity, SES, and age in ways masked by studies looking at the impact of gender alone. For instance, minority male teachers, serving as role models, may have a differential impact on low-income minority males' persistence in school. Such explorations would be worthy of further study.

Given the current political scene, a research agenda focused on the demographic profile of teachers would be incomplete without attention to issues of quality. We discuss the quality profile of teachers in the next chapter.

ACKNOWLEDGMENTS

We are grateful to M. Shelley Thomas of Teachers College, Columbia University, for contributions to the chart and bibliography. In addition to our colleagues on the panel, Jo Mills Braddock, Susan Fuhrmann, Drew Gittomer, and Richard Ingersoll provided helpful comments on drafts of chapters 3 and 4.

REFERENCES: DATA SOURCES[1]

AACTE. (1987). *RATE I: Teaching teachers: Facts and figures*. Washington, DC: American Association of Colleges of Teacher Education.

AACTE. (1988). *RATE II: Teaching teachers: Facts and figures*. Washington, DC: American Association of Colleges of Teacher Education.

AACTE. (1989). *RATE III: Teaching teachers: Facts and figures*. Washington, DC: American Association of Colleges of Teacher Education.

AACTE. (1990). *RATE IV: Teaching teachers: Facts and figures*. Washington, DC: American Association of Colleges of Teacher Education.

AACTE. (1992). *Academic achievement of White, Black, and Hispanic students in teacher education programs*. Washington, DC: American Association of Colleges of Teacher Education.

AACTE. (1994a). *Briefing book 1993*. Washington, DC: American Association of Colleges of Teacher Education.

---

[1]This reference list includes sources for all data (1985–2003) cited in chapter 3. The second reference list (References: Other Works Cited) includes all other sources, including sources for pre-1985 data.

AACTE. (1994b). *RATE VI: The context for the reform of teacher education.* Washington, DC: American Association of Colleges of Teacher Education.

AACTE. (1994c). *RATE VII: Teacher preparation in an urban context.* Washington, DC: American Association of Colleges of Teacher Education.

AACTE. (1999). *Teacher education pipeline IV: Schools and departments of education enrollments by race, ethnicity, and gender.* Washington, DC: American Association of Colleges of Teacher Education.

Adams, G. J., & Dial, M. (1993). Teacher survival: A Cox regression model. *Education and Urban Society, 26*(1), 90–99.

Alexander, K., Entwisle, D., & Thompson, M. (1987). School performance, status relations, and the structure of sentiment: Bringing the teacher back in. *American Sociological Review, 52,* 665–682.

American Association for Employment in Education. (2000). *Educator supply and demand in the United States.* Columbus, OH: Author.

Andrew, M. D. (1990). Differences between graduates of 4-year and 5-year teacher preparation programs. *Journal of Teacher Education, 41*(2), 45–51.

Andrew, M. D., & Schwab, R. L. (1995). Has reform in teacher education influenced teacher performance? An outcome assessment of graduates of an eleven-university consortium. *Action in Teacher Education, 17*(3), 43–53.

Baker, D. P., & Smith, T. (1997). Teacher turnover and teacher quality: Refocusing the issue. *Teachers College Record, 99*(1), 29–35.

Betts, J. R., Reuben, K. S., & Danenberg, A. (2000). *Equal resources, equal outcomes? The distribution of school resources and student achievement in California.* San Francisco: Public Policy Institute of California.

Biraimah, K. (1988). Preservice teachers' career expectations by gender, socioeconomic status, and academic achievement levels. *Florida Journal of Educational Research, 30*(1), 83–91.

Boe, E. E., Bobbitt, S. A., Cook, L. H., Barkanic, G., & Maislin, G. (1998). *Teacher turnover in eight cognate areas: National trends and predictors.* Philadelphia, PA: Center for Research and Evaluation in Social Policy.

Boe, E. E., Bobbitt, S. A., Cook, L. H., Whitener, S. D., & Weber, A. L. (1996). *Predictors of retention, transfer, and attrition of special and general education teachers: Data from the 1989 Teacher Follow-up Survey.* Washington, DC: National Center for Education Statistics, U.S. Department of Education.

Boe, E. E., Cook, L. H., Bobbitt, S. A., & Terhanian, G. (1998). The shortage of fully certified teachers in special and general education. *Teacher Education and Special Education, 21*(1), 1–21.

Boe, E. E., Cook, L. H., Kaufman, M. J., & Danielson, L. C. (1996). Special and general education teachers in public schools: Sources of supply in national perspective. *Teacher Education and Special Education, 19*(1), 1–16.

Book, C., Freeman, D., & Brousseau, B. (1985). Comparing academic backgrounds and career aspirations of education and non-education majors. *Journal of Teacher Education, 36*(3), 27–30.

Bracey, G. W. (2001). Why so few Asian-American teachers? *Phi Delta Kappan, 83*(1), 14–16.

Brookhart, S. M., & Freeman, D. J. (1992). Characteristics of entering teacher candidates. *Review of Educational Research, 62*(1), 37–60.

Brophy, J. (1985). Interactions of male and female teachers with male and female students. In C. Wilkinson (Ed.) *Gender influences in classroom interaction* (pp. 115–142). Madison, WI: University of Wisconsin Press .

Broughman, S. P., & Rollefson, M. R. (2000). *Teacher supply in the United States: Sources of newly hired teachers in the public and private schools, 1987–88 to 1993–94.* Washington, DC: National Center for Education Statistics, U.S. Department of Education.

Casserly, M. (1992). *National urban education goals: Baseline indicators, 1990–91.* Washington, DC: The Council of the Great City Schools.

Chin, E., Young, J. W., & Floyd, B. (2004, April). *Reducing the shortage of teachers in hard-to-staff schools: Do alternate teacher preparation programs make a difference?* Paper presented at the Annual Meeting of the American Educational Research Association, San Diego, CA.

Clewell, B. C., & Puma, M. (2003, April). *Does it matter if my teacher looks like me? The impact of teacher race and ethnicity on student academic achievement.* Paper presented at the Annual Meeting of the American Association of Colleges of Teacher Education, New Orleans, LA.

Cornett, L. M. (1992). Alternative certification: State policies in the SREB states. *Peabody Journal of Education, 67*(3), 55–83.

Darling-Hammond, L., Chung, R., & Frelow, F. (2002). Variation in teacher preparation: How well do different pathways prepare teachers to teach? *Journal of Teacher Education, 53*(4), 286–302.

Darling-Hammond, L., Hudson, L., & Kirby, S. (1989). *Re-designing teacher education: Opening the door for new recruits to science and mathematics teaching.* Santa Monica, CA: Rand Corporation.

Dee, T. S. (2001). *Teachers, race, and student achievement in a randomized experiment.* Cambridge, MA: National Bureau of Economic Research.

Ehrenberg, R. G., & Brewer, D. J. (1994). Do school and teacher characteristics matter? Evidence from *High School and Beyond. Economics of Education Review, 13*(1), 1–17.

Ehrenberg, R. G., & Brewer, D. J. (1995). Did teachers' verbal ability and race matter in the 1960s? Coleman revisited. *Economics of Education Review, 14*(1), 1–21.

Ehrenberg, R. G., Goldhaber, D. D., & Brewer, D. J. (1995). Do teachers' race, gender and ethnicity matter? Evidence from the National Educational Longitudinal Study of 1988. *Industrial and Labor Relations Review, 48,* 547–561.

Evans, M. O. (1992). An estimate of race and gender role-model effects in teaching high school. *Journal of Economic Education, 29*(3), 209–217.

Farkas, G., Grobe, R., Sheehan, D., & Shuan, Y. (1990).*Cultural resources and school success: Gender, ethnicity and poverty groups within an urban school district.* American Sociological Review, 55, 127–142.

Feistritzer, C. E. (1996). *Profile of teachers in the U.S.* Washington, DC: National Center for Education Information.

Feistritzer, C. E. (1999). *The making of a teacher: A report on teacher preparation in the United States.* Washington, DC: National Center for Education Information.

Feistritzer, C. E. (2003). *Alternative teacher certification: A state-by-state analysis 2003.* Washington, DC: National Center for Education Information.

Feistritzer, C. E., Hill, M. D., & Willett, G. G. (1998) *Profile of Troops to Teachers.* Washington, DC: National Center for Education Information.

Ferguson, R. F. (1998). Can schools narrow the Black-White test score gap? In C. Jencks & M. Phillips (Eds.) *The Black-White test score gap* (pp. 318–374). Washington, DC: Brookings Institution.

Goodwin, A. L., Genishi, C., Asher, N., & Woo, K. A. (1997). Voices from the margins: Asian-American teachers' experience in the profession. In D. M. Byrd & D. J. McIntyre (Eds.) *Teacher education Yearbook V* (pp. 219–241). Thousand Oaks, CA: Association of Teacher Educators and Corwin Press.

Gordon, J. A. (1994). Why students of color are not entering teaching: Reflection from minority teachers. *Journal of Teacher Education, 45*(5), 346–353.

Gordon, J. A. (2000). Asian-American resistance to selecting teaching as a career: The power of community and tradition. *Teachers College Record, 102*(1), 173–196.

Grissmer, D. W., & Kirby, S. N. (1987). *Teacher attrition: The uphill climb to staff our nation's schools.* Santa Monica, CA: Rand Corporation.

Grissmer, D. W., & Kirby, S. N. (1997). Teacher turnover and teacher quality. *Teachers College Record, 99*(1), 45–56.

Gruber, K. J., Wiley, S. D., & Broughman, S. P. (2002). *Schools and staffing survey, 1999–2000: Overview of the data for public, private, public charter, and Bureau of Indian Affairs elementary and secondary schools.* Washington, DC: National Center for Education Statistics, U.S. Department of Education.

Guyton, E., Saxton, R., & Wesche, M. (1996). Experiences of diverse students in teacher education. *Teaching and Teacher Education, 12*(6), 643–652.

Hall, B. W., & Carroll, D. (1987). Teachers at risk: A profile of the teacher predisposed to quit. *Florida Journal of Educational Research, 29*(1), 55–72.

Hanushek, E. A. (1992). The trade-off between child quantity and quality. *Journal of Political Economy, 100*, 84–118.

Hanushek, E. A., & Pace, R. R. (1995). Who chooses to teach (and why)? *Economics of Education Review, 14*(2), 101–117.

Hawk, B. P., & Schmidt, M. W. (1989). Teacher preparation: A comparison of traditional and alternative programs. *Journal of Teacher Education, 40*(September–October), 53–58.

Henke, R. R., Chen, X., & Geis, S. (2000). *Progress through the teacher pipeline: 1992–93 college graduates and elementary/secondary school teaching as of 1997.* Washington, DC: National Center for Education Statistics, U.S. Department of Education.

Henke, R. R., Choy, S. P., Chen, X., Geis, S., & Alt, M. N. (1997). *America's teachers: Profile of a profession, 1993–4.* Washington, DC: National Center for Education Statistics, U.S. Department of Education.

Henke, R. R., Choy, S. P., Geis, S., & Broughman, S. P. (1997). *School and Staffing in the U.S.: A statistical profile, 1993–94.* Washington, DC: National Center for Education Statistics, U.S. Department of Education.

Henke, R. R., Geis, S., Giambattista, J., & Knepper, P. (1996). *Out of the lecture hall and into the classroom: 1992–93 college graduates and elementary/secondary school teaching.* Washington, DC: National Center for Education Statistics, U.S. Department of Education.

Heyns, B. (1988). Educational defectors: A first look at teacher attrition in the NLS-72. *Educational Researcher, 17*, 24–32.

Houston, W. R., Marshall, F., & McDavid, T. (1993). Problems of traditionally prepared and alternatively certified first-year teachers. *Education and Urban Society, 26*(1), 78–89.

Huling-Austin, L. (1986). Factors to consider in alternative certification programs: What can be learned from teacher induction research. *Teacher Educator, 8*(2), 51–58.

Humrich, E. (1988, April). *Sex differences in the second IEA science study—U.S. results in an international context.* Paper presented at the Annual Meeting of the National Association for Research in Science Teaching, Lake of the Ozarks, MO.

Ingersoll, R. M. (1999). The problem of underqualified teachers in American secondary schools. *Educational Researcher, 28*(2), 26–37.

Irvine, J. J. (1986). Teacher-student interactions: Effects of student race, sex, and grade level. *Journal of Educational Psychology, 78*(1), 14–21.

Irvine, J. J. (1988). An analysis of the problem of disappearing Black educators. *Elementary School Journal, 88*(5), 503–513.

Jelmberg, J. (1996). College-based teacher education versus state-sponsored alternative programs. *Journal of Teacher Education, 47*(1), 60–66.

Johnson, S. M. (2001). *Research on new teachers shows a changing profession: 43% of new teachers in New Jersey plan to leave classroom teaching; Nearly half are mid-career entrants.* Next Generation of Teachers, Harvard Graduate School of Education. Retrieved from www.gse.harvard.edu/~ngt

Kemple, J. J. (1989, March). *The career paths of Black teachers: Evidence from North Carolina.* Paper presented at the Annual Meeting of the American Educational Research Association, San Francisco, CA.

King, S. (1993a). Why did we choose teaching careers and what will enable us to stay? Insights from one cohort of the African-American teaching pool. *Journal of Negro Education, 62*(4), 475–492.

Kirby, S. N., Berends, M., & Naftel, S. (1999). Supply and demand of minority teachers in Texas: Problems and prospects. *Educational Evaluation and Policy Analysis, 21*(1), 47–66.

Kirby, S. N., Darling-Hammond, L., & Hudson, L. (1989). Nontraditional recruits to mathematics and science teaching. *Educational Evaluation and Policy Analysis, 11*(3), 301–323.

Kirby, S. N., & Grissmer, D. W. (1993). *Teacher attrition: Theory, evidence, and suggested policy options*. Santa Monica, CA: Rand Corporation.

Kirby, S. N., Naftel, S., & Berends, M. (1999). *Staffing at-risk school districts in Texas: Problems and prospects*. Santa Monica, CA: Rand Corporation.

Lankford, H., Loeb, S., & Wykoff, J. (2002). Teacher sorting and the plight of urban schools. *Educational Evaluation and Policy Archives 24*(1), 37–62.

Lewis, L., Parsad, B., Carey, N., Bartfai, N., & Farris, E. (1999). *Teacher quality: A report on the preparation and qualifications of public school teachers*. Washington, DC: National Center for Education Statistics, U.S. Department of Education.

Luekens, M. T., Lyter, D. M., & Fox, E. E. (2004). *Teacher attrition and mobility: Results from the Teacher Follow-up Survey, 2000–01*. Washington, DC: National Center for Education Statistics, U.S. Department of Education.

Lutz, F. W., & Hutton, J. B. (1989). Alternative teacher certification: Its policy implications for classroom and personnel practice. *Educational Evaluation and Policy Analysis, 11*(3), 237–254.

Mantle-Bromley, C., Gould, L. M., McWhorter, B. A., & Whaley, D. C. (2000). The effect of program structure on new teachers' employment and program satisfaction patterns. *Action in Teacher Education, 22*(1), 1–14.

Matthes, W. A., & Carlson, R. V. (1986, April). *Conditions for practice: The reasons teachers selected rural schools*. Paper presented at the Annual meeting of the American Educational Research Association, San Francisco, CA.

McKibbin, M. D., & Giblin, H. (2000). *Report on the teaching internship grant program 1999–2000*. Sacramento, CA: California Commission on Teaching Credentialing.

McKibbin, M. D., & Tyson, S. (2000). *Report on the distribution of pre-internship and internship grant funds for 2000-2001*. Sacramento, CA: California Commission on Teacher Credentialing.

Miller, J. W., McKenna, M. C., & McKenna, B. A. (1998). A comparison of alternatively and traditionally prepared teachers. *Journal of Teacher Education, 49*(3), 165–176.

Murnane, R. J. (1987). Understanding teacher attrition. *Harvard Educational Review, 57,* 177–182.

Murnane, R. J., & Olsen, R. J. (1988, April). *Factors affecting the length of stay in teaching*. Paper presented at the Annual Meeting of the American Educational Research Association, New Orleans, LA.

Murnane, R. J., & Schwinden, M. (1989). Race, gender, and opportunity: Supply and demand for new teachers in North Carolina, 1975–1985. *Educational Evaluation and Policy Analysis, 11*(2), 93–108.

Murnane, R. J., Singer, J. D., Willett, J. B., Kemple, J. J., & Olsen, R. J. (1991). *Who will teach? Policies that matter*. Cambridge, MA: Harvard University Press.

Natriello, G., & Zumwalt, K. K. (1993). New teachers for urban schools? The contribution of the provisional teacher program in New Jersey. *Education and Urban Society, 26*(1), 49–62.

NCES. (2003). *School and Staffing Survey, 1999–2000*. Washington, DC: National Center for Education Statistics, U.S. Department of Education. Retrieved October 3, 2003, from http://www.nces.ed.gov/surveys/sass.

NEA. (1997). *Status of the American public school teacher, 1995–96*. Washington, DC: National Education Association.

NEA. (2003). *Status of the American public school teacher, 2000–2001*. Washington, DC: National Education Association.

Parsad, B., Lewis, L., & Farris, E. (2000). *Teacher preparation and professional development*. Washington, DC: National Center for Education Statistics, U.S. Department of Education.

Pavel, D. M. (1995). Comparing BIA and tribal Schools with public schools: A look at the year 1990–91. *Journal of American Indian Education, 35*(1), 10–15.

Pflaum, S. W., & Abramson, T. (1990). Teacher assignment, hiring, and preparation: Minority teachers in New York City. *Urban Review, 22*(1), 17–31.

Pigge, F. L., & Marso, R. N. (1992). A longitudinal comparison of the academic, affective, and personal characteristics of persisters and nonpersisters in teacher preparation. *Journal of Experimental Education, 61,* 19–26.

Richards, C. E., & Encarnation, D. J. (1986). Teaching in public and private schools: The significance of race. *Educational Evaluation and Policy Analysis, 8*(3), 237–252.

Sedlak, M., & Schlossman, S. (1986). Who will teach? Historical perspectives on the changing appeal of teaching as a profession. *Review of Research in Education* (Vol. 14, pp. 93–131). Washington DC: American Educational Research Association.

Shen, J. (1998a). Alternative certification, minority teachers, and urban education. *Education and Urban Society, 31*(1), 30–41.

Shen, J. (1998b). The impact of alternative certification on the elementary and secondary public teaching force. *Journal of Research and Development in Education, 32*(1), 9–16.

Sherman, J. C. (1991). *Masters degrees for teachers: A study of supply and demand*. Olympia, WA: Washington State Higher Education Coordinating Board.

Smith, G. P., Miller, M. C., & Joy, J. (1988). A case study of the impact of performance-based testing on the supply of minority teachers. *Journal of Teacher Education, 39*(4), 45–53.

Smith, T. (1995). *The condition of education, 1995*. Washington, DC: National Center for Education Statistics, U.S. Department of Education.

Snyder, T. (1998). *Digest of educational statistics*. Washington, DC: National Center for Education Statistics, U.S. Department of Education.

Stafford, D., & Barrow, G. (1994). Houston's alternative certification program. *The Educational Forum, 58*, 193–200.

Stoddart, T. (1990). Los Angeles Unified School District intern program: Recruiting and preparing teachers for an urban context. *Peabody Journal of Education, 67*(3) 84–122.

Su, Z. (1997). Teaching as a profession and as a career: Minority candidates' perspectives. *Teaching and Teacher Education, 13*(3), 325–340.

TEA. (1995). *Texas teacher retention, mobility, and attrition: Teacher supply, demand, and quality policy research project, Report no. 6*. Austin, TX: Texas Education Agency.

Theopold, N. (1990). An examination of the personal, professional, and school district characteristics on public school retention. *Economics of Education Review, 9*, 241–250.

Vegas, E., Murnane, R. J., & Willett, J. B. (2001). From high school to teaching: Many steps, who makes it? *Teachers College Record, 103*(3), 427–449.

Wenglinsky, H. (2000). *Teaching the teachers: Different settings, different results*. Princeton, NJ: Educational Testing Service.

Whitener, S. D., & Gruber, K. (1997). *Characteristics of stayers, movers, and leavers: Results from the teacher follow-up survey: 1994–5*. Washington, DC: National Center for Education Statistics, US Department of Education.

Wong, M. J., & Osguthorpe, R. T. (1993). The continuing domination of the four-year teacher education program: A national survey. *Journal of Teacher Education, 44*(1), 64–70.

Woods, J. E., & Williams, R. A. (1987). *Articulation with two-year colleges to create a multiethnic teaching force*. Paper commissioned for the American Association of Colleges for Teacher Education's Wingspread Policy Forum.

Wright, D. P., McKibbin, M. D., & Walton, P. A. (1987). *The effectiveness of the Teacher Trainee Program: An alternative route into teaching in California*. Sacramento, CA: California Commission on Teacher Credentialing.

REFERENCES: OTHER WORKS CITED

Adelman, N. E. (1986). *An exploratory study of teacher alternative certification and retraining programs*. Washington, DC: Policy Study Associates.

Alston, D. (1988). *Recruiting minority classroom teachers: A national challenge*. Washington, DC: National Governor's Association.

Arends, R., & Winitzky, N. (1996). Program structures and learning to teach. In F. B. Murray (Ed.), *Teacher educator's handbook* (pp. 526–556). Washington, DC: AACTE.

Billingsley, B. S. (1993). Teacher retention and attrition in special and general education: A critical review of the literature. *Journal of Special Education, 27*, 137–174.

Brophy, J., & Good, T. (1974). *Teacher-student relationships: Causes and consequences.* New York: Holt, Rinehart, & Winston.

Brownell, M. T., & Smith, S. W. (1992). Attrition/retention of special education teachers: Critique of current research and recommendations for retention efforts. *Teacher Education and Special Education, 15*(4), 229–248.

Carnegie Fonemon Education and The Economy's Task Force on Teaching as a Profession (1986). A nation prepared: Teachers for the 21st century. NY: Carneqie Corporation of NY.

Coleman, J. S., Campbell, E. Q., Hobson, C. J., McPartland, J., Mood, A. M., Weinfeld, F. D., et al. (1966). *Equality of educational opportunity.* Washington, DC: U.S. Government Printing Office.

Cyphert, F. R., & Ryan, K. A. (1984). Extending initial teacher preparation: Some issues and answers. *Action in Teacher Education, 6*(1–2), 63–70.

Darling-Hammond, L. (1990). Teaching and knowledge: Policy issues posed by alternative certification for teachers. *Peabody Journal of Education, 67*(3), 123–154.

Darling-Hammond, L. (1998, September). *How can we ensure a caring, competent, qualified teacher for every child? Strategies for solving the dilemmas of teacher supply, demand, and standards.* Paper presented at the Shaping the Profession that Shapes the Futures: An AFT/NEA Conference on Teacher Quality, Washington, DC.

Darling-Hammond, L. (2000). *Solving the dilemmas of teacher supply, demand and standards: How can we ensure a competent, caring and qualified teacher for every child?* New York: National Commission on Teaching and America's Future.

Darling-Hammond, L., & Cobb, V. L. (1996). The changing context of teacher education. In F. Murray (Ed.), *Teacher educator's handbook* (pp. 14–62). Washington, DC: AACTE.

Dill, V. S. (1996). Alternative teacher certification. In T. B. J. Sikula & E. Guytor (Eds.), *Handbook for Research on Teacher Education* (pp. 67–101). New York: Macmillan.

Feistritzer, C. E. (1993). National overview of alternative certification. *Education and Urban Society, 26*(1), 18–28.

Funkhouser, C. (1988). Strengthening the rationale for graduate-level preservice teacher education. *Journal of Teacher Education, 39*(6) 40–43.

Gold, D., & Reis, M. (1982). Male teacher effects on young children: A theoretical and empirical consideration. *Sex Roles: A Journal of Research, 8*(5), 493–513.

Goodnough, A. (2002). Half of new teachers lack certificates, data say. *The New York Times*, p. B8.

Holmes Group. (1986). *Tomorrow's teachers: A report of the Holmes Group.* East Lansing, MI: Author.

Howey, K. R., & Zimpher, N. L. (1986). The current debate on teacher preparation. *Journal of Teacher Education, 37*(5), 41–49.

Jorgenson, O. (2000). The need for more ethnic teachers: Addressing the critical shortage in the American public schools [Electronic version]. *Teachers College Record.*

King, S. H. (1993b). The limited presence of African-American teachers. *Review of Educational Research, 63*(2), 115–149.

Kopp, W. (1994). Teach for America: Moving beyond the debate. *The Educational Forum, 58,* 187–192.

Ladson-Billings, G. (1992). Liberatory consequences of literacy: A case of culturally relevant instruction for African-American students. *Journal of Negro Education, 61*(3), 378–391.

Ladson-Billings, G. (1994). *The dreamkeepers: Successful teachers for African-American children.* San Francisco: Jossey-Bass.

Lanier, J. E., & Little, J. W. (1986). Research on teacher education. In M. C. Wittrock (Ed.), *Handbook of research on teaching* (pp. 527–569). New York: MacMillan.

Lortie, D. C. (1975). *Schoolteacher.* Chicago: University of Chicago Press.

National Commission on Excellence in Education. (1983). *A nation at risk: A report to the nation and the Secretary of Education.* Washington, DC: United States Department of Education.

National Commission on Teaching and America's Future. (1996). *What matters most: Teaching for America's Future.* New York: Author.

Popkewitz, T. S., Tabachnick, B. R., & Wehlage, G. (1982). *The myth of educational reform: A study of school responses to a program of change.* Madison, WI: University of Wisconsin Press.

Rist, R. C. (1970). Student social class and teacher expectations: The self-fulfilling prophecy in ghetto education. *Harvard Educational Review, 40*(3), 411–451.

Rosenthal, R., & Jacobson, L. (1968). *Pygmalion in the classroom.* New York: Holt.

Ryan, K. (1987). The wrong report at the right time. *Teachers College Record, 88*(3), 419–422.

Tom, A. R. (1986). The Holmes Groups: Sophisticated analysis, simplistic solutions. *Journal of Teacher Education, 37*(4), 44–46.

Wirt, J., Choy, S., Gerald, D., Provasnik, P. R., Watanabe, S., Tobin, R., et al. (2001). *The condition of education, 2001.* Washington, DC: National Center for Education Statistics, U.S. Department of Education.

Wilson, S. M., Floden, R. E., & Ferrini-Mundy, J. (2001). *Teacher preparation research: Current knowledge, gaps and recommendations.* Seattle, WA: Center for the Study of Teaching and Policy.

Wilson, S. M., Floden, R. E., & Ferrini-Mundy, J. (2002). *Addendum to Teacher preparation research: Current knowledge, gaps and recommendations,* 2001. Seattle, WA: Center for the Study of Teaching and Policy.

Wise, A. E. (1986). Graduate teacher education and professionalism. *Journal of Teacher Education, 37*(September/October), 36–40.

Zeichner, K. M., & Schulte, A. K. (2001). What we know and don't know from peer-reviewed research about alternative teacher certification programs. *Journal of Teacher Education, 52*(4), 266–282.

Zhao, Y. (2002, August 5). Wave of pupils lacking English strains schools. *The New York Times,* p. A1.

Zumwalt, K. K. (1991). Alternate approaches to teacher education. *Journal of Teacher Education 42*(2), 83–92.

4

Teachers' Characteristics: Research on the Indicators of Quality

Karen Zumwalt
Elizabeth Craig
Teachers College, Columbia University

The quality and qualifications of public school teachers have come under increased scrutiny from the public, policymakers, and the profession in the past 2 decades. But efforts to elevate standards for teachers began much earlier in the 20th century, as normal schools gradually were transformed into colleges and universities. Since 1985, every state has raised the bar for entry into the teaching profession in one or more ways: raising minimum grade point averages (GPAs); requiring majors in content areas; instituting teacher tests; requiring master's degrees for permanent certification; raising standards for program registration; and requiring national accreditation of teacher education programs.

While raising standards for candidates and college-based programs, most states also opened alternative routes into teaching. Whether the alternative, graduate, and undergraduate programs attract similar "quality" candidates and provide equally prepared teachers is subject to debate. Additionally, concern about teacher quality has risen now that other professional career paths are fully open to women and people of color.

Teacher quality is currently assessed by such proxies as college entrance tests (SAT and ACT), college GPA, college major, status of the college attended, teacher tests, and state teacher certification status. In this chapter, we look at these quality indicators in relation to the demographic variables described in chapter 3. After describing the quality profile of teachers, we examine differences related to where teachers are prepared, where they teach, and how long they stay in the classroom. We then review research on the impact of two teacher characteristics—academic ability and achievement. In later chapters by Floden and Meniketti and also by Wilson and Youngs (this volume), the impact of other quality indicators (i.e., college majors, teacher tests, and certification) is discussed. This chapter ends with a discussion of a research agenda based on what is known and not known about indicators of teacher quality.

WHO IS TEACHING?

In recent times, interest in the quality of teachers has focused on intellectual competence in comparison to earlier interest in personal qualities and behavioral performance (Lanier & Little, 1986, p. 536). Until recently, the most frequently used measures of quality were academic ability as measured by SAT or ACT scores and academic achievement as measured by college GPA.

Academic Ability and Achievement

The belief in the relative intellectual inferiority of American teachers is not a new phenomenon (Conant, 1963; Flexner, 1930). It was reiterated in recent years by *A Nation at Risk: The Imperative for Educational Reform* (National Commission on Excellence in Education, 1983, p. 22), which stated that "not enough of the academically able students are being attracted to teaching . . . Too many teachers are being drawn from the bottom quarter of graduating high school and college students." The work of Vance and Schlechty (1982), Chapman and Hutcheson (1982), Kerr (1983), Sykes (1983), and Weaver (1983) supported the idea that those who choose teaching are not as academically able as those who choose other careers and that the most academically able are less likely to enter teaching and more likely to leave faster than their peers.

Since the mid-1980s, policymakers, politicians and government officials, leaders of the business and philanthropic communities, and educators at all levels have worked to raise standards for prospective teachers and upgrade teacher education programs. The Carnegie Task Force on Teaching, the Holmes Group (1986; now Holmes Partnership), and the National Commission on Teaching and America's Future (1996) all view professionalization of teaching as the key to improving public education.

Some critics scoff at these improvement efforts. They cite reports, such as *A Nation at Risk* (National Commission on Excellence in Education, 1983), and public dissatisfaction with the schools as evidence that "professional" educators are part of the problem and improvement efforts are not worth the effort. At the extreme are the "deregulators" who believe that the states should get out of the certification business. Theoretically, the argument goes, districts will hire the most qualified candidates. The market will determine whether teachers prepared in teacher education programs are more desirable than academically strong students and second-career people without formal preparation and certification.

Although deregulation represents an extreme position, pragmatic considerations have led most states to create alternatives that open teaching careers up to those who did not prepare by taking pedagogical courses at colleges and universities. Concerns about the quality of those attracted to traditional programs, coupled with predicted teacher shortages due to high teacher turnover and high levels of retirement, gave impetus to the alternate certification movement. The underlying hope is that the quantity and quality of the teaching force will be improved by such efforts.

Teacher educators have been actively engaged in reform efforts, advocating higher standards to enter and exit teacher education programs, improving teacher education programs, and now, in face of growing teacher shortages, working to create quality alternative programs to avoid the cyclical "emergency" backdoor into teaching that undermines efforts to professionalize teaching. Teacher educators and researchers also have challenged some of the reports of the low quality of teachers.

Earlier Research. One flaw researchers found in some earlier studies was the use of high school students who intend to teach as representative of teachers or teacher education students (Barger, Barger, & Rearden, 1988; Gitomer, Latham, & Ziomek, 1999; Hanuchek & Pace, 1995; Henke, Geis, Giambattista, & Knepper, 1996; Latham, Gitomer, & Ziomek, 1999; Olsen, 1985; Pigge, 1985). High school seniors who said they intend to teach had lower SAT and ACT scores than did college students who actually entered and graduated from teacher education programs. Through a process of self- and institutional selection, lower ability students exit from the prospective teaching pool at higher rates. Hence, conclusions about the ability profile of prospective teachers and teachers drawn from studies of high school students who intend to teach presented a misleading picture.

The reports of the early 1980s also spawned initial research efforts at institutional and, less frequently, at state levels to determine how teacher education students compared to other college students in academic ability and performance (American Association of Colleges of Teacher Education [AACTE], 1987; Barger, Barger, & Rearden, 1986; Barger et al., 1988; Fischer & Feldman, 1985; Guyton & Farokhi, 1987; Knight, Duke, & Palcic, 1988; Matczynski, Siler, McLaughlin, & Smith, 1988; Olsen, 1985; Securro, 1992). Academic ability was most often measured by SAT and ACT tests taken during senior year in high school. Academic performance was most frequently measured by college GPA, but sometimes high school GPA and rank were used. Early studies used college GPA, but later studies, sensitive to perception of "grade inflation" in education courses, looked at GPA exclusive of these courses, GPA in content courses, or GPA in lower and upper division courses separately.

These studies indicated that teacher education students had comparable or sometimes better ability and achievement than did other college students at the same institutions. Sometimes they pointed to lower test scores but at higher GPAs for teacher education students. Clark (1989) reconciled these differences by illustrating that many of these studies were conducted at institutions that attracted students with lower test scores than students at other institutions. Because these institutions enrolled teacher education students in large numbers, these students had average or better than average GPAs compared to other students at their institution. Others have noted that few studies controlled for gender. Teacher education students are predominantly female, and females tend to have lower SAT and ACT scores and higher GPAs than do males (AACTE, 1992; Gitomer et al., 1999). Some of the differences between teacher education students and other college students might be explained by the gender imbalance among teacher education students. In studies that did not examine grades in noneducation courses, some differences might have been related to varying grading norms in different subjects.

More Recent Studies.   Studies since the late 1980s have used increasingly sophisticated distinctions and relationships to compare academic ability and achievement of teacher education students. The dismal picture of lower academic ability and achievement of prospective teachers appears modified in the recent research literature, if not in public perception, by better research and policies. Higher minimum GPAs required for entering and graduating from teacher education programs and the more frequent use of teacher testing to screen candidates at entry into teacher education and for licensure have produced a pool of candidates with better credentials.

We look first at three institutional studies that offer some distinctions not found in more comprehensive, national studies. Studying the approximately 10,000 graduates of Eastern Illinois University from 1982 to 1986, Barger et al. (1988) compared ACT scores, high school rank, and college GPA (cumulative, upper division, and adjusted upper division without education courses) for teacher graduates versus nonteacher graduates. The teacher graduates—both those who majored in education and those who pursued a certification option in a noneducation major—scored significantly lower on ACT tests taken in high school than did nonteacher graduates, but there was no difference in high school class rank, which was the best predictor of college GPA. For all three types of college GPAs, teacher graduates were significantly superior to nonteacher graduates. The researchers also compared students in majors that offered certification options. Teacher graduates in these content majors were significantly superior on all three GPAs compared to their peers who majored in the same content. Part of the reason may be that a higher GPA was required for those graduating with certification (2.25) than for those graduating with a "straight" major (2.00).

Exploring whether higher admissions standards altered the profiles of entering teacher candidates, Freeman, Martin, Brousseau, and West (1989) looked at the differences in students who met and those who fell short of the new standards at Michigan State University. To generate comparison groups, they took the 1987 GPA cutoff scores for juniors entering the college of education and applied them to the 1985 cohort. Only 47 of the 157 students in the 1985 cohort would have been admitted under the GPA cutoff in effect 2 years later. The university admitted 129 students in 1987 who met that new GPA requirement.

Freeman et al. (1989) found that teacher candidates who met the new GPA standards scored higher on most, but not all, measures of achievement. A higher proportion of 1985 "denials" said that a significant reason for wanting to become a teacher was their lack of success in courses that would have prepared them for their first choice career. Raising the minimum GPA for entry into teacher education programs made these programs less of a dumping ground for low achievers. Freeman et al. found the same level of commitment to teaching and educational beliefs among both the 1985 and the 1987 groups.

Exploring the perception that teacher education programs were lowering admissions standards for minority students to address the growing shortage of minority teachers, AACTE (1992) examined a random sample of transcripts of teacher education students ($n = 712$) from member institutions in the mid-1980s. Although there were differences in admissions requirements across institutions, there were no differences in admissions criteria within institutions based on race.

On measures of quality, the study (AACTE, 1992) found that teacher education students had higher than national average SAT scores. Whites had significantly higher SAT scores (1012) than Blacks did (724). Females had significantly higher high school GPAs (3.14) than males did (2.89). Whites had the highest high school GPAs,

Hispanics were in the middle, and Blacks had the lowest. Females had significantly higher college GPAs than did males in all years, but the gap between Black and White GPAs narrowed as students moved through the college years, which might be related to differential attrition. By 1989, females (74%) were more likely to have completed the teacher education program than were males (60%). Hispanics (75%) and Whites (72%) were more likely to have completed the program than were Blacks (66%).

High school GPA was the best predictor of college GPA, performance in teacher education courses, and completion of the teacher education program. There was a significant, but weak, relationship between SAT scores and performance in teacher education courses, but not completion of teacher education programs. Using a series of stepwise multiple regression analyses, successful completion of teacher education programs was predicted by a SAT-verbal score of 490 for Whites and 354 for Blacks. Because entry into teacher education programs was heavily dependent on SAT scores and sophomore GPA, the AACTE (1992) concluded: "a bottleneck exists at the front end of the pipeline that tends to choke off minorities who would otherwise perform well in college" (p. 39). If high school GPA were found to be a better predictor of successful completion in other studies, too, they suggested that it be considered along with test scores.

National Data Sets. The next five studies used national longitudinal data to look at how the teacher education pipeline affects the academic profile of prospective teachers.

In a book-length study, Murnane, Singer, Willett, Kemple, and Olsen (1991) explored the question of "who will teach" by looking at career patterns of 50,000 college graduates from 1967 to 1980. One of their concerns was the declining number of high-ability college graduates who entered teaching within 5 years of graduation during this period, which started with high demand for teachers and ended with low demand. They reported that approximately 40% of college graduates with IQs of 100 and those with IQs of 130 became teachers in 1967. By 1980, approximately 5% of those with IQs of 130 became teachers as did approximately 20% of graduates with IQs of 100 (p. 35). They suggested, given the deteriorating job market for teachers at the time, it is reasonable that those with higher IQs would have more opportunities to seek other alternatives, particularly in the professional fields requiring good scores on graduate entrance examinations.

Using the High School and Beyond (HSB) studies, Hanushek and Pace (1995) followed 4,500 high school seniors in 1980 who aspired to be teachers and were in postsecondary institutions in the spring of 1982. They tracked those in teacher education programs in 1982 and 1984, those who graduated prepared to teach by 1986, and those who were teaching in 1986. The admittedly "rough" measure of "ability" was standardized test scores in reading, mathematics, and vocabulary given during senior year in high school.

This longitudinal analysis confirmed that drawing conclusions about the quality of prospective or new teachers from the intentions of high school seniors was misleading. Only 40 percent of the high school seniors who aspired to teach scored in the top half. But only 64 of the 352 original aspirants were teaching as of 1986, while an additional 159 "late aspirants" were teaching as of 1986. Not only were the late aspirants more likely to end up teaching, more (63 percent) were in the top half of the high school ability distribution compared to 52% of the original aspirants who were teaching. Teacher education students and new teachers looked very much like the initial college-going population in terms of SAT/ACT scores. While not the "dregs," as some have suggested (p. 105), they were not as well represented as other college *graduates* in the HSB sample in the top quartile or half of the high school ability distribution.

There were some gender and race and ethnicity differences. At graduation, males who prepared to teach were less likely to be in the top half than were females, but more likely to come from the top quartile. Among those teaching in 1986, for Whites, 54% of the original aspirants and 72% of the late aspirants were in the top half of the ability distribution. Among Hispanic teachers, only 33% of the original aspirants and 21.5% of the late aspirants were in the top half of the ability distribution, but they also became more selective from 1980 to 1986. The same selectivity pattern was not seen for Blacks. Although 17% of the original 66 aspirants were in the top half, none of the 5 teaching in l986 and only 3.5% of the 25 late aspirants were in the top half.

Using Bachelor's and Beyond Survey (BBS) data for 1992 to 1993 college graduates, Henke et al. (1996) confirmed other studies indicating that college students interested in teaching, teacher education students, teachers, and those who remain in teaching had somewhat lower scores on college entry tests, but higher high school and college GPAs. Only 20% of those in the teacher education pipeline were in the top quartile on SAT and ACT tests. Those who majored in liberal arts rather than in education later taught in private schools and did not expect to remain in teaching, were more likely to be in the top quartile. Secondary teachers scored in the top quartile at the same rate as did nonteachers. Using the same data base of l992 to 1993 college graduates, Wirt and Livingston (2002) reported that by 1997, 13% of the top quartile had prepared to teach or taught compared to 20% of the bottom quartile.

Using another HBS cohort, Vegas, Murnane, and Willett (2001) followed 10,584 high school sophomores in 1980 through high school graduation (9,125), college entry (5,924), college graduation (3,037), and entry into teaching (434). Academic skills were measured by a composite score from tests in science, math, reading, vocabulary, and writing in sophomore year of high school. Asian Americans had the highest proportion of high school graduates, college entrants, and college graduates, followed by Whites for high school graduation, Blacks for entry into college, and Whites for college graduation. Tenth-grade academic skills accounted for most of the variation by race and ethnicity in high school graduation, college entry, and college graduation.

Higher proportions of Black, Hispanic, and Native Americans entered teaching compared to Whites and especially compared to Asian Americans. For female college graduates who prepared to teach, those with stronger academic skills were less likely to go into teaching than other fields. There was no discernible difference in academic ability between Whites and Blacks who entered teaching and those who did not, but there was a considerable difference for Hispanic females. Black and White males with high test scores were slightly more likely to teach than those with low test scores.

Since Blacks, Hispanics, and Native-American college graduates entered teaching in proportionately high numbers, Vegas et al. (2001) concluded that the key to increasing the representation of these groups in teaching is increasing the number of students of color who graduate from high school, enroll in college and graduate from college.

Researchers at Educational Testing Service (ETS) and ACT also looked at the academic and demographic profile of those in the teacher education pipeline (Gitomer, et al., 1999; Latham et al., 1999). They explored the relationship between SAT/ACT scores and PRAXIS II scores for 272,000 candidates in 1995 to 1997. Because PRAXIS II tests content and pedagogical knowledge in specific subject areas and is most often used by states to grant initial teaching licenses, it is seen as a proxy for those entering teaching.

As in previous studies, average SAT and ACT scores rose at each successive point in the teacher education pipeline. Those with passing scores on PRAXIS II had comparable or slightly higher SAT scores (1029) than the national average (1016). However, those who passed PRAXIS II had a lower SAT score than the average college graduate (1085; Gitomer et al., 1999, p. 19). Those seeking licensure in elementary, special education, and physical education had substantially lower SAT and ACT scores than those seeking licensure in content areas. With the exception of art and music, those seeking licensure in content areas had comparable or higher scores than other college graduates. Their skills "are substantially higher than many previous researchers have suggested," Latham et al. (1999, p. 5) concluded. The policy implications, they suggested, for elementary teachers should "be one of improving quality, to the extent that SAT and ACT scores are an appropriate measure of quality. For content specialists, the issue appears to be one of increasing quantity" (Gitomer et al., p. 38).

HOW ARE THEY PREPARED?

Concerns about teacher quality also raise questions about the quality of programs that prepare candidates to teach. The quality profile related to preparation includes individual and institutional indicators: (a) academic ability and achievement of students in various types of institutions and programs, (b) status of undergraduate college, (c) accreditation, (d) college major, (e) teacher test performance, and (f) certification status.

Although requiring a master's degree is a frequent reform recommendation, we have not included possession of a master's degree as a quality indicator here. In part, this reflects the focus of this volume on preservice teacher education. It is still more commonly a degree attained in-service, as confirmed by the National Center for Education Statistics (NCES) report that only 16% of teachers with fewer than 3 years' experience held a master's degree (Lewis, Parsad, Carey, Bartfai, & Farris, 1999). Additionally, although the proportion of master's degrees has doubled in the last 4 decades (NEA, 2003), the variation in type and content of these master's degrees makes using them as a quality indicator problematic.

Academic Ability and Achievement

The highest SAT scores were found among prospective teachers at large private universities, followed by small private universities and small public universities (Wenglinsky, 2000). The lowest scores were at small public colleges and small private colleges, with large public universities in the middle. University status appeared more important in attracting students with high SAT scores than either size or public and private control. GPAs present some unexplained variation. White teacher education students had higher GPAs at private liberal arts colleges, whereas Blacks had higher GPAs at research universities, and Hispanics had higher GPAs at doctoral institutions (AACTE, 1992).

Program Structure.   Few studies have compared quality, as measured by GPA and SAT scores, of traditional 4-year-program and extended-program graduates. Generally, graduate study is viewed as more selective and rigorous (Funkhouser, 1988). Research confirms that the GPA cutoff scores for admission are generally higher in postbaccalaureate teacher education programs (Feistritzer, 1999). Some integrated programs even have separate admissions with higher standards for their graduate section (Andrew, 1990). It is no surprise, then, that participants in extended programs tend to be superior students (Andrew, 1990; Coley & Thorpe, 1989). Armstrong, Burlbaw, and Batten (1991) questioned whether this is a useful finding, given that differing entry requirements cloud the issue of whether any other factor, unique to extended programs, attracted superior students. Andrew responded that admissions standards were set higher with the goal of attracting superior students and that achieving that was a mark of success.

Two theoretical concerns have been raised about the impact of extended programs on quality. The first, raised by Howey and Zimpher (1986), suggested that undergraduate teacher education drew students from a wider pool of students and, therefore, had access to a larger group of academically able students. Requiring graduate study to enter teaching might dissuade some high-quality students from entering the field. The second issue was that if extended programs became the norm, weaker institutions would develop them, lowering admissions standards and diluting the quality of master's level education (Knapp, McNergney, Herbert, & York, 1990). No research has demonstrated that either of these possibilities has actually occurred.

Alternative Programs.   Although many alternative programs have the explicit goal of attracting more academically able students, the research regarding differences in the quality of students is inconclusive (Wilson, Floden, & Ferrini-Mundy, 2001, 2002). Several studies found no difference between groups of alternately and traditionally prepared teachers (Hawk & Schmidt, 1989; Jelmberg, 1996). Others reported higher GPAs (Lutz & Hutton, 1989), lower GPAs (Natriello & Zumwalt, 1993), and higher scores on certification tests (Natriello & Zumwalt; Stafford & Barrow, 1994) for alternative candidates. Although not a direct measure of alternative program candidates, the NCES found that among those who taught without formal preparation, 35% came from the top quartile in SAT scores compared to only 14% among teacher education graduates (Wirt et al., 2001). In a review of 21 studies of alternative programs, however, Zeichner and Schulte (2001) found only 4 that compared academic quality of alternately and traditionally prepared teachers. No evidence was found of higher GPAs among alternative candidates.

There are several explanations for these inconclusive findings. First, they represent a very small number of studies, mostly of one program. Additionally, much of the research reports on quality as indicated by evaluations of performance rather than by grades or test scores (see Zeichner and Conklin, this volume). More importantly, many of those that reported on GPAs and test scores did so because they had higher standards for admission than traditional programs. By design, that produced participants with superior academic qualifications. Two studies, however, reported that the average GPA of their participants exceeded the requirement, demonstrating that better students were entering even when less able students could do so (Lutz & Hutton, 1989; Wale & Irons, 1988). No study compared GPAs and SAT scores of alternatively and traditionally prepared students.

Status of Undergraduate College

Prospective teachers are more likely to have received degrees from public, non-doctorate-granting institutions. Some of these master's level universities are the direct descendants of state normal schools. These schools have somewhat lower admissions standards than do doctorate-granting schools and are considered less rigorous. In a study of public school teachers, Ballou (1996) found that they were more likely to have attended colleges and universities ranked as average or below average in selectivity. Only 3% of graduates of selective institutions were teachers compared to 10% of graduates from below-average schools.

Some alternative programs, such as Teach for America, mainly recruit from highly selective colleges. Zeichner and Schulte (2001) do not consider them alternative programs because their aim is to recruit prospective teachers, not to prepare them.

Accreditation

Another indicator of quality may be whether prospective teachers prepared at a college or university accredited by the National Council for Accreditation of Teacher Education (NCATE). In May 2004, there were 575 colleges and universities accredited, and more than 100 others were candidates for accreditation. There are no data comparing the college entry test profile of NCATE versus the non-NCATE institutions. ETS (Gitomer et al., 1999) examined 270,000 candidates who had taken PRAXIS II content tests between 1995 and 1997, and who had earlier taken the SAT or ACT tests. Although 91% of NCATE institution graduates passed PRAXIS II, only 84% of those graduating from non-NCATE institutions passed. Students with comparable college entry scores were more likely to pass the test if they graduated from NCATE institutions. Ballou and Podgursky (2000) questioned the significance of this finding because the study did not report proportions of students not enrolled in teacher preparation programs included in both groups, nor took into account differences in state pass rates and content areas on PRAXIS II exams. A reanalysis by ETS indicated that different state pass rates did not explain the disparity (Darling-Hammond, 2002).

Darling-Hammond (2000) found that more teachers were fully certified in states with higher percentages of NCATE institutions.

College Major

Getting teachers to major in a content area rather than in education has been a part of the teacher education reform movement for the past 20 years. In 1998, Secretary of Education Riley recommended the elimination of the education degree. Some states have done away with the bachelor's in education (Demetrulias, Chiodo, & Dickman, 1990). Thirty-three states now require a content area degree for teachers (U.S. Department of Education, 2003). Opposition to the undergraduate major in education is such that eight states require a noneducation degree regardless of whether it is in the main teaching field (Meyer, Orlofsky, Skinner, & Spicer, 2002).

The 1992 to 1993 BBS data indicated that one third of 142,000 undergraduates who student-taught or became certified were not education majors (Henke et al., 1996). Of those who wound up as classroom teachers, whether or not prepared, 45% did not major in education (Wirt et al., 2001). In 1998, almost two in five public school teachers held a subject matter degree (Lewis et al., 1999). Of noneducation majors, the most common fields among current teachers were in the humanities. Math or science was the second most common among secondary teachers, and the social sciences were second among elementary teachers (Henke, Choy, Chen, Geis, & Alt, 1997). Still, effect of this recent shift is not being felt yet by a majority of students. In 1999, 41% of eighth-graders were taught math by a teacher with a major in mathematics, as opposed to

54% by a teacher with an education degree of whom 37% had a background in math education (Wirt et al., 2001).

The move toward academic degrees is not uniform. Those prepared to teach in secondary schools were far more likely to have academic majors than those prepared for elementary teaching (Feistritzer, 1999; Henke, Choy, Chen, et al., 1997). A greater disparity was found between those who prepared to teach at the undergraduate level and those whose initial work began later. According to Feistritzer, more than 75% of elementary candidates in postbaccalaureate programs had noneducation undergraduate majors compared to fewer than 30% of undergraduates. Similarly, at the secondary level, almost 80% of postbaccalaureate students and fewer than 50% of undergraduates held noneducation degrees. (However, "noneducation" does not necessarily mean an arts and sciences degree.)

Assessing the move toward noneducation degrees is not easy because earlier research on majors often was constructed to determine the extent of out-of-field teaching (Bobbitt, 1989; Ingersoll, 1996; NCES, 1996). Many studies looked at those who have a major or minor in their primary teaching assignment and those who do not. For most, however, the definition of major or minor includes both a content degree (e.g., math) and a subject area education degree (e.g., math education). The best estimate of impact is the proportion of content degrees among teachers with more or less teaching experience. Framed this way, the reforms seem to be making an impact. Half of teachers with 3 years or fewer experience hold a content degree compared to one third of those with 10 to 19 years' experience (Lewis et al., 1999). This is up from 44% of new teachers with content degrees in 1994 and 38% in 1987 (Henke, Choy, Chen, et al., 1997). Perhaps, reflecting previous shortage eras, teachers with 20 or more years experience were more likely that those with 10 to 19 years to have a content major.

By design, alternately prepared teachers usually had noneducation majors. However, Shen (1998b) reported that although proportionately more alternative teachers entered math or science teaching, there were not significantly more math or science majors among them. Natriello and Zumwalt (1993) found that alternative teachers in English and, especially, in math in New Jersey in 1987 were less likely to major in their respective subject areas than teachers prepared in traditional programs that required content majors. Other studies have questioned the assumption that an academic major is enough on its own to prepare teachers to teach the subject well (Gomez & Stoddart, 1991; McDiarmid & Wilson, 1991). McDiarmid and Wilson, analyzing data from math teachers in two alternative programs, found that many had weak comprehension of math concepts and were unable to represent them to students.

Teacher Tests

With teacher testing mandatory in many states, scores on teacher tests now are widely used as another indicator of quality (NCES, 1997b). In a 1998 to 1999 survey, the National Research Council found that 19 states required a basic skills test and a subject matter test for admission to teacher education programs. For licensing, 25 states used a subject matter test, 26 tested pedagogical knowledge, 18 tested basic skills, and 7 tested subject-specific pedagogical knowledge (Mitchell, Robinson, Plake, & Knowles, 2001). These totals do not include additional tests required by specific teacher education programs for entry or exit. In addition, some states have begun in-service testing as a condition of continued employment (Hirsch, Kopich, & Knapp, 1998). Questions have been raised about the objectivity of the tests, the low cutoff scores, their relationship to effective teaching, and the effect on the supply of teachers. This review focuses on the impact of teacher testing on demographics, particularly on the race and ethnicity profile.

Many studies have demonstrated a consistent test score gap on entrance and exit tests between candidates from different racial and ethnic groups (Garibaldi, 1991; Gitomer et al., 1999; Goertz & Pitcher, 1985; Latham et al., 1999; Smith, 1987; Smith, Miller, & Joy, 1988; Texas Education Agency [TEA], 1994). The most extensive research has been conducted by ETS, the developer of PRAXIS I and PRAXIS II tests used in 34 states for entrance, licensure or both. ETS has studied the relationship between measures of teacher quality (SAT and ACT scores and self-reported GPA), demographic characteristics, and success on the teacher tests.

As others have found (Guyton & Farohki, 1987), there is a consistent relationship between passage rates on teacher tests and college GPA. Students in the top quartile of GPAs (3.5 or above) almost always pass the PRAXIS tests. Gitomer et al. (1999) noted, however, that two thirds of the "C" students also passed the tests. Although passing rates of males and females on PRAXIS I and II were similar, there were differences by race and ethnicity. By using the average state passing rate on the basic skills PRAXIS I test, they found that 82% of Whites passed, whereas only 46% of African Americans passed, with Asian (76%) and Hispanic (69%) pass rates falling in between. Because PRAXIS I is an entrance exam, the effect is to limit the diversity of teacher education students. On the PRAXIS II test, there was less of a gap between African-American pass rates (69%) and Whites' pass rates (91%), but more of a gap between Hispanics (59%) and Whites. Because PRAXIS II is used as a licensure requirement, it further limits the diversity of those entering teaching. As the authors noted, however, the pool of test takers is already disproportionately White.

Gitomer et al. (1999) described how lowering the PRAXIS I passing score to the lowest state passing score would decrease the racial and ethnic gap but would lower the average SAT and ACT scores. Raising the score to the highest state passing score in 1997 would increase the racial and ethnic gap but boost average verbal and math SAT scores by 40 points each. They concluded that "...though testing with higher standards holds great promise for ensuring that teachers are academically able, if not used judiciously such testing can also exacerbate already daunting problems with the supply and diversity of potential teachers" (Gitomer et al., p. 38).

Similar to the ETS findings, state studies have demonstrated a link between test mandates and a decline in minority teachers. Most of this work was done in the Southeast where teacher testing got an early foothold (Smith, 1987) and there are large numbers of minority teachers. Concerned about the economic impact of substandard educational systems, Southern boards of education instituted exams for K–12 and entering teachers to improve accountability. Because a large proportion of African-American teachers prepared in the Southeast, these policy changes affected the diversity of the nation's teaching force (AACTE, 1992).

Garibaldi (1991) looked at teacher education graduates from the 21 Louisiana schools, colleges, and departments of education from 1973 to 1986. In 1978, the state required that teacher candidates pass the National Teacher Exam (NTE) to be certified. Garibaldi found a significant decline in the number of African-American education majors who were certifiable after completing a professional education program. Only 3% of education majors from historically Black colleges and universities were certified in 1978 and 1979; that number rose to 6% in 1982. Garibaldi attributed the decline to the fewer than 20% passing rate of African Americans on the NTE. Similar results were found by Murnane and Schwinden (1989) in North Carolina. From 1975 to 1985, they found that a decline in African Americans' entering teaching appeared to be linked to the enforcement of an NTE requirement.

Other studies have looked at the role tests earlier in the career path may play in limiting the presence of minority students in the teacher education applicant pool. Smith et al. (1988) traced the impact of tests in Florida from 1976 to 1986. They found that the six required tests drastically limited access to the next step. Thirty-eight percent of African-American students did not graduate from high school with a standard diploma because they failed 10th-grade competency tests. Only 600 met the SAT cutoff to enter the state university system. Fifty percent of African-American high school graduates went instead to community college. About 1,200 passed the "rising junior" test for university sophomores and transfer students. Approximately 900 met the SAT cutoff used for admission to teacher education programs, but not all were interested. Of those who entered teacher education, only 37% passed the Florida Teacher Competency Exam to obtain provisional certification.

The Texas Education Agency (TEA, 1994) did a similar study of the impact of a basic skills entrance test and a teacher certification exam. Following a cohort of seventh-graders from 1982 to 1983 through college and their application for teacher certification, the agency found college entrance was the biggest hurdle for minority students. Only 37% of minorities entered college compared to 60% of Whites. Again, only a small proportion of those who entered were interested in education as a career. The two exams, however, had a disparate impact on the races. In 1988 to 1989, only 76% of Latinos and 66% of African Americans passed the basic skills test to enter teacher education. Three years later, 85% of Latinos and fewer than 75% of African Americans passed the exam for certification compared to 95% of Whites. As a result, only 3% of those newly eligible to teach in 1993 were Black and 14% were Hispanic.

Researchers debate the effects of race and class in explaining the disparity in test scores. Smith et al. (1988), even after accounting for father's education and family income, found African Americans' scores were still significantly lower than Whites'. Whether these measures adequately measured the low socioeconomic-status (SES) background of many minority students is debatable.

Institutional Types.   Although federal and state data indicate wide variation in mean teacher test scores by institution, there is one large-scale study of the role different teacher education programs and institutions play in teacher test scores. Wenglinsky (2000) looked at 40,000 prospective teachers who had taken the PRAXIS II exam for licensure. Scores were examined in light of the characteristics of the students, the teacher education programs, and the institutions in which they were offered. The initial finding was that students attending large private universities had the highest scores on the PRAXIS II exam. The students at these institutions also had the highest SAT scores and PRAXIS I scores used for admission to teacher education programs; their parents also had the highest education levels. The PRAXIS II results may say more about the entry characteristics of the students than about the value added by the institution. Wenglinsky attempted to isolate school characteristics from student characteristics, using a multilevel structural equation model. He found that student background had the strongest effect on PRAXIS II scores, with SES the most important, followed by prior test scores. Some school characteristics, however, were related, the most important being the status of university, as judged by the proportion of postbaccalaureate students. The second was private rather than public control. Size was not significantly related to PRAXIS scores. He noted that inequitable access to private universities resulted in disadvantaged students not having the opportunity to attend institutions with the potential to have a positive impact on teacher test scores.

Alternative Programs. Research comparing alternately and traditionally prepared teachers' performance on teacher tests is inconclusive. In some studies, the alternative candidates performed better than their counterparts (Cornett, 1992; Natriello & Zumwalt, 1993). Cornett reported that TEA found that alternately prepared teachers in Texas passed the tests at higher rates and that Blacks and Hispanics in the alternative program did much better than minorities who were graduates of traditional teacher education. Hawk and Schmidt (1989), however, found no difference in NTE scores between traditionally and alternatively prepared candidates in North Carolina. In a study of test scores of students conditionally given scholarships for Massachusetts' alternative program, Fowler (2002) found that although their pass rates on the literacy tests were similar to all first time test takers, fewer passed the content tests (44% vs. 66%).

The first Title II report noted that 70% of the 21 reporting states indicate equal or higher pass rates for alternative teachers than for those traditionally prepared (U.S. Department of Education, 2002). In the second year, 65% of the 23 reporting states reported equal or higher pass rates for alternative teachers (U.S. Department of Education, 2003). However, variability was reported on subtests over the 2 years by 10 to 17 states reporting data. In the first year, 80% of states reported equal or high alternative teacher pass rates on basic skills tests, but only 58% in the second year. Conversely, only 45% reported equal or better alternative scores on the professional knowledge tests the first year, whereas the number jumped to 70% the second year. On the academic content tests, 79% of the states reported higher or equal scores for alternative teachers the first year; and 88%, the second year. Although these numbers have been used to show that alternative programs raise teacher quality, the overall pass rates in 2002 were very high for both groups: 93% for the traditionally prepared and 94% for the alternative candidates. Almost everyone passed the basic skills test (98% vs. 99%) as well as the test of professional knowledge (95% for both) and academic content (95% vs. 96%). The problems of data collection and interpretation were described in Appendix C of the Secretary's annual report (U.S. Department of Education, 2003).

Some evidence that teacher education has a value-added impact on teacher test scores is found in an ETS study that examined the scores of all students who took the PRAXIS II exam between 1994 and 1997 (Gitomer et al., 1999). The authors found that 86% had come through traditional teacher education programs and two thirds were still enrolled when they took the exam. Those candidates currently enrolled in a teacher education program had the highest passing rate; those never enrolled in a teacher education program had the lowest rate. This was true, even though the latter group (which may or may not have been in an alternative program) had equal or higher SAT scores. This finding suggests that teacher education provides knowledge beyond the general knowledge and skills necessary to score well on a college entrance test such as the SAT.

Certification Status

As the struggle between professionalization and deregulation takes center stage and in light of federal legislation requiring all classrooms to be staffed by "qualified" teachers, certification status is increasingly debated as an indicator of quality. A major challenge in using it as a quality indicator is that each state has different certification requirements and multiple certificates. Initial certification requirements indicate what a particular state defines as the minimum standards for its "safe-to-practice" criterion. Many states have additional requirements for a permanent certificate, and some now require continuing professional education. Forty-six states also have some form of approved alternative certification program. These various state requirements confound attempts to interpret certification status as a quality indicator for teachers and teacher education programs. What one can say is that being "certified" is an indicator of having met the minimum criteria set by a particular state. Ninety-four percent of teachers held full certification in 2000 to 2001 and 2001 to 2002 (U.S. Department of Education, 2003).

In a 1998, the NCES survey of 3,560 public school teachers from the 50 states and the District of Columbia, 93% of elementary teachers held regular or advanced certification, 3% held provisional certification, 2% held probationary certification, and 1% each held emergency or temporary certification (Lewis et al., 1999). None were uncertified. Teachers of math, science, foreign languages, social studies, and English held standard certification at a slightly lower rate of 92%, with 4% holding provisional certification. Fewer than 0.5% reported teaching with no certification at all in the field in which they taught the most classes. Schools and Staffing Survey (SASS) data from 1993 to 1994 indicated slightly lower rates of certification. That earlier study found 91% of public school teachers had an advanced, regular, standard, or alternative certification; 5% had a probationary, provisional, or temporary certification; 0.5% held an emergency certificate; 3.6% were uncertified (Henke, Choy, Geis, & Broughman, 1997).

Although these results indicate possible improvement over the 5 years between studies, they mask some problems and leave questions unanswered. Only full-time teachers were included. Boe and Barkanic (2000) have linked part-time teaching status to lower rates of certification. The Lewis et al. (1999) study focused on five subject areas, ignoring lower certification rates in special education and bilingual education. Also, these studies indicated how many teachers were certified, not how many teachers were certified in the subject they taught. Last, as an overall assessment of teachers' qualifications, these certification findings miss important distinctions among schools and regions. Because every state sets its own standards for certification, merely knowing that a teacher is certified tells us little about his or her preparation (Darling-Hammond, 2000; Goldhaber & Brewer, 2000). It is not clear from the designation "standard certification" how much, if any, subject matter preparation, pedagogical study, or field work is required, whether a master's degree or major or minor is necessary, and whether a certification test is mandated. Additionally, alternative, provisional, and emergency have different meanings in different states. For example Henke, Choy, Chen et al. (1997) included those with alternative certification as being certified, distinguishing them from those with provisional, probationary, emergency, or no certification. Darling-Hammond (2000a) distinguished those with regular or advanced certification from those with substandard certification including provisional, temporary, emergency, or alternative.

The most problematic debate about certification levels relates to the definition of teachers' certification areas. Most large-scale studies (Henke, Choy, Chen, et al., 1997; Lewis et al., 1999) considered a teacher certified if he or she holds certification in the area in which he or she taught the most classes. Other researchers (Bobbitt & McMillen, 1994; Ingersoll, 1996, 1999) worried that this misses the extent of out-of-field teaching where students were taught by teachers without certification in the courses they teach. For example, Bobbitt and McMillen found that although nationally

86% of math teachers were certified, in 1991 only 67% of all teachers who taught at least one math class were certified. Henke, Choy, Chen et al. found that certification rates dropped sharply when looking at the area in which a teacher spends the second greatest amount of time: Only 51% of all teachers had certification in their second area of teaching compared to 87% in their primary field. For Ingersoll, the issue about teacher quality and certification has less to do with a shortage of prepared teachers than with the utilization of teachers. Many are certified to teach, but not to teach all the courses they are assigned by their principals.

Academic Ability and Achievement

Most studies focus on certification per se as an indicator of quality. Grey et al. (1993) found that "newly qualified teachers" (NQT) in 1991 had higher GPAs than did other bachelor's degree holders. About 50% of NQT had GPAs of 3.25 or above compared to 40% of others. However, the relation of GPA to certification is confounded because NQT included those who had certification, were eligible for certification, or who had taught since graduation whether or not certified.

WHERE DO THEY TEACH?

Although indicators of quality are looked at individually in this section, they are often related. As Lankford, Loeb, and Wykoff (2002, p. 42) stated, "Schools that have low-quality teachers as measured by one attribute are more likely to have low-quality teachers based on other measures. For example, schools with high proportions of teachers who failed exams are more likely to have teachers from less competitive colleges." The variables reviewed as indicators of quality in relation to teacher placement include (a) academic ability and achievement, (b) status of undergraduate college, (c) teacher test scores, (d) certification, (e) "out-of-field" teaching, and (f) experience.

Academic Ability and Achievement

Much of the research regarding teachers' SAT and ACT scores and GPAs focuses on the disparity between public and private school teachers. According to Wirt et al. (2001), public school teachers were nearly twice as likely to be from the bottom quartile in SAT scores than from the top quartile. In comparison, 33% of private school teachers were from the top quartile and 18% were from the bottom quartile. Henke and others (Henke et al., 1996) found that teachers with higher SAT and ACT scores were more likely to teach in private than in public schools. They found no relationship between GPA and where teachers taught.

Secondary teachers are more likely to have higher SAT scores than are other teachers (Gitomer et al., 1999; Henke et al., 1996). They scored in the top quartile at the same rate as other professions. Henke et al. (2000) found that those from the bottom quartile who became teachers taught at the elementary level; teachers from the top quartile were more evenly split between the levels. At the secondary level, those in the top quartile were nearly twice as likely to teach science or math and four times as likely to teach English. Those from the bottom quartile were more likely to teach business, vocational education, fine arts, social sciences and special education. There was less difference related to GPAs, than SAT scores. However, the higher the GPA above 2.75, the lower proportion of teachers were teaching at the elementary level (Henke et al., 2000).

Henke et al. (2000) found some relationship between academic quality and high-minority schools. Twice as many teachers with GPAs below 2.75 were teaching in high-minority schools. Of the teachers who had only taught in high-poverty schools, 31% of teachers from this cohort (high school class of 1992) scored in the bottom quartile of the SAT. Only 10% were from the top quartile (Mayer, Mullens, & Moore, 2000).

Status of Undergraduate College

Ballou (1996) found that teachers who attended colleges listed as more competitive by Barron's were more likely to teach in private schools. In a comprehensive state study, Lankford et al. (2002) found that New York students in urban schools were more likely than were suburban students to have teachers with BAs from less competitive schools. They found that attendance at one of the colleges ranked as competitive or less was highly correlated with at least one failure on a teacher exam and with lack of certification. Statewide, Whites were half as likely as non-Whites to be taught by a teacher from a less competitive school, but there was no difference based on SES. Finally, in schools where 20% or more of students scored in the lowest category on the fourth-grade language arts exam, 26% of the teachers attended less competitive undergraduate schools, whereas only 6% attended most competitive schools.

Teacher Tests

Lankford et al. (2002) also looked at New York teachers' performance on the General Knowledge or Liberal Arts portions of the NTE. Non-White students were three times as likely as White students to have a teacher who had failed a portion of the exam at least once. Twenty-eight percent of low-income students were taught by teachers who had failed once compared to 20% of other students. The biggest difference was in schools serving lower achieving students. In schools where more than one in five students had scored at the lowest level on the fourth-grade language arts exam, 35% of the teachers failed a portion of the NTE at least once compared with 9% in schools where no children scored on the lowest level.

Although an inequitable distribution of teachers with high teacher test scores may seem predictable given varied school district wealth, Strauss, Bowes, Marks, and Plesko (2000), in a comprehensive review of teacher hiring in Pennsylvania in 1997, found that teacher test scores did not weigh heavily in the hiring process. Most districts hired graduates from local institutions. Forty percent of teachers taught in the same district where they attended high school. This "insularity" was positively related to local unemployment rates and inversely to student achievement and to the educational level of adults in the district.

Certification

The single demographic factor most correlated with certification is teaching experience (Boe & Barkanic, 2000; Lewis et al., 1999). New teachers are the largest source of underqualified teachers, especially in public schools. In 1998, Lewis et al. found that approximately 65% of teachers with experience of 3 or fewer years had regular or standard certification. These numbers have dropped since 1993 to 1994 (Henke, Choy, Chen, et al., 1997), but the meaning is unclear. It may be related to changing laws in many states that defer regular certification until a teacher has taught for a few years (Lewis et al.). Teachers with 3 or fewer years' experience have proportionately more provisional or probationary certificates. A growing percentage of newer teachers (12%) hold emergency certificates, which usually signifies a serious gap in preparation. That compared to 1% of teachers with 10 or more years' experience.

These findings are supported by a study of more than 7,000 new teachers hired by New York City in 2001 (Goodnough, 2002). Only 27% had traditional certification and 23% had alternative certification (meaning that they had taught in other countries or were "fast-track" students who had taken a summer course, passed state exams, and were concurrently enrolled in master's programs). Fifty percent of those hired in 2001 had no certification, suggesting that they either had failed or not taken exams or lacked required course work. Only 29% of Hispanics were certified compared with 49% of Blacks and 56% of Whites. The vast majority of certified Blacks were teachers from other countries or those who had participated in the city's alternative teaching fellows program.

Broughman and Rollefson (2000), looking at the 1993 to 1994 SASS data, found that 84% of newly hired public school teachers held some type of certification, but there were notable differences among them. Delayed entrants had the lowest proportion of certified teachers (75%) compared to 82% of newly prepared teachers and 90% of transfers. Using the same data set, Boe and Barkanic (2000) noted that a quarter of all non-fully-certified public school teachers were first-time teachers who had majored in education; 42% were first-time teachers with other majors.

Teaching Field. After experience, the second strongest correlate of certification is subject area. Among new teachers in New York City schools, 34% of those hired to teach elementary school were not certified compared with 70% of those hired to teach in fields with perennial shortages—math, science, special education, Spanish, or bilingual education (Goodnough, 2002). Although these teaching field patterns are typical, these certification levels are below national averages. Using national data and the more rigorous definition of classes taught rather than the main teaching field, Ingersoll (1999) found that in 1993 to 1994, 23% of public school English teachers were not certified in their field, along with 27% of math teachers, 18% of science teachers, and 24% of social studies teachers. These noncertification proportions are all down from 1991 except for social studies, which rose 5% Seastrom, Gruber, Henke, McGrath, and Cohen (2002) looked at the proportion of students taught by teachers with a major and certification in a given subject. They found the percentage of students taught in English, math, and social sciences without a major and certification had decreased 5.8% to 8.4% between 1987 and 1999. Although the decline was less in science (4.1%), the 27% in science who were teaching without a major and certification masked differences by subject. Forty-five percent of biology students, 61% of chemistry students, and 63% of physics students were taught by teachers without a major and certification, as well as 71% of high school students in English as a Second Language (ESL) and bilingual classes and 48% of foreign language students. Even lower percentages of certification were found for middle-school students where general elementary certification is often considered adequate preparation. According to Grey et al. (1993), a third or more of all new teachers assigned to teach math, science, social studies, or special education in 1991 were neither certified nor eligible to become certified.

Special education has the most difficulty filling positions with certified teachers (Billingsley, 1993; U.S. Department of Education, 2003). Boe, Cook, Bobbitt, and Terhanian (1998) found that in a national study of 47,000 public school teachers, schools had a persistent problem hiring and retaining fully certified special education teachers. The effects of low certification levels among new teachers were intensified in special education where the attrition rates among experienced teachers were higher than those in general education. Additionally, a California study found correlation between the growing number of emergency certificates and the increasing stringency of state laws regarding requirements for special education certification (Hart & Burr, 1996).

Type of Students. Public schools with higher proportions of minority or low-income students are more likely to have uncertified teachers (Darling-Hammond & Cobb, 1996; Henke, Choy, Geis, & Broughman, 1997; Pascal, 1987; Zeichner & Schulte, 2001). Data for the 2001 to 2002 year indicates that 8.0% of teachers in high poverty districts were on waivers compared to 4.9% for all other districts (U.S. Department of Education, 2002). Schools with half or more of their students eligible for free or reduced-price lunch had 17.6% of their teachers uncertified in their main field, whereas those with fewer than 5% of low-income students had only 4.4% (Darling-Hammond, 2000b). Smaller studies yield similar data. Kirby, Berends, and Naftel (1999) found that in the average high-risk district in Texas, 5.6% were teaching with no certification compared to 3.2% in low-risk districts. Similarly, in New York State, 16.6% of non-White students had teachers uncertified to teach any of their classes compared with 4% of White students (Lankford et al., 2002). Although Goldhaber and Brewer (2000) questioned the importance of certification, they also noted that teachers with emergency certification were more likely to teach in harder-to-staff, high-poverty areas.

The only significant counterevidence was offered in a 1992 study of the "Great City" schools, which reported that the largest urban districts had a rate of certification among their math and English teachers slightly higher and a rate among science teachers slightly lower than the national averages (Casserly, 1992). Given the high number of low-income and minority students in large cities, these findings contradicted other studies. The apparent discrepancy may lie in differing definitions of certification. Casserly did not define whether "certified" included standard certification only or all forms of certification. The other possibility, pointed out by Lankford et al. (2002), is that there is considerable variation in teacher qualifications within urban districts.

Out-of-Field Teaching

As described earlier, comparing certification status from different studies is confounded not only by different kinds of certification but also by the issue of whether the certification matches the teaching assignment. Studies that use very inclusive definitions (e.g., any certification) tend to underestimate quality issues, whereas studies that use very strict definitions of certification (e.g., certification, major, or minor in each course taught) may overestimate quality issues. Contradictory findings generally come down to how or whether the authors defined "out-of-field" teaching.

According to a study of NCES data, out-of-field teaching is one of the least recognized causes of underqualified teachers (Lewis et al., 1999). These researchers, defining teachers as out-of-field if they did not hold an undergraduate major or minor in the field in which they taught most courses, found no difference between public secondary schools by poverty concentration or proportion of minority students. They found that English, social studies, and science teachers were slightly less likely to be teaching in-field in central cities than in other types of districts, but urban areas were slightly more likely to have in-field foreign language teachers.

Using another definition, Pascal (1987) concluded that student race was a relatively unimportant factor in explaining variance in teacher qualifications in the 1980 to 1984 HSB data set. He defined teacher qualifications as a major in the main subject field taught, courses taken in the main subject field, experience, and advanced degrees. He found that public schools with 25% or greater Black enrollment scored slightly better on measures of teacher qualifications than did schools with no Black students. But higher proportions of low-income students were negatively associated with teacher qualifications. Even here, however, SES was less important than district spending, size, and the percentages of students who were disadvantaged and who were college bound.

Using an even stricter definition, Ingersoll (1996) noted significantly higher rates of out-of-field teaching in high-poverty schools and in central city schools in the 1990 to 2001 SASS data. He examined the data on a class-by-class basis rather than by "main teaching assignment," a method producing greater levels of mismatch. In a later study, using 1993 to 1994 SASS data, he concluded that teachers in high-poverty schools were more likely to be teaching a class out-of-field than in more affluent schools (Ingersoll, 1999, 2001). However, he found school size and school sector were more important in explaining out-of-field teaching. Additionally, variations within school, such as grade level and academic tracks, influenced the amount of out-of-field teaching. Ingersoll's analysis of more recent SASS data (Jerald, 2002) found that the problem had gotten significantly worse by the 1999 to 2000 school year. In high-poverty high schools, 34% of classes were taught by teachers without a college major or minor in the subject compared to 19% in low-poverty schools. In high-minority schools, 29% were taught by out-of-field teachers compared to 21% in low-minority schools.

The U.S. Department of Education (2003), defining "highly qualified" to include teachers with bachelor's degrees, certification and a major in all the courses that they teach, said that 55% of social studies and science teachers, 50% of English teachers, and 47% of math teachers were "highly qualified."

One concern about the greater rate of urban teaching among alternately prepared teachers is that research suggests they were more likely to be teaching out-of-field than traditionally prepared teachers. Houston, Marshall, and McDavid (1993) found that 22% of alternately prepared teachers in Houston taught a grade or subject outside of their license compared with 6% of traditionally prepared teachers. Likewise, Shen (1998b) noted that although alternative routes produced more math and science teachers, they do not bring in more math or science majors.

As the number of limited English-proficient (LEP) students increases, there is concern about whether teachers are prepared to meet their needs. Defining training as any amount of preservice or inservice training, a 1997 NCES report found the proportion of trained teachers varied by region: West (47%), Northeast (21.5%), and Midwest and South (29% each). Teachers of classes with higher proportions of LEP students were more likely to be trained (87%) compared with 20% of teachers who had fewer than 10% LEP students in their classes. Using the most recent SASS data, but defining trained as at least 8 hours of training, Gruber, Wiley, and Broughman (2002) reported that nationally 41% of teachers taught LEP students, but only 12.5% were trained to work with them. In looking at ESL and bilingual education students, Seastrom et al. (2002) found that 36% were taught by a teacher without a major, minor, or certification, and 73% were taught by those without a major and certification. Some of these nonqualified teachers, however, may have been native speakers of another language.

Experience

Experience is often used as a proxy for quality (Murnane & Phillips, 1981; Rivkin, Hanushek, & Kain, 1998). As Mayer et al. (2000, p. 13) said, "Though it is impossible to limit the teaching force only to experienced teachers, the effects of new teachers may be diffused and reduced if new teachers are evenly distributed among the schools and proper assistance is given to new teachers."

Research indicates minority and poor students get a disproportionate number of inexperienced teachers (Lankford et al., 2002; Mayer et al., 2000). According to Mayer et al., schools with 75% or more minority enrollment had one in five teachers with 3 years' or less experience in 1997 to 1998, as did schools with 75% or more low-income students. This was double the percentage found in schools with fewer than 25% minority or low-income students. Data from 1999 to 2000 indicated that the one in five figure continued at these schools, but at schools with low-minority enrollments, one in seven teachers had limited experience, reflecting the recent increases in new teacher hiring in all schools (U.S. Department of Education, 2003).

HOW LONG DO THEY STAY?

Of great concern in the past 2 decades has been the perception that the teaching profession is unable to retain high-quality teachers. Using high school and college GPA and test scores, researchers have attempted to track prospective teachers of presumed higher academic quality through their career. Generally, at each successive step along the teacher education pipeline (high school intent, college entry, teacher education program entry, college graduation, and passing teacher tests) the academic ability and achievement of students become more selective (Gitomer et al., 1999; Hanushek & Pace, 1995; Latham et al., 1999; Vegas et al., 2001). However, Hanushek and Pace found that this pattern was not true for Blacks; the most able exit at higher rates and were not replaced further along the pipeline.

Although passage along the pipeline increases selectivity, those from the top SAT and ACT quartile are less likely to become teachers and stay in teaching. Wirt and Livingston (2002) reported that by 1997, 13% of the top quartile of 1993 college graduates had prepared or taught compared with 20% of the bottom quartile. Of those who became teachers, those in the top quartile were less likely (68%) to still be teaching than those in the bottom quartile (84%).

An indication of what might be happening among higher ability prospective teachers appeared in a 1985 study by Pigge. He looked at whether ability (ACT scores, high school rank, and college GPA) was related to the decisions to enter teaching made by 3,000 graduates from a large college of education in Ohio over two different 3-year periods. Those who chose not to teach because they were continuing their education, had a personal reason, or gave no reason had the highest composite ability scores. Substitute teachers and those who said they did not want to teach because salaries were too low had the lowest scores. Full-time teachers and those who wanted to teach had composite ability scores in the middle.

Once in teaching, teachers with higher scores on tests such as the NTE have a higher rate of attrition (Bobbitt, Faupel, & Burns, 1991). Murnane and Olsen (1988) found the higher the NTE score, the shorter the initial stay in teaching. They pointed out that it was not a linear relationship; the effect was much stronger at the top of the NTE scale than at the bottom. Similarly, a study of special education teachers found that those with higher test scores were at greatest risk of leaving (Singer, 1993). But a study of Texas teachers found no correlation between teacher test scores and likelihood of leaving in the first 5 years (TEA, 1995).

IMPACT OF QUALITY PROFILE

In this chapter, research on the impact of two teacher characteristics—academic ability and achievement—is reviewed. Later chapters by Floden and Meniketti and also by Wilson and Youngs (this volume) address other aspects of the quality profile—content major, teacher test scores, and certification.

Compared to researchers' attention to teachers' academic ability and achievement, there has been less research on whether these indicators of quality really matter in terms of teacher practice and student learning. Reforms that raised minimum required SAT and ACT scores and GPA for students entering and graduating from teacher education programs were predicated on the belief that such steps made a difference. As Vegas et al. (2001) expressed it, "Teaching well is seen as a complex, cognitive challenge requiring the ability to think and reason clearly" (p. 4). The argument is that academically able teachers are more likely to teach well, boosting student achievement.

But the evidence here is not as strong as might be expected. Some look to the Coleman et al. (1966) study from the 1960s or even to research from the 1940s that indicated a relationship between teacher general ability and student test scores (Darling-Hammond, 2000; Murnane et al., 1991; Vegas et al., 2001). About the earlier studies, Darling-Hammond (p. 4) concluded:

> Most relationships are small and insignificant. Two reviews of such studies concluded that there is little or no relationship between teachers' measured intelligence and students' achievement (Schalock, 1979; Soar, Medley, and Coker, 1983). Explanations for the lack of strong relationship have included the lack of variability among teachers in this measure and its tenuous relationship to actual performance (Vernon, 1965; Murnane, 1985).

Other authors have concluded that there is a positive relationship between teachers' verbal ability and student achievement (Bowles & Levin, 1968; Coleman et al., 1966; Ehrenberg & Brewer, 1995; Ferguson, 1991; Ferguson & Ladd, 1996; Greenwald, Hedges, & Laine, 1996; Hanushek, 1971, 1972; Murnane et al., 1991; Strauss & Sawyer, 1986; Vegas et al., 2001). This review looks at the few later studies that relate teachers' academic ability to student achievement.

Reanalyzing the large Coleman et al. (1966) database to address some of the weaknesses of previous studies, Ehrenberg and Brewer (1995) examined whether teachers' verbal ability varied with the race of teachers or students. The original report and subsequent reanalyses had found a positive correlation between teacher's verbal ability (as measured by a 30-item verbal aptitude test) and student test scores. These prior analyses relied on correlations between one point-in-time teacher and student test scores. Ehrenberg and Brewer instead created "synthetic" score gains by using test results for third- and sixth-graders and ninth- and twelfth-graders who had spent their entire careers in the same school.

For elementary students, the authors found that higher teacher verbal scores were associated with higher gains for students. In looking at race, they found that higher verbal scores for Black teachers were associated with higher gains for both Black and White students. But higher verbal scores for White teachers only mattered for White students. For the secondary students, higher teacher verbal scores were associated, on average, with higher gain scores for White students but not for Black students. White teachers' verbal aptitude scores were associated with higher scores for both Black and White students, but Black teachers' verbal aptitude scores did not matter for either group.

Using actual instead of synthetic gain scores, Hanushek (1992) studied achievement gains for students in grades 2 through 6 in Gary, Indiana, public schools. He found that differences in family characteristics (size and birth order) and teacher performance were significantly related to differences in student achievement. In addition, a short word test, used as a proxy for a general IQ test, was administered. There were mixed results between teacher test scores and student achievement test scores. A positive relationship existed between teacher ability and student scores in reading, but not in vocabulary. He concluded, "The ambiguous result . . . is similar to previous studies that find inconsistency in the relationship with teacher tests" (p. 111).

Expanding student outcomes to include the probability of dropping out as well as achievement gains between sophomore and senior year, Ehrenberg and Brewer (1994) used the HSB data to estimate the extent that teacher characteristics were related. Although the HSB did not collect information on teacher intelligence or verbal ability, the authors constructed a "crude" proxy for it by using Barron's college rankings, which are based on SAT and ACT scores of students. They were building on an earlier study by Summers and Wolfe (1977) that found a positive relationship between the status of college teachers attended and the achievement of Philadelphia school students at some grade levels. Ehrenberg and Brewer found that school and teacher characteristics generally related more to achievement gains than to dropout probabilities. Controlling for student and teacher background characteristics, they found gains were significantly related to the selectivity of the teachers' undergraduate alma maters, with the magnitude of the relationship greater for Black students than for White students.

Ferguson and Ladd (1996, p. 266) using district and student-level data from Alabama, found school inputs "did affect educational outcomes" and were "large enough to be relevant for deliberations about educational spending." The results were consistent with their earlier 1991 Texas study. Teacher ACT scores were significantly related to student reading scores and had a positive, but smaller relationship to math scores. They explained that if the teachers' own reading and math scores had been 1 *SD* higher,

> . . . the increase in teacher test scores would offset about two-thirds of the average difference between being African American and being white in a 50 percent urban district. . . . It would take an increase of 25 percentage points . . . to achieve the same gain in reading test scores that could be obtained by substituting teachers with (test scores) higher than those of the school's current teachers. (p. 278)

The school input variables yielding the most explanatory power in predicted differences between top and bottom quartile scoring districts were teachers' ACT test scores, average class size, and teachers with master's degrees.

In a meta-analysis of 60 studies that were longitudinal or controlled for SES, Greenwald et al. (1996) assessed the magnitude and direction of the relationship between school inputs and student achievement. To measure teacher ability, the studies used IQ tests, SAT and ACT scores, and GPA. They found a broad range of school inputs including teacher ability, teacher experience and teacher education all were positively related to student achievement in large enough ways "to be educationally important" (p. 384).

Despite claims that "verbal ability and content knowledge are the most important attributes of highly qualified teachers" (U.S. Department of Education, 2002, p. 19) no studies have compared their relative importance to other knowledge and skills. Although Hanushek (1992) concluded that "the closest thing to a consistent finding... is that 'smarter' teachers who perform well on verbal ability tests do better in the classroom," he also cautioned, "Even for that the evidence is not very strong" (p. 116).

WHAT WE KNOW ABOUT THE QUALITY OF TEACHERS

Although research describing the quality profile of teachers is less conclusive than that describing their demographic profile, the picture painted in the last 15 years is less dismal than that portrayed in the late 1970s and early 1980s, which echoed earlier perceptions of teaching as a "failure belt" (Waller, 1932). Our knowledge about the impact of a particular quality profile, however, is limited. Generally, but not always, teachers' verbal ability scores are positively related to student test scores.

Academic Ability and Achievement

Recent studies of teachers' academic ability and achievement have produced a somewhat more positive picture, probably reflecting both the results of teacher education reform efforts and the better research methods. Studies that followed cohorts of students through the teacher education pipeline have been particularly informative, as has been the recognition of the impact of disproportionate gender and SES profiles of teachers. Although the quality profiles of prospective secondary teachers and teachers in specific subjects are higher, most of those preparing to teach are headed for careers in elementary classrooms, and their preponderance influences the average profile. Race and ethnicity differences, often not adequately acknowledged as confounded by SES, have also illuminated concerns not just about the teaching force, but about the continued gap between high school and college graduation among race and ethnic groups.

Five findings emerge from recent data: (a) Researchers have clearly demonstrated that earlier studies relying on high school students' career intentions are misleading because these students are not the same population that actually prepares to teach or becomes teachers. (b) When differences among college students are reported, prospective teachers tend to have lower college-entry test scores but higher academic achievement as measured by high school GPA and rank and college GPA. However, these differences may largely reflect gender imbalances, because women generally earn higher grades and underperform on entrance tests. (c) More lower ability students exit the teacher pipeline at each successive stage (high school graduation, college entry, entry into teacher education programs, and graduation from college). By graduation, those prepared to teach have higher than average SAT and ACT scores compared to students entering college. (d) Although their average scores are slightly lower than that of all college graduates, those preparing for secondary teaching have comparable scores. (e) Those in the top SAT and ACT quartile are less likely to take jobs as teachers and, once in the classroom, less likely to stay. There are patterns of differences in the ability profiles of Blacks versus Whites, those preparing for elementary versus secondary teaching, and male versus female. Whether any of these demographic differences makes a difference, beyond public perception of teachers and teaching, is uncertain.

Teacher Preparation

Teacher preparation has changed in the past generation. Although most prospective teachers are still prepared in bachelor's level programs, more now graduate with majors in content areas rather than in education, and more enter teaching through alternative programs. Research on the quality profile of alternately prepared candidates is inconclusive. By design, alternately prepared teachers did not major in education, but that does not necessarily mean they majored in the subject they are teaching. As a growing number of colleges—many NCATE-accredited—offer alternative programs, the assumed differential between the quality of alternative and regular programs may diminish.

Teacher Tests

Although the relationship between teacher test scores and attrition is inconclusive, many studies documented a consistent gap on teacher test scores used to enter preparation programs and to gain licensure. The highest SAT and teacher test scores were found among those attending private universities, which generally enroll students with higher SES backgrounds. Teachers graduating from teacher education programs had higher teacher test scores than those who were not prepared at such programs. White applicants had higher passing rates; higher proportions of minorities, particularly Blacks and Hispanics, did not pass the tests. The effect of these tests raises the quality profile but restricts the diversity of the teaching force.

Certification and "Out-of-Field" Teaching

Given the lenient definitions of certification often used, most teachers have been counted as "certified" and deemed qualified. The actual proportion depended on the types of certification counted (e.g., regular, alternative, provisional, transitional, and emergency). The high proportions of certified teachers drops considerably when looking at whether teachers are certified in the area in which they teach most of their classes ("main field") or in the other areas they teach. Most uncertified or partially certified teachers were recent entrants to teaching. Besides its relation to experience, certification status also varied by teaching field. Departmentalized teachers were less likely to be certified than were elementary teachers. Bilingual and special education teachers were least likely to be certified.

Research has confirmed inequities in the distribution of "quality" teachers. Schools serving low-income and minority students had more inexperienced teachers and more without full certification. Some studies also indicated these schools were more likely to have teachers from lower SAT quartiles, teachers from lower status colleges, and teachers more likely to have failed at least one teacher test. Data on out-of-field teaching were less conclusive because of differing definitions, but often indicated more out-of-field teachers taught in poor and central city schools.

As states have raised criteria for certification, as well as entry into and graduation from teacher education programs, it is not surprising that the quality profile of teachers looks better than it did prior to reforms instituted over the past 20 years. There is concern, however, that shortages of teachers may necessitate lowering certification standards and hiring more uncertified or partially certified teachers, particularly in "hard to staff" schools serving lower SES students. To meet new standards for "qualified" teachers, sometimes definitions of who is "certified" have been adjusted to include those who previously would not have been labeled "certified."

Impact of Academic Ability and Achievement

Although the relationship of the ability and achievement profile of teachers and student achievement might seem obvious, the research support for such claims is not strong. Studies exploring the impact of differences in teacher ability, largely measured by test scores, have focused on the relationship to student test scores, rather than on differences in teachers' actual classroom practices. Analyses generally provide mixed results, such as different relationships with reading, vocabulary, or math tests or differences depending on race of teacher and student. Although several recent studies provide stronger evidence of a relationship between teacher verbal ability and student achievement, there is no evidence about the relative importance of teacher verbal ability compared to other aspects of teacher quality.

Despite inconclusive evidence of impact on student achievement, there is concern about the growing mismatch between teachers' race and ethnicity and the increasingly diverse student population. Because of inequities of educational opportunities, there is tension between the goal of increasing diversity of teachers and the goal of increasing the quality profile by establishing higher GPA and SAT and ACT scores for entry and graduation.

WHAT WE DON'T KNOW ABOUT THE QUALITY PROFILE

Knowledge of the quality profile is limited by the lack of comprehensive, comparative data. Breakdowns by gender, race and ethnicity, SES, and age are also limited. Unlike the demographic profile, there are better data on the quality profile of prospective teachers in college than on practicing teachers. Colleges and universities routinely collect these data; school districts do not. The teacher-quality profile is largely limited to what we can learn from looking at such proxies as SAT and ACT scores, GPAs, college major, teacher tests, and certification status. Research on the impact teacher characteristics related to quality has on student learning is limited by the indicators as well as by the measurement of student learning primarily by scores on standardized tests.

Academic Ability and Achievement

Specific concerns about research describing the quality profile relate to limitations of SAT and ACT scores and GPAs as measures of intellectual ability and achievement, how to interpret quality profiles, and whether a focus on narrowly defined intellectual attributes capture the qualities important for good teaching.

Measures of Academic Ability and Achievement.   Most recent research offered caveats about using SAT and ACT scores as indicators of intellectual competence and using GPAs as comparable, credible measures, but concluded they provide the best available data (Ferguson & Ladd, l996; Murnane et al., 1991; Vegas et al., 2001) Whether SAT and ACT tests actually measure intellectual aptitude or achievement, highly correlated with SES, remains debatable. But test scores, unlike GPAs and class rank, do provide comparable, standardized, national data for student cohorts. Unlike teacher tests, they provide data on a more inclusive group, not just on those prepared to teach. However, the fact that these precollege tests are used as an indicator of quality is ironic because their use implies that there is relatively no value added by the college experience or at least that students graduate from college with the same relative abilities with which they entered. The relative ease of collecting SAT and ACT scores and GPA information, however, still makes them a valuable tool for researchers. It is likely that they will remain the most frequently used measures of intellectual competence of teachers, despite their acknowledged limitations.

Interpretation of Quality Profile.   Typically, the GPA of prospective teachers is reported to be average to above average compared to that of their college peers. With grade inflation and minimum GPAs required to enter and graduate from teacher education programs, these results are not surprising. The more robust studies compared the GPAs of those preparing to teach with those of students not preparing to teach, and distinguished between overall GPA, with and without education courses, and GPA in the major. Future teachers appeared to do well in these studies. Whether this is more a reflection of intellectual competence or "knowing how to do school well" remains an open question.

SAT and ACT scores typically are presented in terms of quartiles. These studies generally found that larger proportions of those in the lower quartiles dropped out all along the teacher education pipeline. Concern is expressed, however, that lower proportions of those in the top quartile actually took teaching jobs. These candidates were more likely to continue with their graduate education or pursue more attractive career options. Once teaching, those in the top quartile were more likely to leave.

This raises the question about realistic expectations for raising the ability profile of prospective teachers. As Lanier and Little (1986) pointed out, the annual demand for teachers means that even if all the top quintile of college graduates went into teaching, there still would not be enough teachers for our nation's schools. Obviously, it is completely unrealistic to expect all top college graduates to become teachers, particularly because there are many higher status and better paid careers open to them.

So what would an appropriate profile look like? Should any students in the bottom quartile be permitted to become teachers? Should teacher test cutoffs be raised so that the quality profile of teachers looks better? Should the ability distribution of teachers match the ability profile of all college graduates? Or should it match the distribution of college graduates going into medicine, law, business, journalism, and social work? Lack of comparable data limits our ability to interpret the quality profiles drawn by research.

Definition of Quality.   The intellectual ability of teachers has long dominated discussions of the quality profile. The transition of teacher preparation from normal schools to colleges and universities, not completed until 1940, was not easy because the public perception of normal schools and teachers had been shaped "by the intellectual limitations then commonly believed to be inherent in the female sex" (Lagemann, 2000, p. 6). Although teachers' intellectual competence was questioned, they were seen as possessing compensating personal qualities such as "altruism or idealism . . . in abundance" (p. 16). The perceived intellectual inferiority of teachers and education as a field of study helped make standardized test scores the most used indicator of quality.

When Dewey (1902, pp. 397–398) spoke of the "intellectual equipment" of the teacher being key to the success of teaching, he was not referring to college entrance tests. "[I]t is a question not only of what is known, but of how it is known," he said:

> . . . just in the degree in which the teacher's understanding of the material of the lessons is vital, adequate and comprehensive, will that material come to the child in the same form; in the degree in which the teacher's understanding is mechanical, superficial and restricted, child's appreciation will be correspondingly limited and perverted.

Understanding and appreciation of subject matter and pedagogy are other aspects of intellectual competence critical to teaching. However, such knowledge is not captured in current quality profiles of teachers based on college-entry tests.

Even more broadly defined, intellectual competence is not sufficient for quality teaching. Some prospective teachers from the highest quartile decide not to teach after struggling in student teaching with learners for whom school is not as easy as it was for them. Some, encouraged by others because they are "good with kids," find the organizational and intellectual challenges of teaching overwhelming. The reality is that teaching requires a mix of intellectual and personal qualities. As Howey and Strom (1987, p. 8) suggested:

> Given the complex, interactive and moral nature of teaching and the rapid changes and diversity in schools (and in society), we maintain that the professional preparation of teachers should have as its basic goal the development of teachers as persons who have conceptual systems characterized by the qualities of being adaptable, questioning, critical, inventive, creative, self-renewing and oriented to moral principles.

Profiles based on assessment of all those qualities do not exist. Figuring out how to collect accurate measures of such information about large numbers of college students would be a major challenge. Given these challenges and the public's less complex vision of teaching, it is likely that quality as measured by test scores will continue to dominate research and policy.

College Major

The proportion of teachers who majored in education is declining. Although this change can partly be attributed to the greater number of teachers prepared in graduate and alternative programs, it also reflects changes in undergraduate programs. As a matter of state or institutional policy, more teachers now major in areas other than education. Some are dual majors, with minors or concentrations in education; others pursue certification options within the academic discipline they are majoring in. Whether there is research evidence that supports a content major instead of an education major (see Floden & Meniketti, this volume), it has face validity for policy makers and the public. It serves the purpose of seeming to upgrade teacher quality, whether or not it improves the academic ability profile of teachers, affects the quality of their preparation, or makes them better teachers.

Research that fails to distinguish the relevance of the content major to the teaching field limits quality assessments. For instance, the major, particularly in alternative programs, may not be in the content area for which the teacher is preparing to teach. Whether having math teachers who majored in business or engineering is preferable to having them major in math education is an open question. Additionally, even among those teachers who do major in the content area they teach, many end up teaching in other areas as secondary assignments. Studies that report college majors but do not include teaching assignments provide a limited assessment of quality.

Teacher Tests and Certification

Increasingly, postcollege measures, such as teacher test scores and certification status, are looked to as indicators of teacher quality. Although seemingly more directly related to teacher performance than to GPA and SAT and ACT scores, teacher tests are subject to questions of objectivity and validity. Regardless, mandating teacher tests with minimum cutoff scores has improved the quality profile of the teaching pool, as indicated by traditional measures such as GPA and SAT, but it also made the pool even more homogeneous in terms of race and ethnicity. Because a diverse teaching pool is seen as a critical element of a quality teaching pool, mandated teacher tests can be seen as having contradictory influences on quality.

Data on teacher tests and certification status are both confounded by policy variation at the state level. Not all states test teachers, and not all those that do use the same tests. Even states that use the same tests set different cutoff points. Certification requirements and types of certificates also differ by states. Although teacher tests and certification status provide useful data when looking at the qualifications of the teaching force, there are inherent problems in interpreting such data.

Using certification status as an indicator of quality raises additional issues of interpretation. Some consider only those who have met standard certification as being certified. Others count those with provisional, alternative, transitional, or emergency certification as well. Some consider "out-of-field" teaching as teaching any class out-of-field; some only consider the "main field" when considering certification status. As states clamp down on "noncertified" teachers, these kinds of distinctions become more than academic. Without clear definitions and comparable data across years and across state borders, research on certification status is limited.

Impact of Quality Profile

Besides the messages the quality profile may send to students and the general public, it is widely assumed that teacher quality makes a difference in terms of student achievement. The research evidence about impact, however, is less than conclusive. Although teacher verbal ability appears positively related to student achievement, we do not know conclusively what levels of verbal ability make a difference, nor what contribution verbal ability makes relative to other indicators of quality. Additionally, we know little about the interaction of the quality profile and demographic variables, type of teacher preparation, characteristics of schools and students, and retention rates on student achievement.

Research on the impact of teacher quality has focused on student learning outcomes, as measured by test scores. Acknowledging the limitations of such a narrow measure of student outcomes is almost as ubiquitous as their usage by current researchers. The emphasis on test scores is understandable, but it limits our knowledge about the impact of the quality profile on other cognitive performance measures and student outcomes, such as attitudes, self-concept, motivation, cultural identity, graduation, college entry, and avoidance of risky behavior.

The implication of impact research is that teacher quality influences teacher practice, which in turn influences student learning. Although there was much research in the 1970s and 1980s on teacher attitudes and expectations, little attention has been paid to how quality variables may affect teaching practice and, in turn, student achievement.

Despite inconclusive evidence of impact, there is concern about the mismatch between teachers' race and ethnicity and the increasingly diverse student population. Finding a balance among quality, quantity, and equity in setting teacher education policy is a major challenge. Finding such a balance is limited by our existing knowledge about the interaction among demographic and quality variables.

There is no empirical evidence indicating what GPAs (which are extremely sensitive to institutional variability), SAT and ACT scores, and teacher test scores are minimally acceptable in terms of teacher performance and student achievement. Cutoff scores are largely based on what politically and intuitively seems like a minimal level to convey a message of quality. There is always the danger that cutoffs may keep effective teachers out of the classroom and give a false sense of confidence about those who wind up in the classroom.

In the absence of definitive research, policymakers and institutions set GPA and test score cutoffs based on perceived payoffs between quality and diversity. Supply issues complicate the decision-making process. Regional, state, institutional, subject, and grade level context all play a role in such decisions, making interpreting research evidence about impact very complex. Cutoffs should be set at a level to ensure an adequate supply of qualified teachers of diverse backgrounds. Even if definitive data were available, this decision involves a value judgment about what is viewed as more important at a particular time and place.

RESEARCH AGENDA

In the preceding chapter on teacher demographics, we prefaced our discussion of needed research with some general issues that also apply here. There is a need for a comprehensive, timely database on prospective, current, and reserve-pool teachers. Incorporating such a goal into Title II reports would provide better data about prospective teachers. Because higher education is no longer the sole provider of teachers, State Departments of Education could collect agreed-on demographic, quality, preparation, and job history information as part of their certification process and annual school district reporting. Assuming such data become available, we turn to some questions that research on quality indicators and their impact might address more adequately.

Quality Profile

Regardless of limitations, the use of college entry tests will continue to be used because there are no other common standardized measures widely collected to describe the ability and achievement profile of college students. Comprehensive, accurate data for traditionally and alternatively prepared prospective teachers and practicing teachers are necessary. More needs to be known about SAT quartiles for students who go into other occupations as well as those who choose to teach. Last, research might inform discussion about what a realistic ability and achievement profile for teachers might look like, given the multitude of societal needs, economic realities, and individual preferences.

Pipeline research has been particularly useful in relation to changes in the ability and achievement profile of teachers. As institutional and state policies raise or, in the face of supply issues, lower standards for entry into teacher education programs, graduation, and certification, it will be important to assess the impact on the ability and achievement profile of teachers as well as on the demographic profile of teachers. Given the growing diversity of the student population, the impact of such policy changes on the race and ethnicity composition of teachers needs particular attention in future research.

Quality profiles based on more broadly defined conceptions of intellectual competence than SAT and ACT scores and other personal qualities will be a daunting challenge. Ways must be found (and funded) to operationalize and to collect data in an efficient way for national samples of college students, not just for prospective teachers. For those who believe that SAT and ACT scores are an imperfect measure of ability and achievement, particularly for certain groups of students, and not the best indicator of the intellectual qualities needed for teaching, this research agenda might take priority.

Although the ability and achievement variable has dominated public discussion and research, other indicators of quality are in need of better descriptive research. Current research often pits an education major against a noneducation or content major. Research that includes the relevance of the content major to the teaching field, dual majors, minors, or concentrations in education or content pedagogy would provide a more accurate picture. Data on teacher tests, certification status, "out-of-field" teaching present an array of challenges, particularly given policy variations at the state level and varying definitions by researchers. Studies like the recent work by ETS that looked at data using the lowest, average, and highest state cutoff scores would be particularly informative (Gitomer et al., 1999). The assessment of "qualified" teachers using different definitions for "certified" and "out of field" teaching would be more instructive than current reports of almost universal certification. Given the growing limited-English-proficiency population, collecting data on other-than-English-language abilities of teachers would add another dimension to the quality profile.

Although pipeline and other studies focusing on individual teachers will continue to provide useful information, research that looks at how larger social and economic factors, the ethos of the occupation, and the structure of schools shape the quality profile could also provide valuable guidance to policymakers. These larger factors shape the quality profile by affecting students' interest in teaching, the selectivity of teacher education and alternative programs, whether and where people decide to teach, and how long they stay.

Impact of Quality Profile

The quality profile is important symbolically and important because of its potential impact on students. One could argue that the quality profile should project a strong, positive image about teachers to the general public and particularly to prospective teachers, regardless of the impact of that profile on student learning.

Concerns about the impact of the quality profile on student outcomes, however, could benefit from evidence provided by further research. Expanding the conception of student outcomes beyond standardized test scores to other cognitive measures and other outcomes, such as attitudes, self-concept, cultural identity, graduation, college entry, and avoidance of risky behavior, might reveal different results.

Given the persistent achievement gap among students from different race and ethnicity groups and lower SES backgrounds, there is strong interest in finding out if the nonrepresentative distribution of "quality" teachers might be contributing to an educational system that does not provide all children an equal opportunity to learn. Perhaps, a closer look at teachers and schools that defy the achievement gap would provide new "quality" variables that might make even more of a difference than those now used.

Despite their limitations, GPAs and college entry tests continue to be used to define quality without any clear indication of the ranges that might make a difference in student learning. Institutions and State Education Departments set cutoff scores that have face validity but often represent pragmatic decisions related to issues of teacher supply. Predictive validity studies of GPAs and SAT and ACT and teacher test cutoff scores in terms of teacher performance and student achievement are needed.

Studies on the impact of teachers' academic ability and achievement are difficult to execute. This kind of research demands longitudinal studies with large databases that take into consideration a host of related student, family, teacher, and school variables. Longitudinal research using actual rather than synthetic gain scores would be particularly useful. Using actual SAT and ACT scores rather than proxies, such as status of college, would be more conclusive. This needs to be accompanied by substantial qualitative research probing relationships that are indicated by large-scale data analysis, but are not explained by them. A focus on how quality and demographic variables may relate to teacher knowledge and attitudes and teaching practice might provide new insights into some intractable issues related to student achievement and help teacher educators better prepare teachers who can meet the diverse needs of all students.

As teacher education programs comply with new accreditation demands to collect data on the classroom performance of their graduates and, eventually, student outcomes, a wealth of potential data will be available for analysis. How college entrance tests are related or not related to teacher performance and student learning could inform admissions standards and instruction. Additionally, institutions that alter their admissions standards could compare groups of students who met old and new standards. They could also use different cutoff scores to test their validity with particular student groups.

Finally, given the claims in the first Title II report (U.S. Department of Education, 2002), that the verbal ability and content knowledge of teachers are the most important attributes of highly qualified teachers, there is a need to design research that would support or dispute such claims. If the primacy of these factors is claimed, it is not enough to provide evidence solely of their impact. Evidence is also needed that demonstrates the contribution of a variety of factors including quality indicators that reflect the added value of teacher education programs, workplace context factors, teacher depositions and personality traits.

TABLE 4.1

Teacher Characteristics: Research on the Demographic Profile and the Indicators of Quality: Studies Cited

Studies[a]	Question and Focus	Research Tradition	Research Design	Date of Data[b] Collection
AACTE. (1987)	Study of teacher education programs with a specific emphasis on secondary methods courses	Statistical analysis of survey data	Ninety schools from AACTE membership randomly sampled, 30 each from 3 strata (bachelor's only, master's and bachelor's only, doctoral). Twelve hundred eighty-one preservice teachers, 267 college-based supervisors of student teachers, and 228 school-based cooperating teachers were surveyed. Data were analyzed using SAS.	Collected during spring of 1986 and reflected institutional enrollments for fall of 1985
AACTE. (1988)	Study of teacher education programs with a specific emphasis on foundations courses, faculty, and students	Statistical analysis of survey data	Ninety schools from AACTE membership randomly sampled, 30 each from 3 strata (bachelor's only, master's and bachelor's only, doctoral). Seventy-seven institutions responded: 753 preservice teachers, 153 foundations professors. Data were analyzed using SAS.	Collected during spring of 1987 and reflected institutional enrollments for fall of 1986
AACTE. (1989)	Study of teacher education programs with a specific emphasis on elementary education courses, faculty, and students	Statistical analysis of survey data	Ninety schools from AACTE membership randomly sampled, 30 each from 3 strata (bachelor's only, master's and bachelor's only, doctoral). Twelve	Collected during spring of 1988 and reflected institutional enrollments for fall of 1987

188

			hundred eighty-one preservice teachers, 267 college-based supervisors of student teachers, and 228 school-based cooperating teachers were surveyed. Data were analyzed using SAS.	Collected during spring of 1989 and reflected institutional enrollments for fall of 1988.
AACTE. (1990)	Study of teacher education programs with a specific emphasis on field experiences	Statistical analysis of survey data	Ninety schools from AACTE membership randomly sampled, 30 each from 3 strata (bachelor's only, master's and bachelor's only, doctoral). Twelve hundred eighty-one preservice teachers, 267 college-based supervisors of student teachers, and 228 school-based cooperating teachers were surveyed. Data were analyzed using SAS.	
AACTE. (1992)	This study examined how high school preparation, standardized test scores, and scores on program entrance examinations were indicators of White, Black, and Hispanic students' academic performance and completion of teacher education programs.	Statistical analysis of varied data sources	Teacher education programs were selected through a stratified random sampling (stratified by Carnegie Institution Classification Index). Thirty-four were selected and 23 provided usable data. Institution liasons were advised how to select a representative	1985–1986

(Continued)

TABLE 4.1
(Continued)

Studies[a]	Question and Focus	Research Tradition	Research Design	Date of Data[b] Collection
			sample of fall 1985 and 1986 teacher education sophomores. A combination of the two created a total sample of 712 teacher education students. Data drawn included demographic information, high school GPA, high school rank, SAT and ACT scores, college overall GPA, program entrance examination scores, grades in teacher education courses, and graduation date.	
AACTE. (1994a)	Study of the perceptions of leaders and faculty in teacher education programs across a wide variety of institutional types	Statistical analysis of survey data	Cross-tabulations, ANOVAs, correlations, and regression analyses were conducted to determine relationships among selected variables. Survey to academic leaders (CAO's or chief institutional representatives) and survey to faculty Descriptive statistics reported.	1992

AACTE. (1994b)	Study of teacher education programs in institutions located in cities that are members of the Council of Great City Schools	Statistical analysis of varied data sources	1992	Separate questionnaires distributed to faculty and students from a sample of institutions located in 48 of the 50 largest urban districts in the United States. Stratified by institutional type and drawn from AACTE membership list. Responses are from 58 of 112 institutions. Total of 230 teacher educators, 220 students, and 52 deans or heads of education participated in the survey. Institutional datasets were also used.
AACTE. (1999)	Fourth in a series of reports focusing on diversity in teacher education student enrollments	Statistical analysis of varied data sources	Fall 1995	AACTE membership roster combined with that of the National Association of State Directors of Teacher Education and Certification to identify schools, colleges, and departments of education (SCDEs). Survey instrument mailed to all SCDE's on the combined list requesting fall 1995 enrollments resulted in 1,026 usable responses. Data also from Schools and Staffing Survey, Integrated Postsecondary Education Data System surveys, and

(Continued)

TABLE 4.1
(Continued)

Studies[a]	Question and Focus	Research Tradition	Research Design	Date of Data[b] Collection
Adams, G. J., & Dial, M. (1993)	Survival analysis of teachers in a large urban school district to help administrators decide cost-effective strategies	Statistical analysis of varied data sources	the AACTE teacher education survey. Sample from a large urban school district in the southwest of 2,452 first-year or new teachers. Six and a half years later looked at all teachers excluding those who had left involuntarily (termination, health, or death). Left a sample of 834 who had left voluntarily and 1,493 who were still teaching. Used a regression analysis to link risk of resigning to sex, age, ethnicity, educational level, and certification route.	1985–1991
Andrew, M. (1990)	A comparison of graduates from the 4- and 5-year teacher education programs at a single university in terms of rate of entry, retention, career satisfaction, and effectiveness	Statistical analysis of varied data sources Comparative population	Data was collected from two sources. The first is a study comparing randomly selected graduates of each program over a 10-year period. Each participant received a 70-item questionnaire regarding entry, retention, and background data.	1976–1986; 1981–1989

			1985–1990
Andrew, M., & Schwab, R. L. (1995)	Impact of program structure (4- or 5-year program) on career path and effectiveness (based on principal survey)	Statistical analysis of varied data sources Comparative population	

Total sample was 144 five-year graduates (93.5% response rate) and 163 four-year graduates (70% response rate).

Second, a yearly program evaluation questionnaire was administered to both 4- and 5-year students and cooperating teachers just prior to graduation. Student evaluations from 1981 to 1989 were used in this study with response rate varying from 40% to 95% during that period. Evaluation items produced data on clinical placement, self-rating on instructional tasks, evaluation of clinical supervisors, overall rating of student teaching experience, rating of required certification courses, background data, and career plans.

t-tests and chi-squares were used for analysis.

Thirteen hundred ninety graduates from 11 universities and colleges, 7 of which had 5-year teacher education programs, were

(Continued)

193

TABLE 4.1
(Continued)

Studies[a]	Question and Focus	Research Tradition	Research Design	Date of Data[b] Collection
			surveyed. Four hundred eighty-one principals at schools in which graduates were employed were also surveyed. Locally developed Survey of Graduates and Teacher Effectiveness Survey. Data were analyzed with chi-square tests.	
Ballou, D. (1996)	Do school administrators choose not to hire candidates with superior academic qualifications?	Statistical analysis of varied data sources	Data were gathered as part of the Survey of Recent College Graduates conducted six times over a 15-year period. Questionnaires were sent to bachelor's degree recipients approximately 1-year after graduation. Data were collected on 15,123 graduates who completed teacher training. Data were included information on the experiences of teaching candidate at each stage of the pipeline as well as academic background	1976–1991

Citation	Title/Description	Method	Dates	Notes
				information such as GPA, undergraduate school, and major. Uses an econometric model to analyze the relationship between application and hiring experience and academic quality of candidates.
Barger, J., Barger, R., & Reardon, J. (1986, March)	Comparison of GPAs between teacher education students and other college graduates	Statistical analysis of varied data sources	1982–1985	Sample included all graduates of Eastern Illinois University graduates from 1982 to 1985. $N = 7{,}703$. Divided students into those with degrees offered only with teacher certification, those with degrees that did not include certification, and those with degrees which offered the option of certification. The latter were divided into those students who had attained certification and those who had not. Cumulative GPA was calculated based on all courses taken at Eastern; upper-division major GPA was based on all junior and senior-level classes prescribed for a student's

(Continued)

TABLE 4.1
(Continued)

Studies[a]	Question and Focus	Research Tradition	Research Design	Date of Data[b] Collection
			major; adjusted upper-division GPA was calculated by removing all professional education courses from upper-division GPA calculation. ANOVA analysis of ACT scores, high school class rank, and GPAs.	
Betts, J. R., Reuben, K. S., & Danenberg, A. (2000)	How do school resources, measured in terms of class size, curriculum, teachers' education, credentials, and experience, vary among schools? Do schools serving relatively disadvantaged populations tend to receive fewer of these specific resources? Do existing inequalities in school resources contribute to unequal student outcomes?	Production function analysis	Data drawn from California State CBEDs demographic database. This includes the information collected annually on three forms: Professional Assignment Information Form (gender, age, ethnicity, education level, experience, and credentials for public school personnel as well as assignments and class size for public school teachers), the School Information Form (school-level data on student and teacher counts and program types), and the County and District Information Form (includes	1997–1998

			data on teacher shortages and demand). Student achievement is measured by results of Stanford Achievement Test Series.	
Biraimah, K. (1988)	To what extent are characteristics such as class, gender, or academic achievement associated with career expectations?	Statistical analysis of varied data sources	Multiple regression analyses. Two hundred juniors and seniors randomly selected from 1,200 College of Education students from U. of Florida in 1986–1987. One hundred forty-three female and 57 male students. Student SES determined from parents' level of education. Sample evenly divided among high, middle, and low SES groups. Questionnaire asked about career expectations, GPA, SES, and gender. Simple percentages were used to analyze the data.	1986–1987
Bobbit, S. A. (1989)	Focuses on two questions: What is the distribution of education and noneducation majors among public and private school teachers? Does the distribution of bachelor's	Statistical analysis of survey data	Correlational analysis. Public and private school teachers were asked to indicate whether they majored in an education field or a noneducation field for their bachelor's degree and specify their	1985–86

(Continued)

TABLE 4.1
(Continued)

Studies[a]	Question and Focus	Research Tradition	Research Design	Date of Data[b] Collection
	degree fields differ between public and private school teachers?		major(s) for each type of degree. Education majors were classified by their specific type of education degree, frequency distributions were constructed for private and public schools, and distributions were constructed by subgroups including elementary; secondary; novice (fewer than 5 years experience); midcareer (5–24 years' experience); expert (25+ years' experience); female, male, under 25 years old, 25–49 years old, at least 50 years old; White, non-Hispanic; minority; math and science teachers.	
Bobbitt, S. A., Faupel, E., & Burns, S. (1991)	Looks at the impact of a variety of teacher and school characteristics on the career paths of teachers	Statistical analysis of survey data	Descriptive statistics reported. Teacher Follow-up Survey sample is a subsample of the 1987 to 1988 SASS. Responding public school SASS teachers were sorted by census region by	1987–1988

		urbanicity by teacher subject, by school enrollment. Responding private school teachers were sorted by affiliation by urbanicity by teacher subject by school enrollment. Then teachers were selected within each stratum based on SASS weight. Yielded a total sample of 7,172 teachers, 2,987 leavers and 4,185 stayers and movers.	
Bobbitt, S. A., & McMillen, M. M. (1994)	Four analyses of teacher qualifications using the SASS	Statistical analysis of survey data	One questionnaire was sent to current teachers and another to former teachers. Total response rate was 97.2%. Only examines 1-year change in teacher career choices. Descriptive statistics and frequencies reported. Four analyses of teacher qualifications. Analyses differ in the focus. All look at interaction of academic preparation in the field taught and certification to teach in that field and provide a different window onto the subject of teacher qualifications and out of	1987–1988, 1990–1991

(Continued)

TABLE 4.1
(Continued)

Studies[a]	Question and Focus	Research Tradition	Research Design	Date of Data[b] Collection
			field teaching. The analyses are (a) Are teachers certified in their main assignment field? Did teachers major in their main assignment field? (b) Are teachers certified in their main assignment field? Did teachers major or minor in their main assignment field? (c) Are secondary teachers certified to teach in thee individual subjects they are assigned? Did teachers major or minor in the individual subjects they are assigned? (d) Are students in secondary classes taught by teachers certified to teach in the subject? Are students in secondary classes taught by teachers with a major or minor in the subject? Descriptive statistics and frequencies reported.	
Boe, E. F., & Barkanic, G. (2000, April)	Examines two main facets of teacher qualifications: teacher certification and degree level	Statistical analysis of survey data	A number of predictor variables were created from SASS data in the general categories of teacher	1993–1994

			demographic attributes, teacher working conditions, and broad teaching assignment fields. Following the construction of multivariate models to predict teacher qualification variables, logistic regression was used to construct predictive models.
Boe, E. E., Bobbitt, S. A., Cook, L. H., Barkanic, G., & Maislin, G. (1998)	Examines national trend and predictor data for the turnover of K–12 teachers in eight areas (general elementary education, math and science education, language education, social studies, arts, physical and health education, business and vocational education, other general education, and special education)	Statistical analysis of survey data	1987–89, 1990–92, 1993–1995	Data drawn from three national probability samples taken in the first three SASS and the Teacher Follow-up Survey (TFS). Examined data for three trends: moving to different schools, switching to different assignments, and voluntarily leaving the ranks of public school teaching. Predictor variables used were situational circumstances, teacher characteristics, working conditions, teacher judgments, and changes in such variables from year to year. Logistic regression analyses to the three types of teacher turnover.

(Continued)

TABLE 4.1
(Continued)

Studies[a]	Question and Focus	Research Tradition	Research Design	Date of Data[b] Collection
Boe, E. E., Bobbitt, S. A., Cook, L. H., Whitener, S. D., & Weber, A. L. (1996)	Investigates teacher, school, and district characteristics associated with teacher retention and turnover related to general and special education from a national perspective	Statistical analysis of survey data	Data drawn from 1988–1989 Teacher Follow-up Study of the 1987–88 SASS. Included questionnaires to current and former teachers who were part of the SASS national probability sample. Total sample is 4,789 (639 special education teachers and 4,159 general education teachers). Predictor variables include teacher demographic characteristics including marital status and children; teacher qualifications as measured by degree, certification, and experience; teacher assignment and employment conditions; and school characteristics (size, level, student achievement, minority enrollment and region). Statistical tests for associations were made using a chi-square analysis.	1987–1989

Boe, E. E., Cook, L. H., Bobbitt, S. A., & Terhanian, G. (1998)	The goal of the study is to identify the major sources of teachers who were not fully certified. Compares the certification status of general educators and special educators. How large is the shortage of fully certified teachers? How do entering teachers affect the shortage of fully certified teachers? Is the shortage problem related to the source of supply of entering teachers? Is the shortage problem related to type of continuing teachers?	Statistical analysis of varied data sources	Data on special education teachers taken from annual surveys by the State Special Education Personnel Data Collection and Reporting Systems. Used to describe trends in the annual number of full-time special education teachers and the number of special education teachers needed. Data on general educators come from the Public School Teacher Questionnaire (PSTQ), a component of the 1990–1991 SASS that was used to analyze certification status of teacher from various sources. PSTQ is based on a national probability sample of K–12 teachers ($N = 46,599$) with a response rate of 91%. Used SASS analysis methods and chi-square analysis to compute statistical significance of differences between general and special educators.	1987–1988 to 1992–1993

(Continued)

TABLE 4.1
(Continued)

Studies[a]	Question and Focus	Research Tradition	Research Design	Date of Data[b] Collection
Boe, E. E., Cook, L. H., Kaufman, M. J., & Danielson, L. C. (1996)	Investigates the numbers of individuals drawn from various sources of supply (first-time entrants, delayed entrants, reentering experienced teachers, and private school migrants) for filling the demand for public school special education teachers	Statistical analysis of survey data	Data drawn from the PSTQ of the 1990–1991 SASS. Only public school teachers included in this research. Total sample size of 46,599, reflecting a 91% response rate. The specific information used from the PSTQ allowed for the identification of entering and continuing teachers and for identifying their source of supply. Data were analyzed through special SASS procedures for complex sample survey data. Chi square tests were used to test the significance of differences between special and general education teachers.	1990–1991
Broughman, S. P., & Rollefson, M. R. (2000)	Provides estimates of four types of newly hired teachers (newly prepared, delayed entrants, transfers, reentrants) and their basic demographics, teaching qualifications, career paths, and former occupations	Statistical analysis of survey data	Data from SASS, specifically public and private schools' teacher surveys. Used data from those in the sample who indicated they were newly hired in that state or sector that school year, they taught half-time or more,	1987–1988, 1990–1991, 1993–1994

	they were regular teachers (neither itinerant nor long-term substitute teachers. Sample included 2,479 public and 1,123 private teachers in 1987–1988; 3,458 public and 1,159 private teachers in 1990–1991; and 4,068 public and 1,435 private teachers in 1993–1994. Data were analyzed to produce national estimates of each of the four types of new hires.			
Casserly, M. (1992)	Reports on the status of 40 large urban school districts regarding 6 education goals including graduation rates, teacher quality, academic achievement, post-secondary opportunities, and safe school	Statistical analysis of survey data	Surveys sent to the superintendents and directors of research and evaluation of member districts. Simple percentages and frequencies reported.	1991
Darling-Hammond, L. (2000)	Impact of teacher quality (certification, subject area preparation, graduation from NCATE-accredited teacher education programs) on student achievement (measured by NAEP scores)	Statistical analysis of varied data sources	Teacher data drawn from 1993–1994 SASS. Sample size of 65,000 teachers. Student achievement measurement by state average NAEP scores in mathematics: Grade 4 in 1990, 1996; Grade 8 in 1992,	Teacher data 1993–1994 Student data 1990–1996

(Continued)

TABLE 4.1
(Continued)

Studies[a]	Question and Focus	Research Tradition	Research Design	Date of Data[b] Collection
	State is the unit of analysis.		1996. State average NAEP scores in reading: Grade 4 in 1992, 1994. Multiple regression and partial correlations.	Not available
Darling-Hammond, L., Hudson, L., & Kirby, S. (1989)	Comparison of different special teacher education program for success in preparing nontraditional math and science teachers	Statistical analysis of survey data	Surveyed participants and graduates in nine teacher education programs of varied structures. Survey questions included: training received in program, perceptions of program strengths and weaknesses, future career plans and demographic information.	
Dee, T. S. (2001)	Is there a relationship between own-race teachers and student achievement?	Experimental	Reanalysis of data collected within the Tennessee STAR class-size study. A randomized within school design was used, dividing students in a school into either a class of 15 students, a class of 22 students with a teachers' aide, or a class of 22 students without an	1985–1989

aide. The purely experimental design was considered potentially compromised by class-type shifts and student attrition. For this reanalysis, the data were limited to Black and White non-Hispanic students and teachers. Teacher characteristics included in the model were race, years of experience, education and merit pay status. Analysis was done through an econometric model which related percentile test rank to student, teacher, and classroom traits and fixed effects for grade, entry wave, and school.

Initially interviewed in 1980

| Ehrenberg, R. G., & Brewer, D. J. (1994) | Looks at the impact of school and teacher characteristics on students. Teacher characteristics, measured at the school level, include degree level, experience, and selectivity of undergraduate institution. Student outcome data include test scores (as sophomores and 2 years | Statistical analysis of varied data sources | Data from *High School and Beyond* longitudinal study. Over 30,000 students from more than 1,100 secondary schools Regression analysis |

(Continued)

TABLE 4.1
(Continued)

Studies[a]	Question and Focus	Research Tradition	Research Design	Date of Data[b] Collection
	later) in mathematics, vocabulary, and reading, dropping out, family background.			
Ehrenberg, R. G., & Brewer, D. J. (1995)	A reanalysis of data from the 1966 *Coleman Report*. Asks how, during the mid-1960s, the characteristics of teachers of different races (verbal aptitude, highest degree, experience) influenced an estimate of the change in test scores over a 3-grade-level period, for students of different races.	Statistical analysis of varied data sources.	Original sample included over 570,000 students and 60,000 teachers. This analysis looked at a subsample of 969 elementary schools and 256 high school for which student test data existed for two grades and for which all necessary data were available on teacher characteristics. Most of the analyses reflect the elementary school data because of the larger sample. Measured the "synthetic gain scores" of students as the mean test score of upper-grade students in a school minus the mean test scores of lower grade students in a school using an econometric model.	Mid-1960s

(Continued)

			The relationships between teacher characteristics and student synthetic gain scores were modeled for all teachers and students in a school. They were then modeled for Black and White students separately and then for Black and White teachers separately. A weighted least-squares analysis was done to model several simulated situations.	
Ehrenberg, R. G., Goldhaber, D. D., & Brewer, D. J. (1995)	Impact of teacher characteristics (race, gender, and ethnicity) on student achievement as measured by increase in scores on subject area tests	Statistical analysis of varied data sources	Analysis of the NELS:88 data. Initial data included responses from 24,599 eighth-graders, 22,651 parents, and 5,193 teachers at 1,035 schools. Second wave of data involved 18,221 tenth-graders, 15,908 teachers, and 1,291 school administrators. Cognitive tests were administered to the students. Analysis was limited to White. Black, and Hispanic students enrolled in public schools in both the 8th and	1988, 1990

209

TABLE 4.1
(Continued)

Studies[a]	Question and Focus	Research Tradition	Research Design	Date of Data[b] Collection
			10th grades who took the same subject matter area tests in both years and for whom there were data available on teacher characteristics, school variables, and parent responses. Included 1,776 students who took history, 2,848 students who took reading, 3,029 students who took mathematics, 2,445 students who took science.	
Evans, M. O. (1992)	Attempts to estimate race and gender role-model effects in high school economic courses.	Statistical analysis of varied data sources.	Data collected by the National Association for Economic Education on the education, family background, teacher, school site, and school district of 3,266 high school students. Data analyzed for 1,251 students in 48 classrooms for whom data were available. A knowledge-stock model was used to estimate the relationship between classroom models and economic literacy.	Spring 1987

Economic literacy was measured by students' Test of Economic Literacy scores. The model also included information on students' GPA, school curriculum, quantity of time spent doing economics homework, and family educational background. School characteristics include percentage of students who graduated and the percentage who attended college. Teacher characteristics included economics training, enthusiasm for teaching economics, race, and gender. A gender role model effect was defined as the achievement of a female student in the class of a female teacher, and a race role model effect is the increase in achievement of African-American students if they have an African-American teacher. Seven of the teachers were Black and 18 were female.

(Continued)

TABLE 4.1
(Continued)

Studies[a]	Question and Focus	Research Tradition	Research Design	Date of Data[b] Collection
Farkas, G., Grobe, R., Sheehan, D., & Shuan, Y. (1990)	Impact of teacher race and gender on student performance	Statistical analysis of varied data sources	Stratified random sample (by race) of 486 students in 22 middle school. Student background variables included gender, ethnicity, and poverty. Basic skills measured by the Iowa Test of Basic Skills. Student habits were measured by absenteeism and with a Student Work Ethic Characteristics Questionnaire filled out by teachers. Teacher data collected from school district records of middle school social studies teachers. Variables included gender, race, and years of teaching experience.	Not available
Feistritzer, C. E. (1996)	Survey of the demographic information, preparation, employment, and attitudes of U.S. public school teachers	Statistical analysis of survey data	Surveys sent to 2,998 K–12 teachers selected through systematic random sampling procedure. A response rate of 34% yielded 1,018 usable surveys. Frequency and percentage of responses reported.	1996

Feistritzer, C. E. (1999)	Collected data from Institutions of Higher Education (IHEs) in United States that have programs for the initial preparation of teachers about the nature of these programs	Statistical analysis of survey data	Thirty-six item questionnaire sent to 1,354 IHEs with a teacher preparation program. Six hundred seventy-four returned for a return rate of 50%. Frequency and percentage of responses reported.	Collected in 1999, using data from 1984, 1993–1994, 1998, 1999
Ferguson, R. F., & Ladd, H. F. (1996)	Looks at the impact of teacher quality (as measured by experience, degree level, and college admission ACT scores) on student achievement (as measured by reading and mathematics achievement on SAT)	Statistical analysis of varied data sources	Regression analysis of Alabama state data. Includes 29,544 fourth-graders in 690 schools. Measures impact of teacher characteristics on student achievement on Stanford Achievement Tests (SATs). Analysis accounts for student background characteristics as measured through prior-year scores on Basic Competency Test and family background variables.	1990–1991
Freeman, D. J., Martin, R. J., Brousseau, B. A., & West, B. B. (1989)	Entry-level characteristics of teacher candidates who satisfied higher admission standards at Michigan State University compared with those of candidates who did not in the areas of academic credentials, career orientations, and educational beliefs	Statistical analysis of varied data sources. Comparative population.	Two samples of students, one entering fall 1985 divided into two subgroups: those who would have been admitted under higher standards used for fall 1987 admission (47) and those who would not have been admitted (110). The second sample of students	Fall 1985; fall 1987

(Continued)

213

TABLE 4.1
(Continued)

Studies[a]	Question and Focus	Research Tradition	Research Design	Date of Data[b] Collection
			consisted of 129 students admitted fall 1987. Survey instrument designed by the teacher education faculty at MSU focusing on educational beliefs about students, the curriculum, the social context of education, pedagogy, and teachers. University records of students' GPAs and entrance examination scores also used	
Garibaldi, A. M. (1991)	Focuses on the reduction of Black teachers and delineates the need for these teachers as schools become more diverse	Statistical analysis of varied data sources	Analyses of education degrees awarded between 1976 and 1983 for Louisiana's 21 schools, colleges, and education departments from the Higher Education General Information Survey (HEGIS); estimates of the number of Black education graduates certified to teach shortly after receiving their degrees; surveys and interviews with 101 Black and White education majors and 214 Black and White noneducation	1976–1983

	majors, assessing their attitudes toward the teaching profession and those factors they considered important in enticing them into a teaching career; analyses of passing rates on the NTE for Black and White test takers in Louisiana between 1978 and 1982.	
Gitomer, D. H., Latham, A. S., & Ziomek, R. (1999)	What are the academic and demographic characteristics of the prospective teacher pool and how does teacher testing impact this pool? What is the relationship between academic quality and licensure area? How would raising licensure testing standards affect the academic and demographic profiles of the prospective teaching population?	Statistical analysis of varied data sources	Created a sample of teacher education students for whom both SAT and PRAXIS scores or both ACT and PRAXIS scores were available. Created two parallel samples of 33,866 PRAXIS I and 159,857 PRAXIS II candidates who had taken the SAT and 55,064 PRAXIS I candidates and 112,207 PRAXIS II candidates who had taken the ACT. Another match was made to determine whether candidates had attended an NCATE-accredited college. These were matched with Praxis and SAT and ACT scores. Finally state passing scores were assigned to each candidate.	1975–1995

(Continued)

TABLE 4.1
(Continued)

Studies[a]	Question and Focus	Research Tradition	Research Design	Date of Data[b] Collection
Goertz, M. E., & Pitcher, B. (1985)	Investigated the impact of the NTE Core Battery and Specialty Area tests on the selection of teachers	Statistical analysis of varied data sources	Study examined how states use the NTE tests, distribution of test takers, and test scores by racial and ethnic groups; impact of qualifying scores on passing rates of these groups; implications for the composition of the future teaching force	Core battery data 1982–1984; Specialty Area tests data 1981–1984
Goldhaber, D. D., & Brewer, D. J. (2000)	Relationship of teacher variables (certification status, subject, degree level, and experience) to student variables (demographics, family background, achievement test scores) Adjusted for schooling resources including school-, teacher-, and class-specific variables	Statistical analysis of varied data sources	Data drawn from National Educational Longitudinal Survey 1988. Sample included 3,786 students in mathematics, 2,524 students in science, 2,098 mathematics teachers, and 1,371 science teachers. Student achievement measured by performance on 10th- and 12th-grade standardized math and science tests. Multiple regression analysis	1988
Gordon, J. A. (1994)	Seeks to understand the reason for the lack of minority participation in teacher education	Qualitative analysis of interview data	Part of a larger study on the barriers to minority education. Semistructured interviews conducted with	Not available

Gordon, J. A. (2000)	How can we explain the reluctance of Asian Americans (especially immigrants) in the United States to enter the teaching profession given the high esteem in which the profession is held in many Asian countries? Asks how traditional Asian views on teaching affect immigrants in the context of public school realities.	Qualitative analysis of interview data	140 teachers of color in three cities over 2 years. Interviews were conducted by the authors and nine undergraduate students, all of whom were Asian immigrants or first- or second-generation Asian Americans. They developed a list of the most commonly cited reasons that the students gave for Asians not entering teaching. One prominent theme was the influence of Chinese culture on student attitude. This list was used in later coding of interview data. The 9 students interviewed 49 Asian Americans who varied in age, gender, occupation, and ethnic identities. Students followed a protocol for semistructured interviews. This included questions regarding demographic information, likelihood of entering teaching, view on	Not available

(Continued)

TABLE 4.1
(Continued)

Studies[a]	Question and Focus	Research Tradition	Research Design	Date of Data[b] Collection
			teaching, and images of teachers in the home country.	
Greenwald, R., Hedges, L. V., & Laine, R. D. (1996)	Looks at production function studies of educational inputs and outputs. Teacher variables examined are teacher ability (no description given of the variety of variables so classified), teacher education (possession of a master's degree and sometimes possession of course credits past a master's), and teacher experience (number of years). Outcome variables are student achievement scores in varying subject areas.	Meta-analysis	Meta-analysis of 60 education production function studies collected from literature reviews and electronic databases. Several different analyses, with different numbers of coefficients, were done for each outcome variable. For teacher ability, the number of coefficients ranged from 9 to 24; for teacher education from 24 to 46; and for teacher experience from 20 to 68.	1966–1993
Grissmer, D. W., & Kirby, S. N. (1987)	Attempts to develop a theory of teacher attrition which would improve national and state forecasts of attrition rates. Looks to account for the disparate reasons for attrition and explain the	Statistical analysis of varied data sources.	Data and literature drawn from several selected states. Use of cross-sectional attrition data from two states (samples of 5,000 and 35,000) and time-series evidence from four states (New York, Michigan,	1959–1983

	pattern of attrition unique to each life cycle and career stage			Utah, and Illinois) over 24 years. Bivariate relationship makes interpretation difficult.
Gruber, K. J., Wiley, S. D., & Broughman, S. P. (2002)	Introduces the 1999–2000 SASS data through tables of estimates for traditional public, private, public charter, and Bureau of Indian Affairs (BIA) schools, school library media centers, public school districts, and the principals and teachers that work in these schools	Statistical analysis of survey data	1999–2000	Six survey components: the School District Survey, the School Library Media Specialist/Librarian Survey, the Principal Survey, the School Survey, the Teacher Survey, the Teacher Follow-up Survey administered with slight modifications to meet the needs of public, private, public charter, and BIA schools. Frequency and percentage of responses reported.
Guyton, E., & Farokhi, E. (1987)	Examines the relationship between academic performance and successful teaching	Statistical analysis of varied data sources	1981–1984	Sample for the study drawn from teacher education graduates at a single university from fall 1981 through summer 1984. Participants were excluded for whom Teacher Certification Test (TCT) score or Teacher Performance Assessment Instrument (TPAI) score was unavailable. The study population was 273 students with TPAI scores and 413 with TCT scores.

(Continued)

TABLE 4.1
(Continued)

Studies[a]	Question and Focus	Research Tradition	Research Design	Date of Data[b] Collection
			Academic quality was measured by performance on two statewide tests and GPA. Teacher performance was measured by performance on the TPAI, a statewide assessment procedure. Test scores and GPA were correlated with TCT score and TPAI performance total. TCT and TPAI performance were correlated as well.	
Hall, B. W., & Carroll, D. (1987)	Addresses attrition issues in Florida schools. Compares those who plan to quit to those who plan to continue teaching to "generate a profile" of those in large urban school district who may be at risk of leaving.	Statistical analysis of varied data sources	Stratified (by school) random sample of 10% of teachers from a metropolitan Florida school district with 5,000 teachers. Return rate of 53% gave a sample of 242 teaches under 50 years of age (127 elementary teachers, 70 middle school, 86 high school teachers, 27 adult, vocational technical school (vo-tech), and other). Instruments included Survey of Teacher Characteristics and Activities (variables included long-range teaching plans;	Not available

demographic characteristics; current work conditions; professional activities; attitudes toward education, teaching, and students) and 6-item Teaching Autonomy Scale.

Compared results of those who plan to quit or were undecided and those who plan to continue teaching. Data analyzed through chi-square and ANOVA tests.

Hanushek, E. (1992)	The role of family factors such as birth order and family size in student achievement. The impact of school inputs, especially teacher characteristics, on student achievement.	Production function analysis	1971–1975

Family data were drawn over a 4-year period by the Gary Income Maintenance Experiment. These data were merged with information about student achievement (as measured by Iowa Reading Comprehension and Vocabulary tests) of children in the experimental families between 1971 and 1975. All families were Black and low income.

Includes 1,920 students, Grades 2–6.

Multiple regression analyses.

(Continued)

TABLE 4.1
(Continued)

Studies[a]	Question and Focus	Research Tradition	Research Design	Date of Data[b] Collection
Hanushek, E. A., & Pace, R. R. (1995)	Who enters teaching by demographic information (race and ethnicity and gender) and academic achievement? What roles do salary and certification requirements play in the decision to teach?	Statistical analysis of varied data sources	Study data are drawn from the longitudinal data of the HSB survey. This survey tracks a single cohort beginning in their senior year in high school and continuing for 6 years. The survey produced data on demographics, academic achievement (measured through a composite score on the HSB battery of achievement tests), college entrance, continuation and graduation, and plans or preparations to teach. Data are analyzed to study, in 2-year intervals the progress toward graduation and teaching of the cohort as influenced by race and ethnicity, gender, and achievement scores. In a second analysis, the HSB data are combined with state-level data regarding certification requirements	1980–1986

Citation	Focus	Details	Method	Data sources
Hawk, B. P., & Schmidt, M. W. (1989)	Comparison of graduates of 2 programs (traditional structure vs. 6-week preservice training and 1-year mentored on-the-job training) for quality (measured by NTE scores) and teaching effectiveness	and teacher pay. Examines variation in the probability of preparing to teach by state variation in pay and certification requirements. Multiple analyses of variance. Fifty-three 1st-year science and math teachers who had completed a traditional teacher education program and 16 students who had enrolled in a Lateral Entry Program (LEP) at the same university. Teacher quality measured by scores on NTE Mathematics or Biology Area exams (before school year), NTE Professional Knowledge exam (after school year). Teacher effectiveness measured by ratings across the school year on the Teacher Performance Appraisal Instrument. t-tests used for analysis.	Statistical analysis of varied data sources Population comparison	Not available
Henke, R. R., Choy, S. P., Chen, X., Geis, S., & Alt, M. N. (1997)	State of teachers and teaching in the early to mid-1990s. Reference source for statistical information on teachers in the United States.	The SASS, the TFS, Baccalaureate and Beyond Longitudinal Study (B&B), the National Assessment of Educational Progress (NAEP), and the National	Statistical analysis of varied data sources	1987–1988, 1988–1989 academic years SASS-1993–1994; TFS 1994–1995, B&B 1993–1994; NAEP (1994), NSOPF (1993)

(Continued)

TABLE 4.1
(Continued)

Studies[a]	Question and Focus	Research Tradition	Research Design	Date of Data[b] Collection
			Study of Postsecondary Faculty (NSOPF), as well as data from the Common Core of Data and the 1992 National Adult Literacy Survey were analyzed to provide information to educators at all levels, policymakers, administrators, parents, and the general public about teachers' demographic characteristics, and various characteristics of their schools and students, teachers' preparation and professional development experiences, workloads, teaching practices, compensation, satisfaction with and opinions regarding their working conditions, and the supply and demand of teachers.	
Henke, R. R., Chen, X., & Geis, S. (2000)	Looks at the demographic and quality characteristics as well as the teaching experiences of 1992–1993 college graduates who had	Statistical analysis of survey data	Uses data drawn from the 1994 and 1997 followups of the cohort of college graduates who participated in the Baccalaureate and	1992–1997

taught or prepared to teach in the 4 years following graduation

Beyond Longitudinal study (B&B:93). These include participants in the 1993 National Postsecondary Student Aid Study who received their bachelor's degrees between July 1992 and June 1993. Ninety-two hundred seventy-four participants completed all three phases of the study for an 83% response rate.

Variables examined include demographic characteristics of those who entered the pipeline and those who did not, progress through the pipeline, academic background of entrants, career paths, and experiences of those who had taught, and teaching plans for the future of all participants.

Statistical results were produced using the B&B:93/97 Data Analysis System (DAS). DAS produces simple tables as well as a correlation matrix of selected variables to be used for linear regression models.

(Continued)

TABLE 4.1
(Continued)

Studies[a]	Question and Focus	Research Tradition	Research Design	Date of Data[b] Collection
Henke, R. R., Choy, S. P., Geis, S., & Broughman, S. P. (1997)	Attempts to create a statistical profile of schools and teachers in U. S. public and private schools regarding teacher shortage and demand; characteristics of elementary and secondary teachers; teacher workplace conditions; characteristics of school principals; and school programs and policies.	Statistical analysis of survey data	SASS is a multilevel-linked survey of public and private schools, principals, and teachers, and public school districts. Public school sample is selected from the 1991–1992 NCES Common Core of Data. Private schools were selected from the 1991–1992 Private School Survey Frame. Public schools are selected for sampling by location and private schools by association group. The school is the primary sampling unit. Based on each selected school, samples of districts, administrators, and teachers were created. Each selected school was asked to provide a list of all full-time, part-time, itinerant, and long-term substitute teachers. These were stratified into five types by race and experience and then further sorted by level and subject.	1993–1994

This process created a weighted national probability sample of 68,284 teachers.

Instruments used in the survey include The Teacher Demand and Shortage Survey for Public School Districts, The School Survey, The School Principal Survey, The Teacher Survey, the School Library Media Center Survey, the School Library Media Specialist/Librarian Survey, and the Student Records Survey. Several of these were modified slightly to meet the needs of private schools and BIA schools.

Henke, R. R., Geis, S., Giambattista, J., & Knepper, P. (1996)

Looks at the demographic and quality characteristics of 1992–1993 college graduates who had taught or prepared to teach in the year following graduation

Statistical analysis of survey data

Uses data drawn from the 1994 followup of the cohort of college graduates who participated in the Baccalaureate and Beyond Longitudinal study (B&B:93). These include participants in the 1993 National Postsecondary Student Aid Study who received their bachelor's degrees between July 1992

1992–1994

(Continued)

TABLE 4.1
(Continued)

Studies[a]	Question and Focus	Research Tradition	Research Design	Date of Data[b] Collection
			and June 1993. The 1st followup was conducted approximately 1-year after graduation. Ten thousand eight hundred participants were determined to be eligible and could be contacted for a response rate of 92%. Participants were considered to have entered the teaching pipeline if they had considered teaching, prepared to teach, or had taught. Variables examined include demographic characteristics of those who entered the pipeline and those who did not; progress through the pipeline, academic background of entrants, and school experiences of those who had taught.	
Heyns, B. (1988)	Examines career patterns of teachers from longitudinal data	Statistical analysis of survey data	Data drawn from National Longitudinal Study of the high school class of 1972 (sample size 20,000). Survey sent to past and present	1972–1986

| Houston, W. R., Marshall, F., & McDavid, T. (1993) | Do alternately and traditionally certified teachers differ in their perceptions of the problems they face as 1st-year teachers? Do they differ in their reports of feelings of confidence, satisfaction, and plans to continue teaching? | Statistical analysis of survey data. | elementary and secondary teachers and those who had trained but never taught. Variables included career history, academic data (GPAs, SAT scores), and demographic information. Data collected as part of a 2-year study of 1st-year teachers in Houston schools. Sample composed of 69 traditionally certified teachers (program including education course work and student teaching) and 162 alternatively certified teachers. All participants were elementary school teachers. Study participants completed an instrument after 2-months of teaching and again after 8 months. The instrument collected data regarding demographic information, teaching assignments, perceived problems, support, satisfaction with teaching, and future plans. t-tests and chi-square tests used for analysis. | Not available |

(Continued)

TABLE 4.1
(Continued)

Studies[a]	Question and Focus	Research Tradition	Research Design	Date of Data[b] Collection
Ingersoll, R. (1996)	Looks at the extent to which U.S. secondary students are taught core academic courses by qualified teachers. Also looks at the distribution of qualified teachers across and within schools.	Statistical analysis of survey data	Data drawn from the 1990–1991 SASS. The sample used in this study was limited to secondary-school (7–12) teachers who taught courses in the core departmental areas (English, math, social studies, or science) yielding a total sample of 25,427. For each class period in the school day of each of the sampled teachers, data were collected on the subject taught, grade level, class type or track, student achievement level, student race and ethnicity, and the number of students enrolled. In addition, teachers reported their certification status and their major and minor fields of study for each of their degrees earned, at both the undergraduate and graduate levels.	1990–1991

| Ingersoll, R. (1999) | What is the extent of out-of-field teaching in the United States? What are the main causes of out-of-field teaching? | Statistical analysis of survey data | Out-of-field teaching is measured by the proportion of students being taught by teachers who lack even a minor in the course being taught. Science and social studies are further subdivided into specialties. Data were also collected from school administrators on school minority and poverty levels as well as from class characteristics including student achievement and tracking. Determined the number of those teaching core academic subjects who do not hold either a major or a minor in their fields, using data from the SASS, and considered to what extent it varied across different subjects, different kinds of schools, teachers, and classrooms. Also looked at legitimacy of three widely believed explanations for out-of-field teaching—inadequate training, inflexible teacher unions, or shortages of qualified teachers. | 1987–1988; 1990–1991; 1993–1994 |

(Continued)

TABLE 4.1
(Continued)

Studies[a]	Question and Focus	Research Tradition	Research Design	Date of Data[b] Collection
Jelmberg, J. (1996)	Compares the graduates of college-based teacher education programs with participants in a state sponsored alternate on-the-job training program regarding demographic information, academic background, principal evaluation, and views of preparation and support.	Statistical analysis of survey data. Population comparison.	Survey administered to a random sample of 492 of 660 New Hampshire elementary and secondary teachers of math, science, English, and social studies who had no previous certification and were certified between 1987 and 1990. A 60% response rate yielded 295 responses, of which 236 were usable. Of these, 230 gave permission to survey their principals. Of these, 261 responded and 136 were usable. Data were collected regarding academic credentials, teacher performance, professional courses, and practicum supervision. Differences between the two populations were calculated using z-tests and t-tests.	1987–1990
Kirby, S. N., Berends, M., & Naftel, S. (1999)	Examines the career paths of minority teachers in Texas, particularly Latinos. Subfocus on the role that the proportion of "at-risk"	Statistical analysis of varied data sources	Data taken from a longitudinal data file on public school teachers in Texas obtained from the Texas State Department of	1980–1995

	students in a district plays in issues of supply and demand.		Education. Sample limited to full-time teachers in the Texas public school system from 1980–1981 to 1995–1996. Variety of analysis methods used.	
Kirby, S. N., & Grissmer, D. W. (1993)	Patterns of attrition in all teachers and new teachers. The role of salary in teacher attrition.	Statistical analysis of varied data sources	Database consists of longitudinal records for all full-time teachers in the Indiana public schools from 1965 to 1987. Additionally, they conducted a survey of approximately 1,600 new hires in the 1988 to 1989 school year. Five hundred had participated in a mentor program and were asked about their experiences. Data from other studies were included as well.	1965–1987; 1988–1989
Kirby, S. N., Naftel, S., & Berends, M. (1999)	What defines "at-risk" districts? How do at-risk districts differ from those not at risk in terms of resources and student and teacher characteristics? Given that at-risk districts are staffed largely by minority teachers, what do we know about the likely future demand and supply of such teachers?	Statistical analysis of varied data sources.	Variety of analysis methods. Matched state personnel records (including demographic data and employment history) with district data to create a longitudinal data file on public school teachers in Texas from 1979 to 1995. Using district data on eligibility for the federal free-lunch program, all school districts were	1980–1995

(Continued)

TABLE 4.1
(Continued)

Studies[a]	Question and Focus	Research Tradition	Research Design	Date of Data[b] Collection
			categorized as being low (below 40%), medium (40%–59%) or high risk (60% or above) related to the proportion of children they served deemed at risk for educational failure. Cutoff points were determined based on an analysis of the correlation between percentage of children eligible for free lunch and student achievement as measured by performance on state exams. Looks at differences in demographics, qualifications (certification, degree and experience), and career path of teachers among the three risk categories.	
Lankford, H., Loeb, S., & Wykoff, J. (2002)	How much variation is there in teacher attributes across schools in New York? Which schools have the least qualified teachers? Has the distribution changed over time? How is the distribution affected by attrition and transfer?	Statistical analysis of varied data sources	Sample is all teachers in the New York State system in 1999–2000. Measures of teacher quality were experience, highest degree, certification in current assignment, certification in all assignments, scores on	1999–2000

Citation	Purpose	Method	Description	Year
Latham, A. S., Gitomer, D., & Ziomek, R. (1999)	The study seeks to quantify the academic ability of the teaching force at different points in the pipeline and to ascertain the role that teacher testing plays in shaping the teaching force.	Statistical analysis of varied data sources	NTE or New York State Teacher Certification Examination (NYSTCE), quality of college attended as rated by *Barron's College Guide*. Authors created school level averages of these teacher measures and then looked for variations among regions, among districts within regions, and among schools within districts. Then teacher qualifications were correlated with school and student characteristics. Multiple regression analysis. Sample from the 1995 to 1997 ETS data file including nearly 34,000 PRAXIS I candidates and more than 160,000 PRAXIS II candidates who had also taken the SAT.	1995–1997
Lewis, L., Parsad, B., Carey, N., Bartfai, N., & Farris, E. (1999)	Attempts to provide a national profile of teacher preparation, qualifications, professional development, and school and parental support	Statistical analyses of survey data	Questionnaires were mailed to a nationally representative sample of 4,049 full-time teachers in regular public, elementary, middle, and high schools. Sample was designed to	1998

(Continued)

TABLE 4.1
(Continued)

Studies[a]	Question and Focus	Research Tradition	Research Design	Date of Data[b] Collection
			represent full-time public school teachers in Grades 1–12 whose main teaching assignment is in English and language arts, social studies, foreign language, mathematics, or science or who taught in a self-contained classroom. Data were weighted to national averages. Chi-square tests or *t*-tests were used to test for significance in comparative statements. To make comparisons to 1993 to 1994 SASS data, that data were reanalyzed for a subset of teachers and schools that approximate the sample in this study.	
Lutz, F. W., & Hutton, J. B. (1989)	This is an evaluation of the alternative certification program in the Dallas Independent School District in terms of (a) characteristics of the program, (b) characteristics of the interns, (c) intern attitudes, (d) comparison of	Statistical analyses of varied data sources	Data were collected from many sources to answer research questions. Data sources include intern personnel records (demographic information, GPA, and entrance test scores); personnel records of traditionally certified	1986–1987

				1985
	interns and traditionally certified teachers, (e) teaching performance of interns, (f) predictors of alternately certified teacher success, (g) reaction to the program, and (h) alternate program ability to meet demand.		teachers; Teacher Work-Life Inventory and Teacher Concerns Checklist (attitudes about teaching); SES data of schools in which sample teachers were employed; Texas Teacher Appraisal System, ExCET, and supervisor surveys (performance evaluation); etc. Data were analyzed using chi-square and *t*-tests.	
Matthes, W. A., & Carlson, R. V. (1986, April)	Examines differences in the reasons 1st-year teachers in rural, urban, or suburban schools accepted their present teaching positions. Were the reasons first-year teachers in rural, urban, or suburban schools might consider a teaching position in another school district different?	Statistical analysis of survey data	Ninety-nine respondents who were graduates of either the University of Iowa or the University of Vermont during the 1983–1984 school year and were currently teaching; asked to rate along a 45-item likert-type scale the importance of reasons pertaining to the community, the schools, and salary and benefits in accepting their current teaching position; respondents also asked to choose the 5 most important reasons for considering a position in another school district.	

(Continued)

237

TABLE 4.1
(Continued)

Studies[a]	Question and Focus	Research Tradition	Research Design	Date of Data[b] Collection
McDiarmid, G. W., & Wilson, S. M. (1991)	Investigates whether the subject knowledge of alternate-route mathematics teachers holding a mathematics degree was sufficient for teaching math.	Statistical analysis of survey data	Data were collected as part of a larger National Center for Research on Teacher Education study. For the larger study, researchers collected questionnaire responses from 700 participants in 11 teacher education sites representing a range of program structures. A subsample was chosen for interviews as well. This study reflects only a sample of 55, all of whom were alternate-route participants holding an undergraduate degree in mathematics. Eight (all secondary math teachers) of 55 were chosen for interviews and observations as well. A comparison group of 8 alternate-route teachers whose BAs were in other	Not available

Lastly, respondents rated their teacher education programs on 15 dimensions.

Source	Research questions	Design/method	Data/instruments	Dates
Murnane, R. J., & Schwinden, M. (1989)	What changes took place between 1975 and 1985 in the number and characteristics of college graduates who obtained teacher certification? Do demographic characteristics, subject specialties, and scores on the NTE predict which certificants became teachers in North Carolina and which did not?	Statistical analysis of varied data sources	fields but who taught math on the elementary level. Instruments included a subset of items from a 306-item questionnaire related to mathematics, and the responses to 3 of the mathematics scenarios in the interview. Information from the North Carolina Department of Instruction used to construct database of 47,403 persons with no prior teaching experience in North Carolina and who were classified as either Black or White. Analysis used scores on NTE subject-specific subtests.	1975–1985
Murnane, R. J., Singer, J. D., Willett, J. B., Kemple, J. J., & Olson, R. J. (1991)	Looks at impact of various teacher characteristics (demographics, subject specialty, career status, salary, and entering school districts) on career path. Compares to college graduates in the general population.	Statistical analysis of varied data sources	Teacher data were drawn from state databases. Michigan: 30,614 individuals who entered public school teaching between September 1972 and September 1981. North Carolina: 50,502 individuals licensed by the state for public school teaching between January 1974 and December 1985.	Michigan data from 1972–1981. North Carolina data from 1974–1985. Comparison data from 1967–1985.

(Continued)

TABLE 4.1
(Continued)

Studies[a]	Question and Focus	Research Tradition	Research Design	Date of Data[b] Collection
			Data on individuals who graduated from college between 1967 and 1985 from National Longitudinal Surveys of Labor Market Experience (NLS). Cross-tabulation, logistic regression, and survival analysis.	
NCES. (1997a)	Are public school teachers with LEP students in their classes trained in teaching LEP students? Are teachers with higher percentages of LEP students more likely to receive training? Are teachers of English more likely to have received LEP training than are other subject teachers?	Statistical analysis of survey data	1993 to 1994 SASS data. LEP students defined as those whose dominant language is other than English and who have sufficient difficulty speaking, writing, or reading English as to deny them the opportunity to learn successfully in an English-only classroom. An LEP-trained teacher has either preservice or inservice training (of any amount) in teaching LEP students.	1993–1994
NCES. (2003)	National multilevel survey program designed to create a profile of U.S. schools and teachers regarding teacher shortage and demand; characteristics of	Statistical analysis of survey data	SASS is a multilevel-linked survey of public and private schools, principals, and teachers, and public school districts. Public school sample is selected	1999–2000

240

elementary and secondary teachers; teacher workplace conditions; characteristics of school principals; school programs and policies; school and district performance reports, standards for home-schooled students, charter schools, migrant students, and availability and use of computers and the Internet.

from the 1997–1998 NCES Common Core of Data. Private schools were selected from the 1997 to 1998 Private School Survey Frame. Public schools are selected for sampling by location and private schools by association group. The entire universe of public charter schools and BIA schools was included in the sample.

The school is the primary sampling unit. Based on each selected school, samples of districts (for public, noncharter schools), administrators, and teachers were created. Each selected school was asked to provide a list of all full-time, part-time, itinerant, and long-term substitute teachers. These were stratified into 5 types by race and experience and then further sorted by level and subject. This process created a weighted national probability sample of 72,058 teachers.

(Continued)

TABLE 4.1
(Continued)

Studies[a]	Question and Focus	Research Tradition	Research Design	Date of Data[b] Collection
			Instruments used in the survey include the School District Survey, the Principal Survey, the School Survey, the Teacher Survey, and the School Library Media Center Survey. The questionnaires were modified to meet the needs of private, BIA, and charter schools.	
NEA. (2003)	Report on questionnaire exploring the preparation, experience, assignment, professional development, demographic characteristics, personal background, and attitudes of a sample of public school teachers	Statistical analysis of survey data	Survey participants were selected by means of a two-stage sample design. A sample of public school systems was drawn from the U.S. Department of Education list and classified into nine strata by enrollment. Systems were selected from within each stratum in proportion to the frequency of its occurrence. A systematic sampling of teachers with a random start was done from rosters of teachers from each selected school system. This	2000–2001

(Continued)

			1987–1991
			yielded a sample of 2,826 teachers to receive a 60-item questionnaire. A response rate of 67.4% of usable questionnaires provided a total study sample of 1,467. Data are analyzed with reference to teacher characteristics (sex, age, race, school level, region, and size of school system). Reports frequency and percentage distribution for current participants as well as tabulates historical trends based on similar surveys 1961–1996.
Natriello, G., & Zumwalt, K. K. (1993)	Evaluates the success of 1 New Jersey alternate-route preparation program in producing teachers for urban schools	Statistical analysis of survey data	Data were collected as part of the New Jersey Teacher Education Study, a longitudinal study of individuals entering teaching in 1987. Surveys were initially administered to all individuals completing college-based teacher preparation programs in the fields of secondary English and math, as well as 40% of individuals completing college-based elementary education

243

TABLE 4.1
(Continued)

Studies[a]	Question and Focus	Research Tradition	Research Design	Date of Data[b] Collection
			programs. Yielded a college-prepared sample of 187. For comparison, a sample was drawn of 129 alternate-route teachers. Periodic surveys were administered to both groups over 4 years. Response rates for the initial survey were 87% but declined over time.	
Parsad, B., Lewis, L., & Farris, E. (2000)	Focus on indicators of teacher preparation and qualifications including teacher education, participation in formal professional development, and teachers' feelings of preparedness. Also comparison between 1998 and 2000 survey.	Statistical analysis of survey data	The 1999–2000 SASS database of regular U.S. K–12 public schools was categorized by level, locale, and size, and within each primary category sorted by percentage of minority enrollment. From this universe of 81,405 schools, a sample of 2,209 schools was chosen. Each school was asked to send a list of teachers, and from these lists a sample of 5,253 teachers was drawn at rates from each individual school based on level, subject, and experience. A weighted	2000

			response rate of 84% yielded a study sample (less participants who fell outside the scope of the study) of 4,128. Chi-square tests or t-tests were used to test for significance in comparative statements.	
Pascal, A. (1987)	Statistical analysis of survey data	Describes the qualifications of teachers currently teaching in American public, comprehensive high schools to identify characteristics of schools that have more qualified and less qualified teachers	Teacher survey data files of the HSB study asked a number of questions about teachers' course assignments and educational preparation. Qualifications were defined as intellectual capital acquired, such as college training in subjects most frequently taught, years of experience, and other such characteristics. HSB data from 1980 and 1982 provide information on the attributes of the high schools where these teachers were employed.	1984
Pigge, F. L. (1985)	Statistical analysis of varied data sources	Studies the ability differences between and among certifiable teacher education students who did and did not teach after graduation	Two thousand education graduates from 1972 to 1975 and 1,000 education graduates from 1980 to 1983 from a medium-size university in Ohio divided into 7 independent groups on the basis of their job	1985. Uses data from 1972–1975 and 1980–1983.

(Continued)

TABLE 4.1
(Continued)

Studies[a]	Question and Focus	Research Tradition	Research Design	Date of Data[b] Collection
			placement status after graduation. Compares achievement scores for the placement groups and the interaction of the ability and achievement scores between the years of graduation and the placement status.	
Pigge, F. L., & Marso, R. N. (1992)	Do teacher education persisters and nonpersisters differ in academic, affective, and personal characteristics?	Statistical analysis of varied data sources	Sample of 550 teacher candidates at Bowling Green State University. Data on academic (ACT scores, university GPA, and Comprehensive Tests of Basic Skills scores), personal (demographic information, parent occupation, timing of decision to enter teaching, level of assurance about becoming a teacher, and extent of teacher-like experience), and affective (Teacher Concerns Questionnaire, Attitude Toward Teaching as a Career Scale, and Teacher Anxiety Scale) data were collected on entry to the teacher education program.	1985–1991

			Five years later, those who had completed student teaching were classified as persisters, and those who had not were classified as nonpersisters. MANOVA and ANOVA tests were run to determine statistical differences between the 2 groups.
Seastrom, M. M., Gruber, K. J., Henke, R. R., McGrath, D. J., & Cohen, B. A. (2002)	Examines the extent of out-of-field teaching in U.S. public, middle, and high schools	Statistical analysis of survey data	1999–2000
			Data drawn from 1999 to 2000 School and Staffing Survey. The survey collects data on the educational background, professional credentials, and teaching assignments.
			Defines "out-of-field" in two ways: teachers who lack a major, minor, or certification in the subject taught; and teachers without a major and certification in the subject taught.
			Measures the prevalence of out-of-field teaching by the percentage of teachers' students who are in classes with a teacher teaching outside their field.
			Data were presented separately for middle and high school teachers.

(Continued)

247

TABLE 4.1
(Continued)

Studies[a]	Question and Focus	Research Tradition	Research Design	Date of Data[b] Collection
Shen, J. (1998a)	Investigates the cumulative effect of alternative certification on the elementary and secondary public teaching force and comparative characteristics of those certified traditionally and alternatively	Statistical analysis of survey data	Data were extracted from the Public School Teacher Questionnaire of SASS 1994. Focus on teachers certified in the 10 years prior to the 1993–1994 survey. Sample included 13,601 traditionally certified teachers and 1,118 alternatively certified teachers. Sample weighted to be nationally representative. Arguments for alternative certification policies tested using chi-square test. Data disaggregated by elementary and secondary levels.	1993–1994
Shen, J. (1998b)	An investigation of the cumulative effect of alternative certification on the elementary and secondary teaching force and a comparison of the characteristics of	Statistical analysis of survey data	Makes use of data collected for the 1993 to 1994 SASS, particularly responses to the Public School Teacher Questionnaire. Teachers only included in the sample who had received	1993–1994

	alternatively and traditionally certified teachers. Can alternative certification improve the quality of the teaching force? Does it improve the diversity of the teaching force? Does alternative certification reduce shortages in urban and rural school districts?		certification in the 10 years prior to 1993–1994. Traditionally certified teachers were those with advanced or regular certification. Alternately certified teachers were those who reported that they had received a certificate through an "alternative certificate program." This produced a relative weighted sample of 13,601 traditionally certified teachers and 1,118 alternately certified teachers. Chi-square tests were used for analysis.
Strauss, R. P., & Sawyer, E. A. (1986)	Looks at impact of teacher variables (mean teacher composite NTE scores for a district) on student achievement (as measured by failure rate on state high school competency exam taken in junior year, average achievement on the state Norm Referenced Achievement Test taken in junior year)	Production function analysis	Regression analysis of data from 145 North Carolina school districts. Analyzes impact of teacher quality on student achievement. Adjusts for student background variables including family background and per capita income.	1977–1978
Su, Z. (1997)	Reveals similarities and differences in views of teaching as a profession and as a career among	Qualitative analysis of interview data. Statistical analysis of survey data.	Surveys administered to all teacher candidates toward the end of their preparation. Of the	1993–1994

(Continued)

249

TABLE 4.1
(Continued)

Studies[a]	Question and Focus	Research Tradition	Research Design	Date of Data[b] Collection
	Asian-American, African-American, and Hispanic teacher candidates and their White or Caucasian peers in a state university in the United States		surveys, 90 were White or Caucasian students, 31 Asian Americans, 5 African Americans, 31 Hispanics, and 1 Native American. Interviews were conducted twice—once in the middle of their programs and once at the end with 30 Asian-American students, 17 Hispanics, 4 African Americans, and 15 randomly selected students from the White or Caucasian group. Descriptive statistics reported from survey data.	
T.E.A. (1995)	Analyzes the retention, mobility, and attrition of Texas teaching force by teacher characteristics (demographic information, experience, salary, degree, subject area, and teacher test scores) and school conditions (level, size, diversity, and community type)	Statistical analysis of varied data sources	The sample is 10,381 teachers who began teaching in the Texas public schools 1988–1989. The career paths of these teachers were followed through 1992 to 1993. Survival analysis provides a survival probability and hazard probability in relation to teacher characteristics and school conditions. Discrete-time survival analysis.	1989–1993

| Theopold, N. (1990) | Examines the relationships among the personal and professional attributes of elementary and secondary teachers, the financial, institutional, and demographic characteristics, of school districts, and the retention behavior of teachers employed by those districts. | Production function analysis | Data were gathered from Washington State's Certificated Personnel Reports from 1984–1985 to 1986–1987. Data included demographic, professional, and career characteristics for individual teachers, as well as district level information. $N = 37{,}321$; $37{,}696$; $38{,}378$ respectively for each of the three school years. These data were analyzed using a random utility model to determine the influence of different personal and professional variables on teachers' stay and leave decisions. | 1984–1985 to 1986–1987 |
| Vegas, E., Murnane, R. J., & Willett, J. B. (2001) | Focuses on the roles that race, ethnicity, and academic skills play in predicting whether high school students persist along each of the various steps of the path into teaching | Statistical analysis of survey data | Constructed sample using a sequence of four samples from the High School and Beyond (HSB) to answer the following questions in progression—Who graduates from high school? Who enters college? Who obtains a BA? Who enters teaching—for a final sample of 3,037 | HSB 1992 included longitudinal survey information collected in 1980, 1982, 1984, 1986, 1992. |

(Continued)

TABLE 4.1
(Continued)

Studies[a]	Question and Focus	Research Tradition	Research Design	Date of Data[b] Collection
			participants. At each step the following was explored: (a) whether the conditional probability of moving to the next step differed among individuals of different racial or ethnic origin, (b) whether the conditional probability of moving to the next step is predicted by 10th-grade academic skills, and (c) whether individuals of different racial or ethnic origin but with the same level of 10th-grade academic skills have different conditional probabilities of completing each step of the path into teaching.	
Wenglinsky, H. (2000)	Examines the links among characteristics of teacher education institutions, their	Statistical analysis of varied data sources	Multiple regression analysis. Multilevel structural equation modeling was used with the following data sources.	1994–1997

	programs, and teacher effectiveness measured by scores on teacher licensure tests in southeastern United States		Data from 39,140 perspective teachers who took the PRAXIS II teacher licensure exam. Data from 152 institutions these teachers attended from the U.S. Department of Education database. Data from 76 of 152 institutions from questionnaire sent to deans. SAT scores for 9,078 of the test takers who had also taken the SAT from ETS.	
Whitener, S. D., & Gruber, K. (1997)	Sponsored by NCES to update information on teacher attrition and career patterns	Statistical analysis of survey data	Multiple regression analysis Targeted elementary and secondary teachers who taught in schools that had a first grade or higher in the United States during the 1993–1994 school year. TFS survey of 1994–1995 cohort.	1994–1995 school year

(Continued)

TABLE 4.1
(Continued)

Studies[a]	Question and Focus	Research Tradition	Research Design	Date of Data[b] Collection
Wong, M. J., & Osguthorpe, R. T. (1993)	Investigates program structures of teacher education programs and the relationship between institutional classification (research, doctorate-granting, comprehensive, or liberal arts) and the type of teacher education program? What type of degrees to institutions grant?	Statistical analysis of survey data	A 19-item questionnaire was sent to all 664 institutions listed in *Peterson's Guide to Graduate Programs in Business, Education, Health, and Law* 1989 as having a graduate program in education. Response rate of 61% for a total sample of 407. Institutions were classified according to the Carnegie classification of institutions of higher education based on the degrees granted and the amount of federal research funding. Reports descriptive statistics and frequencies.	1990

[a] Studies included in this chart include post-1985 empirical research studies from which we drew significant data for either chapter 3 or 4. Where full information is not provided under Studies, please see References for this chapter.

[b] Unlike the charts accompanying other chapters, we have not included research findings in the chart because many of the studies were so data intense that it was not possible to adequately summarize them here. The relevant findings are discussed in the text. We have chosen to include information regarding the date of data collection because, in some studies, the age of the data may impact the interpretation of the findings.

REFERENCES: DATA SOURCES[1]

AACTE. (1987). *RATE I: Teaching teachers: Facts and figures*. Washington, DC: American Association of Colleges of Teacher Education.

AACTE. (1992). *Academic achievement of White, Black, and Hispanic students in teacher education programs*. Washington, DC: American Association of Colleges of Teacher Education.

Andrew, M. D. (1990). Differences between graduates of 4-year and 5-year teacher preparation programs. *Journal of Teacher Education, 41*(2), 45–51.

Ballou, D. (1996). Do public schools hire the best applicants? *Quarterly Journal of Economics, 111*(1), 97–133.

Barger, J., Barger, R., & Rearden, J. (1986, March). *The academic quality of teacher certification graduates and their employment histories*. Paper presented at the Annual Meeting of the American Association of Colleges for Teacher Education, Chicago, IL.

Barger, J., Barger, R., & Rearden, J. (1988, February). *Are beginning teachers "Bottom of the barrel?" An institutional study of the academic quality of teacher certification graduates, 1982–1986*. Paper presented at the Annual Conference of the Association of Teacher Educators, San Diego, CA.

Bobbitt, S. A. (1989). *What teachers majored in: Bachelor's degree fields of public and private school teachers*. Washington, DC: National Center for Education Statistics, U.S. Department of Education.

Bobbitt, S. A., Faupel, E., & Burns, S. (1991). *Stayers, movers, and leavers: Results of the 1988–89 Teacher Follow-up Survey, 1991*. Washington, DC: National Center for Education Statistics, U.S. Department of Education.

Bobbitt, S. A., & McMillen, M. M. (1994). *Qualifications of the public school teacher workforce: 1988 and 1991*. Washington, DC: National Center for Education Statistics, U.S. Department of Education.

Boe, E. E., & Barkanic, G. (2000, April). *Critical factors in developing a highly qualified national teaching force*. Paper presented at the Annual Meeting of the American Educational Research Association, New Orleans, LA.

Boe, E. E., Cook, L. H., Bobbitt, S. A., & Terhanian, G. (1998). The shortage of fully certified teachers in special and general education. *Teacher Education and Special Education, 21*(1), 1–21.

Broughman, S. P., & Rollefson, M. R. (2000). *Teacher supply in the United States: Sources of newly hired teachers in the public and private schools, 1987–88 to 1993–94*. Washington, DC: National Center for Education Statistics, U.S. Department of Education.

Casserly, M. (1992). *National urban education goals: Baseline indicators, 1990–91*. Washington, DC: The Council of the Great City Schools.

Clark, J. M. (1989). Reconciliation of data on aptitude test scores and university grades of teachers. *Journal of Teacher Education, July/August*, 49–52.

Coley, R. J., & Thorpe, M. E. (1989). The MAT model revisited: Implications for improving teacher quality. *Teacher Education Quarterly, 16*, 101–110.

Cornett, L. M. (1992). Alternative certification: State policies in the SREB states. *Peabody Journal of Education, 67*(3), 55–83.

Darling-Hammond, L. (2000). Teacher quality and student achievement: A review of state policy evidence. *Education Policy Analysis Archives, 8*(1), 1–29. Retrieved March, 4, 2001, from http://epaa.asu.edu/epaa/v8n1

Demetrulias, D. M., Chiodo, J. J., & Dickman, J. E. (1990). Differential admission requirements and student achievement in teacher education. *Journal of Teacher Education, 41*(2), 66–72.

Ehrenberg, R. G., & Brewer, D. J. (1994). Do school and teacher characteristics matter? Evidence from *High School and Beyond*. *Economics of Education Review, 13*(1), 1–17.

---

[1]This reference list includes sources for all data (1985–2003) cited in chapter 4. The second reference list (References: Other Works Cited) includes all other sources, including sources for pre-1985 data.

Ehrenberg, R. G., & Brewer, D. J. (1995). Did teachers' verbal ability and race matter in the 1960s? Coleman revisited. *Economics of Education Review, 14*(1), 1–21.

Feistritzer, C. E. (1999). *The making of a teacher: A report on teacher preparation in the United States.* Washington, DC: National Center for Education Information.

Ferguson, R. F. (1991). Paying for public education: New evidence on how and why money matters. *Harvard Journal on Legislation, 28*(2), 465–498.

Ferguson, R. F., & Ladd, H. F. (1996). How and why money matters: An analysis of Alabama schools. In H. F. Ladd (Ed.), *Holding schools accountable: Performance based reform in education* (pp. 265–298). Washington, DC: Brookings Institute.

Fowler, C. (2002, August). Fast track . . . slow going. *AACTE Research Brief.*

Freeman, D. J., Martin, R. J., Brousseau, B. A., & West, B. B. (1989). Do higher program admission standards alter profiles of entering teacher candidates? *Journal of Teacher Education, 40*(3), 33–41.

Garibaldi, A. M. (1991). Abating the shortage of Black teachers. In C. V. Willie, A. M. Garibaldi, & W. L. Reed (Eds.), *The education of Africans-Americans* (pp. 148–158). New York: Auburn House.

Gitomer, D. H., Latham, A. S., & Ziomek, R. (1999). *The academic quality of prospective teachers: The impact of admissions and licensure testing.* Princeton, NJ: Educational Testing Service.

Goertz, M. E., & Pitcher, B. (1985). *The impact of NTE use by states on teacher selection.* Research Report No. RR-85–1. Princeton, NJ: Educational Testing Service.

Goldhaber, D. D., & Brewer, D. J. (2000). Does certification matter? High school teacher certification status and student achievement. *Educational Evaluation and Policy Analysis, 22*(2), 129–145.

Gomez, M. L., & Stoddart, T. (1991). Learning to teach writing: The balance of personal and professional perspectives. In R. Clift & C. Evertson (Eds.), *Focal points: Qualitative inquiries into teaching* (pp. 39–64). Washington, DC: American Educational Research Association.

Greenwald, R., Hedges, L. V., & Laine, R. D. (1996). The effect of school resources on student achievement. *Review of Educational Research, 66*(3), 361–396.

Grey, L., Cahalan, M., Hein, S., Litman, C., Severynse, J., Warren, S., et al. (1993). *New teachers in the job market: 1991 update.* Washington, DC: U.S. Department of Education, Office of Educational Research and Improvement.

Gruber, K. J., Wiley, S. D., & Broughman, S. P. (2002). *Schools and staffing survey, 1999–2000: Overview of the data for public, private, public charter, and Bureau of Indian Affairs elementary and secondary schools.* Washington, DC: National Center for Education Statistics, U.S. Department of Education.

Guyton, E., & Farokhi, E. (1987). Relationship among academic performance, basic skills, subject matter knowledge, and teaching skills of teacher education graduates. *Journal of Teacher Education, 38*(5), 37–40.

Hanushek, E. A. (1992). The trade-off between child quantity and quality. *Journal of Political Economy, 100*, 84–118.

Hanushek, E. A., & Pace, R. R. (1995). Who chooses to teach (and why)? *Economics of Education Review, 14*(2), 101–117.

Hawk, B. P., & Schmidt, M. W. (1989). Teacher preparation: A comparison of traditional and alternative programs. *Journal of Teacher Education, 40*(September–October), 53–58.

Henke, R. R., Chen, X., & Geis, S. (2000). *Progress through the teacher pipeline: 1992–93 college graduates and elementary/secondary school teaching as of 1997.* Washington, DC: National Center for Education Statistics, U.S. Department of Education.

Henke, R. R., Choy, S. P., Chen, X., Geis, S., & Alt, M. N. (1997). *America's teachers: Profile of a profession, 1993–4.* Washington, DC: National Center for Education Statistics, U.S. Department of Education.

Henke, R. R., Choy, S. P., Geis, S., & Broughman, S. P. (1997). *School and staffing in the U.S.: A statistical profile, 1993–94.* Washington, DC: National Center for Education Statistics, U.S. Department of Education.

Henke, R. R., Geis, S., Giambattista, J., & Knepper, P. (1996). *Out of the lecture hall and into the classroom: 1992–93 college graduates and elementary/secondary school teaching*. Washington, DC: National Center for Education Statistics, U.S. Department of Education.

Houston, W. R., Marshall, F., & McDavid, T. (1993). Problems of traditionally prepared and alternatively certified first-year teachers. *Education and Urban Society, 26*(1), 78–89.

Howey, K., & Strom, S. (1987). Teacher selection reconsidered. In G. Katz & J. Rath (Eds.), *Advances in Teacher Education* (vol. 3, pp. 1–34). Norwood, NJ: Ablex.

Ingersoll, R. M. (1996). *Out-of-field teaching and educational equality*. Washington, DC: National Center for Education Statistics, U.S. Department of Education.

Ingersoll, R. M. (1999). The problem of underqualified teachers in American secondary schools. *Educational Researcher, 28*(2), 26–37.

Ingersoll, R. M. (2001). *Teacher turnover, teacher shortages, and the organization of schools*. Seattle: University of Washington. Center for the Study of Teaching and Policy.

Jelmberg, J. (1996). College-based teacher education versus state-sponsored alternative programs. *Journal of Teacher Education, 47*(1), 60–66.

Jerald, C. D. (2002). *All talk, no action: Putting an end to out-of-field teaching*. Washington, DC: The Education Trust.

Kirby, S. N., Berends, M., & Naftel, S. (1999). Supply and demand of minority teachers in Texas: Problems and prospects. *Educational Evaluation and Policy Analysis, 21*(1), 47–66.

Knight, R. S., Duke, C. R., & Palcic, R. (1988). *A statistical profile of secondary education teachers at Utah State University at the completion of their teacher education program*. Logan, UT: Utah State University.

Lankford, H., Loeb, S., & Wykoff, J. (2002). Teacher sorting and the plight of urban schools. *Educational Evaluation and Policy Archives, 24*(1), 37–62.

Latham, A. S., Gitomer, D., & Ziomek, R. (1999). What the tests tell us about new teachers. *Educational Leadership, 56*(8), 23–26.

Lewis, L., Parsad, B., Carey, N., Bartfai, N., & Farris, E. (1999). *Teacher quality: A report on the preparation and qualifications of public school teachers*. Washington, DC: National Center for Education Statistics, U.S. Department of Education.

Lutz, F. W., & Hutton, J. B. (1989). Alternative teacher certification: Its policy implications for classroom and personnel practice. *Educational Evaluation and Policy Analysis, 11*(3), 237–254.

Matczynski, T. J., Siler, E. R., McLaughlin, M. L., & Smith, J. W. (1988). A comparative analysis of achievement in arts and science courses by teacher education and non-teacher education graduates. *Journal of Teacher Education, 39*(3), 32–36.

Mayer, D. P., Mullens, J. E., & Moore, M. T. (2000). *Monitoring school quality: Indicators of quality*. Washington DC: National Center for Education Statistics, U.S. Department of Education.

McDiarmid, G. W., & Wilson, S. M. (1991). An exploration of the subject matter knowledge of alternate route teachers: Can we assume they know their subject? *Journal of Teacher Education, 42*(2), 93–103.

Meyer, L., Orlofsky, G. F., Skinner, R. A., & Spicer, S. (2002). The state of the states. *Education Week, 21*(17), 68–80.

Murnane, R. J. (1987). Understanding teacher attrition. *Harvard Educational Review, 57*, 177–182.

Murnane, R. J., & Olsen, R. J. (1988, April). *Factors affecting the length of stay in teaching*. Paper presented at the Annual Meeting of the American Educational Research Association, New Orleans, LA.

Murnane, R. J., & Schwinden, M. (1989). Race, gender, and opportunity: Supply and demand for new teachers in North Carolina, 1975–1985. *Educational Evaluation and Policy Analysis, 11*(2), 93–108.

Murnane, R. J., Singer, J. D., Willett, J. B., Kemple, J. J., & Olsen, R. J. (1991). *Who will teach? Policies that matter*. Cambridge, MA: Harvard University Press.

Natriello, G., & Zumwalt, K. K. (1993). New teachers for urban schools? The contribution of the provisional teacher program in New Jersey. *Education and Urban Society, 26*(1), 49–62.

NCES. (1996). *Are high school teachers teaching core subjects without college majors or minors in those subjects?* Washington, DC: Washington DC: National Center for Education Statistics, U.S. Department of Education.

NCES. (1997a). *Are limited English proficiency (LEP) students being taught by teachers with LEP training?* Washington, DC: Washington DC: National Center for Education Statistics, U.S. Department of Education.

NCES. (1997b). *Credentials and tests in teacher hiring: What do districts require?* Washington, DC: National Center for Education for Statistics, U.S. Department of Education.

NEA. (2003). *Status of the American public school teacher, 2000–2001.* Washington, DC: National Education Association.

Pascal, A. (1987). *The qualifications of teachers in American High Schools.* Santa Monica, CA: Rand Corporation.

Pigge, F. L. (1985). Teacher education graduates: Comparison of those who teach and do not teach. *Journal of Teacher Education, 36*(4), 27–28.

Pigge, F. L., & Marso, R. N. (1992). A longitudinal comparison of the academic, affective, and personal characteristics of persisters and nonpersisters in teacher preparation. *Journal of Experimental Education, 61*, 19–26.

Rivkin, S. G., Hanushek, E. A., & Kain, J. F. (2000).*Teachers, schools, and academic achievement.* Cambridge, MA: National Bureau of Economic Research.

Seastrom, M. M., Gruber, K. J., Henke, R. R., McGrath, D. J., & Cohen, B. A. (2002). *Qualifications of the public school teacher workforce: Prevalence of out-of-field teaching 1987–88 to 1999–2000.* Washington, DC: National Center for Education Statistics, U.S. Department of Education.

Securro, S. (1992). Quality of teacher education and nonteacher education graduates: Fact or fiction. *Journal of Research and Development in Education, 25*(3), 131–135.

Shen, J. (1998a). Alternative certifications, minority teachers, and urban education. *Education and Urban Society, 31*(1), 30–31.

Shen, J. (1998b). The impact of alternative certification on the elementary and secondary public teaching force. *Journal of Research and Development in Education, 32*(1), 9–16.

Singer, J. D. (1993). Are special educators' career paths special? *Exceptional Children, 59*(3), 262–279.

Smith, G. P. (1987). *The effects of competency testing on the supply of minority teachers.* A report prepared for the National Education Association and the Council of Chief State School Offices.

Smith, G. P., Miller, M. C., & Joy, J. (1988). A case study of the impact of performance-based testing on the supply of minority teachers. *Journal of Teacher Education, 39*(4), 45–53.

Stafford, D., & Barrow, G. (1994). Houston's alternative certification program. *The Educational Forum, 58*, 193–200.

Strauss, R. P., Bowes, L. R., Marks, M. R., & Plesko, M. R. (2000). Improving teacher prep and election: Lessons from the Pennsylvania experience. *Economics of Education Review, 19*(4), 387–415.

Strauss, R. P., & Sawyer, E. A. (1986). New evidence on teacher and student competencies. *Economics of Education Review, 5*(1), 41–48.

TEA. (1994). *Texas teacher diversity and recruitment: Teacher supply, demand, and quality policy research project, Report no. 4.* Austin, TX: Texas Education Agency.

TEA. (1995). *Texas teacher retention, mobility, and attrition: Teacher supply, demand, and quality policy research project, Report no. 6.* Austin, TX: Texas Education Agency.

U.S. Department of Education. (2002) *Meeting the highly qualified teachers challenge: The Secretary's annual report on teacher quality.* Washington, DC: Author.

U.S. Department of Education. (2003) *Meeting the highly qualified teachers challenge: The Secretary's second annual report on teacher quality.* Washington, DC: Author.

Vegas, E., Murnane, R. J., & Willett, J. B. (2001). From high school to teaching: Many steps, who makes it? *Teachers College Record, 103*(3), 427–449.

Wale, W. M., & Irons, E. J. (1988). *An evaluative study of Texas alternative certification programs.* Austin, TX: Texas Education Agency, Division of Teacher Education.

Wenglinsky, H. (2000). *Teaching the teachers: Different settings, different results.* Princeton, NJ: Educational Testing Service.

REFERENCES: OTHER WORKS CITED

Armstrong, D. G., Burlbaw, L., & Batten, C. (1991, February). *Extended teacher-preparation programs: What the literature tells us.* Paper presented at the Annual Meeting of the Association of Teacher Educators, New Orleans, LA.

Ballou, D., & Podgursky, M. (2000). Reforming teacher preparation and licensing: Continuing the debate. *Teachers College Record, 102*(1), 5–27.

Billingsley, B. S. (1993). Teacher retention and attrition in special and general education: A critical review of the literature. *Journal of Special Education, 27,* 137–174.

Bowles, S., & Levin, H. M. (1968). The determinants of scholastic achievement—An appraisal of some recent evidence. *Journal of Human Resources, 3,* 3–24.

Chapman, D. W., & Hutcheson, S. M. (1982). Attrition from teaching careers: A discriminate analysis. *American Educational Research Journal, 19,* 93–105.

Coleman, J. S., Campbell, E. Q., Hobson, C. J., McPartland, J., Mood, A. M., Weinfeld, F. D., et al. (1966). *Equality of educational opportunity.* Washington, DC: U.S. Government Printing Office.

Conant, J. B. (1963). *The education of American Teachers.* New York: McGraw-Hill.

Darling-Hammond, L. (2000a). Reforming teacher preparation and licensing: Debating the evidence. [Electronic version]. *Teachers College Record, 102*(1), 28–56.

Darling-Hammond, L. (2000b). *Solving the dilemmas of teacher supply, demand and standards: How we can ensure a competent, caring and qualified teacher for every child.* New York: National Commission on Teaching and America's Future.

Darling-Hammond, L. (2002). Research and rhetoric on teacher certification: A response to "Teacher Certification Reconsidered." *Education Policy Analysis Archives, 10*(36). Retrieved October 26, 2002 from http://epaa.asu.edu/epaa/v10n36.html.

Darling-Hammond, L., & Cobb, V. L. (1996). The changing context of teacher education. In F. Murray (Ed.), *Teacher educator's handbook* (pp. 14–62). Washington, DC: AACTE.

Dewey, J. (1902). The educational situation: As concerns the elementary school. Reprinted in *Journal of Curriculum Studies* [Electronic Version], *34*(3), 387–403.

Fischer, R., & Feldman, M. (1985). Some answers about the quality of teacher education students. *Journal of Teacher Education, 36*(3), 37–40.

Flexner, A. (1930). *Universities: American, English, German.* London: Oxford University Press.

Funkhouser, C. (1988). Strengthening the rationale for graduate-level preservice teacher education. *Journal of Teacher Education, 39*(6), 40–43.

Goodnough, A. (2002). Half of new teachers lack certificates, data say. *The New York Times,* p. B8.

Hanushek, E. A. (1971). Teacher characteristics and gains in student achievement: Estimation using micro-data. *American Economic Review, 61,* 280–288.

Hanushek, E. A. (1972). *Education and race: An analysis of the educational production process.* Lexington, MA: Lexington Books.

Hart, G. K., & Burr, S. K. (1996). *A state of emergency in a state of emergency teachers.* Sacramento, CA: A report for the California State University Institute for Education Reform.

Hirsch, E., Koppich, J. E., & Knapp, M. S. (1998). *What states are doing to improve the quality of teaching: A brief review of current patterns and trends.* Seattle, WA: Center for the Study of Teaching and Policy.

Holmes Group. (1986). *Tomorrow's teachers: A report of the Holmes Group.* East Lansing, MI: Author.

Howey, K. R., & Zimpher, N. L. (1986). The current debate on teacher preparation. *Journal of Teacher Education, 37*(5), 41–49.

Kerr, D. H. (1983). Teaching competence and teacher education in the United States. *Teachers College Record, 84*(3), 525–552.

Knapp, J. L., McNergney, R. F., Herbert, J. M., & York, H. L. (1990). Should a master's degree be required of all teachers? *Journal of Teacher Education, 41*(2), 27–37.

Lagemann, E. C. (2000). *An elusive science: The troubling history of educational research.* Chicago: University of Chicago Press.

Lanier, J. E., & Little, J. W. (1986). Research on teacher education. In M. C. Wittrock (Ed.), *Handbook of research on teaching* (pp. 527–569). New York: MacMillan.

Mitchell, K., Robinson, D. Z., Plake, B. S., & Knowles, K. T. (Eds.). (2001). *Testing teacher candidates: The role of licensure tests in improving teacher quality.* Washington, DC: National Research Council.

Murnane, R. J., & Phillips, B. R. (1981). What do effective teachers of inner-city children have in common? *Social Science Research, 10,* 83–100.

National Commission on Excellence in Education. (1983). *A nation at risk: A report to the nation and the Secretary of Education.* Washington, DC: U.S. Department of Education.

National Commission on Teaching and America's Future. (1996). *What matters most: Teaching for america's future.* New York: Author.

Olsen, D. G. (1985). The quality of prospective teachers: Education vs. noneducation graduates. *Journal of Teacher Education, 36*(5), 56–59.

Summers, A. A., & Wolfe, B. L. (1977). Do schools make a difference? *American Economic Review, 67,* 639–652.

Sykes, G. (1983). Caring about teachers. Response to Donna Kerr. *Teachers College Record, 84*(3), 579–592.

Vance, V. S., & Schlechty, P. C. (1982). The distribution of academic ability in the teaching force: Policy implications. *Phi Delta Kappan, 64*(1), 22–27.

Waller, W. (1932). *The sociology of teaching.* New York: Wiley.

Weaver, W. T. (1983). *America's teacher quality problem: Alternatives for reform.* New York: Praeger.

Wirt, J., Choy, S., Gerald, D., Provasnik, P. R., Watanabe, S., Tobin, R., et al. (2001). *The condition of education, 2001.* Washington, DC: National Center for Education Statistics, U.S. Department of Education.

Wirt, J., & Livingston, A. (2002). *The condition of education 2002 in brief.* Washington, DC: National Center for Education Statistics, U.S. Department of Education.

Wilson, S. M., Floden, R. E., & Ferrini-Mundy, J. (2001). *Teacher preparation research: Current knowledge, gaps and recommendations.* Seattle, WA: Center for the Study of Teaching and Policy.

Wilson, S. M., Floden, R. E., & Ferrini-Mundy, J. (2002). *Addendum to Teacher preparation research: Current knowledge, gaps and recommendations, 2001.* Seattle, WA: Center for the Study of Teaching and Policy.

Zeichner, K. M., & Schulte, A. K. (2001). What we know and don't know from peer-reviewed research about alternative teacher certification programs. *Journal of Teacher Education, 5*(4), 266–282.

5

Research on the Effects of Coursework in the Arts and Sciences and in the Foundations of Education

Robert E. Floden
Marco Meniketti
Michigan State University

Teaching method and field experience courses that focus on teaching make up only a small fraction of the postsecondary coursework required for teachers, especially for prospective secondary teachers. As undergraduates, prospective teachers also take arts and science courses in the subject matter fields they will teach, as well as arts and science courses intended to provide a broad base of knowledge (i.e., courses taken as electives or to fulfill general education requirements), and "foundation of education" courses in areas such as educational psychology, social–philosophical education studies, or history of education.

That college affects students in profound and subtle ways is a generally accepted starting point for most discussions of higher education (e.g., Nussbaum, 1997), despite weak empirical evidence. The expectation—widely held since the 1950s—that teachers should possess a bachelor's degree suggests that this generally accepted belief in the value of higher education also holds for teacher preparation. Discussions about the value of teacher preparation seek empirical evidence about the value of "education" coursework, but seldom ask for empirical evidence about the professional benefit teachers get from the general college requirements for concentrated study in a major field or from broader academic study, whether through distribution requirements or through coursework specifically designed for general education. An examination of the evidence about the benefits of taking such courses is valuable, both in its own right and as a basis for thinking about what mix of "hard" empirical evidence and other grounds is a sufficient basis for decisions about the components of teacher preparation. Examples of "other grounds" include common-sense arguments about the need for teachers to understand how pupils learn and examples of methods experienced teachers use to teach fractions.

The "foundations" courses stem from an arts and sciences tradition, and can thus be included in a general comparison along with arts and sciences courses. These courses use theories and results from psychology, sociology, history, and philosophy to address issues of how children learn, how schooling connects to broad social issues, how U.S. education has changed since Colonial times, and how ethical issues arise in instruction. States may require some courses in education foundations, especially courses about learning and development, as part of licensure requirements. Because these courses serve a special population (i.e., those preparing to teach) and are taught by faculty who specialize in education, our research review treats education foundations courses as a category distinct from other arts and sciences courses.

As with other components of teacher preparation, claims about the value of arts and sciences and foundations coursework are seldom followed by citations of empirical studies that examined the impact of such study on prospective teachers' knowledge, skills and dispositions.[1] As we discuss in the following, the published empirical research work has concentrated on the effects of courses in the subject matter teachers are preparing to teach, with most research done on teaching of mathematics. The literature on what teachers learn from arts and science and foundations courses is scant, particularly for studies that look at effects on knowledge with an obvious connection to future teaching performance. Some ideas for focusing future research, however, can be drawn by examining the literature on what prospective teachers and other students learn by attending college.

CRITERIA FOR INCLUSION

Our intent was to examine the empirical basis for the claims about arts and science and education foundations courses. We selected only articles reporting on original, "rigorous" empirical work, including meta-analyses. As a first screen for rigor, we chose to look at only work that had passed peer review, as indicated by publication in a peer-reviewed journal or book, or in a report from a research organization with an established process for peer review. In keeping with the general approach of this volume, which seeks to summarize what has been found in recent research about teacher preparation in this country, we focused on literature published since 1990 and looked only at studies of teacher education in the United States.

---

[1]The phrase "knowledge, skills, and dispositions" connotes that teachers may learn procedures or attitudes and values, as well as propositional knowledge. To avoid sounding awkward, we reduce the phrase to "knowledge," but we intend that to include the broad range of teachers' learning outcomes.

We use four approaches to identify publications for possible inclusion:

- Drawing on a recent pair of reviews that addressed a similar question and had similar criteria for inclusion (Wilson & Floden, 2003; Wilson, Floden, & Ferrini-Mundy, 2001);
- Doing a hand search of major education journals (listed in the following sections)
- Conducting an electronic search of ERIC and Education Abstracts
- Soliciting nominations from colleagues

First, for the literature on the impact of subject matter study on teaching practice and student achievement, we drew on two published literature reviews which one of us co-authored (Wilson et al. 2001; Wilson & Floden, 2003). The first was completed for the U.S. Department of Education, with a shorter version published in the *Journal of Teacher Education* (Wilson, Floden, & Ferrini-Mundy, 2002). The second, conducted at the request of the Education Commission of the States, was an extension of the first, addressing a broader set of questions and looking at a slightly expanded pool of literature. In both cases, the criteria for inclusion—rigorous, empirical research on U.S. populations—were substantially the same as those for the present review, although the time span went back to 1980, rather than to 1990.

Second, we did a hand search of a sampling of educational journals—refereed journals covering a range of education topics and refereed journals focusing on teacher education—looking for titles relating to research on the influence of these components of teacher preparation on teachers' knowledge. The journals hand searched were *Action in Teacher Education, American Educational Research Journal, American Journal of Education, Anthropology and Education Quarterly, Cognition and Instruction, Educational Forum, Educational Psychologist, Educational Studies, Journal of Educational Psychology, Journal of Educational Research, Journal of Instructional Psychology, Journal of Research and Development in Education, Journal of Research in Science Teaching, Journal of Teacher Education, Review of Educational Research, Sociology of Education, Teaching and Teacher Education, Teaching Psychology, and Theory into Practice.* This phase served to identify candidate articles in these journals, to gather information about other possible articles from the reference lists of articles in these journals, and to identify key words or phrases to be used in the electronic searches that made up the third phase.

Next we used these key words to search ERIC, Education Abstracts, and the JSTOR journals in anthropology, history, and sociology (for studies of foundations of education courses). Common key words, including preservice, liberal arts, foundation courses, and impact were far too broad and appear in numerous studies. It was not uncommon to have hits numbering in the thousands. We refined the search phrasing by combinations of key words to produce lists of hits that numbered 500 or less, an amount we could review in a few hours. Systematic lists were maintained to prevent duplicating key word combinations. With each search, relevant titles were saved. We then read abstracts of articles that seemed likely to meet our other criteria for inclusion. Candidates that met these criteria were recorded for later full text review.

At this stage, we kept references to articles published in journals that lacked peer review, with the hope they might lead us to a related peer-reviewed report. Following up on conference presentations was, however, beyond the scope of our work.

The search for key words and phrases included preservice, teacher preparation, student teachers, teacher education, novice teacher, component, foundational, components of education, foundation courses, educational foundations, general education, liberal arts, liberal education, research, impact, impact on practice, effects, content knowledge, and combinations of these terms.

A fourth source of articles was recommendations from colleagues. We asked those who served on the American Educational Research Association (AERA) panel that sponsored this volume, and others they suggested, whether they knew of articles meeting our criteria that we might have missed.

From this pool of publications, we then did a further screening, drawing on the guiding principles for scientific research formulated in the recent National Research Council (NRC) report on *Scientific Research in Education* (Shavelson & Towne, 2003). We used these principles as a way of thinking about the standards for evaluating research that are shared by empirical research communities in education. The principles in the NRC report are that research should:

- Pose significant questions that can be investigated empirically
- Link research to relevant theory
- Use methods that permit direct investigation of the question
- Provide a coherent and explicit chain of reasoning
- Replicate and generalize across studies
- Disclose research to encourage professional scrutiny

All studies in our pool were consistent with the first principle, because we had selected only empirical studies addressing the impact of arts and science and education foundation courses on teachers' knowledge, a question we considered significant.

In our final selection of studies, the second and fifth principles were not readily applicable. Given that this is an emerging field of study, we included studies even when they lacked a strong basis in prior theory (although building and connecting to theory should help the work progress). The principle regarding replication and generalization applies more to a body of work than to individual studies, so it was not used to eliminate studies.

We did use the other three principles to guide us in selecting studies for this review. We examined studies to see whether they used methods appropriate to the questions they posed and the conclusions they drew, to see whether we could discern a line of reasoning linking the research conducted to conclusions drawn, and to see whether the publication presented enough information about the research to give us (and other readers) a basis for judging the trustworthiness of the conclusions. Because methods and questions in the studies varied, the interpretations of these principles varied as well.

Rather than using rigid rules to evaluate studies, we used our understanding of the standards generally associated with a research method to decide whether to include a study. Many studies were eliminated because they lacked enough detail about methods of data collection and analysis to support scrutiny of the argument from the evidence to the conclusion. We did not insist, however, that a study provide a complete reporting of the data collection methods used and all the specifics of analysis. We included, for example, studies that reported using analyses of prospective teachers' course work (e.g., journals and essays), but did not include details on the coding method or rubric used to judge this coursework. In keeping with current standards for some research approaches, we included studies that had a line of reasoning to support claims about effects of courses on teachers' knowledge, even if the studies were not able to rule out all plausible competing explanations. For example, the regression studies connecting teacher course taking to pupil achievement do not have data that allow them to control for other differences (e.g., family background and differences in knowledge not due to teacher education) among teachers. Studies of the effects of single course experiences on teachers' knowledge often use pretest, posttest, or even posttest-only designs, without comparison groups who had different course experiences.

DESCRIPTION OF THE RESEARCH AND ITS CONCLUSIONS

We discuss results in three areas:

- The impact of subject matter courses in the content area the prospective teacher plans to teach
- The impact of other arts and sciences coursework, such as courses taken to fulfill general education requirements
- The impact of coursework in the foundations of education

In each, we looked for reports of the impact these courses had on prospective teachers' knowledge. In some cases, however, the studies collected data on practicing teachers and their pupils. For these studies, the outcome measure often was pupil achievement, rather than teachers' knowledge, and data about the teacher preparation coursework came from teachers' self-reports, often about past years' experiences. For these studies, we are still interested in effects on teachers' knowledge, which we assume is the way teacher preparation affects pupil learning.

Subject-Specific Preparation

We found three types of studies relevant to the impact content courses in the teaching field have on teachers' knowledge. The first are studies of the correlation between the amount of college subject matter study and either ratings of teacher performance or K–12 pupil achievement. The second type are studies of the subject matter knowledge of prospective teachers, including those near completion of the bachelor's degree. The third type are studies of the impact of individual subject matter courses on the knowledge of the prospective teachers in those courses. Studies in each category offer some evidence relevant to the question of impact of arts and science courses on prospective teachers, but each category also has limitations.

Studies that examine correlations between teachers' subject matter preparation and teacher effectiveness, as measured by either the ratings of teacher performance or the achievement of their pupils, have the limitations generally associated with correlational research. The correlations provide prima facie evidence of the impact of subject matter course taking on teachers' knowledge,[2] but leave open the possibility that these correlations may be spurious, with some other factor causing the association. Given that prospective teachers have some choice about which courses they take— choices that come from selection of college and major, as well as from individual

---

[2]To make the connection to teachers' knowledge, skills, and dispositions, we view the achievement of a teachers' pupils as an indication of the knowledge that teacher possesses. That is, we assume that if a teacher is effective in getting pupils to learn, the teacher must possess knowledge, skills, and dispositions that enable that effectiveness. This way of connecting teachers' knowledge to pupil learning parallels the assumption made in research that uses teachers' knowledge of the subject they teach as an outcome variable. Such studies assume that the knowledge will enable the teachers to be more effective.

courses—associations between amount of coursework and teaching effectiveness may be due to differences in the characteristics of students prior to taking college courses. Prospective teachers who take more subject matter coursework, for example, might enter college with greater enthusiasm for the subject or better high school preparation, either of which might in itself lead to differences in teaching, or to differences in the schools that offer them employment, which in turn would lead to differences in teacher effectiveness. In some studies, statistical modeling is used to adjust for the effects of such other possible influences. When data are available on the other characteristics, the models can be used to give defensible estimates of the effects of subject matter coursework; when data on those other characteristics are not available, conclusions about the causal effects of course taking are contingent on the assumption that these other influences have a comparatively small effect.

The studies of teachers' subject matter knowledge give insight into the impact of the coursework taken during teacher preparation, especially when they measure teachers' knowledge after most or all coursework is complete. The knowledge teachers have after their coursework combines what they learned in subject matter courses with what they learned in other coursework, what they learned outside the college experience, and what they knew on college entry. Thus, studies of teachers' knowledge at the end of college describe what has been learned from a range of sources. To the extent that most opportunities to learn the subject matter come in subject matter courses themselves, as might be reasonably assumed for advanced knowledge of mathematics or physics, the studies describe effects of those courses. When prospective teachers have many other opportunities to learn the subject matter, as might be the case for knowledge of contemporary American literature, it is harder to separate out the effects of coursework. When studies assess teachers' subject matter knowledge and find limitations in knowledge, these studies demonstrate that coursework, despite possibly having positive effects, did not bring all teachers to strong understandings of their subject.

Studies of individual subject matter courses can provide credible evidence about the effects of course experiences, especially when they look at changes occurring during the course and describe features of the course that correspond closely to what was learned. Because the studies found in this category gather data within an individual course, often designed with special (i.e., atypical) content or activities, studies in this category do not answer general questions about the effects that studying subject matter has on teachers' knowledge.

Teachers' Subject Matter Study and Teacher Effectiveness.   All but one of the studies we found that examined correlations between the extent of teachers' subject matter study and teacher effectiveness—as measured by ratings of teacher performance or tests of K–12 student achievement or learning—had been included in the reviews by Wilson and colleagues (Wilson et al., 2001; Wilson & Floden, 2002); the one additional study we found in this category (Wenglinsky, 2002) was published after those reviews were completed. Our conclusions thus resemble those reached in these recent reviews. Those reviews looked at studies back to 1980,[3] so this part of our review has a broader time span than the rest of the chapter.

---

[3]One study in Wilson and Floden (2003) was published in 1977. This study was included in that review because it had been nominated by those who asked for the review. But the review itself was designed to extend work based on a systematic look at research published during or after 1980. Because the systematic search for literature did not extend to the years before 1980, we have decided not to include studies published before 1980 in the present review.

Wilson and colleagues (2001) identified 10 studies that met our criteria for inclusion and addressed the connection between amount of college-level subject matter study and either teacher performance or K–12 pupil achievement (Denton & Lacina, 1984; Druva & Anderson, 1983; Goldhaber & Brewer, 1997, 2000; Hawk, Coble, & Swanson, 1985; Hawkins, Stancavage, & Dossey, 1998; Monk, 1994; Monk & King, 1994; Rowan, Chiang, & Miller, 1997; Rowan, Correnti, & Miller, 2002). Our review summarizes results from those studies, plus the Wenglinsky (2002) study.

These are survey studies, with sample sizes ranging from 3,500 teachers of mathematics and science in the National Education Longitudinal Study (NELS) data to approximately 200 teachers. The set also includes a meta-analysis of 65 studies of science teachers (Druva & Anderson, 1983).

In these surveys, teachers were asked their college major and minor, certification field, or the number of courses taken in a subject area. These questions are all used as indicators for amount of college subject matter study, with teachers who report having a major, minor, or subject-specific certification in mathematics, for example, considered as having taken more coursework in mathematics than those who report some other major or type of certification (e.g., certification as an elementary teacher, with no particular subject matter focus). A statistical procedure, such as regression analysis, was then used to measure the association between the indicator of subject matter study and a measure of teacher effectiveness.

For example, the articles by Monk (1994) and Monk and King (1994) both used data from the Longitudinal Study of American Youth (LSAY). This study used data that began with a base sample of 2,829 students and their teachers, in 51 randomly selected schools. The sample was drawn to permit inferences about students, and subsets of students, representative of the country as a whole. As part of the study, surveys were completed by 608 mathematics teachers and 483 science teachers. The survey asked the number of undergraduate and graduate courses in various curricular areas that teachers had completed. Student achievement was measured by selected National Assessment of Educational Progress (NAEP) items given to 1,492 students in both 10th and 11th grades. Monk and King used these data to draw associations between teachers' courses and gains in their students' achievement.

The research has been concentrated by subject area and grade level. Most focused on mathematics teaching, with eight reports specific to mathematics, two specific to science, one connecting majoring in English to early-elementary school reading achievement, and one comparing teachers with a content area major to those who majored in education. Nine studies looked at secondary school teaching (grades 7-12, including one with grade 6 as well); three examined effects on elementary school (K-6) teaching.

Ten studies measured outcomes on a test of student achievement—NAEP test items, NELS test items, or a locally developed test. These studies usually controlled for student socio-economic characteristics, and sometimes for prior achievement.

For the area most heavily studied – secondary school mathematics teaching—most studies reported a positive correlation between teachers' study of mathematics and the measures of student achievement, but the results were not entirely consistent. When amount of mathematics study was measured by whether the teacher majored or minored in mathematics, five articles reported a positive association (Goldhaber & Brewer, 1997, 2000; Hawkins et al., 1998; Rowan et al., 1997; Wenglinsky, 2002), but two found no significant association (Hawk et al., 1985; Monk, 1994). Two studies, both working with the same dataset, measured teachers' study of mathematics by the number of courses taken (Monk; Monk & King, 1994). These studies found a positive overall association between subject matter study and student achievement, but with differential effects for different types of students. Students in advanced mathematics classes, for example, benefited from teachers with more mathematics preparation, but students in remedial mathematics classes did not perform better when they had teachers who had taken more mathematics. The effect on student achievement varied according to the total number of courses. Course taking had the greatest effect for the first five courses that a teacher took, and then diminished. Most studies labeled the effects small. As a basis for judging the size of effect, Monk reported that courses in undergraduate mathematics pedagogy contributed more to the explanation of student performance gain than did undergraduate mathematics courses.

Looking across studies of secondary mathematics teaching, one sees evidence of a positive effect of studying mathematics, but a relationship with some inconsistency: One study showed the effect leveling off after a handful of courses; the impact of majoring in mathematics was not present in all studies; the effects differed with different types of students.

For other secondary school subjects, four articles reported on science teaching (Druva & Anderson, 1983; Goldhaber & Brewer, 2000; Monk, 1994; Monk & King, 1994), and one compared teachers who majored in education with those who majored in other subjects (Denton & Lacina, 1984). The results were similar to the studies of mathematics teaching. The results generally were positive but varied across studies and teaching situations.

Druva and Anderson (1983) conducted a meta-analysis of 65 studies that linked teacher characteristics to teacher behaviors and student achievement. Fifty-two were dissertations.[4] The meta-analysis found a positive relationship between pupil achievement and both the number of science courses taken (for biology teachers, biology courses in particular). The more science courses taken by the teacher, the more positive the pupil attitudes toward science. As the mathematics studies found, the strength of the association increased when teachers were teaching higher level science courses.

The other three articles reporting results for science teaching also reported results for mathematics teaching (Goldhaber & Brewer, 2000; Monk, 1994; Monk & King, 1994). The mathematics results were generally positive, but inconsistent. In contrast to their results for mathematics, Goldhaber and Brewer found no significant effect of science teachers' having a degree in science. For Monk and King as well, the positive effects of subject matter study were not as strong as those for mathematics. For the life sciences, teachers' undergraduate science course taking had no effect on student achievement; there was a positive effect of taking graduate science courses for teachers of juniors, but not for teachers of sophomores. For the physical sciences, one study found positive effects of teachers' subject matter preparation for both sophomores and juniors; the other found effects for high pretest sophomores, but negative effects for juniors.

Monk and King (1994) also looked at the effects on student achievement of the average amount of teacher subject matter preparation in a school and of the variation

---

[4]For meta-analysis, results of individual studies are treated as data. Meta-analysts often include unpublished studies in their dataset, believing them to contain useful information even if in reports that have not gone through rigorous peer review. Indeed, some analysts argue that the difficulty in finding publication outlets for studies that do not show significant results would lead meta-analyses based only on published work to be biased. For this chapter, our criterion for inclusion is that the meta-analysis appeared in a peer reviewed journal and met the scholarly standards for conducting meta-analyses, not that every study included in the meta-analysis had been through peer review.

in preparation among a school's teachers. For life science teachers, they reported that high variability in the subject preparation of teachers had a positive effect on high pretest students, but a negative effect for low pretest students. For physical science teachers, the more subject matter courses taken, the higher the test scores for low pretest students.

For general effects of subject matter study for secondary school teachers, Denton and Lacina (1984) compared education majors with all other majors. Their outcome measures were ratings of teacher effectiveness in planning and instruction, rather than measures of student achievement. They found no differences in planning effectiveness between the 55 education majors and the 27 other teachers; differences in ratings of instructional competency were small.

For elementary school teaching, one meta-analysis (Druva & Anderson, 1983) looked at effects in science, one study (Hawkins et al., 1998) examined effects on fourth-grade mathematics 1996 NAEP scores, and one (Rowan et al., 2002) looked at effects on reading and math scores on the Comprehensive Test of Basic Skills (CTBS). Druva and Anderson's meta-analysis was the only article to report a positive effect of teachers' study in the subject area tested. They found, as noted previously in the discussion of results for secondary school, that pupils' science achievement test scores and attitudes toward science were positively related to the number of science courses taken by the teachers. The other studies looked at the effect of teachers' subject area major, finding no effects on either the NAEP mathematics scores or the gains on CTBS reading or mathematics tests. Hawkins et al. (1998) grouped teachers by academic major into four categories: mathematics majors, mathematics education majors, education majors, and other majors. For fourth-grade pupils, they found a positive effect on 1996 NAEP mathematics scores of teachers majoring in mathematics education or education, as compared to the 'other majors.' For eighth grade, they found that pupils whose teachers had mathematics majors scored higher than pupils whose teachers had education or "other" majors.

The puzzling result reported by Rowan and colleagues (2002) was that having a teacher with advanced degrees in mathematics was associated with lower growth in mathematics achievement. They raised the possibility that advanced training in mathematics "somehow interferes with effective teaching, either because it substitutes for pedagogical training in people's professional preparation, or because it produces teachers who somehow cannot simplify and clarify their advanced understanding of mathematics for elementary school students" (p. 1541).

In summary, studies of the association between teachers' study in their subject area and measures of teacher effectiveness have focused on secondary school mathematics (and, to a lesser extent, on science). Most studies have used student achievement measures or score gains as the outcome measure, often with large, nationally representative samples. The findings have generally supported claims about the value of subject matter preparation, especially for secondary-school mathematics. But the results are inconsistent, with complex variation by course level and prior student achievement.

Only in secondary-school mathematics do the studies provide a clear answer to questions about connection between amount of teachers' subject matter study and pupil achievement. In other teaching areas, some studies show a positive effect on student achievement for majoring in a subject; others show no effect; one shows a negative effect of elementary school teachers' having a graduate degree in mathematics. For secondary school mathematics, one study showed that the benefit of additional subject matter courses declined after the first five courses, suggesting that, even here, the relationship between subject matter study and student achievement is not as simple as "more is better."[5]

We interpret these studies of impact on pupil achievement as indicators of the effects that subject matter course taking has on those aspects of teachers' knowledge and skills important for teaching. For secondary-school mathematics teaching, the studies show that more subject matter study by teachers has a positive effect on pupils' mathematics achievement. For other subject areas, the evidence is thin. None of these studies addresses questions about *what* professionally valuable knowledge teachers gained through their study. The positive results for pupil achievement showed that whatever it was that teachers gained, it helped foster student learning.

Teachers' Subject Matter Knowledge.   Under the assumption that college subject matter courses are the primary influence on prospective teachers' subject matter knowledge, we can draw inferences about the impact of subject matter courses from studies of the content knowledge of prospective teachers, especially those near the end of their preservice preparation. The assumption is that if prospective teachers have strong content knowledge, then their subject matter courses were effective; if their content knowledge is weak, then their college courses were weak and failed to give prospective teachers a thorough understanding of the subjects they will teach.

Running through this line of research is the assumption that it is important for teachers to understand the central concepts in the subjects they teach. That assumption has considerable common-sense appeal, based on the idea that teachers need a deep and flexible understanding of the subject so they can respond to student questions, interpret unexpected student comments, and devise multiple ways of teaching a concept when the first, second, or third approach does not succeed with all pupils (Ball, 1997; Ma, 1999; McDiarmid, Ball, & Anderson, 1989). The specific relationship between teachers' conceptual understanding and their teaching effectiveness is not clear (Floden, 1997).

Wilson et al. (2001) found 11 studies about teachers' subject matter knowledge that met our review criteria. We located two additional studies that reported on the subject matter knowledge of students at or near the end of teacher preparation (Holt-Reynolds, 1999; Kennedy, 1998). Of these 13 studies, four were intensive studies with a small number (1–4) of preservice teachers (Borko et al., 1992; Holt-Reynolds; Wilson, 1994; Wilson & Wineburg, 1988). The others had sample sizes from 19 to almost 300, with some collecting even more data on subsamples (Adams, 1998; Ball, 1990a, 1990b; Graeber, Tirosh, & Glover, 1989; Kennedy, 1998; McDiarmid & Wilson, 1991; Simon, 1993; Stoddart, Connell, Stofflett, & Peck, 1993; Tirosh & Graeber, 1989). One study focused on knowledge of history; two, on English; the others, on knowledge of mathematics.

The dominant theme in the findings for the mathematics studies was that the prospective teachers who had completed some subject matter coursework had mastered basic skills in school subjects, but lacked a deeper understanding of the concepts they would later teach (e.g., division of fractions). Similar results were found in the study of history teachers.

---

[5]A recent review using an overlapping set of studies came to a similar conclusion (Wayne & Youngs, 2003). That review excluded Monk's (1994) paper, which found no effect of having a mathematics major, because Monk's analysis did not explicitly control for student socioeconomic background. We included the paper, judging that controlling for prior achievement was sufficient. Without Monk's finding of no effect, the evidence for the impact of a mathematics degree on secondary school pupil's mathematics achievement is stronger; Wayne and Youngs's conclusion reflects that greater level of certainty, although they noted that the evidence was strong only for secondary-school mathematics.

A study of a single English teacher found that her subject matter knowledge was strong, although this teacher thought her knowledge to be only average (Holt-Reynolds, 1999). The other study of English and language arts teachers (Kennedy, 1998) found that, although these teachers knew many aspects of English, they lacked the understanding of grammar principles that would allow them to move beyond simple statement of the principles as rules. That level of understanding is parallel to many results about knowledge of mathematics, where students completing teacher education often had mastery of computational rules, but lacked understanding of the underlying concepts.

An elaboration of a few studies will illustrate both the results and the methods used to reach these conclusions. Several mathematics articles report on studies of teachers' understandings of division, especially division of fractions. Division has been used as a focus for examining teachers' subject matter knowledge because it is a central concept in mathematics study in both elementary and secondary school.

Drawing data from interviews completed as part of the larger Teacher Education and Learning to Teach (TELT) study (National Center for Research on Teacher Learning, 1991), Ball (1990b) described the results of interviews with 10 students preparing to teach in elementary school and 9 preparing to become secondary-school teachers. The students were interviewed right before they formally entered their teacher education program, roughly midway through their undergraduate study. Thus, particularly for those preparing to teach secondary-school mathematics, it is possible these teachers learned more mathematics before completing teacher preparation. Given the focus of these questions on topics found in the K–12 curriculum, however, it does not seem likely that they would have taken further coursework that directly addressed the content focused on in these interviews.

Ball (1990b) reports on three different contexts for thinking about division: division by fractions, division by zero, and division in the context of algebraic equations. The context of division by zero illustrates both the questions put to these students and the pattern of response. The students were asked: "Suppose you have a pupil who asks you what 7 divided by 0 is. How would you respond?" In follow-up questions, students were asked to explain *why* they would respond in a particular way. If they said that division by 0 is undefined or that "you can't divide by 0," follow-up questions pushed for an explanation.

Ball (1990b) categorized the responses to these interview questions according to whether the student gave an explanation that involved the meaning of division by 0, gave a correct rule for division by 0, gave an incorrect rule, or said that they didn't know. An example of explaining the meaning of division by 0 would be saying that multiplication and division are inverse operations, so having a number that results from dividing 7 by 0 would mean having a number that, when multiplied by 0, would yield 7, but 0 times any number is 0; hence, there is no number that corresponds to 7 divided by 0. An example of giving a correct rule would be saying that you simply need to remember that division by 0 is undefined. The rule is correct; that is, division by zero is undefined. But this response does not show an understanding of why it is undefined; It even suggests that no explanation is possible: It is simply a rule. An example of giving an incorrect rule is saying that "Anything divided by 0 is 0." An example of "I didn't know" is saying "7 divided by 0? Isn't that—isn't there a term for the answer to that? I can't remember."

Ball (1990b) found that 5 of the 19 prospective teachers gave a meaningful explanation, 7 could only give a rule (albeit a correct rule), 5 gave an incorrect rule, and 2 said that they did not know. The distribution of responses was different for prospective elementary teachers than for prospective secondary teachers. The prospective secondary teachers all gave either meaningful explanations (4) or correct rules (5). The elementary teachers' responses showed less understanding of the mathematics. Only 3 gave a correct rule or meaningful explanation (2 and 1, respectively), whereas the rest either gave an incorrect rule (5) or said they did not know (2). For both groups, these results showed that a large fraction of prospective teachers did not understand basic concepts about division that seem necessary if teachers are in turn to help pupils understand division. The picture was somewhat better for the mathematics majors preparing to teach secondary school, but even there, fewer than half could explain the concept. The results for the other contexts of division paralleled these with secondary teacher candidates understanding more than the elementary candidates, but even the secondary candidates showed weaknesses in their mathematical knowledge that suggest limitations in their ability to explain core mathematical ideas in the K–12 curriculum.

Thus, Ball's (1990b) analysis shows that the content courses in mathematics have not given all teacher candidates mastery of these concepts, which are an important part of the K–12 curriculum, although the content courses may have helped them learn other mathematics content. The other studies of prospective teachers' understandings of mathematics give similar results, showing a mastery of rules and procedures (especially for secondary teacher candidates), but weakness in understanding core concepts that the investigators saw as central in the K–12 curriculum. These analyses should not be taken as an indication that content courses had no effect, for teacher candidates' understandings might have been weaker before they began college; that less than half the secondary candidates could explain division concepts, however, suggests that completion of advanced college-level mathematics courses with passing grades does not imply mastery of the concepts of the K–12 curriculum.

The small number of studies in other subject areas illustrated the type of work that might be carried out, but gave no basis for general conclusions. The study of prospective secondary history teachers found a mix of content knowledge similar to that in the studies of mathematics teachers, with two of the four novice teachers in the study having a rich understanding of history as a discipline, but the other two believing that "they had learned history once they had accumulated the names, dates, and events they read about in textbook accounts" (Wilson & Wineburg, 1988, p. 535). Once again, the college coursework completed as part of teacher preparation may have had positive effects on teachers' understanding, but brought only half of the prospective teachers in the study to the point where they understood concepts underlying the discipline of history.

The studies of English and language arts teachers gave support for a similar pattern (Holt-Reynolds, 1999; Kennedy, 1998). Kennedy (also drawing data from the TELT study) describes the varied responses 72 prospective teachers, from several different programs, gave when asked what they would do if a student asked whether to use "is" or "are" in the sentence, "None of the books —— in the library." As Kennedy explains, this question could be answered by stipulating a choice between the two verbs, or could be answered with a variety of levels of sophistication, showing an understanding of the complex of grammatical principles that are relevant (e.g., subject and verb should agree, but "none" is ambiguous, so proper verb form depends on the object).[6] In classifying the responses, Kennedy counted the number of informative

---

[6]Although the correct answer may seem obvious, Kennedy (1988) notes that grammarians have argued about such examples for at least 2 centuries, with consensus about correct usage varying over time. Although

principles (e.g., subject and verb should agree) mentioned, the number of misinformative principles mentioned (e.g., that "none" always takes "are"), as well as counting the number who mentioned the word, "none" (which is central to any explanation) and the number who said that they did not know how to respond. As in Ball's (1990b) study, the pattern of responses shows that, although some prospective teachers have a strong understanding of these grammatical principles, many do not. The average number of informative principles given was one. (Kennedy argues that at least four are needed to build a complete explanation.) A third of the respondents gave at least one misinformative principle. Less than half mentioned anything about "none." A third did not know what to say. The study found that teacher candidates had limited, and often inaccurate, knowledge of the principles of grammar needed to explain problematic cases. Subject matter courses had left many of them with gaps in the content knowledge needed to teach grammar on the basis of principles.

Holt-Reynolds (1999) reported a similar pattern of limited knowledge for most of the 12 undergraduate literature majors whom she and her colleagues interviewed repeatedly during their teacher preparation. Her study focused on a single teacher who had strong knowledge of subject matter, but did not know how to use it in teaching. Students were asked in the interviews to define "literature," to talk about genre and text types, and to look at 25 texts—ranging from *The Complete Shakespeare* to instructions for operating a coffee maker—and say whether each was "literature." Students were also asked about perspectives in the field of literary studies, reacting to short position papers that represented such common perspectives as New Criticism—criticism based on close analysis of the text—and reader response theory. They were asked to select and justify selections for a literature class, read Poe's *The Raven* and talk about what they did to understand it, then asked to select test questions that might be used in teaching *Romeo and Juliet* to 10th-graders.

Responses to these prompts were used to characterize each student's knowledge of literature as a field of study. The teacher candidate Holt-Reynolds (1999) focused on in her article had an elaborated, consistent scheme for thinking about what counted as literature, seeing literature as text that was intentionally created to invite a variety of interpretations. The teacher candidate distinguished between literature, so defined, and texts written to convey information (e.g., the instruction manual) and used explicit references to literary theories and works of literature to explain her position. She was, in other words, knowledgeable about both works of literature and the concepts used to analyze them. Holt-Reynolds contrasted her level of expertise with the other students in the sample, who "classified everything with words as literature, everything with a plot as literature, everything fictional as literature, or anything that was published as literature" (p. 37). Holt-Reynolds concluded that the courses taken to complete an English major left students without some of the knowledge (e.g., how to think about what distinguishes works of literature from other written work) important to teaching high school English.

Holt-Reynolds (1999) found that despite her considerable knowledge about how to analyze literature, this English major was unable to make maximum use of her subject matter knowledge because she mistakenly thought that her students already

---

one principle of usage is that subject ("none") and verb should agree in number, "none is an ambiguous pronoun. Even knowing that subject and verb should agree, and that none is the subject of this sentence, is not enough to solve this particular problem. Current thinking is that the appropriate verb form depends on the object to which the pronoun none refers. That is, if none refers to a singular noun, the verb should be singular; if it refers to a plural noun, the verb should be plural" (Kennedy, p. 148).

knew as much as she did and she was ready to let students react to literature without her guidance.

In summary, the studies of prospective teachers offered some support for the claim that college content courses, even when they constitute a typical major in a subject area, gave some prospective teachers a strong understanding of central concepts that support K–12 teaching, but left others with a weak command of their subject that remained at the level of memorized facts, rules, and principles, some of them inaccurate.

Impact of Particular Subject Matter Courses.   We found seven studies in which the investigators studied the impact of individual courses on the knowledge of prospective teachers. Four looked at a mathematics course (Civil, 1993; Emenaker, 1996; McNeal & Simon, 2000; Zbiek, 1998); two looked at a science course (Fones, Wagner, & Caldwell, 1999; Smith & Anderson, 1999); one looked at study of literacy (Clark & Medina, 2000). Five studies were interpretive studies of 8 to 26 prospective teachers, in which the course instructor drew on a combination of interviews, observations during the course, and examination of prospective teachers' written papers and reflective journals as the data. One study surveyed 137 prospective teachers (Emenaker) about beliefs about mathematics at the beginning and end of the course. One compared 17 students in an experimental section of a general science class with 97 students in traditional sections, using a survey to ask about knowledge of science concepts, confidence in teaching the concepts, and attitudes toward science.

These studies, all of which focused on a single course, taught at a single institution, using measures unique to the study, provide little support for claims about the typical impact of subject matter courses on prospective teachers. However, they do give a sense of the questions addressed and the research methods used in studies of individual courses. Each highlighted a special feature of the course, such as use of a problem-solving approach, emphasis on changing patterns of discussion, or integration of laboratory and lecture components. For the outcomes measured, some focused on general beliefs about the subject matter (e.g., mathematics problems have only one method of solution, and knowledge in science changes through inquiry), some looked at norms for classroom participation, some looked at prospective teachers' confidence with the subject matter or with teaching it. None of these studies relied on widely used assessments of teachers' knowledge of subject matter or of pedagogy, such as the Praxis exams. And none followed the prospective teachers into their K–12 classrooms.

The studies by Zbiek (1998) and by Fones et al. (1999) illustrate approaches and results from studies of the influence of individual subject matter courses on prospective teachers' knowledge. Zbiek examined the experiences 13 prospective secondary-school mathematics teachers had in an elective mathematics course devoted to mathematical modeling. The course, taught by the researcher, was designed to teach students how to use computer-based modeling tools (e.g., curve fitters and function graphers) to develop and evaluate mathematical models of complex processes. The attempt to connect mathematics representations to real-world processes was, for most students, quite different from what they studied in other mathematics courses. Over the 15-week course, the students used several mathematical representations to answer questions about real-world problems, studied abstract aspects of functions, and, in the final 4 weeks, collected and used computer tools to model empirical data. Zbiek interviewed the students several times and audiotaped students as they worked with the models and software. Student work was also collected and examined. Zbiek went through a process of coding their responses, generating hypotheses, looking for disconfirming evidence, and revising hypotheses. He distinguished among four strategies the students used as they developed models for the phenomena studied during the final part of the course. For example, some students relied on computer tools to determine whether a model was appropriate, whereas others examined graphs of different functions that might be used as models. The overall conclusion about the effect of the course on these prospective teachers' knowledge was that students struggled at times with the unfamiliar task of trying to use mathematics to represent the real world and that few students got beyond complete reliance on the computer tools to tell them whether they had a "good" representation of the empirical phenomena. This conclusion can be seen as a commentary on the prospective teachers' mathematics knowledge, that is, that their mathematical capabilities had not yet reached the point where they could readily connect mathematics to real-world situations and use their own judgment to judge the quality of a mathematical representation.

The study reported by Fones et al. (1999) used a survey with preset questions, rather than the intensive, exploratory approach used by Zbiek (1998). They compared two different ways of structuring the introductory science courses that all prospective elementary teachers completed as part of general education requirements. In one format, 93 students attended a lecture followed by smaller laboratory sections, with lecture and labs taught by different instructors. For the 17 students in the experimental structure, the professor dispensed with the separate lecture but integrated that material instead into instruction solely in the laboratory setting, taught by the professor. All instructors were regarded as highly qualified and had received comparable student evaluations in prior courses.

A pretest and posttest were given to the students in both formats, asking about their attitude toward science, understanding of science, and confidence in teaching science concepts. No significant differences were found between the two groups on the pretest. For both groups of students, scores increased between the beginning and the end of the course. The student gains were equal for perceived understanding and competence, but those in the experimental section scored higher on the attitude measure. Fones et al. (1999) saw these results as evidence of the superiority of a small-section, integrated structure for introductory science courses. Speculating on why this might be so, they said "it is much easier to quietly ask a question as the instructor passes by your lab table than to raise your hand in an auditorium full of people" (p. 235). They acknowledged, however, that the higher cost of the small-section approach would reduce the likelihood of its widespread adoption.

Both these studies (Fones et al., 1999; Zbiek, 1998) illustrate ways in which course instructors in subject matter courses are studying the impact of their courses on prospective teachers' knowledge. The results are probably valuable in local efforts to improve instruction and offer ideas that faculty outside the institutions might see as promising candidates for adaptation at another site, because they had some positive impact in one setting. The studies, however, contain sketchy information about the content of the courses studied and give little basis for understanding how the characteristics of the student body at the institution influence the effects of the course. The link between the knowledge measured and the future teaching practice of these students was not made explicit. Thus, these studies are not well suited to answer broad questions about what prospective teachers typically learn from subject matter courses or how what they learn might contribute to their instructional practice.

Impact of Arts and Sciences Courses Outside the Teaching Field

In our literature search, we found no studies on the impact of arts and science courses outside the prospective teacher's field that met the criteria for inclusion in this review. Such courses, taken as electives or to fulfill general education requirements, typically are part of undergraduate education. Although such coursework is often part of college graduation requirements, thus part of the requirements for teacher certification, we did not locate any publications meeting our selection criteria on how those studies contribute to the quality of teachers currently being prepared.

Because this additional arts and science coursework occupies a large part of college-based teacher preparation, and because it is also a part of alternate certification (which requires new teachers to possess a bachelor's degree), we decided to look outside the studies that met our criteria to get some evidence of the effects of the study of arts and sciences on knowledge that might improve teaching performance. In particular, we looked at the general literature on what students learn in college.

Studies of college learning are not perfectly aligned with our focal questions because they do not focus on the population of prospective teachers or on the knowledge important for teaching. The focus of the studies, however, overlaps with research on college's impact on prospective teachers, both in substance and in respondents. When the studies use analytic ability, knowledge of subject matter and social attitudes as outcomes, they are using outcomes arguably important for teachers. And when the studies report effects on the college-going population, a significant fraction of that population is students pursuing teacher certification. So this general literature offers some indications of how college overall contributes to prospective teachers' knowledge, although the differences in focus require cautious interpretation. We discuss this literature on the assumption that examining what empirical research suggests is better than saying only that we have no sharply focused empirical work. These results also may be useful in formulating studies to address teacher education questions.

A thorough review of the literature on college student learning is beyond the scope of this review. We identify some major results from this literature by examining two central sources: Pascarella and Terenzini's (1991) literature review of research through the 1980s and Astin's two reports (1977, 1993) on his annual surveys of college students.

A Synthesis of Research on the Impact of College Attendance.

Pascarella and Terenzini (1991) synthesized research on college's impact on student development. The authors grouped studies by method, research question, evidentiary strength, theoretical strand, and result. Using a comprehensive search of research abstracts, journals, dissertations, and conference proceedings, the authors claimed that they reviewed every major research report on college impact between 1967 and 1991.[7]

Pascarella and Terenzini synthesized these studies using several criteria for valuing "strength of evidence," paying careful attention to sample size and to whether a study took factors other than college attendance into account. Their book begins with a

---

[7]We consider both this research synthesis and Astin's (1993) book as a category distinct from the studies we have reviewed to this point. Rather then using our selection criteria as a way of choosing these sources, we selected them because they provide a summary of research in another field, which serves mostly as a source to guide future research on the effects that college attendance has on prospective teachers' knowledge.

review of the theoretical models used to conceptualize student development during college. Some theorists see college as a breathing space, where students can try out "new roles, attitudes, beliefs, and behaviors" (p. 58). Others see the move from high school to college as a "culture shock" where new ideas and people are encountered, leading to unlearning of old values and behaviors and to socialization to a new set.

For cognitive outcomes, the theories suggest that it would be "entirely reasonable to expect colleges and universities to promote and facilitate cognitive readiness for development through student encounters with various bodies of knowledge and modes of inquiry, as well as training in logic, critical thinking, and the evaluation of alternative ideas and courses of action. . . . In short, the college environment presumably offers a setting in which the impetus and opportunities for change are substantial, perhaps unsurpassed by those of any other social institution" (Pascarella & Terenzini, 1991, p. 59). The review looks at whether this reasonable expectation is supported by empirical evidence.

Pascarella and Terenzini (1991) organized their discussion around different ways students might be changed by college. The types of change that seem most relevant for the preparation of teachers are changes in subject matter knowledge, in general cognitive skills (e.g., ability to evaluate new ideas), and in attitudes and values.

For changes in subject matter knowledge and academic skills, Pascarella and Terenzini (1991) report that several studies show that students gain knowledge over the course of their college careers, with greater gains in their focal areas of study. For this review, subject matter is treated broadly, using measures of verbal and mathematical skill, rather than measures of content in specific areas. The authors report that the net effect of completing college (as contrasted with no college attendance) on verbal skills is a gain of between .26 and .32 SDs on the various measures used across the studies. The net effect on mathematical skills is a gain of between .29 and .32 SDs.

A question Pascarella and Terenzini (1991) also address is whether the changes produced by college attendance vary by the type of institution attended. They conclude that there is little difference in these net effects across colleges, once differences in entering student characteristics were taken into account.

Pascarella and Terenzini (1991) distinguish between the effects of college on verbal or mathematical knowledge and the effects on developing general cognitive skills, that is, the skills "that permit individuals to process and utilize new information; communicate effectively; reason objectively and draw objective conclusions from various types of data; evaluate new ideas and techniques efficiently; become more objective about beliefs, attitudes, and values; evaluate arguments and claims critically; and make reasonable decisions in the face of imperfect information" (pp. 114–115).

As Pascarella and Terenzini (1991) looked at the studies, they cautioned that the evidence about college's effects on these skills is limited. What evidence there is suggests that college leads to improvement in "written and oral communication . . . , general intellectual and analytical skill . . . , critical thinking . . . , reflective judgment . . . , [and] intellectual flexibility" (pp. 155–156). As with subject matter knowledge, evidence on differences in effects across institutions is scarce. The two studies that give consistent findings indicate that college with "a strong and balanced curricular commitment to general education" has a greater impact on "critical thinking and adult reasoning skills" (Pascarella and Terenzini, p. 157).

Effects on specific cognitive skills were associated with subject area concentration. Science majors perform better on measures that measure reasoning in the context of "science-like tasks or problems" (Pascarella & Terenzini, 1991, p. 157). The results are parallel for social science majors.

For attitudes, the evidence indicates that college increases interest in cultural, aesthetic, and intellectual activities. College-goers place a higher value on these activities. The studies control for race and socioeconomic status, but not for initial level of "cultural sophistication."

Evidence on college's effect on humanitarian values is less clear. "Although the findings are somewhat mixed, we believe the general weight of evidence supports a tentative conclusion that college attendance does have a modest net effect on social conscience and humanitarian values" (Pascarella & Terenzini, 1991, p. 287). Evidence is stronger that college increases students' interest in politics, with effects of college attendance detectable, even as the general political context varies across cohorts.

Astin's Analyses of Annual Surveys.   Astin was a pioneer in the conduct of large-scale, longitudinal survey research to look at the influence of college on affective and cognitive outcomes. *Four Critical Years: Effects of College on Beliefs, Attitudes, and Knowledge* (Astin, 1977) reports on analyses of data collected as part of the Cooperative Institutional Research Program (CIRP), an ongoing, annual student survey initiated by the American Council on Education in 1966. His later book, *What Matters in College? Four Critical Years Revisited* (Astin, 1993), reports on the cohort who entered 4-year colleges in fall 1985.

The CIRP is based on a larger and broader sample than earlier studies had used. Four-year colleges and universities survey more than a quarter-million incoming freshmen each year. The 2002 survey of the Class of 2006 included responses of 282,549 students at 437 institutions. About 300 students from each institution also are given follow-up surveys. The first Astin study (1977) was based on data from the entering classes of 1961 to 1969, for which the size of the follow-up samples ranged from 16,000 to 40,000. The second Astin study (1993) was based on the freshman class of the fall of 1985, where approximately 4,000 students completed the follow-up survey. In reporting, the results from this sample were weighted to approximate the results for the national population of more than 1 million entering freshmen in 1985.

The surveys assess more than 80 cognitive and affective outcome measures, as well as numerous measures of students' entering characteristics and environment measures about their college experience. The survey instruments are intended to extract data on behavior, cognitive and affective outcomes, beliefs, attitudes, and involvement in the college experience of individuals, as well as information on career selection and retention, college type and environment, faculty attributes or orientation, and elements of peer-group influence.

Astin's first surveys (1977) represented an important advance in research on the effects of college, because they included design features to control for other influences on student development. Astin's approach for distinguishing the impact of college attendance from maturational changes was to use variation in degree of exposure to college experience as an independent variable, rather than simply compare those attending college to nonattendees. Degree of exposure included both amount of time in college and intensity, as measured by factors such as belonging to clubs, hours spent studying, and participation in college activities.

With regard to academic and cognitive development, many results in Astin's more recent study (1993) look at effects of differences in college environment, rather than at the overall impact of college attendance. Of relevance for teacher education is his finding that student learning is affected by the area of study. For example, students' quantitative skills are enhanced when they major in quantitative areas, such as mathematics or engineering; verbal skills are enhanced by majoring in subjects such as the social sciences that emphasize such skills. He also noted that performance on general tests of knowledge (e.g., the Graduate Record Examination [GRE]) was enhanced when students report being in a competitive academic environment.

Astin (1977, 1993) also examined growth in student knowledge by using self-report items, which he acknowledged had less validity than direct assessments of knowledge. Students report growth in their knowledge during college, with the greatest growth in a particular field, presumably their major field of study. Regression analyses consistently show that these self-reports of growth in knowledge are associated with amount of time spent studying, both the number of years of college and the number of hours spent.

Growth in general knowledge was linked to taking courses that emphasize writing skills, scientific inquiry, and historical analysis. It also was associated with having instructors critique their written work. Ability to think critically was linked to what Astin (1993) considers the "humanities orientation" of the institution, which includes factors such as emphasis on teaching the classics, heavy faculty involvement in general education teaching, and exams that require essay responses. Astin emphasized that requiring students to write and rewrite papers was an important factor in developing critical thinking ability.

For effects on attitudes, there is a notable difference between Astin's earlier (1997) and later studies (1993). Astin's initial study spanned the Vietnam era, years of civil rights activism, and the early women's liberation movement, social context factors likely to have shaped how college affected students during those years. College had a liberalizing effect on Astin's cohort from the 1960s; that pattern was not replicated in data from students entering college in the 1980s. The first report suggested students became more autonomous, liberal, and open-minded after entering college; the second found greater political and value polarization among students from the 1980s. The fact that Astin could not replicate these results in his follow-up study further supports the implication that strong societal factors, in this case the social unrest of the 1960s, moderated college's effect on students.

The following are findings from the Astin (1977, 1993) reports relevant to teacher education:

- College has a positive effect on development of life philosophy and a negative impact on materialism.
- Peer group strongly affects political and social attitudes as well as self-concept.
- Students who interacted more with faculty had higher retention and completion rates.

Astin (1993) also found that the general education curriculum had only a weak influence on student development; peer group had more influence. Both results suggest that research on the effects that college attendance has on prospective teachers' knowledge should look broadly at the college experience, including interactions with peers as well as completion of course work.

Impact of Education Foundations Courses

In our search for studies about the impact of education foundations courses (e.g., educational psychology, sociology of education, and philosophy of education) on prospective teachers' knowledge, we found five studies that examined the effects of individual courses (Anderson, 1998; Lundeberg, 1997; Lundeberg & Scheurma, 1997; Pankratius, 1997; Vass, Schiller, & Nappi, 2000).

Four studies examined particular approaches (e.g., use of case analysis or lectures on probability, proportion, and correlation) embedded in educational psychology courses (Anderson, 1998; Lundeberg, 1997; Lundeberg & Scheurma, 1997; Vass et al., 2000). The fifth study looked at the use of a psychological test in the context a general foundations course (Pankratius, 1997). These five studies used a range of methods: One was an experiment, with two course sections selected at random to receive the experimental treatment; two used a pretest, posttest design, using informal observations to aid interpretation; One was a posttest-only design, with outcome data from a written self-report; the fifth was an interpretive study in which the outcome data were student journals and course papers. The sample sizes ranged from 22 to 103.

Each study focused on an innovation, with the course serving as the context for this innovation. The experiment (Vass et al., 2000) was designed to see whether brief (20-minute) units on reasoning would improve student performance on a short reasoning test. The pretest, posttest study (Anderson, 1998) looked at the impact on cultural sensitivity of multimedia materials developed for use in the course. The posttest-only study asked whether making students aware of the inaccuracy of their estimates of gender balance in class participation would affect their awareness of gender bias and their intention to attend to the issue. The interpretive study asked whether using a personality inventory to form student groups would affect student awareness of differences in learning styles.

We describe one study to illustrate the methods used and type of conclusions drawn in these studies. Vass et al. (2000) conducted an experiment, using four sections of an educational psychology course as the experimental groups. The students were not assigned to sections at random, but the four sections were assigned to treatment groups at random, with two sections used for two variations on the experimental treatment and two sections serving as the control group.

The investigators developed 20-minute lectures on probability, proportion, and correlation, hoping to improve students' ability to solve problems that involved statistical reasoning. Using two parallel forms of an eight-item paper-and-pencil test that the authors developed, students' reasoning ability was assessed before and after the intervention. In one experimental group, the intervention was three 20-minute lectures, one each on probability, proportion, and correlation. In the second experimental group, the students also heard three lectures, but the third lecture was a review of the first two, rather than addressing correlation. Neither control group received any instruction on statistical reasoning.

The investigators also asked students in the experimental groups to list the college-level mathematics and science courses they had taken. Students who had taken at least two mathematics courses and two science courses were classified as having a science and math background; the other students were classified as lacking a science and math background.

The study analysis looked at differences across groups in both posttest scores and score gains. Because the control group scored slightly lower on the pretest than did the experimental groups, the two analyses gave the same result: The experimental group had higher posttest and score gains. The two experimental groups did not differ significantly in posttest or gain, even for the correlation-focused items, indicating that the lectures on probability and proportion had an effect on correlational reasoning as well.

Looking at differences between students with and without a science and math background, the study reported higher pretest scores for the students with a science and math background. Those students with a science and math background, however, did not gain significantly as a result of the intervention.

Overall, the investigators concluded that explicit instruction on these statistics-related topics could have a positive effect on students who entered with weak understanding of statistics. For students entering with stronger skills in statistical reasoning, some other intervention would be needed to increase their reasoning skills.

In all five studies, the researchers found their focused interventions had a positive effect on prospective teachers' knowledge. These results are consistent with the general result that opportunity to learn is associated with learning. They support the impression that current research on education foundations courses concentrates on particular approaches or exercises within courses, rather than asks questions about the overall impact of foundations courses.

In the search for reports on "foundations" courses, we did not systematically search for studies of the effects of courses on multiculturalism. Including them here would be redundant with another chapter in this book (Hollins & Torres Guzman, this volume). That means that the five studies we located do not represent all the empirical research on the effects of foundations courses. Courses on multiculturalism are also foundational, although they may not highlight their basis in arts and science disciplines in the way that courses in educational psychology, sociology of education, or philosophy of education do.

Two studies of the impact of courses on multiculturalism (Garmon, 1998; Morales, 2000) illustrate the ways in which published research on the effects of multiculturalism courses resembles the other work we found on education foundations courses. Garmon focuses on using dialog journals to change prospective teachers' racial attitudes. He required students in a course on multicultural education to complete weekly dialog journals that were graded not on content but on completion of 30 typed lines. He reasoned that separating grading from the content of the journal would leave students free to express whatever they were thinking as they went through the course.

Garmon (1998) analyzed journals of 21 students, who completed their journals by e-mail. Garmon noted the variety of ways he and the students used the journal entries: as an opportunity for the student to reflect on a course reading, as a chance for Garmon to give students information as prompted by their journal entries, as a forum for Garmon to challenge racial beliefs he considered "problematic" (e.g., the belief that family background has little effect on students' school performance), and as a place for Garmon to use personal comments or rhetorical questions to push students' thinking.

In the article, Garmon (1998) presented an extended analysis of his interactions with a single student. Using numerous quotes from the e-mail exchange, he showed how the student's racial attitudes changed over the semester. The student, in one of her last entries, thanked Garmon for making her more aware of how issues of race ran through education. He offered this exchange as an illustration of the effects dialog journals can have, but cautioned that their use must be adapted to the particular course and instructor.

Morales (2000) presented a case study of her approach to teaching a course, Cultural Diversity in the Early Childhood Classroom. She named the readings used in each session of the course and described the activity that students completed in that session. For one session, students collected materials related to a culture different from their own and wrote a paper about that culture. They also gave an oral presentation on the materials collected. Morales also quoted from a student's journal entry. Her overall conclusion was that the students gained self-confidence, felt that they knew more about how to teach pupils from other cultures, and were more aware of the need to attend to cultural diversity.

Overall, the little research conducted on the effects of foundations courses on teachers' knowledge has shown the potential of particular instructional modules or methods, rather than give any insight into what prospective teachers typically learn from such courses. A similar picture is seen in the studies of individual multicultural courses considered in this chapter. In the individual course studies, instructors report success in the activities whose effects they attempted to measure.

RECAPPING THE RESULTS: WHAT WE KNOW ABOUT IMPACT ON TEACHERS' KNOWLEDGE

It is sobering to look at the amount of empirical research done on what prospective teachers learn from their study of the subjects they will teach, other arts and sciences coursework, and courses in the foundations of education. Sobering because some policymakers forcefully advocate deep subject matter study and a strong liberal education, as well as a grounding in at least the psychological foundations of education. Their stance leaves the impression that here, at least, a strong basis exists for setting course requirements for teachers. Given those unequivocal claims, the small number of empirical studies that met our selection criteria is surprising. Support for arts and science requirements and for foundations based on arts and science work (especially in psychology) appears to depend less on an evidentiary base than does support for courses seen as the province of "educationists."

Perhaps that difference should come as no surprise, given the long history of American skepticism about education as a field of knowledge. As Lagemann (2000) points out in her recent history of educational research, researchers in other fields repeatedly worked to distance themselves from education, even when their work had strong apparent links.

The paucity of research should come as no surprise, given the scarcity of national data about teacher education and the difficulties in conducting research on teaching and learning in the context of higher education. Until the creation of the NAEP, NELS, LSAY datasets in the 1990s, no national databases were available that could link teacher education experiences to pupil achievement, and even those datasets offer only crude measures of teacher education. The variability in college course content, even across sections of the same course at one institution, creates challenges for those who would like to study the effects of higher education. In many disciplines, institutional rewards are given for scholarship within the discipline, rather than for scholarship on how the discipline is taught and learned. Within many teacher education programs, the focus of scholarship is also on the "education" courses, rather than on those in the arts and sciences. Given the data available and the rewards within the field for research in this area, the thinness of the research base is understandable.

Impact of Subject-Specific Study

The studies of secondary mathematics teachers show a positive association between the college study of mathematics and the mathematics learning of high school pupils, with the implication that teachers are gaining knowledge of value for teaching from those mathematics courses. That claim is well supported, although *what* mathematics prospective teachers should study needs further examination. Whether a degree in mathematics is better than a degree in mathematics education, or a degree in physics (which requires substantial mathematical study), remains disputable. No studies address questions about different combinations of college mathematics courses. The recommendations that the mathematical community has put forward about the curriculum for mathematics teachers (e.g., Conference Board of the Mathematical Sciences, 2001; Leitzel, 1991) are based on professional judgment, not on empirical research about what mathematics course work will be of most value to teachers.

For prospective teachers' knowledge of subject matter, the research is less extensive, but the consistent result is that a significant number of prospective teachers have only a "mechanical" understanding of the subject they will teach. They know rules to follow, but cannot explain the rationale behind the rule. Some invoke inaccurate "rules." If the ability to explain basic concepts is important for teaching, then the subject matter courses teachers now typically take leave a large fraction of teachers without important subject matter knowledge.

The number of studies addressing other subject areas and lower grade levels is small, giving little basis for interpreting counterintuitive results like the negative relationship between elementary school teachers' advanced study of mathematics and pupils' achievement. The claim that teachers need to know the subjects they teach has strong intuitive appeal, but exactly what they need to know to teach at various levels, with what desired outcomes, are still topics for debate. Authors may agree on the general principle that some subject matter knowledge is important, yet disagree about the specifics (e.g., Ball, 1997; Floden, 1997; Ma, 1999).

Studies of the impact individual subject matter courses have on prospective teachers also are few in number, with mathematics again the most studied. Given their content specificity, they seem more a source of ideas to be tested through further research than a solid basis for decisions about teacher preparation.

Except for secondary school mathematics, the empirical research about the impact of teachers' subject matter study is richer in questions to be explored than in results to build on. For those looking to support changes in preparation requirements, even the studies of secondary mathematics teachers must be used with caution. Although the studies we included attempt to take account of differences in the characteristics of K–12 pupils, they did not take account of the differences that prospective teachers bring to their preparation programs. Most of the regression analysis studies do not include statistical controls for differences among teachers prior to their entry into teacher education (e.g., teachers' family background or secondary-school academic record).

Although one can use the association between study of mathematics and pupil achievement to identify which teachers in the current system are most likely to achieve higher pupil gains, those associations do not strongly support predictions about the consequences of increasing mathematics coursework for all new teachers. The current greater effectiveness of teachers with more coursework may be due in part to other characteristics of the teachers who chose to study more mathematics. For example, they may enjoy mathematics more or may have had early experiences with mathematics teachers who taught them both a love of mathematics and approaches to teaching, for which formal teacher preparation is not the source.

Impact of Other Arts and Science Coursework

The review of general effect of attending college relied on the two standard references, one of which is a literature review. We did not do a systematic search for other work on the effects of college. Our reasons for including these fairly lengthy discussions of these works were the scarcity of studies specific to prospective teachers and the prevalence of the assumption, as indicated by certification requirements, that students get something valuable from the experience of going to college. The literature on learning from college is particularly relevant in what it says about the development of subject matter knowledge and of general cognitive skills, which have face validity as relevant to teaching.

Although most of the literature we examined provided some evidence about the knowledge that teachers gain, the literature on effects of college also speaks to political and social attitudes, finding general shifts toward greater social conscience and more interest in politics. These results could be tied to goals of education foundations courses, like those in studies we included, which attempted to reduce prejudice and strengthen commitments to social improvement.

Impact of Education Foundations Courses

The research on the impact of foundations courses on teachers' knowledge is scant. As with studies of individual subject matter courses, the studies document cases in which prospective teachers learn content intended by the instructors in special course modules (e.g., about statistical reasoning) or from particular instruction methods (e.g., from analyzing cases in light of course content). That can be helpful to those who taught that course and to those who decide whether to keep the course as it is, revise the syllabus, or drop it altogether. It may help with decisions about which faculty should teach the course. These studies are also starting points for lines of work that examine instructional content or methods in greater depth (e.g., a line of work on approaches to strengthening elementary teachers' skill in scientific reasoning). Like the studies of individual subject matter courses, the benefit for those outside the institution is largely as a source of promising practices, where promise is based on success in one context and on the practical judgment of the college faculty members who invested in the development and study of these approaches.

HOW CAN WE STRENGTHEN THE EMPIRICAL BASIS?

To build greater understanding of the effects on prospective teachers' knowledge of subject matter courses, other arts and science courses, and education foundations courses, researchers must work on three fronts:

- Improving measures of teachers' knowledge, skills, and dispositions
- Creating and making use of national and international datasets
- Drawing on other research on learning to sharpen the vocabulary for describing college coursework

Improving Measures of Teachers' Knowledge. To accumulate knowledge about the effects that college courses have on teachers' knowledge, the research community needs greater agreement on what effects should be studied and how these outcomes can be measured. In the research on the effects of taking mathematics courses, several of the studies used similar measures of effect: adjusted achievement scores of the teachers' pupils. Using similar measures that assess broadly valued outcomes contributes to the sense that these studies can be looked at together to draw conclusions and identify areas for studies that will contribute to a growing understanding. Many of the other studies used measures developed for a single study. However valuable the information, outcomes measured that way clearly are not related to one another. The idiosyncratic nature of these measures impedes accumulation of understanding across studies.

The use of adjusted pupil achievement data as an outcome measure is an important approach to improving measurement of the effects of arts and science courses. The value-added analysis approach Sanders (1994) developed has been well received by policymakers as a way to measure teacher effectiveness. If studies of the effects of teacher education coursework used an outcome measure like Sanders' approach or some other way of measuring teachers' effects on student learning, they could capitalize on this approach's appeal. The current increase in the frequency of state assessments of pupil achievement will create more opportunities to get good measures of pupil learning, although data linking individual teachers with their pupils' test scores will not be available in every state. Where it is available, however, it creates opportunities for research that connects data on teachers' education to outcome measures that have intuitive appeal and that often build on substantial investments on test development.

This approach has two drawbacks. First, it does not make explicit the teacher knowledge that promotes pupil learning. Without making that knowledge explicit, it is more difficult for teacher educators, whether in arts and sciences or in education, to revise their content and methods of instruction to increase pupil learning. Second, the greater the temporal separation between a teacher education experience and the collection of outcome data, the more difficult it will be to distinguish the effects of teacher education from the myriad other sources of teacher learning. The problem may not be insurmountable if data can be collected on teachers in their first or second year on the job, but if those who took part in a foundations course or in some set of arts and science courses scatter geographically after graduation, finding adequate sample sizes may be challenging. State and national databases may include many teachers who went through their preparation at the same institution, but changes in programs over time and variation in teachers' other opportunities to learn may obscure the effects of particular coursework.

Research that uses impact on pupil learning as an outcome measure needs to be coupled with studies that explore the connections between teachers' knowledge and pupil learning and with work that looks at the more immediate effects of teacher education coursework on teachers' knowledge. For the latter, agreement on common measures of teacher knowledge would aid in connecting the results across studies.

Given the current state of research, it may be necessary to begin work on such common measures by working toward measures with content validity based in the professional judgment of the relevant disciplinary and educational communities. Just as various professional communities in various disciplines have developed recommendations for the substance and structure of teacher preparation, these groups could, with the help of measurement experts, develop recommendations for the tools to measure the extent to which teachers are learning the content of these recommended teacher preparation curricula.

If the research we examined is any indication, it will be easier to develop such measures in mathematics than in other fields. To focus assessment development, work in mathematics might begin in one of the areas the RAND Mathematics Study Panel (2002) recommended as a priority for research: mathematical knowledge for teaching, mathematical thinking, problem solving, and algebra.

Making Use of National and International Data Sets.   In the last decade, the strongest empirical research base has come from analyses of large, representative national databases: NAEP, NELS, and LSAY. Even with limitations that come when using survey data not specifically designed to address questions about the effects of teacher preparation, the strength of these studies gives a basis for answering questions about general or typical effects, averaged across the myriad differences among colleges and universities.

Existing databases may support additional analyses, both in mathematics and in other subject areas. Sophisticated statistical procedures can be used to control for differences in the classrooms to which teachers are assigned, giving a credible basis for attributing pupil achievement gains to individual teachers. Investigators should develop comparable controls for differences in college students to provide a less ambiguous basis for attributing prospective teachers' learning either to particular courses or to features of courses.

Work at the course level will likely be more productive than are attempts to attribute teachers' learning to entire programs. For one thing, many programs have multiple versions of every required experience. Prospective teachers may receive credit for courses taken elsewhere. The challenge, then, will be to improve the sophistication of survey questions, or data systems, so that information is available at a level of detail that goes deeper than the number of courses taken or the teacher's academic major.

As international assessments continue to grow in breadth and sophistication, they will also produce datasets that can be analyzed to describe associations between college experiences and teaching effectiveness. Sociologists and economists each bring analytic tools and theoretical models that can undergird informative research.

Sharpening the Vocabulary for Describing College Coursework.   In national surveys, courses are described only by general content area (biological science vs. physical science) and level (undergraduate vs. graduate). Those differences matter, but each category covers an enormous range of variability. In the studies of single courses, when courses were described, the descriptions were idiosyncratic. Authors would mention particular texts or describe the academic tasks they posed to students, in ways that offered detail, but gave scant opportunity for linking to other studies. To build understanding, a more precise, commonly shared vocabulary is needed as much as widely used measures of teacher knowledge.

Research on K–12 classrooms has faced similar problems and made some progress toward greater precision. Work on classroom organization, for example, began by comparing instruction in large groups to instruction in small groups. Although the idea of small groups had great appeal, results of studies were inconsistent. The work began to move forward as attention was paid not only to the number and size of groups but also to the composition of groups (homogeneous or heterogeneous) and to the substance and structure of the activities the groups undertook. The literature on higher education has paid less attention to the organization of instruction. Greater effort to determine which features have potential for influencing learning, and agreement on how those features are described, is needed as a basis for research that can give some sound basis for course design.

CONCLUSION

In debates about the value of preservice teacher education, "teacher education" is sometimes taken to mean the practically-oriented methods classes and field experiences. But teacher education, as defined by certification requirements and program approval standards, also includes arts and sciences coursework and coursework in education foundations that draws as much and perhaps more from the arts and sciences as from education practice. Critiques of teacher preparation sometimes ask what evidence exists to support requirements that teachers complete specialized coursework. The same request for evidence might be made regarding the requirement that teachers complete an academic major in the subject they will teach, be awarded a bachelor's degree, or take courses based on the theories and evidence about education that have been produced by scholars in psychology, sociology, philosophy, and economics.

Our literature search showed that the evidence about the effects of such coursework on teachers' knowledge is extremely thin, with the exception of studies about the connections between secondary-school pupils' mathematics achievement and the amount of college mathematics taken by those pupils' teachers. That thin research base can be explained in part by the dearth of information about teachers' own education and the difficulties of measuring what impact a teacher's education has on pupils' achievement. It can also be attributed to the difficulty of studying effects in the complex context of teachers' learning. But the success that scholars have had in the work on content study for teaching secondary mathematics demonstrates that the challenges of data gathering and analysis can be overcome. Understanding the contributions that mathematics subject matter study makes to teaching will become firmer and richer as more datasets are created, with better measures of teachers' learning and opportunities to learn. Building a similar understanding for other subjects and grade levels may also come with research investments, even if mathematics proves to be the subject area where the relationships are easiest to determine.

The absence of strong empirical support for arts and science and foundations (especially psychological foundations) requirements seems unlikely to lead policymakers to relax these requirements. The intuitive sense that teachers should know their subject and understand how people learn is powerful, perhaps as powerful as the sense that doctors should know anatomy and understand how medicines work. The foundations courses can also lay claim to a strong basis in research, because their content rests on scholarship in their related disciplines. Recognizing that research is unlikely to overthrow general commitments to require coursework in arts and science and foundations is good grounds for focusing future research not on the general question of whether teachers should study the subjects they will teach but on specific questions about what they should study within the subject, how that study can best be drawn on for teaching, and how the study of concepts from psychology, sociology, and other arts and sciences can be taught in ways that make them most valuable for the practice of teaching.

TABLE 5.1

Coursework in the Arts and Sciences and Foundations of Education[a]

Studies[b]	Question and Focus	Research Tradition	Research Design	Findings
Adams (1998)	What is the mathematics knowledge of prospective elementary teachers?	Interpretive and survey research	Ninety-three prospective elementary teachers in elementary methods course in large Southeastern university Self-reported background Open-ended mathematics assessments	Despite having taken multiple college mathematics classes, prospective elementary teachers have limited understanding of the real number system.
Anderson (1998)	What is the effect of using a multimedia multiculturalism unit in an educational psychology course?	Prepost survey comparison	Thirty-two juniors in an educational psychology course that is part of a teacher preparation program Locally developed survey about choice of future work setting, understanding of learning theories, knowledge about cultural diversity	Most students reported that the course increased their understanding of learning theories and their knowledge about cultural diversity. Student preferences for different work settings did not change, though they did indicate a greater interest in having an ethnically diverse mix in their classrooms.
Astin (1977)	What is the effect of college on students?	Regression analysis	Surveys collected on entering college freshmen as part of the Cooperative Institutional Research Program Follow-up surveys on samples from each participating institution, generally 4 years after college entry Data from students entering college from 1961 to 1969 Samples of approximately 17,000–41,000 per year	College leads to increased competencies, especially in areas linked to curricular and extracurricular programs. Engagement in college tends to increase liberalism, interpersonal self-esteem, and artistic interests.

288

Astin (1993)	What is the effect of college on students?	Regression analysis	Surveys collected on entering college freshmen as part of the Cooperative Institutional Research Program Follow-up surveys on sample from each participating institution, generally 4 years after college entry. Data from students entering college in 1985 Normative longitudinal samples of about 4,000 students	Self-reports of growth in knowledge are associated with amount of time spent studying and both the number of years of college, and the number of hours spent. Growth in general knowledge is linked to taking courses that emphasize writing skills, scientific inquiry, and historical analysis. Ability to think critically is linked to factors such as emphasis on teaching the classics, heavy faculty involvement in general education teaching, and use of essay exams. Having students write, and rewrite, papers is important for developing critical thinking ability. Earlier findings on the liberalizing effect of college were not evident.
Ball (1990a)	What is the mathematics knowledge of prospective elementary and secondary teachers?	Survey, interpretive, and longitudinal study	Two hundred fifty-two preservice teachers at 5 institutions (217 elementary, 35 math majors intending to teach high school), from the Teacher Education and Learning to Teach Study (TELT) Questionnaires with all; interviews with a subsample	Elementary and secondary (mathematics majors) prospective teachers had difficulty explaining and articulating their knowledge of division of fractions. Only 30% of elementary and 40% of secondary selected an appropriate representation of a division by fractions problem. Over 30% of the secondary prospective teachers reported that most mathematics cannot be explained. Most elementary and prospective secondary teachers believed that mathematics concerned memorization and understanding standard procedures; few of them thought that mathematics had conceptual dimensions.

(Continued)

TABLE 5.1
(Continued)

Studies[b]	Question and Focus	Research Tradition	Research Design	Findings
Ball (1990b)	What is the mathematics knowledge of prospective elementary and secondary teachers?	Interpretive study	Ten elementary and 9 secondary prospective teachers about to enroll in first education course Elementary prospective teachers majoring in elementary education; secondary students mathematics majors or minors Data from student academic records and interviews about division in various contexts	All but 2 of the prospective teachers could calculate answers to division by fraction problems correctly, but both the elementary and the secondary majors had significant difficulty with the meaning of division by fractions. Only 5 could explain the meaning of division by 0. In a question about algebraic equations, 14 of the students, including all of the mathematics majors, focused on the mechanics of manipulating the equation. In general, most of the prospective teachers—whether they majored in mathematics or not—had fragmented and rule-bound mathematical understanding.
Borko et al. (1992)	What is the mathematics knowledge of prospective middle school teachers?	Interpretive study	Case of 1 middle school mathematics student teacher in the larger database of 8 teachers who participated in the Learning to Teach Mathematics Study Observations, interviews, and observations of university courses	The teacher believed that good mathematics teaching included making mathematics relevant and meaningful. The researchers could not get the teacher to speak about the division of fractions in a meaningful way at the beginning of her student-teaching year, and there was little evidence that she had a conceptual understanding of division by fractions. Although her knowledge of fractions seemed to deepen some throughout her participation in a mathematics methods course, she still could not provide a coherent explanation concerning the division of fractions, even after her

Civil (1993)	What is the influence of a mathematics course that emphasizes small-group discussion on prospective teachers' views about mathematics?	Interpretive study	Eight preservice elementary teachers Observations, interviews, informal discussions, analysis of homework, essays, diaries	student teaching experience. During her student teaching, she was unable to realize her image of good mathematics teaching because her own knowledge of the division of fractions and of how to represent the idea to students in instruction was limited. The teacher education program worked to reinforce the teacher's limited understanding of mathematics and mathematics teaching, rather than question it or help Ms. Daniels reinvent her understanding of division of fractions. The university program did not create the conditions for the teacher to overcome the limitations of her own knowledge. Students developed more reflective critical approaches to teaching and learning mathematics, were more comfortable working in groups, and had a greater feeling that they could learn mathematics.
Clark & Medina (2000)	What is the effect of focused discussion of an autobiographical literacy narrative on prospective teachers' understanding of literacy, multiculturalism, and teaching?	Interpretive study	Eight preservice secondary-school teachers, 2 from social studies education, 2 from English education, and 4 from foreign language education Reporting focused on 3 students, chosen because they had complete data and they were a diverse group: 1 White male, 1 African-American female, and 1 mixed White and Latina female.	The authors presented conclusions, which they characterized as "tentative" because they were based on only three students. The use of narratives supports changes in teachers' views of knowledge, critical understanding of literacy and multiculturalism, disruption of stereotyped conceptions of others, ability to make connections to other people's

(Continued)

TABLE 5.1
(Continued)

Studies[b]	Question and Focus	Research Tradition	Research Design	Findings
			Analysis of student writing in the course, course email, audio tapes of class discussion, field notes from class, and individual student interviews.	narratives, connections to theory, and recognition of the limits of their own perspectives.
Denton & Lacina (1984)	What is the effect of teachers' subject matter study on ratings of teacher effectiveness?	Survey and comparative population study (non parametric sign tests)	Eighty-two secondary-level student teachers: 55 education majors and 27 students seeking teacher certification while majoring in other fields. Education majors had 12 more semester hours (34 vs. 22) of education coursework than majors in other subjects. Locally developed rating scales used by university supervisors to rate student teachers' instructional competencies, personal and professional competencies, and planning effectiveness for 2 curriculum units	No significant difference between education majors and other majors in ratings of planning effectiveness. Between-group differences in ratings of instructional competency were small.
Druva & Anderson (1983)	What is the effect of teachers' subject matter study on pupil achievement?	Meta-analysis	Meta-analysis based on 65 studies of K–12 U.S. science teachers. Fifty-two studies were dissertations; 11 journal articles; 2, unpublished articles. Teacher variables included demographic variables, education, experience, knowledge, and personality variables. Student outcomes included a variety of achievement, performance, and attitude measures.	Student achievement was positively related to the number of biology courses taken (for biology teachers), the number of science courses taken, and attendance at academic institutes. Student attitude toward science was positively related to the number of science courses taken. Student outcomes are positively associated with preparation in education and academic work generally. The relationship between teachers' training in science and cognitive student outcome increases with the level of science course.

Author (Year)	Research question	Method	Description	Findings
Emenaker (1996)	What is the effect of a problem-solving mathematics course on prospective elementary teachers' views about mathematics?	Pre–post survey comparison and interpretive interviews	One hundred thirty-seven students completed a survey at the beginning and end of a mathematics course for elementary teachers. Survey had 5 scales on beliefs about mathematics. 9 students interviewed about changes in beliefs.	Significant change in belief (in the direction intended by the instructor) on four of the five scales. Interviews indicate some increase in students' confidence that they could discover mathematics on their own.
Fones, Wagner, & Caldwell (1999)	What is the effect of integrating lecture and laboratory in a general education science course on prospective teachers' reported understanding of scientific concepts, confidence in teaching those concepts, and attitudes toward science?	Two-sample, pretest posttest comparison	One hundred ten prospective elementary teachers; 97 in a traditionally structured course; 17 in an experimental section in which lecture was done in the context of small lab section. Locally developed self-report survey. Pretest data showed little difference between two groups.	Scores improved both traditional and experimental group. Experimental group improved significantly more on self-reported knowledge of science and attitude toward science. No difference in confidence about teaching.
Garmon (1998)	What is the effect of use of dialog journals on prospective teachers' racial attitudes?	Interpretive study	Analyzed dialog journals of 21 students, but reports on only 1 in detail.	The focal student's attitudes improved, and she became more aware of how racial issues run through education.
Goldhaber & Brewer (1997)	What is the effect of teachers' subject matter study on pupil achievement?	Survey and comparative population study (multiple regression)	Data from the first two waves of 1988 NELS study. Twenty-four thousand 8th-graders in spring 1988; eighteen thousand of these students were surveyed again in 10th-grade (spring 1990). At each survey, students took one or more content knowledge tests in mathematics, science, writing, and history. The researchers focus on students who took the mathematics test in 8th and 10th grades.	Individual and family background variables explain three fourths of the variation in students' 10th-grade math scores. Teachers with a BA in math or an MA in math have statistically significant impact on student achievement; teachers with a nonmath BA or MA have a negative impact on student achievement. Similar results were found with teacher

(Continued)

TABLE 5.1
(Continued)

Studies[b]	Question and Focus	Research Tradition	Research Design	Findings
			Teacher variables include gender, race and ethnicity, degree level, experience, certification. Fifty-one hundred forty-nine 10th-grade students who came from 638 schools and 2,245 mathematics teachers.	certification. Teachers who are certified in mathematics have higher student test scores.
Goldhaber & Brewer (2000)	What is the effect of teachers' subject matter study on pupil achievement?	Survey and comparative population study (multiple regression)	NELS (1988) Thirty-seven hundred eighty-six students in mathematics; 2,524 students in science; 2,098 mathematics teachers; 1,371 science teachers Tenth and 12th-grade standardized test scores in mathematics, and science is the outcome variable. Independent variables are grouped into: • Individual and family background characteristics of students • Schooling resources, which include school, teacher, and class-specific variables. Teacher variables include type of certification (standard subject, probationary subject, private school, none), degree level, and experience.	Students with teachers who had degrees in mathematics were found to have higher test scores relative to those with teachers with out-of-subject degrees. In science, there was no effect. Math students with teachers with bachelor's or master's degrees in mathematics have higher test scores relative to those with out-of-subject degrees. There is no significant relationship between teacher subject matter major and student achievement in science. Having a degree in education had no impact on student science scores, but a BA in education had a negative impact on mathematics achievement.
Graeber, Tirosh, & Glover (1989)	What is the mathematics knowledge of prospective elementary school teachers?	Interpretive study	One hundred twenty-nine college students enrolled in mathematics subject matter or methods courses for early education majors at a large university in southeastern United States Interviews with a subsample and a subject matter knowledge test (26 items) were taken by all participants	Of the preservice teachers, 39% answered 4 or more of the 13 multiplication and division problems incorrectly. All interviewees held various misconceptions about multiplication and division. Preservice teachers demonstrated the weak understanding of multiplication and division. Their

Study	Research question	Method	Sample and measures	Findings
Hawk, Coble, & Swanson (1985)	What is the effect of teachers' subject matter study on pupil achievement?	Comparative and quasiexperimental study (ANOVA, t-tests)	Graduates of East Carolina University Thirty-six mathematics teachers of Grades 6–12 were followed in the study. All were certified. 18 teachers were in-field and 18 were teaching out-of-field; 826 students Teachers matched on school, teaching the same mathematics course, to students of same ability Students tests: Stanford Achievement Test (general math) and Stanford Test of Academic Skills (algebra) Tests of arithmetic and elementary algebra were administered to teachers. Teaching performance was measured by the CTPAS.	knowledge resembled the knowledge of 10- to 15-year-olds in other research on division and multiplication. Significant differences were apparent from the posttest in general mathematics and algebra. Students who had in-field teachers scored higher. In-field teachers scored significantly higher on the Carolina Teacher Performance Assessment System (CTPAS) and the Knowledge test. Chi-square analysis yielded no significant differences due to years of teaching or degree held by teachers in the study.
Hawkins, Stancavage, & Dossey (1998)	What is the effect of teachers' subject matter study on pupil achievement?	Survey	National Assessment of Educational Progress (NAEP; 1996) Thirty-nine states and jurisdictions participated in the 1996 NAEP.	Fourth-grade students whose teacher had a college major in mathematics education or education outperformed students whose teachers had a major in a field other than education, mathematics education, or mathematics. Fourth-graders who were taught by teachers with degrees in mathematics did not outperform students taught by teachers with degrees in education. The type of teaching certificate (mathematics, education, or other) held by the teachers of 4th-graders was not related to 4th-graders' scores on the 1996 NAEP math assessment.

(Continued)

TABLE 5.1
(Continued)

Studies[b]	Question and Focus	Research Tradition	Research Design	Findings
				Eighth-grade students with teachers who had a college major in mathematics (average NAEP scale score of 276) outperformed students whose teachers had a college major in education (average NAEP scale score of 265) or a field other than education, mathematics education, or mathematics (average scale score of 248) on the 1996 NAEP mathematics assessment.
				Eighth-grade students whose teachers had a teaching certificate in mathematics performed better than other 8th-graders.
Holt-Reynolds (1999)	What is preservice secondary English teachers' knowledge about literature?	Interpretive study	Twelve undergraduate literature majors, intending to become certified to teach secondary English. Each interviewed 5 times over the course of teacher preparation. Interview protocol focused on what literature is, why and how respondents read it, what literature they hope to share with future adolescent readers, and what reading actions they intend to teach to their pupils.	Most prospective teachers have superficial or inaccurate view of what literature is. The focal teacher had a strong understanding of literature, but did not plan to use her knowledge in teaching.
Kennedy (1998)	What is preservice teachers' knowledge for the teaching of writing?	Longitudinal survey and interview study	Report based on the TELT study. Data from 75 students for a dozen teacher education programs, 5 of which were preservice programs. Data also collected on faculty in these programs.	Many preservice teachers had procedural knowledge about grammar and writing conventions, but lacked knowledge of underlying principles.

Study	Research question	Design	Sample and data	Findings
Lundeberg (1997)	What effect does a class on gender bias (including comparing perceptions to documented account, viewing videos, and discussion) have on prospective teachers' perceptions of gender bias?	Survey	Variables were teacher education student and faculty beliefs about writing and about teaching writing. Data collected through interviews in which teachers were asked to interpret and respond to a series of hypothetical classroom situations. Forty-eight preservice teachers (21 men and 27 women) enrolled in 2 sections of Educational Psychology Open-response questions about gender bias and how to address in teaching Questions answered after the intervention	Thirteen of the 48 students reported a change in their perception of gender bias in the classroom as a result of the intervention: comparing perception to systematic data collected, viewing videos, and participating in discussion.
Lundeberg & Scheurman (1997)	Do prospective teachers gain from the analysis, and repeated analysis, of dilemma-based cases?	Pre–post analysis of written analyses	Sixty-seven preservice teachers Students analyzed cases both before and after a unit of instruction. Their written analyses were examined for evidence of ability to identify problems, consider others' viewpoints, and make links to theoretical material covered in class.	Students' written analyses showed increased ability to identify problems, consider others' viewpoints, and make links to theory after analyzing cases.
McDiarmid & Wilson (1991)	What is the mathematics knowledge of prospective elementary and secondary teachers?	Interpretive and survey study	N = 55 All in 2 alternate routes Undergraduate degree in mathematics Eight in the intensive sample Another 8 intensive-sample interviewees who majored in something else but were to be elementary-school teachers Questionnaire and interviews	In general, prospective teachers did well on rules of thumb in mathematics but could not explain how those rules worked or represent problems accurately.

(Continued)

TABLE 5.1
(Continued)

Studies[b]	Question and Focus	Research Tradition	Research Design	Findings
McNeal & Simon (2000)	What is the impact of a mathematics class that emphasizes culture of inquiry on preservice teachers' norms and practices for participation in mathematics class?	Interpretive study	Twenty-six prospective elementary teachers Field notes; class meetings videotaped and transcribed; examination of journals, tests, and written work; instructor's reflective journal	Students changed their norms for participating in mathematical inquiry.
Monk (1994)	What is the effect of teachers' subject matter study on pupil achievement?	Survey research and comparative population study (multiple regression)	Longitudinal Study of American Youth Fifty-one randomly selected school sites; base sample of 2,829 students; selected localities nationwide Six hundred eight mathematics teachers, 483 science teachers Sampling rubric included geographic local and community type (rural, suburban, and urban) Teacher survey about number of undergraduate and graduate courses in various curricular areas Student achievement measured by selected NAEP items (1,492 students) at both 10th and 11th grades	Found positive relationships between the number of undergraduate mathematics subject matter courses in a teacher's background and improvement in students' mathematics performance, for both sophomores and juniors. For sophomores, teacher course-taking at the graduate level in mathematics also has a positive effect on student achievement. After 5 mathematics courses, the addition of courses in mathematics has a smaller effect on pupil performance. Mathematics education courses: undergraduate coursework is positively related to improvement in mathematics for sophomores and juniors. Graduate mathematics education courses have a modest positive effect at the junior level. Courses in undergraduate mathematics pedagogy contribute more to student

performance gains than do undergraduate mathematics courses.

Having mathematics major has no apparent bearing in pupil performance.

Teachers' degree level has quite a different effect compared to course-taking variables; there is either a 0 or negative relationship between additional training and student performance.

The number of mathematics courses in a teacher's background has a positive effect on students in advanced courses and a zero effect on students in remedial courses.

Teacher undergraduate preparation in the life sciences has no discernible impact on student performance.

Positive relationships were found between undergraduate coursework in physical sciences and gains in pupil performance, for both sophomores and juniors.

There was a positive relationship between junior gains in achievement and graduate coursework in life sciences.

Graduate courses in science pedagogy were positively related to student achievement for sophomores. Undergraduate coursework in science pedagogy had a positive relationship with student achievement for juniors. The magnitudes of the relationships in science between course taking and student gains were quite small.

(Continued)

TABLE 5.1
(Continued)

Studies[b]	Question and Focus	Research Tradition	Research Design	Findings
				Having a science major was positively related to student gains for juniors.
				The interaction between undergraduate course-taking in the physical sciences and the subject taught is statistically significant for both sophomores and juniors, with the physical sciences sign being positive for pupil's performance in the life sciences.
Monk & King (1994)	What is the effect of teachers' subject matter study on pupil achievement?	Survey research and comparative population study (regression analysis)	Longitudinal Study of American Youth (LSAY)	Found small positive direct effect of mathematics teachers' subject matter preparation during sophomore year for high pretest students.
			Fifty-one randomly selected school sites; base sample of 2,829 students; selected localities nationwide	Looking at 2-year gain, positive effect of subject matter preparation of sophomore year mathematics teacher for low pretest students
			Teacher survey about number of undergraduate and graduate courses in mathematics, life science, and physical science	Positive effect of sophomore- and junior-year mathematics teachers' subject matter preparation for whole sample where the gain in performance is measured over 2 years.
			Student achievement measured by selected NAEP items.	For life sciences, teachers' subject matter preparation had no significant effect on student performance.
				For physical sciences, positive effect of subject matter preparation of sophomore-year teacher for high pretest students
				For physical sciences, negative effect of subject matter preparation of junior-year teacher

Study	Research question	Design	Data/Sample	Findings
				For physical sciences, the mean level of subject matter preparation for teachers in the school had a positive effect on the performance of low-pretest students. For life sciences, a high level of variability in subject matter preparation of teachers in the school had a positive effect for high-pretest students, but a negative effect for low-pretest students.
Morales (2000)	What is the impact of a course on prospective teachers' understanding of culturally appropriate practices?	Interpretive study	Analysis of student work Observation by instructor during class sessions	Students gained self-confidence, felt that they knew more about how to teach pupils from other cultures, and were more aware of the need to attend to cultural diversity.
Pankratius (1997)	How are prospective teachers' views about teaching and learning styles affected learning about the Myers–Briggs Type Indicator and working in groups based on Myers–Briggs type?	Interpretive study	Twenty-two teacher candidates in a course on Perspectives on Secondary Education Data are student journal entries and class papers Themes generated a part of data analysis.	Students gained awareness of differences in learning styles and became more aware of their own assumptions about learning.
Rowan et al. (1997)	What is the effect of teachers' subject matter study on pupil achievement?	Correlational research (correlation, regression, and hierarchical linear modeling)	NELS (1988) Fifty-three hundred eighty-one students in 410 schools Variables for students: NELS 10th-grade math test, course-taking and track, other background	Students who were taught by teachers who had majored in mathematics had higher levels of achievement in mathematics. The effect size was quite small (.015 *SD*).

(Continued)

TABLE 5.1
(Continued)

Studies[b]	Question and Focus	Research Tradition	Research Design	Findings
Rowan et al. (2002)	What is the effect of teachers' subject matter study on pupil achievement?	Survey research and comparative population study (regression analysis)	Variables for teachers: score on NELS math quiz, major in mathematics, emphasis on teaching for higher order thinking, motivation Other school variables Presage variables: special certification in reading or mathematics; BA in English or mathematics; and teacher experience In mathematics, for the cohort beginning in 1st grade, $N = 5,454$ in 1,422 classrooms across 3 years in 138 schools. For the cohort beginning in 3rd grade, $N = 5,926$ students in 1,378 classrooms in 164 schools. In reading, for the cohort beginning in 1st grade, $N = 6,053$ students in 2,033 classrooms in 152 schools. For the cohort beginning in 3rd grade, $N = 6,153$ students in 1,713 classrooms in 166 schools.	The researchers used a 3-level linear hierarchical model of students' growth in academic achievement. In reading, neither teachers' degree status or teachers' certification status had significant effects on student achievement growth, but teacher experience did ($d = .07$ at early grades; $d = .15$ in later grades). In mathematics, teacher certification had no effect, and there was a positive effect of teachers' experience status on student achievement growth in mathematics, but only for the later grades ($d = .18$). Students taught by a teacher with an advanced degree in mathematics did worse than students who were taught by a teacher not having a mathematics degree ($d = -.25$).
Simon (1993)	What is the mathematics knowledge of prospective elementary school teachers?	Interpretive study	Large Eastern teacher education program in large, public state university 33 prospective elementary school teachers for subject matter knowledge test (5-open-response problems)	Prospective teachers demonstrated serious shortcomings in their understanding of division as a model for situations. The teachers had appropriate knowledge of symbols and algorithms associated with division. But their conceptual knowledge

Author/Year	Research question	Type of study	Sample/Context	Findings
				was weak, and they knew little of appropriate connections among different ideas in division.
Smith & Anderson	What is the impact of a physics course designed to engage prospective elementary teachers on their scientific practices and discourses?	Interpretive study	Eight teachers were then interviewed as they worked on problems from the original test. Nine prospective elementary teachers in two sections of a course. Classes videotaped and transcribed. Analysis focused on changes in students' patterns of talk and strategies for making sense.	All students began the course seeing science as static, memorized, and authoritative, but differed in their faith in the authority of science. By the end of the course, students developed "norms and practices that enabled more sophisticated scientific reasoning."
Stoddart et al. (1993)	What is the mathematics and science knowledge of prospective elementary school teachers?	Two parallel interpretive studies: 1 with elementary prospective mathematics teachers, 1 with elementary prospective science teachers	Medium-size university in the western United States. Eighty-three prospective elementary mathematics teachers. Forty-nine prospective elementary science teachers	Future teachers had limited understanding of the mathematics subject matter they would have to teach. The majority could answer simple computational problems. Only half could correctly solve story problems or problems that involved the multiplication, division, and equivalency of fractions. Results show that the majority of teacher candidates entered the course with a poor understanding of science content. Between 60% and 90% of the participants held naive or scientifically naive views of weather phenomena (condensation, temperature, precipitation, etc.). The prospective teachers' knowledge of these phenomena resembled that of the elementary-school children they were to teach.
Tirosh, & Graeber (1989)	What is the mathematics knowledge of prospective	Interpretive study	One hundred thirty-five undergraduate teacher education students enrolled in mathematics subject matter or methods courses at a large university.	Eighty-five percent responded correctly to the statement "In a multiplication problem, the product is greater than either factor." (Correct answer is FALSE.)

(Continued)

TABLE 5.1
(Continued)

Studies[b]	Question and Focus	Research Tradition	Research Design	Findings
	secondary-school teachers?		Mathematics test of beliefs about multiplication and division and computational skills	Ninety percent responded correctly to a statement that could be checked immediately by performing a computation.
			Half were also interviewed about conceptions of multiplication and division	Only 45% responded correctly to "In division problems, the quotient must be less than the dividend." (Correct answer is FALSE.)
				Performance rates on computation tests were generally good.
				Preservice teachers have misconceptions about multiplication and division.
Vass et al. (2000)	Do course exercises focusing on probability and proportionality have an effect on education majors' reasoning skills?	Experimental comparison, with pre- and posttest	One hundred three education majors enrolled in 4 sections of an educational psychology course: 2 sections assigned to experimental treatments; 2, to control	Students in the experimental groups had statistically significant gains on the tests of reasoning. Students in control group did not show a gain.
			Eight-item, pre- and posttests of proportional, probabilistic, correlational reasoning, and Piagetian tasks	Students without science and math background gained significantly in the experimental group; those with science and math background did not gain.
			Student self-report on number of college-level mathematics and science courses taken was used to classify as with science and math background (at least 2 courses of each) or without.	Hence, the treatment had an effect only on students without a math and science background.
			One experimental group received three 20-minute lectures on proportions, probability, and correlations. Second experimental group received three 20-minute lectures: one each on proportions, probability, plus a review lecture. Control groups received no instruction on these topics.	The 2 experimental groups did not differ significantly in their gains, even on the items that focused on correlation.

Study	Research question	Method	Data	Findings
Wenglinsky (2002)	What is the effect of teachers' majoring or minoring in mathematics on their 8th-grade pupils' mathematics achievement?	Regression analysis (multilevel structural equation modeling)	NAEP 1996 data on 8th-grade students. Seventy-one hundred forty-six 8th-grade pupils and their teachers NAEP mathematics assessment and measures of pupil family background NAEP teacher self-reports on education level, major or minor, years of experience, participation in professional development, classroom practices, and class size	In the school-level analysis, the teachers' having major or minor in mathematics had a statistically significant effect on pupil achievement, though the effect of student SES "far outshadows" the effect of teachers' major.
Wilson (1994)	What is the mathematics knowledge of prospective secondary school teachers?	Interpretive study	Case study of one student intending to become a secondary-school mathematics teacher. At the time of the study, she was participating in a secondary mathematics pedagogy course in a university. Written mathematical tasks about functions and seven interviews about functions, technology, and other topics.	The subject sees textbooks as major sources for authority in mathematics, believes it is sufficient for students to only know how to correctly apply procedures and that it is the teacher's responsibility to teach correct rules and procedures in an organized fashion. She understands functions as computational activities and believed that graphs of functions should be continuous. Over the period of the course, her understanding of functions improved.
Wilson & Wineburg (1988)	What is the knowledge of history of prospective secondary-school teachers?	Interpretive study	Four prospective high school social studies teachers Interviews and observations over 1 year	Only 1 of the 3 teachers had an accurate understanding of history as a subject matter
Zbiek (1998)	What do prospective secondary teachers learn from a mathematics class on modeling?	Interpretive study	Thirteen prospective secondary teachers in an elective mathematics course Interviews of students, observations of students working on modeling projects, analysis of student work	Students used four distinct strategies for modeling data. Students struggled at times with the modeling task, despite strong backgrounds in mathematics.

[a] Many of these summaries are drawn, entirely or in part, from the summaries included in the appendices to Wilson et al. (2001) and Wilson and Floden (2003).
[b] Please see References section.

REFERENCES FOR REPORTS INCLUDED IN SUMMARY

Adams, T. L. (1998). Prospective elementary teachers' mathematics subject matter knowledge: The real number system. *Journal for Research in Mathematics Education, 20*, 35–48.

Anderson, S. E. (1998). Integrating multimedia multicultural materials into an educational psychology course. *Journal of Technology and Teacher Education, 6*, 169–182.

Astin, A. W. (1977). *Four critical years: Effects of college on beliefs, attitudes, and knowledge.* San Francisco: Jossey-Bass.

Astin, A. W. (1993). *What matters in college? Four critical years revisited.* San Francisco: Jossey-Bass.

Ball, D. L. (1990a). The mathematical understandings that prospective teachers bring to teacher education. *Elementary School Journal, 90*, 449–466.

Ball, D. L. (1990b). Prospective elementary and secondary teachers' understanding of division. *Journal of Research in Mathematics Education, 21*, 132–144.

Borko, H., Eisenhart, M., Brown, C. A., Underhill, R. G., Jones, D., & Agard, P. C. (1992). Learning to teach hard mathematics: Do novice teachers and their instructors give up too easily? *Journal for Research in Mathematics Education, 23*, 194–222.

Civil, M. (1993). Prospective elementary teachers' thinking about teaching mathematics. *Journal of Mathematical Behavior, 12*, 79–109.

Clark, C., & Medina, C. (2000). How reading and writing literacy narratives affect preservice teachers' understandings of literacy, pedagogy, and multiculturalism. *Journal of Teacher Education, 51*(1), 63–76.

Denton J. J., & Lacina L. J. (1984). Quantity of professional education coursework linked with process measures of student teaching. *Teacher Education and Practice*, Spring, 39–46.

Druva, C. A., & Anderson, R. D. (1983). Science teachers characteristics by teacher behavior by student outcome: A meta-analysis of research. *Journal of Research in Science Teaching, 20*(5), 467–479.

Emenaker, C. (1996). A problem-solving based mathematics course and elementary teachers' beliefs. *School Science and Mathematics, 96*(2), 75–84.

Fones, S. W., Wagner, J. R., & Caldwell, E. R. (1999). Promoting attitude adjustments in science for preservice elementary teachers. *Journal of College Science Teaching, 29*, 231–236.

Garmon, M. A. (1998). Using dialogue journals to promote student learning in a multicultural teacher education course. *Remedial and Special Education, 19*(1), 32–45.

Goldhaber, D. D., & Brewer, D. J. (1997). Why don't schools and teachers seem to matter? Assessing the impact of unobservables on educational productivity. *The Journal of Human Resources, 32*(3), 505–523.

Goldhaber, D. D., & Brewer, D. J. (2000). Does teacher certification matter? High school teacher certification status and student achievement. *Educational Evaluation and Policy Analysis, 22*, 129–145.

Graeber, A. O., Tirosh, D., & Glover, R. (1989). Preservice teachers' misconceptions in solving verbal problems in multiplication and division. *Journal for Research in Mathematics Education, 20*, 95–102.

Hawk, P. P., Coble, C. R., & Swanson, M. (1985). Certification: It does matter. *Journal of Teacher Education, 36*(3), 13–15.

Hawkins, E. F., Stancavage, F. B., & Dossey, J. A. (1998). *School policies and practices affecting instruction in mathematics: Findings from the National Assessment of Educational Progress* (NCES 98-495). Washington, DC: U.S. Department of Education, Office of Educational Research and Improvement.

Holt-Reynolds, D. (1999). Good readers, good teachers? Subject matter expertise as a challenge in learning to teach. *Harvard Educational Review, 69*, 29–50.

Kennedy, M. M. (1998). *Learning to teach writing: Does teacher education make a difference?* New York: Teachers College Press.

Lundeberg, M. A. (1997). You guys are overreacting: Teaching prospective teachers about subtle gender bias. *Journal of Teacher Education, 48*(1), 55–61.

Lundeberg, M. A., & Scheurman, G. (1997). Looking twice means seeing more: Developing pedagogical knowledge through case analysis. *Teaching and Teacher Education, 13*(8), 783–797.

McDiarmid, G. W., & Wilson, S. M. (1991). An exploration of the subject matter knowledge of alternate route teachers: Can we assume they know their subject? *Journal of Teacher Education, 42,* 93–103.

McNeal, B., & Simon, M. A. (2000). Mathematics culture clash: Negotiating new classroom norms with prospective teachers. *Journal of Mathematical Behavior, 18*(4), 475–509.

Monk, D. H. (1994). Subject area preparation of secondary mathematics and science teachers and student achievement. *Economics of Education Review, 13,* 125–145.

Monk, D. H., & King, J. (1994). Multilevel teacher resource effects on pupil performance in secondary mathematics and science: The role of teacher subject-matter preparation. In R. G. Ehrenberg (Ed.), *Contemporary policy issues: Choices and consequences in education* (pp. 29–58). City: ILR Press.

Morales, R. (2000). Effects of teacher preparation experiences and students' perceptions related to developmentally and culturally appropriate practices. *Action in Teacher Education, 22*(2), 67–75.

Pankratius, W. J. (1997). Preservice teachers construct a view on teaching and learning styles. *Action in Teacher Education, 28*(4), 68–76.

Rowan, B., Chiang, F. S., & Miller, R. J. (1997). Using research on employees' performance to study the effects of teachers on students' achievement. *Sociology of Education, 70,* 256–284.

Rowan, B., Correnti, R., & Miller, R. J. (2002). What large-scale survey research tells us about teacher effects on student achievement: Insights from the Prospects Study of Elementary Schools. *Teachers College Record, 104,* 1525–1777.

Simon, M. A. (1993). Prospective teachers' knowledge of division. *Journal for Research in Mathematics Education, 24,* 233–254.

Smith, D. C., & Anderson, C. A. (1999). Appropriating scientific practices and discourses with future elementary teachers. *Journal of Research in Science Teaching, 36*(7), 755–776.

Stoddart, T., Connell, M., Stofflett, R., & Peck, D. (1993). Reconstructing elementary teacher candidates' understanding of mathematics and science content. *Teaching and Teacher Education, 9,* 229–241.

Tirosh, D., & Graeber, A. O. (1989). Preservice teachers' explicit beliefs about multiplication and division. *Educational Studies in Mathematics, 20,* 79–96.

Vass, E., Schiller, D., & Nappi, A. J. (2000). The effects of instructional intervention on improving proportional, probabilistic, and correlational reasoning skills among undergraduate education majors. *Journal of Research in Science Teaching, 37*(9), 981–995.

Wenglinsky, H. (2002, February 13). How schools matter: The link between teacher classroom practices and student academic performance. *Education Policy Analysis Archives, 10*(12). Retrieved January 2, 2004, from http://epaa.asu.edu/epaa/v10n12/

Wilson, M. (1994). One preservice secondary teacher's understanding of function: The impact of a course integrating mathematical content and pedagogy. *Journal for Research in Mathematics Education, 25,* 346–370.

Wilson, S. M., & Wineburg, S. S. (1988). Peering at American history through different lenses: The role of disciplinary knowledge in teaching. *Teachers College Record, 89,* 529–539.

Zbiek, R. M. (1998). Prospective teachers' use of computing tools to develop and validate functions as mathematical models. *Journal for Research in Mathematics Education, 29*(2), 184–201.

OTHER REFERENCES

Ball, D. L. (1997). Developing mathematics reform: What don't we know about teacher learning—but would make good working hypotheses? In S. N. Friel & G. W. Bright (Eds.), *Reflecting on our work: NSF Teacher Enhancement in K-6 mathematics* (pp. 77–111). Latham, MD: University of Press of America.

Conference Board of the Mathematical Sciences. (2001). *The mathematical education of teachers.* Washington, DC: Mathematical Association of America and the American Mathematical Society.

Floden, R. E. (1997). Reforms that call for more than you understand. In N. C. Burbules & D. T. Hansen (Eds.), *Teaching and its predicaments.* Boulder, CO: Westview Press.

Lagemann, E. C. (2000). *An elusive science: The troubling history of educational research.* Chicago: University of Chicago Press.

Leitzel, J. R. C. (Ed.). (1991). *A call for change: Recommendations for the mathematical preparation of teachers of mathematics.* Washington, DC: Mathematical Association of America.

Lortie, D. C. (1975). *Schoolteacher: A sociological study.* Chicago: University of Chicago Press.

Ma, L. (1999). *Knowing and teaching elementary mathematics: Teachers' understanding of fundamental mathematics in China and the United States:* Hillsdale, NJ: Lawrence Erlbaum Associates.

McDiarmid, G. W., Ball, D. L., & Anderson, C. A. (1989). Why staying one chapter ahead doesn't really work: Subject-specific pedagogy. In M. C. Reynolds (Ed.), *Knowledge base for the beginning teacher* (pp. 193–205). New York: Pergamon.

Nussbaum, M. C. (1997). *Cultivating humanity: A classical defense of reform in liberal education.* Cambridge, MA: Harvard University Press.

National Center for Research on Teacher Learning. (1991). *Findings from the Teacher Education and Learning to Teach Study: Final report* (Special Report 6/91). East Lansing, MI: College of Education, Michigan State University. (http://ncrtl.msu.edu/http/sreports/sr691.pdf)

Pascarella, E. T., & Terenzini, P. T. (1991). *How college affects students.* San Francisco: Jossey-Bass.

RAND Mathematics Study Panel. (2002). *Mathematical proficiency for all students: Toward a strategic research and development program in mathematics education* (No. MR-1643.0-OERI). Santa Monica, CA: RAND.

Sanders, W. L., & Horn, S. (1994). The Tennessee value-added assessment system (TVAAS): Mixed-model methodology in educational assessment. *Journal of Personnel Evaluation in Education, 8,* 299–311.

Shavelson, R. J., & Towne, L. (2003). *Scientific research in education.* Washington, DC: National Academy Press.

Wayne, A. J., & Youngs, P. (2003). Teacher characteristics and student achievement gains: A review. *Review of Educational Research, 73,* 89–122.

Wilson, S. M., & Floden, R. E. (2003). *Creating effective teachers—Concise answers for hard questions: An addendum to the report Teacher Preparation Research: Current knowledge, gaps and recommendations.* Washington, DC: ERIC Clearinghouse on Teaching and Teacher Education.

Wilson, S. M., Floden, R. E., & Ferrini-Mundy, J. (2001). *Teacher preparation research: Current knowledge, gaps, and recommendations.* Seattle: Center for the Study of Teaching and Policy.

Wilson, S. M., Floden, R. E., & Ferrini-Mundy, J. (2002). Teacher preparation research: An insider's view from the outside. *Journal of Teacher Education, 53*(3), 190–204.

6

Research on Methods Courses and Field Experiences

Renee T. Clift
Patricia Brady
University of Illinois at Urbana-Champaign

In this chapter we focus on the research procedures and the impact claims of researchers who study the complex phenomenon commonly labeled as a methods course or a teacher-education-related field experience in a school or community. We document the evolution of research in this area from a search for discrete, observable, and measurable teaching behaviors that could impact student attitudes and achievement to more recent investigations of the interactions among thought, intention, belief, behavior, subject matter content, and social and institutional context.

Prior to 1975, most research in this area consisted of psychological studies, conducted under the auspices of large, federally funded research centers, utilizing laboratory-based and field-based designs (Fuller & Bown, 1975; Peck & Tucker, 1973; Turner, 1975). Experimental groups of preservice teachers were trained to exhibit a certain behavior (i.e., asking higher level questions) and use that behavior in laboratory and classroom settings; comparisons were made against an untrained control group. Outcomes (or impact) of these early studies on preservice teachers included short-term gains in professional knowledge, enhanced course grades, desirable behavioral changes, increased knowledge of students, and greater acceptance of children from cultural and racial groups different from those of the preservice teachers. Although researchers were concerned with teaching techniques and intended their research to inform the content of teacher education courses, this early work was not examined within the context of methods courses or teacher education programs.

In the 1970s, as the field of psychology began to move from a focus on observable, measurable behaviors to cognitive studies, many teacher educators expressed considerable skepticism over the early research on training behaviors within teacher education as a base for the content of teacher education programs and as proof for the efficacy of teacher education programs themselves. Reviews of research (e.g., Lanier & Little, 1986) documented that the teacher preparation curriculum itself was fragmented and lacked coherence and that researchers paid scant attention to instruction within the teacher preparation curriculum or the impact of that instruction. Much of the data was based on retrospective interviews or surveys, and the impact of methods courses and field experiences was not systematically studied (beyond training on specified skills). Lanier and Little suggested that teacher education research should not only look at the curriculum for teacher education but should also include teachers' and teacher educators' analyses of their own practice.

The editor of the first *Handbook of Research on Teacher Education* (Houston, 1990, p. ix) noted "the research basis for such important work as educating the nation's teachers is still extremely thin." In the lead chapter, Doyle (1990) acknowledged that although many research frameworks had maintained a technical focus on behavior within teacher education, additional, more complex conceptions of the study of teacher education also were emerging. Programs differed in conceptions of what a good teacher should be, and opinions differed as well in the research community. Doyle attributed this to teacher educators' and researchers' awareness of differences among school contexts. He also argued for a resurgence in the intellectual foundations of method and "an explication of how a practice works and what meaning it has to teachers and students in a particular context" (p. 20).

The chapters that followed documented that although some studies of general teacher education curriculum looked at how teachers were trained to adopt certain behaviors (Cruickshank & Metcalf, 1990), other reviews took a more sociological approach to study of teacher education curriculum. For example, Ginsburg and Clift (1990) suggested that the disjuncture between program components often indicates a view of knowledge that is molecular and fragmented, not designed to develop a holistic view of knowing, doing, or understanding. The chapter summarizing research on field experiences (Guyton & McIntyre, 1990) found that the student teaching experience was seldom connected to program goals and that few structures existed to support cooperation or resolve conflict among supervisors, teachers, and students. In the chapters covering content area research, very few studies looked at methods courses, per se. Instead, much of the research attempted to document what people occupying different role groups did in fulfilling their roles, not what they learned or how their learning was enacted in particular contexts.

In the second *Handbook of Research on Teacher Education* (Sikula, Buttery, & Guyton, 1996), the chapters examining general issues within teacher education did not discuss methods courses but often noted the turn toward standards-based curricula and teaching. The chapter on field and laboratory experiences (McIntyre, Byrd, & Foxx, 1996) concluded that there was a movement toward defining the purpose of field experiences and toward clarifying the goals of teacher education, but that there were still insufficient "quantifiable and qualitative data that will enable teacher educators to determine if these programs are, indeed, preparing more thoughtful, reflective teachers; that is, teachers who are more effective in the classroom than those prepared in more traditional, apprentice-type programs" (p. 173). Although the chapters focusing on teacher preparation within content areas were uneven in the degree to which they focused on empirical research, on balance, the chapters contained more empirical studies and related conceptual analyses than did the 1990 handbook. Cognitive psychological frameworks, wherein teachers' beliefs and intentions were studied, typically informed the research reviewed in these chapters. Several authors noted that the influence of prior beliefs, current beliefs, and instruction within teacher education curricula was bidirectional. Research by teacher education practitioners studying the impact of their own teaching began to appear in the summaries.

A comprehensive, general review published by Wideen, Mayer-Smith, and Moon (1998) summarized research that was largely influenced by cognitive psychology and documented that beginning teachers are often resistant to practices advocated by teacher education curricula because these practices are incompatible with their beliefs. Examining both short- and long-term interventions, Wideen et al. argued that there was evidence that at times teachers' beliefs change, although not always in ways that the researchers viewed as desirable. The authors criticized those who undertook programmatic interventions for assuming that providing knowledge would lead to desirable changes in teacher behavior.

Wideen et al. (1998) also found there were seldom any replications of instructional content or procedures with different groups of prospective teachers, and the commitments of the researcher and the power or ideological relationships between the researcher and the participants were seldom disclosed or reflected on as problematic. In many cases, researchers often failed to report how they built on previous work and often failed to cite relevant prior work. The authors urged researchers to adopt an ecological view in seeking to understand how individuals, institutions, programs, and ideas are interrelated. "We can no longer regard courses, programs, and the other participants and structures of teacher education as unchallengeable and operating in isolation" (p. 169).

Two other reviews (Munby, Russell, & Martin, 2001; Sleeter, 2001) augmented Wideen et al.'s (1998) conclusions. Munby et al. found fundamental tensions within coursework and programs, between academic researchers and teachers, and within the teaching profession itself. Citing both philosophers and empirical researchers, they described the complexity of teachers' knowledge and practice, warning against descriptions that ignored or diminished that complexity. Sleeter concluded that the typical study is small scale, conducted by people trained in a given epistemology who were struggling to publish in journals with their own epistemological slants. She also noted, "It is quite possible that debates about limitations of positivism have produced generations of scholars who have not learned to use tools of positivist research such as gathering quantitative data, having learned to equate such tools with how they have been used historically" (p. 240). She advocated for more longitudinal studies that track students through teacher education programs into actual classroom teaching.

This chapter builds on what we learned from those earlier reviews and examines research not cited in those studies. The main questions we address are the following:

1. Who is conducting research on or within methods courses, field experiences, and student teaching? How was the research designed? What claims of impact were made?
2. What are the contributions and the limitations of this research, within and across content areas?
3. What does this research suggest for future research agendas?

We began by reviewing studies from refereed journals published from 1995 through 2001 that addressed the preparation of teachers within the context of methods courses, early field experiences, and student teaching. We limited our summary to research in English, social studies, mathematics, science, professional development school contexts, and general supervision because of space limitations and because they represent well the state of the research on methods courses and field experiences. We noted, however, that there is a substantial body of work available in other content areas, such as physical education, music, and art.

Beginning with a computer search using the key words "content area" and "preservice teacher" and conducting a manual search of reference lists in relevant reviews of research, we identified subject-matter-specific refereed journals (such as *Research in the Teaching of English*) and more general ones (such as *Teaching and Teacher Education*). We then conducted a manual shelf search of all the journals identified (see Appendix A) and included articles that reported data-based research on methods courses, early field experiences, and student teaching and their impact on preservice teachers. We excluded articles that did not report research on or within methods courses or field experiences, such as general studies of preservice teachers and their beliefs, characteristics, and backgrounds (unless the study looked at how these factors interacted with or were affected by methods courses or field experiences); studies involving other university coursework undertaken by preservice teachers, such as science classes; and descriptions of teacher education programs.

We also eliminated studies that, on careful reading, provided no audit trail or gave insufficient details on participants, data collection, data analysis, and findings, and the relationships among all of these components. We adopted a very generous view of what constituted sufficient detail, and some of the studies we included provided only cursory information about methodology. Even so, many articles were not included because they failed to discuss in any manner how the data were analyzed, a common fault noted by Alton-Lee (1998) in her reflections on serving as an associate editor of *Teaching and Teacher Education*.

We also excluded studies that fell into categories discussed by other panel authors, including those focusing on particular teaching methods, such as use of portfolios or computer–based simulations (see Grossman, this volume), and those focusing on diversity, such as culturally relevant pedagogy and preparing teachers to work in culturally diverse urban schools (see Hollins and Torres Guzman, this volume), or preparation for teaching students with special needs (see Pugach, this volume). Methods instructors who are also researchers are interested in the role of technology, journals, portfolios, and so forth, and are concerned with issues such as teaching for social justice, enabling prospective teachers to work with diverse learners and with special needs, or confronting stereotypes. Thus, our work should be read in conjunction with those of the other chapter authors.

RESEARCH ON METHODS COURSES AND FIELD EXPERIENCES 1995–2001

The authors whose research we included often assumed common agreement on definitions of terms such as methods course, methods instructor, early field experience, student teaching, student teachers, intern, cooperating teacher, and supervisor. We, too, assumed that a tacit assumption exists about how such terms undergird our understanding of teacher education programs. As one external reviewer queried, "What definitional issues arise in trying to study these components in teacher education? What job(s) are methods courses supposed to fulfill?" Seeking to answer these questions, we turned back to the studies themselves.

We noted earlier the shift from a conception of method as a teaching behavior to a focus on methods as engaging and modifying cognition. One's beliefs, intentions, knowledge frames, and skills interact continuously in classroom teaching. The methods courses discussed in this section highlight interaction among instruction, student response, and learning within and, often, outside the methods course. Typically, "outside the methods course" refers to assigned work in communities, schools, or classrooms or working with students one-to-one, in small groups or in whole classes. Much of the research documents how the methods courses and outside assignments are conjoined in an effort to integrate recommended teaching practice with actual teaching practice. These early field experiences occur prior to student teaching and often they are required within the methods course and are evaluated by the methods instructor. Student teaching, however, may or may not be integrated with methods instruction. The evaluation of student teachers is sometimes a joint effort between the supervisor (a university representative) and the cooperating teacher (the teacher to whose classroom a preservice teacher, referred to as student teacher or intern, is assigned with the goal of assuming a major responsibility for designing, implementing, and evaluating children's or adolescents' learning). The supervisor is seldom the methods instructor and may or may not know what occurred in the methods course.

In studying the impact of a methods course on teaching practice, researchers have employed both direct methods (such as classroom observations) and indirect methods (such as interviews or examinations of lesson plans). Seldom did the researchers interrogate the social, political, or cultural contexts in which methods instructors, cooperating teachers, or student teachers worked, although context has become a more salient issue in a handful of studies. Several studies were informed by sociocultural frameworks and look at course work and fieldwork from a more complex perspective. In such studies, researchers examined how social and cultural norms, patterns and histories of institutions, and specific settings impact cognition and behavior.

To prepare the research summaries, we created a table for each content area with columns containing the following information: authors, research participants (and their relationship to researchers or authors), framework or literature base guiding the study, methods for collecting and analyzing data, and major findings. Our purpose was to describe the principal issues examined by the researchers, the frameworks for examining these issues, the impact claims investigated, and the methods for doing so. The tables provide details on the kind and character of the research; the chapter text provides summary and critique.

In discussing frameworks or positions within the field of research, whenever possible we use the same terms used by the authors in identifying the concepts or ideas that guided the study. In studies where the researchers did not connect their work to theoretical stances, we categorize the study according to its focus and the literature referenced. We include information about the researchers' and participants' race, ethnicity, gender, and social class whenever provided in the text, using the researchers' terminology. When the researchers labeled preservice teachers as midcareer, nontraditional, or older students, we include this information.

Using the tables as a reference point, each subsection summarizes the impact of methods courses and field experiences on preservice teachers in four subject areas and in professional development schools or other forms of school–university partnerships. Each subsection ends with a discussion of the studies' contributions to our knowledge as well as their limitations. In the section on professional development schools (PDSs) and general supervision, we further discuss impact claims relating to K–12 teachers, pupils, and schools and on university-based faculty. We do this for two reasons. First, it is integral to understanding the state of research. Most research examines effects on a variety of personnel and stakeholders, not just on preservice teachers. Second, the mission of professional development schools includes having impact on schools, teachers, pupils, and university-based teacher educators. It would have been unrealistic and disingenuous to separate preservice teachers from the other groups affected. Following that, we discuss all the content-area studies as they address impact on field-based and university-based teacher educators because they illustrate the ways in which teacher education researchers are modeling their recommendations to engage in reflective practice and making regular use of data for continuous course and program improvements. We encourage readers to look beyond these summaries and examine the original studies. Our tables and discussions often mask the complexity and quality of the research, its contexts and findings.

English

Five earlier reviews of research on reading and English and language arts teacher education demonstrate how much research in these content areas has increased over time. One of the earliest reviews (O'Donnell, 1990) documented that research on methods and field experiences was limited to surveys of experienced teachers who reflected on the quality of their initial preparation. Alverman (1990), reviewing the research on reading teacher education, concluded there was not much research in this area. She reported that the few naturalistic studies on student teaching indicated that student teachers adapted some instruction so their practice was more congruent with their own theories of reading, but that these adaptations were all situation specific. She attributed the dearth of research on preservice teacher education to its low status as a topic in reading research. Anders, Hoffman, and Duffy (2000) concluded that reading teacher education was not a high priority for researchers, but that such research was increasing and using diverse methodologies. They noted that although few data-based claims could be made on what is effective in preservice reading teacher education, teacher education programs themselves were becoming more complex and that labels such as "courses" had become antiquated.

Fisher, Fox, and Paille (1996) summarized evidence stating that professional course work enabled preservice teachers to examine their own preconceptions about teaching, learning, and content area. They also reported that prospective teachers frequently received differing messages about teaching, learning, and content from university departments and courses, cooperating teachers, and the organization and structure of schools, which led to confusion and discomfort. Preservice teachers often saw cooperating teachers' views, beliefs, and recommended practices as the most salient in field experiences, even when the preservice teachers disagreed with them. Working across institutions and role groups for fieldwork seemed to ameliorate this situation, they concluded.

Grossman, Valencia, and Hamel's (1997) review indicated that secondary teacher preparation coursework, including methods courses, enabled prospective teachers to focus on pedagogical dimensions of teaching that interacted with knowledge of the subject matter and encouraged more focus on students. They found some evidence that elementary methods courses enabled prospective teachers to change their understanding of teaching practice. When in field experiences, however, prospective teachers often abandoned the focus on subject matter and student learning to concentrate on classroom management. These future teachers became disillusioned with students, particularly when working with diverse populations.

We found 24 studies published from 1995 through 2001 that focused specifically on English and language arts methods courses and field experiences. The researchers for the most part shared a commitment to connecting the way one thinks about teaching to how thoughts and beliefs are manifested in practice. Many researchers, although still interested in cognitive issues related to beliefs, reflective practice, and teacher socialization, were beginning to emphasize social and cultural factors embedded within university and P–12 classrooms. We discern a trend in the field of English teacher preparation to conduct research framed by sociocultural views of how practice is created, instead of using frames drawn from cognitive psychology. In this view, teaching practice is seen as a function of the individual and of the contexts in which he or she learns, works, and reflects.

As with the other content areas, in much of the research (16 of the 24 studies), at least one member of the research team worked with the participants in an instructional or supervisory capacity; many of these were acknowledged self-studies. Only one study (Grossman et al., 2000) studied practice beyond student teaching; most studies were conducted over one semester, typically the student teaching semester. Participants were divided between elementary and secondary prospective teachers. Most of the studies provided information on participants' race, and almost all provided information on gender.

What Impacts Do Methods Courses and Field Experiences Have on Preservice English and Reading Teachers' Beliefs and Practices? Eight studies, all using case study methodology, documented that methods courses and field experiences often introduced ideas and concepts that preservice teachers did not accept (Agee, 1997, 1998; Graham, 1997, 1999; Grossman et al., 2000; Newell, Gingrich, & Johnson, 2001; Slick, 1998a; Weaver & Stanulis, 1996; Wolf, Ballentine, & Hill, 1999). The case examples within these studies documented differential change across individuals. Some remained resistant throughout the semester or year; others began to modify their beliefs and practices as a result of engaging with children or adolescents. Wiggins and Clift (1995), Weaver and Stanulis, Denyer and Florio-Ruane (1995), Slick (1997), and Graham (1999) provided evidence that prospective teachers often struggle with contradictions in their ideas about students, teaching, and learning and that they vary in ability to manage these conflicting ideas. In the Weaver and Stanulis case, the student teacher, who was placed in an environment that modeled and reinforced what was taught in the methods course, still struggled with the writing workshop approach. The authors explained that in part this was because she did not know how to manage the workload and in part because she anticipated a first-year teaching position that would not provide her with either the resources or the support for implementing a writing workshop.

Eight studies (Agee, 1997; Boyd, Boll, Brawner, & Villaume, 1998; Mallette, Kile, Smith, McKinney, & Readance, 2000; McMahon, 1997; Mosenthal, 1996; Wolf, Ballentine, & Hill, 2000; Wolf, Mieras, & Carey, 1996; Worthy & Patterson, 2001) investigated the impact of structured and sustained interactions with children or adolescents during early field experiences. They concurred that such interactions can provide an experiential base for prospective teachers through course-based concepts and theories.

In most cases, they also promoted changes in the ways prospective teachers thought about students and about learning in general. The prospective teachers became more accepting of students' ideas and more aware of their strengths and how those strengths interact with literacy development. Boyd et al. also found that the field experience increased the preservice teachers' motivation to become good teachers. One study employed a training design (Bowman & McCormick, 2000) that compared peer coaching to traditional supervision during an early field experience and concluded that peer coaching during interactions with elementary preservice teachers was more effective than traditional supervision.

Interactions alone, however, did not promote such positive changes. Four studies of student teachers who were not engaged with instructors or supervisors around theories and practices of teaching and learning indicated that the student teachers became angry and felt isolated (Bruckerhoff & Carlson, 1995), floundered with respect to planning and implementing instruction (Dooley, 1998), and engaged in debates with the cooperating teacher without much change in practice (Graham, 1997, 1999). Bowman and McCormick's (2000) work, however, suggests that peer coaching holds promise for providing teacher education students with a supportive environment for improving instruction. Fairbanks, Freedman, and Kahn (2000) found that the student and the cooperating teacher learned from each other, but that even in an effective mentoring project it took time for collegial relationships to develop. One study (O'Callaghan, 2001) found that student teachers maintained prior conceptions of teaching while changing in other respects. The researcher attributed such changes to participation in the study, not to student teaching itself.

The single longitudinal study, which followed three teachers through the preservice program into the classroom (Grossman et al., 2000), provided evidence that teachers who completed a program with a strong theoretical base for writing instruction struggled with practical applications of recommended practices evolving from the theoretical constructs. However, within the first 2 years of practice, that base shaped their writing curriculum. The one teacher predisposed toward this program's practice (and who was supported in implementing it both as a student and as a novice teacher) continued to use it to modify and enhance his practice over time. A teacher who did not actively resist the program but who struggled with practice was more able to adapt the district-mandated curriculum package to implement theory-based practice by her second year of teaching. A teacher who actively resisted the methods course instructor also began to implement some of the recommended practices by the end of his second year in the classroom.

Contributions and Limitations. With the exception of Bowman and McCormick's study (2000), these all were qualitative case studies that reinforced the importance of providing support for learning and practice that includes theory as well as multiple opportunities to attempt desired practice and to ask questions about those attempts. The strength of this convergence—across researchers, grade levels, and contexts—is that we can see a trend emerging that emphasizes the importance of planned, guided, and sustained interactions with pupils (children and adolescents) within early field and student teaching settings. Reflecting on learning by working with individuals or small groups can produce changes in preservice teachers' ideas about teaching, learning, and the competence of learners, but only if the prospective teachers are engaged with teacher educators who support theory- and practice-based reflective analyses in relation to what was taught or advocated by the methods course.

The short-term nature of this research limits our ability to understand how teacher education methods courses and fieldwork lead to long-term professional growth. Although the researchers may see changes in one semester or during student teaching, only one study went beyond the teacher education context. Fifteen studies employed some version of self-study methodology and, although in many instances included additional researchers to provide an external viewpoint, the instructor and student evaluative relationship necessitates caution when interpreting the findings. Individual case studies do not lend themselves to aggregations of findings across different individuals, grade levels, and teacher education courses. Finally, as we document in the table, the studies did not all provide the same detail on frameworks, participants, data collection, and methods of analysis. Furthermore, the journals in which these papers were published varied with regard to page limitations and details of methodology. This was the case in all content areas.

Mathematics

Three previous reviews of research on mathematics teacher education (Brown & Borko, 1992; Brown, Cooney, & Jones, 1990; Grouws & Schultz, 1996) found few studies of preservice mathematics teacher education. Those that did exist were predominantly case studies and documented gaps in prospective teachers' knowledge of mathematical principles and procedures and discrepancies between prospective teachers' views of themselves as mathematics learners and their views of students' learning. In addition, the researchers evinced skepticism about how the university-based programs, which sought to produce teachers who were active learners and possessed a conception of good mathematics instruction, were to achieve those goals, given the time and task constraints and other demands on student teachers. Translating university-based recommendations into actual teaching practice seemed difficult at best and filled with conflict at worst. Although not a review, Monk's (1994) analysis of teachers' preservice course work in relation to current students' achievement suggested that courses in undergraduate mathematics pedagogy contribute more to student performance gains than do undergraduate mathematics courses. We found no recent research that drew from Monk's work.

Our search identified 20 studies published from 1995 through 2002. These studies, with the exception of McDevitt, Troyer, Ambrosio, Heikkinen, and Warren's (1995), all examined preservice teachers' beliefs about mathematics, mathematics learning, and mathematics teaching informed primarily by cognitive frameworks, although the socialization literature and the social and cultural factors that affect learning and practice were also represented. Most researchers concurred that what might be termed a constructivist stance toward learning mathematics was desirable and that teachers should be able to implement instruction based on National Council of Teachers of Mathematics (NCTM) standards. The exception, McDevitt et al., conducted a program evaluation of the mathematics and science components of an entire, revised elementary education program. Most studies on beliefs and practices referenced research on teacher socialization, reflective practice, or conceptual change as the framework (or frameworks) for their studies. Two studies, Blanton, Berenson, and Norwood (2001) and Frykholm (1998), referenced sociocultural theories, and the former employed discourse analysis to study preservice teachers' interactions. Kinach (2002), Blanton, Berenson, and Norwood, Langford and Huntley (1999), Frykholm (1996, 1998, 1999), and Cooney, Shealy, and Arvold (1998) studied preservice teachers who focused on high school or middle school. The remainder focused on preservice elementary teachers' beliefs and, in several instances, practices during fieldwork. Steele (2001) was the only researcher who followed teachers beyond the preservice program in her study of graduates in their second year of teaching. In nine studies the researchers were involved with instruction or supervision, but their main intent was to study the preservice teachers, not themselves.

What Impact Do Methods Courses and Field Experiences Have on Preservice Mathematics Teachers' Beliefs and Practices?

As with English methods courses, the answer to this question is mixed. Langrall, Thornton, Jones, and Malone (1996), Mewborn (1999), Kim and Sharp (2000), Steele and Widman (1997), Kinach (2002), Langford and Huntley (1999), Kelly (2001), Rahal and Melvin (1998), and Briscoe and Stout (1996) documented the positive impact of methods courses and field experiences on preservice teachers' beliefs about mathematics, abilities to write lesson plans demonstrating a knowledge of constructivist principles, tendencies to focus on learning as exploratory rather than rote, understanding the importance of the teacher's role, and methods and understandings of problem-solving processes and skills. Kelly also noted the preservice teachers' increased confidence in teaching mathematics, and Harper and Daane (1998) found a reduction in math anxiety. Foss and Kleinhasser (1996), however, documented students' rejection of constructivist messages from the methods instructor.

Studies that focused on beliefs and practices during student teaching were also mixed. Frykohlm (1996, 1999) documented that even though student teachers perceived that the university wanted them to incorporate the NCTM standards into instruction and that they said they were doing so, there was little evidence of that instruction. Furthermore, the cooperating teachers did not seem to place nearly as much emphasis on the standards as did the university. Frykholm (1998) documented that having graduate students in mathematics education mentor student teachers helped both the student teachers and cooperating teachers in terms of bridging theory and practice and becoming more open to standards-based teaching; the mentors reported gaining new insights on mathematics teacher education through the experience. Cooney et al. (1998) found that two student teachers moved toward a more constructivist stance and practice in the methods course and sustained it during student teaching; two did not. Vacc and Bright (1999) reported that although two prospective teachers developed an understanding of the principles of cognitively based instruction (CGI), the one placed with a cooperating teacher experienced in the use of CGI was better able to put the principles to use in practice. The other cooperating teacher, who was aware of but much less experienced with CGI, may not have been able to support her student teacher's emerging understanding or practice. All three students studied by Ebby (2000) moved away from traditional views of mathematics and mathematics learning during a methods course and field experience, but only one had multiple opportunities to apply active engagement with math and multiple teaching approaches during student teaching.

Steele (2001) found only two of four teachers in their second year of teaching were able to sustain the commitment to instruction based on CGI that they showed in their methods courses. Analyzing their schools' differing support for CGI and pressure to follow a curriculum, she concluded that those teaching in ways consistent with CGI were in schools where administrators and teachers actively supported innovation and did nothing to discourage constructivist practices.

Blanton et al. (2001) took a different approach. Through a microanalysis of the discourse during one student teacher's teaching semester, they identified four lessons that tracked her change from more didactic, authority-based teaching to a more dialog-based approach that encouraged students to reflect on and analyze their thinking. Listening to her pupils, the student teacher began to consider their talk as illustrative of their beliefs and problem solving practices. Their misunderstandings frequently became the bases for lessons examining how mathematics problems could be approached, interpreted, and solved. The researchers acknowledged that the open-minded and inquiry-oriented attitudes of the cooperating teacher, who participated in the study, helped this student teacher's development. They also argued that the student's language and discourse also were major influences.

Finally, the evaluation conducted by McDevitt et al. (1995) indicated that a program oriented to inquiry and organized around standards produced a different type of graduate. Comparing two cohorts in the new program with two in the old, they found the new approach enhanced prospective teachers' knowledge of subject matter, based on content-area tests. These students knew more about conducting experiments, strategies for problem solving, and how to teach with inquiry techniques. This study, one of the few program evaluation studies we found, is important in that it provides comparative data on knowledge gains and practical applications of knowledge.

Contributions and Limitations.   There was more agreement within mathematics than in English on what questions were worth investigating. Mathematics education researchers were investigating ways to help preservice teachers change their conception of learning mathematics from one based on providing rules and procedures for working through problems to a more active process. They found that this is possible, but not predictable, across preservice teachers. The researchers shared a view of mathematics teaching and learning as engaging with problems and proposing and testing solutions. They addressed questions about how to prepare teachers to teach in this way. They reported, however, that changing the preservice teachers' views of teacher as authority and provider of knowledge to teacher as facilitator and co-investigator with students is, at best, difficult to put into practice. This line of research indicated that enacting a desirable practice is more likely when there is coherence between the methods courses and the fieldwork. This coherence created a supportive environment for a new teacher. Researchers are just beginning to document progress with these challenging and sometimes changing perspectives on teaching and learning.

Many of the limitations noted in the previous section also apply here, but the mathematics teacher education researchers were less likely to rely on case study methods than were their counterparts in English education. They often relied on researchers' studies of their own students, and most focused on prospective elementary education teachers and ignored those preparing to teach in middle and high school. They provided little information about learning to teach secondary subjects such as geometry or algebra, or about how prospective teachers might be strong in one area and weak in another. The mathematics studies provided less information on the contexts or participant demographics than one would hope for when trying to understand the contexts in which teacher education is taking place. Finally, as noted earlier, the variation among journal parameters impacts how much detail can be covered.

Science

Yager and Penick's (1990) review of science teacher education reported few data-based studies in science teacher education and focused more on recommendations for teacher preparation programs. Anderson and Mitchner (1994) noted that descriptive studies of science teacher education indicated that the field was beginning to move toward a conceptual, inquiry-oriented view of science teaching, but that prospective science education teachers wanted an emphasis on practice and daily teaching concerns. Research on attitudes and on skill acquisition and changes in teacher behavior yielded mixed results; training showed promise but was no guarantee that student teachers would manifest the desired behavior. Cochran and Jones (1998) concluded that students often inferred conflicting messages from within programs. Again, no one seemed to draw from Monk's (1994) analysis of teachers' preservice coursework. Monk found that undergraduate coursework in science pedagogy had a positive relationship with student achievement for juniors, but that the magnitude of the relationships in science between course taking and student gains was quite small.

Twenty-one studies published from 1995 to 2001 documented a wide variation in methodology and theoretical orientation. The focus ranged from prospective teachers' ratings of methods course activities and reports of using certain activities during student teaching (Jarrett, 1998) to studies of an entire program (Hewson, Tabachnik, Zeichner, Blomker, et al., 1999; Hewson, Tabachnik, Zeichner, & Lemberger, 1999) to collaborative, multivocal studies of co-teaching within student teaching (Tobin, Roth, & Zimmermann, 2001). Science education researchers were more likely than researchers in the other content areas to rely on inventories and instruments, and in many of the studies the sample sizes were larger than those in other content areas. Many researchers focused on the ability of teacher education to enable prospective teachers to teach for conceptual change. Three studies focused specifically on how preservice teachers understood the nature of science. This research was typically grounded in cognitive psychology, with references to teacher socialization studies.

A researcher with no instructional or supervisory relationship to the students conducted eight of the studies. Four studies did not specify the nature of the researcher and participant relationship, although we know that in at least one of these the researcher was also the instructor. Only two studies (Adams & Krockover, 1997; Sillman, Dana, & Miller, 2000) collected data after program completion and during the first year of teaching. Few studies identified participants' race or ethnic background.

What Impacts Do Methods Courses and Field Experiences Have on Preservice Science Teachers' Beliefs and Practices?   Eight studies were semester-long investigations of the impact of a methods course, one of which had an accompanying field experience. Five studies investigated prospective elementary teachers' confidence in teaching science and adoption of a conceptual change orientation to teaching. Four studies (Kelly, 2000; Greenwood, 1996; Settlage, 2000; Shapiro, 1996) concluded that methods courses resulted in improved confidence in ability to teach science, but two found no evidence that they led students to adopt a conceptual change model of teaching (Stofflett & Stefanon, 1996) or change their own concepts (Greenwood). Jarrett (1998) asked students to rate methods course activities for fun and for potential to engage student learning, then followed up by asking for self-reports on activities they actually used during student teaching. The study found no clear connection between the two lists of activities except for activities somehow involving working with food. McGinnis and Pearsall (1998) reported on their self-study of a male science teacher educator who attempted to be more gender inclusive. Although the students noted that they were aware of his attempts, they felt uncomfortable being studied and thought the focus on gender detracted from a focus on practical teaching methods.

The eighth study (Abell, Martini, & George, 2001) found that students made some progress, albeit incomplete, toward understanding the nature of science.

Four studies examining methods instruction and fieldwork over the course of an elementary and secondary education program (Lemberger, Hewson, & Park, 1999; Marion, Hewson, Tabachnick, & Blomker, 1999; Meyer, Tabachnick, Hewson, Lemberger, & Park, 1999; Tabachnick & Zeichner, 1999) concurred that the methods courses offered opportunities to learn about and observe teaching for conceptual change, but field experiences did not. Furthermore, although the prospective teachers began to consider students' thoughts and constructions, none of them were able to enact this during student teaching. In three case studies, the prospective teachers had hoped to move from a lecture oriented, knowledge imparting stance, but had no idea how to accomplish it. Anderson, Smith, and Peasley (2000) observed and interviewed faculty and three preservice teachers for a year of methods course work and fieldwork. They documented that each of the preservice teachers entered the program with a different view of teaching and learning, and over time participants moved toward an acceptance of constructivist teaching principles but later struggled to put these ideas into practice in actual classrooms.

Zembal-Saul, Blumenfeld, and Krajcik (2000) studied a pair of students through two methods courses and accompanying fieldwork. The preservice teachers could reflect on their practice during both cycles; during the second cycle their ability to represent content and to support students' learning through questions improved. The researchers also noted that as the pair became more knowledgeable of students as learners, they were better able to represent content as appropriate to the students. Palmquist and Finley (1997), in a yearlong investigation of graduate students in secondary education, found a majority adopted a contemporary view of the nature of science, but two became more traditional. Bryan and Abell (1999), in another yearlong study, found that a preservice elementary teacher became more aware of the inconsistency between her beliefs and practices but still found it extremely difficult to practice what she believed.

The two longitudinal studies (Adams & Krockover, 1997; Sillman et al., 2000) followed selected students into their first year of teaching. The latter was a case study of the third author, who was able to put his skills into practice and continuously improve. They attributed this in part to strong support from the research team and like-minded colleagues. Adams and Krockover found that four new teachers were able to use management and teaching strategies from methods courses, despite inhospitable environments.

Finally, three studies by Tobin and colleagues (Nichols & Tobin, 2000; Tobin, Roth, & Zimmermann, 2001; Tobin, Seiler, & Smith, 1999) investigated ways in which co-teaching might support learning to teach science. Tobin, the teacher educator, was himself attempting to enact the theory-based practices he advocated in his methods courses and, at the same time, to work with student teachers, cooperating teachers, and university supervisors to create classroom communities where reflection on teaching took place and planning and decision making were shared. These studies offer rich, multivoiced accounts of teaching and professional learning. Nichols and Tobin documented the difficulties of breaking a pattern in which student teachers and cooperating teachers go separate ways. Tobin, Seiler, and Smith (1999) documented the importance of learning from all situations—even when a participant was struggling. Tobin, Roth, and Zimmerman (2001) described co-teaching's impact on the professional learning of all participants. In the last two studies, preservice teachers had multiple sources of support to enact increasingly constructivist teaching principles.

Contributions and Limitations.   The difficulty of enacting the practices recommended by methods courses and adopted by prospective teachers tells us that even when preservice teachers believe in teaching a certain way, they often do not know how to act on that desire or how to deal with difficulties they encounter. Moving to action is more difficult than the intention to do so. The studies conducted by Tobin and his colleagues provide an insight not found in the other content areas—that when dedicated and competent teacher education practitioners work in classrooms alongside prospective teachers, they, too, have difficulties with practice. Working, discussing, and revising together may hold promise for reshaping relationships among all trying to improve practice.

In science, the studies were evenly split between students preparing for elementary teaching and those intending to teach in high schools. But here, too, few considered those preparing to teach distinctly different areas of science, such as physics or biology. Curiously, supervision was less a focus for research in science than in other areas. Little effort was made to understand the contributions of cooperating teachers and teacher educators, and the studies focused almost exclusively on short-term effects.

Social Studies

Three previous reviews (Adler, 1991; Armento, 1996; Banks & Parker, 1990) reported that few studies of methods courses or field experiences existed. Adler characterized existing research as particularistic and unsystematic, implying that little was known about what is being done in methods classes and the effects of those classes. She found that field experience studies were seldom linked to courses and that student teachers often acted against espoused beliefs to avoid conflict with cooperating teachers or supervisors.

Three of the 11 studies we found utilized frameworks guided by socialization theory and addressed the impact methods courses or student teaching (or both) had on differences in beliefs and behaviors from experiences preservice teachers recalled from their own secondary social studies classrooms (Fehn & Koeppen, 1998; Koeppen, 1998; Slekar, 1998). Three others (Angell, 1998; Dinkelman, 1999, 2000) adopted more cognitive perspectives with an emphasis on the development of reflection during student teaching. Two focused on prospective teachers' abilities to plan and implement service-learning activities (Donahue, 1999, 2000). Two investigated supervisory practices (Slick, 1998b; Wilson & Saleh, 2000), and one was a collaborative self-study of university-based and field-based instructors (Hohenbrink, Johnston, & Westhoven, 1997) as they reflected on the process of teaching methods courses together over 4 years. All studies employed qualitative methods and included only a small number of participants. Four suggested that the authors assumed the role of researcher, although in the other studies, the researcher occupied the dual role of researcher and instructor or supervisor. With the exception of Hohenbrink et al., Slick, and Wilson and Saleh, the researchers defined impact in terms of changes in preservice teachers' beliefs or abilities to engage in practices recommended by the teacher education program. Most covered a single semester; Dinkelman (2000), Donahue (2000), and Hohenbrink, Johnston, and Westhoven (1997) were exceptions. Most focused on secondary social studies methods courses and field experiences.

What Impacts Do Methods Courses and Field Experiences Have on Preservice Social Studies Teachers' Beliefs and Practices?   Some impact appears in many, but not all, of the case reports. Slekar's (1998) two case studies suggested that student teachers moved away from didactic instruction, although that was how they were taught social studies in high school. Dinkelman's case studies (1999, 2000) indicated that preservice teachers understood and adopted certain critically reflective practices, but that the practice of and topics for reflection varied across individuals. During the student teaching that Dinkelman supervised, the students paid more attention to issues of democratic practice within the classroom—issues they had resisted in the methods course. Fehn and Koeppen (1998) found that 11 preservice teachers incorporated document-based instruction within student teaching, for which they credited their methods course. Donahue (1999) found that students incorporated service learning into lesson plans and understood the ethical as well as practical factors impacting such planning. Implementing service learning in student teaching, however, was more difficult (Donahue, 2000), partly due to variations in preservice teachers' personal commitment and partly due to the cooperating teachers' attitudes toward service learning. Koeppen (1998) and Angell (1998) each reported a case in which no change in beliefs or practices occurred during student teaching. Angell also reported another case in which the student teacher retained a commitment to activity-based teaching, but became more aware of the importance of practicing self-reflection and critique.

The two supervision studies (Slick, 1998b; Wilson & Saleh, 2000) provided interesting contrasts concerning quality of supervision. In Slick's case study, the supervisor had no expertise in secondary social studies, leaving the preservice teacher without support from either the supervisor or the university. Wilson and Saleh summarized the perceptions of field-based clinical master teachers who felt ownership of the supervision process and who believed they were well situated to mediate philosophical and practical differences between the school and the university.

Contributions and Limitations. These studies indicated that there are efforts underway to link social studies methods courses and concurrent field experiences, with instructors paying close attention to what students are learning from both. The studies demonstrated that the practice and research in social studies has adopted a change-oriented focus, but few studies can be aggregated around any change effort (e.g., willingness to engage in service learning or to use primary sources and document-based instruction), and no studies follow graduates into actual teaching. Therefore, it is not possible to link the research to continued practice or beliefs while teaching. Furthermore, because these studies relied so heavily on instructor research and case studies, we cannot say that there is the same amount of convergent evidence of impact across methods and across researcher roles. We can only say that the amount, the focus, and in many cases, the rigor of qualitative studies have improved since the previous published reviews.

Across the Content-Area Research

Recent articles published in refereed journals document that the amount of research on methods courses and field experiences has increased over time, albeit through small case studies. This suggests a cautious but positive conclusion that methods courses and field experiences can impact prospective teachers' thoughts about practice and in some instances actual teaching practices. They reinforce a consideration of the complexities of enacting theory-based practices and provide an array of individual and contextual factors that can enhance or inhibit planning and implementing teaching based on one's beliefs. In several studies, studying the learner (the child or adolescent) in relation to course concepts is paramount. In others, planning, implementing, and reflecting on instruction with small groups or whole classes is the focus. Although many studies focus only on one semester of course work and fieldwork, some researchers are following prospective teachers for a full year and occasionally into the first years of teaching.

Several content-area researchers are learning more about the difficulties of implementing the practices they recommend. This research includes investigations of the impact of methods courses and field experiences on cooperating teachers and on university-based teacher educators, a missing element in much teacher education research identified in earlier reviews (Book, 1996; Lanier & Little, 1986; Wideen et al., 1998). Fecho, Commeyras, Bauer, and Font (2000) were concerned with creating a democratic classroom environment and minimizing issues of power and authority between instructor and preservice students. The instructors found it difficult to abandon their status as professors to enable students to take more control of the class. Newell et al. (2001) showed both the success and the failure of their efforts to assist student teachers in using conceptual and practical tools from methods courses and the ways in which field settings promote and inhibit the practices recommended by the program. The studies conducted by Tobin and colleagues (Nichols & Tobin, 2000; Tobin et al., 1999, 2001) showed that when teacher educators co-teach with students, they learn firsthand how difficult it is to put theory into practice and enact beliefs.

Other studies focused on the relationship of program elements to the teacher educators' practices. Mosenthal (1996) came to trust field-based teacher education more as he learned what a student was learning in a field experience in conjunction with his course. Wolf, working with her student researcher assistants (Wolf et al., 1999), began to critique and revise her own instruction as she learned more about how her preservice teachers were constructing knowledge based on course assignments and interactions. Similarly, Abell et al. (2001) recognized that their instruction did not explicitly help students make desired connections. Zembal-Saul et al. (2000) implied that careful study of a student teaching pair enabled them to better support prospective teachers' learning over two cycles of lesson planning and implementation. Anderson et al. (2000) said that studying a program that was outside of their own university made them more aware of the importance of building relationships among faculty across semesters to understand students' histories and monitor their progress. Hohenbrink et al. (1997), in a 4-year study of their own practice, found that what initially began as a relationship in which school and university instructors competed over whose knowledge was most trustworthy turned into a relationship in which they came to rely on each other's complimentary knowledge. The differences in students' conceptual and practical orientations toward service learning convinced Donahue (1999, 2000) that he needed to keep flexible his expectations in service-learning assignments.

Finally, several studies showed that engaging in research on one's teacher education practice was itself an instructional intervention. Blanton et al. (2001) commented on the impact that their presence as researchers, combined with the supportive actions of the cooperating teacher, had on the student teacher's thinking and acting. Similarly, O'Callaghan (2001) attributed the positive changes experienced by four student teachers to their participation in the research more than to the student teaching itself. The self-study of gender-inclusive practices (McGinnis & Pearsall, 1998) was intriguing in that the issue of most concern to the teacher educator was a nonissue for many of his female students. They did not really appreciate his research focus and felt it provided less time for discussions of practical teaching methods. Dinkelman (2000) found that working closely with students over two semesters enabled him to better understand differences among students in their tendencies to reflect critically and the limits of his ability to influence students' beliefs and practices. The students said the study itself had a major impact on beliefs and practices. Also, two undergraduate co-authors (Wolf et al., 1996) became empowered as researchers through involvement with the study.

Across the four content areas, methods courses are seen as complex sites in which instructors work simultaneously with prospective teachers on beliefs, teaching practices, and creation of identities—their students' and their own. A methods course is seldom defined as a class that transmits information about methods of instruction and ends with a final exam. Content-area researchers, often the course instructors, looked at multifaceted activities such as role adoption, personal relationships, and rationales for appropriating certain tools. Field experiences were increasingly connected to and embedded within methods courses and seen as extending coverage of concepts introduced in the methods courses. The field experiences provide prospective teachers opportunities to practice ideas or gain experience with concepts through small-group observations, tutoring, community experiences, and service learning in addition to observations and more traditional student teaching. They begin to move us from a focus on belief toward a combined focus on belief and action.

Few studies looked at preservice programs' use of specific teaching methods such as CGI in mathematics or process-writing strategies in English. Instead, researchers tended to examine the teacher education students' actions, reactions, and beliefs about the nature of the subject, such as studies of what constitutes mathematics and mathematical learning or studies of students' understandings of children's or adolescents' reading preferences and abilities. The majority of studies looked at how new teachers are socialized into the profession and how beliefs and actions changed (or resisted change) while engaged in methods courses and field experiences.

In summary, teacher education research within content areas has moved from a focus on generic teaching behavior to a focus on thinking about context. Within each area, beliefs about students, teaching, and learning increasingly are investigated in relation to the instructional, interpersonal, social, and historical factors that come into play as one begins teaching practice. Action or actual teaching practice is studied in relation to the content, the individual, and the classroom context. Much research still draws from cognitive theory and cites related concepts or research on the development of the individual, but frameworks drawn from symbolic interactionism, activity theory, cultural capital theory, and discourse theory are appearing across the content areas on a limited basis and move us toward a more complex conceptualization of the interactive and social nature of developing one's practice.

Selected Research on Professional Development Schools and Supervision

This section examines the ways in which research on professional development schools and supervision augment our understanding of the impact of student teaching in relation to the content-area research. In the two earlier handbooks of research on teacher education, supervision was embedded within the two chapters on field experiences, and professional development schools (PDSs) were treated as separate chapters. In the intervening years, the number of professional development schools has grown and so have partnerships between schools and universities. In some cases, the role of supervisor has become more integrated within the total teacher education program. The recent research on supervision is no longer addressing questions of who dominates conferences among teachers, university supervisors, and student teachers and how feedback is provided during those conferences (summarized by Guyton & McIntyre, 1990), but report on some of the issues identified by McIntyre et al. (1996), such as the lack of communication between supervisors and cooperating teachers and the limits of a supervisor's influence. The two reviews of research of professional development schools (Book, 1996; Stallings & Kowalski, 1990) both noted that the studies were mostly descriptive and that the research was focused more on attitudes of participants or on documentation of changes within the schools than on outcomes. Book found some indication that teachers within professional development schools had assumed more leadership roles, which many times led to increased tension within and between teachers and that the opportunity to engage in active decision making was appreciated.

We found 29 studies published between 1995 and 2001 on professional development schools and general supervision. Sixteen studies did not reveal the author's relationship with the participants, but in the studies that provided this information, many authors were PDS coordinators or university liaisons to the PDS or taught courses in supervision; several were PDS instructors or supervisors. Freese (1999) was the only acknowledged self-study. Most of the studies made reference to the literature on partnerships and collaboration. However, few employed an explicitly stated theoretical framework. The methodologies followed in the exceptions were constructivism (Grisham, Laguardia, & Brink, 2000; Stanulis, 1995) and symbolic interactionism (Powell & McGowan, 1996).

Six studies evaluated how well a PDS experience prepared preservice teachers, either by comparing the PDS program to a traditional teacher education program (Blocker & Mantle-Bromley, 1997; Connor & Killmer, 2001; Mantle-Bromley, Gould, McWhorter, & Whaley, 2000; Sandholtz & Wasserman, 2001; Walling & Lewis, 2000) or by surveying both program graduates and administrators in schools where they worked (Van Zandt, 1998). These studies typically had large numbers of participants (42 to more than 200) and used interview or survey and questionnaire data, usually gathered from preservice teachers or recent program graduates. Many studies examined the impact of being in a school–university partnership on various stakeholders, including K–12 teachers and schools, university professors, and preservice teachers; four studies (Brink, Laguardia, Grisham, Granby, & Peck, 2001; Cobb, 2000; Gill & Hove, 2000; Knight, Wiseman, & Cooner, 2000) searched for a link between the PDS and K–12 pupil achievement. Four studies examined some training for supervisors (Daane, 2000; Justen, McJunkin, & Strickland, 1999; Kent, 2001) or peer coaches (Anderson & Radencich, 2001), and two (Knudson & Turley, 2000; Slick, 1997) reported on how supervisors dealt with student teachers perceived to be in difficulty.

What Impacts Do Supervision and Professional Development School Settings Have on Preservice Teachers' Beliefs and Practices?   Six studies compared PDS-based teacher education with a more traditional route at the same university and found the PDS superior on all measures except stress. Connor and Killmer (2001) found supervisors and cooperating teachers gave PDS-trained student teachers higher teaching ratings. Sandholtz and Wasserman (2001) found that student teachers in the PDS were more confident, rated their program more highly, and had more support. Blocker and Mantle-Bromley (1997) found that preservice teachers trained in a PDS were more confident and enthusiastic about teaching and applied theory to practice more frequently. But the PDS group also felt more stressed and had to deal with conflict between high school and university faculty, a similar finding to that of Hopkins, Hoffman, and Moss (1997). Walling and Lewis (2000) found that PDS-trained preservice teachers were more aware of systemic issues in education and focused more on teaching as a career than as a job, as compared to their traditional-route peers. Mantle-Bromley et al. (2000) surveyed 152 recent graduates from three different teacher education programs at one university. The graduates of the postbaccalaureate program were more satisfied with their education and more likely to be teaching than were graduates from the traditional undergraduate program, with PDS graduates falling in the middle. However, no differences were found in job satisfaction.

Three studies examined the strengths of PDS programs and components. Grisham et al. (2000) described preservice teachers' impressions of why the PDS yearlong internship was a valuable experience. van Zandt (1998) found that PDS graduates and employers rated the program highly. The yearlong internship was seen as a strength; however, the quality of professors and mentor teachers was uneven. Wiseman and Nason (1995) found preservice teachers valued relationships with teachers, faculty, and pupils as well as collaboration with teachers. Freese (1999) described the benefits for master's-level preservice teachers of having curricular and philosophical alignment (e.g., using a particular reflective framework) between university-based educators and classroom teachers.

Finally, Allexsaht-Snider, Deegan, and White (1995) noted that preservice teachers found both congruence and incongruence between university coursework and what they observed in the PDS, with congruence increasing over time. After student teaching, they felt better prepared to teach certain subjects, but felt unprepared to address issues they did not see modeled in the schools such as ability grouping and multicultural education.

What Is the Impact of a Professional Development School on University-Based Faculty?   These studies show that professional development schools had a positive impact on university faculty as well as for preservice teachers. Three studies documented the difficulties in making a partnership work and the ultimate rewards in continuing the effort. Wiseman and Nason (1995), for example, described how slowly university faculty and K–12 teachers came to trust each other, although preservice teachers often served as the catalyst to advancing faculty–teacher relationships. Allexsaht-Snider et al. (1995) described 3 years of a PDS that had a similarly challenging beginning; university faculty, however, used the opportunity to revise the teacher education program. A third study (Hudson-Ross, 2001) also found initial communication challenges, but discovered that involvement in the PDS helped teacher educators work collaboratively, despite a lack of university rewards for doing so. Teacher educators were found to play a vital role in the PDS.

A fourth study, by Bullough, Hobbs, Kauchak, Crow, and Stokes (1997), showed similar challenges in a partnership with less overt benefit to the participants. Clinical faculty (K–12 teachers) were hired to free tenure-line faculty from teaching methods courses and working with the new PDS. The clinical faculty felt they were ill-treated by tenure-track faculty, who were concerned with the PDS's perceived high cost and the department's loss of theoretical rigor or, because they perceived the university's reward structure to devalue teacher education research or service, allowed their involvement in the PDS to wane. On a more positive note, Freese's (1999) self-study of her practice as a teacher-educator found that the preservice teachers' practice in their internship reinforced her decision to help them focus on reflection.

What Impact Does a Professional Development School Have on K–12 Schools, Pupils, and Practicing Teachers?   Four studies in this section detailed the positive effects that PDS sites had on practicing K–12 teachers. Hudson-Ross (2001) described positive changes that 30 secondary English teachers experienced in teaching, self-respect, and professional dialog as a result of PDS involvement. Button, Ponticell, and Johnson (1996) showed how teachers evolved from being the objects of research into doing their own inquiry and sharing the results. Sandholtz and Wasserman (2001) documented that cooperating teachers found benefits in the increased availability of the university supervisor and in collaborating with each other and with university faculty. Finally, Powell and McGowan (1995) noted the impact of a PDS on teachers' self-perceptions, from seeing themselves as experts to new roles as learner, collaborator, and social activist.

Three more studies looked at the potentially salutary impact of a PDS on K–12 pupils and other PDS participants. Cobb (2000) found that elementary teachers believed that the PDS positively impacted pupils and preservice teachers and that their own teaching had improved. Knight et al. (2000) examined student achievement directly in a test–posttest design. Teachers attributed pupils' writing and math test score gains to PDS activities and to their own PDS-related professional growth. Gill and Hove's (2000) evaluation of PDSs in West Virginia showed higher basic skills and math gains for students in PDS schools and, also, an increase in learning opportunities for parents.

Stanulis (1995) found that PDS teachers began to engage in program-recommended activities such as modeling reflection; Powell and McGowan (1996) noted that after participation in the PDS, teachers experimented in their classrooms, although one teacher left the PDS because of time issues. Brink et al. (2001) documented that teachers in the PDS benefited from having student teachers through increased time, professional development, and enhanced self-image, although some felt out of touch with colleagues and the curriculum. Allexsaht-Snider et al. (1995) documented that collaboration and communication between teachers and university faculty improved over time, whereas preservice teachers helped the teachers experiment with new approaches.

Three articles examined the mixed effects of PDSs on both teachers and schools. Bullough and Kauchak (1997) and Bullough, Kauchak, Crow, Hobbs, and Stokes (1997) studied three secondary and four elementary PDS sites associated with the same university. The impact was different for each school, depending on principal leadership, continuity, and other factors. Secondary schools' large size worked against program cohesiveness; elementary schools often lacked the critical mass of teachers necessary to carry out PDS duties. Catalysts, usually classroom teachers involved in the PDS, brought about school change; continuity of personnel was important for sustaining change. Although the PDS sites, overall, had positive impacts on teacher practice and interaction, most teachers had different values—such as placing less faith in theory—than did university-based faculty. Wiseman and Nason (1995) suggested that teachers often felt left out of the planning process conducted by university faculty, but came to value the interdisciplinary curriculum developed by the partnership. Teachers also appreciated having a preservice teacher as a "team player" assigned to their classrooms.

Finally, the studies on supervision addressed the importance of relationships among institutions and role groups outside PDS settings. Justen, McJunkin, and Strickland's (1999) survey found that having taken a supervision course made no difference in supervisors' beliefs about supervision. Kent (2001) found that her course enabled cooperating teachers to better engage in clinical supervisory practices and to understand student teachers' abilities to analyze their own practices. Daane (2000) reported that selecting and training clinical master teachers at the school site resulted in closer links between the teacher education program and field practice. Slick's (1997) case study of an elementary education supervisor documented the negative possibilities when there was no programmatic structure to encourage understanding among the university supervisor, student teacher, and cooperating teacher—especially when the student teacher was experiencing severe difficulties in the classroom. Knudson and Turley's (2000) analysis of survey data indicated that in the few cases where student teachers were perceived to be in trouble, supervisors assisted more with planning and instruction and visited the classroom more frequently. The student teachers, not the cooperating teacher or supervisor, were perceived as the owners of the problems. Anderson and Radencich (2001) found that preservice teachers in an early field placement valued feedback from university supervisors and mentor teachers more than from trained peer coaches.

Contributions and Limitations.   These studies are largely atheoretical, and most of the research was done by university-based faculty who were stakeholders in the PDS they studied. There is some evidence that PDS environments are likely to benefit K–12 pupils in measurable ways such as increases in standardized test scores. Preservice teachers also benefit from having more congruence between the program and the field. Partnerships or other structured opportunities for interaction among role groups and across institutions seem to offer that congruence, but at a cost to teachers' and university faculty members' time and other responsibilities.

Detailed case studies of prospective teachers' practice and beliefs in PDS settings or in studies of general supervision were not as prevalent as those in the content areas. Surveys and interviews were the dominant methods used to collect information about perceptions of participants, and most data are limited to perceptual outcomes. There is a curious decrease in research on the nature of supervision since that summarized by McIntyre and colleagues (1996). The content and nature of supervisory conferences, the relations between feedback and subsequent performance, and the struggle among role groups are examples of research topics that seem to have been lost. We have no insight into how PDS environments impact supervisors. There is little evidence from observations or work samples (of student teachers or P–12 students) that documents actual classroom practice. Little research documents impact on P–12 students' work. We found no joint inquiries involving university faculty and classroom teachers trying to understand the impact on students from prospective teachers' presence in their classrooms.

Across the Studies

The 105 empirical studies summarized in this chapter document changes from earlier reviews in both the field and the methods course components of teacher education programs and in the focus and methods of teacher education research. In many instances, methods courses and fieldwork have become inseparable for prestudent teaching experiences. Methods instructors increasingly dismiss conceptions of teaching merely as transmitting information; instead, they attend to the entering beliefs of prospective teachers with the goal of enabling them to rethink their assumptions about teaching and learning and act on those new assumptions. This research suggests that methods courses and field experiences can impact prospective teachers' thoughts about practice and in some instances actual teaching practices, but that practicing one's beliefs is neither linear nor simple. Awareness is growing of the importance of research on the factors that enhance or inhibit planning and implementing teaching based on one's beliefs—whether as a prospective teacher or as a teacher educator.

Many of the studies documented deliberate programmatic attempts to decrease the tensions among program participants and across institutions through individual instructor or researcher actions or through more formal institutional partnerships. Arrangements such as co-teaching methods courses, co-teaching in school settings, and working in professional development schools often succeeded in providing a collaborative, supportive context for learning to engage in practice that differed from typical school settings. Working together across institutions, however, is not something that is automatic or easy. Research within these contexts has the potential for encouraging collaborative reflective practice—or for harming the fragile partnership between educators not accustomed to public self-examination or professional debate surrounding practice. In other words, the contexts for learning to practice and the social forces affecting practice have become salient in the current research on methods classes and field experiences.

We did not find answers to structural or comparative questions such as: Does it matter if there are no field experiences as opposed to intensive field experiences? Does it matter where methods courses are located or positioned within the curriculum? Does it make a difference if the courses (particularly for secondary teachers) are located within the college of education or the colleges of arts and sciences? Do general methods have more impact than do content-specific methods? Do academic or demographic characteristics of those who teach the courses have demonstrable impact on prospective teachers' learning, beliefs, or actions? Some, but by no means all, of these issues are also touched on in Floden and Meniketti (this volume) as they address the research on the components of content-area courses and foundations courses. In general, however, there were almost no comparative studies in the field published in refereed journals at this time.

Our review finds that research within one content area is seldom informed by research in other content areas and that researchers across content areas seldom address common questions. For example, in English and language arts, researchers documented the importance of providing theoretical support plus multiple opportunities to attempt desired practice and to ask questions about those attempts. In contrast, the studies within mathematics focused on enabling preservice teachers to change their conceptions of how one learns mathematics from instruction based on providing rules and procedures for working through problems to a more active process. Research within content areas varies widely in terms of theoretical frameworks; attention to students' race, ethnicity, language, class, age, and educational background; methodology; and coherence across studies.

What We Know About the Nature of Impact and Lack of Impact

Impact, thus far in the evolution of teacher education research on methods courses and field experiences, is almost exclusively defined in terms of preservice teachers' conceptions of the content area, teaching and learning processes, and their ability to translate concepts into actions. Across the content areas, numerous studies report that short-term interventions have a limited impact on enabling prospective teachers to rethink their assumptions about teaching, learning, and students. The research usually attempts to identify factors that move preservice teachers from traditional views—which they experienced as learners—to an emphasis on active, engaged learning and, subsequently, to teaching practices and curriculum development based on these views. Researchers often note or assume a connection between belief and action. They have abandoned the earlier, narrower focus of methods courses and research on instructional practices for a new emphasis on changes of beliefs and conceptions.

We believe that the research at this point supports the following conclusions and possibilities:

- Although researchers report that methods courses and field experiences have an impact on prospective teachers' beliefs about content, learning, and teaching, it is difficult to predict what impact a specific course or experience may have; the impact is often different from what instructors or student teaching supervisors may imagine or wish.
- Although it is well documented that prospective teachers often feel conflict among the messages they receive from differing university instructors, field-based teacher educators, and school settings, it is also the case that prospective teachers resist coherent messages when they find it difficult to engage in recommended practices. When field placements reinforce and support the practices advocated by the teacher education program, individuals may still resist changing beliefs or practices because they are personally uncomfortable with the competing beliefs and practices. Practice and beliefs are mediated by their prior beliefs and experiences, course work, and current perceptions of curriculum, students, pedagogy, and other factors.
- Both prospective teachers and experienced teacher educators often have difficulty translating concepts learned in methods courses into their classrooms. Over time, professional development schools and school–university partnerships can (but do not always) decrease the discrepancies between advocated practice and situated practice, thus increasing the congruence of messages between the school and university contexts.

It seems clear that learning to practice is impacted by individual, instructional, and contextual factors—some of which we are only beginning to understand. Anderson et al. (2000) offered a helpful metaphor for thinking about the interaction between programs and program components: Students enter teacher education programs moving along a certain trajectory, which is acted on by contacts with faculty, peers, cooperating teachers, children, and program materials and tools. "This interaction resulted in continuous reorientation of each student's trajectory, usually aimed closer to the program's goals, but not perfectly oriented" (p. 567). But it is difficult to chart that trajectory in short-term studies.

Current research limits our ability to learn more about how teacher education methods courses and fieldwork lead to long-term professional growth—for teacher educators or for prospective teachers. First, as numerous reviewers have commented, there is not enough information on the long-term development of teaching practice. Although studying one semester of a methods course or even an entire year that includes student teaching enables researchers to build case examples of short-term impact, we have not progressed beyond the conclusion that new teachers are frequently socialized into the practices of their first job and may not base practice on theories and recommended practices from the teacher education programs. Second, most of this research was conducted on only two components of teacher education and failed to take into account the coherence (or lack thereof) of the entire program.

Third, much was based on case studies, which are invaluable when they provide careful analysis of factors impacting practice, but do not permit generalizations beyond an instructor, a course, a situation, or an individual. In some studies, it was impossible to know how much data generated for the case study was an artifact of the prospective teachers' desires to please the instructor. Fourth, the impact and outcome measures we saw were heavily dependent on the instructor, course, or content area. Much research focuses first on belief and then on practice as it relates to belief. We know little about how practice plays out in school settings and what consequence recommended practice has for students. Too few studies included students' work samples. No one built on Monk's (1994) work that investigated the relationships among course work and student achievement.

Still, even with the limitations noted previously, it is clear that there is a growing body of research that can inform future investigations. We identified several findings concerning the relationships among course work and field settings. For example, prospective teachers may have had time in methods courses to focus and reflect on student learning, but this changes when they become full-time teachers. Engaging in tasks associated with full responsibility for instruction such as curriculum planning, time and group management, assessment, and communication with parents (not to mention additional activities required by the student teaching program) may discourage or inhibit continuous attention to individual students. For some, working in field settings can lead to disillusionment with students and with teaching in general. In part, this may be due to the fact that prospective teachers understandably have difficulty integrating knowledge across domains in course work and integrating propositional knowledge with practical knowledge in the field. This seems to hold for the integration of content knowledge with pedagogical knowledge and knowledge about students. It also may hold for prospective teachers' management of conflicting beliefs among courses, field experiences, and individual practices. There is documentation that prospective teachers can act against their beliefs in order to avoid conflict with cooperating teachers or supervisors and they may perceive some conflict even when others involved do not share this perception.

Issues of Research Methodology and Theory Development

As we discussed earlier, we deliberately used a very wide range of acceptability within our criteria for deciding whether authors made specific connections among research questions, data-collection strategies, data analysis, and conclusions. Furthermore, we chose not to critique individual studies in part because of page limitations and because the tables were intended to provide sufficient information for the reader to decide whether to read the actual studies. Our main reason for not critiquing individual studies, however, was because our goal was to identify trends in recent research, analyze its limitations, and offer recommendations for future research. Although many studies in the tables are strong both theoretically and methodologically, many also raise methodological concerns. For example, there is no well-developed theoretical framework for studying the long-term impact of teacher education components on individuals or, even less, on groups or institutions. Indeed, researchers employed multiple frameworks with insufficient articulation among researchers within a content area, much less across content areas. There was a notable absence of quantitative analyses of relationships among teacher education programs, teachers' actions, and students' learning. Moreover, research in areas such as professional development schools remains almost entirely atheoretical. In many studies, the literature reviews did not elaborate on either the theoretical foundations or the relevant content-area research. More troubling was the scarcity of the descriptions of data collection and analysis. These were often so sparse that repeating the studies would be impossible.

Thinking about the directions in which teacher education research might evolve we found it important to keep in mind Grouws and Schultz's (1996, p. 454) argument for the need for theory building in the study of individual practice:

> ...the development of theoretical frameworks for teacher education must take account of the complexity of becoming a teacher, in particular theories must embody not only the complexity of the process but also the fact that it is a continuous process of lengthy duration. Thus, theoretical models must consider experiences prior to formal entry into a teacher education program, the teacher education program with its many components, the induction year of teaching, and subsequent teaching years. The relationships within and among these components must be detailed in the theory with participants' points of view and actions accounted for.

Also, it is important to recognize gender, race, class, and regional differences among prospective teachers. Research participants often were not identified beyond male or female, graduate or undergraduate, elementary or secondary. Teacher educators, researchers, and cooperating teachers were even less identified except for gender and, occasionally, experience. We agree with Wideen et al.'s (1998) caution that researchers must seek to understand how individuals, institutions, programs, and ideas are all interrelated. We are concerned that the research in professional development schools, which has the potential to represent multiple views and give voice to participants across role groups, is conducted by university-based academics, confirming Sleeter's (2001) observation that "most research still constructs White academics as the most legitimate knowers" (p. 209).

Our first recommendation is that journal reviewers and editors work with researchers to ensure that specific information is provided on participants' and researchers' demographics, which may include race, gender, social class, and age. It seems that a large number of participants are White and middle class, which makes sense given the demographics of teacher education in general (see Zumwalt and Craig, this volume). Moreover, the students with whom these prospective teachers work should also be described. The implications of working with different populations should be addressed.

Researchers often did not identify their relationship with those they are studying. Even when they did so, we found few examples of thoughtful discussions of the power dynamics or issues related to drawing valid or meaningful conclusions when the researcher and the course instructor were the same. We also found few examples where someone external to the course or field experience was employed to help collect or analyze data. We applaud the increasing number of identified self-studies that add to our understanding of how methods courses are conducted, instructors' intentions, and the impact on the instructors themselves. But we are concerned that the value of a disinterested researcher is now in danger of being ignored by the large number of instructors who study their own students without similarly examining and critiquing their own practice. We recommend that, in addition to self-studies, researchers work with others, external to the course or even the institution, to interrogate findings and challenge the possibilities of self-fulfilling findings.

Our third recommendation relates to what is, perhaps, an artifact of writing for journals with different expectations for length and detail. An empirical research report should begin with a specific statement of the researchers' conceptual framework and assumptions, as well as an in-depth reference to literature on similar questions.

It should also clearly describe the research questions, the participants, the contexts in which participants work, the data collection and analysis procedures, and the findings, as well as the connections among them. We found that the absence of detail in and the lack of clarity of such links were not limited to any content area or to any identifiable groups of researchers. Additionally, many researchers used terms such as "reflective practice," "constructivist," "conceptual change," and "action research," but did not define these terms or discuss how they related to the study. We concur with Richardson's (2002) concern that the term "constructivism" is a label for a learning theory, not a theory of teaching or teacher education. Too often it is used as a label for teaching practice. We would like to see more precise definitions and fewer *ad hoc* references. We further recommend that more attention be paid to the context of the research—including the policy context and the location of the endeavor within the enterprise of teacher education, whether at the university or at the school. We realize that rich descriptions of context may not adhere to page-length requirements, but we gained a much better understanding of what a methods course was about when the studies summarized the process and dynamics of a particular course (especially when the researchers were studying themselves). Furthermore, when a few reports on professional development schools referenced the historical development of the PDS or described typical days for prospective teachers in PDS settings, we understood more of the richness of the opportunities and challenges of such settings.

The fifth recommendation seeks to overcome the overreliance on conclusions generated by short-term case studies conducted within the confines of the researcher's own course or program, often based at a research-intensive university. We find it problematic that many of the studies purported to examine belief change without moving beyond one course to learn more about how beliefs are shaped and reshaped by practice. The short duration of many studies suggests that some educators intend that beliefs and practices be changeable in a one-semester course or in one carefully designed field experience, or that belief change necessarily impacts future teaching practice. We are troubled by language in some studies that seems to blame the prospective teachers when they did not change quickly. Indeed, studies that implied that resistance to the instructors' ideas was an indication of some inherent personal flaw displayed a lack of respect for the prospective teachers and for the difficulty of change in beliefs or practices. We realize that funding for larger, longer studies is crucial to conducting other forms of research; we realize there are considerable institutional and even ethical barriers to documenting links among teacher education program components, individual practice, practice as modified by teaching context, and P–12 student response. But these barriers are not insurmountable. The teacher education research field should devote at least as much time and effort to removing the barriers to more complex research designs as it currently devotes to explicating and critiquing teacher education programs.

We would welcome more studies using similar frames, questions, and methods in different settings with varying populations, including those currently "missing" from studies of methods courses and field experiences. The voices of university-based, White male and female researchers predominate; voices of cooperating teachers are heard only occasionally; voices of prospective teachers are seldom heard. What is less obvious, and quite troubling, is the absence of school administrators and children and adolescents. We believe this is explained in part by the research questions asked, the methods employed, and the narrow focus on a course or series of courses and field experiences. But we believe that this narrow focus inhibits our understanding of both impact and the potential for the changes advocated by teacher educators (both for teacher education programs and for continuing educational practice).

Finally, researchers should think in terms of not only partnerships for teacher education programs but also partnerships for research, with the partners representing diverse perspectives and orientations. In their review of literature on research related to teachers' knowledge, Munby et al. (2001, pp. 895–896) concluded:

> To the uninitiated, teaching unfolds as sets of skills but, to the initiated, teaching depends on, is grounded in, and constitutes knowledge. The character of this knowledge poses the irony for teacher education: The knowledge is, in part, practical, and that part can only be learned in practice, the very setting over which teacher educators have little direct control.

When we relate this to Cruickshank and Metcalf's (1990) argument in favor of some training within teacher preparation, "training prepares them to do something with what they have come to know, that is, to put knowledge into practice" (p. 471), we conclude that it seems unreasonable for teacher educators to distance themselves from a practice orientation. If we adopt the stance that by providing propositional knowledge of theory-based practice we have accomplished the task, we do our students and the field a grave disservice. Researchers, teacher educators, teachers, administrators, and students must learn more about how to transform propositional knowledge into practice—and how both knowledge and practice must be modified to adapt to different settings.

For us, this implies that frameworks for research should move beyond behavior and cognition, beyond a limited focus on the individual (alone or in a group), and toward a more sophisticated knowledge of how practice is shaped by contexts, materials, and other people. A team approach to research would enable methods that combine internal and external ways of knowing with a sufficient number of studies employing similar methods and relying on common frameworks to generate larger and more consistent studies. We are arguing for multivocal, multidimensional research designs in which temporal and contextual factors are as visible and salient as individual factors are in the current research. If we are to conduct such research, it is important to access relevant data—such as work samples from P–12 students, test scores, and other measures of how practice is enacted at the classroom level.

Such inquiries are necessarily long-term, collaborative, and replete with false starts. They require the gradual redirection of lines of research to accommodate the accumulation of evidence. This implies that we need the financial resources and time to do studies in this manner across teacher-education settings, including teaching without any formal preparation, and programs based in colleges that are not research intensive. We also need teacher education research structures that encourage collaboration and long-term work—structures that are not currently embedded in traditional promotion and tenure arrangements and even less in schools and school districts.

We also argue for funding for teams of researchers—possibly located in centers that cross university, school district, and other organizational lines. Perhaps it is unreasonable to expect a field to create and answer so many questions in the 30 years since Peck and Tucker (1973) first reviewed research on teacher education. And, perhaps, many questions surrounding teacher education are value laden, not empirical. But as our review documents, with limited funding and with researchers often working alone, we have not made sufficient progress toward understanding how individual, instructional, and contextual variables interact with one another at a given time and location. That is why we believe it is imperative to decrease the isolation among teacher education researchers and support more collaborative, cross-institutional, and longitudinal research. This work should be done in concert with research on school contexts, student learning, and educational policy.

We see beginning steps toward such possibilities. For example, the studies that follow teachers into their first years of teaching, such as those conducted by Adams and Krockover (1997), Grossman and colleagues (2000), and Steele (2001), provide models of qualitative methods that move us beyond a focus on belief to research on action and to longer term connections between the teacher education program content and recommended practice and actual teaching practice after graduation. Gill and Hove (2000) enable us to envision a combined qualitative and quantitative study that documents impact on student achievement.

Multivocal studies, such as the work of Weaver and Stanulis (1996), Sillman et al. (2000), Tobin and colleagues (1999, 2001), and Blanton et al. (2001), show how differing views and interpretations can be incorporated into one article. Studies utilizing a team of insiders and outsiders such as Mallette et al. (2000) and studies in which researchers from one institution conduct studies within a similar institution (Anderson et al., 2000) provide examples of how to incorporate carefully conducted qualitative research within teacher education classrooms that is not self-study.

Finally, many teacher educators are living the recommendation to become reflective practitioners through systematic inquiry into their own instruction. This research can be accomplished in large part without external funding. It is clear that research on teacher education has made progress in terms of quantity and quality over the past 30 years, but more progress is imperative. We know little about how practice develops over time and virtually nothing about how that practice is received and understood by children and adolescents. We can draw few conclusions about impact on student learning if we have insufficient knowledge of teachers' transformation from student to student teacher to teacher and the forces that enable them to adopt and adapt recommended practice. Without funding, the field is unlikely to engage in these more complicated studies, and therefore our understanding of impact will remain limited.

APPENDIX A: PEER-REVIEWED JOURNALS THAT SERVED AS SOURCES FOR THIS REVIEW

Action in Teacher Education
Curriculum Inquiry
International Journal of Science Education
Journal for Research in Mathematics Education (NCTM)
Journal of Computers in Mathematics and Science Teaching
Journal of Curriculum Studies
Journal of Education for Teaching
Journal of Literacy Research
Journal of Mathematics Teacher Education
Journal of Research and Development in Education
Journal of Research in Science Teaching
Journal of Teacher Education
Research in the Teaching of English
School Science and Mathematics
Science Education
Teaching and Teacher Education
The Teacher Educator
Theory and Research in Social Education

TABLE 6.1
English

Authors, Date	Relationship With Participants	Theoretical "Framework" or Position in Field of Research	Participants	Data Sources, Duration of Study, and Data Analysis	Impact Claims Examined and Findings
Agee. J. (1997)	Researcher who observed and participated somewhat, but did not teach	Cites socialization theory and cognitive theory, plus competing theories of how to teach literature and the impact of culture on teaching literature	Two middle-class undergraduate secondary-ed female preservice teachers (1 African American, 1 White), 1 male assistant professor	Observations and field notes on the secondary methods class, tapes of whole-class and small-group discussions; interviews with the students and the professor; 3 reading protocols, course syllabi, and assignments during the methods semester; videotapes of student teaching; debriefing interviews; other interviews; and logs during student teaching Data were coded for statements about readers and students of literature and for socialization into teaching based on open coding of data and a constant comparative analysis, preserved in a speaker turn format in the database, followed by axial coding to identify overarching categories and change over time.	The methods instructor had a strong bias against the literary theories with which the students were familiar. He emphasized questioning and reflecting on the status quo. The African American student was receptive to the instructor, especially the focus on multivocal and multicultural literature. During student teaching she encouraged discussion and debate, but learned that students from many races are uncomfortable with discussions of race. The White student initially resisted the instructor, then became more accepting. During student teaching she was initially very controlling, then began to let the students bring their own meaning to literature. Both struggled to learn how to involve students and to listen to them.

(Continued)

TABLE 6.1
(Continued)

Authors, Date	Relationship With Participants	Theoretical "Framework" or Position in Field of Research	Participants	Data Sources, Duration of Study, and Data Analysis	Impact Claims Examined and Findings
Agee, J. (1998)	Researcher who observed and participated somewhat, but did not teach	Cites literature on prior beliefs, teacher socialization, and conceptual change	One male assistant professor (same as in the previous study) Preservice secondary-ed teachers: 13 White females; 7 White males; 1 African-American female; 1 African-American male; 1 Hispanic-American female; 1 Asian-American female Two females and 1 male were older students in their 30s (probably the larger dataset from which the two participants in the previous study were selected)	Observations and field notes on the secondary methods class; audiotapes of whole-class and small-group discussions; interviews with the professor and with preservice teachers; 3-question protocol administered at the beginning and end of the semester; documents including course syllabus, handouts, and assignments; portfolios Same as for previous study with the exception of the 3-question protocol, which documented change over time	The students and the instructor had very different views of teaching at the beginning of the semester. The instructor had a bias against transmissionist views and tried to challenge the students to teach differently from the way they were taught. The students were uncomfortable and most remained confused about how to make the instructor's ideas fit with their instruction, although some conceptual change may have occurred, especially during small-group discussions. The instructor critiqued his own teaching at the end of the semester.

| Wiggins, R. A., & Clift, R. T. (1995) | Wiggins was the researcher; Clift, the methods instructor for the English preservice teachers | References to teachers' beliefs as filters | Complete dataset of 6 secondary-ed student teachers (4 in English, 2 in science); article focused on 2 White female undergraduate student teachers (1 in English; 1 in science) | Interviews at the beginning, middle, and end of the secondary methods course taught in conjunction with student teaching; journals; audiotapes of conferences with cooperating teachers

Cooperative data analysis with the cooperating teachers resulting in identifying 2 student teachers who held onto contradictory beliefs throughout student teaching. | Student teacher in science was conflicted between her role in motivating students and her beliefs that students needed self-motivation in order to learn, and between her belief in individualizing instruction and treating everyone equitably.

Student teacher in English was conflicted between creating a friendly relationship with students and being their evaluator, and between her belief that she should know how to teach already and her wanting to learn from student teaching. |
| Mosenthal, J. (1996) | Instructor and an acknowledged self-study | Situated learning | One female elementary-ed preservice teacher in Mosenthal's field-based methods course, selected after the course ended | Student coursework (including teaching log, child's literacy portfolio, content journal, and teacher portfolio), audiotapes of conferences, end-of-term interviews, field observations and debriefing, instructor journal

Time line of important field experiences was used as a base.

Coded comments directly related to preservice teacher's work with the reading group, historical analysis of her | Although she felt accepted by her cooperating teacher, she found it difficult to generate group discussion (advocated by the methods instructor)—this was resolved by midsemester. Her ability to conduct *cloze* activities was positively influenced by her ability to generate discussion.

Instructor felt that as confidence in practices increased, the issue of when they were appropriate became important. |

(Continued)

TABLE 6.1
(Continued)

Authors, Date	Relationship With Participants	Theoretical "Framework" or Position in Field of Research	Participants	Data Sources, Duration of Study, and Data Analysis	Impact Claims Examined and Findings
				work with the reading group, and analysis of her recorded thoughts and actions surrounding important field experiences	
McMahon, S. I. (1997)	Instructor	Grounded in literature on teacher thinking, reflective practice, and on the ill-structured nature of teaching	Two elementary-ed undergraduate student teachers (1 male, 1 older female who was changing careers), both in their junior year who had successfully completed the methods course and concurrent practicum	Students were selected after the course because the issues they focused on in journals and discussions were similar. Course assignments, field notes, and tapes of course required activities, journals with instructor and supervisor comments, reading lesson plans with supervisor comments, audiotaped small-group discussions, portfolios from a one-semester course with a practicum. Data related to the issues of pullout programs and ability grouping were separated into phases of discussion and analyzed for type of student thinking. Other data sources were used for triangulation.	The younger, male preservice teacher reported disliking pullout programs because they were poorly implemented and seemed to be focused on one race of students. Throughout the experience he seemed to focus on the inconvenience, but only became self-reflective at the end. The older, female preservice teacher was first accepting of ability grouping and then began to question it and to work toward changing her practice. Her reflections became more complex over time.

| Dooley, C. (1998) | Supervisor | Socialization theory and some discussion of constructivism within the text | One elementary-ed male | Field notes of preservice teacher's teaching and his students' reactions for two visits and one videotaped lesson
Journal
Audiotaped interviews
Informal interview with the cooperating teacher
Frequently repeated words and phrases, member checks to verify themes | Preservice teacher struggled with organizing instruction in language arts field experience with very little help from the cooperating teacher in part because the preservice teacher did not provide ideas or plans to discuss. Supervisor sought to provide models; cooperating teacher provided encouragement.
Preservice teacher did not realize the importance of teacher education courses until he reached the field experience.
Preservice teacher's image of teacher as creative and enthusiastic—attributes he believed he already possessed—did not include planning. |
| Weaver, D. & Stanulis, R. N. (1996) | Weaver was the cooperating teacher; Stanulis, the university supervisor. | Social constructivist learning theory and socialization theory with references to collaborative teacher education and mentoring through guided practice | One female undergraduate student teacher, 1 female middle school cooperating teacher, 1 female university supervisor | Transcripts of weekly three-way conferences and individual reflections throughout the student teaching semester; philosophy papers by each participant
Collective discussions of transcripts, and written reflections noting the | Even though course work and the field setting promoted writers' workshops, the preservice teacher did not feel confident about implementing these and was concerned about the workload.
The cooperating teacher and the supervisor both adapted |

(Continued)

TABLE 6.1
(Continued)

Authors, Date	Relationship With Participants	Theoretical "Framework" or Position in Field of Research	Participants	Data Sources, Duration of Study, and Data Analysis	Impact Claims Examined and Findings
				development of the collaborative relationship over time	their expectations so that the preservice teacher could try some ideas of her own—especially planning directly from the textbook, in part because the preservice teacher anticipated not having resources other than a text in her first years of teaching.
Grossman, P. L., Valencia, S. W., Evans, K., Thompson, C., Martin, S., & Place, N. (2000)	Researchers	Activity theory	Ten teachers (followed from graduate-level preservice through in-service) One male high school teacher; 2 elementary teachers (1 male, 1 female) are specific cases, but the report also draws on all of the teachers—5 elementary, 2 middle school, 3 high school).	Classroom observations with pre- and post audiotaped interviews (at least 5 times a year: 2 separate classes at the secondary level; reading and writing observations at the elementary level when possible), including field notes and analytic memos Annual audio- and videotaped group interviews Retrospective interviews with methods instructors Interviews with cooperating teachers, observations of supervisory conferences	The high school teacher did not like his methods course, in part because it was not practical enough, and began a shadow methods course. During student teaching, he adopted a highly structured writing curriculum from a workshop (of which his supervisor was critical), but ultimately rejected it. In his first year of teaching he used writing as a way to generate ideas and as an assessment. In his second year, he began to incorporate peer response (from his methods class).

during student teaching, interviews with mentors, department chairs and principals in the first years of teaching, artifacts for the first 3 years of teaching

Initially focused on writing to develop an understanding of each participant's practice, then examined themes across cases

One elementary-ed teacher began with a struggle to balance skill development and encouraging expression, but student teaching did not resolve this struggle as she taught the way her cooperating teacher expected. In her first year she used the district-mandated curriculum, which she liked, and began to modify it somewhat. She began to adapt it even more in her second year.

One elementary-ed teacher began with a strong background in writing and was able to easily integrate ideas from course work into his teaching—especially because he was in a supportive student teaching placement. In his first year he was able to implement much of what he learned from his methods course and continued to balance some explicit instruction with freedom for the students to experiment in his second year.

(Continued)

TABLE 6.1
(Continued)

Authors, Date	Relationship With Participants	Theoretical "Framework" or Position in Field of Research	Participants	Data Sources, Duration of Study, and Data Analysis	Impact Claims Examined and Findings
					The authors note the importance of practical and conceptual tools and learning to use them in a supportive environment. They note that first-year teachers can encounter curricula that inhibit their learning, but begin to critique them in their second year. The graduates attributed their ability to reflect and to work toward an ideal to the teacher education program.
Newell, G. E., Gingrich, R. S., & Johnson, A. B. (2001)	Supervisors; had taught some of the participants' methods courses	Activity theory with references to situated learning and to teacher socialization	Five graduate students (1 male) and 4 undergraduates (2 male) in secondary English. Eight European-Americans; 1 African-American undergraduate female 2 males, 8 females; European-American cooperating teachers	Audiotaped interviews, 5 classroom observations and debriefings, interviews with the cooperating teachers, journals, lesson plans, retrospective interviews for 1 student-teaching semester Coded for pedagogical content knowledge, appropriation of theoretical and practical tools, and sources of knowledge. Triangulated across data sources. Charts developed on the student teachers' purposes, tools,	There was considerable difference among the students in terms of their appropriation of conceptual as well as of practical tools for teaching and learning. Two were reflective and consistently relied on instructional scaffolding; 5 were interested in practical tools to the exclusion of theoretical tools and relied on student discussion as proof of learning; and 2 did not analyze their own

Citation	Researcher involvement	Focus	Participants	Method	Findings
				and settings, followed by case study reports for each teacher and then by a cross-case analysis	instructional routines and experienced disjuncture between university program and student teaching. The authors concluded that beliefs and understandings change if the activity settings of the program enable change.
Bruckerhoff, C. E., & Carlson, J. L. (1995)	Researchers with no involvement in the teacher education program	Teacher socialization and references to literature on teacher professionalism	One female secondary-ed undergraduate student teacher	The student teacher kept a daily diary. At the end of her first year of teaching she wrote an autobiographical account of her student teaching, based on the diary. The autobiography is contained in the article. The authors discuss it in terms of how the university failed to provide support for her.	The preservice teacher was left on her own throughout student teaching—by her cooperating teacher and her supervisor—and felt angry and isolated.
Wolf, S. A., Ballentine, D., & Hill, L. (1999)	Wolf was the instructor; Ballentine and Hill, her students.	Teaching for conceptual change Conceptual arguments in writing theory in terms of who can speak for which populations	Six graduate preservice teachers, 4 undergraduates; 2 Japanese-European and 6 European-American females (including 2nd and 3rd authors), 2 European-American males. Presumably elementary-ed.	Three formal interviews throughout the year, notes on other conversations, e-mail conversations, all completed assignments. This article focuses on an assignment to create multicultural book handouts and final interviews about authenticity in writing. NUD*IST used to organize data	Due, in part, to class readings and multicultural book reports, preservice teachers' understandings of who has the right to write about various cultures, to examine text authenticity, historical and visual accuracy, aesthetic heat, and children's reactions to the texts changed over the year.

(Continued)

TABLE 6.1
(Continued)

Authors, Date	Relationship With Participants	Theoretical "Framework" or Position in Field of Research	Participants	Data Sources, Duration of Study, and Data Analysis	Impact Claims Examined and Findings
			The group was 80% middle class. Participants were purposefully selected. The university instructor	Interview transcripts coded for hesitations, arguments, support for arguments, changes, and hopes and fears; coded both line-by-line and more holistically Handouts were coded for: qualities of the represented groups, literary elements, illustrations, author's background, responses to and evaluations of the text The team recorded Wolf's changes in instruction and also their own interactions throughout the analysis.	The authors reflected on their own learning, especially Wolf, on what other assignments she could have given, and offered a critique of ways Wolf's teaching could be improved in terms of clarity and holding students accountable for their opinions.
Wolf, S. A., Ballentine, D., & Hill, L. A. (2000)	Wolf was the instructor; Ballentine and Hill were her students.	Discussion of ways of knowing with some references to listening to alternative voices	Three Anglo-American, middle-class elementary-ed preservice teachers (2 females, 1 male) from the group identified previously	Course assignments: reading autobiographies, field notebooks for Child as Teacher project, analytic papers Interviews at the beginning, middle, and end of the academic year Construction of a narrative relying on literary theory and story structure, including the following analytic categories: features	All preservice teachers were enthusiastic, successful readers working with students from cultural backgrounds different from their own. One preservice teacher worked with an African-American 3rd grade male and learned that he was insightful and enjoyed reading, but that his school did not realize these strengths.

One preservice teacher worked with an African-American male and became involved in the family. He learned about their hectic lifestyle and his student's difficulties with homework. He further learned that when the student was interested in a text he became involved in reading, but that his teacher did not realize this or recognize much about the boy and his family.

One preservice teacher worked with a 2nd-grade Mexican-American student and learned that she had to learn to ask good questions to encourage her student to respond. She also learned that the Spanish language was important to her student and that her family valued education. She learned that her student enjoyed teaching her Spanish and that she was a very insightful reader. All preservice teachers learned that school for their students was not the same as it had been for them and that their students' views of books were different from their

of language marking construction of self, influences on thinking, cognitive or emotional responses, understandings of child's literary engagement, understandings of children in their communities

Participants read through article before publication.

(Continued)

TABLE 6.1
(Continued)

Authors, Date	Relationship With Participants	Theoretical "Framework" or Position in Field of Research	Participants	Data Sources, Duration of Study, and Data Analysis	Impact Claims Examined and Findings
					own—but that it was possible and enjoyable to engage the students in reading.
Wolf, S. A., Mieras, E. L., & Carey, A. A. (1996)	Wolf was the instructor: Mieras and Carey were her students.	Reader-response theory; literature on teacher questioning	Forty-three undergraduate elementary-ed preservice teachers, including 2nd and 3rd authors; 37 females, 6 males; predominantly European American (in 2 separate classes with same instructor and assignments)	Participants' field notes and final papers for case study assignment, with instructor's comments for a semester; class lecture notes and handouts Researchers jointly determined codes based on *a priori* and emerging themes, then did 3 iterations of data coding, and narrowing, with 1st author doing a 4th iteration. Specifically coded questions participants asked case study pupils (known information; opinion; connection; conditional) in search of change over time	Through course emphasis on questioning and through direct experiences reading with young children, participants' literary questions shifted from teacher dominance to child–teacher dialog; participants also reflected on their questions and on creating a balance between comfort and challenge. Meanwhile, the children moved from hesitancy to confidence. Undergraduate co-authors became empowered as researchers.
Fecho, B., Commeyras, M., Bauer, E. B., & Font, G. (2000)	Fecho, Commeyras, and Bauer were instructors in their own	Critical theory	Undergraduate reading methods instructors: 1 White, working-class male; 1 European	Data collection varied across instructors, but all wrote reflective notes after each class and e-mailed them to the team based on student conferences, class	Using a dance metaphor, 1 instructor focused on interactions with 3 students—first establishing her authority, then moving to an inquiry-oriented

discourse for the students, then allowing the students to make sense of ownership of their work, then establishing synchrony with some students but not others as they vied for control. She ultimately realized that teacher and students must take on authority in a synchronous fashion, that students must challenge teachers' authority, and that teachers cannot force a liberation of students' thinking.

One instructor used inquiry as a frame, but with no set syllabus. In discussions of race with the students he began to argue with the students instead of asking clarifying questions, thus setting himself up as the authority, followed by an attempt to reestablish dialog. One instructor worked toward redirecting authority back to the students, but became concerned when students did not react positively. Her students did not like the ambiguity.

interaction, student responses to readings, students' written coursework, and course syllabi for 1 semester E-mailed reflections served as the basis for challenging one another to consider alternative explanations throughout the semester. After the semester ended, group analysis around the question of authority in a critical-inquiry classroom. Each created stories around this and the 4th author provided a cross-story analysis.

female who came to the U.S. at age 3; 1 Haitian female who came to the U.S. at age 10; 1 male graduate student (not an instructor) with family ties to Cuba

courses working collaboratively to better understand their own practice; Font had no course involvement.

(Continued)

TABLE 6.1
(Continued)

Authors, Date	Relationship With Participants	Theoretical "Framework" or Position in Field of Research	Participants	Data Sources, Duration of Study, and Data Analysis	Impact Claims Examined and Findings
Graham, P. (1999)	Supervisor	References to power relationships during student teaching and to socialization theory	Two junior high cooperating teachers (1 female, 1 male) One secondary-ed male preservice teacher	Interviews at the beginning and end of the student-teaching semester, student teacher journal, classroom observations and postobservation conferences, evaluations, lesson plans, tapes of student-teaching seminars, notes on informal conversations Beginning with conference tapes and interviews, themes, dilemmas, and tensions were identified and mapped against other sources.	The preservice teacher began with an image of teaching as athletic coaching and was very teacher centered. The female cooperating teacher fit his image, but he began to disrespect her teaching. The male cooperating teacher was very student centered and immersed in the state Writing Project. The preservice teacher bonded with the male cooperating teacher, and both argued and negotiated views; the student teacher changed his views somewhat on teaching and on power relations with the cooperating teacher, and both men respected their disagreements with one another.
Mallette, M. H., Kile, R. S., Smith, M. M., McKinney, M., & Readence, J. E. (2000)	Mallette was the course instructor; Kile was her faculty mentor; Smith taught a second section	Symbolic interactionism and social constructivism	Six female elementary-ed preservice teachers: 5 White, 1 Hispanic. Two of the White preservice teachers were in their early 40s.	Written assignments plus the instructor's comments; class-discussion notes; instructional notes; preservice teachers' semester-long study of 1 child who was having reading difficulties, which	Stances toward reading difficulties predispose preservice teachers to construct reading difficulties in different ways. The stances are typically unknown to the preservice teachers until they reflect on

Author	Relationship	Method	Sample	Data sources and analysis	Findings
	of the course; McKinney led the cohort program; and Readance served as the external reactor.			included field notes, a case study, and reflective writing Descriptive coding of each data source related to the child study collapsed into a broader coding system subsuming the descriptions Case studies were prepared for each student, followed by a cross-case analysis.	their own data. Once they acknowledged the limitation of their views they were free to make changes. Preservice teachers became more critical of classroom practices over time and began to see reading difficulty as an instructional issue as opposed to a problem with the child or family. Multiple and continuous assessments became important as a monitor of their student's learning and their own learning.
Denyer, J., & Florio-Ruane, S. (1995)	Denyer was the supervisor; Florio-Ruane's relationship was not specified.	Discourse analysis	One elementary-ed preservice female	Field notes during weekly observations, audiotapes of conferences with the cooperating teacher, videotapes of writing conferences with children, audiotapes of the debriefing, and course materials during the student teaching semester Analysis of turn taking and question and answer sequences during 1 writing conference episode, triangulated with other data sources	The preservice teacher struggled among exploring ideas, evaluating child's knowledge, and directing behavior. After student teaching, the preservice teacher critiqued herself and was able to offer concrete suggestions on better supporting the child's voice in writing as opposed to managing her behavior.

(Continued)

TABLE 6.1
(Continued)

Authors, Date	Relationship With Participants	Theoretical "Framework" or Position in Field of Research	Participants	Data Sources, Duration of Study, and Data Analysis	Impact Claims Examined and Findings
Bowman, C. L., & McCormick, S. (2000)	Not specified	References to peer coaching literature and to Vygotsky's social–developmental theory	Thirty-two elementary-ed preservice teachers: 5 males; 27 females; 2 aged between 28 and 30; others, between 19 and 22	Half assigned to peer coaching dyads; half assigned to traditional supervision during an early field experience Preassessment videotapes and an audiotaped postconference Postassessment videotapes and an audiotaped postconference plus an attitude scale rating dimensions of the field experience Clarity Observation Instrument used with videotapes to determine frequency of clarity skill use and ANOVAs computed Audiotapes analyzed for evidence of pedagogical reasoning and action processes and ANCOVAs were computed because preassessment means were not equal. t-tests were computed for the attitude measure.	Those in the peer coaching group were significantly higher in frequency and quality of clarifying skills in their postassessments and in pedagogical reasoning and action. Those in the peer coaching group provided more technical feedback, analysis of applications, adaptation to students, and personal facilitation. There were no differences in collegiality or in overall rating.

| Slick, S. K. (1998a) | Researcher | References to student-teaching supervision literature | 45-year-old experienced teacher, now a graduate student and university supervisor
Female cooperating teacher
Male high school student teacher | Interviews with the supervisor, student teacher, and cooperating teacher; transcripts and field notes of student teaching seminars; conferences at the beginning and end of the semester; informal discussions
Analysis of tensions, ambiguities, and power dynamics | The student teacher experienced a conflict between what he had been taught and expected in classroom practice. Although the supervisor felt estranged from the actual field site, she could use her experience to help the student teacher understand the classroom dynamics. Gradually she established rapport with the cooperating teacher—even though she still needed to deal with issues of power and negotiation at both the university and the school. |
| Graham, P. (1997) | Supervisor | References to literature on supervision | Two female cooperating teachers
Two male secondary-ed graduate student teachers | Repeated, in-depth phenomenological interviews, participant observation and field notes, nonparticipant observation and field notes, written documents
Constant comparative analysis with a focus on the dynamics within student teaching resulting in two case studies of the development of the cooperating teacher–student teacher relationships | Case Study 1. At first the cooperating teacher felt that she needed to handle problems with the student teacher by herself, then in exasperation called in the supervisor, and together they worked with the student teacher. Student teacher attempted to implement recommended practice, but struggled with classroom management and reverted back to habits of teacher centered authority. |

(Continued)

TABLE 6.1
(Continued)

Authors, Date	Relationship With Participants	Theoretical "Framework" or Position in Field of Research	Participants	Data Sources, Duration of Study, and Data Analysis	Impact Claims Examined and Findings
					The cooperating teacher began to question her own beliefs, but used teacher research to examine the impact of student centered practice. When the teacher research showed that the student teacher's practice was problematic for student learning, their working relationship broke down completely.

Case Study 2. The philosophical disagreement between student teacher and cooperating teacher was more open than that in Case Study 1. The student teacher had substitute-taught in the school and considered his cooperating teacher as the expert. She resisted this and refused to give "pat" answers. The supervisor used their seminar to explore alternatives in decision making and to deal—somewhat—with uncertainty. The uncertainty never resolved. |

| O'Callaghan, C. (2001) | Not specified | Review of literature on reflective, narrative inquiry | Four early childhood female undergraduate student teachers, all seniors. 3 traditional-age: Hispanic American, Jewish American, Italian American; 1 non-traditional-age immigrant from Guyana | Theoretical Orientation to Reading Profile; vignettes of primary-grade reading problems with think-aloud protocols; literacy narratives; interviews; teaching metaphors; teaching observations using the Classroom Analysis of Teachers' Theoretical Orientation to Reading Instrument

Data collected at the beginning, middle, and end of the semester

Descriptive data reduced by categorizing and pattern matching; data display through matrices; conclusion drawing and verifying. Initial codes based on critical incidents in early childhood and school, and metaphors and instructional approaches

Think-aloud protocols codified using categories of the sources of preservice teachers' pedagogical knowledge: received knowing; subjective knowing; and procedural knowing

Cross-validation method and multiple coders used to validate data analysis | Student teachers maintained conceptualizations of teaching based on their early learning experiences, at school and at home. All four showed increases in reflective thinking and in procedural reasoning; two changed their teaching metaphors; and one changed her theoretical orientation toward teaching reading from phonics to skills learning. The researcher attributed these changes to participation in the study more than to student teaching itself. |

(Continued)

TABLE 6.1
(Continued)

Authors, Date	Relationship With Participants	Theoretical "Framework" or Position in Field of Research	Participants	Data Sources, Duration of Study, and Data Analysis	Impact Claims Examined and Findings
Worthy, J. & Patterson, E. (2001)	Reading course instructors and field placement supervisors (acknowl-edged self-study)	Review of literature on active, situated learning and reflection; personal relationships, especially involving caring	Seventy-one preservice elementary teachers in 4 cohorts; 75% undergraduate, 25% already had college degrees; 67 women, 4 men; 47% European American, 33% Hispanic American, 10% African American, 10% Asian American. Twenty-two working toward bilingual endorsement, 4 toward ESL endorsement. Mostly middle class. Two instructors: both White, female, middle-class former teachers. First author is a professor and cohort coordinator; 2nd author has a PhD	Students' formal and informal written reflections on tutoring; researchers' notes Researchers wrote summaries of student reflections; looked for patterns, themes, and categories using constant comparative analysis and analogy of qualitative research as improvisational jazz music. Final categories included tutors' concerns; assessing; instruction; tutor learning; and relationships. Independently analyzed 25% of the reflections for 82% interrater reliability Used anecdotal notes and research journals as contextual data	In the field component of their reading methods course, preservice teachers tutored elementary pupils in a high-poverty school. During the semester, the preservice teachers shifted their attention from pupil behavior to pupil learning; they were better able to assess their tutees' needs; they moved from talking about how to teach their individual tutee to lessons learned for teaching in general; and some initial deficit labeling was replaced by a language of respect. The tutoring involved complex personal relationships that took time and effort to develop; preservice teachers felt emotionally invested and believed that the relationship motivated their tutees to learn.

| Fairbanks, C. M., Freedman, D., & Kahn, C. (2000) | Not specified | References to literature on mentoring relationships | Fifteen student teachers Fifteen cooperating teachers: 8 middle school, 7 high school; with 4–20 years of teaching experience | Dialog journals; interviews; videotapes of mentoring conferences; artifacts from weekly seminars Participants and researchers together sorted through data and determined the following categories: helping student teachers survive the experience and define their teaching lives; establishing relationships based on dialog and reflection; building professional partnerships. | Mentor teachers in the Effective Mentoring in English Education (EMEE) project shared craft knowledge and advice on balancing responsibilities; provided models of interpersonal relationships; and helped student teachers negotiate professional relationships. To do this, mentor teachers shared reflections with student teachers; made their practices explicit; posed questions; and acted as both mentor and teacher to student teachers. In mentoring relationships, student teachers raised their own questions to foster dialog and broached broader issues of teaching and learning. In the classroom, learning to teach involved observing, questioning, experimenting, and reflecting. During the student-teaching semester, relationships were increasingly defined as collegial, and partners learned from each other; however, developing this collaborative relationship took time. |

(Continued)

TABLE 6.1
(Continued)

Authors, Date	Relationship With Participants	Theoretical "Framework" or Position in Field of Research	Participants	Data Sources, Duration of Study, and Data Analysis	Impact Claims Examined and Findings
Boyd, P. C., Boll, M., Brawner, L., & Villaume, S. K. (1998)	Instructors	References to literature on educational reform and on reflection	Forty-seven elementary education preservice teachers (40 female, 7 male; 45 Caucasian, 2 African American) in 2 sections of a reading and language arts methods course	Observation of preservice teachers' interactions and reactions in university classes and field placements; learning log and journal entries; written responses to open-ended midterm and final exam questions; questionnaire on teaching concerns; semi-structured interviews on categories identified from questionnaire. Researchers met weekly to analyze the data using a constant-comparative method; grouped preservice teacher behaviors in 3 categories: questioning as a way of learning, constructing a coherent philosophy, and committing to professional and ongoing inquiry.	Preservice teachers had varying levels of comfort with questioning their assumptions and practices regarding education. Questions generated in the university classroom were often answered or confirmed in field placements, and the field placements generated more questions and problems to be solved. The university classroom provided the groundwork for the participants' educational philosophy, and the field placements allowed the participants to integrate theory and practice. Most participants had internal motivation—enhanced through the field experience—to develop the knowledge and skills of a good teacher.

TABLE 6.2
Mathematics

Authors, Date	Relationship With Participants	Theoretical "Framework" or Position in Field of Research	Participants	Data Sources, Duration of Study, and Data Analysis	Impact Claims Examined and Findings
Cooney, T. J., Shealy, B. E., & Arvold, B. (1998)	Shealy and Arvold were instructors in the fall; Cooney's relationship is not identified.	Grounded in the literature on reflective practice with references to beliefs, the psychological and social construction of knowledge, subordination to authority, and the interplay between the individual and the situation	Cohort of 15 preservice secondary math undergraduates as initial dataset. Four participants (2 males, 2 females) purposefully selected to represent a wide range of positions on mathematics teaching and learning	Early fall survey, secondary methods class field notes, and assignments of 15 preservice undergraduates Narrowed from 15 to 4 participants Interviews during the fall methods course with a survey at the end, followed by another interview prior to the 2nd methods course and field experience One more interview before and 2 after student teaching Yearlong observation field notes Weekly meetings to discuss fieldnotes, with a focus on belief statements and an active search for disconfirming evidence Themes were informed by theoretical framework of belief structures and were analyzed over time.	All experienced some conflict among beliefs, and all sought affirmation for their thinking about self. One preservice teacher became more open ended in his activities and connected mathematics more to life and to students. One left teaching after graduation, but seemed to have a view of teaching as exploring and increasingly challenged other students' views. One had a cooperating teacher who supported his views; he showed no change over time and wanted to be the authority in the classroom; wanted to teach high-level math to affluent students. One still relied on the authority of others to know the right way to teach. They varied in tendencies to be reflective and to rely on beliefs about authority and sources of knowledge.

(Continued)

359

TABLE 6.2
(Continued)

Authors, Date	Relationship With Participants	Theoretical "Framework" or Position in Field of Research	Participants	Data Sources, Duration of Study, and Data Analysis	Impact Claims Examined and Findings
Mewborn, D. S. (1999)	Instructor for a special section of a methods course	Reflective thinking as both individual and social. Later references to teacher socialization	Four Caucasian female Early Childhood education undergraduates—the only students in the special section. An experienced 4-grade teacher, chosen because her beliefs about mathematics and teaching were similar to the instructor's	Interviews at the beginning and mid-point of the semester, class-group discussions, journals, observations of the 4th-grade teacher, preservice teacher interviews with children, and small group teaching. Use of HyperRESEARCH to analyze interactions and continuous coding of data throughout the study using categories influenced by John Dewey's phases of reflective thought	After the field experience, the preservice teachers increased in their intellectual curiosity concerning teaching and learning and shifted their locus of authority from external to internal. They began to think reflectively about mathematics teaching and learning over time in a nonlinear manner. Conferences with the classroom teacher were important to the process.
Kim, M. K., & Sharp, J. (2000)	It is not clear if one of the researchers was also the instructor.	Constructivist theory with references to teacher socialization	Twenty-eight elementary-ed undergraduates: 2 male, 26 female	Lesson plans developed during a methods course. Three independent analyses (scoring) of lesson plans using the Teaching Strategy Test	After 6 hours of multimedia-enhanced instruction in technology, problem solving, and ratios and proportions as part of a constructivist-based methods course, participants demonstrated the ability to write lesson plans using some constructivist

					principles. There was wide variance in the dimensions and categories identified by the Teaching Strategy Test, such as the willingness to encourage their future students to communicate mathematically with the teacher and their classmates; to plan student-centered instruction; and to use manipulatives, diagrams, and other alternative representations.
Frykholm, J. A. (1996)	Supervisor	Teachers' beliefs with references to cognitive psychology and teacher socialization	Twenty-five female, 19 male secondary-ed student teachers, representing 4 separate cohorts across 2 years	Classroom observations, postlesson conferences, lesson plans, audiotaped seminars, questionnaire, informal conversations References to the NCTM standards categorized by pressures to implement, own teaching practice, observations of standards in practice, and perceptions of cooperating teachers' implementation of the standards; domain analysis to examine relationships among themes	The preservice teachers regarded the NCTM standards highly, and perceived that although the university pressured them to implement standards, the cooperating teachers did not—and cooperating teachers were the most significant influence on the participants' philosophies and practices. The preservice teachers expressed the belief that they were implementing the standards in their own teaching, but the supervisor did not see evidence of this.

(Continued)

TABLE 6.2
(Continued)

Authors, Date	Relationship With Participants	Theoretical "Framework" or Position in Field of Research	Participants	Data Sources, Duration of Study, and Data Analysis	Impact Claims Examined and Findings
Frykholm, J. A. (1999)	Not specified; presumably the supervisor	Review of literature on mathematics education reform and implementation; teacher knowledge and beliefs	Sixty-three secondary-ed student teachers, representing 6 separate cohorts across 3 years. (Some of these participants are the same as in the previous study.)	Classroom observations, postlesson conferences, interviews, survey (half of questions Likert-scale; half free-response), seminar sessions, informal conversation and interactions—for a 1-semester student-teaching experience Data were read; themes were identified and labeled; data coded by theme and subtheme. Data analyzed by cohort group; iterative search for relationships between themes and across datasets	Student teachers reported that their cooperating teachers were the most significant influence on their teaching philosophy and instructional practices. Although methods courses had emphasized the NCTM standards, and preservice teachers reported valuing them, the cooperating teachers often did not model or discuss the standards. Student teachers suggested that they needed more information on how to implement the standards; lesson observations showed that the majority of student teachers used traditional, teacher-centered methods, although a few reported concern with the mismatch between how they taught and how they wanted to teach.
Langrall, C. W., Thornton, C. A., Jones,	Researchers	References to teacher change and reflective practice	Seventy-one elementary-ed undergraduates in	Beliefs About Teaching Mathematics Inventory administered before and	The mean change on the Beliefs About Teaching Mathematics Inventory

G. A., &
Malone,
J. A. (1996)

3 methods classes with a focus on 6 females as case examples

after the methods course and field experience to all preservice teachers. Researchers used a Teacher Talk/Student Talk Frequency Survey for participants' 6 days of practicum experiences. A Reflective Teaching Analysis was completed by the 6 case study participants on a lesson taught at beginning and end of the course, and they participated in a stimulated recall session based on videotapes of teaching at beginning and end of the course.

Videos of the lessons were coded for overall patterns of change in teacher actions, percentage of open-ended questions, and the quality of the mathematics teaching

The entire group of 71 preservice teachers' responses to the Beliefs About Teaching Mathematics Inventory was submitted to multivariate analysis and subsequent univariate analyses.

subcluster was significant, although there was positive movement on all other subclusters. The 6 focus students' lessons demonstrated a change from modeling problem solving to encouraging children to engage with problems. Another change was a shift toward having higher expectations for the children in generating and justifying solutions to problems.

(Continued)

TABLE 6.2
(Continued)

Authors, Date	Relationship With Participants	Theoretical "Framework" or Position in Field of Research	Participants	Data Sources, Duration of Study, and Data Analysis	Impact Claims Examined and Findings
Blanton, M. L., Berenson, S. B., & Norwood, K. S. (2001)	Participant observation	Vygotskian sociocultural theory with an emphasis on discourse analysis	Female student teacher in a middle school paired with a nurturing cooperating teacher	Audio- and videotaped observation followed by an interview followed by a second observation each week, lesson plans, journal, and an exit interview Two clinical interviews with the cooperating teacher Questions and comments entered into transcripts Analysis of conversational turns within changes in the sequence of classroom events. Sections from 4 representative classes were analyzed for routines and patterns with discourse analyzed as univocal or dialogic. Other data sources used for triangulation	Preservice teacher moved from univocal discourse and teacher-provided routines and methods to increased attention to students' problem-solving strategies and mathematical thinking and to greater reliance on dialog and a balance between dialog and transmission. The researchers noted that their presence was an intervention.
Foss, D. H., & Kleinsasser, R. C. (1996)	Participant observation by Foss	Teachers' practical knowledge and beliefs	One male and 21 female elementary-ed preservice teachers (average age 26) Their female methods instructor, a self-defined constructivist	Three interviews during the methods course with preservice teachers and instructor, field notes during the methods course, videotapes of 18 of the preservice teachers teaching, observations, lesson plans, students' written work, course evaluations, survey,	Preservice teachers' views of mathematics as computational applications related to everyday life and to solving problems in class remained unchanged during methods course; they also rejected the methods instructor's emphasis on knowledge construction.

Study	Role	Participants	Framework	Methods	Findings
Briscoe, C., & Stout, D. (1996)	Presumably instructors	Eight male, 54 female elementary-ed majors	References to knowledge construction, the socialization of experience, and knowledge of problem-solving processes	and demographic questionnaire Triangulation across data sources; ETHNOGRAPH used to identify categories of views of mathematical knowledge and pedagogical content knowledge Interviews, portfolios, and problem solutions with accompanying explanations throughout the integrated mathematics–science methods courses Categories were negotiated between instructors and sorted into attitudes toward and knowledge of problem solving and applications to classroom teaching	Preservice teachers believed that children have innate abilities for mathematics and best learn math on their own; they also saw repetition and drill as appropriate teaching techniques. Experience with problem solving increased the students' understanding of the nature of problem solving and confidence in their own problem-solving skills. Solution strategies became more sophisticated over time, and preservice teachers became more favorable toward problem-solving activities as a means toward teaching children science and mathematics.
Steele, D. F., & Widman, T. F. (1997)	Steele was both researcher and instructor.	Five traditional age elementary-ed females were randomly selected for close analysis from among 19 elementary-ed and middle school preservice teachers	Constructivist learning principles with references to conceptual change and to the use of cognitively guided instruction (CGI) to help understand children's thinking	Interviews at the beginning and the end of the methods course, written assignments, math logs, researcher's journals, field notes of observations during course, group-discussion notes Described as a cyclical process of questioning and collecting, recording, and analyzing data (Developmental Research Sequence)	Preservice teachers' understanding of mathematics learning shifted from math as passive through drill and practice to learning as problem solving and exploration of concepts

(Continued)

TABLE 6.2
(Continued)

Authors, Date	Relationship With Participants	Theoretical "Framework" or Position in Field of Research	Participants	Data Sources, Duration of Study, and Data Analysis	Impact Claims Examined and Findings
Steele, D. F. (2001)	Researcher and former instructor	Teacher socialization with references to the framework in the study described previously	Four of the 5 preservice teachers in the previous study, 2 years into their teaching career (and 4 years after the methods course in the previous study)	Data cited previously and an interview after student teaching. Six audio- and videotaped formal interviews with the teachers, informal interviews with the principal and other teachers at the schools, 2 full days of observation, researcher's journal and field notes, lesson plans, questionnaire Themes of personal commitment, professional strength, curriculum, planning, assessment, beliefs, knowledge, and support from school administration were identified.	Two of the teachers had internalized cognitively based strategies, used multiple sources, and evidenced reflection on their teaching. Two became procedure oriented, and instruction was teacher directed and based on textbooks. Administrative and school culture factors were cited as possible explanations for the differences.
Vacc, N. N., & Bright, G. W. (1999)	Vacc was cohort leader and instructor	Beliefs about mathematics instruction in light of interventions based on CGI	Thirty-four elementary-ed preservice teachers were in a 2-year cohort program. Study focused on 2 female students who student-taught in a Professional	CGI Belief Scale administered 4 times across the 2 years, 8 observations during student-teaching, journals, videotaped lessons, and 3 interviews across the 2 years Repeated measures ANOVA with paired *t*-tests to	Both preservice teachers increased in their understanding of CGI principles, became somewhat more constructivist in their orientation, and moved away from teaching as telling. One appeared to use some of the

Study	Focus	Role of researcher	Participants/Setting	Data collection/Analysis	Findings
			Development School (PDS) environment, but only 1 had a cooperating teacher with extensive experience in CGI.	determine change on the Belief Scale Descriptions of lessons during student teaching that described use or nonuse of CGI principles in practice	CGI principles in her instruction; the other did not. The differences in the cooperating teachers' knowledge and implementation of CGI was one possible factor in the participants' differences.
Ebby, C. B. (2000)	Teacher socialization with references to conception of mathematics and mathematics learning	Researcher	One Hispanic American, 1 Korean, and 1 African/Hispanic American female elementary-ed graduate-level preservice teachers, selected as contrasts	Interviews, observations, and document analysis (journals, essays, and course projects) during a 1-semester methods course and 1 semester of student teaching Analytic induction, followed by coding data using constant comparisons between data and assertions, followed by the development of narrative case studies	All began with a view of mathematics teaching as a process of explaining concepts and how to work through problems. Through course activities and fieldwork, all moved away from their initial conceptions, but in different ways. The 2 participants who were confident in math became empowered through the course's emphasis on active engagement with math and diversity in approaches to teaching, although only 1 had multiple opportunities to work this out in practice; the other participant had her negative views of herself as a mathematics learner strengthened through the course, but had her assumptions disconfirmed during fieldwork.

(Continued)

TABLE 6.2
(Continued)

Authors, Date	Relationship With Participants	Theoretical "Framework" or Position in Field of Research	Participants	Data Sources, Duration of Study, and Data Analysis	Impact Claims Examined and Findings
McDevitt, T. M., Troyer, R., Ambrosio, A. L., Heikkinen, H. W., & Warren, E. (1995)	Evaluators of preservice teacher performance in a new model program in elementary-ed mathematics and science—referred to as "project" students	Not acknowledged	Two cohorts of project elementary-ed preservice teachers compared with 2 cohorts of nonproject elementary-ed preservice teachers. The groups were demographically similar, although the project group contained a slightly larger proportion of women. Neither group had a large number of minority students.	A comparison across 8 courses in math, science, educational psychology, and pedagogy using tests of content knowledge and alternative assessments such as questionnaires ANOVA	Project students were no different from controls on content knowledge. Project students also were stronger in inquiry orientation and toward inquiry-oriented teaching and learning strategies; they were also more oriented toward equity.
Frykholm, J. A. (1998)	Program coordinator and organizer of whole-team meetings	Constructivism combined with sociocultural theories	Two male and 1 female secondary-ed undergraduate student teachers Two male and 1 female graduate students in mathematics education, serving	Weekly observations, lesson plans, audiotaped pre- and postlesson conferences, interviews, audiotaped meetings with all participants, journals, and notes from informal conferences Domain analysis organized around semantic	The student teachers felt that their mentors and the whole-group meetings helped them bridge theory and practice. Mentors reported new insights on mathematics education and teacher education. The cooperating teachers became more involved in

368

Citation	Concept / Framework	Role	Participants	Data collection and analysis	Findings
			as mentors and supervisors	relationships, establishing taxonomic relationships within codes and thematic relationships between codes	discussions of reform-based pedagogy and became more open to new ways of teaching.
Kinach, B. M. (2002)	Pedagogical content knowledge; belief transformation	Instructor	Twenty-one secondary education students: 20 preservice, 1 in-service; 16 female, 5 male; 18 undergraduate, 3 graduate	Journals, homework assignments, videotaped classroom discussions Analyzed data using Levels of Understanding framework (coded for content, concept, problem-solving, epistemic, and inquiry-level understanding) after students completed each of 3 tasks; instructor modified approach on Tasks 2 and 3 based on this data analysis.	Through methods course activities, preservice teachers moved from instrumental to relational pedagogical content knowledge.
Langford, K., & Huntley, M. A. (1999)	References to literature on development of content knowledge	Not specified	Seventeen female preservice teachers; 15 traditional-age, 2 older; preparing to teach math and science to Grades 4–8.	Archived listserve discussions; pre- and post-Likert-scale survey on knowledge and beliefs of mathematics and science, including learning, teaching strategies, and importance of; artifacts from orientation, student forum, and presentation day, including preservice teachers' research summaries Used analytical induction for listserve and artifact data: read data, identified themes,	After a summer internship involving collaboration with professional mathematicians and scientists, preservice teachers changed their thinking on the nature of math and science—albeit in individual ways—and became more willing to tolerate ambiguity.

(Continued)

TABLE 6.2
(Continued)

Authors, Date	Relationship With Participants	Theoretical "Framework" or Position in Field of Research	Participants	Data Sources, Duration of Study, and Data Analysis	Impact Claims Examined and Findings
				and coded data in an iterative process. Final themes: nature of math and science; teaching of math and science; nature of the professional workplace. For survey questions: identified questions for which there was the most change over time	
Kelly, C. (2001)	Not specified	Constructivism	Eighty-three elementary-ed preservice teachers (12 male, 71 female) in 2 consecutive semesters of a mathematics and science methods course. Twenty-eight already held baccalaureate degrees; age range from 22 to 52, mean of 30. 37% identified as minorities.	Twenty-item pre- and posttest; individual interviews; informal classroom observations; review of student work Pre- and posttest analyzed using *t*-test; interviews and observations used as secondary data sources	After a 1-semester course that emphasized discipline integration and inquiry, preservice teachers reported feeling more confident about teaching mathematics and science; they also attributed greater importance to the teacher's role and choice of methods, to the use of manipulatives, and to the integration of disciplines.

Harper, N. W., & Daane, C. J. (1998)	Not specified	Review of literature on math anxiety	Fifty-three undergraduate elementary-ed preservice teachers in 3 sections of a mathematics methods course	Ninety-eight item Mathematics Anxiety Rating Scale (MARS) distributed at beginning and end of methods course; checklist on factors influencing mathematics anxiety; reflection on methods course; interviews with 11 participants who showed the greatest differences between their MARS pretest and posttest. Analysis of variance of MARS; noting frequency of answers on other instruments.	Forty-four participants showed a decrease in math anxiety after the course, whereas 9 showed an increase. The course decreased math anxiety through working with peers, using manipulatives, writing about mathematics, and doing fieldwork in an elementary school.
Rahal, B. F., & Melvin, M. J. (1998)	Instructors	References to literature on mathematics discourse	One hundred thirty-nine undergraduate preservice elementary, early childhood, and special education teachers in four 1-semester mathematics methods classes. Twenty-five percent were nontraditional (25 years of age or older)	Journal responses to structured prompts on the teachers' role Assessed journals for knowledge level and level of understanding for discourse instructional strategies and mathematical discourse, using a rubric prepared by the researchers; grouped journal responses by discourse category	During the course, participants showed increased knowledge of the teacher's role in questioning, listening, using writing, providing information and modeling, and initiating and monitoring student participation.

371

TABLE 6.3
Science

Authors, Date	Relationship With Participants	Theoretical "Framework" or Position in Field of Research	Participants	Data Sources, Duration of Study, and Data Analysis	Impact Claims Examined and Findings
Hewson, P. W., Tabachnick, B. R., Zeichner, K. M., Blomker, K. B., Meyer, H., Lemberger, J. (1999)	Researcher (Note: This is the first of 6 articles devoted to 1 large study of a program and provides the details of the study for all of the following articles. The first 5 are summarized in this table. The last one (Hewson, Tabachnick, Zeichner, & Lemberger, 1999) summarizes across the first 5 and is not included).	Constructivist learning with references to teaching for conceptual change and to reflective practice and action research	Two cohorts of students in the elementary-ed and secondary-ed science education programs at 1 university. There were no minority students. There were only a few males in elementary-ed, but secondary-ed was more evenly balanced between males and females. Elementary-ed students were mostly traditional age; two thirds of secondary-ed students were traditional age Methods instructors	Field notes and some audio and videotapes of observations in methods courses plus an action research seminar for 11 elementary-ed and 8 secondary-ed students (There was a comparison elementary-ed group that did not take the action research seminar, but no comparison group for secondary-ed) in a practicum, and during student teaching (which paralleled the action research seminar). Written documents from the action research seminar students (journals, action research projects, and instructor comments) Interviews with methods instructors Interviews with preservice teachers at the beginning of the methods course and at the end of student teaching	See following

(one on ideas about teaching science and one on biological concepts)

When possible, there was a 3rd interview after full-time teaching had begun

Teaching observations during practicum and student teaching

Conceptions of teaching science interviews with preservice teachers were coded as science, learning, instruction, and teaching, entered into Ethnograph and organized by preservice teacher views, then themes representing relationships between categories were identified.

Biology interviews analyzed for content knowledge, conceptual ecology, and affective responses—again using Ethnograph.

Audiotapes were analyzed for affective responses.

Methods instructor interviews were analyzed for goals and expectations and summarized by answer.

Course and seminar observations were analyzed

(Continued)

TABLE 6.3
(Continued)

Authors, Date	Relationship With Participants	Theoretical "Framework" or Position in Field of Research	Participants	Data Sources, Duration of Study, and Data Analysis	Impact Claims Examined and Findings
				for activities that were representative of practice or that were significant events and used to identify opportunities for preservice teachers to learn about teaching for conceptual change. Two observations during the practicum and 2 during student teaching were analyzed in terms of significant features of conceptual change teaching noted. Written documents from action research seminar analyzed for features of conceptual change	
Marion, R., Hewson, P. W., Tabachnick, B. R., & Blomker, K. B. (1999)	Researcher	See previous	See previous	See previous	Both the elementary-ed and secondary-ed preservice teachers had many opportunities to observe conceptual change lessons modeled by the methods instructor and conceptual

				change lessons were planned by students. The elementary-ed students saw lessons start to finish; the secondary-ed students did not, but had more resources available to them. The elementary-ed preservice teachers may not have had many opportunities to see science lessons in classrooms, and opportunities to teach science lessons were also limited. For both groups, opportunities to put plans and ideas into practice were limited.
Tabachnick, B. R., & Zeichner, K. M. (1999)	Instructors	See previous	See previous	See previous	Versions of some elements of conceptual change teaching were present in the 1st-semester cohort but not in the 2nd-semester cohort of the action research seminar. Although all students collected data on and were interested in students' thinking, they did not use that knowledge to move from a transmissionist view of teaching.

(Continued)

TABLE 6.3
(Continued)

Authors, Date	Relationship With Participants	Theoretical "Framework" or Position in Field of Research	Participants	Data Sources, Duration of Study, and Data Analysis	Impact Claims Examined and Findings
Meyer, H., Tabachnick, B. R., Hewson, P. W., Lemberger, J., & Park, H.-J. (1999)	Researcher	See previous	Focus on 3 female elementary-ed preservice teachers (1 traditional-age undergraduate; 2 nontraditional)	See previous	One preservice teacher retained views of science as information to be discovered through observation and remembered, but there was some change in her willingness to listen to students' ideas and accept differences.
One preservice teacher moved somewhat from a view of science as facts to a more ambiguous idea of what science is, but teaching as the presentation of information stayed constant.
One preservice teacher began with a view of learning as reciprocal and, even though she treated the curriculum as given, she encouraged discussion. She moved to a more complex view of how to construct her role and her students' roles in developing conceptual change teaching,

| Lemberger, J., Hewson, P. W., & Park, H.-J. (1999) | Researcher | See previous | Focus on 3 female traditional-age secondary-ed preservice teachers | See previous | but her teaching itself did not change. |

One preservice teacher began with an idea of science as teaching facts, but moved somewhat more to a conceptual change orientation in terms of being more aware of her students' conceptions—but with no ideas on how to help them revise them.

One preservice teacher began with the idea of teaching science as getting students to think and giving knowledge to students, but began to diagnose students' conceptions—although with no idea of how to implement conceptual change teaching.

One preservice teacher began with a view of teaching science as making ideas interesting and developed 3 facets of conceptual change teaching over time—but still felt responsible for moving students toward the right answer.

(Continued)

TABLE 6.3
(Continued)

Authors, Date	Relationship With Participants	Theoretical "Framework" or Position in Field of Research	Participants	Data Sources, Duration of Study, and Data Analysis	Impact Claims Examined and Findings
Palmquist, B. C., & Finley, F. N. (1997)	Palmquist was the teaching assistant for 2 methods courses and practica; Finley's role is not specified.	References to conceptual change and differing views on nature of science	Fifteen secondary-ed graduate-level preservice science teachers from 23 to 45 years old. Sixty percent had experience in science related work.	Survey and interview prior to the beginning of the methods course and practicum and after the 1st methods course; work samples (including lesson plans and journals); in-depth interview with 8 students before and after the 2nd methods course and practicum Surveys, interviews, lesson plans, and curriculum coded for contemporary or traditional views of science and examined for change over time	Mixed views on the nature of science at the beginning of the program, with 9 out of 15 moving toward a more contemporary (i.e., postpositivist) view of science at the end of the program. Two, however, became more traditional in their views.
Shapiro, B. L. (1996)	Instructor	Differing views on the nature of science with some references to the language of science and to changes in personal constructs	Thirty-four female, 4 male elementary-ed student teachers; 12 were graduate students. The article focuses on 1 female as an examplar.	Repertory grids were constructed by 38 preservice teachers at the beginning and end of the methods course. Twenty-one of these were interviewed. One female and her partner were selected as an example. Repertory grids and interviews were analyzed for change over time.	Preservice teacher began with little confidence in her ability to teach science, but became more knowledgeable of scientific terms and project oriented in her teaching.

| Anderson, L. M., Smith, D. C., & Peasley, K. (2000) | Researchers | Cognitive theory with references to conceptual change | Two female Caucasian, elementary-ed undergraduates, 1 Caucasian male elementary-ed graduate | Observations of university classrooms for the 1st year of a 2-year program (coursework and practica), conversations with program faculty, 10 interviews across the year Journals, 1 interview, lesson plans, and conversations during the student-teaching semester the following year Observations and conversations served only as background information. Interviews were analyzed for instructional responsibilities emphasized in the program. Each responsibility was coded separately for each student and individual; chronological case studies were developed. | One female began with an image of science as learner centered, but her early teaching was teacher directed. By the 2nd semester, she became more concerned about learners' cognitive activity, but still fell back on teacher-centered instruction. By the end of the year she began to struggle with knowing how students learned. One female began with an image of teaching as entertaining, and her early teaching emphasized students as active responders. By the end of the year she began to attribute learning to students' experiences and the construction of meaning. The male continuously complained about the teacher education program and began with a teacher-centered model of instruction. He moved to a model of engaging student interest, but still believed that the teacher was the primary source of knowledge. |

(Continued)

379

TABLE 6.3
(Continued)

Authors, Date	Relationship With Participants	Theoretical "Framework" or Position in Field of Research	Participants	Data Sources, Duration of Study, and Data Analysis	Impact Claims Examined and Findings
					The 2 females did well in student teaching and obtained jobs in a nearby district. The male student taught at a grade level outside of his practicum preparation and spent little time on science; he was evaluated as satisfactory. He did not seek a job immediately because he was still in school.
Bryan, L. A., & Abell, S. K. (1999)	Researcher, but worked with the methods instructor to design a conceptual change oriented curriculum	Cognitive theory with references to the complexity of learning from experience, socialization theory, and constructivist learning theory	One female undergraduate elementary-ed preservice teacher	Written reflections, audiotapes of 5 large and small group discussions, 6 interviews during the methods class Observations of her 1st student-teaching placement, interviews throughout both placements Written summaries throughout the study were shared with the preservice teacher. Data coded for experiences that influenced thinking, beliefs, tensions, and analytical frames	Preservice teacher developed greater self-knowledge of her beliefs and how her practice was not consistent with those beliefs. These became more consistent over time, but practice was much more difficult than thinking about the way one should teach.

| Zembal-Saul, C., Blumenfeld, P., & Krajcik, J. (2000) | Zembal-Saul was the university supervisor; Blumenfeld taught the educational psychology course; Krajcik taught the science methods course. | Pedagogical content knowledge—specifically the ability to represent content knowledge—and literature on reflection | Two (1 teaching pair) elementary-ed undergraduate female preservice teachers | Planning data, videotapes of classroom teaching with audiotaped debriefings, written lesson plans, and reflections for 2 semesters of the methods course and practicum
A framework organized data by the representation of science concepts and consideration of the learner's needs. Interviews and teaching episodes were coded and summarized with comparisons across 2 teaching cycles | Content representation improved over time, as did the preservice teachers' ability to support learners and ask questions. In both cycles they were able to identify strengths and weaknesses. Developing knowledge of learners appeared to impact changes in content representation. |
| Adams, P. E., & Krockover, G. H. (1997) | Researcher | Cognitive theory with an emphasis on the development of knowledge with references to constructivism and to pedagogical content knowledge | Three male, 1 female secondary-ed science teachers who had graduated from the same teacher education program
Two science education faculty (1 female, 1 male) | Teachers' Pedagogical Philosophy Interview given twice to each participant, observation of teaching with post-observation interviews, classroom documents, videotapes of classroom interaction collected during the 1st, 2nd, or 3rd year of classroom teaching
Videotapes analyzed using the Secondary Science Teachers Analysis Matrix, daily inductive analysis of observations and interviews, identification of knowledge structures. Faculty data were | Methods courses cited as sources of instructional strategies, but the teachers varied in the degree to which they had developed a framework for teaching. One course was consistently cited as a source for knowledge of classroom control.
Two students reported no program resources for management routine; 2 reported on experiences as undergraduate teaching assistants as helpful—even though the program did |

(Continued)

TABLE 6.3
(Continued)

Authors, Date	Relationship With Participants	Theoretical "Framework" or Position in Field of Research	Participants	Data Sources, Duration of Study, and Data Analysis	Impact Claims Examined and Findings
				similarly analyzed. Triangulation and searches for disconfirming evidence across data sources, development of cases and cross-case analysis	provide such instruction. Three teachers credited the methods course for knowledge of student centered learning. Generally, methods courses seemed to confirm teachers' prior beliefs.
Kelly, J. (2000)	Not specified	Constructivism with references to national science standards	Two hundred thirty elementary-ed students in 9 different sections of the science methods course over 4 years: 11 male (1 minority), 219 female (9 minorities) Elementary-ed preservice teacher	Pre–post questionnaires on attitudes toward science, confidence in teaching, and understanding of pedagogical knowledge and teaching strategies; pre–post tests on content knowledge and pedagogy; course assignments; interviews with program graduates who were teaching Percentages of responses were tabulated for the questionnaires and assessments, percentage of unit plans meeting criteria. No information on the number or analysis of the interviews with graduates	The percentage reporting positive attitudes, confidence in teaching science, and knowledge of science and pedagogical strategies improved from the pre- to postassessment. Practicing teachers reported using materials obtained from the course.

Stofflett, R. T., & Stefanon, L. (1996)	Stofflett was the instructor (but this was not disclosed in the article).	Constructivism	Seventy-six elementary-ed preservice teachers in the same course at 2 different universities, taught by the same instructor	Reflective writing assessing their own performance on a lesson they taught in conjunction with their methods course and concurrent practicum Master list of preservice teachers' success criteria was created and then grouped into teacher- and student-oriented factors. Independently coded and all discrepancies were negotiated to consensus.	The majority of preservice teachers defined success as children's learning of content, positive attitudes, on task behavior, attainment of objectives, and a positive evaluation from a cooperating teacher or supervisor. Only 25% of preservice teachers saw conceptual change (the focus of the course) as a success criterion.
Greenwood, A. (1996)	Researcher instructor	Teachers' content knowledge and constructivism	Twenty-three elementary-ed graduate students: 22 females, 1 male	Pre- and delayed test of preservice teachers' knowledge of density after being taught using the Density Constructivist Teaching Sequence and journals throughout the methods course Paired *t*-tests comparing students' pre- and postscores. No information on how the journals were analyzed	Although there was improvement in mean scores on knowledge of density, as many as 19 out of 23 showed no firm evidence of conceptual change. Preservice teachers reported feeling more confident about teaching science.
McGinnis, J. R., & Pearsall, M. (1998)	McGinnis was the instructor engaged in a self-study; Pearsall, his co-researcher.	Symbolic interaction theory with references to gender differences between a male professor and female students	One male professor and 2 African-American, 6 White, 1 Chinese-American female, and 4 White male (out of 28 total, with 23 female) elementary-ed	Co-researcher interviewed the instructor and the preservice teachers at the beginning of the semester and a subset of the female students at the end of the semester; she observed all classes; the instructor and preservice	McGinnis felt that his attempts to be very gender inclusive were uncomfortable for the males. The females noted his attempts, and some (but not all) appreciated them, but he felt that he could have done much more.

(Continued)

383

TABLE 6.3
(Continued)

Authors, Date	Relationship With Participants	Theoretical "Framework" or Position in Field of Research	Participants	Data Sources, Duration of Study, and Data Analysis	Impact Claims Examined and Findings
			students in his science methods class	teachers kept journals. Formal course evaluations were also used. Analytic induction was used to categorize interviews by item, and separate accounts were written by each researcher. These accounts were shared with selected preservice teachers as a form of member checking.	Pearsall felt that the gender of the professor was not important to the students, but that male preservice teachers have different expectations of the science class climate. Even when they noted gender bias, preservice teachers seldom speak out; they also believe that females process science information differently from males. Member checks suggested that the students felt uncomfortable by being part of the study—that it diverted attention from the focus of teaching science.
Tobin, K., Seiler, G., & Smith, M. W. (1999)	Tobin was the teacher educator; Seiler, the doctoral student and supervisor; Smith, the	Hermeneutic, phenomenological theory with references to theories of habitus and cultural capital	One male professor; 1 female doctoral student and supervisor; and 1 male graduate secondary-ed student teacher	Field notes, narratives on field experiences, artifacts, interviews, and assistance from a student as a participant on the research team. The article is a conversation (metalog), based on the data,	Co-teaching (in which the methods instructor, cooperating teacher, student teacher, and others plan and teach in the same class) moved methods classes from talk to action, and the problems of enactment are

		student teacher	about the methods course and the role of the cooperating teacher.	shared and discussed across participants. The issue of quality as it relates to any one participant becomes increasingly irrelevant as all became learners with one another.
Tobin, K., Roth, W.-M., & Zimmer-mann, A. (2001)	Hermeneutic, phenomenological theory with references to theories of cultural capital	One male professor; 1 male external participant and researcher; 1 female, graduate, secondary-ed student teacher. Tobin was the teacher educator and supervisor; Roth, the external researcher; and Zimmermann, the student teacher	Videotapes, recorded debriefings, videotapes of the analysis sessions, journals, e-mail, face-to-face interactions during student teaching. Recursive dialogical analysis and discussion of data as a base for further action. Part of the article focuses on 1 lesson and presents a multivocal interpretation of that lesson, followed by a metalog on the co-teaching experience in general.	In the lesson example, gaps within 1 teacher's instruction were supplemented by another's. All co-teachers debriefed the lesson and talked about where to go next (short term and long term). The metalog on co-teaching represented the different and complex interpretations of the participants.
Nichols, S. E., & Tobin, K. (2000)	Discursive practices and co-participatory learning experiences, with some references to situated learning	One female, elementary-ed undergraduate, her cooperating teacher, and the supervisor—all in a PDS. Nichols was the university supervisor; Tobin's relationship is not specified	Observations and interviews throughout student teaching with some participation by the supervisor, teacher-learning environment questionnaire, journals by the preservice teacher and the supervisor. Narrative construction of a case summary	Instead of the creation of a learning community during student teaching, the preservice teacher and cooperating teacher carried out separate responsibilities and tasks.

(Continued)

TABLE 6.3
(Continued)

Authors, Date	Relationship With Participants	Theoretical "Framework" or Position in Field of Research	Participants	Data Sources, Duration of Study, and Data Analysis	Impact Claims Examined and Findings
Settlage, J. (2000)	Not specified	Efficacy theory	Seventy-six elementary-ed students in 2 different methods courses	Science Teaching Efficacy Beliefs Inventory and the Zuckerman Affect Adjective Checklist completed before and after the methods course *t*-tests	Overall improvement in teaching efficacy and reduction in science anxiety after methods course
Sillman, K., Dana, T., & Miller, M. (2000)	Sillman was the science methods instructor; Dana was a researcher; Miller, the teacher	Socialization theory with references to situated learning	One male elementary-ed major followed into his 1st year of teaching	Twelve formal and informal interviews, 20 reflective journals, 15 pieces of reflective writing, collected during the final year of the teacher education program and the 1st year of full-time teaching Inductive approach to developing an interpretive case study, with an external researcher to increase validity and reliability	Teacher was able to put his beliefs into practice in his 1st year of teaching, using reflection and inquiry to analyze classroom actions, in part because his colleagues and roommate shared his philosophy of teaching and learning.
Jarrett, O. S. (1998)	Not specified	References to inquiry science and playfulness	Thirty-six elementary-ed undergraduate preservice teachers,	Survey given at the end of the methods course that asked participants to rate the course activities on levels of	Preservice teachers reported an intention to use activities rated highly on fun, interest, and learning potential.

Citation	Framework / Role	Participants	Methods / Data	Findings
		most with weak backgrounds in science	fun, interest, and learning; and rate which activities they would use. Two quarters later, after student teaching, participants reported on science activities implemented during student teaching. Correlations of rating of activities with intentions to use them. Frequencies reported for activities used during student teaching	Activities they reported using were cooking, plant observation and classification, and activities with the senses and magnets. There was no clear connection between activities considered fun in the course and activities implemented in student teaching.
Abell, S., Martini, M., & George, M. (2001)	References to literature on the nature of science. Abell and George were instructors (acknowledged self-study); Martini was a participant-observer.	Eleven elementary-ed preservice teachers in 2 sections of a science methods course	Field notes of class sessions; audiotape of small group discussions; student journals and written reflections; interviews. Research team iteratively read the dataset to search for common patterns; analyzed data according to features of the nature of science (empirically based; subjective; involves invention; socially and culturally embedded). Student journals used for triangulation	After doing an extensive moon investigation project, preservice teachers better understood the nature of science as empirically based. They were able to invent explanations and work socially themselves, but did not articulate these as activities of scientists. Instructors realized that they did not explicitly help students make connections between the students' activities in class and the nature of science and scientists' activities.

TABLE 6.4
Social Studies

Authors, Date	Relationship With Participants	Theoretical "Framework" or Position in Field of Research	Participants	Data Sources, and Duration of Study	Impact Claims Examined and Findings
Wilson, E. K., & Saleh, A. (2000)	Wilson was clinical master teacher coordinator; Saleh, assistant coordinator (presumably at the same time).	References to the student teaching supervision literature	Four secondary teachers (1 African-American and 2 Caucasian females; 1 Caucasian male) serving as school-based clinical master teachers	Questionnaires, observations and assessment forms, and meeting minutes for 1 year, plus a final interview Constant comparative analysis for patterns, triangulated across the research team and across data sources.	Participation in the Clinical Master Teacher program gave teachers a greater ownership of the entire process of supervision; enabled examination of philosophical links and discrepancies between the school and university. There was no real change in communication styles. They reported feeling that their knowledge was respected by the university community.
Slick, S. K. (1998b)	Researcher and participant observer	References to the student teaching supervision literature	One female supervisor (taught public school 1 year, college 4 years) One female secondary-ed student teacher One male cooperating teacher (36 years' teaching experience)	Interviews with preservice teacher, cooperating teacher, and supervisor; transcript of conferences and the student-teaching seminar; and informal discussions Constant comparative analysis resulting in a case study	The university supervisor had no background in the content area, no guidance from the university, and the ambiguity surrounding expectations resulted in feelings of isolation, an unwillingness to be an interventionist, and in letting the student teacher resolve her own problems with the cooperating teacher. She tried to support the cooperating teacher while counseling the student teacher.

Slekar, T. D. (1998)	Researcher did not discuss	Teacher socialization, with references to an apprenticeship of observation and reflexive conservatism in P–16 education	One female preservice undergraduate and 1 "nontraditional" (older, career change) male preservice undergraduate; both elementary-ed	Three interviews recalling the preservice teachers' instruction in school and the university and current conceptions of teaching and learning social studies, conducted at the end of the teacher education program that occurred during the 1st semester of their senior year Data were categorized by recollections, anticipating approaches, and indications of reflexive tendencies.	Relationship between earlier educational experiences and current thoughts on teaching. Both preservice teachers recalled objectivist-style presentations of history and didactic teaching, but questioned this approach and indicated that they would teach differently from the way they were taught—a view reinforced by teaching internships and exposure to resources.
Fehn, B., & Koeppen, K. E. (1998)	Not specified	Teacher socialization with references to the development of pedagogical content knowledge	Nine preservice undergraduates; 2 preservice postbaccalaureate students: 7 male, 4 female, all Caucasian (presumably secondary-ed)	Interviews completed after student teaching; lesson plans during student teaching; reflections written during the student-teaching seminar Interviews, lesson plans, and reflections analyzed for references to attitudes toward and use of primary sources and for credit to the methods course for either.	All used primary sources at least once to enliven classes or supplement texts and to give students practice in interpreting documents. Even though they were enthusiastic, they felt constrained by time, lack of school support, or student response or ability. Credit for use was given to the methods instructor and course.
Koeppen, K. E. (1998)	Researcher—any role as instructor not discussed.	Student teacher planning with references to differences between experts and novices and to the literature	Study referenced 6 participants, but only 1 case study (Anglo-American male preservice secondary-ed	Interviews, think-aloud protocols, questionnaires, journals, lesson plans and teaching observations during the student teaching semester	Perceptions of instructional planning and planning activities seemed to be guided by a metaphor of teaching as performing a monologue, with few

(Continued)

TABLE 6.4
(Continued)

Authors, Date	Relationship With Participants	Theoretical "Framework" or Position in Field of Research	Participants	Data Sources, and Duration of Study	Impact Claims Examined and Findings
		on teacher socialization	undergrad) is presented.	Dataset analyzed for recurrent themes and patterns and then summarized by case. Reported out as planning experiences and the metaphors that guided the student teacher's planning.	attempts to actively engage students. This was based on his prior schooling experiences and his cooperating teacher's style and was in contradiction to his methods course (which emphasized student-centered instruction). Planning was also constrained by content coverage and time constraints imposed by cooperating teacher. No flexibility or versatility was built into plans.
Angell, A. V. (1998)	Researcher taking the role of participant observer	Cognitive theory with an emphasis on teacher cognition and domain-specific beliefs and references to the constructivist process of learning to teach	Two female White, middle-class, elementary-ed undergraduates	Reflective writing, teaching observations, interviews, concept maps of social studies for 1 semester that included methods courses and student teaching Case summaries compiled from analysis of recurrent expressions, episodic memories, metaphorical language, etc., as indicators of beliefs and then shared	Through coursework and student teaching, 1 preservice teacher reinforced her beliefs about creating meaningful activities for pupils but added the importance of reflection and critique. Beliefs about social studies began to emphasize a more global perspective. One preservice teacher retained beliefs about the

Study	Context	References	Participants	Methods	Findings
				with participants. Comparison across cases for changes and connections between changes and attributions to the teacher education program	importance of correct answers and moved away from beliefs about emphasizing tolerance and appreciation for diversity.
Dinkelman, T. (1999)	Acknowledged, purposeful study of his efforts as the course instructor to promote critical reflection	References to critical reflection and to democratic practice. Teacher socialization research is also mentioned.	One Euro-American undergraduate female and 2 postgraduate Euro-American males, one of whom was over 40; all secondary-ed	Interviews, observations of work and class participation, field notes and assignments during a 1-semester methods course that also included a field assignment. Discussion of his intentions and practices were presented. Data from students were categorized into topics and actions evaluated as critical reflection and triangulated across data sources, followed by construction of case summaries.	Extent, nature, development of critical reflection, and commitment to democratic education were evidenced in 2 subthemes: democratic education and rationales for social studies. All of the preservice teachers showed evidence of understanding and practicing critical reflection, but the course emphasis on critical democracy did not make much of an impact.
Dinkelman, T. (2000)	Instructor and student-teaching supervisor	Critical reflective teaching	The same students as previously cited	Interviews, classroom observations, field notes, and written artifacts during the student-teaching semester. Constant comparative analysis of evidence of critical reflection, critically reflective teaching, social studies rationales, and democratic education resulted in case	All of the preservice teachers showed evidence of understanding and practicing critical reflection, in part because of interactions with the researcher and supervisor. They all engaged in active teaching during student teaching and began to develop a somewhat

(Continued)

TABLE 6.4
(Continued)

Authors, Date	Relationship With Participants	Theoretical "Framework" or Position in Field of Research	Participants	Data Sources, and Duration of Study	Impact Claims Examined and Findings
				summaries for each preservice teacher, followed by cross-case analysis.	stronger emphasis on democratic education. One preservice teacher's critical reflection was restricted by lack of time and her limited subject matter understanding; another preservice teacher's critical thinking may not have influenced his practice, perhaps because of classroom difficulties and his overconfidence in his reflective abilities.
Donahue, D. M. (1999)	Instructor	Moral and political foundations for service learning	Four female, White middle-class undergraduates (presumably secondary-ed)	Reflective writing, curriculum plans, field notes, and interviews with field-based educators and administrators for 1 semester Analyzed for examples of dilemmas and then connected to belief statements, experiences, and the teacher education program	Curriculum written for the Third World Women's Center provided evidence that students became more competent on how to address issues of race and class and not put pupils at risk as a result of the project. They attained a higher degree of understanding links between advocacy and action and they wrestled with the ethical role of the

Donahue, D. M. (2000)	Instructor	Personal, practical knowledge and a continued emphasis on the political foundations for service learning	Two female White middle-class secondary-ed undergraduates—1 may have been in the earlier study	Reflective writing, audiotaped class discussions, interviews, curriculum developed by the preservice teachers over 1 year. Coded for experiences; context; and purpose, method, and meaning of beliefs about service. Written as case summaries. Thoughtful discussion of safeguards against biasing the data	teacher in addressing moral and political issues. One preservice teacher embraced an activist, change-oriented approach to service learning and used it extensively in student teaching in part because of her family history, the methods course, and the receptiveness of her cooperating teacher. One defined service learning as charity, based in part because of camp counselor experiences and early career experiences. She did not use service learning in student teaching in part because of lack of support from her team.
Hohenbrink, J., Johnston, M., & Westhoven, L. (1997)	Self-study by all 3 participants	Poststructural feminist; interpretive and hermeneutic theories	University-based and field-based instructors in a social studies methods course: 1 university faculty, 1 graduate student, and 1 classroom teacher—all female (presumably secondary-ed)	Tapes of conversations, journals, and group interviews for 4 years. Periodic, joint analysis of data for themes and changes in understandings, which guided future conversations	Co-teaching over time resulted in diminished competition for whose knowledge counts and a concurrent increase in the trusting and valuing of one another's knowledge. Fear of one another also decreased.

393

TABLE 6.5
PDS Partnerships and General Supervision

Authors, Date	Relationship With Participants	Theoretical "Framework" or Position in Field of Research	Participants	Data Sources, and Duration of Study	Impact Claims Examined and Findings
Gill, B., & Hove, A. (February, 2000)	External evaluators	Not stated	Preservice teachers from West Virginia University (WVU); the pupils in their classes, grades 5–11; and pupils in comparison schools.	ACT scores, High School GPA, and WVU GPA on all WVU preservice teachers, plus impressions on their abilities from the PDS sites. Stanford 9 scores, ACT scores for PDS and non-PDS pupils. Interviews, observations, meeting notes, and surveys of PDS staff	Preservice teachers in the new, PDS program had higher high school GPAs and WVU GPAs than those in the old program. Gain scores on the Stanford 9 for pupils in the PDS schools showed higher basic skills gains and math gains. There was no difference in reading gains. Pupils who transferred in to PDS schools at the beginning of high school showed higher math gains than those who remained in non-PDS schools. Longer term analysis of older PDSs suggests higher ACT scores. PDS teachers felt empowered and respected. Parental learning opportunities increased. Collaborative research with WVU faculty and PDS faculty happened at only a few PDSs.
Blocker, L. S., & Mantle-Bromley, C. (1997)	Unknown	Cites literature on PDS evaluations and self-efficacy theory	Secondary-ed preservice teachers, both graduate and undergraduate: 22 (14 male) from	One structured interview using open-ended questions—by a researcher not involved with teaching or supervising preservice	Preservice teachers in the PDS were more involved with and in a greater variety of field experiences; were more satisfied with the program

Citation	Role	Theoretical framework	Participants	Methods	Findings
			the first PDS cohort; 20 (11 male) from the traditional program	teachers—with each participant; use of purposive sampling to achieve data redundancy Responses categorized under each of 5 interview questions for the 2 groups of participants	and confident in their teaching, and made more connections between theory and practice. Negatives for the PDS preservice teachers included stress as well as conflicts among PDS staff and between PDS and university staff. Traditional-program preservice teachers most valued their microteaching course and asked for more hands-on experiential learning; they cited fewer examples of using theory in classroom practice.
Grisham, D. L., Laguardia, A., & Brink, B. (2000)	Participant observers; exact role in program not specified	Constructivist; also cites NCTAF and literature on collaboration	Five female elementary graduate-level preservice teachers, traditional age and older	Interviews at 3 points during the PDS year; comparison interviews with 5 preservice teachers at non-PDS schools; classroom journals; classroom observations and some videotapes; audiotapes of steering committee meetings; action research projects of preservice teachers and their teachers Triangulation within and across data sources and search for disconfirming evidence	Preservice teachers identified 8 factors that make a quality student teaching experience within a PDS setting: yearlong experience and feeling like a part of the school; clustering of preservice teachers for a support system; on-site literacy classes; participation in teacher study groups and action research; enhanced supervision; communication as a function of the Steering Committee; potential of having 2 different placements at the PDS; status as "co-teacher."

TABLE 6.5
(Continued)

Authors, Date	Relationship With Participants	Theoretical "Framework" or Position in Field of Research	Participants	Data Sources, and Duration of Study	Impact Claims Examined and Findings
Mantle-Bromley, C., Gould, L. M., McWhorter, B. A., & Whaley, D. C. (2000)	Unknown	Reference to literature on PDSs	One hundred fifty-two program completers who could be located and agreed to be interviewed: 79 undergrads in the traditional program (mean age: 31); 36 undergrads in the 1-semester PDS experience, within the traditional program (26); 37 grads in the 10 month postbaccalaureate program (34.5)	Thirty-six-question telephone interview, conducted between 1.5 and 3 years after graduation: mostly forced-choice, on job search characteristics, employment status, future plans, factors in attrition, and program satisfaction Descriptive statistics of employment patterns: chi-square analysis of program route and employment status and of actual employment in teaching; one-way ANOVA to assess program satisfaction	Study is limited in scope of comparison because of the numbers not interviewed. 78% of those interviewed were working for a school system; only 58% as full-time teachers. Graduates of postbaccalaureate program were most satisfied with the program and were most likely to still be teaching or working in schools; PDS came next; traditional undergrad was least. No differences found in job satisfaction, number of jobs held, or numbers who were seeking new employment.
Stanulis, R. N. (1995)	Unknown	Social constructivism Focus on collaboration, reflective practice, and mentoring	Five Caucasian female elementary teachers and their student teachers	Mentor and student teacher dyads videotaped up to 8 times each over 5 months during conferences about language arts; these videotapes used in stimulated recall interviews Seven standardized open-ended interviews with	Teachers drew from 3 main sources of knowledge: the PDS, the teacher education program, and their classroom teaching. They modeled reflection and encouraged preservice teachers to reflect; they also reflected about their own

Study		Literature	Participants	Data/Methods	Findings
				each participant; observation data from mentor and preservice teacher conferences and PDS seminars Data across the 5 cases were examined to define 3 categories (views about learning; sources of knowledge; nature of reflection). Themes were then labeled; data were coded per the themes.	work with the preservice teachers. Their views on mentoring included helping the preservice teachers become independent thinkers; matching their philosophy with instruction; connecting the subject matter with children; and seeing student teachers as colleagues. Four teachers played prominent roles as teacher educators and developed collaborative relationships with preservice teachers and university faculty. One teacher felt that her teaching wasn't affected by the PDS or the teacher education program.
Walling, B., & Lewis, M. (2000)	First author was a PDS instructor; second author was the PDS coordinator	Cites literature on professional development of teachers	Twenty-six elementary-ed preservice teachers in the PDS's 1st cohort A comparison group of randomly selected elementary volunteers in the traditional teacher ed program	Open-ended questionnaires in 1st semester, end of 3rd semester, and end of student teaching (4th and final) semester; questions asked about significant issues facing American education, characteristics of a professional educator, their own motives for becoming a teacher, and professional goals for next 10 years.	Preservice teachers in the PDS were more aware of systemic issues in education (e.g., school funding; testing procedures) and saw professional educators as multidimensional. Their goals shifted from "job" to "career" and they placed increased emphasis on caring for students and teaching.

(Continued)

TABLE 6.5
(Continued)

Authors, Date	Relationship With Participants	Theoretical "Framework" or Position in Field of Research	Participants	Data Sources, and Duration of Study	Impact Claims Examined and Findings
				Responses to questions listed, sorted into categories, frequencies calculated, and presented by category over time	Preservice teachers in the traditional program had less focus on systemic issues; identified personal characteristics as most important for professional educators; and maintained their "job" orientation.
Wiseman, D. L., & Nason, P. L. (1995)	Unknown	Cites literature on school–university partnerships	Middle-school teachers and principal, university faculty, grad students Two cohorts of middle-school preservice teachers (25 in the first cohort, 14 in the second)	Audiotaped small and larger group evaluation discussions, observations of curriculum planning and teaching, minutes, journals, interviews with key members of the partnership; data collected over a 2-year period The researchers separately grouped responses from the evaluation meetings, then met to agree on categorizations. Themes (personal and professional development; collaboration and communication; curricular restructuring; resources) were elaborated from other data sources.	Teachers and university faculty slowly developed trust during 2 years, although teachers often felt left out of the university's planning process. Allocating money and space in the school was a source of frustration. Teachers came to value the interdisciplinary units created through the partnership. Preservice teachers valued relationships with teachers, faculty, and pupils; collaboration and teamwork with teachers; and the field-based experience. Teachers and preservice teachers seemed to bond

Allexsaht-Snider, M., Deegan, J. G., & White, C. S. (1995)	Review of literature on partnerships and collaboration	Three cohorts of early childhood preservice teachers, aged 21-35: 8 European-Americans, 7 female; 11 Euro-American females; 21 Euro-American females, 1 African-American female Seventeen cooperating teachers for the 3rd cohort, at 3 schools Early childhood faculty and supervisors in program, and members of partnership	Data collected from preservice teachers: focused interviews; open-ended questionnaires in the 1st and 3rd quarters of the program; daily journal entries; meeting minutes. Questionnaires for cooperating teachers Speculative analysis; analysis of journals, surveys, questionnaires with triangulation across sources and across individuals Analysis of discrepant examples	closer with one another than either did with faculty; teachers valued having a preservice teacher as a "team player" in their classrooms. Preservice teachers were sometimes catalysts in enhancing faculty–teacher relationships. Two phases in the university–school partnership were identified: partial alignment initially, then expanded collaboration between both sites. Communication improved over time; roles for cooperating teachers and university faculty were reconceptualized. School and university influenced each other. University faculty and preservice teachers influenced school's literacy practices; then school's focus on developing new assessments and its constructivist and child-centered practices influenced the university. Preservice teachers saw fits and discontinuities between

(Continued)

TABLE 6.5
(Continued)

Authors, Date	Relationship With Participants	Theoretical "Framework" or Position in Field of Research	Participants	Data Sources, and Duration of Study	Impact Claims Examined and Findings
					university course work and schools; partnership saw discontinuities as opportunities for growth. At the end of their student teaching, preservice teachers felt prepared to teach reading and language arts, but had concerns about ability grouping, multicultural education, and special education because of discontinuities and lack of modeling.
Bullough, R. V., Jr., Hobbs, S. F., Kauchak, D. P., Crow, N. A., & Stokes, D. (1997)	Unknown	Review of literature on PDSs and clinical faculty (current or former K–12 classroom teachers)	Twelve faculty (including department chair; dean; 3 clinical faculty members; and faculty from the major divisions within the teacher education program)	Audiotaped interviews using protocol to explore the department's increasing reliance on clinical faculty in the teacher-ed program Five-person research team collectively identified patterns and themes from the interview data.	Discipline-driven researchers were concerned about perceived high cost of PDSs and that the department had lost theoretical rigor. They believed that teacher-ed is not related to their work. Field-focused researchers' initial involvement in the PDS waned because of university and professional reward structure. They realized importance of clinical faculty, but believed

Author/Year			Sample	Method	Findings
					that good teacher-ed programs require tenure-line faculty too. Clinical faculty members felt like second-class citizens, questioned university priorities and withdrawal of tenure-line faculty from PDS. They took great pride in their work and believed they had improved preservice teacher-ed. Junior tenure-line faculty believed that discipline-driven researchers do not value teacher-ed research or service of any kind, including PDS work.
Bullough, R. V., Jr., & Kauchak, D. (1997)	Unknown	Review of literature on higher education and public school partnerships	Six to seven teachers at each of 3 PDSs (2 high schools, 1 junior high) Administrators in PDSs Note: PDS is involved with the same university as that in the previous study	Interviews with teachers and administrators; questionnaire for teachers Analysis of data through coding and a matrix; initial categories identified, then iterations Comparison of codes across research team members	Teachers at all 3 sites believed that good teacher education involves extensive fieldwork, and that good teachers are born not made. At all sites, the importance of principal leadership and the complexity involved in creating partnerships was noted. Differences existed across the sites, including: At HS1 there was goodwill toward university and its efforts. The teachers were

(Continued)

TABLE 6.5
(Continued)

Authors, Date	Relationship With Participants	Theoretical "Framework" or Position in Field of Research	Participants	Data Sources, and Duration of Study	Impact Claims Examined and Findings
					positively influenced by their involvement. There were changes in some departments' requirements. In the junior high faculty and principal turnover created communication problems with the university. There was evidence of increased teacher reflection and some enhanced teacher–teacher communication. Teachers called for more cooperating teacher training. At HS2 a strong principal made all PDS decisions. There were competing, simultaneous reform initiatives, which meant that the PDS had limited influence on teachers and on the school.
Bullough, R. V., Jr., Kauchak, D., Crow, N. A., Hobbs, S., & Stokes, D. (1997)	Unknown	Review of literature on PDSs	Forty-nine teachers and principals at 7 PDS sites (3 middle-class suburban schools—2 elementary, 1 high	Audiotaped interviews focusing on demographics, participants' views of PDS successes and failures and how the PDS concept played out in each school. An initial set of interviews was	Many teachers reported that they grew more reflective about teaching, that their classroom practice changed, and that there was more faculty interaction.

			school; 3 working class urban schools—2 elementary, 1 high school; 1 working-class suburban junior high) Note: The secondary PDSs are the same as those in the previous study.	conducted, transcribed, and analyzed; then the protocol was revised. Analysis of data through coding and a matrix that sought to reveal similarities and differences between interviews. Initial categories identified, then data coded, then iterations. Comparison of codes across team members. Data collapsed into school matrices (sample matrix included in an appendix); case studies were written of each site.	Most teachers discounted the value of theory, thought professors were "out of touch," and saw the university-based inservice programs as superficial and irrelevant. Many teachers had only simplistic conceptions of the PDS's aims. Secondary schools' large size worked against program cohesiveness; elementary schools' small size meant they didn't have a critical mass of teachers. School change arose from catalysts, who were usually very involved cooperating teachers; principals were less effective as catalysts. Continuity of university personnel was essential for effective communication.
Button, K., Ponticell, J., & Johnson, M. J. (1996)	University liaisons to PDS sites and participant observers	Review of literature on culture differences between school and university	Teachers and administrators at 6 PDS sites (5 urban: 2 elementary, 2 junior high, 1 high school; and 1 rural K–12) University faculty	Audiotaped interviews with principal and 2 teachers from each school Participant–observer field notes from informal school visits and scheduled faculty meetings Archival records (e.g., meeting minutes) Researchers used case study methodology; coded data	Prior to formation of the PDSs, schools had been studied but had not been involved in doing research. Through the PDSs, some teachers began doing inquiry in their own classrooms and sharing the results. Teachers and professors served as resources for each other.

(Continued)

TABLE 6.5
(Continued)

Authors, Date	Relationship With Participants	Theoretical "Framework" or Position in Field of Research	Participants	Data Sources, and Duration of Study	Impact Claims Examined and Findings
				with no predetermined themes; constant comparative analysis and independent analysis by researchers were then combined; member checking.	
Cobb, J. (2000)	Unknown	Review of literature on effectiveness of PDSs	Thirty-five teachers at an elementary PDS	An anonymous survey of all participating teachers administered after 3rd and 4th year of PDS. Respondents responded to various statements on a 5-point scale. Seventy-eight percent of teachers responded in Year 3; 61%, in Year 4. Researchers tallied survey items, calculating percentages based on the number of teachers who responded to each question. Year 3 responses were compared to those in Year 4.	Teachers believed the PDS positively impacted students and that it did not have a negative impact on standardized test scores; that it prepared preservice teachers better than did non-PDS programs; that it helped their own teaching and professionalism; and they were appreciative of the materials and technology that the PDS grant bought for them. Year 4 responses seemed slightly more positive, but that may be an artifact of who responded and the difference in response rate.
Freese, A. R. (1999)	Instructor in program who works with	Review of literature on reflection	Eleven secondary-ed preservice teachers in a 2-year Master's	One audiotaped interview, which did not focus specifically on reflection,	Despite complaining about reflective activities during 3 semesters of coursework,

preservice teachers and the PDS. This is an acknowledged self-study.		of Education in Teaching program cohort; aged 22–38; 7 males; 2 math, 4 science, 2 English, 3 social studies. Six had professional work experiences prior to entering the program—3 of which involved teaching in private schools. Female course instructor and researcher	with each participant during the 4th-semester internship when they were in their own classrooms and were not required to keep journals or complete other assignments. Comments related to reflection were categorized; search for recurring patterns was undertaken.	the preservice teachers reported that they used the reflective framework during their teaching and that they valued it for self-evaluation, "on-the-spot" decision making, and collaboration. Preservice teachers had relatively sophisticated understandings of reflection. This study reinforced Freese's decision to continue using Loughran's reflective framework collaboratively with preservice teachers and cooperating teachers, seeing herself as co-inquirer, and making her thinking public.
Knight, S. L., Wiseman, D. L., & Cooner, D. (2000)	Unknown Collaborative teacher research Review of literature on PDS's impact on K–12 pupils	Writing study: 750 pupils, Grades 1–4 Math study: 284 pupils, Grades 2–4 Teachers, preservice teachers, administrators	Single-group pretest-posttest design: pre- and postwriting samples and pre- and postmath problem-solving test, given in fall and spring of a single academic year Focus group interviews with teachers Evaluation of writing samples per a teacher- and university researcher-designed rubric; grading of math test A focus group of teachers, preservice teachers, and administrators helped interpret data	One hundred fifty preservice teachers were trained in helping children with creating, revising, and sharing their writing; they worked with individual elementary students or small groups on hands-on process writing. On the posttest, 1st-grade students showed increases of 1/3 SD overall; 2nd- 3rd-, and 4th-grade students showed more modest increases of about 1/5 SD.

(Continued)

TABLE 6.5
(Continued)

Authors, Date	Relationship With Participants	Theoretical "Framework" or Position in Field of Research	Participants	Data Sources, and Duration of Study	Impact Claims Examined and Findings
				Repeated-measures MANOVA with follow-up univariate analyses; effect sizes calculated for each subscale at each grade level.	On the 3rd-grade state criterion-referenced test for writing, students showed an increase from 77% mastery in the fall to 90% mastery in the spring. Forty preservice teachers in a math methods course participated in the elementary school's math and technology lab. At each grade level, students scored significantly higher on the math posttest. Teachers attributed the students' gains directly to the PDS activities and indirectly to the opportunities provided for professional growth when the teachers developed and validated the scoring rubrics.
Powell, J. H., & McGowan, T. M. (1995)	Powell was professor-in-residence at PDS; McGowan was grad student with some	Review of literature on teacher roles at PDSs	Twelve elementary teachers at a new urban PDS	Earlier, biographical interviews were analyzed as a basis for this study; those interviews did not focus specifically on the PDS. After analysis of first interviews for statements	Teachers rejected the role of "teacher as expert" in favor of 3 other roles: teacher-as-learner; teacher-as-collaborator (with fellow teachers, administrators, and

Citation	Theoretical framework	Participants	Data collection and analysis	Findings
		duties at PDS. Participant observers	on PDSs, researchers conducted follow-up interviews specifically on the PDS. Participant observations Document review (e.g., meeting agendas and minutes of PDS meetings) Creation of categories concurrent with the beginning of data collection on behaviors and activities Member checking	university faculty); and teacher-as-social-activist in their desire to care for the whole child.
Powell, J. H., & McGowan, T. M. (1996)	Symbolic interactionist Review of literature on PDSs with an emphasis on participant collaboration	University representatives to the PDS (see previous) Twelve elementary teachers at a new urban PDS (same participants and dataset as previous study)	Audiotaped biographical interviews; follow-up interviews to probe earlier responses Participant observations of PDS meetings for 6 months Creation of categories and assertions about teachers' beliefs about their roles and responsibilities Search for disconfirming evidence	External events or conditions were responsible for the teachers' initial exploration of teaching in a PDS. Teachers decided to join because they hoped to have more control over their environment, not because of any specific information they had received about their role in this PDS. They wanted to have the freedom to take risks and to experiment with instruction, methods, and assessment. This desire increased throughout their participation. One teacher felt that PDS participation inhibited her ability to help children because of the time commitment.

(Continued)

407

TABLE 6.5
(Continued)

Authors, Date	Relationship With Participants	Theoretical "Framework" or Position in Field of Research	Participants	Data Sources, and Duration of Study	Impact Claims Examined and Findings
van Zandt, L. M. (1998)	Unknown	Unacknowledged Cites literature on PDSs and collaboration	Phase I: 189 MAT program graduates (elementary, middle, and secondary-ed) from 4 cohorts surveyed with a 67% response rate; 89% female Phase II: survey of school administrators in the university's county and administrators in other states who had program graduates (total = 652). Only 91 administrators returned completed surveys.	Likert-scale and open-ended survey questions—designed to assess components of the teacher education curriculum—mailed to recent graduates and administrators who had worked with the graduates Cronbach's alpha for internal consistency Quantitative data: t-test, ANOVA, chi-square analyses of significant differences among subgroups of graduates Qualitative data: organized by item, coded by frequency of response	Graduates—particularly those who had taught for several years—and administrators alike rated the 5-year MAT program very highly. The main program strength was its 1-year PDS internship, which allowed for the connection between theory and practice; other strengths—and some weaknesses—related to issues of quality (e.g., of professors and mentor teachers).
Hopkins, W. S., Hoffman, S. Q., & Moss, V. D. (1997)	Not specified	Review of literature on teacher education reform, PDSs, and preservice teacher stress	64 elementary education student teachers assigned to either traditional or PDS-based student teaching	Pre- and posttest Teacher Stress Scale with subscales to measure role-related stress (through role ambiguity, role overload, and role preparedness), job	Student teachers in the traditional program experienced less stress during the semester than did PDS-based student teachers, and student teachers in both

Study	Research design	Theoretical framework	Sample	Data collection and analysis	Findings
				satisfaction, and illness symptoms ANCOVA performed for overall stress and its subscales	groups developed a greater capacity for dealing with stress.
Connor, K. R., & Killmer, N. (2001)	Not specified	References to literature on effective teacher preparation	One hundred ninety-six elementary and early childhood education student teachers: 158 in the traditional program, 38 in Project Opportunity Cooperating teachers and university supervisors	Likert-scale and open-ended questionnaires: 1 for student teachers on 12 constructs (prediction of success; confidence; professional background; preparation; personal attributes; instructional skills; classroom management; application of knowledge; holistic understanding; student interactions; university faculty interactions; professional opportunities); and one for university supervisors and cooperating teachers on the first 8 constructs t-Tests used to establish p-values for each construct	Student teachers in Project Opportunity—a collaboration among university faculty and classroom teachers that involved student cohorts, redesigned courses, and extended field experiences—had higher ratings on the 12 constructs than did student teachers in the traditional program. Respondents cited the main strengths of Project Opportunity as student cohorts; articulated, interdisciplinary courses and field experiences; research and program development; and technology.
Sandholtz, J. H., & Wasserman, K. (2001)	Not specified	References to literature on teacher education programs and PDSs	Twenty-six postbaccalaureate elementary-ed student teachers: 18 in the traditional program, 8 in the PDS; mostly females aged 22–24	Scaled-response and open-ended questionnaires (for cooperating teachers, based on problems, benefits, and program evaluation; for student teachers, based on developmental concerns of self, task, and impact, and	Both the traditional and professional development school programs were rated highly by cooperating and student teachers, but those in the traditional program offered more suggestions for improvement.

(Continued)

TABLE 6.5
(Continued)

Authors, Date	Relationship With Participants	Theoretical "Framework" or Position in Field of Research	Participants	Data Sources, and Duration of Study	Impact Claims Examined and Findings
			Thirty-three cooperating teachers: 20 in the traditional program, 13 in the PDS; with 1–10 years experience	on main problems); exit interviews conducted as part of the teacher education program; observations by university supervisors For the questionnaires: descriptive statistics and ANOVA For the qualitative data: organized according to 4 categories (problems, benefits, program strengths, and recommendations for improvement), sorted by 4 groups (student and cooperating teachers in traditional and professional development school programs)	Cooperating teachers faced similar problems including disruption of classroom management and increased responsibilities. Cooperating teachers in the PDS, however, found benefits in the increased availability of the university supervisor and in collaborating with one another and with university faculty. Student teachers faced similar problems in the process of learning to teach, but those in the PDS had extra support to deal with these problems (e.g., full-year student teaching; problem-solving seminars; classroom observations by peers; increased availability of university supervisor). PDS student teachers had lower levels of concern and higher confidence by the end of the program.

| Brink, B., Laguardia, A., Grisham, D. L., Granby, C., & Peck, C. A. (2001) | Not specified | Review of literature on impact of PDSs on mentor teachers and K–12 students | Ten female postbaccalaureate elementary education student teachers at 2 PDSs (5 in a primary, 5 in a middle school): 4 nontraditional age, including 1 from Iran; 1 from the Netherlands
Ten female mentor teachers, with 10–30 years' teaching experience
Students at the PDS schools: majority White, middle class | Audiotaped and transcribed interviews with student teachers, mentors, and principals; field notes from university supervisors' classroom observations; samples of K–8 student work; action research reports by the student teachers
Case summaries written for each student teacher
Data coded according to impact on K–8 students, mentor teachers, and the school as a whole. Search for thematic patterns and disconfirming evidence
Two case summaries elaborated into case portraits | Having student teachers provided benefits for mentor teachers including: increased reflection and professional development, including learning new techniques and skills; increased time for planning; improvement in self-image. However, a few mentor teachers reported that they felt isolated from their colleagues and out of touch with the curriculum because of having a student teacher. K–8 pupils also benefited from having a student teacher through increased individualized instruction, enhanced curriculum, and increased literacy skills. Student teachers had a positive impact on schools' climate and activities. |
| Anderson, N. A., & Radencich, M. C. (2001) | First author was university supervisor. | References to literature on peer coaching | Thirty-four elementary education preservice teachers in an early field placement: 25 Caucasian females, 3 Hispanic females, | Peer coaching data forms, dialog journals with university supervisor, course evaluations, quantitative survey
Analyzed data forms for behaviors targeted for observation; observed | In a field-experience model that emphasized coaching over evaluation, preservice teachers were taught peer coaching methods and weaker preservice teachers were paired with stronger peers. Participants reported |

(Continued)

TABLE 6.5
(Continued)

Authors, Date	Relationship With Participants	Theoretical "Framework" or Position in Field of Research	Participants	Data Sources, and Duration of Study	Impact Claims Examined and Findings
			2 African-American females, 3 Caucasian males, and 1 African-American male	students' concerns and perceptions on strengths of the lesson; overall evaluation of the peer observation process in the current situation and for the future Analyzed journals for value of each source of feedback (peer, teacher, and supervisor) Course evaluations were not formally analyzed.	that they valued feedback more from mentor teachers and university supervisors than from peer coaches. They most often asked for feedback on classroom management and pedagogy. Participants generally expressed agreement with feedback, regardless of the source.
Knudson, R. E., & Turley, S. (2000)	Unknown	References to the literature on supervisors' roles and activities	Thirty secondary-ed supervisors, 16 female, 14 male Seventeen elementary-ed supervisors, 13 female, 4 male One hundred forty-five secondary-ed student teachers, 87 female, 58 male; 13.5% Asian; 4% African American; 12% Hispanic, 65% Anglo; 5% Other	Supervisors answered Likert-scale and open-ended questions on success or lack of success for each of their student teachers and ranked the importance of events challenging them to go beyond standard operating procedures, when they did so, and why. The answers were compiled in relation to students who were identified as being at risk by the supervisors.	Ten percent of secondary-ed student teachers were considered at-risk, 70% of whom were identified as at-risk by the end of the 4th week of student teaching; the others, by the 9th week. Indicators included the match between student teacher, cooperating teacher, and supervisor; poor classroom management; poor rapport with children; and poor communication with the cooperating teacher. To work with these student teachers, they changed their

412

standard operating procedures by moving students to another placement, helping students in specific areas, and visiting and conferring more often with the student teacher. 9.5% of elementary-ed student teachers were considered at-risk (92% of these were identified as at-risk by the end of the 4th week of student teaching, the others by the 9th week). Indicators included ineffective use of strategies and difficulty assuming the role of teacher. To work with these student teachers they changed their standard operating procedures by increasing feedback, visiting more often, and spending more time with the student teacher outside of school. In 50% of cases, the supervisor—not the cooperating teacher or student teacher—initially identified the problem. No agency for problems was ascribed to the cooperating teacher or the university supervisor.

Two hundred twenty-three elementary-ed student teachers, 193 female, 30 male; 74% Anglo; 11% Hispanic; 7% Asian American; 4% African American

(Continued)

TABLE 6.5
(Continued)

Authors, Date	Relationship With Participants	Theoretical "Framework" or Position in Field of Research	Participants	Data Sources, and Duration of Study	Impact Claims Examined and Findings
Slick, S. K. (1997)	Researcher	References to the literature on supervision of student teaching	Female elementary-ed supervisor—an experienced teacher and cooperating teacher and current graduate student Female experienced elementary-ed teacher Male elementary-ed student teacher	Interviews with cooperating teacher, student teacher, and supervisor Field notes of seminars, transcripts of postobservation conference, midterm and final 3-way conferences, informal discussions Constant comparative analysis of themes and patterns in perceptions and interactions, resulting in a case study	Mixed messages for the student teacher from the supervisor and the cooperating teacher. Student teacher not meeting expectations by the end of student teaching, but cooperating teacher and supervisor didn't work collaboratively with him. The supervisor was expected to handle tensions and ambiguities throughout the semester, which she resolved by working to maintain a positive relationship with the cooperating teacher. They both passed the student with an "A."
Justen, J. E., III, McJunkin, M., & Strickland, H. (1999)	Researchers	References to supervisory styles	One hundred fifty-seven cooperating teachers: 103 elementary-ed, 40 secondary-ed, 14 special ed; 38 had taken a	Supervisor Beliefs Inventory mailed to 195 cooperating teachers, 80% return rate The inventory was also given to university supervisors at one state university Two-way ANOVA—grade level by belief and style	No grade-level differences were found, but more teachers reported nondirective styles than directive or collaborative styles. There were no significant differences between those

			student-teaching supervision course Thirty-three university supervisors	Two-way ANOVA—supervisory training by belief and style Two way ANOVA—role by belief and style	who had taken a course and those who had not. There were no significant differences in style between university supervisors and cooperating teachers.
Kent, S. I. (2001)	Instructor	References to the literature on supervision and cooperating teachers	Sixteen elementary-ed and middle-school teachers in a graduate-level course on supervising student teachers; only 1 had previous experience as a cooperating teacher	Student teaching observation forms, conference notes, weekly reflective journals, final interview Comparative content analysis of positive and problematic aspects of implementing clinical supervision—actual practice compared to statements of intended practice. Frequencies and averages calculated of types of observation techniques—categorized as objective or evaluative	Intended implementation of clinical supervision cycle was far greater than actual implementation. Teachers who had been evaluated through clinical supervision themselves had higher intentions and higher levels of implementation. The teachers used a variety of observation techniques drawn from the course and often adapted techniques to fit the particular situation. Advantages included less judgmental observations and learning more about one's own students through observation. Disadvantages included the time-consuming nature of clinical supervision and the necessity of refraining from direct intervention and remaining objective.

(Continued)

TABLE 6.5
(Continued)

Authors, Date	Relationship With Participants	Theoretical "Framework" or Position in Field of Research	Participants	Data Sources, and Duration of Study	Impact Claims Examined and Findings
					In all cases but one, student teachers were able to identify their own weaknesses and to help focus observations and reflective analyses.
Daane, C. J. (2000)	Unknown	References to the literature on supervision	Fifty-five elementary-ed Clinical Master Teachers Ten elementary-ed preservice teachers (and 10 Clinical Master Teachers) from 10 different schools	Survey of all Clinical Master Teachers Interviews with 10 randomly selected teachers and interns from 10 different schools Responses were summarized by question.	The Clinical Master Teachers were able to implement most program requirements and generally liked the input and responsibility they had over interns' progress. The interns enjoyed the field control over the evaluations (as opposed to university control) and the consistency of having a single mentor during student teaching.
Hudson-Ross, S. (2001)	A university teacher–educator and partnership founder	Cites literature on partnerships and collaboration	Thirty-five secondary English teachers from 7 participating PDS sites Two European-American female university professors,	Surveys; audiotaped focus group and individual interviews; documents (e-mails, weekly bulletins, field notes, group reports and publications) from 5 years Interview data coded to locate patterns; patterns and	Teachers identified 4 sites for professional development: individual classrooms (through self-examination and having student teachers); the secondary school and college departments; the teacher network (through its

including the author

categories member-checked, and triangulated with other data.

positive culture and leadership opportunities); and the field of teacher education locally and beyond.

Individual changes included considering multiple intelligences, providing more choice and opportunities for independent learning, more hands-on activities, and more consideration of equity and diversity.

Teachers reported changed daily interaction and increased professional dialog through having student teachers; they began to recognize and respect their own expertise.

Teacher educators felt similar challenges as did secondary teachers; they learned to better work collaboratively, despite lack of university rewards. In the partnership, they provided resources and structure and sustained communication.

Learning communities evolved over time and required leadership, a critical mass of participants, and balancing of safety and disruption.

REFERENCES: STUDIES REVIEWED

Abell, S., Martini, M., & George, M. (2001). "That's what scientists have to do": Preservice elementary teachers' conceptions of the nature of science during a moon investigation. *International Journal of Science Education, 23,* 1095–1109.

Adams, P. E., & Krockover, G. H. (1997). Beginning science teacher cognition and its origins in the preservice secondary science teacher program. *Journal of Research in Science Teaching, 34,* 633–653.

Agee, J. (1997). Readers becoming teachers of literature. *Journal of Literacy Research, 29,* 397–431.

Agee, J. (1998). Negotiating different conceptions about reading and teaching literature in a preservice literature class. *Research in the Teaching of English, 33,* 85–124.

Allexsaht-Snider, M., Deegan, J. G., & White, C. S. (1995). Educational renewal in an alternative teacher education program: Evolution of a school-university partnership. *Teaching and Teacher Education, 11,* 519–530.

Anderson, N. A., & Radencich, M. C. (2001). The value of feedback in an early field experience: Peer, teacher, and supervisor coaching. *Action in Teacher Education, 23*(3), 66–74.

Anderson, L. M., Smith, D. C., & Peasley, K. (2000). Integrating learner and learning concerns: Prospective elementary science teachers' paths and progress. *Teaching and Teacher Education, 16,* 547–574.

Angell, A. V. (1998). Learning to teach social studies: A case study of belief restructuring. *Theory and Research in Social Education, 26,* 509–529.

Blanton, M. L., Berenson, S. B., & Norwood, K. S. (2001). Using classroom discourse to understand a prospective mathematics teacher's developing practice. *Teaching and Teacher Education, 17,* 227–242.

Blocker, L. S., & Mantle-Bromley, C. (1997). PDS versus campus preparation: Through the eyes of the students. *The Teacher Educator, 33,* 70–89.

Bowman, C. L., & McCormick, S. (2000). Comparison of peer coaching versus traditional supervision effects. *Journal of Educational Research, 93,* 256–61.

Boyd, P. C., Boll, M., Brawner, L., & Villaume, S. K. (1998). Becoming reflective professionals: An exploration of preservice teachers' struggles as they translate language and literacy theory into practice. *Action in Teacher Education, 19*(4), 61–75.

Brink, B., Laguardia, A., Grisham, D. L., Granby, C., & Peck, C. A. (2001). Who needs student teachers? *Action in Teacher Education, 23*(3), 33–45.

Briscoe, C., & Stout, D. (1996). Integrating math and science through problem centered learning in methods courses: Effects on prospective teachers' understanding of problem solving. *Journal of Elementary Science Education, 8*(2), 66–87.

Bruckerhoff, C. E., & Carlson, J. L. (1995). Loneliness, fear and disrepute: The haphazard socialization of a student teacher. *Journal of Curriculum Studies, 24,* 431–444.

Bryan, L. A., & Abell, S. K. (1999). Development of professional knowledge in learning to teach elementary science. *Journal of Research in Science Teaching, 36,* 121–139.

Bullough, R. V., Jr., Hobbs, S. F., Kauchak, D. P., Crow, N. A., & Stokes, D. (1997). Long-term PDS development in research universities and the clinicalization of teacher education. *Journal of Teacher Education, 48,* 85–95.

Bullough, R. V., Jr., & Kauchak, D. (1997). Partnerships between higher education and secondary schools: Some problems. *Journal of Education for Teaching, 23,* 215–233.

Bullough, R. V., Jr., Kauchak, D., Crow, N. A., Hobbs, S., & Stokes, D. (1997). Professional development schools: Catalysts for teacher and school change. *Teaching and Teacher Education, 13,* 153–169.

Button, K., Ponticell, J., & Johnson, M. J. (1996). Enabling school-university collaborative research: Lessons learned in professional development schools. *Journal of Teacher Education, 47,* 16–20.

Cobb, J. (2000). The impact of a professional development school in preservice teacher preparation, inservice teachers' professionalism, and children's achievement: Perceptions of inservice teachers. *Action in Teacher Education, 22*(3), 64–76.

Connor, K. R., & Killmer, N. (2001). Cohorts, collaboration, and community: Does contextual teacher education really work? *Action in Teacher Education, 23*(3), 46–53.

Cooney, T. J., Shealy, B. E., & Arvold, B. (1998). Conceptualizing belief structures of preservice secondary mathematics teachers. *Journal for Research in Mathematics Education, 29,* 306–333.

Daane, C. J. (2000). Clinical master teacher program: Teachers' and interns' perceptions of supervision with limited university intervention. *Action in Teacher Education, 22,* 93–100.

Denyer, J., & Florio-Ruane, S. (1995). Mixed messages and missed opportunities: Moments of transformation in writing conferences and teacher education. *Teaching and Teacher Education, 11,* 539–551.

Dinkelman, T. (1999). Critical reflection in a social studies methods semester. *Theory and Research in Social Education, 27,* 329–357.

Dinkelman, T. (2000). An inquiry into the development of critical reflection in secondary student teachers. *Teaching and Teacher Education, 16,* 195–222.

Donahue, D. M. (1999). Service-learning for preservice teachers: Ethical dilemmas for practice. *Teaching and Teacher Education, 15,* 685–695.

Donahue, D. M. (2000). Charity basket or revolution: Beliefs, experiences, and context in preservice teachers' service learning. *Curriculum Inquiry, 30,* 429–450.

Dooley, C. (1998). Teaching as a two-way street: Discontinuities among metaphors, images, and classroom realities. *Journal of Teacher Education, 49,* 97–107.

Ebby, C. B. (2000). Learning to teach mathematics differently: The interaction between coursework and fieldwork for preservice teachers. *Journal of Mathematics Teacher Education, 3,* 69–97.

Fairbanks, C. M., Freedman, D., & Kahn, C. (2000). The role of effective mentors in learning to teach. *Journal of Teacher Education, 51,* 102–112.

Fecho, B., Commeyras, M., Bauer, E. B., & Font, G. (2000). In rehearsal: Complicating authority in undergraduate critical-inquiry classrooms. *Journal of Literacy Research, 32,* 471–504.

Fehn, B., & Koeppen, K. E. (1998). Intensive document-based instruction in a social studies methods course and student teachers' attitudes and practice in subsequent field experiences. *Theory and Research in Social Education, 26,* 461–484.

Foss, D. H., & Kleinsasser, R. C. (1996). Preservice elementary teachers' views of pedagogical and mathematical content knowledge. *Teaching and Teacher Education, 12,* 429–442.

Freese, A. R. (1999). The role of reflection on preservice teachers' development in the context of a professional development school. *Teaching and Teacher Education, 15,* 895–909.

Frykholm, J. A. (1996). Pre-service teachers in mathematics: Struggling with the Standards. *Teaching and Teacher Education, 12,* 665–681.

Frykholm, J. A. (1998). Beyond supervision: Learning to teach mathematics in community. *Teaching and Teacher Education, 14,* 305–322.

Frykholm, J. A. (1999). The impact of reform: Challenges for mathematics teacher preparation. *Journal of Mathematics Teacher Education, 2,* 79–105.

Gill, B., & Hove, A. (2000, February). *The Benedum collaborative model of teacher education: A preliminary evaluation.* Retrieved November 3, 2003, from http://www.rand.org/publications/DB/DB303/

Graham, P. (1997). Tensions in the mentor teacher-student teacher relationship: Creating productive sites for learning within a high school English teacher education program. *Teaching and Teacher Education, 13,* 513–527.

Graham, P. (1999). Powerful influences: A case of one student teacher renegotiating his perceptions of power relations. *Teaching and Teacher Education, 15,* 523–540.

Greenwood, A. (1996). When it comes to teaching about floating and sinking, preservice elementary teachers do not have to feel as though they are drowning. *Journal of Elementary Science Education, 8*(1), 1–16.

Grisham, D. L., Laguardia, A., & Brink, B. (2000). Partners in professionalism: Creating a quality field experience for preservice teachers. *Action in Teacher Education, 21*(4), 27–40.

Grossman, P. L., Valencia, S. W., Evans, K., Thompson, C., Martin, S., & Place, N. (2000). Transitions into teaching: Learning to teach writing in teacher education and beyond. *Journal of Literacy Research, 32,* 631–662.

Harper, N. W., & Daane, C. J. (1998). Causes and reduction of math anxiety in preservice elementary teachers. *Action in Teacher Education, 19*(4), 29–38.

Hewson, P. W., Tabachnick, B. R., Zeichner, K. M., & Lemberger, J. (1999). Educating prospective teachers of biology: Findings, limitations, and recommendations. *Science Education, 83,* 373–384.

Hewson, P. W., Tabachnick, B. R., Zeichner, K. M., Blomker, K. B., Meyer, H., & Lemberger, J. (1999). Educating prospective teachers of biology: Introduction and research methods. *Science Education, 83,* 247–273.

Hohenbrink, J., Johnston, M., & Westhoven, L. (1997). Collaborative teaching of a social studies methods course: Intimidation and change. *Journal of Teacher Education, 48,* 293–300.

Hopkins, W. S., Hoffman, S. Q., & Moss, V. D. (1997). Professional development schools and preservice teacher stress. *Action in Teacher Education, 18*(4), 36–46.

Hudson-Ross, S. (2001). Intertwining opportunities: Participants' perceptions of professional growth within a multiple-site teacher education network at the secondary level. *Teaching and Teacher Education, 17,* 433–454.

Jarrett, O. S. (1998). Playfulness: A motivator in elementary science teacher preparation. *School Science and Mathematics, 98*(4), 181–187.

Justen, J. E., III, McJunkin, M., & Strickland, H. (1999). Supervisory beliefs of cooperating teachers. *The Teacher Educator, 34*(3), 173–180.

Kelly, C. (2001). Creating advocates: Building preservice teachers' confidence using an integrated, spiral-based, inquiry approach in mathematics and science methods instruction. *Action in Teacher Education, 23*(3), 75–83.

Kelly, J. (2000). Rethinking the elementary science methods course: A case for content, pedagogy, and informal science education. *International Journal of Science Education, 22,* 755–777.

Kent, S. I. (2001). Supervision of student teachers: Practices of cooperating teachers prepared in a clinical supervision course. *Journal of Curriculum and Supervision, 16,* 228–244.

Kim, M. K., & Sharp, J. (2000). Investigating and measuring preservice elementary mathematics teachers' decision about lesson planning after experiencing technology-enhanced methods instruction. *Journal of Computers in Mathematics and Science Teaching, 19,* 317–338.

Kinach, B. M. (2002). A cognitive strategy for developing pedagogical content knowledge in the secondary mathematics methods course: Toward a model of effective practice. *Teaching and Teacher Education, 18,* 51–71.

Knight, S. L., Wiseman, D. L., & Cooner, D. (2000). Using collaborative teacher research to determine the impact of professional development school activities on elementary students' math and writing outcomes. *Journal of Teacher Education, 51,* 26–38.

Knudson, R. E., & Turley, S. (2000). University supervisors and at-risk student teachers. *Journal of Research and Development in Education, 33,* 175–186.

Koeppen, K. E. (1998). The experiences of a secondary social studies student teacher: Seeking security by planning for self. *Teaching and Teacher Education, 14,* 401–411.

Langford, K., & Huntley, M. A. (1999). Internships as commencement: Mathematics and science research experiences as catalysts for preservice teacher professional development. *Journal of Mathematics Teacher Education, 2,* 277–299.

Langrall, C. W., Thornton, C. A., Jones, G. A., & Malone, J. A. (1996). Enhanced pedagogical knowledge and reflective analysis in elementary mathematics teacher education. *Journal of Teacher Education, 47,* 271–282.

Lemberger, J., Hewson, P. W., & Park, H. J. (1999). Relationships between prospective secondary teachers' classroom practice and their conceptions of biology and of teaching science. *Science Education, 83,* 347–371.

Mallette, M. H., Kile, R. S., Smith, M. M., McKinney, M., & Readence, J. E. (2000). Constructing meaning about literacy difficulties: Preservice teachers beginning to think about pedagogy. *Teaching and Teacher Education, 16,* 593–612.

Mantle-Bromley, C., Gould, L. M., McWhorter, B. A., & Whaley, D. C. (2000). The effect of program structure on new teachers' employment and program satisfaction patterns. *Action in Teacher Education, 22,* 1–14.

Marion, R., Hewson, P. W., Tabachnick, B. R., & Blomker, K. B. (1999). Teaching for conceptual change in elementary and secondary science methods courses. *Science Education, 83,* 275–307.

McDevitt, T. M., Troyer, R., Ambrosio, A. L., Heikkinen, H. W., & Warren, E. (1995). Evaluating prospective elementary teachers' understanding of science and mathematics in a model preservice program. *Journal of Research in Science Teaching, 32,* 749–775.

McGinnis, J. R., & Pearsall, M. (1998). Teaching elementary science methods to women: A male professor's experience from two perspectives. *Journal of Research in Science Teaching, 35,* 919–949.

McMahon, S. I. (1997). Using documented written and oral dialogue to understand and challenge preservice teachers' reflections. *Teaching and Teacher Education, 13,* 199–213.

Mewborn, D. S. (1999). Reflective thinking among preservice elementary mathematics teachers. *Journal for Research in Mathematics Education, 30,* 316–341.

Meyer, H., Tabachnick, B. R., Hewson, P. W., Lemberger, J., & Park, H.-J. (1999). Relationships between prospective elementary teachers' classroom practice and their conceptions of biology and of teaching science. *Science Education, 83,* 323–346.

Mosenthal, J. (1996). Situated learning and methods coursework in the teaching of literacy. *Journal of Literacy Research, 28,* 379–403.

Newell, G. E., Gingrich, R. S., & Johnson, A. B. (2001). Considering the contexts for appropriating theoretical and practical tools for teaching middle and secondary English. *Research in the Teaching of English, 35,* 302–343.

Nichols, S. E., & Tobin, K. (2000). Discursive practice among teachers co-learning during field-based elementary science teacher preparation. *Action in Teacher Education, 22*(2A), 45–54.

O'Callaghan, C. (2001). Social construction of preservice teachers' instructional strategies for reading. *The Teacher Educator, 36,* 265–281.

Palmquist, B. C., & Finley, F. N. (1997). Preservice teachers' views of the nature of science during a postbaccalaureate science teaching program. *Journal of Research in Science Teaching, 34,* 595–615.

Powell, J. H., & McGowan, T. M. (1995). Adjusting the focus: Teachers' roles and responsibilities in a school/university collaborative. *The Teacher Educator, 31,* 1–22.

Powell, J. H., & McGowan, T. M. (1996). In search of autonomy: Teachers' aspirations and expectations from a school-university collaborative. *Teaching and Teacher Education, 12,* 249–260.

Rahal, B. F., & Melvin, M. J. (1998). The effects of modeling mathematics discourse on the instructional strategies of preservice teachers. *Action in Teacher Education, 19*(4), 102–118.

Sandholtz, J. H., & Wasserman, K. (2001). Student and cooperating teachers: Contrasting experiences in teacher preparation. *Action in Teacher Education, 23*(3), 54–65.

Settlage, J. (2000). Understanding the learning cycle: Influences on abilities to embrace the approach by preservice elementary school teachers. *Science Education, 84,* 43–50.

Shapiro, B. L. (1996). A case study of change in elementary student teacher thinking during an independent investigation in science: Learning about the "face of science that does not yet know." *Science Education, 80,* 535–560.

Sillman, K., Dana, T., & Miller, M. (2000). The first year of teaching science: Ready or not? *Action in Teacher Education, 22*(3), 56–63.

Slekar, T. D. (1998). Epistemological entanglements: Preservice elementary school teachers' "apprenticeship of observation" and the teaching of history. *Theory and Research in Social Education, 26,* 485–507.

Slick, S. K. (1997). Assessing versus assisting: The supervisor's roles in the complex dynamics of the students teaching triad. *Teaching and Teacher Education, 13,* 713–726.

Slick, S. K. (1998a). A university supervisor negotiates territory and status. *Journal of Teacher Education, 49,* 306–315.

Slick, S. K. (1998b). The university supervisor: A disenfranchised outsider. *Teaching and Teacher Education, 14,* 821–834.

Stanulis, R. N. (1995). Classroom teachers as mentors: Possibilities for participation in a professional development school context. *Teaching and Teacher Education, 11,* 331–344.

Steele, D. F. (2001). The interfacing of preservice and inservice experiences of reform-based teaching: A longitudinal study. *Journal of Mathematics Teacher Education, 4,* 139–172.

Steele, D. F., & Widman, T. F. (1997). Practitioner's research: A study in changing preservice teachers' conceptions about mathematics and mathematics teaching and learning. *School Science and Mathematics, 97*(4), 184–191.

Stofflett, R. T., & Stefanon, L. (1996). Elementary teacher candidates' conceptions of successful conceptual change teaching. *Journal of Elementary Science Education, 8*(2), 1–20.

Tabachnick, B. R., & Zeichner, K. M. (1999). Idea and action: Action research and the development of conceptual change teaching of science. *Science Education, 83,* 309–322.

Tobin, K., Roth, W. M., & Zimmermann, A. (2001). Learning to teach science in urban schools. *Journal of Research in Science Teaching, 38,* 941–964.

Tobin, K., Seiler, G., & Smith, M. W. (1999). Educating science teachers for the sociocultural diversity of urban schools. *Research in Science Education, 29,* 69–88.

Vacc, N. N., & Bright, G. W. (1999). Elementary preservice teachers' changing beliefs and instructional use of children's mathematical thinking. *Journal for Research in Mathematics Education, 30,* 89–110.

van Zandt, L. M. (1998). Assessing the effects of reform in teacher education: An evaluation of the 5-year MAT program at Trinity University. *Journal of Teacher Education, 49,* 120–131.

Walling, B., & Lewis, M. (2000). Development of professional identity among professional development school preservice teachers: Longitudinal and comparative analysis. *Action in Teacher Education, 22,* 65–72.

Weaver, D., & Stanulis, R. N. (1996). Negotiating preparation and practice: Student teaching in the middle. *Journal of Teacher Education, 47,* 27–36.

Wiggins, R. A., & Clift, R. T. (1995). Oppositional pairs: Unresolved conflicts in student teaching. *Action in Teacher Education, 17,* 9–19.

Wilson, E. K., & Saleh, A. (2000). The effects of an alternative model of student teaching supervision on clinical master teachers. *Action in Teacher Education, 22*(2A), 84–90.

Wiseman, D. L., & Nason, P. L. (1995). The nature of interactions in a field-based teacher education experience. *Action in Teacher Education, 17*(3), 1–12.

Wolf, S. A., Ballentine, D., & Hill, L. (1999). The right to write: Preservice teachers' evolving understandings of authenticity and aesthetic heat in multicultural literature. *Research in the Teaching of English, 34,* 130–184.

Wolf, S. A., Ballentine, D., & Hill, L. A. (2000). "Only connect!": Cross-cultural connections in the reading lives of preservice teachers and children. *Journal of Literacy Research, 32,* 533–569.

Wolf, S. A., Mieras, E. L., & Carey, A. A. (1996). What's after "What's that?": Preservice teachers learning to ask literary questions. *Journal of Literacy Research, 28,* 459–497.

Worthy, J., & Patterson, E. (2001). "I can't wait to see Carlos!": Preservice teachers, situated learning, and personal relationships with students. *Journal of Literacy Research, 33,* 303–344.

Zembal-Saul, C., Blumenfeld, P., & Krajcik, J. (2000). Influence of guided cycles of planning, teaching, and reflection on prospective elementary teachers' science content representations. *Journal of Research in Science Teaching, 37,* 318–339.

REFERENCES CITED IN TEXT

Adler, S. A. (1991). The education of social studies teachers. In J. P. Shaver (Ed.), *Handbook of research on social studies teaching and learning* (pp. 210–221). New York: MacMillan.

Alton-Lee, A. (1998). A troubleshooter's checklist for prospective authors derived from reviewer's critical feedback. *Teaching and Teacher Education, 14,* 887–890.

Alverman, D. E. (1990). Reading teacher education. In W. R. Houston, M. Haberman, & J. Sikula (Eds.), *Handbook of research on teacher education* (pp. 687–704). New York: MacMillan.

Anders, P. L., Hoffman, J. V., & Duffy, G. G. (2000). Teaching teachers to teach reading: Paradigm shifts, persistent problems and challenges. In M. L. Kamil, P. B. Mosenthal, P. D. Pearson,

& R. Barr (Eds.), *Handbook of reading research* (Vol. 3, pp. 719–742). Mahwah, NJ: Lawrence Erlbaum Associates.

Anderson, R. D., & Mitchener, C. P. (1994). Research on science teacher education. In D. L. Gabel (Ed.), *Handbook of research on science teaching and learning* (pp. 3–44). New York: Macmillan.

Armento, B. J. (1996). The professional development of social studies educators. In J. Sikula, T. Buttery, & E. Guyton (Eds.), *Handbook of research on teacher education* (2nd ed., pp. 485–502). New York: Simon & Schuster Macmillan.

Banks, J. A., & Parker, W. C. (1990). Social studies teacher education. In W. R. Houston, M. Haberman, & J. Sikula (Eds.), *Handbook of research on teacher education,* (pp. 674 – 686). New York: Macmillan.

Book, C. L. (1996). Professional Development Schools. In J. Sikula, T. Buttery, & E. Guyton (Eds.), *Handbook of research on teacher education* (2nd ed., pp. 194–210). New York: Macmillan.

Brown, C. A., & Borko, H. (1992). Becoming a mathematics teacher. In D. A. Grouws (Ed.), *Handbook of research on mathematics teaching and learning* (pp. 209–239). New York: Macmillan.

Brown, S. I., Cooney, T. J., & Jones, D. (1990). Mathematics teacher education. In W. R. Houston, M. Haberman, & J. Sikula (Eds.), *Handbook of research on teacher education* (pp. 639–656). New York: Macmillan.

Cochran, K. F., & Jones, L. L. (1998). The subject matter knowledge of preservice science teachers. In B. J. Fraser & K. G. Tobin (Eds.), *International handbook of science education* (pp. 707–718). Boston: Kluwer.

Cruickshank, D. R., & Metcalf, K. K. (1990). Training within teacher preparation. In W. R. Houston, M. Haberman, & J. Sikula (Eds.), *Handbook of research on teacher education* (pp. 469–497). New York: Macmillan.

Doyle, W. (1990). Themes in teacher education research. In W. R. Houston, M. Haberman, & J. Sikula (Eds.), *Handbook of research on teacher education* (pp. 3–24). New York: Macmillan.

Fisher, C. J., Fox, D. L., & Paille, E. (1996). Teacher education research in the English language arts and reading. In J. Sikula, T. Buttery, & E. Guyton (Eds.), *Handbook of research on teacher education* (2nd ed., pp. 410–441). New York: Macmillan.

Fuller, F. F., & Bown, O. H. (1975). Becoming a teacher. In K. Ryan (Ed.), *Teacher education* (74th Yearbook of the National Society for the Study of Education, Part II, pp. 25–52). Chicago: University of Chicago Press.

Ginsburg, M. B., & Clift, R. T. (1990). The hidden curriculum of preservice teacher preparation. In W. R. Houston, M. Haberman, & J. Sikula (Eds.), *Handbook of research on teacher education* (pp. 450–465). New York: Macmillan.

Grossman, P. L., Valencia, S. W., & Hamel, F. L. (1997). Preparing language arts teachers in a time of reform. *Handbook of research on teaching literacy through the communicative and visual Arts* (pp. 407–416). New York: Macmillan.

Grouws, D. A., & Schultz, K. A. (1996). Mathematics teacher education. In John Sikula, Thomas Buttery, & Edith Guyton (Eds.), *Handbook of research on teacher education* (2nd ed., pp. 442–458). New York: Simon & Schuster Macmillan.

Guyton, E., & McIntyre, D. J. (1990). Student teaching and school experience. In W. R. Houston, M. Haberman, & J. Sikula (Eds.), *Handbook of research on teacher education* (pp. 514–534). New York: Macmillan.

Houston (1990). Preface. In W. R. Houston, M. Haberman, & J. Sikula (Eds.), *Handbook of research on teacher education* (pp. ix–xi). New York: Macmillan.

Lanier, J. E., & Little, J. W. (1986). In M. C. Wittrock (Ed.) *Handbook of research on teaching* (3rd ed., pp. 527–569). New York: Macmillan.

McIntyre, D. J., Byrd, D., & Foxx, S. M. (1996). Field and laboratory experiences. In J. Sikula, T. Buttery, & E. Guyton (Eds.), *Handbook of research on teacher education* (2nd ed., pp. 171–193). New York: Macmillan.

Monk, D. H. (1994). Subject matter preparation of secondary mathematics and science teachers and student achievement. *Economics of Education Review, 13*(2), 125–145.

Munby, H., Russell, T., & Martin, A. K. (2001). Teachers' knowledge and how it develops. In V. Richardson (Ed.), *Handbook of research on teaching* (4th ed., pp. 877–904). Washington, DC: American Educational Research Association.

O'Donnell, R. C. (1990). English language arts teacher education. In W. R. Houston, M. Haberman, & J. Sikula (Eds.), *Handbook of research on teacher education* (pp. 705–716). New York: Macmillan.

Peck, R. F., & Tucker, J. A. (1973). Research on teacher education. In R. M. W. Travers (Ed.), *Second handbook of research on teaching* (pp. 940–978). Chicago: Rand McNally.

Richardson, V. (2002, April). *Research on teaching: Recent past, current conditions, and future.* Invited address to the annual meeting of the American Educational Research Association, New Orleans, LA.

Sikula, J., Buttery, T., & Guyton, E. (Eds.). (1996). *Handbook of research on teacher education* (2nd ed.). New York: Simon & Schuster Macmillan.

Sleeter, C. E. (2001). Epistemological diversity in research on preservice teacher preparation for historically underserved children. In W. G. Secada (Ed.), *Review of Research in Education.* (Vol. 25, pp. 209–250). Washington, DC: American Educational Research Association.

Stallings, J. A., & Kowalski, T. (1990). Research on professional development schools. In W. R. Houston, M. Haberman, & J. Sikula (Eds.), *Handbook of research on teacher education* (pp. 251–263). New York: Macmillan.

Turner, R. L. (1975). An overview of research in teacher education. In K. Ryan (Ed.), *Teacher education* (74th Yearbook of the National Society for the Study of Education, Part II, pp. 87–110). Chicago: University of Chicago Press.

Wideen, M., Mayer-Smith, J., & Moon, B. (1998). A critical analysis of learning to teach: Making the case for an ecological perspective on inquiry. *Review of Educational Research, 68,* 130–178.

Yager, R. E., & Penick, J. E. (1990). Science teacher education. In W. R. Houston, M. Haberman, & J. Sikula (Eds.), *Handbook of research on teacher education* (pp. 657–673). New York: Macmillan.

7

Research on Pedagogical Approaches in Teacher Education

Pamela Grossman
Stanford University

Most reports about teacher education focus more on curricular issues, such as what prospective teachers should learn, or on structural issues, such as the uses of professional development schools or the length of programs, than on issues of instruction. Neither the research literature nor the reform reports of the 1980s (Carnegie Forum on Education and the Economy, 1986; Holmes Group, 1986) had much to say about how prospective teachers should be taught.[1] Yet in teacher education, attention to pedagogy is critical; *how* one teaches is part and parcel of *what* one teaches (Loughran & Russell, 1997). In the professional preparation of teachers, the medium *is* the message. This chapter summarizes the research on how we teach prospective teachers and on how various approaches used by teacher educators might affect what teachers learn about teaching, including what they come to know or believe about teaching, as well as how they engage in the practice of teaching itself.

What do we mean by the pedagogy of teacher education? What might be included in investigations of pedagogy? The initial prompt for this review focused on discrete

---

[1]The third Holmes Group report, published in 1995, did begin to address issues of how we might teach teachers.

instructional strategies, such as case methods, action research, and microteaching, that are commonly used in teacher education. However, pedagogy might be defined more broadly to include the following:

- Classroom instruction and interaction: Instruction includes all interactions among faculty, students, and content during class time. This includes various instructional strategies used by faculty, the nature of instructional discourse, and the representations of content. Within this category, I would include such instructional approaches as case-based teaching, simulations, role-plays, and use of video cases. Also included in this aspect of pedagogy are the more relational aspects of teaching and learning such as the relationships established among teachers and students and how they shape what prospective teachers learn (e.g., Kessels, Koster, Lagerwerf, Wubbels, & Korthagen, 2001).
- Tasks and assignments: Tasks or assignments represent a crucial ingredient in the pedagogy of teacher education, as they focus students' attention on particular problems of practice and introduce them to ways of reasoning or performing. This category includes student journals, case reports, portfolios, and practitioner research.

Although all of these aspects of pedagogy are significant in the preparation of teachers, the research literature in the United States has focused primarily on the uses of various pedagogical approaches or instructional strategies.[2] This chapter reviews the research on five broad approaches used in preservice teacher education: uses of laboratory experiences, including microteaching and computer simulations; uses of case methods; uses of video and hypermedia materials; uses of portfolios; uses of practitioner research. These certainly do not exhaust the universe of possibilities for how we teach teachers. This list leaves out, for example, the use of student journals (e.g., Bolin, 1990; Roe & Stillman, 1994)—a widespread practice in teacher education—as well as the use of popular films and other media (e.g., Torchon, 1999). Despite the prevalence of some of these approaches, we found relatively few empirical studies that met the criteria for inclusion. The list also does not include the use of modeling in teacher education, another widespread practice about which there is little systematic research. In focusing on these five broad approaches, I have chosen pedagogical approaches that are both prevalent in teacher education programs and about which there are a number of systematic studies that met the criteria established by the Panel.

This review also focuses on studies that focused primarily on the professional component of teacher education. Teacher education, however, extends well beyond experiences in the professional component to include subject matter and general education courses offered by faculty in the arts and sciences. The pedagogy of such courses is most certainly a part of the pedagogy of teacher education. However, few studies have examined the pedagogy of arts and sciences courses as they connect to teacher education (cf. Marshall & Smith, 1997; McDiarmid, 1996; Thompson, 2002, for counterexamples). Because of the paucity of such studies, and because studies of

---

[2]This is less true of European research on teacher education, as Fred Korthagen reminds us. This is also less true of the self-studies conducted by teacher educators (e.g., Loughran & Russell, 1990), in which teacher educators study their practice more holistically.

subject matter preparation are addressed in a separate chapter (Floden & Meniketti, this volume), the pedagogy of arts and sciences courses is not included in this review.

PROCESS AND CRITERIA FOR SELECTING STUDIES FOR INCLUSION IN THIS REVIEW

The original question that framed this review read as follows: "What does the research say about the impact of instructional strategies (e.g., cases, action research, teacher research, technology, portfolios, community immersion, inquiry, biography, microteaching, and videos) on professional practice, teacher learning, and student learning? Under what conditions or in what contexts are these instructional strategies effective?"

Because so few studies in this area make the difficult connection between the instructional strategies used in teacher education and what is learned by the students of prospective teachers, this review focuses more on outcomes of instructional strategies for the preservice teachers themselves, rather than for their students. These outcomes include changes in preservice teachers' beliefs, knowledge, attitudes, or classroom practice. The nature of the question also focuses explicitly on discrete instructional strategies rather than on more general descriptions of pedagogy.

To answer this question, we conducted an extensive search of the empirical research literature between the years of 1985 and 2001. We extended these dates to include some earlier research on microteaching from the 1970s, in part because of the historical importance of this line of research. We used a variety of strategies for our search, including ERIC searches on specific pedagogies, a handsearch of the most relevant national peer-reviewed journals, and careful examinations of published reviews of related literature. We conducted a hand search of *Journal of Teacher Education, Teaching and Teacher Education,* and *Journal of Education for Teaching.* We did ERIC searches using the following key words in conjunction with research in teacher education: case methods, case-based teaching, action research, practitioner research, teacher research, microteaching, simulations, journals, portfolios, modeling, technology, video, and apprenticeship. We also did searches combining seven subject areas (English, math, foreign language, social studies, science, art, and health) with the terms teacher education pedagogy, in order to catch research conducted on the pedagogy of teacher education within those subject areas. Finally, we looked at reviews of teacher education in the *Handbook of Research on Teacher Education* (1990, 1996), *The Handbook of Research on Teaching* (2001), and *The International Encyclopedia of Teaching and Teacher Education* (1987).

Employing these strategies, we found more than 200 articles related to the pedagogy of teacher education. We then winnowed this list down to studies that met the Panel's criteria. These were adapted from the criteria used by Wilson, Floden, and Ferrini-Mundy (2001) for a review of research on teacher education. For example, for interpretive studies, criteria include "description of their processes for data collection and analysis that include evidence, such as samples of interview responses or detailed descriptions of events as part of the report." We excluded studies that did not supply information about methods for both data collection and analysis.

Researchers have used a wide range of research genres to study the pedagogy of teacher education (Kennedy, 1996). Studies range from surveys, to experimental or quasi-experimental studies of particular strategies, to qualitative studies of other's practices, to studies of one's own practice. The studies differ with respect to the following questions:

- Who conducts the research?
- What aspects of pedagogy are addressed?
- What outcomes are investigated?
- How is the research designed and conducted?

One theme of this review concerns the variability in both the outcomes under investigation and the instruments used in the research. I return to this topic in the conclusion.

In this area of research, the modal study consists of researchers' studies of their own students or programs. There are many reasons to study one's own practice in teacher education. In most instances, research in teacher education is poorly funded; absent support for travel or research assistance, studying one's own students is a logical step, as generations of psychology professors have discovered. Funding aside, there are other reasons for studying one's own practice. Perhaps the predominant reason is to enable professors to learn from their own experiences in the classroom and improve subsequent instruction. Much of the work characterized as self-study in teacher education falls into this category. The researchers or instructors are less concerned with what their investigations can contribute to broader, generalizable claims about teacher education than they are in learning from the careful study of their own practice (Loughran & Russell, 2002). Because their own learning and the improvement of their own practice are the primary motivations for the work, researchers in this area may be less concerned about providing detailed, explicit descriptions of their methods of data collection and analysis. However, others who study their own students do so for the explicit purpose of contributing to broader understandings of teacher education. These authors may be more likely to write for peer-refereed journals and to include detailed information regarding the studies, including how data were collected and analyzed.

For inclusion in this review, all research had to meet the criteria relevant to the particular methodology chosen by the researcher, as outlined in the general criteria established by the Panel. To be included, therefore, interpretive studies needed to "include a description of their processes for data collection and analysis that include evidence, such as samples of interview responses or detailed descriptions of events as part of the report." Similarly, self-studies that used surveys needed a return rate of 60% and needed to address, in some way, the possible differences between those who responded to the surveys and those who did not.

In addition to these general criteria, for studies of the researcher's own practice, we examined how researchers addressed the dual role they played as researchers and instructors. For example, how do researchers deal with the problem of interviewing their own students about what they have learned in class, particularly when researchers have the power to evaluate the students' performance in their role as instructors? How do researchers address issues involved with the use of student work, produced for the course and evaluated by the instructor, as data? Researchers varied widely in how they dealt with these issues in the published accounts of their work. In some instances, researchers may have been studying their own classrooms but did not identify themselves as the instructors. At the other extreme, some researchers were explicit about their role as both instructor and researcher and how they addressed issues of evaluation. In one study, for example, the researchers stated that they "interviewed preservice and in-service teacher volunteers after the course grades had been submitted to diminish the effect of power relations and thus encourage unbiased feedback" (Moje & Wade, 1997, p. 695).

PEDAGOGY AS PREPARATION FOR PROFESSIONAL PRACTICE

Considerations of pedagogy for professional education must begin with a consideration of the nature of professional practice itself. In *The Lost Lawyer*, Anthony Kronman (1993) describes the common features of lawyers' work and how the case method widely used in law schools prepares future lawyers to engage in this work. Similarly, descriptions of the Harvard Business School's model of case-based teaching (Barnes, Christensen, & Hansen, 1994) locate the pedagogy of cases within a discussion of the practice of business administration. Mike Rose (1999) situates his description of a course to prepare physical therapists in an understanding of the practice of physical therapists within a particular domain. David Cohen (in press) illuminates the challenges of preparing practitioners for professionals of human improvement, challenges that are rooted in the very nature of practice.

The plethora of pedagogies used in teacher education reflects, in part, the different conceptions of teaching practice that exist. Teaching has been described as a set of techniques or behaviors, as a form of clinical decision making, as a cognitive apprenticeship based in disciplinary understanding, as a therapeutic relationship, and as a process of continuing inquiry. Each of these views of the nature of practice might lead to a different form of pedagogy in professional education. Training models such as microteaching, for example, are closely linked to the technical view of teaching, in which teachers are trained in the discrete skills of teaching. Case methods have been advocated to develop teachers' capacities to make informed decisions in the face of uncertainty, whereas others advocate the use of teacher research to prepare teachers to adopt an inquiry-stance into their teaching.

As Merseth and Lacey (1993) argue, although the pedagogical activities of teacher education are linked implicitly to conceptual orientations toward teaching, learning, and learning to teach, the goals of particular pedagogies and the ways they are tethered to particular conceptual orientations are often left tacit. Part of this review will address the conceptions of teaching and learning to teach embedded within the various pedagogies of teacher education, and how these conceptions are reflected in the outcomes researchers choose to study.

Microteaching and Laboratory Experiences

One of the earliest research programs on the pedagogy of teacher education investigated the uses and effects of microteaching during teacher education. Originally developed at Stanford University in the 1960s, microteaching has been defined as "a laboratory training procedure aimed at simplifying the complexities of regular teaching-learning processes" (Perlberg, 1987). Microteaching grew out of the process–product line of research, which identified particular teaching skills that correlated with gains in student achievement and then tried to teach these discrete skills to teachers (Gage, 1978).

Although the theoretical underpinnings of microteaching were never completely specified, the approach is certainly aligned with a behavioral model of learning; one of its creators specifically saw it as an attempt to use behavior modification in teacher education (McDonald, 1973, cited in Perlberg, 1987). Most forms of microteaching focus on discrete skills of teaching and involve videotaping prospective teachers' efforts to enact these skills and then providing them with feedback on their performance. Early forms of microteaching also included models of master teachers demonstrating the skill to be learned. Despite the depiction of microteaching as behavior modification, the model as enacted is quite complex, involving the close observation of master teachers, the formation of concepts related to teaching, practice and feedback, as well as opportunities to learn from experience. The use of videotape, which allows repeated viewing of one's teaching episode, also distinguishes this form of pedagogy.

Most research on microteaching took place in the 1960s and 1970s and has been reviewed elsewhere (Copeland, 1982; MacLeod, 1987, 1984; McIntyre, Byrd, & Foxx, 1996). However, there have been several more recent studies (Vare, 1994; Wilkinson, 1996; Winitzky & Arends, 1991). Here we summarize the findings of earlier research and explore how more recent work fits into these findings.

In a review of laboratory experiences that included microteaching, Copeland (1982) concluded that although microteaching may increase the initial acquisition of target skills, prospective teachers do not necessarily use these skills in the classroom. He also concluded, however, that microteaching can improve teachers' feelings of self-confidence. Another review of the literature suggested that the initial phase of microteaching, in which prospective teachers view master teachers modeling a skill, may be as powerful as the actual practice of microteaching itself (MacLeod, 1987). The more recent work on video cases and simulations can be seen as an extension of this line of work on microteaching.

Much research on microteaching also looked at the nature and form of feedback provided to students after the teaching episode (MacLeod, 1987), but it is difficult to make firm conclusions based on the research. A more recent study (Wilkinson, 1996) followed up on the question of feedback by conducting a study in which students in an experimental group received additional feedback on their videotape from experienced teachers who were also preservice administrators. Using questionnaire data, the researchers examined how this feedback affected student teachers' perceptions of their teaching ability and the value of professional development. The author concluded that students who received feedback from the preservice administrators reported placing greater value on supervision as part of professional development and appreciating the specific feedback they received as part of learning to teach. This study confirms the importance of feedback as part of the process of microteaching found in earlier research.

Research on microteaching is closely related to other research on the uses of laboratory experiences in teacher education (Copeland, 1982). Although laboratory experiences have been critiqued as artificial and overly focused on the development of skills, researchers have continued to investigate the potential of various laboratory models to promote both teacher thinking and practice. Metcalf (1992) developed a training model to teach preservice teachers the skills involved in "clear teaching." Building on earlier work, Metcalf investigated how involvement in a training model affected preservice teachers' ability to use the behaviors taught and how their participation in clarity training affected their peers' learning. In a quasi-experimental and carefully controlled study, students were divided into experimental and control groups, based on their prior enrollment in a section. The experimental group received training in instructional clarity, which included viewing videotaped demonstrations, reading and discussing a manual on clarity, and engaging in practice teaching exercises. Other than the focus on instructional clarity, the content of the two sections was the same. In the second and final weeks of the semester, students were asked to teach one of six reflective teaching lessons to a group of peers in a 15-minute segment. Following the videotaped lessons, the learners completed a brief test on lesson content and rated their satisfaction with the lesson. Researchers coded the videotapes for use of behaviors related to clarity. Not surprisingly, students who received the clarity training received higher ratings on clarity than did control teachers; they also used a broader range of behaviors related to clear teaching. The students of teachers in the experimental group also scored higher on the tests given at the end of the brief lessons. One limitation of the study, however, has to do with the use of small peer groups for the lessons, rather than actual classrooms; we do not know whether the preservice teachers would use the same behaviors in a regular classroom situation.

Other research has tried to compare laboratory experiences including forms of microteaching to early field experiences or other forms of laboratory experience (Metcalf, Hammer, & Kahlich, 1996; Winitzsky & Arends, 1991). In a carefully designed study of the differences between field experiences and laboratory experiences, researchers investigated the comparative effects of each experience on preservice teachers' ability to identify and reason about complex pedagogical issues in written cases and to plan and implement organized, meaningful lessons (Metcalf et al., 1996). Researchers assigned two sections of a general methods class to one of these two treatments; the content of the course was similar in both cases, but students had different clinical experiences. One section was assigned to a field placement in which students were required to complete a series of teaching activities and to keep observation logs. The students assigned to the laboratory experience participated in a series of clinical activities including preparing and implementing videotaped lessons and participating in role-play exercises. For both pre- and posttests, students were asked to respond to a written case study, one on the first day of class and one in the final week and to prepare and implement a 15-minute lesson to a small group of peers.

In their analysis, researchers (Metcalf et al., 1996) found differences between the two groups in their ability to analyze the written cases and in their instructional behavior. Although the students in the field experience section were superior to students in the laboratory section on pretest measures, students in laboratory experiences showed more improvement both in instructional performance and in ability to reflect on written cases. However, researchers also found there was only a small correlation between teachers' pedagogical cognition and pedagogical behavior. The authors concluded that laboratory experiences are a promising alternative to field experiences, and can be at least as effective in developing students' ability to reason about teaching and to teach small groups of peers. However, the study did not examine the effects of either experience on actual classroom teaching.

In a series of comparative studies, Nancy Winitzky and Richard Arends (1991) compared various ways in which preservice teachers could learn from experienced teachers. The project attempted to build teaching laboratories—or clinical classrooms—in regular public schools in order to make field experiences more effective. Clinical teachers were trained in five instructional approaches: direct instruction, presentation with advanced organizers, concept teaching, cooperative learning, and classroom management. A set of three experimental studies investigated how to take advantage of clinical teachers' expertise to promote the knowledge and teaching skill of preservice teachers and to help them become more reflective about their practice. In one study, the researchers compared microteaching to clinical teacher-led discussion as ways to increase preservice teachers' knowledge, skill, and ability to reflect. Researchers used an experimental design that used repeated measures and alternating treatments across two randomly assigned groups. The groups alternated using microteaching as a way to learn about an instructional strategy, with clinical discussion in which preservice teachers analyzed a videotape with clinical teachers and practiced components of the strategy through role-plays. Instruments included multiple-choice tests of knowledge about the strategy, lesson plans developed by the preservice teachers and scored by clinical teachers, and preservice teachers' analyses of videotaped lessons. Raters scored these analyses on the basis of quality and completeness of responses. Finally, researchers collected data on preservice teachers' verbal ability to check for interactions between reflection and verbal ability.

Winitzky and Arends (1991) found no significant differences across treatment groups, suggesting that microteaching and clinical discussion are equally effective at promoting not only knowledge but also skill acquisition. However, the research did not look at the effects of either intervention on actual classroom teaching. In addition, because the clinical discussions also included role-plays of aspects of the instructional strategy, the treatments may not have been that different. As the researchers noted, these measures have not been validated in other studies. They concluded, "the findings reported here must be considered tentative until reliability and validity of the instruments are better established and until replication of these studies using other measures can be completed" (p. 64). Despite these limitations, the study suggests that microteaching is not necessarily more effective than other forms of instruction in helping prospective teachers develop understanding and skill.

The research on microteaching provides a compelling example of both the promise and the pitfalls of research on the pedagogy of teacher education. While it lasted, this line of research represented the closest thing to an extended program of research that exists in this area. Microteaching was investigated from a number of different angles, and researchers attempted to tease out the effects of subject matter and grade level, forms of feedback, and the importance of models in the success of microteaching. Although somewhat separate lines of research existed in the United States and Great Britain, the researchers were aware of and cited each other's work. Some more recent work on microteaching (Winitzsky & Arends, 1991) also has tried to take an explicitly comparative approach, comparing microteaching to other pedagogical approaches used in teacher education.

At the same time, the research on microteaching illustrates some of the shortcomings of the field in general. First, as many have observed, the research on microteaching was largely atheoretical. In fact, some early creators of microteaching explicitly rejected the idea of a unified theory, preferring an eclectic stance, and focusing on what works rather than trying to explain why. Second, although numerous studies of microteaching were conducted, only a small percentage found their way into peer-reviewed journals. The vast majority of the research consists of doctoral dissertations, book chapters, papers presented at conferences, and technical reports. As a result, relatively little of this research went through a rigorous process of review and revision. Finally, despite the numerous studies in this area, few definitive claims can be made about the value of microteaching. As one researcher concluded, "Despite the enormity of the research endeavour, there are few definite conclusions which can be drawn about the effects and effectiveness of microteaching" (MacLeod, 1987, p. 538).

Computer Simulations

One extension of research on the role of laboratory experiences in learning to teach involved the use of computer simulations. Early studies used computer-based simulations to assist preservice teachers in the acquisition of such teaching skills as classroom management, feedback to students, questioning, and the use of wait time. These researchers argued that computer simulations can simplify the unpredictability of actual classrooms, which makes the classroom such a challenging learning environment for student teachers, and can focus students' attention on discrete, specified skills.

Underlying the earlier research in this field is a view of teaching that emphasizes the technical components of teaching practice. Harold Strang, one of the most active researchers in this area, and his colleagues (e.g., Strang, Badt, & Kaufmann, 1987; Strang, Landrum, & Lynch, 1989) identified a set of six basic assumptions that underlie the use of computer simulation in teacher education. These assumptions include the need to define fundamental skills required for teaching practice; the importance of practice in skill acquisition; the need for prompting in skill acquisition; the value of reinforcement for the use of targeted skills; the inclusion of feedback that provides information on the use of the skill; and finally, the need to attend to conditions of transfer between the simulation and real-world classrooms.

Drawing on these assumptions, Strang and his colleagues (Strang et al., 1987, 1989) created a simulation that focused on three areas of teaching skills: (a) giving feedback to students during a spelling lesson, (b) managing time through pacing of questioning and use of wait time, and (c) managing disruptive behavior during a spelling lesson. In each area, researchers defined optimal responses.

The simulation consisted of images of students projected on a 3- × 4-foot screen. Students' facial expressions represented behavior and changed in response to teacher actions. These "simulated" students also responded to teacher questions with yes or no answers and correct or incorrect spellings of words, and simulated misbehaviors such as daydreaming, wandering around the room, making noise, and whispering. A systems operator converted the teacher's actions into codes entered into the computer, which in turn prompted student responses. The computer was programmed so that if teachers gave "helpful clues" to a student who misspelled a word, the student would spell the word correctly on a second try. If the teacher provided no assistance, the student would spell the word incorrectly again. Similarly, "effective" and "ineffective" responses to student misbehavior resulted in either a decrease or increase in misbehavior. Following each simulated spelling lesson, the student teachers were given feedback comparing their responses to norms for both inexperienced and experienced teachers. The study followed 61 prospective teachers in a required course on learning and development at the University of Virginia's 5-year teacher education program. The prospective teachers completed back-to-back simulated lessons in the fall, and then a single follow-up lesson in the spring. Data consisted of printouts of the complete sequential record of pupil–teacher interactions, as well as a questionnaire given to students. Researchers (Strang et al., 1987, 1989) analyzed the data for changes in prospective teachers' performances over the three sessions.

Strang et al. (1987, 1989) found that over time prospective teachers gave more encouragement, provided more feedback on inaccurate spelling, and used more content-oriented prompts. However, they showed no change in involvement of other pupils in the lesson. Prospective teachers also decreased their use of "ineffective" behaviors. These changes persisted into the third follow-up session in the spring. Analyses of questionnaire data revealed that the vast majority of prospective teachers rated the simulation as very useful. The authors suggested that the realism of the task and the provision of immediate feedback contributed to the success of the computer simulation. However, the researchers did not collect data on these prospective teachers' practices in student teaching to see if they continued to use these interventions in teaching spelling to actual students.

In another study on the use of computer simulations in an undergraduate educational psychology course, researchers investigated how computer simulations could help train prospective teachers to use psychological principles to solve classroom problems (Gorrell & Downing, 1989). In this experimental study, 64 volunteers were randomly assigned to four groups, including a computer simulation group, a problem-solving group, an extended instruction group, and a control group. In the three experimental groups, students spent 90 minutes with activities related to the procedures of behavior analysis. Researchers assessed knowledge of behavior analysis through a 30-item multiple choice test, and application of these principles through a written test in which students responded to classroom problems. Researchers also assessed the self-efficacy of students through a questionnaire.

Although there were no significant differences on the test of knowledge or on measure of self-efficacy, the computer simulation group scored higher than the control group on the application measure, using more of the behavior analysis principles to solve problems. In a secondary analysis of targeted subskills, researchers (Gorrell & Downing, 1989) also found that the computer simulation group outperformed other groups, which is not surprising because the computer simulation specifically targeted these subskills. As in the previous study, the researchers (Gorrel & Downing, 1989) did not follow these prospective teachers to see how they applied these principles in an actual classroom.

A third study focused on the use of computer simulation to help preservice elementary teachers develop science process skills (Baird & Kobala, 1988), particularly hypothesis formation. The researchers were also interested in whether having preservice teachers work on simulations in small group contexts would affect teachers' learning. The sample consisted of 87 elementary education students enrolled in four sections of a teacher education course. These intact classes were assigned to one of four conditions: cooperative learning groups with computer simulation, cooperative learning groups with textual exercises, individual work with computer simulation, and individual work with textual exercises. The computer simulation consisted of commercially developed products, and the textual exercise was taken from a science textbook and presented on the computer. Both the simulation and the textual exercise focused on formal reasoning and hypothesis formation and testing. Researchers also used the Group Assessment of Logical Thinking to measure students' formal thinking and to place students into heterogeneous groups. To assess hypothesis-testing skills, researchers used items from tests of science process skills. Researchers found that formal reasoning ability was strongly correlated with hypothesizing skills; they found a strong aptitude–treatment interaction between the level of prior reasoning ability and the treatment. The researchers concluded that computer simulations are not necessarily more effective for all types of learning in acquiring skills of forming and testing hypotheses, nor was cooperative group learning necessarily more effective in this particular study. As the researchers noted, this was a brief 2-hour treatment, which may have lessened the potential effects of either the simulation or group work.

A more recent study investigated the use of a computer simulation to help prospective elementary teachers develop an understanding of physics concepts (Otero, Johnson, & Goldberg, 1999). This study looked at how a group of prospective elementary teachers used a computer simulation in collaborative inquiry to construct their understanding of a variety of physics concepts. As part of a physical science course at San Diego State University, groups of three students engaged with a set of activities that were linked to the computer. The activities first elicited their prior knowledge and assumptions about a concept and then guided them to develop and test explanatory models. Finally, students were asked to apply their ideas to solve new problems. Using videotapes of these small groups and of whole-class discussion, computer records, and student interviews as data, researchers investigated how the computer simulation supported students' understanding. They argued that the computer provided a shared representational space that supported students' evaluation and modification of ideas and that the simulation facilitated the process of model building, as students could test their emerging ideas through computer experiments. This study represents a departure from the earlier studies of computer simulations in that it focuses on the development of teacher cognition, rather than on behavior, as an outcome. The conceptual framework focuses both on the tool of the computer simulation and what it offers, as well as on the process of collaborative inquiry; in fact, the researchers noted that they were unable to untangle the power of collaborative inquiry from the specific use of the simulation.

The majority of studies on computer simulation focuses on training preservice teachers to use specific skills that researchers posit are related to effective teaching. In two studies, skills are strongly rooted in principles of behavioral psychology, reflecting in part the historical context of these studies. The behavioral model also underlies the pedagogical approach, with its emphasis on feedback and targeting of specific skills. Two studies suggest that computer simulations can be effective in helping prospective teachers develop targeted skills within the simulation. However, neither study looked at how the preservice teachers might use these skills in actual classrooms. Similar to the research on microteaching, the primary outcome investigated in the earlier two studies was teacher behavior, although the final study reviewed looked at teacher cognition as the outcome.

Uses of Video Technology and Hypermedia

One effect of the research on microteaching was the realization that videotapes could be a powerful mode of instruction for prospective teachers. Videotape technology allowed teacher educators to capture classroom practice in a form that could be replayed, unlike regular classroom teaching. Videotaped segments of classroom teaching also provided prospective teachers with common examples of teaching, something they were unlikely to find in their varied field experiences. Researchers became intrigued with the question of what prospective teachers could learn from viewing and responding to videotapes of classroom teaching.

This interest in video technology occurred at the same time as the shift to more cognitive views of teaching and learning, which resulted in a corresponding shift in the outcomes being investigated. Although earlier research on microteaching generally looked at effects on teacher behaviors and acquisition of discrete teaching skills, research in the 1980s and 1990s focused on the effects of pedagogy on various forms of teacher cognition, including teachers' reasoning ability, decision making, and reflection.

An early example of research on the uses of video tried to tease out differences between having students participate in a role-play on an instructional strategy for teaching reading and having students watch a videotape of a teacher using the same strategy with students (Anderson, Frager, & Bolin, 1982). Although the results did not reach significance in most areas, teachers viewing the videotape did score higher than those who participated in the role-play in their ability to use the instructional strategy with elementary children.

Later work focused less on skills acquired through the use of videotape and more on the development of preservice teachers' reasoning and thinking. Copeland and Decker (1996), for example, investigated how nine preservice elementary teachers "made meaning" from watching a brief video clip of instruction and discussing the clip with peers. Through analyses of interviews and peer discussions, researchers looked both at the number of topics raised by individuals and at how their thinking about a topic may have changed. Although the authors concluded that video discussion contributed to the meaning making of preservice teachers, it was not clear whether viewing the tape multiple times or discussions of the tape with peers contributed to their changes in thinking.

A number of studies have investigated the uses of video technology of various kinds in elementary mathematics. Researchers have studied how the use of videotapes affects prospective teachers' beliefs and attitudes toward the teaching of math. Building on a long-term professional development project, Daniel (1996) studied how preservice teachers interacted with an interactive, multimedia environment that included a video database of experienced math teachers. Using think-aloud and interview data, as well as observations, Daniel hoped to understand how students interacted with the database and what they learned. Although some students were dissatisfied with the materials, most felt that the videos helped them make connections between theories of constructivist teaching and actual practice. In a study on the effects of using videotapes to affect preservice teachers' beliefs about the teaching of math (Friel & Carboni, 2000), instructors of a math methods class used videotape to focus students' attention on reform-based teaching of mathematics. On the basis of interviews conducted with a sample of five student teachers, researchers suggest that these preservice teachers began to adopt more student-centered beliefs about the teaching of math. They also claimed that videos provided students with a common case for reflection and an image of what a productive reform classroom might look like. However, as the authors noted, it was difficult to isolate the effect of the video cases from other aspects of the methods class. The study also did not include observations of student teaching, so we do not know how or whether student teachers used these images in their own practice.

Another group of researchers (Lambdin, Duffy, & Moore, 1997) also explored how the uses of interactive videodisc technology affected eight prospective teachers' visions of teaching, learning and assessment in elementary mathematics. The materials included three representations of exemplary practice along with commentaries from diverse perspectives. The researchers investigated prospective teachers' uses of the materials, as captured in keystroke data and students' reflective journals. Based on these data, researchers concluded that preservice teachers used all components of the videodisc materials, but only during one component of the course, in which they were directed to use them. Students seemed to value the commentaries and multiple models but wanted more lessons included in the materials. Finally, although students valued the opportunity to view the materials, they believed that direct classroom observation was more valuable.

Another study conducted in elementary math looked at preservice teachers' uses of videodisc materials (Goldman & Barron, 1990). The researchers used hypermedia materials funded by the National Science Foundation that linked text to videoclips.

They looked at preservice teachers' reactions to the materials, the extent to which the use of these materials affected teachers' retention of facts, and the influence of materials on student teaching. Using questionnaires, interviews, and an observation instrument, authors concluded that preservice teachers were generally positive about the materials, but the materials had no effect on students' recall of information. The authors also reported that in a comparison of observations of student teaching of students who did not experience hypermedia materials and of students who did, students who experienced the materials outperformed the comparison group in six areas. However, as means were not provided and the data analysis was not fully explained, these results are difficult to interpret.

In the comparative study conducted by Winitzky and Arends (1991) mentioned earlier, researchers compared the effects of viewing live and videotaped models of cooperative learning on preservice teachers' knowledge of cooperative learning, skill in teaching a cooperative lesson, and their ability to reflect on a cooperative lesson. Using only a posttest with a multiple treatment-group design, the researchers randomly assigned 37 preservice teachers to three treatment groups that varied according to whether preservice teachers had the opportunity to observe a live demonstration or to watch a demonstration on videotape. Using a test of knowledge of cooperative learning, a test of reflectiveness, and coding of videotaped microteaching lessons as instruments, the researchers found there were no significant differences in any of the outcomes, suggesting that videotaped models of practice may be just as effective as live ones. Another study investigating elementary preservice teacher education (Carlson & Falk, 1990) compared what elementary education students learned about cooperative learning from written materials to what they learned from using interactive videodisc materials. Using a test of content knowledge and a task that assessed observation skills, researchers found that the students using the videodisc materials scored significantly higher on the test of content knowledge and on the assessment of observation skill than did students who used the written materials. Again, this study did not look at students' ability to implement cooperative learning in classrooms. Finally, Overbaugh (1995) looked at how the use of interactive video materials affected what preservice teachers learned about classroom management and their concerns about teaching. The materials allowed students in a teacher education class to experiment for 3 hours with various solutions to classroom management problems and to learn eight basic principles. The research assessed students' knowledge and concerns before and after the use of the materials; knowledge of classroom management was assessed using a researcher-constructed test, whereas concerns were assessed with a questionnaire. The author found significant differences in achievement from pre- to posttest, although the difference was not dramatic.

One of the most extensive examples of hypermedia materials for teacher education was created by Deborah Ball and Magdalene Lampert. Based on their own teaching of elementary mathematics in a local elementary school, Lampert and Ball (1998) created a set of hypermedia materials that included video of an entire year of instruction in third and fifth grades, transcripts of these videos, records of student work, including their math notebooks, teachers' daily journals, and other classroom records. In their roles as teacher-educators, Ball and Lampert used these materials with prospective elementary teachers, asking them to investigate questions about the teaching of mathematics using these hypermedia materials. Lampert and Ball then analyzed 68 of these student investigations. They found that two thirds of the investigations focused on the teacher or some aspect of the teaching, seven focused on students, and several focused on policy. Despite the emphasis on content in these materials, very few students focused on mathematics. Although Lampert and Ball offer conjectures rather than conclusions about student learning, they talk about the importance of the particular tasks assigned to students and how these tasks focus students' attention on aspects of teaching that otherwise may be invisible.

What can we conclude on the basis of these studies? A number of studies found that preservice teachers were positive about the uses of videodisc and hypermedia materials (Daniel, 1996; Goldman & Barron, 1990; Lambdin et al., 1997; Overbaugh, 1995), and several studies found that viewing videotapes can improve preservice teachers' understanding of a teaching strategy or concept (Carlson & Falk, 1990; Daniel; Overbaugh). A few studies tried to untangle what preservice teachers learned from videotapes as opposed to what they learned from other approaches, such as role-plays, live observation, or written materials (Anderson et al., 1982; Carlson & Falk; Winitzky & Arends 1991). These studies suggest that video materials can be at least as effective as other approaches in helping students develop knowledge about instructional approaches. However, the studies cannot help us understand whether preservice teachers are better able to implement these approaches in classrooms.

In other instances, it is difficult to untangle the effects of video materials from other aspects of the class and program in which the materials are used. So, for example, are the videos themselves the catalyst for the kinds of changes described in these studies, or is the instruction around the videos? As Lampert and Ball (1998) ask about students' uses of hypermedia, "Did listening to one another's presentations, or working together in project groups, influence what they learned? Did they change one another's resources for interpretation? Did they develop habits of mind from one another?" (p. 160). These questions begin to address how professors' instructional decisions around the uses of hypermedia, not just the materials themselves, may affect student learning.

We also have little sense of the features of video materials themselves that might matter to student learning. Although it is difficult to tell from some descriptions, it seems that many of these videoclips were quite brief. How is viewing a videoclip selected as a discrete example of cooperative learning, for example, different from being able to watch videotape of one class over an entire year of instruction, in which many forms of cooperative learning might be seen? (Lampert & Ball, 1998) What kinds of learning are possible, given these different uses of video and hypermedia technology?

Somewhat surprisingly, we did not find recent studies that investigated what prospective teachers learn from watching videos of their own classroom practice (one feature of the microteaching tradition). As many programs now require student teachers to videotape their practice, this lacuna in the research seems surprising.

As was true of the research on microteaching, much of the work on video technology lacks a strong theoretical framework to guide the research. Although the materials seem to hold tremendous promise, we need a much richer understanding of the features of video materials that matter most in helping prospective teachers learn from others' practice, as well as the kinds of instruction that must be orchestrated around video materials to support the learning of preservice teachers.

Case Methods

As the paradigm for research on teaching shifted from behavioral psychology to cognitive psychology, researchers shifted their focus from teachers' behaviors to teachers' thinking and knowledge. Teacher educators responded by focusing less on training models than on models that attempted to improve teachers' ability to reason and reflect on teaching. In the early 1990s, teacher educators began to explore the use of case methods. Kathy Carter (Carter & Unklesbay, 1989) and Lee Shulman (1986) among others, proposed that the case method could help prospective teachers learn to think pedagogically, to reason through classroom dilemmas, and to explore possible actions. Work on knowledge acquisition in complex domains (Spiro, Coulson, Feltovich, & Anderson, 1988) is one of the primary theoretical foundations for the use of cases, as is the work on situated cognition. Researchers in this area have argued that because teaching is so complex and uncertain, novices must have the opportunity to view practice from multiple perspectives. In addition, because teachers' decisions are intimately tied to the specifics of the situation, novices need opportunities to examine how principles play out in the particulars of teaching.

As many writers note (Lundeberg, Levin, & Harrington, 1999; McAninch, 1993; Merseth, 1996; Merseth & Lacey, 1993; Shulman, L., 1996; Shulman, J., 1992), teacher educators have expressed tremendous enthusiasm for the "case idea" (Sykes & Bird, 1992) and a number have written about using case methods in their classrooms (Kleinfeld, 1992; LaBoskey, 1992; Richert, 1992; Wade, 1992). Consistent with the stated purposes of case methods, these authors focus primarily on how the use of cases helps develop prospective teachers' ability to reason pedagogically and to reflect about practice.[3]

In a study conducted in an introductory undergraduate course, Anderson and Bird (1995) looked for what impact one course's use of cases had on students' conceptions of teaching. The undergraduate participants were taking an introductory teacher education course built around three video case studies, each paired with a related reading. Bird, who taught the course, hoped the cases would challenge and broaden students' conceptions of teaching. The data came from 8 of 31 students who either volunteered or were chosen for unidentified reasons. After interviewing participants and analyzing their written work, the researchers offer three students as case studies, providing evidence of some growth, but little change in fundamental conceptions of teaching. According to the researchers, students viewed cases through the lenses of their largely unchanged initial conceptions. Their findings offer a cautionary note to those seeking to use cases to help student teachers change deeply held views and beliefs.

In a study designed to explore the potential for case-based pedagogy to promote reasoning skills, Harrington (1995) looked at 26 elementary education students' first and last case analyses to understand their development of pedagogical reasoning. These students wrote a total of four case analyses as part of an introductory course. The author defined pedagogical reasoning in terms of five discrete skills: framing problems, considering multiple perspectives, warranting solutions, considering consequences of proposed action, and the reflectiveness of students' critique of their analysis and solution for the case. Harrington coded students' written work to determine each student's level of ability in the first and last written analysis for each skill. Harrington concluded that students were able at least to begin to engage in each of these five elements of reasoning; thus, she finds that "case-based pedagogy can be used to gain access to student's professional reasoning and may, as well, foster that reasoning" (p. 212). The author does not provide much information about the instruction around the use of cases, nor the criteria used in coding students' skill levels. One alternative hypothesis not addressed is that students simply improved

---

[3]Tom Levine contributed to both the analysis and prose of this section.

on the assignment with practice; they learned how to "do" cases, that is, to meet an instructor's requirements, without necessarily internalizing habits and skills that would enhance practice. Elsewhere, Harrington noted that "there was little change" in students' ability to take perspectives other than the one offered in the case; her data support the conclusion that students made some progress in the other four skills, but not in this one. As in much teacher education research, it is difficult to isolate the effects of this particular pedagogy and class from the other teacher education experiences of students; Harrington acknowledges that students were taking three other courses concurrently. Still, Harrington's findings begin to build an empirical base for the claim that case-based pedagogy can contribute to preservice teachers' ability to make reasoned decisions under conditions of uncertainty.

Harrington and her colleagues (Harrington, Quinn-Leering, & Hodson, 1996) conducted a similar study looking at how the use of case-based pedagogy can provide opportunities for critical reflection. Based on the literature on life-span development, the researchers define critical reflection as the ability to identify and acknowledge different perspectives (open-mindedness), the ability to consider the moral and ethical consequences of choices (responsibility), and the ability to identify and clarify the limitations in one's assumptions when making decisions (wholeheartedness).[4] Using a set of case analyses completed by 21 students enrolled in an introductory class on elementary school teaching, the authors asked how these case analyses provided "insight into the development of different aspects of critical reflection" (p. 26). The case analyses, the third written by these students in a semester course, were coded across four levels of coding, looking particularly for patterns related to open-mindedness, responsibility, and wholeheartedness. The authors identified three patterns within each of these elements of critical reflection and concluded that these case analyses provided evidence of students' development of critical reflection in all three areas. The authors did not argue that case-based pedagogy helped foster the development of these perspectives; rather, they use this study as a way to demonstrate the value of using case analyses as data.

A later study looked at the kinds of mediational tools and reasoning processes student teachers employ, the issues they identify, and the images of teaching and learning they create as they work with cases in teacher education (Moje & Wade, 1997). Locating their research in sociocultural theories of learning, the authors studied a preservice class on content-area literacy and an in-service class on a similar topic, both taught by the first author. In these classes, preservice teachers worked with three published cases and wrote two cases based on their experience, although the research seems to focus on the published cases. The authors describe the case discussions as including analysis, role-plays, and the generation and evaluation of possible actions. Data sources included audiotapes of case discussions and debriefing sessions, in which students discussed what they learned from the case discussion, focus group interviews with students conducted after the course had ended, and individual interviews with ten preservice and three in-service teachers, following the focus group interviews. Data analysis focused on the tools, images, and issues that teachers identified. The authors found that student teachers used their experiences as students, texts and concepts from their university courses, and role-play activities as tools for analyzing the cases, whereas experienced teachers relied almost exclusively on their own teaching experience. Student teachers identified teacher resistance and

---

[4]The researchers are drawing upon Dewey's constructs in this analysis.

the diverse needs of future learners as two of the primary issues in the cases. The authors claimed that student teachers developed images of teaching as technical and learner abilities as fixed.

Other research focuses less on the overall impact of case methods than on the appropriate pedagogy for using cases with teachers. Levin (1995) used an experimental study design with two groups of a dozen preservice teachers. The control group read and wrote an analysis of a case, then wrote a second analysis a few days later. One month later, the group wrote about a second case which experts identified as raising five of the same core issues as the first case. The experimental group did the same reading and writing, but met in two separate groups of six within two days of reading the first case to discuss it. The experimental group then wrote about the second case one month later. Using a scoring rubric, Levin found that the control and experimental group's first written case analyses were equal; the control group's scores declined when they wrote a second analysis of the same case and then declined again upon writing about a second, similar case. The experimental group's scores remained about the same in their second written analysis of the same case, and declined to the same level as the control group upon writing about the second case. Qualitative analysis of the second analyses showed several impacts of discussion: Student teachers improved their understanding of the issues and offered more explicit and elaborated analyses. The study provides evidence of teachers picking up ideas and even ways of analyzing a case from other teachers after discussion, providing support to the findings of Copeland and Decker (1996). The authors also found that teachers' backgrounds, experiences, and interests appear to affect their view of cases, because some participants ignored a key aspect of the second case. This finding resonates with Anderson's and Bird's (1995) finding regarding the strength of deeply held conceptions in shaping what participants see in a case. In the final analysis, when the authors focused on qualitative analysis rather than their own quantitative rubric, they were able to find evidence suggesting that discussion improved preservice and beginning teachers' understandings drawn from cases, although it was not clear how these understandings might affect their practice.

Another study began with a friendly argument between two teacher educators over the best use of cases in the classrooms (Lundeberg & Scheurman, 1997). Unable to resolve their disagreement over the pedagogical value of using a case more than once, they conducted action research to investigate the effects of analyzing a case before and after instruction on students' learning about educational psychology. The research took place in the instructors' undergraduate educational psychology courses, in which different kinds of cases were used, including short textbook cases, open-ended dilemma cases taken from a casebook, a hyper-card case developed for the class, and video cases. Classroom discussion of cases focused initially on the issues raised in the case, different perspectives on the issues, a discussion of the concepts or principles embedded within the case, and finally an effort to generate possible actions. The study covered two units of study, one on motivation and one on learning, both of which are described in the article. Following the motivation unit, the instructor gave students a case and asked them to analyze it with a peer and to identify issues using psychological concepts, justify their reasoning, and propose possible solutions. In the following unit on learning, the instructor did not explicitly refer to the case, but at the end of the unit, students analyzed the same case a second time with a different peer. Data consisted of the students' written analyses, which were coded using a list of potential psychological concepts from the textbook, and students' written reflections on the differences between their two case analyses. The authors found that in the second case analysis, students identified more concepts about both motivation and learning, but especially about learning. An ANOVA conducted on the coded data showed a significant difference between the two analyses and an interaction effect between the timing of the analysis and content learned. The authors conducted a replication in the second author's classroom, altering only the order of the units, the follow-up question asked of students, and the peer analysis. In the second study, students worked with the same peer on both case analyses. The authors found very similar results. The authors concluded that "when cases are used as an anchor, they serve to stimulate students' background knowledge and to increase their receptivity to subsequent instructional efforts aimed at developing their pedagogical knowledge" (Lundeberg & Scheurman, p. 795). The authors do not, however, address how the results may have been affected by the greater familiarity of the task; as students reported in their reflections, in the second analysis, they had a better idea of the task.

Despite the enthusiasm for "the case idea," there is still relatively little empirical research on the uses of cases in teacher education. As is true for much research in this area, more descriptive work exists on what people are doing in teacher education classrooms than do systematic studies of the outcomes of various aspects of case-based pedagogy. As was also true for research on microteaching, much of the research did not make it into peer-reviewed journals; a number of often-cited studies on case methods were presented at conferences but were never written up for publication in peer-reviewed venues, which meant they did not meet the criteria established by the Panel.

The studies reviewed provide initial evidence that cases may help improve reasoning skills of preservice teachers, enabling them to identify issues and analyze an educational problem more effectively, although how reasoning skills are defined differs from study to study. It is also clear that the instruction around a case matters, not just the use of case materials (Copeland & Decker, 1996; Levin, 1995; Lundeberg & Scheurman, 1997). This raises the importance of looking more carefully at the instructional interactions around case methods. A smaller body of research has looked at the substantive knowledge preservice teachers can gain from reading cases (Lundeberg & Scheurman). Finally, several researchers argue that case-based analyses and discussions can reveal the thinking of preservice teachers, giving teacher educators a better window into how their students think (Harrington et al., 1996; Moje & Wade, 1997). Most research in this area focuses on cognitive outcomes; there is no evidence that the use of case-based pedagogy affects preservice teachers' classroom practice.

Researchers need to be more explicit in describing the characteristics of cases used in teacher education classrooms. We do not yet have a rich vocabulary for describing the genres of cases used in teacher education (Grossman, 1992), yet features of the case itself are likely to matter to student learning. One possible research program in this area might provide a better sense of what kinds of cases are most useful for which instructional purposes. We also need more detail about how cases are actually used in case-based pedagogy (Grossman, 1993; Lundeberg et al., 1999). With more research, it may become possible to theorize about the most appropriate uses and contexts for analyzing cases. At this point, we cannot make strong claims about the use of cases; continued research focusing on measurable impacts on students' understandings, reasoning skills, beliefs, and classroom practice is still needed to provide more evidence of when and how this approach can be used effectively.

Portfolios in Teacher Education

At roughly the same time teacher educators became interested in the uses of case-based pedagogy, they also began to explore the use of teacher portfolios (Bird, 1990). In part, this enthusiasm grew from the uses of student portfolios in public schools, as part of efforts to create more authentic forms of performance assessment. The movement also reflected the desire to document teachers' work more carefully and to make the work of teaching more public. Portfolios in public school were used both for assessment purposes and as an opportunity to enable students to reflect on their own progress; the legacy of these twin purposes continued into their use in teacher education, in which portfolios are used both to stimulate preservice teachers' reflections on their development, as well as to assess that development, often in a summative way. Teacher portfolios are now the capstone project in a large number of teacher education programs (Zeichner & Wray, 2001). Despite the numerous claims made about the potential benefits of teacher portfolios, "there have been very few systematic studies of the nature and consequences of their use for either assessment or development purposes" (Zeichner & Wray, p. 615). In this section, I review the few systematic studies that exist, most of which look at student perceptions of the process of constructing portfolios.

Studies have looked at the process of portfolio construction and the effects of using portfolios on some aspect of preservice teachers' beliefs or reflective ability. Loughran and Corrigan (1995) describe how portfolios are used in a preservice science methods course at Monash University. They investigated how preservice teachers approached the process of constructing portfolios and the value they saw in the task. They gave 22 students a questionnaire at the end of the course and conducted interviews with eight of these students both midway through and at the end of the course. A research assistant conducted the interviews "to minimize the likelihood that participants would feel obliged to tell us what they thought we (as their teacher) might want to hear" (p. 569). Findings from the survey suggest that roughly a third of students initially had no clear idea of the purposes of the portfolio assignment, a third saw it as an assessment tool, and another third perceived the portfolio in terms of its employment purposes. Three fourths of the students felt that the portfolio was valuable, with participants equally split between those who saw its primary use in employment interviews and those who saw its use in demonstrating what they had learned.

In one study of portfolios in a community service-learning project for a social studies methods course, researchers investigated how preservice teachers responded to portfolio construction, how they perceived the usefulness of the portfolios, and how portfolios assisted the reflective process (Wade & Yarbrough, 1996). The researchers, who were also the instructors, detailed the required components of the portfolios, which included a lesson plan, a research paper, a reflection on their experiences during service learning, and two reflective letters on preservice teachers' experiences with the portfolio. Data were collected over several semesters, leading to an initial sample of 212 elementary teacher education students enrolled in six different sections of the course across three semesters. Data sources included a survey of 136 students, in-depth interviews with seven students, and students' final reflective essays. The authors coded the essay for uses of the portfolio, struggles with the portfolio process, and learning through reflection and analyzed interview data with similar codes. Finally, descriptive details were provided on students' responses to the ten items on the survey relating to portfolio use. The researchers found that more than a third of the students felt frustrated in trying to represent their learning through the portfolio, and 45% reported not understanding the purposes of the portfolio assignment. Although 63% of the students reported learning something from the portfolio process, most reported learning about themselves. Researchers tested for the effect of the instructor on survey results and found significant differences between the responses of students taught by different instructors on 5 of the 10 items analyzed. Although the authors do not describe the teaching of the portfolio process in the various sections of these courses, they hypothesize that how the instructors "prepare, interact with students or present information about the portfolio process can have a sizeable influence on the value of the portfolio as a reflective tool, the overall value and enjoyment of the portfolios and the uses made of them" (p. 75). The researchers do not look at the quality of reflection or explain what they counted as evidence of reflection.

Another study tried to look at the factors that students perceived as facilitating or hindering the process of constructing portfolios (Borko, Michalec, Timmons, & Siddle, 1997). Researchers described how student-teaching portfolios were used for both reflection and exploration, on one hand, and for evaluation, on the other. Using action research to study their own program, the authors collected written reflections from the 21 students in their graduate teacher education program and interviewed eight of them. University supervisors conducted the interviews four to five months after the completion of the portfolios. Researchers found the majority of students saw the portfolio as a tool for reflection, and half reported that it enabled them to link theory and practice. Six of the 21 student teachers, however, felt that the process of constructing the portfolios drew their attention away from student teaching. Students identified support and guidance from the university, support from their cooperating teacher, and support from peers as facilitating factors. They saw the restrictiveness of the portfolio guidelines, the status of the portfolio as a course assignment, the emphasis on reflection, and the timing of the assignment as hindrances. The study did not look directly at what students learned from this process, concentrating instead on student reports of their experiences with the portfolios.

In a carefully designed study that looked at how program structures, such as portfolios and teaching partners, affected preservice teachers' reflections, Anna Richert (1990) asked student teachers to reflect under four conditions: alone, without the aid of a partner or portfolio; reflecting with a portfolio; reflecting with a partner; and reflecting with both a partner and a portfolio. The study included 12 preservice teachers, each of whom was asked to reflect under two of the four conditions. The preservice teachers were allowed to determine the content of their teaching portfolio, which represented one week of their teaching. Richert collected both process data, including questionnaires and self-report interviews on the process of reflection, and product data, which included their journal entries, essays, portfolios, and interviews. Data were coded for content of reflections and categories of teacher knowledge. Richert found that preservice teachers who used the teaching portfolios in talking with partners were more likely to reflect about content and the teaching of content. The preservice teachers also reported that the portfolios helped them remember teaching events more accurately and that the process of constructing the portfolio provoked them to think more specifically about their teaching.

In most instances, researchers have studied the use of portfolios in their own teacher education settings. Because both the goals and approaches for using portfolios vary across these programs, the studies are difficult to compare. However, most of the portfolios described in these studies share common elements (lesson plans and reflective pieces), and most serve at least the dual purposes of helping students reflect on their practice and of assessing their learning. How portfolios are used in teacher education influences students' perceptions of their value (Borko et al., 1997; Loughran & Corrigan, 1995; Wade & Yarbrough, 1996). Even within the same program, students experience the process of portfolio development differently depending on the particular instructor (Wade & Yarbrough) and the quality of the feedback provided by supervisors and cooperating teachers (Borko et al; Wade & Yarbrough). Despite the challenges of implementing teaching portfolios, most students seemed to value the process of constructing a portfolio (Borko et al.; Loughran & Corrigan; Wade & Yarbrough). Despite the often-repeated claim that portfolios can contribute to preservice teachers' ability to reflect on their practice, only one study carefully looked at how the structure of a portfolio assignment might affect the content of students' reflections (Richert, 1990).

Practitioner Research

Although the practice of school- or classroom-based research among teachers has a long history (e.g., Corey, 1953), and teacher educators began to use forms of action research as early as the 1950s (cf. Beckman, 1957; Perrodin, 1959), over the past 20 years many teacher educators have begun to include various forms of practitioner research in the preparation of teachers. Although there are different nuances in how authors define forms of practitioner research, including action research and teacher research, we have chosen to group these studies under the broader rubric of practitioner research. In their review of the field, Zeichner and Noffke (2001) provide an overview of the multiple traditions that have contributed to the evolution of practitioner research.

In most examples of practitioner research reviewed here, prospective teachers are required to study and analyze some aspect of their classroom practice, either by themselves or with others. The research results in either a plan for action or deeper understandings of practice. Definitions range from an emphasis on the nature and processes of the inquiry itself to an emphasis on its outcomes. Price (2001), for example, defines action research as "intentional, collaborative, and democratic in its intent and process" (p. 43), a definition that focuses more on the nature of the inquiry than on its outcomes. Drawing from early definitions of action science, Clift, Veal, Johnson, and Holland (1990) suggest that the goal of action research is "to change practice or sets of practices" (p. 54). How researchers define practitioner research connects to the types of outcomes they might choose to study.

The choice of practitioner research as a pedagogy for teacher education reflects assumptions about the nature of teaching practice. Most researchers in this area explicitly connect their choice of this approach to their definition of teaching as a practice centered around inquiry. As Tabachnik and Zeichner (1999) state, "It is not so much a matter of doing action research *on* teaching as it is of viewing teaching itself as a form of inquiry or experimentation" (p. 311). Similarly, Cochran-Smith (1991b) sees teacher research as providing opportunities for preservice teachers "to learn to think like teachers and reformers" (p. 111).

Despite the many descriptions of teacher educators using some form of practitioner research in their courses, relatively few empirical studies in this area met the Panel criteria. Most of these studies focus on the process of using practitioner research in the teacher education curriculum and its attendant challenges, rather than looking at what prospective teachers learned from their inquiries. In a description of an effort to create collaborative action research as the basis of the reform of teacher education, Clift and her colleagues (1990) studied their efforts to create a collaboration between the University of Houston and five local public schools and to design a teacher education program centered around action research and inquiry. In several articles, Cochran-Smith (1991a, 1991b) describes an innovative teacher education program at the University of Pennsylvania built around collaborative teacher research opportunities that were part of student teaching. All these authors value building forms of practitioner research into teacher education and emphasize the need to establish new partnerships with school-based teacher educators to create and sustain such opportunities.

Connecting the use of action research with a social–reconstructionist perspective on teaching, Gore and Zeichner (1991) described how they use action research in the elementary teacher education program at the University of Wisconsin, Madison, as a "vehicle for structuring the reflections of student teachers" (p. 125). One author, in her role as a supervisor for 18 students during their student-teaching semester, introduced the students to the action research project they were to conduct while student teaching. The authors analyzed the 18 written reports of the students' action research projects, looking for concerns about moral and political issues and evidence of critical reflection. They found that only a small group of projects revealed a "clear concern for moral and political issues as integral to the project" (p. 129), whereas more than half of the projects revealed no explicit concern for these issues at all. Many students focused their projects on issues of discipline and classroom management, whereas others focused on their relationships with the cooperating teacher or other adults.

In another study of action research in the University of Wisconsin, Madison, teacher education program, Tabachnik and Zeichner (1999) studied an action research seminar that was designed to help teachers develop a conceptual change orientation to the teaching of science. This study focused on how the seminar and action research projects facilitated learning to teach for conceptual change. The researchers collected and transcribed audiotapes of all class sessions, videotapes of students' project presentations, and student and instructor course journals. They analyzed the data for prospective teachers' personal understandings of conceptual change and what it means to teach for conceptual change, and for their thoughts about aspects of the school environment that supported or hindered their efforts to teach for conceptual change. The authors found that the action research projects helped prospective teachers understand more about students' thinking and helped them focus on students as learners. However, the prospective teachers did not use the information they elicited from students to plan for instruction.

Valli (2000) and Price (2001) provided detailed descriptions of courses in action research taught in the context of a preservice teacher education program. Valli described her attempts to rethink her action research class to focus more directly on issues of school improvement. Using participant observation, verbatim transcripts of audiotaped class sessions, questionnaires, and other data sources, Valli set out to document how her efforts to make an explicit connection between action research and school improvement might affect students' understandings of action research. Valli's analysis suggested that, despite her efforts, students found it difficult to make connections between the concept of action research as professional development and action research as a tool for school improvement.

In his inquiry into his course, Price (2001) explored what it means for preservice teachers to engage in action research; what constitute key experiences in learning about teaching, action research, and change; and what kinds of changes preservice teachers imagine undertaking as beginning teachers. Using transcripts of audiotapes of classroom conversations, questionnaires from the beginning and end of the course, action-research journals, writing, informal interviews with preservice teachers, videotapes, and policy documents as data, Price looked for changes in what these 11 preservice teachers knew and were able to do, their view of themselves as change agents, and other more personal changes. Price also analyzed the focus of preservice teachers' inquiries, and their views of action research. Price found that most preservice teachers used action research to pursue their own specific pedagogical issues, whereas several used action research to "strengthen their confidence in an area in which they felt uneasy" (p. 47). Not surprisingly, the preservice teachers in the course developed slightly different definitions of action research based on their own experiences and inquiry. Price also identified challenges to preservice teachers' engagement with action research, including the difficulty in finding time to reflect and in negotiating their research agendas with mentor teachers. Although the preservice teachers saw themselves as able to effect some change within their own classrooms, few felt they could make changes in their schools or communities. Finally, most of these 11 teachers wanted to pursue changes in their first year of teaching that were directly related to the topic of their action research projects.

Although these three studies focused on practitioner research conducted in university-based courses, others have examined prospective teachers' experiences with research during field experiences. Nath and Tellez (1995) studied eight preservice teachers placed with teacher researchers as part of their early field experience in the University of Houston teacher education program (see Clift et al., 1990, for a description of the program). The researchers collected 176 assignments, 88 from students placed with teacher researchers and another 88 randomly selected from other students in the course who were not placed with teacher researchers. The assignments were coded for level of satisfaction with the field experience, as well as ideas, attitudes, and knowledge developed in the field. Following the required 45 hours of early field experience, researchers interviewed each of the eight students. They concluded that students placed with teacher researchers felt more welcomed and supported in their field experience, and were more likely to report observations of good teaching. These students also reported interacting with children more frequently than did students with other placements and could envision themselves engaging in teacher research once they became teachers. Although it is hard to disentangle the particular benefits of placements with teacher researchers from benefits of a placement with a carefully selected group of cooperating teachers, the authors concluded that placing preservice teachers with teacher researchers can help them see teaching as inquiry oriented and student centered.

Although many teacher educators proclaim the value of various forms of practitioner research in preservice teacher education, we are still at the early stages of being able to bolster these claims with empirical evidence. Studies reviewed here suggest that it can be difficult for preservice teachers to find the time to engage in sustained inquiry while student teaching (Gore & Zeichner, 1991; Price, 2001) and that negotiating research agendas with their cooperating teachers can be challenging. Placing student teachers with more experienced teacher-researchers (e.g., Clift et al., 1990; Cochran-Smith, 1991a, 1991b; Nath & Tellez, 1995) can ease the difficulty of such negotiations and provide prospective teachers with both support and an inquiry-oriented perspective on teaching. However, there is, as yet, little evidence that engaging in practitioner research affects dimensions of the actual classroom practice of preservice teachers (Tabachnik & Zeichner, 1999).

Having reviewed the research in five areas of the pedagogy of teacher education, I now turn to a consideration of some of the broader issues that cut across research on the pedagogy of teacher education.

The Question of Context

One dilemma that haunts the literature on the pedagogy of teacher education is how to address the interrelationship of any particular pedagogy to the larger context of the teacher education program. Many of the studies included in this review do not address how the effects of a particular pedagogy used in a specific class connect to other aspects of the class, to use of the same pedagogy in other classes, or to the cumulative effects of the program as a whole. In some instances, researchers noted that students were having many other experiences in teacher education that either contributed to or diluted the impact of the particular pedagogy they were studying. Yet few designs look at the pedagogy of programs as a whole or try explicitly to disentangle the power of particular pedagogies from overall program effects.

The effort to make claims about the effects of particular pedagogical approaches is also hampered by lack of information on instructional context. As mentioned earlier, the research reports often provide relatively little information about the instruction that surrounds the use of a case or a teaching portfolio, making it difficult to determine what aspects of the pedagogical approach have contributed to the described outcomes. For example, to understand the pedagogy of case methods, we would need to know more about the features of the written or video case, how the case was introduced, the nature of interaction around the case, and any tasks students were asked to do in conjunction with the case discussion. One critical feature of instructional context has to do with the time allotted to a particular pedagogy. Some studies included in this review, particularly those on microteaching and computer simulation, relied on very short interventions, sometimes as short as a few hours. I doubt that any pedagogy is powerful enough to make an impact in such a limited amount of time. Most studies of instructional approach also do not specify features of the relationships among teachers and students in teacher education that might either intensify or dilute the power of a particular approach, yet we know that these relationships affect the quality of student experiences in every educational program.

Making Methods Explicit

Research on the pedagogy of teacher education is still a relatively new field of inquiry, and one that includes a wide array of disciplinary perspectives. As a result, researchers in this area lack a common tradition for describing how data were analyzed and collected. In their discussion of research on the use of case methods, Lundeberg, Levin, and Harrington (1999, p. 236) concluded:

> Although definitions may be given, rarely are coding schemes shared that include examples from the data. What distinguishes a student from a teacher perspective? If we are to advance knowledge in this area, we need to better understand one another's

interpretations of data. This is particularly true with research in an area such as case pedagogy, given the variety of research paradigms and disciplines of the researchers. Teacher-educators' goals and methods of using cases vary considerably and need to be made explicit in their research, regardless of methods selected.

The lack of common traditions for the description of approaches to data collection and analysis makes it difficult for readers to interpret the results of studies in this research area. For example, many qualitative researchers state that they engaged in the "constant comparative method" advocated by Glaser and Strauss (1967) but provide few details in their reports about how they conducted their analyses. Similarly, as the previously cited authors noted, researchers may state that they used a coding scheme but do not provide examples of either the scheme itself or instances of coded data. If readers are to make judgments about the credibility or trustworthiness of the study and its claims, the processes of data collection and analysis must be more transparent. Much of this may be due to the relative youth of the field of research in teacher education. As this area of research continues to develop, however, researchers will need to be more explicit about how they analyze data and how they provide warrants for their claims.

The Role of Practitioner Research

Much of the research reviewed in this chapter was conducted by university teachers studying their own students and programs. Many reasons might account for this situation, including the paucity of funding for research in teacher education and the demands to publish placed on teacher education faculty with heavy teaching loads. As mentioned earlier, there are also terrific advantages to having faculty research their own practice; they can provide more of an insider's perspective on their students and their goals, than an outsider could hope to provide. However, researchers have not completely addressed the complications that result from occupying a dual role in the classroom as researcher and teacher, nor have they established criteria for explaining and addressing how they negotiate these joint roles. If the primary purpose of self-study is to improve the practice of teacher-educators themselves, such criteria would not be necessary; the most important aspect of validity in such studies would be whether the self-study resulted in the improvement of practice (Hamilton & Pinnegar, 2001). But if the intent is to contribute to broader understanding of the pedagogies of teacher education, then closer attention must be paid to the circumstances under which data are collected, the relationship between researcher and students, and the manner in which data are analyzed (see Zeichner & Noffke, 2001, for an in-depth discussion of these issues).

The Problem of Outcomes

One of the most pressing problems facing research on the pedagogy of teacher education is the lack of a common tradition for conceptualizing and assessing outcomes. The outcomes investigated in these studies range from shifts in perceptions, changes in knowledge and beliefs, changes in the ability to reflect or identify issues—all cognitive outcomes—to attitudes toward the pedagogy or feelings of self-efficacy—more affective outcomes. The kinds of outcomes under investigation are loosely tied to the time period in which the research was conducted. For example, the early work on microteaching tried to look at the effects of this pedagogy on the use of particular teaching skills, whereas later work on microteaching looked more at cognitive outcomes. Much of the research conducted in the 1990s focused almost exclusively on cognitive outcomes, such as teachers' reasoning or knowledge, and avoided the issue of how the pedagogies of teacher education might influence prospective teachers' classroom practice. Few, if any, studies attempted to investigate the difficult problem of the relationships among the pedagogical approaches used in teacher education, the practices of beginning teachers, and the learning of their students (Wilson et al., 2001).

The shifting nature of outcomes in this research makes any form of meta-analysis or aggregation of results difficult if not impossible. The studies simply are not looking for the same thing. But even when different researchers attempt to study a common outcome, they generally use different instruments or analytic procedures, leading to a wide variability in methodology. Our field does not yet have a tradition of using similar instruments or common ways of analyzing data, and few common tools exist for studying the learning of student teachers.

Professional education aims at multiple goals, including the development of understanding, the ability to reason and reflect, the disposition to care about one's students and to work for equitable access to education, as well as the cultivation of skills entailed in teaching. Keeping a wide array of possible outcomes of teacher education in mind is a virtue (e.g., Cochran-Smith, 2001). However, to understand more about how different forms of pedagogy result in different kinds of outcomes, we need better tools for understanding distinct facets of teacher learning. If researchers could draw from a common set of toolkits for looking at teacher learning, we could approach problems in ways that allow us more easily to build on each other's work.

The Role of Theory: Past as Prologue?

Much of the early work on mictroteaching was atheoretical. The approach was grounded not in a well-defined theory of teacher or adult learning, but rather in a kind of gritty empiricism, building on what seemed to work and discarding what did not. Not surprisingly, a similar charge was leveled against research on teaching during this same time period. Although recent studies nod more to theory, often the theory invoked covers only the specific pedagogy under investigation, not the larger problem of the relationship between how we teach in teacher education and what our students learn. For example, although theories of knowledge acquisition in domains of uncertainty (Spiro, et. al., 1988) are used to support case methods in teacher education, this framework is not evoked to help us understand why portfolios might be valuable for teacher learning.

In addition to better tools, we need better theory, which is itself a different kind of tool. Such a theory would go beyond the particulars of a specific pedagogical approach to help us understand more broadly the relationship between the pedagogies of professional education and features of professional practice. One way of viewing the different pedagogies included in this chapter, for example, is that all involve either learning from one's own experience or learning from someone else's experience. The use of video-cases represents an example of efforts to learn from someone else's classroom practice, whereas writing a case based on student teaching represents a form of learning from one's own experience. Microteaching is also a variety of learning from one's own experience, but the nature of the experience differs dramatically from the experience of teaching 30 or so students in a real classroom.

If we accept this approach to parsing the pedagogies of teacher education, then what we need are more robust theories of what it means to learn from experience, both one's own and others. Deborah Ball and David Cohen (1999) began to articulate such a theory, arguing for the need for teachers to learn in and from practice and suggesting ways in which practice, and records of practice, might be used in professional education. They also recognized the need to conceptualize a pedagogy for professional development that would include "the sorts of tasks in which teachers would engage around materials of practice, the nature of the discourse that would be needed to support learning with and from these tasks and materials, and the role and capabilities of teacher educators and leaders who would provide guidance for this work" (Ball & Cohen, p. 25). Others have also tried to articulate theories of teacher learning that cut across a range of pedagogical approaches (Borko & Putnam, 1996; Feiman-Nemser, 2001; Grossman, 1991; Grossman, Smagorinsky, & Valencia, 1999). Such theoretical work can help both guide research design and data analysis and provide a broader framework within which to interpret the disparate findings in this area of research.

For example, a framework of professional education as rooted in practice suggests a research program in which researchers begin to investigate what teachers learn through specific tasks based on particular records of practice. Much of the research I have reviewed in this chapter could be usefully placed in such a framework, if researchers provided sufficient detail about the nature of the task, the nature of the materials, the nature of classroom discourse, and the role and interactions of teachers and students. As we begin to develop a more robust program of research around the pedagogy of teacher education, we first need theoretical frameworks of professional learning that might guide such research.

TOWARD A RESEARCH PROGRAM ON THE PEDAGOGY OF TEACHER EDUCATION

As suggested by the need for a theoretical framework that goes beyond single pedagogies, a program of research in the pedagogy of teacher education should encompass a broader territory and explore that territory more deeply and systematically. For example, the emerging research on case-based pedagogy might develop into a program of research in which researchers investigate how different kinds of cases—textual, video, and hypermedia cases—used in different contexts influence what prospective teachers learn with regard to a variety of outcomes, including cognitive outcomes such as ability to reason through a classroom dilemma as well as outcomes related to classroom practice. Part of developing such a research program would involve developing a more precise language to talk about features of a case, or genres of cases, and about the instruction surrounding the case. Similarly such a program would depend on the use of some common tools or ways of looking at outcomes. As a field, research on teacher education has expended relatively little effort in building the tools of the trade. Yet, as work in the biological sciences and genetics suggests, having the right tools for investigating complex phenomena can make all the difference in what we are able to see.

Such a research program might enable us to understand what prospective teachers can learn from representations of others' practices. If a written case helps prospective teachers reason through a classroom dilemma, is the case also able to help them learn to enact certain practices in the classroom? What habits of mind are developed as prospective teachers interact with different kinds of cases? How do prospective teachers learn from brief written representations of practice? What do they need to have observed to fill out these descriptions of practice? How does their learning differ when they have the opportunity to investigate a hypermedia case of a full-year of classroom instruction? How do their interactions with such extensive records from a single classroom inform prospective teachers' own classroom practices? One might hypothesize that prospective teachers learn quite different things from different kinds of cases, but as of yet, we lack an empirical basis for making such claims.

Another promising line of research involves questions related to pedagogical approaches designed to help people learn from their own practice. Under this category would fall research on portfolios, practitioner research of various kinds, student-written cases, as well as forms of microteaching and supervision. Again, a research program might investigate how a particular pedagogical approach structures opportunities to learn from one's own experience—what particular artifacts of practice (videotapes, student work, etc.) are available, the kinds of tasks and activities in which prospective teachers engage, the nature of feedback they receive, and how these all contribute to learning. Within a larger program of research, researchers could look at multiple outcomes, including the development of knowledge, skill, dispositions, and identity across a variety of structures. Anna Richert's (1990) research on reflection and portfolios provides an example of the start of such a research program by suggesting that, with access to different artifacts and under different conditions, teachers reflect about quite different things.

Teacher education has always encompassed a wide range of pedagogical approaches, from traditional lecture and recitation formats to investigations of practice, to experimentation and feedback, to reflective formats including the uses of autobiographies and journals. Given the complex and multidimensional nature of teaching practice, no single pedagogical approach is ever likely to suffice in preparing teachers. Setting individual pedagogies within a broader framework of research on learning from one's own and others' experiences may provide teacher educators with greater insight into the kinds of experiences most likely to help prospective teachers develop the knowledge, skill, dispositions, integrity, and identities that will inform their future practice.

ACKNOWLEDGMENTS

I am deeply indebted to Chauncey Monte-Sano, Danielle Igra, and Tom Levine, all of Stanford University, for their assistance with this review. They helped locate the articles for this review, culled through numerous studies to find those that met our criteria, provided reviews of the articles, helped create the table, and offered helpful feedback and support along the way. I would also like to thank Gloria Ladson-Billings, Jeremy Price, and Linda Valli for their helpful feedback on an earlier draft of this chapter, as well as my internal reviewers, Ann Lieberman and Ana Maria Villegas.

TABLE 7.1

Studies of Pedagogical Approaches in Teacher Education

Studies[a]	Question and Focus	Research Tradition and Research Context	Research design	Findings	Pedagogy
Anderson, L., & Bird, T. (1995)	Do prospective teachers' entering beliefs affect their interpretation of cases? If so, how? Does working with cases change prospective teachers' conceptions of teaching? If so, how?	Qualitative study Drawn from class of 31 undergraduates beginning their teacher training at Michigan State.	N = 8 undergraduate teacher education students (3 presented). Data sources = interview transcripts, written case conversations, and essays. Analysis = coding.	The authors conclude that in spite of Bird's efforts to raise new perspectives through cases, readings, and class activities, prospective teachers' entering beliefs were "sturdy and central in their interpretation of the cases."	Case method
Anderson, G., Frager, A., & Bolin, C. (1982)	Are there differences in the performance of four teacher competencies between preservice teachers who view a videotape protocol and those who participate in a role-play demonstration?	Quasi-experimental. No random assignment. Practicum course required of elementary education undergraduates at Arizona State University	N = 74. Data sources = audiotapes of preservice teachers using targeted strategy. Analysis = data scored by looking at behavior. Four 2-way ANOVAs conducted to determine main interaction effects.	"For each of the four teaching competencies, the three groups who viewed the videotape protocols achieved higher mean scores on performance measures than the groups which had a role-play simulation of the comprehension strategy." Teachers reached "conventional level of significance" with one competency (reciprocal questioning) yet did not reach this level with two competencies.	Video technology

(Continued)

TABLE 7.1
(Continued)

Studies[a]	Question and Focus	Research Tradition and Research Context	Research design	Findings	Pedagogy
Baird, W. E., & Kobala, T. R., Jr. (1988)	What is the impact of different kinds of computer simulations on students' learning?	Quasi-experimental. No random assignment. Elementary education majors at large southwestern university	N = 87. Data sources = GALT pretest, hypothesis testing skills pre-posttest. Computer simulation with visual and auditory stimuli. Computer simulation with text-only survey of perceived success.	Different kinds of learners seem to benefit from different kinds of methods. Specifically, working alone and textual presentations help those with high levels of formal reasoning skills.	Computer simulation
Borko, H., Michalec, P., Timmons, M., & Siddle, J. (1997)	What are the factors that facilitate and hinder the process of portfolio construction?	Qualitative research. MAT program at UC Denver where students earn certification and MA in elementary education in 2 years.	N = 21 (entire program cohort). Data sources = written reflections from 21 students, structured interviews with 8 students.	Most students reported that portfolios were a tool for reflection and for linking theory and practice. Support from peers, CT, and professor helped. Timing and status as course assignment hindered.	Portfolio
Carlson, H. L., & Falk, D. R. (1989)	How can videodisc technology be used effectively to help elementary education candidates develop the ability to faciliate	Quasi-experimental. No control group. Random assignment. Elementary education majors in 3rd field experience course at	N = 66. Data sources = content test, observation skills assessment, observation of students in practicum,	Students who learned about cooperative learning through videodisc instruction scored higher than did students in lecture,	Videodisc technology

	cooperative learning in social studies?	midwestern university.	measurement of satisfaction with instruction, assessment of thinking skills.	reading, and discussion group. Of those, students who learned from videodisc using an inductive model learned more than those who learned from a videodisc using a deductive model.	
Carlson, H. L., & Falk, D.R. (1990)	How can teacher education candidates acquire background knowledge about and learn to observe cooperative learning functions? How do changes in conditions affect this process?	Quasi-experimental. No control group. Random assignment. Elementary education majors in 3rd field experience course at midwestern university.	N = 65. Data sources = Content knowledge measured by 25 items on paper-and-pencil test. Observation skills assessment. Satisfaction survey. Analysis = ANOVA with Scheffe comparisons. No pretests.	Content knowledge: Videodisc inductive group scored higher than reading groups. Videodisc deductive working in pairs scored higher than reading groups. Observation skills: Video-inductive (pairs and alone) and video-deductive (pairs) scored higher than reading groups. Satisfaction: Videodisc deductive group significantly more satisfied. Efficiency: Videodisc deductive groups used significantly less time than others.	Videodisc technology

(Continued)

TABLE 7.1
(Continued)

Studies[a]	Question and Focus	Research Tradition and Research Context	Research design	Findings	Pedagogy
Clift, R., Veal, M. L., Johnson, M., & Holland, P. (1990)	What are the factors that enable teachers and administrators to work together for school improvement and staff development?	Qualitative study. A project that evolved from a 4-year collaboration in the context of the University of Houston's preservice teacher education program.	N = 5 schools. Data sources = interviews, shadowing administrators, and observations of meetings and classrooms.	Five dimensions influence opportunities to learn in professional school communities: leadership, structures that facilitate collaboration, individual contributions and needs, interpersonal relationships, and synergy (harmony).	Practitioner research
Cochran-Smith, M. (1991a)	What are the most effective approaches to preparing teachers? How can we prepare teachers so that they are inclined toward reforming teaching and education?	Interpretive case study. Project START at University of Pennsylvania. Fifth-year teacher education program (TEP) in elementary education.	Data sources = classroom participation and conversations with participants.	Placing student teachers with teachers focused on reforming teaching is an effective way to foster reform-mindedness in preservice teachers.	Practitioner research
Cochran-Smith, M. (1991b)	What is the most effective type of student teaching program?	Interpretive case study. Project START at University of Pennsylvania. Fifth-year TEP in elementary education.	The author uses "data and program literature collected over 3 years" (p. 104). Otherwise, the methodology and sample are unclear.	Teacher education programs based on collaborative resonance are the best way to prepare teachers and to alter their outlooks and practices.	Practitioner research

Copeland, W., & Decker, L. D. (1996)	What is the impact of video case-based instruction on prospective teachers' cognition?	Qualitative study. Content analysis of interviews. Elementary credential program, UC Santa Barbara.	$N = 9$ preservice teachers. Data sources = transcriptions of interviews before and after case discussion. Analysis = identification of ideas that are carried, changed, adopted by others, or dropped in later interview.	The analysis revealed that over one third (28 of 72) of the topics students discussed were adopted, changed, or created in the process of discussing a video case and then checking for meaning-making 3 weeks later.	Video cases
Daniel, P. (1996)	How does the "Cview," a multimedia tool, help students build connections between learning theory and teaching practice based on cognitive flexibility theory?	Qualitative study including think-aloud protocols. Four math and science methods courses in a TEP in a southern university.	$N = 39$. Data sources = pre-interviews of students, think-aloud protocols of students, post-interviews, student writing, questionnaires, observations. Analysis = coded and analyzed data from 27 student think-aloud protocols.	Students felt teaching episodes connected with course work and made it more comprehensible. Most students felt positively about "Cview."	Multimedia technology

(Continued)

TABLE 7.1
(Continued)

Studies[a]	Question and Focus	Research Tradition and Research Context	Research design	Findings	Pedagogy
Friel, S. N., & Carboni, L. W. (2000)	How does video-based technology impact preservice teachers' cognition about teaching mathematics?	Qualitative case studies. Elementary math methods course taken during senior year of TEP.	N = 19. Case studies of 3 students presented. Data sources = written work, journals, 3 interviews with 5 students.	Teachers moved from teacher-centered view of teaching mathematics to student-centered view. Teachers did not see value of listening to children's thinking or how this could inform instruction. Video episodes were a common point for reflection.	Video technology
Goldman, E., & Barron, L. (1990)	How do students react to the use of videodisc? What is the influence of videodisc technology on retention of facts, and on teaching?	Mixed method. Elementary TEP at Vanderbilt. Math methods course.	N = 30. Data sources = written questionnaires, interviews with students, observation and rating instrument. One control group and one treatment group.	Group who learned from video learned more basic skills, higher order problem-solving skills, management practices, and positive attitudes towards math. They also had greater pupil involvement and on-task behavior in their classrooms.	Videodisc technology
Gore, J., & Zeichner, K. (1991)	How does engagement in action research contribute to reflective teaching practice?	Qualitative study. The 5th year of a 5-year preservice TEP program at University of Wisconsin.	N = 18 student teachers. Data sources = written reports of the action research projects conducted by	Though the authors did not see much evidence of reflective thinking, student teacher reports suggest	Practitioner research

		students. Gore supervised these students and taught them to do action research in a 2-semester course.	that action research helped them be more thoughtful about their teaching, aware of their own practices, aware of the gap between practices and beliefs, aware of their students' thinking and learning (p. 131). Little evidence of critical reflection.	
Gorrell, J., & Downing, H. (1989)	What is "the feasibility of using computer simulations as realistic training in the use of psychological principles to solve classroom problems"?	Experimental study. Forty percent of students in an undergraduate educational psychology course at a comprehensive state university volunteered.	$N = 64$. Data sources = "Knowledge of Behavior Analysis" multiple choice test, "Application of Behavioral Principles" written test. "Self-Efficacy" pre- and post-questionnaire. Three treatments: computer simulation, extended instruction, group problem solving, control group.	Significant differences between groups on the application measure. Simulation group scored higher than other 3 groups. No significant difference among groups in knowledge of concepts or in measure of self-efficacy.	Computer simulation

(Continued)

TABLE 7.1
(Continued)

Studies[a]	Question and Focus	Research Tradition and Research Context	Research design	Findings	Pedagogy
Harrington, H. (1995)	Can dilemma-based cases be used to gain insight into the development of students' professional reasoning?	Qualitative study. University of Michigan course: Teaching in the Elementary School. Part of 1st block of education courses students take. Unclear who taught course.	N = 26. Data sources = set of case analyses completed as assignments for the course. Analysis = coding of responses for evidence in 5 categories	The majority of students were "able to begin to" do 5 elements of reasoning identified; suggests that "case-based pedagogy can be used to gain access to students' professional reasoning and may, as well, foster that reasoning."	Case method
Harrington, H. L, Quinn-Leering, K., & Hodson, L. (1996)	Do students' written analyses of cases provide insight into the development of different aspects of critical reflection?	Qualitative study. University of Michigan course: Teaching in the Elementary School. Unclear who taught course.	N = 21. Data sources = students' 3rd written case analysis completed in 8th week of semester. Coded data for 4 levels of reflection.	Case analyses are valuable data. Case analyses provide evidence that students developed critical reflection skills in 3 areas: open-mindedness, responsibility, and wholeheartedness.	Case method
Lambdin, D.V., Duffy, T. M., & Moore, J. A. (1997)	How does the use of an interactive videodisc information system help preservice teachers expand their visions of teaching, learning, and	Mixed methods. Preservice field experience course on the teaching of elementary mathematics in Elementary Education	N = 8. Data sources = keystroke data, students' reflective journals, teaching videos, and reflections on teaching.	Students used all 3 information sources of the technology (video, commentaries, and databases). Students valued accessibility of multiple models	Videodisc technology

460

assessment in mathematics?	Graduate Program at Indiana University.		and access to teacher thinking, but felt direct experience in classroom was still more valuable. Students used the videodisc lessons in developing their own lessons, used the videodisc teachers as "mental models" and learned about specific teaching techniques.	Multimedia technology
Lampert, M., & Ball, D. L. (1998) — What is the impact of hypermedia materials on teaching and students' learning?	Qualitative study. Hypermedia materials used in elementary teacher education program at the University of Michigan.	N = 68 elementary preservice teachers.. Data sources = student investigations using hypermedia materials; class observations. Authors analyzed these investigations.	Two thirds of the investigations focused on the teacher and teaching, 7 focused on students, and several focused on policy. Few focused on mathematics.	
Levin, B. B. (1995) — What do teachers understand from reading and writing about a case compared with reading, discussing, and writing about a case?	Qualitative study. Graduates of, or student teachers at, UC Berkeley Developmental Teacher Education Program (elementary education).	N = 8 experienced teachers; 8 beginning teachers; 8 student teachers. Data sources = written case analyses and audiotaped case discussions.	The opportunity to discuss, as well as read and write about, a case affected teacher thinking. For experienced teachers, more reflection and metacognition. For	Case method

(Continued)

TABLE 7.1
(Continued)

Studies[a]	Question and Focus	Research Tradition and Research Context	Research design	Findings	Pedagogy
			Analysis = constant comparative analysis and discourse analysis.	less experienced teachers, clarity, understanding of multiple perspectives. One case discussion and 2 case analyses did not result in observable transfer of new knowledge or skills to another case 1 month later.	
Loughran, J. L., & Corrigan, D. (1995)	How did teachers approach portfoliio construction? To what extent and how did teachers value this task?	Survey and qualitative study. Preservice methods class for prospective science teachers at Monash University.	N = 30. Data sources = questionnaire filled out by 22 teachers. Open-ended survey at end of class. 2 interviews with 8 volunteers (middle and end of class) by research assistant.	Seventy-five percent thought task was valuable but for different reasons. Tension among different purposes for portfolios	Portfolio
Lundeberg, M. A., & Scheurman, G. (1997)	What is the pedagogical value of using a case more than once—both before and after a unit of instruction? Do students learn more when case comes first and theory	Qualitative study. Educational Psychology class in an undergraduate preservice program.	N = 48. Data sources = students' 1st and 2nd case analyses, students' reflections on changes between 2 cases (self-report). Analysis = ANOVA on coded data.	When cases are used as an anchor, they serve to stimulate students' background knowledge and to increase their receptivity to subsequent instructional efforts	Case method

462

	comes second or vice versa?			aimed at developing their pedagogical knowledge.	Laboratory
Metcalf, K. K. (1992)	Do prospective teachers' entering beliefs affect their interpretation of cases? If so, how? Does working with cases change prospective teachers' conceptions of teaching? If so, how?	Quasi-experimental study using intact groups. Two intact sections of an undergraduate secondary general methods class.	N = 54. Data sources = videotaped lessons, coded for behaviors representing instructional clarity. Tests of content developed for reflective teaching lessons. Survey of satisfaction. Analysis used MANCOVA & ANCOVA	Teachers trained in instructional clarity received higher ratings on clarity than control teachers and used a broader range of behaviors related to clarity. Students of teachers in experimental group also scored higher on tests and expressed greater satisfaction with the lessons.	Laboratory
Metcalf, K. K., Hammer, M. A. R., & Kahlich, P. A. (1996)	What are the effects of laboratory and field placement on reflection, complex understanding, and pedagogical behavior?	Quasi-experimental. No random assignment. Two intact sections of general methods for undergraduates pursuing secondary teacher certification.	N = 37. Data sources = student analysis of written case studies; videotapes of students' minilessons; student journals; student essays; student self-reflection. Analysis = coded case study analysis, rated videotape performance, read journals, t-tests.	Field students score higher on both pretests. Lab students make greater gains and are stronger on both posttests.	Laboratory vs. field placement

(Continued)

TABLE 7.1
(Continued)

Studies[a]	Question and Focus	Research Tradition and Research Context	Research design	Findings	Pedagogy
Moje, E. B., & Wade, S. E. (1997)	What mediational tools and processes of reasoning do preservice and in-service teachers employ in dealing with cases? What range of issues do cases raise for them? What images of teaching and learning do teachers create as they read and discuss cases?	Qualitative study. One preservice university course in secondary literacy methods and one in-service university course in secondary literacy. Western metropolitan university. Study of one author's classrooom.	N = 13. Data sources = tape-recorded case discussions and debriefing sessions, interviews of teacher volunteers in focus groups and of individuals. Analysis focused on the tools, images, and issues that teachers identified.	Preservice teachers used their experiences as students, theories and texts from university course work, and role-playing activities as tools to understand cases. Preservice teachers identified teacher resistance and diverse needs of future learners as key issues in cases. Preservice teachers saw teaching as technical, teacher as responsible, and learner abilities as fixed.	Case method
Mokhtari, K., Yellin, D., Bull, K., & Montgomery, D. (1996)	How much do preservice teachers know about porfolio assessment and how do they feel about portfolios as a means of evaluation?	Survey. Elementary education majors at comprehensive midwestern university. One of the authors was also an instructor.	N = 66 juniors and seniors. Data sources = instructor's weekly log of class, questionnaire using 5-point scale (assessed cognitive and attitudinal knowledge about portfolios).	Students had general knowledge of purposes of portfolio and felt positively about porfolio assessment.	Portfolio

464

| Nath, J. M., & Tellez, K. (1995) | What is the impact of placing preservice teachers with teacher researchers during their field placement? | Qualitative study. University of Houston teacher education program field placement. | N = 176 preservice teachers; 8 presented. Data sources = 176 assignments and interviews with 8 students. Analysis = coding for level of satisfaction with the field experience, as well as ideas, attitudes, and knowledge being developed in the field. | Students placed with teacher researchers felt more welcomed and supported in their field experience and were more likely to report observations of good teaching. These students also reported interacting with children more frequently than did students with other placements and could envision themselves engaging in teacher research once they became teachers themselves. | Practitioner research |
| Otero, V. K., Johnson, A., & Goldberg, F. (1999) | How do a group of prospective elementary teachers use a computer simulation in the context of collaborative inquiry to construct their understanding of a variety of physics concepts? | Mixed methods. Required physical science course for prospective elementary teachers at San Diego State University. | N = not stated. Data sources = videotapes of small groups and of whole-class discussion, computer records, student work, and student interviews. Analysis = video transcriptions, tested hypotheses against data. Triangulated data from interviews, videos, and hypotheses. | The computer provided a shared representational space that supported students' evaluation and modification of ideas.

The simulation facilitated the process of model building, as students could test their emerging ideas through computer experiments. | Computer simulation |

(Continued)

TABLE 7.1
(Continued)

Studies[a]	Question and Focus	Research Tradition and Research Context	Research design	Findings	Pedagogy
Overbaugh, R.C. (1995)	What effects does an interactive video classroom management simulation have on the achievement of preservice teachers representing 2 class ranks and 2 learning styles? What effects does simulation have on the concerns of teachers? What are the relationships between class ranking, level of computer anxiety, and GPA with achievement?	Quasi-experimental. No control group. Teacher education students at West Virginia University.	N = 88 (59 enrolled in first ed. class; 29 enrolled in final ed. class before student teaching). Data sources = student responses to and interaction with Hypercard program, self-evaluation questionnaire, classroom management achievement test, learning modality test. Analysis = 2×2 ANOVA, paired t-tests.	No differences for class rank or learning modality, but differences in achievement. No significant effects on students in last class. Some effects on students in initial class including drop in concern over management and increase in concern over collaboration and refocusing. Positive responses to simulation game.	Video technology
Price, J. (2001)	What does it mean for preservice teachers to engage in action research? What counts as curriculum in an action-research course?	Qualitative study. Preservice teachers in an action research course in a year-long, full-time masters and certification program at the University of Maryland.	N = 11. Data sources = transcripts of audiotapes of classroom conversations, questionnaires conducted at the beginning and end of	Most of the preservice teachers used action research to pursue their own pedagogical interests and several used action research in areas in which they	Practitioner research

	What are some key experiences that promote learning about teaching, action research and change? What kinds of changes do preservice teachers embrace and imagine that they would undertake as beginning teachers?		the course, action-research journals, preservice teachers' and their students' writing, informal interviews with preservice teachers, videotapes of classroom work, school, district, and state policy documents. Analysis of the kinds of changes evident in data.	lacked confidence. Student teachers' response to action research is shaped by their contexts, resources, and experiences.
Richert, A. E. (1990)	How do program structures such as portfolios and teaching partners affect student teachers' reflections?	Qualitative study. Secondary TEP in Northern California. Fifth-year graduate program.	$N = 12$ preservice teachers. Data sources = questionnaires, self-report interviews on the process of reflection, journal entries, essays, portfolios, and interviews. Analysis = data were coded for content of reflections and categories of teacher knowledge.	Preservice teachers who used the teaching portfolios were more likely to reflect about content and the teaching of content. Portfolio

(Continued)

TABLE 7.1
(Continued)

Studies[a]	Question and Focus	Research Tradition and Research Context	Research design	Findings	Pedagogy
Strang, H. R., Badt, K. S. & Kauffman, J. M. (1987)	Can microcomputer simulations of teaching exercises train teachers in fundamental instructional and behavior management skills?	Mixed methods. Curry School of Education, University of Virginia.	Examined education students' pretraining proficiency in employing the 3 fundamental teaching skills—time management, feedback and behavior management—during a computer simulation. Design included a followup with students 2 months after training.	"Once trained, a person maintained at least two of the skills over at least a two-month period." In self-evaluations, trainees overestimated their skills at the beginning and estimated their performance accurately after the simulations. Seventy-seven percent of the students said using the simulation was enjoyable. Ninety percent said the simulation was helpful.	Computer simulation
Strang, H. R., Landrum, M. S., & Lynch, K. A. (1989)	What is the impact of a computer simulation on the acquisition of knowledge, teaching skills, and sense of efficacy?	Mixed methods. Curry School's 5-year teacher preparation program learning and development course.	N = 61 (whole-class participation required). Data sources = spelling lesson simulation results,	Increased use of encouragement and offers of information. Decrease in direct spelling feedback. No change in	Computer simulation

			posttraining questionnaire, anecdotal evidence from system operator and teachers.	involvement of other students to assist students. Increase in spellers. Increase in involvement and success with poor spellers. Decrease in ineffective practices. Some increase and decrease in effective practices. Little sign of decay and some increase in effective behaviors in followup. Students find simulation useful, effective, and realistic.	
Tabachnick, B. R., Zeichner, K. M. (1999)	How does action research enact a "conceptual change" approach to teaching?	Qualitative study. Two-semester course in action research in which students were introduced to action research and completed their own project.	Data sources = audiotapes of all class sessions; videotapes of the final class sessions in which students presented their action research projects; written reports of action research projects of some course	"The action research seminar helped prospective teachers understand their students' thinking and preferences" (p. 309). "Although most of the prospective teachers became practiced in eliciting students' prior knowledge,	Practitioner research

(Continued)

TABLE 7.1
(Continued)

Studies[a]	Question and Focus	Research Tradition and Research Context	Research design	Findings	Pedagogy
			members; prospective teachers' journals; course instructors' written responses to journal entries; course instructors' journals.	only a few were able to use their knowledge of their students' thinking to plan their teaching" (p. 309).	
Valli, L. (2000)	How does strengthening the connection between action research as professional development and as school improvement affect preservice teachers' conceptions of action research?	Qualitative study Course on action research for preservice teachers in the University of Maryland teacher education program.	Fourteen preservice teachers enrolled in the class. Data sources = audiotapes of class sessions, field notes, interviews with key informants, analysis of syllabus and texts, and analysis of students' action research projects.	Students found it difficult to make connections between action research as a form of personal professional development and action research as a tool for school improvement. Students focused either on their own classrooms or on the school as the unit of analysis.	Practitioner research
Wade, R. C., & Yarbrough, D. B. (1996)	What are students' perceptions of their experience with and value of portfolios? What is the effect of	Mixed methods. Elementary undergraduate teacher education program in large	N = 212. Data sources = survey of 212 students in 4 sections. Interview with	Mixed responses to portfolio experience. Majority (63%) said they learned; 35% reported frustrations	Portfolio

	portfolios on the reflective process?	midwestern university. Self-study by teacher educators.	7 students. Student essays. Researchers coded data for uses of portfolio.	with portfolio; 45% did not understand purposes of portfolio. Significant difference in students taught by different instructors.	Microteaching
Wilkinson, G. A. (1996)	How does additional feedback from preservice administrators affect preservice teachers' perceptions of their teaching ability, process of learning and teaching, and value of supervision in professional development?	Experimental study. General methods class at urban, midwestern university. Three years of data. Author and 2 other professors taught experimental group; 2 other professors taught control group.	$N = 104$ in experimental group; $N = 98$ in control group. Data sources = responses of preservice teachers to administrator feedback, open-ended questionnaire about feedback. Analysis = ANCOVA to compare pre- posttest.	Experimental group reported placing greater value on supervision for professional development (means not shown). Specific feedback helped them learn to teach. Comments from administrators gave them specific ways to improve lessons.	
Winitzky, N., & Arends, R. (1991)	How effective is microteaching in promoting knowledge and skill acquisition in prospective teachers?	Experimental study. Random assignment. Preservice teachers in a general secondary methods class at University of Maryland at College Park.	$N = 37$. Data sources = multiple choice test, observational instrument used to assess microlesson, test of reflectiveness. Analysis = ANOVA.	No significant differences in preservice teachers' learning among live observation with discussion, watching a videotape, and watching a videotape with discussion.	Microteaching

[a] Please see References.

REFERENCES: WORKS REVIEWED

Anderson, L., & Bird, T. (1995). How three prospective teachers construed three cases of teaching. *Teaching and Teacher Education, 11*(5), 479–499.

Anderson, G., Frager, A., & Boling, C. (1982). Developing instructional competence in field-based programs: Videotape protocols versus role-play simulations. *Teacher Educator, 18,* 16–25.

Baird, W. E., & and Kobala, T. R., Jr. (1988). Changes in pre-service elementary teachers' hypothesizing skills following group or individual study with computer simulations. *Science Education, 72*(2), 209–223.

Borko, H., Michalec, P., Timmons, M., & Siddle, J. (1997). Student teaching portfolios: A tool for promoting reflective practices. *Journal of Teacher Education, 48,* 345–357.

Carlson, H. L., & Falk, D. R. (1989). Effective use of interactive videodisc instruction in understanding and implementing cooperative group learning with elementary pupils in social studies and social education. *Theory and Research in Social Education, 17*(3), 241–258.

Carlson, H. L., & Falk, D. R. (1990). Effectiveness of interactive videodisc instructional programs in elementary teacher education. *Journal of Educational Technology Systems, 19*(2), 151–163.

Clift, R., Veal, M. L., Johnson, M., & Holland, P. (1990). Restructuring teacher education through collaborative action research. *Journal of Teacher Education, 41*(2), 52–62.

Cochran-Smith, M. (1991a). Learning to teach against the grain. *Harvard Educational Review, 61*(3), 279–310.

Cochran-Smith, M. (1991b). Reinventing student teaching. *Journal of Teacher Education, 42*(2), 104–118.

Copeland, W., & Decker, L. (1996) Video cases and the development of meaning making in pre-service teachers. *Teaching and Teacher Education, 12*(5), 467–481.

Daniel, P. (1996). Helping beginning teachers link theory and practice: An interactive multimedia environment for mathematics and science teacher preparation. *Journal of Teacher Education, 47*(3), 197–204.

Friel, S. N., & Carboni, L. W. (2000). Using video-based pedagogy in an elementary mathematics methods course. *School Science and Mathematics, 100*(3), 118–127.

Goldman, E., & Barron, L. (1990). Using hypermedia to improve the preparation of elementary teachers. *Journal of Teacher Education, 41*(3), 21–31.

Gore, J., & Zeichner, K. (1991). Action research and reflective teaching in pre-service teacher education: A case study from the United States. *Teaching and Teacher Education, 7*(2), 119–136.

Gorrell, J., & Downing, H. (1989). Effects of computer-simulated behavior analysis on pre-service teachers' problem solving. *Journal of Educational Computing Research, 5*(3), 335–347.

Harrington, H. (1995). Fostering reasoned decisions: Case-based pedagogy and the professional development of teachers. *Teaching and Teacher Education, 11*(3), 203–214.

Harrington, H., Quinn-Leering, K., & Hodson, L. (1996). Written case analyses and critical reflection. *Teaching and Teacher Education, 12*(1), 25–37.

Lambdin, D. V., Duffy, T. M., & Moore, J. A. (1997). Using an interactive information system to expand pre-service teachers' visions of effective mathematics teaching. *Journal of Technology and Teacher Education, 5*(2/3), 171–202.

Lampert, M., & Ball, D. L. (1998). *Teaching, multimedia, and mathematics: Investigations of real practice.* New York: Teachers College Press.

Levin, B. B. (1995). Using the case method in teacher education: The role of discussion and experience in teachers' thinking about cases. *Teaching and Teacher Education, 11*(1), 63–79.

Loughran, J., & Corrigan, D. (1995). Teaching portfolios: A strategy for developing learning and teaching in pre-service education. *Teaching and Teacher Education, 11,* 565–577.

Lundeberg, M. A., & Scheurman, G. (1997). Looking twice means seeing more: Developing pedagogical knowledge through case analysis. *Teaching and Teacher Education, 13*(8), 783–797.

Metcalf, K. K. (1992). The effects of guided training experience on the instructional clarity of preservice teachers. *Teaching and Teacher Education, 8*(3), 275–286.

Metcalf, K. K., Hammer, M. A. R., & Kahlich, P. A. (1996). Alternatives to field-based experiences: The comparative effects of on-campus laboratories. *Teaching and Teacher Education, 12*(3), 271–283.

Moje, E. B., & Wade, S. E. (1997). What case discussions reveal about teacher thinking. *Teaching and Teacher Education, 13*(7), 691–712.

Mokhtari, K., Yellin, D., Bull, K., & Montgomery, D. (1996). Portfolio assessment in teacher education: Impact on pre-service teachers' knowledge and attitudes. *Journal of Teacher Education, 47*, 245–252.

Nath, J. M., & Tellez, K. (1995). A room of one's own: Teaching and learning to teach through inquiry. *Action in Teacher Education, 16*(4), 1–13.

Otero, V. K., Johnson, A., & Goldberg, F. (1999). How does the computer facilitate the development of physics knowledge by prospective elementary teachers? *Journal of Education, 181*(2), 57–89.

Overbaugh, R. C. (1995). The efficacy of interactive video for teaching basic classroom management skills and pre-service teachers. *Computers in Human Behavior, 11*(3/4), 511–527.

Price, J. (2001). Action research, pedagogy and change: The transformative potential of action research in pre-service teacher education. *Journal of Curriculum Studies, 33*(1), 43–74.

Richert, A. E. (1990). Teaching teachers to reflect: A consideration of programme structure. *Journal of Curriculum Studies, 22*, 509–527.

Schuck, S. (1997). Using a research simulation to challenge prospective teachers' beliefs about mathematics. *Teaching and Teacher Education, 13*(5), 529–539.

Strang, H. R., Badt, K. S., & Kauffman, J. M. (1987). Microcomputer-based simulations for training fundamental teaching skills. *Journal of Teacher Education, 38*(1), 20–26.

Strang, H. R., Landrum, M. S., and Lynch, K. A. (1989). Talking with the computer: A simulation for training basic teaching skills. *Teaching and Teacher Education, 5*(2), 143–153.

Tabachnick, B. R., & Zeichner, K. M. (1999). Idea and action: Action research and the development of conceptual change in the teaching of science. *Science Education, 83*(3), 309–322.

Valli, L. (2000). Connecting teacher development and school improvement: Ironic consequences of a pre-service action research course. *Teaching and Teacher Education, 16*(7), 715–730.

Wade, R. C., Yarbrough, D. B. (1996). Portfolios: A tool for reflective thinking in teacher education? *Teaching and Teacher Education, 12*, 63–79.

Wilkinson, G. A. (1996). Enhancing microteaching through additional feedback from pre-service administrators. *Teaching and Teacher Education, 12*(2), 211–221.

Winitzky, N., & Arends, R. (1991). Translating research into practice: The effects of various forms of training and clinical experience on pre-service students' knowledge, skill, and reflectiveness. *Journal of Teacher Education, 42*(1), 52–65.

REFERENCES: WORKS CITED

Ball, D. L., & Cohen, D. K. (1999). Developing practice, developing practitioners: Toward a practice-based theory of professional development. In L. Darling-Hammond & G. Sykes (Eds.), *Teaching as the learning profession: Handbook of policy and practice* (pp. 3–32). San Francisco: Jossey-Bass.

Barnes, L. B., Christensen, C. R., & Hansen, A. J. (1994). *Teaching and the case method* (3rd ed.). Boston, MA: Harvard Business School Press.

Beckman, D. (1957). Student teachers learn by action research. *Journal of Teacher Education, 8*(4), 369–375.

Bird, T. (1990). The schoolteacher's portfolio: An essay on possibilities. In J. Milman & L. Darling-Hammond (Eds.), *The new handbook of teacher evaluation: Assessing elementary and secondary school teachers*. Newbury Park, CA: Sage.

Bolin, F.S. (1990). Helping student teachers think about teaching: Another look at Lou. *Journal of Teacher Education, 41*(1), 10–19.

Borko, H., & Putnam, R. (1996). Learning to teach. In D. C. Berliner & R. C. Calfee (Eds.), *Handbook of educational psychology* (pp. 673–708). New York: Macmillan.

Carnegie Forum on Education and the Economy. (1986). *A nation prepared: Teachers for the 21st century.* New York: Carnegie Forum on Education and the Economy.

Carter, K., & Unklesbay, R. (1989). Cases in teaching and law. *Journal of Curriculum Studies, 21,* 527–536.

Cochran-Smith, M. (2001). The outcomes question in teacher education. *Teaching and Teacher Education, 17,* 527–46.

Cohen, D. K. (in press). Professions of human improvement: Predicaments of teaching. In *Educational deliberations: Studies in education dedicated to Shlomo (Seymour) Fox.* Israel: Keter Publishers.

Copeland, W. (1982). Laboratory experiences in teacher education. In *Encyclopedia of Educational Research*, (Vol. 2, 5th ed., 1008–1019). New York: Free Press.

Corey, S. (1953). *Action research to improve school practices.* New York: Teachers College Press.

Feiman-Nemser, S. (2001). From preparation to practice: Designing a continuum to strengthen and sustain teaching. *Teachers College Record, 103*(6), 1013–1055.

Gage, N. L. (1978). *The scientific basis of the art of teaching.* New York: Teachers College Press.

Grossman, P. L., Smagorinsky, P., & Valencia, S. (1999). Appropriating tools for teaching English: A theoretical framework for research on learning to teach. *American Journal of Education, 108,* 1–29.

Grossman, P. L. (1991). Overcoming the apprenticeship of observation in teacher education coursework. *Teaching and Teacher Education, 7*(4), 345–357.

Grossman, P. L. (1992). Teaching and learning with cases: Unanswered questions. In J. Shulman, *Case methods in teacher education*. New York: Teachers College Press.

Hamilton, M. L., & Pinnegar, S. (2000). On the threshold of a new century: Trustworthiness, integrity, and self-study in teacher education. *Journal of Teacher Education, 51*(3), 234–240.

Holmes Group. (1986). *Tomorrow's teachers*. East Lansing, MI: The Holmes Group.

Kennedy, M. M. (1996). Research genres in teacher education. In F. B. Murray (Ed.), *The teacher educator's handbook: Building a knowledge base for the preparation of teachers* (pp. 120–152). San Francisco: Jossey-Bass.

Kessels, J. Koster, B., Lagerwerf, B., Wubbels, T., & Korthagen, F. (2001). *Linking practice with theory: The pedagogy of realistic teacher education*. Mahweh, NJ: Lawrence Erlbaum Associates.

Kleinfeld, J. (1992). Learning to think like a teacher. In J. H. Shulman (Ed.), *Case methods in teacher education* (pp. 33–49). New York: Teachers College Press.

Kronman, A. (1993). *The lost lawyer: Failing ideas of the legal profession*. Cambridge, MA: Harvard University Press.

LaBoskey, V. K. (1992). Case investigations: Pre-service teacher research as an aid to reflection. In J. H. Shulman (Ed.), *Case methods in teacher education* (pp. 175–193). New York: Teachers College Press.

Loughran, J., & Russell, T. (Eds.). (1997). *Teaching about teaching: Purpose, passion and pedagogy in teacher education*. London: Falmer Press.

Loughran, J., & Russell, T. (Eds.). (2002). *Improving teacher education practice through self-study.* London: Falmer Press.

Lundeberg, M. A., Levin, B. B., & Harrington, H. (1999). *Who learns what from cases and how?* Mahwah, NJ: Lawrence Erlbaum Associates.

MacLeod, G. (1987). Microteaching: End of a research era? *International Journal of Educational Research, 11*(5), 531–541.

Marshall, J., & Smith, J. (1997). Teaching as we're taught: The university's role in the education of English teachers. *English Education, 29*(4), 246–271.

McAninch, A. R. (1993). The case method in teacher education. In A. McAninch (Ed.), *Teacher thinking and the case method.* New York: Teachers College Press.

McDiarmid, G. W. (1996). Challenging prospective teachers' understandings of history: An examination of a historiography seminar. In L. Schauble & R. Glaser (Eds.), *Innovations in learning: New environments for education.* Mahwah, NJ: Lawrence Earlbaum Associates.

McIntyre, D. J., Byrd, D. M., & Foxx, S. M. (1996). Field and laboratory experiences. In Sikula, J., T. Buttery, & E. Guyton (Eds.), *Handbook of research on teacher education* (2nd ed.). New York: Macmillan.

Merseth, K. K., & Lacey, C.A. (1993). Weaving stronger fabric: The pedagogical promise of hypermedia and case methods in teacher education. *Teaching and Teacher Education, 9*(3), 283–299.

Merseth, K. (1996). Cases and case methods in teacher education. In J. Sikula, T. Buttery, & E. Guyton (Eds.), *Handbook of research on teacher education* (2nd ed.). New York: Macmillan.

Perlberg, A. (1987). Microteaching: Conceptual and theoretical bases. In M. Dunkin (Ed.), *The international encyclopedia of teaching and teacher education* (pp. 715–720). Oxford: Pergamon Press.

Perrodin, A. (1959). Student teachers try action research. *Journal of Teacher Education, 10*(4), 471–474.

Richert, A. E. (1992). Writing cases: A vehicle for inquiry into the teaching process. In J. H. Shulman (Ed.), *Case methods in teacher education* (pp. 155–174). New York: Teachers College Press.

Roe, M. F., & Stillman, A. C. (1994). A comparative study of dialogue and response journals. *Teaching and Teacher Education, 10*(6), 579–588.

Rose, M. (1999). "Our hands will know": The development of tactile diagnostic skill—teaching, learning, and situated cognition in a physical therapy program. *Anthropology and Education Quarterly, 30,* 133–160.

Shulman, J. H. (1992). *Case methods in teacher education.* New York: Teachers College Press.

Shulman, L. S. (1996). Just in case: Reflections on learning from experience. In J. Colbert, P. Desberg, & K. Trimble (Eds.). *The case for education: Contemporary approaches to using case methods.* Boston: Allyn & Bacon.

Shulman, L. S. (1986). Those who understand: Knowledge growth in teaching. *Educational Researcher, 15*(2), 4–14.

Spiro, R. J., Coulson, R. L., Feltovich, P. J., & Anderson, D. K. (1988). Cognitive flexibility theory: Advanced knowledge acquisition in ill-structured domains. In *Tenth Anniversary Conference of the Cognitive Science Society* (pp. 375–383). Hillsdale, NJ: Lawrence Erlbaum Associates.

Sykes, G., & Bird, T. (1992). Teacher education and the case idea. In G. Grant (Ed.), *Review of research in education* (Vol. 18, pp. 457–521). Washington DC: American Educational Research Association.

Thompson, C. (2002). *Pedagogy and prospective teachers in three college English courses.* Unpublished dissertation, Seattle, WA: University of Washington.

Torchon, F. V. (1999). *Video study groups for education, professional development, and change.* Madison, WI: Atwood Publishing.

Vare, J. W. (1994). Partnership contrasts: Microteaching activity as two apprenticeships in thinking. *Journal of Teacher Education, 45*(3), 209–217.

Wade, S. (1992). On becoming a consulting teacher: Overcoming role conflicts and misperceptions. In J. H. Shulman (Ed.), *Case methods in teacher education* (pp. 90–110). New York: Teachers College Press.

Wilson, S. M., Floden, R. E., & Ferrini-Mundy, J. (2001). Teacher preparation research: Current knowledge, gaps, and recommendations. Seattle, WA: Center for the Study of Teaching and Policy.

Zeichner, K. M., & Noffke, S. E. (2001). Practitioner research. In V. Richardson (Ed.), *Handbook of research on teaching* (4th ed.). Washington DC: American Educational Research Association.

Zeichner, K. M., & Wray, S. (2001). The teaching portfolio in U.S. teacher education programs: What we know and what we need to know. *Teaching and Teacher Education, 17*(5), 613–621.

8

Research on Preparing Teachers for Diverse Populations

Etta R. Hollins
University of Southern California

Maria Torres Guzman
Teachers College, Columbia University

Among the most important challenges facing the nation is providing high-quality schooling for all students, especially those presently underserved by the educational system, including students of color, low-income students, English-language learners, and students in rural and urban settings. A recent report from the National Center for Educational Statistics (NCES, 2003a) indicated that the 100 largest public school districts in the nation enroll 23% of all public school students. Sixty-nine percent of those were students of color, and 54% were eligible for free and reduced-price lunches. The challenge of providing a high-quality education to the increasingly diverse student population is not just a challenge faced by large cities, however. According to national data reported by NCES (2003b) in *The Condition of Education*, the percentage of all public school students from ethnic minority groups increased dramatically from 22% in 1972 to 39% in 2000. In 2000, African-American students represented 17% of public school enrollment, up 2 percentage points from 1972. During this same time period, Hispanic student enrollment increased from 6% to 17%, up a full 11 percentage points. In addition, from 1979 to 1999, the percentage of 5- to 24-year-olds who spoke a language other than English at home increased 118% and the percentage of those who spoke English with difficulty increased by 110%. Demographers predict that children of color will constitute the statistical majority of the student population by 2035 and account for 57% by 2050 (U.S. Department of Commerce, 1996, in Villegas & Lucas, 2002).

It is important to make clear here that it is not the changing demographic profile of the nation's schoolchildren in and of itself that is an obstacle to providing high-quality schooling for all. The United States has long been a nation of immigrants, and there have long been students of various colors and ethnicities in the schools. The problems are the persistent and pernicious disparities that exist in educational achievement, resources, and life chances between students of color and their White peers. On the 2000 National Assessment of Educational Progress (NAEP) reading assessment, for example, 40% of White fourth-graders scored at or above the "proficient" level, although this was true for only 12% of African American students, 16% of Hispanic students, and 17% of Native-American students. In mathematics 35% of White fourth graders scored at or above the "proficient" level, while only 5% of African American students, 10% of Hispanic students and 14% of Native-American students did that well (NCES, 2002). Disparities in educational achievement are also reflected in disparate high school graduation rates, which are consistently higher for White students than for their African-American, Hispanic, and Native-American peers (Educational Research Service, 1995; National Educational Goals Panel, 1994). In addition, in city schools, where there are such large numbers of students of color and students in poverty, the pupil-to-teacher ratio is higher than average (NCES, 2003a); teacher shortages are greater than those in other areas (Ingersoll, 2003); there are larger numbers of new, out-of-field and underqualified teachers (Darling-Hammond, 2000; Darling-Hammond & Sclan, 1996); and there are major deficiencies in the allocation of resources.

Although many factors influence educational outcomes in schools serving diverse student populations, there is increasing agreement among members of the educational community that teacher quality is a major factor, as discussed in chapter 2 of this volume. In an analysis of 1996 NAEP data, for example, Wenglinsky (2000) concluded that "one aspect of schools, the quality of their teaching force, does have a major impact on student test scores—indeed an impact that is comparable in size to that of student socioeconomic status" (p. 31). Some researchers take this point even further. Sanders (1998) and Sanders and Horn (1998), for example, who judge teachers by their value—added to pupils' test scores, argue that teacher quality is the single most important influence on school success and students' achievement, surpassing socioeconomic status, class size, family background, school context, and all other factors that influence achievement.

Over the past 2 decades in response to continuing disparities in achievement and resources between students of color and their White peers, and partly in response to growing recognition of the teacher's role in influencing achievement, there has been growing attention to the knowledge, skills, and dispositions of today's teachers. Critics from both inside and outside teacher education have suggested that traditional preservice and in-service teacher education has not done an adequate job preparing teachers to teach diverse populations (Ladson-Billings, 1999; Zeichner & Hoeft, 1996). Over the last decade, teacher preparation programs at colleges and universities across the country have attempted to respond to these challenges by altering courses, curriculum, fieldwork experiences, and other policies to include attention to diversity and multicultural education. A sizeable research literature has developed that documents and analyzes a number of key issues in this area.

This chapter begins with a general discussion of issues and trends in the study of the preparation of teacher candidates. Then the chapter analyzes the empirical research on four aspects of the preparation of preservice teachers: candidates' predispositions, preservice preparation of prospective teachers, the experiences of teacher candidates of color, and program evaluations. The chapter concludes with a discussion of implications for further research. The major argument of this review is straightforward. Although there are a number of promising lines of research and several patterns in the evidence that is available, we need more research that goes beyond single-site studies, that looks beyond short-term effects, and that examines the links among teacher preparation, teacher candidates' growth in knowledge and disposition, teachers' performances, and their pupils' learning. Although research along these lines is vital, it requires more funding, capacity, and attention than is currently being devoted to the topic.

STUDYING THE PREPARATION OF TEACHERS FOR DIVERSE POPULATIONS

The preparation of teachers for diverse populations has been the subject of a growing body of research over the last 2 decades. This chapter provides a review of that literature. Some of this literature is also included in chapter 5 on general education and educational foundations, chapter 6 on methods courses and fieldwork, and chapter 7 on the pedagogy of teacher education. It is important to note, as was stated in chapter 1, that the panel's decision to include the diversity and multicultural research in its own chapter was made partly to avoid redundancy. As also stated in chapter 1, however, there is a paradox involved in this decision. In setting apart the research on diversity and multicultural teacher education, the panel takes the risk of marginalizing this work and bolstering the status quo which has traditionally divided issues of diversity from the rest of the curriculum. We want to make a point of noting that this is not the intent. As pointed out in chapter 1, this literature is included in its own chapter to call attention to the critical importance of this work given the changing population of school children and the continuing disparities in the achievement of groups from different racial and cultural groups. The panel wanted to mark the fact that this work represents a topic in its own right in teacher education research.

Previous Reviews

The research related to the preparation of teachers for diverse student populations has been reviewed in a number of previous syntheses (Cochran-Smith, Davis, & Fries, 2003; Grant & Secada, 1990; Haberman, 1996; Ladson-Billings, 1999; Sleeter, 2001a, 2001b; Weiner, 1993, 2000; Zeichner & Hoeft, 1996). As Cochran-Smith, Davis and Fries point out, there has been remarkable consistency in the conclusions of previous reviews: Basic changes in teacher education for diversity are necessary, but have not occurred despite 25 years of attention; although some studies, suggest a positive impact of teacher preparation approaches, the findings about preparing teachers for diversity are generally inconsistent and inconclusive; outcome measures are not well developed; and, there are few longitudinal or large-scale studies, whereas there are many short-term and small-scale studies that have little general application. These critiques notwithstanding, the previous syntheses consistently identify two critical reasons for the weaknesses in the research that are important and illuminating: the research reflects the current state of the larger field of teacher education practice itself and there has been consistent marginalization and underfunding of research on issues related to diversity.

In teacher education programs and curricula, issues of diversity have generally been separated from the rest of teacher education. Often diversity has been addressed in optional or add-on "diversity" or "multicultural" courses (Ladson-Billings, 1995a; Zeichner & Hoeft, 1996), whereas the rest of the teacher education curriculum has remained unchanged (Gollnick, 1992; Villegas & Lucas, 2002). Often the pedagogy of teacher education, particularly as played out in methods courses and fieldwork experiences, has been separated to a great extent from the foundations of teacher education (Villegas & Lucas). Although the last decade has seen a fairly consistent call from multicultural curriculum theorists for teacher preparation that challenges the ideological and epistemological underpinnings of traditional programs (Ladson-Billings, 1999; Sleeter, 2001a; Weiner, 1993, 2000), it is clear that the multicultural teacher education envisioned by the theorists is not in place in practice, at least if we judge by the research. In addition, as Grant and Secada (1990) pointed out a decade and a half ago in the first major synthesis of research on preparing teachers for diversity, research on these issues has been consistently marginalized and underfunded. Because a problem exists does not mean that researchers will conduct research about it. Rather these decisions are integrally tied to the ideological climate and to economic conditions (Weiner, 2000). Consistent marginalization in mission, funding, and urgency helps to explain the lack of longitudinal studies and concentrated efforts to develop clear impact measures related to the preparation of teachers for diversity. Recognition of these conditions also sheds light on the large number of small-scale, short-term studies that are conducted by individual teacher educators often using either pre- and posttest attitude surveys or qualitative analyses of prospective teachers' written assignments.

Regardless of research methods, the most important thing previous syntheses reveal is that the research on teacher preparation for diversity reflects the state of teacher education more generally and is strongly influenced by lack of funding and other necessary infrastructure and resources. There are many small studies conducted in individual courses or seminars because diversity issues are generally not well integrated into teacher preparation as a whole. There are very few longitudinal studies or analyses based on national databases because diversity has been neither a priority for funding agencies nor a focus of well-supported programmatic research. What this suggests is that there is a dynamic and reciprocal relationship between research and practice in preservice teacher education. Problems and issues in preservice teacher preparation provide the impetus for scholarly inquiry, the results of the inquiry advance practices and informs subsequent research. This dynamic relationship advances both research and practice. However, when the research is underfunded, progress in the field of teacher education is hampered.

Selection and Evaluation Procedures

In the present review of the literature on preparing teachers for diverse students we have attempted to take these conditions into account even as we provide a critique of the current state of the field. We attempted to diminish the problem of studies with many methodological weaknesses noted in previous reviews by including only those studies reported in referred journals.

This review focused on empirical studies on the preparation of teachers for underserved populations, that is, students of color, those from low-income backgrounds, language minorities, and those living in urban and rural settings. In identifying the studies for review, initially we combined the descriptors of teacher education, preservice, diversity, and multicultural to search three databases: ERIC, Psych Lit, and Sociological Abstracts. Also, we conducted a hand search of the last 5 years for *Action in Teacher Education*, the *Journal of Teacher Education*, and *Teaching and Teacher Education* and a computer search of specialized areas such as English as a second language and bilingual education. We also examined the bibliographies of recent studies to identify publications that might have been overlooked. The studies included in this review are not exhaustive, but they are representative of what exists in the field.

The criteria in our initial review of studies were: (a) published between 1980 and 2002 in a refereed journal; (b) clearly presented outcomes, not purely descriptive; and (c) conducted within the United States. Our search yielded 101 studies that met the criteria. We then used, where appropriate, the guiding principles for scientific research in education developed by the National Research Council (2001) as a kind of framework to help us evaluate the studies: (a) poses significant questions that can be investigated empirically; (b) links research to relevant theory; (c) uses methods that permit direct investigation of the question; (d) provides coherent, explicit chain of reasoning; (e) replicates and generalizes across studies, and (f) discloses research to encourage professional scrutiny and critique.

It is important to note what this review does and does not include. We focused only on studies that dealt directly with the preparation of candidates for teaching diverse students within the context of teacher preparation programs in the United States. Thus, we did not include the literature on recruiting a diverse teaching force, the literature on the in-service education of teachers, or the major body of work that has emerged over the last 15 years on successful teaching practices for diverse students. The research on the successful teaching of diverse students offers major insights and has influenced the content of the preservice curriculum and raised expectations for teaching practices of preservice candidates. However, the focus of this review is on the preparation and learning of preservice teachers rather than on practices that enhance the learning of K–12 pupils. In addition, in keeping with the American Educational Research Association (AERA) Panel's charge to review the empirical research, this review also does not include the conceptual and theoretical literature on multicultural teacher education.

Our review of the literature is organized around four questions that are central in the existing literature: (a) What are the predispositions of candidates entering teacher preparation? (b) What are the outcomes of various practices used in the preparation of candidates for teaching diverse students, and under what conditions do these occur? What claims can be made based on these investigations? (c) What are the experiences and perspectives of candidates of color within preservice programs? (d) How have preservice programs for teaching diverse populations been evaluated? These four categories are subdivided into clusters of related studies. For the studies in each category we analyzed the underlying theories, perspectives, and ideologies that guided the studies; the research methods used; the findings; and strengths and weaknesses. To locate studies with a number of foci within a particular group, we concentrated on the major intention of the study. For example, we included in the field experience category several studies that examined the use of biography and storytelling during student teaching as a way to increase prospective teachers' cultural awareness.

RESEARCH ON CANDIDATES' PREDISPOSITIONS

The studies in this category focused on the attitudes, beliefs, predispositions, and prior experiences with diversity of those entering teacher preparation programs. Research on prospective teachers' attitudes, beliefs, and predispositions is in keeping with developments in learning theory over the last quarter century (National Research Council, 2000) and, more specifically, with studies of learning to teach and teachers' learning over time. As noted in chapter 2, this line of research is based on the premise that teachers' knowledge frames and belief structures are the filters through which their practices, strategies, actions, interpretations, and decisions are made. This means that knowledge and beliefs play an important mediating role in what candidates learn during their teacher education programs and also how and what they teach once they are in classrooms (Borko & Putnam, 1996; Wideen, Mayer-Smith, & Moon, 1998).

With regard to prospective teachers' beliefs and attitudes about teaching diverse populations, it has been argued that there are often marked differences between the bi-ographies and experiences of teachers who are White, middle class, and from English-only backgrounds in comparison with the experiences and perspectives of students of color, English-language learners, or students living in poverty (Gay, 1993; Irvine, 1997). White mainstream teachers tend not to have the same cultural frames of reference and points of view as their diverse students and may have difficulty serving as role models or cultural brokers between home and school (Goodwin, 2000; Villegas & Lucas, 2002). In addition, when teachers believe that diversity is a deficit to be over-come or when they hold low expectations for their students, or both, they often have difficulty teaching in ways that are both culturally responsive and academically chal-lenging (Irvine, 2001; Ladson-Billings, 1995b). Coupled with the general mismatch between teachers' and students' cultural, language, and socioeconomic backgrounds, as noted previously and in chapter 1, this may mean that unless prospective teachers have opportunities to rethink and change their attitudes and beliefs, the students who are in the greatest academic need may also be the ones least likely to have access to rich learning opportunities (Gay, 1993; Villegas & Lucas, 2002).

Most of the studies we reviewed in this category were quantitative with 13 of the 15 studies relying on surveys and questionnaires. Collectively, these studies provide a profile of candidates' experiences with diverse populations and their awareness of and attitudes toward diversity. We discuss the studies in three clusters: (a) candidate's prior experiences with diversity, (b) their attitudes and beliefs related to diversity, and (c) the experiences of candidates of color in teacher education programs.

Candidates' Prior Experiences With Diversity

Two studies examined teacher candidates' background characteristics and previous experiences with diversity. Not surprisingly, it was found that incoming teachers were predominately female, White, middle-class, and with limited interaction with those from backgrounds different from their own. Hadaway and Florez (1987–1988) ad-ministered a researcher-developed questionnaire to 125 candidates enrolled in meth-ods courses at Texas A&M University. They found that most candidates had limited experience with those from cultures other than their own and few had long-term in-teraction with people of other races and cultures. Findings indicated that these teacher candidates did not feel prepared to teach students from diverse backgrounds.

Green and Weaver (1992) administered a researcher-developed survey to some 1,600 freshmen who entered teacher education between 1987 and 1991 at Ball State

University. In keeping with national trends (see chap. 3), they found that more than 91% were White and middle class and that a majority were females from small or rural communities. Despite their own demographic profile, the respondents in this study were interested in developing the competencies needed to teach diverse groups, had idealistic reasons for becoming teachers, and had often been influenced by a high school teacher to choose teaching as a career.

Candidates' Attitudes Toward Diversity

Studies of candidates' predispositions and attitudes toward diversity had mixed results. Although teacher candidates were generally open to the idea of cultural diversity, they lacked confidence in their ability to do well in diverse settings, and many preferred not to be placed in situations where they felt uncomfortable and inadequate.

Martin and Williams-Dixon (1994) used the "Social Distance Scale" to investigate the perceptions of 266 undergraduates at a predominately White university in the South. They found that most were willing to make accommodations for diversity and, realizing the high probability of teaching in a culturally diverse setting, wanted to be able to communicate with children from different ethnic groups. They supported parental participation in schools, but felt uncomfortable interacting with parents from diverse backgrounds. On the other hand, they rejected nonstandard English and accepted ethnic jokes. Almost half thought racial statements should simply be ignored and believed minorities tended to overreact to racial statements. Barry and Lechner (1995) used a researcher-developed questionnaire with open-ended and forced answer responses to investigate candidates' awareness and perceptions of their preparation for teaching students from diverse backgrounds. The 73 teacher candidates in the study (97% White) were enrolled in three sections of an undergraduate elementary methods course at a large rural university in the Southeast. All had completed an orientation to education course and most (83%) had completed at least one course on global and multicultural education. Results indicated that candidates were aware of multicultural issues and anticipated having diverse students in their classrooms. However, they felt inadequately prepared to teach diverse students, and a majority thought it was difficult to change peoples' biases through multicultural education.

Easter, Shultz, Neyhart, and Reck (1999) used a similar survey to investigate the beliefs of 80 predominately White candidates enrolled in an introductory course at Kutztown University in Pennsylvania. Ninety-six percent of respondents said they respected cultural differences and believed they could successfully teach diverse populations despite a lack of life experience in diverse settings. Terrill and Mark (2000) also administered a researcher-developed survey to 97 undergraduates in an education foundations course at Central Michigan University. Fifty-two percent of respondents had never been in classrooms with students of color, and 75% had spent 10 hours or fewer. Seventy-five percent said they were interested in working in a school where all teachers were required to take Spanish to communicate better with Hispanic students and parents, but when asked to indicate their first choice for student teaching, 64% chose a White suburban school. Similarly Hlebwitsh and Tellez (1993) used a researcher-developed questionnaire to study the attitudes toward diverse groups of 235 predominantly White undergraduates in their first education course at the University of Houston. Although they found that respondents accorded higher levels of respect to Black, female, and low-socioeconomic-status (SES) students than to others, they also indicated that there were other plausible explanations, including sympathy.

Shultz, Neyhart, and Reck (1996) also administered a researcher-developed questionnaire with open-ended questions on attitudes and beliefs about culturally diverse students to 300 predominantly White candidates at Kutztown University. They found that despite negative attitudes toward urban students, teacher candidates were willing to teach in urban schools. Gilbert (1995) found similar results with a researcher-developed survey of knowledge and beliefs about diversity, which was administered to 193 undergraduate candidates, primarily White and female, enrolled in methods courses at a rural university in the Midwest. Although the candidates lacked both knowledge and experience, they said they planned to look for jobs in urban schools to be sure they would find a position. Gilbert (1997) also surveyed candidates at six urban and rural universities in Georgia, Illinois, Missouri, Ohio, Oklahoma, and Texas about their school experiences, preferences for schools, and perceptions of urban schools. Only 10% of respondents had urban experience. Almost half said they absolutely would not teach in an urban school. Respondents said they respected urban teachers, but thought urban students were uninterested in learning and urban schools were plagued with violence.

Along somewhat different lines, Richman, Bovelsky, Kroovand, Vacca, and West (1997) investigated ethnic bias by randomly assigning 20 teacher candidates at Wake Forest University to two groups that examined photographs of White and African-American children of similar ages and dress. They were asked to guess grade point average (GPA), IQ, leadership potential, likelihood of engaging in criminal behavior, likelihood of drug use, honesty, self-confidence, and initiative using a 6-point Likert scale. One group was shown the photographs of four African-American children, and the other group was shown these same photographs plus photographs of four similarly dressed European-American children. Candidates in both groups rated African Americans as inferior on GPA and IQ scores ($p < .01$). In terms of students' personal characteristics, the teachers rated the African-American students to be less ambitious, less self-confident, and to have little initiative when compared to European students ($p < .05$).

In a second study eight weeks later, the researchers used an autobiography and photographs of a writer and a poet in a similar way with 58 White candidates who volunteered to participate in the experiment. The results were similar. The study did not examine whether and how the candidates acted on these biases in classroom settings.

Using structured autobiographies as a tool of inquiry, Smith, Moallem, and Sherrill (1997) analyzed the source of the attitudes of 20 teacher candidates at a medium-size, predominately White university in the Southeast. Candidates were given a description of how people are socialized into oppressive beliefs and then asked to examine their own autobiographies. Analysis revealed that 35% were socialized to believe in gender equality, and 33% were socialized to believe in racial equality. In addition, 20% said they were socialized to believe in equality and had retained that belief; 30% were socialized to believe in discrimination but had rejected that belief; 14% were socialized to believe in discrimination and had subsequently developed mixed views; and 12% were socialized to believe in discrimination and had retained that belief. The factors the candidates reported as changing their beliefs included exposure to individuals from different cultural and experiential backgrounds, education, travel, and personal experience with discrimination.

Comparison of White and Minority Candidates' Attitudes

A few studies have compared the attitudes and dispositions of White and minority teacher candidates with the general conclusion that the two groups differ in interest in teaching as a career, perceptions, and experiences. Using data from the National Educational Longitudinal Study Follow-up in 1992, Cardina and Roden (1998) found that teaching had stronger career appeal for White candidates than for other racial groups. Su (1996) used surveys adapted from the national "Study of the Education of Educators" and interviews to compare 90 White and 58 minority teacher candidates at a major public university in California. He found that minorities were generally from lower socioeconomic groups and that their parents had less education and income and lower job status than their White peers. In a related study, Su (1997) also investigated the attitudes of Asian-American, African-American, and Hispanic teacher candidates at a state university in California. He found that unlike most White candidates, minority candidates came into teacher education programs with social justice goals and saw their own roles as change agents in the schools and society.

Research on Predispositions: Overview and Comment

The studies of candidates' predispositions are generally consistent with national trends, indicating that the majority of teacher candidates are White, female, middle class, from suburbs or small towns, and have limited experience with those from cultures different from their own. Many candidates hold negative attitudes and beliefs about those different from themselves. Although many are willing to teach in urban areas despite lack of experience and skill, some are unwilling to teach in cities or preferred suburban schools. Many candidates feel inadequately prepared to teach in urban areas. Candidates of color and their White counterparts have different experiences and different interests in teaching as a career.

The reliability and validity of the survey instruments used in many of the studies reviewed here are problematic because they are researcher-developed and inadequately described. Validation procedures are often not explained. In addition, the content of courses is often not adequately described nor is the context of the teacher preparation programs. In a number of instances, the initial dispositions of the candidates are not reported, nor is there any reference to growth. This means that although we have some information about candidates' attitudes, it is difficult to know how generally applicable this information is and, as the following sections suggest, it is difficult to know whether and how coursework and fieldwork affects attitudes or prompts growth and development.

THE PREPARATION OF CANDIDATES

This section reviews research on the preparation of teacher candidates for teaching diverse students as well as candidates' responses to these practices. The majority of the studies are qualitative, and many were conducted within the context of college- and university-based teacher education programs, especially in courses and field experiences. Four groupings of studies are included: prejudice reduction, equity pedagogy, field experiences, and the preparation of candidates of color.

Prejudice Reduction

The studies in this category focused on teacher education practices intended to reduce prejudice or increase awareness and sensitivity to diversity. According to Banks (2003, p. 21), prejudice reduction in the K–12 curriculum "describes lessons and activities teachers use to help students develop positive attitudes toward different racial, ethnic and cultural groups." Similarly, we use this term to describe investigations of the impact of particular practices in teacher preparation intended to help candidates develop positive attitudes toward groups and individuals different from themselves. Studies that addressed prejudice reduction but concentrated on equity pedagogy, field experiences, or candidates of color were not included. We discuss studies with a positive impact on reducing prejudice first and then turn to those with negative outcomes.

Studies With Generally Positive Results.   A majority of the studies reported a positive short-term impact of various course-based prejudice reduction activities on candidates' attitudes and beliefs. Marshall (1998) investigated the use of an "issues exchange" approach to multicultural education by assigning candidates to present opposing positions on diversity (e.g., either antimulticultural education or pro-multicultural education) to classmates. Surveys of 15 students who had previously completed the course indicated that candidates reported that they better understood the perspectives of others and their own perspectives. Nathenson-Mejía and Escamilla (2003) studied the introduction of children's literature in a fieldwork seminar. Based on group debriefings, observations of lessons, and participant reflections from 70 teacher candidates, of whom 16 were from linguistic and ethnic minority groups, the researchers found that teacher candidates used the books in their classrooms to make connections with their students' lives and to extend the pupils' verbal, reading, and writing skills. Over 3 years, candidates' attitudes toward their students changed, and they were motivated to teach in multicultural communities.

Similarly, Laframboise and Griffith (1997) reported positive outcomes using literary narratives as teaching cases. The participants were 22 White, middle-class candidates enrolled in a reading language arts course with a field-experience component located in a professional development school, during their first semester of a five-semester teacher education program at the University of South Florida. Using the Bogardus Social Distance Scale as a pre–post test with 178 predominately White candidates enrolled in a multicultural education course at Indiana University, Bennett, Niggle, and Stage (1990) investigated the impact of subject matter that addressed historical perspectives, cultural consciousness, prejudice reduction, and successful teaching of multicultural students. The researchers reported gains in multicultural knowledge and reductions in social distance for students in all six sections of the course.

Based on content analysis of dialogue journals, Garmon (1998) investigated 21 teacher candidates' learning about racial issues in a one-semester multicultural teacher education course at Western Michigan University. The researcher concluded that candidates learned through self-reflections, information provided by the instructor, and class discussion. McFalls and Cobb-Roberts (2001) also focused on pedagogy by investigating the use of cognitive dissonance as a means of reducing resistance to diversity with 124 majority White, undergraduate candidates in two sections of a course on diversity education at a large predominantly White university in the Southeast. One group read about White privilege and, following discussion, were asked about what had been learned. A second group received a lecture on cognitive dissonance and then wrote about connections between the content of the article on White privilege and the content of the lecture on cognitive dissonance theory. The authors suggested that cognitive dissonance created an awareness of dissonance and had the potential for reducing resistance to diversity issues. Along somewhat similar lines, Anderson (1998) investigated the impact of a unit of study in a junior-level educational psychology course that addressed culture, stereotypes, racism, and prejudice on the attitudes and beliefs of 32 undergraduate White female candidates at a small private university in the Southwest. The researcher used modeling of applied learning theory and the integration of multimedia technology into instruction to increase candidates' sensitivity to cultures different from their own. The candidates indicated in a survey that their understanding of cultural difference increased.

Several additional studies also reported positive outcomes for a multiple strategies approach to prejudice reduction and racial identity development. Lawrence and Bunche (1996) used readings, discussions, films, projects, and writing assignments in a course in multicultural education to influence the racial identity of five White female candidates at a college in the Northeast. Data sources were written course assignments and interviews before and after the course conducted by an individual not affiliated with the class. These researchers found that all participants had advanced beyond Helms's (1990) "contact stage" (low level of awareness of institutional racism) by the end of the course, with two candidates at the "reintegration stage," and three at either the "pseudo-independent" or "immersion" stages where they rejected previously held beliefs but did not assume responsibility for learning more about racism.

Obidah (2000) conducted a self-study in a multicultural education course with 29 candidates (17 White, 9 Black, and 3 biracial and bicultural), which focused on helping students critically reflect on their ideas and beliefs about education and culture. The course included readings, discussions, exercises, films, e-mail exchanges, debates, and individual meetings with the instructor. Data sources included candidates' written assignments, notes kept by the professor on conversations with students, student e-mails to the professor, and student course evaluations.

Obidah (2000) reflected on her course in terms of several outcomes: helping students' reconceptualize their identities in relation to multiculturalism, creating an atmosphere of empowerment in the class, and learning the challenges of practicing critical multiculturalism as a professor. Based on her analysis of her student data sources, Obidah concluded that students' perspectives on multiculturalism broadened, their understanding of bias and cultural assumptions in teaching and learning increased, and their ability to critique their own beliefs and assumptions about different groups of people also increased.

In terms of her own role as the instructor, Obidah (2000) concluded that she became more aware of the challenges of mediating and disrupting dominant norms of teaching and learning in university classrooms in order to be able to deal with issues of race and social class in education (e.g., deciding when student discomfort adds to or gets in the way of students' learning about multiculturalism).

Peterson, Cross, Johnson, and Howell (2000) also used a multiple strategies approach to influence the attitudes of 26 candidates in a foundations of education course at Governors State University in Illinois. A researcher-developed posttest questionnaire indicated that 87% of candidates reported that their views regarding intolerance and multicultural issues were greatly changed by viewing and discussing a film, group presentations, and the instructor's and classmates' stories. Similarly, Arias and Poynor (2001) studied the change in attitudes of three ESL and two bilingual pre-service teachers at Arizona State University who were in a reading and language arts course block held in a professional development school. The researchers used Banks's (1984) developmental stages of ethnic behaviors to assess the three English-as-second-language (ESL) teacher candidates' growth. The researchers observed and participated with the teacher educators in developing the syllabus, observing the teacher candidates in the course and field placement in the professional development school (PDS) classrooms, and conducted semistructured interviews with three candidates and the two course instructors. They found all candidates had reached Level 3 of Banks's (1984) states of ethnic behaviors (ethnic identity clarifi-cation) where "they seemed to accept themselves and their ethnic identity as well as accept and respect the cultural and linguistic diversity of others" (p. 418).

The studies discussed so far in this category on prejudice reduction have inves-tigated practices in a single course or field experience. A few researchers, however, compared the effects of different courses and arrangements. Sparks and Verner (1995) compared the impact of four different multicultural education courses on 228 teacher candidates' perceptions of their personal knowledge and attitudes at a public univer-sity in Illinois: a discipline-specific course, an integrated course that focused on generic multicultural concepts, a discipline-specific field experience, and an integrated field experience. Based on data from a researcher-developed and validated Multicultural Physical Education Instrument, researchers found that candidates' perceptions of their multicultural knowledge increased significantly in the discipline-specific course and the integrated course, but not in the other two. In the discipline-specific field experi-ence, perceptions of multicultural knowledge actually decreased.

Grottkau and Nickolai-Mays (1989) investigated the infusion of a "broad-based multicultural paradigm" (p. 29) across the curriculum. Using a pre–post test of the Bogardus Social Distance Scale for 122 predominately White candidates at a liberal arts college in Wisconsin, researchers found that exposure to multicultural education experiences over time decreased overall levels of bias toward specific groups.

Studies With Mixed Results.   Three studies suggested a dynamic interaction among candidates' experiential backgrounds, subject matter, and the practices used in teacher preparation programs. Drawing on demographic data, an initial position paper, journals, and a capstone assignment that required candidates to evaluate solu-tions for African-American pupils' underachievement, Cockrell, Placier, Cockrell, and Middleton (1999) found that a multicultural foundations course at a large Midwestern research university had little impact on students' views of diversity. To explore why, the teacher educators considered the 128 candidates' identities, experiences, and be-liefs to learn more about their negative responses to a multicultural foundations course they taught. They concluded that candidates held different views of diversity based on personal experience, political ideologies, and beliefs about the roles of schools and teachers. Some of their resistance to multicultural education was related to a strong affinity for individualism and monoculturalism. Along somewhat similar lines, Greenman and Kimmel (1995) investigated the extent to which candidates, teachers, and school counselors-in-training embraced an American Association of Colleges for Teacher Education- (AACTE)-endorsed stance on multiculturalism, equity and cul-tural differences. The 96 majority White participants in this study, including counselor trainees as well as preservice and in-service teachers, attended a week-long mul-ticultural education workshop. A researcher-developed questionnaire indicated no change in definitions of culture for the majority of the participants, and only 43% of the students showed growth in their definitions of multicultural education.

Katz (2000) studied the impact of a bilingual education course on the attitudes and beliefs of 200 teacher candidates (70% White) at the University of San Francisco, using as data written reflections, written field observations, reports about bilingual and ESL classrooms and families, and an original self-initiated project. They found growth in students' knowledge, but not a change in attitudes nor a reduction in prejudice. When exposed to policies, research, and theory related to language acquisition, candidates who were already supportive of bilingualism became more articulate in their sup-port, whereas those who were already skeptical rejected the research and looked for evidence to support their belief in English-only education. Each of three studies in this cluster with mixed results reported a dynamic relationship between candidates' experiential backgrounds and perceptions and subject matter and practices in the courses or experiences in which they participated. A multiple-strategies approach was used in each study.

Studies With Negative Results. Three studies in this category reported negative results. They were conducted under a variety of conditions that included a series of multicultural in-service training sessions, eight 2-hour seminars and a 10-week methods course with a 3-week field experience.

McDiarmid (1992) investigated the impact of a series of state department of education sponsored in-service training sessions intended to influence trainees' attitudes toward children culturally different from themselves as well as provide information about culture, pedagogical techniques, and the effects of teacher behaviors. Questionnaires with scenarios keyed to workshop objectives were distributed to 110 trainees at the beginning of the program, the end of the first year of teaching, and during the second year of teaching. Twelve trainees were interviewed and observed. Researchers concluded that multicultural workshops neither reduced candidates' acceptance of stereotypes nor diminished their use of culturally inappropriate assignments.

McIntyre (1997) explored what it means to be a "White teacher" with 13 White female undergraduate candidates at a private Northeastern university enrolled in a one-semester prepracticum field experience. Study volunteers attended eight 2-hour sessions on White privilege, field experiences, and daily encounters with race led by the researcher. Data were drawn from transcriptions of group sessions and semi-structured interviews. The researcher found that participants understood multicultural education to be dialogue about "other people" and were unable to connect racism and Whiteness to multicultural education or to oppression and inequality in society and the schools.

In the third study, Causey, Thomas, and Armento (2000) investigated the impact of an undergraduate middle-grades social studies methods class that included three weeks in an urban school. Data sources included autobiographical and post-experience essays, reflection journals, and action plans developed by the candidates. Researchers found that most candidates retained their original beliefs about diversity. A longitudinal follow-up with two candidates who seemed to experience cognitive change during the course revealed that one candidate seemed to have retained her new perspective in the classroom, whereas the other, who was teaching in an urban school, had become more cynical.

The single factor that these three studies seemed to have in common was a short time period of one year or less or an interrupted time interval where the study started, stopped, and restarted. Additionally, the practices in these studies with negative results did not appear consistent with those in studies reporting positive outcomes such as the use of a model or interpretive framework, introducing dissonance and discontinuity, cognitive coaching, or the use of critical text analysis.

Research on Prejudice Reduction: Overview and Comment

A majority of the studies examining prejudice reduction reported positive short-term impacts on candidates' attitudes and beliefs. Although this is promising, it is difficult to determine the sustainability of these outcomes over time. Very few studies were longitudinal or included follow-up investigations. Three studies reported mixed results in terms of prejudice reduction, but also revealed a dynamic interaction among candidates' experiential backgrounds, course content, and pedagogical strategies (Cockrell et al., 1999; Greenman & Kimmel, 1995; Katz, 2000). Three studies reported no impact from the intervention (McDiarmid, 1992; McIntyre, 1997; Causey et al., 2000). One study reported a longitudinal follow-up with two candidates who seemed to have experienced cognitive change during the program only to find that teaching context influenced the sustainability of gains (Causey et al.).

There are a number of methodological concerns about most of the studies on prejudice reduction. They have small sample sizes and usually occur over very short time frames. In addition, they are based primarily on self-reported data rather than on direct observation or documentation. In addition the studies provide little information about the context in which prejudice reduction activities occurred or how they fit into larger teacher preparation program arrangements and structures. Several studies lacked adequate description of the courses or practices that were being investigated (Anderson, 1998; Bennett et al., 1990; Greenman & Kimmell, 1995; McDiarmid, 1992; Sparks & Verner, 1995), and in some cases, information about the participants was incomplete (Marshall, 1998; Nel, 1992). In two studies, the researchers acknowledged the possibility of selection bias due to lack of randomized sampling in assigning candidates to groups or due to voluntary status of participants (Grottkau & Nickolai-Mays, 1989; McIntyre, 1997). In some instances, the findings were not adequately described. For example, in the study by Nathenson-Mejía and Escamilla (2003), it was unclear how many students exhibited the behavioral change claimed as a finding in the investigation. LaFramboise and Griffith (1997) did not explain the extent to which attitudes, beliefs, and responsiveness to diverse student populations were changed.

Equity Pedagogy

Banks (1991, 2003) suggests that "equity pedagogy" exists when teachers employ methods and materials that support the academic achievement of students from diverse and minority groups. This includes creating curriculum and instruction based on students' backgrounds, fostering self-determination, and attending to oppressed and underserved groups. A number of the studies we reviewed investigated teacher education courses intended to prepare teacher candidates to provide equity pedagogy in their K–12 classrooms.

Based on a "social-objective constructivist" view that focused on how individuals make sense of science, Southerland and Gess-Newsome (1999) engaged 21 second-career candidates in a science methods course in writing reflective journal entries, conducting science interviews with children, teaching lessons, and planning units of instruction. This "social-objective constructivist" view referred to experience with the physical world, prior knowledge, and the influence of cultural experiences and social interaction on how individuals make sense of science. Using as data sources transcriptions of class discussions, journal entries, interviews, plans, and case-based teaching, the teacher-educator researchers found that positivistic views of knowledge and authority interfered with candidates' development of inclusive approaches to science. In another science methods course with 18 candidates at New Mexico State, Rodriguez (1998), used a "socio-transformative constructivist orientation" to link multicultural education and social constructivist theoretical frameworks. Rodriguez identified two types of resistance among candidates—resistance to ideological change and to pedagogical change. Four White candidates who were seemingly more open and had contrasting views of science were selected for further examination through interviews, class assignments, field notes, and videotaped lessons. These practitioner researchers concluded that a "counter-resistance strategy" incorporating dialogue, a focus on metacognition and reflexivity, and the use of authentic science activities helped candidates overcome resistance and begin to see science teaching and learning as a socially constructed process.

Greenleaf, Hull, and Reilly (1994) had similar findings about the inflexibility of candidates' thinking. Based on analysis of the responses of 36 primarily White teachers, tutors, and candidates in different settings, the researchers found two barriers to productive problem solving: a belief in "right" answers and methods and the belief that diversity is an obstacle to pupils' learning. The researchers concluded that a group inquiry, problem-solving-type process encouraged critical thinking and prompted participants to reconsider their expectations for diverse students. In an introductory literacy and culture course, Clark and Medina (2000) had candidates work in self-selected reading groups where they chose from among book-length narratives. Three candidates (one White, one Black, one Latina White) who chose the same book were studied using as data sources e-mail conversations, group discussions, and individual reading logs. The practitioner researchers concluded that during the course, candidates began to understand multiple perspectives, contexts, and influences on how individuals construct literacy. This enabled candidates to correct their own overgeneralized conclusions about those from cultural and experiential backgrounds different from their own and to better understand cultural conditions.

Candidates' ability to engage equity pedagogy may be influenced by their ability to communicate with the learners. The level of candidates' language competence for teaching English-language learners was the subject of a pilot study conducted by Johanessen and Bustamante Lopez (2002). They focused on the development of a language assessment test that examined the Spanish-language usage of candidates within a teaching domain. Based on interviews and surveys of 60 students seeking a bilingual credential in a California university, the researchers found that about one fourth of the candidates engaged in activities that helped develop academic language proficiencies in Spanish when they were provided with opportunities for academic exchanges in the language.

Two studies investigated candidates' ability to consider students' cultural and experiential backgrounds when planning lessons. Xu (2000) found that during a literacy course with an eight-week field experience at a diverse school, 20 primarily White middle-class candidates learned to plan instruction that took learning styles, background knowledge, and life experiences into consideration. Morales (2000) studied primarily minority candidates who were taking a course employing a constructivist philosophy with a Developmentally Appropriate Practices framework. Drawing on pre- and post-course surveys, journals, and reflections, the researcher concluded that the majority of candidates acquired an understanding of cultural and experiential differences and the construction of developmentally appropriate strategies for young children and also gained confidence working with children and families different from themselves.

Research on Equity Pedagogy: Overview and Comment

Several of the studies that we grouped in this category reported problems in candidates' thinking as barriers to implementing equity pedagogy. In three of these studies, inflexibility and rigidity appeared to be the heart of the problem (Greenleaf et al., 1994; Rodriguez, 1998; Southerland & Gess-Newsome, 1999). In one study, early socialization seemed to shape candidates' thinking in ways that made it difficult for them to consider cultural and experiential differences in planning instruction (McCall, 1995). Two studies reporting problematic thinking were conducted in science courses (Rodriguez, 1998; Southerland & Gess-Newsome, 1999) and one study was conducted with individuals involved in five different types of teacher training or professional development (Greenleaf et al.). A multiple-strategies approach was used in each of the three studies. Four studies in this category reported positive outcomes without mention of interference from problematic thinking (Ball, 2000; Clark & Medina, 2000; Morales, 2000; Xu, 2000). Three of those studies reporting positive outcomes were conducted in literacy methods courses (Ball; Clark & Medina; Xu). The fourth involved a majority (87%) of candidates of color (Morales, 2000). The pedagogical approaches varied in the studies reporting positive outcomes from a single focus on literary narratives (Clark & Medina) to the multiple strategies approaches used in the other studies.

Collectively, these studies help us understand some of the factors that interfere with candidates' ability to acquire knowledge and skills related to the development of equity pedagogy. Studies conducted in science methods courses seem to suggest that how candidates have constructed understanding of the subject matter may interfere with their openness to equity pedagogy. This was not evident in studies conducted in language arts methods courses. The multiple strategies approaches that generated positive outcomes in language arts methods courses did not consistently generate the same effect in science methods courses. Studies in methods courses with positive outcomes tell us that candidates can learn and apply knowledge of equity pedagogy in planning instruction; however, they do not tell us the extent to which candidates were enabled to apply equity pedagogy to raise the academic performance of students.

We need to exercise caution in interpreting the findings from these studies because of their methodological shortcomings. With one exception, all the studies in this group were conducted in methods courses, and the researcher was the course instructor. The relationship between the researcher as instructor and the candidates as students may have influenced the outcomes. Candidates' responses may have been influenced by their perceptions of the instructor's expectations. Additionally, the dual role of instructor and researcher may have influenced the interpretation of the findings from the study. There is nothing inherently limiting in teacher educators studying their own courses. The problem is that in these studies the researchers did not discuss how they dealt with the dual role of instructor and researcher to protect the validity of their results. In one study (Greenleaf et al., 1994) the relationship between the researcher and the participants was unclear.

All of the studies had small samples of 2 to 36 participants with the exception of Johanessen and Bustamante Lopez (2002), who administered a language assessment to 60 participants. None of the studies randomly selected participants. In some cases the participants were selected because they displayed attributes the researcher wished to investigate (McCall, 1995; Rodriguez, 1998), or the participants volunteered (Southerland & Gess-Newsome, 1999), or an entire class was studied (Morales, 2000). These selection procedures raise questions about whether the samples were representative of the larger population from which they were selected. These studies documented short-term outcomes usually over the regular term of a course with the exception of Xu (2000), where the study was conducted over an 8-week field experience. The sustainability of these outcomes needs to be examined. Only one study in this category (Morales) provided adequate description of the context to allow the reader to understand how the course fit into the teacher education program and to consider other factors that may have contributed to the findings. What this means is that although we have many descriptions of teacher educators working to help their students develop pedagogies that will meet the needs of their diverse student populations, we know very little about the conditions and contexts in which this occurs or whether graduates actually use what they have learned once they are in schools.

Field Experiences

Field experiences have long been identified by both teacher educators and prospective and experienced teachers as a major, if not the most important, part of preservice teacher preparation. It is broadly assumed that field experiences are the key components of preparation where prospective teachers learn to bridge theory and practice, work with colleagues and families, and develop pedagogical and curricular strategies for meeting the learning needs of a diverse population. How experienced teachers do or do not teach African-American and other minority students effectively are among the most well-researched questions in the multicultural literature on K–12 schools. Although this substantial literature on what has been referred to as culturally relevant pedagogy, culturally responsive teaching, and culturally competent teaching (e.g., Gay, 2000; Irvine, 2001; Irvine & Armento, 2001; Ladson-Billings, 1994, 1995a, 1995b; Villegas, 1991) is not part of the present review, it has had a major impact on the ways teacher education programs organize fieldwork opportunities and requirements for prospective teachers, including student teaching and other community experiences.

In teacher preparation programs, field experiences are organized in various ways and for a variety of purposes. The varieties of field experiences that have been studied include introductory field experiences designed for exposure and observations in classrooms, practicum courses that simultaneously engage teacher candidates in field experiences along with methods courses, community-based field experiences intended to familiarize candidates with diverse populations, and student-teaching placements in contexts with diverse student populations. The duration of field experiences varied from a few hours a week for several weeks to daily full-time work across two semesters.

We organized this group of studies according to the focus of the research: community-based field experiences, relocation of candidates from rural or monocultural settings to diverse or urban settings for field experiences, candidates' responses to urban settings, a comparison of benefits from different settings, the use of personal biographies and story telling, the application of training in multicultural education, and candidates' attention during field experiences.

Community-Based Field Experiences. Several studies investigated community-based field experiences, including tutoring low-income students, working in community agencies in locations with diverse populations, internships in a Christian school, work as participant observers in a community study, and other experiences. Although these community experiences provide different types of contact with diverse populations, their common objective was to increase candidates' awareness, understanding, and acceptance of those different from themselves.

In several of these studies, the teacher candidate's role was knowledge broker or service provider, such as tutoring a school child. Bollin (1996) studied 40 elementary candidates enrolled in a group processes course at West Chester University, West Chester, PA, where tutoring low-income children from an ethnic group different from the candidates' was required. Content analysis of candidates' reflective journals revealed an increase in understanding of candidates' own ethnic identity, ethnicity and social class as factors in students' school experiences, and the complexities of teaching in culturally diverse classrooms.

Bondy and Davis (2000) studied the experiences of nine White, middle-class elementary candidates at the University of Florida who tutored African-American children in a public housing neighborhood, concentrating on their strategies for negotiating caring relationships with children. Tutor-child pairs met weekly for an hour at a tutoring site within the neighborhood. Based on qualitative analysis of interviews, they found that candidates who stuck with the tutoring sought information about the students from various sources, observed and listened to the students, and planned activities that incorporated this information. Some of the students had to overcome initial relationship problems to develop connections with their pupils. By the end of the 10-week program, eight of the nine prospective teachers had demonstrated forms of caring that allowed them to connect with pupils with whom they initially felt little connection.

Burant and Kirby (2002) studied candidates' community-based work in an urban school and how these experiences were integrated with the educational foundations and methods course taught by the researchers. The participants, 26 candidates enrolled at a university in the Southwest, nine of whom were people of color, engaged in a variety of activities with children, parents, and school staff. Data sources included candidates' weekly reflective papers and action reports as well as field notes, interviews, and focus groups conducted by the researchers. The researchers found that although just under half of the students had "deepening" or "transformational" experiences that led them to desire teaching positions in urban schools, just over half had "masked," "partially miseducative," or "escaping" experiences (p. 565) and retained their preference for teaching White, middle-class children in urban schools.

In two studies, candidates were placed in community service agencies. Mahan (1982) reported a 9-year longitudinal evaluation of a one-semester cultural immersion experience completed by 293 candidates in the teacher preparation program at Indiana University—Bloomington. Participants were prepared for the cultural immersion experience in a course focused on the cultural group in the particular community to which they were assigned. During the cultural immersion experience candidates completed an internship with a community agency, attended community meetings, interacted with families, and completed student teaching. The evaluation was based on a Likert scale instrument and content analysis of the reports written by candidates after each experience. The researcher found that the benefits of the immersion experience included new relationships between candidates from different backgrounds, increased self-awareness, better understanding of how to promote cultural pluralism in the classroom, and the candidates' performance of a valuable service in the community. Potthoff et al. (2000) used a researcher-developed survey to study majority White, undergraduate candidates enrolled in a community-based field experience at the University of Nebraska. They found that experience in human services agencies helped candidates acquire positive attitudes toward diversity, promoted empathy for persons different from themselves, and promoted communication skills for interacting with those from diverse populations.

Narode, Rennie-Hill, and Peterson (1994) studied the experiences of 26 majority White graduate candidates in a cohort at Portland State University who served as participant observers in an urban community study where they interviewed community members and parents, shadowed middle school and high school students, and interviewed classroom teachers. Based on content analysis of candidates' documentation of their experiences, the researchers concluded that the experience had a positive impact on candidates' views about urban settings. Seidl and Friend (2002) investigated the influence of a cross-cultural, equal-status internship on the perspectives and identities of a group of predominantly White candidates in a fifth-year, graduate-level teacher education program at The Ohio State University, Columbus. The researchers were the primary mediators of a partnership between the university and a Christian school. The participants in the internship met and worked with African-American adults who were their peers, economically and professionally. Data sources included field notes of community and university meetings, classroom dialogue and candidates' course assignments. These researchers concluded that although there was some resistance, many of the students developed more sophisticated understandings of culture, race, and education.

These studies suggest short-term benefits for teacher candidates in community-based field experiences that include better understanding of diverse populations and learning how to communicate and build relationships with those from cultures different from their own. Although former experiences remained a strong influence on attitudes and beliefs, some candidates made significant shifts in knowledge and perspectives about diversity regardless of the status assumed during the field experience. The significance of the roles of knowledge broker and service provider, investigator and equal-status relationships need further investigation. The studies are limited in terms of confirmability and transferability of findings. None provided a rich description of the settings for the community-based field experiences, the particular assignments or activities in which candidates participated, the framework for the teacher preparation program that housed the field experience, or the roles of those who facilitated or guided the experience. None made clear how the community-based field experiences were linked to the larger teacher education programs, or how these experiences might inform classroom practices. In addition, because the candidates volunteered for the field experience or the study, it is not clear that they were representative of the larger population in the preparation programs. Other omissions of information make the studies difficult to evaluate methodologically.

Relocation to Urban Settings.   Several studies focused on the relocation of teacher candidates from rural or monocultural settings to urban or culturally diverse settings for a field placement. These studies revealed some of the complexities, practices, and outcomes of providing candidates from rural universities with an urban field experience.

Canning (1995) explored the experiences of 39 majority White candidates from a rural Midwestern university who volunteered to student teach in an urban, multicultural setting in the Southwest between 1993 and 1994. Concurrent with the student teaching, the students completed a course in multicultural education emphasizing interpersonal and cross-cultural communication skills. Student teachers also participated in written reflections and conducted action research and worked with Mexican-American and African-American teachers in their schools who served as bicultural mentors. In addition, ideas from local Mexican-American consultants were routinely incorporated into seminar meetings and site-based supervision conferences. Drawing on the researcher's observations in classrooms, candidates' reports, and interviews, Canning concluded that although "open-mindedness" seemed to be an important aspect of candidates' success in the classroom, only one student teacher applied knowledge gained from theory and methods courses to provide content based on the cultural heritage of the students.

Lopez Estrada (1999) conducted a qualitative study using observations and interviews with six interns at the University of Indiana—Bloomington who volunteered to complete a 6- to 15-week practicum in schools in the Rio Grand Valley of Texas. The researcher found that although the experience seemed to affect the viewpoints of all participants, the three interns who were members of ethnic minority groups (Hispanic or African-American) achieved higher levels of cultural consciousness and cross-cultural awareness and were more likely to end up in language minority communities than were their White counterparts in the same field work experience.

Along somewhat similar lines, Sconzert, Iazzetto, and Purkey (2000) studied the experiences of 12 student teachers at Lawrence University in Wisconsin who were enrolled in an Urban Education Program sponsored by the Associated Colleges of the Midwest. Data sources were interviews with the candidates before and after their student teaching experience in Chicago and a reflective essay about the experience. Although candidates reported they had learned that instruction should be adapted to the needs and cultural experiences of students, they felt inadequately prepared to teach in an urban setting and were surprised by the negative attitudes of veteran teachers. These researchers cautioned that their data did not allow for the sorting out of program, self-selection, and context factors.

Cooper, Beare, and Thorman (1990) used the Self-Assessment in Multicultural Education instrument to compare the experiences of 18 candidates from Morehead State University in northwest Minnesota who went to south Texas to student teach (and had three courses in multicultural education) with the experiences of 85 Morehead classmates who student-taught in Minnesota. Both groups of student teachers, those who went to Texas and those who did not completed three courses in multicultural education prior to student teaching. In a comparison of the students who taught in Texas and Minnesota, in the Texas group there were statistical differences in 9 of the 20 items in the survey. The Texas group felt more comfortable discussing racial issues, were more likely to encourage a variety of viewpoints when they were teaching, and held higher expectations for the learning of students of color. The researchers concluded that this opportunity to student-teach in Texas in this program led to the development of multicultural competencies to a greater degree than for the student teachers who remained in Minnesota.

McCormick (1990) reported a follow-up study of candidates in the Cooperative Urban Teacher Education Program (CUTE), a collaborative of 20 colleges and universities, which was initiated by the Mid-Continent Regional Educational Laboratory and was intended to prepare teachers to teach in urban settings. Data came from a questionnaire sent to 172 of the 234 participants from Iowa State University who had completed a 17-week semester of student teaching in Kansas City, Kansas, between 1970 and 1984. Sixty percent of the questionnaires were returned; 95% of respondents were White. Forty-seven percent of respondents were still teaching, primarily in urban settings. They indicated that student teaching in an urban setting had a profound impact on their development as teachers and identified various strengths of the program including the multicultural experiences it provided for them. They also identified several program weaknesses including the lack of awareness about the program on the Iowa State campus.

These studies about relocation for field experience seem to suggest that rural candidates student teaching in an urban setting can learn about students from diverse cultural and experiential backgrounds as well as about school conditions in urban settings. The researchers indicated that frames of mind such as open-mindedness, playfulness, and a social justice orientation as well as previous experiences with diverse populations had a positive influence on the experience. Some candidates felt inadequately prepared and uncomfortable in urban settings but most identified aspects of the urban experience that were helpful and useful to them as teachers. All of these relocation studies had small sample sizes, volunteer participants, and researchers who were either the field experience supervisor or the instructor for the course linked to the field experience. These study characteristics raise questions about the degree to which the participants in these studies were representative of the larger population of their peers in other programs. In addition, these practitioner researchers did not provide information about how they managed the tensions associated with their dual roles or about the relocation settings or home program.

Candidates' Responses to Diverse Settings.   Some studies focused on candidates' cognitive and emotional responses to early field experiences or internships, or both, in unfamiliar situations in school settings with diverse students, including impact on cultural awareness, sensitivity, attitudes, their concerns, and strategies. Deering and Stanutz (1995) used the "Cultural Diversity Awareness Inventory" as a pre- and posttest to investigate the impact of field experiences in diverse settings on the cultural sensitivity of 16 secondary candidates at a suburban, private liberal arts university who had not yet had multicultural education courses. The survey was designed to assess an individual's attitudes, beliefs, and behavior toward children of culturally diverse backgrounds. The candidates took the survey prior to and after a 10-week field experience in a middle school with a predominately Hispanic and Black student population. Although there was some evidence of growth in the student teachers after the 10-week field experience (e.g., more student teachers said at the end that they would like to teach students different from themselves, fewer said at the end that they were uncomfortable with people who speak nonstandard English), the researchers concluded that one field experience without coursework in multicultural education did not significantly improve the cultural sensitivity of these preservice teachers.

In a similar study at a university in the Southeast, Marshall (1996) used the "Multicultural Teaching Concerns Survey" to identify candidates' concerns about working with diverse student populations during their first education course, which was linked to an 8-week practicum. The 64-item survey addressed concerns related to family group knowledge, strategies and techniques, interpersonal competence, and school bureaucracy. Based on an analysis of the responses from 90 education students, it was concluded that the teaching candidates were most concerned about how their students would perceive them as teachers, instructional methods for diverse students, dealing with attitudes of intolerance, and whether diverse students had appropriate adult role models at home. Marshall suggests that the teacher education curriculum should be designed to address candidates' concerns related to teaching diverse students.

Olmedo (1997) examined the impact of a course that she taught at a large urban university in the Midwest where candidates spent one day per week for eight to ten weeks observing and helping a teacher in an elementary classroom. The course also consisted of readings, discussions, and assignments related to teaching in an urban multicultural environment. Content analysis of the journals and essays written by 16 of the 24 White students in the class of 29 revealed that all 16 expressed more favorable views of urban schools at the end of the experience than at the beginning. However, they continued to express concern about institutional limitations of teaching in a large urban school district with large classes in tight spaces and limited resources. The researcher observed that the expression of changing views of candidates about teaching culturally diverse students did not necessarily indicate real changes in attitudes or in classroom practices and that these changes need to be reinforced by other parts of the teacher education program Olmedo identified several aspects of her course such as small group discussions and assignments that focused her students' attention on particular things during their fieldwork as important in helping her students to question their assumptions about teaching in urban schools.

Tiezzi and Cross (1997) examined the attitudes and beliefs toward teaching in urban schools of 48 of the 54 students who were enrolled in a 50-hour early field experience observing in urban classrooms as part of an introduction to an urban teaching course at the University of Wisconsin—Milwaukee. They also looked closely at the experiences of two White elementary candidates in the course. While in the field, the candidates completed several assignments including observation logs, and journals focused primarily on the school and classroom organization and learning environment.

Based on content analysis of several written assignments such as reflective journals and personal history essays, the researchers concluded that the prospective teachers brought firmly held beliefs about teaching in urban schools to their program that were based on their educational and life experiences. Common beliefs that students brought to the program included a belief that inner-city children could not learn and were poor, hostile, and unmotivated and that their parents did not care. The researchers concluded that these beliefs often persisted throughout the course and that the continued focus of their students on the problems of urban contexts, urban children, and urban families was much more prevalent than a focus on teaching and learning.

Tiezzi and Cross (1997) discussed the experiences of two students in the course whose profiles illustrate the similarities and differences in the experiences of the students in the course. One student entered the field experience with a positive view of urban schools and ended with frustration and disillusionment about urban school personnel, students, and their families. The other entered the field experience with a negative view of urban schools, which was unchanged by the experience. The researchers cautioned about the impact of field experiences in urban schools where little support or preparation is provided to students and planned to use their findings to redesign their course.

The next set of studies examined the influence of internships and student teaching experiences on teaching candidates. In the first study, Goodwin (1997) conducted a seminar where 83 full-time candidates (27% were candidates of color) in a childhood education program at Teachers College, Columbia University, were instructed to generate vignettes about their experiences with multicultural issues or dilemmas during student teaching. The candidates had basic instruction in multicultural curriculum models and materials, but not in general issues of diversity. A content analysis of the student teachers' vignettes revealed that during student teaching in New York City, these candidates were surprised to see inequitable and racist behavior, expressed indecisiveness about the issues and about how they should respond to particular situations, and were concerned about children who were victimized. Goodwin concluded that her findings showed a general feeling of helplessness in student teachers in the face of multicultural dilemmas, and their support for an assimilationist ideology that located the problems in the students and not in the schools. She saw the idea of placing student teachers in urban classrooms as a way of multiculturalizing them as naïve and called for a variety of teacher education practices to supplement student teaching in urban schools.

Mahan (1984) used the "Frequent Concerns of Student Teachers" survey to determine 42 Anglo student teachers' concerns at different intervals during student teaching in Navajo, Apache, and Hopi elementary schools in the southwestern United

States. The student teachers were part of Indiana University's American Indian Reservation Project. The categories on the survey, which candidates completed three times prior to and during the student teaching period, included instructional and curricular knowledge and skills and cultural knowledge and skills. Mahan found that three concerns ranked within the top eight at all three survey points: motivating pupils to work, understanding the culture of students, and adapting teaching to fit the local culture.

A number of researchers have used case studies to examine White teacher candidates' experiences in urban and diverse settings. In a case study of one White female candidate at a university in the Southeast, Luft, Bragg, and Peters (1999) used in-depth interviews, classroom observations, and journal reflections to study her student-teaching experience in an urban setting. The candidate attempted to negotiate personal and professional challenges, but because she was unfamiliar with the students and their life experiences, she was marginalized when she tried to enact student-centered instruction. Because she was committed to teaching science to underserved students, she persisted. In a similar case study at the University of Tennessee, Rushton (2001) examined one candidate's year-long internship at a city school. Drawing on interviews and reflections, the researchers found that the candidate experienced culture shock and emotional and cognitive dissonance. She worried about her relationship with her mentor teacher, but relied on her sense of purpose and "higher self" to adapt and eventually emerged with a positive attitude. Mason (1999) studied the field experiences of two undergraduates at an eastern urban university using written assignments, classroom observations, evaluation materials, and interviews. Working from psychological learning theories, they found that the support and assistance of the cooperating teachers was more important than candidates' personal characteristics such as confidence and persistence in determining classroom success, although both candidates later became successful teachers.

Other researchers have studied candidates placed in urban PDSs where university faculty and school personnel collaborated in organizing and planning the field experience. Groulx (2001) used a pre- and post-fieldwork survey of Texas Christian University candidates' attitudes and beliefs about working in urban schools. The initial sample included 112 candidates (98% White and 89% female); 29 White females were surveyed a second time. Researchers concluded that positive shifts in attitudes occurred more frequently for candidates in the elementary program, which was linked to fieldwork in urban professional development schools. Using the Stallings Observation Instrument, interviews, and records of discussions, Stallings, Bossung, and Martin (1990) compared the performance of 44 University of Houston candidates assigned to urban professional development schools with those of 25 candidates assigned to urban and suburban schools that were not part of professional development schools. Researchers found that the PDS group showed greater increases in the use of academic statements during class periods, increased supportive feedback to student responses, and showed greater reduction in off-task behavior for students. Although these two studies suggest that PDSs might enhance the preparation of teachers for work in diverse urban schools, little information is provided about the nature of the PDS partnerships. Because of the great variation in what it means to be a PDS (e.g., Levine & Trachtman, 1997), these studies tell us little about the particular conditions under which PDSs have positive effects.

Studies of early field experiences in urban settings indicate that candidates had similar apprehensions and concerns. Commitment and persistence were important, but insufficient factors in their ability to negotiate positive outcomes. Quality of supervision and school context also appear to be important factors in influencing success.

However, because many of these studies are case studies involving one or two candidates (Luft et al., 1999; Mason, 1999; Rushton, 2001; Tiezzi & Cross, 1997), their findings cannot be generalized to a larger population, and a number of the studies do not include adequate information about school context or the relationships among the candidates, researchers, and cooperating teachers. In three studies (Groulx, 2001; Mahan, 1984; Marshall, 1996) where surveys were used, the descriptive data on content and pedagogical practices in the programs lacked the detail necessary for replication and confirmation of effects. In two studies (Groulx; Marshall), validation procedures for the researcher-developed instruments were not described. Groulx pointed out that this study was limited by its focus on beliefs without inquiry into candidates' field experiences or how beliefs might be manifested in practices in the classroom.

The studies discussed so far indicate that candidates had similar concerns whether or not they had course work in multicultural education prior to a field experience in an urban setting. Three of the studies (Luft et al., 1999; Mason, 1999; Rushton, 2001) suggest that commitment and persistence are important variables in a successful urban field experience, but one cautions that these may be insufficient and the quality of support and guidance during the field experience also plays an important role. The remaining four studies had small samples, and the descriptions of the approaches and data analysis procedures were lacking in details. In the study conducted by Deering and Stanutz (1995), the ethnicity of the participants was not disclosed and the field experience was not described. Olmedo (1997) provided a rich description of the course and the related field experience, but not of the teacher education program in which the course was located. Goodwin (1997) did not describe the teacher education program in which the field experience was located. Stallings et al. (1990) pointed out that weaknesses in their study included an inadequate control group (candidates placed in similar urban school settings were not included), and there was follow-up to determine the placement of those in the experimental group, but not of the control group, on completion of the program.

Comparing Different Settings and Approaches in Field Experiences.   Three studies compared the impact of field experiences in different settings. Using an experimental approach with random sampling and a post-test-only control group design, Gipe, Duffy, and Richards (1989) compared an experimental group that had an immersion-type field experience in an urban school and a control group placed in a suburban or parochial school. Participants were 52 female elementary candidates enrolled in three sections of the language arts and reading methods courses and a field experience. The majority of the candidates were White, middle class, and 20 years of age. Data were collected using the Language Attitude Scale (Taylor, 1972), the Theoretical Orientation to Reading Profile (Deford, 1985), and a survey instrument developed by the researchers to assess their perceptions of the value of the practicum in relation to various aspects of teaching. The experimental (urban) and control (suburban) groups were randomly developed by course scheduling. There were 12 students enrolled in the experimental group and 20 students in each of two control groups. Beyond reporting increased knowledge of teaching techniques and classroom routines, the experimental group indicated a greater awareness of the connection between oral and written language, felt more comfortable in an inner-city school situation, and became more familiar with the customs, values, and language of children from a low socioeconomic environment, most of whom were dialect speakers (Gipe, Duffy, & Richards, 1989, p. 260).

Cook and Van Cleaf (2000), at Washburn University in Kansas, used a questionnaire to compare the impact of student teaching in different contexts on first-year teachers' understanding of students' sociocultural needs. The respondents were 59 first-year teachers selected on the basis of having completed student teaching in urban schools using the Comer reform model, or urban schools not using the Comer model, or rural and suburban schools. Researchers found that candidates who completed student teaching in an urban school (regardless of the Comer model) felt that they better understood the sociocultural needs of their students and felt better prepared to interact with parents from diverse backgrounds than those who completed student teaching in a suburban or rural setting. Ross and Smith (1992), at the University of Florida, used written assignments, journals, and interviews to investigate the perspectives on diverse learners of six White candidates (five female) enrolled in a research course with two field placements, one a "transmission" and one a "constructivist" classroom. Researchers found that with the guidance of university supervisors, candidates benefited from both settings in developing a contextual orientation toward curriculum and in constructing more complex understandings of diversity.

Although these studies indicate that urban field placements have the potential to help candidates develop complex understandings of teaching and learning for diverse students, more research is needed to determine the particular elements in school settings that support candidates' learning. These studies are somewhat limited in their generalizability. Gipe et al. (1989), for example, used a post-test-only design, and the impact of the field experience or other aspects of the program on changes in the candidates' attitudes was not revealed. Cook and Van Cleaf (2000) did not describe the student-teaching experiences in each context or the teacher preparation program in which each was located, nor did they describe how their questionnaire was validated. Additionally, each of the three studies had small sample sizes.

Personal Biographies and Storytelling.   Three studies focused on the use of personal biographies and storytelling as tools for developing cultural awareness during field experiences with diverse students and in urban settings. Using dialogue journals, beginning- and end-of-semester candidate interviews, assignments, and class discussions as data, Fry and McKinney (1997) found that the use of personal biographies during a language arts methods course that included a 4-week field experience in an urban school with a predominately African-American population at the University of Oklahoma increased the cultural awareness and sensitivity of 10 White female candidates who were between 21 and 29 years old and who had little experience with cultural diversity.

In a study using similar data sources at Penn State University, Johnson (1994) found that prior experiences influenced the beliefs about second-language teachers and second-language teaching of four ESL teachers in a practicum experience.

Gomez, Walker, and Page (2000) at the University of Wisconsin, Madison, used a qualitative case study approach to investigate the impact of storytelling on the perceptions and practices of seven candidates in the Teach for Diversity program. Drawing on field notes, candidates' written stories, interviews, observations, and postobservation conferences, the researchers found that narratives did not support self- and peer critique but reinscribed personal experiences as teaching guidelines.

The four studies in this group had mixed results. Two studies indicate positive outcomes when using personal biographies and storytelling to increase cultural awareness and sensitivity and to increase candidates' awareness of their own strengths and limitations in an urban field experience (Gomez, 1996). Two studies had negative outcomes where candidates' "episodic memories" interfered with their ability to alter classroom practices to meet the learning needs of their students (Johnson, 1994) and personal biographies were reinscribed as authentic guidelines for teaching diverse students (Gomez et al., 2000).

In the study with positive outcomes (Fry & McKinney, 1997), it was difficult to determine how the findings were derived. For the two studies with negative outcomes, one involved four ESL teachers whose ethnic identity was not revealed (Johnson, 1994), and the other focused on five of seven White participants (Gomez et al., 2000). Case studies provide rich descriptions of the experiences of the candidates and help reveal new questions, but they have limited generalizability. Additional research is needed to explore the general applicability of the findings in these studies and to raise questions about the role of ethnicity in the use of personal biographies and storytelling, especially in light of the conclusion (Villegas & Lucas, 2002) that majority institutions generally do not make use of the insider knowledge of candidates of color.

Research on Field Experiences: Overview and Comment

Redesigning or enhancing field experiences is one of the major ways teacher preparation programs have attempted to improve the preparation of teachers for work with diverse populations. Research in this area focuses on the experiences in and impact of community-based field experiences, the relocation of candidates from rural to urban settings for field experiences, candidates' responses to urban settings, a comparison of benefits from different field experience settings, the use of personal biographies and storytelling, and the application of training in multicultural education. These studies show the short-term positive impact of community-based field experiences on candidates' awareness and acceptance of students from culturally diverse backgrounds. Field placements in urban settings increased rural candidates' cultural awareness and sensitivity. Candidates in urban school placements had many concerns about understanding and motivating their students, providing meaningful instruction, and developing positive relationships with students and mentors. They dealt with these challenges with a variety of approaches and levels of effectiveness. Some of the research suggests that candidates in urban settings acquired more complex understandings and awareness of cultural and experiential differences than did their peers in suburban settings. The small number of studies on using personal biographies and storytelling showed inconsistent outcomes.

Most of these studies were qualitative, and many were self-studies in which the researchers were also instructors or supervisors for the participants. As was the case in the other categories, these researchers generally did not discuss how they handled the tensions associated with the dual role of researcher and teacher educator. Most studies were not contextualized within a teacher education program and lacked descriptions of the field placement sites. The sample size was small in most of the studies, and some provided incomplete demographic data on participants.

THE EXPERIENCES OF TEACHER CANDIDATES
OF COLOR

A number of studies focused on aspects of the preparation of candidates of color for teaching diverse student populations, including retention in preparation programs, experiences in programs, and alternative program arrangements that accommodated the needs of candidates of color. (Chapter 3 reviews studies dealing with the reasons candidates of color do or do not choose teaching as a career and with the diversity of the teacher workforce.

Retention of Candidates of Color in Teacher Preparation Programs

As chapter 3 indicates, teacher candidates of color, particularly African Americans, were more likely than Whites to prefer urban and diverse teaching settings and to cite making a contribution to society, working as activists to change the lives of children of color, and serving as role models as a reason for entering teaching. Some studies also indicated that some people of color may not choose teaching because of lack of respect for the profession, although this varied among minority groups. Once candidates of color have entered preparation programs, however, retention is a problem.

Root, Rudawski, Taylor, and Rochon (2003), for example, examined the retention of Hmong paraprofessionals and college-age students in teacher education. Twenty-three teacher certification candidates from two federally funded programs in Wisconsin were the initial subjects of this study, which used analysis of student files, exit interviews, records of interactions with students while in the program, and student assessments. An additional researcher-constructed questionnaire was administered to 14 of the 23 former participants. Researchers found that dropouts were disproportionately male and nontraditional candidates for reasons related to financial, social and personal issues. Candidates who dropped out cited difficulty juggling job and student responsibilities, lack of money and family responsibilities.

Waldschmidt (2002) conducted ethnographic research on three bilingual and bicultural teacher interns at a local community college, drawing on interviews, essays written for the scholarship applications, field notes from classroom visits, audio taped focus groups, and a survey of program participants conducted by an outside evaluator. Walschmidt, who was program coordinator as well as researcher, had anticipated that these low-income Mexican American teacher candidates would have financial, family and personal issues, but was surprised by the unanticipated barriers of difficulty passing licensure exams and their student teaching placement in schools with English immersion programs. In these placements, the teacher candidates were unable to participate in the kinds of programs for which they were preparing, and their assigned mentor teachers had no formal education in either ESL or bilingual education. These barriers caused the teacher candidates to became discouraged about the teaching profession. The practitioner researcher raised questions about the paternalistic attitudes that she found were engrained in the system and the limitations of White teacher educators in programs for Mexican American candidates. Bustos Flores and Riojas Clark (1999) also studied the impact of high-stakes testing on prospective bilingual and minority teachers. Using Texas state data on bilingual teacher exams and the two case studies of Mexican-American women, the researchers found that although both women were recognized by peers and school administrators as good teachers, they were unable to pass the test. The researchers called for program support structures for prospective bilingual teachers until successful completion of licensure tests.

In an effort to accommodate the financial and social challenges faced by many candidates of color, some colleges and universities now offer alternative teacher preparation programs. Becket (1998) found that two nontraditional teacher-preparation programs were able to attract minorities, the Latino Teacher Project at the University of Southern California and the Navajo Nation Teacher Preparation program at Fort Lewis College. To address the special academic needs of the candidates, university courses were scheduled at convenient times and locations that allowed teacher candidates to continue in their roles as classroom paraprofessionals where they were able to learn from their own practice. Researchers found that these programs increased the numbers of minorities in hard-to-staff schools and that the candidates developed a sense of community and reaffirmed their sense of ethnic identity and commitment to working for social justice.

At the University of Wisconsin—Milwaukee, Haberman (1993) used the Urban Teacher Selection Interview to predict the success of a group of primarily ethnic minority candidates enrolled in an alternative certification program. The 38 participants were over 30 years old, had undergraduate degrees in subjects other than education, had experience as teacher aides and paraprofessionals, and were assigned to teach in urban schools. Based on previous work (Haberman & Post, 1998), the interview instrument identified characteristics of successful urban teachers that were not identified among teachers who quit or failed in urban schools, including persistence, response to authority, application of ideas to practice, approach to at-risk students, the development of teacher–student rapport, and particular responses to bureaucracy and fallibility. Haberman concluded that candidates who ranked in the top half of teachers on the Urban Teacher Selection Interview were also ranked in the top half of teachers on performance by their principals, and, inversely, those ranked in the bottom half of the interview were also ranked in the bottom half for performance by their principals.

Candidates' Program Experiences

A number of studies examined the experiences of teacher candidates of color within teacher preparation programs. A significant issue suggested by many of these studies is the extent to which candidates of color were invited or allowed to use their insider knowledge to facilitate students' learning. At the University of Houston, Tellez (1999) conducted extensive interviews with four Mexican-American candidates randomly selected from a population of 25. The researcher concluded that although experiences varied, these candidates were committed to incorporating aspects of their insider cultural knowledge into their teaching. Because they found the formal curriculum impenetrable, they tried to include Mexican-American culture in the informal curriculum. In addition the veteran teachers they worked with tended to regard them as resources or as ambassadors to explain why children were failing without examining their own teaching practices. Walker de Felix and Cavazos Pena (1992) examined the benefits of studying Spanish in Mexico for 15 volunteer teacher candidates of Mexican descent who had successful teaching evaluations and were able to communicate in Spanish. Data sources included pre- and post-Modern Language Association (MLA) Spanish reading and writing tests, semantic differential instrument measuring attitudes related to self as well as to Mexicans and Americans, journals, and observations. All but one candidate passed the state-required Language Proficiency Interview exam in Spanish. All changed significantly in their attitudes toward both Mexicans and Americans, but not toward self.

In a related study, Bustos Flores, Keehn, and Perez (2002) compared Texas teacher candidates from two Chicano or Mexican groups—foreign-trained *normalistas* and currently employed paraprofessionals—to investigate the extent to which a teacher education program could help teacher candidates respond to the linguistic, cultural, and cognitive needs of language minority children. Seven candidates from each cohort were interviewed and observed in the classroom, and their narrative and reflective writing was collected. The researchers found that the *normalista* cohort provided knowledge of the strengths of the educational system of the sending country and began to understand the differences in the sending and receiving educational systems. The paraprofessionals began to question both the deficit model in relation to the Latino and Mexican students that was pervasive in many schools and their own stance toward authority. The researchers concluded that a "grow-your-own" recruitment approach was a viable way to address the shortage of cultural and linguistic diversity among the teaching force.

Although special programs or cohort groups for teacher candidates of color exist in a few places across the country, most candidates of color are prepared in programs where the majority of their peers are White. In these programs, candidates of color often express feelings of discomfort and isolation within the group (Villegas & Lucas, 2002). Not all candidates of color share these feelings. Guyton, Saxton, and Wesche (1996), for example, interviewed seven candidates of color in a master's-level initial teacher preparation program in early childhood education at a predominately White urban university. They found that these candidates valued their own role in the educational process, perceived themselves as role models for children of similar cultural backgrounds, preferred teaching diverse student populations, and had been discouraged from entering teaching. Overall these candidates reported they had experienced only limited racism from their peers, did not experience racism on the part of faculty members, and appreciated the attention to issues of diversity in the program. Smolkin and Suina (1999) focused on instructional practices. They reported that learning was reciprocal among paired American-Indian and non-Indian candidates in a cross-cultural partnership program at the University of New Mexico where they taught together in an Indian school and then at an urban school. The American-Indian candidates learned how to utilize their own cultural resources to facilitate learning in the classroom as well as how non-Indian candidates identified and used resources. The non-Indian candidates became more culturally sensitive and knowledgeable.

In special programs or cohorts for candidates of color, the intention is to build the camaraderie that supports candidates' learning that is missing in many programs where candidates of color are in the minority. In a longitudinal action research study of 45 candidates in three cohorts at Indiana University, Bloomington, Bennett, Cole, and Thompson (2000) used as data sources a questionnaire, autobiographical interviews, focus group interviews, course assignments, and journals. They found that when placed in a separate cohort, candidates of color developed a sense of community, a stronger sense of ethnic identity, and an affirmed commitment to working for social justice. Similarly, Sheets and Chew (2002) examined 32 Chinese-American candidates' perceptions of the value of a course in diversity taught by seven different instructors at San Francisco State University. Data sources included questionnaires, participant profiles, surveys, interviews, focus groups, course syllabi, and classroom observations. Exit questionnaires were mailed to all participants at the end of the second year, and 15 participated in focus group meetings. The researchers found that candidates reported that the cohort group increased opportunities for students to learn from each other, created a comfortable academic climate, and sustained a sense of group belonging. Once in classrooms, the candidates' knowledge and consciousness of diversity were measured with the Diversity Pedagogical Behaviors Observations Tool. The candidates showed weakness in the area of culturally relevant content knowledge acquisition and diversity consciousness and awareness of differences.

Fisher (1980) studied the impact on the performance of 52 African-American candidates at historically Black colleges and universities (HBCU) randomly assigned to either a group whose supervisors were trained in generic teaching skills or to a group whose supervisors had not had this training. Supervisors used the Student Teacher

Elementary Feedback form to evaluate the candidates' performance. They found that supervisors trained in generic teaching skills performed better on a test of these skills than those not trained, and that candidates supervised by the trained teachers performed better in the classroom than the control group whose supervisors had not received such training, the researcher refers to 10 teaching competencies believed to be important for beginning teachers which were not specified.

Research on the Experiences of Candidates of Color: Overview and Comment

Collectively studies about the preparation of candidates of color provide insights into the challenges faced by this group when pursuing teaching as a career and some of the approaches used in teacher preparation programs to accommodate their needs. Several studies indicate that many candidates of color face financial, social, and personal issues, as well as inadequate academic preparation for college. Approaches that have been used in teacher preparation programs to accommodate the needs of candidates of color include nontraditional programs (Becket, 1998; Haberman, 1993), separate cohorts (Bennett et al., 2000; Sheets & Chew, 2002), pairing candidates of color and White candidates (Smolkin and Suina, 1999), drawing on the insider cultural knowledge of candidates of color to facilitate learning in the classroom (Bustos Flores et al., 2002; Riojas Clark & Bustos Flores, 2001; Tellez, 1999), and providing additional training for fieldwork supervisors (Fisher, 1980). Candidates of color often feel alienated in majority White institutions where their perspectives are not incorporated and their knowledge is not regarded as a resource for meeting the needs of the diverse school population (Villegas & Lucas, 2002). The studies reviewed here suggest that the experiences and retention of candidates of color can be increased by placement in cohorts or programs where they feel their sense of commitment to social justice is valued and that make use of the unique experiences and knowledge they bring to the program for teaching diverse and underserved student populations.

The limitations in the generalizability of the findings of these studies are similar to those previously discussed, including small sample sizes, inadequate description of the teacher preparation program, and inconsistency in acknowledging other factors that may have contributed to or influenced the findings. One study did not describe the relationship between the researcher and the candidates (Walker de Felix & Cavazos Pena, 1992). Waldschmidt (2002) acknowledged that her position as coordinator and faculty advisor as well as researcher put her in a position in which distancing was difficult. Riojas Clark and Bustos Flores (2001) acknowledged the limitations of a static notion of ethnicity, the lack of control of the candidates' coursework and convenience sampling. Gordon's study on teaching as a career choice did not indicate how many individuals were interviewed from specific ethnic groups, nor were responses disaggregated according to ethnic group membership. In studies by Root, Rudawski, Taylor, and Rochan (2003) and Sheets and Chew (2002) validation procedures for the instrument were not discussed.

EVALUATION STUDIES OF PROGRAMS TO PREPARE TEACHERS FOR DIVERSITY

Reed and Simon (1991) studied teacher education practices in 10 HBCUs in Maryland, Virginia, North Carolina, Kentucky, Louisiana, and Mississippi. Surveys, followed by telephone interviews with deans and directors of education, indicated that nine of the ten required student teaching in an urban school and provided opportunities for experiences in urban educational settings outside of schools. Johnson (1987) studied a representative sample of 56 colleges and universities that required a linguistic course in their bilingual preparation programs. Data sources included faculty interviews during 95 program visits and examination of 328 course syllabi and exams. Johnson found inconsistencies in program content and emphasis across institutions, with teacher candidates in programs funded by the U.S. Department of Education's Title VII Bilingual Education Act receiving less emphasis on formal aspects of linguistics and more on sociolinguistic and cultural aspects. The unfunded programs placed more emphasis on social and psychological factors in second language and on code switching in language use. The Title VII master's programs were slightly broader (p. 905).

Wiggins and Follo (1999) used a researcher-developed questionnaire and interviews with candidates at different stages in the undergraduate elementary education program at Oakland University to determine the impact of the program on candidates' readiness and willingness to teach in culturally diverse schools. They found that although candidates perceived that the program had prepared them with instructional skills for teaching in culturally diverse classrooms and with experience in multicultural settings, they were not comfortable teaching in diverse cultural settings and did not seem to understand the cultural norms and expectations of diverse communities. Cabello and Eckmier (1995) studied 26 graduates of the Comprehensive Teacher Institute at California State University, Northridge, a program specifically intended to prepare teachers for diversity. Drawing on content analysis of questionnaire and interview data, they found that school–university collaboration, a cadre of faculty, extensive pre-student-teaching fieldwork, and opportunities to reflect with a cohort group were factors in success; systemic differences between school and university cultures were obstacles.

Noordhoff and Kleinfeld (1993) examined candidates' development in the Teachers for Alaska program at the University of Alaska–Fairbanks, a fifth-year program preparing teachers for secondary schools in remote Eskimo and Indian villages. The 15 candidates admitted annually were required to be strong academically, have experience with adolescents, and have experience living or working in cross-cultural or multicultural settings. The program consisted of six tightly integrated units each of which included a teaching case study, an apprenticeship with a master teacher for two periods each day during the first five units, 12 weeks of student teaching during the final unit, and a concluding seminar. Researchers compared candidates' teaching by examining 10-minute reflective teaching lessons at the beginning of the program, after the campus-based semester and at the end of the program after student teaching to determine changes in level of responsiveness to teaching diverse populations. In addition to the observations of the lessons, the researchers asked the candidates why they chose the lesson, what they thought about in planning the lesson, and what they might do differently if they taught it again.

They found indications of substantial growth in candidates' orientations. The most dramatic shift was in the candidates' conceptions of teaching moving from an initial view of teaching as telling and covering as much material as possible to one of teaching as engaging students with subject matter. The analyses of the lessons also revealed gains in candidates' dispositions to take into account their students' background knowledge, frames of reference, communication styles, and vocabulary. Despite this evidence of consistent growth by student teachers during the course of their fifth-year program, the researchers caution that program selection rather than the curriculum may account for some of this growth.

The studies described thus far examine the quality of teacher preparation programs and the development of candidates in programs. A few studies have also looked at the extent to which candidates apply the knowledge they gain in preparation programs after completion. Sleeter (1989) investigated how teachers appropriated the multicultural content that the state of Wisconsin required in teacher education programs beginning in 1974. In survey of 1,552 Wisconsin teachers (37% return rate) who had completed a teacher education program between 1981 and 1985, 98% of respondents were White; 78% taught classes that were 95% White. The researcher concluded that teachers attended to differences among their students through instruction and improving social relationships and included nonsexist materials. Few reported doing much else to make their curriculum multicultural.

Cabello and Burstein (1995) reported a follow-up case study of two candidates to determine how teachers' beliefs and practices evolved during the program and how this influenced their practices in the classroom. These candidates were enrolled in a 2-year graduate program at a small urban liberal arts college for elementary and secondary teachers who wanted a master's degree in special education and a credential for teaching students with learning disabilities. The data sources for this study included pre- and post-questionnaires; course assignments such as reflective logs, a teaching strategies project, a case study on a culturally diverse student, and an exit interview. The researchers found that over time both candidates modified their practices, although not radically. The African-American female candidate learned that sharing the same race or culture with students did not automatically provide understanding, empathy, and an ability to effectively work with them, and she learned new strategies for working with the students. The European-American female candidate changed her description of the students from "deficit" to "different" and indicated that she had learned different approaches to teaching students from different cultural and experiential backgrounds.

In a longitudinal investigation, Artiles, Barreto, Pena, and McClafferty (1998) studied the relationship among the knowledge, beliefs, and decisions of two White bilingual candidates when teaching diverse populations after completing their 1-year graduate teacher education program at an unidentified university. Data sources, included concept maps, interviews, surveys, and stimulated recall sessions before and after the completion of the program and during their first and second years of teaching. The teacher preparation program completed by these candidates included urban teaching placements and a multicultural education course designed to provide a complex view of teaching culturally diverse students and encourage personal reflection on diversity issues. This 3-year follow-up study, which examined the teachers' beliefs and practices before and after the multicultural education course and during their first and second years of inservice teaching, revealed that the participants' decisions were not always congruent with their pedagogical knowledge. Rather they dichotomized teaching subject matter and teaching multiculturally. Both used an incidental approach to multicultural education where they dealt with multicultural issues as they arose in the classroom. The researchers found that a variety of factors in addition to the teacher education program influenced the teaching perspectives and practices that they documented in this study. These included the teachers' developmental needs and the school and classroom contexts in which teachers worked. This study did not enable the researchers to disaggregate the effects of these various influences.

Evaluation Studies: Overview and Comment

These program evaluation studies addressed different questions, used different perspectives, and varied in completeness when describing teacher education programs. However, they tell an instructive story. A few university programs appeared to offer a carefully crafted program that prepared candidates to teach students from diverse populations (Cabello & Eckmier, 1995; Noordhoff & Kleinfeld, 1993). Most university programs were at various stages in developing the capacity to address issues of cultural and linguistic diversity (Baca, Bransford, Nelson, & Ortiz, 1994; Johnson, 1987; Wiggins & Follo, 1999). Many universities have hardly begun to address issues of diversity in certain program areas (Redican, Stewart, Johnson, & Frazee, 1994). Although candidates deal with multicultural issues in the teacher education programs, this does not always translate to changes in school practices once they leave these programs (Artiles et al., 1998; Cabello & Burnstein, 1995; Sleeter, 1989).

The findings from the studies included in this category must be interpreted in relationship to their methodological limitations. Seven of the ten studies were qualitative and were expected to provide rich descriptions for developing grounded theory. Only one study provided a rich description of the teacher education program (Noordhoff & Kleinfeld, 1993). These researchers acknowledged limitations such as selection of candidates, the conditions of videotape recording, the sustainability of the outcomes, and the potential impact of being socialized as beginning teachers. In the Baca et al., study (1994), the quality of the teacher preparation programs was judged from self-reports from faculty and administrators, not the candidates enrolled in the programs. In the study by Wiggins and Follo (1999) on candidates' readiness and willingness to teach diverse students, the researchers acknowledged that candidates' responses might have been influenced by the need to be politically correct. Johnson (1987) cautioned the reader about the findings from this study by stating that "what graduate students gain from programs is also a result of their background knowledge as well as information and insights gained though other courses and experiences" (p. 905).

Three studies in this category primarily used surveys or questionnaires (Redican et al., 1994; Reed & Simon, 1991; Sleeter, 1989). All of the studies used self-reported data. One (see Sleeter, 1989) had a very low rate of return on usable surveys, which raises serious questions about whether the sample was representative. A similar question could be raised about the Reed and Simon study concerning the sample of HBCUs included. Additionally, all studies in this category had small sample sizes.

RESEARCH ON PREPARING TEACHERS FOR DIVERSITY: STRENGTHENING THE RESEARCH BASE

Fifteen years ago when Grant and Secada (1990) completed the first major review of the literature on preparing teachers for work with diverse populations, they concluded that there was a surprising and unacceptable paucity of empirical research on the topic. That situation has now changed. As our review suggests, research has been conducted on a wide array of topics related to the preparation of teachers for diversity. However, there are very significant gaps in the literature, as we discuss in the following section.

Gaps in the Research Base

As this chapter has made clear, a growing amount of the research on preparing teachers for diversity has been conducted by teacher educators themselves who have engaged in self-study and other forms of practitioner inquiry by taking their own professional programs and projects as sites for inquiry. This is good news in a certain sense. This means that many teacher educators take their work seriously, self-consciously posing questions and then investigating those questions by gathering and analyzing the data of practice. The focus of most of this work is what preservice teachers learn from course and program experiences—how their knowledge, attitudes, and beliefs may change; how they interact with program content; and how particular pedagogies provide different kinds of learning opportunities.

On the other hand, many small studies carried out in the courses and seminars of individual instructors do not lead to a strong empirical research base that can be generalized across programs and institutions, and there are significant gaps in the research in each of the categories of studies we reviewed. These gaps limit our understanding of the process of learning to teach diverse populations and of the design and structure of teacher preparation programs that support candidates' learning in this area.

In the area of candidates' predispositions, we identified studies that addressed the attitudes and beliefs of those entering teacher preparation, but we did not find studies of how these influence candidates' actions in the classroom. Nor did we find studies of how candidates' predispositions are related to the admission and selection processes used to identify applicants most responsive to learning to teach diverse students. Almost all of the studies that focused on prejudice reduction were conducted in various courses and field experiences and as a group showed mixed results. None of these studies investigated the relationship between prejudice or negative attitudes toward diverse students and candidates' effectiveness in the classroom.

Similarly, the studies on helping teacher candidates develop equity pedagogy did not investigate the extent to which candidates were able to enact this pedagogy in classrooms with a positive impact on the learning of diverse students. None of the studies we reviewed investigated candidates' ability to apply theories of learning when planning and conducting instruction for diverse students. The studies in the category on field experiences were conducted in various settings and under a variety of conditions. However, little is known about these settings, the process for selecting field-experience sites, and the role of mentors and supervisors who work in the field. Again, studies of field experiences did not examine the extent to which candidates were able to plan and execute instruction that had a positive impact on diverse students' learning. Evaluations of teacher preparation programs also did not address the extent to which candidates could apply what had been learned to produce a positive impact on learning for diverse students.

Methodological Issues

All the studies we reviewed addressed questions and issues that are important to the preparation of teachers for diverse populations. However, the quality of studies was rather uneven, and some studies were reported in a summary format that made it difficult to judge their quality. As noted earlier, many studies did not provide full information about the context of the teacher education program being studied; omitting important details about the theoretical framework for the program, its structure, the extent to which the question under investigation permeated the entire program, or the extent to which the particular practice or intervention being studied was supported by other components of the program. Similarly many studies did not provide information about the relevant institutional and state policy contexts. This made it difficult to know much about the contexts and conditions under which teacher candidates learned or performed in particular ways.

The majority of the quantitative studies in this review employed surveys or questionnaires as research tools. Some of these were self-constructed or did not include information about validation procedures, or both. In addition, in many of the studies surveys and questionnaires were administered at only one point in time, which does not provide information about growth or change.

As we have noted several times, the majority of the qualitative studies in this review were conducted in a single course or field experience and drew on narrative data from course assignments, journals, field notes, and classroom observations. Because these studies were not contextualized within a teacher education program, it was difficult to distinguish the effects of the course or field experience under study from those of other aspects of the teacher education program. In the case of field experiences, as with course experiences, very little information was given about the field site itself or the larger culture of the schools and classrooms in which teacher candidates had experience. There was also very little information overall about the experiences and preparation of the practitioners who served as supervisors and cooperating teachers in teacher education programs. This information is important in accounting for the impact of a particular intervention and for looking at the impact of an intervention across studies.

Directions Forward: Promising Lines of Research

What then do we know about preparing teachers for diversity based on the empirical research? We see a number of patterns in the evidence reported in this review. However, for the conceptual and methodological reasons noted previously, we caution readers that our conclusions are tentative and in need of confirmation or disconfirmation in future research.

Many of the studies in this chapter confirm what we already know about prospective teachers. (See chap. 3 as well as previous reviews of the literature on teacher preparation for diversity.) Teacher candidates are a homogeneous population, the large majority of whom are White and middle-class, female, from suburban or rural backgrounds, and with limited experiences with those from backgrounds different from their own. Many of these candidates seem to enter teacher preparation programs with negative or deficit attitudes and beliefs about those different from themselves. Interestingly, however, they often express a willingness to teach in urban areas despite limited experience and conflicting attitudes and beliefs.

Some of the studies we reviewed for this chapter suggest that some candidates of color, particularly African-Americans, find teaching a less attractive career than do their White counterparts and confront more barriers to admission and licensure. In addition candidates of color prepared primarily in White majority institutions often feel alienated, in part because their cultural and experiential knowledge is not treated as a resource or valued as a way to provide high-quality instruction to children of color. Candidates of color are also more likely than are their White peers to come from working-class backgrounds and to have had negative school-ing experiences themselves. Perhaps for these reasons they also often have better understandings of inequities in society and stronger commitments to social justice. There is some evidence that candidates of color benefit from placement in cohorts or programs where they feel comfortable and supported, are given opportunities to make use of the unique experiences and knowledge they bring to the program, and are part of programs focused on teaching diverse and underserved student populations.

Second, studies about the preparation of teacher candidates for diversity suggest that activities intended to reduce prejudice have mixed results. Although many stud-ies report short-term positive gains, there is little evidence about whether these gains are sustained over time. Looking across the studies suggests that there is a com-plex interaction among candidates' experiential backgrounds, the content offered in courses, and the pedagogical strategies candidates learn (or not). Barriers to candi-dates' increased knowledge growth about cultural differences and ways of providing appropriate and responsive pedagogy to students from cultures other than their own included positivistic thinking, dualistic thinking, a belief in one right answer, and relying on personal biographies as guides to how to teach others.

Studies comparing the impact of different fieldwork settings suggest that candi-dates placed in urban community and school settings with diverse students acquire more complex understandings and awareness of cultural and experiential differences than do their peers placed in suburban settings.

Third, program evaluation research suggests that universities are at different points in their preparedness for addressing issues of cultural and linguistic diversity. Some university programs seem to be in the process of becoming more inclusive and multi-cultural in their approaches to teacher education. Some report no changes or shifts in candidates' attitudes and practices, whereas others report significant changes. Even in situations where candidates deal with multicultural issues in their teacher preparation programs, this training does not always translate to implementing appropriate class-room practices once candidates leave the programs.

It is very clear that empirical examination of the relationship between teacher prepa-ration for diversity and pupils' learning and other outcomes is largely unchartered territory in the field of research on teacher education. This is a particularly promising line of inquiry. We need research that examines the links among teacher preparation for diversity, what teacher candidates learn from this preparation, how this affects their professional practices in schools, and what the impact is on their pupils' learn-ing. This is not a new conclusion. Grant and Secada (1990) called for "more information about the scope of effective educational practice and the combinations of practice that result in optimal outcomes" (p. 413). They recommended research that went beyond changing teachers' attitudes on a self-reported, short-term basis and instead examined the impact of teachers' expectations on students' learning. Every major review of the literature since that time has reached a similar conclusion. This suggests that studies of outcomes are generally missing from the literature. One needed program of research is that of longitudinal studies that track teachers from initial preparation to their early career experiences, focusing on classroom performance and pupils' learning as well as studies that begin with successful teaching performance, as indicated by pupils' learning, and then tracks back to teacher-learning experiences and varying modes of teacher preparation.

Sleeter (2001a) suggests that instead of starting with questions about what good teacher education ought to be, we should start with good teaching and ask research questions that work backward to teacher preparation. There is a significant gap in the literature in this area. Although we know a great deal about effective teaching practices for diverse students (e.g., Au, 1980; Foster, 1997; Irvine, 1990; Ladson-Billings, 1994; Lee, 1995; Lipka, 1991; McCarty, 1993; Moll, 1986), not much is known about how teachers who are effective with diverse students acquired the skills, knowledge, and dispositions needed. Examining the practices and teacher preparation history of effective teachers could provide insights into what candidates need to know.

Although the kind of research that connects teacher preparation to pupil and other outcomes is sorely needed, it is very difficult to do well. We need sophisticated notions of teaching outcomes that take into account the social and cultural contexts of schools and that are informed by local meanings. In contrast, many studies that focus on outcomes are intended to produce evidence of the impact of isolatable variables that generalize across contexts and conditions. A particular challenge is to design studies that link teacher preparation and educational outcomes but avoid reductionist studies of single factors (Weiner, 2000).

Another promising line of research is that on well-designed urban field experiences contextualized within a teacher education program with clearly stated purposes, theoretical frameworks, and carefully thought out practices and procedures. Action research studies within such a context have potential for providing insight into the developmental trajectories of candidates in learning to teach, relationships among the different components of a teacher preparation program, and the role of these components in preparing candidates to teach diverse students.

To get around the problem of many small-scale studies with results that are not generalizable, one possibility is linking individual studies into multisite research programs, which Wilson, Floden, and Ferrini-Mundy (2001) suggest is one of "strategic investments" needed to move forward teacher education research generally. The possibility of linking individual studies is very applicable to research on teacher preparation for diversity, particularly in light of the increasing number of teacher educators who are interested in doing self-studies and other forms of practitioner research on their own practice.

There are many promising lines of research and important questions to be addressed about the preparation of America's teachers for diverse populations. Many members of the educational community agree that these are among the most important questions facing education today. Longitudinal studies of the kind mentioned previously, studies of the teacher preparation histories of successful teachers of diverse populations, sophisticated studies of the impact of preparation on pupil and other outcomes, and multisite research studies require considerable funding and research capacity. These are not readily available at most of the sites where teacher educators have been struggling to research their own programs. Like most forms of research on teacher education, research on the preparation of teachers for diversity has been consistently marginalized and underfunded. Nonetheless, with appropriate funding and capacity building, there is great potential.

ACKNOWLEDGMENTS

The authors would like to acknowledge the assistance of Jesse Kass, Byron Delgado, and Kimberly S. Hollins.

TABLE 8.1
Studies Reviewed

Studies[a]	Question	Research Design	Findings
Anderson, S. E. (1998)	How might candidates benefit from a course at the beginning of the program focused on increasing sensitivity to diversity; applying learning theories in teaching, and integrating technology into instruction?	Survey, questionnaire, informal observations. Thirty-two undergraduate, White female candidates at a private university. Administered a questionnaire describing 4 hypothetical schools. Intervention was a unit addressing the concepts of culture, stereotypes, racism, and prejudice.	The unit increased candidates' understanding of learning theories, helped them gain a better understanding of cultural differences, increased appreciation for diversity, but did not change preferences for teaching contexts.
Arias, B., & Poynor, L. (2001)	What do ESL and bilingual preservice teachers in a progressive, transactional reading and language arts methods course at an urban PDS learn and understand about teaching culturally and linguistically diverse children?	Participants were in a cohort of 3 ESL and 2 bilingual preservice teachers whose field experience would occur at the PDS. Data collected were documents, course observations, interviews, placement observations.	All preservice teachers were able to understand that cultural and linguistic diversity is a resource that should be valued and respected.
Artiles, A. J., Barreto, R. M., Pena, L., & McClafferty, K. (1998)	What is the relationship between bilingual education teachers' knowledge and beliefs and their interactive decisions during lessons in multicultural classrooms? And how do their interactive decisions change over time?	Case Study of 2 White teachers. Used quantitative and qualitative procedures and analysis. In-depth interviews, concept maps, video tapes, and survey. Analysis of mean centrality level, proportional frequencies, contextual information about videotapes of teaching.	The relationship among teachers' knowledge, beliefs, and decision making is complicated and dynamic. Prior beliefs as well as the teacher education program and teachers' own developmental needs contributed to the ways in which they learned to teach.
Baca, L., Bransford, J., Nelson, C., & Ortiz, L. (1994)	How is the University of Colorado Training, Development, and Improvement (TDI) program being implemented? What progress are the participating institutions of higher education (IHEs) making	Participant–observer evaluation of program's 1st year, including surveys, direct observation, interviews, and document review.	Survey responses from IHE participants were very positive. IHEs were making progress toward some objectives, such as developing and improving courses. Less progress was being made in recruiting and

514

	toward the objectives of strengthening their bilingual education and ESL teacher training programs?		retaining minority students, assessing student and faculty needs, and developing understanding of the importance of parental involvement.
Ball, A. F. (2000)	How do candidates move beyond surface level use of theory and best practices to transformative practice for culturally and linguistically diverse students?	Qualitative study. Data were collected from over 100 teacher candidates from the United States and South Africa. Four candidates were selected for case studies. Sources of data included literacy biographies, transcripts of classroom discussions, journal entries, and reflections they wrote in response to carefully selected course readings and course experiences.	The data revealed qualitative and quantitative differences in the candidates' pre- and postdefinitions of literacy which suggested that they had broadened after the course. Candidates began to expand their understanding of the different ways that an individual can be considered literate and of the different ways of expressing literacy.
Barry, N. H., & Lechner, J. V. (1995)	What are teacher candidates' attitudes about and awareness of aspects of multicultural teaching and learning?	Questionnaire administered to 73 undergraduate candidates in 3 different sections of elementary teaching methods	Candidates are aware of various issues related to multicultural education and anticipate having culturally diverse students in their classrooms; however, they are undecided as to how well their teacher preparation has developed their abilities to teach diverse students.
Becket, D. R. (1998)	How do traditional and nontraditional teacher preparation programs compare?	Qualitative study involving 27 respondents from 9 groups who were interviewed. Reviewed recorded documents and program proposals.	Most traditional programs attract fewer minorities. Two programs in Los Angeles were found to attract minorities, increase minority teachers in hard-to-staff schools, and concentrate on providing quality programs for participants.
Bennett, C., Cole, D., & Thompson, J. N. (2000)	How do teachers of color benefit when placed in a special program cohort for teachers of color?	Qualitative, longitudinal action research study involving 45 candidates in 3 cohorts. Candidates were invited to participate in the research project.	The candidates developed a sense of community, a stronger sense of ethnic identity, and an affirmed commitment to working for social justice.

(Continued)

515

TABLE 8.1
(Continued)

Studies[a]	Question	Research Design	Findings
Bennett, C., Niggle, T., & Stage, F. (1990)	Do candidates in a multicultural education program exhibit a range of dualism in their thinking?	Data were collected from questionnaire, autobiographical interviews, focus-group interviews, selected course assignments, meta-comment paper, and a process journal. A questionnaire was administered to 178 candidates enrolled in a multicultural education course. Bogardus Social Distance Scale was administered at beginning and end of semester to measure students' acceptance of diverse ethnic and racial groups.	Dualism varied by content area—English majors were least dualistic, and physical education majors were the most dualistic. Males were more dualistic than females. The least dualistic candidates had the strongest multicultural knowledge base before and after the course. The least dualistic, the least social distance.
Bollin, G. G. (1996)	How do teacher candidates benefit from tutoring ethnic minority students?	Qualitative study of 40 elementary candidates' participation in a field experience that included tutoring low-income students. Data sources: reflective journals.	Candidates' understanding of their own ethnic identity and the complexities of teaching in culturally diverse classrooms increased.
Bondy, E., & Davis, S. (2000)	How do tutors establish positive relationships in a culturally unfamiliar community?	Qualitative study involving 10 tutors who volunteered to participate in the study. One left the program after the first interview.	Eight of the 9 tutors who remained in the program provided extensive evidence of caring that enabled them to remain committed to students with whom they initially felt little connection. Tutors sought information about their work and their students.

Burant, T. J., & Kirby, D. (2002)	How do teacher candidates benefit from community based field experiences?	Qualitative study of 26 candidates enrolled in a Southwestern university providing community-based work. Data sources: reflective papers and action reports, field notes, interviews, and focus groups.	Candidates' responses to community-based field experiences fell into 5 categories: deepening multicultural, eye-opening, transformative, masked multicultural, partially miseducative, and escaping.
Bustos Flores, B., Keehn, S., & Perez, B. (2002)	To what extent could a teacher preparation program, specifically designed to assist both foreign trained *normalistas* and currently employed paraprofessionals recruited from the Chicano and Mexicano community, develop appropriate knowledge and skills to effectively teach language minority children? To what extent are the 2 student cohorts attuned to the linguistic, cultural, and cognitive needs of language minority children, and thus, prepared to provide equitable learning environments?	Seven individuals from a pool of 32 were chosen to participate in an in-depth study. Students were observed in their field sites; they were interviewed at various points in the program, personal narrative writing, reflective writing from a course in literacy education and field experience reflections were collected. Triangulation and team briefings were employed to ensure trustworthiness of interpretations of data.	The *normalista* cohort provided knowledge of the strengths of the educational system of the sending country and began to understand the differences in the sending and receiving educational systems. The paraprofessionals began to question both the deficit model in relation to the Latino and Mexican students pervasive in many schools and their own stance toward authority. The "grow-your-own" recruitment approach used in this Texas teacher education program was found viable in addressing the shortage of cultural and linguistic diversity among the teaching force.
Bustos Flores, B., & Riojas Clark, E. (1999)	What is the impact of high-stakes testing on prospective bilingual and minority teachers?	Literature review and 2 case studies of Mexican American females who were good teachers but could not initially pass the test.	Prospective bilingual teachers in Texas have a higher failure rate on high-stakes tests. Studies on the relationship between test scores and teacher performance have shown little correlation. For Hispanic students, particular sections of the tests seem to present greater difficulty than do others.

(Continued)

TABLE 8.1
(Continued)

Studies[a]	Question	Research Design	Findings
Cabello, B., & Burstein, N. D. (1995)	How do teacher attitudes and beliefs influence the approaches and practices they use?	Follow-up case study of 2 candidates enrolled in a 2-year undergraduate program at a small liberal arts college in the inner city. Data sources: pre- and postquestionnaires; course assignments, case study, exit interview.	The African-American female candidate learned that the same race or culture did not automatically provide understanding, empathy, or ability. The European-American female did not change her beliefs. Both candidates learned different approaches for teaching students from diverse cultures and backgrounds.
Cabello, B., & Eckmier, J. (1995)	What is the developmental trajectory for candidates in a comprehensive teacher institute?	Program evaluation: 38 candidates entered the cohort, 26 candidates completed the final year of the program. Bilingual candidates were hired before completing the program.	All candidates began the program with a sense of mission. As teachers, the concern shifted to instruction, classroom management, the shortage of materials, and transience of the students.
Canning, C. (1995)	What do Anglo teachers need to know in order to effectively teach Mexican-American students?	Qualitative study with faculty member as participant observer. Thirty-nine candidates from a rural Midwestern university volunteered to participate in a field experience in an urban setting in the southwest 1,200 miles from the university campus.	Findings were in three categories: enabling attitudes—open-mindedness, not knowing, and asking questions; ways to open doors—honesty and authenticity; and observations from the inside—seeing differences and similarities.
Cardina, C. E., & Roden, J. K. (1998)	What is the distribution of the academic proficiency level of high school students who choose to major in education as compared with those indicating other academic majors?	An analysis of survey data from the National Education Longitudinal Study (NELS) follow-up (1992). 16,842 (91%) completed questionnaires, 13,276 (76.6%) completed the cognitive tests.	Education majors appeared less prepared in mathematics, science, and reading than those choosing other majors. White students showed more interest in education as a major than did ethnic minority students.

Causey, V. E., Thomas, C. D., & Armento, B. J. (2000)	What is the impact of a specific approach to diversity issues that includes structured dialog, goal setting, and action plan development on candidates' knowledge, understanding, and application of diversity issues?	Qualitative, longitudinal case study. Twenty-four participants; 2 candidates were selected for longitudinal study from among 24 undergraduate candidates in a middle-grades social studies methods class in an urban university. Data sources included a reflective journal, lesson plans, postexperience essays, and diversity plans.	One candidate restructured her diversity beliefs after the TE program, then reverted to a less culturally sensitive stance during her three years of teaching in an urban setting. The second candidate restructured her diversity beliefs after the teacher education (TE) program, then acted on her new schema over the 3 years of teaching in an upper-middle-class suburban school.
Clark, C., & Medina, C. (2000)	How are candidates' understandings of literacy and multiculturalism mediated through the acts of teaching and writing literacy narratives?	Qualitative, self-study by 2 teacher educators. Eight candidates were, selected from a pool of 60, in secondary English, social studies, and foreign language who chose to focus on literacy narratives. Three candidates were selected for further study. Data sources included e-mail conversations, group discussions, reading logs, interviews, observations, and selected course work.	Literacy narratives supported candidates epistemological development, critical understanding of literacy and multiculturalism, disrupted overgeneralizations and stereotypes, established links between their personal narratives and other people's narratives and a personal connection to theory.
Cockrell, K. S., Placier, P. L., Cockrell, D. H., & Middleton, J. N. (1999)	How do candidates appropriate knowledge acquired in a multicultural foundations course?	Qualitative, self-study by 4 teacher educators. One hundred twenty-eight candidates in 4 sections of a foundations of education course. Data sources included a demographic questionnaire, initial position paper, reflective journals, and a capstone paper.	Candidates held different positions based on personal experience, political ideologies, and beliefs about the roles of schools and teachers. Most students held some belief in multiculturalism, but few believed it could be realized in practice. The course had weak effects on candidates' beliefs.

(Continued)

TABLE 8.1
(Continued)

Studies[a]	Question	Research Design	Findings
Cook, D. W., & Van Cleaf, D. W. (2000)	What is the impact of student teaching in different settings—urban Comer, urban non-Comer, rural, suburban?	Survey, questionnaire administered to 51 first-year teachers.	Teachers who completed student teaching in urban Comer and non-Comer schools felt they had a better understanding of the sociocultural needs of students and were better prepared to interact with parents from multiracial settings than teachers from suburban or rural schools.
Cooper, A., Beare, P., & Thorman, J. (1990)	How are candidates' attitudes influenced by cross-cultural experiences?	Quasi-experimental study. MN group immersed in Hispanic culture with only general training in multicultural education. TX group had more training and cross-cultural experiences. Eighteen TX student teachers and 85 MN student teachers administered a Likert-type attitude assessment scale.	TX teachers were more comfortable discussing racial issues and encouraging different points of view, and were more comfortable visiting students' homes.
Deering, T. E., & Stanutz, A. (1995)	What are school districts and teacher education programs doing to enhance cultural sensitivity among teachers and how successful are these attempts?	Survey inventory. Sixteen secondary teacher candidates were given a 28-item self-administered questionnaire—cultural diversity awareness inventory prior to and at the end of a 10-week urban field experience.	The field experience did not significantly raise the cultural sensitivity of the participants.
Easter, L. M., Shultz, E. L., Neyhart, T. K., & Reck, U. M. (1999)	What interpersonal and intrapsychic beliefs influence candidates?	Eighty candidates in a Perspectives on American Education course were administered Teacher Beliefs Survey.	These candidates believed in their efficacy to deal with diversity in spite of the fact that very few had urban experience and exposure to other cultures.

Citation	Research question	Methodology	Findings
Fisher, A. (1980). The effects of feedback	What is the impact of supervisors' training in generic teaching skills on candidates' performance and the use of a feedback instrument by supervisors on candidates' attitudes and achievement?	Quantitative study with control and experimental groups. Fifty-two African American undergraduate teacher candidates and their cooperating teachers at an HBCU.	Supervisors who study generic teaching skills perform significantly better on a generic teaching skills test than teachers who did not receive training in this area.
Fry, P. G., & McKinney, L. J. (1997)	What are candidates' attitudes toward culturally diverse people, career expectations, and sense of preparedness?	Qualitative self-study. Ten White, female elementary candidates in a language arts methods course. Data sources included dialog journals, interviews, class discussions and assignments, biographies, and surveys.	Candidates' attitudes and practices were positively affected, cultural awareness was increased through the use of biographies, and 9 of the 10 candidates would consider urban teaching.
Garmon, M. A. (1998)	How can dialog journals be used to promote candidates' learning about racial issues in a multicultural education course?	Qualitative self-study. Twenty-one of 22 students enrolled in a multicultural education course taught by the researcher. The primary data source for this study was the e-mail journals submitted by the students.	Candidates learned from the journals through their own self-reflection, through instructor's comments, and by having their ideas challenged by the instructor.
Gilbert, S. L. (1995)	How do rural candidates respond to teaching in an urban setting?	Survey, questionnaire with open-ended questions. One hundred ninety-three candidates responded to a survey regarding their knowledge of, and expectations about, teaching in urban schools. Content analysis	49.2% of the respondents indicated that they would teach in an urban school. Thirteen of the 19 candidates who attended urban schools would return to teach there. Of the students who attended rural schools, 42.3% would teach in urban schools.
Gilbert, S. L. (1997)	What knowledge and beliefs do candidates have about the elements of schooling, the students, the teachers, the subject matter, and the context of urban schools?	Survey, author-developed instrument. Three hundred forty-five candidates in 6 universities responded to survey regarding their knowledge of, and expectations about, teaching in urban schools. Survey. Questionnaire: Teaching in Urban Schools Questionnaire	Candidates described teachers in urban schools in a positive way, but described students as "self-determining perpetrators of violence." They believed that the disruptive nature of urban schools required a restricted curriculum.

(Continued)

TABLE 8.1
(Continued)

Studies[a]	Question	Research Design	Findings
Gipe, J. P., Duffy, C. A., & Richards, J. C. (1989)	What is the impact of 2 different types of early field experiences on candidates' attitudes, beliefs, and perceptions of teaching reading and language arts to urban, low-SES, dialect-speaking students?	Quantitative study with experimental and control groups. Fifty-two female elementary candidates enrolled in 3 sections of a language arts methods course. Instruments included, The Language Attitude Scale, The Theoretical Orientation to Reading Profile, and a researcher-devised questionnaire.	The immersion field experience for the experimental group resulted in positive responses to dialect-speaking students and change in theoretical perspective on reading by moving from a phonics perspective to a more holistic perspective.
Gomez, M. L. (1996)	What is the impact of telling and interrogating stories about themselves and their teaching on preservice teachers understanding and practices in teaching diverse students?	One White middle-class student enrolled in a student teaching seminar.	Candidates increased their understanding of their strengths and limitations for teaching students from diverse backgrounds and their understanding of the students in their classrooms.
Goodwin, A. L. (1994)	What are preservice teachers' conceptions of the goals of multicultural education? What do preservice teachers identify as multicultural practices?	Researcher-developed survey completed by 80 candidates who completed their teacher preparation program, 59% White.	Forty-one percent of respondents indicated that learning about others is the most important goal of multicultural education. Also, the majority of respondents indicated a need for more knowledge about information, techniques, materials, and models for implementing multicultural education.
Goodwin, A. L. (1997)	What multicultural diversity issues are of concern to student teachers?	Survey, Questionnaire. Eighty-three candidates, 27% people of color. A critical incident sheet was used to solicit descriptions of observations or involvement in dilemmas that raised questions related to race, gender, or class.	The categories that emerged from the data were rejection, internalization, derision, suspicion and attack, discomfort, disregard, and ambivalence. 50% of the vignettes identified race as the main variable; 9% identified class and language. Candidates were confused about how to deal with such issues.

Green, J. E., & Weaver, R. A. (1992)	What are the characteristics of candidates who choose teaching as a career?	Sixteen hundred entering freshmen at Ball State University were surveyed over a 4-year period.	The general characteristics of recent high school graduates entering teacher education are predominantly female, Caucasian, middle class, and come from small or rural communities.
Greenleaf, C., Hull, G., & Reilly, B. (1994)	What is the impact of using teaching cases to engage candidates' in rethinking problematic teaching and learning situations in literacy instruction?	Qualitative self-study by 3 teacher educators involving 36 teacher candidates in 10 discussion groups. Data sources included audiotaped discussion sessions, written conclusions drawn by participants.	Candidates engaged in an inquiry mode with the case materials by trying to account for student performance in each instance. Candidates differed in the degree to which they located the problem in the student, the teacher, the task, or the instructional context.
Greenman, N. P., & Kimmel, E. B. (1995)	To what extent do candidates, teachers, and school counselors-in-training embrace the AACTE-endorsed multiculturalism, multilingualism, multidialectism, empowerment, equity, and cultural and individual inequities?	Survey, researcher-developed instrument. Participants were 33 preservice counselors, 38 teacher candidates, and 25 teachers. Research developed instrument used for data collection.	Teacher educators experience tension and difficulties when conducting multicultural training.
Grottkau, B. J., & Nickolai-Mays, S. (1989)	To what extent does exposure over time to ongoing multicultural education experiences effect change in bias toward culturally different groups?	Quantitative study. One hundred twenty-two candidates were administered a pre- and post-treatment, a Revised version of the Social Distance Scale.	Exposure to multicultural education experiences over time does contribute to a statistically significant difference in overall levels of bias, as well as levels of bias towards specific groups.
Groulx, J. G. (2001)	What impact does student teaching in a PDS with underserved students have on candidates' attitudes and perceptions?	Survey completed prior to student teaching. One hundred twelve candidates were given a 2-part questionnaire with a Likert scale that	Initially, candidates had difficulty seeing themselves as teachers for urban minority students. Greater shifts in attitude and perception

(Continued)

TABLE 8.1
(Continued)

Studies[a]	Question	Research Design	Findings
		asks for a response to 4 types of schools and their level of comfort and interest in each before and after student teaching. Twenty-nine candidates were surveyed a 2nd time.	occurred for elementary certification candidates than for secondary and all level certification candidates.
Guyton, E., Saxton, R., & Wesche, M. (1996)	What are the experiences of diverse candidates in teacher education?	Qualitative study with semi-structured interviews. Seven candidates: 4 African Americans, 2 White males, and 1 Asian American. Each candidate was interviewed individually 3 times over a 1-year time period.	Overall satisfaction with the program. Experienced limited racism from peers and none from faculty. Valued diversity in program content, comfortable in urban school settings, perceived themselves as role models, and felt pressure not to choose teaching as a career.
Haberman, M. (1993)	To what extent does an interview assessing candidates' responses to 7 functions common to "star" teachers predict their potential for successful teaching in urban settings?	Quantitative correlational study. Thirty-eight teacher candidates, 29 African Americans, 4 Hispanics, 5 Whites.	Candidates who ranked in the top half on The Urban Teacher Selection Interview also ranked in the top half in practice. Those who ranked in the bottom half on the interview also ranked in the bottom half in practice.
Hadaway, N. L., & Florez, V. (1987–1988)	Do candidates have relevant experiences in multicultural settings and value multicultural training, and have a willingness to participate in such training?	Survey questionnaire involving 125 candidates responded to the survey.	Candidates had limited experiences with those from cultures different from their own, felt inadequately prepared, and were desirous of additional training in multicultural education.
Hlebowitsh, P. S., & Tellez, K. (1993)	What level of respect do candidates award to students on the basis of race, gender, and social class?	Quantitative, questionnaire. Two hundred thirty-five undergraduate candidates in their 1st teacher education course.	Higher levels of respect were awarded to Black, low-SES students, and to females.

Reference	Research question	Method	Findings
Johanessen, G. G., & Bustamante Lopez, I. (2002)	Are bilingual teacher candidates' abilities in basic interpersonal communicative skills (BICS) and Cognitive Academic Language Proficiency (CALP) being adequately tested to enable them to conduct instruction in a Spanish–English bilingual context? Do teachers with acceptable BICS but limited CALP need more opportunities to engage in academic exchanges in Spanish?	The article reports on a pilot study of a new test to assess the proficiency in Spanish of teacher candidates. The assessment was administered to 60 participants. The authors focused on inferences about the test-taker's ability to use Spanish to perform tasks in an academic domain.	Findings confirmed the need to provide students with opportunities to engage in academic exchanges in Spanish, both within and beyond the boundaries of the university. They also suggest that improved language testing is preferable to just simply raising the bar on teacher credential testing.
Johnson, K. E. (1994)	How do candidates' beliefs about 2nd-language learning and teaching influence how they conceptualize instructional practice during the practicum?	Qualitative study. Four ESL teacher candidates in a Master of Arts program in Teaching English as a Second Language (TESL). Data sources included reflective journals, observations, interviews, and researchers' conceptual memos.	All 4 candidates focused on their own practice, had difficulty seeing what students were learning from instruction, focused less on ways to promote learning and more on ways to keeping the flow of instruction.
Katz, S. R. (2000)	How do candidates for teaching bilingual children grapple with the complex relationship of research, policy, and practice within the field of bilingual education?	Qualitative self-study by a teacher educator involving 200 teacher candidates at the University of San Francisco. Data sources included weekly written reflections based on readings and class discussions, written field observations, linguistic history charts, oral debate on policy issues, and a final paper.	Those who were previously supportive of bilingualism became more articulate in their support once they were exposed to the research in the field. Those who were previously skeptical of bilingual tend to refute the research and look for evidence to support their belief in English-only education.
LaFramboise, K. L., & Griffith, P. L. (1997)	How do undergraduate teacher candidates make meaning from instances of cultural conflict that are portrayed in juvenile novels,	Qualitative self-study by 2 teacher educators with 22 intern teachers in the 1st semester of a 5-semester undergraduate teacher education	Six categories emerged within the meaning-making dimension: paraphrasing, connecting to own knowledge, comparing,

(Continued)

TABLE 8.1
(Continued)

Studies[a]	Question	Research Design	Findings
	and how is this helpful in delineating appropriate practice for case-based instruction in teacher education courses?	program engaged in an early field experience at a professional development school. Data sources included literature logs, audiotape recording of group discussions, candidates' exit memos following each discussion session, classroom observations, and a final written project.	inferring, critiquing, and connecting to course content.
Lawrence, S. M., & Bunche, T. (1996)	To what extent can a course in multicultural education help White candidates develop a White antiracist identity?	Qualitative self-study by a teacher educator involving 5 of the 23 teacher candidates enrolled in a multicultural education course who were selected for the case study. Data sources: interviews at the beginning and end of the course, weekly written response papers, and a formal paper submitted at the end of the semester.	These cases indicate that a race-focused multicultural education course can help white students unlearn misinformation and provide guidelines for relearning that can facilitate their reflecting on the effects of racism. All 5 women in the study seemed to move through Helms' stages of racial identity.
Lopez Estrada, V. (1999)	How did the interns' experience in the Rio Grande Valley contribute to their development of cultural consciousness and cross-cultural awareness?	The study is qualitative. It divided 6 interns in 2 cohorts—one of minority teacher candidates with bicultural experiences and the other with candidates who considered themselves mainstream. Participant observations, interviews, and site documents were collected and analyzed.	Interns who were members of ethnic minorities (Hispanic or Black) achieved higher levels of cultural consciousness and cross-cultural awareness than the White interns. For all participants, the experience affected their teaching philosophies. Attributes such as "playfulness" and "world-traveling" seem to facilitate cross-cultural awareness.

Citation	Research question	Method	Findings
Luft, J. A., Bragg, J., & Peters, C. (1999)	What constraints does an Anglo candidate in a culturally diverse field placement face?	Qualitative case study of 1 student teacher in a culturally diverse secondary science class. The researcher was the university supervisor. The approach included in-depth interviews, classroom observations with pre- and postconferences conducted by university supervisor, and notes from the candidate's journal.	The challenges the candidate faced were a lack of familiarity with students and their life experiences, feeling personally marginalized when implementing a student-centered science lesson, and making the science lessons more relevant to her students.
Mahan, J. M. (1982)	How do teacher candidates benefit from engaging in community-based experiences with members of a culture different from their own?	Nine-year longitudinal study of 293 candidates who participated in a cultural immersion experience by engaging in community-based activities. Data sources: Likert-scale instrument and synthesis reports.	Benefits from the emersion experience included new relationships, increased self-awareness, and an understanding of how to promote cultural pluralism in the classroom.
Mahan, J. M. (1984)	What are the cultural and methodological concerns of candidates serving Navajo, Hopi, and Apache elementary schools?	Used Frequent Concerns of Student Teachers Survey with 42 participants in an American-Indian Reservation Project. Data Sources were two categories of concerns from the survey.	The 3 top concerns were (a) motivating pupils to work, (b) understanding the culture of the people, and (c) adapting teaching to fit the culture.
Marshall, P. L. (1996)	What concerns do candidates have about teaching culturally diverse students?	Survey, questionnaire administered to 103 teacher candidates in the Introduction to Teaching in the Humanities and Social Sciences course, 103 teachers. Data sources: The Multicultural Teaching Concerns Survey.	Concerns were found in each of the 3 categories of the survey used: cross-cultural competence, strategies and techniques for teaching diverse populations, familial and group knowledge, and school bureaucracy.
Marshall, P. L. (1998)	How does an issues-exchange approach to multicultural education affect candidates' understanding of diverse perspectives?	Surveys administered to 7 of 15 students from a course taken 1 year before and 8 of 21 students from a course taken two years before.	Candidates reported a better understanding of the perspectives of others' and of their own perspectives.

(Continued)

TABLE 8.1
(Continued)

Studies[a]	Question	Research Design	Findings
Martin, O., & Williams-Dixon, R. (1994)	What is the social distance perspective of candidates and what implications does this have for preservice teacher education?	Social Distance Scale administered to 266 preservice teachers enrolled in undergraduate education courses at a predominately White university in the Southern United States.	A distinct social distance does exist by dominant group from diverse racial and ethnic groups. Candidates in all age ranges and from various ethnic groups displayed significant social distance toward certain racial and ethnic groups.
Mason, T. C. (1999)	What factors contribute to one candidate's success and to another's frustration?	Case study of 2 teacher candidates enrolled in a senior-level general methods course with a field experience in an urban school. Note: Competence was not directly tied to students' background experiences.	One candidate contended that a major factor in her success was the support and guidance provided by her cooperating teacher. The unsuccessful candidate received very little feedback from his cooperating teacher.
McCall, A. L. (1995)	What meaning do candidates construct regarding multicultural, social reconstructionist ideology in a social studies methods course?	Case study of 2 candidates. Julie was from a large middle-class family; her father was a high school graduate; her mother was not. Rick was from a working-class family with limited resources, father was deceased; mother—a registered nurse. Data sources: interviews, reflective journals, and other course assignments.	These candidates' background experiences influenced their commitment to multicultural education. Julie was concerned about reinforcing existing social conditions by teaching about power, prejudice, and racism; her own lack of experience with discrimination; and about her childhood experiences. Rick viewed multicultural education as a form of social activism, a way to disrupt discrimination.
McCormick, T. E. (1990)	What can be learned from a follow-up study of graduates of a teacher education program?	Survey, questionnaire—103 respondents from Iowa State University placed in the Cooperative Urban Teacher Education (CUTE) Program at Kansas City, KS. The Program was designed	In 1990, less than half of the participants from 1970 to 1984 were still teaching. Those that were teaching were employed in predominantly urban school districts and planned to stay in

528

		to prepare teachers for urban settings with ethnically and economically diverse students.	the same positions. Respondents indicated that student teaching in an urban setting had a profound impact on their development.
McDiarmid, G. W. (1992)	To what extent does a series of multicultural in-service training sessions impact candidates' thinking and understanding of cultural diversity?	One hundred ten trainees given a 306-item questionnaire at the beginning of their program, at the end of the 1st year of teaching, and during the 2nd year of teaching. Additionally, 12 randomly selected from among 110 were interviewed and observations conducted in their classrooms. The participants responded to vignettes related to multicultural teaching.	Training did not reduce acceptance of stereotypes and discrepancies in assignments given to students based on race or ethnicity.
McFalls, E. L., & Cobb-Roberts, D. (2001)	To what extent does cognitive dissonance theory reduce resistance to diversity?	One hundred twenty-four undergraduate candidates, majority White, enrolled in 2 sections of a diversity education course. Researchers introduced cognitive dissonance theory to 1 section. Self-reported data.	Incorporating cognitive dissonance theory into a diversity course created an awareness of dissonance and may potentially reduce resistance to diversity issues.
McIntyre, A. (1997)	What is the meaning of Whiteness in the daily lives of white teacher candidates?	Participatory action research methodology was used with 13 White undergraduate middle-class females engaged in a practicum field experience at a private Northeastern university. Data sources: Semi-structured interviews, group discussions audiotaped	Many described multicultural ed as about "awareness of different cultures." They did not situate racism and Whiteness within multicultural ed, knowledge of the power and influence of racism on others' lives brought feelings of guilt and defensiveness, acted as "White knights" in urban schools, held stereotypes about children of color, & shared stories among participants that maintained myths.

(Continued)

TABLE 8.1
(Continued)

Studies[a]	Question	Research Design	Findings
Morales, R. (2000)	What knowledge do candidates bring to the teacher education program concerning group differences, educational resources, and teacher preparation, and what is the impact of a course in early childhood education on their knowledge?	Qualitative self-study by a teacher educator. Pre- and postsurveys administered to 23 students enrolled in an early childhood education course. Data sources: survey, candidates' journals, and class discussions and activities.	The candidates' reflections and the postsurvey indicate that they gained confidence in themselves, believed that they had increased their knowledge and ability to teach culturally and linguistically diverse students, and were more aware of the need to critically examine issues related to cultural diversity.
Narode, R., Rennie-Hill, L., & Peterson, K. D. (1994)	How does an urban community perceive quality education, and how might this perception inform beginning teachers? How do candidates benefit from such inquiry?	Qualitative self-study involving 26 graduate teacher education candidates (1 person of color) at a West-coast urban public university. A content analysis was conducted on participant observer narratives, and significant themes and examples were extracted.	It was found that these experiences had a positive influence on the candidates' views of all participants in the educational process in urban settings. Expectation for schools is influenced by early experiences with schools, education, comfortableness with schools, physical and emotional safety, involvement, and the effects of tracking.
Nathenson-Mejía, S., & Escamilla, K. (2003)	How does using Latino children's literature in seminars with predominantly White teacher candidates help broaden their perspectives of the multicultural student population with which they would be working?	Qualitative analysis of the 3-year project, working with total of 70 teacher candidates. Data were drawn from participant observation, group debriefings, observations of lessons taught by the student teachers using the books, and participant reflections.	Candidates used the books in their classrooms to make connections with their students' lives and to extend their verbal, reading, and writing skills. Over the course of the program, candidates' attitudes toward their students changed. Participants became more motivated to teach in multicultural communities.

Author (Year)	Research Question	Methods	Findings
Nel, J. (1992)	What is the impact of using Cummins' framework for empowering minorities on candidates' cultural sensitivity?	Qualitative self-study with candidates enrolled in a multicultural education course. Data sources: Pre- and postadminstration of the cultural Diversity Inventory, goal selection instrument, and candidates testimonies.	An increase in cultural sensitivity and awareness of the necessity to incorporate minority students' culture and home language into the school program, to foster parent and community involvement, and to help students actively construct knowledge.
Noordhoff, K., & Kleinfeld, J. (1993)	What is the impact of a program designed to prepare teachers to teach for schools in Eskimo and Indian villages on the candidates' orientation toward teaching culturally diverse students?	Qualitative study of 15 candidates admitted to a 1-year program. Pre- and postsample lessons were analyzed to determine amount of change.	Researchers found indication of substantial growth in candidates' orientations toward teaching culturally diverse populations.
Obidah, J. E. (2000)	What effect does critical reflection have on candidates' perceptions and beliefs about culture?	Qualitative self-study of 29 candidates in a multicultural education course. Data sources: written assignments, professor notes, course evaluation.	Students reported that their perceptions and beliefs about culture were changed during the course.
Olmedo, I. M. (1997)	What is the impact of fieldwork and related readings on the views of candidates about teaching in urban culturally diverse schools?	Qualitative self-study with 29 teacher candidates in a fieldwork course. Results reported for 16 candidates. Data sources: journals and essays—assignments for the course. In all of the assignments, candidates made meaningful connections between their readings and their field experiences.	Candidates developed new perspectives such as children want to learn; good teaching can take place even in inner city schools; there is diversity within diversity; being colorblind is not good pedagogy.
Peterson, K. M., Cross, L. F., Johnson, E. J., & Howell, G. L. (2000)	To what extent are candidates' attitudes regarding diversity issues expanded by classroom instructional activities, and what types of instructional strategies are the most influential in eliciting changes?	Survey administered by 4 teacher educators. Instrument was a posttest measuring the impact of the class on candidates' attitudes regarding diversity issues. Twenty-six candidates in a foundations of education course.	The course had a positive impact on candidates attitudes regarding diversity issues. The film The Color of Fear seemed to have the greatest impact on the candidates.

(Continued)

TABLE 8.1
(Continued)

Studies[a]	Question	Research Design	Findings
Potthoff, D. E., Dinsmore, J., Eifler, K., Stirtz, G., Walsh, T., & Ziebarth, J. (2000)	What are the perceptions of preservice teachers, faculty, and community personnel as to how the community-based field experience in human services agencies impacts candidates' growth in knowledge, skills, and attitudes?	Survey of 136 candidates in the course "Community based Human Services Field Experience," 65 community agencies, and 26 faculty who taught the course. Researcher-developed survey. Data source: a 53-item Likert scale survey.	Results of the survey indicate that the course helped foster appropriate knowledge, skills, and attitudes toward diversity; warm, caring candidates with a willingness to serve others; empathy for persons different from self; self-understanding; interpersonal communication skills; confidence; self-esteem.
Redican, K., Stewart, S. H., Johnson, L. E., & Frazee, A. M. (1994)	To what extent are colleges and universities preparing teacher candidates in health education for urban schools?	One hundred fifty of 215 professional programs contacted responded to the survey questionnaire.	Many colleges and universities preparing health educators do not actively provide for or incorporate cultural sensitivity experiences as part of the professional preparation.
Reed, D. F., & Simon, D. J. (1991)	How do historically Black colleges and universities respond to the critical need to prepare teachers for urban school settings?	Surveys and telephone interviews were administered to deans and directors of education at 10 HBCUs in 6 states.	HBCUs have a clear mission based on the need to prepare teachers for urban school settings. Courses and field experiences support this mission.
Richman, C. L., Bovelsky, S., Kroovand, N., Vacca, J., & West, T. (1997)	What are the racial attitudes of European-American candidates in a small, Southern liberal arts university?	Quantitative, random sampling with 20 White college students in a 4th-year teacher education course at a small, Southern liberal arts university. Data sources: Multifactor Racial Attitudes Inventory, candidates' responses to autobiography and photograph of a short-story writer and photograph of a poet. Race was variable.	When European-American candidates were shown pictures of African-American and European-American students, they judged African-American students as inferior. The findings were similar when the autobiographies and photographs of a short-story writer and a poet were used.

Riojas Clark, E., & Bustos Flores, B. (1997)	How can an observational tool, such as Instructional Snapshot, serve teacher education students to identify and reflect on instructional strategies used in Spanish in sending and receiving countries? How can knowing about the sending country's educational system help service immigrant students in the United States?	Eight undergraduate and 2 graduate students from a university in Texas, accompanied by their professor and student-teaching supervisors, visited 2 school sites in Monterrey, Mexico, during their spring break. They observed the classroom physical environment, the teacher-student interaction, the instruction, the teacher-questioning and motivational strategies, and classroom management using the Instructional Snapshot (IS) observation form. Dyads of students were formed based on grade-level interests.	The authors found that the pre-service teachers affirmed their commitment to teach language minority students, their understanding and knowledge base of differing socio-cultural contexts, and self-confidence as teachers of bilingual/bicultural education.
Riojas Clark, E., & Bustos Flores, B. (2001)	How do bilingual teachers candidates identify themselves ethnically, and what are their self-conceptualizations? And is there a within-group difference in how these Latino teacher candidates identify themselves?	The participants were Latino students, mainly Mexican-American, in a bilingual teacher education preparation program in Texas. Profiles of how they identify themselves were gathered in an attempt to measure ethnic identity as a psychological construct. Data were taken and coded in 18 identity categories.	The findings indicate that there is a strong association between ethnic identity and self-concept and that there are group differences. The authors suggest a developmental transformative process that requires teacher preparation programs to model the value of cultural knowledge and to provide teachers with the skills necessary to enhance their own and, consequently, their future students' ethnic identity.

(Continued)

TABLE 8.1
(Continued)

Studies[a]	Question	Research Design	Findings
Rodriguez, A. J. (1998)	What would be the impact on candidates' resistance to ideological change and pedagogical change when linking multicultural education, sociotransformative constructive orientation, and pedagogical strategies?	Qualitative self-study by a teacher educator employing focus groups, survey, classroom observations of 18 students in a secondary science methods course. Four candidates selected from initial 18 for closer study. Data sources: interviews, field notes, candidate-produced artifacts, and videotaped lessons.	Linking multicultural education and sociotransformative constructivist orientation in pedagogical strategies for counter-resistance supported candidates in learning to teach for diversity and understanding.
Root, S., Rudawski, A., Taylor, M., & Rochon, R. (2003)	What are some causes of attrition among Hmong participants in projects designed to help them work toward teaching certification or graduate degrees?	Analysis of 23 teacher-candidate student files, exit interviews, records of interactions with students while they were in the program, and student assessments. An additional questionnaire was prepared and administered to 14 of the 23 former participants in the study.	More nontraditional-age students left the program than traditional-age students. The main reasons for leaving were related to employment and finances. Other reasons included family issues, relocation, and low academic performance.
Ross, D. D., & Smith, W. (1992)	To what extent does candidates' understanding of diversity change over the course of the teacher preparation program?	Case study of 6 candidates enrolled in a research course and their 1st field placement seminar experience. Data sources: Interviews, written course work, reflective journals, supervisors' notes.	The candidates' orientation to diversity became more complex. They focused on the role of curriculum and the individual teacher in creating and maintaining the low achievement of diverse learners rather than on the role played by the context of schooling, the work conditions faced by teachers, or the social context of U.S. society.

534

Rushton, S. P. (2001)	The focus of this study is a narrative of a candidate's experiences in a yearlong internship in an inner-city school.	Case study of 1 candidate's experiences in a yearlong internship in an inner-city school located in Knoxville, TN. Data sources: The researcher used four 2-hour semi structured interviews, weekly 2-page reflections, and weekly taped group discussions over a 1-year time period.	During this internship in an inner-city school, the candidate experienced culture shock and cognitive dissonance, worried about relationship with mentor teacher, doubted her own abilities, and relied on a personal sense of purpose to support her transition from student to teacher.
Sconzert, K., Iazzetto, D., & Purkey, S. (2000)	What do candidates from a rural liberal arts university learn from an urban student teaching experience?	A qualitative study involving 12 student teachers from a liberal arts college in the Midwest located in a rural setting.	The changes that occurred were that the reality of teaching was different than what candidates expected; course work was inadequate preparation; negative attitudes of veteran teachers were unexpected and frustrating, teaching requires building relationships with students; instruction needs to be adapted to the needs and experiences of the students; learning from students and being aware of their ethnicity and background experiences are critical.
Seidl, B., & Friend, G. (2002)	What is the influence of a cross-cultural, socioeconomically diverse, equal-status internship on a group of predominantly White candidates' perspectives and identities?	Candidates enrolled in a 5th-year graduate level teacher education program. Data sources: field notes, classroom dialogue, and course assignments.	Many students developed deepening understandings of culture, racism, and education issues; whereas some students exhibited little growth, resisting personal and social transformation.

(Continued)

TABLE 8.1
(Continued)

Studies[a]	Question	Research Design	Findings
Sheets, R. H., & Chew, L. (2002)	What is the value, to Chinese-American students, of a course in diversity, and how do they apply the knowledge gained in the classroom?	Thirty-two Chinese-American candidates in a diversity course. Data sources: questionnaires, profiles, surveys, interviews, focus groups (15 of 32 participated), syllabi, course and school documents, classroom observations.	Candidates reported positive experiences and a sense of belonging; however, using the Diversity Pedagogical Behaviors Observations Tool, researchers found that candidates showed weakness in the area of culturally relevant content knowledge acquisition and diversity consciousness and awareness of differences.
Shultz, E. L., Neyhart, K., & Reck, U. M. (1996)	What are the attitudes and beliefs of candidates in teacher education?	Survey of 300 teacher candidates enrolled in a course called Perspectives on American Education. Data sources: survey questionnaire developed by the researcher.	Candidates in this teacher preparation program indicate a willingness to teach in urban schools; however, this is inconsistent with their beliefs and attitudes about urban students.
Sleeter, C. E. (1989)	How do teachers use what was learned in their teacher education program about multicultural education?	Analysis of data from the 416 of 1,552 surveys sent to teachers licensed in Wisconsin between 1981 and 1985 that were returned.	Generally, teachers reported responding to differences among students through instruction, creating positive social relationships among groups, and incorporating diversity into the curriculum.
Smith, R., Moallem, M., & Sherrill, D. (1997)	What factors influence candidates' beliefs about equity?	A qualitative study of 20 of 80 papers (autobiographies) submitted by candidates enrolled in the Secondary Social Studies Methods course was analyzed.	Some candidates were taught equality as part of their early socialization; others were influenced by exposure to individuals of different cultural backgrounds, education, travel, and other personal experiences with discrimination.

Smolkin, L. B., & Suina, J. H. (1999)	What do candidates learn from cross-cultural partnerships in a rural/urban American-Indian teacher education program?	In the first 2 years of the project, data were collected from 10 Indian/non-Indian pairs of candidates. Data sources were weekly logs completed by candidates and audiotaped group discussions, and audiotaped and transcribed interviews with mentor teachers.	American-Indian candidates became more aware of how to identify and utilize their own cultural resources to facilitate learning in the classroom and how non-Indian candidates identify and use resources. Non-Indian candidates and teachers became more culturally sensitive and knowledgeable.
Southerland, S. A., & Gess-Newsome, J. (1999)	How do science teacher candidates make sense of inclusive science teaching for diverse student populations?	Qualitative self-study by a teacher educator involving 22 science teacher candidates in a cohort. Data sources: Candidates' written work and audiotapes of classroom discussions related to inclusion.	Candidates held positivistic views of knowledge, learning, and teaching through which they understood and reacted to ideas of teaching science to diverse student populations.
Sparks, W. G., III, & Verner, M. E. (1995)	Given 4 approaches to multicultural education in preservice teacher education, which generates the greatest impact on candidates' knowledge and attitudes?	Quantitative, pre- and postassessments using the Multicultural Physical Education Instrument (MPEI). Two hundred twenty-eight candidates in courses designated for 4 treatment groups: Discipline-specific course, integrated course, discipline-specific field-based experience—public school, integrated field-based experience in urban setting.	Multicultural knowledge and attitudes were enhanced in the discipline-specific and integrated course approach. However, the traditional discipline-specific field-based group declined in their perception of multicultural education.
Stallings, J. A., Bossung, J., & Martin, A. (1990)	How does the experience of candidates placed in an urban professional development school compare with that of their peers with field placements in other settings?	Administered Stallings Observation Instrument, conducted interviews, and observed discussions of 44 participants in an experimental student-teaching group placed in urban professional development	The experimental group showed greater increases in the use of academic statements during class periods, increased supportive feedback to student responses, and greater reduction in off-task behavior.

(Continued)

TABLE 8.1
(Continued)

Studies[a]	Question	Research Design	Findings
		schools, and 25 control group participants placed in urban and suburban schools serving middle-class, diverse populations.	
Su, Z. (1996)	How do the characteristics and perspectives of minority and White candidates compare?	Conducted interviews and administered surveys to 148 teacher candidates: 90 Whites and 58 minorities. Data sources: survey and interviews.	A comparison of minority and White students' characteristics and perspectives revealed that minorities were from lower SES, had less positive educational experiences, and encountered more obstacles in making career choices than Whites.
Su, Z. (1997)	What are ethnic minority candidates' views on teaching as a profession and as a career?	Qualitative case study of candidates from 3 different ethnic groups: Asian American, African American, and Hispanic. Forty-one candidates from 3 different ethnic minority groups. Data source: survey instrument adapted from the American national study, The Study of the Education of Educators.	Minority candidates were motivated to enter teaching for altruistic reasons and awareness of educational and social inequities. Many minorities held a clear vision of their roles as change agents in the schools.
Tellez, K. (1999)	How do Mexican-American candidates use their ethnicity during student teaching?	Qualitative, interviews with 4 Mexican-American student teachers in a yearlong teacher education program. Data sources: extensive interviews.	These student teachers used their cultural knowledge to communicate with students, explain students' actions to other teachers, and to communicate with parents. They did not use their cultural knowledge to make adjustments to the curriculum or instruction.

Terrill, M., & Mark, D. L. H. (2000)	Do candidates at a Midwestern university hold significantly different expectations for students of color in different settings than for White students in suburban schools?	Survey, questionnaire with 97 undergraduate students: 89% White and 65% female. Administered a 2-part questionnaire with descriptions of similar schools with variations in the race of the students and the type of community. Participants were to indicate their preference.	Sixty-four percent preferred student teaching in a majority White school; 52% had never spent time in a classroom with students of color; 70% said they would allow the use of Ebonics in the classroom. Candidates held different expectations for students in different settings. Expectations were not different for curriculum.
Tiezzi, L. J., & Cross, B. E. (1997)	Do candidates hold significantly different expectations for learners in different racial and linguistic backgrounds?	Qualitative study that included a Quantitative procedure. Friedman test used as a nonparametric alternative to analysis of variance. Subjects were 48 of 54 candidates enrolled in 3 sections of an Introduction to Teaching course. Two students were selected for case study analysis. Data sources: reflective journals, in-class writings, observational field assignments, personal history essays, and a final survey.	Candidates held significantly different expectations for learners in different school settings and from different racial and linguistic backgrounds.
Vavrus, M. (1994)	How do Anglo candidates appropriate knowledge about multicultural education?	Survey questionnaire administered to 120 out of 170 candidates in a teacher education program shared among 3 private liberal arts colleges in the Midwestern part of the United States.	Seventy percent reported activities within the additive approach; 30% of activities were in contributions category; 31% attempted curriculum transformation; 10% attempted a social action approach; 62% mentioned minority groups; and 23% mentioned women.

(Continued)

TABLE 8.1
(Continued)

Studies[a]	Question	Research Design	Findings
Waldschmidt, E. D. (2002)	A study on the efforts to diversify the teaching force, to avoid the common danger of neocolonialism, and to overcome the bilingual and bicultural interns' propensity, as members of a subordinate group, to accept and propagate racism.	Ethnographic study of 3 bilingual and bicultural teacher interns at a local community college. Open-ended interviews, essays written for the yearly scholarship applications, field notes from classroom visits, audiotaped focus groups, and survey results from a survey of program participants conducted by an outside evaluator were used as data.	The findings of the study suggest that efforts to diversify the teaching force must not be informed solely by the living experiences of individuals from underrepresented groups, these efforts ought to be critiqued and transformed.
Walker de Felix, J., & Cavazos Pena, S. (1992)	Do bilingual teachers of Mexican descent benefit from a program in which they study Spanish in Mexico?	Sixteen candidates of Mexican descent. Pre- and posttests included the Modern Language Association Spanish reading and writing test and a Semantic Differential instrument measuring attitudes toward the concepts of Mexican, American, and Self. Other sources of data included participant journals and observations.	Participants showed a significant positive change in their attitudes toward Mexicans, as well as some negative change toward Americans. Their overall attitudes toward Self did not change significantly, although they saw themselves as more powerful after the program. Participants performed better on a Spanish cloze test, but their reading scores unexpectedly declined. Teachers felt more confident in their Spanish fluency and felt a stronger connection to their Mexican roots.

(Continued)

TABLE 8.1
(Continued)

Studies[a]	Question	Research Design	Findings
Wiggins, R. A., & Follo, E. J. (1999)	What aspects of the teacher preparation program had the most impact on preservice teachers' preparation to teach diverse students?	One hundred twenty-six candidates enrolled in 2 sections of 3 different program courses responded to pre- and postsemester questionnaires. Data sources: Wald Test of Significance of Fixed Effects and Covariates.	Candidates are well prepared for the academic responsibilities in a culturally diverse classroom. Their experiences do not seem to help them feel comfortable with students from cultures other than their own.
Xu, H. (2000)	What is candidates' understanding of their own cultural backgrounds and those of their students, and how are these understandings integrated into literacy instruction?	A qualitative self-study of 20 candidates in their early 20s; 4 identified as ethnic minorities; 4, low SES. Data sources: autobiographies, case study students' biographies, cross-cultural analysis charts, case study reports, strategy and literature sheets, and field notes of observations and class discussions.	The model used in this study fostered respect for students' cultural, linguistic, and life experiences. Candidates used strategies such as multicultural integration and cooperative learning, during reading and writing instruction with case study students to maximize student active engagement and promote success.

[a] Please see References.

541

BIBLIOGRAPHY OF RESEARCH STUDIES

Anderson, S. E. (1998). Integrating multimedia multicultural materials into an educational psychology course. *Journal of Technology and Teacher Education, 6*(2–3), 169–182.

Arias, B., & Poynor, L. (2001). A good start: A progressive, transactional approach to diversity in pre-service teacher education. *Bilingual Research Journal,25*(4), 417–434.

Artiles, A. J., Barreto, R. M., Pena, L., & McClafferty, K. (1998). Pathways to teacher learning in multicultural contexts: A longitudinal case study of two novice bilingual teachers in urban schools. *Remedial and Special Education, 19*(2), 70–90.

Baca, L., Bransford, J., Nelson, C., & Ortiz, L. (1994). Training, development, and improvement (TDI): A new approach for reforming bilingual teacher preparation. *The Journal of Educational Issues of Language Minority Students,14*, 1–22. Retrieved July 9, 2003, from Ingenta database.

Ball, A. F. (2000). Preparing teachers for diversity: Lessons learned from the U.S. and South Africa. *Teaching and Teacher Education, 16*(4), 491–509.

Barry, N. H., & Lechner, J. V. (1995). Preservice teachers' attitudes about and awareness of multicultural teaching and learning. *Teaching and Teacher Education, 11*(2), 149–161.

Becket, D. R. (1998). Increasing the number of Latino and Navajo teachers in hard-to-staff schools. *Journal of Teacher Education, 49*(3), 196–205.

Bennett, C., Cole, D., & Thompson, J. N. (2000). Preparing teachers of color at a predominantly White university: A case study of project TEAM. *Teaching and Teacher Education, 16*(4), 445–464.

Bennett, C., Niggle, T., & Stage, F. (1990). Preservice multicultural teacher education: Predictors of student readiness. *Teaching and Teacher Education*, 6(3), 243–254.

Bollin, G. G. (1996). Using multicultural tutoring to prepare preservice teachers for diverse classrooms. *The Educational Forum, 61*, 68–76.

Bondy, E., & Davis, S. (2000). The caring of strangers: Insights from a field experience in a culturally unfamiliar community. *Action in Teacher Education, 22*(2), 54–66.

Burant, T. J., & Kirby, D. (2002). Beyond classroom-based early field experiences: Understanding an "educative practicum" in an urban school community. *Teaching and Teacher Education*, 18, 561–575.

Bustos Flores, B., Keehn, S., & Perez, B. (2002). Critical need for bilingual education teachers: The potential of *normalistas* and paraprofessional. *Bilingual Research Journal, 26*(3), 501–524.

Bustos Flores, B., & Riojas Clark, E. (1999). High-stakes testing: Barriers for prospective bilingual education teachers. *Bilingual Research Journal, 21*(4), 335–357.

Cabello, B., & Burstein, N. D. (1995). Examining teachers' beliefs about teaching in culturally diverse classrooms. *Journal of Teacher Education, 46*(4), 285–294.

Cabello, B., & Eckmier, J. (1995). Looking back: Teachers' reflections on an innovative teacher preparation program. *Action in Teacher Education, 17*(3), 33–42.

Canning, C. (1995). Getting from the outside in: Teaching Mexican Americans when you are an "Anglo." *High School Journal, 78*(4), 195–205.

Cardina, C. E., & Roden, J. K. (1998). Academic proficiency of students who reported intentions of majoring in education. *Journal of Teacher Education, 49*(1), 38–46.

Causey, V. E., Thomas, C. D., & Armento, B. J. (2000). Cultural diversity is basically a foreign term to me: The challenges of diversity for preservice teacher education. *Teaching and Teacher Education, 16*(1), 33–45.

Clark, C., & Medina, C. (2000). How reading and writing literacy narratives affect preservice teachers' understandings of literacy, pedagogy, and multiculturalism. *Journal of Teacher Education, 51*(1), 63–76.

Cockrell, K. S., Placier, P. L., Cockrell, D. H., & Middleton, J. N. (1999). Coming to terms with "diversity" and "multiculturalism" in teacher education: Learning about our students, changing our practice. *Teaching and Teacher Education, 15*(4), 351–366.

Cook, D. W., & Van Cleaf, D. W. (2000). Multicultural perceptions of 1st-year elementary teachers' urban, suburban, and rural student teacher placements. *Urban Education, 35*(2), 165–174.

Cooper, A., Beare, P., & Thorman, J. (1990). Preparing teachers for diversity: A comparison of student teaching experiences in Minnesota and South Texas. *Action in Teacher Education, 12*(3), 1–4.

Deering, T. E., & Stanutz, A. (1995). Preservice field experience as a multicultural component of a teacher education program. *Journal of Teacher Education, 46*(5), 390–394.

Deford, D. E. (1985). Validating the construct of theoretical orientation in teading instruction. *Reading Reasearch Quarterly, 20,* 351–367.

Easter, L. M., Shultz, E. L., Neyhart, T. K., & Reck, U. M. (1999). Weighty perceptions: A study of the attitudes and beliefs of preservice teacher education students regarding diversity and urban education. *The Urban Review, 31*(2), 205–220.

Fisher, A. (1980). The effects of feedback instruction during student teaching on performance and attitudes of prospective Black elementary school teachers. *Negro Educational Review, 31*(2), 83–88.

Fry, P. G., & McKinney, L. J. (1997). A qualitative study of preservice teachers' early field experiences in an urban, culturally different school. *Urban Education, 32*(2), 184–201.

Garmon, M. A. (1998). Using dialogue journals to promote student learning in a multicultural teacher education course. *Remedial & Special Education 19*(1), 32–45.

Gilbert, S. L. (1995). Perspectives of rural prospective teachers toward teaching in urban schools. *Urban Education, 30*(3), 290–305.

Gilbert, S. L. (1997). The "four commonplaces of teaching": Prospective teachers' beliefs about teaching in urban schools. *The Urban Review, 29*(2), 81–96.

Gipe, J. P., Duffy, C. A., & Richards, J. C. (1989). A comparison of two types of early field experiences. *Reading Improvement, 26*(3), 254–265.

Gomez, M. L. (1996). Telling stories of our teaching, reflecting on our practices. *Action in Teacher Education, 28*(3), 1–12.

Gomez, M. L., Walker, A. B., & Page, M. L. (2000). Personal experience as a guide to teaching. *Teaching and Teacher Education, 16*(7), 731–747.

Goodwin, A. L. (1994). Making the transition from self to other: What do preservice teachers really think about multicultural educaton? *Journal of Teacher Education, 45*(2), 119–131.

Goodwin, A. L. (1997). Multicultural stories: Preservice teachers' conceptions of and responses to issues of diversity. *Urban Education, 32*(1), 117–145.

Green, J. E., & Weaver, R. A. (1992). Who aspires to teach? A descriptive study of preservice teachers. *Contemporary Education, 63*(3), 234–238.

Greenleaf, C., Hull, G., & Reilly, B. (1994). Learning from our diverse students: Helping teachers rethink problematic teaching and learning situations. *Teaching and Teacher Education, 10*(5), 521–541.

Greenman, N. P., & Kimmel, E. B. (1995). The road to multicultural education: Potholes of resistance. *Journal of Teacher Education, 46*(5), 360–368.

Grottkau, B. J., & Nickolai-Mays, S. (1989). An empirical analysis of a multicultural education paradigm for preservice teachers. *Educational Research Quarterly, 13*(4), 27–33.

Groulx, J. G. (2001). Changing preservice teacher perceptions of minority schools. *Urban Education, 36*(1), 60–92.

Guyton, E., Saxton, R., & Wesche, M. (1996). Experiences of diverse students in teacher education. *Teaching and Teacher Education, 12*(6), 643–652.

Haberman, M. (1993). Predicting the success of urban teachers (The Milwaukee Trials). *Action in Teacher Education, 15*(3), 1–5.

Haberman, M., & Post, L. (1998). Teachers for multicultural schools: The power of selection. *Theory Into Practice, 37*(2), 96–104.

Hadaway, N. L., & Florez, V. (1987–1988). Diversity in the classroom: Are our teachers prepared? *Teacher Education & Practice, 4*(1), 25–30.

Hlebowitsh, P. S., & Tellez, K. (1993). Pre-service teachers and their students: Early views of race, gender, and class. *Journal of Education for Teaching, 17*(1), 41–52.

Johanessen, G. G., & Bustamante Lopez, I. (2002). Bilingual academic Spanish proficiency tests: Assessment of bilingual cross-cultural language and academic development teacher candidates. *Bilingual Research Journal, 23*(3), 563–574.

Johnson, D. M. (1987). Linguistics and applied linguistics curricula in graduate programs in bilingual education. *Hispania, 70*(4), 900–907.

Johnson, K. E. (1994). The emerging beliefs and instructional practices of preservice English as a second language teachers. *Teaching and Teacher Education, 10*(4), 439–452.

Katz, S. R. (2000). Promoting bilingualism in the era of Unz: Making sense of the gap between research, policy, and practice in teacher education. *Multicultural Education, 8*(1), 2–7.

LaFramboise, K. L., & Griffith, P. L. (1997). Using literature cases to examine diversity issues with preservice teachers. *Teaching and Teacher Education, 13*(4), 369–382.

Lawrence, S. M., & Bunche, T. (1996). Feeling and dealing: Teaching White students about racial privilege. *Teaching and Teacher Education, 12*(5), 531–543.

Lopez, I. (2002). Bilingual academic spanish proficiency tests: Assessment of bilingual cross-cultural language and acadmeic development teacher candidates. *Bilingual Research Journal, 23*(3), 563–574.

Lopez Estrada, V. (1999). Living and teaching along the U.S./Mexico border: Midwestern student intern's cultural adaptation experiences in Texas schools.

Luft, J. A., Bragg, J., & Peters, C. (1999). Learning to teach in a diverse setting: A case study of a multicultural science education enthusiast. *Science Teacher Education, 83*(5), 527–543.

Mahan, J. M. (1982). Community involvement components in culturally-oriented teacher preparation. *Education, 103*(2), 163–172.

Mahan, J. M. (1984). Major concerns of Anglo student teachers serving in Native American communities. *Journal of American Indian Education, 23*(3), 19–24.

Marshall, P. L. (1996). Multicultural teaching concerns: New dimensions in the area of teacher concerns research? *The Journal of Educational Research, 89*(6), 371–379.

Marshall, P. L. (1998). Toward developmental multicultural education: Case study of the issues exchange activity. *Journal of Teacher Education, 49*(1), 57–65.

Martin, O., & Williams-Dixon, R. (1994). Overcoming social distance barriers: Preservice teachers' perceptions of racial ethnic groups. *Journal of Instructional Psychology, 21*(1), 76–82.

Mason, T. C. (1999). Predictors of success in urban teaching: Analyzing two paradoxical cases. *Multicultural Education, 6*(3), 26–32.

McCall, A. L. (1995). Constructing conceptions of multicultural teaching: Preservice teachers' life experiences and teacher education. *Journal of Teacher Education, 46*(5), 340–350.

McCormick, T. E. (1990). Collaboration works! Preparing teachers for urban realities. *Contemporary Education, 61*(3), 129–134.

McDiarmid, G. W. (1992). What to do about difference? A study of multicultural education for teacher trainees in the Los Angeles Unified School District. *Journal of Teacher Education, 43*(2), 83–93.

McFalls, E. L., & Cobb-Roberts, D. (2001). Reducing resistance to diversity through cognitive dissonance instruction: Implications for teacher education. *Journal of Teacher Education, 52*(2), 164–172.

McIntyre, A. (1997). Constructing an image of a White teacher. *Teachers College Record, 98*(4), 653–681.

Morales, R. (2000). Effects of teacher preparation experiences and students' perceptions related to developmentally and culturally appropriate practices. *Action in Teacher Education, 22*(2), 67–75.

Narode, R., Rennie-Hill, L., & Peterson, K. D. (1994). Urban community study by preservice teachers. *Urban Education, 29*(1), 5–21.

Nathenson-Mejía, S., & Escamilla, K. (2003). Connecting with Latino children: Bridging cultural gaps with children's literature. *Bilingual Research Journal, 27*(1), 101–116.

National Center for Education Statistics (2002). *The Nation's Report Card Reading 2002.* Washington, DC: Institute of Education Sciences, U.S. Department of Education.

National Center for Education Statistics (2003a). *Results of the NAEP 2003 Trial Urban District Assessment* Washington, DC: Institute of Education Science, U.S. Department of Education.

National Center for Education Statistics (2003b). *The Condittion of Education 2003.* Washington, DC: Institute of Education Sciences, U.S. Department of Education.

Nel, J. (1992). The empowerment of minority students: Implications of Cummins' model for teacher education. *Action in Teacher Education, 14*(3), 38–45.

Noordhoff, K., & Kleinfeld, J. (1993). Preparing teachers for multicultural classrooms. *Teaching and Teacher Education , 9*(1), 27–39.

Obidah, J. E. (2000). Mediating boundaries of race, class, and professorial authority as a critical multiculturalist. *Teachers College Record, 102*(6), 1035–1060.

Olmedo, I. M. (1997). Challenging old assumptions: Preparing teachers for inner city schools. *Teaching and Teacher Education, 13*(3), 245–258.

Peterson, K. M., Cross, L. F., Johnson, E. J., & Howell, G. L. (2000). Diversity education for preservice teachers: Strategies and attitude outcomes. *Action in Teacher Education, 22*(2), 33–38.

Potthoff, D. E., Dinsmore, J., Eifler, K., Stirtz, G., Walsh, T., & Ziebarth, J. (2000). Preparing for democracy and diversity: The impact of a community-based field experience on preservice teachers' knowledge, skills, and attitudes. *Action in Teacher Education, 22*(1), 79–92.

Redican, K., Stewart, S. H., Johnson, L. E., & Frazee, A. M. (1994). Professional preparation in cultural awareness and sensitivity in health education: A national survey. *Journal of Health Education, 25*(4), 215–217.

Reed, D. F., & Simon, D. J. (1991). Preparing teachers for urban schools: Suggestions from historically Black institutions. *Action in Teacher Education, 13*(2), 30–35.

Richman, C. L., Bovelsky, S., Kroovand, N., Vacca, J., & West, T. (1997). Racism 102: The classroom. *Journal of Black Psychology, 23*(4), 378–387.

Riojas Clark, E., & Bustos Flores, B. (1997). Instructional Snapshots (IS) in Mexico: Pre-service bilingual teachers take pictures of classroom practices. *Bilingual Research Journal, 21*(2 & 3), 273–282.

Riojas Clark, E., & Bustos Flores, B. (2001). Who am I? The social construction of ethnic identity and self perceptions in Latino pre-service teachers. *The Urban Review, 33*(2), 69–86.

Rodriguez, A. J. (1998). Strategies for counterresistance: Toward sociotransformative constructivism and learning to teach science for diversity and for understanding. *Journal of Research in Science Teaching, 35*(6), 589–622.

Root, S., Rudawski, A., Taylor, M., & Rochon, R. (2003). Attrition of Hmong students in teacher education programs. *Bilingual Research Journal 27*(1), 137–148.

Ross, D. D., & Smith, W. (1992). Understanding preservice teachers' perspectives on diversity. *Journal of Teacher Education, 43*(2), 94–103.

Rushton, S. P. (2001). Cultural assimilation: A narrative case study of student-teaching in an inner-city school. *Teaching and Teacher Education, 17*, 147–160.

Sconzert, K., Iazzetto, D., & Purkey, S. (2000). Small-town college to big-city school: Preparing urban teachers from liberal arts colleges. *Teaching and Teacher Education, 16*(4), 465–490.

Seidl, B., & Friend, G. (2002). Leaving authority at the door: Equal-status community-based experiences and the preparation of teachers for diverse classrooms. *Teaching and Teacher Education, 18*, 421–433.

Sheets, R. H., & Chew, L. (2002). Absent from the research, present in our classrooms: Preparing culturally responsive Chinese American teachers. *Journal of Teacher Education, 53*(2), 127–141.

Shultz, E. L., Neyhart, K., & Reck, U. M. (1996). Swimming against the tide: A study of prospective teachers' attitudes regarding cultural diversity and urban teaching. *Western Journal of Black Studies, 20*(1), 1–8.

Sleeter, C. E. (1989). Doing multicultural education across grade levels and subject areas: A case study of Wisconsin. *Teaching and Teacher Education, 5*(3), 189–203.

Smith, R., Moallem, M., & Sherrill, D. (1997). How preservice teachers think about cultural diversity: A closer look at factors which influence their beliefs towards equality. *Educational Foundations, 11*(2), 41–61.

Smolkin, L. B., & Suina, J. H. (1999). Cross-cultural partnerships: Acknowledging the "equal other" in the rural/urban American Indian teacher education program. *Teaching & Teacher Education, 15*(5), 571–590.

Southerland, S. A., & Gess-Newsome, J. (1999). Preservice teachers' views of inclusive science teaching as shaped by images of teaching, learning, and knowing. *Science Education, 83*(2), 131–150.

Sparks, W. G., III, & Verner, M. E. (1995). Intervention strategies in multicultural education: A comparison of pre-service models. *Physical Educator, 52*(4), 170–186.

Stallings, J. A., Bossung, J., & Martin, A. (1990). Houston teaching academy: Partnership in developing teachers. *Teaching and Teacher Education, 6*(4), 355–365.

Su, Z. (1996). Why teach: Profiles and entry perspectives of minority students as becoming teachers. *Journal of Research and Development in Education, 29* (3), 117–133.

Su, Z. (1997). Teaching as a profession and as a career: Minority candidates' perspectives. *Teaching and Teacher Education, 13*(3), 325–340.

Taylor, O. L. (1972). *Black language: The research variable.* New York: Speech Communication Association (ERIC Document Reproduction service No. ED082 262).

Tellez, K. (1999). Mexican-American preservice teachers and the intransigency of the elementary school curriculum. *Teaching and Teacher Education, 15*(5), 555–570.

Terrill, M., & Mark, D. L. H. (2000). Preservice teachers' expectations for schools with children of color and second-language learners. *Journal of Teacher Education, 51*(2), 149–155.

Tiezzi, L. J., & Cross, B. E. (1997). Utilizing research on prospective teachers' beliefs to inform urban field experiences. *Urban Review, 29*(2), 113–125.

Waldschmidt, E. D. (2002). Bilingual interns' barriers to becoming teachers: At what cost do we diversify the teaching force? *Bilingual Research Journal, 26*(3), 537–561.

Walker de Felix, J., & Cavazos Pena, S. (1992). Return home: The effects of study in Mexico on bilingual teachers. *Hispania, 75*(3), 743–750.

Wenglinsky, H. (2000). *How teaching matters: Bringing the classroom back into discussions of teacher quality.* Princeton, NJ: Educational Testing Service.

Wiggins, R. A., & Follo, E. J. (1999). Development of knowledge, attitudes, and commitment to teach diverse student populations. *Journal of Teacher Education, 50*(2), 94–105.

Xu, H. (2000). Preservice teachers integrate understandings of diversity into literacy instruction: an adaptation of the abc's model. *Journal of Teacher Education, 51*(2), 135–142.

OTHER REFERENCES

Au, K. (1980). Participation structures in a reading lesson with Hawaiian children: Analysis of a culturally appropriate instructional event. *Anthropology and Education Quarterly, 11*(2), 91–115.

Banks, J. A. (1984). *Teaching strategies for ethnic studies* (3rd. ed.). Boston: Allyn & Bacon.

Banks, J. A. (2003). Multicultural education: Characteristics and goals. In J. A. Banks & C. A. Banks (Eds.), *Multicultural education: Issues & perspectives* (pp. 3–30). New York: Wiley.

Borko, H., & Putnam, R. (1996). Learning to teach. In D. Berliner & R. Calfee (Eds.), *Handbook of research on educational psychology* (pp. 673–699). New York: Macmillan.

Cochran-Smith, M., Davis, D., & Fries, M. K. (2003). Multicultural teacher education: Research, practice and policy. In J. A. Banks & C. M. Banks (Eds.), *Handbook of research on multicultural education.* San Francisco: Jossey-Bass.

Darling-Hammond, L. (2000). Teacher quality and student achievement: A review of state policy evidence. *Education Policy Analysis Archives, 8*(1).

Darling-Hammond, L., & Sclan, E. (1996). Who teaches and why. In J. Sikula (Ed.), *Handbook of research on teacher education* (pp. 67–101). New York: Simon & Schuster Macmillan.

Educational Research Service. (1995). *Demographic factors in American education.* Arlington: VA: Educational Research Service.

Foster, M. (1997). *Black teachers on teaching.* New York: New Press.

Gay, G. (1993). Building cultural bridges: A bold proposal for teacher education. *Education and Urban Socity, 25*(3), 285–299.

Gay, G. (2000). *Culturally responsive teaching: Theory, research and practice.* New York: Teachers College Press.

Gollnick, D. (1992). Multicultural education: Policies and practices in teacher education. In C. Grant (Ed.), *Research and multicultural education: From the margins to the mainstream* (pp. 218–239). London: Falmer Press.

Goodwin, A. (2000). Teachers as (multi)cultural agents in schools. In R. Carter (Ed.), *Addressing cultural issues in organizations: Beyond the corporate context* (pp. 104–114). Thousand Oaks, CA: Sage.

Grant, C., & Secada, W. (1990). Preparing teachers for diversity. In W. R. Houston, M. Haberman, & J. Sikula (Eds.), *Handbook of research on teacher education* (pp. 403–422). New York: Macmillan.

Haberman, M. (1996). Selecting and preparing culturally competent teachers for urban schools. In J. Sikula, T. Buttery, & E. Guyton (Eds.), *Handbook of research on teacher education* (2nd ed., pp. 747–760). New York: Macmillan.

Helms, J. E. (Ed.). (1990). *Black and White racial identity: Theory, research and practices.* Westport, CT: Greenwood Press.

Ingersoll, R. (2003). *Is there really a teacher shortage? A report co-sponsored by the Center for the Study of Teaching and Policy and the Center for Policy Research in Education.* Seattle, WA: Center for the Study of Teaching and Policy, University of Washington.

Irvine, J. J. (Ed.). (1997). *Critical knowledge for diverse teachers and learners.* Washington, DC: American Association of Colleges for Teacher Education.

Irvine, J. J. (1990). *Black students and school failure.* New York: Greenwood Press.

Irvine, J. J. (2001, March 2). *Caring, competent teachers in complex classrooms. The 41st Charles W. Hunt Memorial Lecture.* Paper presented at the AACTE 53rd Annual Meeting, Dallas.

Irvine, J. J., & Armento, B. J. (2001). *Culturally responsive teaching.* New York: McGraw-Hill.

Ladson-Billings, G. (1994). *The dream keepers: Successful teachers of African American children.* San Francisco: Jossey-Bass.

Ladson-Billings, G. (1995a). Multicultural teacher education: Research, practice, and policy. In J. A. Banks & C. A. Banks (Eds.), *Handbook of research on multicultural education* (pp. 747–761). New York, NY: Macmillan.

Ladson-Billings, G. (1995b). Toward a theory of culturally relevant pedagogy. *American Educational Research Journal, 32*(3), 465–491.

Ladson-Billings, G. (1999). Preparing teachers for diverse student populations: A critical race theory perspective. In A. Iran-Nejad & D. Pearson (Eds.), *Review of research in education* (Vol. 24, pp. 211–248). Washington, DC: American Educational Research Association.

Lee, C. D. (1995). Signifying as a scaffold for literary interpretation. *Journal of Black Psychology, 21*(4), 357–381.

Levine, M., & Trachtman, R. (Eds.). (1997). *Making professional development schools work: Politics, practice, and policy.* New York: Teachers College Press.

Lipka, J. (1991). Toward a culturally based pedagogy: A case study of one Yup'ik Eskimo teacher. *Anthropology and Education Quarterly, 22,* 203–223.

McCarty, T. (1993). Language, literacy and the image of the child in American Indian classrooms. *Language Arts, 70*(3), 182–192.

Moll, L. C. (1986). Writing as communication: Creating strategic learning environments for students. *Theory into Practice, 25*(2), 103–108.

National Education Goals Panel. (1994). *Data volume for the National Education Goals Report: Volume 1—National data.* Washington, DC: U.S. Government Printing Office.

National Research Council. (2000). *How people learn.* Washington, DC: National Academy Press.

National Research Council. (2001). *Scientific research in education.* Washington, DC: National Academy Press.

Sanders, W. (1998). Value-added assessment. *The School Administrator*, 24–27.

Sanders, W., & Horn, S. (1998). Research findings from the Tennessee Value-Added Assessment System (TVAAS) database: Implications for educational evaluation and research. *Journal of Personnel Evaluation in Education, 12*(3), 247–256.

Sleeter, C. (2001a). Epistemological diversity in research on preservice teacher preparation for historically underserved children. In W. Secada (Ed.), *Review of research in education* (Vol. 25, pp. 209–250). Washington, DC: American Educational Research Association.

Sleeter, C. (2001b). Preparing teachers for culturally diverse schools: The overwhelming presence of Whiteness. *Journal of Teacher Education, 52*(2), 94–106.

U.S. Department of Commerce. (1996). *Current population reports: Population projections of the United States by age, sex, race and Hispanic origin, 1995–2050.* Washington, DC.

Vavrus, M. (2002). *Transforming the multicultural education of teachers: Theory, research and practice.* New York: Teachers College Press.

Villegas, A. M. (1991). *Culturally responsive pedagogy for the 1990's and beyond.* Princeton, NJ: Educational Testing Service.

Villegas, A. M., & Lucas, T. (2002). *Educating culturally responsive teachers: A coherent approach.* Albany, NY: SUNY Press.

Weiner, L. (1993). *Preparing teachers for urban schools, lessons from 30 years of school reform.* New York, NY: Teachers College Press.

Weiner, L. (2000). Research in the 90s: Implications for urban teacher preparation. *Review of Educational Research, 70*(3), 369–406.

Wideen, M., Mayer-Smith, J., & Moon, B. (1998). A critical analysis of the research on learning to teach: Making the case for an ecological perspective on inquiry. *Review of Educational Research, 68*(2), 130–178.

Wilson, S. M., Floden, R. E., & Ferrini-Mundy, J. (2001). *Teacher preparation research: Current knowledge, gaps, and recommendations.* Seattle: University of Washington, Center for the Study of Teaching and Policy.

Zeichner, K. M., & Hoeft, K. (1996). Teacher socialization for cultural diversity. In J. Sikula, T. J. Buttery, & E. Guyton (Eds.), *Handbook of research on teacher education* (2nd ed., pp. 525–547). New York: Macmillan.

9

Research on Preparing General Education Teachers to Work With Students With Disabilities

Marleen C. Pugach
University of Wisconsin-Milwaukee

It is no longer remarkable or unusual, as it was 30 years ago, to talk about the importance of preparing all teachers to work with students with disabilities. Although in 1980 only 15 states required general education teachers to complete coursework on educating students with disabilities (Smith & Shindler, 1980), today teacher education programs in 45 states and the District of Columbia have such requirements (National Association of State Directors of Teacher Education and Certification, 2004). Either through dedicated special education coursework or content integrated into other preservice coursework, the majority of today's new teachers are expected to know something about working with students with disabilities.

This change in state requirements stems from the normative practice, anchored by the legislative imperative of the Individual with Disabilities Education Act (IDEA), which places the majority of students with disabilities in general educational settings for over 40% of their school day (U.S. Department of Education, 2002). A report from the Study of Personnel Needs in Special Education (SPeNSE, 2000) indicates that 95% of all general education teachers currently teach students with disabilities or have done so in the past, with an average case load of 3.5 students with disabilities. Although the special education community remains divided over how much inclusive education is appropriate for students with disabilities, the need to prepare all teachers to create classrooms that embrace students with disabilities and teach them well is no longer contested.

SCOPE AND FRAMEWORK

The scope of this chapter is to review the literature on what we know about preparing general education teachers to work with students with disabilities, drawing principally on research conducted since 1990. This period has been marked by widespread collaboration between special and general education, not only at the P–12 level but also in higher education. Underlying this trend is the substantial increase in the practice of inclusive education, supported by the 1997 amendments to IDEA, which underscored the general education curriculum as the appropriate curriculum for most students with disabilities. No longer are we simply talking about moving students with disabilities into general education classrooms under the practice of mainstreaming, as was the case starting in the mid-1970s. Instead, today the expectation is that most students with disabilities will attend general classrooms as much as is appropriate and that while they are there, they will learn the general education curriculum. Although this goal was implied under mainstreaming, in the 1990s it represented a legislative mandate that unequivocally favored the general education setting and emphasized the role of the general education teacher in achieving this goal, an emphasis that was retained in the reauthorization of IDEA in 2004.

In both policy and practice, the 1990s represented an era of vibrant reform in teacher education. The challenge of preparing general education teachers to work with students with disabilities is situated within this national context of teacher education reform. An unmistakable feature of this continuing reform activity is that national standards promulgated to improve teacher education now generally include the expectation that all teachers should be prepared for working with students with disabilities, for new teachers (e.g., National Council for Accreditation of Teacher Education [NCATE], 2000; Interstate New Teacher Assessment and Support Consortium [INTASC], 1992, 2001) and veterans alike (National Board for Professional Teaching Standards [NBPTS], 2004). Preparing teachers to work with this population is no longer a concern solely of the special education community, isolated from considerations that face all teacher educators. This national reform context is an important consideration in how we think about how all teachers are prepared as regards special education.

For this chapter, the principal source of studies was a hand search of the most relevant national, peer-reviewed journals. These included: *Action in Teacher Education, Education and Training in Mental Retardation and Developmental Disabilities, The Educational Forum, Elementary School Journal, Exceptional Children, Journal of Learning Disabilities, Journal of Special Education, Journal of Teacher Education, Learning Disability Quarterly, Multiple Voices, Remedial and Special Education, Teacher Education and Special Education, The Teacher Educator, Teacher Education Quarterly* and *Teaching and Teacher Education*. As much as possible this review has been limited to available empirical studies that meet the criteria established by the American Educational Research Association (AERA) Panel on Research and Teacher Education. Studies using survey methodology were included if they met a 60% return rate criterion.

Studies on the preservice preparation of general education teachers to work with students with disabilities are sparse. Table 9.1 summarizes 17 empirical studies on the preservice preparation of general education teachers. These studies primarily use survey techniques or qualitative research methods. Many represent teacher educator self-studies of preservice courses or programs at the institutions in which they taught.

A small number of references relating to program descriptions or to potentially promising programs of research have been included in this analysis to provide a view of current trends in the field. In the absence of research on accountability processes, the chapter also includes a review of national standards documents as they relate to the preparation of general education teachers to work with students with disabilities. Finally, studies related to practicing teachers have been included as occasional points of reference, specifically in the section on teacher attitudes and in providing direction for new research.

The scope of this chapter is limited to the preparation of general education teachers. It does not address literature on the preservice preparation of special education teachers. Always hovering over the goal of greater inclusion of students with disabilities and its implications for the work of general classroom teachers, however, is the struggle to redefine the responsibilities and contributions of special education teachers themselves. The level at which we expect general education teachers to perform—and the level of their preservice preparation in anticipation of these responsibilities—has direct implications for the roles for which new special education teachers are prepared. Raising the bar so that general education preservice teachers possess an adequate level of knowledge and skill to educate students with disabilities in their classrooms also necessitates a redefinition of what preservice special education teachers are prepared to do.

New state certification requirements mandated in relationship to changes in legislation and in educational practice, as well as changes in national teacher education standards, indicate that teacher education has been responsive to including special education in general preservice programming and to sharing responsibility for this aspect of the curriculum. We can think of this new relationship between special and general teacher education in two phases. In the first, in the late 1970s, many schools, departments, and colleges of education (SCDEs) adopted a "disability of the week" approach, often requiring a traditional introductory course in special education or a course in mainstreaming, both focused on traditional categories of disability (Jones & Messenheimer-Young, 1989).

Today we are in a second phase that emphasizes collaboration and classroom accommodations. Jones and Messenheimer-Young (1989) also documented the shift toward emphasizing curriculum modifications and adaptations within designated courses on mainstreaming. Today there is a growing trend for SCDEs to create collaborative relationships across preservice faculty in general and special teacher education, who typically share some level of responsibility for preparing general education teachers to work with students with disabilities (Voltz, 2003). These collaborations range along a continuum and may include fully integrated programs with no dedicated coursework in special education, a combination of dedicated special education coursework and integrated content, or the continuation of a single course requirement in special education. Both general and special education faculty are likely to have a say in the content of these courses and their coordination with the entire program. Some collaborative programs result in dual certification in general and special education; others do not. Blanton, Griffin, Winn, and Pugach (1997) described the conceptual frameworks and structures of 10 early collaborative programs along with a cross-site analysis. Characteristics of collaborative programs in early childhood education have been described by Miller and Stayton (1998), Dunne (2002) and LaMontagne et al. (2002). Descriptions of individual collaborative programs have appeared with regularity in a special feature of the journal *Teacher Education and Special Education* (see Rosenberg, 1999), which represents the Teacher Education Division of the International Council for Exceptional Children. These descriptions indicate that in such programs preservice students are taught how to work collaboratively with professional peers, to be careful in applying labels and making assumptions about disability for minority children, and to make accommodations and modifications for students with disabilities as they prepare and implement lesson plans.

As structures to prepare all teachers to learn to work with students with disabilities, these collaborative preservice activities are becoming more recognizable at the national level and are beginning to represent well-practiced features of the teacher education curriculum. Collectively we can think of them as a familiar, relatively stable, and enduring response to the goal of preparing general education teachers to work with students with disabilities. These current practices stand in contrast to the complete separation of special and general preservice programs and the absence of discussion of students with disabilities that characterized general teacher education prior to the mid-1970s. Prospective teachers frequently demand this preparation if it is not already a part of their preparation program (Van Zandt, 1998).

Outcomes of this high level of teacher education activity to prepare general education teachers to work with students with disabilities, however, are not as well documented. As a backdrop, this chapter begins with a brief description of the earliest systematic effort to alter the fundamental nature of teacher education as it relates to preparing teachers to work with students with disabilities, namely, the Deans' Grants projects. This is followed by a review of available research on current efforts to achieve this goal. Next, a comparison of national standards for the preparation of teachers to work with students with disabilities is presented. The chapter concludes with a proposal for a new conceptual framework to guide future research at the preservice level.

INITIAL EFFORTS TO PREPARE GENERAL EDUCATION TEACHERS—THE DEANS' GRANT PROJECTS

Preparing general education teachers to work with students with disabilities was acknowledged as a critical need from the outset of modern special education practice. In 1975, when the Education of All Handicapped Children Act (Public Law 94-142) was first enacted, the Bureau of Education for the Handicapped[1] launched a federal grant competition to support the preservice preparation of general education teachers (Kleinhammer-Trammill, 2003). Entitled *The Deans' Grant Projects*, the underlying concept was to grant deans of schools, colleges, and departments of education modest funding (averaging $40,000 per year) to support curricular reform in teacher education to prepare all new teachers to work with students with disabilities (Grosenick & Reynolds, 1978; National Support Systems Project, 1980). In 1975, 39 projects were supported (Kleinhammer-Trammill). From 1975 to 1980, some 205 Deans' Grants were awarded across 45 different states, virtually assuring a national effort. The institutions

---

[1] The Bureau was the predecessor of the U.S. Department of Education Office of Special Education and Rehabilitative Services.

prepared approximately 38% of all new teachers nationwide (National Support Systems Project, 1980). To support their work and promote national dialogue and dissemination, Deans' Grants staff participated in six regional networks and a national network, The National Support Systems Project (Kleinhammer-Trammill & Fiore, 2003).

In 1978, *The Journal of Teacher Education* devoted a special issue to the preparation of general education teachers in special education. Authors included several deans whose institutions were engaged in these efforts (e.g., Corrigan, 1978; Haisley & Gilberts, 1978), as well as a guest editorial by Senator Edward M. Kennedy (1978). On a practical level, these projects underscored the new reality of teachers' lives under mainstreaming, namely, that students with disabilities would increasingly be educated in general education classrooms.

The explicit goal of these projects was to reform teacher education practice (Behrens & Grosenick, 1978), with an emphasis on faculty and curriculum development. Ten clusters of capabilities were identified as essential for teachers to be successful with students with disabilities. These clusters read more like present-day standards for teacher education than the decontextualized competencies that typically drove teacher education in the 1970s (Urban, 1990). They were:

- *Curriculum*—A broad orientation to curriculum and how to modify it
- *Basic skills*—Preparation to teach literacy and basic life skills
- *Consultation*—Using consultation to study children and design alternative programs
- *Parent–School Relationships*—Understanding and communicating with families, with emphasis on minority group families
- *Classroom management*—Maintaining a favorable climate in the classroom
- *Individualized teaching*—Diagnostic procedures and systematic approaches in individualized instruction
- *Exceptional conditions*—Basic knowledge of exceptional conditions and an orientation to working collaboratively with special education teachers
- *Referral and observation*—Procedures and obligations for using specialized resources
- *Student–student relationships*—Helping students understand and accept classmates with disabilities
- *Legal requirements and professional values*—Training in due process and ethical issues (National Support Systems Project, 1980).

At the national level the Deans' Grant Projects represented an external perspective on the part of special education. They operated on the principle that serious collaboration among teacher educators in special and general education was essential and mandated such partnerships. Through the Deans' Grants, teacher educators at the national and local levels acknowledged that curricular reform in teacher education was an institution-wide responsibility. Although notions of institutional responsibility and standards-based reform are common parlance in teacher education today, in 1975 these concepts were novel.

The last Deans' Grants were funded in 1982 (Kleinhammer-Trammill, 2003). Afterwards applicants could apply for grants related to the preparation of general educators, but only as an invitational priority under competitions such as Special Projects or Projects of National Significance rather than as an absolute priority (Kleinhammer-Tramill, Peters, & Fiore, 2001). This decision represented a shift in policy on the part of the national special education community, at least as represented by the Personnel

Preparation Division of the Office of Special Education Programs (Kleinhammer-Tramill, 2003). This less aggressive funding status for the preparation of general education teachers effectively ended the federally mandated national dialogue about teacher education curriculum reform related to special education as well as the formal national and regional networks across institutions of higher education.

The Deans' Grants raised a fundamental question about where responsibility lies for preparing general education teachers to work with students with disabilities (Pugach, 2001). In so doing, they were ahead of their time in foreshadowing essential features of current teacher education reform, for example, faculty development across departments, joint ownership of reform efforts, and active institutional responsibility for the teacher education curriculum. But they existed in a vacuum of reform in general teacher education (Pugach, 2001), ending just as *A Nation at Risk* (National Commission on Excellence in Education, 1983) and later the first report of The Holmes Group, *Tomorrow's Teachers* (1986), focused new, national attention on teacher preparation.

As Kleinhammer-Trammill notes (2003), preservice projects continued to be funded with federal special education dollars after 1982, but these subsequent projects supported a smaller percentage of programs that prepare general education teachers nationwide. Although 111 Dean's Grants projects were funded on average in each of the last 5 years of their existence, from 1997 to 2001 only 15 projects were funded each year that addressed the preparation of general education teachers, including preservice and in-service education (Kleinhammer-Trammill, 2003). Today's funding most often go to programs preparing special education teachers alone. However, with national reform efforts in teacher education firmly established, teacher educators in special and general education continue to be engaged in the types of dialogue and activity foreshadowed by the Dean's Grants. The Deans' Grants appear to have seeded the fertile ground of reform that was to come, preparing a generation of special and general teacher educators to participate actively, often in leadership roles, once the reform context had been firmly established (Pugach, 2001).

Although the Deans' Grant Projects were not designed to support research on the preparation of general education teachers, they did provide an opportunity for such research to take place. But little occurred. In the next section, we review the research evidence that exists on preparing general education teachers to work with students with disabilities.

THE RESEARCH EVIDENCE

In almost every instance the research on the preparation of general education teachers to work with students with disabilities has been conducted by special education faculty, sometimes with allies from general teacher education. These studies fall into four categories: (a) research on attitudes and beliefs about inclusive education and working with students with disabilities, (b) research on program structures and pedagogies in teacher education, (c) research on the effects of preservice programs, and (d) research on the relationship between diversity and disability.

Research on Teacher Attitudes and Beliefs

Historically special educators have been deeply interested in the attitudes and beliefs of general education teachers about the integration of students with disabilities.

Studies on this topic, chiefly surveys, have appeared regularly over several decades in the special education literature (see, e.g., Scruggs & Mastropieri, 1996). This line of research has documented the attitudes and beliefs of practicing teachers as a global disposition in favor of or against the integration of students with disabilities. The early work often focused on attitudes and beliefs of general education teachers who were not actually teaching students with disabilities.

Later studies, however, shifted to studying the experiences of practicing teachers working in inclusive environments who had direct, sustained contact with students with disabilities (Giangreco, Dennis, Cloninger, Edelman, & Schattman, 1993; Minke, Bear, Deemer, & Griffin, 1996; McLeskey, Waldron, So, Swanson, & Loveland, 2001; Waldron, McLeskey, & Pacciano, 1999). These studies demonstrated that the perspectives and attitudes of teachers involved in inclusive education are more positive than those with no such professional experience. Rather than merely speculating about problems a teacher might encounter working in an inclusive classroom (McLeskey et al., 2001), or taking a stark position in favor or against inclusion, practicing teachers who participate in inclusive classrooms are likely to express more positive attitudes. They also express more practical concerns about working with students with disabilities based on their experience.

Giangreco et al. (1993) used interviews and a brief survey to determine the attitudes of 19 general education teachers who worked with students with severe disabilities. Seventeen had what the authors called a "transformative" experience and held positive attitudes toward their students. Their transformations "were gradual and progressive rather than discrete and abrupt" (p. 365). These teachers spoke about the importance of building supportive relationships with special education teachers and paraprofessionals, as well as being able to question colleagues' decisions and still work as a team. Minke et al. (1996) surveyed almost 500 teachers to compare attitudes of general classroom teachers in traditional settings with those of general and special education teachers who taught students with mild disabilities in inclusive settings. Based on a response rate of 65%, teachers who worked in inclusive settings reported greater feelings of efficacy. They identified developing sound working relationships among co-teachers as important and were particularly concerned about the ratio of students with and without disabilities in a single classroom. In a survey of 174 teachers who were primarily in general education, an analysis based on a response rate of 75% documented teachers' concerns about the need for supports for the small number of students with extreme behavior needs (McLeskey et al., 2001). Treder, Morse, and Ferron (2000) studied the attitudes of 106 general education teachers who had earned membership in the Florida League of Teachers compared with 150 teachers who did not belong to the honorary group. Using a survey that measured attitudes regarding acceptable student behavior, and based on a response rate of 60%, they found that the League teachers identified fewer negative student behaviors as unacceptable—indicating a higher level of tolerance for difference.

Finally, it also appears that teachers' beliefs about their ability to work with students with disabilities can be influenced by their views about the quality of their preservice preparation. Brownell and Pajares (1999) conducted a teacher efficacy study based on a survey of 200 second-grade teachers in a school district where students with disabilities typically were integrated at that grade level. Sixty-four percent of these teachers responded to a survey designed specifically for general education teachers working with students with disabilities. As a general result they found that high levels of teacher efficacy were related to perceived success in working with the targeted population. In addition, teachers who felt their preservice education had prepared them to work with students with disabilities showed higher levels of efficacy.

Although authors of the earlier studies tended to be wary of inclusion, the latter studies are more supportive, with several described as having been designed to offer a countervailing view of teachers' attitudes and beliefs when compared to prior research (e.g., McLeskey et al., 2001; Treder et al., 2000). In the studies, teachers seemed more concerned with how to make inclusion happen, how to support general education teachers as they participate in inclusive settings, how to collaborate with special education team teaching partners, and how best to meet the needs of students. This shift to studying the attitudes of teachers in inclusive classroom environments has important implications for the preparation of preservice teachers. First, not only have most of today's preservice candidates probably attended P–12 schools with students who have disabilities, but also today many are likely to experience some degree of inclusive teaching during their field placements—whether by design or chance (Ford, Pugach, & Otis-Wilborn, 2001). These experiences can provide them a basis to inquire into practical questions regarding inclusion; they may be more likely to come to their professional programs with the expectation that they will be responsible for meeting the needs of students with disabilities and require the knowledge and skills to do so.

For example, Hutchinson and Martin (1999a) reported on a qualitative analysis of preservice candidates' concerns about working with students with disabilities during a 4-month practicum and related field-based *Critical Issues* course at Queen's University in Ontario, Canada. The data source for these concerns were dilemma cases, defined by the author as cases without a right or wrong response, or cases where one response might cause another problem to emerge. Five preservice students assigned to one K–8 school raised these concerns:

- Is providing appropriate individual attention to one child, with successful results, inequitable?
- Is it appropriate to remove a disruptive student to an isolated location if doing so prevents the student from working on his relationship with the teacher?
- How do you overcome the influence of negative beliefs others have about students, even if the students admittedly are very challenging?
- How do you continue to work with a very challenging student in a classroom of 30-plus students, especially when the student is not likable?

The issues define domains of knowledge and skills candidates believed they would need to meet their responsibilities. In responding to these cases, peers encouraged colleagues not to write students off and to re-examine their commitments to the most challenging students.

In a related study, Taylor and Sobel (2001) examined beliefs about disability and equity among 129 preservice teachers entering a graduate program at the University of Colorado at Denver. These data anchored a longitudinal study of teacher beliefs for this cohort of students. Responding to a survey and open-ended questions, candidates indicated strong beliefs that it was their job to provide equitable education to all children and to hold high expectations for achievement across special education and racial and ethnic diversity. However, they also believed that as beginning teacher education students, they did not yet know how to adapt instruction appropriately or create classrooms that promoted learning across learning styles and abilities. These results suggest that in addition to the positive dispositions they may hold about working with a wide range of students, entering teacher education students readily acknowledge the specific knowledge and skills they believe they will need to be successful with students who have different abilities and different racial and ethnic backgrounds.

Cook (2002) surveyed 181 undergraduate preservice students in general education on attitudes toward inclusion according to various categories of disability. Students were enrolled in four required seminars in which issues related to special education were integrated; only one instructor had special education experience, and none of the others received preparation to carry out their special education responsibilities. No specific materials were identified and no procedures were in place to ensure that special education topics were addressed. Based on a return rate of 98%, students perceived their ability to teach students with learning disabilities as significantly higher than for other disability categories. Asked to gauge their own strengths and weaknesses, these prospective teachers often questioned whether their preservice program had prepared them adequately for inclusive teaching. Class standing did not affect their comments.

In combination with the work on attitudes and beliefs of practicing general education teachers, the modest body of research on the attitudes of preservice general education teachers signals a shift in focus about what is important to study. The problem of teacher attitudes and beliefs about inclusion has been reframed away from documenting the global disposition to be in favor or against inclusion. Research on attitudes seems to have shifted to what it is preservice teachers need to know and be able to do to provide successful learning environments for their students and the specific dispositions they will need to demonstrate to carry out these responsibilities. This trend appears to have freed research from the skepticism that may have led to the longstanding interest in studying attitudes in the first place. Further, these recent studies seem to be based on the assumption that the disposition to be responsible for students with disabilities is in place. However, when preservice programs do not adequately provide the requisite knowledge and skills, the attitudes of intending teachers may be likely to suffer.

Evidence From Research on Pedagogical Practices and Program Structures in Teacher Education

Given the near universal mandate to prepare all teachers to work with students with disabilities, along with attitude research that is more concerned with what candidates know and can do, what do we actually know from research on specific practices within teacher education programs? This section focuses on a modest body of research on studies of various pedagogies and structures used in preservice programs to prepare general educators. Studies that use attitude as a dependent measure are included here when they represent interventions in teacher education pedagogy and structure.

Reconfiguring Coursework in Conjunction With Student Teaching.   Three studies looked at configurations of coursework offered in conjunction with internships or student teaching. Two involved students assigned to Professional Development School (PDS) sites.

A study designed to consider how novice teachers develop an understanding of and ability to respond to the needs of academically diverse learners was conducted by Tomlinson et al. (1997). Seventy preservice general education students across six universities participated in a six-hour workshop preceding a one-semester student teaching experience; half of the participants also received the support of a curriculum coach (an experienced teacher who provided support at least weekly during the semester). The workshop focused on how to adapt and modify content, process and products for a broad range of learners. Data were collected via interviews and observations.

The authors found no difference between the workshop-only and workshop-plus-coach groups. They reasoned that student teachers were already so overwhelmed with advice that it may have been difficult for them to integrate yet another source of support into their lives. Both groups articulated their responsibility for differentiating instruction and accepted it as part of their work. Finally, the data suggested that the pull of the normative school culture favored standardization of instruction and that novices would need direct, explicit support to develop the skills and dispositions to practice differentiated instruction.

Rademacher, Wilhelm, Hildreth, Bridges, and Cowart (1998) considered the question of how different special education course structures affect general education student teachers' attitudes toward inclusion. They administered a pre-post survey with two open-ended questions to 78 student teachers who were assigned to three groups: (a) 35 participated in a 1-hour special education course prior to conventional student teaching that included observing a student with disabilities in a general education classroom and interviewing special and general education teachers; (b) 20 were assigned to one-semester, full-day student teaching experience in a professional development school (PDS) preceded by a 4-week professional development institute that was co-taught by faculty in general and special education, and a weekly seminar during student teaching; and (c) 23 participated in a two-semester student teaching program at a PDS with half-days in the classroom the first semester and full days the second semester and coursework on site, including a one-credit course in special education. All groups understood student characteristics better in the posttest; the two PDS groups better understood the need for students with disabilities to lead economically independent lives and the importance of general education teachers' making modifications for students with disabilities. Students in the university course demonstrated a significant decrease in positive attitude for the belief that every child, regardless of disability, should have the opportunity to participate in a general education classroom, whereas the two-semester PDS students showed a significant gain.

Levin, Hibbard, and Rock (2002) investigated the effects of problem-based learning (PBL) on 44 preservice students completing a 10-hour per week internship in a PDS. PBL activities that focused on working with students with disabilities constituted the only special education-related instruction in the program. In a weekly seminar the problem posed was whether to accept a position teaching in an inclusive classroom. PBL activities included studying specific categories of disability, interviewing professionals in the school, observing inclusive classrooms, and visiting agencies supporting the transition of students with disabilities into work settings. These activities took place individually, in pairs and in small groups. Data sources included pre- and postreaction papers to the problem and a survey on beliefs about inclusion.

Prior to the intervention 19 students said that they would teach in the inclusion classroom, 15 would not and 10 were undecided. Following PBL activities, 32 stated they would accept the position, 11 would not, and 1 student was undecided. No student changed from affirmative to negative; 7 students changed from negative to affirmative; half cited lack of knowledge and teaching experience as reasons for declining. Attitudes toward inclusive education were more positive after the PBL activities. Reaction papers were also analyzed for perceptions of which PBL activities were valued most. Responses included having many opportunities to conduct research on specific disability categories, observing in inclusive classrooms and identifying specific instructional strategies, adaptations, and modifications.

Reconfiguring Individual Courses.   In a quasi-experimental study, Nowacek and Blanton (1996) investigated the effects of a collaboratively taught methods course on preservice students' attitudes and knowledge of learning characteristics. Methods included gathering responses to a videotaped vignette of a student with disabilities. Senior students were enrolled in a 10-week, generic methods course prior to an internship. Seventeen elementary education majors took the course with 10 special education majors; the control group consisted of 12 elementary education majors who took the course alone. The experimental course was co-taught by general and special education faculty.

No significant differences on the attitude scale were obtained. Analysis of concept maps indicated that the experimental group shifted from little to greater emphasis on lesson plans and instructional processes, whereas the control group shifted from little to greater emphasis on classroom management and instructional materials. Asked to name strengths and weaknesses of the student in the videotape, 70% of both groups identified weaknesses; the only strengths were academic readiness and reading skills. The authors had hoped that students would demonstrate greater variety in their discussion of students' academic strengths. They interpreted these weak results in light of the difficulty of creating and implementing collaborative teaching, arguing that careful attention must be paid to faculty involvement in such planning, the culture of the academy, and how the role of special education is defined.

Marlowe and Maycock (2001) deliberately altered the preservice curriculum in a required course, *Introduction to Teaching*, to determine the effects of using literature about the lives of individuals with disabilities on the attitudes of preservice students. During the 6-week course on disabilities, students were randomly assigned to use as primary texts either trade books containing vivid stories about individuals with disabilities or traditional textbooks.

The students who used the books containing vivid stories showed more positive attitudes toward students with disabilities. In a prior study using random assignment of intact groups of preservice students in special education, similar results were obtained (Marlowe, Maycock, Palmer, & Morrison, 1997).

Cases.   Interest in case study pedagogy related to special education is growing. More than three fourths of 257 members of the Teacher Education Division of the Council for Exceptional Children surveyed by Elksnin (1998) used case studies in their instruction of preservice students, and they were overwhelmingly positive about the effectiveness of this method. Based on a response rate of 56%, 78% reported employing cases in their work, and of those, 90% were positive about using cases effectively in their teaching.[2] This study did not specify the courses in which cases were used; however, cases appear to be used often in special education courses required for general education teachers. Similarly, McNaughton, Hall, and Maccini's (2001) interviews

---

[2]Although the response rate for this survey was below the 60% criterion, it provided a viable picture of the trend toward the use of cases in pre-service programming.

with 15 special education faculty members indicated that the primary benefit of using cases was to assist students in solving practical teaching problems. A secondary benefit was to foster students' consideration of multiple perspectives, whereas a third was to promote reflective thinking.

The teacher education program reported by Hutchinson and Martin (1999b), which immersed preservice students in the field at the start of teacher preparation, elevating the role of experience in pedagogical learning, also used cases as a primary pedagogical strategy (see also Hutchinson & Martin, 1999a; Munby & Hutchinson, 1998). Hutchinson and Martin applied the concept of communities of practice, typically used with practicing teachers, as a structure for this 1 year, graduate-level program, with the expectation that preservice candidates "are learning through action, sharing their expertise and socially constructing knowledge formally and informally" (Hutchinson & Martin, 1999b, p. 236). During their initial 4-month practicum, students met 1 hour per day; concurrently they took two university courses, one including substantial coverage of issues related to teaching students with disabilities. As a central activity for this course, students responded to and wrote cases.

The authors defined *dilemma cases* as those in which a solution either caused another problem, or the number of solutions made it difficult to choose one. *Vignettes* were described as cases that were "memorable or critical incidents free of paradox" (Hutchinson & Martin, 1999b, p. 240). Preservice candidates who were successful writing cases that represented real dilemmas of practice almost universally presented inclusive and intense adaptations for their students. Students who wrote vignettes as opposed to dilemma cases presented what the authors identified as adaptations that only scratched the surface, for example, describing a personal reaction to a student who required adaptations. Therefore, understanding what it meant to write a specific type of case was instrumental in how the students conceptualized what it meant to intervene with students with disabilities. This program was unique in its structure and use of case method as pedagogy.

At the University of South Florida, the use of case-based methodology served two purposes (Cranston-Gingras, Raines, Paul, Epanchin, & Roselli, 1996). Like Hutchinson and Martin (1999b), the authors reported anecdotally that cases enabled students to discuss dilemmas of practice in depth and with a reflective, critical stance. Equally important, however, was that the introduction of case-based pedagogy constituted an important rationale for reforming the teacher education program itself across general and special education. A Teaching Cases Collaborative Research Group (TCRG) was formed and met for 2 hours weekly to discuss cases and jointly write case reviews. The TCRG engaged faculty across departments and served four reform agendas: (a) providing an interdisciplinary administrative structure for collaboration; (b) setting an agenda for change by bringing together faculty in a "dynamic working alliance" (Cranston-Gingras et al., p. 164); (c) brokering change in the culture of teacher education at the university toward a community of learners, particularly in sharing academic projects related to case study pedagogy; and (d) enabling development of a shared scholarly agenda as cases were developed, revised, and studied.

Peer Coaching and Tutoring in Early Field Experience.   To improve the methodological skills of general education preservice teachers for working with students with learning problems, Mallette, Maheady, and Harper (1999) studied peer coaching as part of a course entitled *Introduction to Exceptional Learner*. Based on prior research on peer coaching with preservice special education teachers (Hasbrouck, 1997;

Morgan, Gustavson, Hudson, & Salzberg, 1992; Pierce & Miller, 1994; Hudson, Miller, Salzberg, & Morgan, 1994), the authors studied three pairs of undergraduate preservice students assigned to a tutor for eight weeks in an after-school program. This early field experience was part of a sequence of highly structured field experiences within a reformed teacher education program (Maheady, Mallette, & Harper, 1996; Maheady, 1997).

Pairs of preservice students alternated roles, with one tutoring a third-grade pupil identified as learning disabled for two 1-hour sessions each week and the other serving as an observer, data collector, and peer coach. Peer coaching took place following each tutoring session. Using a multiple baseline design across subjects, results indicated that preservice students' accuracy implementing the tutoring model increased after peer coaching, attesting to the viability of coaching at the preservice level to enhance preservice students' methodological skills.

Evidence From Research on Program Effects

The teacher education literature in special education is replete with descriptions that demonstrate the trend toward developing collaborative preservice programs between special and general education. Despite this heavy emphasis on program description, however, only three studies were located that provided empirical evidence on the effects of teacher education programs that integrate general and special education at the preservice level. The third study, which is a formative program evaluation, is included in this section to illustrate the challenges related to discerning who delivers special education content.

Corbett, Kilgore, and Sindelar (1998) examined an experimental, federally funded teacher education program at the University of Florida known as Project PART, in which general education elementary students took additional courses in special education and were dually certified in general and special education. Preservice programs in special and general education were located in separate departments, and the additional coursework was added without creating a unified programmatic approach across faculty. Six of 11 students in the first cohort of graduates volunteered for the study. Data sources included interviews with students, classroom observations, videotaped lessons, interviews with cooperating teachers, and analysis of planning documents.

The authors identified three themes in the data. In the first, "The more we know, the better we teach" (Corbett et al., 1998, p. 297), students dealt with theoretical conflicts between instructors in special and general education. Students used a pragmatic approach and drew on whatever strategies constituted, in their words, good teaching. They perceived their preparation as coming from two separate knowledge bases and believed they benefited from both sets of knowledge and skills. The second theme was "Our kids not their kids." Students felt well prepared to take responsibility for students with challenging learning and behavior needs within their classrooms. Examples of accommodations they reported using included reading materials matched to children's levels, the What I know, What I want to know, What I learned (KWL) strategy, student selection of topics of study and adapting writing levels. They also utilized cooperative learning, clear communication of instructions, advanced organizers, and reduced assignment length. In the third theme, "Classroom management doesn't puzzle us," students attributed their ability to manage classrooms to a required special education course where they learned to provide clear expectations, set classroom rules, and provide clear directions. They also learned behavior management approaches that stressed extrinsic motivation.

The authors' interpretation of the findings indicated that the students "were not overwhelmed by the different viewpoints they encountered in their courses. Rather, they seemed to benefit from the diversity of points of view about teaching and learning" (Corbett et al., 1998, p. 303). The authors valued students acquiring these varied knowledge bases and skills; a unified, programmatically consistent approach was not their goal.

Project PART was the precursor of the now fully integrated PROTEACH program (Bondy & Ross, 2005), a 5-year teacher education program at the University of Florida that provides students with the choice of receiving dual certification in special and general education or general elementary certification. All students, whether they elect dual certification, are prepared "to work effectively with diverse student populations and . . . use research-based practices." Students are taught "alternative instructional strategies (e.g., direct instruction, cognitive strategy instruction, inductive instruction, cooperative learning) and the theories that support each strategy" (Ross, Lane, & McCallum, 2005). How students make sense of these various strategies and whether the strategies are placed in a broader, more comprehensive view of instruction was not described.

Maheady et al. (1996) reported initial data on the effects of the *Reflective and Responsive Educator Program* (RARE) at the State University of New York at Fredonia (see also Maheady, 1997), a field-based program for the preparation of general educators in early childhood, elementary, and secondary education. It is based on two assumptions: (a) that children's learning is maximized when teachers evaluate the consequences of their teaching and adjust it based on an analysis of student learning, and (b) that preservice teachers need more direct opportunities to teach in highly structured field experiences using a small number of validated teaching practices applicable to students with special needs. These validated, peer-mediated practices include ClassWide Peer Tutoring, Peer Assisted Learning Strategies, and Numbered Heads Together (Maheady, 1997). In other words, this program selectively focused on a small number of instructional practices and requires candidates to evaluate their effectiveness based on student outcome data. Students also had the opportunity, in peer groups, to discuss, get feedback to assist each other in improving their skills in each instructional strategy (Maheady et al., 1996).

Candidates participated in five field experiences during the RARE program, each requiring progressively more responsibility on the student's part. Initial outcome data were reported for the 1994 academic year for paired tutoring, the first field experience. Students provided 2,682 hours of tutoring, which included tutoring in content-area literacy at the middle and secondary levels. Two thirds of the tutor pairs graphed student progress in a usable, readable fashion according to the curriculum-based measurement approach they were taught; 62% of individual tutors did the same. The course and the field experience both were rated very highly by the students. The authors argued that direct service to students with disabilities using validated instructional programs with built-in requirements for evaluating outcomes, as well as reflecting on one's teaching practice, were consistent with the goals of reform efforts in teacher education and also provided a reciprocal service to the public schools that housed the field experience.

Finally, Lombardi and Hunka (2001) studied a 5-year teacher education program at West Virginia University that merged special and general education into a single administrative unit. Graduates received both a bachelors and masters degree. Ten jointly identified special education outcomes were fully integrated into required core courses in the general education preservice curriculum and were taught exclusively by general teacher education faculty. Students and faculty were asked to provide confidence and competence ratings on each of the 10 outcomes, as well as an indication of the level of coverage for each outcome. Only response data for faculty, based on a response rate of 92%, are addressed here. Although the number of faculty in this study is small, the data raise important issues about how collaboration is carried out when responsibility for special education content rests with general teacher educators alone.

Four faculty reported feeling competent and confident teaching the outcomes, and four felt competent but not confident. Two reported feeling confident but not competent, and one felt neither competent nor confident. The authors' principal recommendation in response to these data was to reactivate a committee to monitor how well special education content was covered in the program to ensure that students would be prepared to work inclusive settings.

SUMMARY AND IMPLICATIONS OF THE RESEARCH ON PEDAGOGICAL PRACTICES, PROGRAM STRUCTURES AND PROGRAM EFFECTS

This body of work on program pedagogy, structures and effects primarily provides data from the perspective of candidates and instructors and measures of their own perceived effectiveness. Such evaluative judgments from the participants can be an important source of information to suggest directions for program improvement. However, they constitute a limited definition of what is meant by teacher effectiveness. Only the RARE study, which taught candidates how to graph student progress, attempted to measure the impact on student learning of teaching practices taught in a preservice program.

Together these studies do provide an important departure point for considering how we define the relationship between special and general teacher education. Collectively they raise two central issues: (a) how "good teaching" is defined and (b) how a legitimate role for general teacher education faculty is developed in relationship to special education preservice content.

When Is Good Teaching Actually Good Teaching?

The phrase "Teaching students with disabilities well is only good teaching" is frequently heard in discussions about preparing all teachers to work with students with disabilities. But what exactly do we mean when we say "Good teaching is good teaching"? Whose view of good teaching is being promoted? And more importantly, how do preservice students understand what they and their instructors mean by good teaching?

Students in the Corbett et al. (1998) study appeared to define good teaching as whatever worked for them. Drawing on disparate methods and approaches learned separately from special and general teacher educators, these graduates believed that good teaching was having at their command as many teaching methods and strategies as possible and selecting from them based on their immediate, pragmatic needs. Disdaining a "one-size-fits-all" model, they made the argument that for them what constitutes good teaching is finding a strategy that will meet the needs of students with disabilities. As novice teachers, they were flexible enough to alter assignments, developed interventions for challenging behaviors, or used flexible or cooperative grouping structures. They appeared to tolerate multiple sets of materials and juggled groups of students with varying needs. They valued collaborative work with colleagues and were willing to work together to find a strategy that worked for their students.

The willingness to accommodate, modify, and collaborate with professional peers enhanced their potential to create classrooms where differences among students are viewed as normative. Insofar as prospective teachers are routinely disposed to accept the need to be flexible to meet the needs of students with disabilities through accommodation, modification, and collaboration—and to understand that their basic teaching responsibilities will include these practices—the traditional relationship between special and general education has changed markedly. Several of these studies indicate that change of this type has taken place.

A question that can be raised in relationship to these studies, however, is whether accommodation, modification, and collaboration are adequate proxies for good teaching. As evidenced in the Corbett et al. study (1998), where any strategy "that works" is deemed appropriate, preservice candidates justify their choices of pedagogy based on this strictly pragmatic definition of what it means to teach all students well. From this perspective, where good teaching is what works and what works is good teaching, it seems that students in the PART study at the University of Florida embraced the proverbial "bag of tricks," that is, the disparate methods and curricula they learned in special or general education courses. Extrapolating from the participants' perspective, the larger the bag of tricks, the more secure they are likely to feel in the classroom. What these data did not indicate, however, was whether or not these students possessed a conceptual framework that guided how they justified their pedagogical choices from among the array they had mastered.

In his discussion of coherent and effective preservice programs, Howey (1996) noted that the role of a conceptual framework in teacher education is to orient students to what is important. In the absence of a negotiated conceptual framework across special and general teacher education, the *de facto* orientation of the PART program was that a teacher should accommodate and modify curriculum and instruction for students with whatever approach they can without necessarily asking the question "To what end?" By failing to provide candidates with a unifying conceptual framework within which to consider the curricular and instructional goals that drive their work, instructors may have encouraged their graduates to define good teaching without considering curricular and methodological choices that might best foster their students' long-term achievement. A unifying conceptual framework should lead preservice teachers to make thoughtful, informed instructional decisions and to articulate the relationship among the pedagogies they choose within that framework. The "bag-of-tricks" approach suggests, in contrast, that program graduates have no explicit framework from which to make such decisions. Tom (2005) raised similar concerns about the absence of programmatic coherence in the Florida PROTEACH program.

A different view of "good teaching" was offered by Maheady and colleagues (1996; Maheady, 1997). In their restructured program, good teaching was defined as providing candidates with explicit, peer-assisted instructional methods for imparting basic skills to students with disabilities. These researchers stressed the importance of teachers' reflecting and making decisions based on data regarding student progress. These validated strategies were taught to general education candidates as the preferred way to instruct students with disabilities.

Maheady (1997) stated that because the RARE program is based on an improvement-oriented approach dependent on student progress data, it can be implemented either with a constructivist or a behaviorist instructional model. In other words, student progress became the framework for good teaching. Advancing the idea that teachers should judge the effects of their work based on careful analyses of student progress data is appropriate and consistent with the national emphasis on the analysis of student work samples as an indicator of teacher education effectiveness (see, e.g., Schalock, 2002). Despite this claim, however, it appears that the RARE program offered students a relatively limited view of instructional methods based primarily on teaching basic skills. As such, it may have limited preservice students' conceptions of what constitutes appropriate instruction for students with disabilities. In so doing, it runs counter to the views of other special educators (e.g., Blanton, 1992; Englert, Tarrant, & Mariage, 1992; Hindin, Morocco, & Aguilar, 2001), who emphasize the role of meaningful and authentic instruction for students with disabilities and who argue that learning basic skills is not an absolute prerequisite for making instruction meaningful and authentic. In the RARE program, the idea of being "reflective and responsive" was meant to apply to any validated strategy, and certainly peer-assisted approaches have the potential for wide applicability beyond basic skills. But within the program, students appeared to reflect on a small number of highly explicit strategies related to the acquisition of basic skills. As a consequence, this approach may limit what they believe students with disabilities are capable of learning, especially with regard to a more complex, challenging curriculum.

Absent from the studies on program effects is documentation regarding the difference between what teacher educators in special education mean when they say "good teaching" and what teacher educators in general education may mean. Historically, a persistent dichotomy has existed between a more behaviorist view of instruction on the part of special educators and a more constructivist view often said to characterize general education. Likewise, a dichotomy has existed between a remediation view of learning in special education and learning meaningful content in general education. Whether conceptions of what constitutes good teaching continue to echo these historic dichotomies in preservice preparation today—even as efforts to collaborate increase—has yet to be documented. Efforts to move toward a more inclusive view of instruction with concepts like comprehensive literacy and comprehensive mathematics suggest that these dichotomies no longer need dominate discussions of method and instruction. But failing a public, negotiated definition of good teaching, it is possible that the traditional dichotomies between special and general education may form a persistent subtext, even in teacher education programs that strive to be collaborative. As we find out more about the capacity of students with disabilities to learn complex subject matter (see, e.g., Feretti, MacArthur, & Okolo, 2001; Morocco, 2001; Morocco, Hindin, Mata-Aguilar, & Clark-Chiarelli, 2001; Palincsar, Magnusson, Collins, & Cutter, 2001; Woodward, Monroe, & Baxter, 2001), it seems critical to ensure that definitions of good teaching explicitly address learning authentic content and not limiting the curriculum that is taught to students with disabilities.

The Assumption of Universal Applicability

A different but related set of questions regarding the relationship between special and general education at the preservice level was raised by Levin, Hibbard, and Rock (2002), Lombardi and Hunka (2001), and Cook (2002). In these studies, it was expected that general teacher education faculty would take full responsibility for teaching special education content. In the Lombardi and Hunka study, however, faculty responsible for teaching this curriculum did not feel uniformly confident or competent to teach to the required outcomes. In the Cook study, faculty had not been prepared for this content; student perceptions suggested that they did not feel prepared to work with students with disabilities. In the Levin et al. (2002) study, faculty took it upon themselves to focus problem-based learning activities on working with students with disabilities because the issues were not addressed elsewhere in the preservice curriculum.

Although it seems fitting to strive for a seamless preservice curriculum in which the needs of most students with disabilities are covered within general education courses, the ability of general teacher education faculty to deliver that content effectively remains tenuous. Is it reasonable to expect general teacher educators to deliver instruction that may be outside their teaching experience and expertise? Is it necessary for all special education content to be embedded in the general teacher education curriculum in the first place?

Applying a Vygotskian perspective, it can be argued that many general teacher educators may not feel ready to address working with students with disabilities independently and that their zone of proximal development may require a scaffold to achieve this goal. In higher education, that scaffold is currently provided by teacher educators in special education, at least as documented in the preservice program delivery and team teaching collaborations reported earlier. Lombardi and Hunka's (2001) solution, monitoring how general education faculty address these issues, is problematic insofar as seems to contradict the trend toward collaboration. How they intend to carry out the monitoring has important implications for the evolving relationship between general and special teacher education. Does "monitor" mean a summative accounting of coverage or a formative faculty development effort to support general teacher education faculty in carrying out new instructional responsibilities? Requiring a summative accounting in the absence of faculty development does not seem to meet the spirit of what is meant by collaboration between special and general education faculty. Furthermore, it may be that a combination of embedded content, and carefully defined coursework in special education taught by special education faculty, could be an effective combination as long as there is ongoing dialogue, framed within a shared conceptual framework, for how the range of content across special and general teacher education fits together.

A related issue is: What is actually being taught when general teacher educators are teaching special education material in their courses? Are faculty teaching what they consider to be good practice for all students from their traditional repertoires of instructional methodology, or are they teaching specific content that formerly appeared in special education courses? An important concern is how faculty are making connections between pedagogical practices presented as legitimate for all students and their applicability to students with disabilities.

Much taught within the general education curriculum is likely to be good pedagogy for many students, including those with disabilities, and it may be powerful in counteracting the low expectations often set for what special education students can achieve (Englert et al., 1992). General education faculty, however, may be (a) unable to provide specific, cogent examples of such pedagogies being used successfully with students with disabilities; (b) unable to articulate the relationship between a particular pedagogy and the needs of students with disabilities for meaningful instruction, or; (c) lack familiarity with research on successful applications of these approaches to students with disabilities. Even if well intended and highly committed general teacher education instructors assume that they are introducing methods for working with all students, preservice candidates may fail to make the appropriate connections to students with disabilities. Thus, although we may appropriately assume that much of what goes on in the preparation of general classroom teachers is universally applicable to students with disabilities, prospective teachers are likely to require a specific understanding of how this application works. The studies in which special education content is integrated fail to provide enough detail to enable us to understand how the content and concepts are taught, what examples related to students with disabilities are offered, and the degree to which faculty may be relying on the assumption of universal applicability of good pedagogy.

The quality of preparation for those preparing to be general education teachers receive in the name of inclusion should not be left to chance. Rather, it should be discussed and deliberated on as a function of faculty collaboration and reflect a fundamental level of shared understanding across special or general faculty who are delivering special education content and concepts. The early study by Nowacek and Blanton (1996) foreshadowed the challenges in redesigning teacher education as a collaborative enterprise.

EVIDENCE FROM RESEARCH ON PREPARING TEACHERS FOR DIVERSITY AND DISABILITY

Another critical area related to preparing general education teachers to work with students with disabilities is how preservice students view the relationship between diversity and disability. Preparing teachers to work effectively with diverse populations is a prominent goal for teacher education programs and remains central, especially given the persistent achievement gap between racial and ethnic minority students and students from low-socioeconomic-status (SES) levels and White, middle-class students. Although this relationship is central to a deep understanding of diversity, how issues related to disability intersect with the more general focus on diversity has not been explored well. The intransigence of the disproportionate number of racial and ethnic minority and low-SES students in special education (see Donovan & Cross, 2002) is emblematic of the need for greater, more sophisticated understanding of the relationship between diversity and disability as an overarching goal of pre-service teacher education.

Disability typically is presented as a parallel marker of diversity in a series of many different diversities. When this occurs, disability is not presented in relationship to diversity in terms of race, ethnicity, language and social class; the concepts are not nested. Many special educators have criticized this approach because it can easily lead to the inappropriate assumption that students who are not white, or whose first language is not English, or who are poor are more likely to have disabilities (Artiles & Trent, 1994; Ball & Harry, 1993; Cloud, 1993; Ford, 1992; Pugach & Seidl, 1996, 1998; Rueda, 1989).

The most common reference point for addressing the relationship between diversity and disability is the disproportionate representation of racial and ethnic minority students in special education. At the preservice level, this issue is often addressed as an important set of caveats about problems with the overuse of labeling, inappropriate interpretations of culturally appropriate behavior, and misinterpreting problems of second-language acquisition as a disability. Labeling theory and theories of cultural mismatch between teachers and students tend to drive this work. These issues represent critical aspects of the relationship between diversity and disability.

In the preservice special education literature, analyses of issues related to diversity are more prominent than are empirical studies. In these analyses, the reader is educated about aspects of multicultural education, calls are made for teaching prospective and practicing special educators about culturally responsive teaching, or specific theories are explored (e.g., Campbell-Whatley & Comer, 2000; Day-Vines, 2000; Ford, 1992; Harry, 2002; Obiakor, 2001; Patton & Townsend, 1999; Trent, Artiles, Fitchett-Bazemore, McDaniel, & Coleman-Sorrell, 2002; Voltz, 1998; Voltz, Dooley, & Jefferies, 1999). Two empirical studies regarding preservice teacher education were located that link multicultural and special education. Although the number of studies that deliberately address diversity and disability together is limited, they begin to provide perspective on the urgency of the challenge.

Applying a strategy from research in general teacher education, Trent, Pernell, Mungai and Chimedza (1998) used pre- and postconcept maps and explanatory essays to measure conceptual change for 30 preservice students enrolled in a course on multicultural and special education. The required course addressed special education issues from the perspective of multicultural education. For example, the 1975 passage of Public Law 94-142 was studied alongside the 1955 Supreme Court decision in *Brown v. Board of Education*—a relationship that is not always drawn.

Twenty students showed conceptual change. Their postconcept maps included a greater number of categories of diversity, demonstrating a greater recognition of the complexity of teaching. Postmaps showed a move away from focusing exclusively on teacher or student variables and toward conceptualizing teaching as multidimensional and involving highly diverse groups of students. In contrast to premaps including race, ethnicity, and religion as instances of diversity, postmaps included disability and learning styles as well. The authors noted that many students went beyond simply adding categories of diversity and addressed the need for teachers to continually question their own attitudes and value the full range of diversities.

Results also demonstrated a move toward discussing specific instructional strategies and away from making general comments about teaching in a diverse class of learners. Examples of strategies included holding discussions about diversity in class and making sure students from various groups worked together. Finally, results also indicated the appearance of new concepts that had not appeared on the premaps. These new items referred to the provision of services to students with disabilities. In particular, students included concepts such as collaboration and team teaching on their postmaps.

The authors discussed the results in relationship to their own pedagogical practices in the course, ascribing student changes to consistent discourse between faculty instructors and their teaching assistants, levels of interaction with students, and how past student evaluations of the course were used. They argued that faculty should make explicit their aims for multicultural education and assist students to integrate and expand their conceptions of what it means to teach diverse groups of learners.

The Trent et al. (1998) study represented an attempt to document what happens when diversity and disability are addressed together. Many students appeared to question their own biases across several categories of diversity, among which disability was one. The instrumentation, however, was not complex enough to determine the extent to which students may actually have transcended a simple categorical understanding of diversity—which was a concern expressed by the authors.

In the second study, Sobel, Taylor, Kalisher, and Weddle-Steinberg (2002) analyzed the content of reflective journals for seven postbaccalaureate preservice candidates enrolled in the Initial Teacher Education Program at the University of Colorado—Denver who had specialty areas in inclusion and bilingual education. These seven volunteer students agreed, over the course of their internship year working in low-SES schools with high Latino student populations, to respond to a general journal prompt on "how beliefs regarding diversity issues were revealed in their classroom interactions, practices and observations" (p. 2). Five were White, one was African American, and one was Asian American. Based on the work of Gollnick and Chinn (1998, p. 4), this program posited "a broader definition of diversity that includes factors of culture, language, ethnicity, race, ability, gender, socioeconomic level, religion, age and sexual orientation."

The authors identified three dominant themes in the journals: (a) the value of equity in classroom planning and practices, (b) the value of family involvement and interactions, and (c) the value of cultural sensitivity and understanding in classroom instruction and interaction. The authors provided verbatim examples of each theme from student journals. For equity, examples included cooperative learning, accommodating a student for a mathematics text, modifying a spelling test list, providing combs to all children to accommodate one child's need for a comb, and discussing a teacher's gender preference. For family involvement, examples included empathizing with a young working mother, parents' asking advice about a child's behavioral needs, and the importance of becoming familiar with students' home contexts because the students have such "difficult lives." For cultural sensitivity, examples included learning about cultural holidays and foods and figuring out how to celebrate multiple winter holidays in December. One teacher noted that in discussing holidays with her class, she learned that some of her pupils had never been to a "sit down" restaurant.

Sobel and her colleagues (2002) concluded that "the reflective focus of this project aided in preparing preservice teachers to critically examine the educational structures in which they worked with regard to issues of equity" (p. 11). The journal entries the authors chose to highlight focused more on exceptionality than on race and ethnicity. When they were focused on race and ethnicity, examples were primarily about foods and festivals—not on the need to transform schools to achieve equity in education (see Banks, 1995). Additionally, the journal entry that referenced a Native-American student also noted a traditional Thanksgiving activity, but with no discussion of the issues posed for many Native American students by the traditional interpretation of the Thanksgiving story.

Preservice students' entries did not engage in any depth with issues like the achievement gap, institutionalized practices that lead to it in the schools, or the question of privilege in our society. This journal study seems to bear out the concerns voiced by Taylor and Sobel (2001) that the students in their baseline study expressed only a surface level understanding of diversity.

Students' general sensitivity to issues of diversity and their need to be aware of their own biases increased in the Trent et al. (1998) study, and without question this is a useful outcome for preservice education, as is the fact that students in the Sobel et al. (2002) study wrote about issues related to diversity. However, we might ask whether these outcomes are sufficient. At the preservice level, disability is usually treated as another category of diversity analogous to race, class, culture, language, and gender—as it was in the teacher education program at UC-Denver. This approach may foster an atmosphere where preservice students pick and choose which of these many "diversities" they wish to focus on and learn about—and in the process may ignore some of the most crucial issues related to diversity that trouble our schools. Students in both studies appeared to have gained only a surface understanding of the complex issues surrounding diversity and appeared unfamiliar with critical concepts like privilege. They did not ask questions about language and dialect issues relative to standard English, nor did they seem to understand how inequity is institutionalized in the schools.

Discussing the various markers of diversity as equivalent diminishes the possibility that students and faculty will consider them in relationship to one another (Artiles & Trent, 1997; Pugach & Seidl, 1998). A challenge for preservice teacher education faculty is to figure out how to move beyond isolated, serial discussions of categories of diversity and embed the discussion of disability within the larger framework of diversity. For example, faculty and students will need to understand that when real disabilities do exist, they are always embedded in individual student's identity based on their race, class, language, and culture (Artiles & Trent, 1997; Pugach & Seidl, 1998), making it crucial to consider how the two interact. In other words, every student with a disability also has sociocultural characteristics that teachers must consider carefully. Faculty and students need to understand that looking at disability and diversity only as isolated, parallel categories can lead to devaluing or ignoring the positive contributions that race, culture, and language represent in the classroom. If these complexities are not part of preservice preparation, it is possible to lose the valuable ground that has started to be gained in how teachers view their students' sociocultural and sociolinguistic backgrounds. In the process we may end up ignoring some of the most critical issues related to race and ethnicity that are especially challenging for White, middle-class teachers working with racial and ethnic minority, low-income students.

ACCOUNTABILITY PROCESSES FOR PREPARING GENERAL EDUCATION TEACHERS TO WORK WITH STUDENTS WITH DISABILITIES

All national standards address the need to prepare general education teachers to work with students with disabilities. Although the various standards documents use different language, each underscores the importance of this issue for novice teachers and, in the case of the National Board for Professional Teaching Standards, for accomplished teachers as well. While several standards across the documents have important implications for working with students with disabilities, the standards cited in Table 9.2 represent only those with language that directly addresses working with this population.

NCATE Standards

The 1995 and 2000 National Council for Accreditation of Teacher Education (NCATE) standards in Table 9.2 differ in scope, but both treat diversity as a unitary umbrella for all categories of difference, including exceptionality. Both emphasize the need for teachers to base curricular decisions on the diverse life experiences and backgrounds of their students. Interestingly, Standard 4 of NCATE 2000, although subsuming all forms of diversity, makes specific reference to "knowledge bases for, and conceptualizations of, diversity and inclusion . . . " indicating some level of differentiation between diversity and inclusion. No elaboration is provided to describe this differentiation. These standards specify that, although teachers should challenge all students instructionally, they should engage students with disabilities using instructional conversation as a methodology (see Tharp & Gallimore, 1988). No other category of diversity is singled out with a recommendation for a specific instructional methodology.

The reference to *instructional conversation* emphasizes an expectation that teachers will not rely solely on rote, decontextualized programs of instruction, which historically have been favored for disabilities, but rather should provide students with more challenging, more engaging forms of instruction. As such, the NCATE 2000 standards give deliberate weight to moving away from a singularly technical view of teaching for students with disabilities. These standards also support a view of diversity based on mutually exclusive categories of diversity rather than recognize the interaction between diversity and disability.

Finally, several NCATE standards reference approaches to instruction that today are considered state-of-the art teaching *for all students* and that have potential as well for working with students with disabilities. Although there is an assumption of universal applicability of these methods, the connection to working with students with disabilities is not made explicitly.

INTASC 1992 and 2001

The original 1992 Interstate New Teacher Assessment and Support Consortium (INTASC) standards were designed to describe what every new teacher should know and be able to do well. Disability is addressed by inference in Principle 3, which reads: "The teacher understands how students differ in their approaches to learning and creates instructional opportunities that are adapted to diverse learners." The knowledge item in this principle is related to "knowing about areas of exceptionality," signifying the importance of knowledge about discrete categories of disability. The related disposition and performance statements address individual difference from a perspective of building a unified classroom community and modifying instruction to meet students' needs. Similar to the NCATE standards, many INTASC principles reference currently accepted approaches to instruction that may apply to students with disabilities, but without explicit statements connecting the two.

By contrast, the 2001 INTASC *Model Standards for Licensing General and Special Education Teachers of Students with Disabilities: A Resource for State Dialogue* (INTASC, 2001) are comprehensive, addressing standards not only for general education teachers but also for special education teachers. These are not a new set of standards per se, but build on the 10 Core Principles in the 1992 INTASC document by describing the explicit implications of how those principles apply to general and special education teachers' working with students with disabilities. The 2001 standards begin to address where the responsibility of general education teachers ends and where that of special education teachers begins. This document serves a unique role as a scaffold and begins to solve the problem that exists when we make—but fail to articulate explicitly—assumptions about the universal applicability of various pedagogical approaches for teaching students with disabilities.

Regarding the relationship between disability and diversity, the newer INTASC standards state that "teachers understand students with disabilities within the broader context of their families, cultural backgrounds, socioeconomic classes, languages, communities and peer/social groups" (INTASC, 2001, p. 17). The document goes on to state that "all teachers reflect on the potential interaction between a student's cultural experiences and their disabilities. Teachers generally question the extent to which they may be interpreting student responses on the basis of their own cultural values versus the cultural perspectives of the students or the student's family or community" (p. 36). With statements like these, disability is placed within the larger diversity framework, going beyond the idea that disabilities are merely another category of diversity.

The 2001 INTASC standards represented a turning point for defining the relationship between general and special education. Prior to this document, discussions about what all teachers need to know and be able to do were interpreted locally within individual SCDEs, often as a part of grassroots efforts to create more collaborative relationships between special and general education. These standards make explicit the connections between general views of good teaching as defined by the original INTASC principles and their specific implications for preparing new teachers to work with students with disabilities.

National Board for Professional Teaching Standards

The items on Table 9.2 from the National Board for Professional Teaching Standards are drawn from two of its five Core Propositions. Although specific NBPTS standards exist for many different age levels and subject or specialty areas, including teachers of students with special needs, the Core Propositions represent the overarching philosophy of the NBPTS.

References to working with students with disabilities appear in Core Propositions 1 and 4. The section titled *Teachers Treat Students Equitably* addressed the importance of teachers' not holding biases based on disability or all other categories of diversity—including social, cultural, language, race, religion, or gender differences. The emphasis is squarely on not holding biases and not treating certain students as favorites. It states explicitly that equitable teaching does not mean treating all members of a class equally, but demands different practices based on individual student needs.

Core Proposition 5 focuses on collaboration among professionals. It defines collaboration as fundamental to a productive relationship between general and special education. The need for coordination of services is described as an essential part of the practice of accomplished teachers. These two Core Propositions are based on the assumption that (a) accomplished teachers teach students with disabilities and (b) they collaborate with colleagues to ensure that their students receive the appropriate services. The tone of the Core Propositions strongly supports the role of the general education teacher in working with students with disabilities.

ESTABLISHING NEW RESEARCH FRAMEWORKS FOR STUDYING THE RELATIONSHIP BETWEEN GENERAL AND SPECIAL TEACHER EDUCATION

Given the state of this research base, as well as the expectations set by the national standards, how might we focus future research to best serve teacher education as it strives to prepare all teachers to work with students with disabilities? In general, the research shows that the progress that has been made in preparing general education teachers for this responsibility centers on improving attitudes and on content and experiences related to special education within the general teacher education curriculum. Some studies also suggest that concepts of accommodation and modification are becoming better embedded into teacher education programs.

However, this level of success and comfort with including special education in the general preservice curriculum—as well as the trend toward collaborative preservice programming—may mask the complexity of the relationship between special and general education at the preservice level. The degree of progress achieved thus far may be acceptable but it may also subvert the importance of asking deeper and more challenging questions about this relationship. Thinking about the preparation of general education teachers as it relates to students with disabilities demands a more sophisticated view of the relationship between general teacher education and special education. Creating a research agenda based on a deeper level of questioning can be thought of as a legitimate third phase in the evolving relationship between general and special teacher education in relationship to the two phases described at the start of this chapter.

But what might research in this third phase actually look like? In an effort to create more powerful frameworks, future research needs to transcend the questions that have driven research to date, questions like: Are preservice students learning to accommodate and modify curriculum? Are they collaborating with professional peers? Is special education content covered in a particular course or program? Does instruction in diversity include disability as one kind of diversity? These appear to have been critical, important issues in the first two phases of the relationship between special and general teacher education. To create more cogent frameworks, research might proceed in the following areas.

Interrogating Pedagogy and Its Universal Applicability

One important potential line of research involves documenting what conceptual frameworks drive preservice programs that aspire to integrate general and special education methodologies. Do faculty present multiple philosophies and instructional methods in the absence of coherent programmatic frameworks, as appeared to be the case in Florida's Project PART? Or do comprehensive conceptual frameworks drive preservice programs that are explicitly designed to prepare general education teachers to work with students with disabilities? If well-defined conceptual frameworks are driving these programs, what are they, and from a comprehensive viewpoint, how are students making sense of—and implementing in practice—the full range of methodologies required to teach a wide range of students?

Teacher educators in general and special education, for example, have not typically engaged in sustained discourse about the relationship between more explicit forms of instruction that often focus on basic skills and the larger goals of the curriculum in terms of meaningful and authentic instruction for students with disabilities. This discourse becomes critical in light of IDEA's commitment to the general education curriculum as the goal for students with disabilities. Although newly emerging collaborative programs of teacher education may attempt to bridge this gap, dialogue within programs revealing the way issues actually are addressed has not been well documented (Otis-Wilborn & Pugach, 2002). An exception is a description offered by Lowenbraun and Nolen (1998) of their negotiations as they team-taught a course in adolescent development.

Such studies could make an important contribution to increasing programmatic coherence in collaborative teacher education programs. Specific research might include the following:

- Survey research to document the pedagogical strategies taught in collaborative teacher education programs and the frameworks that connect them in relationship to teaching students with disabilities
- Classroom-based qualitative research in collaborative teacher education programs to describe discourse around pedagogy and particularly the role of explicit, skills-based instruction vis-à-vis more complex curricular goals for students with disabilities
- Case studies of student teacher, intern, and resident decision making about pedagogical and curricular choices for students with disabilities in general education classrooms, especially regarding how participants justify their choices
- Observational studies of preservice students in classrooms describing their instructional practices with students with disabilities
- Systematic analyses of pupil work on the part of student teachers, interns, and residents for how closely aligned the outcomes are in relationship to complex curricular goals.

In addition to the importance of studying pedagogical and curricular frameworks that guide teacher preparation, it will be important to conduct other classroom-based research at the preservice level to determine how general faculty view and carry out their roles in preparing candidates to work with students with disabilities. In reality, the success of collaborative preservice models is founded on a complex relationship among faculty members' area of expertise, their knowledge about working with students with disabilities and the way they connect their expertise to issues related to educating students with disabilities. In the course of their teaching, faculty may not be sending consistent messages about how to work with students with disabilities. To what degree do general teacher education faculty rely on their special education colleagues, who may bring a rich experiential base with difficult-to-teach students but may be less skilled in contextualizing their own work within the general education classroom?

For example, the general teacher education curriculum may emphasize the importance of building strong classroom communities. Done correctly, a true classroom community would provide a positive environment for all students, including those with disabilities. To a teacher educator in special education, however, building classroom community might mean taking explicit steps to make sure that students with disabilities are included in every aspect of classroom life. Faculty members who lack experience in special education may not be able to provide, or may not feel comfortable with, providing examples of community building as it pertains to students with disabilities. So although it might be true that what is indeed good pedagogy in relationship to building classroom community is applicable to students with disabilities, if the connection is not made explicitly, the nuances of applications for students with disabilities may be lost on preservice students.

Multiple studies of classroom practice could be conducted either by content area or by standards for beginning teachers. Specific studies on this topic might include the following:

- Survey research on who is responsible for delivering instruction about working with students with disabilities

- Classroom-based qualitative research on how general education faculty connects pedagogy to working with students with disabilities
- Classroom-based qualitative research on how general education faculty talk about students with disabilities in their classes
- Implementing systematic variations across cohorts in how content related to working with students with disabilities is addressed based on different configurations of instructors (e.g., teaming and development of general education faculty)

These might be conducted as traditional qualitative studies to describe classroom practice or as action research on the part of teacher education faculty.

Interrogating the Relationship Between Diversity and Disability

A serious effort needs to be launched to study how teacher education students and faculty view the relationship between diversity and disability. What aspects of the relationship between diversity and disability may be appropriate for study?

The need to establish a more sophisticated understanding of disability embedded within—not parallel to—diversity exists at the same time that teacher education struggles to embrace a multicultural agenda. Therefore, any study of the relationship between these two concepts will require research across special and general teacher educators, including those who identify themselves as multicultural teacher educators. Complicating this goal as it relates to preparing candidates to work with students with disabilities is the fact that few teacher educators who specialize in multicultural education appear to address special education. Perhaps this is so because faculty who identify themselves with multicultural education may not wish to legitimize the inappropriate association between diversity and disability—and understandably so. However, critical to the success of the multicultural preservice agenda will be asking faculty to interrogate themselves about disability in relationship to multicultural education, rather than continuing to address them separately.

How is the issue of disability addressed, for example, in classes on multicultural education? Conversely, how is diversity of race, class, culture, and language addressed in classes on special education?

Studies of what actually constitutes classroom discourse in SCDEs in this regard do not exist. Another potential line of research involves how preservice teachers view the identities of students of color who also have disabilities. For example, how do they make distinctions between students of color who have low-incidence disabilities and those who may have been labeled inappropriately as having a behavior disorder due to cultural mismatches between teachers and students?

Further, as the field moves into performance-based assessment, what kinds of assessments are being used to capture preservice students' commitments to diversity, and how do those assessments address disability? Do faculty members accept portfolio entries on disability, for example, as indicators of a students' competence in the more general area of diversity, or do students demonstrate their knowledge, skills, and dispositions in diversity by explicitly addressing issues of race, class, culture, language, and gender? In other words, do programs say that preservice students have met standards regarding diversity if they are sensitive to students who have disabilities but have failed to confront their beliefs about diversity of race, class, culture, and language? If as part of preservice education students are charged to become more reflective about diversity and equity, it seems inappropriate to accept isolated discussions of disability as a stand-in for addressing the challenge of providing equitable education in the schools as it relates to race, class, culture, language, and gender.

This aspect of future research could serve to open up a much-needed dialogue on new representations of the relationship between diversity and disability as a means of promoting the equity agenda for teacher education. By considering disability and multicultural education in relationship to each another, teacher educators in special education are challenged to match their commitment to disability with a commitment to diversity in terms of race, class, culture, and language (Pugach & Seidl, 1998).

National Standards and the Next Generation of Research

How do national standards help or hinder the evolution of more complex frameworks for how we conceptualize preparing all teachers to work with students with disabilities? The analysis offered in this chapter might also inform how future research is conceptualized as it relates both to what is meant by good teaching and to the relationship between diversity and disability.

As a general pattern, the national standards do not make explicit the relationship between what is generally thought to be good pedagogy and what it means to teach students with disabilities well. Further, they are generally weighted in favor of a definition of diversity that treats disability as a parallel category rather than as a construct nested within sociocultural, socioeconomic, and sociolinguistic diversity. When standards diverge from this, they do so inconsistently. The NCATE 2000 standards emphasize instructional conversation for students with disabilities, for example, but other documents do not address instructional methodology explicitly.

It should be noted that several standards other than those that appear in Table 9.2 use language that makes explicit reference to meeting the needs of "all students." That phrase is often used so that a list of various markers of diversity does not need to be included in every standard. As another example of the problem of universal applicability, however, "all students" treats all diversities as equivalent and fails to help preservice students or teacher education faculty move beyond the generality that good teaching applies to all students. This is a tricky issue. As noted earlier, a lot of what is considered to be good teaching is in fact applicable to all students. However, in its application, teachers must make decisions about how they teach specific strategies and content to which students and with what level of explicitness. Therefore, applying the beliefs that underlie the phrase "all students" is more challenging than it may at first appear.

Let us say, for example, that a standard addressed the importance of moving all students to self-regulation and independence. We know this represents a particular challenge for many students with mild disabilities and needs to be emphasized by their teachers. If we embed this goal as being good for all students and preservice candidates read this as good for students of all diversities, they may conclude that they need to teach self-regulation explicitly to all racial and ethnic minority students, all students with disabilities, and all students whose first language is not English. However, not all children need to be taught self-regulation explicitly. The absence of nuance in the relationship between diversity and disability may mask how students interpret the standard and fails to draw attention to the need for unpacking this relationship and its subtleties.

Longitudinal Studies of Teacher Education

The increasing number of collaborative teacher education programs across general and special education constitute a logical resource for conducting longitudinal studies on the preparation of general education teachers for their work with students with disabilities. Faculties that deliberately join ranks to make preparation for working with students with disabilities a central feature of their work are poised to collect important data regarding their graduates' effectiveness with students with disabilities. Further, as they engage in team teaching, they have a natural means of fostering dialogue about what is valued and how it will be addressed. They have within their grasp important data that could be mined to produce penetrating analyses of these issues.

However, such longitudinal studies should be undertaken in conjunction with support for induction-year programming that can help graduates consolidate the fragile new knowledge and skills they acquire during teacher preparation. The effects of teacher education can wash out in the absence of support at the school level for implementing high-quality teaching practices (Zeichner & Gore, 1990). Longitudinal studies of graduates who do not receive induction support are, in essence, studies of the socialization process to the specific schools and school districts in which students work, rather than studies of the effectiveness of teacher preparation. Data need be collected not only on how well students with disabilities are performing in the classrooms of program graduates but also on how graduates work with students who are struggling but not labeled as having a disability and also on their practices with regard to referral and placement in special education—especially for students of color and students whose first language is not English. An important feature of such studies would be to document the degree to which P–12 students are engaging in complex curricula that challenge their thinking in the classrooms of program graduates. If faculty in these and similar programs worked on a collective research agenda, the data from such studies would be powerful.

In addition, it will be important to engage in quantitative documentation of how many teacher education programs are engaging in collaboration and exactly what they mean when they say they are collaborative. What do they have in common and what do they do differently? Descriptive data of this kind would provide an important historical marker of preservice trends.

Research on Differentiated Roles for General and Special Education Teachers

Finally, given the near universal preparation of general education teachers for working with students with disabilities, it will be important to launch studies that inquire into how the roles of special and general education teachers are differentiated. How are their jobs defined not only in terms of services provided but also in terms of instructional strategies and curriculum approaches? How have roles been renegotiated at the preservice level? What is the demarcation line, if any, between what a prospective general education teacher is prepared to do and what a prospective special education teacher is prepared to do?

Also, how much interaction is there between candidates in special and general teacher education programs? Do programs build on one another, with general education as the basis for special education preservice work? Do the knowledge expectations differ for candidates in general and special education? It will also be important to document the number of dual-certification programs and the success of dually certified graduates who take special education positions.

CONCLUSION

As this review illustrates, there is a great deal of research activity around preparing teachers to work with students with disabilities. This is the result of major changes in legislation and practice, as well as the promulgation of national standards that set new expectations for how teachers are prepared. However, more hard data are needed to drive the development and improvement of preservice programs. Capturing the quality of the commitment to prepare all teachers to work with students with disabilities will require a sustained research effort. Mining the current practice of teacher education to document its effectiveness is one of the most important tasks at hand.

If we are to gauge the value of teacher education in improving the lives of students with disabilities, it is essential to generate questions that capture a more sophisticated view of what it means to prepare general education teachers to work with them. At the least, this will require nesting disability within overarching concepts in teacher education and then teasing out the nuances of those concepts as they apply directly to students with disabilities. For this reason, proposed studies and lines of research identified in this chapter focus on placing the specific concerns of special education within broader, more universal concepts outside of special education.

Finally, it will be critical to take advantage of the natural progression toward collaborative preservice programs and to use these programs as the basis for studies that will answer questions about their effectiveness. However, in studying program effectiveness, those who conceptualize the research also must ask more sophisticated questions.

This work can be enriched immeasurably if it is conducted in joint fashion, in teams comprised of teacher educators from special and general teacher education, across content areas and multicultural education. These partnerships can constitute a natural, on-the-job form of faculty development, which ultimately can serve the goal of shared responsibility for teaching the preservice curriculum. By joining forces in this manner, we can begin to provide answers to a new generation of questions about how best to achieve the goal of delivering instruction of the highest quality to students with disabilities.

ACKNOWLEDGMENTS

The author would like to thank Melanie Agnew, University of Wisconsin—Milwaukee, for assistance locating the literature for this chapter; and to Carol Sue Englert, Michigan State University; Dan Fallon, Carnegie Corporation of New York; Susan Fuhrman, University of Pennsylvania; and Annemarie Palincsar, University of Michigan, who read drafts of the manuscript and provided invaluable insight, critique, and suggestions.

TABLE 9.1
Preservice Studies Reviewed in Pugach Chapter

Studies[a]	Question and Focus	Research Tradition	Research Design	Findings
Cook, B. (2002)	What attitudes toward inclusion are held by preservice students in a completely infused teacher education program?	25-item survey of attitudes	Survey of intact group of students using Opinions Related to Integration Scale (ORI); instrument modified to measure attitudes toward specific categories of disability; 181 undergraduate students in required seminar courses.	Significant main effect of disability category on perceived ability to teach favoring learning disabilities; ratings of benefits of inclusion did not differ across 4 classes (freshman–senior); analysis of comments: students did not feel prepared and were concerned about lack of preparation.
Corbett, N. L., Kilgore, K. L., & Sindelar, P. T. (1998)	How do students in a collaborative program make sense of diverse perspectives they are taught, and how do these diverse perspectives affect their teaching practice?	Qualitative study; thematic analysis of observation, interview, and document data	Six volunteer preservice students, all female; 10-week internship; observation with follow-up interview, structured interview, stimulated recall interview using video, cooperating teacher interview	Three themes: The more we know the better we teach; we take responsibility for students with disabilities; we have management down. Participants overlooked theoretical conflicts.
Elksnin, L. K. (1998)	Preliminary investigation of use of case method of instruction by special education teacher educators	Twenty-four-item survey on case method of instruction developed for study including forced choice, checklist, and open-ended responses	Two hundred fifty-seven members of Teacher Education Division of Council for Exceptional Children; 141 respondents	Seventy-eight percent used cases; 15% used commercial cases; 49% used combination of own, student-generated and commercial cases; used most frequently in methods and assessment classes
Hutchinson, N. L., & Martin, A. K. (1999a)	Document and interpret case studies of 5 preservice students regarding beliefs and practices teaching students with disabilities	Self-study: qualitative, thematic analysis of 5 written cases generated by preservice students	Five general education students placed at one elementary school for 14-week practicum; course topic on critical issues in education with emphasis on special education; cases written by preservice students	All candidates tried to accommodate students; presented complexity of cases and their own tensions in decision making; were not defeated by existing school culture

(Continued)

TABLE 9.1
(Continued)

Studies[a]	Question and Focus	Research Tradition	Research Design	Findings
Hutchinson, N. L., & Martin, A. K. (1999b)	Cross-case analysis of case studies across as cohort of students; primarily interested in beliefs and practices of inclusive education for pupils with disabilities	Self-study; qualitative thematic analysis across all written cases generated by preservice students	Twenty-eight general education students enrolled in 14-week field-based course with seminar 1 hour/week as community of practice; course topic on critical issues in education with emphasis on special education; cases written by pre-service students	Twenty-one dilemma cases written, students took a critical stance; 7 vignettes written, students accepted status quo; 25 questioned own assumptions about working with students with disabilities; adaptations of students who wrote dilemma cases were intensive; students who wrote vignettes created adaptations that scratched the surface only.
Levin, B., Hibbard, K., & Rock, T. (2002)	What is effect of problem-based learning (PBL) on preservice student learning to teach student with disabilities? What knowledge, skills, and attitudes do students gain as they move through PBL?	Self-study, mixed-method; qualitative analysis of pre- and postreaction papers; 28-item survey on beliefs about inclusion	Forty-four preservice teachers in second semester of program; 10 hour/week field experience with 2-hour weekly seminar; PBL activities on special education integrated into seminar; focus on responding to request to accept position in an inclusive classroom	Increase from 19 to 32 students accepting position in inclusive classroom post-PBL activities; decrease from 15 to 11 declining position; decrease from 10 to 1 undecided; 50% of reasons for declining offer related to lack of knowledge; change toward more positive beliefs significant on survey
Lombardi, T. P., & Hunka, N. J. (2001)	What levels of competence and confidence exist among students and faculty in an integrated program as an indication of strength of special education program strand?	Six-item survey with closed and open-ended questions on 10 special education outcomes and 28 special education competencies	Seventy-two preservice teacher education students in first 4 years of a 5-year program; 11 general education faculty	Significant differences between 2nd-year, and 3rd-, and 4th-year students, on acquisition of outcomes and competencies favoring 3rd- and 4th-year students; much learning on topic took place in PDS; lack of consistency of faculty coverage of specific outcomes in classes; range of faculty perceptions of competence and confidence

Study	Research question	Method	Sample	Findings
Maheady, L., Mallette, B., & Harper, G. (1996)	How effectively do general education preservice students' implement a pair tutoring model, and what effect does the model have on pupils with disabilities?	Analysis of tutoring journals for descriptive data on quality and quantity of field experience; surveys of consumer satisfaction with 7-point scale; reading rate data (curriculum based assessments)	Two hundred sixty-four preservice general education students participating in required tutoring field experience, for two 1-hour weekly sessions, as part of Introduction to Exceptional Learner course; 118 tutored students in after school program, 72 with disabilities	Twenty-six hundred eighty-two hours of tutoring over 1 academic year; average increases of over 50% in oral reading rates for 72 tutor pairs; mean satisfaction ratings all above 6.03.
Mallette, B., Maheady, L., & Harper, G. F. (1999)	What effect does reciprocal peer coaching have on preservice general education students' ability to implement an educational intervention? How does coaching affect pupil learning?	Single subject, multiple baseline with reciprocal peer coaching intervention	Intro to special education course with required 8-week field experience; 3 dyads of preservice students tutoring in after-school program using Peer Assisted Learning Strategies (PALS); in dyads, 1 teaches, 1 observes and collects data	Fidelity of implementation improved 15% following training; improvement on comprehension measures for pupils ranging from 2% to 20% on daily measures; greater gains by dyads who had better implementation skills; inconsistent use of feedback across dyads, with most on how to implement PALS
Marlowe, M., & Maycock, G. (2001)	Is there a relationship between reading literature about children with disabilities and attitudes of preservice students about working with students with disabilities?	Quasi-experimental; random selection of intact groups; 7-point semantic differential instrument as pre- and postmeasure of attitudes	Two sections of Introduction to Teaching classes; same instructor; $n = 20$ for experimental group, and $n = 18$ for control group; module on reducing stereotypes of students with disabilities; control group used conventional texts; experimental group used trade books	Significant positive effect of using literary texts on preservice students' attitudes toward characteristics of children with disabilities
McNaughton, D., Hall, T. E., & Maccini, P. (2001)	What is the perceived impact, benefits, and barriers to using case-based instruction (CBI) in teacher education?	Survey on demographics followed by telephone or e-mail interview; qualitative, thematic analysis of interviews	In-depth interviews with faculty in special education who had made professional presentations on use of case-based instruction;	Cases used in classes ranging from 7 to 38 students; 87% had goal of knowledge and skill acquisition; 87% use cases because they are a decision-making model;

(continued)

TABLE 9.1
(Continued)

Studies[a]	Question and Focus	Research Tradition	Research Design	Findings
			thematic analysis	benefits include solving "real-world" problems, consideration of multiple perspectives; barriers include time, classwide acquisition of fundamental skills
Nowacek, E. J., & Blanton L. P. (1996)	What is the effect of a collaborative course on attitudes and knowledge of general education preservice students?	Quasi-experimental, pre- and postdesign on 22-item attitude scale, concept map, and response to video vignette	Seventeen elementary and 10 special education majors in experimental group; 12 elementary majors in control group; experimental form of methods course team taught with collaboration content included	No significant differences in attitude; concept maps showed shifts to greater emphasis on lesson plans and instructional processes for experimental group, and to classroom management and instructional materials for control group; more weaknesses than strengths identified for student with disabilities in video vignette
Rademacher, J. A., Wilhelm, R. W., Hildreth, B. L., Bridges, D. L., & Cowart, M. F. (1998)	How do different special education course configurations affect attitudes toward inclusion of general education preservice students?	Seventeen-item survey plus content analysis of 2 open-ended questions	Seventy-eight interns in 3 conditions: on campus class, professional institute with 1-semester PDS placement, onsite coursework with 2-semester PDS placement	Significant positive change for all groups on knowledge of student characteristics; for both PDS groups on understanding special education programs; students with disabilities becoming economically independent, and general education teachers making modifications
Sobel, D. M., Taylor, S. V., Kalisher, S. M., & Weddle-Steinberg, R. A. (2002)	How are preservice teachers' beliefs regarding diversity revealed and realized in classroom interactions, practices, and observations?	Self-study; interpretive, critical content analysis of preservice student journals	Seven graduate preservice students in large urban school; 1-year internship; 1 journal entry per week required; responding to prompts about cultural diversity	Three themes: value of equity in classroom instruction and practices; value of family involvement; value of cultural sensitivity.

Reference	Research question	Method/analysis	Sample	Findings
Taylor, S. V., & Sobel, D. M. (2001)	What are entering beliefs of cohort of preservice students regarding needs of students whose backgrounds and abilities are not the same as their own?	Descriptive data on demographics of cohort and responses to 34-item questionnaire including Likert scale, definition of terminology, and open-ended responses	One hundred twenty-nine newly admitted graduate preservice students in collaborative teacher education program	Strong belief in teachers' responsibility to provide equitable education for all students and to believe in ability of all students to learn; capable of confronting prejudices; need to learn more to be able to meet students' needs
Tomlinson, C. A., Callahan, C. M., Tomchin, E. M., Eiss, N., Imbeau, M., & Landrum, M. (1997)	How do student teachers come to understand and address the needs of learners who are academically diverse?	Qualitative study: structured observation protocols, field notes, semistructured interviews; preordinate codes for thematic analysis	Seventy preservice students in 6 IHEs, randomly selected; 6-hour required workshop or 6-hour workshop with curriculum coach on adaptations and modifications for students with disabilities	No difference between workshop-only and workshop-plus-coach groups in thematic analysis. Students articulated their responsibility for differentiating instruction, accepted it as part of their work, and were committed to developing skills, but did not have skills yet. Pull of normative school culture favored standardization of instruction; novices need direct support to develop the skills and inclination to differentiate instruction well.
Trent, S. C., Pernell, E., Mungai, A., & Chimedza, R. (1998)	How do students' cognitions about teaching diverse special education students change in a course on special and multicultural education?	Mixed method. Qualitative, thematic analysis of content of pre- and postconcept maps on effective teaching for culturally diverse learners, rationale for premap, and essay comparing maps; quantitative analysis of measures of centrality and specificity	Thirty general education students randomly selected from 140 in course; 1-semester course with lecture and lab	Broader definitions of diversity, shift from general to specific techniques, strategies, and service delivery models in postmaps; service delivery as new concept on postmaps; significant quantitative differences for relationships among concepts, hierarchies, and links across concepts

[a] Please see References.

TABLE 9.2
How National Standards Explicitly Address the Role of General Education
Teachers With Students With Disabilities

NCATE (1995)	**Standard I.D.2.** Candidates complete a well-developed sequence of courses and experiences in pedagogical studies that help develop understanding and use of *different student approaches to learning for creating instructional opportunities adapted to learners from diverse cultural backgrounds and with exceptionalities (p. 17). Collaboration with school colleagues, parents, and agencies in the larger community for supporting students' learning and well being* (p. 18).
	Standard I.E.2. The learning experiences created by teacher candidates build on students' prior experiences, exceptionalities, and cultural backgrounds based on membership in ethnic, racial, gender, language, socioeconomic, community, and family groups to help all students achieve high levels of learning (p. 18).
	Standard I.G.3. Teaching reflects knowledge about and experiences with cultural diversity and exceptionalities (p. 19).
	Standard I.H.1. The unit selects field experiences, including student teaching and internships, to provide candidates with opportunities to *study and practice in a variety of communities, with students of different ages, and with culturally diverse and exceptional populations* (pp. 19–20).
	Standard III.A.1. Higher education faculty are knowledgeable about, and have experience with, teaching and learning, cultural differences and exceptionalities and their instructional implications (p. 24).
NCATE (2000)	**Standard 4. Diversity. Design, implementation, and evaluation of curriculum and experiences.** Curriculum, field experiences, and clinical practice help candidates to demonstrate knowledge, skills, and dispositions related to diversity. They are based on well-developed knowledge bases for, and conceptualizations of, diversity and inclusion so that candidates can apply them effectively in schools. Candidates learn to contextualize teaching and to draw on representations from students own experiences and knowledge. They learn how to challenge students toward cognitive complexity and engage all students, including students with exceptionalities, through instructional conversation. Candidates and faculty review assessment data that provide information about candidates' ability to work with all student and develop a plan for improving their practice in this area (p. 29). **Experiences working with diverse students in P–12 schools.** Extensive and substantive field experiences and clinical practices are designed to encourage candidates to interact with exceptional students and students from different ethnic, racial, gender, socioeconomic, language, and religious groups. The experiences help candidates confront issues of diversity that affect teaching and student learning and develop strategies for improving student learning and candidates' effectiveness as teachers (p. 31).
INTASC (1992)	**Principle 3.** The teacher understands how students differ in their approaches to learning and creates instructional opportunities that are adapted to diverse learners. [The specific knowledge item related to disability under this principle is as follows: *The teacher knows about areas of exceptionality in learning—including learning disabilities, visual and perceptual difficulties, and special physical or mental challenges.*] (p. 14).
INTASC (2001)	**Model Standards for Licensing General and Special Education Teachers of Students with Disabilities** (entire document)

(Continued)

TABLE 9.2
(Continued)

National Board for Professional Teaching Standards (2004)	**Core Proposition 1: Teachers are committed to students and their learning.** Fundamental to the teacher's credo is the belief that all students can learn. Furthermore, they act on that belief. Accomplished teachers like young people and are dedicated to and skilled at making knowledge accessible to all students, even as they acknowledge their distinctive traits and talents. Success depends on teachers' belief in the dignity and worth of all human beings and in the potential that exists within each child. Teachers typically do not work one-on-one with students for extended periods of time because they are responsible for groups. But within this constraint, they are attentive to human variability and its influence on learning.

Teachers treat students equitably. As stewards for the interests of students, accomplished teachers are vigilant in ensuring that all pupils receive their fair share of attention and that biases based on real or perceived ability differences, handicaps or disabilities, social or cultural background, language, race, religion, or gender do not distort relationships between themselves and their students. This, however, is not a simple proposition. Accomplished teachers do not treat all students alike, for similar treatment is not necessarily equivalent to equitable education. In responding to differences among students, teachers are careful to counter potential inequities and avoid favoritism. This requires a well-tuned alertness to such matters and is difficult, as we have only modest knowledge of human differences and how best to respond to them. Hence, accomplished teachers employ what is known about ineffectual and effective practice with diverse group of students, while striving to learn more about how best to accommodate those differences.

Core Proposition 5: Teachers are members of learning communities.

Teachers contribute to school effectiveness by collaborating with other professionals. Accomplished teachers attend to issues of continuity and equity of learning experiences for students that require schoolwide collaboration across the boundaries of academic tracks, grade levels, special and regular instruction and disciplines. Such boundaries, constructed as much out of traditional patterns of school organization as out of instructional rationales, are often dysfunctional and damaging to student learning. National Board Certified teachers cultivate a critical spirit in appraising such schooling commonplaces, together with a willingness to work with administrators toward schoolwide improvements that can include revision of organizational as well as instructional features of schooling.

Accomplished teachers also participate in the coordination of services to students. Today's schools include a wide variety of educational specialists, and with increasing specialization has come the need for coordination, lest pupils' educational experiences become fragmented. The increased practice of "mainstreaming" special-needs students to assure that they are being educated in the least restrictive environment has meant that general and special education teachers need to work with one another. Compensatory education programs typically involve teaching pupils outside regular school settings. The various forms of English as a second language, bilingual and English-immersion programs often require cooperation among teachers of non- and limited-English-speaking youth. National Board Certified teachers are adept at identifying students who might benefit from such special attention and at working in tandem with specialists. (www.hbpts.org) |

REFERENCES

Artiles, A. J., & Trent, S. C. (1994). Overrepresentation of minority students in special education: A continuing debate. *The Journal of Special Education, 27,* 410–437.

Artiles, A. J., & Trent, S. C. (1997). Forging a research program on multicultural pre-service teacher education in special education: A conceptual scheme. In J. W. Lloyd, E. Kameenui, & D. Chard (Eds.), *Educating students with disabilities* (pp. 275–304). Hillside, NJ: Lawrence Erlbaum Associates.

Ball, E. W., & Harry, B. (1993). Multicultural education and special education: Parallels, divergences and intersections. *The Educational Forum, 57,* 430–436.

Banks, J. A. (1995). Multicultural education: Historical development, dimensions, and practice. In J. A. Banks & C. M. Banks (Eds.), *Handbook of research on multicultural education* (pp. 3–24). New York: Simon & Schuster Macmillan.

Behrens, T., & Grosenick, J. K. (1978). Deans' grants projects: Supporting innovation in teacher education programs. In J. K. Grosenick & M. C. Reynolds (Eds.), *Teacher education: Renegotiating roles for mainstreaming* (pp. 1–5). Minneapolis: National Support Systems Project, University of Minnesota and the Council for Exceptional Children.

Blanton, L. P. (1992). Pre-service education: Essential knowledge for the effective special educator. *Teacher Education and Special Education, 15*(2), 87–96.

Blanton, L. P., Griffin, C. G., Winn, J. A., & Pugach, M. C. (Eds.). (1997). *Teacher education in transition: Collaborative programs to prepare general and special educators.* Denver: Love Publishing Company.

Bondy, E., & Ross, D. (2005). *Preparing for inclusive teaching: Meeting the challenges of teacher education reform.* Albany, NY: SUNY Press.

Brownell, M. T., & Pajares, F. (1999). Teacher efficacy and perceived student success in mainstreaming students with learning and behavior problems. *Teacher Education and Special Education, 22,* 154–163.

Campbell-Whatley, G. D., & Comer, J. (2000). Self-concept and African-American student achievement: Related issues of ethics, power and privilege. *Teacher Education and Special Education, 23,* 19–31.

Cloud, N. (1993). Language, culture and disability: Implications for instruction and teacher preparation. *Teacher Education and Special Education, 16,* 60–72.

Corrigan, D. (1978). Political and moral contexts that produced P. L. 94-142. *Journal of Teacher Education, 29*(6), 10–14.

Cranston-Gingras, A., Raines, S., Paul, J., Epanchin, B., & Roselli, H. (1996). Developing and using cases in a partnership teaching environment. *Teacher Education and Special Education, 19,* 158–168.

Day-Vines, N. L. (2000). Ethics, power and privilege: Salient issues in the development of multicultural competencies for teachers serving African-American students with disabilities. *Teacher Education and Special Education, 23,* 3–18.

Donovan, M. S., and Cross, C. T. (Eds.). (2002). *Minority students in special and gifted education.* Washington, DC: National Research Council.

Dunne, L. F. (2002). Characteristics of unified and separate early childhood education and early childhood special education programs: A national study. *Teacher Education and Special Education, 25,* 219–235.

Englert, C. S., Tarrant, K. L., & Mariage, T. V. (1992). Defining and redefining instructional practice in special education: Perspectives on good teaching. *Teacher Education and Special Education, 15,* 62–86.

Feretti, R. P., MacArthur, C. D., & Okolo, C. (2001). Teaching for historical understanding in inclusive classrooms. *Learning Disability Quarterly, 24,* 59–72.

Ford, B. A. (1992). Multicultural training for special educators working with African-American youth. *Exceptional Children, 59,* 107–114.

Ford, A., Pugach, M. C., & Otis-Wilborn, A. (2001). Preparing general educators to work with students who have disabilities: What's reasonable at the pre-service level? *Learning Disability Quarterly, 24,* 275–285.

Giangreco, M. F., Dennis, R., Cloninger, C., Edelman, S., & Schattman, R. (1993). "I've counted Jon": Transformational experiences of teachers educating students with disabilities. *Exceptional Children, 59,* 359–372.

Gollnick, D. M., & Chinn, P. (1998). *Multicultural education: Education in a pluralistic society* (5th ed.). Upper Saddle River, NJ: Merrill/Prentice Hall.

Grosenick, J. K., & Reynolds, M. C. (Eds.). (1978). *Teacher education: Renegotiating roles for mainstreaming.* Minneapolis: National Support Systems Project, University of Minnesota and the Council for Exceptional Children.

Haisley, F. B., & Gilberts, R. D. (1978). Individual competencies needed to implement P. L. 94-142. *Journal of Teacher Education, 29*(6), 30–33.

Harry, B. (2002). Trends and issues in serving culturally diverse families of children with disabilities. *Journal of Special Education, 36,* 131–139.

Hasbrouck, J. E. (1997). Mediated peer coaching for training pre-service teachers. *The Journal of Special Education, 31,* 251–271.

Hindin, A., Morocco, C. C., & Aguilar, C. M. (2001). "This book *lives* in our school:" Teaching middle school students to understand literature. *Remedial & Special Education, 22,* 204–213.

Howey, K. (1996). Designing coherent and effective teacher education programs. In J. Sikula (Ed.), *Handbook of research on teacher education* (2nd ed., pp. 143–170). New York: Simon & Schuster Macmillan.

Hudson, P., Miller, S., Salzberg, C., & Morgan, R. (1994). The role of peer coaching in teacher education programs. *Teacher Education and Special Education, 17,* 224–235.

IDEA. 20 U. S. C. Secs. 1400–1485.

Interstate New Teacher Assessment and Support Consortium. (1992). *Model standards for beginning teacher licensing and development: A resource for state dialogue.* Washington, DC: Council of Chief State School Officers.

Interstate New Teacher Assessment and Support Consortium. (2001, May). *Model standards for licensing general and special education teachers of students with disabilities: A resource for state dialogue.* Washington, DC: Council of Chief State School Officers.

Jones, S. D., & Messenheimer-Young, T. (1989). Content of special education courses for pre-service general education teachers. *Teacher Education and Special Education, 12,* 154–159.

Kennedy, E. M. (1978). P. L. 94-142 poses lofty challenge. *Journal of Teacher Education, 29*(6), 7.

Kleinhammer-Tramill, J. (2003). An analysis of federal initiatives to prepare regular educators to serve students with disabilities: Deans' Grants, REGI and beyond. *Teacher Education and Special Education, 26,* 230–245.

Kleinhammer-Tramill, J., & Fiore, T. A. (2003). A history of federal support for preparing special educators and related services personnel to serve children and youth with disabilities. *Teacher Education and Special Education, 26,* 217–229.

Kleinhammer-Tramill, P. J., Peters, J. T., & Fiore, T. A. (2001, March). The federal role in preparation of special education personnel: An historical perspective. *Policy Perspectives* (Vol. 2, No. 3, pp. 1–8). Washington, DC: American Association of Colleges for Teacher Education.

LaMontagne, M. J., Johnson, L. J., Kilgo, J. L., Stayton, V., Carr, V., Bauer, A. M., et al. (2002). Unified early childhood personnel preparation programs: Perceptions from the field. *Teacher Education and Special Education, 25,* 236–246.

Lowenbraun, S., & Nolen, S. B. (1998). Implementing change in a research university: Constructivist team teaching in a general education teacher education program. *Teacher Education and Special Education, 21,* 34–36.

Maheady, L. (1997). Preparing teachers for instructing multiple ability groups. *Teacher Education and Special Education, 20,* 322–339.

Maheady, L., Harper, G. F., & Mallette, B. (2001). Peer-mediated instruction and interventions and students with mild disabilities. *Remedial and Special Education, 22,* 4–14.

Marlowe, M., Maycock, G., Palmer, L., & Morrison, W. F. (1997). Using literary texts in teacher education to promote positive attitudes toward children with emotional and behavioral disorders. *Behavioral Disorders, 22,* 152–159.

McLeskey, J., Waldron, N. L., So, T. H., Swanson, K., & Loveland, T. (2001). Perspectives of teachers toward inclusive school programs. *Teacher Education and Special Education, 24*, 108–115.

Miller, P. S., & Stayton, V. D. (1998). Blended interdisciplinary teacher preparation in early education and intervention: A national study. *Topics in Early Childhood Education, 18*, 49–58.

Minke, K. M., Bear, G. G., Deemer, S. A., & Griffin, S. M. (1996). Teachers' experiences with inclusive classrooms: Implications for special education reform. *The Journal of Special Education, 30*, 152–186.

Morgan, R. L., Gustafson, K. J., Hudson, P., & Salzberg, C. L. (1992). Peer coaching in a preservice special education program. *Teacher Education and Special Education, 15*, 249–258.

Morocco, C. (2001). Teaching for understanding with students with disabilities: New directions for research on access to the general education curriculum. *Learning Disability Quarterly, 24*, 5–14.

Morocco, C. C., Hindin, A., Mata-Aguilar, C., & Clark-Chicarelli, N. C. (2001). Building a deep understanding of literature with middle-grade students with learning disabilities. *Learning Disability Quarterly, 24*, 47–59.

Munby, H., & Hutchinson, N. (1998). Using experience to prepare teachers for inclusive classrooms: Teacher education and the epistemology of practice. *Teacher Education and Special Education, 21*, 75–82.

National Association of State Directors of Teacher Education and Certification. (2004). *The NASDTEC manual 2004: Manual on the preparation and certification of educational personnel* (5th ed.). Sacramento, CA: School Services of California, Inc.

National Board for Professional Teaching Standards. (2004). *About NBPTS: Five core propositions.* Retrieved April 19, 2005, from http://www.nbpts.org/about/coreprops.cfm.

National Commission on Excellence in Education. *A nation at risk: The imperative for educational reform.* (1983). Washington, DC: Author.

National Council for Accreditation of Teacher Education. (2000). *Professional standards for the accreditation of schools, colleges and departments of education.* Retrieved April 19, 2005, from http://www.ncate.org.

National Council for Accreditation of Teacher Education. (1995). *Standards, procedures and policies for the accreditation of professional education units.* Washington, DC: Author.

National Support Systems Project. (1980). *The Deans' Grant projects: Descriptive analysis and evaluation.* Minneapolis: College of Education, University of Minnesota.

Obiakor, F. E. (2001). Multicultural education: Powerful tool for preparing future general and special educators. *Teacher Education and Special Education, 24*, 241–255.

Otis-Wilborn, A., & Pugach, M. C. (2002). Beyond standards: Creating depth in teacher education reform. In G. G. Griffin & Associates (Eds.), *Rethinking standards through teacher preparation partnerships* (pp. 141–164). Albany, NY: SUNY Press.

Palincsar, A. S., Magnusson, S. J., Collins, K. M., & Cutter, J. (2001). Making science accessible to all: Results of a design experiment in inclusive classrooms. *Learning Disability Quarterly, 24*, 15–32.

Patton, J. M., & Townsend, B. L. (1999). Ethics, power and privilege: Neglected considerations in the education of African American learners with special needs. *Teacher Education and Special Education, 22*, 276–286.

Pierce, T., & Miller, S. P. (1994). Using peer coaching in pre-service practica. *Teacher Education and Special Education, 17*, 215–223.

Pugach, M. C. (2001). A deans' grant initiative for the twenty-first century? *Teacher Education and Special Education, 24*, 256–261.

Pugach, M. C., & Seidl, B. L. (1996). Deconstructing the diversity-disability connection. *Contemporary Education, 68*(1), 5–8.

Pugach, M. C., & Seidl, B. L. (1998). Responsible linkages between diversity and disability: A challenge for special education. *Teacher Education and Special Education, 21*, 319–333.

Rosenberg, M. (1999). Descriptions of new and innovative personnel training programs. *Teacher Education and Special Education, 22*, 287–288.

Ross, D. D., Lane, J., & McCallum, C. (2005). In E. Bondy & D. Ross (Eds). *Preparing for inclusive teaching: Meeting the challenges of teacher education reform* (pp. 51–67). Albany, NY: SUNY Press.

Rueda, R. (1989). Defining mild disabilities with language-minority children. *Exceptional Children, 56,* 121–128.

Schalock, H. D. (2002). Teacher work sample methodology with a standards orientation. In G. R. Girod (Ed.), *Connecting teaching and learning: A handbook for teacher educators on teacher work sample methodology* (pp. 33–64). Washington, DC: American Association of Colleges for Teacher Education, ERIC Clearinghouse on Teaching and Teacher Education and Western Oregon University.

Scruggs, T. E., & Mastropieri, M. A. (1996). Teacher perceptions of mainstreaming/inclusion, 1958-1995: A research synthesis. *Exceptional Children, 63,* 59–74.

Smith, J. E., & Schindler, W. J. (1980). Certification requirements of general educators concerning exceptional pupils. *Exceptional Children, 46,* 394–396.

Study of Personnel Needs in Special Education. (2000). *General education teachers' role in special education* (fact sheet). Retrieved April 19, 2005 from http://ferdig.coe.ufl.edu/spense/

Tharp, R. G., & Gallimore, R. (1988). *Rousing minds to life: Teaching, learning and schooling in social context.* Cambridge, England: Cambridge University Press.

The Holmes Group. (1986). *Tomorrow's teachers: A report of the Holmes Group.* East Lansing, MI: Author.

Tom, A. R. (2005). A general teacher educator's reflections. In E. Bondy & D. Ross (Eds.), *Preparing for inclusive teaching* (pp. 257–271). Albany, NY: SUNY Press.

Treder, D. W., Morse, W. C., & Ferron, J. M. (2000). The relationship between teacher effectiveness and teacher attitudes toward inclusion. *Teacher Education and Special Education, 23,* 202–210.

Trent, S. C., Artiles, A. J., Fitchett-Bazemore, K., McDaniel, L., & Coleman-Sorrell, A. (2002). Addressing theory, ethics power and privilege in inclusion research and practice. *Teacher Education and Special Education, 25,* 11–22.

Urban, W. J. (1990). Historical studies of teacher education. In W. H. Houston (Ed.), *Handbook of research on teacher education* (pp. 59–71). New York: Macmillan.

U. S. Department of Education, Office of Special Education Programs. (2002). To assure the free, appropriate public education of all children with disabilities. *Twenty-fourth Annual Report to Congress on the Implementation of the Individuals with Disabilities Education Act* (IDEA). Washington, DC: U.S. Government Printing Office.

Van Zandt, L. M. (1998). Assessing the effects of reform in teacher education: An evaluation of the 5-year MAT program at Trinity University. *Journal of Teacher Education, 49,* 120–131.

Voltz, D. J. (2003). Collaborative infusion: An emerging approach to teacher preparation for inclusive education. *Action in Teacher Education, 25,* 5–13.

Voltz, D. L. (1998). Cultural diversity and special education teacher preparation: Critical issues confronting the field. *Teacher Education and Special Education, 21,* 63–70.

Voltz, D. L., Dooley, E., & Jefferies, P. (1999). Preparing special educators for cultural diversity: How far have we come? *Teacher Education and Special Education, 22,* 66–77.

Waldron, N. L., McLeskey, J., & Pacciano, D. (1999). Giving teachers a voice: Teachers' perspectives regarding elementary inclusive school programs (ISP). *Teacher Education and Special Education, 22,* 141–153.

Woodward, J., Monroe, K., & Baxter, J. (2001). Enhancing student achievement on performance assessments in mathematics. *Learning Disability Quarterly, 24,* 33–47.

Zeichner, K. M., & Zore, J. M. (1990). Teacher socialization. In R. Houston (Ed.), *Handbook of research on teacher education* (pp. 329–348). New York: Macmillan.

PRESERVICE TEACHER EDUCATION STUDIES CITED

Cook, B. (2002). Inclusive attitudes, strengths and weaknesses of pre-service general educators enrolled in a curriculum infusion teacher preparation program. *Teacher Education and Special Education, 25,* 262–277.

Corbett, N. L., Kilgore, K. L., & Sindelar, P. T. (1998). "Making sense" in a collaborative teacher education program: Lessons from Project PART students. *Teacher Education and Special Education, 21,* 293–305.

Elksnin, L. K. (1998). Use of the case method of instruction in special education teacher preparation programs: A preliminary investigation. *Teacher Education and Special Education, 21,* 95–108.

Hutchinson, N. L., & Martin, A. K. (1999a). The challenge of creating inclusive classrooms: Experiences of teacher candidates in a field-based course. *Teacher Education Quarterly, 26*(2), 51–70.

Hutchinson, N. L., & Martin, A. K. (1999b). Fostering inclusive beliefs and practices during pre-service teacher education through communities of practice. *Teacher Education and Special Education, 22,* 234–250.

Levin, B., Hibbard, K., & Rock, T. (2002). Using problem-based learning as a tool for learning to teach students with special needs. *Teacher Education and Special Education, 25,* 278–290.

Lombardi, T. P., & Hunka, N. J. (2001). Preparing general education teachers for inclusive classrooms: Assessing the process. *Teacher Education and Special Education, 24,* 183–197.

Maheady, L., Mallette, B., & Harper, G. (1996). The pair tutoring program: An early field-based experience to prepare pre-service general educators to work with students with special needs. *Teacher Education and Special Education, 19,* 277–297.

Mallette, B., Maheady, L., & Harper, G. F. (1999). The effects of reciprocal peer coaching on pre-service general educator's instruction of students with special learning needs. *Teacher Education and Special Education, 22,* 201–216.

Marlowe, M., & Maycock, G. (2001). Using literary texts in teacher education to promote positive attitudes toward children with disabilities. *Teacher Education and Special Education, 24,* 75–83.

McNaughton, D., Hall, T. E., & Maccini, P. (2001). Case-based instruction in special education teacher preparation: Practices and concerns of teacher educator/researchers. *Teacher Education and Special Education, 24,* 84–94.

Nowacek, E. J., & Blanton, L. P. (1996). A pilot project investigating the influence of a collaborative methods course on pre-service elementary education teachers. *Teacher Education and Special Education, 19,* 298–312.

Rademacher, J. A., Wilhelm, R. W., Hildreth, B. L., Bridges, D. L., & Cowart, M. F. (1998). A study of pre-service teachers' attitudes toward inclusion. *The Educational Forum, 62,* 154–163.

Sobel, D. M., Taylor, S. V., Kalisher, S. M., & Weddle-Steinberg, R. A. (2002). A self-study of diversity: Pre-service teachers' beliefs revealed through classroom practices. *Multiple Voices* 5(1), 1–12.

Taylor, S. V., & Sobel, D. M. (2001). Addressing the discontinuity of students' and teachers' diversity: A preliminary study of pre-service teachers' beliefs and perceived skills. *Teaching and Teacher Education, 17,* 487–503.

Tomlinson, C. A., Callahan, C. M., Tomchin, E. M., Eiss, N., Imbeau, M., & Landrum, M. (1997). Becoming architects of communities of learning: Addressing academic diversity in contemporary classrooms. *Exceptional Children, 63,* 269–282.

Trent, S. C., Pernell, E., Mungai, A., & Chimedza, R. (1998). Using concept maps to measure conceptual change in pre-service teachers enrolled in a multicultural education/special education course. *Remedial and Special Education, 19,* 16–31.

10

Research on Accountability
Processes in Teacher Education

Suzanne M. Wilson
Peter Youngs
Michigan State University

The past decade has seen a strong push by states, the federal government, foundations, and national organizations for more accountability in teacher education. The states in particular have mandated teacher certification tests, changed accreditation procedures, and imposed other accountability measures in an attempt to raise the quality and qualifications of the teacher workforce. This chapter explores the history of accountability processes in teacher education and summarizes the contemporary research in that domain.

Whether teachers need to be certified to teach—and if so, how—is a politicized, often contentious matter of debate (see, e.g., Walsh, 2001a, 2001b; Darling-Hammond, 2001). Several themes run through these debates, including questions about the merit of teacher preparation, about the skills and knowledge teachers must possess, and about who has jurisdiction over certifying and licensing teachers.

Critics of the education establishment see traditional approaches to certification as an obstacle in the path of talented college graduates eager to enter teaching. Recent criticisms call for the elimination of bureaucratic obstacles, optional attendance at schools of education, and streamlined requirements (focusing largely on higher standards for verbal ability and content knowledge) (U.S. Department of Education, 2002; Walsh, 2001a).

For supporters of traditional teacher certification, certification bolsters public confidence that everyone hired to teach in a public school possesses necessary professional knowledge, skill, and experience. Supporters of traditional certification sometimes argue for more preparation and more regulation; critics often argue for less or no regulation.

Complicating matters further are questions about jurisdiction. Who has the right to control teacher certification and licensure? For those who argue that teaching and teacher education are professions, teachers and teacher educators should police their own ranks. But public school teachers are also seen as civil servants who must be held accountable by the state (Mitchell & Kerchner, 1983). The education establishment's critics believe that the public, through the state, should control teacher certification and licensure. This struggle over control of the terrain is a classic problem across professions (Abbott, 1988). For example, treatment of the mentally ill originally fell under the jurisdiction of the law until the medical profession—specifically the arm that emerged as psychiatry—claimed jurisdiction and redefined the problem not as one of maintaining order, but as one of treating disease (Abbott). Given contemporary debates about accountability in teacher education, questions of jurisdictional competition are helpful in considering arguments over what constitutes preparation for teachers and whether and who (schools of education, K–12 schools, or the state) should certify teachers' competence.

To inform those debates, this chapter offers a thorough examination of the peer-reviewed literature concerning the impact of accountability processes in teacher education on teachers' knowledge, skill, and behaviors and on student achievement. The question underlying this analysis is: What is the research base for the accountability processes currently used in teacher preparation, specifically teacher testing, certification, and accreditation? What is known about the impact of these processes on teachers' learning, knowledge, professional practices, and students' learning?

We consider this question by reviewing literature on teacher testing, initial certification, and accreditation. The chapter's arguments are easily summarized: The literature on teacher testing is outdated, focusing primarily on tests no longer in use. The research that does exist suggests that such tests have content and concurrent validity, but there is little evidence that such tests have predictive validity; that is, that a relationship exists between teachers' scores on such tests and their teaching success (measured in terms of teacher behavior, principal ratings, or student achievement). The literature on certification is also limited, but the trend is in favor of certification over noncertification or undercertification. With regard to the literature on accreditation, it is usually informational: Articles describe the process of participating in accreditation review or feature recommendations for other institutions as they prepare for reviews. Empirical studies on the impact of accreditation policies and processes are almost nonexistent.

Given the impassioned debates about whether accountability processes lead to higher teacher quality, we need much more research—rigorously conducted with sophisticated measures of teacher quality characteristics and designed with a sharper eye toward the complexities of teacher certification and licensure across the states—before we can confidently assert that certain accountability processes enhance or compromise teacher quality.

We examine first the historical and contemporary contexts of accountability in teacher education before summarizing the research.

A BRIEF HISTORY OF TEACHER CERTIFICATION AND PROGRAM ACCREDITATION

Let us begin by defining our terms. *Certification*, or licensing, is the process by which states assess the qualifications of *individuals* to teach. Currently, tests for making certification decisions include tests of basic skills and general academic ability, subject matter knowledge, and pedagogical knowledge, as well as performance-based assessments of teachers' instructional practices. Certification, however, does not have to involve such tests; in some states, teachers can become certified by attending recognized programs of teacher preparation or submitting evidence of completing certain requirements (e.g., an undergraduate degree in a relevant subject matter). In other states, candidates must complete teacher preparation and pass one or more certification tests.

Accreditation is the process by which an institution (a college or university) convinces the public and other institutions of its program's soundness and rigor. Accreditation, as van Vught (1994) suggests, may "be the most fully developed institutionalization of the idea of accountability in higher education" (p. 42). Program accreditation is:

> A quality assurance process based on program review . . . a means to verify the quality of academic programs and of institutions to external stakeholders. The accreditation process most often involves a formal review, with self-study of a specific academic program, evaluations by peers and external constituents and a report to the agency, association or organization that will certify program quality. (Lubinescu, Ratcliff, & Gaffney, 2001, p. 8)

Accreditation procedures within teacher education include those developed by individual states, as well as the National Council for the Accreditation of Teacher Education and, more recently, the Teacher Education Accreditation Council.

Historically, neither teacher certification nor teacher education program accreditation have inspired much public confidence. For instance, in the last 20 years, most states have added basic skills tests—tests that most people presume would be a prerequisite for college, not a prerequisite for a professional credential—to the battery of requirements for teacher certification. In its 1998 reauthorization of Title II of the Higher Education Act (Public Law 105–244), Congress mandated that each state report annually the percentage of teaching candidates who passed state certification tests. In so doing, it "federalized teacher testing" (Ludlow, Shirley, & Rosca, 2002, p. 1). As a result, Congress singled out teaching as the only profession required to do so; business, law, medicine, physical therapy, and nursing schools were not asked to report on the percentage of candidates who were passing professional certification exams (Murray, 2001).

To understand contemporary certification and accreditation practices, let us briefly consider their history. According to Angus (2001), the U.S. movement to centralize state authority of teacher certification was clearly visible by the late 19th century, with roots in traditions established in colonial America. For instance, in the colonies, many communities required that teachers be approved by their ministers, who were most concerned with a potential teacher's moral fiber.

Gradually, authority for approving teachers shifted from the community's spiritual leader to the state. According to Sedlak (1989), by the 1840s, the majority of U.S. teachers received their teaching certificate from local officials based on their performance on an examination. The first examinations were most often short, oral examinations given by community members that focused on the candidate's character; these evolved into longer, written examinations that assessed the candidate's subject matter knowledge. Occasionally, a few questions would be asked concerning pedagogy and child development. This certification system—which granted local officials the power to appoint teachers—was often used inappropriately, favoring family relatives or political supporters. Over time, the practice faced growing opposition from the public, state administrators, and teachers, who argued that to raise educational standards, the state had to centralize control over the field by introducing state licensure requirements (Sedlak, 1989).

As the demand for teachers grew, so did normal schools, teacher education institutions that provided a high school education (sometimes extending into the first two years of college) for prospective teachers. Over time, some states moved away from direct assessments of candidate knowledge and integrity. Angus (2001) reported that, by 1897, "twenty eight states certified teachers based on graduation from a normal school" (p. 5). Other states continued to require normal school graduates to sit for state or county examinations.

Even in these early stages, there was wide variation among the states over who had jurisdiction for preparing teachers and what teachers were supposed to know. For instance, the rapid growth of urban centers during the mid-1800s led to teacher shortages in elementary schools in cities. Angus (2001) noted that city high schools or normal schools—controlled by local boards of education—were often empowered to issue teaching certificates. Urban boards of education "were able to control the supply of teachers for the city schools by raising and lowering entrance requirements, by issuing certificates only to those who had received their training in those schools, and even by suspending the training programs during brief periods of oversupply" (p. 6). Teachers graduating from normal schools and urban programs were expected to have a high school subject matter education (or first two years of college), as well as some foundational and pedagogical knowledge. What constituted foundational and pedagogical knowledge expanded, becoming better articulated as normal schools expanded.

Meanwhile, rural schools, lacking the urban centers' ready supply of high school students, also struggled to find teachers. Several Midwestern legislatures created "teacher institutes" to supply these schools with teachers. State-subsidized, the institutes were run by county superintendents. Some normal school faculty were suspicious of the quality of these early "alternative routes." Angus (2001) suggested that these institutes were "despised" by the professional teacher educators housed in the normal schools, because they largely helped candidates simply brush up on basic subjects and attend a few lectures on good teaching provided by locally respected teachers. Expectations were minimal and county teacher licensing examinations were given at the institute's conclusion. These examinations, too, were considered suspect by the normal school faculty who saw them as unprofessional shortcuts into teaching. In summary, throughout the 19th century, "there were as many approaches to the certification of teachers as there were states" (Angus, p. 11).

State departments of education grew rapidly during the first third of the 20th century, and normal schools evolved into teacher colleges (Labaree, 1998). A consensus about what constituted teacher preparation began to emerge within the so-called progressive educational establishment (Angus, 2001; Ravitch, 2000). Competition arose between the universities and normal schools for who should teach the teachers. Although most Eastern normal schools eventually ceded to the universities in the domain of preparing high school teachers, in the Midwest, the normal schools fought to remain the dominant preparer of both elementary and secondary teachers.

Teacher certification became increasingly centralized. Frazier (1938, as quoted in Angus, 2001) reports the data found in Table 10.2.

Throughout this period, Angus (2001) argues that teacher colleges and universities were united in supporting three trends: an increase in formal requirements for teacher education, a decline in the use of examinations, and an increase in the number of teaching specializations (and requisite certificates). Gradually, views of what constituted professional knowledge expanded further. Preparation came to include courses in the history of education, educational psychology, principles of education, teaching methods, and assessment. By the 1930s, states also began specifying requirements for liberal education, although in 1930, 27 states had no academic requirements for high school teachers other than graduation from a recognized college. This led to the first public outcry about teachers' teaching out of field. One study found that in 1933 to 1934, fewer than 30% of high school teachers in Kansas were teaching in their major (Angus).

At the same time, examinations began to disappear from the teacher certification landscape. By 1937, 28 states had abolished teacher testing, relying solely on graduation from a professional training program for certification. Angus (2001) argues that the education establishment "vilified" such examinations, seeing them "as a 'back door' into teaching through which people with inferior training and talents 'infiltrated' the profession" (p. 19).

Post-World War II America witnessed the most severe crisis in teacher supply to date (Angus, 2001; Sedlak & Schlossman, 1986). The number of emergency certified teachers rose from 2,305 in 1940–1941 to 69,423 in 1943–1944. By war's end, there were over 108,000 emergency-credentialed teachers (Angus). Despite these shortages, 23 states increased requirements for elementary teacher certification between 1943 and 1953 to a minimum of a 4-year college degree. Examinations disappeared and most states discontinued the local issuance of teaching certificates.

Simultaneously, serious concerns about the quality of teacher preparation were voiced. In 1946, the National Education Association created the National Commission on Teacher Education and Professional Standards (TEPS), which was to develop professional standards in teaching (teachers would then control entry into teaching) and give teachers more say in professional preparation. TEPS aimed to sponsor conferences about relevant topics, which would lead to proposals for change, disseminated through a network of state affiliates. One important objective was to push for the delegation of authority for teacher certification to state departments of education. Another mission included arguing for the "approved program" approach to program oversight. Instead of requiring certain courses and hours of study, the state department would approve an institution, leaving the program details to the institution.

TEPS leaders were sharply critical of existing teacher preparation programs, both at universities and teacher colleges. Ralph MacDonald, the first TEPS Executive Secretary, proclaimed:

> The teacher education system of the United States, with the exception of a very few states, is a hodgepodge of programs which are in the main a travesty upon professional education. . . . We even provide a better-planned and better-financed system of professional education for those who raise pigs than we do for those who teach children. (MacDonald, quoted in Angus, 2001, p. 24)

In response to the rising concern about teacher preparation, the National Council for the Accreditation of Teacher Education (NCATE) began to take shape. In 1948, the American Association of Colleges of Teacher Education (AACTE) was formed from the merger of the National Association of Colleges and Departments of Education, the National Association of Teacher Education Institutions in Metropolitan Districts, and the American Association of Teachers Colleges, a department of the National Education Association (NEA). In 1952, AACTE, TEPS, and the National Association of State Directors of Teacher Education and Certification (NASDTEC) created NCATE as the central body for accreditation. Although the organization was conceptualized as a way to give practicing teachers and liberal arts and sciences faculty more voice in teacher education policy and practice, Angus (2001) claimed that the teacher education establishment gradually took over the governing body through iterative reorganizations that marginalized teachers. By 1959, five years after NCATE began accrediting programs, 17 states had included some provision for NCATE accreditation in their reciprocity agreements for teachers moving across state lines. By 1961, NCATE had approved only 342 of the then 1,100 teacher education programs nationwide.

Meanwhile, criticism of teacher quality and teacher education continued. Rudolf Flesch's (1955) *Why Johnny Can't Read—And What You Can Do About It* was a widely read critique of teaching and teacher quality. In 1963, James Koerner's *The Miseducation of American Teachers* characterized teachers as a sincere and humanitarian lot, but badly educated and ineffective. In the same year, James Conant (1963) declared in *The Education of American Teachers* that the only essential portion of professional preparation was a high quality field experience.

These criticisms of teaching, when joined with the increased militancy of teachers and push for unionization in the 1960s, seriously undercut the TEPS' professionalization agenda with its standards, standards boards, and controlled entry into the profession. Although efforts to professionalize teaching were heard again in the 1980s and 1990s, especially in discussions concerning both the Holmes Group and the National Board for Professional Teaching Standards (NBPTS), the political and intellectual contexts in which these discussions took place had significantly changed. The public had a deeper suspicion of teacher quality and demanded more accountability. This is perhaps seen most clearly in the reemergence of teacher tests. By 2002, 37 states required teaching candidates to pass basic skills tests to earn a teaching certificate; 33 states required them to pass tests of subject matter knowledge; and 26 states required them to pass tests of pedagogical knowledge (Youngs, Odden, & Porter, 2003).

Moreover, we have witnessed a significant shift away from a "hands-off" federal role in defining teacher quality, including requirements for teacher preparation (Ramirez, 2003). Although the Clinton administration largely supported the teacher professionalism agenda (consider its significant support of NBPTS), when Congress reauthorized Title II of the Higher Education Act in October 1998, it sought to hold institutions of higher education accountable for teacher preparation by requiring them to report candidate pass rates on state licensure exams. At the same time, critics of the Title II reauthorization questioned whether teacher quality could be assessed by such examinations, especially when education schools had no control over what candidates were taught in disciplinary departments.

In 2002, the No Child Left Behind Act called for "highly qualified teachers" (HQTs) in every classroom. HQTs would have state certification and pass a required licensing examination. In the Secretary's Annual Report on Teacher Quality in June 2002, U.S. Secretary of Education Rod Paige argued that teacher verbal ability and subject matter knowledge were the primary characteristics of the HQT (U.S. Department of Education [USDE], 2002). The Bush administration's belief that traditional teacher education and certification were obstacles for promising teacher candidates was also reflected in its withdrawal of NBPTS support and considerable financial support ($5 million in 2002) for the newly created American Board for Certification of Teacher Excellence (ABCTE), which was designed to ease entry into teaching by allowing teacher candidates with an appropriate undergraduate degree to take a certification examination and bypass teacher preparation (Metzger, 2004).

In summary, in over a century and a half, we have shifted from local control to centralization of teacher certification. We have had an ambivalent relationship with teacher testing, with early suspicions concerning the capacity of tests to be trustworthy measures of an individual's capacity to teach and as inappropriate "shortcuts" into teaching. From the start, there have been serious concerns about the quality and rigor of teacher preparation. The accreditation movement arose in attempts to monitor and enhance program quality, but fewer than 40% of existing programs are nationally accredited. Further, the accreditation process was taken over by the very people—teacher educators—who some critics blamed for teachers' poor preparation (Angus, 2001). These themes resonate with contemporary discussions of accountability processes in teacher education, including such questions as: Should teacher certification and licensure be a local or centralized process? Who should make decisions about teacher certification? What should certified teachers know and be able to do? How can we best demonstrate that teacher candidates possess that knowledge and skill?

CURRENT ACCOUNTABILITY PRACTICES
IN TEACHER EDUCATION

In a comparative study, Wang, Colement, Coley, and Phelps (2003) found that the U.S. system of teacher education and certification is much more decentralized that those of several other countries. It is, as Angus (2001) noted, a "national non-system" (p. 1). Nonetheless, there are generalizations that we can make about the current practices of teacher certification and program accreditation, the primary institutional means the field has to hold teacher education accountable.

Certification and Licensure

Individual states are responsible for certifying and licensing teachers; most states award an initial teaching certificate after successful completion of an approved program. All states require that teacher candidates possess a bachelor's degree in education or a content area. Most states also require that teacher candidates have some supervised student teaching experience, which varies from nine to 18 weeks. Fourteen states have professional standards boards or commissions that establish state licensure requirements.

Forty-two states require some form of teacher testing (NASDTEC, 2000). Teacher tests can include tests of basic skills, general knowledge, subject matter knowledge, or pedagogical knowledge. The two primary test development companies are Educational Testing Service (ETS) and National Evaluation Systems (NES), although some states have created their own certification tests. In part because different tests are used to evaluate candidates within and across more than 25 credential areas (e.g., elementary education, chemistry, art, and special education), there are more than 600 teacher tests of basic skills, subject matter knowledge, and teaching knowledge currently in use (Mitchell, Robinson, Plake, & Knowles, 2001).

States vary in terms of other requirements, which can include character recommendations, oaths of allegiance, U.S. citizenship, or a minimum age (NASDTEC, 2000). Once they receive a bachelor's degree, pass any required tests, and meet these other requirements, teacher candidates receive a license.

Most states have a staged licensure process. Thirty-one states require an initial license that is valid for two to five years, with a permanent license to follow when additional requirements are fulfilled (e.g., completing advanced degrees or continuing professional development). To earn a full license, some states require teachers to pass assessments of classroom performance. These assessments include the Connecticut/ Interstate New Teacher Assessment and Support Consortium (INTASC) content-specific portfolios and Praxis III, an observation instrument developed by ETS. Only 13 states offer advanced certification; in 2004, only two states were using Praxis III. Teachers may also receive advanced certification through NBPTS.[1]

At the beginning of this decade, approximately 45 states and the District of Columbia offered alternative certification programs. On entry, most participants in these programs have bachelor's degrees in a subject other than education and have completed little or no education school coursework or student teaching. Requirements for alternative route candidates to earn initial or full licensure vary across the states, although most require candidates to complete additional coursework and pass state licensing exams before receiving a teaching credential (see Zumwalt and Craig (this volume) and Zeichner and Conklin (this volume)).

Accreditation

All states require that teacher preparation programs receive state approval, which is typically based on state standards; approval standards and licensure requirements are unique to each state. Unlike professions such as architecture, medicine and law, national accreditation is not required in teacher education (Mitchell et al., 2001). Over half of the 1,300 U.S. teacher education programs are regionally accredited. Less than 40% are accredited by NCATE or TEAC, the two national organizations.

The content and character of state accreditation vary. Some states do paper reviews of program curricula; others have on-site reviews conducted by teams of professionals. Some states have performance or competency-based processes, requiring that programs demonstrate how they ensure that prospective teachers have acquired necessary knowledge and skill; others examine program outcomes, examining graduation, job placement, and retention rates.

In more than 40 states, teacher education programs can also obtain national accreditation in addition to state approval. In some states, programs can substitute national accreditation for state accreditation. Twelve states require their teacher education

---

[1]Because this volume focuses on research on teacher preparation, we do not include research on advanced certification, including research on permanent licensure (which typically occurs 2 to 5 years after initial licensure), INTASC assessments (intended for teachers with approximately 2–3 years of experience), or NBPTS assessments.

programs to use NCATE standards; more than 40 states encourage national accreditation through partnerships (Mitchell et al., 2001). Current estimates are that NCATE has accredited approximately 550 institutions, with 100 others in process. State processes are also influenced by standards for beginning teachers issued by various organizations, including INTASC.

An alternative accreditation body, the Teacher Education Accreditation Council (TEAC), was created in 1997 by a group of education school deans and college presidents. Officially recognized by the U.S. Department of Education as a specialized accreditor in 2003, TEAC plans to accredit teacher education programs based on their performance in relation to internally derived objectives and standards (Murray, 2000, 2001). As Murray (2001) noted: "TEAC . . . answered questions more about the program than the institution. Is there credible reason to believe the faculty has accomplished what it thinks it has accomplished, how does it know, and is the evidence strong enough to convince disinterested experts?" (p. 54). TEAC currently works with both private and public universities; approximately 70 programs have satisfied TEAC's eligibility requirements and currently have candidate status in TEAC. To date, the council has accredited 7 programs (TEAC, 2003).

Finally, as already noted, Congress, in its 1998 reauthorization of the Higher Education Act, directed each state to report the percentage of teaching candidates who pass state certification tests. In addition, these requirements include a mechanism for limiting access to federally funded student financial aid in programs whose students perform poorly. It was within this historical and contemporary context that we reviewed the relevant research literature. We now turn to that review, beginning with a brief discussion of our search process and then summarizing and commenting on the literature.

EMPIRICAL RESEARCH ON ACCOUNTABILITY PROCESSES IN TEACHER EDUCATION: TEACHER TESTING, TEACHER CERTIFICATION, AND ACCREDITATION

Search Strategies and Decision Rules

In searching for published, peer-reviewed literature on teacher accountability processes (defined here to include teacher testing, traditional teacher certification, and accreditation policies and processes), we searched electronic databases in education, psychology, and economics. We used extensive literature reviews to identify other relevant articles. We followed procedures similar to those summarized by Cochran-Smith and Fries (this volume).

Three electronic databases were searched extensively: (a) the ERIC database, which indexes journals and technical literature from *Resources in Education* and *Current Index to Journals in Education;* (b) PsycLit, which houses the American Psychological Association's *Psychological Abstracts;* and (c) EconLit, which corresponds to the American Economic Association's *Journal of Economic Literature* and the *Index of Economic Articles.*[2] We also drew on other literature reviews to identify articles, including Allen

---

[2]The following search terms were used with all three electronic databases: accredit*; certificat*; licens*; student achievement; student performance; teach* practices; teacher assessment; teacher education; teacher preparation; teacher quality; teacher test; and Title II.

(2003), Darling-Hammond and Youngs (2002), Rice (2002), Wayne and Youngs (2003), Wilson, Floden, and Ferrini-Mundy (2001), and Wilson and Floden (2002).

In determining which studies to include, we followed these decision rules: (a) the data concerned U.S. teachers; (b) the outcome measure was some form of student achievement or teacher classroom performance; and (c) prospective and practicing teachers were included as subjects. Because the literature was so limited, we broadened our search. Instead of examining only literature published since 1990, we examined literature published in peer-reviewed journals or the equivalent between 1975 and 2003. We did not include in the review any research on the validity of state teacher tests that had not been submitted for peer review.

We then read the full pool of potential manuscripts and included only those that met the standards identified by the Panel, 23 reports in all. We start with a review of literature on teacher testing, and then move to a review of research on the effects of teacher certification. Finally, we consider the limited literature on accreditation before laying out recommendations for future research.

Research on Teacher Testing

As we have seen, the history of teacher testing is uneven: After an initial reliance on teacher examinations through the mid-19th-century, states moved away from such tests. Only in the last 20 years have we seen a gradual return to their use.

Teacher tests range from tests of basic skills to tests of liberal arts or general knowledge, subject matter knowledge, and pedagogical knowledge. Some variation in states' use of tests is due to differing conceptions of teacher professional knowledge. Most are multiple-choice examinations; states set their own cutoff scores for both basic skills and teaching examinations.

Despite this variation, we can make some generalizations about these tests. For the most part, the tests set minimum standards for teacher knowledge: They are not designed to distinguish between minimally competent and "highly qualified" teachers. Nor are they designed to predict teaching success (Mitchell et al., 2001).

Two vendors dominate the market for teacher licensure tests: ETS and NES. Of the states that require tests, approximately 80% use some portion of ETS's Praxis Series: Professional Assessments for Beginning Teachers (a three-part assessment including Praxis I—tests of basic academic skills; Praxis II—tests of content knowledge and professional knowledge; and Praxis III—assessments of classroom performance) (ETS, 2003). Approximately 400,000 prospective teachers take some part of Praxis II each year (Latham, 2004). NES has developed over 400 different teacher tests for various states (Mitchell et al., 2001). Because of the recent rebirth of interest in teacher tests, it is difficult to get stable and up-to-date statistics on use. Table 10.3 describes what the landscape looked like in 1998–1999.

In 1998, more states used basic skills tests than any other kind of test; 38 states required teachers to pass such tests for initial licensure. Fourteen states also required some test of general knowledge, typically presumed to be an assessment of a liberal arts education. Twenty-one states required subject matter knowledge tests. The Praxis II tests included 126 different subject matter tests; for its part, NES has developed over 360 tests (see Table 10.4; Mitchell, Robinson, Plake, & Knowles, 2001).

In 1988, 28 states used tests to assess teacher candidates' pedagogical knowledge, including the professional knowledge tests from ETS. These assessments cover areas like planning instruction, evaluating instruction, classroom management, and assessment. INTASC is developing a new test for pedagogical knowledge, the Test of

Teaching Knowledge (TTK). As of 2003, two secure forms of the test were being developed to measure domains aligned with INTASC standards, including knowledge of theories of teaching and learning; cognitive, social, and physical development; diagnostic and evaluative assessments; language acquisition; and the role of student background in learning (INTASC, 2003).

Finally, a growing number of states also require an assessment of prospective teachers' pedagogical content knowledge (Shulman, 1986). The Praxis II series includes tests of pedagogical content knowledge in several domains.

The plethora of tests available for teacher testing presents considerable challenges for researchers interested in the impact of those assessments on teachers and their students, a matter we discuss later in this chapter. Another complicating factor is that states use the tests at different points in a prospective teacher's journey through certification and licensure.

A final complicating factor is that passing scores are determined by states, not by the testing houses. Thus, what constitutes passing in one state is not comparable to another, even when states use the same examinations.

We found 14 studies that examined issues related to teacher tests. We begin with research involving tests developed by ETS.

Research on the National Teacher Examination

For years, the National Teacher Examination (NTE) was the dominant force in the teaching landscape, and several researchers inquired into both its concurrent and predictive validity. On the matter of concurrent validity, Egan and Ferre (1989) examined the relationship between sophomore grade point average (GPA), ACT subtest scores (in English, math, social science, science, and composite), and NTE Core Battery scores for 94 undergraduates who completed majors in education at a Midwestern public state institution. The NTE Core Battery included tests of general knowledge, professional knowledge, and communication skills. For each teacher, the researchers performed a stepwise regression analysis for each of their NTE Core Battery test scores.[3] They found that ACT English and ACT composite scores were the best predictors of NTE communication skills scores; the ACT composite score was the best predictor of NTE general knowledge scores; and ACT English and GPA were the best predictors of NTE professional knowledge scores. Similar results were found with the cross-validation group.

But that tells us little about the predictive validity of the NTE; that is, whether it is related to measures of teacher effectiveness or student learning. We found six relevant studies related to this question: All but one found no significant relationships between the test and successful teaching. Before examining that literature, we note that ETS does not claim that its tests predict future teaching success. ETS has a well-articulated process for checking its tests' content validity, based on literature reviews, interviews with experts, and expert panels. Even after ETS establishes that its tests have content validity, it requires that any state interested in adopting the examinations conduct its own content validity studies, using their own state teaching standards.

Although these teacher tests are not promoted as predicting future teaching success, the current policy context—with its increasing press for accountability—involves the increased use of such tests and, often, the implicit assumption is that a passing score

---

[3]Correlations computed for GPA, ACT subtest scores, and NTE Core Battery test scores showed a significant correlation for each pair of variables at the .01 level.

is related to teacher quality and signifies the capacity to teach successfully. For that reason, we examine the limited, although outdated, literature on the NTE's predictive validity.

Ayers (1988) examined the NTE's concurrent and predictive validity by correlating teachers' performance on the NTE Core Battery tests with GPA, ACT scores, principals' ratings, student ratings, and observer ratings. Forty-six teachers in Grades 1 to 7 participated in the study. GPA was the best predictor of NTE scores in most areas except for General Knowledge. ACT scores correlated significantly with all the NTE Core Battery Tests and appeared to be a better predictor of success on the NTE than did GPA. In terms of predictive validity, no significant correlations were found between the NTE scores and principal ratings, student ratings, or observer ratings, except for a significant relationship between the principals' ratings for overall performance of elementary teachers and their NTE scores on the specialty area test. No information was provided about the reliability of the principals' evaluations. We also note that the researcher did not control for student, school, or community characteristics.

Lawrenz (1975) examined the relationship between five teacher characteristics and student achievement in science: knowledge of subject matter and teaching methods, experience, attitude toward science, professional self-improvement, and type of learning environment created. Lawrenz obtained a random sample of 236 secondary science teachers from 14 states. Eighty-four teachers taught biology, 111 taught chemistry, 41 taught physics. The 14 states were stratified by city size and a percentage of schools from each population were randomly selected. The participating teachers completed a questionnaire, the NTE science exam, the Science Process Inventory (SPI), and the Science Attitude Inventory (SAI). Lawrenz obtained measures of teachers' subject matter knowledge from their NTE and SPI scores and measures of teachers' attitudes toward science from their SAI scores. Each teacher randomly selected one class of students to complete four instruments: the Learning Environment Inventory (LEI), the Test on Achievement in Science (TAS), the SPI, and the SAI.

The study used data disaggregated at the classroom level. The three teacher tests and the student tests all had high levels of reliability. In terms of the issue of reverse causation (i.e., the possibility that better schools get better teachers), Lawrenz controlled for the effects of family and community background characteristics through use of a stratified random sample. In terms of sensitivity of students' performance on tests to teacher effects, the NTE and SPI measured teachers' knowledge of science, whereas the SPI and TAS assessed students' knowledge and skills in science. In other words, the NTE and SPI measured teacher skills closely related to the skills measured by the SPI and TAS tests.

The author reported that the selected teacher characteristics were significantly related to student attitude toward and achievement in science. In particular, Lawrenz's (1975) analysis indicated that teachers' scores on the SPI were significant predictors of student achievement on the TAS and the SPI. However, teachers' subject matter knowledge, as measured by the NTE, was negatively correlated with student achievement. The author suggested that teachers' knowledge of the scientific process might be distinct from their knowledge of scientific substance and that the former might be more important for teaching effectiveness.

Sheehan and Marcus (1978) examined the relationship between teachers' performance on the Weighted Common Examinations Total (WCET) and student math and vocabulary achievement. The WCET was part of the NTE and measured general academic and professional knowledge. The sample consisted of 119 first-grade teachers and 1,836 first-grade students from a large urban school district in 1973 to 1974.

The researchers used stepwise regression analyses to determine the predictive power of teacher WCET scores for student mathematics and vocabulary achievement. Teachers' WCET scores ranged from 333 to 732, with a mean of 516. The pretest measures were the Metropolitan Reading Tests (MRT) word meaning and number tests, administered by the district in September 1973. The posttest measures were the Iowa Tests of Basic Skills (ITBS) vocabulary and mathematics subtests administered by the district in September 1974. The dependent variables in the regression analyses were the class-average ITBS mathematics and vocabulary raw scores. The researchers found that WCET scores were significant, positive predictors of student mathematics and vocabulary achievement.

When race was entered into the regression analysis, the magnitude of the contributions of the WCET scores lessened; they were no longer significantly related to student achievement in either mathematics or vocabulary. In this study, the researchers did not control for the effects of students' socioeconomic status. Overall, their findings suggested that the teacher characteristics measured by the WCET component of the NTE might not have been related to student achievement.

Ayers and Qualls (1979) conducted a longitudinal study of the relationship between NTE scores and undergraduate success (GPA), other test scores (ACT), certain personal characteristics, principal and pupil ratings, and classroom observations. The data were aggregated at the level of teacher type (elementary vs. secondary). In general, no significant relationships were found between principal ratings and NTE scores, with the exception of a single significant positive relationship ($p < .05$) between principals' rating of secondary teachers' subject matter knowledge and the NTE. In terms of pupil ratings, few significant relationships were found. In general, the correlations between NTE scores and observational data were low, although there was a positive correlation between teachers' NTE scores and how alert, responsible, and confident their students were. However, no information was provided about the reliability of the principals' evaluations. The researchers did not control for the possibility that school quality could have affected the quality of teachers' practices.

Andrews, Blackmon, and Mackey (1980) reported results for 269 teacher education students who completed the NTE Common Examinations and the NTE Subject Area Examinations. Results were reported for only 4 of the 26 NTE subject areas: elementary education, secondary English, special education, and physical education. Supervising teachers' ratings of teacher education students on 22 teaching performance items were used.

The authors found a highly significant relationship for elementary teacher education students between the WCET and only 3 of the 22 student teaching performance ratings: appearance, enthusiasm, and English usage. Similarly, relationships between candidate performance on the NTE elementary examination and student teaching performance were significant for only four items. Finally, composite NTE score and GPA correlated at the .0001 level of significance.

For secondary English majors who took the NTE English language and literature area examination, Andrews, Blackmon and Mackey (1980) reported significant relationships between the WCET and only two performance measures during student teaching: subject matter knowledge and supervisors' rating of the students' general information. At the same time, there was a significant relationship between the WCET and students' cumulative GPA. In addition, the subject matter and general information ratings were significantly related to the broader NTE composite score.

The researchers found a significant relationship between the WCET and GPA for special education majors as well as a significant, negative relationship between the weighted common examination and their overall performance ratings in student teaching. Finally, a highly significant negative relationship was found between their scores on the NTE area examination and their overall student teaching performance ratings.

Andrews et al. (1980) concluded that the significant relationships found between the NTE weighted common scores and cumulative GPA for three of the four subject areas (all but physical education) suggested that academic performance was a useful predictor of NTE scores. They added that this conclusion was supported by the similar significant relationships found between the NTE composite scores and the grade-point averages. They noted, however, the following:

> ... the data in this study indicate that the NTE is valid for what is taught in the college classroom but not necessarily for predicting teacher performance, a conclusion in keeping with the NTE literature ... [T]he sparsity in this study of significant positive relationships between the NTE scores and teaching performance ratings, when coupled with the presence of a few significant negative relationships, tends to undermine confidence in the relationship of NTE scores to teaching performance ratings. (p. 359)

The study had some limitations. No information was provided about the reliability of the outcome measures (undergraduate GPA, supervising teachers' ratings of student teaching performance). Nor did the authors control for the effect of K–12 students' socioeconomic status on ratings of student teaching performance.

In the one study that found positive relationships between the NTE and impact measures, Strauss and Sawyer (1986) examined the determinants of average student performance on standardized tests and the extent to which students failed such tests, using data from 145 North Carolina school districts for 1977 to 1978. The study looked at six inputs: number of teachers in the district, number of students, number of high school students interested in postsecondary education, racial composition of schools, insured value of district's capital stock (for 105 districts), and average NTE scores for new teachers in each district. The researchers used two measures of student performance: (a) percentage of high school juniors who failed the reading and math competency examinations in spring 1978, and (b) average achievement of students on the Norm Referenced Achievement (NRA) Test administered to the same group of high school juniors in 1978.

When estimating their first model, Strauss and Sawyer (1986) found that more than 83% of the variation in the student failures in reading and math was explained by the six inputs. The most significant and sizable variable that influenced failures was the average level of teacher quality (as measured by average NTE scores). In contrast, the effects of class size, number of teachers, and number of students with post-high school educational intentions were not significant. Employing a second model to explain the variance in the rate of student failures, Strauss and Sawyer found that more than 37% of the variation was explained by the six inputs; teachers' NTE scores again were the largest, most significant variable.

In their third model (which explained the variance in students' average reading and math scores), the researchers found that teachers' NTE scores had a more modest effect on student achievement. Finally, Strauss and Sawyer (1986) substituted per capita income for the capital variable and found that teachers' NTE scores still had large, statistically significant effects on students' failure rates and average reading and math scores.

As was the pattern in this body of research, no information was provided about the reliability of the outcome measures (student performance on the competency and

NRA tests). In terms of reverse causation, Strauss and Sawyer included a capital variable (to control for community background factors), but only had district capital data for 105 of the 145 districts. In terms of sensitivity of students' performance on tests to teacher effects, the researchers did not indicate which components of the NTE were taken by the teachers (i.e., subject area, professional knowledge, and/or general knowledge). As a result, one can only say that the teacher tests measured teacher skills that were related to the skills measured by the student tests (reading and mathematics competency exams and NRA tests). The teacher tests would have measured teacher skills closely related to the skills measured by the student tests if the teachers had taken the NTE subject area tests in English/language arts and mathematics.

Off the topic of the relationship between the NTE and teacher effectiveness, we found one study (Murnane, Singer, Willett, Kemple, & Olsen, 1991) in which the investigators were able to take advantage of changing certification requirements to draw conclusions about the effects of differing certification requirements on who applies for certification or licensure. In North Carolina, removal of the licensure requirement for a minimum NTE test score increased the number of college graduates who applied for a teaching license. Reinstatement of the requirement reduced the number of applicants. The effect was more pronounced for Blacks than for Whites. During the period in which the NTE requirement was eliminated, those licensees who nevertheless took the NTE examination (even though not required) were more likely to enter teaching in North Carolina within three years than those who did not take the exam. Among the licensees who took the NTE during the period when it was not required, those with higher scores were less likely than those with lower scores to enter teaching within three years of licensure.

In sum, six of the eight studies that we examined concerning the NTE explored relationships between the NTE and measures of teacher effectiveness (measured by pupil and principal ratings, teacher behaviors and student achievement on standardized tests). Most found no relationship. Only one study found that teachers with higher NTE scores had a significant, albeit modest, impact on student reading and mathematics achievement and significantly lower student failure rates (Strauss & Sawyer, 1986). Only one study that included measures of teacher effectiveness also controlled for students' socioeconomic status.

In addition, one study found that the removal of the NTE requirement for licensure increased the number of licensure applications; however, during the 3 years when the requirement was suspended, prospective teachers with higher NTE scores were less likely to join the teaching force. Based on this research, we are inclined to believe that although the NTE might be correlated with success in university coursework or teacher candidates' performance in those courses, it did not predict teacher effectiveness.

Research on the Praxis Series Examinations

In the 1990s, there was a gradual shift away from the NTE to the Praxis Series. This transition took place during a time of increased concern about articulating the professional knowledge base of teaching and requiring teachers to demonstrate much more than basic knowledge. Shulman (1986) had argued persuasively for a more fully elaborated understanding of teacher knowledge; INTASC and NBPTS were created to develop standards and assessments that would reflect and measure these new notions of professional knowledge. ETS was a significant actor during this period, sponsoring discussions about teacher professional knowledge and teacher assessment. And the shift away from the NTE to Praxis reflected a substantial shift along numerous dimensions, including both what to assess and how.

The transition from the NTE to Praxis took place in the second half of the 1990s and was completed by 2000. As noted above, more than 30 states use Praxis I and/or II in granting admission to teacher education programs and making licensure decisions. Given their recent arrival on the educational landscape, there is not yet an extensive research literature about the Praxis tests; however, there are now a few studies that have investigated the relationship of Praxis tests to various outcome measures. We found three relevant to this review.

Wenglinsky (2000) selected a sample of 40,000 teaching candidates from the Southeast United States who had taken Praxis II tests of professional knowledge. The database provided Praxis II scores as well as background information including parents' educational levels, candidates' ethnicity, the teacher education institution (TEI) they had attended and their scores on Praxis I or the SAT (if they had taken them). The researcher also collected data on the schools, colleges, and departments of education (SCDEs) where the teachers were trained.

The author compared candidates' scores on six Praxis II assessments among seven types of teacher education institutions. The assessments were elementary education, early childhood education, educational leadership, communication skills, general knowledge, and professional knowledge. Communication skills, general knowledge, and professional knowledge form the core battery, which is given to prospective teachers in some states regardless of the subject they intend to teach. Tests in specific subjects were not included due to the small numbers of candidates who had taken any given one of these tests. The study also examined the relationship between SCDE characteristics and Praxis II scores, including (a) whether the percentage of minority faculty was greater in the SCDE than in the TEI in which it was located, (b) the SCDE's scope, that is, the percentage of undergraduates who major in education and the percentage of the institution's budget spent on the SCDE; (c) whether most education majors had a traditional undergraduate experience; and (d) whether the SCDE was involved in the local community.

For all six Praxis II assessments, Wenglinsky (2000) found that prospective teachers from private institutions scored higher than those from public institutions; prospective teachers from universities scored higher than those from colleges; and prospective teachers from larger institutions scored higher than those from smaller institutions (all of these findings were significant at a $p < .05$ level). The author added that more advantaged students (in terms of parents' education and SAT scores) attended institutions that were larger, private, and enrolled a greater percentage of graduate students. When students' socioeconomic status (SES) and prior test scores were controlled, the study still found that university students outperformed those who attended colleges and that students at private institutions outperformed those at public ones.

Wenglinsky (2000) also reported that more affluent students were more likely to attend private institutions and universities and that they were more likely to be exposed to diverse faculty and engage in traditional college experiences. In sum it appeared that two characteristics of teacher education institutions and three characteristics of schools, colleges, or departments of teacher education had an impact on licensure: private institutions outperform public ones; universities outperform colleges; SCDEs with more diverse faculty outperform SCDEs that are largely White; SCDEs with more traditional students outperform those with fewer traditional students; and SCDEs that are smaller in relationship to the larger institution outperform SCDEs where the role of that unit plays a large role in the overall institution.

In another study sponsored by ETS, Gitomer, Latham, and Ziomek (1999) examined the relationship between college applicants' SAT and ACT scores and their performance on the Praxis I and Praxis II assessments. The researchers analyzed data for all individuals who took the SAT and/or ACT between 1977 and 1995, and also took Praxis I or Praxis II between 1994 and 1997. For the SAT, math and verbal scores were included. For the ACT, English and math scores were included. The dataset included 33,866 Praxis I candidates and 159,857 Praxis II candidates who had taken the SAT and 55,064 Praxis I candidates and 112,207 Praxis II candidates who had taken the ACT. The researchers also considered whether candidates had attended an NCATE-accredited institution as undergraduates.

The researchers assigned a state passing status to each candidate. For each candidate who took a Praxis test, they applied the passing scores in effect in the state in which the candidate took the test. In each case, the respective state's passing standard in 1997 was applied, even though some states may have changed their passing rates between 1994 and 1997. In related analyses, the researchers also assigned passing status based on two hypothetical passing standards: high and low. The high standard employed in the study was the highest passing score used by any state in 1997, whereas the low standard was the lowest passing score used by any state in 1997. The researchers then considered each candidate's passing status in light of the test requirements of the state and these hypothetical passing standards.

Gitomer et al. (1999) reported several findings. First, candidates who passed Praxis I had higher average scores on the SAT (Math, 514; Verbal, 525) and the ACT (Math, 20.4; English, 21.6) than those who failed Praxis I (Math, 414; Verbal, 427; Math, 16.5; English, 16.1). Second, passing rates for Praxis I differed substantially by race and ethnicity (White, 82%; Asian American, 76%; Hispanic, 69%; African American, 46%). Third, candidates who passed Praxis II had lower SAT rates (Math, 507; Verbal 522) than all college graduates (Math, 542; Verbal, 543). Fourth, passing rates for Praxis II differed substantially by race/ethnicity (White, 91%; Asian American, 75%; African American, 69%; Hispanic, 59%).

Among those who had taken the SAT, the study found that current teacher education students had the highest passing rate on the licensure tests (compared to recent preparation program graduates and to those who reported that they had never enrolled in a teacher education program). Those who had never been enrolled in a teacher education program had the lowest passing rates, even though their mean SAT scores were as high as those who were or had been enrolled in teacher preparation programs when they took the licensure tests.

Candidates who had taken the ACT and who had never enrolled in teacher preparation also passed the licensure tests at a lower rate, though their ACT scores were lower than those who were in teacher education programs at the time of testing, but almost identical to those enrolled in such programs in prior years. Finally, the authors noted that increasing the passing scores for Praxis I and Praxis II to their hypothetical standard would result in a group of teaching candidates with higher mean SAT and ACT scores that was less racially and ethnically diverse (Gitomer et al., 1999).

This research suggested that the Praxis exams may very well align with the content of teacher preparation programs. But what about their predictive validity? While no published research on this topic is yet available, it is useful to consider research on related tests. Dybdahl, Shaw, and Edwards (1997) investigated the relationship between the subscores of the Pre-Professional Skills Test (PPST, the precursor to Praxis I) and its predictive validity in a causal comparative study of 375 education majors from 1986 to 1992 at a medium-size urban university. Correlations were computed among the PPST subtests. Outcome measures included GPA, student teaching ratings, local school district interview scores, and postgraduation employment as a teacher.

Correlations between the subtests ranged from .42 to .58; all were significant at the .05 level. Correlations were also significant between the subtest scores and sophomore English and general education mathematics course grades ($p < .001$). Correlations calculated to examine predictive validity were mixed: Correlations between the subtest scores and overall GPA ranged from .32 to .39 (all of which were significant at the .05 level); the correlation between the subtest scores and the composite score was .42 ($p < .001$), which accounts for about 16% of the variance. There appeared to be no significant correlations among the subtest scores and the three other measures of program success: student teaching, district interviews, and employment.

The little research that exists suggests that Praxis might have concurrent and content validity. However, we know nothing about the relationship between prospective teachers' performances on these certification tests and their later effectiveness as teachers, as measured by student achievement, pupil ratings, classroom observations, employment history, or principal ratings. The one study we did find reported no relationship between PPST scores and teaching success.

Research on Other Teacher Tests

On the matter of teacher testing, other studies bear consideration. Ferguson (1991) examined the influence of various schooling inputs on student test scores, while controlling for student background and district characteristics. He analyzed data from almost 900 of Texas's more than 1,000 districts.

For each district, Ferguson (1991) examined teachers' performance on the Texas licensing test, the Texas Examination of Current Administrators and Teachers (TECAT); teachers' years of experience; the percentage of teachers with master's degrees; the average school size; total district enrollment; and number of students per teacher. The TECAT had sections on reading and writing skills, which featured 55 multiple-choice items, and questions about professional knowledge were integrated into several items in both sections. Passing required earning at least 47 points from a possible score of 55.

In his analysis, Ferguson (1991) used the TECAT reading scores; therefore, his results should be interpreted as applying to a test that measured teachers' reading skills and professional knowledge. Students' reading and math scores came from the Texas Educational Assessment of Minimum Skills (TEAMS) exams. These multiple-choice tests were administered to students in grades 1, 3, 5, 7, 9, and 11. The TEAMS results used in the analysis were from the spring semester of the 1985–1986 school year. To control for family and community influences, data from the 1980 U.S. Census were used to calculate school district averages for various socioeconomic indices.

When family and background characteristics were controlled, Ferguson (1991) found that four variables had statistically significant effects on students' scores: TECAT scores, teachers' experience, the number of students per teacher, and the percentage of teachers with master's degrees. Of particular relevance to this review, after first grade, teachers' TECAT scores accounted for 20% to 25% of all variation across districts in students' average scores on the TEAMS exams, suggesting that higher literacy and higher levels of professional knowledge among teachers were significantly related to higher student achievement. In fact, of these four variables, TECAT scores accounted for the largest percentage (20%–25%) of all variation across districts in students' average scores on state assessments.

Again, no information was provided about the reliability of the outcome measures (student TEAMS performance). Regarding reverse causation, Ferguson (1991) controlled for the effects of teacher salaries and socioeconomic status of families in the district, as well as for other socioeconomic and contextual factors. In terms of sensitivity of students' performance on tests to teacher effects, the TECAT measured teachers' reading and writing skills, including verbal ability and research skills, and the TEAMS exams measured students' basic skills in reading and math. In other words, the TECAT measured teacher skills related to the skills measured by the student tests.

Guyton and Farokhi (1987) investigated the relationships between Georgia teachers' performance on a basic skills test and subject matter tests, GPA, and the quality of their instructional practices as measured by the Teacher Performance Assessment Instrument (TPAI). The researchers studied graduates from Georgia State University between 1981 and 1984; samples ranged between 151 and 411 graduates, depending on the availability of data. The researchers found that knowledge of basic skills was correlated with tests of subject matter knowledge, but not with on-the-job performance. Both GPA at the sophomore level and GPA at the upper level (i.e., senior year) were positively correlated with subject matter test scores and TPAI scores, although the upper-level GPA had a much stronger correlation with TPAI scores than the sophomore GPA. There was no significant correlation between performance on the subject matter test (TCT) and on-the-job performance (TPAI).

In terms of the reliability of the outcome measures, the researchers noted that extensive reliability studies had been conducted on the TPAI. Guyton and Farokhi (1987) also noted that the reliability estimates for the TCT ranged from .84 to .93. In terms of reverse causation, the researchers did not control for the possibility that school quality could affect the quality of teachers' practices (i.e., the possibility that teachers might perform better on the TPAI because they were employed in schools with higher teacher salaries and/or that served families from higher socioeconomic backgrounds).

Examining another teacher test, Cobb, Shaw, Millard, and Bomotti (1999) examined the concurrent, systemic, and consequential validity of Colorado's high-stakes teacher tests, Program for Licensing Assessments for Colorado Educators (PLACE). PLACE, which recently was replaced with another testing system, included four test batteries: basic skills (three tests of reading, mathematics, and writing), liberal arts and sciences (one test of broad knowledge), professional knowledge (three tests for elementary, middle, and high school), and content areas (42 tests in specific content areas). Prospective teachers had to pass the basic skills tests, the liberal arts and sciences test, as well as the professional knowledge test for the level they planned to teach and the content test(s) for the subject matter(s) they intended to teach. The data were aggregated at the level of institution of higher education.

Conducting analyses on 1,772 examinees from 4 of the 17 four-year institutions in Colorado that prepare teachers, the researchers identified a number of correlations. The correlations between the basic skills mathematics test and other data (ACT, SAT, and GRE mathematics scores) were relatively consistent and high (.66–.68). Basic skills reading and writing tests had very low correlations with other verbal measures (ranging from .25 to .49 on reading tests and .25 to .39 for writing tests). The liberal arts and sciences test had correlations between .50 and .65 with SAT and ACT scores.

The correlations between the tests of professional knowledge and test takers' GPAs in methods classes and student teaching were very low, ranging from .05 to .25 with the exception of a .66 correlation between student teaching and scores on the middle school professional knowledge exam. Correlations between undergraduate GPA and content area examinations scores were also low, as were correlations between GPA in major and performance on the content area examination (with the exception of mathematics which had a .63 correlation between GPA in major and passing score on content area exam). The authors concluded that the examinations appeared to have reasonable construct validity in how much they represented the domains of knowledge required for teaching as reflected in teacher education programs. At the same time, they noted the tests' construct validity was threatened by the consistently lower performance of non-White individuals. In their view, the basic skills tests may be essential from the perspective of the general public, but they were inefficient (i.e., they have very low failure rates) and yielded the least amount of usable information.

Taking a step back, we ask, what does this research tell us about our original question: What is the research base for the accountability processes currently used in teacher preparation, specifically teacher testing, certification, and accreditation? What is known about the impact of these processes on teachers' learning, knowledge, professional practices, and students' learning? When carefully devised, teacher tests can have construct and concurrent validity, but simply because a published test is used does not guarantee that it meets professional standards for reliability or validity (Haney, Fowler, Wheelock, Bebell, & Malec, 1999; Melnick & Pullin, 2000). There is little evidence that such tests have predictive validity; only 2 studies of the 14 we reviewed found positive correlations (Ferguson, 1991; Strauss & Sawyer, 1986). However, those two studies were also much better designed than the other research reviewed. Nonetheless, we concur with Hanushek (1992) who, while arguing that there was evidence for teacher skill differences, went on to assert that "measured characteristics of teachers do not capture skill differences very well, corroborating previous analyses of the overall inconsistency of results for individual teacher characteristics" (p. 113). That observation certainly holds true here.

The literature suffers from significant weaknesses. First, the research focuses on a defunct examination—the NTE. Second, the literature lacks powerful research designs that reflect an understanding of the variability in teacher tests and their use. Recall especially the fact that teacher tests measure different domains of knowledge and skill, and those measures vary considerably across states. In addition, tests are used at different decision points in a teacher's path toward licensure, and states use different cutoff scores, even when using the same test. Candidates take these tests at different times in their careers—in terms of how much professional preparation they had, whether they completed student teaching, and whether they completed their subject matter majors and minors. The research was not designed to accommodate for these variations. Third, we know very little about the content and concurrent validity of many of the more than 600 tests currently in use.

We know next to nothing about certification tests' predictive validity. Measures of impact were limited in a number of ways. When student test scores were used, it was not clear whether they were aligned with the standards and assessments of teachers; further, they varied across states, making comparisons impossible. Measures of instruction were equally flawed, with many locally developed measures that included observations of teaching, principals' and supervisors' evaluations, hiring and retention rates, job satisfaction analyses, and student questionnaires. Future research will need to make substantial investments in the development of sophisticated designs that reflect the complexity of the testing landscape and appropriate measures of impact. We return to the implications for future research in our conclusion.

RESEARCH ON TEACHER CERTIFICATION

A second approach to examining the literature on the impact of accountability processes is to consider the relationships between the global decision that a teacher is certified and teacher behavior or student achievement. Two approaches dominate the literature: researchers contrast teachers with certification with those who are not certified (or undercertified), or researchers compare teachers with traditional certification and those with alternative certification. Here we focus on the research on certification; readers interested in research on alternative certification should consult Zumwalt and Craig (this volume) and Zeichner and Conklin (this volume).

We found eight studies that shed light on the relationships between certification status (certified, uncertified, and undercertified) and teacher effectiveness. Seven found in favor of certified teachers; one did not. However, what counted as "certified" was a bone of contention with the research community. We address this issue shortly.

Fetler (1999) examined the relationship between school average mathematics achievement test scores (SAT-9) and high school staff characteristics at 795 regular California high schools. The data were aggregated at the school level. More than 1 in 10 mathematics teachers in regular high schools were teaching with emergency permits. Fetler reported a strong negative correlation between student poverty and mathematics achievement. Controlling for the effects of poverty, he found a strong negative relationship between percentage of teachers with emergency certificates and achievement. In particular, there was a consistent negative and significant (.001) correlation among 9th-, 10th-, and 11th-graders' performance on the SAT-9 and the percentage of teachers with emergency certificates, as well as a consistent and significant (again at the .001 level) relationship between teaching experience and student achievement. Higher percentages of emergency permit teachers were consistently associated with lower test scores. The average number of years of teaching experience was positively related to student test scores. In terms of the issue of reverse causation, Fetler controlled for the effects of poverty on student test scores. The study did not involve pre- and posttesting.

Hawk, Coble, and Swanson (1985) used analysis of variance (ANOVA) to examine differences between 18 teachers certified in mathematics (in-field) and 18 who held certification in areas other than mathematics (out-of-field). For the study, each in-field teacher was paired with an out-of-field teacher in the same school, teaching the same mathematics course to students of the same general ability level. Matching certified and noncertified teachers by subject area, student ability level, and school allowed the researchers to control for reverse causation. The student sample included 826 middle and high school students. The Stanford Achievement Test (general math) and the Stanford Test of Academic Skills (algebra) were used to measure student achievement.

Pretest scores were not significantly different for students taught by in-field versus out-of-field teachers. The same Stanford Tests were administered as posttests of achievement after 5 months of instruction. Teachers' mathematical knowledge was measured by their performance on the Descriptive Tests of Mathematical Skills. In addition, the Carolina Teacher Performance Assessment System (CTPAS) was used during two classroom observations to assess teachers' performance in five areas: management of instructional time, management of student behavior, instructional presentation, instructional monitoring, and instructional feedback.

The researchers found that student achievement gains were greater in general mathematics and algebra classes taught by in-field teachers. In addition, the authors found that the teachers certified in mathematics scored significantly higher on the instructional presentation function of the CTPAS. The generalizability of the findings from this study was limited by the small sample size.

Darling-Hammond (2000) used data from the 1993 to 1994 Schools and Staffing Survey (SASS) and the 1990, 1992, 1994, and 1996 National Assessment of Educational Progress mathematics and reading assessments to examine the relative contributions of teaching policies and student characteristics to student achievement. She reported that teacher quality characteristics such as certification status and degree in the field were significantly and positively correlated with student outcomes. The relationship between teachers with master's degrees and student achievement was positive, but not significant.

In the multivariate analyses, Darling-Hammond (2000) reported that "in all cases, the proportion of well-qualified teachers (i.e., those with full certification status) is by far the most important determinant of student achievement" (p. 30). As some observers have noted, when data are aggregated at the state level (as in this study), the variables omitted may bias the coefficients of school input variables upward (Hanushek et al., 1995). Further, the response categories for the question about certification status in the 1993–1994 SASS were not clearly defined, which could have affected the reliability of the item.

Mandeville and Liu (1997) investigated the relationship between the kind of certification status of 7th-grade teachers in South Carolina and their students' achievement, as measured by the Stanford Achievement Test. Schools in which all 7th-grade teachers had secondary mathematics certification or who had 12 or more credit hours in mathematics beyond initial certification were classified as high MATHPREP; schools in which all 7th-grade teachers had elementary certification or were teaching out of field were classified as low MATHPREP. Thirty-three high MATHPREP schools were matched with 33 low MATHPREP schools on SES, size, location, and school-grade organization.

Mean student achievement scores were higher for the high MATHPREP schools than for the low MATHPREP schools. Seventh-grade students tended to perform better on higher level thinking tasks in mathematics when their teachers had advanced certification in mathematics. The differences in student achievement were small and not significantly different when performance was measured on low-level mathematics problems. There was a significant difference in student achievement when students were assessed on thinking skills problems.

In terms of reverse causation, the researchers controlled for students' socioeconomic backgrounds, school size, school location, and school-grade organization. In terms of sensitivity of students' performance on tests to teacher effects, teachers in high MATHPREP schools all had secondary certification or 12 or more credit hours in mathematics beyond initial certification. This level of training made it likely that teachers had acquired teaching skills related to the skills measured by the student tests. On the other hand, it was less likely that teachers in low MATHPREP schools had acquired teaching skills related to those skills.

Laczko-Kerr and Berliner (2002) investigated the relationship between teachers' certification status and student achievement (as measured by SAT-9 class means). They matched 109 undercertified teachers with 109 certified teachers in five districts on grade level and highest degree attained. The undercertified teachers included those who had emergency, temporary, and provisional teaching certificates. To control for such variables as student SES, curriculum, and school characteristics, the researchers matched each pair of teachers based on grade level and highest degree attained.

The researchers found that, for 1998–1999, the students of certified teachers outperformed—in both reading and language—peers taught by undercertified teachers. Levels of performance in mathematics were not significantly different, although the students of certified teachers had higher scores than those of undercertified teachers. In 1999–2000, students of certified teachers outperformed students of undercertified teachers by about 2 months on a grade-equivalent scale in all three areas. Put another way, they concluded that students of undercertified teachers made about 20% less academic growth per year than did students of teachers with regular certification. However, save for matching the teachers, the researchers did not otherwise control for students' prior achievement.

Using data from the National Educational Longitudinal Study of 1988 (NELS:88), Goldhaber and Brewer (2000) examined the relationship between teachers' certification status and the achievement of 12th-grade students in public schools in mathematics and science. Their sample consisted of 3,786 students in mathematics and 2,524 students in science as well as 2,098 math teachers and 1,371 science teachers. The teacher sample included math and science teachers with standard certification (1,695 and 1,106), probationary certification (21 and 23), emergency certification (34 and 24), private school certification (34 and 27) and no certification (52 and 21). The vast majority of the teachers had standard certification (86% in mathematics and 82% in science). The researchers used multiple regression to estimate the determinants of individual students' 12th-grade standardized test scores. Four sets of explanatory variables were included in each model: individual and family background, school, teacher, and class. In their models, they measured the impact of certification type relative to those who held standard certification in the subject.

In mathematics, Goldhaber and Brewer (2000) found that students of teachers who were either not certified in their subject or held a private school certification did less well than students whose teachers held a standard, probationary, or emergency certification in math. Having a teacher with standard certification in mathematics rather than a private school certification or a certification out of subject resulted in at least a 1.3-point increase on the mathematics test. This was equivalent to about 10% of the standard deviation on the 12th-grade test. The results in science were similar, but not as strong in magnitude or statistical significance. The study did find that the students of emergency certified science teachers had the highest gain scores, but this was based on only 24 such teachers out of a sample of 1,201.

Goldhaber and Brewer (2000) controlled for the effects of family background and school characteristics by using data from NELS:88, a nationally representative survey of students. At the same time, they noted that teachers with standard certification and private school certification had students who had higher achievement on the 10th-grade tests and higher levels of parental education and family income.

It is important to note here that there were differences across these studies in how researchers "sort" on the issue of certification. For some researchers, the distinction is dichotomous: One is either fully certified or not. Within the "not-certified" category, these researchers include emergency-credentialed teachers, out-of-subject teachers, probationary teachers, and teachers with private school certification. Across states, however, these labels can mean very different things, for the process by which one receives a preliminary or emergency credential depends on state policies and local school district adaptations. Further, it matters where a particular respondent is in the certification "pathway": One might have an emergency credential and have completed almost all required courses for full certification, or one might have an emergency credential and have no intention of completing the necessary requirements.

In the specific case of the Goldhaber and Brewer (2000) analysis, Darling-Hammond, Berry, and Thoreson (2001) objected to the claims the researchers made concerning the quality of emergency credentialed teachers in the sample. Reanalyzing the data, Darling-Hammond and her colleagues argued that many of the emergency-credentialed teachers had both subject matter preparation and preparation in teacher education or education coursework (see also Goldhaber & Brewer, 2001, for a response to this critique).

Finally, in an earlier study that also employed NELS:88, Goldhaber and Brewer (1997) limited their analysis to students who took the mathematics test in grades 8 and 10; the 10th-grade mathematics test score was the dependent variable. Again, explanatory variables were grouped in four clusters: individual and family background, school, teacher characteristics, and classroom. The researchers found that students with more experienced teachers had significantly higher test scores. Teachers with a BA or an MA in mathematics or who were certified to teach mathematics had a statistically significant positive effect on student achievement.

Again, we return to our original charge: What is the research base for the accountability processes currently used in teacher preparation, specifically teacher testing, certification, and accreditation? What is known about the impact of these processes on teachers' learning, knowledge, professional practices, and/or students' learning? With regard to the literature on certification, the trend is toward favoring certified teachers (i.e., those who have gone through traditional routes to certification, including university-based teacher preparation), particularly in the area of mathematics. Seven of the eight studies reviewed found positive correlations between certification and student achievement; largely these results pertain to mathematics, with one study that included science teachers and another that examined reading and language scores as well.

Clearly, more research is needed. First, the exchange between Goldhaber and Brewer (2000) and Darling-Hammond, Berry, and Thoreson (2001) reminds us of Angus's (2001) observation of mid-19th-century policies on teacher certification: There are as many approaches to teacher certification as there are states. Indeed, given the distinctions between probationary and provisional, permanent and full, emergency and preliminary, research on teacher certification needs designs that explore and illuminate those differences. Second, although student achievement data are an important aspect of impact, research would also benefit from a broader conceptualization of impact that included other measures of effective instruction.

Finally, we know next to nothing about the impact of certification across different grade levels and across the full array of subject areas in which teachers are certified.

RESEARCH ON PROGRAM ACCREDITATION

Our final approach to the question of accountability in teacher education examines research on program accreditation. The literature on accreditation is most often informational: Most published articles describe the process of participating in an accreditation review and feature recommendations for other institutions as they prepare for reviews (e.g., Barnette & Gorham, 1999; Black & Stave, 2001; Cochran-Smith, 2001; Coombs & Allred, 1993; Elliott, 1997; Gorrell, Kunkel, & Ossant, 1993; Samaras et al., 1999; Troutman, Jones, & Ramirez, 1997; Wilkerson, Searls, & Uprichard, 1993). Others present arguments in support of NCATE (e.g., Darling-Hammond, 2000; Gardner, Scannell, & Wisniewski, 1996; NCTAF, 1996) or TEAC (e.g., Murray, 2000, 2001), whereas others suggest or explain changes in the goals of accreditation (e.g., Dill, 1998; Elliott, 1997; Graham, Lyman, & Trow, 1995; Tom, 1999). There is little empirical research on the impact of accreditation. We found two relevant studies.

Goodlad (1990) and his team made visits to 29 teacher education institutions during 1987–1988, spending 10 to 14 researcher days per site. They surveyed faculty and students; interviewed students, faculty, and administrators; and reviewed documents. Their book presents results as a narrative, with no systematic attempt to present specific results from surveys or observations. The researchers reported that, in higher education, teacher education was the field most affected by outside forces, especially state agencies. In Goodlad's view, this has eroded the curricular autonomy of teacher preparation programs. Heads of teacher education programs, more or less resigned to circumstances beyond their control, commonly adjust their curricula to conform to the most recent list of state requirements. Furthermore, Goodlad claimed that the current system of state dictates of teacher education curriculum have a "stultifying impact" on program improvement. In effect, the state focus on regulation tends to lower program quality. (If this is true, the subsequent sharp increase in regulation—both on the national and state levels—does not bode well for improving teacher education.) Finally, the researchers reported that NCATE was seen as important by regional institutions, less so for flagship and major public and private universities and private liberal arts institutions.

As already discussed, Gitomer et al. (1999) analyzed data for all individuals who took the SAT or ACT between 1977 and 1995 and who took Praxis I and/or Praxis II between 1994 and 1997. The study reported that passing rates on Praxis I and II were higher for those who had attended NCATE-accredited institutions than for those who attended institutions not accredited by NCATE.

These two studies do not provide a basis on which to make claims about the effects of accreditation. One study suggested that NCATE approval was associated with higher quality graduates (as measured by Praxis I and Praxis II); the other study suggested that NCATE approval was important to institutions in inverse relationship to their size and status.

Certainly, one complicating factor is that the accreditation processes used by both NCATE and TEAC continue to change. NCATE, not surprisingly given its longer history, has responded to several waves of criticism. Its last major redesign occurred in the 1990s when it responded to suggestions for change from its parent organization, the AACTE, and other sources (see Gardner, Scannell, & Wisniewski, 1996). Current work involves exploring what kinds of publicly credible, professionally responsible assessments might be used across institutions to track prospective teacher learning over time (see NCATE, 2003). This ever-shifting landscape of accreditation makes it difficult to conduct timely, relevant research.

In addition to this churning, there is also a concern about the relationship between internal and external purposes of accreditation. Graham, Lyman, and Trow (1995) argued that internal accountability should focus on teaching and learning and address whether the institution was meeting its own standards. In contrast, in their view, external accountability should involve audits of the internal review procedures used by institutions of higher education. The purpose of these audits would be to determine whether the institution had in place procedures and practices enabling it to understand and address its own weaknesses. According to this argument, if teacher tests established and used by states or the federal government do not measure the knowledge, skills, and dispositions that teacher preparation programs hope to develop in graduates, then such external forms of accountability are not aligned with internal accountability. The authors suggest that misalignment can undercut educational quality.

In an investigation of how institutions of higher education responded to their students' high failure rates on the Massachusetts teacher tests, Ludlow et al. (2002) found that the public disclosure of their graduates' failure prompted a wide range of institutional responses. At the most besieged institutions with the highest failure rates, prospective teachers were offered test preparation workshops (ranging from 2 to 24 hours in length); faculty were offered professional development to realign their courses with the examinations; new courses were offered; the alignment of the state curriculum standards for K–12 students and the teacher tests was emphasized in methods classes; and prospective teachers were encouraged to study middle and high school textbooks to enhance their subject matter knowledge.

At less threatened institutions, prospective teachers were offered orientation sessions or workshops on test preparation and at-risk prospective teachers were offered extra support. Although some responses might have led to program improvements, only research can tell us that, and in this case, we do not know whether this response led to improved teacher education or compromised program quality. This study suggests the need for sustained research on the effects of various accountability policies, a topic we return to in the next section.

IMPLICATIONS FOR FURTHER RESEARCH

Given the impassioned debates around accountability in teacher education, it is both surprising and troubling that there is so little relevant empirical research. This is a research domain in need of sustained, intensive work.

Teacher Testing

As noted earlier, future research will need to redress the serious weaknesses in the research base and extant literature. First, there is an urgent need for more and better research about the teacher tests currently in widespread use. Although previous research suggested that the NTE and the other tests examined had content and concurrent validity, teacher education researchers, policymakers, and funders all should feel obliged to assess the content and concurrent validity of all such tests. Given the increasingly high stakes associated with these tests, such vigilance is a moral and practical necessity.

Clearly, we also need research on the predictive and consequential validity of all teacher tests. That is, we need to know how well tests predict teaching success, as gauged by a host of tools for measuring instruction, from student assessments to teacher observations to ratings by principals and supervisors. We also need to know whether mandating these tests has an impact on instruction and leads to improved teaching performance. The ABCTE tests should be included in these studies.

Further, we need research that explores alternative formats and arrangements for teacher testing. In response to the shortcomings of current tests of basic skills, subject matter knowledge, and professional knowledge, a number of states and organizations have developed, piloted, and implemented performance assessments for use in licensing beginning teachers. These assessments, which include the Connecticut portfolios and Praxis III, may have the potential to better measure and promote effective instructional practices than the existing, widely used teacher tests. Given the research in industrial and organizational psychology, which suggests that work samples are sound predicators of on-the-job success (e.g., Schmidt & Hunter, 1998), future research needs to investigate the validity and reliability of these assessments as well.

Over the past decade, Connecticut has created and implemented content-specific portfolios for use with second-year teachers in 10 content areas—science, mathematics, English/language arts, social studies, elementary education, special education, visual art, music, physical education and world languages. For each portfolio, teachers complete several entries that are integrated around one or two units of instruction, including a description of their teaching context, lesson plans, videotapes of instruction during the unit(s), student work samples, and teachers' written reflections (Pecheone & Stansbury, 1996). Each completed portfolio reveals information about the logic and coherence of the teacher's curriculum, the appropriateness of instructional decisions for students, the range of pedagogical strategies used effectively, the quality of assignments, skill in assessing student learning, and ability to reflect on one's own teaching and make changes based on evidence of student learning (Wilson et al., 2001).

The Praxis III series, developed and piloted by ETS in the 1990s, recently has been implemented in two states. Praxis III is a generic assessment; that is, the same assessment procedures are used with all teachers regardless of grade level and content area. For Praxis III, teachers complete class and instruction profiles and are interviewed and observed by trained assessors. In a preobservation interview, teachers discuss their goals, instructional methods, activities, and materials. During the observation, assessors record key aspects of what the teacher and students say and do that are related to the 19 criteria that underlie Praxis III. After a postobservation interview, the assessor selects the most salient evidence of performance for each of the 19 criteria from the observation and interview data, writes a summary statement for each criterion (linking the evidence to the scoring rules for that criterion), and assigns a score for each criterion.

All activities associated with the assessment of a single lesson comprise an assessment cycle. ETS requires that states that use Praxis III in making licensure decisions administer the assessment at least twice during each candidate's first year of teaching. We hardly need to add that research is needed on the validity and reliability of novel assessments such as Praxis III and the Connecticut portfolios.

This new generation of assessments, based on observation of actual practice, may have the potential to more authentically measure teachers' ability to plan instruction, analyze student learning, and reflect on practice. At the same time, states face several challenges in implementing such assessments in professional licensure decisions, including costs, collecting evidence of validity and reliability, ensuring fairness, and staving off pressure to lower standards for entry into the profession due to teacher shortages (Youngs et al., 2003). The challenges suggest that we will also need to conduct research on the policy requirements and implications of such teacher testing.

All research on teacher testing needs to be more sophisticated and subtle in recognizing important variations in tests and their use. This includes variations in content (basic skills, general knowledge, subject matter knowledge, pedagogical knowledge, and pedagogical content knowledge); variations in candidate background (undergraduate, postbaccalaureate, and less or more professional education or experience); and variations in purpose (admission, certification, or licensure). In particular, we need research on how different state policies concerning teacher testing impact student achievement and effective instruction. The research reviewed here sheds little light on the effects of teacher testing policies, save for the one study that demonstrated that the pool of prospective teachers increased when the NTE requirement was lifted although the quality of the new candidates was unclear (Murnane et al., 1991). This is especially troubling given calls for more teacher tests, as well as calls to raise passing scores.

Teacher Certification

We have already noted two serious gaps in the research on teacher certification. First, research designs need to be conceptualized to accommodate the complexity of certification practices and policies currently used across the country. We need to understand the multiple forms of certification that exist within and across states, including the variability that exists within individual categories of certification (e.g., emergency credentials). A teacher with an emergency credential can be someone with little or no teaching experience, or it may be a veteran, fully certified teacher from another state who has not yet fulfilled the requirements for a full credential in her new state. Developing databases that provide information on the multiple relevant factors will be an important step in expanding and enriching research on certification.

In addition, there are few findings on the impact of teacher certification in areas other than mathematics teaching. We need to broaden the fields investigated to include all subjects in which teachers are certified and the full range of grade levels. This research will also benefit from the development of a full array of measures of impact, as discussed in the previous section. Further, because certification is most often the combination of a number of different requirements (completion of a subject matter major or BA, completion of a teacher education program, teacher testing, and other requirements), future research should investigate the relative contributions of the individual proxies used to make the certification decision.

Finally, it is important for researchers to acknowledge and account for the fact that the size of measured effects of different variables often varies at different levels of the system. On one hand, data disaggregated at the individual teacher or school level can exhibit greater measurement error. At the same time, as noted earlier, omitted variables can bias the coefficients of school inputs upward when data are aggregated at the district or state level (Hanushek et al., 1995). Due to concerns about aggregation bias, we recommend that researchers aggregate and analyze data at multiple levels (Darling-Hammond & Youngs, 2002).

Program Accreditation

With so little existing research, almost any research in the area of accreditation would help. In particular, the field would benefit from studies that linked program accreditation with impact measures, including student learning and effective instruction. As Murray (2001) noted, "A large problem with accreditation and the other quality assurance measures is that the teaching profession has not grounded its work in scholarly evidence" (p. 61). Accreditation is changing, however, and much more attention is being paid to collecting evidence that is both publicly credible and professionally responsible.

Murray (2001) proposed a host of measures, including prospective teachers' grades and GPAs, portfolios and work samples, prospective teachers' scores on licensing examinations, prospective teachers' scores on admission tests for graduate study, job placement rates, program completion rates; employer evaluations; alumni follow-up studies, professional recognition of graduates (e.g., awards), rates of advanced study; professional activities (e.g., participating in national or regional organizations, participating in standards development or textbook adoption processes), and academic achievements of program graduates' students.

No form of evidence is without flaws and researchers might need to conceptualize the measurement of impact from what Shulman (2004) termed "a marriage of insufficiencies." The development of a portfolio of reasonable measures that could be used across studies would be a particularly valuable contribution to the field.

Given the coexistence of several different models of accreditation (TEAC, NCATE, and state reviews that involve paper reviews or visiting teams), we might also conduct research on the relative effectiveness of different models. Important questions to be pursued include: Does participation in a national accreditation program have a differential effect? What is the effect of aligning a teacher education program with various standards (e.g., state developed, national subject-matter organization)? Do some forms of accreditation have more impact on student learning?

CONCLUSION: RESEARCH WILL NOT SUFFICE

In an international study of teacher education, Gitomer (in Wang, Colement, Coley, & Phelps, 2003) noted, "Every high performing country in this study employs significant regulatory controls on their teaching force, almost all more rigorous that the United States" (p. 2). Our regulatory system needs improvement. Of that, there is little doubt. Better research will help.

But such a system needs to be built with a clear sense of what the important underlying issues are. The issues are not simply about empirical data. Three present themselves for consideration here. First is the issue of what certified teachers are expected to know and be able to do. Second is the issue of jurisdiction, that is, who ought to be making these decisions. Third, we need to attend to the purposes of accountability.

Although empirical research can inform these issues, research is not the only basis on which to make decisions about accountability in teacher education. We conclude with a brief discussion of some of the associated normative issues that cannot be addressed solely with empirical data.

On the matter of expectations for beginning teachers: Although many educational researchers have attempted to argue for and delineate a knowledge base of teaching, all such discussions are predicated on a normative view of teaching and what it takes to be a teacher. The views of educators, policymakers, and the American public on the nature of teaching as work vary widely, and these differences have implications for assumptions about teacher qualifications. Some argue that teachers are civil servants; others, that teachers are professionals. Some argue that teaching is moral work; others, that it is technical. Teaching is alternatively seen as an art or a science. Although some might say that these discussions are only of interests to academics, presumptions about what teaching is—as work—are inextricably woven into our decisions about what teacher tests should assess, what the requirements for teacher certification and licensure are, and how programs should be accredited.

Becker, Kennedy, and Hundersmarck (2003) offered one conceptual framework that helps illuminate the problem. They argued that three rival hypotheses currently exist about the necessary background characteristics for teachers: the bright well-educated person hypothesis, the professional-knowledge hypothesis, and the educational-values hypothesis. Each hypothesis carries with it different assumptions about what teachers should be like—and, presumably, what the basis of their preparation, certification, and licensure should be. The bright, well-educated person needs a respectable undergraduate degree and high verbal ability. The professional knowledge perspective would presume that teachers need content and pedagogical knowledge, as well as general and foundational knowledge. Someone coming from the educational-values perspective, on the other hand, would want to know that a prospective teacher was committed to the learning of all children; that a teacher was patient and tolerant, that a teacher valued diversity and had faith in students.

Although empirical data on the relationship between teacher knowledge and skill and student learning might inform the development of such conceptions, on some level, these views about what teachers need to know or who they need to be are normative. Indeed, they resonate with the history of teacher testing, starting with ministers and local community boards using oral examinations of prospective teachers' moral fiber to the contemporary disagreements about whether to test teachers on basic skills, general knowledge, subject matter knowledge, pedagogical knowledge, or some subset of those domains.

Similarly, issues of jurisdiction are not readily amenable to persuasion with data. Who should control teacher education, certification, and licensure is another value-laden decision. Of particular importance is an understanding of how state and federal mandates play an increasingly dominant role in teacher education accountability and the consequences of that encroachment. Historically, the state has always been antagonistic toward what Krause (1996) called "guilds"—associations (including professions) and "institutions created by groups of workers around their work, their skill or craft" (p. 3). Guilds exercised power through association by controlling both the workplace and the market. The state sees this guild power as "the enemy and . . . as a plot against the consumer" (Krause, p. 6).

In the case of teacher quality policies, conceptions of teaching as profession or vocation resonate with the notion of guilds or associations. In the current political climate, marked as it is with a free market ideology, such associations are seen as the "enemy" of the state. Krause (1996) argued that, "Guild power . . . is declining as state power and capitalist power encroach upon it. Where state and capitalist power have won out, they and not the profession control the aspects of professional life that we call "the workplace" and "the market" and determine to a large extent how much associational group power the profession has left vis-à-vis the state and capitalism" (Krause, p. 22). As the "state," both in the form of state policies and federal legislation like No Child Left Behind and the reauthorization of Title II, increasingly encroaches on teacher preparation and professional development, teachers are pressed more and more into civil service and labor orientations toward teaching in their daily work and further away from conceptions of teaching as professional work.

The third issue, the purposes of accountability, is also largely normative. As already noted, Graham et al. (1995) argued that our voluntary accreditation processes in higher education are sometimes compromised by the tensions between the purpose of internal improvement and the purpose of gaining external credibility and trust. These purposes are not rooted in empirical research; instead, they have arisen in the political, intellectual, organizational world of higher education. They have been shaped by cultural norms and expectations, not determined by data. Similarly, when NBPTS was in early stages of development, it set forth five criteria for its assessment system: that it be administratively feasible, professionally acceptable, publicly credible, legally defensible, and economically affordable. Although some criteria were based on political and economic grounds, the decision to make the assessments both professionally acceptable (teachers would agree that they assessed good teaching) and publicly credible was, again, a normative decision.

Our point here is a simple one: Research will help inform discussions of accountability in teacher education, but it will never deliver the last word. Issues of conceptions of good teachers and their necessary background characteristics, ideas about jurisdiction, and assumptions about the purposes of accountability will also be shaped by our collective normative assumptions. Thus, educational researchers have a dual obligation. First, to conduct rigorous, sophisticated, and relevant research. Second, to participate—with open minds and ears—in deliberative discussions concerning our individual and collective normative assumptions about what teachers should know, how they should be prepared and certified, who has the right to control those processes, and to what ends we embrace the need for accountability processes in teacher education.

ACKNOWLEDGMENTS

We thank Scott Metzger and Eran Tamir for their assistance in understanding the history of teacher certification and program accreditation. We also thank Robert Floden, Susan Fuhrman, Andrew Gitomer, Mary Kennedy, and Brian Stecher for their careful review of earlier drafts.

TABLE 10.1
Accountability Processes in Teacher Education

Studies[a]	Question/Focus	Research Tradition	Research Design	Findings
Andrews, J. W., Blackmon, C. R., & Mackey, J. (1980)	Teachers' knowledge as measured by teacher test scores. Relationships among undergraduate grade point averages, student-teaching performance, and National Teacher Examination (NTE) scores. The study used scores for 4 groups of teachers on the NTE Common Exams or NTE subject area exams.	Correlational analyses	The sample included 269 teacher education students who completed student teaching and took the NTE between 1975 and 1978.	Significant positive relationships between measures of teaching performance and elementary student teachers' NTE Common Exam and subject exam scores and English student teachers' NTE Common Exam and subject exam scores; negative relationships between NTE exam scores and measures of teaching performance for prospective physical education and special education teachers.
Ayers, J. B. (1988)	Teachers' knowledge as measured by teacher test scores. Relationships between teachers' performance on the NTE, teachers' scores on the American College Test (ACT), teachers' GPA, and principals' ratings, student ratings, and ratings by other observers. NTE scores included scores from 3 parts of the NTE Core Battery—Communication Skills, General Knowledge, and Professional Knowledge—as well as scores from the NTE Specialty Area test, Education in the Elementary School (EES)	Correlational analyses	The sample included 46 teachers who had graduated from Tennessee Technological University in 1984 and 1985.	Mean ACT scores for the 46 teachers indicated that they performed at or above the national mean on the test. ACT scores correlated significantly with scores derived from the four tests of NTE; also significant relationships between GPA and NTE scores although ACT scores seemed to be a better predictor of success on NTE than GPA. Correlation of .37 between principal rating of overall effectiveness of teachers and EES scores; other correlations between principal ratings and NTE scores were low and not significant.

Citation	Description	Method	Sample	Findings
Ayers, J. B., & Qualls, G. S. (1979)	Teachers' knowledge as measured by teacher test scores. Relationships between teachers' scores on the NTE Weighted Common Examinations (WCET) and the Education in the Elementary School (TAE) test and principals' ratings of the teachers' knowledge and practices. The WCET measured general academic knowledge and professional knowledge).	Correlational analyses	The sample included 84 elementary school teachers and 49 secondary school teachers, all of whom graduated from Tennessee Technological University and entered teaching between 1973 and 1977.	The authors found a correlation of .27 between principals' ratings of secondary teachers' subject matter knowledge and secondary teachers' performance on the WCET. All other correlations were low and nonsignificant.
Cobb, R. B., Shaw, R., Millard, M., & Bomotti, S. (1999)	Teachers' knowledge as measured by teacher test scores. The authors compared the average performances on several measures of individuals who passed the Colorado licensure tests (Program for Licensing Assessments for Colorado Educators) with those who failed the tests. The measures included ACT reading test, SAT verbal test, GRE verbal test, GPA of undergraduates, and GPA of graduate students.	Multiple regression analyses	The sample included more than 5,500 prospective teachers from 5 of the 17 institutions in Colorado that train teachers. Of these 5 institutions, 2 were from urban areas, 1 was from a suburban area, and 2 were from rural areas. All of the institutions were public and representative of both graduate and undergraduate licensure programs.	Correlations between Basic Skills math test and ACT, SAT, and GRE math tests were consistent and relatively high (.68, .66, .66); correlations between Basic Skills reading test and ACT reading test, and SAT and GRE verbal tests were all less than .50 (.25, .49, .46). Liberal Arts and Science test was correlated with SAT verbal and total and ACT reading and total test scores; correlations ranged from .50 to .65 (.50, .57, .58, .65). Correlations between PLACE tests and SAT, ACT, and GRE total test scores were consistent and fairly high. The authors found "a reasonably large differential between the GPAs of those who passed and those who failed the PLACE tests; the differential was in the right direction (1999, p. 169). Strong correlations between 4 content area tests (math,

(Continued)

623

TABLE 10.1
(Continued)

Studies[a]	Question/Focus	Research Tradition	Research Design	Findings
				science, English, social studies) and several measures include SAT math test, SAT verbal test, ACT reading test, ACT math test, ACT English test, ACT verbal test, and ACT science test.
Darling-Hammond, L. (2000)	Author examined the relative contributions of teacher qualifications, other school inputs, and student characteristics to student achievement across the states.	Multiple regression analyses	The analyses involved data on teacher characteristics and school inputs from 1993–1994 Schools and Staffing Survey (SASS) and data on student characteristics and achievement from the NAEP reading and math assessments (administered in 1990, 1992, 1994, and 1996).	Author found that measures of teacher preparation and certification were the strongest correlates of average student achievement in reading and math, whereas class size had very modest additional effects. The most strongly significant predictor of achievement was the proportion of well-qualified teachers, defined as the proportion holding both full certification and a major in the field being taught. The proportion of teachers holding master's degrees exerted a small positive effect on achievement and the proportion on emergency credentials exerted a small negative effect.
Darling-Hammond, L., Berry, B., & Thoreson, A. (2001)	Response to Goldhaber & Brewer (2000)	Multiple regression analyses	The sample included more than 3,400 teachers from NELS:88.	The authors analyze the same data from NELS:88 that Goldhaber & Brewer (2000) analyzed to examine the relationship between teachers' certification status in math and science and student achievement gains between 10th grade and 12th

Reference	Methodology	Variables	Sample	Findings
				grade. The authors question Goldhaber and Brewer's statement that "students who have teachers with emergency credentials do no worse than students whose teachers have standard teaching credentials" (2000, p. 141) The authors note that (a) Goldhaber and Brewer had a small number of teachers in their sample with emergency certification, and (b) many teachers with emergency certification are experienced teachers moving into new states or new teaching assignments.
Dybdahl, C. S., Shaw, D. G., & Edwards, D. (1997)	Correlational analyses	Teachers' knowledge as measured by teacher test scores Relationships among prospective teachers' scores on ETS' Pre-Professional Skills Test (PPST) and GPA, student teaching ratings, local school district interview score, and postgraduation employment as a teacher. The PPST assessed teachers' reading, writing, and math skills.	The sample included 375 elementary, secondary, and physical education student teachers.	The authors reported that correlations between measures of the subtest ranged from .42 to .58, and that all three intratest correlations were significant at the .05 level; correlations between the three subscores on the PPST and cumulative GPA ranged from .32 to .39. All correlations were statistically significant, but accounted for only 10% to 15% of the variance. No correlations between the 3 subscores on the PPST and the other 3 outcome measures.
Egan, P. J. & Ferre, V. A. (1989)	Correlational analyses	Teachers' knowledge as measured by teacher test scores. Relationships among GPA, ACT scores, and NTE Core Battery test scores.	The sample included 94 elementary and secondary school teachers who had graduated from Peru College. The authors	Regression analyses, using the reference group, indicated that ACT English and ACT composite scores were the best predictors of NTE communication skills scores; the

(Continued)

625

TABLE 10.1
(Continued)

Studies[a]	Question/Focus	Research Tradition	Research Design	Findings
			divided the sample into a reference group and a cross-validation group. The reference group included 73 elementary and secondary education students who completed their programs between May 1984 and fall 1985. The cross-validation group included 21 elementary and secondary education students who completed their programs in spring 1986.	ACT composite subtest score was the best predictor of NTE general knowledge scores; and the ACT English subtest score and GPA were the best predictors of NTE professional knowledge scores.
Ferguson, R. F. (1991)	Teachers' professional knowledge as measured by teacher tests; student learning as measured by synthetic gains. Relationships among teacher characteristics (performance on TECAT licensure test, teachers' degree level, and teachers' experience); school size; and student performance. The TECAT measured teachers' verbal ability and professional knowledge. This was a district-level analysis.	Multiple regression analyses	The sample included more than 900 districts in Texas; the analyses involved teachers' scores on the TECAT licensure exams and students' reading scores on the Texas Educational Assessment of Minimum Skills (TEAMS) — for students in Grades 1, 3, 5, 7, 9, and 11.	The following 4 variables had statistically significant effects on students' tests scores: TECAT scores, teachers' experience, number of students per teacher, and percentage of teachers with master's degrees. After 1st grade, teachers' TECAT scores accounted for about 20%–25% of all variation across districts in students' average scores on the TEAMS exams. Teachers' experience accounted for just over 10% of the interdistrict variation in student test scores. The 2 experience variables were the percentage of teachers with

5–9 (i.e., to 8.99) years of experience and the percentage with 9 or more. Both had statistically significant effects on test scores. The percentage of teachers with master's degrees accounted for about 5% of the variation in student's scores across districts for Grades 1 through 7. This variable had no predictive power after 7th grade.

Fetler, M. (1999)	Relationships among percentage of teachers on emergency permits, teachers' experience, teachers' education level, and average student scores on state mathematics examination (Stanford 9). This was a school-level analysis.	Correlational analyses	The sample included 795 California high schools.	Fetler (1999) reported a significant negative relationship between average student scores on the Stanford 9 (the state math exam) and percentage of teachers on emergency permits. He also found a smaller positive relationship between student test scores and teacher experience levels, after controlling for student poverty rates and test participation rates. He concluded that "After factoring out the effects of poverty, teacher experience and preparation are significantly related to achievement" (p. 13). Fetler (1999) notes that the requirements for a full credential in California include demonstration of subject matter knowledge and completion of a set of teacher education requirements. The majority of teachers with emergency permits in California are ones who have either demonstrated subject

(Continued)

627

TABLE 10.1
(Continued)

Studies[a]	Question/Focus	Research Tradition	Research Design	Findings
				matter knowledge, but not completed teacher education requirements; or who have passed a basic skills test, but not completed either the subject matter or teacher education requirements required for a full credential.
Gitomer, D. H., Latham, A. S., & Ziomek, R. (1999)	Teachers' knowledge as measured by teacher test scores (Praxis II); accreditation status of teachers' preparation program (NCATE vs. non-NCATE).		The researchers analyzed data for all those individuals (a) who took the SAT and ACT between 1977 and 1995, and (b) who took Praxis I and Praxis II between 1994 and 1997. For the SAT, math and verbal scores were included. For the ACT, English and math scores were included. The dataset included 33,866 Praxis I candidates and 159,857 Praxis II candidates who had taken the SAT, and 55,064 Praxis I candidates and 112,207 Praxis II candidates who had taken the ACT. The researchers also considered whether candidates had attended an NCATE-accredited	The study reported that Praxis II passing rates for those who had attended NCATE-accredited institutions were higher than for those who attended institutions not accredited by NCATE. For teaching candidates who had previously taken the SAT, 91% of candidates from NCATE-accredited institutions passed Praxis II compared to 83% of those who attended non-NCATE institutions. For teaching candidates who had previously taken the ACT, 91% of candidates from NCATE-accredited institutions passed Praxis II compared to 87% of those who attended non-NCATE institutions. The authors note, "It is especially noteworthy that the NCATE rates are higher because candidates at NCATE institutions have somewhat lower SAT or ACT scores than do candidates at non-NCATE schools.

			Thus, NCATE-accredited institutions appear to increase the likelihood that candidates will meet state licensing requirements" (p. 25).
Goldhaber & Brewer (1997)	Teacher characteristics and student achievement	Production function study	Individual and family background variables explain three quarters of the variation in students' 10th grade math scores.
			Findings concerning teacher characteristic variables: Students of more experienced teachers have higher scores. Female teachers have higher student test scores; Black teachers have lower student test scores.
		Gain score production function study	Teachers with a BA in math or an MA in math have statistically significant impact on student achievement; teachers with a nonmath BA or MA have a negative impact on student achievement. Similar results were found with teacher certification.
		Data from the first two waves of National Educational Longitudinal Study of 1988 (NELS) 24,000 eighth-graders in spring 1988; 18,000 of these students were surveyed again in 10th grade (spring 1990). At each survey, students took one or more content knowledge tests in mathematics, science, writing and history. The researchers focus on students who took the mathematics test in 8th and 10th grades.	Teachers who are certified in mathematics have higher student test scores.
		Teacher variables include gender, race and ethnicity, degree level, experience, certification.	Student achievement models using teacher degree (BA or MA) without specifying the subject matter of the degree shows teacher's degree as statistically insignificant. This was also true of teacher certification.
		5,149 tenth-grade students who came from 638 schools and who were taught by 2,245 mathematics teachers.	Findings concerned teacher behavior variables: Teachers ho have little or no control over their teaching

institution as undergraduates.

(Continued)

TABLE 10.1
(Continued)

Studies[a]	Question/Focus	Research Tradition	Research Design	Findings
				strategies have students with significantly lower test scores. Teaching in small groups and emphasizing problem solving appear to lower student test scores on traditional tests.
Goldhaber, D. D., & Brewer, D. J. (2000)	Relationships between teachers' certification status and student achievement gains.	Multiple regression analyses	The sample included more than 3,400 teachers from NELS:88.	The researchers found that fully certified teachers have a statistically significant positive impact on student performance as compared to teachers who are not certified in their subject area (no certification, private school certification, teaching out-of-field), as do teachers who hold a degree in math or math education—relative to teachers who do not hold such degrees (Goldhaber & Brewer, 2000). The same trends were evident in science, but the influences were somewhat smaller. In the authors' words, "Roughly speaking, having a teacher with a standard certification in mathematics rather than a private school certification or a certification out of subject results in at least a 1.3-point increase in the mathematics test. This is equivalent to about 10% of the standard deviation on the 12th-grade test,

			"a little more than the impact of having a teacher with a BA or MA in mathematics. Though the effects are not as strong in magnitude or statistical significance, the pattern of results in science mimics that in mathematics. Teachers who hold private school certification or are not certified in their subject area have a negative (though not statistically significant) impact on science test scores" (2000, p. 139).
Goodlad (1990)	Teacher education program accreditation	Cross-case field study Interpretive study using surveys, interviews, and observations Visits to 29 teacher education institutions during 1987–1988, spending 10–14 researcher days per site. Used surveys for faculty and students, interviews with students, faculty, and administrators, and review of documents.	In higher education, teacher education is the field most affected by outside forces, especially state agencies. This has eroded curricular autonomy. Heads of teacher education commonly square their curricula with the most recent list of state requirements, more or less resigned to circumstances beyond their control. The current system of state dictates of teacher education curriculum have a "stultifying impact . . . on program renewal" (p. 100) State focus on regulation tends to lower program quality. NCATE is seen as important by regional institutions, less so for flagship and major public, major private, and liberal arts private institutions.

(Continued)

TABLE 10.1
(Continued)

Studies[a]	Question/Focus	Research Tradition	Research Design	Findings
Guyton, E., & Farokhi, E. (1987)	Teachers' knowledge as measured by assessments of teachers' classroom practices. Relationships among teachers' performance on basic skills tests, subject matter tests (required for initial certification), and grade point averages, and the quality of their instructional practices (measured by the Georgia Teacher Performance Assessment Instrument, which must be passed to earn certification).	Correlational analyses	The sample included more than 270 teachers from the same teacher education program.	The authors reported consistently strong, positive relationships between teacher education coursework performance and classroom performance as measured by the TPAI. Relationships between classroom performance and subject matter test scores were positive, but insignificant and relationships between classroom performance and basic academic skill scores were negligible.
Hawk, P. P., Coble, C. R., & Swanson, M. (1985)	The effects of teacher certification	Comparative quasi-experimental study (ANOVA, t-tests)	Graduates of East Carolina University Thirty-six mathematics teachers of Grades 6–12 were followed in the study. All were certified. Eighteen teachers were in-field, and 18 were out-of-field. Eight hundred twenty-six students Teachers matched on school, teaching the same mathematics course to students of the same approximate ability Student tests: Stanford Achievement Test (general math) and Stanford Test of Academic Skills (algebra)	Significant differences were apparent from the posttest in general mathematics and algebra. Students who had in-field teachers scored higher. In-field teachers scored significantly higher on the CTPAS and the knowledge test. Chi-square analysis yielded no significant differences due to years of teaching or degree held by teachers in the study.

		Tests of arithmetic and elementary algebra were administered to teachers Teaching performance was measured by the CTPAS	For both 1998–1999 and 1999–2000, Laczko-Kerr and Berliner (2002) found that students of certified teachers had significantly higher scorers on the SAT 9 in reading and language than students of under-certified teachers. Students of certified teachers had significantly higher SAT 9 mathematics scores in 1999–2000.
Laczko-Kerr, I., & Berliner, D. C. (2002)	Multiple regression analyses	Teachers' certification status The study examined the relationship between teachers' certification status and student performance in Grades 3–8 on the Stanford Achievement Test 9th ed. (SAT 9). The sample included 109 certified teachers and 109 undercertified teachers in Grades 3–8 in Arizona. The undercertified teachers included those with emergency, temporary, and provisional certification. Some of the emergency certified teachers were in Teach For America (TFA).	The researchers found that students of certified teachers had significantly higher scores in reading, language, and mathematics in 1999–2000 than did students of TFA teachers. Although the pattern of results was similar for the 1998–1999 sample, the differences in achievement were not statistically significant.
Lawrenz, F. (1975)	Correlational analyses	Teachers' knowledge as measured by the NTE science exams and the Science Process Inventory (SPI); student achievement was measured by the Test of Achievement in Science and the SPI. Relationships among teacher characteristics and student achievement in science. The teacher characteristics included knowledge of subject matter and teaching methods, experience, attitude toward science, The sample included 236 secondary science teachers from 14 states. Eighty-four teachers taught biology, 111 taught chemistry, and 41 taught physics. The 14 states were stratified by city size and a percentage of the schools from each population were randomly selected.	The author reported that the selected teacher characteristics were significantly related to student achievement in and attitude toward science with a canonical correlation of .61. In particular, Lawrenz's regression analysis indicated that teachers' scores on the SPI were significant predictors of student achievement on the TAS and the SPI.

(Continued)

TABLE 10.1
(Continued)

Studies[a]	Question/Focus	Research Tradition	Research Design	Findings
	professional self-improvement, and type of learning environment created.			
Mandeville, G. K., & Liu, Q. (1997)	Relationship between teachers' certification status and student achievement. Student achievement was measured by the Stanford Achievement Test in math, which was administered to all 7th-graders in South Carolina in the spring of 1991. The test items were designed to assess 3 levels of thinking. At the lowest level, there were 43 items dealing with "knowledge and recognition"; at the next level, there were 52 items dealing with "understanding"; and at the highest thinking level, there were 23 items dealing with "thinking skills."	Correlational analyses	The sample included 122 middle schools: 31 high MATHPREP schools and 91 low MATHPREP schools. High MATHPREP schools were those where all of the 7th-grade math teachers had secondary certification or had 12 or more credit hours in math beyond initial certification. In contrast, low MATHPREP schools were those where all of the 7th-grade math teachers had elementary certification or were teaching out-of-field.	When performance was measured by high-level math problems, Mandeville and Liu found statistically and practically significant differences between 7th-graders taught by teachers with more specialized math training and those taught by teachers with less specialized training. When performance was measured by intermediate-level math problems, the differences favored the students of teachers with more specialized training, but they were not statistically significant. When performance was measured by low-level math problems, the differences between the two groups were small and not statistically significant.
Murnane, Singer, Willett, Kemple, & Olsen (1991)	Teacher characteristics	Survey research and comparative population analysis (cross-tabulation, logistic regression, survival analysis)	State databases from Michigan (30,614 individuals who entered public school teaching in Michigan between September 1972 and September 1981) and North Carolina (50,502 individual licensed by North Carolina for public	In North Carolina, removal of the licensure requirement for a minimum NTE test score increased the number of college graduates who applied for a teaching license. Reinstatement of the requirement reduced the number of applicants. The effect was more pronounced for Blacks than for Whites.

		school teaching between January 1974 and December 1985) National Longitudinal Surveys of Labor Market Experience (NLS; 2,539 individuals who graduated from college between 1967 and 1985) Demographic characteristics, education, subject matter specialty, career status, salary	During the period in which the NTE requirement was eliminated, those licensees who nevertheless took the NTE examination even though it was not required were more likely to enter teaching in North Carolina within 3 years than those who did not take the exam. Licensees with higher NTE scores were less likely to enter teaching in North Carolina within 3 years of licensure.
Sheehan, D. S., & Marcus, M. (1978)	Regression analyses	The sample included 119 first-grade teachers and 1,836 first-grade students in a large urban district. Teachers' knowledge as measured by teacher tests; student achievement in mathematics and vocabulary. Relationships between teachers' NTE scores and students' math and vocabulary achievement.	After controlling for initial levels of achievement, and for teacher degree and years of experience, the authors found that WCET scores accounted for 3% of the variance of the class-average mathematics posttest scores and for 2% of the variance of the class-average vocabulary posttest scores. When race was controlled, though, the magnitudes of the contributions of the WCET scores were reduced. In these regressions, the WCET scores accounted for 1% of the variance of the class-average mathematics posttest scores and for none of the variance of the class-average vocabulary posttest scores. In addition, the WCET scores were no longer significant predictors of student math and vocabulary achievement.

(Continued)

TABLE 10.1
(Continued)

Studies[a]	Question/Focus	Research Tradition	Research Design	Findings
Strauss, R. P., & Sawyer, E. A. (1986)	Teachers' knowledge as tests by the NTE Core Battery; student achievement as measured by students' performance on reading and math competency examinations and students' dropout rates. Relationships among teachers' performance on teacher tests and student achievement in reading and math and students' dropout rates.	Correlational analyses	The sample included 145 North Carolina school districts.	When the authors controlled for per-capita income, student race, student–teacher ratios, student plans to attend college, and district capital assessment, they found that teachers' NTE scores had a significant and large effect on students' failure rates on the state competency examinations in reading and math. In particular, they reported that a 1% increase in district average NTE score was associated with a 3% to 5% decline in district failure rate on the competency exams. The authors found that teachers' NTE scores mattered more for rates of failure on the competency exams than for average student achievement, and that in both sets of estimates, teacher quality had more influence on these outcomes than the proportion of Black students in the district—which had a noticeable, but smaller effect. The authors conclude: "Of the inputs which are potentially policy-controllable (teacher quality, teacher numbers via the student–teacher ration and capital stock), our analysis indicates quite clearly that improving the quality of teachers in the classroom will do

Author/Year	Focus/Measures	Analysis	Sample	Findings
				more for students who are most educationally at risk, those prone to fail, than reducing the class size or improving the capital stock by any reasonable margin which could be available to policy makers" (p.47).
Summers, A., & Wolfe, B. (1977)	Teachers' knowledge as measured by NTE Common Examinations; student learning as measured by ITBS composite score gains. The NTE Common Exams measure general academic ability. Relationships among teachers' NTE scores, teachers' experience, and student achievement gains.	Multiple regression analyses	The sample included 627 sixth-grade students and their teachers in 103 public elementary schools in Philadelphia.	Controlling for the effects of teachers' experience and ratings of their undergraduate institutions, the authors reported a negative relationship between teachers' NTE Common Exam scores and students' achievement gains.
Wenglinsky, H. (2000)	Teachers' knowledge as measured by Praxis II Relationships among teachers' performance on Praxis II and characteristics of their teacher education programs. The study compared candidates' scores on 6 Praxis II assessments.	Multiple regression analyses	The sample included more than 40,000 teachers who had taken Praxis II. To obtain information about the prospective teachers' schools, colleges, and departments of education (SCDEs), the researcher sent questionnaires to the deans of the 152 institutions under study. One-half of the deans responded, representing 66% of 40,000 prospective teachers in the study.	For all 6 Praxis II assessments, the author found that (a) prospective teachers from private schools scored higher than those from public schools; (b) prospective teachers from universities scored higher than those from colleges; and (c) prospective teachers from larger schools scored higher than those from smaller schools. The author added that more advantaged students (in terms of parents' education and SAT scores) attend institutions that are larger, private, and enroll a greater percentage of graduate students. When student SES and students' prior test scores were controlled, the study found that students who attended

(Continued)

TABLE 10.1
(Continued)

Studies[a]	Question/Focus	Research Tradition	Research Design	Findings
				universities still outperformed those who attended colleges and that students who attended private institutions still outperformed those who attended public ones. The author also reported that candidates scored higher on Praxis II if the percentage of minority students in their school, college, or department of education (SCDE) was higher than in their institution and if high percentages of students in their SCDE had a traditional college experience. At the same time, the greater the scope of the SCDE, the lower the licensure scores of its teacher candidates. SCDE involvement in the local community was unrelated to Praxis II scores. The study also reported that more affluent students were more likely to attend private institutions and universities, and that these students were more likely to be exposed to diverse faculty and engage in traditional college experiences.

[a] Please see References.

TABLE 10.2
Type and Number of State Systems of Teacher Certification, 1898–1937

	1898	1911	1921	1926	1937
State systems					
State issues all certificates.	3	15	26	36	41
State-controlled systems					
State sets rules, conducts exams, county issues some certificates.	1	2	7	4	3
Semi-state systems					
State sets rules, writes questions, county grades papers, issues certificates.	17	18	10	5	1
State–county systems					
Both issue certificates, county controls some certificates.	18	7	3	2	2
State–local system					
Full control by town committees.	2	2	2	2	1

TABLE 10.3

Numbers of States Using Different Types of Initial Licensure Tests, by Test Developer, 1998–1999 (Mitchell et al., 2001, p. 49)

				Test Type		
Test Developer	Basic Skills	General Knowledge	Subject Matter Knowledge	Subject-Specific Pedagogical Knowledge	Pedagogical Knowledge	Total Number of States
ETS	28	10	20	20	7	32
NES	9	4	9	6	—	8
State	1	—	2	2	—	2
Total	38	14	31	28	7	42

TABLE 10.4

Number of Different Initial Licensure Tests, by Test Type and Test Developer, 1998–1999 (Mitchell et al., 2001, p. 50)

				Test Type		
Test Developer	Basic Skills	General Knowledge	Subject Matter Knowledge	Subject-Specific Pedagogical Knowledge	Pedagogical Knowledge	Total Number
ETS	7	10	126	4	6	144
NES	27	4	362	12	—	405
State	6	—	69	1	—	76
Total	40	5	557	17	6	625

TABLE 10.5
Numbers of States Using Initial Teacher Licensure Tests to Support
Decisions About Candidates in 1998–1999

	Basic Skills	Subject Matter Knowledge	Pedagogical Knowledge	Subject-Specific Pedagogical Knowledge
Admission to teacher education	19	3	0	0
Eligibility for student teaching or degree conferral	1	3	2	2
Licensure	18	25	26	5
Total	38	31	28	7

REFERENCES

Andrews, J. W., Blackmon, C. R., & Mackey, J. (1980). Preservice performance and the National Teacher Exams. *Phi Delta Kappan*, 61(5), 358–359.

Ayers, J. B. (1988). Another look at the concurrent and predictive validity of the National Teacher Examinations. *Journal of Educational Research*, 13–17.

Ayers, J. B., & Qualls, G. S. (1979). Concurrent and predictive validity of the National Teacher Examinations. *Journal of Educational Research*, 73(2), 86–92.

Cobb, R. B., Shaw, R., Millard, M., & Bomotti, S. (1999). An examination of Colorado's teacher licensure testing. *Journal of Educational Research*, 92(3), 161–175.

Darling-Hammond, L. (2000). Teacher quality and student achievement: A review of state policy evidence. *Educational Policy Analysis Archives*, 8(1). Retrieved October 15, 2003, from http://epaa.asu.edu/epaa/v8n1

Darling-Hammond, L., Berry, B., & Thoreson, A. (2001). Does teacher certification matter? Evaluating the evidence. *Educational Evaluation and Policy Analysis*, 23(1), 57–77.

Dybdahl, C. S., Shaw, D. G., & Edwards, D. (1997). Teacher testing: Reason or rhetoric. *Journal of Research and Development in Education*, 30(4), 248–254.

Egan, P. J., & Ferre, V. A. (1989). Predicting performance on the NTE Core Battery. *Journal of Educational Research*, 82(4), 227–230.

Ferguson, R. F. (1991). Paying for public education: New evidence on how and why money matters. *Harvard Journal on Legislation*, 28(2), 465–498.

Fetler, M. (1999). High school staff characteristics and mathematics test results. *Education Policy Analysis Archives*, 7. Retrieved August 1, 2003, from http://epaa.asu.edu/epaa/v7n9

Gitomer, D. H., Latham, A. S., & Ziomek, R. (1999). *The academic quality of prospective teachers: The impact of admissions and licensure testing.* Princeton, NJ: Educational Testing Service.

Goldhaber, D. D., & Brewer, D. J. (2000). Does teacher certification matter? High school teacher certification status and student achievement. *Educational Evaluation and Policy Analysis*, 22(2), 129–145.

Goldhaber, D. D., & Brewer, D. J. (1997). Why don't schools and teachers seem to matter? Assessing the impact of unobservables on educational productivity. *The Journal of Human Resources*, 32, 505–523.

Goodlad, J. (1990). *Teachers for our nation's schools.* San Francisco: Jossey-Bass.

Guyton, E., & Farokhi, E. (1987). Relationships among academic performance, basic skills, subject matter knowledge and teaching skills of teacher education graduates. *Journal of Teacher Education*, 38(5), 37–42.

Hawk, P. P., Coble, C. R., & Swanson, M. (1985). Certification: It does matter. *Journal of Teacher Education*, 36(3), 13–15.

Laczko-Kerr, I., & Berliner, D. C. (2002). The effectiveness of Teach for America and other under-certified teachers on student academic achievement: A case of harmful public policy. *Educational Policy Analysis Archives, 10*(37). Retrieved January 2, 2003, from http://epaa.asu.edu/epaa/v10n37/

Lawrenz, F. (1975). The relationship between teacher characteristics and student achievement and attitude. *Journal of Research in Science Teaching, 12*(4), 433–437.

Mandeville, G. K., & Liu, Q. (1997). The effect of teacher certification and task level on mathematics achievement. *Teaching and Teacher Education, 13*(4), 397–407.

Murnane, R. J., Singer, J. D., Willett, J. B., Kemple, J. J., & Olsen, R. J. (1991). *Who will teach? Policies that matter.* Cambridge, MA: Harvard University Press.

Sheehan, D. S., & Marcus, M. (1978). Teacher performance on the National Teacher Examinations and student mathematics and vocabulary achievement. *Journal of Educational Research, 71,* 134–136.

Strauss, R. P., & Sawyer, E. A. (1986). Some new evidence on teacher and student competencies. *Economics of Education Review, 5*(1), 41–48.

Wenglinsky, H. (2000). *Teaching the teachers: Different settings, different results.* Princeton, NJ: Educational Testing Service.

REFERENCES: OTHER SOURCES CITED

Abbott, A. (1988). *The system of professions: An essay on the division of expert labor.* Chicago: University of Chicago Press.

Allen, M. (2003). *Eight questions on teacher preparation: What does the research say?* Denver, CO: Education Commission of the States.

Angus, D. L. (2001). *Professionalism and the public good: A brief history of teacher certification.* Washington, DC: The Fordham Foundation.

Barnette, J. J., & Gorham, K. (1996). Evaluation of teacher preparation graduates by NCATE accredited institutions: Techniques used and barriers. *Research in the School, 6*(2), 55–62.

Becker, B. J., Kennedy, M. M., & Hundersmarck, S. (2003). *Communities of scholars, research and debates about teacher quality.* Paper presented at the annual meeting of the American Educational Research Association, Chicago, IL.

Black, A., & Stave, A. (2001). Action research: A model for teacher leadership through the NCATE review process. *Educational Horizons, 79*(3), 130–134.

Cochran-Smith, M. (2001). Constructing outcomes in teacher education: Policy, practice and pitfalls. *Education Policy Analysis Archives,9*(11). Retrieved December 10, 2002, from http://epaa.asu.edu/epaa/v9n11

Conant, J. B. (1963). *The education of American teachers.* New York: McGraw-Hill.

Coombs, C. G., & Allred, R. A. (1993). NCATE accreditation: Getting the most from the self-study. *Journal of Teacher Education, 44*(3), 165–169.

Darling-Hammond, L. (2001). *The research and rhetoric on teacher certification: A response to "Teacher certification reconsidered."* New York: National Commission on Teaching and America's Future. Retrieved October 15, 2003, from http://www.nctaf.org/publications/abell_response.pdf

Darling-Hammond, L., & Youngs, P. (2002). Defining "Highly Qualified Teachers": What does "Scientifically-Based Research" actually tell us? *Educational Researcher, 31*(9), 13–25.

Dill, W. R. (1998). Guard dogs or guide dogs? Adequacy vs. quality in the accreditation of teacher education. *Change, 30*(6), 12–17.

Educational Testing Service. (2003). *The Praxis Series.* Retrieved December 10, 2003, from http://www.ets.org/praxis/index.html

Elliott, E. J. (1997). Performance: A new look at program quality evaluation in accreditation. *Action in Teacher Education, 19*(2), 38–43.

Flesch, R. F. (1955). *Why Johnny can't read—And what you can do about it.* New York: Harper.

Gardner, W. E., Scannell, D., & Wisniewski, R. (1996). The curious case of NCATE redesign. *Phi Delta Kappan, 82*, 622–629.

Goldhaber, D. D., & Brewer, D. J. (2001). Evaluating the evidence on teacher certification: A rejoinder. *Educational Evaluation and Policy Analysis, 23*(1), 79–86.

Gorrell, J., Kunkel, R. C., & Ossant, D. M. (1993). Using Lasswell's decision seminars to assure appropriate knowledge base in teacher education programs. *Journal of Teacher Education, 44*(3), 183–189.

Graham, P. A., Lyman, R. W., & Trow, M. (1995). *Accountability of colleges and universities*. New York: Columbia University Press.

Haney, W., Fowler, C., Wheelock, A., Bebell, D., & Malec, N. (1999). Less truth than error? An independent study of the Massachusetts Teacher Tests. *Education Policy Analysis Archives,7*(4). Retrieved December 15, 2003, from http://epaa.asu.edu/epaa/v7n4

Hanushek, E. A. (1992). The trade-off between child quantity and quality. *Journal of Political Economy, 100*, 84–117.

Hanushek, E. A., Rivkin, S. G., & Taylor, L. L. (1995). *Aggregation bias and the estimated effects of school resources*. Rochester, NY: University of Rochester, Center for Economic Research.

Interstate New Teacher Assessment and Support Consortium. (2003). *Test of teaching knowledge*. Retreived December 15, 2003, from http://www.ccsso.org/projects/Interstate_New_Teacher_Assessment_and_Support Consortium/Projects/Test_of_Teaching_Knowledge/

Koerner, J. D. (1963). *The miseducation of American teachers*. Boston: Houghton Mifflin.

Krause, E. A. (1996). *Death of the guilds: Professions, states and the advance of capitalism, 1930 to the present*. New Haven, CT: Yale University Press.

Labaree, D. (1998). *How to succeed in school without really learning*. New Haven: Yale University Press.

Latham, A. (2004, January). *The Praxis Series*. Presentation at the Consortium for Policy Research in Education conference, The Measurement of Instruction, Washington, DC.

Lubinescu, E. S., Ratcliff, J. L., & Gaffney, M. A. (2001). Two continuums collide: Accreditation and assessment. *New Directions for Higher Education, 113*, 5–21.

Ludlow, L. H., Shirley, D., & Rosca, C. (2002). The case that won't go away: Besieged institutions and the Massachusetts teacher tests. *Education Policy Analysis Archives, 10*(50). Retrieved December 16, 2002, from http://epaa.asu.edu/epaa/v10n50/

Melnick, S. L., & Pullin, D. (2000). Can you take dictation? Prescribing teacher quality through testing. *Journal of Teacher Education, 51*(4), 262–275.

Metzger, S. (2004). *Teacher qualification historical timeline*. Unpublished manuscript. Michigan State University, East Lansing, MI.

Mitchell, K. J., Robinson, D. Z., Plake, B. S., & Knowles, K. T. (Eds.). (2001). *Testing teacher candidates: The role of licensure tests in improving teacher quality*. Washington, DC: National Academy Press.

Mitchell, D. E., & Kerchner, C. T. (1983). Labor relations and teacher policy. In L. S. Shulman & G. Sykes (Eds.), *Handbook of teaching and policy* (pp. 214–237). New York: Longman.

Murray, F. B. (2000). The role of accreditation reform in teacher education. *Educational Policy,14*(1), 40–59.

Murray, F. B. (2001). From consensus standards to evidence of claims: Assessment and accreditation in the case of teacher education. *New Directions for Higher Education, 113*, 49–66.

National Association of State Directors of Teacher Education and Certification. (2000). *The NASDTEC manual on the preparation and certification of educational personnel* (5th ed.). Dubuque, IA: Kendall/Hunt.

National Commission on Teaching and America's Future. (1996). *What matters most: Teaching for America's future*. New York: Author.

National Council for Accreditation of Teacher Education. (2003). *Assessing education candidate performance: An early look at changing practices*. Washington, DC: Author.

Pecheone, R. L., & Stansbury, K. (1996). Connecting teacher assessment and school reform. *The Elementary School Journal, 97*(2), 163–177.

Ramirez, H. (2003, October). *The shift from hands-off: The federal role in supporting and defining teacher quality*. Presentation at the A Qualified Teacher in Every Classroom: Appraising Old Answers and New Ideas, sponsored by the American Enterprise Institute.

Ravitch, D. (2000). *Left back: A century of failed school reforms*. New York: Simon & Schuster.

Rice, J. K. (2002). *Quality counts, but what counts as teacher quality? Evidence to enhance productivity, equity and adequacy of public education*. Paper prepared for the Economic Policy Institute.

Samaras, A. P., Francis, S. L., Holt, Y. D., Jones, T. W., Martin, D. S., Thompson, J. L., et al. (1999). Lived experiences and reflections of joint NCATE-state reviews. *Teacher Educator, 35*(1), 68–83.

Schmidt, F. L., & Hunter, J. E. (1998). The validity and utility of selection methods in personnel psychology: Practical and theoretical implications of 85 years of research findings. *Psychological Bulletin, 124,* 262–274.

Sedlak, M. (1989). "Let us go and buy a school master": Historical perspectives on the hiring of teachers in the United States, 1750–1980. In D. Warren (Ed.), *American teachers: Histories of a profession at work* (pp. 257–290). New York: Macmillan.

Sedlak, M., & Schlossman, S. L. (1986). *Who will teach? Historical perspectives on the changing appeal of teaching as a profession*. Santa Monica, CA: RAND.

Shulman, L. S. (1986). Those who understand: Knowledge growth in teaching. *Educational Researcher, 15*(2), 4–14.

Shulman, L. S. (2004). *The wisdom of practice: Essays on teaching, learning and learning to teach*. San Francisco: Jossey-Bass.

Summers, A. A., & Wolfe, B. L. (1977). Do schools make a difference? *American Economic Review, 67,* 639–652.

Teacher Education Accreditation Council. (2003). *Teacher Education Accreditation Council*. Retrieved December 20, 2003, from http://www.teac.org/about/index.asp

Tom, A. R. (1999). NCATE: Is lowering the standards the way to go? *Action in Teacher Education, 21*(3), 57–66.

Troutman, P., Jones, W. P., Ramirez, M. G. (1997). Cultural diversity and the NCATE standards. *Multicultural Education, 4*(3), 30–33.

U.S. Department of Education. (2002). *Meeting the highly qualified teachers challenge: The Secretary's Annual Report on Teacher Quality*. Washington, DC: U.S. Department of Education, Office of Postsecondary Education, Office of Policy, Planning and Innovation.

van Vught, F. A. (1994). Intrinsic and extrinsic aspects of quality assessment in higher education. In D. F. Westerheijden, J. Brennan, & P. A. M. Massen (Eds.), *Changing contexts of quality assessment*. Utrecht: Lemma.

Walsh, K. (2001a). *Teacher certification reconsidered: Stumbling for quality*. Baltimore, MD: Abell Foundation.

Walsh, K. (2001b). *Teacher certification reconsidered: Stumbling for quality. A rejoinder*. Baltimore, MD: Abell Foundation.

Wang, A. H., Colement, A., B., Coley, R. J., & Phelps, R. P. (2003). *Preparing teachers around the world*. Princeton, NJ: Educational Testing Service.

Wayne, A. J., & Youngs, P. (2003). Teacher characteristics and student achievement gains: A review. *Review of Educational Research, 73*(1), 89–122.

Wilkerson, J. R., Searls, E. F., & Uprichard, A. E. (1993). The effectiveness of SIDPASS: A research-based self-study model for seeking NCATE accreditation and program improvement. *Journal of Teacher Education, 44*(3), 190–199.

Wilson, S. M., Darling-Hammond, L., & Berry, B. (2001). *A case of successful teaching policy: Connecticut's long-term efforts to improve teaching and learning*. Seattle, WA: Center for the Study of Teaching and Policy.

Wilson, S., Floden, R. E., & Ferrini-Mundy, J. (2001). *Teacher preparation research: Current knowledge, gaps and recommendations*. Seattle, WA: Center for the Study of Teaching and Policy.

Wilson, S. M., & Floden, R. E. (2002). *Addendum to Teacher preparation research: Current knowledge, gaps and recommendations*. Paper commissioned by the Education Commission of the States.

Youngs, P., Odden, A., & Porter, A. C. (2003). State policy related to teacher licensure. *Educational Policy, 17*(2), 217–236.

11

Teacher Education Programs

Kenneth M. Zeichner
Hilary G. Conklin
University of Wisconsin–Madison

This chapter examines the evidence related to the impact of different forms of preservice teacher education programs on various aspects of teacher recruitment, retention, and quality. Although our analysis will include comparisons of research on traditional and alternative teacher education programs and 4-year and 5-year programs, this mode of analysis is primarily a result of how the empirical research on teacher education programs has been organized and conducted. We review the research as it has been structured and then seek to identify a more productive direction for inquiries into the nature and impact of teacher education programs.

The chapter begins with a look at how teacher education programs have been discussed in the literature and some conceptual problems with how these discussions have been framed. Following this general analysis and discussion of the outcomes assessed in teacher education program research, we examine the empirical evidence on the impact of different kinds of preservice teacher education programs. In doing so, we will examine studies of 4-year versus 5-year programs and studies that compared various kinds of traditional and alternative programs. We summarize what we know and do not know about the efficacy of different program models on the basis of the extant empirical research. Finally, we discuss a group of case studies of preservice programs that illustrate a way to do research about teacher education programs that we think will be more useful to the field in the long run than the comparisons of programs according to their general labels. We also discuss the implications for understanding teacher education programs of other chapters in this volume that have examined particular program components such as methods courses and field experiences.

THE IDEA OF A TEACHER EDUCATION PROGRAM

Teacher education programs have been distinguished from one another in several different ways in the literature. The most common distinction that has been made among programs has been in terms of their structure. Programs have been distinguished according to their length (e.g., 1, 4, and 5 years), when they are offered (e.g., at the graduate level and undergraduate level), and by the institutions that sponsor them (e.g., college or university, school district, state education department, or for-profit company). Programs have also been defined in terms of their admissions requirements and curricular emphases, such as the amount of credits in arts and sciences courses versus education courses, whether they require an academic major, the amount of time spent working in schools as opposed to that spent in classes on campus, and according to when courses are offered in the program. Teacher education programs have also been distinguished from one another in terms of their conceptual orientations. Several frameworks have been proposed for describing the different conceptual orientations of programs based on their view of teaching, learning, what teachers need to know, and the process of learning to teach (e.g., Feiman-Nemser, 1990; Tom, 1997; Zeichner, 1993). Barnes (1987) also distinguished programs according to whether they have coherent themes that tie together the various courses and field experiences. Barnes argued that organizing programs around themes strengthens their socializing power. Others have defined programs in terms of whether they have particular features such as student cohort groups or professional development school partnerships (e.g., see Arends & Winitzky, 1996).

Most of the discussion about teacher education reform has focused on the impact of teacher education programs' structural characteristics. For example, there have been numerous proposals to lengthen teacher education to 5 or more years or move it to the graduate level entirely (e.g., Carnegie Forum on Education and the Economy, 1986; Denemark & Nutter, 1984; Holmes Group, 1986; Scannell, 1986; Smith, 1980; Joyce & Clift, 1984). On the other hand, there have been arguments to preserve the traditional four–year undergraduate model as the dominant path into teaching (e.g., Conant, 1963; Hawley, 1987; Mehlinger, 1986; Tom, 1987; Travers & Sacks, 1987; Winetrout, 1963).[1]

The emergence of proposals for extended 5-year and graduate programs was an outgrowth in part of the American Association of Colleges for Teacher Education (AACTE) Commission on Education for the Profession of Teaching's widely read bicentennial report *Educating a Profession* (Howsam, Corrigan, Denemark, & Nash, 1976),

---

[1]According to Feistritzer (1999), although nearly two thirds (65%) of teacher education institutions she surveyed in 1998 indicated that they have at least one teacher education program where candidates enter at the postbaccalaureate level, only 28% of those who completed teacher education began their preparation at the postbaccalaureate level. Most teachers still begin their teacher education programs at the undergraduate level, although they do not necessarily finish in 4 years. Mayer, Decker, Glazerman, and Silva's (2003), analysis of the 1999, 2000, Schools and Staffing Survey (SASS) data showed that for teachers with 3 or fewer years of experience, 69% of elementary, 62% of middle, and 58% of high school teachers received their certification as part of a bachelor's degree program. The practice and public advocacy for extending preservice teacher education to five years dates from at least 1905 (Von Schlichten, 1958).

the follow-up report by the AACTE Commission on Extended Programs (1982) and several other widely discussed reports issued over the subsequent decade that called for extended or graduate programs. The growth in calls for alternative certification programs was associated with the beginnings of state sponsored alternative programs in the early 1980s and continuing shortages of qualified teachers in urban and rural schools.[2]

These calls for extended, graduate, and alternative programs emanated from long-standing debates in teacher education programs about the existence of a knowledge base for teaching, the adequacy of teachers' content and pedagogical preparation, the low status of teacher education in college and universities, the lack of integration across various courses and between the courses and field experiences, and the best ways to deal with the lack of fully prepared teachers in urban and rural schools. One motivation for those who argued for extended or graduate programs has been to up-grade the status of teacher education in higher education and the status of teaching in society. One motivation of many who have advocated alternative certification programs has been to ameliorate the teacher shortages that have plagued urban and rural schools and all districts in particular subject areas and provide a qualified teacher to every student. Advocates of alternative certification have also argued that these programs will bring more teachers of color into teaching (see Cochran-Smith & Fries, 2001; Zeichner, 2003).[3]

DIFFERENT TEACHER EDUCATION PROGRAM STRUCTURES

In a review of the literature on teacher education program structures, Arends and Winitzky (1996), identified five structural types of teacher education programs other than the 4-year undergraduate model: (a) the extended and integrated 5-year program leading to a bachelor's degree, (b) the extended and integrated 5-year program leading to a bachelor's and master's degree, (c) the fifth-year program leading to a master's degree, (d) the 6-year program leading to a master's degree, and (e) alternative certification programs.[4] The literature makes further distinctions between different kinds of graduate programs such as the master of arts in teaching (MAT) program developed at Harvard in the 1930s with a strong liberal arts focus (Coley & Thorpe, 1986) and other programs such as the 2-year graduate programs at the University of California, Los Angeles, and the University of California, Berkeley, that focus on such things as developmental theory and preparing teachers who will work for social justice (Oakes, 1996; Snyder, 2000).

---

[2]Virginia was the first state to establish a statewide alternative certification program in 1982. California began its district-based intern program in 1983, and Texas and New Jersey began their statewide alternative programs in 1984.

[3]See chapter 3 for a discussion of the data related to the demographics associated with alternative certification programs.

[4]The definition of alternative certification programs given by Arends and Winitzky is vague, but it does suggest that alternative programs shorten the time spent in professional studies and that they are not normally associated with higher education. As is pointed out in this chapter, however, higher education has been involved in private-, state-, and school-district-sponsored programs to varying degrees. The higher education versus non-higher-education "contest" that has been set up in policy debates is inconsistent with the reality of how programs are sponsored and staffed.

The most common arguments about programs made in the teacher education literature over the last 30 years have been either for the lengthening of programs beyond
4 years, removing them from the undergraduate years entirely, or for the establishment of alternative routes into teaching. The warrants for these proposals have come
mostly from the logical arguments made by the advocates for different models. For
example, advocates of extended 5-year programs have often argued that the 4-year
model cannot give adequate attention to all that a teacher needs to know to begin
teaching (the "life space" argument) or that the extension of programs to 5 years will
help enhance the status of teaching in the society (the "professionalization" argument). It is not common for arguments about the efficacy of programs to draw on
empirical research that has systematically examined the impact of different program
structures. Feiman-Nemser (1990) concluded: "The dominance of a given program
structure at a particular historic moment depends as much on compelling social
forces as it does on the demonstrated strengths or weaknesses of the form itself"
(p. 220).

Several problems exist with the way in which the debates about programs have
been framed in the literature. One issue is the problems associated with "naming" a
program according to its structural characteristics alone, because different definitions
may be used for particular program types. For example, the literature on alternative
certification discussed in the following pages reflects the use of different definitions
of an alternative certification program, some that include university postbaccalau-
rate programs and some that do not. Generally, there is so much variety within each
type of teacher education program (e.g., graduate, alternative, and traditional) that
it does not make sense to compare general types without discussing the substantive characteristics and policy contexts of these programs (Weinstein, 1989; Zeichner,
1989).

There is also variation within specific national programs assumed to have a shared
set of practices. For example, "Teach for America" (TFA) is often discussed in the
literature as if it has the same meaning in all parts of the country. In reality, although
there is consistency in the summer preservice phase of the program prior to the
point where TFA teachers assume responsibility for a classroom, subsequently there
is much variation in the experience of TFA teachers depending on their location.
TFA teachers in some sites such as Baltimore and New York City, for example, now
complete university-based graduate-level teacher education programs, whereas TFA
teachers in other locations do not. TFA teachers' access to high-quality mentoring and
other forms of support also varies by location.

Another issue in the naming of program structures is that a program as described
by teacher educators may be different from the one experienced by teacher education students. For example, in the "Teacher Education and Learning to Teach" (TELT)
study conducted by researchers at the National Center for Research on Teacher Education between 1986 and 1990 researchers found that in one of the 5-year programs
in their sample, relatively few of the students actually were enrolled in the program
for 5 years. Many students spent their first 2 years in a community college and transferred to the university in their third year; some either could not get admitted to the
graduate school for the fifth year or left to complete student teaching as teachers of
record because of a severe teaching shortage in the state (Kennedy, 1998). Howey and
Zimpher (1989) reported data from a national survey of a sample of teacher education
students that indicated that about 50% of teacher education students attended at least
two institutions to complete their teacher education programs. To understand the
impact of different structures of teacher education programs under these conditions

of high mobility, one needs to look at programs from the perspective of the students who experience them.

TELT researchers also included two alternative teacher education programs in their sample. One was run by a large urban school district, whereas the other was sponsored by a state education department but staffed by college and university faculty from around the state. Kennedy (1998) noted that these two programs enrolled teachers who were very similar to those enrolled in the traditional university-based programs in their sample and that the types of courses taken in the two programs were very similar. These program similarities illustrate the difficulty of assuming that we know what an alternative or traditional or a 5-year program is like and that we can make comparisons among program types based on these structural labels alone.

Finally, the descriptions of programs included in this review represent those reported by researchers at the time the research was conducted. Given the evolving nature of teacher education programs in response to changing contexts, people, and purposes (Liston & Zeichner, 1991), it is important to recognize that these descriptions may not be accurate depictions of the current status of these programs. Furthermore, the program information provided in most studies was based on either descriptions of the programs by those associated with them or on an analysis of program documents, not on close study of the implementation of the programs. There is the possibility that programs as described in documents and by their faculty were not accurate reflections of the complex reality of these programs.

THE OUTCOMES OF TEACHER EDUCATION PROGRAMS

The studies reviewed in this chapter investigate various outcomes from participation in different kinds of teacher education programs. One type of outcome is concerned with teacher or principal perceptions of the quality of preservice teacher education programs. In studies measuring this outcome, teachers were asked to rate the overall quality of their preparation program or how well they thought it prepared them to do such things as adapt curriculum to meet individual learner needs. Teachers also were asked to rate the value of particular aspects of their preservice programs such as specific types of courses or the quality of the supervision they received in clinical experiences.

A second type of outcome investigated in these studies is the ratings of principals, supervisors, mentors, and sometimes superintendents of the quality of teaching and leadership of teachers who completed different kinds of teacher education programs. Sometimes the specific criteria used in these ratings were unclear, and the ratings were expressed in terms of overall teaching quality; other times the ratings were done in relation to specific aspects of teaching (e.g., instructional planning) or to a set of teaching standards. Most often these ratings were done on teachers in relation to a vague comparison group such as "other beginning teachers" or "the average first-year teacher." Another type of teacher education outcome included in some studies were teachers' statements about their beliefs about particular aspects of teaching in general or in relation to specific hypothetical situations presented to them. Teachers were also asked in these studies to report on their teaching and leadership practices, to rate their own teaching abilities, and to report the problems they have experienced in the classroom in general or at particular points in time. Sometime the self-reports of teachers were compared to those of principals and supervisors.

Teachers also were asked in some studies about their satisfaction with teaching, if they would choose teaching again, and to project whether they might remain in the classroom for particular periods of time such as 3 years, 10 years, or longer. These projections were said to reflect teachers' commitment to teaching. A few studies asked teachers how successful they felt in influencing student learning (teacher efficacy) or about their expectations for the learning of particular kinds of students (e.g., from low-income or middle-class families). In one study, pupils were asked to assess the quality of their classroom learning environment along several dimensions.

In other studies, researchers documented the percentages of teachers from different programs who entered teaching after completing a program, whereas other authors reported where teachers taught (e.g., in hard to staff schools in low-socioeconomic-status (SES) neighborhoods). A number of studies also reported the percentages of teachers from different programs who remained in teaching for periods of time ranging from 1 to 10 years. Sometimes teacher retention data were reported by teacher characteristics in addition to the type of program attended (e.g., their ethnicity and subject area). Sometimes the kind of schools where teachers taught was reported in the retention data and sometimes it was not reported.

Beyond measures of teacher entry and retention there have been various efforts to assess teacher quality that examined the knowledge and practices of teachers. These included comparisons of teachers' scores on tests of content and professional knowledge and evaluations of teacher performance based on classroom observations. Sometimes these observations have been "blind" where the observer was unaware of the type of teacher education program completed by the teacher. Sometimes single observations were used as the basis for the assessment, and sometimes multiple observations were used. Also, sometimes the ratings were presented as overall ratings in relation to a set of general teaching criteria. In other studies, observers used structured classroom observation instruments such as the "Texas Teacher Appraisal System" or otherwise assessed the extent to which certain practices believed to be effective were present in a teacher's practice.

Finally, in a few studies an attempt was made to connect experience in a particular type of teacher education program to student learning as defined by standardized test scores. Sometimes the researchers attempted to rule out alternative explanations for differences in pupil test scores by such tactics as controlling for the previous year's scores or matching teachers for comparisons. We next comment on the strengths and limitations of these various outcome measures in our discussion of the research studies.

THE SELECTION OF STUDIES

We followed the general guidelines adopted by the American Educational Research Association (AERA) Panel on Research and Teacher Education for the selection of studies to review and included only studies that had been peer reviewed and that provided adequate descriptions of the data collection and data analysis methods. We did not eliminate any studies because of their failure to adequately describe the context for the research. We have included U.S. research in this review published from 1986 to 2002 that met these criteria. We chose to begin with studies in 1986 because of the emergence at that time of the most recent incarnation of the extended program literature and of alternative program literature. Hand searches were conducted of the major peer-reviewed educational journals that we thought would likely contain

U.S. studies on teacher education programs.[5] We also examined both editions of the *Handbook of Research on Teacher Education* (Houston, 1990; Sikula, 1996), the chapter on teacher education in the third edition of the *Handbook of Research on Teaching* (Lanier & Little, 1986), peer-reviewed yearbooks of the Association of Teacher Educators, publications of the American Association of Colleges for Teacher Education (AACTE), reports from the federally funded research center on Teacher Education and Teacher Learning at Michigan State University from 1985 to 1995; reports from the Rand Corporation and the Educational Testing Service, and publications of the U.S. Department of Education. We conducted an archival analysis of these studies that led us to other peer-reviewed studies.

For this review, we have grouped the studies into three major categories: 4-year versus 5-year programs, alternative versus traditional certification, and the case studies of teacher education programs. Following an analysis of each of these groups of studies, we offer some generalizations about teacher education programs based on these three categories of research and on the implications of the analyses in the previous chapters of this report for the program level.

RESEARCH ON 4-YEAR VERSUS 5-YEAR PROGRAMS

Despite the voluminous literature arguing for or against the extension of teacher education programs to 5 years, there are relatively few empirical studies that have examined the consequences of extending teacher education beyond the 4-year undergraduate model. Four studies were located that met our criteria for inclusion. The first two (Andrew, 1990, and Andrew & Schwab, 1995) are frequently cited in debates about teacher education reform. We have given much attention to these two studies in this chapter because of the frequency with which they are referred to in the literature and in public debates.

Andrew (1990) studied graduates of both 4- and 5-year programs at the University of New Hampshire. Two data sources were used for this research: (a) random samples of 4- and 5-year program graduates from 1976 to 1986; and (b) yearly program evaluation questionnaires sent to all students at the end of their 4- or 5-year program between 1981 to 1982 and 1988 to 1989. Comparisons were made among graduates of programs offering certification in different subject areas. The 4-year program included students in home economics, mathematics, and physical education, whereas the 5-year program was for students in all other certification areas. In addition to subject matter differences, there were various differences in the admission requirements and content of the two programs. For example, the extended program had higher academic standards for admission and a yearlong internship instead of the one-semester student teaching experience in the 4-year program.

The 10-year study of random samples of graduates from the two programs was based on a 70-item questionnaire that included responses from 144 5-year program graduates and 163 4-year program graduates. These represented 93.5% and 70% return rates, respectively. Comparisons were made between the two programs of the entry and retention rates of graduates, their career satisfaction, and their evaluations

[5]These were: *Action in Teacher Education, American Educational Research Journal, American Journal of Education, Education & Urban Society, Educational Evaluation and Policy Analysis, Educational Policy, Educational Policy Archives, Journal of Teacher Education, Peabody Journal of Education, Review of Educational Research, Review of Research in Education, Teachers College Record,* and *Teaching and Teacher Education.*

of their teacher education programs. The findings indicated that the graduates of the 5-year program entered teaching at a higher rate than the 4-year graduates (93% vs. 86%). Retention was also higher for graduates of the 5-year program. At the time of the study, 56% of the 4-year program graduates were still teaching, whereas 74% of the 5-year graduates were still teaching ($p < .01$).

Additionally, there were significant differences in the career satisfaction of graduates. Only 56% of the 4-year teachers said that they would choose teaching again compared to 82% of 5-year teachers ($p < .001$). Seventy-five percent of 5-year graduates planned to be teaching in 10 years compared to 54% of 4-year graduates ($p < .01$). Finally, graduates of the 5-year program evaluated the overall quality of their teacher education program more favorably than did graduates of the 4-year program ($p < .001$).

In the yearly comparisons of the surveys completed by graduates of both programs, teachers rated their own teaching abilities using a 4-point scale, and rated the effectiveness of their program coursework and clinical experiences. On 11 of the 12 items on this scale related to teaching ability, 5-year program graduates consistently rated their abilities higher than their 4-year counterparts rated theirs. No statistical analyses were performed on these data. The overall ratings of clinical experiences were very similar for the two programs. It was reported that 5-year graduates found education faculty more supportive and their course work more valuable in 9 of 12 categories, but no details were provided about the courses and about whether the more favorable ratings were related to courses only taken by the 5-year graduates or those that they took along with 4-year program students.

Despite the apparent support for 5-year programs in this study, there were various limitations of this research that restrict its usefulness in furthering our understanding of the influence of program structure in teacher education. Andrew (1990) was aware of and discussed some of these limitations. For example, because the academic qualifications of students in the two programs differed, "We cannot eliminate the possibility that differences observed between 4-year and 5-year graduates in this study are not simply the result of differences in academic ability" (p. 50). Andrew also acknowledged that differences in the subject matter and grade levels taught by the teachers may have influenced the findings.

There is evidence in other research on the retention of teacher education program graduates that the subject and grade taught by teachers play significant roles in mediating the effects of program structure. In Natriello and Zumwalt's (1993) research on alternative certification in New Jersey, for example, elementary teachers from both the traditional and alternative programs were the most likely to remain in teaching after 3 years and alternatively certified teachers of mathematics had the lowest retention rates among the five groups. The significance of the content area in teacher retention was supported by other research done in Michigan and North Carolina (Murnane, Singer, Willett, Kempe, & Olsen, 1991). Murnane et al. argued that accurate statements about teacher retention and career patterns must differentiate among subject specialties because of the different opportunities outside of teaching that are available to people in various fields of study. These analyses suggest that the findings of research like Andrew's that compare teacher retention across content areas are confounded by the effects of the different costs and opportunities associated with teacher retention in these different content areas and do not necessarily reflect the effects of different program structures.

Another issue that limits the usefulness of the retention findings in Andrew's study is that the contexts in which the teachers taught were not described. Andrew (1990) asserted that his data "support the conclusion that the nature of the one-year internship and the additional coursework required for the master's degree result in more effective learning about teaching." This conclusion may be true in New Hampshire but may not hold up in teaching contexts different from those in which University of New Hampshire graduates work, such as urban districts in Illinois, California, and New York.[6]

Andrew and Schwab (1995) and Baker (1993) reported the results of a study of an 11-institution consortium of teacher education institutions that joined together to study the outcomes of their programs. Seven of these institutions had 5-year extended programs in at least some subject areas.[7] The subject areas and grade-level specializations included in the sample were not reported except for the statement that 57% of the teachers were certified as elementary teachers and 43% as secondary teachers.

In this research, 1,390 surveys were analyzed from 1985 to 1990 graduates of teacher education programs in the 11 institutions (response rate of 48%).[8] Each of the 11 institutions had initially identified a random sample of 300 graduates for the years included in the study. Forty nine percent of the sample completed 4-year programs, 36% graduated from 5-year programs, and 14% completed fifth-year programs. Of the 72% who were currently teaching, 25% were teaching in urban districts, 27% in rural districts, and 48% in suburban districts. Sixty-eight percent of the sample agreed to have their principals contacted to rate their teaching, and 70% of these principals (481) returned usable surveys.

The results indicated that 90% of the 5-year graduates entered teaching as compared to 80% of the 4-year graduates ($p < .001$). The 5-year graduates also displayed a greater commitment to teaching in that a significantly greater proportion indicated that they would choose teaching again ($p < .007$) and thought they would be teaching in 5 years ($p < .01$). At the time of the study, 87% of the 5-year graduates were still teaching as compared to 78% of the 4-year graduates ($p < .001$).

The teacher self-reports indicated that 5-year program graduates were engaged in more leadership activities than their 4-year counterparts in three areas ($p < .05$): serving as committee heads, serving as workshop presenters, and taking on professional leadership responsibilities beyond their school. According to these self-reports, significantly more 4-year than 5-year program graduates had moved partially or wholly out of the classroom into some kind of nonteaching or administrative position. The principals' ratings of teacher leadership activities contradicted the teachers' self-reports and did not show any significant differences across program types.

With regard to teacher self-reports of how often they used selected strategies in their teaching, 4-year graduates appeared somewhat more likely to use learner-centered approaches such as experiential learning ($p < .002$), student-initiated planning ($p < .0001$), discovery learning ($p < .0001$), and were less likely to lecture ($p < .001$). Principals of the graduates were asked to rate the performance of the graduates compared to "teachers of similar teaching experience," and although it was reported that initial analyses found no significant differences between principals' ratings of 4- and 5-year graduates (all of the ratings were relatively high) "graduates of five-year programs clustered at the top of the principal's ratings" (Baker, 1993, p. 32). When the frequency of the top ratings were compared on all 35 items on the

---

[6]Research on the spatial geography of teacher labor markets (e.g., Boyd, Grossman, Lankford, Loeb, & Wyckoff, 2003a) suggests that graduates of the University of New Hampshire program will likely take teaching positions close to home.

[7]The 11 institutions were Austin College, Drake University, University of Florida, University of Kansas, University of Nebraska-Lincoln, University of New Hampshire, Oakland University, Texas A&M University, University of Virginia, University of Rhode Island-Kingston, and the University of Vermont.

[8]There are some minor discrepancies in the data presented by Baker (1993) and Andrew and Schwab (1995). When these differences exist we have used the figures presented by Andrew and Schwab.

survey, only 2 items showed significant institutional differences, both favoring 5-year program graduates: "subject matter knowledge" ($p < .01$), and "teaches in a clear and logical manner" ($p < .05$).

Here, as in the first study by Andrew (1990), several limitations restrict the usefulness of the research in informing us about the impact of program structure. Because of the differences in the students in the different programs due in part to different program admission requirements, we do not know the degree to which selection (i.e., the specific admissions requirements) rather than socialization within the programs was responsible for the differences reported. Also, because no information was provided about the contexts in which the graduates taught (except for broad percentages indicating who worked in urban, rural, and suburban), the meaning of the entry and retention data is unclear. Finally, it was likely as in the first study that the retention comparisons made among teachers are questionable because they ignored subject matter and grade-level differences.

In the final study comparing graduates of 4-year and extended programs, Breidenstein (2002) studied the perceptions of second-year teachers in San Antonio, Texas, about their teacher preparation, current teaching practices, and plans to remain in teaching. This study employed a variety of qualitative and quantitative methods: a survey of teachers and individual and focus group interviews with some of the teachers who completed the survey. The survey sample consisted of 84 second-year elementary and secondary teachers teaching in the San Antonio schools who had graduated from either a 4- or 5-year extended preservice teacher education program. This represents 57% of all of the second-year teachers in the district during the 1997 to 1998 year. The 84 survey participants attended 25 four-year programs and seven extended programs. None of these programs was described in the research report. Following the surveys, individual and focus group interviews were conducted with 16 elementary and secondary survey respondents who agreed to be interviewed (35.5% of the survey sample). Each focus group (there were two elementary and three secondary groups) consisted of teachers who had graduated from 4- and 5-year programs. The 16 teachers who participated in the interviews represented seven 4-year programs and four extended programs.

A survey instrument developed for the National Commission on Teaching and America's Future (NCTAF) case studies of exemplary teacher education programs (Darling-Hammond, 2000) was employed in this research. Teachers responded to 61 Likert-scale questions regarding the structure and content of their teacher education program, their current teaching context and practices, and their plans for remaining in teaching. The semistructured individual interview protocol consisted of 16 questions that focused on gathering descriptions of the teacher education and teaching experiences of the teachers. The focus group protocol consisted of 6 questions that encouraged teachers to describe their first year of teaching, their perceptions of their preparation for teaching, and other matters including reasons why they might leave the profession.

Although the survey indicated that both the 4- and 5-year program graduates were confident of what they knew and could do as teachers, there were a number of differences between the graduates of the different program structures that, according to Breidenstein (2002), indicate a perception of a stronger preparation in the 5-year programs. The survey indicated that there were statistically significant differences ($p < .05$) between the 4- and 5-year graduates regarding their preparation for teaching on 20 of the 37 items on the survey dealing with teacher preparation. These items dealt with various aspects of pedagogy, curriculum, development, and assessment such as understanding how different students in the classroom are learning, and developing a curriculum that builds on students' experiences, interests, and abilities. Fewer than one half (47%) of the 4-year graduates said that their program prepared them "very well" or "well" for teaching, whereas 66.7% of the 5-year graduates felt that way.

In terms of teaching practices, the survey indicated that there were two areas of self-reported classroom differences between 4- and 5-year graduates favoring the 5-year program: Students more often participated in setting goals for their learning ($p = .029$), and students more often revise their work for reevaluation ($p. = .00002$). Five-year program graduates also agreed more often that a lot of their ideas about teaching come from their teacher education program ($p = .002$). There were no significant differences in perceptions of teaching practice that favored the 4-year graduates. The interviews indicated that the 5-year program graduates felt better prepared and able to assume leadership responsibilities in their school and plan and solve problems with colleagues. The only area in the whole study where the results favored the 4-year program graduates was in teachers' plans to remain in teaching. Here the interview data indicated that 62.7% of 4-year graduates said that they planned to remain in teaching more than 10 years compared with only 17.6% of 5-year graduates. This later finding contradicted the teacher commitment data in Andrew's (1990) study that favored 5-year graduates.

In summary, these four studies of the relative impact of 4- and 5-year programs on various outcome indicators provided some evidence favoring 5-year extended programs over 4-year programs in terms of the percentage of graduates who entered teaching, remained in teaching over time, were committed to a career in teaching, in self-reports of teaching abilities and how well their programs prepared them to do particular things in the classroom, and in teacher self-reports of involvement in leadership activities in schools. At the same time, principal ratings of the teachers did not show many differences in either the competence of the teachers or their assumption of leadership roles. There were only a few instances in this research where the 4-year program graduates exceeded or equaled the 5-year graduates in the outcomes, but some potentially important differences (e.g., engaging in more learner-centered teaching) were not explained.

However, as mentioned earlier, many factors greatly limit the usefulness of the findings from these studies. A basic problem in drawing conclusions from these studies is the wide variation that exists within the categories of 4- and 5-year programs. Goodlad's (1990) national study of teacher education has shown significant differences in the nature and quality of preservice teacher education programs in different kinds of institutions (e.g., liberal arts college and research university). There is also evidence that teacher education programs vary within institutions according to the diverse goals of program faculty (Liston & Zeichner, 1991). State policy contexts also greatly affect the content and quality of a program. For example, a 4-year program in a state like Texas that has drastically limited the amount of professional education courses in the curriculum of teacher education programs differs vastly from 4-year programs in states that have not done so. Also, as discussed earlier in reference to the research of Natriello and Zumwalt (1993) and others, the subject matter area of the program has been shown to influence the nature of program outcomes such as teacher retention. Lumping all 4- and 5-year programs together in two groups without paying attention to the subject area majors of the candidates and to the nature and quality of the different programs is likely to distort the findings. Additionally, the lack of description of the contexts in which teacher candidates and program graduates teach greatly limits the usefulness of conclusions about teacher retention and teaching effectiveness.

Furthermore, the comparison of graduates from programs with different admission requirements and the lack of attention by researchers to the entering characteristics of the teachers when they began the different programs prevents us from disentangling the effects of student characteristics from those of the programs.

Finally, with regard to the follow-up surveys of the quality of teacher preparation, there is reason to believe from a recent international comparison of teacher education systems (Wang, Coleman, Coley, & Phelps, 2003) that in the United States, teachers' perceptions of the quality of their teacher preparation programs and their level of confidence in specific areas of teaching may not correspond to their actual level of teacher competence in these areas.[9] These findings suggest that we need to be cautious about teachers' self-reports of the quality of teacher preparation in these and other studies discussed in this chapter.

ALTERNATIVE VERSUS TRADITIONAL TEACHER EDUCATION PROGRAMS

The next set of studies is concerned with comparisons of various outcomes associated with teachers who have been certified in alternative versus traditional teacher education programs. Alternative certification has become a major policy issue in the United States. According to Feistritzer and Chester's (2003) report on alternative certification in the United States, 46 states and the District of Columbia currently have some type of alternative teacher certification program, whereas in 1983, only 8 states reported that they had alternative routes to teaching. Feistritzer and Chester estimated that over 200,000 individuals have been licensed to teach through non-college-based alternative programs and that thousands more have been licensed through college-based alternatives. State requirements concerning alternative certification programs vary. For example, only 13 states require any classroom training prior to a teacher's assuming full responsibility for a classroom, and only 19 states require a mentoring component (Education Week, 2003).

It is clear that there is no agreement about the definition of alternative certification and there is some confusion as well about what constitutes traditional certification (Dill, 1996; Humphrey, Wechsler, Bosetti, Wayne, & Adelman, 2002). Fenstermacher (1990) noted that the meaning of alternative certification "is obscure and its forms of implementation are many" (p. 155). Some researchers have defined alternative programs as those programs other than those that are offered by colleges and universities, whereas others have defined traditional programs as undergraduate college and university programs and have considered university postbaccalaureate programs as alternative. Darling-Hammond (1990), recognizing the great diversity in alternative programs, made a distinction between "alternative certification" programs where standards for entry into teaching were reduced and "alternative routes," which were alternatives to college and university undergraduate or postbaccalaureate programs that required candidates to meet the same standards as those of the college and university programs.

The use of different definitions of alternative and traditional certification in the literature has created problems in interpreting the research findings (e.g., Wilson, Floden, & Ferrini Mundy, 2001; Zeichner & Schulte, 2001). In the current review, we have

---

[9] Also see Katz, Raths, Mohanty, Kurachi, and Irving (1981) for a discussion of the limitations of graduates' evaluations of their preservice preparation programs.

adopted Adelman's (1986) definition of alternative certification as "those teacher education programs that enroll noncertified individuals with at least a bachelor's degree offering shortcuts, special assistance, or unique curricula leading to eligibility for a standard teaching credential" (p. 2). This definition includes college and university postbaccalaureaute programs within the definition of alternative and defines traditional certification as a 4-year undergraduate or 5-year integrated program offered by a college and university. Under this definition, alternative certification programs may or may not require lower standards for entry to teaching than do traditional programs. It should be emphasized that both traditional and alternative programs vary widely in terms of purposes and goals, structure and processes, and in their institutional and policy contexts.[10]

The common practice in public debates about teacher education of defining as alternative those programs sponsored by an institution other than a college or university does not work very well in reality, because a number of these programs (e.g., sponsored by school districts and states) utilize university faculty as instructors in varying degrees and may be very similar in substance to university-based programs. It will be concluded from the review that follows that comparisons of traditional and alternative, however defined, are not very productive without attention to specific program characteristics. The definition of alternative and traditional programs adopted for use in this chapter is imperfect, but so, too, are the alternatives.

Stoddart and Floden (1996) provided a potentially more useful way than did Adelman (1986) to distinguish alternative from traditional programs. Their analysis was based on the identification of the assumptions underlying different programs about what teachers need to know to be effective instructors and how they can best acquire that knowledge. For example, one source of disagreement among program proponents is the amount of preparation needed before teachers begin teaching full-time. According to Stoddart and Floden, advocates of traditional programs argue that teachers need some amount of coursework and supervised practice before assuming responsibility for a classroom, whereas advocates of alternative certification outside of colleges and universities believe that individuals with a college degree can pick up much of what they need to learn on the job with mentoring and support. Stoddart and Floden correctly argued that the choice between a traditional program and alternative route is not, as public discussions often imply, a choice between some professional preparation and no preparation. They noted that the arguments are really about the timing and institutional context for teacher education and about the best mix of professional knowledge and skills required. Ideally, we would have structured this review of alternative and traditional program comparisons around these and other substantive differences in programs rather than on the basis of structural characteristics alone. We could not do this, however, because of the limited information about the substance of programs presented in the studies.[11]

---

[10]A recent report on alternative certification by the National Association of State Boards of Education (Roach & Cohen, 2002) also defined alternative certification in this same way as did a discussion of alternative certification by Berry (2000). Finally, Feistritzer and Chester's (2003) influential typology of alternative routes into teaching also includes university postbaccalaureate programs in their alternate route directory of programs.

[11]Stoddart and Floden (1996) identify several assumptions about what knowledge teachers need and how and when they should acquire that knowledge that differentiate proponents of alternative and traditional certification. Those underlying alternative certification are (a) if one knows a subject one can teach it, (b) one learns to teach by doing it, and (c) mature individuals with prior work experience make better teachers.

The following review examines studies that compared preservice preparation in alternative and traditional programs and examined a variety of outcomes of this preparation for the teacher graduates and their students. We examine issues of teacher recruitment in hard to staff areas, retention, and teacher quality as related to traditional and alternative certification.[12] The studies below investigated how traditional and alternative programs influenced entry to and retention in teaching (both anticipated and actual retention), and indicators of teacher quality based on ratings by principals, supervisors and mentor teachers, observations of teaching, teachers' sense of efficacy, and student achievement. The studies reviewed have been organized into five categories based on program sponsorship: (a) comparisons of state-sponsored alternative programs and traditional programs, (b) comparisons of university-sponsored alternative programs and traditional programs and studies of university-based alternative programs, (c) comparisons of school-district-sponsored alternative programs and traditional programs, and (d) studies involving TFA as a comparison group, and (e) studies comparing multiple programs.[13]

COMPARISONS OF STATE-SPONSORED ALTERNATIVE PROGRAMS AND TRADITIONAL PROGRAMS

The first group of studies compared outcomes for the graduates of several state-sponsored programs in Connecticut, Georgia, New Hampshire, and New Jersey with outcomes for graduates of traditional university-based programs. These studies examined the impact of different programs on attracting teachers to hard to staff schools, teachers' ratings of the quality of their preparation, teachers' projected commitment to teaching, teacher retention, teacher efficacy, and aspects of teacher performance as assessed by ratings of supervisors and principals and classroom observation.

Natriello and Zumwalt (1992, 1993) studied various aspects of the state-sponsored alternative certification program in New Jersey ("The Provisional Teacher Program") that began operation in 1985 to 1986. The program included 200 hours of instruction at a regional teaching center established by the state and run by a local college or university. Eighty hours of the 200 were supposed to take place before the beginning of the school year, and the rest was to occur during the first year.[14] There also was supposed to be a 20-day period of limited teaching responsibility at the start of the school year where the interns received intensive supervisory support. The research involved comparisons of teachers who graduated from college-based programs in the state with those in the Provisional Teacher program. This discussion will focus on the data about the settings in which teachers from different teacher education programs taught and their retention in teaching. Natriello and Zumwalt also addressed the demographic and quality profiles of teachers from the college-based and the state-alternative program, and these data are discussed in this volume by Zumwalt and Craig.

Surveys were completed by teachers between spring 1987 and spring 1990. In 1987, the survey was administered to all teachers completing college-based teacher education programs in English education and secondary mathematics and to 40% of those

---

[12]Chapters 3 and 4 of this report have examined the demographic and quality profiles of teachers who enter teaching through alternative and traditional routes.

[13]These categories do not imply that conceptual or substantive differences among programs necessarily exist because of who sponsors them. The sections are merely for the convenience of the readers and break down a rather lengthy analysis into more manageable chunks.

[14]For those teachers hired immediately prior to the start of the school year, the 80 hours of instruction need to be completed during the first 30 days of teaching.

completing elementary education programs. This college-based sample included 121 elementary teachers, 36 secondary English teachers, and 30 secondary mathematics teachers. The same survey was administered in the summer and fall of 1987 to all teachers entering the Provisional Teacher program including 75 elementary teachers, 24 secondary English teachers, and 30 secondary mathematics teachers. These same individuals were surveyed again in the spring of 1988 and 1989. The response rate for the initial survey was 87% or higher and over 80% were retained in the study over the three years.

One set of findings addressed the issue of staffing urban schools. During the first survey administration, alternative route teachers expressed a greater preference than college-prepared teachers in all three subject areas for teaching in typically hard to staff urban areas. In elementary education, the percentages expressing this preference were 26% alternative versus 8.3% traditional. The percentages for English were 17.4% alternative versus 5.6% traditional; and for mathematics, 20.6% alternative versus 0% traditional. Surveys with this same sample of teachers from 1987 to 1991 were reported by Natriello and Zumwalt (1993). In elementary education, alternative teachers were more likely than traditional teachers to report teaching in an urban school district. The figures were 1988, 42.6% versus 17.9%; 1989, 43.2% versus 22.6%; 1990, 33.9% versus 17.4%; and 1991, 34.9% versus 17.4%.

Throughout the 3 years of the study, alternatively certified teachers were more likely than college-prepared teachers to be teaching in low-SES districts, especially elementary alternatively certified teachers who were twice as likely as their traditionally certified counterparts to be teaching in low-SES districts. In the spring of 1990, for example, about one third of the college-prepared elementary and English teachers and slightly less than half of college-prepared math teachers were in low-SES districts. Among the alternatively certified, more than three fourths of the elementary teachers, almost half of the English teachers, and more than half of the math teachers were teaching in low-SES districts. The differences noted previously between alternatively and traditionally teachers in their preferences for teaching in urban schools or in schools serving low-SES pupils may reflect more about where the alternatively certified teachers could find jobs than about their actual preferences. The majority of districts that hire teachers in the Provisional Teacher Program are urban districts serving disadvantaged students. Natriello and Zumwalt (1993, p. 59) concluded:

> In view of this, it is impossible in our present analysis to disentangle the preferences of teachers from an acceptance of the reality of teaching positions open to them. Alternate route teachers in New Jersey have been more successful in securing positions in urban districts where the need for teachers is more pronounced than in suburban districts, and so they may be adjusting their preferences to be consistent with their actual positions.

Teachers were also asked about their plans to remain in teaching over time. Eighty percent or more of traditionally and alternatively certified teachers reported that they expected to be teaching for at least 3 years. In terms of long-range plans to remain in schools, 81.7% of elementary traditionally certified teachers had long-range plans to remain in schools. Sixty-five to 73.8% of all of the other groups had such plans. The only exception to this general trend was that only 40% of mathematics teachers who were alternatively certified intended to remain in schools over the long term. Based on these data, Natriello and Zumwalt (1992, p. 72) concluded the following:

> The most striking differences are not those between college-prepared and alternative route teachers in general, but between alternative route mathematics teachers and the other five groups. These differences suggest that viewing alternative route programs

generically may be misleading . . . subject matter and grade level differences are important in considering the consequences of alternative route programs.

Finally, retention of the teachers was also tracked over the 3 years. About 85% of both the alternatively and traditionally certified elementary teachers remained in teaching, but differences existed in the secondary areas. Here about three fourths of the secondary English teachers from alternative routes stayed in teaching through the third year compared to about two thirds of English teachers from traditional programs. In the case of mathematics, 80% to 90% of the traditionally certified teachers stayed in teaching as compared to about 60% of the alternatively certified math teachers. Once again with regard to actual teacher retention, the importance of grade level and subject matter becomes important in understanding the consequences of alternative and traditional programs.

Guyton, Fox, and Sisk (1991) studied 23 first-year teachers who participated in the 1988 to 1989 alternative certification program in Georgia and 26 first-year teachers who had been prepared through traditional university-based programs at various colleges and universities. All of the teachers were either certified or in the process of becoming certified in mathematics, science, or foreign language. The schools where they taught did not differ in terms of size and racial and socioeconomic background of the students. The state-sponsored alternative program included an 8-week resident summer program with coursework in human development and the identification and education of children with special learning needs. During the following academic year, participants completed an internship under the supervision of a mentor teacher. Applicants needed a 2.5 GPA and a bachelor's degree to be admitted, and the mentors were provided with a weeklong training program. No information was provided about the preservice preparation of the traditionally certified teachers, but it was noted that they did not have mentors during their first year.

Comparisons were made between the alternatively and regularly certified teachers on a number of dimensions related to teacher retention and teacher quality. The traditionally certified were more positive at the end of the year about staying in the profession. The results consisted of responses to two questions—"I plan to teach next year," and "I view teaching as my career choice." However, all but two of the alternatively certified teachers completed the year and 83% of these planned to return to the same schools the following year.

Several different comparisons were made of aspects of teacher quality. First, using portions of Gibson and Dembo's "Teacher Efficacy Scale" (16 of the 30 items) for which an acceptable level of reliability was achieved, no differences were found on teaching efficacy or personal efficacy.[15] Two observations were also completed of each teacher after 1 month of teaching by a variety of people including principals, assistant principals, mentors, and peers. No significant differences in the quality of teaching were found in these observations. Little information was given about the content of the beginning teacher evaluation form used except for mention of its attention to the use of classroom time, enthusiasm, and an overall rating of teacher performance. Finally, an educational attitude inventory was administered at the beginning of the year, after 5 months of teaching, and at the end of the school year. This instrument described teacher attitudes in terms of their student-centeredness and teacher-centeredness. At the beginning of the year, the teachers from traditional programs had significantly

---

[15]Teaching efficacy is the degree to which teachers believe students can be taught given such factors as family background, school conditions, and so forth. Personal efficacy is teachers' evaluations of their own abilities to bring about positive student change and motivation.

higher teacher centeredness scores, but these differences disappeared at midyear and did not reappear. There were no differences at anytime during the year in student-centeredness which was high for both groups. Finally, the alternatively certified teachers were significantly more positive than traditionally certified teachers about their teacher education program and the improvement of their teaching abilities over the first month of teaching. This improvement was not surprising because these teachers began teaching with less formal preparation than traditionally certified teachers.

The general lack of differences throughout this research led Guyton et al. (1991) to conclude that "the findings of this study generally support the contention that condensed pedagogical preparation and a supervised internship are a reasonable alternative to traditional teacher preparation programs for persons with degrees in the subject they will teach" (p. 7). On the other hand, the authors lamented the high cost of the program in comparison with traditional programs. In this study, the cost of preparing 23 teachers in the alternative route exceeded a quarter million dollars.

Several aspects of this study limit its usefulness. First, because of the omission of information about the preservice preparation programs attended by the teachers, it was unclear what kind of preparation the alternative preparation is being compared against. This same limitation applies to all of the other studies in this section. Furthermore, the lack of information about the criteria used to assess the teachers' performance made it difficult to understand how teachers were rated. On the other hand, it should be noted that in this study, unlike most other studies assessing teacher performance, an effort was made to equate the schools in which the teachers taught according to the ethnic and racial and socioeconomic background of the pupils. This added to the usefulness of the teacher evaluation data in that we knew that teacher performance was compared in similar kinds of schools.

Bliss (1990) conducted a study comparing the teaching performance of teachers licensed through Connecticut's alternative certification program to that of teachers licensed through college- and university-based programs. The alternative program involved an 8-week summer program consisting of an integrated curriculum rather than separate courses, and 2 years of mentoring and assessment. Teachers licensed through traditional routes were mentored for only 1 year.

Two pieces of empirical evidence were presented related to the teaching competence of alternatively certified teachers. First, when asked whether alternatively teachers were "stronger than other beginning teachers" (left for the responders to define), 88% of the supervisors felt that the alternatively certified teachers were stronger than the other beginning teachers. All but three supervisors indicated that they would gladly rehire the alternatively certified teacher in question. Information about how many supervisors completed the ratings was not provided. The use of the vague term *other beginning teachers* for comparison purposes provided little help in interpreting these findings.

Also, in late spring 1990, a report was presented on the required state assessments of all the alternatively and traditionally certified teachers in relation to the state teaching competencies. These assessments were based on six observations made by trained observers. In the elementary education group, all five of the alternatively certified teachers met the state standard, whereas 29 of the 32 traditionally prepared teachers (91%) did so. In the secondary group, 18 of the 25 alternatively certified teachers (72%) met the standard, whereas 9 of the 13 traditionally prepared teachers (69%) did so. Although the sample sizes were too small to conduct meaningful tests of statistical significance, Bliss (1990) concludes: "The percentages passing seem equivalent and thus support the contention that comparable proportions of alternatively certified teachers are meeting the standards expected of beginning teachers in Connecticut" (p. 50). These ratings were supported by a survey of school personnel responsible for supporting the alternatively certified teachers and for preparing them for the assessments. These supervisors, mentors, and principals rated the teachers' preparation as good to excellent for each of the state's 15 teaching competencies. As was the case in the Georgia study discussed earlier, the vagueness of the criteria in the assessments of teacher performance, both those done by ratings and classroom observations, detracted from the usefulness of the findings. Also, the small sample sizes limit the value of the study.

In the final comparison between a state-sponsored alternative certification program and traditional programs, Jelmberg (1996) studied graduates from various college-based preparation programs in New Hampshire and from an alternative program sponsored by the state where teachers become the teachers of record before any preparation and then have 3 years to complete a professional development plan and demonstrate proficiency on 14 state teacher competencies. The college-based programs were either 4-year undergraduate programs, fifth-year programs, or extended 5-year programs.[16] The research consisted of two surveys: one completed by teachers about the quality of their preparation program; and the other, by principals evaluating teachers' teaching performance.

Jelmberg (1996) surveyed a random sample of 492 of 660 elementary and secondary teachers of math, science, English and language arts, and social studies certified between 1987 and 1990 and who had no prior certification. Some 295 teachers responded (60%), and 236 surveys were usable after those teachers with prior certifications were removed. One hundred thirty-six principals of these teachers returned usable teacher evaluations. About two thirds of the sample had been teaching for 2 to 3 years.

The principals rated teachers on both instructional skills and instructional planning. The ratings of the 107 traditionally prepared teachers were significantly higher than those of the alternatively prepared teachers on both instructional planning and instructional skills ($p < .05$). Additionally, the traditionally certified teachers rated their preparation programs significantly higher than did the alternatively certified teachers with regard to professional courses, practicum supervision, and overall preparation ($p < .05$). These teacher surveys indicated that the traditional teachers rated their programs higher than did the alternatively certified teachers on 11 of the 14 competencies used by the state education department to certify teachers. Since 6 of these 11 were the same competencies rated highly by the principals, Jelmberg (1996) concluded that "there was considerable agreement among teachers and principals that teachers from traditional teacher education programs were better prepared in these 6 competencies" (p. 65).

This research report provided little information about the teacher competencies included in the surveys. Jelmberg's (1996) overall conclusion that "these findings suggest that experienced teachers who have undergone preparation through college-based teacher education programs are better performers than experienced teachers from state-sponsored alternative programs ... " (p. 63) went beyond the data presented, because only one alternative program in one state was involved in this study. Furthermore, this state-sponsored program, unlike a number of others, provided no preparation for teaching prior to the assumption of responsibility for a classroom.

---

[16]Given our definition of alternative certification, some alternatively certified teachers (in fifth-year programs) were included in the group of traditionally certified teachers. It was not stated how many teachers graduated from 4-year, 5-year, or fifth-year programs.

Finally, because not much information was provided about the specific competencies involved in the teacher evaluation data, the process of evaluation used, and about the schools in which the teachers taught, the value of this study was very limited.

In summary, the four studies that compared graduates from state-sponsored alternative programs and university-based programs provided some evidence in the case of New Jersey that alternatively certified teachers are more willing than traditionally certified teachers to teach in low-SES urban schools, but these data may reflect more where teachers can get jobs than actual teacher preferences. The subject areas and grade levels taught by teachers appeared to influence how long they planned to and actually remain in teaching. There were no differences between alternatively and traditionally certified teachers in terms of teacher efficacy or in teaching competence as measured by classroom observations. Principal and supervisor ratings of teacher competence were mixed, favoring alternative certification in one case and traditional certification in the other. The value of these observations and ratings are extremely limited, however, due to the lack of specificity with regard to the evaluation criteria and the schools in which the graduates taught.

In all four cases, although some details were provided about the alternative programs, traditional programs from an unknown number of different institutions were lumped together into a single category ignoring any differences in the programs. Because of the lack of information about the preparation received by the comparison group and the characteristics that they brought to this preparation, it was not possible to disentangle the influence of teacher characteristics from those of their preparation programs. Even if we assume the preparation made the difference in the reported outcomes, it was impossible to determine which characteristics of the teacher education programs might have accounted for these differences.

COMPARISONS OF UNIVERSITY-SPONSORED ALTERNATIVE PROGRAMS AND TRADITIONAL PROGRAMS AND A STUDY OF A UNIVERSITY-BASED ALTERNATIVE PROGRAM

The next group of eight studies examined the outcomes of teacher education in university-based alternative and traditional programs in Georgia, Tennessee, North Carolina, Colorado, California, and Virginia, and in MAT programs across the country. First, in one of the few instances in the literature in which researchers examined the impact of the type of certification program on pupil achievement, Miller, McKenna, and McKenna (1998) conducted three different studies to examine the relative effects of an alternative certification program for middle school teachers at a state university in Georgia and traditional university teacher preparation on teachers' perceptions of the value of their training, perceptions of their teaching ability, classroom practice, and the achievement of their pupils. Three years after completing the program, 41 of 67 teachers who were placed as alternative program interns in the fall of 1989 were matched with 41 who taught the same subjects in the same schools and had the same amount of teaching experience.

The alternative program included summer coursework prior to a yearlong internship where the intern was the teacher of record from the beginning of the school year. Interns received extensive mentoring from both a university supervisor (eight visits) and a school-based mentor. Interns participated in a biweekly seminar in which they analyzed their teaching. They continued to take courses throughout the year. The traditionally certified teachers had graduated from a variety of unspecified university-based, preservice programs.

A 15-item rating scale was used to evaluate observed lessons taught by the 41 alternatively certified and 41 traditionally certified teachers. This scale included two dimensions: "effective lesson components" (e.g., focus, objective, and purpose) and "effective teacher–pupil interaction" (e.g., high pupil participation). Two experienced teachers were trained as observers, and each observed all 82 of the teachers without knowing how they were certified. The observations were conducted without prior notice to the teachers. These observations showed no significant differences between the two groups of teachers on the behaviors examined.

The two observers interviewed each of the 82 teachers, exploring the teachers' perceptions of their teaching abilities when they began teaching,[17] perceptions of their current level of teaching competency, and perceptions of the problems they experienced across their 3-year careers. Generally, these interviews revealed greater differences within the alternatively and traditionally certified groups than those across the categories. Neither group felt that they were particularly well prepared to teach after their preservice program. There also was no difference between the groups in their views of their current level of teaching competence and problems they perceived to have faced in their teaching over 3 years. Both groups felt that they were now very competent as a result of teaching experience and mentoring. The two groups were indistinguishable on the basis of the problems they said they had faced as teachers. Not surprisingly, discipline and classroom management were cited as the major problems they had faced in the classroom.

Finally, nine alternatively certified and nine traditionally certified teachers who taught in self-contained fifth and sixth-grade classrooms were selected from the original sample of 82 teachers. Pupils who had been present in these 18 classes the whole year were selected for comparisons of achievement test scores using the Iowa Test of Basic Skills. There were no pretest differences between these two groups (188 pupils taught by alternatively certified teachers and 157 pupils taught by traditionally certified teachers) on the total mathematics and reading tests and on the mathematics subtests of concepts, problem solving, and computation. The end–of-year comparisons between the test scores of the pupils taught by the two groups of teachers showed no significant differences on either the total reading and math tests or the math subtests.

Miller et al. (1998) concluded that after 3 years, there appeared to be no significant differences between the alternatively and traditionally certified teachers in terms of teaching behaviors and the results for pupils. They saw these results as supporting the development of "carefully constructed alternative certification programs with extensive mentoring components, post graduation training, regular inservice classes, and ongoing university supervision" (p. 174).

Although this study had several of the same limitations as others in which comparisons were made (e.g., vague criteria for assessing teaching performance, lack of description of the characteristics of the traditional programs), the blind observations where the observers did not know which type of program the teacher had attended and the matching of teachers who taught the same subjects in the same schools are positive design features that strengthened the usefulness of the findings.

Mayer, Decker, Glazerman, and Silva (2003) raised several additional concerns about this study. They argued that because the analysis of student achievement score

---

[17]Strang, Badt, and Kauffman (1997) provide some evidence that teachers cannot accurately recall their prior teaching capability.

differences involved only nine teachers in each group from one state, the findings were of limited value. They also questioned how teachers were matched, arguing that there could be factors other than the teacher education program such as class size differences between the alternatively certified and traditionally certified teachers' classrooms that may have accounted for the findings.[18] Mayer et. al. contended that randomly assigning pupils to teachers who received different types of preparation would be the only way to ensure that the findings were attributable to the preparation teachers received. Practical obstacles involved in doing this kind of study (e.g., high student mobility) make this kind of randomized experiment extremely difficult and complex to carry out. There are also ethical issues involved in randomly assigning pupils to teachers who have received different amounts of preparation that we think warrant careful deliberation. We discuss the conditions under which we think randomized trials are appropriate later in this chapter.

In the second study in this group, Boser and Wiley (1988) surveyed superintendents, principals, and mentor teachers who worked with graduates of the University of Tennessee-Knoxville's 12-month alternative certification program, its 4-year undergraduate program, and its fifth-year postbaccalaureate program. All three programs prepared teachers for the secondary level. In both of the "traditional" programs,[19] students completed a semester of student teaching. In the alternative program they completed a full-year internship (three-course teaching load). In the alternative program, students also completed 10 weeks of intensive course work before the school year and attended seminars and courses throughout their internship year. Interns were mentored by experienced public school teachers, but no preparation in supervision and mentoring was provided to the mentors.

An unspecified number of superintendents, principals, and mentor teachers who worked with the alternative program in 1984 to 1985 were surveyed about their opinions of the program's quality. They were given four options for comparing the quality of the different teacher education programs: Interns were better prepared, traditional students were better prepared, there was no difference between the programs, and the advantages of the two programs were balanced. The survey indicated that most thought that the preparation received in the alternative program was comparable to, as good as, or better than that received by students in the traditional program. Only 21% of the principals and 6% of the mentors thought that the students in the traditional program were better prepared. Because these ratings were made in a general way without specification of criteria of teaching quality, they are of limited value. No tests of the statistical significance of the identified differences in perceptions of the quality of teacher preparation were reported. The authors cautioned readers that it was not possible from their study to distinguish program effects from participant effects. The traditionally and alternatively certified teachers were similar in their undergraduate GPA and PPST reading scores, but the authors noted that there may have been other differences in the students rather than in the program that would explain the more positive ratings of the alternative program.

---

[18]Mayer et al. (2003) point out that the 9 alternatively certified teachers taught 188 students and the 9 traditionally certified teachers taught 157 students resulting in class size differences on the average of 3.5 students.

[19]According to our definition of traditional and alternative, the fifth-year program is an alternative program. The University of Tennessee defines the fifth year program as traditional and distinguishes it from the alternative program on the basis of the nature of the final clinical experience (student teaching or internship).

Hawk and Schmidt (1989) of East Carolina University in North Carolina conducted a study of 16 students seeking mathematics or science certification who were enrolled in a 12-month alternative certification program conducted by East Carolina University, the "Lateral Entry Program" (LEP). These students were compared to a group of first-year teachers certified through traditional university-based teacher education both at East Carolina University and elsewhere.

The alternative certification program included 6 weeks of summer coursework in "essential teaching skills" and a 1-year paid internship in a rural North Carolina school. The interns were supervised by a mentor certified in the same content area. They attended weekly seminars led by university staff. To be certified, teachers needed to pass the National Teacher Examination professional knowledge and appropriate content area exams. No information was provided about the preparation received by the traditionally prepared teachers except that it occurred in a variety of institutions. It was stated that the alternative program included 255 contact hours of classroom instruction versus 312 hours in the regular math and science certification programs at East Carolina University.

Comparisons were made of the National Teacher Examination scores of the 16 alternatively certified teachers and 7 math and 11 science teacher education graduates from the same institution. No significant differences were found when comparing their NTE content area and professional knowledge scores.

An unspecified number of observations of both groups of teachers was conducted throughout the year by school district personnel using the "Teacher Performance Appraisal Instrument" (TPAI). Although this is a validated research-based instrument that assesses 28 observable teaching practices in five major areas, interrater reliability could not be established for this study because of time and distance constraints. The traditionally certified teachers observed included the 18 mathematics and science teachers noted above plus 35 first-year mathematics and science teachers who were certified in a variety of other preservice programs. The observation data were reported in terms of the percentages of teachers below standard, at standard, and above standard in the five major areas assessed by the instrument: management of time, management of students, instructional presentation, instructional monitoring, and instructional feedback. Here, although the range of difference between alternatively and traditionally certified teachers was very small with regard to below standard ratings (0%–5%), there was a larger difference between the two groups in terms of their above standard ratings (10%–28%). Fewer alternatively certified teachers received above standard ratings than traditionally certified teachers in all of the areas except for instructional monitoring. In instructional monitoring, 23.1% more alternative teachers than traditional teachers were rated at above standard. The meaning of the specific categories in this observation instrument was not explained in the report of the study. Although the traditionally certified teachers received more above standard ratings than alternatively certified teachers, Hawk and Schmidt (1989) concluded that "the LEP prepared competent at standard teachers whose NTE scores were equal to those of traditionally prepared teachers" (p. 57). No tests of the statistical significance of the identified differences in teacher performance were reported.

In a study of a 1-year, master's level, fast track certification program for secondary teachers at Colorado State University (CSU; "Project Promise"), Paccione, McWhorter, and Richburg (2000) examined the comparative effects of this alternative certification program and two versions of the regular undergraduate program on teacher entry and retention, teachers' perceptions of the quality of their teacher preparation, and principal satisfaction. In Project Promise, carefully selected cohorts of 20 students completed intensive coursework and five field experiences in a variety of urban and rural schools and communities. In the traditional undergraduate program, students completed 100 hours of prestudent teaching field experiences and 15 weeks of student teaching. In the Professional Development School option within the traditional program, during the semester prior to student teaching, students completed a methods course co-taught at a local high school by university staff and teachers along with a one-credit field experience and seminar.

Of the students who completed Project Promise in 1994, 87% secured teaching positions within 4 months of completing the program. Only 60% of those students who completed the regular undergraduate program were able to secure teaching positions within 4 months of graduation. A follow-up study was conducted after CSU added a Professional Development School option to its teacher education programs. Teachers included in this study were 36 graduates of Project Promise, 36 graduates of the Professional Development School option, and 78 graduates of the traditional program. On the issue of retention, significantly more Project Promise completers (92%) were working for a school system 2 years after completing the program than were completers of the traditional CSU programs (71%), or the PDS option (81%). The meanings of "working for a school system" and of "significantly more" were not made clear in the report of the study.

The same CSU graduates then completed a survey evaluating how well they thought they were prepared in five areas of teaching: classroom management, diversity, lesson planning, technology, and teaching strategies. Here the alternatively certified teachers were significantly (level of significance not defined) more positive than graduates of the PDS and the traditional program about the quality of their preparation in the areas of classroom management, diversity, technology, and teaching strategies. Only in the area of lesson planning was there no statistically significant difference.

Finally, the 16 principals of the 17 alternatively certified program completers in 1995 to 1996 completed a 28-item survey where they were asked to compare them with an "average teacher of equal teaching experience." On each of the survey's 28-items, principals rated the alternatively certified teachers' performance higher. The 28 items included such things as teacher professionalism, planning, organizing and delivering instruction, and creating a learning environment. Whether these differences were statistically significant was not reported.

Mantle-Bromley, Gould, McWhorter, and Whaley (2000) reported on a study of graduates of the same programs during the fall and spring semesters of 1994 and 1995. The sample included 79 graduates of the traditional 4-year undergraduate program, 37 graduates of "Project Promise" and 36 graduates of the Professional Development School (PDS) option within the undergraduate program. This sample represented 31% of the traditional program graduates during this period, 92.5% of the Project Promise graduates, and 48% of the Professional Development School option graduates. The sample probably includes many if not most of the same teachers in the Paccione et al. (2000) study, but the relationship between the two samples was not discussed or explained.

The graduates had completed student teaching from 18 months to 3 years before completing the telephone survey. Of the 152 in the sample, 57.9% were working as full-time teachers at the time of the survey. They included 36 of the 79 graduates (45.6%) of the undergraduate program, 23 of the 36 PDS program completers (63.8%), and 29 of the 37 Project Promise completers (78%). A chi-square analysis indicated that the retention rate for Project Promise was significantly greater than that for the undergraduate program ($p = .001$). None of the other differences was statistically significant. The teachers were also asked how long they planned to remain in their current teaching positions: The "more than 3 years" category was selected the most. Differences across the programs were not statistically significant.

Teachers were also asked to rate how well their program prepared them in five areas: classroom management, diversity, lesson planning, technology, and teaching strategies. The Project Promise teachers gave significantly higher ($p < 01$) ratings to their preparation in all areas except lesson planning where there were no differences by program. The Project Promise teachers' ratings were also significantly higher ($p < 01$) than those of the graduates of the PDS program in the areas of diversity, and teaching strategies, but were not significantly different in technology or classroom management. The researchers speculated that several factors in the Project Promise program may account for the more positive ratings including cohesive cohort groups, closely supervised field experiences prior to student teaching, courses that were integrated across content areas and team-taught, scholarships for most students that paid for their tuition, selective admissions, the frequency of faculty supervision, and help from the faculty in securing employment. The report presented no evidence demonstrating the links between these program characteristics and the outcomes. The differences in outcomes could have been a result of differences in the students choosing the different programs rather than of the programs themselves.

Sandlin, Young, and Karge (1992) compared the classroom teaching practices of 58 teachers enrolled in an intern program at a California State University campus (alternatively certified teachers) and 66 first-year teachers who were recent graduates of the traditional certification program at the same California State University campus. All teachers were randomly selected for this study and taught in grades K–6. Little information was provided about both the alternative and traditional certification programs, beyond that the university provided the coursework, seminars, and classroom supervision of the alternatively certified teachers, and the school district provided them with a mentor and a salaried teaching position. All interns were required to present evidence to faculty of 2 years' paid work in schools prior to admission to the alternative certification program. It was also reported that all the teachers taught in seven southern California school districts. The only information provided about the traditionally certified teachers' preparation was that they recently completed coursework and traditional student teaching under the direction of a master teacher and university supervisor.

The "Teacher Evaluation Scale" was used to assess the teaching of both groups of teachers. This instrument has a Pearson correlation coefficient of .96 and interrater reliability coefficients ranging from .91 to .95 (Hawthorne Educational Services, 1990). Three observations were conducted of each teacher (fall, winter, and spring) by an experienced supervisor. The observers did not know whether the teachers were in the alternatively or traditionally certified group. The observation scale included 16 items that were concerned with instruction and classroom management. The research report provided no specific information about these items. In the fall and winter observations, the scores of the traditionally certified teachers were lower than those of the alternatively certified teachers on five and two of the items, respectively ($p < .05$). By the end of the school year, however, the two groups scored at virtually the same level, and there were no significant differences on any of the items. The researchers concluded that at the end of their first year, there appeared to be no differences in the classrooms of intern and traditionally prepared beginning teachers. Although the blind observations were helpful, it would have been useful for the research report to include information about the schools in which the teachers taught and about the meaning of the components of the observation instrument.

In another study of graduates of an alternative certification program with no comparison group, Shannon (1990) examined both teachers' satisfaction with their alternative certification program and principal evaluations of their teaching performance. The program was a 1-year alternative route for career switchers offered by Virginia Wesleyan College that included three courses, a brief observational practicum, and a 10-week student-teaching experience under the supervision of a cooperating teacher. Thirty-six of the 63 graduates of the program's first four cohorts responded to a survey that asked them to rate the quality of their preparation for the nine teaching competencies required by the Virginia Department of Education (these were not described in the paper). All of the graduates rated their preparation in these nine areas good or excellent.

Seventeen of the teachers employed for at least a year gave permission for their employers to be contacted for a teaching evaluation on the nine state teaching competencies. Fifteen of these principals returned the survey: 14 reported the performance of the teachers to be good or excellent in all of the competencies. The other principal rated the teacher as excellent or good in eight categories and fair in classroom management. The fact that these evaluations were only from those principals where beginning teachers gave permission for them to be contacted limited the usefulness of the ratings. The author limited her claims about generalizing from the success of the program to a more mature population of career switchers.

Finally, Coley and Thorpe (1986), in a study of graduates of Master of Arts in Teaching (MAT) programs, examined where these teachers taught, how long they stayed in teaching, and other issues. MAT programs are postbaccalaureate programs that are designed to attract and prepare bright liberal arts graduates for teaching. In its original conception, the distinctive feature of the MAT program was that students continued to take courses in their disciplines as well as professional education courses, and arts and sciences faculty were closely involved in the program. In many postbaccalaureate programs, students take only professional education courses, and the program is administered solely by a school or college of education. In recent years, programs that offer an MAT degree have not always emphasized content courses or involved faculty from outside the department, school, or college of education.

In the spring of 1985, surveys were sent to the 1968 and 1969 graduates of the MAT programs at nine institutions[20] and to the most recent graduates from MAT programs in four institutions.[21] Some 751 completed surveys were returned which represented an 81% return rate for the 1968 and 1969 graduates and a 90% return rate for recent graduates.

As discussed in the literature on graduate teacher education (e.g., Zeichner, 1989), the students in these MAT programs were in the upper ranges of academic quality on such measures as the Miller Analogy Test and the Graduate Record Examination. Coley and Thorpe (1986) point out that these students "came from selective undergraduate schools, earned high grades, and received a substantial number of academic honors as undergraduates" (p. 7). These data strongly suggested that the MAT model for graduate teacher education was effective in attracting academically superior students to prepare for teaching.

Of the 715 MATs from the 1960s who prepared to teach, 83% entered elementary or secondary school teaching following their MAT program. About one third of these

---

[20]Converse College, Duke, Harvard, Johns Hopkins, Notre Dame, Stanford, the University of Chicago, the University of Massachusetts, and Vanderbilt. Many of the 1960s MAT programs were funded by the Ford Foundation and were referred to as "Breakthrough" programs (Stone, 1968).

[21]Brown, Stanford, Vanderbilt, and the University of Chicago.

individuals held a teaching position at the time of the study. The 1960s MATs taught for an average of 5 years before leaving teaching. A similar pattern of entry emerged for the 1980s MATs. Eighty-eight percent of this group indicated that they planned to enter teaching following completion of their program. Of those who planned to enter, one third said that they planned to make teaching their career. Coley and Thorpe (1986) concluded that the MAT program compared favorably with other forms of teacher education in terms of the proportion of graduates who entered and remained in teaching. Although these programs have brought academically capable individuals into teaching who have stayed at least as long as teachers in general this study also indicated that the majority of the MATs taught in suburban public secondary schools in which the majority of the students are White, middle to upper middle class, and above the mean in academic ability. There was no evidence from this study that the MAT model has been successful in preparing teachers who will ameliorate the serious and long-standing shortages of qualified teachers in rural and urban schools. Furthermore, because the teachers who participated in these programs have been predominately White, the MAT model has not demonstrated its ability to attract and keep academically talented teachers of color.

In summary, the findings of this research that compared university-sponsored alternative programs to traditional programs show very little difference between alternatively and traditionally certified teachers. Although differences emerged in the individual studies, such problems as vague definitions of the criteria used to define teaching effectiveness, a lack of discussion of the settings where graduates taught, and a dearth of information about the traditional teacher education programs greatly limited the value of the findings. One interesting feature that was used in two studies was that the observers of program graduates did not know whether the teachers being observed had completed an alternative or traditional program. This practice is an improvement over the usual situation where the rater of teaching effectiveness has a stake in a program and knows which teachers are associated with particular programs. In five of the eight studies, statistical tests were not performed on the data largely because of small sample sizes. Because of the methodological problems with these studies, they do not provide a basis for determining whether there are important differences between the programs under study.

COMPARISONS OF SCHOOL-DISTRICT-SPONSORED
PROGRAMS AND TRADITIONAL PROGRAMS

The next group of five studies examined various outcomes associated with district-sponsored alternative programs in Houston, Dallas, and Milwaukee in comparison with those of traditional university-based programs.

Two studies were conducted on the alternative certification program in and around Houston, Texas. In the Houston Independent School District's 1-year alternative program participants assumed full responsibility for a classroom at the beginning of the school year following a summer of coursework in how to teach reading. During the year interns were assigned a mentor teacher, and completed six credit hours in the teaching of reading and a number of school-based workshops designed for program participants.[22]

---

[22]In a study of the Houston program, Stevens and Dial (1993) report that although mentors were assigned to all Houston interns and some were perceived as helpful, many of the new teachers they interviewed did not even know who their assigned mentor was.

In the first study, Knight, Owens, and Waxman (1991) compared the perceptions of students taught by alternatively certified and traditionally certified teachers of the nature of instruction and of their classroom environments. A sample of 676 elementary and middle school students and their 24 teachers in Houston and nearby districts with similar demographic profiles was selected from a pool of 1,100 students and 50 teachers. Half the students were taught by alternatively certified teachers, and half, by traditionally certified teachers. None of the teachers in the sample had a master's degree. No information was provided about the differences in the preparation programs attended by the teachers in the sample except statements that the traditionally certified teachers had completed a student teaching experience and the alternatively certified teachers had not done so.

An adapted version of the "My Classmates" inventory (Fisher & Frasier, 1981) was administered to all students. How the original instrument was adapted was not stated. This 43-item instrument consists of 10 subscales including satisfaction with and enjoyment of school work and the classroom, degree of friction among students in the class, the degree of cohesiveness and cooperation among students, and students' perceptions of instruction at the lower and higher levels of thinking as defined by Bloom's taxonomy. The report made assertions about the instrument's reliability and validity and provided a citation (Fraser, 1986), but provided no specific information on these matters in the research report.

A multivariate analysis of variance was performed to investigate overall differences in the perceptions of learning environments between the two groups of students. Statistically significant differences were found on 5 of the 11 subscales. Students in classes of traditionally certified teachers perceived significantly more instruction and opportunities to engage in higher thought processes than students taught by alternatively certified teachers ($p < .01$). These students also thought that their teachers moved them through class work at a more appropriate pace than students in classes taught by alternatively certified teachers ($p < .05$). Finally, students in classes taught by traditionally certified teachers perceived significantly more group cohesiveness ($p < .01$) and cooperation ($p < .001$) and significantly less friction among students ($p < .01$) than students in classes taught by alternatively certified teachers.

The authors cautioned readers about the meaning of these differences, all of which favored the traditionally certified teachers, because they suspected that other factors not investigated in this study may have contributed to students' perceptions. Also, they noted that students' perceptions of the nature and quality of instruction and the classroom environment may not correspond to the reality of what existed or to the quality of student learning. When in the school year these surveys were administered is not reported. This information is important to know in interpreting the findings because the alternatively certified teachers started the year with less professional preparation and would be expected to have more problems in their teaching at the onset.

In the second study, Houston, Marshall, and McDavid (1993) studied problems experienced by first-year teachers who had completed the Houston Independent School District alternative route and those who had completed unidentified college or university programs. Among the traditionally certified teachers, no distinction was made between teachers who graduated from 4- or 5-year programs. The sample consisted of 69 traditionally certified teachers and 162 alternatively certified teachers. Both groups taught in schools with predominately minority enrollments.

The study examined teachers' perceptions of the importance of various problems that could be experienced by teachers and their level of confidence and satisfaction with teaching. Teachers were asked to rate the importance of these problems after two months of teaching and again after eight months. After two months of teaching, the alternatively certified teachers perceived greater problems than the traditionally certified teachers in six areas: student motivation ($p = .0001$), managing teacher time ($p = .0006$), the amount of paperwork ($p = .043$), lack of personal time ($p = .009$), grading students ($p = .016$), and problems with school administration ($p = .02$). After 8 months of teaching, these differences disappeared and the only difference that existed was that traditionally certified teachers perceived significantly greater problems with classroom management ($p = .05$) than alternatively certified teachers.

After two months of teaching, traditionally certified teachers were more satisfied with their jobs than alternatively certified teachers, but these differences disappeared by the end of the year. Thus, although those from the traditional route had fewer problems and more satisfaction after two months of teaching, the two groups were essentially equivalent on these dimensions by the end of the year. These findings are not surprising given that the traditionally certified teachers started the year with much more coursework and clinical preparation. (Houston et al., 1993) concluded that "This study-supports those who indicate that there are no differences between those who have spent two or more years completing a traditional certification program and those who have spent a few weeks preparing for their first job in the classroom" (p. 88).

The fact that alternatively certified teachers appeared to "catch up" to traditionally certified teachers by the end of the year in classroom performance contradicts this conclusion of the researchers that there is no difference in the effects of alternative and traditional programs. The students taught by the alternatively certified teachers when they assume responsibility for a classroom at the beginning of the year with little professional preparation may suffer academic losses while their teachers are "catching up" to the traditionally certified teachers.

A study was conducted on the alternative certification program in the Dallas, Texas, Independent School District (DISD). Hutton, Lutz, and Williamson, (1990); and Lutz and Hutton (1989) compared the content knowledge, teaching performance, and retention rates of 110 alternative certification interns during the 1986 to 1987 school year to that of 62 first-year teachers certified through university-based programs. The alternative certification program in the Dallas Independent School District sought to alleviate teacher shortages in areas such as early childhood, bilingual and ESL education, mathematics, and science. The instruction and classroom supervision was provided by a combination of DISD staff and faculty from East Texas State University. One distinctive characteristic of this alternative program was that interns taught under the direct supervision of a supervising teacher for the first weeks of school and did not become the teachers of record in a classroom until October. Twenty experienced teachers in the district were released from their classrooms and served as teacher advisors participating in instruction and classroom supervision of the interns. The program admitted individuals who had a bachelor's degree, at least a 2.8 GPA in a content area and who passed a basic skills exam. The schools to which the interns and beginning teachers in the comparison were assigned did not differ from one another in terms of the percentage of pupils eligible for free and reduced lunch.

A comparison was made of teachers' expectations for remaining in teaching. Here 72% of the traditionally certified teachers reported a long-term commitment, whereas only 40% of the alternatively certified teachers did so (Lutz & Hutton, 1989). However, the meaning of these data is unclear because the response rate from the traditionally certified group was only 10%.

The teaching performance of alternatively certified interns was compared to that of the traditionally certified teachers using the "Texas Teacher Appraisal System" (TTAS; Texas Education Agency, 1986) and the Teacher Advisor Comparison Rating Form (TACRF; Hughes & Hukill, 1982). The TTAS consists of standards grouped under five major areas: instructional strategies, classroom management and organization, presentation of subject matter, learning environment, and growth and responsibilities. Each intern was rated four times during the school year, twice by the principal or supervising teacher and twice by another trained rater including teacher advisors. Each observation was for 45 minutes. All but one of the alternatively certified interns was rated satisfactory or above, and 62 received exceptional or clearly outstanding ratings. The principals' ratings counted for 60% of the score in each domain. There was a high level of agreement among the principals, supervising teachers, and teacher advisors about the classroom performance of the interns.

The teacher advisors (experienced DISD teachers released from the classroom to work with the interns) were asked to compare the alternatively certified interns with "the average first year teacher" using the TACRF. The advisors were in a position to make these comparisons because they worked with both interns and traditionally certified teachers. The TACRF consists of 50 items including a global rating of teaching effectiveness. The ratings on the global question comparing the classroom performance of alternatively certified interns to the average first-year teacher indicated that 91.8% of the interns were rated as performing "as well as," "superior to," or "very superior to" the average first-year teacher, and almost half the interns were rated "superior" or "very superior." The ratings of the other 49 items in the scale were not reported, although it was stated that "The alternatively certified interns compared favorably to the first year teachers on all 50 items" (Hutton et al., 1990, p. 46).

The two groups of teachers were also compared based on their scores on the required state content examinations, the "ExCET," in seven different areas: elementary and early childhood, ESL, bilingual, English, mathematics, physical science, and physics. Of the 99 alternatively certified interns who completed the program, 90 had taken one or more of the ExCET exams, and 84 (93%) passed at least one. Comparisons of these scores to those of all teacher candidates statewide indicated that a larger percentage of alternatively certified interns passed the exams on five of the seven comparisons (mathematics and physical science were the exceptions), and the alternatively certified interns had higher mean scores on all seven comparisons. The statistical significance of these differences was not reported. Finally, it was noted that 59 of the original 110 interns (53.6%) were successful completing all program requirements, passing at least one ExCET exam and being recommended by the district for certification. Eleven interns had dropped out during the year, 15 were asked to complete another semester or year of an internship, and 1 was not recommended for certification.

Despite the lack of success of almost half of the original group of interns, the authors were optimistic about the teaching ability of the alternatively certified teachers. When they asked themselves the question, "Are alternative certification teachers good teachers," they concluded:

> The answer is an unqualified yes. On virtually every indicator examined in this study, the alternatively certified interns did as well as first-year teachers were doing. They were rated as high or higher than were first-year teachers by their principals and mentor teachers. They scored as high or higher on standardized measures of teaching ability/performance. (Lutz & Hutton, 1989, p. 252)

Lutz and Hutton (1989) then identified the programmatic conditions that they felt were responsible for the interns' success in the classroom. The value of claims about the teaching performance of alternatively certified teachers was limited by the lack of information presented about the specifics of the performance assessment instruments, the vagueness of who the alternatively certified teachers were being compared against (i.e., "other beginning teachers"), and the unreliable nature of principal ratings of teachers especially when the raters have a stake in the programs involved (Hawley, 1990). The data on projected teacher retention were not very helpful because of the low response rate of the comparison group.

In a study of an alternative certification program in Milwaukee, Wisconsin, Haberman (1999) examined the retention rate in the Milwaukee Public Schools for teachers certified through the Metropolitan Milwaukee Teacher Education Program (MMTEP). This program involved 7 weeks of summer work prior to the school year in which students complete an internship as the teachers of record in an elementary or middle school classroom. Experienced Milwaukee teachers released from their classrooms full time provide mentoring, with four interns to one mentor.

During 1990 to 1999, 137 individuals completed the program (20 did not), and of these, 94% were still teaching in Milwaukee Public Schools in 1999. Seventy-eight percent of these teachers were minorities, and of these, 71% were African American. Haberman also asked the principals of the program graduates still teaching to evaluate their teaching performance; the rating scale was not described. Fifty-one percent of the 129 principals evaluated the teachers' work as satisfactory; 45% said it was exemplary. Only 1% evaluated the teaching of MMTEP graduates as needing improvement; 3% did not respond.

The performance evaluations were of limited value because of the lack of information about the specific aspects of teaching that were evaluated and the lack of a comparison group. Nothing was said in the report about the specific program characteristics that may be responsible for the higher than normal retention rate for an urban school district.

In summary, these studies of the alternative certification programs in Houston, Dallas, and Milwaukee school districts indicate inconclusive results. Pupils of traditionally certified teachers in Houston perceived a more favorable academic and interpersonal environment than pupils of alternatively certified teachers in about one half of the areas they rated. The researchers did not rule out various possible explanations for why these differences existed other than the type of preparation received by teachers. Also, by the end of the academic year in Houston there were no significant differences between alternatively certified and traditionally certified teachers' perceptions of the problems they faced in the classroom which suggested that the programs were equally effective. More traditionally certified teachers in Dallas projected that they would remain in the classroom for at least 10 years, but in Milwaukee an alternative program demonstrated the ability to retain teachers of color in the classroom over a 10-year period at a rate higher than typical in urban districts. Finally, with regard to teacher performance, in both Milwaukee and Dallas, principals and other supervisors rated alternatively certified teachers as effective as those who traditionally certified, but the vagueness of the criteria for evaluation and of the comparison group (e.g., "compared to the average first- year teacher") limited the value of the findings. Here as in the previous groups of studies, the lack of description of the characteristics of the traditional programs attended prevented the linking of reported differences to program characteristics.

STUDIES INVOLVING THE TEACH FOR
AMERICA PROGRAM

In the next group of program comparisons, four studies examined the relative effectiveness of TFA, a mostly privately financed national program to attract noneducation majors into the classroom in schools located in areas of poverty.

In the first of the four studies, Darling-Hammond, Chung, and Frelow (2002) surveyed approximately 3,000 beginning teachers in New York City public schools who had entered the system through different routes. The survey was sent to all teachers in the district with 4 or fewer years experience, and 2,956 teachers returned usable surveys (33% response rate). For the purposes of this report of the study, only teachers with three or fewer years were included in the analysis, and there were 2,302 surveys in this group.[23] The survey assessed teachers' sense of teaching efficacy, asked them to rate their preparedness for teaching in 40 different areas, and asked for information about their views on a variety of teaching issues. The 40 areas of teaching assessed were grouped into five factors: promoting student learning, teaching critical thinking and social development, using technology, understanding learners, and developing instructional leadership. There were no significant differences in student poverty rates and proportions of minority students in the schools where teachers who entered from the different pathways worked.

Differences in teachers' perceptions about the quality of their preparation were examined for those from university-based preparation programs, those who entered without prior preparation on an emergency credential, and those who came in through a transcript review, or through various alternative routes operating only in New York City. The alternative routes included those in Teach for America who entered after a few weeks' training, and those in the Peace Corps and Teacher Opportunity Corps who were enrolled in master's degree certification programs. Very little information was provided about teacher education programs completed by the teachers except for the two programs whose graduates indicated a high level of satisfaction with their preparation: Bank Street College and Wagner College.

Teachers who entered through one of the three alternative routes rated their initial preparation for teaching significantly lower than did graduates of teacher education programs on 25 of the 40 items, including designing curriculum and instruction, teaching subject matter content, and understanding the needs of learners. The overall ratings of the alternative route teachers fell below a 3 (adequately prepared), which suggested that they felt insufficiently prepared to teach upon entry.

When the responses of teachers from different programs were analyzed, the TFA teachers—the sole alternative program with a sample size large enough to include in the analysis—felt significantly less well prepared than teacher education program graduates overall and on 19 of the 40 items ($p < .05$). Their ratings were consistently lower than those of teachers from the lowest rated teacher education program (significantly lower on five items, including overall preparation to teach) and even were consistently lower than teachers from the other two alternative routes that enrolled teachers in master's degree programs and provided them with coursework and university supervision of their teaching.

TFA teachers felt unprepared for many of the core tasks of teaching. For example, only 12 percent of the TFA teachers rated themselves as well or very well prepared

---

[23]The percentage of teachers with 3 or fewer years who responded to the survey is not reported.

to "teach subject matter concepts, knowledge and skills in ways that enable students to learn." On 25 of the 40 items, including "overall preparation for teaching," TFA teachers felt inadequately prepared. Although no attempt was made to analyze the relationship between teachers' perceptions of the effectiveness of their teacher preparation and their actual effectiveness in the classroom, teachers' overall perceptions of their programs (item 40) were correlated with their sense of efficacy about whether they were able to make a difference in student learning. This analysis indicated that teachers who felt better prepared were significantly more likely ($p < .001$) to believe that they could reach all of their students, handle problems in the classroom, teach all students to high levels, and make a difference in students' lives. Although teachers' sense of efficacy was influenced by their years of experience, and other factors, when these were controlled in a regression analysis, sense of preparedness was still the strongest predictor of teaching efficacy.

Teachers' views of teaching as an occupation also were strongly related to their sense of preparedness. Teachers who felt poorly prepared were significantly less likely to say they would choose teaching again and significantly less likely to say that they planned to remain in teaching ($p < .0001$). The researchers concluded that this study demonstrated that beginning teachers who took different pathways into teaching felt differently about the quality of their preparation and that these feelings had consequences for their efficacy as teachers and for their commitment to teaching. Teachers' sense of preparedness was relatively stable within pathways with substantial variation across pathways. Those prepared in the alternative route programs consistently had a less favorable sense of preparedness than those prepared in traditional university-based programs.

However, these findings indicating the superiority of traditional teacher education programs over TFA teachers were not as clear as they may seem. TFA teachers in New York City now and to some extent in the past have participated in graduate-level certification programs at a number of institutions including Bank Street College, which is one of the university-based exemplars in this study. Darling-Hammond et al. (2002) provided no information about the nature of the preparation received by the TFA teachers in New York City at the time of this study. As pointed out earlier, there is a 5-week summer preservice component that is relatively consistent across the country, but beyond this, there is much variation in the nature of the mentoring and support received by TFA teachers. This, together with the lack of all but general information on the university-based licensure programs in the study, made it hard to know exactly what was being compared.

Significantly, the researchers in this study overcame some limitations discussed earlier in teacher ratings of their preparation by correlating these with their sense of efficacy. We still do not know whether the teachers' reported levels of preparation correspond to their actual levels of teaching competence, but this linking of the ratings of preparedness to teacher efficacy, which has been shown to be associated with student learning (e.g., Ashton & Webb, 1986), made these preparedness ratings more useful than those in the studies discussed earlier.

In the second study that used TFA as a comparison group, Laczko-Kerr and Berliner (2002) compared the achievement of pupils in Grades 3 to 8 in Arizona who were taught by fully certified teachers from a variety of programs and by TFA teachers.[24] The TFA and comparison groups were drawn from 1998 to 1999 and 1999 to 2000

---

[24]They also included comparisons with a variety of other undercertified teachers that will not be discussed here.

data from five urban Arizona school districts, all serving largely minority student populations, employing large numbers of undercertified teachers, and participating in the TFA program. Pupils' reading, math, and language arts scores on the Stanford Achievement Test 9th ed., (SAT9) were aggregated at the classroom level for each of 109 matched pairs of teachers. The alternatively certified and traditionally certified teachers were matched on the basis of grade level and the highest degree attained first within schools, then within districts, and finally between similar districts. As discussed earlier, the TFA program includes 5 weeks of summer training prior to the school year and some support of an unspecified nature during the school year. No information was provided either about that support for teachers or about the teacher education programs completed by the fully certified teachers.

Student test scores were compared using correlated t-tests to determine if pupils taught by certified teachers outperformed those taught by TFA teachers. Laczko-Kerr and Berliner (2002) argued that there was no reason to believe that other factors such as pupil SES, class size, the curriculum, and so forth differed for TFA and certified teachers. For 1999 to 2000, the data indicated that pupils taught by certified teachers outperformed those taught by TFA teachers in reading ($p = .04$), math ($p = .02$), and language arts ($p = .04$). The 1998 to 1999 data showed the same pattern of results, but the differences were not statistically significant.[25] When the seventh- and eighth-grade classes were removed from the comparison to eliminate the effects of any departmentalization that would dilute the effects of individual teachers, the differences in the achievement scores were statistically significant in both years for all of the tests except in math in 1998 to 1999. The researchers concluded that TFA produced teachers whose students did not achieve as well as those pupils taught by fully certified teachers. They made the general claim that "the present research study supports the assertion that university prepared teachers are of a higher quality than those prepared without an approved program of preparation" (Laczko-Kerr & Berliner, p. 42).

One complication in interpreting these findings is that in many parts of the country including Arizona where this study took place, TFA teachers currently are required to enroll in certification programs. As was the case with the Darling-Hammond et al. (2002) study discussed earlier, the researchers provided no information about the specific training that the TFA teachers in this study received. Beyond a common summer preservice component, there has been great variability in different parts of the country in the mentoring and other support received by TFA teachers. The researchers also provided no information about the training received by the fully certified teachers except general information about the approximate numbers of credits completed in general areas. This lack of specificity makes it very difficult to identify the program characteristics that may explain in part, differences in student achievement.

Similarly, the lack of specificity with regard to the nature of the preparation received by the fully certified teachers implied that any sort of preparation that leads to full certification is better than that provided by TFA. In addition to the variability within TFA, there is much variation in substance and quality in traditional university-based teacher preparation programs (Kennedy, 1999). Furthermore, some teachers in this

---

[25]Several ANOVA analyses were performed to determine if the students' SAT9 test scores differed by the school they attended or by school district. The ANOVA that examined school differences found with one exception (1999 mathematics scores) that the school attended did not affect achievement scores. The ANOVA to examine school district differences found that the district level mean SAT9 scores were statistically different from one another. The researchers argue however, that since "only 38% of all teachers had to be matched with teachers from another district, it is likely, therefore, that only a small percent of those matches could have been problematic, totaling less than 10% of the matches made" (p. 32).

research sample who were considered fully certified could have been prepared in alternative programs in Arizona or other states. Together with the fact that the researchers did not control for the students' prior year achievement, this all suggests that one should interpret the findings of this study with caution.

Although matching is a legitimate alternative to controlling for prior year student achievement scores in some cases, Mayer et al. (2003) criticized the way in which the matching was done in this particular study. They argued that although the teachers were matched according to grade level taught, highest degree attained, and year of test administration, the researchers did not substantiate their assumption that the teachers matched within and across schools in a district and across districts[26] taught similar students. Mayer et al. (2003) suggested that other factors such as differences in class size and student ability rather than the type of teacher education may have accounted for the findings.

It should be noted that this was one of the few studies in our entire review that has attempted to link teacher education to student learning. The complexities of doing this are apparent in this study, and the efforts made by these researchers to rule out alternative explanations for the differences in student achievement scores should be commended and made a part of all studies that attempt to link teacher education programs to student learning.

In the third study that used TFA teachers as a comparison group, Raymond, Fletcher, and Luque (2001) and Raymond and Fletcher (2002) examined student learning in the classes of TFA teachers versus the student learning in classes taught by other teachers in Houston, Texas. Unlike the other two studies that focused on TFA teachers, these researchers provide a fairly clear description of the program in Houston at the time the research was conducted.[27] Following 5 weeks of summer training, TFA teachers who were selected based on a good academic record in an academic discipline and some type of leadership experience were placed in city schools for 2 years and were provided with ongoing professional development sponsored by TFA and by the Alternative Certification Program (ACP) in the Houston schools.[28] The summer program consisted of coursework on curricular planning, lesson planning, classroom management, student assessment and literacy development and a student teaching experience in the Houston summer school program.

During the school year, TFA teachers were assigned a mentor at their school and attended weekly training sessions. They also met with and were observed by an ACP specialist each month. Additionally the teachers received release time each month to observe their mentor or another teacher. They needed to complete 12 ACP training sessions and two courses provided by a local university to fulfill certification requirements. Finally, in addition to the professional development provided by the ACP, all TFA teachers in Houston met together once a month to discuss the practical aspects of teaching and other issues. They also met an additional 10 times each year in grade-specific groups organized by TFA to discuss instructional issues.

The research focused on the question of how well TFA teachers performed compared to other beginning teachers and involved analysis of the year-end learning gains

---

[26]Thirty-eight percent of the teachers were matched across districts.

[27]This description, like all of the other descriptions in this chapter with the exception of the case studies to be discussed here are based on reports by program staff and written materials about what goes on. Here and in all of the studies that rely on this secondhand information about program realities there is probably some difference between what is supposed to go on and what actually goes on.

[28]In Houston, TFA teachers must enroll in the district alternative certification program at the beginning of their first year.

on the Texas Assessment of Academic Skills (TAAS) of students who had a Teach for America teacher as opposed to those students whose teachers were not in the TFA program in the years 1996 to 2000. Two kinds of comparisons were conducted, one with all Grades 3 to 8 teachers in the Houston SD from 1996 to 2000 and another with all Grades 3–8 beginning teachers in the district (in their first or second year) during this period. The variability in student achievement scores within the TFA and non-TFA groups was also assessed. A comparison of the schools where teachers taught indicated that TFA teachers were assigned to higher poverty schools than other new teachers as measured by the percentages of pupils on free and reduced-cost lunch.

One part of the research was concerned with teacher retention. Here it was found that the percentage of TFA teachers who left teaching after 1 year was significantly less than the attrition rate for other new teachers after 1 year ($p < .05$) between 1996 and 1999.[29] However, after 2 years, the attrition rate for TFA teachers ranged from 60% in 1997 to 100% in 1998. The rate for other new teachers varied from a low of 43% in 1998 to a high of 51% in 1997. TFA teachers initially committed to teach in Houston for 2 years, so the high rate of attrition after this period was not surprising. The researchers pointed out that with the exception of 1998 when 100% of the TFA teachers left the district, from 16% to 40% of TFA teachers stayed in the district beyond 2 years. This high attrition rate, together with other data presented that showed both TFA and other new teachers transferring to higher achieving schools within the district after 2 years raised questions about the long-term benefit that these high-poverty schools received from the current arrangement.

The researchers also performed regression analyses that controlled for a variety of school, social class, teacher, and student characteristics, such as years of teaching experience, percentage of students receiving free or reduced-cost lunch, and students' TAAS scores the previous year. Controlling for students' TAAS scores from the previous year enabled a focus on learning that occurred during the particular year under study. The controls for various school, social class, teacher, and student characteristics attempted to eliminate explanations for differences in student achievement other than whether a student was taught by a TFA or other new teacher. Separate analyses were performed on student achievement test scores in mathematics, reading, and English language arts. All elementary and many middle school students in Houston were matched with a teacher for instruction in these three areas.[30]

The findings at the elementary level indicated that new TFA teachers produced greater gains in their students' achievement in both reading and mathematics than other teachers, and the effect was statistically significant in mathematics ($p. = .01$). In comparison to all teachers, TFA teachers also produced greater gains, but none of these was statistically significant.

The examination of the variance in elementary teacher quality between the two groups assessed how closely clustered the teacher groups were around their group average and how the two distribution curves of student test scores differed from each other. In reading, although the overall difference in student test scores was not statistically significant, 60.61% of TFA teachers did better than the median performance for all teachers, and TFA teachers were more closely distributed around the median than were their peers (i.e., did better than the average peer teacher). In comparison

---

[29]The attrition rates after one year were 8.3%, 5%, 29.3%, and 34.5% for TFA teachers and 35.7%, 37.3%, 21%, and 34.5% for non-TFA teachers.

[30]Some middle school students could not be matched with a single teacher and were eliminated from the analyses.

with all new teachers in reading, 63.46% of TFA teachers exceeded the median. These comparisons were statistically significant at $p < .04$ and $p < .02$, respectively.

In mathematics, 64.15% of TFA teachers were above the median score for the other new teachers, and 57.58% of TFA teachers were above the median for all teachers. Both of these were significant at $p < .02$. The researchers argued that these analyses demonstrated that TFA teachers were more consistent in improving student test scores than were other teachers.

At the middle school level, the analysis was more complicated because of the common practice of students' having more than one teacher in reading and English language arts. In mathematics, 80% of the students had a single teacher for the entire year; the analyses eliminated those students with multiple teachers. Although students of TFA teachers scored on average 4.4% of a standard distribution higher than students with other new teachers, the difference was not statistically significant. In the comparison with all middle school mathematics teachers, students with Teach for America teachers scored on average 11% of a standard deviation higher than students with other new teachers ($p < .025$). The analysis of the consistency of the effect for middle school mathematics teachers paralleled those of the general analysis. Here 64.5% of TFA teachers outperformed the mean student score achieved by all middle school mathematics teachers in Houston ($p < .008$).

In middle school reading and English language arts, the researchers concluded that students of TFA teachers did no worse than other students in reading achievement, but the results were by their own admission ambiguous because of the very limited number of cases where students had a single teacher throughout the year.

Raymond and Fletcher (2002) concluded that their analyses "dispel the notion that TFA is inferior to other sources of teachers" (p. 10) and that only traditional routes of teacher preparation can prepare good teachers. They asserted that although statistical significance was not always achieved in their analyses, the effect of having a TFA teacher was always positive. Raymond and Fletcher also argued that the lack of statistical significance can be explained by the small number of TFA teachers in comparison to other new teachers in Houston which made the TFA groups more vulnerable to variation across students. The size of the TFA effect varied from less than 2% of a standard deviation to more than 10%, depending on the grade, peer group, and subject. The effect was strongest for mathematics where statistical significance was achieved for some of the comparisons at both the elementary and the middle school levels. They also concluded that their analyses showed that TFA teachers were more alike (i.e., showed less variation in quality) than all other groups except new middle school mathematics teachers to whom they were equivalent.

This study, like the other two that involved TFA comparisons, had a number of methodological problems that limited the usefulness of its findings. The researchers were aware of and commented on some of these. First, although the study provided a description of the TFA program, it provided no information about the teacher preparation experienced by the other new teachers. All of the new teachers were required to participate in the Houston ACP, but it is not known whether the non-TFA teachers came to teaching via alternative routes or traditional programs. Nothing was known about the specific programs they completed. This prevented the researchers from being able to link the differences in student achievement to any specific program characteristics. In fact, because of the lack of information about the characteristics of the teachers, one cannot differentiate the effects of teacher characteristics from those of their teacher education programs. Raymond and Fletcher (2002) concluded:

Many questions remain and it would be imprudent to extrapolate too generally from this analysis. We cannot say, for example, what aspects of TFA and other teachers account for differences in the performance of their students. The evaluation focused on TFA as a whole, so we do not know if the effectiveness of TFA teachers is due to the type of people being recruited, the difference in academic background, the support provided by TFA, the ACP training, or a combination of factors. (p. 11)

With regard to the differences in academic background between the TFA group and other groups, it should be noted that in 4 of the 5 years studied, from 6% to 35% of the new teachers who were not in TFA did not have bachelor degrees. Although hiring teachers without bachelor degrees may be a reality in some large urban school districts in the United State, this lack of academic qualifications in the comparison group raises questions about the usefulness of these comparisons between the TFA and non-TFA new teachers. Additionally, the researchers acknowledged that there are a variety of other factors not accounted for in their models that influenced what went on in schools at the time of the study. Finally, although the attrition rate for TFA teachers was lower than that of the comparison group after 1 year of teaching, the fact that so many TFA teachers either left the district or stayed and transferred to higher achieving schools after 2 years raises questions about the long-term impact of the program on the high-poverty schools where TFA teachers are initially placed.

In the fourth and final study that focused on comparisons with TFA teachers, Decker, Mayer, and Glazerman (2004)[31] compared the reading and mathematics test scores of pupils taught by TFA teachers and by other teachers. This study was focused in elementary schools (Grades 1–5), began with a pilot in Baltimore in 2001 to 2002 and then expanded to Chicago, Los Angeles, Houston, New Orleans, and the Mississippi Delta in 2002 to 2003. Two types of comparisons were made in this research. First, test scores of pupils taught by TFA teachers were compared to scores of pupils taught by all of the other teachers in the sample, both novices and veterans. Then, classes taught by novice TFA teachers were compared to those of other novice teachers. A novice was defined as a teacher in his or her first 3 years of teaching. Because the non-TFA or control group teachers included those who were traditionally certified, alternatively certified, and uncertified, this study was not a comparison between TFA and any specific route to teaching. The researchers also stated that this study was not designed to disentangle the separate influences on student outcomes of the recruitment effects of TFA from the effects of the training received in the program.

The main question that guided this research was: Did TFA teachers improve student outcomes relative to what would have happened to students in their absence? This is the only study reviewed in this chapter that used random assignment of students to classrooms of teachers who were prepared in different ways. Students were randomly assigned to classes taught by TFA teachers or other teachers in the same grades in the same schools in an attempt to isolate program and selection effects from the influence of other contextual factors. The researchers contended that this method of pupil assignment ensured that "any differences in average outcomes between the classes can be attributed to differences in the teachers" (Decker et al., 2004, p. 7).

The sample included 17 schools, 100 classrooms, and 1800 students. The schools were randomly selected from those in the designated districts that had the staffing to

---

[31]This study was released just before this volume went to press. We decided to include it in our review even though it had not yet been published in a peer-reviewed journal because of its use of random assignment and its high visibility in the national press.

support the research design. All of the schools involved in the study served an economically disadvantaged student population and faced substantial teacher shortages.
For example, student eligibility for free and reduced-cost lunch in these schools was
greater than 95% compared to a national average of around 41%. Overall the students
in the sample were about 67% African American and 26% Hispanic, but the student
demographics varied in the different school districts. The schools were chosen to be
broadly representative of the schools where TFA teachers were placed at the time of
the study.

Decker et al. (2004) did a better job than those in any of the other TFA studies reviewed in this chapter of describing the admissions process to the TFA program, the
curriculum of the 5-week summer institute, personal characteristics of the TFA and
control teachers, and the characteristics of the schools in which the teachers taught.
They also described a variety of induction and support mechanisms for TFA teachers
regardless of where they were placed. Despite these methodological improvements
over other studies, no information was provided about the certification programs
enrolled in by the TFA teachers in the different regions studied or about the alternative and traditional teacher education programs completed by those control teachers
who had completed programs. As was pointed out earlier, TFA teachers are often
required to meet the state certification requirements in existence in their regions or
to comply with the requirements for "highly qualified teachers" under the No Child
Left Behind Act and, in some cases (e.g., Baltimore), these teachers complete traditional university-based programs. Overall, more than 51% of the TFA teachers had
earned a regular or initial certification by the end of the study year as compared
to 38% of novice control teachers. Thus, unlike the Darling-Hammond, Chung, and
Frelow (2002) study where TFA teachers were compared with teachers prepared in
traditional university-based programs, the novice control group teachers had less
teacher preparation than their TFA counterparts. The lack of specificity about the
actual preparation received by both the TFA and control group teachers makes it difficult to interpret the meaning of any differences in student outcomes between the two
groups.

One part of the study included data from a survey of teachers that attempted to
assess the teaching philosophies and instructional practices of teachers in reading
and mathematics. Usable surveys were returned by 98 of the 100 teachers in the
sample. These included 41 TFA teachers and 57 control teachers (18 novices and 39
veterans). With regard to instructional modes, teachers were asked to indicate the
percentage of time they spent in reading and mathematics using various instructional
modes such as "teacher-directed whole class" and "teacher-directed small group"
activities as well as what percentage of the time they spent on academic instruction
versus managing classroom tasks and behavior. In both mathematics and reading,
the TFA and control teachers utilized each instructional mode for similar amounts
of time. The most popular mode in both groups was "teacher-directed whole-class"
activities followed by "teacher-directed small group" activities and "students working
independently in small-groups."

Although the general modes for delivering instruction were similar for the two
groups of teachers, the teachers differed in their philosophies of mathematics and
reading instruction. Survey responses suggested that the control teachers were more
likely than the TFA teachers to embrace a phonics orientation to reading instruction.
In mathematics, both groups of teachers placed a major emphasis on understanding
mathematics in an applied fashion, but the control teachers were more likely than the
TFA teachers to believe that "emphasizing getting the right answer and memorizing

mathematical rules is important" (Decker et al., 2004, p. 22). The findings indicated that novice control teachers were more likely to use a "basic skills approach" in teaching mathematics as compared to the TFA teachers teaching in the same schools ($p = 0.07$).

Measures of student achievement were based on the Iowa Test of Basic Skills (ITBS) in reading and mathematics. A baseline achievement test was administered in the fall, and a follow-up test in the spring to each of the classes was included in the study. In academic performance, the students in the sample started off the year achieving far below the level of children in the same grade nationally, with baseline scores of the average sample member in the 14th percentile in mathematics and the 13th percentile in reading. The percentage of students who took the baseline test and completed the test in the spring was over 90% and was nearly the same for the TFA and control groups.

The impact of the TFA program was determined by comparing the test scores of students in control and TFA classes at the end of the school year. Because students were randomly assigned to the two types of teachers, test score differences at the beginning of the year were very small and were controlled for in the analyses.[32] By the end of the school year, average student test scores in TFA classrooms were higher than those in control group classrooms in mathematics and were the same as control group classrooms in reading. In mathematics, the average control class student scored in the 15th percentile in the fall and remained in the 15th percentile in the spring. On the other hand, the average TFA class students increased their ranking from the 14th percentile to the 17th percentile. The difference in growth rates was statistically significant ($p = 0.002$) and was estimated by the researchers to be equivalent to 1 month of instruction. These differences were also significant for a comparison of the TFA classes with the novice control teachers ($p = 0.009$),[33] and for different groups of students (e.g., in different grades and different ethnic backgrounds). For reading achievement, the average student in TFA and control classes experienced the same growth rate. The average pupil score increased by the equivalent of 1 percentile point during the school year.[34]

In addition to administering achievement tests the researchers examined other student outcomes using data from school and district records and teacher reports. Assessments were made of differences between the control and TFA groups in retention in grade, assignment to summer school, disciplinary incidents, tardiness, chronic absence, and the extent to which student behavior disrupted the class. Differences with regard to summer school attendance and grade retention using both the whole control group and novice control teachers as the comparison were not significant. With regard to the student behavioral outcomes, the school records showed that TFA and the control classes did not differ in absenteeism or disciplinary incidents. Teacher reported experiences, on the other hand, indicated that TFA teachers were significantly more likely to report that student disruptions and physical conflicts were a serious problem and reported significantly more class interruptions to deal

---

[32]The researchers used a hierarchical regression model to control for students' baseline achievement, age, gender, race, ethnicity, and eligibility for free and reduced-price lunch.

[33]Despite the statistical significance here, the researchers concluded that because of the limited sample size in the comparison of the two groups of novice teachers, they were reluctant to draw definitive conclusions on this point.

[34]TFA class students increased from the 14th to 15th percentile and the control classroom teachers increased from the 13th to 14th percentile.

with student disruptions. Because of the differences in behavioral outcomes between school-reported and teacher-reported data sources, the researchers stated that these findings were inconclusive.

Decker et al. (2004) concluded that despite the fact that this study showed that TFA recruitment and training had a positive impact on mathematics achievement, the results "should not be interpreted as evidence that traditional teacher preparation routes provide training inferior to that provided by Teach for America" (p. 47). As pointed out earlier, the TFA teachers in this study had more preparation than the comparison group of novice teachers. Despite the methodological improvements in this study over other research, there are several major problems involved in interpreting the results. First, because of the lack of description of the diverse preparation experienced by the control teachers and the certification programs in which Teach for America teachers enrolled during the study year, it was not clear what in the preparation of the teachers may have accounted for the mathematics achievement differences. The researchers also were not able to link these changes to differences in the instruction that students experienced. Teacher self-reports of their teaching practices in reading and mathematics did not show any significant differences in how teachers taught these subjects. Finally, as discussed earlier, the researchers estimated the impact of the entire TFA program and did not attempt to disentangle selection effects from training effects.

Overall this study underlined how poorly students in the kinds of schools where Teach for America teachers are placed are achieving compared to their peers nationwide. It also showed how little access these students have to teachers who begin their teaching careers with more than a minimum of formal teacher preparation.

In summary, these four studies that involved comparisons with the TFA program presented mixed evidence. TFA teachers in New York City felt less prepared and less successful than did other new teachers, although actual teacher performance and student learning were not assessed. The studies in Houston and Arizona and the national study presented conflicting results about how much students achieved in reading and mathematics when taught by TFA versus those taught by other new teachers. In the case of Arizona, TFA teachers were shown to be less effective. In Houston, the students of TFA teachers had better achievement test results in some instances. In the national study, the students taught by TFA teachers experienced greater growth in mathematics achievement, but not in reading. These studies, like much of the research reviewed in this chapter, were limited to "black box" analyses of the outcomes of TFA and other programs without significant attention to the characteristics of the preparation received by teachers, which means it was not possible to link their findings to the features of the programs. The studies employed a variety of methodological tools such as random assignment, matching and controlling for students' prior year achievement to rule out alternative explanations for differences in outcomes. Both the focus on linking teacher education with student learning and the efforts to get an accurate reading of the influence of particular teachers on student learning are unusual in the research on teacher education programs and should be continued. It is critical, however, that researchers begin to gain an understanding of the character and quality of the actual preparation received by teachers in these comparisons if their findings are going to illuminate the impact of different program characteristics. These four studies comparing TFA with other programs clearly do not settle the issue of the efficacy of the TFA program in comparison with that of other programs.

COMPARISONS OF MULTIPLE ALTERNATIVE
AND TRADITIONAL PROGRAMS

Stoddart (1990, 1993) and Gomez and Stoddart (1992) studied the retention of teachers in the Los Angeles Unified School District's Internship program and compared the teaching perspectives and practices of teachers certified through this program in secondary mathematics and English with those of teachers certified in these same content areas in university-based programs in the Southeast (English) and the Midwest (mathematics).[35] First, an analysis of data provided by the Los Angeles Unified School District (LAUSD) indicated that for the cohort of teacher interns that began the program in 1987, the attrition rate after 3 years was 18%. Stoddart (1990) argued that this rate was lower than would be expected given national data on teacher retention in urban schools. This attrition rate for Los Angeles interns rose sharply after 4 years to 35%, and to 48% after 5 years.

In 1990, the Los Angeles intern program consisted of a 15-day preservice orientation, weekly 2-hour seminars for 2 years led by experienced Los Angeles teachers, a 1-week institute on multicultural education after the first year, and support from mentor teachers. Interns became the teachers of record immediately after the 15- day preservice orientation. Although the number of clock hours of classes in this alternative program was equivalent to that found in California's college-based programs at that time, Stoddart (1990) asserted that the substance and rigor of the program were different from those of traditional college-based programs because, for example, there were no formal assignments or examinations in the alternative program courses. Additionally, she concluded that the program focused on the practicalities of teaching in the Los Angeles school district and did not emphasize theory or different teaching approaches. The university-based program in mathematics education was a 4-year undergraduate program and the English education program was a fifth-year program. Both programs included several practicum experiences and a semester of student teaching.

Stoddart (1990) concluded on the basis of a survey that alternatively certified interns in the Los Angeles program held higher expectations for the learning of low-income and minority students than a sample of students enrolled in traditional university-based programs included in the Teacher Education and Learning to Teach study (TELT) conducted by the National Center for Research on Teacher Education. Ninety-five percent of elementary and secondary English interns and 81% of secondary mathematics interns believed that low-income and minority students were capable of learning higher order concepts in the subject areas they taught. Only 76% of English and 60% of mathematics teaching candidates in traditional university-based programs held the same expectations. The statistical significance of these differences was not reported. At least one-third of the traditional program candidates believed that these students should only be taught basic skills in reading, writing, grammar and arithmetic.

Stoddart (1993) studied three cohorts of teacher candidates who entered their programs in the fall of 1987: 19 secondary English and 37 secondary mathematics interns from the Los Angeles alternative route, 26 English education graduates from a fifth-year university-based program in the Southeast, and 22 secondary mathematics

---

[35]The secondary English program was a fifth-year program and is considered "alternative" in this review. The secondary mathematics program was a traditional 4-year undergraduate program.

graduates from a 4-year undergraduate university-based program in the Midwest. This report utilized data from the second year of the study: the first year of independent teaching for the university program graduates and the second year of intern teaching for the alternative route teachers. The study was part of the Teacher Education and Learning to Teach Study (TELT) of the National Center for Research on Teacher Learning at Michigan State University and utilized the data collection methods employed in all of the TELT study sites: a survey, semistructured interviews, and classroom observations (Kennedy, Ball, & McDiarmid, 1993).

One aspect of the study dealt with teachers' expectations for the learning of different students. They were asked about their learning expectations for pupils in two different schools: one school located in an inner-city neighborhood serving mostly low-income and minority students and the other in a White suburban community serving pupils whose parents were mostly college educated and in professional positions. The findings indicated that the alternative route teachers held higher expectations for the low-income and minority students when compared to the traditional certification program graduates. Between 85% and 95% of the alternatively certified English teachers believed that both middle-class and low-income students would effectively use writing in their learning compared to 77% of the traditionally certified teachers. The statistical significance of these differences was not reported. Additionally, the alternatively certified teachers were more likely than the traditionally certified teachers (70% to 47%) to attribute student failure to teachers rather than to the students.

Stoddart (1993) also reported a series of case studies of 16 teachers (4 teachers from each of the 4 groups) that reinforced the findings related to the higher expectations of alternatively certified teachers for low-income and minority pupils. She summarized the case studies as follows: "The university certified novice teachers found it difficult to relate to students who were different than themselves . . . Most held a 'cultural deficit' perspective on student achievement and believed that poor and minority students lack enriching life experiences (p. 47).

Gomez and Stoddart (1992) reported case studies of eight English teachers, all of whom were part of the sample in the Stoddart (1993) study. Four were interns in the second year of their alternative route program, and the other four were graduates of a fifth-year program in the Southeast. Interviews were conducted with the teachers at the beginning of their first year of teaching and at the midpoint of the year, and interviews and observations were conducted toward the end of the year. The interviews dealt with teachers' knowledge about the teaching of writing and their understanding of diverse learners. All eight of the teachers spent their first year of teaching in schools with diverse pupil populations.

The findings of these case studies generally supported the conclusions reported by Stoddart (1993) about expectations for student learning. All four of the traditionally certified teachers were White females in their 20s who grew up in mainstream, middle-class, suburban homes. The four alternatively certified teachers (two males and two females) all spent considerable time living in Los Angeles. Three of the four traditionally certified teachers emphasized the social class differences between themselves and their students and viewed their students as having cultural and learning deficits that made them difficult to teach. Three of the four alternatively certified teachers identified with the students they taught and did not view them as suffering from cultural deficits. "They expect students to be able to achieve in school and life and value the experiences that students bring with them to school and believe it is important to make instruction culturally and personally relevant" (p. 47).

All four of the traditionally certified teachers taught classes of low-income learners in schools that emphasized a skills-based curriculum focusing on grammar and writing mechanics although their teacher education program had stressed a process approach to teaching writing. All four of the alternatively certified teachers began their first year of teaching without any formal instruction in the teaching of writing and worked in schools emphasizing a skills-based approach focusing on grammar and mechanics. Three of the four traditionally certified teachers developed a clear understanding of their program's process orientation to the teaching of writing, but they were unable to adapt it to teaching low-income and minority students unlike themselves. They quickly moved to adopt the teacher-directed and skills-based approach used in their schools, and when they were not successful, they located the source for their students' low achievement in their students' family backgrounds and social class positions. One of the four traditionally certified teachers who had high expectations for her students' learning was successfully able to adapt the process approach in her school even though it was in conflict with the focus on grammar and mechanics emphasized throughout her school. The alternatively certified teachers who had begun the school year with no formal instruction in the teaching of writing drew on their own personal views about writing and their experiences as writers and human beings. Three of the four emphasized making writing meaningful to their students and various successes were reported of their attempts to motivate students to write and discuss each other's work. The other alternatively certified teacher was less successful and when his personal pedagogy failed he resorted to blaming his students for their lack of motivation.

In summary, these studies comparing the Los Angeles alternative route and other university-based programs are the only ones discussed thus far that got past surface descriptions of the kinds of courses and field experiences in a program to describe the rigor and focus of the curriculum and its helpfulness for preparing teachers to teach diverse students with backgrounds very different from their teachers'. These studies are also the only ones thus far that went beyond a rating scale or use of a classroom observation system to probe more deeply into teachers' dispositions and skills related to the teaching of specific content to diverse learners. The links made in these studies between teachers' expectations for their students' learning and the extent to which they utilized the kind of teaching encouraged in their preparation add an important dimension to the research on program effects. Attempting to establish links between programs and teacher performance without attending to teacher cognitions and dispositions is unlikely to be a productive strategy in the long run. The sample sizes were relatively small in these studies as is the case in most of the research on programs, but the researchers probed more deeply into both the programs and the outcomes.

In a widely cited study using a nationally representative sample of 14,721 teachers who were certified between 1984 to 1985 and 1993 to 1994 and still teaching in 1993 to 1994, Shen (1997) compared various aspects of traditionally and alternatively certified teacher characteristics.[36] There were 13,602 traditionally certified and 1,119 alternatively certified teachers in the sample. Although retention was not directly investigated, one aspect of this study had potential implications for teacher retention. The teachers were asked: "If you could go back to your college days and start over again, would you become a teacher or not?" There was no difference between

---

[36]The American Educational Research Association (AERA) issued a policy brief on alternative certification based exclusively on Shen's work (AERA, 1997).

the alternatively certified and traditionally certified teachers in their plans to become teachers again. However, when teachers were asked about their plans to remain in teaching, some group differences emerged. Specifically, a lower percentage of alternatively certified teachers (19.7%) than of traditionally certified teachers (22.7%) said that they saw themselves remaining in teaching until retirement, and a higher percentage of alternatively certified teachers (26%) than of traditionally certified teachers (22.3%) responded that they were undecided as to future career plans. Shen used these findings to question alternatively certified teachers' intentions to regard teaching as a lifelong career and concluded that policies that encourage alternative certification are "likely to exacerbate teacher attrition" (p. 281). In addition to the obvious limitation that actual teacher retention was not studied, Shen's findings were of limited value because of his failure to differentiate among various alternative certification programs. In this study those who indicated that they had received a teaching certificate through "what their state calls an alternative certification program" were classified as alternatively certified teachers. The wide range of variation in these programs from those that closely resemble traditional university-based programs to those that include minimal preparation makes analyses like Shen's that lump all alternative programs together problematic.

Furthermore, Ballou (1998) raised additional questions about Shen's data and asserted that Shen did not accurately identify those teachers who actually were alternatively certified. One piece of evidence cited by Ballou was that 52% of those who chose the alternative certification option indicated elsewhere on their survey that they had undergraduate majors in education. All of these problems make Shen's (1997) research of very limited value. Nonetheless, Shen was the only researcher in this group who took on the complex task of using a large national database to understand the relative outcomes of different kinds of teacher education programs for teacher retention. The problems noted previously were mostly a reflection of the definitional problems related to alternative certification and preparation more generally across the different states than of the quality of the research. Until there is more consistency across the country in the definitions that are used for various teacher education models and until the national databases include more information about the specifics of the preparation received by teachers, these databases will be of limited value in helping us understand the effects of different program models.

Finally, Adelman (1986) conducted telephone interviews with 16 participants in seven alternative certification programs,[37] with their supervisors and with teachers in their schools who prepared for teaching in traditional university-based programs.[38] Among the issues addressed in the interviews were the evaluations of the teaching competence of the alternatively certified teachers. The supervisors were asked to assess these teachers on a variety of dimensions such as mastery of subject matter and knowledge of a variety of teaching strategies as well as providing an overall rating. The findings indicated that all of the alternatively certified teachers were rated above

---

[37]The programs included those sponsored by the state, by universities and by school districts. They are the Arizona Partners Project, Harvard Mid Career Math and Science program, Houston Alternative Certification Program, Los Angeles Unified School District Teacher Trainee Program, New Jersey Provisional Teacher Program, University of New Mexico/Santa Fe Public Schools Intern Program, and the University of Southern Maine Teachers for Secondary Schools Program.

[38]The supervisors interviewed included university supervisors, principals, and mentor, and supervising teachers.

average or superior in the mastery of subject matter. A need for improvement was identified in several areas for the majority of these teachers (e.g., classroom management and expectations for students). Adelman (1986) concluded that the pattern of strengths and weaknesses "parallels that of traditionally trained first-year teachers" and that on the whole, there was a noticeable lack of criticism of the alternate route teachers. The overall assessments showed that 14 alternatively certified teachers were rated above average or superior. In addition to the lack of specificity about evaluation criteria, the usefulness of the results of this study were greatly limited by the fact that the teachers included in the sample were recommended to Adelman by the program directors. Adelman acknowledged that a selection effect "undoubtedly affected" her findings.

In summary, the studies that compared the impact of multiple teacher education programs on various dimensions of teacher quality have suggested that alternatively certified teachers may in some circumstances have higher expectations for the learning of students of color living in poverty than teachers who have been traditionally certified. The data with regard to teacher retention were mixed. In one case we saw higher than normal retention rates for alternatively certified teachers in Los Angeles after the first year of teaching. However, in a national study, we saw a suggestion that alternatively certified teachers may be less committed to a career in teaching over time. In another study we were told that alternatively certified teachers rate the quality of their teacher education programs less favorably than traditionally certified teachers in terms of how well they were prepared for the tasks of teaching.

All of this is of very limited value in helping us understand the relative impact of different kinds of teacher education programs on aspects of teacher quality. Although in a few cases, descriptions were provided of some aspects of the alternative programs involved (e.g., the Los Angeles intern program), for the most part the nature of the preparation received by alternatively and traditionally certified teachers was not adequately described. This made it difficult to link the differences in outcomes to particular program characteristics.

CASE STUDIES OF TEACHER EDUCATION PROGRAMS

In addition to the studies discussed previously that compared the effects of different program types on various outcomes for prospective teachers, there were a few large-scale comprehensive case studies of teacher education programs where researchers closely examined programs in action and studied their consequences in terms of a variety of outcomes. Although these studies, like those reviewed earlier, have certain methodological problems that limit their usefulness in identifying effective program characteristics, we argue that they suggest a direction for research on teacher education programs likely to be more productive in the long run than attempts to discover which structural model for teacher education is most effective.

The direction for research that these studies suggest involves close examination of the characteristics within teacher education programs that make a difference with regard to teacher recruitment, retention, and quality. They suggest that gaining an in-depth understanding of the complex reality of the implementation of a teacher education program, the contexts in which it is embedded, and what teachers learn from the program is important to being able to link specific program characteristics to various outcomes.

The TELT Study

Between 1986 and 1990, researchers at the National Center for Research on Teacher Education at Michigan State University conducted detailed studies of teacher education and the process of learning to teach writing and mathematics to diverse learners in a variety of teacher education programs across the United States including seven preservice programs that had different conceptual emphases and structural characteristics. The seven preservice programs in the sample were one 5-year program, four 4-year programs, and two alternative certification programs for individuals who had already completed a bachelor's degree. In addition to their structural variation, there was also variation in the institutions with which the programs were connected: liberal arts college, research university, historic teacher education institution turned multipurpose university, historically Black university, urban school district, and state department of education. There was also substantive variation in the programs' views on what teachers needed to learn, what teaching was like, and how teachers learn. For example, some programs emphasized pedagogy as a generic concept, whereas others stressed content-specific pedagogies. Some programs emphasized liberal arts knowledge, whereas others stressed knowledge from research on teaching or craft or skill knowledge gained through exposure to teachers in schools. The research focused on preservice programs in elementary education, English education, and mathematics education.

The study followed teachers from their entry into the program through their completion of the program. It illuminated how their ideas about teaching changed, if at all, during this time. Data were collected at different points depending on the program's structure. One part of the study design focused on what opportunities for teacher learning were available in a program. Faculty were surveyed and interviewed about their goals for their programs and courses; documents such as syllabi, exams, and policies were collected and examined; and instruction was observed both in campus classes and in guided clinical practice in schools. Similar kinds of courses were observed across the different programs (e.g., a child development course and mathematics methods course). A second part of the design focused on teacher learning at different points in the program. Here many teacher education students were repeatedly surveyed, and some were repeatedly interviewed about hypothetical classroom situations related to the teaching of writing and mathematics to diverse learners. The situations were constructed to include concepts central to the K–12 curriculum in mathematics and writing. In addition, student teachers were observed in their field placements and interviewed before and after each observation.

Several types of findings emerged from this comprehensive study. One of the main findings was that contrary to the emphasis in the literature on the importance of program structure, the substance of a teacher education program rather than its structure was the most important consideration in impacting teacher education students. TELT researchers differentiated programs by their substance and identified two basic kinds: traditional programs and reform programs. The traditional programs emphasized how to organize students and to maintain an orderly flow of classroom activities. Little or no attention was given in the traditional programs to the teaching of particular subject matter (e.g., what aspects of the subjects to teach and how to teach subject matter). The reform programs, on the other hand, were oriented toward altering traditional teaching practices and encouraging the more learner-centered practices advocated in the literature. There was much emphasis on these programs on subject-specific teaching consistent with the emphasis in the literature on reform-oriented teaching practices (see Kennedy, 1998).

Two kinds of influences of teacher education programs on their students were identified. First, in some cases, teacher education programs appeared to influence students by changing their interpretations of the situations presented in the interviews toward those views emphasized in the program curriculum. Kennedy (1998) referred to these cases as "learning influences." In other cases, the programs did not change students' ideas toward those stressed in the curriculum, but they recruited students whose ideas were already compatible with the program's orientation. Kennedy referred to these situations as "enrollment influences." The detailed attention in this project to both the program and entering student characteristics enabled the researchers to disentangle the effects of the students from those of their programs. The failure to do this has been a major limitation of most studies reviewed in this chapter.

The TELT researchers concluded that the main factor determining a program's learning influence on its students was its substance, reform or traditional. They found that programs that had similar structures sometimes had remarkably different influences on both enrollment and teacher learning. On the other hand, they sometimes found that programs with different structures had very similar influences on teachers depending on their substantive orientation. Kennedy (1998, p. 21)[39] concluded:

> The single most important finding of this study is that these substantive orientations made a difference. Teachers who participated in traditional management-oriented programs became even more concerned about prescriptions by the end of their programs than they had been in the beginning, while teachers in reform-oriented programs reduced their concerns about prescriptions and increased their concerns about students' strategies and purposes.... Virtually all of the changes in teachers' interpretations of these particular situations were consistent with the programs' substantive orientation.

Program impact on students was defined in several different ways in this study. The interviews asked students their general ideas about different issues related to subject matter, teaching, and students (espoused ideals) and asked them to respond to hypothetical classroom situations (immediate concerns). Despite changes that occurred in students' ideas about the teaching of subject matter in some programs that showed movement toward the adoption of reform-oriented practices, follow-up studies of students sometimes indicated that the students were inclined to teach in more traditional ways (e.g., Wilcox, Schram, Lappan, & Lanier, 1991). This finding demonstrated the importance of going beyond teachers' self-reports to directly observe their classroom practices.

Based on the findings where changes in students' orientations toward teaching were found to occur, TELT researchers identified four factors they argued were associated with fundamental changes in teachers' beliefs. They said their research showed that teachers needed (a) a chance to consider why the new practices were better than more conventional approaches, (b) opportunities to see examples of these new practices, (c) the experience of learning these practices firsthand, and (d) on-site assistance and support in learning to put the new practices in place.

Although these factors sound sensible, the report did not elaborate on them, nor did it establish a clear link between the data presented and the four factors. Given

---

[39]Kennedy's (1998) analysis focuses on the TELT data related to learning to teach writing.

this lack of specific evidence related to the links between the data and these program characteristics, one should interpret the claim about their importance cautiously. They provide a good starting place though for further research into the aspects of teacher education programs that make a difference in influencing teachers and their pupils.

The NCTAF Case Studies

In the late 1990s, the National Commission on Teaching and America's Future (NCTAF) sponsored case studies of seven preservice teacher education programs identified as being successful in preparing teachers for "learner-centered" and "learning-centered" practice.[40] In selecting the seven exemplary programs for study,[41] researchers considered program reputation among local and national educators, and employer data on hiring. The sample includes undergraduate, extended 5-year programs, and fifth-year programs, programs that had established professional development school partnerships and those that had not done so, and programs that used student cohort groups and those without them.

The case studies attempted to document the goals, strategies, content, and processes in the teacher education programs as well as the teaching capabilities of program graduates. Recent program graduates completed a survey of how well they felt prepared in specific aspects of teaching associated with a learning-centered and learner-centered approach. These data were compared with a national random sample of beginning teachers who completed the same survey. To gain an understanding of the program, program documents were collected and analyzed, and teacher educators were interviewed and observed in the classroom. Both students currently enrolled in the program and a few program graduates also were interviewed and observed. Finally, the principals of program graduates completed a survey indicating how well they thought the teachers were prepared in the same areas included in the graduate survey. A sample of principals also was interviewed.

Darling-Hammond (2000) identified six features that she concluded were common characteristics across all seven programs. The first was a shared and clear understanding among faculty, students, and school personnel of good teaching that permeated all courses and field experiences in a program. Next, Darling-Hammond noted that all seven programs had a clear set of practice and performance standards against which candidates' coursework was guided and evaluated. Additionally, all the programs had a curriculum that included extensive work on child and adolescent development, learning theory, and theories about cognition, motivation, and subject matter pedagogy. This material was taught in a manner that integrated it into the context of practice. The fourth program feature was the existence of extended field experiences (of at least 30 weeks) in schools and communities that were carefully chosen to support the ideas covered in concurrent coursework. The fifth program characteristic was strong relationships and a set of shared beliefs among school and university-based faculty and staff. Finally, all seven programs extensively utilized pedagogical

---

[40]Learner-centered practice means that teachers are able to meet the needs of diverse learners. Learning-centered practice means that teachers are able to teach for understanding and in ways that promote active and in-depth learning for students.

[41]The seven programs are Bank Street College of Education (elementary and middle school education), the University of California-Berkeley's Developmental Teacher Education program, The University of Southern Maine's extended teacher education program, Wheelock College (early child care and education), Alverno College (elementary education), Trinity University, and the University of Virginia (secondary English and mathematics).

strategies such as case studies, teacher research, performance assessments, and port-folio evaluations that related learning to real problems of practice. All six program characteristics were defined and implemented in various ways in the seven different programs.

A major limitation of the usefulness of this work was that the programs were identified as examples of excellence based on nominations by educators and not on empirically demonstrated effects on measures of teacher quality. The findings are reported in the form of seven individual case studies. The individual studies vary in terms of how clearly links were made between the evidence presented and the general program characteristics identified by Darling-Hammond (2000) in her general introduction to each volume. In no case was a strong link identified between the program characteristics and teacher effectiveness. We know that the school districts looked to hire teachers from these programs and that the teachers thought highly of the quality of their preparation, but these factors alone do not demonstrate the efficacy of the programs in preparing effective teachers. We discussed earlier the problems that have been raised with teacher evaluations of the quality of their preparation.

As with the TELT study, these NCTAF program design principles proposed in the summary of these case studies provided good ideas for further research into program characteristics that make a difference in terms of teacher and learner outcomes.

The Study of the Education of Educators

In the first national study of teacher education in the United States since the survey conducted by the U.S. Office of Education in the 1930s (Evenden, 1933), John Goodlad (1990, 1994) and colleagues, at the Center for Educational Renewal at the University of Washington, conducted a study of a representative sample of 29 programs from across the United States[42] in 1987 to 1988. At each institution, relevant documents were collected and analyzed, and faculty and students completed questionnaires. Interviews were also conducted with students, faculty, administrators, and school-based educators, and observations were conducted of both campus classes and classes taught by student teachers in the field. Researchers spent from 10 to 14 days at each teacher education institution.

Unlike the TELT and NCTAF case studies where assertions about criteria for good teacher education programs were made after the fact from the study of programs, Goodlad (1990, 1994) and his research team went into the field at the onset with a set of hypotheses about the necessary conditions for effective teacher education pro-grams. These 19 postulates were based on a conception of education, teaching, and learning in democratic societies and on a set of "reasonable expectations" for teachers within these societies: providing access to knowledge for all students, ensuring the responsible stewardship of schools, enculturating the young in a social and political democracy, and teaching in a nurturing way (Goodlad, 1994). The postulates were framed as a statement of a comprehensive set of interrelated conditions that, taken to-gether, describe the conditions needed for good teacher education in colleges and uni-versities.[43] Goodlad (1990, 1994) argued that the removal of any one condition would weaken the whole.

---

[42]These programs were located in eight states that account for about 30% of the population of the United States: California, Colorado, Georgia, Illinois, Iowa, Massachusetts, Oklahoma, and Pennsylvania.

[43]About one half of the original postulates stated in Goodlad (1990) were slightly reworded in Goodlad (1994) based on feedback from teacher educators across the United States. This chapter uses the original formulation of the postulates that were in existence at the time the research was conducted.

Prior to enumerating the programmatic conditions that he felt were needed for successful teacher education, Goodlad (1990, 1994) described the context in which a teacher education program must exist to successfully educate teachers for the mission defined within the conception of democratic education guiding this project. Goodlad posited that teacher education programs require the trust, support, and promotion of their institutions and deserve the full backing of their institutional leaders as a major responsibility to society. Similarly, teacher education programs should have equal standing with other programs at an institution, and teacher education faculty should have comparable status and rewards to other members of the faculty. Goodlad further argued that the success of a teacher education program was contingent on its establishing secure resources, autonomy, and boundaries similar to those of other professional schools.

A number of the postulates centered around the requirements for faculty of teacher education programs. First was the assertion that teacher education needs to be the top priority of a group of academic and clinical faculty. This group must be able to oversee and coordinate all aspects of program admission, curriculum, and program evaluation. They need to be fully committed to educating teachers to assume the full range of responsibilities required (e.g., serving as stewards of schools in addition to educating pupils in the classroom). Finally, institutions should carefully select candidates for a predetermined number of places in its teacher education programs who display an initial commitment to the moral and ethical aspects of the responsibilities they will be prepared to assume.

Next, Goodlad (1990) elaborated on a set of program level conditions that he felt were necessary for success. First, to ensure that their graduates have strong literacy and critical thinking abilities, he argued that programs must have entry minimums to be met by examinations, counseling to help students remedy deficiencies, and a requirement that candidates moving through a program demonstrate the "intellectual traits associated with continued development as educated persons" (1990, p. 58). Programs need to have a socialization process to help students transcend their self-oriented concerns as students to become more other-oriented and identify with a culture of teaching. Programs must be conducted in a way to help future teachers move beyond being consumers of educational knowledge developed by others to become teachers who also inquire into knowledge, the teaching of knowledge, and schooling.

One aspect of the intellectual quality of good teacher education programs according to Goodlad (1990, 1994) was that they help prospective teachers think about and constructively deal with the ongoing tensions between the interests and desires of individual parents and groups and the role of schools in a democracy to transcend narrow special interests. These programs need to prepare teachers who are committed to ensuring access to and engagement in the best possible education for all students. Given that this equity in educational provision is not now a reality, these programs must also prepare teachers to analyze the frequent disconnect between what is often advocated in the educational literature and practice in schools, to think beyond the status quo, and to be knowledgeable of various alternatives to what now exists and be capable of bringing about needed changes.

For teacher education programs to be able to succeed at these tasks, Goodlad (1990, 1994) argued that they should be characterized in all respects by conditions for learning that are consistent with those advocated for use by prospective teachers in their K–12 classrooms. Another needed element is the availability of a diverse array of exemplary classroom and school settings where students can observe and practice in their internships and other clinical experiences. Goodlad argued that programs should not admit more students than can be supplied with these exemplary field placements.

Finally, teacher education programs need to establish and maintain contact with their graduates to inform program improvement and to ease their transition into teaching. To be continually renewing, these programs must be free from excessive curricular specifications from licensing agencies and protected from state policies that would allow the hiring of unqualified individuals because of teaching shortages.

The Study of the Education of Educators was designed to determine the extent to which these conditions were present in a representative sample of teacher education institutions that included private liberal arts colleges, public and private regional universities, and "flagship" research universities. Although the conditions felt to be necessary for good teacher education were present to varying degrees in the different types of institutions (e.g., liberal arts institutions offered the most favorable environment for teacher education), Goodlad (1994) and his colleagues consistently found that many of these conditions were absent or minimally present in the settings they studied. "We looked for well designed, well constructed houses of teacher education and found roofs missing, doors hanging loose, and windows broken" (p. 7).

Although the study of the Education of Educators did not resolve the issue of the validity of the postulates, it provided information on the extent to which these conditions, based on a particular view of teaching in a democratic society, were present in different kinds of institutions. The evidence supporting the conclusions about the extent of existence of the postulates in the programs studied was not always developed in the published accounts of the research project. References were made to various unpublished technical reports where the details supporting the conclusions supposedly could be found.[44]

Goodlad (1990) correctly argued that statements about the conditions needed for exemplary teacher education are inevitably tied to moral positions about the desired nature of teaching and learning, schooling and society and not subject to "proof" by empirical tests. He said that there is no such thing as a neutral and value-free position on teacher education that can be validated by research alone. The visions of teaching and learning embraced by those who conducted many of the studies reviewed in this chapter were not clearly articulated. On the one hand, we have seen vague comparisons in studies where teachers have been compared as to who is "better." On the other hand, some studies compared teachers on specific criteria such as classroom management and lesson planning, but the overall visions of teaching underlying these various lists of discrete components were not clearly described. Only Goodlad (1990, 1994) and Darling-Hammond (2000) presented clear and elaborated descriptions of the kind of teaching that they were looking for when they examined the impact of teacher education programs on teacher performance.

The value of the Education of Educators study to future research on teacher education programs was to underline the importance of researchers' taking into account the vision of teaching, learning, and schooling that underlies statements about program effectiveness. It also underlined the importance of situating the examination of teacher education programs within the various institutional, political, and social contexts within which they are embedded. Both of these principles can become valuable parts of an agenda for future research on teacher education programs.

---

[44]We decided to include this work in our sample even though it was not peer reviewed because of the enormous influence it has had on the field over the last decade (Sirotnik & Associates, 2001).

A Study of Exemplary and Distinctive Elementary Teacher Education Programs

In the final case study research to be examined in this review, Howey and Zimpher (1989) conducted studies of six Midwestern elementary teacher education programs that had been identified as exemplary or distinctive by having received national program awards, by state education department personnel, and in the research journals. The institutions included research universities, state universities that emphasized teaching over research, and a liberal arts college.[45] Data were collected in 1985 in multiple visits or extended visits to the sites. Interviews were conducted with faculty, prospective teachers, cooperating teachers, and principals; campus classes were observed; and program documents were analyzed. The researchers sought to describe the scope, nature, and quality of program curricula; the conceptual orientations and pedagogical practices of program faculty; and the background, experiences, and teaching orientation of the teacher education students. Howey and Zimpher (1989) were careful to point out that they had not collected data that would enable them to confirm that these programs were successful in accomplishing their goals for teacher learning or that the teachers who left these programs were effective teachers as measured by pupil outcomes. They also pointed out that these six programs were not necessarily representative of teacher education programs generally or even of elementary education programs.

Based in part on the case studies of the six programs designated as exemplary by peer nomination, Howey and Zimpher (1989) offered a set of program attributes that they thought represented manifestations of best practice and contributed to program coherence in elementary teacher education programs. The first characteristic was a clear set of shared ideas and values about schooling and teaching. Next, they pointed out that the faculty in these programs tended to come together around experimental programs that have distinctive identities beyond the general "elementary" designation. These distinctive identities (e.g., the multiple program strands at Michigan State) contributed to greater collegiality among the program faculty and to faculty investment in and ownership of the program. The goals of these programs were clear, explicit, and reasonable, and as a result, students were able to articulate the goals of their programs. These program goals were developed into a set of themes that permeated all courses and field experiences and that tied work together.

The programs were also characterized by high levels of rigor and academic challenge and by an appropriate balance between general knowledge and pedagogical knowledge, avoiding narrow and purely technical definitions of teaching methods. In several programs, student cohort groups were identified as a strength by students and faculty and seemed to create a collective sense of pride and public accountability among the students. In some programs, particular milestone or benchmark points deliberately built into the program contributed to strengthening an individual and collective sense of pride in accomplishment and to reinforcing students' commitment to teaching as a career. These programs also allowed for an integrated or interdisciplinary approach to curriculum that addressed such core teaching functions as planning across subject disciplines. There was also strong articulation between the campus-based and school-based activities in the programs.

---

[45]The institutions studied were Ball State University, Indiana University, Luther College, Michigan State University, University of Toledo, and the University of Wisconsin-Eau Claire.

Howey and Zimpher (1989) concluded their empirically based statement of the manifestations of excellence in elementary teacher education programs by arguing several general points. The first was that adequate life space be provided within the curriculum to accomplish all that needs to be done to prepare teachers to begin their teaching careers and that adequate resources (e.g., curriculum, instructional, communication, and information technology) be made available to support the work of educating teachers. They also felt it was important that teacher education programs have close connections to research and development into teacher education and that they have plans for systematically evaluating their work. To some extent these six programs exemplified these characteristics, although Howey and Zimpher noted areas where the programs fell short. Here as in the other case studies, it was hard at times to trace a clear link between the data and conclusions. The statements about manifestations of program excellence make sense, but it was not possible to establish an evidentiary warrant for them based on the data presented in the research report.

All four of these case studies of teacher education programs represented efforts by researchers to probe more deeply into the inner workings of teacher education programs as actually implemented and, in the cases of Darling-Hammond (2000) and Goodlad (1990), into the contexts in which the programs were embedded. Although the researchers' assertions about the characteristics of program effectiveness were weakened by their failure to establish clear links between evidence in their data and program characteristics of excellence, and between the program characteristics and teacher and student outcomes (i.e., the programs were deemed to be exemplary mostly by peer nomination), the studies represented an important sign of progress in attempts to link program characteristics with teacher and student outcomes. The main thing that they offered the field were examples of ways that the complexities of preservice teacher education programs can be examined. These methods can be used alone or in conjunction with systematic quantitative analyses of the effects of different types of teacher preparation.

We will never be able to identify the features of effective teacher education programs in terms of any measures of teacher quality or pupil learning without close study of the characteristics teachers bring to their programs, of the complexities of programs as they are actually implemented, of what students learn from their programs, and of the schools in which they teach. We know from research on the process of learning to teach that the initial beliefs of entering preservice teachers about teaching, learning, and learners are very difficult to change and that they influence what teachers learn from their preservice programs (Wideen, Mayer-Smith, & Moon, 1998). We also know from all of the case studies discussed previously that preservice programs as actually implemented usually are more complex and contradictory than as described in the literature. Furthermore, it is clear that the schools where teachers teach and that the districts and states where they are located both exert a powerful influence on teachers' actions (Zeichner & Tabachnick, 1981).

Wasley and McDiarmid (2003, p. 8) nicely captured some of the complexities involved in trying to link teacher education programs to teacher and pupil outcomes:

> Teachers may or may not act on the knowledge and practices that they were taught in their preservice programs. If we are to determine the effects of different types of teacher preparation on student learning, we must first determine the extent to which what teachers do in the classroom is shaped by their preservice training . . . The extent to which test scores of students reflect the consequences of their teacher's preservice preparation is difficult to determine. They might well reflect the socialization into a particular school culture and attendant practices or the power of the "apprenticeship of observation."

A second thing that the aforementioned cases also offered the field was the potential to develop a tradition of using common instrumentation across studies to investigate teacher education programs and their effects. All these studies have developed detailed ways of studying the intentions of teacher educators, the opportunities for teacher learning that are made available in programs, how the intentions and actions of teacher educators are interpreted and given meaning by teacher education students, and how this all connects to teacher and pupil outcomes during and after the program. The researchers in the NCTAF case studies closely examined and incorporated aspects of the instrumentation used in TELT. This was the one of the few instances in all of the research on teacher education programs of a deliberate building on the methodological work of others. This practice should become more common.

CONCLUSION

This chapter examines peer-reviewed empirical research related to the impact of teacher education programs on various aspects of teacher retention, teacher quality, and student learning. The research examined is concerned with comparisons of the efficacy of 4-year versus 5-year programs, and with comparisons of different kinds of alternative versus traditional programs. The various outcomes examined in these studies include how many teachers completing particular kinds of programs entered teaching and what kinds of schools they entered, teachers' ratings of the effectiveness of their preparation in relation to particular tasks of teaching (e.g., teaching English-language learners), and the professional teaching knowledge of graduates from different programs. In addition, various aspects of teaching quality after program completion are examined including self-ratings by teachers of their own teaching abilities; teaching practices and problems in the classroom; observations and ratings of teaching by principals, supervisors, and other trained observers using particular classroom observation instruments; pupil ratings of the nature and quality of instruction; and measures of pupil learning. Teachers' commitment to teaching, their sense of efficacy, their career satisfaction (e.g., would they choose teaching again), and their actual retention are also assessed. Finally, teacher engagement in various activities is assessed both through teacher self-report and by principal ratings.

Although the studies examined in this chapter have provided us with some potentially useful information about the ways in which aspects of teacher education programs influence teachers' entry into teaching and retention, and about various aspects of teacher quality, few definitive statements can be made about the effects of different structural models of preservice teacher education based on this body of research. Inconsistent and contradictory outcomes across studies and various conceptual and methodological problems with the existing research have been discussed that limit the usefulness of their findings including the lack of description of programs, the state policy contexts in which programs are embedded, and the school and community contexts in which program graduates teach; the use of vague criteria and comparison groups in the evaluation of teacher performance; and the failure to distinguish effects of programs from the influence of the characteristics that prospective teachers bring to the programs. We know from this research that teacher education programs and those who enroll in them matter in terms of teacher and pupil outcomes, but because of the lack of close study of what teachers brought to the programs, the programs themselves and the contexts in which they operated, the inconsistencies in the findings cannot be adequately explained. Kennedy (1999, p. 104) summarized these problems with research on teacher education programs as well as the limits of small samples in many of the studies:

> By failing to document the content and character of teacher education programs, they confuse quantity with quality. By failing to consider what teacher candidates know or think prior to participating in teacher education, they may over- or underestimate the contributions of teacher education. By failing to consider the context in which teachers are teaching, they may confuse the effects of the current teaching context with the effects of the earlier teacher preparation. When they only study a handful of teachers, they cannot tell us how widespread their observed changes are likely to be.

Research on the various components of teacher education programs reviewed in several other chapters in this volume also has been characterized by many of these same problems of lack of attention to the contexts in which the components were embedded. Trying to isolate the effects of a particular methods course or field experience, foundations course, or pedagogical strategy apart from the teacher education program in which these existed or from the characteristics of the particular students in the program will not yield much useful knowledge. Both the components of teacher education programs and the programs themselves need to be described and studied in a way that acknowledges their complexity and their ties to the settings in which they are located and the people who inhabit them. The fragmented nature of teacher education programs and differences in substance and context within courses with the same titles even in the same institution (Zeichner, 1993) underline the importance of researchers' fully describing the situations they are studying at both the course and program level.

With few exceptions, neither the studies on program components nor programs have been able to disentangle the effects of courses and programs from the characteristics, perspectives, and abilities that prospective teachers bring to teacher education and from the settings in which they go on to teach. The literature on teacher learning is very clear about the power of what prospective teachers bring to teacher education in shaping what they learn and do as teachers (e.g., Feiman-Nemser & Remillard, 1996). Research on teacher education needs to be able to distinguish enrollment from learning effects and to distinguish learning effects within teacher education programs from the influence of the settings in which graduates teach. It is possible with certain improvements in research designs to do both of these things, but it will not be inexpensive to do the kinds of observations and interviews necessary. For example, studies of matched pairs of teachers in the same schools and at similar grade levels or in similar subject areas who came from different teacher education programs can help to begin to sort out the effects of the current school from those of the preservice program. Similarly, careful study of the characteristics of prospective teachers in different teacher education programs can begin to disentangle enrollment from learning effects.

Also, as was pointed out in this review, more attention needs to be paid to the subject area specializations of the teachers being compared and to the socioeconomic characteristics of the schools in which teachers teach. We need to know more about the program content and structures that enable teachers to be successful in different types of schools.

One necessary component in studying the impact of different models of preservice preparation is for researchers to spend time in the programs observing program activities and talking with participants. Even when research studies provided a description of the various kinds of programs being compared, they often were based on a reading of program documents and not on firsthand experience in the program over time to understand its complexity. There is some evidence that the reality of teacher education programs is much more complex and contradictory than that reported in the literature (Kennedy, 1998). Close study of the inner workings of a teacher education program will help illuminate the critical features of programs that make a difference in producing desired outcomes. A study in progress of the effects of different pathways into teaching in New York City (Boyd et al., 2003b) combines this kind of qualitative probing of the substance and meaning of teacher education programs with systematic quantitative analyses of the effects of different types of preparation.

Even with improvements in these and other areas, however, future research is not likely to determine in an unambiguous way which structural model of teacher education is the most effective. There will always be a wide range of quality in any model of teacher education such as a 4- or 5-year program. The state policy context, type of institution, and institutional history and culture in which the program is located; the goals and capabilities of teacher education faculty; and many other factors will affect the character and quality of programs. There is no such thing as a 4- or 5-year or alternative program that means the same thing regardless of contexts in which it exists. Courses, field experiences, and programs differ along a number of dimensions including the substance and academic rigor of the curriculum and the vision of teaching, learning, schooling, and society that underlies it; and the degree to which this vision is elaborated, understood, and shared by those campus- and field-based teacher educators who work with prospective teachers.

Although studies reviewed in this chapter are cited in support of particular program structures such as 5-year or alternative programs, the evidence as a whole does not support the uniform adoption of a particular structural approach. For example, although some evidence gathered in a limited number of programs suggested that graduates of 5-year programs stayed in teaching longer than graduates of 4-year programs in some contexts, there was no evidence that this was the case in high-poverty urban schools or that the characteristics that teachers brought to the programs and the program admission requirements rather than the programs themselves were responsible for the higher teacher retention.

Also, although in some cases alternatively certified teachers were evaluated to be as competent or more competent than traditionally certified teachers, the particular characteristics of both the alternative and traditional programs inevitably influenced the results. There is a big difference, for example, between the alternative program studied by Jelmberg (1996) in New Hampshire where teachers were given full responsibility for a classroom with no prior training and the alternative programs elsewhere where there was a significant preservice component. Also, as pointed out earlier, when assessing the quality of teaching of the graduates of different models of teacher education, the characteristics of the schools in which teachers teach needs to be taken into account. If this research is to provide us with useful information, researchers need to compare teachers who are teaching in the same or similar kinds of schools and in similar grade levels and subject areas. Generally there has been a lack of attention in the research reviewed to describing the schools and communities in which program graduates teach. Rice (2003) pointed out the importance of careful attention by researchers to describing the teaching context in studies of teacher quality. More attention to describing teaching contexts in research on teacher education programs would enable us to disentangle the impact of the schools and communities from those of teacher preparation and individual teacher characteristics.

We have also seen that the amount and quality of program characteristics often identified as important such as the mentoring provided to alternatively certified teachers varied both across and within programs. A case in point was the situation in Houston noted earlier where a substantial number of interns had never met their mentors. All the program characteristics identified in the literature on both traditional and alternative programs vary in how they are defined and implemented. It is important for researchers to begin to understand more about the particular qualities of mentoring and other program features that are related to desired outcomes.

Rather than continuing the futile search for the most effective program model, a more productive direction for research on teacher education programs to take would be to build on the work done in the comprehensive program case studies sponsored by the National Center for Research on Teacher Education and the National Commission for Teaching and America's Future discussed earlier to further identify the substantive features of programs that make a difference in influencing teacher quality and student learning. We need to learn more about the characteristics of effective programs and how they are enacted in different kinds of teacher education programs and in different state policy contexts. Given the large number of teachers that we need to prepare for the public schools, there will likely continue to be a need for multiple pathways into teaching that address the different circumstances of people wanting to teach. Effective program characteristics that are suggested but not necessarily warranted by the evidence present in the case studies reviewed in this chapter can be present in programs with different structures (e.g., a clear and common vision of teaching and learning that is present in all courses and field experiences, carefully supervised clinical experiences, and strong preparation in content knowledge).

Kliebard (1973) noted that research in teacher education has often been structured as a horse race: "Sometimes one horse wins, sometimes the other; often, it is a tie" (p. 21). The research on teacher education programs reviewed in this chapter resembles Kliebard's characterization, and we agree with his conclusions that this kind of inquiry does not result in findings with much explanatory value. More of a focus on the substance of teacher education programs and better conceptualization of the research problems in relation to existing theories (e.g., of teacher learning) will potentially enable researchers to offer explanations as to why particular components and aspects of teacher education programs have the effects or lack of effects that are identified in research studies.

As discussed previously, the TELT study showed that it is program substance not structure that is key in influencing prospective teachers. We need research that focuses more on the substance of programs and that goes beyond surface-level assertions about good program features (e.g., the importance of coherence, partnerships, mentoring, and modeling) to elaborate what these characteristics mean in practice and the particular configurations of these features (e.g., what good mentoring practice means) that enable the realization of desired outcomes.[46]

To enhance our understanding of the substantive aspects of effective teacher education programs, researchers must address many of the methodological problems that are present in the extant research. It is very important that research on teacher education programs and their components help us understand the difference between the effects of what candidates bring to the program and those influences that can be

---

[46]A study currently in progress by researchers at SRI (Humphrey et al., 2002) is using survey items used in other research including the TELT study and will result in case studies of seven alternative certification programs. The goal of this research is to illuminate the features of effective alternative programs.

attributed to the programs themselves. It is also important that researchers begin to develop a common set of ways to assess outcomes related to teacher retention and teacher quality. Currently, it is hard to aggregate findings across studies of teacher education programs because researchers have used different measures of teaching performance. In the TELT study and NCTAF case studies, researchers developed ways of assessing such things as graduates' perceptions of how well they were prepared by their teacher education programs in different areas, the nature and quality of the various components of teacher education programs, and of teaching performance that overcome the historic limitations of principal ratings. It is important for researchers to begin to use these and similar methodological tools so that we can look across individual studies more easily.

A critical element needed in future research on teacher education programs is explicit articulation of the vision of teaching that the preparation aims for. The characteristics of exemplary programs that seek to develop teachers able to teach all students in a way that promotes student understanding will be different from those of a program that effectively prepares teachers to pass on information to students to be digested and regurgitated. The characteristics of programs that effectively prepare teachers to exercise their judgment about matters of curriculum and instruction will differ from those of programs that successfully prepare teachers to follow the dictates of a scripted curriculum. Currently there is a lack of agreement about what vision of teaching should be emphasized in preservice preparation programs. Research on teacher education programs needs to be explicit about the visions of teaching and learning underlying the programs under study.

One obvious way to move beyond a situation of extreme relativism with regard to the aims that should be emphasized in teacher education programs is to begin to examine how the realization of certain aims in the preparation of teachers influences student learning. Only four studies reviewed in this chapter attempted to examine the links between preservice teacher preparation and student learning. In one case, the standardized achievement test scores of pupils taught by graduates of different programs were compared, and no differences among traditional and alternative programs were found. In two other cases the students taught by traditionally certified teachers appeared to do better, and in the final study the students of the alternatively certified teachers had higher score gains. Although the studies sought to establish the equivalency of the schools in which the different teachers taught, none adequately described the differences in the specific characteristics of the traditional and alternative programs that may have accounted for those differences in student test scores.

Comparing the standardized test scores of pupils taught by graduates of different kinds of programs is one approach to examining the links between preservice preparation and pupil learning. Mayer et al. (2003) proposed a study of teachers who have completed different teacher education programs that vary by specific characteristics (e.g., entrance requirements and extent of preparation prior to assuming responsibility for a classroom) that would involve randomly assigning pupils to classrooms. They argued that random assignment of students to teachers prepared under different conditions is the only way to ensure that student learning differences are attributable to the program alone and not to other factors.

As we mentioned previously, we think that there are potential ethical and practical problems involved in randomly assigning pupils to classrooms that necessitate caution when using this approach. As Gueron (2002), an advocate of random trials points out, it is particularly important to avoid any assignment procedures "that would deny people access to a service to which they are legally entitled" (p. 22). It seems ethically acceptable to us, but still practically difficult and very expensive[47] to randomly assign pupils to classrooms taught by qualified teachers who have completed different teacher education programs. We believe, however, that it is not ethically acceptable to randomly assign pupils to the classrooms of teachers who have not received *any* formal professional preparation for teaching in addition to a bachelor's degree prior to becoming teachers of record. This is based on evidence discussed earlier that in some cases teachers with no or minimal amounts of preservice preparation performed during the year at a lower level of effectiveness than did teachers who had more substantial professional preparation before becoming teachers of record. Although the former group appears to "catch up" to the later group by the end of the year in some cases, the pupils who are assigned to these teachers during the period of catching up may suffer academic losses.

Teaching is not alone in the ethical and practical complications and the great expense associated with random trials, and we support their use as one part of an agenda for research on teacher education programs. We do not agree, however, that random trials are the only way that researchers can systematically investigate the impact of different programs and program components.

A study in progress of a number of alternative pathways into teaching in New York City (Boyd et al., 2003b) does not employ randomization; instead, it uses a combination of qualitative and quantitative methods to better understand the effects of individual teacher attributes, teacher education program features, and school context on various aspects of teacher quality and student learning.[48] This study identifies a number of individual teacher attributes (e.g., academic ability), and school context, school district, and state policy features (e.g., class size, induction, and mentoring support) that are examined in relation to various teacher and student outcomes (e.g., teacher entry and retention and student test scores). It also identifies a number of teacher education program features (e.g., the nature and quality of field experiences and preparation for working with diverse students) that will be examined in relation to the same outcomes. One goal of this study is to distinguish the individual attribute and context effects from those of the teacher education pathways. One potential danger in specifying up front what factors will be employed in the value-added econometric models is that the most important factors could be missed. A particular strength of this research, in addition to its longitudinal design, is that the quantitative work is supplemented and informed by interviews, observations, and document analysis within the teacher education programs that will enable the researchers to produce rich portraits of how elementary teachers are prepared to teach mathematics and reading in the different programs.

The few studies in our data set that examined the impact of teacher education or its components on student learning used gains in standardized test scores as the measure of learning. The use of pupil growth in standardized test scores as the only measure of learning is very limited because these tests only illuminate limited aspects of learning. Researchers should utilize a variety of measures (e.g., student work samples and

---

[47]Practical difficulties include gaining parental permission for these studies, and managing the high student mobility rates in most urban schools.

[48]The researchers use a variety of statistical techniques for dealing with potential selection bias that are common in nonexperimental program evaluations. They also focus on improving the quality of the data that they have available to identify how attributes of teacher preparation programs affect specific teacher and student outcomes.

teacher-designed tests) to understand teacher education's connection to other aspects of academic learning and also investigate links to other kinds of learning such as social, emotional, and civic learning.

One approach to examining student learning other than through standardized tests is provided by the NCTAF case studies of exemplary programs that included (in addition to an in-depth study of the programs themselves) a component where graduates of the programs were observed and interviewed in their beginning years of teaching. Documenting the teaching practices and student learning in classrooms of graduates of different programs through in-depth classroom observations that involve the use of student work samples and teacher-designed tests also are very complex and expensive to carry out, but so too are the other approaches that deal with the complexity of the issue. Researchers need to ensure that measures of student learning used in these studies are aligned with the curriculum and instruction that students actually receive. However done, more attention needs to be given by researchers to linking teacher education programs and measures of teacher quality to the quality of student learning.

The lack of success in finding empirical support for a particular model of teacher education at the preservice level is consistent with other analyses of research on teacher education programs (e.g., Allen, 2003; Wilson, et al., 2001). Evertson, Hawley, and Zlotnik (1985), in a widely cited review of the research concluded: "Hundreds of studies related to teacher education are available, but the lessons they teach do not add up to a particular model for improvement around which teacher educators should rally" (p. 9).

Although there may be good moral, ethical, and political reasons for promoting the availability of particular models of preservice teacher preparation, it is not possible at this time to settle the debates about program models on the basis of empirical research alone. With improvements in the way studies on teacher education programs are designed and carried out, research clearly can become more useful to informing policy and practice with regard to the design of teacher education programs.

Finally, there is a danger that in the current highly charged ideological debates about teacher quality in the current political context of the United States that supporters of specific positions will go into this review and pull out selected findings that support their particular point of view, ignoring other findings. For example, those who want to argue that there is no difference in terms of teacher quality between an alternative program sponsored by a school district or other nonuniversity agency and traditional university-based programs can find examples in this review that taken out of context could wind up being used as "evidence" that non-university-sponsored alternative certification is justified. Those who want to find examples of how traditional university-based teacher education is superior to programs sponsored by some other agencies also could distort the findings of this review.

This selective use of evidence from particular studies to support a particular policy direction without regard to the complexities of the analysis of the studies would be a distortion of what the research as a whole shows. This review does not support an uncritical adoption of either alternative or traditional programs or resolve the issue of whether particular programs like TFA are more effective than particular alternatives. The weight of the evidence of peer-reviewed research on teacher education programs in the United States suggests certain characteristics of programs that may be important in terms of teacher quality and student learning. It remains for future research, however, to establish an evidentiary warrant for the validity of these claims about program excellence.

TABLE 11.1

AERA Panel Program Structure

Studies[a]	Question and Focus	Research Tradition and Research Context	Research Design	Findings	Program Structure
Adelman, N. (1986)	How competent are alternatively certified teachers in terms of mastery of subject matter, knowledge of a variety of teaching strategies, and overall?	Survey: Participants in 7 alternative certification programs: Arizona Partners Project, Harvard Mid Career Math and Science program, Houston Alternative Certification program, Los Angeles Unified School District Teacher Trainee Program, New Jersey Provisional Teacher Program, University of New Mexico/Santa Fe Public Schools Intern Program, and University of Southern Maine Teachers for Secondary Schools Program.	$N = 16$ program participants. Data sources = telephone interviews with program participants, supervisors, and teachers in participants' schools prepared through traditional university-based programs. Analysis = Descriptive data.	All of the AC teachers earned above-average or superior ratings in mastery of subject matter. Although the majority of AC teachers needed improvement in areas such as classroom management and student expectations, alternate route teachers were very similar to traditionally prepared first-year teachers in these areas. Overall, 14 of the AC teachers were rated above average or superior.	Traditional vs. alternative programs
Andrew, M. D., & Schwab, R. L. (1995)	Are there differences in performance levels of graduates of 4-year programs and graduates of extended programs?	Survey: Teacher education program graduates from 11 institutions: Austin College (TX), Drake University (IA), Oakland University (MI), Texas A&M; Universities of Florida, Kansas, Nebraska-Lincoln, New Hampshire, Rhode Island, Virginia, and Vermont.	$N = 1,390$ graduates; $N = 481$ principals. Data sources = survey of graduates and teacher effectiveness survey (35 items; 4 indicators: entry into the profession, retention, classroom performance, and leadership behavior). Analysis = factor analysis, content analysis of principal surveys, chi-square, ANOVA.	Graduates of extended programs had higher rates of entering teaching and had higher retention rates than 4-year program graduates. Extended program graduates reported higher rates of involvement in teacher leadership roles.	Four-year vs. 5-year programs

(Continued)

TABLE 11.1
(Continued)

Studies[a]	Question and Focus	Research Tradition and Research Context	Research Design	Findings	Program Structure
Andrew, M. D. (1990)	Are there significant differences in the rates of entry into the teaching profession, retention, job satisfaction, and program satisfaction between graduates of 4-year teacher education programs and graduates of 5-year programs?	Survey and Comparative Study: University of New Hampshire teacher education program graduates	Two data sources: $N = 144$ five-year graduates; $N = 163$ four-year graduates. Data sources = 70-item questionnaire. Analysis = frequencies of response, chi-square, t-tests. AND $N =$ (not reported) Data sources = program evaluation questionnaire of 4- and 5-year program completers. Analysis = comparison of questionnaire responses.	Graduates of the 5-year teacher education program had higher rates of entry into the teaching profession and higher retention rates than graduates of the 4-year program. Five-year program graduates also had greater job satisfaction and greater satisfaction with their teacher education program than the 4-year program graduates did.	Four-year vs. five-year programs
Baker, T. E. (1993)	Are there significant differences between graduates of 4-year programs and graduates of 5-year programs in terms of academic qualifications, commitment to the profession, sense of efficacy, and preferred	Survey: Teacher education program graduates from 11 institutions: Austin College, Drake University, Oakland University, Texas A&M; Universities of Florida, Kansas, Nebraska-Lincoln, New Hampshire, Rhode Island, Virginia, and Vermont.	$N = 1,394$ graduates; $N = 70\%$ of principals whose graduates agreed to have principals contacted. Data sources = surveys. Analysis = comparison of survey responses, factor analysis, chi-square, t-tests.	Program graduates have strong academic preparations, are highly committed to teaching, prefer non-traditional teaching techniques, and have confidence in their classroom abilities. Five-year program graduates were more likely to enter and remain in teaching; more involved in curriculum development,	Four- vs. 5-year programs

Author (year)	Research question	Method	Sample/analysis	Findings	Category
	teaching techniques?			and more interested in collaboration with colleagues than 4-year program graduates. Four-year graduates were slightly more likely to use innovative, student-centered teaching techniques.	Traditional vs. alternative programs
Bliss, T. (1990)	In its first 3 years, to what extent has the Alternate Route to Certification in Connecticut realized its objectives of bringing exceptionally qualified individuals with diverse backgrounds into the profession?	Survey: Connecticut alternate route teachers and "other beginning teachers."	N = 30 ARC teachers; N = 45 regular teachers. Data sources = surveys with principals, supervisors, and mentors of alternate route teachers; formal classroom observations. Analysis = Comparison of ARC teachers and regular teachers.	Eighty-eight percent of supervisors felt AC teachers were stronger than other beginning teachers, and all but 3 of the supervisors said they would rehire the AC teacher. From observation assessments, all 5 of the elementary AC teachers met the state standard, whereas 29 of 32 regular teachers did. In the secondary group, 18 of the 25 AC teachers met the standard, whereas 9 of 13 regular teachers did.	Traditional vs. alternative programs
Boser, J. A., & Wiley, P. D. (1988)	Do educators perceive the alternative program to be comparable to traditional programs?	Survey: Superintendents, principals, and mentor teachers who worked with graduates of University of Tennessee-Knoxville's secondary alternative certification program, 4-year undergraduate program, and 5th year postbaccalaureate program.	N = unspecified number of superintendents, principals, and mentor teachers. Data sources = Interviews and questionnaires with superintendents, principals, and mentor teachers. Analysis = response frequencies and percentages.	Most superintendents, principals, and mentor teachers thought the alternative program preparation was comparable to, as good as, or better than the preparation from the traditional programs.	Traditional vs. alternative programs

(Continued)

TABLE 11.1
(Continued)

Studies[a]	Question and Focus	Research Tradition and Research Context	Research Design	Findings	Program Structure
Breidenstein, A. (2002)	How do the perceptions of graduates of 4-year and extended teacher preparation programs compare regarding their teaching preparation and teaching experience?	Mixed Methods: Second-year elementary and secondary teachers in San Antonio, Texas, from 4- or 5-year teacher education programs.	$N = 84$ teachers (for surveys); $N = 16$ teachers (for interviews). Data sources = surveys (61 Likert-scale items); individual and focus group interviews (16 and 6 questions, respectively). Analysis = SPSS analysis; chi-square; category analysis; coding by theme.	All program graduates had confidence in their knowledge and abilities, but graduates of extended programs feel better prepared on all indicators. In teaching experiences, there were also differences that favored graduates of extended programs on all but 1 indicator.	Four-year vs. 5-year programs
Coley, R. J. & Thorpe, M. E. (1986)	Where do graduates of MAT programs teach, and how long do they stay in teaching?	Survey: 1968 and 1969 graduates from MAT programs at Converse College, Duke, Harvard, Johns Hopkins, Notre Dame, Stanford, University of Chicago, University of Massachusetts, Vanderbilt; most recent graduates (1985) of MAT programs at Brown, Stanford, Vanderbilt, and University of Chicago.	$N = 715$ 1960s graduates of MAT programs; $N = 36$ 1980s graduates of MAT programs. Data sources = Mail survey. Analysis = Descriptive data.	83% of the 1960s MAT graduates entered K–12 teaching after their program, 1/3 of these held a teaching position at the time of the study, and they stayed in teaching for an average of 5 years. Eighty-eight percent of the 1980's MAT graduates said they planned to enter teaching after completing their program, and 1/3 said they intended to teach for their career. The majority of the MATs taught in suburban	Traditional vs. alternative programs

| Darling-Hammond, L. (2000) | What are the characteristics of exemplary teacher education programs? | Case study Seven preservice teacher education programs identified as successful in preparing "learner-centered" and "learning-centered" teachers: Bank Street College of Education, University of California-Berkeley's Developmental Teacher Education program, University of Southern Maine's Extended teacher education program, Wheelock College, Alverno College, Trinity University, and University of Virginia. | public secondary schools with primarily White, upper-middle-class, and academically above-the-mean students. N = 7 institutions. Data sources = Surveys of recent program graduates, program document collection, interviews with teacher educators, observations of teacher educators in classrooms, interviews, and observations with current students and recent graduates, surveys and interviews with principals of recent graduates. Analysis = varied quantitative and qualitative | The 7-programs shared 6 common features: a shared, clear understanding among faculty, students, and school personnel of good teaching that permeates all courses and field experiences; a clear set of practice and performance standards against which students' work is guided and evaluated; a curriculum with extensive work in child and adolescent development, learning theory, and theories of cognition, motivation, and subject matter pedagogy; carefully selected field experiences of at least 30 weeks that support the ideas in concurrent coursework; strong relationships and shared beliefs among school and | Characteristics of effective teacher education programs |

TABLE 11.1
(Continued)

Studies[a]	Question and Focus	Research Tradition and Research Context	Research Design	Findings	Program Structure
				university-based faculty and staff; and extensive use of various pedagogical strategies that relate learning to real problems of practice.	
Darling-Hammond, L., Chung, R., & Frelow, F. (2002)	Are there differences in how prepared teachers feel in the classroom depending on the pathway through which they entered teaching? Are there some programs whose graduates rate their preparation significantly higher or lower than those of other programs?	Survey: Teachers with 3 or fewer years experience teaching in New York City public schools.	$N = 2,302$ teachers. Data sources = surveys (40 items: views on preparation for teaching, beliefs and practice, and plans to stay in teaching). Analysis = t-tests, correlations, regression analyses, chi-square.	Graduates of teacher education programs felt better prepared on most dimensions of teaching than teachers with either alternative preparation or no program preparation. Teachers' ratings of their preparation varied by individual program; some program graduates felt significantly better prepared. Teachers' senses of preparation are significantly related to their sense of teaching efficacy.	Traditional vs. alternative programs
Decker, P. T., Mayer, D. P., & Glazerman, S. (June, 2004)	"Do Teach for America teachers improve student outcomes relative to what would have happened	Random Assignment: Elementary (Grades 1–5) TFA teachers and other teachers in economically disadvantaged schools in Baltimore, Chicago, Los	$N = 17$ schools; $N = 100$ classrooms; $N = 1,800$ students. Data sources = teacher surveys on teaching philosophies and instructional practices in	In reading and math, TFA and control teachers used similar instructional practices for similar amounts of time. In reading, control teachers	Traditional vs. alternative programs

in their absence?" (p. xi)

Angeles, Houston, New Orleans, and the Mississippi Delta.

math and reading; fall and spring student achievement scores on Iowa Test of Basic Skills in reading and math; data from schools, districts, and teacher reports on retention in grade, assignment to summer school, disciplinary incidents, tardiness, chronic absence, and student disruptions. Analysis = descriptive statistics; statistical comparisons.

were more likely than TFA teachers to endorse phonics. In math, both groups emphasized understanding math in an applied fashion, but control teachers were more likely than TFA teachers to believe in the importance of getting correct answers and memorizing mathematical rules. At the end of the year, average student math test scores in TFA classrooms were higher than in control group classrooms, and average student reading scores were the same in both sets of classrooms. There were no significant differences in summer school attendance, absenteeism, disciplinary incidents, or grade retention between the two groups of teachers. TFA teachers were significantly more likely to report problems with student behavior and

(Continued)

TABLE 11.1
(Continued)

Studies[a]	Question and Focus	Research Tradition and Research Context	Research Design	Findings	Program Structure
				disruptions than control teachers.	
Gomez, M. L., & Stoddart, T. (1992)	What are the relative influences of personal perspectives and professional pedagogy on instructional practice, comparing graduates of a 5th-year university-based teacher education program and candidates from a school-district-based alternative route?	Case study: English-teaching interns from a school-district-based alternative route and English-teaching graduates of a 5th-year university-based teacher education program in the Southeast.	N = 4 alternative route interns; N = 4 university-based program graduates. Data sources = TELT study of the National Center for Research on Teacher Education. Semistructured interviews; observations. Analysis = Analytic induction of transcripts.	The university-educated teachers could not apply their program's subject-specific pedagogy to students who were not like themselves, focused on the social and cultural differences between themselves and their students, and believed students' social class and family backgrounds explained their low achievement. The alternative route interns used their personal views and experiences to make writing meaningful to their students, and held high expectations for their students.	Traditional vs. alternative programs
Goodlad, J. (1990)	What are the conditions necessary for effective teacher education?	Case study: Twenty-nine teacher education programs from across United States: programs located in California, Colorado,	N = 29 programs. Data sources = document collection; faculty and student questionnaires; interviews with students, faculty,	There are certain interrelated conditions necessary for teacher education based on a conception of democratic	Characteristics of effective teacher education programs

712

teaching and learning. Teacher education programs should have full institutional support; equal standing with other programs and comparable faculty status and rewards; secure resources, autonomy, and boundaries like other professional schools. There must be 1 group of faculty whose top priority is teacher education; they must coordinate and oversee all aspects of the program; they must be fully committed to educating teachers for all responsibilities; and programs must carefully select teaching candidates who show moral and ethical commitment to the responsibilities they will assume. Programs must ensure that graduates have strong literacy and critical thinking abilities; provide a socialization process that enables

administrators, and school-based educators; observations of campus classes and classes taught by student teachers in the field. Analysis = varied quantitative and qualitative

Georgia, Illinois, Iowa, Massachusetts, Oklahoma, and Pennsylvania.

(Continued)

TABLE 11.1
(Continued)

Studies[a]	Question and Focus	Research Tradition and Research Context	Research Design	Findings	Program Structure
				students to become other-oriented and identify with a culture of teaching; and help teachers inquire into knowledge, the teaching of knowledge, and schooling. Programs should help teachers deal with ongoing tensions of different interest groups; prepare teachers who are committed to ensuring the best education for all students; and prepare teachers to analyze the disconnect between current practice and needed changes. Programs should be characterized by the same type of learning advocated for K–12 classrooms; diverse and exemplary field experiences; and admittance for only the number of students for whom exemplary field placements are available. Programs should maintain contact with	

	See Goodlad (1990)	See Goodlad (1990)	See Goodlad (1990)	program graduates to ease their transition and improve the program. Finally, programs should be free of excessive curricular requirements from licensing agencies and must be protected from state policies that would permit unqualified teachers to teach because of shortages.	Characteristics of effective teacher education programs
Goodlad, J. (1994)	See Goodlad (1990)	See Goodlad (1990)	See Goodlad (1990)		
Guyton, E., Fox, M. C., & Sisk, K. A. (1991)	What are the attitudes, performance, and experiences of 1st-year teachers who have been prepared through Georgia's alternative certification program and those prepared through traditional teacher education programs?	Mixed Methods: Beginning teachers prepared through the state of Georgia's alternative certification program and those prepared through traditional teacher education.	$N = 23$ alternatively prepared teachers; $N = 26$ traditionally prepared teachers. Data sources = Background information on participants; survey of attitudes, influences, and concerns (14 open-ended items); Educational Attitudes Inventory; Teaching Attitude Inventory (43 Likert-scale items); Teacher Efficacy Scale (16 items); and Beginning Teacher Evaluations (15 items). Analysis = descriptive statistics, t-tests, Mann-Whitney U test.	Regularly certified and alternatively certified teachers were similar on almost all measures. The alternatively certified teachers rated their program more highly after the 1st month of teaching. The regularly certified teachers felt better about teaching at the end of the year and about remaining in teaching.	Traditional vs. alternative programs

(Continued)

TABLE 11.1
(Continued)

Studies[a]	Question and Focus	Research Tradition and Research Context	Research Design	Findings	Program Structure
Haberman, M. (1999)	How successful is the School of Education at University of Wisconsin-Milwaukee in recruiting and preparing more minority teachers? What is the retention and success of these teachers? How do they rate their preparation?	Survey: Graduates of Metropolitan Milwaukee Teacher Education Program (alternative certification program in Milwaukee, WI).	$N = 137$ graduates; $N = 125$ principals. Data sources = Telephone survey; principal questionnaire. Analysis = not specified.	MMTEP prepares 78% minority teachers, most of whom remained in Milwaukee Public Schools over 10 years. Graduates earned high principal ratings and expressed high satisfaction with their preparation.	Traditional vs. alternative programs
Hawk, P., & Schmidt, M. W. (1989)	How do National Teacher Exam results and classroom performance compare among participants in a traditional teacher preparation program and those of a Lateral Entry Program (LEP)?	Mixed Methods: East Carolina University School of Education Lateral Entry Program participants and traditionally certified teachers in science and math.	$N = 16$ Lateral Entry participants; $N = 18$ traditionally prepared teachers (NTE score comparisons); $N = 53$ 1st-year math and science teachers (TPAI comparisons). Data sources = NTE math or biology exam scores; NTE Professional Knowledge Exam scores; Teacher Performance Appraisal Instrument (28 observable teaching practices); questionnaires. Analysis = t-tests, comparison of TPAI ratings.	Students prepared through the Lateral entry/alternative certification program were as successful on NTE exams as traditionally prepared students. LEP participants received fewer "above-standard" ratings on most classroom performance measures than did traditionally prepared teachers.	Traditional vs. alternative programs

Reference	Study focus	Sample/Data	Findings	Category
Houston, W. R., Marshall, F., & McDavid, T. (1993)	Survey: First-year alternatively and traditionally certified teachers in Houston, TX. Are there differences in the problems faced by alternatively certified elementary teachers and those faced by 1st-year traditionally certified elementary teachers? Are there differences in confidence, satisfaction, and plans to continue teaching between these two groups of teachers?	$N = 69$ regularly certified elementary school teachers; $N = 162$ alternatively certified elementary school teachers. Data sources = Survey instrument after 2 months of teaching; survey instrument after 8 months of teaching. Analysis = Descriptive data; statistical analysis not specified.	After 2 months of teaching, the AC teachers perceived greater problems than the TC teachers in 6 areas: student motivation, managing teacher time, amount of paperwork, lack of personal time, grading students, and problems with school administration. After 8 months, these differences disappeared, and TC teachers perceived greater problems with classroom management than did AC teachers. After 2 months of teaching, TC teachers expressed greater job satisfaction than did AC teachers, but after 8 months, these differences disappeared.	Traditional vs. alternative programs
Howey, K. R., & Zimpher, N. L. (1989)	Case study: Six elementary teacher education programs in the Midwest identified as exemplary: Ball State University, Indiana University, Luther College, Michigan State University, University of Toledo, At exemplary teacher education programs, what are the scope, nature and quality of program curricula; the conceptual	$N = 6$ institutions. Data sources = Interviews with faculty, prospective teachers, and cooperating teachers and principals; observations of campus classes; collection of documents. Analysis = varied quantitative and qualitative	Certain program attributes represent manifestations of best practice and contribute to program coherence. These are a clear set of shared ideas and values about schooling and teaching;	Characteristics of effective teacher education programs

(Continued)

TABLE 11.1
(Continued)

Studies[a]	Question and Focus	Research Tradition and Research Context	Research Design	Findings	Program Structure
	orientations and pedagogical practices of program faculty; and the background, experiences and teaching orientation of the teacher education students?	and University of Wisconsin-Eau Claire.		faculty with strong collegiality who have investment in and ownership of the program; program goals that are clear, explicit, and reasonable; and themes derived from these goals that permeate all courses and field experiences. Programs have high levels of rigor and academic challenge, a good balance between general and pedagogical knowledge, an interdisciplinary curriculum approach, and a strong link between campus and school-based activities. Some programs have strong cohort groups and benchmarks that contribute to student pride and collective senses of accomplishment. Programs need to provide adequate life	

	How do AC interns compare to traditionally prepared 1st-year teachers on performance measures and certification exams?	Mixed Methods: Dallas, TX, Independent School District/East Texas State University Alternative Certification interns.	$N = 110$ AC interns; $N = 62$ traditionally certified 1st-year teachers. Data sources = ExCET exams; Texas Teacher Appraisal System; Teacher Advisor Comparison Rating Form (TACRE) (50 items). Analysis = t-tests, chi-square analysis.	space and adequate resources to support the education of teachers, and also must have close connections to teacher education research and development in order to improve and evaluate their work. Principals rated all but 1 AC intern as "satisfactory" or above; 62% were rated as "exceptional" or "clearly outstanding." The TACRF ratings of AC interns "compared favorably" to those of the 1st-year teachers. A larger percentage of AC interns passed the ExCET exams than all teacher candidates statewide on 5 of 7 comparisons. The AC interns had higher mean scores.	Traditional vs. alternative programs
Hutton, J. B., Lutz, F. W., & Williamson, J. L. (1990)					
Jelmberg. J. (1996)	How do college-based teacher education programs compare to state-sponsored Alternative 4 certification programs?	Survey: College-based and alternative teacher certification programs in New Hampshire.	$N = 236$ teachers; $N = 136$ principals. Data sources = Two questionnaires: Teacher program evaluations and principal performance evaluations. Analysis: z-tests and t-tests.	There were significant differences between college-based teacher education programs and Alternative 4 programs across 27 measures, all but one favoring the college-based programs.	Traditional vs. alternative programs

TABLE 11.1
(Continued)

Studies[a]	Question and Focus	Research Tradition and Research Context	Research Design	Findings	Program Structure
Kennedy, M. M. (1998)	How do preservice teachers learn to teach writing to diverse learners? How do preservice teachers' ideas about teaching change through their program?	Case study: Seven preservice programs: one 5-year program, four 4-year programs, and 2 alternative certification programs connected to a liberal arts college, research university, historic teacher education institution turned multipurpose university, historically Black university, urban school district, and state department of education.	$N = 7$ institutions. Data sources = Faculty surveys and interviews; document review; observations in campus classes and in clinical practice in schools; teacher education student surveys and interviews; observations of student teachers in field placements. Analysis = varied quantitative and qualitative	The substance of a teacher education program rather than its structure is the most important consideration in impacting teacher education students. In some cases, teacher education programs influenced students by changing students' views toward ideas emphasized in the program, whereas in other cases, programs recruited students who already shared ideas that the program emphasized. Fundamental changes in teachers' beliefs were associated with teachers having a chance to consider why new practices are better to conventional approaches; being able to see examples of the new practices; being able to experience these practices firsthand as learners; and having	Characteristics of effective teacher education programs

Source	Research Question	Method/Sample	Findings	Category
			on-site support to implement the new practices.	
Knight, S. B., Owens, E. W., & Waxman, H. C. (1991)	How do students perceive the learning environments of classes taught by traditionally certified teachers compared with the classes of alternatively certified teachers?	Survey: Elementary and middle school students in public school districts in and around a large Southwestern city.	$N = 676$ elementary and middle school students; $N = 24$ teachers. Data sources = Adapted version of *My Class Inventory* (Fisher & Fraser, 1981) with 43 items. Analysis = Descriptive statistics; MANOVA.	Students in classes taught by traditionally certified teachers perceived significantly more instruction and opportunities to engage in higher thought processes; more appropriate pacing of classwork; more group cohesiveness; more group cooperation; and significantly less friction among students than students in classes taught by alternatively certified teachers.	Traditional vs. alternative programs
Laczko-Kerr, I. & Berliner, D. C., (2002)	Do students of "TFA" teachers (i.e., undercertified teachers) learn as much or achieve as well as students taught by fully certified teachers?	"Ex-post-facto Archival Research Design:" Fully certified teachers and "TFA" teachers in 5 urban Arizona school districts.	$N = 109$ matched pairs of teachers. Data sources = Stanford Achievement Test scores, school district data on teacher certification status. Analysis = correlated t-tests on student test scores; ANOVA for matching analysis.	In reading, mathematics, and language arts, students of fully certified teachers performed better on achievement tests than students of TFA teachers. "Students of undercertified teachers make about 20% less academic growth per year than do students of teachers with regular certification."	Traditional vs. alternative programs

(Continued)

TABLE 11.1
(Continued)

Studies[a]	Question and Focus	Research Tradition and Research Context	Research Design	Findings	Program Structure
Lutz, F. W., & Hutton, J. B. (1989)	How do AC interns compare to traditionally certified teachers? What is the teaching performance of AC interns?	Mixed Methods: Alternative certification program in the Dallas, TX, Independent School District.	$N = 110$ AC interns; $N = 62$ first-year teachers. Data sources = questionnaire; Teacher Work-Life Inventory; Teacher Concerns Checklist; Organizational Climate Description Questionnaire; Teacher Expectation Scale; Texas Teacher Appraisal System; ExCET exam; Teacher Advisor Comparison Rating Form; surveys. Analysis = chi-square, t-tests.	The AC interns did as well as 1st-year teachers on almost every indicator. AC interns earned performance ratings that were as high or higher than 1st-year teachers, and scored as high or higher on standardized measures of teaching ability and performance.	Traditional vs. alternative programs
Mantle-Bromley, C., Gould, L. M., McWhorter, B. A., & Whaley, D. C. (2000)	What is the impact of program structure on new teachers' employment and program satisfaction?	Survey: Graduates of "Project Promise," a 1-year master's-level certification program for secondary teachers, graduates of the regular undergraduate teacher education program, and graduates of the Professional Development School program at "a large land-grant, Carnegie I research institution in the intermountain west."	$N = 79$ traditional program graduates; $N = 37$ "Project Promise" graduates; $N = 36$ PDS graduates. Data sources = telephone survey (36 questions). Analysis = ANOVA; chi-square; descriptive statistics.	Project Promise graduates had significantly greater retention rates than the undergraduate program graduates. Project Promise graduates rated their preparation significantly higher than did traditional program graduates in all areas but one, and Project Promise graduates also gave significantly higher ratings to their preparation than did graduates of the PDS program in 2 areas.	Traditional vs. alternative programs

Source	Research Question	Method and Sample	Findings	Focus
Miller, J. W., McKenna, M. C., & McKenna, B. A. (1998)	How are teaching practices and perceptions of practice different between AC and TC teachers? How are the achievement results of students in AC and TC teachers' classrooms different?	Mixed Methods: Middle-level Alternative Certification program at a Georgia university and traditionally certified teachers from varied institutions in and out of Georgia.	$N = 41$ AC teachers; $N = 41$ TC teachers; $N = 18$ classrooms of students for test score analysis. Data sources = classroom observations (15-item rating scale), interviews, student achievement test scores (Iowa Test of Basic Skills). Analysis = MANOVA; content analysis of interviews.	There were no significant differences in teaching behavior, perceptions of teaching abilities, and student achievement between AC and TC teachers.	Traditional vs. alternative programs
National Center for Research on Teacher Education. (1991)	How do preservice teachers learn to teach mathematics and English to diverse learners? How do preservice teachers' ideas about teaching change through their program?	Case study: Seven preservice programs: one 5-year program, four 4-year programs, and two alternative certification programs connected to a liberal arts college, research university, historic teacher education institution turned multipurpose university, historically Black university, urban school district, and state department of education.	$N = 7$ institutions. Data sources = Faculty surveys and interviews; document review; observations in campus classes and in clinical practice in schools; teacher education student surveys and interviews; observations of student teachers in field placements. Analysis = varied quantitative and qualitative	The substance of a teacher education program rather than its structure is the most important consideration in impacting teacher education students. In some cases, teacher education programs influenced students by changing students' views toward ideas emphasized in the program, whereas in other cases, programs recruited students who already shared ideas that the program emphasized. Fundamental changes in teachers' beliefs were associated with teachers	Characteristics of effective teacher education programs

(Continued)

TABLE 11.1
(Continued)

Studies[a]	Question and Focus	Research Tradition and Research Context	Research Design	Findings	Program Structure
				having a chance to consider why new practices are better to conventional approaches; being able to see examples of the new practices; being able to experience these practices firsthand as learners; and having on-site support to implement the new practices.	
Natriello, G., & Zumwalt, K. (1992)	How do alternate route programs, such as the Provisional Teacher Program in New Jersey, address 4 challenges: maintaining and enhancing the quality of people entering teaching, meeting staffing needs of certain schools, contributing to efforts to professionalize teaching, and retaining teachers?	Survey: Participants in New Jersey college-based teacher education programs in secondary English and math and elementary education; participants in the Provisional Teacher Program in New Jersey.	$N = 121$ elementary, 36 secondary English, and 30 secondary math college-based teacher education program completers; $N = 75$ elementary, 24 secondary English, and 30 secondary math Provisional Teacher Program completers. Data sources = Initial survey, tracking surveys, and follow-up surveys over 3 years. Analysis = Comparison of survey responses related to recruitment, placement, and retention.	Alternate route teachers were more likely to be teaching in low-SES urban districts and in middle grades than college-prepared teachers. Retention data showed little difference between alternate route and college-prepared teachers, but a significantly lower proportion of alternate route math teachers expressed long-range interest in staying in teaching and a significantly lower percentage of the alternate route math	Traditional vs. alternative programs

Natriello, G. & Zumwalt, K. (1993)	What potential do alternate route preparation and certification programs, such as the Provisional Teacher Program in New Jersey, hold for meeting the needs of urban schools?	Survey: Participants in New Jersey college-based teacher education programs in secondary English and math and elementary education; participants in the Provisional Teacher Program in New Jersey.	$N = 121$ elementary, 36 secondary English, and 30 secondary math college-based teacher education program completers; $N = 75$ elementary, 24 secondary English, and 30 secondary math Provisional Teacher Program completers. Data sources = Initial survey, tracking surveys, and follow-up surveys over 3 years. Analysis = Comparison of survey responses related to staffing in urban schools.	teachers actually stayed in teaching over 3 years. Alternate route teachers were more likely to prefer teaching in urban settings, prefer teaching disadvantaged students, and be working in urban districts in their first year of teaching than college-prepared teachers.	Traditional vs. alternative programs
Paccione, A. V., McWhorter, B. A., & Richburg, R. W. (2000)	How do "Project Promise" graduates compare to traditional education program graduates in terms of entry into teaching, retention, ratings of program satisfaction, and principal ratings?	Survey: Graduates of "Project Promise," a 1-year master's level certification program for secondary teachers, graduates of the regular undergraduate teacher education program, and graduates of the Professional Development School program at Colorado State University.	$N = 36$ Project Promise completers; $N = 78$ graduates of traditional program; $N = 36$ graduates of PDS program; $N = 16$ principals. Data sources = Likert-scale questionnaires; "data from both programs"; 28-item principal questionnaire. Analysis = NOVA.	Graduates of the "Project Promise" program were working in schools and remained in teaching at significantly higher rates than graduates of the traditional program. "Project Promise" graduates also were significantly more satisfied with their preparation and earned higher principal ratings than graduates of traditional programs.	Traditional vs. alternative programs

(Continued)

TABLE 11.1
(Continued)

Studies[a]	Question and Focus	Research Tradition and Research Context	Research Design	Findings	Program Structure
Raymond, M., Fletcher, S. H., & Luque, J. (2001)	How do the performance and retention rates of TFA teachers compare to performance and retention rates of non-TFA teachers?	Econometric Analysis: All Grades 3–8 teachers in the Houston, TX, School District from 1996 to 2000 and their students; all grads 3-8 1st- or 2nd-year teachers in the district from 1996 to 2000 and their students.	N = 36 TFA and 330 non-TFA new teachers in 1996; 20 TFA and 293 non-TFA new teachers in 1997; 21 TFA and 334 non-TFA new teachers in 1998; 19 TFA and 395 non-TFA new teachers in 1999; 21 TFA and 333 non-TFA new teachers in 2000. N = 80, 608 students in elementary reading TFA vs. all teacher comparison; 11,107 students in elementary reading TFA vs. new teacher comparison; 81,814 students in elementary math TFA vs. all teacher comparison; 11,321 students in elementary math TFA vs. new teacher comparison. N = 132, 021 students in middle school reading TFA vs. all teacher comparison; 11,347 students in middle school reading TFA vs. new teacher comparison; 96,276 students in middle school math TFA vs. all teacher comparison; 19,494 students in middle school math TFA vs. new teacher comparison.	TFA teachers left the profession after 1 year at a lower rate than non-TFA teachers. After 2 years, TFA teachers left the profession at a higher rate than non-TFA teachers. The effect of having a TFA teacher relative to student achievement was always positive, though this effect was not always statistically significant. There is less variation in quality among TFA teachers than among non-TFA teachers except new middle school math teachers to which TFA teachers were equivalent.	Traditional vs. alternative programs

Study	Research question	Sample/data sources	Findings	Focus
Raymond, M., & Fletcher, S. (2002)	See Raymond et al. (2001)	Data sources = student characteristics (school attended; school year; minority status; free and reduced lunch eligibility; birth date; teacher; English language proficiency; testing exemption status; Texas Assessment of Academic Skills (TAAS) test scores); teacher characteristics (academic degree; certification status; ExCET test scores; years of teaching experience, grade taught; school assignment); TFA status; student scores on TAAS Analysis = Tabular summaries; regression analysis; econometric analysis	See Raymond et al. (2001)	Traditional vs. alternative programs
Sandlin, R. A., Young, B. L., & Karge, B. D. (1992)	What differences, if any, exist between beginning teachers and intern teachers during their 1st-years of teaching in the elementary classroom?	Survey: California State University campus alternatively and traditionally certified teachers. $N = 58$ AC teachers; $N = 66$ 1st-year teachers. Data sources = Teacher Evaluation Scale; Teacher Concern Survey; telephone interviews. Analysis = ANOVA, MANOVA.	At the end of the teachers' 1st-year, there were no apparent differences in the classrooms of alternatively and traditionally prepared beginning teachers.	Traditional vs. alternative programs

(Continued)

TABLE 11.1
(Continued)

Studies[a]	Question and Focus	Research Tradition and Research Context	Research Design	Findings	Program Structure
Shannon, I. L. (1990)	How satisfied are graduates of Virginia Wesleyan College's alternative route with the quality of their program? How do school administrators and external evaluators evaluate program graduates?	Survey: Graduates of Virginia Wesleyan College alternative route program for career switchers.	$N = 36$ program graduate survey respondents; 15 administrator respondents. Data sources = Candidate satisfaction survey; administrator questionnaire. Analysis = analysis of survey responses, descriptive statistics.	All graduates rated their preparation in 9 teaching competencies as good or excellent. Fourteen of 15 administrators rated the graduates' teaching performance as excellent or good in all of the teaching competencies. The additional administrator rated the teacher fair in classroom management but excellent or good in all other competencies.	Traditional vs. alternative programs
Shen, J. (1997)	How do the characteristics of TC and AC teachers in public schools compare along the dimensions of intent to stay in teaching and intent to become teachers if starting over again?	Survey: Nationally representative sample of public school teachers.	$N = 13,602$ traditionally certified teachers; $N = 1,119$ alternatively certified teachers. Data sources = SASS 1993–1994. Analysis = descriptive statistics.	A lower percentage of AC teachers reported that they planned to teach until retirement, and a higher percentage of AC teachers were undecided about remaining in teaching. There was no difference between the AC and TC teachers in their intent to become teachers if starting over again.	Traditional vs. alternative programs

| Stoddart, T. (1990) | "How effective is an alternative route to teacher certification in recruiting academically qualified individuals to teach in urban schools? What kind of professional education is provided by an alternative route to teacher certification? How do teachers in the alternative route program compare to university-educated teachers?" | Mixed Methods: Los Angeles Unified School District Intern Program and national samples of traditional teacher education programs. | $N = 1, 100$ interns (attrition rates); N for other comparisons not specified. Data sources = data (including interviews and tape recordings of teacher education classes) from (TELT) study of National Center for Research on Teacher Learning at Michigan State University; LAUSD Personnel Division demographic data; AACTE RATE III study; National Center for Educational Statistics data. Analysis = descriptive statistics; other analysis not specified. | In one cohort of LAUSD interns, there was a lower attrition rate in the first 3 years of teaching than national rates would predict. The alternative program was not as rigorous as traditional university-based programs. LAUSD interns hold higher expectations for low-income and minority students than a national sample of teachers enrolled in traditional teacher education programs do. | Traditional vs. alternative programs |

(Continued)

TABLE 11.1
(Continued)

Studies[a]	Question and Focus	Research Tradition and Research Context	Research Design	Findings	Program Structure
Stoddart, T. (1993)	How do 1st-year alternative route math and English interns compare to traditionally prepared 1st-year math and English teachers in terms of beliefs about urban education and interactions with students?	Mixed Methods: Alternative route interns from a school-district-based program in the western United States, graduates from 5th-year university-based program in the Southeast, and graduates from 4-year university-based program in the Midwest.	$N = 19$ alternative route English interns; $N = 37$ alternative route math interns; $N = 26$ English university-based program graduates; $N = 22$ math university-based program graduates. Data sources = TELT study of National Center for Research on Teacher Learning at Michigan State University (questionnaire, semi-structured interviews, classroom observations) Analysis = descriptive statistics; analytic induction of interview and observation transcriptions.	Alternative route teachers hold higher expectations for low-income and minority students than do graduates of traditional programs. Alternative route teachers are more likely than traditional program graduates to attribute student failure to teachers rather than students.	Traditional vs. alternative programs

[a] Please see References.

730

REFERENCES

Adelman, N. (1986). *An exploratory study of teacher alternative certification and retraining programs.* Washington, DC: U.S. Department of Education.

Andrew, M. D. (1990). Differences between graduates of 4-year and 5-year teacher preparation programs. *Journal of Teacher Education, 41*(2), 45–51.

Andrew, M. D., & Schwab, R. L. (1995). Has reform in teacher education influenced teacher performance? An outcome assessment of graduates of an eleven-university consortium. *Action in Teacher Education, 17*(3), 43–53.

Baker, T. E. (1993). A survey of four-year and five-year program graduates and their principals. *Southern Regional Association of Teacher Education Journal, 2*(2), 28–33.

Bliss, T. (1990). Alternate certification in Connecticut: Reshaping the profession. *Peabody Journal of Education, 67*(3), 35–54.

Boser, J. A., & Wiley, P. D. (1988). An alternative teacher preparation program: Is the promise fulfilled? *Peabody Journal of Education, 65,* 130–142.

Breidenstein, A. (2002). Examining the outcomes of four-year and extended teacher education programs. *Teacher Education and Practice, 15*(3), 12–43.

Coley, R. J., & Thorpe, M. E. (1986). *A look at the MAT model of teacher education and its graduates: Lessons for today.* Princeton, NJ: Educational Testing Service.

Darling-Hammond, L. (2000). *Studies of excellence in teacher education.* New York: National Commission on Teaching and America's Future.

Darling-Hammond, L., Chung, R., & Frelow, F. (2002). Variation in teacher preparation: How well do different pathways prepare teachers to teach? *Journal of Teacher Education, 53*(4), 286–302.

Decker, P., Mayer, D., & Glazerman, S. (2004, June). *The effects of Teach for America on students: Findings from a national evaluation.* Princeton, NJ: Mathematica Policy Research Inc.

Gomez, M. L., & Stoddart, T. (1992). Personal perspectives and learning to teach writing. In R. T. Clift & C. M. Evertson (Eds.), *Focal points: Qualitative inquiries into teaching and teacher education.* Washington, DC: ERIC Clearinghouse on Teacher Education.

Goodlad, J. (1990). *Teachers for our nation's schools.* San Francisco: Jossey-Bass.

Goodlad, J. (1994). *Educational renewal: Better teachers, better schools.* San Francisco: Jossey-Bass.

Guyton, E., Fox, M. C., & Sisk, K. A. (1991). Comparison of teaching attitudes, teacher efficacy, and teacher performance of first year teachers prepared by alternative and traditional teacher education programs. *Action in Teacher Education, 13*(2), 1–9.

Haberman, M. (1999). Increasing the number of high-quality African American teachers in urban schools. *Journal of Instructional Psychology, 26*(4), 208–12.

Hawk, P., & Schmidt, M. W. (1989). Teacher preparation: A comparison of traditional and alternative programs. *Journal of Teacher Education, 40*(5), 53–58.

Houston, W. R., Marshall, F., & McDavid, T. (1993). Problems of traditionally prepared and alternatively certified first-year teachers. *Education and Urban Society, 26*(1), 78–89.

Howey, K. R., & Zimpher, N. L. (1989). *Profiles of preservice teacher education: Inquiry into the nature of programs.* Albany, NY: State University of New York Press.

Hutton, J. B., Lutz, F. W., & Williamson, J. L. (1990). Characteristics, attitudes, and performance of alternative certification interns. *Educational Research Quarterly, 14*(1), 38–48.

Jelmberg, J. (1996). College-based teacher education versus state-sponsored alternative programs. *Journal of Teacher Education, 47*(1), 60–66.

Kennedy, M. M. (1998). *Learning to teach writing: Does teacher education make a difference?* New York: Teachers College Press.

Knight, S. B., Owens, E. W., & Waxman, H. C. (1991). Comparing the classroom learning environments of traditionally and alternatively certified teachers. *Action in Teacher Education, 12*(4), 29–34.

Laczko-Kerr, I., & Berliner, D. C. (2002). The effectiveness of "Teach for America" and other under-certified teachers on student academic achievement: A case of harmful public policy. *Education Policy Analysis Archives, 10*(37). Retrieved March 23, 2003, from http://epaa.asu.edu/epaa/v10n37/

Lutz, F. W., & Hutton, J. B. (1989). Alternative teacher certification: Its policy implications for classroom and personnel practice. *Educational Evaluation and Policy Analysis, 11*(3), 237–254.

Mantle-Bromley, C., Gould, L. M., McWhorter, B. A., & Whaley, D. C. (2000). The effect of program structure on new teachers' employment and program satisfaction patterns. *Action in Teacher Education, 22*(1), 1–14.

Miller, J. W., McKenna, M. C., & McKenna, B. A. (1998). A comparison of alternatively and traditionally prepared teachers. *Journal of Teacher Education, 49*(3), 165–176.

National Center for Research on Teacher Education. (1991). *Findings from the Teacher Education and Learning to Teach study.* East Lansing, MI: The National Center for Research on Teacher Learning.

Natriello, G., & Zumwalt, K. (1992). Challenges to an alternative route for teacher education. In A. Lieberman (Ed.), *The changing contexts of teaching.* Chicago, IL: The University of Chicago Press.

Natriello, G., & Zumwalt, K. (1993). New teachers for urban schools? The contribution of the provisional teacher program in New Jersey. *Education and Urban Society, 26*(1), 49–62.

Paccione, A. V., McWhorter, B. A., & Richburg, R. W. (2000). Ten years on the fast track: Effective teacher preparation for nontraditional candidates. In D. J. McIntyre & D. M. Byrd (Eds.), *Research on effective models for teacher education.* Thousand Oaks, CA: Corwin Press.

Raymond, M., & Fletcher, S. (2002). The Teach for America evaluation. *Education Next, 2*(1), 62–69.

Raymond, M., Fletcher, S. H., & Luque, J. (2001). *Teach for America: An evaluation of teacher differences and student outcomes in Houston, Texas.* Stanford, CA: Center for Research on Education Outcomes.

Sandlin, R. A., Young, B. L., & Karge, B. D. (1992). Regularly and alternatively credentialed beginning teachers: Comparison and contrast of their development. *Action in Teacher Education, 14*(4), 16–23.

Shannon, I. L. (1990). ASEP—An alternative certification program for career switchers that works. *Action in Teacher Education, 12*(2), 38–42.

Shen, J. (1997). Has the alternative certification policy materialized its promise? A comparison between traditionally and alternatively certified teachers in public schools. *Educational Evaluation and Policy Analysis, 19*(3), 276–283.

Stoddart, T. (1990). Los Angeles Unified School District Intern Program: Recruiting and preparing teachers for an urban context. *Peabody Journal of Education, 67*(3), 84–122.

Stoddart, T. (1993). Who is prepared to teach in urban schools? *Education and Urban Society, 26*(1), 29–48.

REFERENCES: OTHER SOURCES CITED

Adelman, N. (1986). *An exploratory study of teacher and alternative certification and retraining programs.* Washington, DC: U.S. Department of Education.

Allen, M. (2003, April). *Eight questions on teacher preparation: What does the research say?* Denver: Education Commission of the States.

American Association of Colleges for Teacher Education. (1982, February). *Taskforce report on extended programs.* Washington, DC: Author.

American Educational Research Association. (1997). *The promise of alternative certification: Has it materialized?* Washington, DC: Author.

Arends, R., & Winitzky, N. (1996). Program structures and learning to teach. In F. Murray (Ed.), *The teacher educator handbook* (pp. 526–556). San Francisco: Jossey-Bass.

Ashton, P., & Webb, R. B. (1986). *Making a difference: Teachers' sense of efficacy and student achievement.* New York: Longman.

Ballou , D. (1998). Alternative certification: A comment. *Educational Evaluation & Policy Analysis,* 20(4), 313–315.

Barnes, H. (1987). The conceptual basis for thematic teacher education programs. *Journal of Teacher Education, 38*(4), 13–18.

Berry, B. (2000). Quality alternatives in teacher education: Dodging the "silver bullet" and doing what's right for students. *The State Education Standard, 1*(2), 21–25.

Boyd, D., Grossman, P., Lankford, H., Loeb, S., & Wyckoff, J. (2003a, July). *Examining teacher preparation: Does the pathway make a difference?* Retrieved March 15, 2004, from http://www.teacherpolicyresearch.org

Boyd, D., Lankford, H., Loeb, S., & Wyckoff, J. (2003b, March). *The draw of home: How teachers' preferences for proximity disadvantage urban schools.* Retrieved March 15, 2004, from http://teacherpolicyresearch.org

Carnegie Forum on Education and the Economy, Task Force on Teaching as a Profession. (1986). *A nation prepared: Teachers for the 21st century.* New York: Author.

Coley, R., & Thorpe, M. (1986). *A look at the MAT model of teacher education and its graduates: Lessons for today.* Princeton, NJ: Educational Testing Service.

Conant, J. (1963). *The education of American teachers.* New York: McGraw-Hill.

Cochran-Smith, M., & Fries, M. K. (2001). Sticks, stones, and ideology: The discourse of reform in teacher education. *Educational Researcher, 30*(8), 3–15.

Darling-Hammond, L. (1990). Teaching and knowledge: Policy issues posed by alternative certification for teachers. *Peabody Journal of Education, 67*(3), 123–154.

Darling-Hammond, L. (2000). *Studies of excellence in teacher education* (3 volumes). Washington, DC: American Association of Colleges for Teacher Education.

Denemark, G., & Nutter, N. (1984). The case for extended programs of initial teacher preparation. In L. Katz & J. Raths (Eds.), *Advances in teacher education* (Vol. 1, pp. 203–246). Norwood, NJ: Able.

Dill, V. (1996). Alternative teacher certification. In J. Sikula (Ed.), *Handbook of research on teacher education* (2nd ed., pp. 932–960). New York: Macmillan.

Education Week. (2003). *Quality counts: If I can't learn from you. Ensuring a highly qualified teacher for every classroom.* Bethesda, MD: Author.

Evenden, E. S. (1933). *National survey of the education of teachers* (6 volumes). Washington, DC: U.S. Office of Education, Department of the Interior.

Evertson, C., Hawley, W. D., & Zlotnick, M. (1985). Making a difference in educational quality through teacher education. *Journal of Teacher Education, 36*(13), 2–12

Feiman-Nemser, S. (1990). Teacher education: Structural and conceptual alternatives. In W. R. Houston (Ed.), *Handbook of research on teacher education* (pp. 212–223). New York: Macmillan.

Feiman-Nemser S., & Remillard, J. (1996). Perspectives on learning to teach. In F. Murray (Ed.), *The teacher educator's handbook* (pp. 63–91). San Francisco: Jossey-Bass.

Feistritzer, E. (1999). *The making of a teacher.* Washington, DC: Center for Educational Information.

Feistritzer, E., & Chester, D. T. (2003). *Alternative certification: A state by state analysis:* 2003. Washington, DC: National Center for Educational Information.

Fenstermacher, G. (1990). The place of alternative certification in the education of teachers. *Peabody Journal of Education, 67*(3), 155–185.

Fisher, D. L., & Frasier, B. F. (1981). Validity and use of My Class Inventory. *Science Education, 65,* 145–156.

Fraser, B. J. (1986). *Classroom environment.* London: Croom Helm.

Gueron, J. (2002). The politics of random assignment: Implementing studies and affecting policy. In F. Mosteller & R. Boruch (Eds.), *Evidence matters: Randomized trials in education research.* Washington, DC: Brookings Institution Press.

Hawley, W. D. (1987). The high costs and doubtful efficacy of extended teacher preparation programs. *American Journal of Education, 95,* 275–313.

Hawley, W. D. (1990). The theory and practice of alternative certification: Implications for the improvement of teaching. *Peabody Journal of Education,* 67(3), 3–34.

Hawthorne Educational Services. (1990). *The teacher evaluation scale*. Columbia, MO: Author.

Holmes Group. (1986). *Tomorrow's teachers*. East Lansing, MI: Author.

Houston, W. R. (Ed.). (1990). *Handbook of research on teacher education*. New York: Macmillan.

Howey, K., & Zimpher, N. (1989). *Profiles of preservice teacher education: Inquiry into the nature of programs*. Albany, NY: SUNY Press.

Howsam, R., Corrigan, D., Denemark, G., & Nash, R. (1976). *Educating a profession*. Washington, DC: American Association of Colleges for Teacher Education.

Hughes, R., & Hukill, H. (1982, July). *Participant characteristics, change and outcomes in preservice clinical teacher education*. Austin, TX: Research and Development Center for Teacher Education. (ERIC Document Reproduction Service No. ED240096).

Humphrey, D., Wechsler, M., Bosetti, K., Wayne, A., & Adelman, N. (2002, October). *Alternative certification: Design for a national study*. Menlo Park, CA: SRI.

Joyce, B., & Clift, R. (1984). The Phoenix agenda: Essential reform in teacher education. *Educational Researcher, 13*(4), 5–18.

Katz, L., Raths, J., Mohanty, C., Kurachi, A., & Irving, J. (1981). Follow-up studies: Are they worth the trouble? *Journal of Teacher Education, 32*(2), 18–24.

Kennedy, M. (1998). *Learning to teach writing: Does teacher education make a difference?* New York: Teachers College Press.

Kennedy, M. (1999). The problem of evidence in teacher education. In R. Roth (Ed.), *The role of the university in the preparation of teachers* (pp. 87–107). London: Falmer Press.

Kennedy, M., Ball, D., & McDiarmid, G. W. (1993). *A study package for examining and tracking changes in teachers' knowledge*. TS-93-1. East Lansing, MI: National Center for Research on Teacher Learning.

Kliebard, H. (1973). The question in teacher education. In D. McCarty & Associates (Eds.), *New perspectives on teacher education* (pp. 8–24). San Francisco: Jossey-Bass.

Lanier, J., & Little, J. W. (1986). Research on teacher education. In M. Wittrock (Ed.), *Handbook of research on teaching* (3rd ed., pp. 527–569). New York: Macmillan.

Liston, D., & Zeichner, K. (1991). *Teacher education and the social conditions of schooling*. New York: Routledge.

Mayer, D., Decker, P., Glazerman, S., & Silva, T. (2003, April). *Identifying alternative certification programs for an impact on teacher preparation*. Cambridge, MA: Mathematica Policy Research Inc.

Mehlinger, H. (1986). A risky venture. *Kappan, 67*, 33–36.

Murnane, R., Singer, J., Willett, J., Kempe, J., & Olsen, R. (1991). *Who will teach? Policies that matter*. Cambridge, MA: Harvard University Press.

National Center for Research on Teacher Education. (1991). *Findings from the Teacher Education and Learning to Teach Study*. East Lansing, MI: National Center for Research on Teacher Education.

Natriello, G., & Zumwalt, K. (1993). New teachers for urban schools? The contribution of the provisional teacher program in New Jersey. *Education and Urban Society, 26*(1), 49–62

Oakes, J. (1996). Making the rhetoric real. *National Association of Multicultural Education Journal, 4*(2), 4–10.

Rice, J. K. (2003). *Teacher quality: Understanding the effectiveness of teacher attributes*. Washington, DC: Economic Policy Institute.

Roach, V., & Cohen, B. (2002). *Moving past the politics: How alternative certification can promote comprehensive teacher development reforms*. Alexandria, VA: National Association of State Boards of Education.

Scannell, D. P. (1986). Extending teacher preparation programs. In E.C. Gallegos (Ed.), *Improving teacher education* (pp. 17–26). San Francisco: Jossey-Bass.

Sikula, J. (Ed.). (1996). *Handbook of research on teacher education* (2nd ed.) New York: Macmillan.

Sirotnik, K., & Associates. (2001). *Renewing schools and teacher education*. Washington, DC: American Association of Colleges for Teacher Education.

Smith, B. O. (1980). *A design for a school of pedagogy*. Washington, DC: U.S. Department of Education.

Snyder, J. (2000). Knowing the children—Understanding the teaching: The Developmental Teacher Education Program at the University of California-Berkeley. In L. Darling-Hammond (Ed.), *Studies of excellence in teacher education: Preparation at the graduate level* (pp. 97–172). Washington, DC: American Association of Colleges for Teacher Education.

Stevens, C. J., & Dial, M. (1993). A qualitative study of alternatively certified teachers. *Education and Urban Society, 26*(1), 63–77.

Stoddart, P., & Floden, R. (1996). Traditional and alternative routes to certification: Issues, assumptions, and misconceptions. In K. Zeichner, S. Melnick, & M. L. Gomez (Eds.), *Currents of reform in preservice teacher education* (pp. 80–108). New York: Teachers College Press.

Stone, J. (1968). *Breakthrough in teacher education.* San Francisco: Jossey-Bass.

Strang, H. R., Badt, K. S., & Kauffman, J. M. (1997). Micro-computer based simulations for training fundamental teaching skills. *Journal of Teacher Education, 38*(1), 20–26.

Texas Education Agency. (1986, May). *Appraisal queries get answers. Direct line: A Texas Education Agency Report to Teachers.* Austin: Texas Education Agency.

Tom, A. (1987). A critique of the rationale for extended teacher preparation. *Educational Policy, 1*(1), 43–56.

Tom, A. (1997). *Redesigning teacher education.* Albany, NY: SUNY Press.

Travers, E., & Sacks, S. (1987, February). *Teacher education and the liberal arts.* Swarthmore, PA: Consortium for Excellence in Teacher Education.

Von Schlichten, E. W. (1958). Idea and practice of a fifth-year requirement for teacher certification. *Teachers College Record, 60*(1), 41–53.

Wang, A., Coleman, A., Coley, R., & Phelps, R. (2003). *Preparing teachers around the world.* Princeton, NJ: Educational Testing Service.

Wasley, P., & McDiarmid, G. W. (2003, July). *Tying the assessment of new teachers to student learning and teacher preparation.* Paper presented at a meeting of The National Commission on Teaching and America's Future, Denver, CO.

Weinstein, C. (1989). Case studies of extended teacher preparation. In A. Woolfolk (Ed.), *Research perspectives on the graduate preparation of teachers* (pp. 30–50). Englewood Cliffs, NJ: Prentice Hall.

Wideen, M., Mayer-Smith, J., & Moon, B. (1998). A critical analysis of learning to teach: Making the case for an ecological perspective on inquiry. *Review of Educational Research, 66*(2), 130–178.

Wilcox, S. K., Schram, P., Lappan, G., & Lanier, P. (1991). *The role of a learning community in changing preservice teachers' knowledge and beliefs about mathematics education.* Research Report 991. East Lansing, MI: National Center for Research on Teacher Education.

Wilson, S., Floden, R., & Ferrini Mundy, J. (2001). *Teacher preparation research: Current knowledge, gaps, and recommendations.* Seattle: University of Washington Center for the Study of Teaching and Policy.

Winetrout, K. (1963). In defense of the four-year program of teacher education. *Phi Delta Kappan, 44*(4), 183–184.

Zeichner, K. (1989). Learning from experience in graduate teacher education. In A. Woolfolk (Ed.), *Research perspectives on the graduate preparation of teachers* (pp. 12–29). Englewood Cliffs, NJ: Prentice Hall.

Zeichner, K. (1993). Traditions of practice in North American teacher education. *Teaching and Teacher Education, 9*(1), 1–13.

Zeichner, K. (2003). The adequacies and inadequacies of three current strategies to recruit, prepare and retain the best teachers for all students. *Teachers College Record, 105*(3), 490–515.

Zeichner, K., & Schulte, A. (2001). What we know and don't know from peer-reviewed research about alternative teacher certification programs. *Journal of Teacher Education, 52*(4), 266–282.

Zeichner, K., & Tabachnick, B. R. (1981). Are the effects of university teacher education washed out by school experience? *Journal of Teacher Education, 32,* 7–11.

12

A Research Agenda for Teacher Education

Kenneth M. Zeichner
University of Wisconsin-Madison

This chapter looks across the preceding chapters that reviewed the empirical research on selected topics concerning preservice teacher education in the United States and suggests a research agenda for the field that seeks to overcome some of the major limitations in the existing research and build on promising lines of work. It also discusses the conditions needed to support the implementation of this research agenda. I begin by reviewing the charge to the panel and the general direction of our recommendations. After reviewing some the limitations in our work, I offer a research agenda that we the panel believe addresses the research designs, methodologies, and topics that offer promise to raise the quality of research in the field.

THE WORK OF THE PANEL

At the onset, let me reiterate several important points about the work of the panel and our views of the relationship between educational research and teacher education policy and practice. First, a central element of our deliberations has been a vigorous effort to maintain neutrality on the highly visible and intense debates about teacher education and teacher quality that have occurred during the 4 years of our work. Throughout internal and external reviews of each chapter as well as the volume as a whole, we gave priority to producing a rigorous and evenhanded analysis of peer-reviewed research on questions of critical importance to preservice teacher education in the United States. Our work has focused on analyzing the empirical research on the relationships between aspects of teacher education and teacher education policies and different outcomes: teacher recruitment and retention, teachers' own learning, teachers' practices, and student learning.

Consistent with the diverse disciplinary and methodological perspectives represented on the panel, we also took pains to present an analysis of research and proposals for improving research that draw on and benefit from a variety of methodological approaches including research conducted by teacher educators on their own practices and programs. We recognize that particular research approaches have different strengths and drawbacks; we sought to evaluate the research included in this review according to criteria for rigor appropriate for particular research genres. We recommend attention to the full variety of research approaches available; we rule out no approaches *a priori*. The main issue in our view is to develop a research program in teacher education that can address the variety of questions that investigators seek to answer about teacher education and its connections to various kinds of outcomes of importance to society.

We believe that a multidisciplinary and multimethodological research approach to studying problems in teacher education is needed because the range of questions that are practically and theoretically important can best be answered by using a comparable range of framing concepts and research designs. Individual questions and problems call for different research approaches, and the portfolio of studies that we have proposed in this volume lend themselves to study through different and complementary disciplinary and methodological approaches. We agree with Florio Ruane's (2002) assertion about the importance of looking both within and outside of the areas illuminated by a single approach to research.

The implementation of the research agenda that we suggest will require greater resources than have ever been available for teacher education research. These resources should come from new investments in teacher education research and from the reallocation of existing resources. More money for research in teacher education, however, will not automatically result in better research. These additional resources need to be targeted to the study of particular questions and issues and to studies that employ methodologies capable of dealing with the complexity of what is being studied, and that result in credible and persuasive evidence and deeper understanding. Given the importance of teacher quality in the current discourse on educational reform in the United States, and the need for sound evidence, a well-financed program of strong teacher education research is urgently needed.

LIMITATIONS IN OUR WORK AND OF RESEARCH

The analyses presented in this volume have several major limitations. For example, although we focused on empirical research related to several topics we felt are important to preservice teacher education, we recognize that some important research has not been included within the scope of our work. This includes conceptual, historical, and comparative scholarship on preservice teacher education and all kinds of research conducted on preservice teacher education outside of the United States. Limiting our focus to U.S. empirical studies on certain topics does not imply that these other kinds of scholarship on teacher education are unimportant.

Also, as mentioned in the introduction to this volume, although we believe that empirical research can make important contributions to practice and policy in teacher education, we also believe that decisions about policy and practice are mediated by moral, ethical, and political considerations and that practice in teaching and teacher education as in other fields is inherently complex. Research can help us think about teacher education in more useful ways and can offer guidance as to practices effective in accomplishing particular goals, but it cannot tell us everything to do in teacher education programs or in the policy arena. Schon (1984) has described the dynamic and uncertain nature of practice and the limits of research in framing and solving the problems of practice in fields outside teaching including engineering meteorology, and psychotherapy. Gawande's (2002, p. 7), reflections on the state of scientific research in medicine reinforce our view about the limits involved in connecting research to practice and policy:

> We look for medicine to be an orderly field of knowledge and procedure. But it is not. It is an imperfect science, an enterprise of constantly changing knowledge, uncertain information, fallible individuals, and at the same time lives on the line. There is science in what we do, yes, but also habit, intuition, and sometimes plain old guessing. The gap between what we know and what we aim for persists. And this gap complicates everything we do.

Although research has the potential to help us more effectively manage and reduce the complexity and uncertainty of teaching, it will never be able to eliminate it. Empirical research is one source, among others, that should be considered in determining the worth of a teacher education activity.

ELEMENTS OF A RESEARCH AGENDA

This section outlines the elements of a research agenda for teacher education that is based on our analysis and discussion of the existing empirical research. First, it discusses features of research design, methodology, and research topics that we think need to be priorities in future teacher education research. Following this, it discusses the development of a stronger infrastructure for research on teacher education that is needed to support the implementation of our proposed research agenda. This discussion of infrastructure support will address the development of research networks, the preparation and training of educational researchers, and the peer-review and publication process.

It is important to point out that despite the critiques of existing research we have offered throughout this volume, each of the reviews we have undertaken identifies promising lines of work and insights about aspects of the effects of preservice teacher education. These are detailed in the individual chapters and in the executive summary. The research agenda that we propose here seeks to build on what we have learned from the existing research in this relatively young area of inquiry (see chap. 2).

For example, although there appears to be a relationship between coursework taken by teachers in mathematics and student learning at the secondary level (see chap. 4), we know very little about this relationship at the elementary level, about the specific kinds of coursework preparation in mathematics that matter, and about teachers' subject preparation in other disciplines. Also, as pointed out in chapter 7, although we have learned some things about the impact of particular instructional approaches on teachers' knowledge and beliefs, there have been few systematic comparisons of the impact of different instructional methods and the effects of instructional methods on future teachers' practices. Rather than focus on what we know from existing research, however, this chapter focuses on what we need to know and how we can design and support research to help get us there.

RESEARCH DESIGN AND METHODOLOGY

We highlight several aspects of research design and methodology in our proposals for strengthening research in teacher education. Some are standards that apply to all good research; others are more specific to research on teacher education. Some of these recommendations are concrete examples of the principles for scientific inquiry recently offered by a National Research Council Report on educational research (Shavelson & Towne, 2002). Our recommendations include:

1. Clear and consistent definition of terms
2. Full description of data collection and analysis methods and the contexts in which research is conducted
3. Research situated in relation to relevant theoretical frameworks
4. Development of more programs of research
5. More attention to the impact of teacher education on teacher learning and teacher practices
6. Research that connects teacher education to student learning
7. Total portfolio of studies that includes multidisciplinary and multimethodological approaches to studying the complexities of teacher education
8. Development of better measures of teacher knowledge and performance
9. Research that examines teacher preparation in different subjects in addition to mathematics and science and takes the subjects taught into account when examining the effects of teacher education components and programs
10. More systematic analysis of clearly identifiable alternatives in teacher education using matching controls or random trials as separate studies or in conjunction with in-depth case studies
11. More in-depth multiinstitutional case studies of teacher education programs and their components

Definition of Terms

The first area of research is concerned with the *definition of terms*. As pointed out in our analysis of the individual topics covered in this project, there is a great deal of inconsistency and confusion with regard to the definition of terms currently used in research studies such as "alternative" and "traditional" certification, "professional development school," "portfolio," and "action research." Researchers define these and other terms differently. Some studies attempt comparisons between categories (e.g., alternative certification and traditional certification) without clearly defining what is being compared. All aspects of teacher education including instructional approaches, curriculum, and organizational arrangements should be defined clearly, consistently, and with enough specificity to enable the accumulation of knowledge across studies about the nature and impact of different aspects of teacher education. For example, research on the impact of particular instructional approaches such as case studies and action research needs to discuss the ways in which these strategies are conceptualized and introduced to prospective teachers and how their use is facilitated and supported. Greater attention to the particular purposes and conditions of use for various teacher education strategies will enable us to understand more about the conditions that matter in achieving particular outcomes.

Description of Data Collection, Analysis, and Research Contexts

A second aspect of research design that should be emphasized in teacher education research is the *fuller description of methods of data collection and analysis and the contexts in which the research was conducted*. Many studies reviewed in this volume provide inadequate information about how data were collected and analyzed. That makes it difficult if not impossible to evaluate the credibility of the conclusions reached by researchers. Similarly, many studies conducted within individual courses did not situate the courses within the programs, institutions, and state policy contexts in which they were embedded. A number of studies that discussed teacher retention for those who completed different kinds of teacher education programs provided no description of the characteristics of the schools and communities in which the teachers taught. Greater attention to contexts in the reporting of research will enable a better understanding of the conditions under which teacher education and its components relate to various outcomes.

More attention should also be paid in research reports to the validity and reliability of research instruments and data collection protocols. Many studies reviewed in this volume provide no information about how instruments used for data collection were developed and, validated or how their reliability was assessed. This lack of information in the published reports of research necessarily weakens the claims that researchers can make about the effects of what was examined.

Connect Research to Theoretical Frameworks

Another aspect of design that we think is important for future research is to better *situate research studies in relation to relevant theoretical frameworks*. Failure to do this will result in continued difficulties in explaining findings about the effects or lack of effects of particular teacher education practices. For example, one area that has received much attention in recent years is research on teacher learning (e.g., Borko & Putnam, 1996; Richardson & Placier, 2001; Whitcomb, 2003; Wideen, Mayer-Smith, & Moon, 1998). Currently there are a variety of conceptualizations available from research conducted from cognitive psychological, sociological, and anthropological perspectives that offer often quite different explanations for how teachers learn to teach. Particular conceptions of teaching and learning to teach are also embedded in the curriculum, social relations, instructional strategies, and organizational structures of teacher education programs. Empirical research on teacher education programs, their components, and policies affecting teacher education can potentially contribute to the elaboration and refinement of these frameworks and to greater understanding of the process of teacher learning in different contexts (e.g., in different kinds of teacher education institutions and in different subject areas). Framing research in relation to relevant theoretical frameworks is necessary for researchers to be able to explain their findings.

Develop Research Programs

We think that it is also important to develop more *programs of research* in teacher education where researchers consciously build on each other's work to pursue a line of inquiry (e.g., the conditions of mentoring student teachers that facilitate certain kinds of teacher learning and case studies as a tool for teacher learning). One positive feature of a productive research program is that researchers pursue different aspects of particular problems and questions accumulating and extending knowledge with each new study.

Another benefit to be expected of systematic research programs in teacher education is the use of more common data collection methods and instruments. This wider use of data collection methods and instruments would make it easier to accumulate knowledge across individual studies. Some of the clearest examples of research programs in teacher education are the research on microteaching described in chapter 6, the research on pedagogical content knowledge discussed in chapter 4, and the research on teacher labor markets discussed in chapters 2 and 3. These exceptions aside, there is very little evidence in the studies reviewed of researchers' building on others' work in establishing chains of inquiry around particular questions and consistently defined outcomes, and of researchers using the same outcome measures across studies.

There are a handful of examples in the studies we reviewed of research protocols and instruments that have been used in a variety of research projects such as the use of the Teacher Education and Learning to Teach (TELT) study protocols (Kennedy, Ball, & McDiarmid, 1993) in the case studies of teacher education programs sponsored by the National Commission for Teaching and America's Future (NCTAF; Darling-Hammond, 2000) and the NCTAF protocols used by individual researchers (Breidenstein, 2002). We think that there should be more pooling of data collection instruments among researchers so that it will be easier to accumulate knowledge across individual studies.

Connect Teacher Characteristics, Teacher Education, Teacher Learning, and Teacher Practice

The next issue is that across studies, research needs to focus more on *the connections among teacher characteristics, teacher education, teacher learning, and teaching practices*. Our analyses indicated that the focus in much of the existing research on teacher education program components is on how methods courses, field experiences, instructional strategies, and the like influence teachers' beliefs and attitudes. These studies pay little attention to how teachers' *knowledge and practices* are influenced by what they experience in teacher education programs and even less attention to how teachers are affected over time by their preparation. There is a clear need to look more at how teachers' knowledge and practices are shaped by their preparation including after they have completed their programs. More longitudinal studies that examine the effects of preparation on teachers over time such as Grossman et al.'s (2000) study of teachers learning to teach writing during and after their preservice teacher education program are needed.

Some studies have sought to connect teacher characteristics or teacher education directly with student outcomes without giving attention to teacher learning or teacher practices. These studies that bypass teacher learning and teachers' practices will have very little explanatory power even if they detect relationships between teacher education and student outcomes. We need to know how teacher characteristics and teacher education programs and their components interact with teacher learning to mediate these effects on students. There are multiple varieties of practice within particular kinds of courses and programs. A research focus on teacher learning and practice is necessary to illuminate the particular qualities of a course or program that are connected to desired outcomes and for the research to prove useful to practitioners and policymakers (Kennedy, 1999).

Connect Teacher Education to Student Learning

One critical outcome that has been largely neglected in the teacher education research literature is *student learning*. In the few studies that address this issue, student learning has been assessed using growth in standardized achievement tests, a limited measure of what students learn. Given the current political context discussed in chapter 2 where pressures on teacher education programs have intensified to demonstrate the connection of their work to student learning, we think that greater efforts need to be made by researchers to connect teacher education to student learning. In doing so, researchers need to explore measures of other aspects of academic student learning in addition to that which is assessed in standardized achievement tests. The work on teacher work sample methodology is one example of efforts by researchers to develop other valid measures of teachers' ability to promote student learning (McConney, Schalock, & Schalock, 1998).[1]

Although national attention is currently focused on cognitive measures of academic performance, a look at the broader history of our country shows a strong recurrent interest of the public in other outcomes (e.g., Goodlad, 1984). Researchers should address these other aspects of student learning such as students' social, emotional, aesthetic, and civic development. We need broader conceptions of how to measure student competence or success. Testing alone cannot measure nor tell us all we need to know about student learning.

Teacher Education Research is Multidisciplinary and Multimethodological

We also think that a *multidisciplinary* and *multimethodological approach* to studying issues in teacher education offers the best hope for producing knowledge that is useful for policy and practice. Student learning in schools is affected by a number of different but interrelated factors in addition to the general type of preparation for teaching received by their teachers. Among these are the individual attributes brought by prospective teachers to their teacher education programs; the specific features of these programs and their components and the institutions in which they are situated; the nature of instruction in teacher education programs, what prospective teachers learn in these programs; the schools in which teachers teach before, during, and after they complete their preparation; school district policies and practices; and state and federal policies. Given the complexity of teacher education and its connections to various aspects of teacher quality and student learning, no single methodological or theoretical approach will be able to provide all that is needed to understand how and why teacher education influences educational outcomes. Obviously, no single study will be able to address all of the various factors that influence aspects of teacher quality and student learning. These are characteristics that should be addressed in full programs of research (Shulman, 2004).

---

[1] In teacher work samples, teachers document over a 3- to 5-week period their effectiveness in fostering student learning.

Many different research questions have been identified in the chapters in this volume that we think are ripe for further study by researchers. Each of these questions is best studied through particular kinds of research methodologies. For example, if the issue is how prospective teachers interpret and make use of knowledge gained from a methods course about how to teach reading, it is important for researchers to examine the inner workings of the course to illuminate how the instruction was implemented, what candidates brought to the course in terms of the knowledge and skills under study, what they learned from this instruction, and then how and why they applied in their classrooms what they learned. This issue—developing a better understanding of how a methods course contributes to the acquisition of particular knowledge and skills by prospective teachers and to their subsequent use in the classroom—calls for an in-depth examination of the course and practice setting in order to be able to distinguish the effects of the course from selection effects and from the influence of the settings in which teachers teach. On the other hand, if the question concerns the overall relative effectiveness of two different kinds of reading methods courses, researchers might also want to do a systematic comparison of course outcomes using an experimental or quasiexperimental design.

We also believe that researchers need to use *better measures of teacher knowledge and skills* than has been evident in existing studies. First, much of the research examining teacher outcomes has focused on attitudes and beliefs, not on how teacher education and its components influence teachers' knowledge acquisition and use of knowledge. In terms of teacher knowledge, some researchers have used tests to assess what professional knowledge teachers have acquired. More focus is needed on what teacher candidates actually learn from the opportunities provided them in their preparation (including attention to what knowledge they bring to the program) to increase our knowledge about how particular components and programs contribute to the development and use of teacher knowledge. Measures of teacher knowledge that are linked to the teacher education curriculum are called for.

More reliable and valid measures of teacher performance also are needed in research that attempt to connect teacher education components and programs and policies to the teaching of candidates and program graduates. Instruments and rating scales that assess teaching performance should use clear, specific criteria and address multiple aspects of teaching with multiple indicators of performance. The existing research on assessing teaching performance is weakened by studies that either use vague criteria or criteria so specific and fragmented that the mutually reinforcing components of coherent teaching are lost (Zeichner, 2005).

Most preservice teacher education programs now are required to use performance-based assessment linked to a set of teaching standards. Studies that examine the impact of particular teacher education components and strategies on teacher performance should begin to utilize new advances in teacher assessment that are now available such as structured teaching portfolios, assessment center exercises, and classroom observation systems that pay attention to both the cognitive and the behavioral dimensions of teaching (see Porter, Youngs, & Odden, 2001).

Conduct Research on the Preparation of Teachers to Teach Different Subjects

Although there is research that has examined the preparation of teachers in particular disciplines (in part as a result of the availability of funding), we need *more research in a variety of different disciplines*. Our review of research shows that the subject area taught by teachers influences teacher retention. On topics such as teachers' subject matter preparation, we have many more studies in some areas (e.g., mathematics teaching) than others. The analysis of the research on the subject matter preparation of teachers in chapters 5 and 6 and the review of research on teacher preparation for underserved populations in chapter 8 indicate that we cannot assume that findings with regard to the preparation of teachers in one subject area hold true for teachers of other subjects.

We saw in chapter 11 that the preparation of teachers for different content areas has sometimes been lumped together in studies of the impact of different teacher education program structures. For example, the preparation of mathematics teachers in one kind of program was compared against the preparation of elementary or social studies teachers in another type of program. We need to design research in ways that enable us to distinguish the effects of the programs or program components from those of the subject areas in which teachers are teaching and from the characteristics of individual teachers.

Conduct Systematic Analyses of Distinct Alternatives in Teacher Education

There has been increased attention in recent years to the contributions that can be made by *systematic analyses of clearly identifiable alternatives in teacher education* using quasi-experimental designs with various forms of matching and controls and experimental designs with randomized assignment (e.g., Mosteller & Boruch, 2002; Shavelson & Towne, 2002; Whitehurst, 2002). Although we encourage more studies that systematically examine the effects on teachers and their pupils of distinctly different preparation routes, it is the view of the panel that there is a variety of ways to conduct these studies. Although we support more random trials and quasiexperimental designs using matching or controls in teacher education research, we believe that funding and other practical issues will continue to limit how much teacher education research will be conducted in this manner. This kind of work is very expensive, and the high pupil and teacher mobility rates in many urban schools and informed-consent issues involved in random assignment make this research complicated to implement. Despite these difficulties, we believe that this kind of work needs to become more common in teacher education research. The recent study of Teach for America that used random assignment of pupils to teachers who were prepared in different ways (Decker, Mayer, & Glazerman, 2004) is an example of this genre of research on the effects of alternative forms of teacher preparation.

When random assignment is not feasible, we think that the use of various forms of matching and controls are reasonable alternatives. We particularly recommend research designs that combine quantitative and qualitative analyses like the study on different pathways into teaching currently underway in New York City (Boyd, Grossman, Lankford, Loeb, & Wyckoff, 2003).

Conduct In-Depth Case Studies of Teacher Education Programs

Finally, in chapter 11, we review two large-scale multiinstitutional case studies of teacher education programs across the country, the TELT and the NCTAF studies. Case study research of programs, like the systematic comparative analyses discussed earlier, are extremely expensive and complicated to carry out and inevitably will be a limited part of the full spectrum of teacher education research. Both these kinds of studies, systematic comparisons of program alternatives and in-depth case studies of programs, are good candidates for targeted resource allocations to teacher education research (see following section).

RESEARCH TOPICS

In the previous discussion of research design and methodology, several recommendations were made for improving teacher education research from a design perspective that also have implications for the content of research. These recommendations when considered from the perspective of research content, suggest that a top priority for teacher education research should be to further our knowledge about the connections between particular aspects of teacher education (e.g., curriculum, instruction, programs, and policies) and teacher learning, teacher practices, and student learning under various conditions and in different contexts. The discussion of methodological issues was intended to improve the ability of teacher education research to be able to distinguish the effects of teacher education from those attributable to individuals and contexts, and to be able to explain the conditions under which various effects occur and why they occur.

In addition to this general recommendations for research content, design, and methodology, our analyses of research in this volume identified several important issues or topics that we think teacher education research also needs to address. These include:

1. Research on preparing teachers to successfully teach the diverse students who are in U.S. public schools and on recruiting a diverse teaching force
2. Research on teacher educators, teacher education students, and graduates, and on the context of instruction
3. Research on teacher education curriculum and program of study, and instructional interactions
4. Research on organizational arrangements within programs
5. Research on the predictive validity of teacher education program admissions standards
6. Research on important overlooked topics

CONDUCT RESEARCH ON PREPARING TEACHERS FOR CULTURAL DIVERSITY AND ON RECRUITING A MORE DIVERSE TEACHING FORCE

First, because of the relative neglect of research on the preparation of teachers for the cultural diversity that they will encounter in U.S. public schools and on recruiting a more diverse teaching force, we believe that research in teacher education *needs to contribute in a more central way to the narrowing of the achievement gap in U.S. public education.* As mentioned numerous times in this volume, one problem with the existing research (e.g., about methods courses and instructional strategies) is that the contexts in which teachers work (e.g., the characteristics of the students taught and the communities in which they live) often are not described in the research reports. This lack of explicit attention to teaching contexts by researchers makes it very difficult to interpret data about teaching performance and teacher retention and about the effectiveness of different teacher education components and programs.

We concur with Wilson, Floden, and Ferrini-Mundy's (2001) recommendation that researchers should be much more explicit about the contexts in which teachers work. We need to ensure that our definitions of teaching effectiveness and student learning include the many students of color and students living in poverty who are currently underserved by our public schools, and that our definition of high-quality teachers includes the development of a diverse teaching force that more adequately reflects the diversity of our population (Villegas & Lucas, 2004).

Research in teacher education needs to make the narrowing of the achievement gap a priority concern by documenting how the status quo in the preservice preparation of teachers has fallen short in recruiting a diverse teaching force and preparing teachers to teach diverse learners. It should also play a greater role in illuminating how we can do a better job of preparing candidates who will choose to teach in the schools where they are most needed, will be successful once they arrive, and will stay there, and in documenting ways to recruit a more diverse teaching force. This research on the preparation of teachers to teach underserved populations should pay special attention to the preparation of teachers to teach English-language learners because almost no research has been conducted on this aspect of diversity in teacher education.

Conduct Research on Teacher Educators, Teacher Education Students and Graduates, and on the Instructional Context in Teacher Education

Second, there is a need for *studies of teacher educators, teacher education students, graduates, and of the context in which instruction is delivered.* Our reviews do not include attention to research on teacher educators. Although there was some research on teacher educators in the 1980s (e.g., see Lanier & Little, 1986; Wisniewski & Ducharme, 1989), much of this work is outdated. This question bears new research scrutiny. More research is needed examining the consequences of who is teaching a particular program component (e.g., a methods course or foundations course), who is using a particular instructional strategy, or who is supervising a student engaged in a field experience in a school. In what ways does it matter if the instructors and supervisors in preservice programs are permanent faculty, academic staff, and adjunct faculty, or doctoral students? What are the characteristics of teacher educators, and how do various demographic and quality indicators associated with teacher educators (e.g., years of teaching experience and type of graduate education) influence the character and quality of instruction in teacher education programs?

We also need to build more comprehensive and up-to-date databases on prospective teachers, teachers, and the reserve pool of teachers, including information on race and ethnicity, social class background, gender, measures of academic performance, and personal qualities. These databases should include attention to such things as how teachers with different demographic and quality profiles are prepared, where they teach, and how long they stay in teaching.

Also, we know very little from the existing research about how the context of instruction in teacher education programs influences what opportunities are made available to teacher education students, what they learn from these opportunities, and how this learning impacts teacher quality and student learning. Examples of questions related to the context of teaching in teacher education that should be explored by researchers include the following. Does it matter if the instruction takes place in a school or on a university campus, in person or online via distance education? Are there particular conditions for conducting distance teacher education related to the achievement of certain goals for teacher learning? Is the character and quality of supervision and support provided to student teachers and interns by graduate student university supervisors different from that provided by faculty, doctoral students, or adjuncts? How do particular kinds of professional development opportunities for teacher educators influence the instruction and supervision provided to students (e.g., training and support for field supervisors)? What staffing patterns in a teacher education program are effective in preparing teachers for work in schools serving pupils on the short end of the achievement gap?

Conduct Research on Teacher Education Curriculum, Instructional Practices, and Organizational Arrangements Within Programs

A third area in need of research is the *teacher education curriculum and instructional practices and organizational arrangements within programs.* Very little work has documented the nature and quality of the teacher education curriculum, the variety of requirements, the content of preparation programs at different levels (e.g., elementary and secondary) and in different subject areas (e.g., Smagorinsky & Whiting, 1995), and the academic rigor of the preparation as assessed by such means as analyses of course syllabi and assignments (e.g., Steiner & Rozen, 2004).

There is also the issue of the consequences of organizing the teacher education curriculum in particular ways. Tom (1997) has discussed teacher education programs as involving principles of both conceptual and structural design. More research is needed on the conditions under which different conceptual and structural arrangements within programs are connected to various outcomes. For example, what are the implications of organizing methods courses as subject-specific courses or as generic courses? What are the implications of integrating content on topics like multiculturalism and technology into a whole program as opposed to isolating it in specific courses? What are the most useful ways to organize methods instruction for individuals to be successful in different pathways into teaching?

With the exception of the few case studies of programs that are discussed in chapter 11, and in some of the self-study research, we know very little about the nature of instructional interactions between teacher educators and their students in teacher education classrooms. We need research that explores the process of teacher education both within the teacher education classroom and in the supervisory situations that exist in internship settings. Questions about instructional interactions and social relations in teacher education that need to be explored include the following: What views of knowledge and level of academic demands are evident in classroom discussions in teacher education programs? To what extent do teacher educators teach prospective teachers in ways consistent with what they advocate in their classes? How does the ethnic, racial, and social class composition of teacher education classes influence classroom discourse?

We also need research on *organizational issues related to teacher education programs* such as the effects of student cohort groups on teacher learning and performance. What are the outcomes associated with different patterns of prospective teachers taking coursework together? There are also issues related to timing in relation to the teacher education curriculum. With the growth of alternative routes into teaching, the question of what the consequences are of different types of preparation prior to individuals' becoming teachers of record fully responsible for classrooms is critical. We see in chapter 11 that programs vary according to the nature and amount of preparation in the preservice phase and that sometimes when there is minimal or no preservice professional preparation, there is a process of "catching up" for teachers that occurs during the year that may cause academic losses for pupils. What are the knowledge and skills and dispositions needed by teachers to be entrusted to begin practice as full-time teachers? [2]

Closely related to the study of program organizational characteristics, further research is needed to elaborate and refine our understanding of the characteristics of teacher education programs related to their success in accomplishing program goals. In chapter 11, several large-scale case study projects are discussed (e.g., Darling-Hammond, 2000) that identified program characteristics that appeared related to program effectiveness. Much more research is needed to understand these characteristics and how they influence various aspects of teacher and pupil learning.

Conduct Research on the Predictive Validity of Admissions Criteria

A fourth area in which research is needed is with regard to the *predictive validity of criteria used for admission to teacher education programs*. How well do particular measures of the academic potential and performance (e.g., GPA, ACT and SAT, and teacher tests) and personal qualities of preservice teachers (e.g., cultural sensitivity) predict their success in different pathways into teaching and in classrooms after they complete their programs as well as their longevity in teaching, particularly in the urban and remote rural schools where they are most needed? States and teacher education institutions have created admissions policies with relatively little evidence about what such criteria mean in terms of both recruiting a diverse teaching force and the quality of teaching performance over time. Research needs to identify the relationships between particular admissions criteria and processes and aspects of teacher quality and retention as well as the trade-offs involved in the use of particular kinds of admissions criteria (e.g., between the use of standardized tests for selection and the recruitment of teachers of color).

Conduct Research on Other Neglected Topics

Finally, as noted in the individual chapters, there are whole aspects of teacher education that remain virtually unexplored by researchers and need careful study. These include the nature and impact of subject matter and general education preparation of teachers, the role of psychological and social foundations, and the impact of different policies that affect teacher education. Although the idea of teacher education as the responsibility of the whole institution has been advocated in several recent national reports (American Council of Education, 1999) research on teacher education has largely ignored the role of the general education and subject matter preparation of teachers and has focused more narrowly on methods courses and field experiences. Given that much of the coursework of prospective teachers is taken outside of education schools and departments, for both alternatively and traditionally certified teachers, it is important for researchers to broaden the scope of research to include these neglected areas.

---

[2]The National Academy of Education Teacher Education Committee has produced a report that addresses this question (Darling-Hammond & Bransford, 2005).

Also as pointed out in chapter 10, despite intense debates over the value of different forms of accountability such as national accreditation and different policies affecting teacher education programs, very little research has been done about the impact of these policies. Much of what has been done (e.g., research on teacher tests) is outdated (e.g., on tests that are no longer used) and of little use in the current policy context. Finally, almost no research has been conducted on the preparation of general education teachers to work with students with disabilities, which is a serious omission given that currently most teachers work with these students.

DEVELOPING AN INFRASTRUCTURE FOR RESEARCH ON TEACHER EDUCATION

Much of the empirical research reviewed in this project involves individual or small groups of teacher educators studying aspects of their own courses and programs.[3] Whereas there are advantages to this "insider" and local perspective on teacher education,[4] there are also limitations in a research literature based largely on small sample studies within single courses and programs. It is not surprising that most of the research is conducted in relation to individual teacher education courses and programs.[5] The heavy teaching loads of faculty who do the work of teacher education have been clearly documented (e.g., Liston, 1995). These differences in teaching loads exist within schools and colleges of education as well as between education units and other college and university departments (Schneider, 1987). Heavier teaching loads means that teacher education faculty often have less time available for research than do many other faculty. Much of the research on preservice teacher education is undertaken on top of an already full teaching load (Koehler, 1985).

It should not be inferred from these comments that we think that the lack of resources to conduct research is the major reason why self-study research by teacher educators has grown in the last decade. Many teacher educators who conduct research on their own courses and programs argue that they benefit greatly from these inquiries and that this visible commitment to self-inquiry provides a model for their students. They also argue that improvements in their work as teacher educators and their programs result from these self-studies (e.g., Cochran-Smith, 1994; Hamilton, 1998; Loughran, Hamilton, & Russell, 2004).

Even with these advantages, however, it is important that more research be conducted that looks at the nature and impact of different components of teacher education across different program, institutional, and state policy contexts. Because teacher education is embedded in contexts with particular constellations of admissions criteria, program requirements and goals, staffing patterns, institutional cultures, state policies, and community demographics, it is important to understand how different contexts affect the efficacy of components like courses, field experiences, and specific teaching strategies that are used within these components. We cannot assume that evidence about successful practices in one setting with a particular group of teacher

---

[3]Some, but not all of the research by teacher educators in their own classes and programs is "self-study" research that focuses on the teacher educators' own practices. Some of this insider research, however, involves a focus on teacher education students and what they are and are not learning in their programs and does not include a focus on the teacher educators' own practices.

[4]It has been argued, for example (e.g., by Cochran-Smith & Lytle, 1993) that insiders can illuminate aspects of teaching practice that are not accessible to outside researchers.

[5]Koehler (1985) refers to this research as "bootstrap research."

educators or in one type of pathway into teaching is meaningful in other kinds of settings.

Resources for Research

It is clear that except for studies that focus on mathematics and science instruction, resources to support research in teacher education are extremely limited. As Lagemann (1999) pointed out, the funding base for educational research in general is "dangerously insufficient." Referring to a report by the President's Panel on Education and Technology (Panel, 1997), she argued that the percentage of education spending that is invested in research and development is far less than the proportions of expenditure that are invested in other areas such as prescription and nonprescription medications. The resources invested in educational research have been meager, and teacher education research has received only a small proportion of that allotment.

This lack of investment in teacher education research has had understandable consequences. For example, the neglect of content areas other than mathematics and science in the research reviewed in this volume can in part be explained by the lack of research funding in these other areas. Limited time and funding also explains why existing research on how teacher education influences beliefs and attitudes tends to use small samples and focus on short-term effects. It also explains the reliance on evaluations of teaching that do not involve direct observation of teaching by researchers during or after program completion. Most research in teacher education is not funded by outside agencies, and this lack of access to funding has clearly influenced the research in the field.

As pointed out in chapter 2, the federal government for 3 decades supported national Centers for Teacher Education Research first at the University of Texas (1965–1986) and then at Michigan State University (1986–1995). Since the Center for Research on Teacher Learning at Michigan State University closed its doors in 1995, there have been only a few large-scale studies of teacher education sponsored by private foundations or outside agencies such as the NCTAF case studies of exemplary teacher education programs (Darling-Hammond, 2000). The federal government in recent years has retreated from its role in supporting research in teacher education. One important requirement in moving research on teacher education forward is to provide the resources that are needed to support an ambitious research agenda. Both the federal government and the foundations need to play a more active role in supporting a variety of different kinds of research in teacher education. This increased support should be targeted at particular topics and specific kinds of studies that will likely produce a high payoff. Following the discussion of the preparation of researchers, peer review of research, and research networks, we will recommend certain areas in our proposed research agenda for targeting new funding and the redirection of existing funding.

The Peer-Review Process

In addition to the need for more resources for research, there is also a need for rethinking *how studies are reviewed for publication*. Much of the research that is cited in reviews in teacher education (e.g., in the two *Handbooks of Research on Teacher Education*) is unpublished and did not undergo peer review. These include numerous conference papers, dissertations, and articles published in non-peer-reviewed journals. Even with the elimination of these studies and with our limited focus on peer reviewed studies, we reviewed studies that did not adequately describe the contexts in which the research was conducted, the characteristics of that teacher education students brought to their preparation programs, and the nature of the schools in which program graduates taught.

Empirical research on the nature and effects of different approaches to educating teachers is obviously only one aspect of teacher education scholarship. Although the methodological recommendations made in this report may not be appropriate for some kinds of research in teacher education such as conceptual, historical, and comparative research or for studies that are primarily aimed at improving practice in a local setting, we strongly recommend tightening the peer-review process for empirical studies that seek to make contributions to our collective knowledge about teacher education, both for publication in academic journals and in books distributed by commercial and university presses.

One way to do this is to provide reviewers with more explicit guidance than is now common about the kinds of things that should be present in empirical research for it to be published. In addition to coming to agreement within the teacher education research community on general standards for good research like those proposed by the recent National Research Council Committee on Scientific Research in Education (Shavelson & Towne, 2002), and those discussed in this chapter such as full description of the conditions under which findings were produced, and situating research in relation to theoretical frameworks, these should be more precisely specified in reviewers' instructions.

Although we recognize the space limitations in print journals, we need to find ways to enable researchers to include the necessary information in their research reports that enable readers to judge whether the findings are warranted by evidence. Publishing empirical research in teacher education in electronic peer-reviewed formats should be explored as a way to address the problem of space limitations in print journals. As Shulman (1999) pointed out, disciplined scholarship that meets academically rigorous yet flexible standards is necessary if research is going to be credible and useful to other researchers, practitioners and policymakers.

Even though individual teacher education researchers may not have the time and resources to conduct large sample or multiinstitutional studies that involve direct observations of teaching during and after the teacher education program under study, there are ways to improve the quality of research. Researchers can do a better job in describing the teacher education students and the teacher education components under study and the program, institutional, and state policy contexts in which the preparation is embedded. Studies that describe the use of particular instructional strategies need to describe the ways in which these strategies are conceptualized and used with students. Researchers can also better utilize the research protocols and instruments used by other researchers and define their terms in ways that are consistent within particular programs of research.

The Preparation of Educational Researchers

The preparation and training of educational researchers in graduate schools is an issue currently receiving much discussion and debate (e.g., Pallas, 2001; Schoenfeld, 1997; Siddle Walker, 1999; Young, 2001). Although efforts have been made to improve the quality of researcher preparation in education, very little of this effort has been focused on teacher education research. For example, the Spencer Foundation has implemented a number of institutional and individual grant programs directed at promoting high-quality educational research such as their predissertation, dissertation, and postdoctoral research fellowships and their institutional Research Training Grant Program and Discipline-Based Scholarship in Education Program.[6] An examination of the annual reports of the Spencer Foundation listing the research studies funded under their grant programs clearly shows that teacher education research has not been a priority in funding.[7] As pointed out earlier, since 1995, the federal government has not sponsored a research center that is focused on teacher education and learning to teach.

It is the belief of our panel that if significant improvement in the field of teacher education research is going to occur, greater investments must be made in the preparation of researchers, in the funding of studies that will advance our knowledge about teacher education, and in tightening the process through which research findings are vetted. Focusing some portion of researcher preparation programs like Spencer's Research Training Grant Program on teacher education research is one way to provide additional support to teacher education researchers. This program often provides students with carefully structured experiences in faculty research projects and with interdisciplinary seminars that help broaden students' preparation beyond their own specialty areas. Participation in these interdisciplinary activities helps prospective researchers understand the complexity of research issues as they interact with peers who see the issues through different disciplinary lenses. In addition to Spencer, other major foundations with an interest in the quality of U.S. public education such as Annenberg, Carnegie, Ford, Gates, Hewlett, Rockefeller, and MacArthur should make new, targeted investments in the preparation of education researchers who will be concerned with issues of teacher education and in the kind of research outlined in this chapter. Because there is a limited amount of research competence that can be acquired by researchers during their doctoral education, some of this support for preparing researchers should be focused on postdoctoral fellowships that enable recent graduates to work on research projects with more experienced researchers and expand their repertoires of research skills (Grossman, 2004).

The Organization of Teacher Education Research: Research Partnerships

As mentioned in chapter 2, The National Research Council (NRC) recently issued a report on educational research that proposed the development of "Strategic Research Partnerships" (Donovan, Wigdor, & Snow, 2003) that involve collaborative teams of practitioners and researchers working on coherent and highly focused programs of research. Although the proposal for three initial networks in learning and instruction, schools as organizations and educational policy and the volume as a whole do not give much attention to teacher education, we are attracted to the ideas outlined in this report as one way to build greater capacity for research in teacher education.

Currently, several projects are underway that involve networks of teacher educators and researchers studying aspects of their own; and others' teacher education

---

[6]To date, Spencer has invested in Research Training Grant Programs in 12 U.S. research universities and in five universities for their Discipline-Based Scholarship in Education program.

[7]It should be pointed out that in a general research support program like Spencer's, the low number of teacher education research proposals funded is partly a consequence of the kind of proposals that are submitted.

programs. These include the Teachers for a New Era project (TNE; Carnegie Corporation, 2004), the New York City Pathways study (Boyd et al., 2003), a multiinstitutional study in Massachusetts (Maloy, Pine, & Sideman, 2002), and the Ohio Partnership for Accountability (Ohio Teacher Quality Partnership, 2005). Although these projects differ from one another in significant ways and are at different stages of development, they all involve networks of teacher educators and researchers pursuing focused assessment agendas concerning teacher education and its connection to outcomes including student learning. Research protocols are being developed and will be shared within and across these networks that other researchers can utilize. Each initiative involves teacher education programs in multiple institutions. These projects aim to improve teacher education by making it more attentive to evidence and making systematic assessment internal to teacher education programs.

In addition to these special initiatives, every teacher education program in the United States is required to conduct some form of self-study and graduate follow-up study for state program approval, national accreditation, or for the reporting requirements of the Higher Education Act. In addition, many colleges and universities require regular evaluation and review of all academic programs including teacher education. In a recent case, a state university system has begun coordinating the collection of data on teacher education and its impact (California State University, 2001). The data accumulated in these self-study efforts offer much potential for building a comprehensive national database for teacher education research. Many of these efforts at program self-study currently display the problems that exist in the formal research literature and fail to deal with the complexity involved in explaining the influences on teacher and pupil outcomes. For the most part, these accreditation reports and self-studies do not enable us to distinguish the effects of teacher education programs from those of individuals' attributes or contextual factors. It is important for teacher educators and others to begin to tap into the research potential in these program reviews and assessments and to preserve the data produced for further use by other researchers. We agree with Shulman's (2004) recommendation that long-term programs of research should be embedded within ongoing programs of teacher education.

The data on program variations that are part of these self-studies and external reviews include the characteristics of students who enter and complete various kinds of teacher education programs, the curriculum requirements, and information about who teaches prospective teachers. There is a need for more precise, up-to-date information from different kinds of programs in different areas of the country. These databases (e.g., on the demographic and quality profiles of teachers and on the substance and timing of specific teacher education program requirements) can be used by researchers to link particular characteristics of prospective teachers to a variety of outcomes.

In the past, the American Association of Colleges for Teacher Education (AACTE) compiled limited data of this type in its "Research About Teacher Education" (RATE) reports (Howey, 1997; Lee & Yarger, 1990). Each of these reports focused on particular aspects of teacher education such as field experiences, faculty, and program requirements. What is needed now is the construction of more comprehensive national datasets on teacher education students, teacher educators, curriculum, and instruction. These databases would include information about such things as who preservice teachers are, where they receive their teacher preparation, the components of this preparation, where they teach, how long they stay, and the quality of learning for their students. It is important that this data be updated regularly so that the information accurately reflects the current realities of U.S. teacher preparation.

The issue of who would coordinate the development of these databases is an important one. AACTE includes only about 780 of the approximately 1,300 college and university programs involved in teacher education. There is an increasing number of preservice programs run by school districts, state education departments, and for-profit providers. One possibility is to coordinate the compilation of these data through the state education departments that approve all teacher education programs in their states (including alternative routes) and their umbrella group the National Association of State Directors of Teacher Education and Certification (NASDTEC). Other possibilities are for the National Center for Educational Statistics or the Education Commission of the States to play a role in compiling data on teacher education programs supplied by state departments of education.

Coordinated efforts to pursue coherent and focused research agendas in teacher education through researcher–practitioner partnerships offer many advantages over the more local research that has dominated the field. Although we still see a place for individual researchers in the overall landscape of teacher education research, we would like to see more researcher–practitioner networks developed like those mentioned previously. Research that deals with the complexities of teacher education is often expensive and time consuming. We think that the pooling of resources and researchers in the form of practitioner–researcher partnerships will help move teacher education forward to where it can deal more adequately with the complexities of studying the relationships between teacher education and outcomes. It will also help address the limitations of small sample size studies in single teacher education programs and classrooms. Self-studies and small sample case studies have an important role to play in the teacher education research landscape, but we also need to have more studies that involve multiple teacher education programs and larger sample sizes. As pointed out earlier in this volume, we think that this combination of large and small sample studies will enable us to better understand the larger patterns that exist in the relationships between teacher education or its components and various outcomes and the nuances and complexities of these patterns in different contexts.

The formation of more research partnerships in the study of teacher education goes against the grain of individual accomplishment that dominates the culture of U.S. higher education (Gumport, 1997; Lagemann, 2000). For the idea of research partnerships to be realized to a degree that will have a noticeable impact on research in teacher education, cultural changes will need to occur in the academy that support engagement in collaborative research partnerships like those outline previously.

CONCLUSION

Despite the many problems that we note in the existing research on preservice teacher education in the United States, there is reason to be optimistic about the future. Scholars from a variety of disciplines are conducting more research than ever on teacher education. More teacher educators are carefully examining their practices and attempting to improve their work based on these self-studies. Teacher educators and policymakers recognize the importance of moving toward a situation in which decisions about teacher education programs and policies affecting teacher education are made with greater confidence based on consultation of research evidence.

Teacher education research is a relatively young field of study that draws on many different disciplines and responds to an evolving policy context (Zeichner, 1999). Despite the problems with the research noted and explained in this volume, the field is evolving positively. Not only have we already learned some things of importance from this research that are detailed in the chapters of this volume, but also this work has identified the key dimensions that need to be taken into account to understand how teacher education contributes to the achievement of particular outcomes. We can see more clearly now what approaches must be taken to answer the range of important questions about teacher education.

Given the scope of the research agenda proposed in this chapter, one could legitimately ask, where should we begin? There are several critical pieces of what we recommend that should receive priority attention in the allocation of new resources for teacher education research. First, the construction of the up-to-date and specific national database detailing information about who goes into various kinds of preservice programs, the curricular requirements in these programs, and where graduates from various programs teach and how long they stay, is the logical place to target new resources right away. There is ample data on teacher education already out there that needs to be coordinated and made available to researchers. Intensive examination of databases constructed on representative samples of teacher education programs would also be useful to the field.

A second place to focus initially is for foundations and government funding agencies to make strategic investments in some of the studies that are proposed in this chapter. Systematic comparisons of distinct alternatives in teacher education such as the current study in New York City (Boyd et al., 2003) and in-depth case studies aimed at illuminating how particular characteristics of preparation programs influence educational outcomes for teachers and students (e.g., Darling-Hammond, 2000) are in particular need of support because of their high cost.

A third area of immediate priority is to focus some of the effort now directed at improving the preparation of researchers in education in general to the preparation of teacher education researchers. More new programs to support the graduate and postgraduate training of future researchers should be launched along the lines of the Spencer Foundation research training grant program and the National Academy of Education Spencer postdoctoral fellowships. A portion of these efforts should be targeted at training a new generation of educational researchers interested in studying critical issues in teacher education.

Finally, efforts should be made immediately to provide more detailed guidance to reviewers of research in the major peer-reviewed journals in teacher education so that the methodological concerns outlined in this report are addressed in the peer-review process. Given space limitations in peer-reviewed journals, efforts should be mounted to explore the possibilities of greater use of electronic publishing of reports of research so that researchers will be able to include the necessary information about research methods and contexts.

There is widespread agreement that teacher education research has had very little influence on policymaking and on practice in teacher education programs. Both teacher educators and policymakers go about their work in designing and implementing policies and programs without much regard to the kind of research reviewed in this volume. Houston (1990) argued in the first *Handbook of Research on Teacher Education* that each teacher education institution rediscovers its own best way of educating teachers with little or no attention to other institutions or to the research literature. One underlying goal of the work represented in this volume is to move us closer toward a world where both teacher education practitioners and policymakers regularly consult and find useful guidance in a research literature that addresses their deepest concerns about preparing teachers for our nation's schools.

We hope that our work over the last 4 years in reviewing the research discussed in this volume, our recommendations for a research agenda for the field, and our suggestions for strengthening the infrastructure for research will contribute toward vigorous discussion and debate about how research can better inform practice, policy, and new research related to teacher education. It must not be forgotten though that empirical research is only one means by which we can determine the worth of teacher education. In addition to discussion and debate about teacher education research, we must continue to deliberate about the moral, ethical, and political issues that provide the anchor for the work of teacher education.

Although research can illuminate what elements and kinds of teacher education are successful, and in what ways and under what conditions they work to accomplish particular goals (Fenstermacher, 2002), it cannot tell us what goals we ought to seek to accomplish. Given the very different views of the purposes of teacher education and of the role of education in our society that underlie proposals for teacher education reform today (e.g., Cochran-Smith & Fries, 2001; Zeichner, 2003), we must continue to openly discuss and debate the role of teacher education in a democratic society such as the United States.

REFERENCES

American Council on Education. (1999). *To touch the future: Transforming the ways teachers are taught*. Washington, DC: Author.

Borko, H., & Putnam, R. (1996). *Learning to teach*. In R. C. Calfee & D. Berliner (Eds.), *Handbook of educational psychology* (pp. 673–708). New York: Macmillan.

Boyd, D., Grossman, P., Lankford, H., Loeb, S., & Wyckoff, J. (2003, July). *Examining teacher preparation: Does the pathway make a difference?* Retrieved April 28, 2004 from http://www.teacherpolicyresearch.org

Breidenstein, A. (2002). Examining the outcomes of four-year and extended teacher education programs. *Teacher Education Programs and Practice, 15*(3), 12–43.

California State University. (2001). *First systemwide evaluation of teacher education programs*. Sacramento: Office of the Chancellor, California State University.

Carnegie Corporation. (2004). *Teachers for a new era: Prospectus*. Retrieved from http://carnegie.org/sub/program/teachers_prospectus.html

Cochran-Smith, M. (1994). The power of teacher research in teacher education. In S. Hollingsworth & H. Sockett (Eds.), *Teacher research and educational reform* (pp. 142–165). Chicago: University of Chicago Press.

Cochran-Smith, M., & Fries, K. (2001). Sticks, stones, and ideology: The discourse of reform in teacher education. *Educational Researcher 30*(8), 3–15.

Cochran-Smith, M., & Lytle, S. (1993). *Inside outside: Teacher research and knowledge*. New York: Teachers College Press.

Darling-Hammond L. (Ed.). (2000). *Studies of excellence in teacher education* (3 volumes). Washington, DC: American Association of Colleges for Teacher Education.

Darling-Hammond, L., & Bransford, J. (Eds.). (2005). *Preparing teachers for a changing world*. San Francisco: Jossey-Bass.

Decker, P., Mayer, D., & Glazerman, S. (2004, June). *The effects of teach for America on students: Findings from a national evaluation*. Princeton, NJ: Mathematica Policy Research, Inc.

Donovan, M. S., Wigdor, A. K., & Snow, C. E. (Eds.). (2001). *Strategic education research partnership*. Washington, DC: The National Academies Press.

Florio-Ruane, S. (2002). More light: An argument for complexity in studies of teaching and teacher education. *Journal of Teacher Education, 53*(2), 205–215.

Gawande, A. (2002). *Complications: A surgeon's notes on an imperfect science*. New York: Picador.

Goodlad, J. (1984). *A place called school: Prospects for the future.* New York: Rand McNally.

Grossman, P. (April, 2004). *The research we want, the research we need: A teacher educator's perspective.* Division K Vice Presidential address, San Diego.

Grossman, P., Valencia, S., Evans, K., Thompson, C., Martin, S., & Place, N. (2000). Transitions into teaching: Learning to teach writing in teacher education and beyond. *Journal of Literacy Research, 3*(2), 631–662.

Gumport, P. J. (1997). Public universities as academic workplaces. *Daedalus, 126*(4), 113–136.

Hamilton, M. L. (Ed.). (1998). *Reconceptualizing teaching practice: Self-studies in teacher education.* London: Falmer Press.

Houston, W. R. (Ed.). (1990). *Handbook of research on teacher education.* New York: Macmillan.

Howey, K. (1997, March). *Preservice teacher education in the United States: The RATE project, teacher education reform and teacher education policy.* Paper presented at the annual meeting of the American Educational Research Association, Chicago.

Kennedy, M. (1999). The problem of evidence in teacher education. In R. Roth (Ed.), *The role of the university in the preparation of teachers* (pp. 87–107). London: Falmer Press.

Kennedy, M., Ball, D., & McDiarmid, G.W. (1993). *A study package for examining and tracking changes in teachers' knowledge.* East Lansing, MI: National Center for Research on Teacher Learning.

Koehler, V. (1985). Research on preservice teacher education. *Journal of Teacher Education, 36,* 23–30.

Lagemann, E. (1999). An auspicious moment for educational research. In E. Lagemann & L. Shulman (Eds.), *Issues in educational research: Problems and possibilities.* (pp. 3–16). San Francisco: Jossey-Bass.

Lagemann, E. (2000). *An elusive science: The troubling history of educational research.* Chicago: University of Chicago Press.

Lanier, J., & Little, J. W. (1986). Research in teacher education. In M. Wittrock (Ed.), *Handbook of research on teaching* (pp. 527–569). New York: Macmillan.

Lee, O., & Yarger, S. (1990). Modes of inquiry in research on teacher education. In W. R. Houston (Ed.), *Handbook of research on teacher education* (pp. 14–37). New York: Macmillan.

Liston, D. (1995). Work in teacher education: A current assessment of U.S. teacher education. In N. Shimahara & I. Holowinsky (Eds.), *Teacher education in industrialized nations* (pp. 87–124). New York: Garland.

Loughran, J., Hamilton, M. L., & Russell, T. (2004). *International handbook of research of self-study of teaching and teacher education.* Amsterdam: Kluwer.

Maloy, R., Pine, G., & Seidman, I. (2002). *Massachusetts teacher education and induction study report: First-year findings.* Washington, D.C.: National Education Association.

McConney, A., Schalock, M., & Schalock, H. D. (1998). Focusing improvement and quality assurance: Work samples as authentic performance measures of prospective teachers' effectiveness. *Journal of Personnel Evaluation in Education, 11,* 343–363.

Mosteller, F., & Boruch, R. (2002). *Evidence matters: Randomized trials in education research.* Washington, DC: Brookings Institution Press.

Ohio Teacher Quality Partnership (January, 2005). *Teacher Education Matters:* Mt. Vernon, OH: Mt. Vernon Nazarene University.

Pallas, A. (2001). Preparing education doctoral students for epistemological diversity. *Educational Researcher, 30*(5), 6–11.

Panel on Educational Technology (1997). President's Committee of Advisors on Science and Technology. *Report to the president on the use of technology to strengthen K-12 education in the U.S.* Washington, DC: U.S. Government Printing Office.

Porter, A., Youngs, P., & Odden, A. (2001). Advances in teacher assessment and their uses. In V. Richardson (Ed.), *Handbook of research on teaching* (4th ed., pp. 259–297). Washington, DC: American Educational Research Association.

Richardson, V., & Placier, P. (2001). Teacher change. In V. Richardson (Ed.), *Handbook of research on teaching* (4th ed., pp. 905–947). Washington, DC: American Educational Research Association.

Schneider, B. (1987). Tracing the provenance of teacher education. In T. Popkewitz (Ed.), Critical studies in teacher education (pp. 211–241). London: Falmer Press.

Schoenfeld, A. (1997). The core, the canon, and the development of research skills: Issues in the preparation of educational researchers. In E. Lagemann & L. Shulman (Eds.), *Issues in educational research: Problems and possibilities* (pp. 166–202). San Francisco: Jossey-Bass.

Schon, D. (1984). *The reflective practitioner.* New York: Basic Books.

Shavelson, R., & Towne, L. (2002). *Scientific research in education: Report of the National Research Council's Committee on Scientific Principles in Education Research.* Washington, DC: National Academy Press.

Shulman, L. (1999). Professing educational scholarship. In E. Lagemann & L. Shulman (Eds.), *Issues in educational research: Problems and possibilities* (pp. 159–165). San Francisco: Jossey-Bass.

Shulman, L. (2004). Truth and consequences: Inquiry and policy in research on teacher education. *Journal of Teacher Education, 53*(3), 248–253.

Siddle Walker, V. (1999). Culture and commitment: Challenges for the future training of educational researchers. In E, Lagemann & L. Shulman (Eds.), *Issues in educational research: Problems and possibilities.* San Francisco: Jossey-Bass.

Smagorinsky, P., & Whiting, M. (1995). *How English teachers get taught: Methods of teaching the methods class.* Urbana, IL: National Council of Teachers of English.

Steiner, D., & Rozen, S. (2004). Preparing tomorrow's teachers. In F. Hess, A. Rotherham, & K. Walsh (Eds.), *A qualified teacher in every classroom? Appraising old answers and new ideas.* (pp. 119–148). Cambridge, MA: Harvard Education Press.

Tom, A. (1997). *Redesigning teacher education.* Albany, NY: SUNY Press.

Villegas, A. M., & Lucas, T. (2004). Diversifying the teacher workforce: A retrospective and prospective analysis. In M. Smylie & D. Miretzky (Eds.), *Developing the teacher workforce* (pp. 70–104). Chicago: University of Chicago Press.

Whitcomb, J. A. (2003). Learning and pedagogy in initial teacher preparation, In W. M. Reynolds & G. E. Miller (Eds.), & I. B. Weiner (Edition-in-cheif), *Handbook of psychology, Volume 7: Educational Psychology* (pp. 533–556). New York: John Wiley and Sons.

Whitehurst, G. (2002). *Scientifically-based research on teacher quality: Research on teacher education and professional development.* Paper presented at the White House Conference on Preparing Tomorrow's Teachers.

Wilson, S., Floden, R., & Ferrini-Mundy, J. (2001). *Teacher preparation research: Current knowledge, gaps, and recommendations.* Seattle: Center for the Study of Teaching and Policy.

Wisniewski, R., & Ducharme, E. (Eds.). (1989). *The professors of teaching.* Albany, NY: SUNY Press.

Wideen, M., Mayer-Smith, J., & Moon, B. (1998). A critical analysis of the research on learning to teach. *Review of Educational Research, 68*(2), 130–178.

Young, L. J. (2001). Border crossings and other journeys: Re-envisioning the doctoral preparation of educational researchers. *Educational Researcher, 30*(5), 3–5.

Zeichner, K. (1999). The new scholarship of teacher education. *Educational Researcher, 28*(9), 4–15.

Zeichner, K. (2003). The adequacies and inadequacies of three current strategies to recruit, prepare, and retain the best teachers for all students. *Teachers College Record, 105*(3), 490–515.

Zeichner, K. (2005). Learning from experience with performance-based teacher education. In F. Peterman (Ed.), *Assessment in urban teacher education programs* (pp. 3–20). Mahwah, NJ: Lawrence Erlbaum Associates.

BIOGRAPHICAL SKETCHES

CO-CHAIRS

Marilyn Cochran-Smith (Co-Chair of the Panel and Author of chapters 1 and 2)
is the John E. Cawthorne Professor of Education at the Lynch School of Education at
Boston College. She is the President of AERA, 2004–2005, as well as the editor of the
Journal of Teacher Education and co-editor of the *Practitioner Inquiry Series* published by
Teachers College Press. Her research interests include teacher education policy and
reform, teachers' knowledge, and teacher inquiry as well as diversity, equity, and social
justice in teaching and teacher education. Dr. Cochran-Smith is the author of many
award-winning books and articles and is a frequent keynote speaker in the United
States and across the world. Her publications include *The Making of a Reader* (Ablex
Publishing Corporation, 1984), *Learning to Write Differently: Beginning Writers and World
Processing* (with Cynthia Paris and Jessica Kahn, Ablex Publishing Corporation, 1991),
Inside/Outside: Teacher Research and Knowledge (with Susan L. Lytle, Teachers College
Press, 1993) and *Walking the Road: Race, Diversity, and Social Justice in Teacher Education*
(Teachers College Press, 2004).

Kenneth M. Zeichner (Co-Chair of the Panel and Author of chapters 11 and 12)
is Hoefs-Bascom Professor of Teacher Education and Associate Dean of the School of
Education at the University of Wisconsin-Madison. He has served as Vice President
of AERA (Division K) and is a member of the Board of Directors of AACTE and a
member of the National Academy of Education Teacher Education Committee. His
publications include *Reflective Teaching and Culture and Teaching* (Lawrence Erlbaum
Associates, 1996, with Dan Liston), *Currents of Reform in Preservice Teacher Education*
(Teachers College Press, 1996), *Democratic Teacher Education Reform in Africa* (Westview, 1999), *Teacher Education and the Social Conditions of Schooling* (Routledge, 1991),
and *Issues and Practices in Inquiry-Oriented Teacher Education* (Falmer, 1991). From 1985
to 1995, Zeichner worked as a principal investigator in the National Center for Research on Teacher Education/Teacher Learning at Michigan State University. He has
recently completed a Spencer-Foundation-funded study of teacher education reform
in Namibia and was a Fulbright Senior specialist in Australia in 2004.

PANEL MEMBERS, AUTHORS, AND CO-AUTHORS

Patricia Brady (Co-Author of chapter 6) is a doctoral student in Curriculum and Instruction at the University of Illinois at Urbana-Champaign. She formerly taught English in urban and suburban high schools. Her research interests focus on preparing teachers to meet the needs of diverse students.

Renee T. Clift (Panel Member and Co-Author of chapter 6) is professor of education in the Department of Curriculum and Instruction at the University of Illinois at Urbana-Champaign. She received her PhD in Curriculum and Teacher Education from Stanford University and was on faculty at the University of Houston before moving to Illinois. She has authored or edited several books on reflective practice and teacher leadership, as well as numerous articles on reflective practice, the uses of technology in teacher education, and the factors that enhance or inhibit learning to teach. Her current research includes longitudinal case studies of graduates from an English teacher education program and the use of technology in induction and mentoring programs.

Hilary Conklin (Co-Author of chapter 11) is a doctoral candidate in Curriculum and Instruction at the University of Wisconsin-Madison. Her current research focuses on the preparation of middle school social studies teachers.

Elizabeth Craig (Co-Author of chapters 3 and 4) is a doctoral candidate in Curriculum and Teaching at Teachers College, Columbia University. Her current research focuses on the preparation of teachers to respond to student resistance.

Mary E. Dilworth (Panel Member) is Senior Vice-President for the American Association of Colleges for Teacher Education (AACTE), the largest national organization dedicated to the preparation and professional development of teachers. Dilworth is nationally known for her research and program development work in the areas of teaching, teacher education, teachers' professional development, and teacher and learner diversity. In her current position, she is responsible for the coordination of policy and research across the Association. In addition, she directs the activities of the Association's research, technology, and equity projects and activities. Dilworth holds and has held a number of elected and appointed positions on national educational boards including ETS's Visiting Panel on Research, the National Association of State Boards of Education-Panel on Teacher Education & Accountability, Interstate New Teacher Assessment & Support Consortia (INTASC) Higher Education Panel, American Council on Education/NCES—Panel on Postsecondary Education, National Center for Research on Teacher Education & National Center for Research on Teacher Learning, the Danforth Foundation Compton Fellows, and Annenburg—QEM Teacher Leadership Corps.

Dan Fallon (Panel Member) is Chair of the Education Division of Carnegie Corporation of New York, supervising the award and administration of grants in support of teacher education reform, urban school reform, advancing literacy (ages 8 through 18), and other areas of education important to the national interest. He is Professor Emeritus of Psychology and of Public Policy at the University of Maryland, College Park, where he also served as Vice President for Academic Affairs and Provost. Dr. Fallon served earlier as Dean of the College of Liberal Arts at Texas A&M

University, Dean of the College of Liberal Arts Sciences at the University of Colorado at Denver, and Associate Dean of Arts and Sciences of Harpur College at Binghamton University. As President of the Council of Colleges of Arts and Sciences, he led an effort to explore the joint contribution of arts and sciences faculty and education faculty in the education of teachers, which was known as *The Project 30 Alliance*. Dr. Fallon has published widely on learning and motivation through his work in experimental psychology, on academic public policy, and on comparative higher education. He is the author of a prize-winning book, *The German University*.

Robert E. Floden (Panel Member and Co-Author of chapter 5) is Professor of Teacher Education, Measurement & Quantitative Methods, Educational Psychology, and Educational Policy at the Michigan State University College of Education, where he is also Director of the Institute for Research on Teaching and Learning. Floden has an AB in philosophy from Princeton University and an MS in mathematical statistics and PhD in philosophy of education from Stanford University. Floden's work has been published in the *Handbook of Research on Teaching*, the *Handbook of Research on Teacher Education*, and many journals. He is co-PI of MSU's Teachers for a New Era initiative and co-PI on a project developing measures of teachers' mathematical knowledge for teaching algebra. He has been studying teacher education and other influences on teaching and learning for almost 3 decades. He is currently president of the Philosophy of Education Society.

Kim Fries (Project Director and Co-Author of chapters 1 and 2) is an Assistant Professor in the Department of Education at the University of New Hampshire. Prior to completing her PhD at Boston College, Kim taught in a variety of educational settings (K–12). She is presently the Vice President of the New England Educational Research Organization (NEERO), a member of the Publications Committee for the American Educational Research Association, and the Director of the AERA Panel on Research and Teacher Education that has put together this volume. Her research interests include teacher education, research on teaching, and teacher research.

Susan Fuhrman (Panel Member) is the Dean and George and Diane Weiss Professor of Education at the University of Pennsylvania's Graduate School of Education. She is also Chair of the Management Committee of the Consortium for Policy Research in Education (CPRE). CPRE conducts research on state and local education policies and finance, bringing together the resources of Penn, Harvard University, the University of Michigan, Stanford University, and the University of Wisconsin-Madison. Dr. Fuhrman received bachelor's and master's degrees in history from Northwestern University in Chicago, IL, and a PhD in political science and education from Columbia University, New York. She has written widely on education policy and finance; among her edited books are *Redesigning Accountability Systems for Education* (co-edited with Richard Elmore, 2004), *From the Capitol to the Classroom: Standards-Based Reform in the States* (2001), and *Rewards and Reform: Creating Educational Incentives that Work* (co-edited with Jennifer O'Day, 1996). Her many professional involvements include membership on the Board of Trustees of the Carnegie Foundation for the Advancement of Teaching, and the Coca-Cola Council for Corporate and School Partnerships. She is also a member of the National Academy of Education, a former Vice President of the American Educational Research Association, and a non-executive-Director of Pearson plc, the international education and publishing company. Her research interests include state policy design, accountability in education, deregulation, intergovernmental relationships, and standards-based reform.

Drew Gitomer (Panel Member) is Senior Fellow at NORC. He joined NORC in 2004 after spending 20 years at Educational Testing Service (ETS) as a researcher. From 1999 to 2004, Gitomer was Senior Vice-President for Research and Development. His primary research interests have been in the design of assessments to support improved instructional practice. His current research interests include policy and evaluation issues related to teacher education, licensure, induction, and professional development.

Pamela Grossman (Panel Member and Author of chapter 7) is a Professor and Chair of Curriculum and Teacher Education in the School of Education at Stanford University. She received her BA from Yale University and her PhD from Stanford University. Her research interests include the content and pedagogy of teacher education, the connection between professional knowledge and professional preparation in teaching and other professions, the teaching of English in secondary schools, and the role of subject matter in high school teaching. Her articles have appeared in *Teachers College Record*, *Educational Researcher*, *Educational Evaluation and Policy Analysis*, and the *American Educational Research Journal*, among other publications. Her most recent research projects include a large-scale study of pathways into teaching in New York City Schools and a study of the teaching of practice in professional preparation programs for teaching, the clergy, and clinical psychology. She has served as Member at Large and Vice President of Division K—Teaching and Teacher Education—for the American Educational Research Association.

Etta Hollins (Panel Member and Co-Author of chapter 8) is professor of teacher education and co-chair of the Teacher Education for a Multicultural Society in the EdD program at the University of Southern California. Her research interests are on the professional development of teachers for underserved and urban school students. She is presently conducting a longitudinal study on the use of structured dialogs in a study group format as professional development for urban teachers. Dr. Hollins' important contributions to the field of teacher education include the books *Culture in School Learning* (author, 1996), *Teaching Diverse Populations* (co-editor, 1994), *Preparing Teachers for Cultural Diversity* (co-editor, 1997), and *Transforming Curriculum for a Culturally Diverse Society* (editor, 1997).

Jacqueline Jordan Irvine (Panel Member) is the Charles Howard Candler Professor of Urban Education at Emory University. Dr. Irvine's specialization is multicultural education and urban teacher education, particularly the education of African Americans. Her books include *Black Students and School Failure*, *Growing Up African American in Catholic Schools*, *Critical Knowledge for Diverse Students*, *Culturally Responsive Lesson Planning for Elementary and Middle Grades*, *In Search of Wholeness: African American Teachers and Their Culturally Specific Pedagogy*, and *Educating Teachers for Diversity*. In addition these books, she has published numerous articles, book chapters, and presented papers to professional and community organizations.

Ann Lieberman (Panel Member) received her EdD at UCLA. She is well known in the United States and internationally for her work on and sensitivity to issues of teaching and school improvement. She has written scores of articles and books on these issues.

Her well-known book *Teachers: Their World and Their Work,* written with Lynne Miller, and its sequel are used in a variety of classes and professional development projects throughout the United States and the United Kingdom. She is a frequent consultant and speaker and is on many international boards. Her research interests range from teacher leadership to networks and coalitions.

Marco Meniketti (Co-Author of chapter 5) is an assistant professor of archaeology in the department of Social Sciences at Michigan Technological University. He received his PhD in Anthropology from Michigan State University, where he studied the evolution of capitalism and environmental change in colonial plantation systems. Meniketti is a former science and history teacher and served as research assistant on numerous projects concerning teacher preparation and educational leadership while at MSU. His interests encompass educational anthropology, learning environments, cultural influences on learning, and issues of identity transformation in postcolonial societies.

Marleen Pugach (Panel Member and Author of chapter 9) is Professor of Teacher Education in the Department of Curriculum and Instruction at the University of Wisconsin-Milwaukee, where she directs the Collaborative Teacher Education Program for Urban Communities. She received her PhD from the University of Illinois at Urbana-Champaign. Her scholarly interests include building collaborative relationships between the preparation of special and general education teachers, the preparation of teachers for urban schools, and school–university partnerships. She is author of the forthcoming book *Because Teaching Matters* (Wiley), co-author of *Collaborative Practitioners, Collaborative Schools* (2002, Love Publishing) and co-editor of *Teacher Education in Transition: Collaborative Programs to Prepare General and Special Educators* (1997, Love Publishing), *Curriculum Trends, Special Education, and Reform* (1996, Teachers College Press), and *Encouraging Reflective Practice in Education* (1990, Teachers College Press). Dr. Pugach was the 1998 recipient of the Margaret Lindsey Award for Distinguished Research in Teacher Education from the American Association of Colleges for Teacher Education.

Maria Torres Guzman (Co-Author of chapter 8) is an Associate Professor of Bilingual/Bicultural Education in the Department of International and Transcultural Studies at Teachers College, Columbia University. She has published extensively, and among her latest publications are a co-authored article for the *International Bilingualism and Bilingual Education Journal* entitled, *Modelo B/Dual Language Programs in the Basque Country and the US*; a co-authored article with Morales-Rodriguez (2003) entitled *A Profile of Dual Language Programs in New York City: A subset of six stable programs*; and a sole-authored article (2003) entitled "Preparing Teachers to Recognize and Confront Symbolic Violence in Bilingual Education," published in B. C. Wallace, & R. T. Carter (Eds.), *Understanding and Dealing with Violence: A Multicultural Approach.*

Ana Maria Villegas (Panel Member) is Professor of Education at Montclair State University, where she teaches courses on culturally responsive teaching and urban education. She specializes in the education of racial and ethnic and language minority students and in the preparation of teachers for diversity. She has conducted studies of culturally responsive teaching, policies and practices in the education of immigrant students, effective instructional practices in bilingual classrooms, increasing the diversity of the teaching force, and strategies for transforming teacher education for diversity. Her publications include a co-authored book entitled *Educating Culturally Responsive Teachers: A Coherent Approach* (SUNY Press), and numerous book chapters and journal articles. Villegas is the 2004 recipient of the Margaret B. Lindsay Award for Distinguished Research in Teacher Education given by the American Association of Colleges for Teacher Education.

Suzanne M. Wilson (Panel Member and Co-Author of chapter 10) is currently Professor of Teacher Education and Director of the Center for the Scholarship of Teaching at Michigan State University. Three major interrelated strands form the nucleus of her work: teacher knowledge and its relationship to teaching, curricular policy and its relationship to teaching, and teacher learning and its relationship to teaching. Her undergraduate degree is in history and American Studies from Brown University; she also has a MS in Statistics and a PhD in Educational Psychology from Stanford University. Prior to joining the faculty at MSU, Wilson was the first director of the Teacher Assessment Project (PI, Lee Shulman), which developed prototype assessments for the National Board for Professional Teaching Standards. While at Michigan State, she has collaborated on several large-scale research projects, including the National Center for Research on Teacher Education, the Educational Policy and Practice Study, and the National Partnership for Excellence and Accountability in Teaching.

Peter Youngs (Co-Author of chapter 10) is on the faculty in the Department of Teacher Education at Michigan State University. His research interests focus on the effects of policy related to teacher education, induction, and professional development on teaching quality and school reform. Recent publications have appeared in *Educational Researcher, Educational Policy, Educational Administration Quarterly, Review of Educational Research*, and the *Handbook of Research on Teaching*.

Karen Zumwalt (Panel Member and Co-Author of chapters 3 and 4) is the Edward Evenden Professor of Education in the Department of Curriculum and Teaching at Teachers College, Columbia University. From 1995 to 2000, she served as Dean of the College and Vice President for Academic Affairs. Her writings and research have focused on curriculum and teacher education. Her chapter on the policy implications of research on teaching for teacher education won AERA's first Interpretive Scholarship Award in 1983. She received her initial teacher preparation at the Harvard Graduate School of Education, where she student taught in the Boston public schools. After teaching middle school in the Cleveland, OH, and Glencoe, IL, public schools, she earned her PhD in curriculum and philosophy from the University of Chicago. Before coming to Teachers College as the Director of the preservice program in elementary education, she was a teacher educator at Smith College, Northampton, MA.

Author Index

Page numbers followed by t indicate a table
Page numbers in *italics* indicate pages with complete bibliographic information

G

N

Subject Index

Page numbers followed by t indicate a table

A

AACTE. *See* American Association of Colleges for Teacher Education (AACTE)
ABCTE (American Board for Certification of Teacher Excellence), 597
Abell Foundation, 95
Academic ability and achievement
  quality of teachers and, 179–180, 181
  teachers' characteristics and, 158–163
  teachers' placement and, 171–172
  teachers' preparation and, 163–164
Academic background, TFA group and, 681
Academic development, college's impact on, 278–279
Academic institutions, training of teachers and, 39
Academic skills, studies on measurement of, 162
Accountability in teacher education
  certification and, 593–597, 611–615
  current practices, 597–599
  definition of, 599
  description of research, 26–28
  empirical research, 599–611
  further research on, 616–619
  guiding questions on, 26, 57–58
  important issues in, 619–620
  overview of, 591–592
  program accreditation and, 593–597, 615–616
  studies on, 622–638t
Accountability movement, 39
Accreditation. *See* Program accreditation
ACE (American Council on Education), 73, 278
ACP. *See* Alternative Certification Program (ACP)
Action in Teacher Education, 113, 481
Action research, 445–447, 513
ACT/SAT scores/tests. *See* SAT/ACT scores/tests
Adjusted pupil achievement scores, 285
Adjusted upper division GPA, 160

Admission
  to teacher education programs, 749
  for Teach for America (TFA) program, 682
Advanced degrees, students achievement and teachers', 269
AERA. *See* American Educational Research Association (AERA)
AERA panel on Research and Teacher Education. *See* American Educational Research Association (AERA) panel on Research and teacher Education
Affective outcome measures, assessment of, 278–279
African-Americans
  age of teachers, 116
  colleges attended by, 118
  enrollment in teacher education programs, 41
  enrollment of public school students, 477
  passing rates for Praxis I and II, 607
  percentage of teachers in public schools, 114
  prospective teachers, 128–129
  teaching at the elementary level, 124
  teaching jobs preferred by, 125. *See also* Black teachers; Teachers of color
AFT (American Federation of Teachers), 113
Age
  attrition and, 139
  of elementary and high school teachers, 124
  knowledge about, 141
  mobility of teachers and, 131–132
  of new teachers, 123, 129
  of prospective teachers, 116, 141, 146
  research needs about, 146, 149
  school level, subject, and, 124
  socioeconomic background and, 116
  of students in alternative programs, 122
  teacher education program structure and, 120
  of teachers, 116, 146
Alabama, 178
Alternative Certification Program (ACP), 678
"Alternative instructional strategies," 562